THE
ECONOMY
TODAY

Fifth Edition

Bradley R. Schiller
The American University

McGraw-Hill, Inc.

New York St. Louis San Francisco Auckland Bogotá Caracas Hamburg
Lisbon London Madrid Mexico Milan Montreal New Delhi Paris
San Juan São Paulo Singapore Sydney Tokyo Toronto

2 3 4 5 6 7 8 9 0 DOW DOW 9 5 4 3 2 1

ISBN 0-07-056164-8

This book was set in Cheltenham Book by Waldman Graphics, Inc.
The editors were Jim Bittker, Scott D. Stratford, and Elaine Rosenberg;
the designer was Charles A. Carson;
the cover illustrator was Roy Wiemann;
the production supervisor was Leroy A. Young.
R. R. Donnelley & Sons Company was printer and binder.

Library of Congress Cataloging-in-Publication Data

Schiller, Bradley R., (date).
    The economy today / Bradley R. Schiller. — 5th ed.
        p.   cm.
    Includes index.
    ISBN 0-07-056164-8
    1. Economics.   I. Title.
HB171.5.S292   1991
330—dc20   90-13209

ABOUT THE AUTHOR

Bradley R. Schiller has two decades of experience teaching introductory economics at The American University, the University of California (Berkeley and Santa Cruz), and the University of Maryland. Dr. Schiller's unique contribution to teaching is his ability to relate basic principles to current socioeconomic problems, institutions, and public policy decisions. This perspective is evident throughout *The Economy Today*.

Dr. Schiller derives this policy focus from his extensive experience as a Washington consultant. He has been a consultant to most major federal agencies, many congressional committees, and political candidates. In addition, he has evaluated scores of government programs and helped design others. His studies of discrimination, employment and training programs, tax reform, pensions, welfare, and Social Security have appeared and been cited in both professional journals and popular media. Dr. Schiller is also a frequent commentator on economic policy for television, radio, and newspapers.

Dr. Schiller received his Ph.D. from Harvard in 1969. His B.A. degree, with great distinction, was completed at the University of California (Berkeley) in 1965. He is now a professor of economics in the School of Public Affairs at The American University.

PREFACE

*T*he economy today doesn't stand still. Within a year of publication of *The Economy Today*'s fourth edition, the foundations of communism began to tremble. By the time most students got to the chapter on socialist planning, central planners were looking for new jobs. And teachers of introductory economics were looking for new textbooks. Today's students want explanations for the collapse of communism. They are newly motivated to understand how the "invisible hand" of the marketplace works and why central planners look with envy at its efficiency. This changing world requires a new approach to economics, going "back to basics" and highlighting the comparative appeal of free markets.

The collapse of communism was not the only headline story of recent years. The financial markets have also figured prominently in the news. First there was the crash of 1987. Then came the tremor of October 13, 1989, which sent the Dow Jones Industrial Average plunging 190 points. In early 1990 the Japanese stock market also took a tumble, dropping more than 20 percent. Continuing volatility along with insider trading scandals raise basic concerns about the stability and integrity of all financial markets. The growth of the financial-services sector, together with the central role of financial markets in allocating resources, makes these concerns important *economic* issues that can no longer be ignored in a principles course.

This fifth edition of *The Economy Today* responds fully to these challenges. Both the appeal and the shortcomings of central planning are vividly assessed in a new chapter on the collapse of communism. Market and command economies are compared throughout the text, in areas as diverse as commodity pricing, labor relations, environmental protection, and trade. These perspectives are reinforced with a basic issue that recurs through the entire text, namely, the alternate risks of *market failure* and *government failure*. This same theme is apparent in the new chapter on financial markets, which focuses on the *economic* functions of stock, bond, and futures markets.

The Economy Today doesn't just follow the headlines. Pedagogy changes as well. We all try to make every lecture a little better, every test a bit more discriminating. The fifth edition strives for the same kinds of improvement. *The Economy Today* seeks to make the study of economics as dynamic and exciting as the world economy itself.

PRODUCT DIFFERENTIATION

What most clearly differentiates *The Economy Today* from other texts are the following features.

Global Vision To understand economics today, students must learn to think in global terms. In *The Economy Today* this global vision is manifest in:

World views   Interspersed throughout the text are boxed illustrations of economic issues in a global setting. Many of the World Views offer comparative perspectives on key economic indices (e.g., debt, GNP growth, labor productivity). Others provide current or historical illustrations of core ideas (e.g., the role of markets in financing Columbus's voyages, the role of central planning in creating a shortage of soap in the Soviet Union). All eighty-two World View boxes have a distinctive logo and light blue background (e.g., see p. 17) and are explicitly referenced in the body of the text.

Global macro   Chapter 18 provides an opportunity to introduce students to the realities of internationalized economics, without the necessity of first studying trade and finance theory. This "one-stop shopping" innovation has proven to be particularly valuable to instructors who are pressed for course time but want to offer some global insights in the macro sequence. This policy-oriented chapter can also be used as a capstone to the more traditional (and extended) sequence of trade theory (Chapter 35) and international finance (Chapter 36).

Real-World Relevance

The global vision of *The Economy Today* is an integral part of the "real world." In addition to international illustrations, the relevance of economic principles is demonstrated through examples of today's policy debates, current institutional structures, and real firms and industries.

Actual case studies   Fanciful stories about widget production won't motivate students who are mastering high-tech and wondering how software prices are determined; the real-life applications of economic principles featured in *The Economy Today* will. The evolution of the personal computer industry (Chapters 22–24) is a classic illustration of (changing) industrial structure. The product- and firm-specific concentration data in Table 25.2 (p. 634) contrast sharply with the more generalized (and therefore less meaningful) industry data provided in other texts. The new discussion of cable TV is the basis for a revised discussion of natural monopoly and government regulation (Chapter 26). And Chapter 17, Theory and Reality, offers students a meat-and-potatoes explanation of why economic performance doesn't always measure up to the expectations of economic theory. *Every* chapter of *The Economy Today* conveys the conviction that economic principles are important and relevant to what's happening in the world today.

In the news   This second set of boxes has its own distinctive logo and design; thus each box is instantly distinguished from World Views and the body of the text (e.g., see p. 4). The purpose of these brief news stories is to illustrate specific principles while underscoring the real-world relevance of economic theory. In the News applications are explicitly referenced in the body of the text and are often the subject of questions at the end of a chapter or in the accompanying *Study Guide*. In the brief period between the last edition and this, ninety-two of the In the News and World View boxes were replaced or updated.

Policy insights   Every chapter in the theory sequences includes a final section on Policy Insights. These sections, identified by a distinctive red banner, apply basic principles to actual policy issues. These applications test student ability to think critically about the relevance and validity of economic concepts.

Hot Issues   Given the real-world orientation of this text, readers can expect the most widely discussed issues of the 1990s to command substantial attention. They won't be disappointed. Among the "hot issues" are:

The collapse of communism   The emerging transition from "command-driven" to "demand-driven" economies in Eastern Europe, the Soviet Union, and China is the most significant economic event of the 1990s. Two years ago this cataclysmic change was unforeseen; today everyone is trying to explain it. *The Economy Today* offers a new chapter that looks at the promise of communism, the defects of central planning, and the continuing difficulties of the transition to freer markets. Chapter 38 explains these revolutionary changes succinctly and contrasts market and centrally planned economies perceptively. Many instructors may want to assign this chapter immediately after Chapter 2, thereby highlighting the unique (but often mysterious) character of the market mechanism.

Discussion of the collapse of communism is not confined to Chapter 38. The contrast of East German prices and West German prices at the time the Berlin Wall was dismantled introduces the basics of supply and demand (Chapter 2). The resultant shifts in the demand and supply of Deutche marks and Ostmarks are a good starting point for consideration of foreign-exchange markets (Chapter 36). The pervasive neglect of environmental protection in Eastern Europe illustrates the tradeoffs inherent in pollution control (Chapter 27). And the long line of eager job applicants at McDonald's new Pushkin Square outlet demonstrates basic principles of labor supply (Chapter 29).

The cold war peace dividend   The collapse of communism has led to a worldwide reassessment of the "guns vs. butter" decision. As the cold war dwindles, demands for a military build-down intensify. The resulting "peace dividend" will create unparalleled opportunities for new investment, consumption, or other (nonmilitary) public-sector activity. David Wyss of Data Resources, Inc., developed expressly for *The Economy Today* some illustrative estimates of the actual terms of the guns vs. butter tradeoff (see p. 7).

Financial markets   One of the fastest growing sectors of the global economy is financial services. Yet introductory courses, following the cursory descriptions of corporate structure, stock market averages, and stock market quotations which appear in other textbooks, have largely ignored this industry. *The Economy Today* offers a more compelling alternative. Chapter 34 emphasizes the basic *economic* functions of the financial markets in mobilizing and allocating real resources. Illustrations include the financing of Columbus's exploration, the new EuroDisney World outside of Paris, and the new interest expressed in the Soviet Union and Eastern Europe in this fundamental tool of capitalism.

In addition to this chapter-length treatment of financial markets, a brief discussion of venture capitalism is included in Chapter 31, Rent, Interest, and Profit. This particular Policy Insight emphasizes the relation between risk and profit as well as the role of venture capitalists in resource allocation.

Environmental protection   Concerns about the earth's warming, ozone depletion, toxic wastes, and other environmental damages affect the way we live and conduct business. The Clean Air Act amendments of 1990 stipulate substantial behavioral changes in the years ahead. To comprehend these changes, students need to understand both the consequences of pollution and the costs of environmental protection. Chapter 27 provides this perspective as it seeks to illustrate the core problem of externalities and to develop the concept of *optimal* pollution.

Government failure vs. market failure   Environmental protection is just one dimension of a much broader issue. At the core of most policy debates is the question of market failure. If unregulated markets always generated the optimal mix of output, full employment, and an equitable distribution of income, there would be no need for government intervention. In reality, of course, markets do fail and the government is called upon to move the economy closer to desired outcomes.

But does government intervention succeed? Does intervention move us closer to the optimal mix of output or the optimal distribution of income? If not, government intervention fails as well. In the real world, the choice is not between imperfect markets and perfect intervention, but between imperfect markets and imperfect policies. The nature and cost of these real-world choices is a unifying theme throughout *The Economy Today*.

Balanced Macro Theory

The Economy Today offers no simple answers. Indeed, a familiar lament of students who read this text is that they don't know which theory is the correct one. This is particularly evident in macro, where students are exposed to the competing advice of Keynesians, Monetarists, Supply-siders, and the new breed of Rational Expectationists. Rather than try to "sell" one of these theories, *The Economy Today* presents and discusses each of these perspectives. Students are introduced to the controversies of economic theory and policy at the outset. They are also shown how the different schools of thought would respond to specific policy questions. In this way, students gain not only a sense of major theoretical debates, but also an appreciation for conflicting policy advice. This is part and parcel of critical thinking.

This macro balance is first evident in Chapter 5, where competing explanations of the business cycle are introduced. In Chapter 14, separate sections are provided for Keynesian and monetarist views of monetary policy. Tables 14.1 and 14.2 offer explicit, contrasting interpretations of both fiscal and monetary policy. A graphical contrast of fiscal, monetary, and supply-side perspectives is offered in Chapter 15. Finally, Chapter 17 provides a roster of competing theories (p. 432) and their differing prescriptions for our economic ills (pp. 410–417). This capsule summary is an excellent review tool.

Careful Pedagogy

Economic principles were put to use in designing *The Economy Today*. The opportunity cost of trying to cover everything was crystal clear. Encyclopedic texts leave the average student floundering. The choice made here was to cover less material but cover it thoroughly. The emphasis is on step-by-step development of core concepts, with a generous dose of real-world illustrations.

The emphasis on *teaching* basic principles is evident in an assortment of pedagogical features, including:

• *Clear Graphs* All of the graphs are clearly labeled, fully annotated, and highlighted with colors. The time dimension is always included when *flows* are being examined.

• *Annotated Tables* This shouldn't be a differentiating feature but it still is. *All* of the tables in *The Economy Today* include self-contained explanations.

- *Running and Repeated Glossary* Most other texts have now adopted *The Economy Today*'s pioneering in-margin glossary. This remains, however, the only text that *repeats* in-margin definitions in subsequent chapters. Unfortunately, few people grasp and retain core concepts after only one exposure. *The Economy Today* recognizes this real-world limitation and offers students some additional support. Learning and retention are further encouraged by end-of-chapter key-term reviews and a complete glossary (with chapter references) at the end of the book.

- *Motivating Questions* Every chapter starts out with a few questions to pique student interest. A brief introduction highlights the general coverage of the chapter. This is followed by key questions, which forge a direct link between the introductory illustration and the core objectives of the chapter.

Lively Style   Pedagogy is more than just technique and organization. Style is also important. Dull writing dulls the learning process. The *motivation* to learn must be reinforced with interesting examples, sharp wit, and clever phrases. This isn't a novel, but it is a very readable economics text—students actually *enjoy* it.

MACRO HIGHLIGHTS

There are several important changes in the macro portion of this fifth edition. Among these are:

Unifying Model of Aggregate Supply and Demand   A new diagrammatic summary of the macro economy has been introduced as a unifying framework for the entire macro sequence. An overview of the model—depicting the major determinants, mechanisms, and outcomes of the macro economy—is introduced in Chapter 5 (see figure on p. 109). This diagram is then used with appropriate color highlighting to introduce each part of the macro sequence. Notice in the figure on p. 181, for example, how the Keynesian focus on aggregate demand, fiscal policy, and jobs and output is highlighted. The accompanying annotation gives students a sense of how the subsequent four chapters relate to the general model. Similar introductions are provided for monetary policy, supply-side approaches, policy issues, and international economics. These unifying diagrams should help students see how all the pieces of the macro puzzle fit together.

A succinct overview   A riveting account of the Great Depression introduces students to the business cycle—the core concern of macro theory. Chapter 5 also provides "previews" of macro policy options and the theoretical controversies about their use. Separate chapters on unemployment (Chapter 6) and inflation (Chapter 7) can be used either at the outset of the course or later. These chapters are designed to increase student awareness of why unemployment and inflation are major policy concerns; explanations for these macro ills are contained in the theory sequences.

Repositioning of debt and deficits   The chapter on debt and deficits has now been placed immediately after the discussion of fiscal policy (Chapter 10). This facilitates a more complete discussion of budget policy while providing a smoother transition to monetary issues. This chapter still traces the origins of the national debt, examines its current dimensions, and assesses its real costs. The Policy Insights section assesses the nature and appropriateness of debt- and deficit-limitation legislation.

Short- vs. long-run aggregate supply More space is devoted in this edition to the nature and position of the aggregate supply curve. The distinction between short- and long-run aggregate supply is made in Chapter 5. The "eclectic" aggregate supply curve—an amalgam of Keynesian, monetarist, and supply-side perspectives—is also introduced at the outset as a practical reconciliation of competing views. Chapter 16, Economic Growth, now immediately follows the supply-side chapter and is more closely integrated with it.

Capstone chapter on theory vs. reality Students never fail to recognize that the world doesn't work nearly so well as theory. Indeed, they often raise the question "If economic theory is so good, why is the economy so messed up?" There's usually an unstated implication that our theories are wrong or, worse still, irrelevant.

Chapter 17 addresses the apparent gap between theory and reality. It starts with a summary of the major macro theories and a review of their potential use in different economic settings (recession, inflation, stagflation). Then the discussion turns to real-world impediments, including measurement, design, and implementation problems. The message of this chapter is there is no *ceteris paribus* in the real world—economic policy is not as easy as economic theory often seems. The chapter ends with a discussion of policy expectations and the Bush administration's emphasis on policy credibility.

A global perspective The global vision of *The Economy Today* has already been noted. Some further explanation of Chapter 18, Global Macro, is called for, however. This chapter was expressly written for instructors who want to cover some international topics in macro but don't have time for chapter-length treatments of trade theory and finance theory. Chapter 18 offers a shortcut. This is a self-contained explanation of how international markets impinge on macro policy (and vice versa). The chapter may be used as the only discussion of global macro, without first mastering trade and finance theories, or used as a capstone to the traditional trade and finance sequence.

MICRO HIGHLIGHTS

The micro portion of *The Economy Today* has been revised extensively. The major revisions include a strengthening of the introduction to supply and demand (Chapters 2 and 19), a reconfiguration of the basic theory of the firm sequence (especially Chapters 21 and 22), an expansion of the discussion of antitrust and regulation (Chapters 25 and 26), a consolidation of the labor chapters (Chapter 29), and new discussions of financial markets (Chapters 31 and 34).

Competitive firms and industries The traditional chapter on competitive behavior has been expanded to two chapters. Chapter 21 focuses on the competitive *firm,* showing how it makes production, shutdown, and investment decisions. Chapter 22 focuses on a competitive *industry,* emphasizing the role of entry and exit in changing market outcomes. This extended treatment should help students grasp the unique characteristics of both competitive firms and the market (industry) environment in which they function. Explicit contrasts to the behavior and outcomes of monopoly and other industry structures are provided in subsequent chapters (e.g., see p. 607). Contrasts with centrally planned economies are also included (e.g., see World View on p. 573).

Antitrust and regulation   The antitrust and regulatory discussions have been placed in sequence (Chapters 25 and 26) and expanded. The antitrust discussion makes a sharp distinction between market *structure* and *behavior* and introduces the Herfindahl-Hirshman Index as a pragmatic guide to antitrust policy. The chapter on regulation begins with a review of the sources of market failure, then focuses on the unique regulatory choices posed by natural monopoly. The cable TV industry and World Views on European and Japanese telephone monopolies enliven the discussion.

Consolidated labor sequence   This edition combines the discussions of labor supply and demand into a single chapter (Chapter 29). The new labor market chapter provides a capsule explanation of labor supply, based on substitution and income effects, and a longer discussion of labor demand. The impacts of new minimum wage rates and the influx of immigrants into American and Western European labor markets are examined.

Risk and entrepreneurship   Rather than take risk and entrepreneurship for granted, *The Economy Today* emphasizes their critical role in allocating resources, innovating new products, and expanding our production possibilities. This greater visibility is apparent in Chapter 31, Rent, Interest, and Profit (including a discussion of venture capitalism); Chapter 32, Taxes and Inequality (including the pros and cons of a capital gains tax cut); and the all-new Chapter 34, Financial Markets. The failure of centrally planned economies to exploit the power of entrepreneurship is discussed in Chapter 38.

INTERNATIONAL HIGHLIGHTS

The global vision that epitomizes *The Economy Today* is apparent throughout the text. The final four chapters, however, focus exclusively on international topics. In this revision, highlights for these chapters include:

United States as a net debtor   In 1987 the international position of the United States was reversed, making this country a net debtor in the world economy. This change in investment flows has been accompanied by increasing anxiety over foreign investments in the United States. Indeed, in a recent Harris poll for *Business Week,* two out of three Americans said they expected foreign companies to dominate the American economy in the 1990s. These concerns are addressed in Chapters 35 and 36. In addition to developing and illustrating basic trade and finance theories, these chapters discuss the competing interests that seek to alter trade and finance outcomes.

Eastern Europe and Third World development   The consequences of slow growth became apparent when the Iron Curtain was dismantled. Like the Third World, the countries of Eastern and Central Europe are desperately seeking mechanisms that will accelerate growth. Although Eastern Europe enjoys much higher living standards than the Third World, both groups of nations face common obstacles (e.g., bloated state enterprises, weak currencies, consumer subsidies, and high debt). Chapter 37 examines these common growth barriers and alternative strategies for overcoming them.

Collapse of Communism   The final chapter provides a cautious, analytical assessment of the revolutionary changes taking place in the Eastern bloc. In addition to spotlighting the defects of central planning, Chapter 38 emphasizes the political, social, and economic forces that are setting the pace of transition. Examples are drawn from Eastern Europe, the Soviet Union, China, and Cuba. The chapter was designed for use either as a capstone to the macro or micro sequences or, alternatively, as an earlier contrast to the robustness of the market mechanism (e.g., after Chapter 2).

PEDAGOGICAL HIGHLIGHTS

The fifth edition of *The Economy Today* is a bit more rigorous than earlier editions. This added rigor has been made possible by the deletion or consolidation of secondary topics, with more space devoted to the development of basic principles. This is most evident in Chapters 2 and 19, the foundations of supply and demand. More visible revisions to the pedagogy include:

- *Chapter-Opening Questions* As noted earlier, every chapter now starts with questions designed to guide and stimulate the learning process.

- *More End-of-Chapter Problems* Additional numerical problems have been included, giving instructors more choices of homework or in-class assignments. Answers to all problems are in the *Instructor's Manual.*

- *Greater Integration of Tables and Graphs* The Economy Today was the first book to tie tables and related graphs closely together by synchronizing the labeling of table rows and points on corresponding graphs. The fifth edition takes this innovation a step further by incorporating more tables and graphs into the same figure (see, for example, p. 37).

- *Functional Use of Color* This is the first edition of *The Economy Today* to be published in four colors. The goal of this "colorization" has been *functional,* not merely aesthetic. Consistent use of color screening and logos sets off key features (e.g., World Views). Consistency in the use of broken and smooth curves, together with color screening, highlights shifts of supply and demand curves (e.g., p. 128).

- *Integrating Theme* The various sections of the text are explicitly related to the overriding issue of government intervention. Can markets do the job? Or is government intervention needed? This broad issue is restated repeatedly throughout the text, giving students a consistent framework in which to learn and apply economic principles.

- *Critical Thinking* By confronting students with the recurrent use of market vs. government failure, *The Economy Today* stimulates students to apply economic principles. Rather than just memorizing terminology, students are encouraged to think critically about the use of economic theory in the world today.

A COMPLETE TEACHING AND LEARNING PACKAGE

The various parts of the teaching and learning package to accompany *The Economy Today* have been closely coordinated with one another and include a new and unique focus on critical thinking through reading newspapers and periodicals. In addition, painstaking efforts were made to keep *The Economy Today* error-free, from beginning to end, with a consistency of style, level, and approach throughout the text.

Paperbacks In this edition, the text is again available in paperback splits. The macro half contains Chapters 1–18 and 34–38. The micro half contains Chapters 1–3 and 19–38.

Student Learning Aids *Study Guide*   Several supplements accompany the text. From the student's perspective, the most important of the supplements is the *Study Guide,* prepared by Professors Michael Tansey at Rockhurst College and Lawrence Ziegler at the University of Texas (Arlington). There is a full-text *Study Guide* and, once again, macro and micro versions are also available. The *Study Guide* develops skills in mathematics and the use of economic terminology and enhances critical thinking capabilities. Each chapter of the *Study Guide* contains these features:

QUICK REVIEW   Key points in the text chapter are restated at the beginning of each *Study Guide* chapter. The reviews are parallel to and reinforce the chapter summaries provided in the text.

LEARNING OBJECTIVES   The salient lessons of the text chapters are noted at the outset of each *Study Guide* chapter. These objectives focus the student's study and help to ensure that key points will not be overlooked. The objectives are keyed to the exercises in the *Study Guide* to help reinforce learning.

KEY-TERM REVIEW   Early in each chapter the students are asked to match definitions with key terms. This relatively simple exercise is designed to refresh the student's memory and provide a basis for subsequent exercises.

TRUE–FALSE QUESTIONS   Twenty or so true–false questions are provided in each chapter. These questions have been class tested to ensure their effectiveness in highlighting basic principles.

MULTIPLE-CHOICE QUESTIONS   Approximately fifteen multiple-choice questions per chapter are provided. These questions allow only one correct answer and also focus on basic principles.

PROBLEMS AND APPLICATIONS   There are more than forty exercises in the *Study Guide,* most of which stress current issues and events.

MEDIA ASSIGNMENTS   Refined from the previous edition and with extensive classroom testing, media assignments have been included for most chapters in the textbook. Each assignment requires the student to find and copy a newspaper or magazine article, and then underline a few words that illustrate the required economic idea. Because each assignment is carefully and precisely specified following an example provided in the *Study Guide,* the assignments require a minimum of explanation, and grading is fast and easy.

COMMON ERRORS   In each chapter of the *Study Guide,* errors that students frequently make are identified. The bases for those errors are then explained, along with the correct principles. This unique feature is very effective in helping students discover their own mistakes.

ANSWERS   Answers to *all* problems, exercises, and questions are provided at the end of each chapter. Difficult problems have annotated answers. These answers make the *Study Guide* self-contained, thus allowing students to use it for self-study.

Student software   For those interested in computer-assisted instruction, several economic software programs are available.

INTERACTIVE GRAPHICS TUTORIAL II   Interactive Graphics Tutorial II is an upgraded version of McGraw-Hill's very successful economics software program developed by H. Scott Bierman at Carlton College and Todd Proebsting (University of Wisconsin). Thousands of students have used the Interactive Graphics Tutorial to learn, understand, and reinforce their study of economic graphics. This updated and technically advanced version includes microcomputer simulations.

GRAPHICS TUTOR   The Graphics Tutor is available in three packages: microeconomics, macroeconomics, and principles of economics. Each package presents tutorials that help students learn fundamental ideas in economics through the extensive and dynamic use of graphs.

VIZECON   For users of MacIntosh computers, there is an exciting new tutorial program, *VizEcon.* Developed by Professor William A. Phillips at the University of Southern Maine, this innovative package uses Apple's HYPERCARD programming environment to produce an extremely interactive learning experience. Dynamic shifts of curves, screen animation, sound effects, and simple-to-use command keys are features of this program. Its development was underwritten by grant funds and consultation from Apple Computer Inc.

Instructor Teaching Aids

Why not try to make the learning process easier for teachers as well as students? To this end, the teaching package includes several items valued by instructors:

News Flashes   As up-to-date as *The Economy Today* is, it can't foretell the future. As the future becomes the present, however, Bradley Schiller writes News Flashes describing major economic events and relating them to specific text references. For this edition, adopters of *The Economy Today* have the option of receiving News Flashes nearly instantaneously via FAX. Four to six News Flashes are sent to adopters each year.

Instructor's Resource Manual   Donald Pearson at Eastern Michigan University has fully revised his *Instructor's Resource Manual* for this edition, with new sections designed to make the test more effective and easier to use. It has several innovations. First, an introductory chapter is devoted entirely to instructional tools and contains references to instructional handbooks, workbooks, newspapers, magazines, student subscription programs, and customized readings. Second, a chapter-by-chapter review of the text provides tools, suggestions, and hints for effective use of classroom time devoted to each chapter. Features include:

CONTENTS IN BRIEF   A brief outline gives a quick overview of the chapter.

WHAT IS THIS CHAPTER ALL ABOUT?   New and unique features of each chapter are explained and key critical thinking goals are stressed.

LECTURE SUGGESTIONS   General suggestions for the direction lecturers might take and one or more *lecture launchers* for introducing the material are offered.

SOME COMMON PROBLEMS   Topics in each chapter which tend to be problematic for students are reviewed. The section has drawn on the expertise of instructors who have used previous editions of the text in both small classes and large lectures.

ANNOTATED CONTENTS IN DETAIL   An outline of each text chapter is completely annotated. It can be used for building lectures or it can be distributed to students as a study guide.

TAKE A STAND   A controversial question is posed about one issue in the chapter which is illustrated by either an In the News or World View box. The question is followed by one paragraph in support of the issue and one paragraph in opposition. No resolution of the issue is offered. Take a Stand is intended to motivate classroom discussion or to form the basis for essay questions.

QUESTIONS FOR DISCUSSION   The questions from the end of the text chapter are repeated and answers or guidelines for answers are provided to all questions.

ANSWERS TO PROBLEMS   Here you will find the answers to problems at the end of the text chapters.

SUPPLEMENTARY RESOURCES   This final section provides two kinds of information. First, it contains annotated references of videotapes or films relevant to the text chapter. Second, it contains a brief bibliography of articles and books that can be used for additional reading assignments or suggestions for students. These also provide a quick guide of sources to use for expanding lecture materials.

MEDIA EXERCISES   These tear-out assignments require the student to find an example from the media to illustrate an economic concept. There is approximately one per chapter. After each exercise, professor's notes and lecture opportunities are provided.

Test Bank   The Test Bank to accompany *The Economy Today* follows the lead of the textbook in its application of economic concepts to worldwide economic issues, current real-world examples, and the role of government in the economy. Now prepared by the *Study Guide* authors, Michael Tansey and Lawrence Ziegler, together with Bruce Kelley at Florida International University, the Test Bank has been significantly strengthened. The new authorship team helps assure not only a high level of quality and consistency of the test questions, but the fullest possible correlation with the content of the text and *Study Guide.* The Test Bank will be published in two separate volumes, each with over 3,000 objective, predominantly multiple-choice, questions; either volume can be used to construct tests to cover all the material in a chapter.

Computerized testing   Computerized versions of the Test Bank are available for both IBM-PC computers and compatibles and MacIntosh computers. The programs allow instructors to view, edit, and test questions to create exams.

Customized test   Instructors may have tests custom prepared by the publisher by calling the publisher's special test service. Masters prepared from the Test Bank will be mailed out within seventy-two hours.

Overhead Transparencies   One hundred of the key tables and graphs in the text have been reproduced as full-color overhead transparency acetates. These are made available to adopters by the publisher.

ACKNOWLEDGMENTS

The Economy Today continues to benefit from the advice and suggestions of users and reviewers. I am particularly grateful to those individuals who scrutinized the fourth edition or reviewed drafts of this fifth edition. With my profound appreciation for their contributions, I thank

Thomas Anderson
Montgomery Community College

Masato Aoki
University of Massachusetts at Amherst

John Azer
Normandale Community College

Andrew Barnett
Auburn University

Erwin Blackstone
Temple University

Wallace Broome
Community College of Rhode Island

E. Ray Canterbery
Florida State University

Basil Cooil
Tompkins Cortland Community College

Duane Eberhardt
Missouri Southern State College

Ray Egan
Pierce College

John Farrell
Oregon State University

John Fizel
Pennsylvania State University–Erie

Roger Frantz
San Diego State University

Carl Guelzo
Catonsville Community College

Robert Harris
Economics Consultant to the
Superintendent of Education in
California

Elizabeth Hill
Pennsylvania State University–
Mont Alto

Christopher Inya
Monroe Community College

Walter Johnson
University of Missouri

M. W. Keil
Northeastern University

Bruce Kelley
Florida International University

William Kerby
California State University–Sacramento

Stephen E. Lile
Western Kentucky University

W. L. Loh
Mohawk Valley Community College

Carol McDonough
University of Lowell

Farhang Niroomand
University of Southern Mississippi

John Pearce
North Georgia College

Donald Pearson
Eastern Michigan University

Ronald Schuelke
Santa Rosa Junior College

Augustus Shakelford
El Camino College

Marsha Shelburn
University of South Carolina at Aiken

Dorothy Siden
Salem State College

Larry Singell
University of Colorado–Boulder

Donald Smith
Boston University

Gary Sorenson
Oregon State University

Richard Spivack
Bryant College

Michael M. Tansey
Rockhurst College

Peter Turner
Herkimer County Community College

Jack Wegman
Santa Rosa Junior College

William Zeis
Bucks County Community College

Lawrence F. Ziegler
University of Texas at Arlington

Publishing Team This is the first edition of *The Economy Today* to be published by McGraw-Hill, which, I was told, acquired the Random House college division just to get this text. I don't believe that, but have been very impressed by the care and attention McGraw-Hill has devoted to this book. Jim Bittker in particular has been instrumental in generating ideas, mobilizing reviewers and resources, and attending to the quality and timeliness of every stage of production. Editing Supervisor Elaine Rosenberg kept the project rolling and made sure I didn't take any days off. Chuck Carson created a distinctive cover and text design. Leroy Young oversaw the production process. Lastly, thanks are due to Carole Schwager, copy editor, for her meticulous work on both the text and *Study Guide.*

Personals Thanks again to Tricia, Justin, and Ashley, who helped me in many tangible ways and inspired me in countless intangible ways.

Bradley R. Schiller

THE ECONOMY TODAY

BASICS

CHAPTER 1

An Overview

People worry about love, the weather, and the economy. But not necessarily in that order. According to public-opinion polls, the economy is always one of our foremost concerns. Government deficits, taxes, unemployment, and rising prices are consistently at the top of our collective list of worries. A Yankelovich poll taken in 1990 illustrates this concern. When asked what the country's most important problem was, three out of four Americans pointed to the drug problem. However, four out of ten cited economic concerns, including unemployment, government spending, budget deficits, and inflation.

Another poll showed just how much people worry about the economy. As the following In the News box reveals, nearly half the population is "very concerned" about inflation, unemployment, foreign competition, and economic growth in the 1990s. Few people claim to be unconcerned.

Even more remarkable is the response to a Gallup poll taken in October 1943. That poll asked people what they thought the greatest problem facing the country would be in the year ahead. Although the nation was deeply involved in World War II, most Americans thought jobs and economic readjustment would be our greatest problems. Little concern was expressed for the prospects of peace.[1]

For many people, of course, concern for the economy goes no further than the price of tuition or the fear of losing a job. Many others, however, are becoming increasingly aware that their job prospects and the prices they pay are somehow related to national trends in prices, unemployment, and economic growth. Although few people think in terms of price indexes, graphs, or economic cycles, most of us now recognize the importance of major economic events. And that is why so many people worry about such abstractions as unemployment rates, inflation, economic growth, trade deficits, and budget deficits.

Despite the widespread concern for the economy, few people really understand how it works. You can hardly blame them. For one thing, the very dimensions of the economy tend to obscure its relevance. The annual output of our economy is now measured in trillions of dollars. For those of us who rarely see a $100 bill, it is difficult to comprehend such figures. The significance of billion-dollar changes in output is easily lost on people who are trying to figure out how to pay this month's rent or next semester's tuition.

[1]George H. Gallup, *The Gallup Poll: Public Opinion 1935–1971* (New York: Random House, 1972), vol. 1, p. 410.

In The News

ECONOMIC CONCERNS

Worried About Wealth

Responses to a Harris poll of 1,250 adults reported in *BUSINESS WEEK*.

Question: How concerned are you about each of these threats to prosperity in the 1990s—very concerned, somewhat concerned, not very concerned, or not concerned at all?

BUSINESS WEEK, SEPTEMBER 25, 1989, p. 175.

	Very concerned	Somewhat	Not very	Not at all	Not sure
Inflation	49%	36%	9%	5%	1%
Unemployment	49%	29%	12%	9%	1%
Foreign competition	47%	31%	10%	9%	3%
Decline in economic growth	42%	40%	10%	7%	1%
Another stock market crash	31%	29%	19%	20%	1%

However abstract "the economy" might seem, it is very much a part of our everyday lives. We spend much of our lives working to produce the goods and services that flow from our factories and offices. We spend a good part of the remaining time consuming those same goods and services. And during much of the time left over, we worry about what to produce or consume next. Even such simple things as reading this book, going to school, and lying on the beach can be described as economic activities.

Interest in the workings of the economy intensifies when we have some immediate stake in its performance. The loss of a job, for example, can rivet one's attention on the causes of unemployment. A tuition increase may start you thinking about the nature and causes of inflation. And high rents can start you thinking about the demand for housing in relation to its supply.

What we seek to determine, then, is not simply whether we are involved in the economy—a fact nearly everyone can accept with a shrug—but more important, *how* we are involved and where our interests lie.

Two key questions must be answered:

• **What forces shape the economy?** What determines how many jobs will be available? how much income people will receive? what goods will be produced? how much pollution will be created?

• **What, if anything, can we do to improve the economy's performance?** Can government policy create more jobs, raise incomes, or reduce prices? Can individual consumers, workers, or producers affect economic outcomes?

THE ECONOMY IS US

In seeking to figure out how the economy works, it is useful to start with a simple truth—namely, that *the economy is us*. "The economy" is simply an abstraction that refers to the sum of all our individual production and consumption activities. What we collectively produce is what the economy produces; what we collectively consume is what the economy consumes. In this sense, the concept of "the economy" is no more difficult than the concept of "the family." If someone tells you that the Jones family has an annual income of $22,000, you know that the reference is to the collective earnings of all the Joneses. Hence when someone reports that the nation's income exceeds $5 trillion per year—as it now does—we should recognize immediately that the reference is to the sum of our individual incomes. If we work fewer hours or get paid less, family income and national income both decline. Thus to understand our own economic behavior is to understand the economy.

The same relationship between individual behavior and aggregate behavior applies to specific outputs as well. If we as individuals insist on driving cars rather than walking or taking public transportation, the economy will produce millions of cars each year and consume vast quantities of oil. In a slightly different way, the economy produces and consumes billions of dollars of military hardware to satisfy our desire for national defense. In each case, the output of the economy reflects the collective efforts and demands of the 250 million individuals who participate in the economy. In these very tangible dimensions, the economy is truly us.

We may not always be happy with the output of the economy, of course. But we cannot deny the essential link between individual action and collective outcomes. If the highways are clogged and the air is polluted as a consequence of our transportation choices, we cannot blame someone else for our predicament. If we are disturbed by the size of our military arsenal, we must still accept responsibility for our choices (or nonchoices, if we failed to vote). In either case, we continue to have the option of reallocating our efforts or rearranging our priorities. We can create a different outcome the next day, month, or year.

"Meaningless statistics were up one-point-five per cent this month over last month."

Drawing by Dana Fradon; © 1977 The New Yorker Magazine, Inc.

THE NATURE OF ECONOMIC CHOICE

factors of production: Resource inputs used to produce goods and services, e.g, land, labor, capital.

Although we can change economic outcomes, we cannot have everything we want. In order to produce anything, we need resources, or factors of production. **Factors of production** are the inputs—land, labor, and capital (buildings and machinery)—we use to produce final goods and services (output). To produce this textbook, we needed paper, printing presses, a building, and lots of labor. To produce the education you are getting in this class, we need not only a textbook but a classroom, a teacher, and a blackboard as well. Without factors of production, we simply cannot produce anything.

Unfortunately, the quantity of available resources is limited. We cannot produce everything we want in the quantities we desire. Resources are scarce relative to our desires. This fact forces us to make difficult choices. The building space we use for your economics class cannot be used to show Charlie Chaplin movies at the same time. Your professor cannot lecture (produce education) and repair a car simultaneously. Likewise, the more labor and machinery used to dig holes in the ground for missiles, the less is available to dig holes for swimming pools. Hence the more missiles we build, the less of other goods and services we can produce at the same time. This is the classic "guns vs. butter" problem. It is especially relevant to the economy today. If American defense output (guns) is curtailed in response to easing East–West tensions in Europe, we will have more resources available for producing other goods and services (butter). The accompanying In the News box indicates some of the goods and services that might be included in such a "peace dividend." Notice how many homes could be built with just the resources needed to produce a single B-2 bomber.

Opportunity Costs

opportunity cost: The most desired goods or services that are forgone in order to obtain something else.

The dilemma of guns vs. butter typifies our economic problem. ***Because our resources are limited, we are compelled to choose among goods and services.*** Even the time you spend reading this book illustrates the problem. The labor time you devote to reading this book reduces the amount of time you have for other activities. You could be sleeping, watching television, or using your time in some other way. The true cost of reading this book, then, is whatever you would really like to be doing right now but can't because you have to complete this reading assignment. As long as you continue to read this book, you are sacrificing the *opportunity* to use your time in some other way. This sacrifice is your **opportunity cost** of reading these pages.[2]

Opportunity costs exist in all situations where available resources are not abundant enough to satisfy all our desires. In all such situations, we must make hard decisions about how to allocate our scarce resources among competing uses. Because our wants and desires generally exceed our resources, ***everything we do involves an opportunity cost.***

Opportunity costs are relevant not only to personal decision making, but also to the decisions of an entire economy. Consider the guns vs. butter dilemma again. The production of a nuclear attack submarine uses land, labor, and capital worth roughly $600 million. That same quantity of resources could build 100 miles of electrified railroad (or thousands of other things). But those resources cannot be used to produce *both* goods at once. Hence if we choose

---

[2]By the way, if you continue reading, we can conclude that you expect the benefits of doing this homework to exceed their opportunity cost, and thus that doing your homework will be "worthwhile."

In The News

OPPORTUNITY COSTS

The Peace Dividend

The current easing of Cold War tensions gives Congress and the Bush administration a chance to reverse the military buildup of the 1980s. During the 1980s defense buildup, the percentage of GNP allocated to nondefense investment fell to a post–World War II low.

Defense Secretary Richard Cheney has said that the fall of the Iron Curtain could allow the United States to cut $120 billion from the defense budget over five years. This "peace dividend" represents resources that could be allocated to other uses. Here are some possible uses of the peace dividend:

8% of estimated military spending	$120 billion	Cost of cleaning up and modernizing nuclear weapons plants
Advanced technology fighter	$40 billion	Cost of repairing the nation's 240,000 deficient bridges
Navy's V-22 Osprey program	$25 billion	Cost of modernizing the air-traffic control system
SDI expenditures (1991)	$5 billion	50% increase in all university research budgets
One B-2 bomber	$532 million	Cost of buying housing for 8,000 families
One M-1 tank	$2.6 million	Full four-year college costs for 50 students
One Phoenix air-to-air missile	$1 million	Cost of nursing home care for 35 elderly citizens

Source: Data Resources, Inc.

Produce this . . .

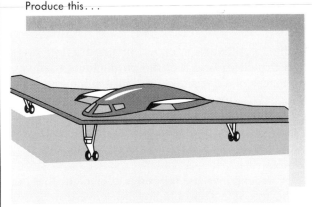

or this?

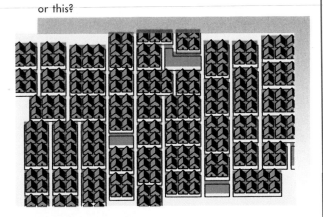

to build the sub, we forsake the opportunity to build an additional 100 miles of railroad. The 100 miles of forgone railroad is the *opportunity cost* of building one nuclear attack sub. If we make the opposite choice—that is, build more railroads and fewer subs—then the forgone sub would be the opportunity cost of the additional 100 miles of railroad. The opportunity cost of anything is the best forgone alternative.

economics: The study of how best to allocate scarce resources among competing uses.

The concept of opportunity cost is basic to economic decision making. Indeed, **economics** is often defined as the study of how to allocate scarce resources. The study of economics focuses on "getting the most from what we've got," on making the *best* use of our scarce resources. In these terms, reading this book right now represents the *best* use of your time if it ultimately yields greater satisfaction (from higher grades, if nothing else) than any other use of the same time. Production of additional nuclear submarines represents the *best* use of society's resources only if the additional subs are more highly valued than any other goods or services that could be produced with the same factors of production.

PRODUCTION POSSIBILITIES

The opportunity costs implied by our every choice can be easily illustrated. Imagine for the moment that labor (workers) is the only factor of production used to produce either submarines or railroads and that no other goods are desired. Although other factors of production (land, machinery) are also needed in actual production, ignoring them for the moment does no harm. Let us assume further that we have a total of 1,000 workers (labor) available in a given year, and that they can be used to produce either subs or railroads. Our initial problem is to determine how many subs or railroads can be produced in a year under such circumstances.

Before going any further, notice how opportunity costs will affect our answer. If we employ all 1,000 workers in the production of nuclear submarines, then no labor will be available to build railroads. In this case, forgone railroads would become the opportunity cost of a decision to use all our resources in the production of submarines.

We still do not know how many submarines could be built with 1,000 workers or exactly how many railroads would be forgone by such a decision. To get these answers, we must know a little more about the production process involved—specifically, how many workers are required to build a nuclear sub or a railroad.

production possibilities: The alternative combinations of final goods and services that could be produced in a given time period with all available resources and technology.

Table 1.1 summarizes the hypothetical choices, or **production possibilities,** that we confront in this case. Row *A* of the production-possibilities schedule shows the consequences of a decision to produce submarines only. With 1,000 workers available and a labor requirement of 200 workers per sub, we can build a *maximum* of five subs per year. By so doing, however, we use up all our available resources, leaving nothing for railroad construction. If we want railroads, we have to cut back on submarine construction; this is the essential choice we must make.

The remainder of Table 1.1 describes the full range of choices that confronts us. By cutting back the rate of sub production from five to four subs per year (row *B*), we reduce labor use from 1,000 workers to 800. The remaining 200 workers are then available for other uses, including railroad construction. If we in fact employ these workers to lay rails, we can build one new railroad per year. In this case, we end up with four new subs and one new railroad per year. What is the opportunity cost of that railroad? It is the one additional submarine that we could have built but did not, in order to make factors of production (labor) available for railroad construction.

As we proceed down the rows of Table 1.1, the nature of opportunity costs becomes apparent. Each additional railroad built implies the loss (op-

TABLE 1.1 Production-Possibilities Schedule
(for one year)

So long as resources are limited, their use entails an opportunity cost. In this case, resources (labor) used to produce nuclear submarines cannot be used to produce railroads at the same time. Hence forgone railroads are the opportunity cost of additional subs. If all of our resources were used to produce subs (row *A*), no railroads could be built.

| | Total available labor | Submarines | | | Railroads | | |
		Number × of subs	Labor needed per sub	= Total labor required for subs	Labor not used for subs	÷ Labor needed per railroad	= Number of potential railroads
A	1,000	5	200	1,000	0	200	0
B	1,000	4	200	800	200	200	1
C	1,000	3	200	600	400	200	2
D	1,000	2	200	400	600	200	3
E	1,000	1	200	200	800	200	4
F	1,000	0	200	0	1,000	200	5

portunity cost) of one nuclear submarine. Likewise, every sub built implies the loss of one railroad.

These tradeoffs between railroads and submarines are illustrated in the production-possibilities curve of Figure 1.1. ***Each point on the production-possibilities curve depicts an alternative mix of output*** that could be produced. In this case, each point represents a different combination of railroads and submarines that we could produce, using all available resources (labor in this case) and technology.

Notice in particular how points *A* through *F* in Figure 1.1 represent the choices described in each row of Table 1.1. At point *A*, we are producing five

FIGURE 1.1
A Linear Production-Possibilities Curve

A production-possibilities curve describes the various combinations of final goods or services that could be produced in a given time period with available resources and technology. It represents a "menu" of output choices an economy confronts. Point *B* indicates that we could produce a *combination* of four submarines and one railroad per year. By giving up one sub, we could produce a second railroad, and thus move to point *C*. Points *A, D, E,* and *F* illustrate still other output combinations that could be produced. This curve is a graphic illustration of the production-possibilities schedule provided in Table 1.1

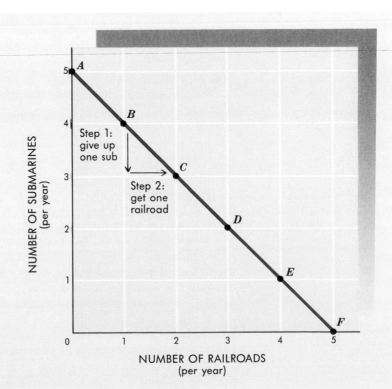

subs per year and no railroads. As we move from point *A* to point *B*, we are decreasing submarine production from five to four subs per year while increasing railroad construction from zero to one. In other words, we are giving up one sub to get one railroad. The opportunity cost of the railroad is the one sub that is given up. A production-possibilities curve, then, is simply a graphic summary of production possibilities, as described in Table 1.1. The purpose of the production-possibilities table and graph is to illustrate the hard choices we must make when resources are scarce. They illustrate the alternative goods and services we could produce—and the implied opportunity costs of each choice.

In summary, ***the production-possibilities curve illustrates two essential principles:***

- ***Scarce resources.*** There is a limit to the amount we can produce in a given time period with available resources and technology.

- ***Opportunity costs.*** We can obtain additional quantities of any desired good only by reducing the potential production of another good.

Increasing Opportunity Costs

Although Figure 1.1 illustrates the principles of scarcity and opportunity costs, it depicts an overly optimistic view of our production possibilities. When we reduce the rate of output of one good in order to get more of another, we have to reallocate factors of production from one industry to another. In order to get more railroads, for example, we have to take workers out of nuclear submarine construction and put them to work laying rails. No magic wand is available to transform nuclear subs into railroads. Instead, the rails must be laid with the same factors of production that would otherwise be used in submarine production. As a consequence, ***our ability to alter the mix of output depends in part on the capability of factors of production to move from one industry to another.***

As we contemplate the possibilities of moving resources from one industry to another, two issues arise. First, can the resources be moved? Second, how efficient will the resources be in a new line of production?

In our example, it is probably safe to assume that workers can move from submarine construction to railroad construction. We have made this kind of move after every modern war. But it is also likely that some efficiency will be lost in the process. Workers who have been constructing submarines for several years will probably not be as adept at building railroads. As a result, we will not be able to "transform" subs into railroads so easily. Instead, we may discover that sooner or later *more* than 200 submarine workers are needed to construct one railroad. If so, the opportunity cost of one new railroad will be more than one potential sub.

One reason for this higher opportunity cost is the different skills required for submarine and railroad construction. Both industries need welders, for example. But in railroad construction a weld must be secure, not necessarily airtight. The welds on nuclear subs, on the other hand, must be completely airtight, or the sub may never resurface. So when we start to move welders out of submarine construction and into railroad development, we will move the worst welders first. That will minimize our losses in submarine production while increasing our output of railroads.

As we continue to move labor from sub production to railroad construction, the remaining sub builders are likely to be the least adept at laying rails or the most adept at building subs. This has important implications for opportunity costs. Each additional worker allocated to railroad construction will produce less output. Conversely, each worker taken out of submarine construction will cause an even greater reduction in sub output. In either case, we are likely to get fewer railroads for each potential sub given up. The opportunity cost of railroads increases as more railroads are produced.

Increasing opportunity costs are illustrated in Figure 1.2. We still have 1,000 workers available, all of whom are initially employed in submarine production (row *A* of the schedule). When we cut back submarine production to only four per year (row *B*) we release 200 workers for railroad construction, as before. Now, however, those first 200 workers are assumed to be capable of producing two railroads (rather than only one, as in Table 1.1).

This high rate of submarine-to-railroad transformation does not last long. When sub production is cut back from four to three per year, another 200 workers are made available for railroad construction (row *C*). But now railroad output increases by only one, from two to three roads per year. Now we are getting fewer railroads for each sub given up. The opportunity cost of railroads is increasing.

This process of increasing opportunity costs continues. By the time we give up the last sub (row *F*), railroad output increases by only 0.5. We get only half a railroad for the last sub given up.

Increasing opportunity costs alter the shape of the production-possibilities curve. The linear "curve" in Figure 1.1 suggested that factors of production could be moved effortlessly from one industry to another. In reality, such transformations are more difficult, and the production-possibilities curve will usually bend outward, as in Figure 1.2.

Suppose that we start again at point *A,* using all our labor to produce five nuclear submarines per year, leaving no resources for railroad construction. We then decide (Step 1) to reduce the rate of submarine construction in order to free resources for railroad production. According to the production-possibilities schedule in Figure 1.2, we can produce two railroads per year with the labor initially taken out of submarine production. Thus Step 2 takes us to point *B,* where we produce four subs and two railroads per year. The two railroads are the first "peace dividend" from the reduction in military output (see earlier News).

The peace dividend increases as we continue cutting back on submarine construction. If we cut the number of new subs from four to three per year (Step 3), how many additional railroads can we produce with the released labor? According to Figure 1.2, we can obtain only one more railroad per year with the additional labor (Step 4). Hence the opportunity cost of a railroad has risen. The newest (third) railroad "cost" one sub, whereas we earlier obtained *two* railroads by forgoing one sub (i.e., one railroad previously cost only half a nuclear submarine).

Nonlinear production-possibilities curves like the one in Figure 1.2 are so universal that they have become a basic "law" of economics, the **law of increasing opportunity costs.** According to this law, we must give up ever-increasing quantities of other goods and services in order to get more of a particular good.

The law of increasing opportunity costs is not based solely on the limited versatility of individual workers. In most production processes, some amount of land and capital works with labor. If they had to, railroad workers could lay rails with picks, shovels, and sledgehammers. The construction of nuclear submarines requires much more capital (equipment), of far greater complex-

law of increasing opportunity costs: In order to get more of any good in a given time period, society must sacrifice ever-increasing amounts of other goods.

FIGURE 1.2
Increasing Opportunity Costs

Resources are not perfectly adaptable from one industry to another. As a consequence, we are unlikely to get one additional railroad for every sub given up. Instead, opportunity costs *increase*. Notice that we get two railroads for the first sub given up (moving from row *A* to row *B* in the schedule) but only one railroad for the second sub given up (row *B* to row *C*). The third sub is "transformed" into only 0.8 railroad.

Increasing opportunity costs bend the production-possibilities curve outward, as in the graph. In this case, we get two railroads (Step 2) by giving up the fifth submarine (Step 1). When we give up the next sub (Step 3), however, we get only one additional railroad (Step 4). Each additional railroad "costs" more submarines.

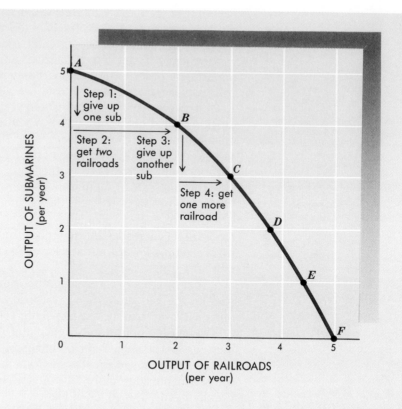

	Submarines					Railroads	
	Total available labor	Output of subs	× Labor needed per sub	= Total labor required for subs	Labor not used for subs	Potential output of railroads	Changes in output
A	1,000	5	200	1,000	0	0	
							> 2.0
B	1,000	4	200	800	200	2.0	
							> 1.0
C	1,000	3	200	600	400	3.0	
							> 0.8
D	1,000	2	200	400	600	3.8	
							> 0.7
E	1,000	1	200	200	800	4.5	
							> 0.5
F	1,000	0	200	0	1,000	5.0	

ity. Hence the productivity of workers moved from the railroad industry to nuclear submarine construction depends on how much capital equipment we supply them with. With little capital—or the wrong kind of capital—they won't be able to produce many nuclear submarines. Accordingly, our ability to alter the mix of output does not depend on the talents of individual workers alone. It also depends on the adaptability of land and capital and the availability of each in the right proportions.

Points Inside and Outside the Curve

Points X and Y in Figure 1.3 illustrate two additional combinations of submarines and railroads. One of these combinations is unattainable, however, while the other is undesirable. Consider point X, which represents a combined output of five submarines and two railroads per year. Point X is clearly better than point A, because it includes just as many subs and two more railroads. It appears, in other words, that by moving from point A to point X we could get two additional railroads *without* giving up any potential submarines. Unfortunately, point X lies *outside* our production possibilities and is beyond our grasp. In order to produce five nuclear submarines per year, we have to use *all* our available resources and technology, leaving none to produce railroads. We cannot have five new submarines every year *and* two new railroads; point X represents an unattainable output combination. In fact, **all output combinations that lie outside the production-possibilities curve are unattainable with available resources and technology.**

Point Y represents a very different situation. At point Y, three submarines and two railroads are being produced each year. This output combination is easily attainable with our available resources and technology. But if we produced at point Y, we would be wasting resources. Either some labor is completely idle (unemployed), or workers are not employed efficiently (underemployed). This is evident from the fact that we could produce at point C, with one more railroad and no fewer submarines each year. Or we could move to point B and have one more sub and no fewer railroads. By choosing

FIGURE 1.3
Points Inside and Outside the Curve

Points outside the production-possibilities curve (e.g., point X) are unattainable with available resources and technology. Points inside the curve (e.g., point Y) represent the incomplete use of available resources. Only points on the production-possibilities curve (e.g., A, B, C) represent maximum use of our production capabilities.

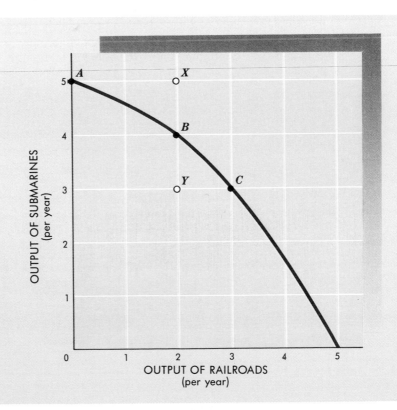

to stay at point *Y*, we would be forsaking the opportunity to use all our resources to the fullest, in effect giving up potential output for nothing in return. So long as either more submarines or more railroads (or any other good) are desired, it is wasteful to leave workers idle when they could be producing one of those goods. Thus point *Y* and ***all points inside the production-possibilities curve are undesirable because they imply the waste (nonuse) of available resources.***

Growth and Technology

The production possibilities illustrated in Figure 1.3 are not fixed for all time. As time passes, we will acquire more resources and improve our knowledge of how to use them. Until the 1950s, no one even knew what a nuclear submarine was. Advances in both nuclear technology and submarine design since that time have made nuclear submarines both feasible and familiar. In other words, our technology has improved. As a result, we can produce more subs today than we could fifty or even five years ago, with the same quantity of resources.

Over time, the quantity of resources available for production has also increased. Each year our population grows a bit, thereby enlarging the number of potential workers. Our stock of capital equipment has increased even faster. In addition the *quality* of our labor and capital resources has improved, as a result of more education (labor) and better machinery (capital).

All of this adds up to an ever-increasing capacity to produce goods and services. This is illustrated in Figure 1.4 by the outward *shift* of the production-possibilities curve. Before the appearance of new resources or better technology, our production possibilities were limited by the curve PP_1. ***With more resources or better technology, our production possibilities increase.*** This greater capacity to produce is represented by curve PP_2. This outward shift of the production-possibilities curve is the essence of **economic growth.** As we shall see in later chapters, much of our recent growth has come from continuing improvements in technology.

economic growth: An increase in output (real GNP); an expansion of production possibilities.

"There's no such thing as a free lunch."

Drawing by Dana Fradon; © 1975 The New Yorker Magazine, Inc.

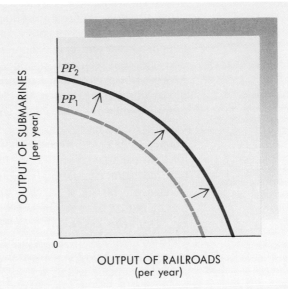

**FIGURE 1.4
Increasing Production
Possibilities**

A production–possibilities
curve is based on *available*
resources and technology. If
more resources or better
technology becomes available,
production possibilities will
increase. This is illustrated by
the *shift* from PP_1 to PP_2.

HOW CHOICES ARE MADE

However promising the prospects for growth may be, we still have to live within our current production constraints. There is still a limit to how much we can produce in any year. The fact that those limits may expand in future years does not make our current choices any easier. Each year we still have to choose some mix of output that is consistent with our existing production possibilities. ***Choosing WHAT to produce—a mix of output—is one of our most important economic decisions.***

Our menu of choices is illustrated by the prevailing production-possibilities curve. Because those points that lie *outside* the production-possibilities curve are unattainable and those *inside* the curve are undesirable, only those points *on* the curve represent our immediate choices. But which of these many points should we choose? What goods and services should the economy produce?

Although the consequences of alternative output choices can be illustrated with a production-possibilities curve, the curve itself says nothing about the desirability of any particular combination of goods and services. Why do we choose fewer railroads and more nuclear submarines? Or, for that matter, why do you choose—and it is a choice!—to do more homework and get less sleep? If we are really to understand economic outcomes, we have to know more than just what the choices are. We also have to know how we make such choices.

The Market Mechanism

market mechanism: The use of market prices and sales to signal desired outputs (or resource allocations).

The actual choices individual consumers and firms make are expressed for the most part in market purchases and sales. The use of the **market mechanism** to express your desires is as familiar as grocery shopping. If you desire ice cream and have sufficient income, you simply buy ice cream. Your purchases act as a signal to producers that ice cream is desired. By expressing the *ability and willingness to pay* for ice cream, you are effectively telling ice cream producers that their efforts are going to be rewarded. If enough consumers feel the same way you do—and are able and willing to pay the price of ice cream—ice cream producers will produce more ice cream.

The same kind of interactions influence the choice we must make between houses and cars. There are many alternative combinations of houses and cars that we *could* produce. But we must choose only one. How do we express our preference? Consumers express their preference for houses simply by purchasing houses, that is, by expressing a willingness to pay for such output. Similarly, consumers who would prefer to see more new cars can express their desires by buying cars. In this way, the debate over cars versus houses boils down to a question of who is willing and able to pay the most for the available factors of production. If potential homeowners are willing to pay more for our limited resources than are potential drivers, then more houses will be supplied. Why? Simply because suppliers will provide those products that offer the highest profit.

Thus ***the essential feature of the market mechanism is the price signal.*** If you want something and have sufficient income, you buy it. If enough people do the same thing, the total sales of that product will rise, and perhaps its price will as well. Producers, seeing sales and prices rise, will be inclined to increase production. To do so, they will attempt to acquire a larger share of our available resources and use it to produce the goods we desire. No direct communication between us and the producer is required; market sales and prices convey the message and direct the market, much like an "invisible hand." Although producers and sellers have a variety of reasons for offering their wares, and consumers have myriad motives for buying, prices are used as a common means of communication. It is this price or market mechanism that translates the disparate interests and desires of our 250 million selves into a producing and consuming whole. From this perspective, the price system is a very efficient method of communication.

Command Economies

The market mechanism is not the only way to choose a mix of output. Many countries have in fact rejected the market mechanism in favor of central planning. In so-called *command economies,* the government's central planners choose the mix of output. They then allocate the economy's scarce resources to assure that the planned combination of goods and services is produced.

The motivation for command economies is the conviction that central planning is more likely to produce the "right" mix of output than a decentralized market mechanism. The market mechanism gives undue weight to the desires of the rich. As a result, a market economy may produce lots of frivolous goods while neglecting greater social needs. Central planning creates the opportunity to direct resources to the society's most pressing needs, without the distractions of conspicuous consumption.

Although the goals of central planning may be worthy, their implementation is fraught with difficulty. To begin with, one must assume that the wisdom of the central planners is greater than the collective wisdom of the marketplace. In other words, one must assume that the planners are better positioned than the mass of consumers to pick the "right" mix of output. But even this is not enough. The central planners must also know how to produce that right mix efficiently. Specifically, they must know how many resources to allocate to each industry. If they make a mistake, resources will be wasted and the wrong mix of output will be produced (see World View).

W🌐RLD VIEW

COMMAND ECONOMIES

Where Communist Economies Fell Short

It's not over till it's over, Yogi admonished. But with Muscovites salivating over the arrival of McDonald's and Hungary celebrating the embrace of General Electric, it is hard to deny that the long ideological war between capitalism and socialism has ended in a decisive win for the home team.

Economists across the political spectrum agree that central planning has proved a bust in recent decades. Most would also agree that decentralized economic decision-making offers Communist countries the best hope for catching up with the affluent West.

Under the purest versions of centralized planning, administrators decide what goods will be produced and what economic resources will be used to make them. Unemployment is, in effect, abolished by decree. And inflation is suppressed, with excess demand showing up as shortages rather than as rising prices.

But in practice, the performance of planned economies is mixed. Their inherent strength, the ability to mobilize resources for a few national goals, is familiar to anyone who remembers the way the American economy rallied to support the Allied armies in World War II. By organizing what amounts to a permanent war economy, Stalin was able to transform a backward land into a great military power with an impressively large industrial base. And by forcing Soviet citizens to invest a high percentage of income, planners could maintain very high growth rates through the 1960's.

Drowning in Detail

Soviet economists once thought they could use computer models to simulate the decentralized workings of markets, but that idea has proved far beyond the capacities of the speediest supercomputer. As the Soviet economy grew more complex, the lack of accurate signals of cost and value began to cut more deeply. Production goals set in tons, for example, have led Soviet pipe manufacturers to use far more steel than necessary. Consumer prices held far below cost have led to colossal waste: it often pays farmers to sell their grain to the state, and then buy back the subsidized bread made from the grain, to use as animal feed.

Correcting such obvious misincentives is not easy. Planners, with thousands of interdependent production sectors to coordinate, drown in detail. Even the Soviet Congress, convened last week to debate momentous issues of policy, was reduced to quarreling over the poor quality of washing machines and the scarcity of school desks.

Scale and complexity seem to magnify another weakness of planned economies—the lack of financial incentives for personal initiative. In Stalin's day it might have been sufficient to set quotas for numbers of tractors assembled or tons of coal dug, rewarding overachievers with New Years' vodka and punishing shirkers with holidays in the gulag.

But in a modern economy whose long-term prospects depend on the creation and rapid diffusion of technology, such crude incentives cannot work.

—Peter Passell

The New York Times, December 17, 1989, p. E3. Copyright © 1989 The New York Times Company. Reprinted by permission.

The difficulties of formulating and implementing central plans have made many command economies look with envy to the efficiency of the market mechanism. The Soviet Union and China have both tried to harness some of the efficiency of the market mechanism. The countries of Eastern Europe— Poland, East Germany, Yugoslavia, Czechoslovakia—have moved even further away from central planning in an effort to gain more economic efficiency. This economic restructuring—sometimes referred to as the "collapse of communism"—reflects a recognition of how well decentralized markets can communicate consumption desires and production possibilities.

Market Imperfections   Although the market mechanism is an efficient method for choosing the mix of output, it is not without blemishes. One of the foremost objections to the market mechanism concerns equity. Use of the price system presumes allegiance to certain standards of fairness. In particular, reliance on prices as a mechanism for distributing goods and resources implies that we believe such a distribution is "fair." For example, goods and services distributed through the market mechanism go disproportionately to those with the greatest ability to pay. Rich people live in comfortable homes, while some poor people sleep in abandoned cars. Whether this system of allocating shelter is "fair" depends on how one views the distribution of wealth and income and the importance of basic shelter. It is at least conceivable that the efficiency of the price system may conflict with standards of equity or fairness. If so, we may choose to distribute housing or other goods in different ways. Shelter for the homeless, medical and legal assistance provided for the poor, not to mention public schools, all illustrate departures from the price mechanism prompted by our concern for equity.

Another problem that strikes at the very heart of the market mechanism is that some very valuable things are not priced. Clean air, for example, is something nearly everyone considers precious. Nevertheless, it is difficult to imagine how we could *buy* clean air, much less reserve the cleanest air for those who are most eager and able to purchase it. Air, unlike videotapes or soap, cannot be packaged and marketed. Hence to leave the quality of the air we breathe to the determination of the market mechanism is like tightening one's own noose. The final outcome is foreseeable, but not necessarily desirable. Just breathing in New York City, Los Angeles, or Chicago can be dangerous to your health.

Clean air is not alone among unpackageable and unmarketable goods. On the contrary, the list of such goods is long, including such diverse products as national defense, traffic congestion, and the vibrations from your next-door neighbor's stereo. In every such case, we are sidestepping the market mechanism: benefits or costs are being exchanged without direct payment. These kinds of interactions are referred to as **externalities.**

externalities: Costs (or benefits) of a market activity borne by a third party; the difference between the social and private costs (benefits) of a market activity.

Externalities violate the basic market dictum that everything must be packaged, marketed, and exchanged for a negotiated price. Because they sidestep the market, externalities impede the market mechanism's ability to generate the right mix of output. If we rely exclusively on market prices to allocate resources, we will end up with too much pollution. This is an example of **market failure**—that is, the inability of the market to deliver the most desired economic outcomes. When the market fails, the production and consumption of such goods must often be controlled by other mechanisms. These mechanisms may be public laws (such as those to fight pollution), taxes (to pay for common defense), or threats against neighbors (to muffle their stereos). In almost all cases, we seek to alter market choices by intervening directly in the production or consumption process.

market failure: An imperfection in the market mechanism that prevents optimal outcomes.

Mixed Economies

Because of such imperfections, no country relies exclusively on the market mechanism to make its economic decisions. The United States and most other countries rely instead on the market for some decisions and on centralized decision making (the government) for others. The use of both market signals and nonmarket directives is the hallmark of a **mixed economy.**

mixed economy: An economy that uses both market and nonmarket signals to allocate goods and resources.

Although economies use some mix of market signals and government intervention to fashion economic outcomes, there are profound differences in those mixes. The U.S. economy is distinguished by a heavy reliance on the market mechanism. Other "mixed" economies include a heavier dose of government intervention.

Our heavy reliance on the market mechanism is based on its efficiency in allocating resources and goods in accordance with consumer preferences.

At the same time, our apparent commitment to government intervention reflects the judgment that market outcomes are not always best. The market mechanism is only a means to an end, not an end in itself. When we find the mechanism or the outcomes incompatible with our visions of the good and proper life, we can and do seek to change them. This explains why we formulate public policies to reduce unemployment, to slow the rate of inflation, to foster economic growth, and to redistribute incomes. If the market mechanism could itself ensure fulfillment of these goals, economic policy would be unnecessary.

We should not embrace market interference too hastily, however. We have no assurance that public policy is *capable* of improving our economic performance or that such policy will be properly implemented. That is to say, nonmarket signals are imperfect, too. Accordingly, we cannot assume that all our economic problems are attributable to the market mechanism or that public policy will always provide a solution. On the contrary, experience has taught us that the government may fail too.

government failure: Government intervention that fails to improve economic outcomes.

We speak of **government failure** when government intervention fails to improve economic outcomes—or makes them worse. Identifying a market problem is not the hardest part of formulating economic policy; devising an intervention strategy that will not worsen the problem is far more difficult. This is the core dilemma that the countries of Eastern Europe have come to recognize as they assess the failures of central planning. It is the same dilemma that U.S. policymakers must confront on a smaller scale at every turn. Should we try to fix every market blemish? Can we be sure that our policy intervention will improve economic outcomes? These basic concerns—the competing risks of market failure and government failure—are emphasized throughout the remainder of this book.

WHAT ECONOMICS IS ALL ABOUT

Understanding how various economies work is the basic purpose of studying economics. We seek to know how an economy is organized, how it behaves, and how successfully it achieves its basic objectives. Then, if we are lucky, we can discover better ways of attaining those same objectives.

End vs. Means

Economists do not formulate an economy's objectives. Instead, they focus on the *means* available for achieving given *goals.* In 1978, for example, the U.S. Congress identified "full employment" as a major economic goal. The Congress then directed future presidents (and their economic advisers) to formulate polices that would enable us to achieve full employment.

Four major economic goals are generally accepted. These goals are

• Full employment

• Price stability

• Economic growth

• An equitable distribution of income

In each case, the goal itself is formulated through the political process. The economist's job is to help design policies that will allocate the economy's resources in ways that best achieve these goals. The nature and significance of our major economic goals, as well as the means available for attaining them, are discussed in later chapters.

Macro vs. Micro

The study of economics is typically divided into two parts: macroeconomics and microeconomics. Macroeconomics focuses on the behavior of an entire economy—the "big picture." In macroeconomics we worry about such national goals as full employment, control of inflation, and economic growth, without worrying about the well-being or behavior of specific individuals or groups. The essential concern of **macroeconomics** is to understand and improve the performance of the economy as a whole.

Microeconomics is concerned with the details of this "big picture." In microeconomics we focus on the individuals, firms, and government agencies that actually comprise the larger economy. Our interest here is in the behavior of individual economic actors. What are their goals? How can they best achieve these goals with their limited resources? How will they respond to various incentives and opportunities?

A primary concern of macroeconomics, for example, is to determine the impact of aggregate consumer spending on total output, employment, and prices. Very little attention is devoted to the actual content of consumer spending or its determinants. Microeconomics, on the other hand, focuses on the specific expenditure decisions of individual consumers and the forces (tastes, prices, incomes) that influence those decisions.

The distinction between macro- and microeconomics is also reflected in discussions of business investment. In macroeconomics we want to know what determines the aggregate rate of business investment and how those expenditures influence the nation's total output, employment, and prices. In microeconomics we focus on the decisions of individual businesses regarding the rate of production, the choice of factors of production, and the pricing of specific goods.

The distinction between macro- and microeconomics is a matter of convenience. In reality, macroeconomic outcomes depend on micro behavior, and micro behavior is affected by macro outcomes. Hence one cannot fully understand how an economy works until one understands how all the participants behave and why they behave as they do. But just as you can drive a car without knowing how its engine is constructed, you can observe how an economy runs without completely disassembling it. In macroeconomics we observe that the car goes faster when the accelerator is depressed and that it slows when the brake is applied. That is all we need to know in most situations. There are times, however, when the car breaks down. When it does, we have to know something more about how the pedals work. This leads us into micro studies. How does each part work? Which ones can or should be fixed?

Our interest in microeconomics is motivated by more than our need to understand how the larger economy works. The "parts" of the economic engine are people. To the extent that we care about the welfare of individuals in society, we have a fundamental interest in microeconomic behavior and outcomes. In this regard, we examine the goals of individual consumers and business firms, seeking to explain how they can maximize their welfare in the economy. In microeconomics, for example, we spend more time looking at which goods are produced, who produces them, and who receives them. In

---

macroeconomics: The study of aggregate economic behavior, of the economy as a whole.

microeconomics: The study of individual behavior in the economy, of the components of the larger economy.

macroeconomics we tend to focus only on how much is produced or how many people are employed in the process.

Theory and Reality

The distinction between macroeconomics and microeconomics is one of many simplifications we make in studying economic behavior. The economy is much too vast and complex to describe and explain in one course (or one lifetime). Accordingly, we focus on basic relationships, ignoring annoying detail. In so doing, we isolate basic principles of economic behavior, then use those principles to predict economic events and formulate economic policies. What this means is that we formulate theories, or *models,* of economic behavior, then use those theories to evaluate and design economic policy.

Because all economic models entail simplifying assumptions, they never *exactly* describe the real world. Nevertheless, the models may be useful. If our models are *reasonably* consistent with economic reality, they may yield good predictions of economic behavior. Likewise, if our simplifications do not become distortions, they may provide good guidelines for economic policy.

Our theory of consumer behavior assumes, for example, a distinct relationship between the price of a good and the quantity people buy. As prices increase, people buy less. In reality, however, people *may* buy *more* of a good at increased prices, especially if those high prices create a certain "snob appeal" or if prices are expected to increase still further. In predicting consumer responses to price increases, we typically ignore such possibilities by *assuming* that the price of the good in question is the *only* thing that changes. This assumption of "other things remaining equal (unchanged)" (in Latin, **ceteris paribus**) allows us to make straightforward predictions. If instead we described consumer responses to increased prices in any and all circumstances (allowing everything to change at once), every prediction would be accompanied by a book full of exceptions and qualifications. We would look more like lawyers than economists.

ceteris paribus: The assumption of nothing else changing.

Although the assumption of *ceteris paribus* makes it easier to formulate economic theory and policy, it also increases the risk of error. Obviously, if other things do change in significant ways, our predictions (and policies) may fail. But, like weather forecasters, we continue to make predictions, knowing that occasional failure is inevitable. In so doing, we are motivated by the conviction that it is better to be approximately right than to be dead wrong.

Policy

Politicians cannot afford to be quite so complacent about predictions, however. Policy decisions must be made every day. And a politician's continued survival may depend on being more than approximately right. Economists can contribute to those policy decisions by offering measures of economic impact and predictions of economic behavior. But in the real world, those measures and predictions will always contain a substantial margin of error. That is to say, economic policy decisions are always based on some amount of uncertainty. Even the best economic minds cannot foretell the future.

Even if the future were known, economic policy could not rely completely on economic theory. There are always political choices to be made. The choice of more submarines or more railroads, for example, is not an economic decision. Rather it is a sociopolitical decision based in part on economic tradeoffs (opportunity costs). The "need" for more subs or more railroads must be expressed politically—ends versus means again. Political forces are a necessary ingredient in economic policy decisions. That is not to say that all "political" decisions are right. It does suggest, however, that economic policies may not always conform to economic theory. We shall explore the interaction of policy and theory, highlighting those forces that contribute to disappointing economic performance.

Controversy

One last word of warning before you go further. Economics claims to be a science, in pursuit of basic truths. We want to understand and explain how the economy works without getting tangled up in subjective value judgments. This may be an impossible task. First of all, it is not clear where the truth lies. For over 200 years economists have been arguing about what makes the economy tick. None of the competing theories has performed spectacularly well. Indeed, few economists have successfully predicted major economic events with any consistency. Even annual forecasts of inflation, unemployment, and output are regularly in error. Worse still, there are never-ending arguments about what caused a major economic event long after it has already occurred. In fact, economists are still arguing over the causes of the Great Depression of the 1930s!

The most persistent debate in economics has focused on the degree to which the government can improve the economy's performance. Two hundred years ago, Adam Smith convinced most of the world that the economy worked best when it was left alone. In the throes of the Great Depression, the British economist John Maynard Keynes forced people to rethink that conclusion. He convinced people that active government intervention in the marketplace was the only way to ensure economic growth and stability. For nearly thirty years his theory dominated the economics profession and public policy. A decade of disappointing economic performance ended Keynes's overwhelming dominance. The 1970s were fraught with repeated recessions, slow growth, and high inflation. "Supply-siders" and "Monetarists" laid much of the blame on Keynesian theory. Specifically, they argued that we got into economic trouble because we permitted too much government intervention. Excessive government intervention had stifled the market mechanism, they claimed; Keynes's call for active government policy had to be rejected.

The Reagan administration was persuaded by these arguments and sought to reduce government intervention. At first, the economy was wracked by back-to-back recessions that threw millions of Americans out of work. From 1983 to the end of the decade, however, the American economy prospered. Supporters of Reagan's policy claimed victory; critics said he was lucky and pointed to lingering problems of poverty, homelessness, bloated budget deficits, and inadequate public services.

The Bush administration has tried to extend the economic successes of the 1980s while tending to some of those lingering problems. Bush's initial promises of a "kinder, gentler" nation took substance in more spending for education, income transfers, and medical research. As the economy slowed, President Bush also had to confront *macroeconomic* choices about whether and how to intervene. Conservatives advocated a continued "hands-off" policy; liberals urged him to make greater use of the government's tax and spending powers to finance additional public services.

In part, this enduring controversy reflects diverse sociopolitical views on the appropriate role of government. Some people think a big public sector is undesirable, even if it improves economic performance. But the controversy has even deeper roots. There are still important gaps in our understanding of the economy. We know how much of the economy works, but not all of it. We are adept at identifying all the forces at work, but not always successful in gauging their relative importance. In point of fact, we may *never* find an absolute truth, because the inner workings of the economy change over time. When economic behavior changes, our theories must be adapted.

Modest Expectations   In view of all these debates and uncertainties, you should not expect to learn everything there is to know about the economy today in this text or course. Our goals are more modest. We want to develop a reasonable perspective on economic behavior, an understanding of basic principles. With this foundation, you should acquire a better view of how the economy works. Daily news reports on economic events should make more sense. Congressional debates on tax and budget policies should take on more meaning. You may even develop some insights that you can apply toward running a business or planning a career.

SUMMARY

• Scarcity is a basic fact of economic life. Available resources (factors of production) are scarce in relation to our desires for goods and services.

• Scarcity necessitates difficult choices. Factors of production (resources) used to produce one output cannot simultaneously be used to produce something else. Accordingly, when we choose to produce something, we forsake the opportunity to produce some other good or service.

• A production-possibilities curve illustrates the kinds of opportunity costs an economy confronts. It shows the alternative combinations of final goods and services that could be produced in a given time period with available resources and technology.

• The bent shape of the production-possibilities curve reflects the law of increasing opportunity costs. This law states that increasing quantities of any good can be obtained only by sacrificing ever-increasing quantities of other goods.

• Production possibilities expand (shift outward) when additional resources or better technologies become available. This is the essence of economic growth.

• The market mechanism facilitates the actual choice of output combinations. Consumers indicate their preference for specific outputs by expressing an ability and a willingness to pay for desired goods. Their actual purchases act as signals to producers, who in turn assemble factors of production and produce the desired outputs.

• The market mechanism does not work efficiently when externalities exist— that is, when market interactions between two parties impose costs or benefits on third parties. Market outcomes may also conflict with accepted standards of equity. In these cases, the market may fail to deliver the best possible economic outcomes.

• Command economies rely on central planning rather than decentralized markets to allocate resources. To succeed, central planners must know what mix of output is best and how to produce that mix.

• Government intervention (including the extreme of central planning) may make outcomes worse—a result referred to as government failure.

• A mixed economy relies on a combination of market signals and nonmarket intervention to allocate goods and services. The critical problem for both economic theory and public policy is to determine the mix of market and nonmarket directives that will best fulfill our social and economic goals.

• The study of economics focuses on the broad question of resource allocation. Macroeconomics is concerned with allocating the resources of an entire economy to achieve aggregate economic goals (e.g., full employment). Microeconomics focuses on the behavior and goals of individual market participants.

Terms to Remember   Define the following terms:

factors of production	**externalities**
opportunity cost	**market failure**
economics	**mixed economy**
production possibilities	**government failure**
law of increasing opportunity costs	**macroeconomics**
economic growth	**microeconomics**
market mechanism	*ceteris paribus*

Questions for Discussion

1. What opportunity costs did you incur in reading this chapter?

2. If you read four more chapters of this text today, would your opportunity costs (per chapter) increase? Explain.

3. What is the real cost of the "free lunch" advertised in the cartoon on page 14?

4. If all consumers desire clean air, why doesn't the market mechanism produce it?

5. How much is the federal government spending on defense (see tables inside front cover)? If defense spending is cut by 10 percent, how should the "peace dividend" be spent? Who should decide?

Problems

1. Assume that the schedule at the left describes the production possibilities confronting an economy. Using the information from the table:
    (*a*) Draw the production-possibilities curve. Be sure to label each alternative output combination (*A* through *E*).
    (*b*) Calculate and illustrate on your graph the opportunity cost of producing one stereo per week.
    (*c*) What is the cost of producing a second stereo? What accounts for the difference?
    (*d*) Which point on the curve is the most desired one? How will we find out?
    (*e*) What would happen to the production-possibilities curve if additional factors of production became available? Illustrate.

Potential Weekly Output Combinations Using All Resources

	Pianos	Stereos
A	10	0
B	9	1
C	7	2
D	4	3
E	0	4

Potential Weekly Output Combinations Using All Resoures

Combi-nation	Number of students (millions per year)	Number of defense programs
A	0	27
B	2	24
C	4	18
D	6	10
E	8	0

2. Engineers are in short supply in the United States. This forces a choice between employing engineers to produce defense goods and employing them as professors to educate students. Suppose the accompanying schedule describes the tradeoff between the number of students trained by scientists each year and the number of defense programs undertaken.
   (*a*) Draw the production-possibilities curve showing the tradeoff between the number of students educated and the number of defense programs. Label each of the five output combinations (*A* through *E*).
   (*b*) Calculate and illustrate on your production-possibilities curve the opportunity cost of educating 2 million, 4 million, 6 million, and 8 million students per year.
   (*c*) Why does the opportunity cost change?

APPENDIX

USING GRAPHS

Economists like to draw graphs. In fact, we didn't even make it through the first chapter without a few graphs. The purpose of this appendix is to look more closely at the way graphs are drawn and used.

The basic purpose of a graph is to illustrate a relationship between two *variables.* Consider, for example, the relationship between grades and studying. In general, we expect that additional hours of study time will lead to higher grades. Hence we should be able to see a distinct relationship between hours of study time and grade-point average.

Suppose that we actually surveyed all the students taking this course with regard to their study time and grade-point averages. The resulting information can be compiled in a table such as Table A.1.

According to the table, students who don't study at all can expect an F in this course. To get a C, the average student apparently spends 8 hours a week studying. All those who study 16 hours a week end up with an A in the course.

These relationships between grades and studying can also be illustrated on a graph. Indeed, the whole purpose of a graph is to summarize numerical relationships.

We begin to construct a graph by drawing horizontal and vertical boundaries, as in Figure A.1. These boundaries are called the *axes* of the graph. On the vertical axis we measure one of the variables; the other variable is measured on the horizontal axis.[1]

In this case, we shall measure the grade-point average on the vertical axis. We start at the *origin* (the intersection of the two axes) and count upward, letting the distance between horizontal lines represent half (0.5) a grade point. Each horizontal line is numbered, up to the maximum grade-point average of 4.0.

The number of hours each week spent doing homework is measured on the horizontal axis. We begin at the origin again, and count to the right. The *scale* (numbering) proceeds in increments of 1 hour, up to 20 hours per week.

When both axes have been labeled and measured, we can begin to illustrate the relationship between study time and grades. Consider the typical student who does 8 hours of homework per week and has a 2.0 (C) grade-point average. We illustrate this relationship by first locating 8 hours on the horizontal axis. We then move up from that point a distance of 2.0 grade points, to point *M*. Point *M* tells us that 8 hours of study time per week is typically associated with a 2.0 grade-point average.

**TABLE A.1
Hypothetical Relationship of Grades to Study Time**

Study time (hours per week)	Grade-point average
16	4.0 (A)
14	3.5 (B+)
12	3.0 (B)
10	2.5 (C+)
8	2.0 (C)
6	1.5 (D+)
4	1.0 (D)
2	0.5 (F+)
0	0 (F)

[1]The vertical axis is often called the *Y* axis; the horizontal axis, the *X* axis.

FIGURE A.1
The Relationship of Grades to Study Time

The upward (positive) slope of the curve indicates that additional studying is associated with higher grades. The average student (2.0, or C grade) studies 8 hours per week. This is indicated by point *M* on the graph.

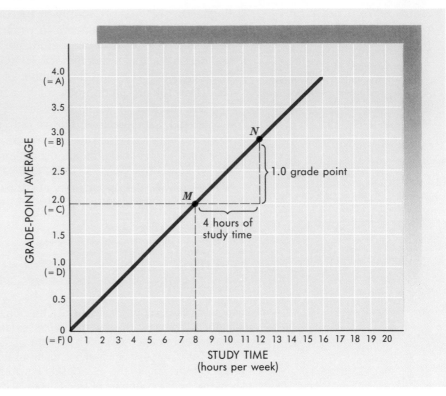

The rest of the information in Table A.1 is drawn (or *plotted*) on the graph in the same way. To illustrate the average grade for people who study 12 hours per week, we move upward from the number 12 on the horizontal axis until we reach the height of 3.0 on the vertical axis. At that intersection, we draw another point (point *N*).

Once we have plotted the various points describing the relationship of study time to grades, we may connect them with a line or curve. This line (curve) is our summary. In this case, the line slopes upward to the right—that is, it has a *positive* slope. This slope indicates that more hours of study time are associated with *higher* grades. Were higher grades associated with *less* study time, the curve in Figure A.1 would have a *negative* slope (downward from left to right).

Slopes   The upward slope of Figure A.1 tells us that higher grades are associated with increased amounts of study time. That same curve also tells us *by how much* grades tend to rise with study time. According to point *M* in Figure A.1, the average student studies 8 hours per week and earns a C (2.0 grade-point average). In order to earn a B (3.0 average), students apparently need to study an average of 12 hours per week (point *N*). Hence an increase of 4 hours of study time per week is associated with a 1-point increase in grade-point average. This relationship between *changes* in study time and *changes* in grade-point average is expressed by the steepness, or *slope*, of the graph.

The slope of any graph is calculated as

$$\bullet \quad \text{Slope} = \frac{\text{vertical distance between two points}}{\text{horizontal distance between two points}}$$

In our example, the vertical distance between points M and N represents a change in grade-point average. The horizontal distance between these two points represents the change in study time. Hence the slope of the graph between points M and N is equal to

$$\text{Slope} = \frac{3.0 \text{ grade} - 2.0 \text{ grade}}{12 \text{ hours} - 8 \text{ hours}} = \frac{1 \text{ grade point}}{4 \text{ hours}}$$

In other words, a 4-hour increase in study time (from 8 to 12 hours) is associated with a 1-point increase in grade-point average (see Figure A.1).

Shifts

The relationship between grades and studying illustrated in Figure A.1 is not inevitable. It is simply a graphical illustration of student experiences, as revealed in our hypothetical survey. The relationship between study time and grades could be quite different.

Suppose that the university decided to raise grading standards, making it more difficult to achieve every grade other than an F. To achieve a C, a student now would need to study 12 hours per week, not just 8 (as in Figure A.1). Whereas students could previously expect to get a B by studying 12 hours per week, now they have to study 16 hours to get that grade.

Figure A.2 illustrates the new grading standards. Notice that the new curve lies to the right of the earlier curve. We say that the curve has *shifted* to reflect a change in the relationship between study time and grades. Point R indicates that 12 hours of study time now "produces" a C, not a B (point N on the old curve). Students who now study only 4 hours per week (point S) will fail. Under the old grading policy, they could have at least gotten a D. ***When a curve shifts, the underlying relationship between the two variables has changed.***

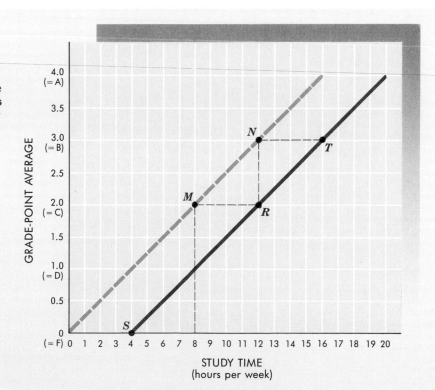

**FIGURE A.2
A Shift**

When a relationship between two variables changes, the entire curve *shifts*. In this case a tougher grading policy alters the relationship between study time and grades. To get a C one must now study 12 hours per week (point R), not just 8 hours (point M).

A shift may also change the slope of the curve. In Figure A.2, the new grading curve is parallel to the old one; it therefore has the same slope. Under either the new grading policy or the old one, a 4-hour increase in study time leads to a 1-point increase in grades. Therefore, the slope of both curves in Figure A.2 is

$$\text{Slope} = \frac{\text{vertical change}}{\text{horizontal change}} = \frac{1}{4}$$

This, too, may change, however. Figure A.3 illustrates such a possibility. In this case, zero study time still results in an F. But now the payoff for additional studying is reduced. Now it takes 6 hours of study time to get a D (1.0 grade point), not 4 hours as before. Likewise, another 4 hours of study time (to a total of 10) raises the grade by only two-thirds of a point. It takes 6 hours to raise the grade a full point. The slope of the new line is therefore

$$\text{Slope} = \frac{\text{vertical change}}{\text{horizontal change}} = \frac{1}{6}$$

The new curve in Figure A.3 has a smaller slope than the original curve and so lies below it. What all this means is that it now takes a greater effort to *improve* your grade.

Linear vs. Nonlinear Curves

In Figures A.1–A.3 the relationship between grades and studying is represented by a straight line—that is, a *linear curve*. A distinguishing feature of linear curves is that they have the same (constant) slope throughout. In Figure A.1, it appears that *every* 4-hour increase in study time is associated with a 1-point increase in average grades. In Figure A.3, it appears that every 6-hour increase in study time leads to a 1-point increase in grades. But the relationship between studying and grades may not be linear. Higher grades may be more difficult to attain. You may be able to raise a C to a B by studying 4 hours more per week. But it may be harder to raise a B to an A.

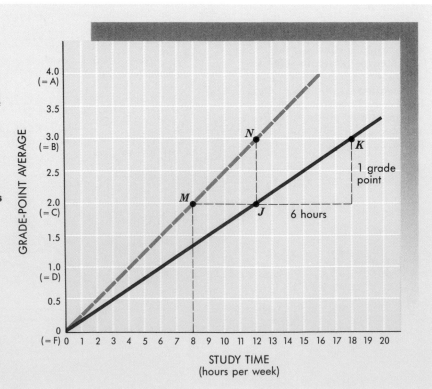

FIGURE A.3
A Change in Slope

When a curve shifts, it may change its slope as well. In this case, a new grading policy makes each higher grade more difficult to reach. To raise a C to a B, for example, one must study **6 additional hours** (compare points *J* and *K*). Earlier it took only 4 hours to move up the grade scale a full point. The slope of the line has declined from 0.25 (= 1 ÷ 4) to 0.17 (= 1 ÷ 6).

FIGURE A.4
A Nonlinear Relationship
Straight lines have a constant slope, implying a constant relationship between the two variables. But the relationship (and slope) may vary. In this case, it takes 6 extra hours of study to raise a C (point *W*) to a B (point *X*) but 8 extra hours to raise a B to an A (point *Y*). The slope is decreasing as we move up the curve.

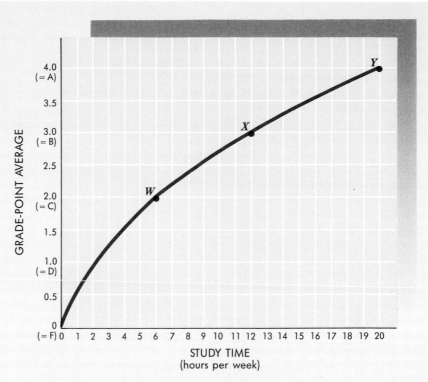

According to Figure A.4, it takes an additional 8 hours of studying to raise a B to an A. Thus the relationship between study time and grades is *nonlinear* in Figure A.4; the slope of the curve changes as study time increases. In this case, the slope decreases as study time increases. Grades continue to improve, but not so fast, as more and more time is devoted to homework. You may know the feeling.

Causation

Figure A.4 does not itself guarantee that your grade-point average will rise if you study 4 more hours per week. In fact, the graph drawn in Figure A.4 does not prove that additional study ever results in higher grades. The graph is only a summary of empirical observations. It says nothing about cause and effect. It could be that students who study a lot are smarter to begin with. If so, then less able students might not get higher grades if they studied harder. In other words, the *cause* of higher grades is debatable. At best, the empirical relationship summarized in the graph may be used to support a particular theory (e.g., that it pays to study more). Graphs, like tables, charts, and other statistical media, rarely tell their own story; rather, they must be *interpreted* in terms of some underlying theory or expectation.

Supply and Demand

*T*he dismantling of the Berlin Wall in November 1989 was a symbol of the Cold War's end and the reintegration of Europe. It also provided a quick lesson in the economics of supply and demand. Millions of East Germans flocked to West Berlin to buy goods that were not available in the East. Electronic toys, radios, cosmetics, tropical fruit, and chocolate were at the top of the shopping list. The East Germans had to pay high prices, but at least they had the chance to buy the goods they desired.

West Berliners went on a shopping spree as well. Fewer goods were available in East Berlin, but the prices of those necessities were kept low by the East German government. So West Berliners rushed into East Berlin to buy boots, sausages, women's lingerie, children's clothes, and Christmas geese. So much merchandise was being carted off to West Berlin that the East German government had to halt sales to foreigners and impose border controls to slow the outflow of available goods.

The cross-border shopping frenzy reflected a basic difference in the way production and prices were established in the two Germanys. West Germany had relied on *decentralized markets* to determine the production and prices of consumer goods: it was a *market economy*. East Germany relied instead on *central planners* to determine which goods to produce and at what prices to sell them; it was a *command economy*. When the Berlin Wall fell, consumers on both sides got a clear view of the differences between market and command economies.

The central economic concerns on both sides of the Berlin Wall were the same:

- WHAT goods and services should the economy produce?

- HOW should they be produced?

- FOR WHOM should they be produced?

These same basic economic questions confront every country.

Although the questions asked are always the same, the answers vary tremendously. Some countries want more consumer goods in their mix of output; others want more machinery. Some countries want more income equality; others accept inequality.

31

Just as important as the answers are the mechanisms used for making these decisions. The Soviet Union and China rely heavily on *central planners* to determine WHAT, HOW, and FOR WHOM. By contrast, the United States relies heavily on the *market mechanism* to allocate resources and distribute incomes.

Our commitment to the market mechanism reflects a conviction that the marketplace can run efficiently without central direction. Even socialist countries have gained a certain respect for decentralized markets. Rather than leaving all production decisions to central planners, the Soviet Union and China have given farmers and manufacturers increasing authority to make their own output decisions. The move toward decentralized markets is occurring even faster in Eastern Europe. Although vast differences remain between "capitalist" and "communist" countries, the efficiency of markets is acknowledged in both.

In this chapter we take a first look at how markets actually work. How does the market mechanism decide WHAT to produce, HOW to produce, and FOR WHOM to produce? Specifically:

- What determines the price of a good or service?

- How does the price of a product affect its production or consumption?

- Why do prices and production levels often change?

MARKET PARTICIPANTS

Over 250 million individual consumers, about 18 million business firms, and tens of thousands of government agencies participate directly in the U.S. economy. Millions of foreigners also participate by buying and selling goods in American markets. Fortunately, we can summarize much of this activity by classifying market participants into four distinct groups—consumers, business firms, government agencies, and foreigners—and then analyzing their behavior.

Goals Individual consumers, business firms, and government agencies participate in the market in order to achieve certain goals. Consumers strive to maximize their own happiness by purchasing the most satisfying bundle of goods and services with their available incomes. For their part, businesses try to maximize profits by using the most efficient combination of resources to produce the most profitable products. Government agencies are supposed to maximize the general welfare by using available resources to produce desired public goods and services and to redistribute incomes. Foreigners pursue these same goals, as consumers, producers, or governmental agencies.

Market participants sometimes lose sight of their respective goals. Consumers, for example, sometimes buy something impulsively and later wish they had used their income more wisely. Likewise, a producer may take a two-hour lunch, even at the sacrifice of maximum profits. A foreign tourist may belatedly decide that Las Vegas is not worth a visit. And vested economic or political interests can easily cause a government agency to neglect the public's general welfare. In all sectors of the economy, however, the basic goals of utility maximization, profit maximization, or welfare maximization explain most economic activity.

Constraints   The tendency of all participants in the economy to try to maximize something, be it profits, private satisfaction, or social welfare, is not their only common trait. Another element common to all participants is their *limited resources*. You and I cannot buy everything we desire; we simply don't have enough income. As a consequence, we must make *choices* among available products, always hoping to get the most satisfaction for the few dollars we have to spend. Likewise, business firms and government agencies must decide how *best* to use their limited resources to maximize profits or public welfare.

Specialization and Exchange   Our desire to maximize the returns on our limited resources leads us to participate in the market, buying and selling various goods and services. Our decision to participate in these exchanges is prompted by two considerations. First, most of us are incapable of producing everything we desire to consume. Second, even if we *could* produce all our own goods and services, it would still make sense to specialize, producing only one product and trading it for other desired goods and services.

Suppose you were capable of growing your own food, stitching your own clothes, building your own shelter, and even writing your own economics text. Even in these idyllic circumstances, it would still make sense to decide how *best* to expend your limited time and energy, and to rely on others to fill in the gaps. If you were *most* proficient at growing food, you would be best off spending your time farming. You could then exchange some of your food output for the clothes, shelter, and books you desired.

Our economic interactions with others are thus necessitated by two constraints:

- Our absolute inability as individuals to produce all the things we need or desire

- The limited amount of time, energy, and resources we possess for producing those things we could make for ourselves

Together, these constraints lead us to specialize and interact. Most of the interactions that result take place in the market.

MARKET INTERACTIONS

Figure 2.1 summarizes the kinds of interactions that occur among market participants. Note first of all that we have identified four separate groups of participants, each containing many individuals. Domestically, the rectangle marked "Consumers" includes all 250 million consumers in the United States. In the "Business firms" box we have grouped all of the domestic business enterprises that buy and sell goods and services. The third participant, "Governments," includes the many separate agencies of the federal government, as well as state and local governments. Figure 2.1 also illustrates the role of foreigners.

FIGURE 2.1
Market Interactions

Business firms participate in markets by supplying goods and services to product markets and purchasing factors of production in factor markets. Individual consumers participate in the marketplace by supplying factors of production (e.g., their own labor) and purchasing final goods and services. Federal, state, and local governments also participate in both factor and product markets. Foreigners also participate by supplying imports, purchasing exports, and buying and selling resources.

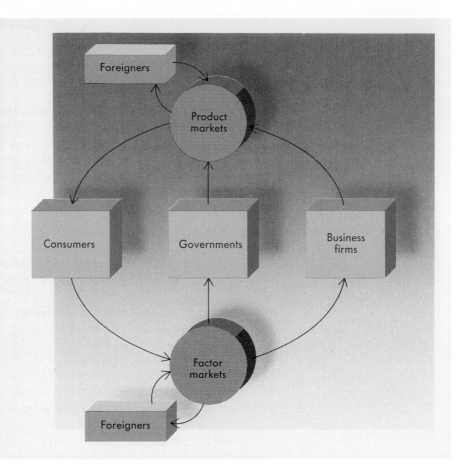

The Two Markets

factor market: Any place where factors of production (e.g., land, labor, capital) are bought and sold.

The easiest way to keep track of all this market activity is to distinguish two basic markets. Figure 2.1 does this, by portraying separate circles for product markets and factor markets. In **factor markets,** factors of production are exchanged. Market participants buy or sell land, labor, or capital that can be used in the production process.[1] When you go looking for work, for example, you are making a factor of production—your labor—available to producers. The producers will hire you—purchase your services in the factor market— if you are offering the skills they need at a price they are willing to pay. The same kind of interaction occurs in factor markets when the government enlists workers into the armed services or when the Japanese buy farmland in Montana.

Interactions within factor markets are only half the story. At the end of a hard day's work consumers enter the grocery store (or bar) to purchase desired goods and services—that is, to buy *products.* In this context, consumers again interact with business firms, this time purchasing goods and services those firms have produced. These interactions occur in **product markets.** Foreigners also participate in the product market by supplying goods and services (imports) to the United States and buying some of our output (exports).

product market: Any place where finished goods and services (products) are bought and sold.

[1]Factor markets are also called *resource markets:* "resources" and "factors of production" are often used synonymously.

Governments also supply goods and services to product markets. The consumer rarely buys national defense, schools, or highways directly; instead, such purchases are made indirectly through taxes and government expenditure. In Figure 2.1, the arrows running from the government through product markets to consumers serve to remind us, however, that all government output is intended "for the people." In this sense, the government acts as an intermediary, buying factors of production and providing certain goods and services consumers desire.

In Figure 2.1 the arrow connecting product markets to consumers emphasizes the fact that consumers, by definition, do not supply products. To the extent that individuals produce goods and services, they do so within the government or business sector. An individual who is a doctor, a dentist, or an economic consultant functions in two sectors. When selling services in the market, this person is regarded as a "business"; when away from the office, he or she is regarded as a "consumer." This distinction is helpful in emphasizing the role of the consumer as the final recipient of all goods and services produced.

Locating markets   Although we will refer repeatedly to two kinds of markets, it would be a little foolish to go off in search of the product and factor markets. Neither a factor market nor a product market is a single, identifiable structure. The term "market" simply refers to any place where an economic exchange occurs—where a buyer and seller interact. The exchange may take place on the street, in a taxicab, over the phone, by mail, or through the classified ads of the newspaper. In some cases, the market used may in fact be quite distinguishable, as in the case of a retail store, the Chicago Commodity Exchange, or a state employment office. But whatever it looks like, *a market exists wherever and whenever an exchange takes place.* The market is simply a place or medium where buyer and seller get together; which market they are in depends on what they are buying or selling.

Dollars and Exchange   Figure 2.1 is a useful summary of market activities, but it neglects one critical element of market interactions: dollars. Each of the arrows depicted in the figure actually has two dimensions. Consider again the arrow linking consumers and product markets. It is drawn in only one direction because consumers, by definition, do not provide goods and services directly to product markets. But they do provide something: dollars. If you want to obtain something from a product market, you must offer to pay for it (typically, with cash, check, or credit card). Consumers exchange dollars for goods and services in product markets.

The same kinds of exchange occur in factor markets. When you go to work, you are exchanging a factor of production (your labor) for income, typically a paycheck. Here again, the path connecting consumers to factor markets really goes in two directions, one of real resources, the other of dollars. Consumers receive wages, rent, and interest for the labor, land, and capital they bring to the factor markets. Indeed, nearly *every market transaction involves an exchange of dollars for goods (in product markets) or resources (in factor markets).*[2] Money thus plays a critical role in facilitating market exchanges and the specialization they permit.

[2]In the rare cases where one good is exchanged directly for another, we speak of *barter* exchanges.

Supply and Demand

supply: The ability and willingness to sell (produce) specific quantities of a good at alternative prices in a given time period, *ceteris paribus*.

demand: The ability and willingness to buy specific quantities of a good at alternative prices in a given time period, *ceteris paribus*.

The two sides of each market transaction are called **supply** and **demand**. As noted earlier, we are *supplying* resources to the market when we look for a job—that is, when we offer our labor in exchange for income. But we are *demanding* goods when we shop in a supermarket—that is, when we are prepared to offer dollars in exchange for something to eat. Business firms may *supply* goods and services in product markets at the same time that they are *demanding* factors of production in factor markets.

Whether one is on the supply side or the demand side of any particular market transaction depends on the nature of the exchange, not on the people or institutions involved.

DEMAND

Although the concepts of supply and demand are useful for explaining what's happening in the marketplace, we are not yet ready to summarize the countless transactions that occur daily in both factor and product markets. Recall that *every market transaction involves an exchange and thus some element of both supply and demand.* Then just consider how many exchanges you alone undertake in a single week, not to mention the transactions of the other 250 million or so consumers among us. The daily volume of market transactions is truly awesome; to keep track of so much action, we need to summarize the activities of many individuals.

Individual Demand

We can begin to understand how market forces work by looking more closely at the behavior of a single market participant. Let us start with Tom, a sophomore at Clearview College. Tom is currently experiencing the torment of writing a paper for his English composition class. To make matters worse, Tom's professor has insisted on typed papers, and Tom cannot type with his fingers much better than he can write with his toes. Under the circumstances, Tom is desperate for a typist.

Although it is apparent that Tom has a strong desire for a typist, his demand for typing services is not yet evident. *A demand exists only if someone is willing and able to pay for the good*—that is, exchange dollars for a good or service in the marketplace. Is Tom willing and able to pay for typing?

Let us assume that Tom has some income and is willing to spend some of it to get his English paper typed. Under these assumptions, we can claim that Tom is a participant in the *market* for typing services.

But can we say anything about his demand? Surely Tom is not prepared to exchange *all* his income for the typing of a single English paper. After all, Tom *could* use his income to buy more desirable goods and services; to give up everything for the typing of just one paper would imply an extremely high **opportunity cost**. It would be more reasonable to assume that there are *limits* to the amount Tom is willing to pay for any given quantity of typing. These limits will be determined by how much income Tom has to spend and how many other goods and services he must forsake in order to pay for typing services. If the price of typing exceeds these limits, Tom may end up typing all or part of the paper himself.

opportunity cost: The most desired goods or services that are forgone in order to obtain something else.

**FIGURE 2.2
A Demand Schedule
and Curve**

A demand schedule indicates the quantities of a good a consumer is able and willing to buy at alternative prices (*ceteris paribus*). The demand schedule (*above*) indicates that Tom would buy 5 pages of typing per semester if the price of typing were $3.50 per page (Row *D*). If typing were less expensive (rows *E–I*), Tom would purchase a larger quantity.

A demand curve is a graphical illustration of a demand schedule. Each point on the curve refers to a specific quantity that will be demanded at a given price. If, for example, the price of typing were $3.50 per page, this curve tells us the consumer would purchase 5 pages per semester (point *D*). If typing cost $3 per page, 7 pages per semester would be demanded (point *E*). Each point on the curve corresponds to a row in the schedule.

	Price of typing (per page)	Quantity of typing demanded (pages per semester)
A	$5.00	1
B	4.50	2
C	4.00	3
D	3.50	5
E	3.00	7
F	2.50	9
G	2.00	12
H	1.50	15
I	1.00	20

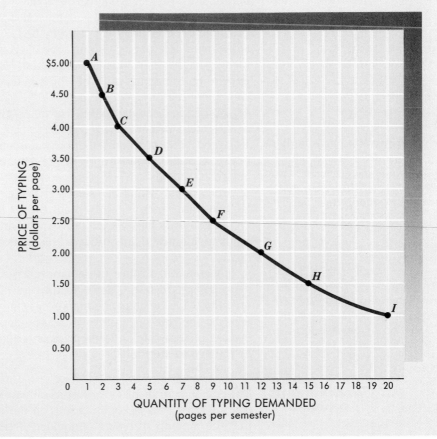

demand schedule: A table showing the quantities of a good a consumer is willing and able to buy at alternative prices in a given time period, *ceteris paribus*.

We assume, then, that when Tom starts looking for a typist, he has in mind some sort of **demand schedule** like that described in Figure 2.2. According to row *A* of this schedule, our tormented English compositionist is willing and able to buy only 1 page of typing per semester if he must pay $5 per page. At such an outrageous price, he will have only the first page of his paper typed professionally and will peck out or print the remaining pages himself. That way, the paper will make a good first impression, and Tom won't have to sacrifice so many other goods and services for his paper.

At lower prices, Tom would behave differently. According to Figure 2.2, Tom would get more pages typed if the price of typing were less. At lower prices, he would not have to give up so many other goods and services for each page of professional typing. The reduced opportunity costs implied by lower typing prices increase the attractiveness of professional typing. Indeed, we see from row *I* of the demand schedule that Tom is willing to have 20 pages per semester—an entire paper—typed professionally if the price per page is as low as $1.

Notice that the demand schedule doesn't tell us anything about *why* this consumer is willing to pay specific prices for various amounts of typing. Tom's expressed willingness to pay for typing may reflect a desperate need to finish his paper, a lot of income to spend, or a relatively small desire for other goods and services. All the demand schedule tells us is what the consumer is *willing and able* to buy, for whatever reasons.

Also observe that the demand schedule doesn't tell us how many pages of typing the consumer will *actually* buy. Figure 2.2 simply states that Tom is *willing and able* to pay for one page of typing per semester at $5.00 per page, for two pages at $4.50 each, and so on. How much typing he purchases will depend on the actual price of typing in the market. Until we know that price, we cannot tell how much typing will be purchased. Hence **"demand" is an expression of consumer buying intentions, of a willingness to buy, not a statement of actual purchases.**

demand curve: A curve describing the quantities of a good a consumer is willing and able to buy at alternative prices in a given time period, *ceteris paribus.*

A convenient summary of buying intentions is provided by the **demand curve,** a graphical illustration of the demand schedule. The demand curve in Figure 2.2 tells us again that this consumer is willing to pay for only one page of professional typing per semester if the price is $5.00 per page (point *A*), for two if the price is $4.50 (point *B*), for three pages at $4.00 a page (point *C*), and so on. Once we know what the market price of typing actually is, a quick look at the demand curve tells us how much typing this consumer will buy.

law of demand: The quantity of a good demanded in a given time period increases as its price falls, *ceteris paribus.*

A common feature of demand curves is their downward slope. As the price of a good falls, people tend to purchase more of it. In Figure 2.2 the quantity of typing demanded increases (moves rightward along the horizontal axis) as the price per page decreases (moves down the vertical axis). This inverse relationship between price and quantity is so common we refer to it as the **law of demand.**

Determinants of Demand

The demand curve in Figure 2.2 has only two dimensions—quantity demanded (on the horizontal axis) and price (on the vertical axis). This seems to imply that the amount of typing demanded depends only on the price of typing. This is surely not the case. A consumer's willingness and ability to buy a product at various prices depends on a variety of forces. **The determinants of demand include**

- **Tastes** (desire for this and other goods)
- **Income** (of the consumer)
- **Other goods** (their availability and price)
- **Expectations** (for income, prices, tastes)

If Tom didn't have to turn in a typed English composition, he would have no taste (desire) for typing services and thus no demand. If he had no income, he would not have the ability to pay and thus would still be out of the typing market. Other goods shape the opportunity cost of typing, while expectations for income, grades, and graduation prospects would all influence his willingness to buy typing services.

Ceteris Paribus

If demand is in fact such a multidimensional decision, how can we reduce it to only two dimensions? This is one of the most common tricks of the economics trade. To simplify their models of the world, economists focus on only one or two forces at a time and *assume* nothing else changes. We know a consumer's tastes, income, other goods, and expectations all affect the decision to buy typing services. But we want to focus on the relationship between quantity demanded and price. That is to say, we want to know what *independent* influence price has on consumption decisions. To find out, we must isolate that one influence, price, and assume that the determinants of demand remain unchanged. Formally, this assumption is referred to by the Latin expression **ceteris paribus** ("all other things remaining equal").

ceteris paribus: The assumption of nothing else changing.

The *ceteris paribus* assumption is not as far-fetched as it may seem at first. In the short run, people's tastes, income, and expectations do not change very much. Also, the prices and availability of other goods remain fairly constant. Hence a change in the *price* of a product may be the only thing that prompts a change in quantity demanded.

Shifts in Demand

The determinants of demand do change, of course, particularly as the time frame is expanded. Accordingly, ***the demand schedule and curve remain unchanged only so long as the underlying determinants of demand remain constant.*** If the *ceteris paribus* assumption is violated—if tastes, income, other goods, or expectations change—the ability or willingness to buy will change. When this happens, the demand curve will **shift** to a new position.

shift in demand: A change in the quantity demanded at any (every) given price.

Suppose, for example, that Tom won the state lottery. This increase in his income would greatly increase his ability to pay for typing services. Figure 2.3 shows the effect of this windfall on Tom's demand for typing. The old demand curve, D_1, is no longer relevant. Tom's lottery winnings enable him to buy more pages at any price. This is illustrated by the new demand curve, D_2. According to this new curve, lucky Tom is now willing and able to buy 11 pages per semester at the price of $3.50 per page (point d_2). This is a large increase in demand, as previously (before winning the lottery) he demanded only 5 pages at that price (point d_1).

With his higher income, Tom can buy more typing at every price. Thus ***the entire demand curve shifts to the right when income goes up.*** Both the old (prelottery) and the new (postlottery) demand curves are illustrated in Figure 2.3.

Income is only one of four basic determinants of demand. Changes in any of the other determinants of demand would also cause the demand curve to shift. Tom's taste for typing might increase dramatically, for example, if his parents promised to buy him a new car for passing English composition. In that case, he might be willing to forgo other goods and spend more of his income on typing. ***An increase in taste (desire) also shifts the demand curve to the right.***

FIGURE 2.3
A Shift in Demand

A demand curve shows how the quantity demanded changes in response to a change in price, *if* all else remains constant. But the determinants of demand may themselves change, causing the demand curve to shift. In this case, an increase in income increases demand from D_1 to D_2. After this shift, Tom demands 11 pages (d_2), rather than 5 (d_1), at the price of $3.50. The quantity demanded at all other prices increases as well.

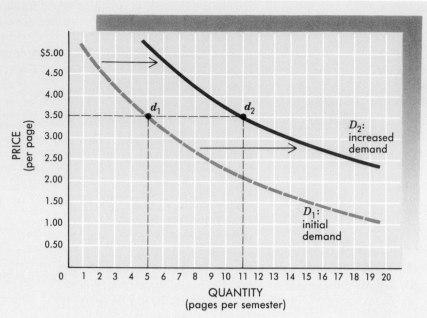

Movements vs. Shifts

It is important to distinguish shifts of the demand curve from movements along the demand curve. ***Movements along a demand curve are a response to price changes for that good.*** Such movements assume that determinants of demand are unchanged. By contrast, ***shifts of the demand curve occur when the determinants of demand change.*** When tastes, income, other goods, or expectations are altered, the basic relationship between price and quantity demanded is changed (shifts).

For convenience, the distinction between movements along a demand curve and shifts of the demand curve have their own labels. Specifically, take care to distinguish:

- ***Changes in quantity demanded:*** movements along a given demand curve, in response to price changes of that good

- ***Changes in demand:*** shifts of the demand curve due to changes in tastes, income, other goods, or expectations

Tom's behavior in the typing market will change if either the price of typing changes or the underlying determinants of his demand for typing are altered. Demand curves help us predict those behavioral changes.

Market Demand

What we can say about demand for typing on the part of one harassed English major we can say about the demand of all other market participants. That is, we can identify the demand for typing services associated with every student at Clearview College (or, for that matter, with all 250 million consumers in the United States). Some students, of course, have no need or desire for professional typing and are not willing to pay anything for such services: they do not participate in the typing market. Other students have a desire for such services but not enough income to pay for them; they, too, are excluded from the typing market. A large number of students, however, not only have a need (or desire) for typing services but also are willing and able to purchase such services.

What we start with in product markets, then, is many individual demand curves. Fortunately, it is possible to combine all the individual demand curves into a single **market demand** for typing services. The aggregation process is no more difficult than simple arithmetic. In fact, simple arithmetic is all that's needed, once you know the buying intentions of all consumers. Suppose you would be willing to buy 1 page of typing per semester at a price of $8 per page. George, who is desperate to make his English essays at least *look* good, would buy 2 at that price; and I would buy none, since I only grade papers and needn't type the grades. What would our combined (market) demand for typing services be at that price? Clearly, our individual inclinations indicate that we would be willing to buy a total of 3 pages of typing per semester if the price were $8 per page. Our combined willingness to buy—our collective market demand—is nothing more than the sum of our individual demand schedules. The same kind of aggregation can be performed for all consumers, leading to a summary of the total market demand for typing services at Clearview College. This *market demand is determined by the number of potential buyers and their respective tastes, incomes, other goods, and expectations.*

What is nice about the market-demand concept is that it permits us to ignore some of the idiosyncrasies of our friends and neighbors. With thousands of students at Clearview College, the typing market is large. Accordingly, we don't have to consider whether George's roommate will move out if George starts doing his own typing, or whether you will buy more typing if you win the state lottery. The market demand for typing services will be little affected by these great moments in your lives. In so large a market, the demand for typing services tends to be more stable and predictable than the demands of the separate individuals who participate in that market. In still larger markets—say, the total U.S. market for typewriters—the predictability of market demand is important to the businesspeople and bureaucrats who make output and price decisions.

We cannot completely ignore the factors that mold and shape the buying habits of individual consumers, however. First of all, we are likely to be as interested in the welfare and happiness of specific individuals as in the dimensions of the whole market. Second, we must recognize that the whole is nothing more than the sum of its parts. In other words, individual decisions determine market outcomes. We need to understand consumer motivations and behavior if we want to forecast larger economic outcomes.

market demand: The total quantities of a good or service people are willing and able to buy at alternative prices in a given time period; the sum of individual demands.

The Market Demand Curve

Table 2.1 provides the basic market demand schedule for a situation in which only four people participate on the demand side of the market. Figure 2.4 illustrates the same market situation with demand curves. The four individuals who participate in the market demand for typing at Clearview College obviously differ greatly, as suggested by their respective demand schedules. Tom has to turn in several papers each semester, has a good income, and is willing to purchase typing services. His demand schedule is portrayed in the first column of Table 2.1 (and is identical to the one we examined in Figure 2.2). George, as we already noted, is desperate to improve the appearance of his papers and is willing to pay relatively high prices for typing services. His

TABLE 2.1 The Market Demand Schedule for Typing

Market demand represents the combined demands of all market participants. To determine the total quantity of typing demanded at any given price, we add up the separate demands of the individual consumers. Row *G* of this schedule indicates that a *total* quantity of 39 pages per semester will be demanded at a price of $2 per page.

| | Price per page | Quantity demanded (pages per semester) | | | | Total demand |
		Tom +	George +	Lisa +	Me =	
A	$5.00	1	4	0	0	5
B	4.50	2	6	0	0	8
C	4.00	3	8	0	0	11
D	3.50	5	11	0	0	16
E	3.00	7	14	1	0	22
F	2.50	9	18	3	0	30
G	2.00	12	22	5	0	39
H	1.50	15	26	6	0	47
I	1.00	20	30	7	0	57

demand schedule is summarized in the second column under "Quantity demanded" in Table 2.1. The third consumer in this market is Lisa. She has a very limited budget and can do her own typing if she must; is not willing to buy any typing at higher prices. As prices drop below $3.50 per page, however, her demand schedule indicates that she will get some of her work professionally typed. Finally, there is my demand schedule (the fourth column under "Quantity demanded" in Table 2.1), which confirms that I really don't participate in the local typing market.

The differing personalities and consumption habits of Tom, George, Lisa, and me are expressed in our individual demand schedules and associated curves, as depicted in Table 2.1 and Figure 2.4. To determine the *market*

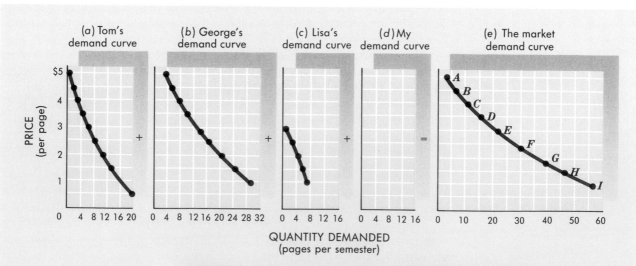

FIGURE 2.4 Construction of the Market Demand Curve

The market demand curve expresses the *combined* demands of all market participants. At a price of $3 per page, the total quantity of typing demanded would be 22 pages per semester (point *E*): 7 pages demanded by Tom, 14 by George, and 1 by Lisa.

demand for typing from this information, we simply add up these four separate demands. The end result of this aggregation is, first, a *market* demand schedule (the last column in Table 2.1) and, second, the resultant *market* demand curve (the curve in Figure 2.4e). These market summaries describe the various quantities of typing that Clearview College students are *willing and able* to purchase each semester at various prices.

How much typing will be purchased each semester? Knowing how much typing Tom, George, Lisa, and I are willing to buy at various prices doesn't tell you how much we are actually going to purchase. To determine the actual consumption of typing services, we have to know something about prices and supplies. What is the price of typing in this market, and how is it determined?

SUPPLY

market supply: The total quantities of a good that sellers are willing and able to sell at alternative prices in a given time period (*ceteris paribus*).

To understand how the price of typing is established we have to look also at the other side of the typing market—namely, the supply side. We need to know how many pages of typing people are willing and able to sell at various prices—that is, the **market supply.** As on the demand side, the *market* supply depends on the behavior of all the individuals who are willing and able to supply typing services at some price.

Determinants of Supply

Generally speaking, people don't like to type. Word processors and computers have made the job easier, but they haven't made it fun. So few people offer to supply typing services just for the fun of it. People who supply typing services do it for money. Specifically, they do it to earn income that they, in turn, can spend on goods and services they desire.

How much income one can make from typing depends on a number of things. As a consequence, the *determinants of market supply include*

- *Technology*
- *Factor costs*
- *Other goods*

- *Taxes*
- *Expectations*
- *Number of sellers*

Word processors, for example, are a technological improvement over standard typewriters. By making it easier to "produce" typing, they induce people to supply more typing services at every price.

In The News

MARKET SUPPLY

Typing Services

PROFESSIONAL TYPING COMPANY. Dissertations, theses, manuscripts. $2/page. Campus pickup. Jane Davis, 840-8854.

PROF. TYPING—$1.50 page, exp. Zena 589-2419.
Computer-scripted dissertations, texts, papers. Perfect. $2 per page. Anita 686-2479.
24-hour service (4 typists) Masters theses, term papers, etc. Professionally typed and corrected. 653-2880.

How many pages of typing are offered at any given price also depends on the cost of factors of production. If ribbons, software, or paper costs are high, typists will have to charge more per page in order to earn some income.

Other goods can also affect the willingness to supply typing services. If you can make more income waiting tables than you can typing, why type? As the prices paid for other goods and services change, they will influence people's decision about whether to offer typing services.

In the real world, the decision to supply goods and services is also influenced by the long arm of Uncle Sam. Federal, state, and local governments impose taxes on income earned in the marketplace. When tax rates are high, people get to keep less of the income they earn. Some people may conclude that typing is no longer worth the hassle and withdraw from the market.

Expectations are also important on the supply side of the market. If typists expect higher prices, lower costs, or reduced taxes, they may be more willing to perfect their typing skills. On the other hand, if they have bad expectations about the future, they may just sell their word processors and find something else to do.

Finally, we note that the number of available typists will affect the quantity of typing offered for sale at various prices. If there are lots of willing typists on campus, a large quantity of typing will be available.

The Market Supply Curve

law of supply: The quantity of a good supplied in a given time period increases as its price increases, *ceteris paribus*.

Figure 2.5 illustrates the market supply curve of typing at Clearview College. Like market demand, the market supply curve is the sum of all the individual supplier decisions about how much to produce at any given price. The market supply curve slopes upward to the right, indicating that *larger quantities will be offered at higher prices.* This basic **law of supply** reflects the fact that increased output typically entails higher costs and so will be forthcoming only at higher prices. Higher prices may also increase profits and so entice producers to supply greater quantities.

Note that Figure 2.5 illustrates the *market* supply. We have not bothered to construct separate supply curves for each person who is able and willing to supply typing services on the Clearview campus. We have skipped over

FIGURE 2.5
The Market Supply Curve

The market supply curve indicates the *combined* sales intentions of all market participants. If the price of typing were $2.50 per page (point *e*), the *total* quantity of typing supplied would be 62 pages per semester. This quantity is determined by adding together the supply decisions of all individual producers.

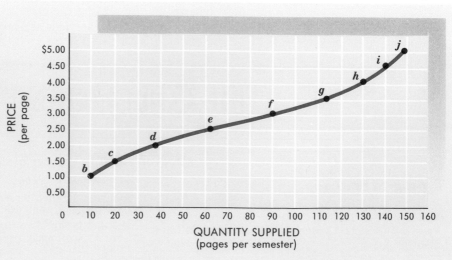

that first step and gone right to the market supply curve. Like the market demand curve, however, the market supply curve is based on the supply decisions of individual producers. The curve itself is computed via simple arithmetic, by adding up the quantities each producer is willing and able to supply at every given price. Point *f* in Figure 2.5 tells us that those individuals are collectively willing and able to produce 90 pages of typing per semester at a price of $3 per page. The rest of the points on the supply curve tell us how many pages of typing will be offered at other prices.

None of the points on the market supply curve (Figure 2.5) tells us how much typing is actually being sold on the Clearview campus. ***Market supply is an expression of sellers' intentions, of the ability and willingness to sell, not a statement of actual sales.*** My next-door neighbor may be *willing* to sell his 1982 Honda Civic for $8,000, but it is most unlikely that he will ever find a buyer at that price. Nevertheless, his *willingness* to sell his car at that price is part of the *market supply* of used cars.

Shifts in Supply

As with demand, there is nothing sacred about any given set of supply intentions. Supply curves *shift* when the underlying determinants of supply change. Thus we again distinguish

- ***Changes in quantity supplied:*** movements along a given supply curve

- ***Changes in supply:*** shifts of the supply curve

Our Latin friend *ceteris paribus* is once again the decisive factor. If the price of typing is the only thing changing, then we can ***track changes in quantity supplied along the supply curve*** in Figure 2.5. But if *ceteris paribus* is violated—if technology, factor costs, other goods, taxes, or expectations change—then ***changes in supply are illustrated by shifts of the supply curve.***

The accompanying In the News box illustrates a shift in the supply of condos in New York City. When one of the determinants of supply—in this case, taxes—changed, the supply curve *shifted* to the right, pushing condo prices down.

EQUILIBRIUM

We can now determine the price and quantity of typing being sold at Clearview College. The market supply curve expresses the *ability and willingness* of producers to sell typing at various prices. The market demand curve illustrates the *ability and willingness* of Tom, George, Lisa, and me to buy typing at those same prices. When we put the two curves together, we see that ***only one price and quantity are compatible with the existing intentions of both buyers and sellers.*** This **equilibrium** occurs at the intersection of the two curves in Figure 2.6. Once it is established, typing will cost $2 per page. At that price, campus typists will sell a total of 39 pages of typing per semester—the same amount that students wish to buy at that price.

An important characteristic of the equilibrium price is that it is not determined by any single individual. Rather it is determined by the collective behavior of many buyers and sellers, each acting out his or her own demand or supply schedule. It is this kind of impersonal price determination that gave rise to Adam Smith's characterization of the market mechanism as "the in-

equilibrium price: The price at which the quantity of a good demanded in a given time period equals the quantity supplied.

In The News

Condo Prices in New York

More than 1.5 million people live on the 22.2-square-mile island of Manhattan, New York City's central borough. The resulting demand for housing creates astronomical prices for living quarters. In January 1985 the average price of a new two-bedroom condominium apartment was $450,000. This price was determined by the intersection of the "old" supply curve with the market demand curve.

The supply of any good, including condo apartments, depends on technology, factor costs, other goods, taxes, expectations, and the number of sellers. If any of these determinants changes, the supply curve will shift.

That is exactly what happened in the New York City condo market. To spur additional construction, the state gave builders a special tax break for units constructed prior to November 1985. This tax reduction made it more profitable to supply condo apartments. The result was a dramatic, rightward shift of the condo supply curve: in January 1985, 13,359 apartments were under construc-

tion, compared with only 3,952 apartments in all of 1984. This increase in supply caused condo prices to fall—to an average of merely $380,000.

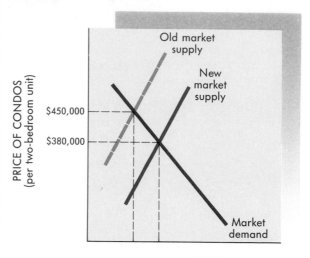

visible hand." In attempting to explain how the market mechanism works, the famed eighteenth-century economist noted a certain feature of market prices. The market behaves as if some unseen force (the invisible hand) were examining each individual's supply or demand schedule, then selecting a price that assured an equilibrium. In practice, of course, the process of price determination is not so mysterious; rather it is a simple process of trial and error.

Surplus and Shortage

Suppose for the moment that campus typists believed typing could be sold for $2.50 per page rather than the equilibrium price of $2.00 and offered it only at this higher price. From the demand and supply schedules depicted in Figure 2.6 we can readily foresee the consequences. At $2.50 per page, campus typists would be offering more typing services (point Y) than Tom, George, and Lisa were willing to buy (point X) at that price. A **market surplus** of typing services would exist, in the sense that more typing was being offered for sale (supplied) than students cared to purchase at the available price.

As Figure 2.6 indicates, at a price of $2.50 per page, a market surplus of 32 pages per semester exists. Under these circumstances, campus typists would be spending many idle hours at their typewriters, waiting for customers to appear. Their waiting will be in vain, because the quantity of typing demanded will not increase until the price of typing falls. That is the clear message of the demand curve. The tendency of quantity demanded to increase as price falls is illustrated in Figure 2.6 by a movement along the

market surplus: The amount by which the quantity supplied exceeds the quantity demanded at a given price; excess supply.

FIGURE 2.6
Market Surplus or Shortage

Only at equilibrium is the quantity demanded equal to the quantity supplied. In this case, the equilibrium price is $2 per page, and 39 pages is the equilibrium quantity. At higher prices, a market surplus exists—the quantity supplied exceeds the quantity demanded. At prices below equilibrium, a market shortage exists.

The intersection of the demand and supply curves in the graph represents equilibrium price and output in this market.

Price per page	Quantity supplied (pages per semester)		Quantity demanded (pages per semester)
$5.00	148		5
4.50	140		8
4.00	130	market surplus	11
3.50	114		16
3.00	90		22
2.50	62		30
2.00	39	equilibrium	39
1.50	20	market shortage	47
1.00	10		57

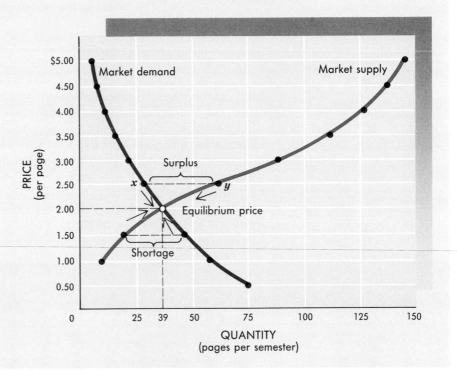

demand curve from point *X* to lower prices and greater quantity demanded. As we move down the market demand curve, the desire for typing does not change, but the quantity people are able and willing to buy increases.

Typists at Clearview would have to reduce price from $2.50 (point *Y*) to $2.00 per page in order to attract enough buyers. Oil producers confronted the same dilemma in the mid-1980s. The accompanying In the News box shows how a surplus of oil in world markets forced sellers to reduce the price of oil.

A very different sequence of events would occur if a market shortage existed. Suppose someone were to spread the word that typing services were available at only $1.50 per page. Tom, George, and Lisa would be standing in line to get their papers typed, but campus typists would not be willing to

In The News

MARKET SURPLUS

Surplus Punches Hole in Oil Price

The law of supply and demand caught up with oil prices Tuesday, sending them plunging on the spot market.

West Texas intermediate, the USA's highest quality grade of crude, plunged $1.55, to $15.35 a barrel.

On the futures market, the benchmark crude fell 49 cents, to $15.10 a barrel.

That's down from a three-month high of $17.16 a barrel May 19, but nowhere near the eight-year trading low of $9.75 on April 1.

Fueling the earlier price rally: expected strong demand for gasoline for this summer's driving season and a tem-porary shortage of light crude after a three-week Norwegian oil strike. But the current 2 million barrel-a-day world surplus brought prices back to earth.

"That's a heck of a drop," says analyst Jack Carney of Pace Consultants Inc.

"The price of crude was bid up higher than anybody could explain as far as supply and demand," he says. "We were sort of astounded when it went up."

Houston oil expert Dale Steffes said oil will hover around $15 a barrel for the short term. . . .

—David Landis

USA Today, May 28, 1986, p. 1. Copyright © 1986 USA TODAY. Excerpted with permission.

---

market shortage: The amount by which the quantity demanded exceeds the quantity supplied at a given price; excess demand.

supply the quantity desired at that price. As Figure 2.6 confirms, at $1.50 per page, the quantity demanded (47 pages per semester) would greatly exceed the quantity supplied (20 pages per semester). In this situation, we may speak of a **market shortage,** that is, an excess of quantity demanded over quantity supplied. At a price of $1.50 a page, the shortage amounts to 27 pages of typing.

When a market shortage exists, not all consumer demands can be satisfied. In other words, some people who are *willing* to buy typing at the going price ($1.50) will not be able to do so. To assure themselves of sufficient typing, Tom, George, Lisa, or some other consumer may offer to pay a *higher*

In The News

MARKET SHORTAGE

U2 Fans and the Longest Five Days

Vigil for RFK Tickets Winds Up in a Sellout

Last Wednesday night, a dozen people trudged to RFK Stadium and slumped beneath ticket windows, eager for them to open. Five days later, they did.

At 10 A.M. yesterday, $19 tickets for U2's Sept. 20 concert at RFK finally went on sale. There were 44,000 seats available. Three hours later, there were none.

"These tickets went faster than any concert around here all summer, and quicker than any I can remember, except for Springsteen in 1985," said Patti Pacak, spokeswoman for the RFK Stadium ticket office.

"The phones were ringing constantly, and the lines were real long, but we weren't surprised by the response. We knew it was going to be like this when we saw a small group of people start lining up out here last Wednesday night about 10 P.M."

More than 4,600 people—3,900 outside RFK—endured overnight and weekend vigils at Ticket Center offices in metropolitan Washington, Pacak said.

—Rene Sanchez

Washington Post, August 25, 1987, p. D1. Copyright © 1987 The Washington Post.

price, thus initiating a move up the demand curve of Figure 2.6. The higher prices offered will in turn induce other enterprising students to type more, thus ensuring an upward movement along the market supply curve. Thus a higher price tends to call forth a greater quantity supplied, as reflected in the upward-sloping supply curve. Notice, again, that the *desire* to type has not changed; only the quantity supplied has responded to a change in price.

What we observe, then, is that **whenever the market price is set above or below the equilibrium price, either a market surplus or a market shortage will emerge.** To overcome a surplus or shortage, buyers and sellers will change their behavior—that is, the prices charged or paid and the quantities demanded or sold. Only at the *equilibrium* price will no further adjustments be required. The equilibrium price is the only price at which the amount consumers are willing to buy equals the amount producers are willing to sell. We can count on market participants to find this equilibrium.

Business firms can discover equilibrium market prices in the same way. If they find that consumer purchases are not keeping up with production, they may conclude that their price is above the equilibrium price. They will have to get rid of their accumulated inventory. To do so they will have to lower their price (by a Grand End-of-Year Sale, perhaps) or convince consumers (via advertising) that they have underrated a most indispensable product. In the happy situation where consumer purchases are outpacing production, a firm might conclude that its price was a trifle too low and give it a nudge upward. Or it might expand production facilities. In any case, the equilibrium price can be established after a few trials in the marketplace.

Changes in Equilibrium

The collective actions of buyers and sellers will quickly establish an equilibrium price for any product. We should not regard any particular equilibrium price as permanent, however. The equilibrium price established in the Clearview College typing market, for example, was the unique outcome of specific demand and supply schedules. Those schedules themselves were based on our assumption of *ceteris paribus.* Specifically, we assumed that the "taste" (desire) for typing was given, as were consumers' incomes, the price and availability of other goods, and expectations. But any of these determinants of demand could change. When one does, the demand curve has to be redrawn. Such a shift of the demand curve will lead to a new equilibrium price and quantity. Indeed, **the equilibrium price will change whenever the supply or demand curve shifts.**

We can illustrate how equilibrium prices change by taking one last look at the Clearview College typing market. Our original supply and demand curves, together with the resulting equilibrium (point E_1), are depicted in Figure 2.7. Now suppose that the professors at Clearview begin assigning additional papers and homework, all of which must be typed. The increased need (desire) for typing services will affect market demand. Tom, George, and Lisa are suddenly willing to buy more typing at every price than they were before. That is to say, the *demand* for typing has increased. We can represent this increased demand by a rightward *shift* of the market demand curve, as illustrated in Figure 2.7.

Note that the new demand curve intersects the (unchanged) market supply curve at a new price (point E_2); the equilibrium price is now $3 per page. This new equilibrium price will persist until either the demand curve or the supply curve shifts again.

FIGURE 2.7
A New Equilibrium

A rightward shift of the demand curve indicates that consumers are willing and able to buy a larger quantity at every price. As a consequence, a new equilibrium is established (point E_2), at a higher price and greater quantity. A shift of the demand curve occurs only when the assumption of *ceteris paribus* is violated—when one of the determinants of demand changes.

The equilibrium would also be altered if the determinants of supply changed, causing a shift of the market supply curve.

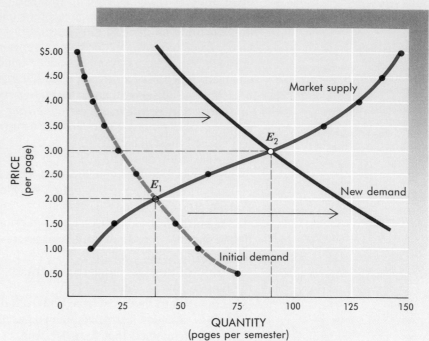

The kinds of price changes we are describing here are quite common. Indeed, equilibrium prices change as often as significant changes occur in the behavior of buyers or sellers. A few moments in a stockbroker's office or a glance through the stock pages of the daily newspaper should be testimony enough to the fluid character of market prices. If thousands of stockholders decide to sell IBM shares tomorrow, you can be sure that the market price of that stock will drop. The accompanying World View illustrates how even a single restaurant can use the principles of supply and demand to ensure that all of the items on the menu are ordered.

DISEQUILIBRIUM PRICING

The ability of the market to achieve equilibrium price and quantity is evident. Nevertheless, people are often upset with those outcomes. At Clearview College, the consumers of typing services are likely to feel that the price of typing is too high. On the other hand, campus typists may feel that they are getting paid too little for their services.

Price Ceilings Sometimes consumers are able to convince the government to intervene on their behalf by setting a limit on prices. In many cities, for example, poor people and their advocates have convinced local governments that rents are too high. High rents, they argue, make housing prohibitively expensive for the poor, leaving them homeless or living in crowded, unsafe quarters. They ask government to impose a *limit* on rents in order to make housing affordable for everyone. Two hundred local governments—including New York City, Bos-

W🌐RLD VIEW

EQUILIBRIUM PRICES

Dining on the Downtick

Americans aren't the only consumers who fall for packaging. Since late January, Parisians (not to mention TV crews from around the world) have been drawn to 6 rue Feydeau to try La Connivence, a restaurant with a new gimmick. The name means "collusion," and, yes, of course, La Connivence is a block away from the Bourse, the French stock exchange.

What's the gimmick? Just that the restaurant's prices fluctuate according to supply and demand. The more a dish is ordered, the higher its price. A dish that's ignored gets cheaper.

Customers tune in to the day's menu (couched in trading terms) on computer screens. Among a typical day's options: *forte baisse du haddock* ("precipitous drop in haddock"), *vif recul de la côte de boeuf* ("rapid decline in beef ribs"), *la brochette de lotte au plus bas* ("fish kabob hits bottom"). Then comes the major decision— whether to opt for the price that's listed when you order or to gamble that the price will have gone down by the time you finish your meal.

So far, only main dishes are open to speculation, but co-owners Pierre Guetta, an ex-professor at a top French business school, and Jean-Paul Trastour, an ex-journalist at *Le Nouvel Observateur,* are adding wine to the risk list.

La Connivence is open for dinner, but the midday "session" (as the owners call it) is the one to catch. That's when the traders of Paris leave the floor to push their luck *à table.* But here, at least, the return on their $15 investment (the average price of a meal) is immediate— and usually good.

—Christina de Liagre

New York, April 7, 1986, p. 30.

---

price ceiling: Upper limit imposed on the price of a good.

ton, Washington, D.C., and San Francisco—have responded with rent controls of varying severity. In all cases, rent controls are a **price ceiling**—an upper limit imposed on the price of a good or service.

Rent controls have the immediate effect of making housing more affordable. But such controls are *disequilibrium* prices and will change housing decisions in unintended ways. Figure 2.8 illustrates the problem. In the absence of government intervention, the quantity of housing consumed (q_e) and the prevailing rent (p_e) would be established by the intersection of market supply and demand curves. Not everyone would be housed to their satisfaction in this equilibrium. As the demand curve indicates, more housing would be consumed if rents were lower. Some of those people on the low end of the demand curve simply do not have enough income to pay the equilibrium rent p_e. They may be homeless.

To remedy this situation, the city government imposes a rent ceiling of p_c. This lower price seemingly makes housing more affordable for everyone, including the poor. At the controlled rent p_c, people are willing and able to consume a lot more housing: the quantity demanded increases from q_e to q_d.

But what about the quantity of housing supplied? Rent controls do not increase the number of housing units available. On the contrary, price controls tend to have the opposite effect. Notice in Figure 2.8 how the quantity *supplied* falls from q_e to q_s when the rent ceiling is enacted. There is now less housing available than there was before. Thus *price ceilings tend to*

- *Increase the quantity demanded*
- *Decrease the quantity supplied*
- *Create a market shortage*

FIGURE 2.8
Price Ceilings Create Shortages

Many cities impose rent controls to keep housing affordable. Consumers respond to the below–equilibrium price ceiling (p_c) by demanding more housing (q_d vs. q_e). But the quantity of housing supplied diminishes as landlords convert buildings to other uses (e.g., condos) or simply let rental units deteriorate. New construction also slows. The result is a housing shortage ($q_d - q_s$) and an actual reduction in available housing.

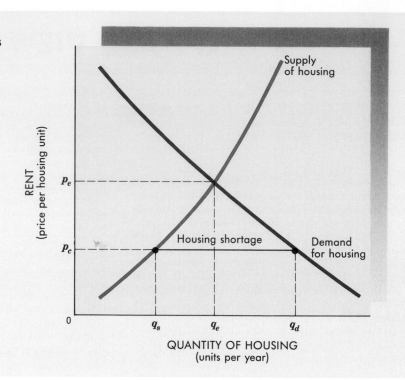

You may well wonder where the "lost" housing went. The houses did not disappear. However, some landlords decided that renting their units was no longer worth the effort. They chose instead to sell the units, convert them to condominiums, or even live in them themselves. Other landlords stopped maintaining their buildings, letting the units deteriorate. The rate of new construction slowed, too, as builders decided that rent control made new construction less profitable. Slowly but surely the quantity of housing declines from q_e to q_s. Hence *there will be less housing for everyone when rent controls are imposed to make housing more affordable for some.*

Figure 2.8 illustrates another problem. As we have seen, the rent ceiling p_c has created a housing shortage—a gap between the quantity demanded (q_d) and the quantity supplied (q_s). Who will get the increasingly scarce housing? The market would have settled this FOR WHOM question by permitting rents to rise and allocating available units to those consumers willing and able to pay the rent p_e. Now, however, rents cannot rise and we have lots of people clamoring for housing that is not available. A different method of distributing goods must be found. Vacant units will go to those who learn of them first, patiently wait on waiting lists, or offer a gratuity to the landlord or renting agent. In New York City, where rent control was the law for forty years, people "sold" their rent-controlled apartments when they moved elsewhere. In Poland, people stood in line for hours to get price-controlled food (see World View) before price ceilings were eliminated.

Price Floors

Artificially high (above-equilibrium) prices create similar problems. A **price floor** is a minimum price imposed by the government for a good or service. The objective of such intervention is to raise the price of the good and create more income for the seller. Federal minimum wage laws, for example, forbid most employers from paying less than $4.25 an hour for labor.

price floor: Lower limit imposed on the price of a good.

W✪RLD VIEW

DISEQUILIBRIUM PRICES

Fed Up with the Food Fight

Forced to Queue Endlessly for Supplies, the Poles Are Boiling

It is 4 A.M. The sun will not rise for almost three hours, but already the line has begun to form in front of the austere, dimly lit shop. A panel truck pulls up to the rear entrance, and two burly workers, their white smocks spattered with red stains, deliver their precious cargo: a day's supply of meat. Within three hours, the choicest cuts—pork chops, ham, boneless beef—will be gone. The late arrivals will have to make do with sausage, soup bones or chicken. Or perhaps nothing at all.

The government officially maintains that the average Pole spends four hours queuing up each day. That estimate drew derisive laughter from most shoppers. Says one retired woman: "I spend half my time in lines. I do all the shopping for my daughter and her family." Indeed, the elderly are one of the Polish family's most valuable assets, since they have more free time for waiting in line. . . .

With the state-run supply system on the verge of collapse, most Poles must turn to alternate sources for food and other scarce items. Those with friends or relatives abroad may get some of what they need via parcel post.

Others resort to barter: a mechanic might trade two quarts of motor oil to a salesgirl for a pound of coffee; in Silesia, the miners are reportedly trading coal to farmers for meat. For exorbitant prices, or hard Western currency, almost anything can be gotten on the black market. Sample prices: blue jeans, $180; one pint of vodka, $24.

More affordable to the average Pole are the so-called free markets, which the government traditionally has ignored. These extralegal bazaars are operated as private enterprises by farmers or nimble entrepreneurs who offer abundant quantities of fruits and vegetables at prices slightly higher than the state stores. A free-market egg costs about 40¢, for example, compared with 30¢ for one in a state store. The more wealthy city dweller may drive out into the country and buy meat directly and illegally from a farmer. One Gdansk bureaucrat admits that he and a neighbor buy whole pigs and then salt the meat down in barrels. Such stratagems have become so common that the government last month prohibited the sale of meat outside state stores. Reason: farmers were refusing to sell their pigs to the government at the official price of $1.30 per lb. when they could get half again as much from individuals.

Time, September 28, 1981. Copyright © 1981 Time Inc. Reprinted by permission.

Price floors are also common in the farm sector. To stabilize farmers' incomes while ensuring a steady flow of food, the government offers price guarantees for certain crops. In 1990, for example, the government set a price guarantee ("target price") of $2.75 per bushel for corn. If the market price of corn were to fall below $2.75, the government promised to pay farmers the difference. Hence farmers knew they could sell their corn for $2.75 per bushel, regardless of market demand.

Figure 2.9 illustrates the consequences of the price floor. The price guarantee p_f lies above the equilibrium price p_e (otherwise it would have no effect). At that higher price, farmers supply more corn (q_s vs. q_e). However, consumers are not willing to buy that much corn: at the price p_f they demand only the quantity q_d. Hence ***a price floor***

* ***Increases the quantity supplied***

* ***Reduces the quantity demanded***

* ***Creates a market surplus***

The problem now is to dispose of all that excess corn. For years, the U.S. government simply purchased the surplus corn and stored it. This got too expensive, and tons of corn were wasted through spoilage and rat pillage. We even tried giving it to poor countries, but the surplus disrupted their own

FIGURE 2.9
Price Floors Create Surplus

The U.S. Department of Agriculture sets a "target price" for corn (p_f). If the market price drops below p_f, the government pays farmers the difference. Hence the target price is a guaranteed price floor for farmers.

Farmers respond by producing the quantity q_s. Consumers will purchase the quantity q_s, however, only if the market price drops to p_m (point a on the demand curve). The government thus must either purchase and store the surplus $q_s - q_d$ or pay farmers the difference between p_f and p_m for each bushel of corn.

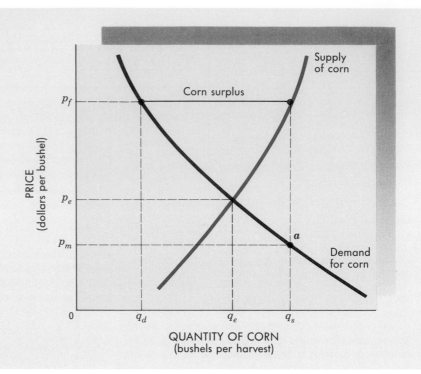

agricultural markets. Finally, we decided to sell it. But notice what happened to the market price. Consumers would purchase the quantity q_s only if the price of corn fell to p_m (point a in Figure 2.9). Hence corn prices in the marketplace have to fall *below* the true equilibrium (p_e) in order to dispose of the excess corn grown for sale at the guaranteed price p_f. That sounds like a great deal for both consumers (now paying a below-equilibrium price) and farmers (now receiving an above-equilibrium price). But the outcome is not as good as it looks. The government must collect enough taxes to pay farmers the difference between the price floor (p_f) and the resulting market price (p_m). Furthermore, the mix of output now includes more corn than people would want if they had to pay the true costs of corn (p_f) directly. This is a classic case of **government failure**: society ends up with the wrong mix of output, an increased tax burden, and an altered distribution of income.

government failure: Government intervention that fails to improve economic outcomes.

POLICY INSIGHTS:

LAISSEZ FAIRE

The apparent inefficiencies of price ceilings and floors imply that market outcomes are best left alone. This is a conclusion reached long ago by Adam Smith, the founder of modern economic theory. In 1776 he advocated a policy of **laissez faire**—literally, "leave it alone." As he saw it, the market mechanism was an efficient procedure for allocating resources and distributing incomes. Interference with the market—through price ceilings, floors, or other regulation—was likely to cause more problems than it could hope to solve.

The policy of laissez faire is motivated not only by the potential pitfalls of government intervention, but also by the recognition of how well the market

laissez faire: The doctrine of "leave it alone," of nonintervention by government in the market mechanism.

market mechanism: The use of market prices and sales to signal desired outputs (or resource allocations).

mechanism can work. Recall our visit to Clearview College, where the price and quantity of typing services had to be established. There was no central agency that set the price of typing or determined how much typing would be done at Clearview College. Instead, both the price of typing and its quantity were determined by the **market mechanism**—the interactions of many independent (decentralized) buyers and sellers.

What, How, for Whom

Notice how the market mechanism resolved the basic economic questions of WHAT, HOW, and FOR WHOM. The WHAT question refers to how much typing to include in society's mix of output. The answer at Clearview College was 39 pages per semester. This decision was not reached in a referendum, but instead in the market equilibrium (Figure 2.6). In the same way but on a larger scale, millions of consumers and a handful of auto producers decide to include 6 million to 7 million cars in each year's mix of output.

The market mechanism will also determine HOW these goods are produced. Profit-seeking producers will strive to produce typing and automobiles in the most efficient way. They will use market prices to decide not only WHAT to produce, but also what resources to use in the production process.

Finally, the "invisible hand" of the market will determine who gets the goods produced. At Clearview College, who got their papers typed? Only those students who were willing and able to pay $2 per page for that service. FOR WHOM are all those automobiles produced each year? The answer is the same: those consumers who are willing and able to pay the market price for a new car.

Optimal, Not Perfect

Not everyone is happy with these answers, of course. Tom would like to pay only $1 a page for his typing. And some of the Clearview students do not have enough income to buy any typing. They think it is unfair that they have to type their own papers while richer students can have someone else do their typing for them. Students who cannot afford cars are even less happy with the market's answer to the FOR WHOM question.

Although the outcomes of the marketplace are not perfect, they are likely to be optimal. Optimal outcomes are the best possible, *given* our incomes and scarce resources. In other words, we expect the choices made in the marketplace to be the best possible choices for each participant. Why do we draw such a conclusion? Because Tom and George and everybody in our little Clearview College drama had (and continue to have) absolute freedom to make their own purchase and consumption decisions. And also because we assume that sooner or later they will make the choices they find most satisfying. The results are thus *optimal,* in the sense that everyone has done as well as they can, given their income and talents.

The optimality of market outcomes provides a powerful argument for *laissez faire.* In essence, the laissez-faire doctrine recognizes that decentralized markets not only work, but also give individuals the opportunity to maximize their satisfaction. In this context, government interference is seen as a threat to the attainment of the "right" mix of output and other economic goals. The evident efficiency of the market mechanism in allocating scarce resources seems to dictate against government intervention. Since its development by Adam Smith in 1776, the laissez-faire doctrine has had a profound impact on the way the economy functions and what government does (or doesn't do).

SUMMARY

- Individual consumers, business firms, government agencies, and foreigners participate in the marketplace by offering to buy or sell goods and services, or factors of production. Participation is motivated by the desire to maximize utility (consumers), profits (business firms), or the general welfare (government agencies).

- All interactions in the marketplace involve the exchange of either factors of production or finished products. Although the actual exchanges can take place anywhere, we may say that they take place in product markets or factor markets, depending on what is being exchanged.

- People who are willing and able to buy a particular good at some price are part of the market demand for that product. All those who are willing and able to sell that good at some price are part of the market supply. Total market demand or supply is the sum of individual demands or supplies.

- Supply and demand curves illustrate how the quantity demanded or supplied changes in response to a change in the price of that good, if nothing else changes (*ceteris paribus*). Demand curves slope downward; supply curves slope upward.

- The determinants of market demand include the number of potential buyers and their respective tastes (desires), incomes, other goods, and expectations. If any of these determinants changes, the demand curve shifts. Movements along a demand curve are induced only by a change in the price of that good.

- The determinants of market supply include technology, factor costs, other goods, taxes, expectations, and the number of sellers. Supply shifts when these underlying determinants change.

- The quantity of goods or resources actually exchanged in each market will depend on the behavior of all buyers and sellers, as summarized in market supply and demand curves. At the point where the two curves intersect, an equilibrium price—the price at which the quantity demanded equals the quantity supplied—will be established.

- A distinctive feature of the equilibrium price and quantity is that it is the only price–quantity combination that is acceptable to buyers and sellers alike. At higher prices, sellers supply more than buyers are willing to purchase (a market surplus); at lower prices, the amount demanded exceeds the quantity supplied (a market shortage). Only the equilibrium price clears the market.

- Price ceilings and floors are disequilibrium prices imposed on the marketplace. Such price controls create an imbalance between quantities demanded and supplied.

- The market mechanism is a device for establishing prices and product and resource flows. As such, it may be used to answer the basic economic question of WHAT to produce, HOW to produce it, and FOR WHOM. Its apparent efficiency prompts the call for laissez faire—a policy of government nonintervention in the marketplace.

Terms to Remember Define the following terms:

factor market
product market
supply
demand
opportunity cost
demand schedule
demand curve
law of demand
ceteris paribus
shift in demand
market demand

market supply
law of supply
equilibrium price
market surplus
market shortage
price ceiling
price floor
government failure
laissez faire
market mechanism

Questions for Discussion

1. In our story of Tom, the nontypist confronted with a typing assignment, we emphasized the great urgency of his desire for typing services. Many people would say that Tom had an "absolute need" for typing and was therefore ready to "pay anything" to get his paper typed. If this were true, what shape would his demand curve have? Why isn't this realistic?

2. Illustrate the market situation for the U2 concert (p. 48). Why didn't the concert promoters set an equilibrium price?

3. Word-processing machines make typing easier and improve the appearance of the final product as well. How have word processors altered the supply and demand for typing services?

4. Can you explain the practice of "scalping" tickets for major sporting events in terms of market shortages? How else might tickets be distributed?

5. If rent controls are so counterproductive, why do cities impose them? How else might the housing problems of poor people be solved?

Problems

1. Given the following data, (*a*) construct market supply and demand curves and identify the equilibrium price; and (*b*) identify the amount of shortage or surplus that would exist at a price of $4:

Participant	Quantity demanded or supplied (per week)				
	$5	$4	$3	$2	$1
A. Price					
B. Demand side					
Al	1	2	3	4	5
Betsy	0	1	1	1	2
Casey	2	2	3	3	4
Daisy	1	3	4	4	6
Eddie	1	2	2	3	5
Market total	—	—	—	—	—

Participant	Quantity demanded or supplied (per week)				
	$5	$4	$3	$2	$1
C. Supply side					
Alice	3	3	3	3	3
Butch	7	5	4	4	2
Connie	6	4	3	3	1
Dutch	6	5	4	3	0
Ellen	4	2	2	2	1
Market total	—	—	—	—	—

2. Suppose that the good described in problem 1 became so popular that every consumer demanded one additional unit at every price. Illustrate this increase in market demand and identify the new equilibrium. Which curve has shifted? Along which curve has there been a movement of price and quantity?

3. (a) According to Figure 2.9, how much would the government have to pay to purchase the entire corn surplus created by the target price p_f?

   (b) How much would the government have to pay if it let farmers sell the entire surplus in the markets and simply paid them the difference between the market price and the guaranteed price?

   (c) How could the government maintain the true equilibrium price p_e? How much would it have to spend in this case?

4. The following events shift either the supply or the demand curve for American-made automobiles. Draw an initial set of market supply and demand curves, then illustrate each of the following events:

   (a) In 1929 a depression began in the United States that severely curtailed purchases of automobiles.

   (b) Serious strikes hit the auto industry during the 1930s.

   (c) During World War II, producers of automobiles converted their factories to war production.

   (d) In the 1960s small, inexpensive foreign cars began to appear and gain market share in the U.S. market.

   (e) In 1973 and again in 1978, oil prices rose dramatically.

   (f) From 1982 to 1985, the U.S. government imposed quotas on the number of Japanese cars that could be imported into the United States.

   (g) To gear up to foreign competition, American car producers began to automate so as to increase productivity in the automobile industry.

   (h) Pickup trucks, minivans, and recreation vehicles gained popularity in the 1980s, and many families bought such vehicles rather than automobiles.

   (i) During the late 1970s and early 1980s, foreign producers set up new plants in the United States in order to produce foreign-model cars.

The Public Sector

*The market has a keen ear for private wants,
but a deaf ear for public needs.*

–Robert Heilbroner

*A*n overwhelming majority of Americans believe that the government wastes their tax dollars. Taxpayers perceive government agencies as bloated and inefficient and bureaucrats as more interested in their own well-being than in the welfare of the general public. Nevertheless, the public sector keeps growing. Year in and year out government budgets increase—not just the federal budget, but also those of the 50 state governments, 3,000 counties, 18,000 cities, 17,000 townships, 21,000 school districts, and over 20,000 special districts that make up the public sector.

Ironically, few Americans are prepared to cut these government budgets. Although taxpayers grumble about "excessive" government spending, they are quick to complain whenever any specific cutbacks in government services are proposed. Proposals to "privatize" government programs—turn them over to the private sector—bring even louder cries of anguish.

This schizophrenia about government spending reflects an unease about the role of government. On the one hand, people worry that the government has too much control over the economy. On the other hand, there is a deep-rooted conviction that some government functions are essential to our well-being.

The purpose of this chapter is to examine the economic role of the public sector. What functions does the government perform? What functions *should* it perform? Our inquiry focuses on these basic questions:

- Do we need a public sector?

- What goods and services are best produced by the government?

- How large a public sector is desirable?

We shall see that there are a number of economic functions only government can fulfill. We shall also observe how the public sector has grown and what goods and services it now produces. Finally, we shall consider whether taxpayers are "getting their money's worth" for the resources allocated to the public sector.

MICRO FAILURE

optimal mix of output: The most desirable combination of output attainable with existing resources, technology, and social values.

As we noted earlier, every country must decide WHAT to produce, HOW to produce, and FOR WHOM to produce. The objective is always to fashion the best possible answers to these questions. With respect to the WHAT questions, for example, we want to produce the **optimal mix of output**—the most desirable combination of goods and services on our production-possibilities curve.

In Chapter 2 we observed that the market mechanism can help us find this desired mix of output. The **market mechanism** moves resources from one industry to another in response to consumer demands. If we demand more typing services—offer to buy more at a given price—more resources (labor) will be allocated to typing. Similarly, a fall in demand will encourage producers to stop typing and offer their services in another industry. Changes in market prices direct resources from one industry to another, moving us along the perimeter of the production-possibilities curve.

market mechanism: The use of market prices and sales to signal desired outputs (or resource allocations).

The Big Question is whether the mix of output selected by the market mechanism is the one most desired by society. If so, we don't need government intervention to change the mix of output. If not, we may need government intervention to guide the "invisible hand" of the market.

market failure: An imperfection in the market mechanism that prevents optimal outcomes.

We use the term **market failure** to refer to less-than-perfect (nonoptimal) outcomes. If the invisible hand of the marketplace produces a mix of output that is different from the one society most desires, then it has failed. *Market failure implies that the forces of supply and demand have not led us to the best point on the production-possibilities curve.* Such failure implies that government intervention is needed to achieve an optimal mix of output.

There are several reasons why the market might fail. The sources of market failure reside in the nature of some goods and the structure of some markets.

Public Goods

The market mechanism has the unique capability to signal consumer demands for various goods and services. By offering to pay higher or lower prices for some goods, we express our collective answer to the question of WHAT to produce. However, the market mechanism works efficiently only if the benefits of consuming a particular good or service are available only to the individuals who purchase that product.

Consider doughnuts, for example. When you eat a doughnut, you get the satisfaction from its taste and your fuller stomach—that is, you derive a private benefit. No one else reaps any significant benefit from your consumption of a doughnut: the doughnut you purchase in the market is yours alone to consume. Accordingly, your decision to purchase the doughnut will be determined by your anticipated satisfaction as well as your income and opportunity costs.

Most of the goods and services produced in the public sector are different from doughnuts—and not just because doughnuts look, taste, and smell different from nuclear submarines. When you buy a doughnut, you effectively exclude others from consumption of that product. If Dunkin' Donuts sells a particular pastry to you, it cannot supply the same pastry to someone else. If you devour it, no one else can. In this sense, the transaction and product are completely private.

The same exclusiveness is not characteristic of national defense. If you buy a nuclear submarine to patrol the Pacific Ocean, there is no way you can exclude your neighbors from the protection your submarine provides. Either the submarine deters would-be attackers or it doesn't. In the former case, both you and your neighbors survive happily ever after; in the latter case, we are all blown away together. In that sense, you and your neighbors either consume or don't consume the benefits of nuclear submarine defenses *jointly*. There is no such thing as exclusive consumption here. The consumption of nuclear defenses is a communal feat, no matter who pays for them. Accordingly, national defense is regarded as a **public good** or product, in the sense that *consumption of a public good by one person does not preclude consumption of the same good by another person.* By contrast, a doughnut is a **private good,** because once I eat it, nobody else can have it.

The free-rider dilemma The "communal" nature of public goods leads to a real dilemma. If you and I will *both* benefit from nuclear defenses, which one of us should buy the nuclear submarine? I would prefer, of course, that *you* buy it, thereby providing me with protection at no direct cost. Hence I may profess no desire for nuclear subs, secretly hoping to take a **free ride** on your market purchase. Unfortunately, you, too, have an incentive to conceal your desire for national defenses. As a consequence, neither one of us may step forward to demand nuclear subs in the marketplace. We will both end up defenseless.

Police and fire protection also exhibit this free-rider phenomenon. If your neighbors pay for improved police and fire services, you will benefit from their purchases even if you don't contribute a penny. Would-be burglars are apt to be deterred from both your house and your neighbors' houses by the presence of more police on the street. By the same token, your house is in less danger of fire if your neighbor's house is protected. In both these cases, your neighbors are unable to confine all the benefits of their expenditure to themselves. Consumption of these goods is nonexclusive—that is, public. Even streets and highways have the characteristics of public goods. Although we could theoretically restrict the use of streets and highways to those who paid for them, a toll gate on every corner would be exceedingly expensive and impractical. Here again joint or public consumption appears to be the only feasible alternative.

To the list of public goods we could add the administration of justice, the regulation of commerce, and the conduct of foreign relations. These services—which cost tens of *billions* of dollars and employ thousands of workers—provide benefits to everyone, no matter who pays for them.

The free riders associated with public goods upset the customary practice of paying for what you get. If I can get all the highways, defenses, and laws I desire without paying for them, I am not about to complain. I am perfectly happy to let you pay for the services while all of us consume them. Of course, you may feel the same way. Why should you pay for these services if you can consume just as much of them when your neighbors foot the whole bill? It might be regarded as selfish or unseemly not to pay your share of the cost of providing public goods, but you would be better off in a material sense if you spent your income on doughnuts, letting others pick up the tab for public services.

Because the familiar link between paying and consuming is broken, public goods cannot be peddled in the supermarket. People are reluctant to buy what they can get free, a perfectly rational response for a consumer who has

public good: A good or service whose consumption by one person does not exclude consumption by others.

private good: A good or service whose consumption by one person excludes consumption by others.

free rider: An individual who reaps direct benefits from someone else's purchase (consumption) of a public good.

production possibilities: The alternative combinations of final goods and services that could be produced in a given time period with all available resources and technology.

limited income to spend. Hence *if public goods were marketed like private goods, everyone would wait for someone else to pay.* The end result might be a total lack of public services.

The **production-possibilities** curve in Figure 3.1 illustrates the dilemma created by public goods. Suppose that point *A* represents the optimal mix of private and public goods. It is the mix of goods and services we would select if everyone's preferences were known and reflected in production decisions. The market mechanism will not lead us to point *A*, however, because the demand for public goods will be hidden. If we rely on the market, nearly everyone will withhold demand for public goods, waiting for a "free ride" to point *A*. As a result, we will get a smaller quantity of public goods than we really want. The market mechanism will leave us at a mix of output like that at point *B*, with few, if any, public goods. Since point *A* is assumed to be optimal, point *B* must be *suboptimal* (inferior to point *A*). The market fails: we cannot rely on the market mechanism to allocate resources to the production of public goods, no matter how much they might be desired.

Note that we are using "public good" in a different way than most people use it. To most people, the term "public good" refers to any good or service the government produces. In economics, however, the meaning is much more restrictive. The term "public good" refers only to those goods and services that are consumed jointly, both by those who pay for them and by those who don't. Public goods can be produced by either the government or the private sector. Private goods can be produced in either sector as well. The problem is that *the market tends to underproduce public goods and overproduce private goods.*

Externalities

The free-rider problem associated with public goods provides one justification for government intervention into the market's decision about WHAT to produce. It is not the only justification, however. Further grounds for intervention

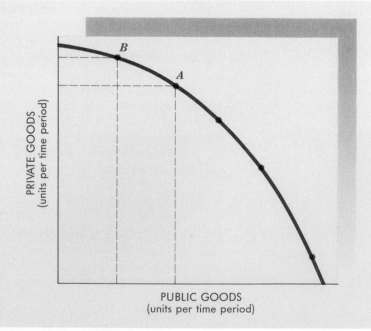

**FIGURE 3.1
Underproduction of
Public Goods**

Suppose point *A* represents the optimal mix of output, i.e., the mix of private and public goods that maximizes society's welfare. Because consumers will not demand purely public goods in the marketplace, the price mechanism will not allocate so many resources to the production of public goods. Instead, the market will tend to produce a mix of output like point *B*, which includes fewer public goods and more private goods than is optimal.

arise from the tendency of costs or benefits of some market activities to "spill over" onto third parties.

Your demand for a good reflects the amount of satisfaction you expect from its consumption. The price you are willing and able to pay for it acts as a market signal to producers of your preferences. Often, however, your consumption may affect others. The purchase of cigarettes, for example, expresses a smoker's demand for that good. But others may suffer from that consumption. In this case, smoke literally spills over onto other consumers, causing them discomfort and possibly even ill health (see In the News). Yet their loss is not reflected in the market—the harm caused to nonsmokers is *external* to the market price of cigarettes.

externalities: Costs (or benefits) of a market activity borne by a third party; the difference between the social and private costs (benefits) of a market activity.

The term **externalities** refers to all costs or benefits of a market activity borne by a third party, that is, by someone other than the immediate producer or consumer. Whenever externalities are present, the preferences expressed in the marketplace will not be a complete measure of a good's value to society. As a consequence, the market will fail to produce the right mix of output. Specifically, ***the market will underproduce goods that yield external benefits and overproduce those that generate external costs.*** Government intervention may be needed to move the mix of output closer to society's optimal point.

Externalities also exist in production. A steel plant that burns high-sulfur coal tends to destroy the surrounding environment. Yet the damage inflicted on neighboring people, vegetation, and buildings is external to the cost calculations of the firm. Because the cost of such pollution is not reflected in the price of steel, the firm will tend to produce more steel (and pollution) than is socially desirable. To reduce this imbalance, the government has to step in and somehow change market outcomes.

In The News

EXTERNALITIES

Beverly Hills Outlaws Smoking in Restaurants

It's like the Old West. Whoever draws his gun first wins. Someone lights a cigarette, and another person says, "You can't smoke here." Then the first says, "I dare you to do something about it." And there goes the peace and tranquillity of an evening meal.

–Joe Patti, owner of La Famiglia restaurant

On April 3 a new era began in Beverly Hills: smoking was banned in restaurants and retail stores. Three weeks later many cigarettes remain unlit but scorched tempers are flaring. In cafés and restaurants throughout this clean, orderly city, known for its per capita wealth and celebrity residents, vociferous smokers are shrieking that the new ordinance is fascist, communist and tyrannical. . . .

The Beverly Hills ban is part of a pulmonary consciousness sweeping the land, fueled by Surgeon General C. Everett Koop's report that secondhand, or "sidestream," smoke can have a negative effect on the health of nonsmokers. Two years ago Aspen, Colo., passed the first law to prohibit smoking in most dining rooms. On May 7 New York State will join the trend, restricting smokers in restaurants with 51 or more seats to designated areas. The Beverly Hills ordinance, passed unanimously by the city council, penalizes disobedient smokers—and restaurants that fail to display no-smoking signs—with fines of up to $500. . . .

Time, April 27, 1987, p. 78. Copyright © 1987 Time Inc. Reprinted by permission.

Externalities may also be beneficial. Education, for example, enriches not only the individual who goes to school but also the student's community. Basic literacy assures a better-informed electorate and a more viable democracy. Higher education often stimulates scientific and humanitarian discoveries that improve the well-being of millions of people. Educators also like to think that educated people make better neighbors! In these respects, the *social* benefits of education generally exceed the *private* benefits reaped by those who attend school: education generates beneficial externalities. Those external benefits justify government support for education.

Market Power

In the case of both public goods and externalities the market fails to achieve the optimal mix of output because the price signal is flawed. The price consumers are willing and able to pay for a specific good does not reflect all the benefits or cost of producing that good.

The market may fail, however, even when the price signals are accurate. The *response* to price signals, rather than the signals themselves, may be flawed.

monopoly: A firm that produces the entire market supply of a particular good or service.

Market power is often the cause of a flawed response. Suppose there were only one airline company in the world. This single seller of airline travel would be a **monopoly**—that is, the only producer in that industry. As a monopolist, the airline could charge extremely high prices without worrying that travelers would flock to a competing airline. At the same time, the high prices paid by consumers would express the importance of that service to society. Ideally, such prices would act as a signal to producers to build and fly more planes—to change the mix of output. But a monopolist does not have to cater to every consumer whim. It can limit airline travel and thus obstruct our efforts to achieve an optimal mix of output.

market power: The ability to alter the market price of a good or service.

Monopoly is the most severe form of **market power.** More generally, market power refers to any situation where a single producer or consumer has the ability to alter the market price of a specific product. If the publisher (McGraw-Hill) charges a high price for this book, you will have to pay the tab. McGraw-Hill has market power because there are relatively few economics textbooks and your professor has required you to use this one. You don't have power in the textbook market because your decision to buy or not will not alter the market price of this text. You are only one of the million students who are taking an introductory economics course this year.

The market power McGraw-Hill possesses is derived from the copyright on this text. No matter how profitable textbook sales might be, no one else is permitted to produce or sell this particular text. Patents are another common source of market power, because they also preclude others from making or selling a specific product. Market power may also result from control of resources, restrictive production agreements, or efficiencies of large-scale production.

Whatever the source of market power, the direct consequence is that one or more producers attain discretionary power over the market's response to price signals. They may use that discretion to enrich themselves rather than to move the economy toward the optimal mix of output. In this case, the market will again fail to deliver the most desired goods and services.

antitrust: Government intervention to alter market structure or prevent abuse of market power.

regulation: Government intervention to alter the behavior of firms, e.g., in pricing, output, advertising.

Government intervention to curb the abuse of market power may take one of two forms. **Antitrust** activity is intended to reduce or eliminate market power—to change the structure of the markets. Alternatively, government **regulation** is designed to limit the use of market power—to change the behavior, rather than the structure, of markets. When the Justice Department blocks a merger between two companies, it is influencing market structure. When the local utility commission prevents the phone company from raising rates, it is limiting the use of market power.

Equity

Public goods, externalities, and market power all cause resource misallocations. Where these phenomena exist, the market mechanism will fail to produce the optimal mix of output.

Beyond the question of WHAT to produce, we are also concerned about FOR WHOM output is to be produced. Is the distribution of goods and services generated by the marketplace "fair"? If the market fails to reflect our notions of equity, government intervention may be needed to redistribute income.

In general, the market mechanism tends to answer the basic question of FOR WHOM to produce by distributing a larger share of total output to those with the most income. Although this result may be efficient, it is not necessarily equitable. Individuals who are aged or disabled, for example, may be unable to earn much income yet still be regarded as "worthy" recipients of goods and services. In such cases, we may want to change the market's answer to the basic question of FOR WHOM goods are produced. Instead of relying exclusively on the market mechanism to determine people's income, we provide income transfers. **Transfer payments** are income payments for which no goods or services are exchanged. They are used to bolster the incomes of those for whom the market itself provides too little.

transfer payment: Payments to individuals for which no current goods or services are exchanged, e.g., Social Security, welfare, unemployment benefits.

To some extent, government intervention in the distribution of income can also be explained by the theory of public goods. If the public sector did not provide help to the aged, the disabled, the unemployed, and the needy, what would they do? Some might find a little extra work, but many would starve, even die. Others would resort to private solicitations or criminal activities to fend off hunger or death. This would mean more homeless people and muggers on the streets. In nearly all cases, the general public would be beset with much of the burden and consequences of poverty and disability, either directly or through pangs of conscience. Because the sight or knowledge of hungry or sick neighbors is something most people seek to avoid, the elimination of poverty creates some satisfaction for a great many people.

But even if the elimination of poverty were a common objective, it could be accomplished by individual action. If I contributed heavily to the needy, then you and I would both be relieved of the burden of the poor. We could both walk the streets with less fear and better consciences. Hence you could benefit from my expenditure, just as was possible in the case of national defense. In this sense, the relief of misery is a *public* good. Were I the only taxpayer to benefit substantially from the reduction of poverty, then charity would be a private affair. As long as income support substantially benefits the public at large, then income redistribution is a *public* good, for which public funding is appropriate. This is the *economic* rationale for public income-redistribution activities. To this rationale one can add such moral arguments as seem appropriate.

MACRO FAILURE

The micro failures of the marketplace imply that we are at the wrong point on the production-possibilities curve or inequitably distributing the output produced. There is another basic question we have swept under the rug, however. How do we get to the production-possibilities curve in the first place? To reach the curve, we must utilize all available resources and technology. Can we be confident that the invisible hand of the marketplace will use all of our resources? Or will some people remain **unemployed**—that is, willing to work, but unable to find a job?

And what about prices? Price signals are a critical feature of the market mechanism. But the validity of those signals depends on some stable measure of value. What good is a doubling of salary when the price of everything you buy doubles as well? Generally, rising prices will enrich people who own property while impoverishing people who rent. For many such reasons we strive to avoid **inflation**—a situation where the *average* price level is increasing.

Historically, the marketplace has been wracked with bouts of both unemployment and inflation. These experiences have prompted calls for government intervention at the macro level. ***The goal of macro intervention is to stabilize the economy—to get us on the production-possibilities curve (full employment) and to maintain a stable price level (price stability).***

unemployment: The inability of labor-force participants to find jobs.

inflation: An increase in the average level of prices of goods and services.

GROWTH OF GOVERNMENT

The potential micro and macro failures of the marketplace provide specific justifications for government intervention. The question then turns to how well the activities of the public sector correspond to these implied mandates.

Federal Growth

Until the 1930s the federal government's role was largely limited to national defense (a public good), enforcement of a common legal system (also a public good), and provision of postal service (equity). The Great Depression of the 1930s spawned a new range of government activities, including welfare and Social Security programs (equity), minimum wage laws and workplace standards (regulation), and massive public works (public goods and externalities). In the 1950s the federal government also assumed a greater role in maintaining macroeconomic stability (macro failure), protecting the environment (externalities), and safeguarding the public's health (externalities and equity).

These increasing responsibilities have greatly increased the size of the public sector. In 1902 the federal government employed fewer than 14,000 people and spent a mere $650 *million*. Today the federal government employs 5 million people and spends over $1 *trillion* a year.

Figure 3.2 summarizes the growth of the public sector since 1930. World War II caused a massive increase in the size of the federal government. Federal purchases of goods and services for the war accounted for over 40 percent of total output in 1943–44. The federal share of total U.S. output fell abruptly after World War II, rose again during the Korean War, and has declined slightly since then.

The decline in the federal share of total output is somewhat at odds with most people's perception of government growth. This discrepancy is explained by two phenomena. First, people see the *absolute* size of the government growing every year. But we are focusing here on the *relative* size of the

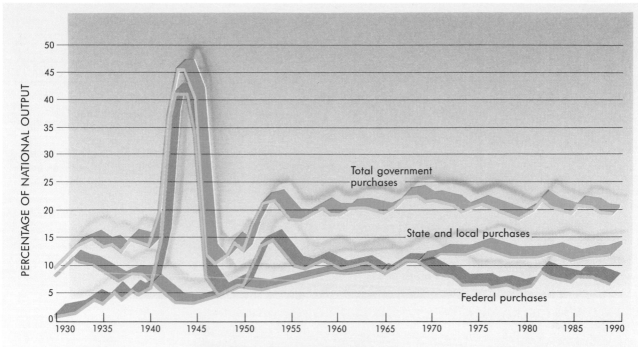

FIGURE 3.2 Government Growth

During World War II the public sector purchased nearly half of total U.S. output. Since the early 1950s the public-sector share of total output has remained about 20 percent. Within the public sector, however, there has been a major shift. The state and local claims on resources have grown, while the federal share has declined.

Source: *Economic Report of the President,* 1990.

public sector. Since the 1950s the public sector has grown at the same rate as the private sector, leaving its relative size unchanged. As the accompanying World View shows, other countries tend to have significantly larger public sectors.

Figure 3.2 is deceiving because it refers to spending on goods and services only, not to all items in the federal budget. Specifically not included in Figure 3.2 are government transfer payments—that is, financial assistance (e.g., welfare, Social Security, unemployment benefits) paid out by Uncle Sam. Income transfers redistribute incomes among households but allocate no real resources to the public sector. Nevertheless, income-transfer programs have grown tremendously and now account for over one-third of the federal budget.

State and Local Growth

State and local spending on goods and services has followed a very different path than federal expenditure. Prior to World War II, state and local governments dominated public-sector spending. During the war, however, the share of total output going to state and local governments fell, hitting a low of 3 percent in that period (Figure 3.2).

State and local spending caught up with federal spending in the mid-1960s and has exceeded it ever since. Today more than 80,000 state and local government entities buy much more output than Uncle Sam and employ nearly three times as many people.

W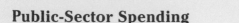RLD VIEW

RELATIVE SIZE

Public-Sector Spending

The public sector in the United States is relatively small compared to that of other industrial countries. The figures below reflect *total* public-sector spending, including both expenditures on goods and services and income transfers. Spending is shown as a proportion of total output.

Source: Organization for Economic Cooperation and Development (1988 data).

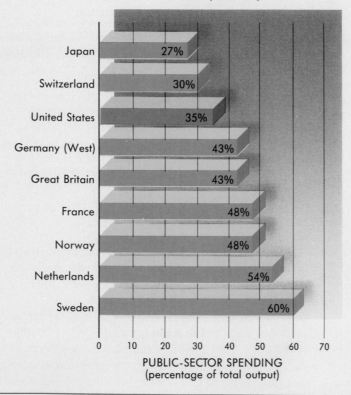

Japan	27%
Switzerland	30%
United States	35%
Germany (West)	43%
Great Britain	43%
France	48%
Norway	48%
Netherlands	54%
Sweden	60%

PUBLIC-SECTOR SPENDING
(percentage of total output)

GOVERNMENT SPENDING

Government spending on goods and services accounts for most, but not all, public-sector expenditure. As noted earlier, a lot of public spending is for income-transfer payments rather than for the purchase of goods and services. This is an important distinction, since government purchases directly affect the rate and mix of output, whereas income transfers have more indirect effects on the question of WHAT to produce. In the last thirty years, transfer payments have increased faster than direct purchases. As a result, government budgets have grown disproportionately, even though the public sector's direct share of output (Figure 3.2) has remained fairly constant.

The Federal Budget

fiscal year (FY): The twelve-month period used for accounting purposes; begins October 1 for federal government.

A complete accounting of federal expenditures is contained in the federal budget. At the beginning of each year, the president, with the assistance of the Office of Management and Budget (OMB), prepares a statement of desired expenditures for the next **fiscal year (FY),** which begins on October 1. The president then submits this budget to Congress for review. After amending the proposed budget to its own liking, the Congress returns it to the president, with authorization to spend federal revenues. In January 1990, for example, President Bush submitted his proposed FY 1991 budget to Congress. The Congress then reviewed his proposals, revised them, and ultimately gave the president permission (budget authorization) to spend over $1.2 trillion in the fiscal year beginning October 1, 1990.

The complete budget of the U.S. government is a document encompassing nearly 1,600 pages and weighing nearly 5 pounds. A brief summary of its contents is provided in Table 3.1.

Expenditures on Goods and Services

Much of the federal budget is devoted to the purchase of goods and services. In FY 1991, for example, the federal government spent $292 billion on national defense, $30 billion on transportation, and $13 billion on the administration

TABLE 3.1 Projected Federal Expenditures, Fiscal 1991

The federal government spent over $1.2 trillion in fiscal 1991. Only 52 percent of this ($658 billion) was for goods and services. The rest represents transfers to individuals ($436 billion) and interest payments ($173 billion). All of these expenditures influence our collective answers to the questions of WHAT, HOW, and FOR WHOM to produce.

Expenditures	Amount (in billions)
A. Goods and Services	
National defense	$292
Transportation	30
Education, training, and social services	41
Commerce and housing	17
International affairs	18
Science, space, and technology	17
Energy	3
Natural resources and environment	18
Agriculture	15
Community and regional development	8
Administration of justice	13
Health	162
Veterans' services	13
General government	11
Total purchases of goods and services	658
B. Income Transfers	
Social Security	265
Federal employees' retirement benefits	54
Public assistance	81
Unemployment insurance	19
Veterans' benefits	17
Total income transfers	436
C. Interest (net)	173
D. Offsetting Receipts	(34)
E. Total Expenditures	$1,233

Source: Office of Management and Budget, fiscal 1991 estimates.

of justice (Table 3.1). In many cases—for example, the purchase of new weapons—these expenditures look just like any other purchases in product markets. In reality, however, the government itself typically *produces* the good or service in question. The judges and clerks who comprise the federal judicial system, for example, are employed by the U.S. government to "produce" $13 billion worth of "administration of justice." Similarly, the 2 million men and women who serve in the armed forces are employed to "produce" national defense. Although the federal government directly pays for such goods and services, the government's basic role is really to produce these outputs for the use of consumers.

To produce all the goods summarized in Table 3.1, the federal government must have access to factors of production. These resources may be purchased directly in factor markets, as in the case of labor employed in the armed forces or the halls of justice. Or they may be purchased indirectly, as when the government pays a building contractor to build a highway or a government building. In either case, **expenditures of the federal government imply vast command over our available resources and thus our decisions on WHAT to produce and HOW to produce it.** The inner arrows in Figure 3.3 highlight the role of government in acquiring resources in factor markets to produce desired services.

Income Transfers

Although the federal government is the single largest participant in U.S. product and factor markets, expenditures on goods and services account for only 52 percent of the federal budget. A large fraction of the budget represents income transfers to individuals. The most familiar transfer payments are Social Security benefits. More than 40 million Americans receive Social Security checks every month. Most of these individuals are retired; others are either

**FIGURE 3.3
Government in the Marketplace**

The public sector is a major participant in both factor and product markets. Federal, state, and local governments hire labor, capital, and land in factor markets. They use these resources to produce goods and services for consumers (taxpayers).

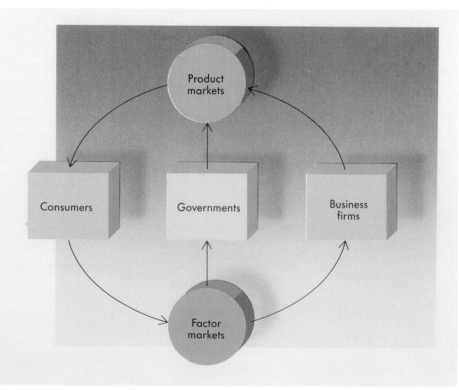

disabled or the children of workers who died before retirement. As Table 3.1 indicates, $265 billion was spent on Social Security benefits in fiscal 1991, making them the second-largest single item in the federal budget.

Social Security benefits are financed by payroll taxes imposed on those who are still working. Thus Social Security retirement benefits *transfer* income from those who are currently working to those who are retired.

Welfare benefits and unemployment insurance benefits serve the same income-transfer purpose but are distributed to those who are poor or unable to find work. In all of these cases, the income transfers are not paid in return for any current product or service. Rather, they represent an explicit attempt to alter the distribution of income and hence access to goods and services.

Interest

interest: Payments made for the use of borrowed money.

The last major expenditure category in the federal budget consists of **interest** payments. Federal expenditures usually exceed federal revenues causing a budget deficit. In FY 1991 the budget deficit exceeded $130 billion. To finance this deficit—to pay for expenditures in excess of tax revenues—the U.S. Treasury must borrow money. Because the government has been running a deficit every year for over two decades, the total debt of the U.S. government now exceeds $3 trillion. Like all borrowers, the U.S. government must pay interest on its debts. In FY 1991 alone, the federal government had to pay $173 billion in interest on its accumulated debt.

State and Local Spending

As much as Uncle Sam spends, federal spending on goods and services is outstripped by the expenditures of state and local governments. Most people don't realize this because state and local spending is fragmented among 80,171 government units, whereas federal spending is summarized in a single budget.

Table 3.2 provides an overview of the content of state and local expenditures. Education accounts for 40 percent of state and local budgets. State governments tend to split their school expenditures between higher education (state colleges and universities) and state aid to local school systems. For their part, local governments focus nearly all education expenditures on ele-

---

TABLE 3.2 State and Local Expenditures, 1987

Most direct state expenditures (excluding transfers to local governments) are for education, welfare programs, and highways. Local governments also spend more on education than anything else.

Expenditures	State governments (in millions)	Percentage	Local governments (in millions)	Percentage
Education	$53	22	$176	48
Transportation	42	17	27	7
Public welfare	65	27	18	6
Health and hospitals	30	12	31	9
Housing and community services	1	—	12	3
Recreation	2	1	9	2
Public safety	16	7	40	11
Interest (net)	−1	—	9	2
Other	33	14	42	12
Total	$241	100.0	$364	100.0

Source: U.S. Department of Commerce.

mentary and secondary school systems. States devote other large portions of their resources to highways and welfare programs. At the local level, non-education expenditures tend to be concentrated on police protection, health services, fire protection, and streets.

TAXATION

Whatever we may think of any specific government expenditure, we must recognize one basic fact of life: we pay for government spending. In real terms, the cost of government spending can be measured by the private goods and services that are forsaken when the public sector takes command over factors of production. Factors of production used to produce national defense or schools cannot be used at the same time to produce private goods or services.

opportunity cost: The most desired goods or services that are forgone in order to obtain something else.

The **opportunity costs** of public spending are not always apparent. We don't directly hand over factors of production to the government. Instead, we give the government part of our income in the form of taxes. Those dollars are then used to buy factors of production or goods and services in the marketplace. Thus *the primary function of taxes is to transfer command over resources (purchasing power) from the private sector to the public sector.* Although the government also borrows dollars to finance its purchases, taxes are the primary source of government revenues.

Federal Taxes

As recently as 1902, much of the revenue collected by the federal government came from taxes imposed on alcoholic beverages. The federal government did not have authority to collect income taxes. As a consequence, *total* federal revenue in 1902 was only $653 million.

Income taxes　All that has changed. The Sixteenth Amendment to the U.S. Constitution, enacted in 1915, granted the federal government authority to collect income taxes. The government now collects over $500 *billion* in that form alone. Although the federal government still collects taxes on alcoholic

---

TABLE 3.3　Federal Revenues, Fiscal 1991

Taxes transfer purchasing power from the private sector to the public sector. The largest federal tax is the individual income tax. The second-largest source of federal revenue is the Social Security tax.

Source	Amount (in billions)
Individual income taxes	$ 528
Social Security taxes	421
Corporate income taxes	130
Excise taxes	38
Custom duties	19
Estate and gift taxes	10
Other	24
Total	$1,170

Source: Office of Management and Budget, fiscal 1991 estimates.

beverages, the individual income tax has become the largest single source of government revenue (see Table 3.3).

progressive tax: A tax system in which tax rates rise as incomes rise.

In theory, the federal income tax is designed to be **progressive**—that is, to take a larger *fraction* of high incomes than of low incomes. In 1990, for example, a single person with less than $5,000 of income paid no federal income tax. A person with $5,000 to $24,000 was obligated to turn over 15 percent of each additional dollar of income to Uncle Sam. People with over $24,000 in income confronted a 28 percent tax rate on their additional income. Thus people with high incomes not only pay more taxes but also pay a larger *fraction* of their income in taxes.

Social Security taxes   The second major source of federal revenue is the Social Security payroll tax. As noted earlier, people now working transfer part of their earnings to retired workers by making "contributions" to Social Security. There is nothing voluntary about these "contributions"; they take the form of mandatory payroll deductions. In 1990 each worker paid 7.65 percent of his or her wages to Social Security and employers contributed an equal amount.[1] As a consequence, the government collected $421 billion.

Corporate taxes   The federal government taxes the profits of corporations as well as the incomes of consumers. But there are far fewer corporations than consumers, and their profits are small in comparison to total consumer income. In fiscal 1991, the federal government collected only $130 billion in corporate income taxes, despite the fact that it imposed a tax rate of 34 percent on corporate profits.

Excise taxes   The last major source of federal revenue is excise taxes. Like the early taxes on whiskey, excise taxes are sales taxes imposed on specific goods and services. The federal government taxes not only liquor ($12.50 per gallon) but also gasoline (9 cents per gallon), cigarettes (16 cents per pack), telephone service (3 percent), and a variety of other goods and services. Such taxes not only discourage production and consumption of these goods—by raising their price, and thereby reducing the quantity demanded—but also raise a substantial amount of revenue.

[1]In 1990 this tax rate was imposed on the first $51,300 of income; the income ceiling increases every year and the tax rate is increased occasionally as well.

"I can't find anything wrong here, Mr. Truffle . . . you just seem to have too much left after taxes."

GRIN AND BEAR IT by George Lichty. © *Field Newspaper Syndicate,* 1978. Reprinted with special permission of NAS, Inc.

State and Local Revenues

Taxes State and local governments also levy taxes on consumers and businesses. In general, cities depend heavily on property taxes, and state governments rely heavily on sales taxes (see Figure 3.4). Although nearly all states and many cities also impose income taxes, effective tax rates are so low (averaging less than 2 percent of personal income) that income tax revenues are much less than sales and property tax revenues.

One feature of state and local tax structures is important to note. State and local taxes tend to be **regressive**—that is, they take a larger share of income from the poor than from the rich. Consider a 4 percent sales tax, for example. It might appear that a uniform tax rate like this would affect all consumers equally. But people with lower incomes tend to spend most of their income on goods and services. Thus most of their income is subject to sales taxes. By contrast, a person with a high income can afford to save part of his or her income and thereby shelter it from sales taxes. A family that earns $20,000 and spends $15,000 of it on taxable goods and services, for example, pays $600 in sales taxes when the tax rate is 4 percent. In effect, then, they are handing over 3 percent of their *income* ($600 ÷ $20,000) to the state. By contrast, the family that makes only $6,000 and spends $5,800 of it for food, clothing, and shelter pays $232 in sales taxes in the same state. Their total tax is smaller, but it represents a much larger *share* (3.9 vs. 3.0 percent) of their income.

regressive tax: A tax system in which tax rates fall as incomes rise.

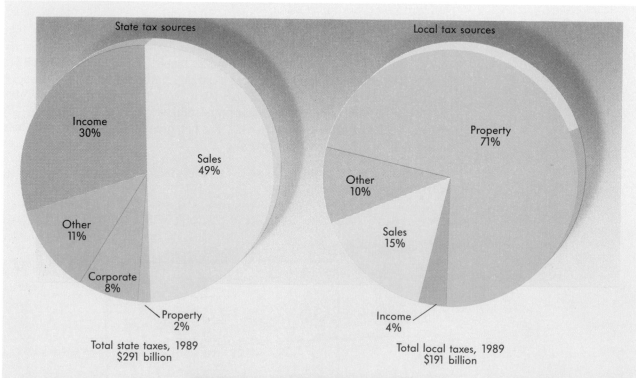

Total state taxes, 1989
$291 billion

Total local taxes, 1989
$191 billion

FIGURE 3.4 State and Local Tax Sources

State governments get half of their tax revenue from sales taxes. By contrast, local governments depend heavily on property taxes.

Source: U.S. Department of Commerce

Local property taxes are also regressive, because poorer people devote a larger portion of their incomes to housing costs. Property taxes directly affect housing costs. Hence a larger share of a poor family's income is subject to property taxes. According to the Advisory Council on Intergovernmental Relations, a family earning $50,000 a year devotes only 2.5 percent of its income to property taxes, whereas a family earning $5,000 pays out 4.6 percent of its income in property taxes. State lotteries are also regressive, for the same reason (see In the News).

Federal aid   Up until 1986, the federal government gave state and local governments some of its revenues for whatever purposes those entities desired. But such general "revenue sharing" was always small. Most grants to state and local governments are for specific purposes and included in the federal budget under the appropriate category. For example, Table 3.1 indicates that the federal government spent $18 billion on natural resources and environment. But one-fifth of this amount was simply given to local communities for the construction of sewage-treatment plants. The local governments actually purchased or built these plants; the federal government only provided the necessary revenue. Accordingly, control over WHAT to produce was maintained by the federal government, but local governments exercised some judgment on HOW to produce it.

categorical grants: Federal grants to state and local governments for specific expenditure purposes.

This "strings-attached" nature of most federal aid is the distinguishing feature of **categorical grants.** Funds bestowed on state and local governments in the form of categorical grants have to be used for specific purposes. If a city government needs street lighting but federal grants are available only for sewage treatment or job training, the city must choose between one of the latter or do without federal aid. Categorical grants cannot be shifted from one use to another.

In fiscal 1991 the federal government gave over $130 billion to state and local governments in the form of categorical grants (including those for welfare benefits, Medicaid, schools, and highways). These federal grants accounted for about one-fifth of all state and local revenues.

In The News

REGRESSIVE TAXES

Some Taxing Facts About Lotteries

In 1964 New Hampshire started the first modern state lottery. By 1990, 32 states and the District of Columbia had taken in over $80 billion in state lottery revenues. In 1990 alone, these states collected over $16 billion in lottery revenues. Per capita ticket sales averaged $120, up from $23 in 1975.

The transfer of these revenues to state treasuries is an implicit tax on lottery bettors, and that tax is "decidedly regressive," an NBER study concludes. Furthermore, the implicit tax rate on lottery purchases is higher than the total tax on cigarettes or alcohol according to NBER Research Associate Charles Clotfelter and Philip Cook. . . .

Clotfelter and Cook observe that since "average lottery expenditures exhibit no consistent relationship to income," the implicit tax on those expenditures (as a percentage of income) generally falls as incomes increase. For example, average yearly lottery expenditures in California in 1986 fell from 1.4 percent of income in the lowest income class (under $10,000) to only 0.1 percent in the $50,000–$60,000 class. . . .

NBER Digest, National Bureau of Economic Research, July 1987 and August 1989.

user charge: Fee paid for the use of a public-sector good or service.

User charges The third major source of state and local revenues consists of **user charges.** The tuition that college students (or their parents) pay for attending a state university or community college is a familiar user charge that generates billions of dollars in state and local revenues. But tuition fees never cover the full costs of maintaining public colleges. Part of the costs of providing higher education are borne by all state taxpayers, whether or not they attend college. Public hospitals and highways are financed in the same way, with users paying part of the costs directly and all taxpayers paying the remaining costs through state and local taxes. Hence user charges are not identical to market prices, because they are not intended to cover the full costs of supplying a particular good.

POLICY INSIGHTS:

GOVERNMENT FAILURE?

We have answered two of the three questions posed at the beginning of this chapter. First, we *do* need a public sector. Government intervention is necessitated by the micro and macro failures of the market. As efficient as the market mechanism is, it cannot assure optimal outcomes in every instance.

In The News

PERCEIVED WASTE

Rising Doubts About Government Waste

Question: Do you think that people in government waste a lot of the money we pay in taxes, waste some of it, or don't waste very much of it?

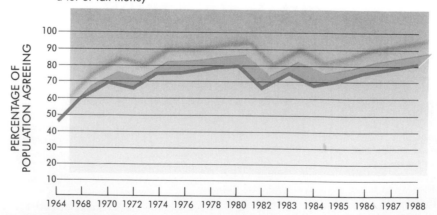

The government wastes a lot of tax money

Source: *Public Opinion,* 1987. Reprinted with permission of American Enterprise Institute for Public Policy Research.

Second, the specific sources of micro and macro failure dictate the kinds of activities appropriate for the public sector. We have also reviewed the kinds of services the government actually provides.

But what about the third question? Has the government grown too large? Just because some intervention is justified doesn't mean that any and all government activity is desirable. Should there be some limits to the size and scope of government intervention? Is the public sector now too big? Has it gone beyond the mandate we gave it in remedying market failures? If so, then we have to consider the possibility of government failure as well as market failure. In this context, **government failure** means that government intervention fails to move us closer to our economic goals.

government failure: Government intervention that fails to improve economic outcomes.

Perceptions of Waste

Taxpayers seem to have strong opinions about government failure. When asked whether the government "wastes" their tax dollars or uses them well, the overwhelming majority see waste in government. Moreover, perceptions of waste have increased along with the size of the public sector. The average taxpayer now believes that state governments waste 29 cents out of each dollar, while the federal government wastes 42 cents out of each tax dollar!

In 1982 President Reagan asked Peter Grace and 164 other business executives to "roll up their sleeves and search out waste and inefficiency" in the federal government. For nearly two years, the Grace Commission examined every nook and cranny of the federal bureaucracy. What they discovered confirmed the public's worst perceptions. The commission members concluded that "one-third of all taxes is consumed by waste and inefficiency in the federal government" and stated that the government could save over $400 billion in three years by adopting the 2,287 specific recommendations that the commission proposed.

The commission's report filled 41 volumes. There were 267 specific recommendations for the Department of Defense alone (representing a saving of $92 billion). The catalog of wasteful practices ranged from negligent inventory controls for Air Force spare parts to the fact that 64 Indians were not old enough to qualify for the pensions they were receiving.

Opportunity Costs

The Grace Commission's report was essentially a management study of government operations. It compared government operations to the current practices of the private sector and labeled the differences as "waste." The commission essentially concluded that the government could provide the same services we now get at a significantly lower cost than we now pay.

But important as efficiency in government may be, it begs the larger question of how many government services we really *want*. To address this question we must refer to the economic concept of opportunity cost.

The taxes people pay are used by governments to purchase scarce resources. As a consequence, fewer resources are available for the production of private goods and services. The more police officers or schoolteachers employed by the public sector, the fewer workers available to private producers and consumers. Similarly, the more typewriters, pencils, and paper consumed by government agencies, the fewer accessible to individuals and private companies. In other words, ***everything the public sector does involves an opportunity cost.***

When assessing government's role in the economy, then, we must consider not only what governments do, but also what we give up to allow them to do it. The theory of public goods tells us only what activities are appropriate for government, not the proper *level* of such activity. National defense is clearly a proper function of the public sector. Not so clear, however, is how much government should spend on tanks and aircraft carriers. The same is true of environmental protection or law enforcement.

The concept of opportunity costs puts a new perspective on the whole question of government size. Before we can decide how big is "too big," we must decide what we are willing to give up to support the public sector. A military force of 2 million men and women is "too big" from an economic perspective only if we value the forgone private production and consumption more highly than we value added strength of our defenses. The government has gone "too far" if the highway it builds is less desired than the park and homes it implicitly replaced. In these and all cases, the assessment of bigness must come back to a comparison of what is given up with what is received.

The consequences of an expanding public sector are illustrated by the production-possibilities curves in Figure 3.5. In any year, our resources and technology set limits to the quantity of public and private goods we can produce. In 1980 we chose a mix of output such as point *A*, devoting 20 percent of our resources to public-sector output. The opportunity cost of those public-sector goods and services was the *private* goods and services we could have produced in that year but chose not to, as represented by the line *BC*.

Over time, the quantity of available resources has increased and our technology has advanced, expanding our production possibilities. The public sector, however, has expanded as well. Accordingly, we have moved from point *A* toward point *D*, producing more public and private goods alike, but still devoting one-fifth of our resources to the public sector.

FIGURE 3.5
Private vs. Public Goods

The public sector of the United States has grown as production possibilities have expanded. In 1980 we produced at point *A*, devoting one-fifth of our output to the public sector. In 1990 we moved toward point *D*, with more goods produced in both sectors.

If the government wastes resources—produces fewer services than possible with the resources at its disposal—we are at a point such as *E*. If both the public sector and the private sector are being efficient, we are at point *D*. In either case, *FG* represents the opportunity cost of government services.

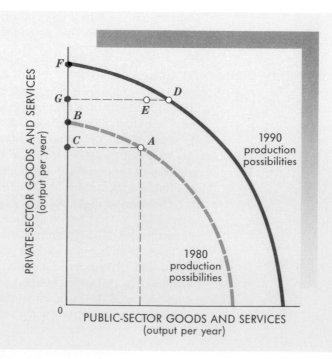

We would be at point D only if the government were operating at full efficiency. If perceptions of government waste are accurate, we are *inside* the production-possibilities curve, at a point such as E. In either case, we are still devoting about one-fifth of our resources to the government, as we have for the last twenty years or so.

The issue of government "waste" then really encompasses two questions:

- *Efficiency:* Are we getting as much service as we could from the resources we allocate to government (i.e., are we at point D or point E)?

- *Opportunity cost:* Are we giving up too many private-sector goods in order to get those services (i.e., does point D represent the optimal mix of public-sector and private-sector goods)?

Public Choice   To answer these questions, we need to know whether point D is optimal. Would we be better off allocating more of our resources to the private sector and less to the public sector (i.e., moving from point D toward point F in Figure 3.5)? Where is the optimal mix of output? How will we know when we've found it?

Cost–benefit analysis   In principle, the search for the optimal mix of output is simple. The concept of opportunity cost provides the necessary clues. *Additional public-sector activity is desirable only if the benefits from that activity exceed its opportunity costs.* In other words, we compare the benefits of a public project to the value of the private goods given up to produce it. By performing this calculation repeatedly along the perimeter of the production-possibilities curve, we could locate the optimal mix of output—the point at which no further increase in public-sector spending activity is desirable.

This same principle can be used to decide *which* goods to produce within the public sector. A public project is desirable only to the extent that it promises to yield some benefits (or utility). But all public projects involve some costs. Hence a project should be pursued only if it can deliver a satisfactory *ratio* of benefits to costs. Otherwise we would not be making very good use of our limited resources. In general, we would want to pursue those projects with the highest cost–benefit ratio. They will maximize the amount of utility we get from the resources we devote to the public sector.

Although the principles of cost–benefit analysis are simple enough, they are deceptive. How are we to measure the potential benefits of improved police services, for example? Should we estimate the number of robberies and murders prevented, calculate the worth of each, and add up the benefits? And how are we supposed to calculate the worth of a saved life? By a person's earnings? value of assets? number of friends? And what about the increased sense of security people have when they know the police are patrolling in their neighborhood? Should this be included in the benefit calculation? Some people will attach great value to this service; others will attach little. Whose values should we use?

When we are dealing with (private) market goods and services, we can gauge the benefits of production by the amount of money consumers are willing to pay for some particular output. In the case of public goods, however, we must make crude and highly subjective estimates of the benefits yielded by a particular output. Accordingly, cost–benefit analyses are valuable only to the extent that they are based on broadly accepted perceptions of benefits (or costs). In practice, consensus on the value of benefits is hard to reach, and cost–benefit calculations are subject to great controversy.

Ballot-box economics   In practice, we rely on political mechanisms, not cost–benefit calculations, to decide what to produce in the public sector. ***Voting mechanisms substitute for the market mechanism in allocating resources to the public sector and deciding how to use them.*** Some people have even suggested that the variety and volume of public goods are determined by the most votes, just as the variety and volume of private goods are determined by the most dollars. Thus governments choose that level and mix of output (and related taxation) that seem to command the most votes.[2]

Sometimes the link between the ballot box and output decisions is very clear and direct. State and local governments, for example, are often compelled to get voter approval before building another highway, school, housing project, or sewage plant. *Bond referendums* are direct requests by a government unit for the authority and purchasing power to expand the production of particular public goods. In 1988, for example, governments sought voter approval for $6 billion of new borrowing to finance public expenditure. Eighty percent of those requests were approved (some examples are provided in In the News).

Although the direct link between bond referendums and spending decisions is important, it is more the exception than the rule. Bond referendums account for less than 1 percent of state and local expenditures. As a consequence, voter control of public spending is much less direct. Although federal agencies must receive authorization from Congress for all expenditures, consumers get a chance to elect new representatives only every two years. Much

[2]In the absence of unanimity, this means that some people will end up paying for public goods and services they do not want. The majority will thus benefit at the expense of the minority, a familiar consequence of democratic rule. Is there any other way to share the costs of public goods and services?

In The News

BALLOT BOX ECONOMICS

A Sampling of 1988–1989 State Referendums

- *California:* Voters approved $800 million in construction for the University of California, $1.3 billion for jails and detention centers, $300 million to house the homeless.

- *Maine:* Voters rejected $35 million for jails, but approved $17 million for sewage facilities and $3 million for a statewide emergency 911 system.

- *New York:* Approved $3 billion for highway and bridge repair.

- *Michigan:* Voters rejected a state sales tax increase to finance $400 million aid to low-income schools.

- *Texas:* Approved $500 million for water supply and flood control.

- *Oregon:* Voters turned down a tax on beer and cigarettes intended to finance state university sports programs.

Free Congress Foundation, Washington, D.C.

the same is true at state and local levels. Voters are in a position to dictate the general level and pattern of public expenditures but have little direct influence on everyday output decisions. In this sense, the ballot box is a poor substitute for the market mechanism.

Even if the link between the ballot box and allocation decisions were stronger, the resulting mix of output might not be optimal. A "democratic" vote, for example, might yield a 51 percent majority for approval of new local highways. Should the highways then be built? The answer is not obvious. After all, a large minority (49 percent) of the voters have stated that they don't want resources used in this way. If we proceed to build the highways, we will make those people worse off. Even the voters who voted for the highways may end up worse off, depending on how the benefits and costs of the highway are distributed and what other opportunities exist. The basic dilemma is really twofold. ***We do not know what the real demand for public goods is, and votes alone do not reflect the intensity of individual demands.*** Moreover, real-world decision making involves so many choices that a stable consensus is impossible.

Self-interest   In the midst of all this complexity and uncertainty, another factor may be decisive—namely, self-interest. In principle, government officials are supposed to serve the people. It doesn't take long, however, before officials realize that the public is indecisive about what it wants and takes very little interest in the day-to-day activities of government. With such latitude, government officials can set their own agendas. Those agendas may give higher priority to the personal advancement of public officials than to the needs of the public. Agency directors may foster new programs that enlarge their mandate, enhance their visibility, and increase their prestige or income. Members of Congress may likewise pursue legislative favors (e.g., tax breaks) for supporters more diligently than they pursue the general public interest. In such cases, the probability of attaining the optimal mix of output declines.

The recognition of self-interest raises concerns about the whole question of public-sector decision making. Many citizens would prefer to believe that elected officials selflessly pursue the "public good" rather than narrow, selfish goals. But the "public good" is ill-defined and the motivations for such public service are uncertain. It is also evident that some public-policy decisions harm rather than help us. In this context, the notion of self-interest as a basic motivation for public policy has a seductive appeal.

public choice: Theory of public-sector behavior emphasizing rational self-interest of decision makers and voters.

The theory of **public choice** emphasizes the role of self-interest in public decision making. Public-choice theory essentially extends the analysis of market behavior to political behavior. Public officials are assumed to have specific personal goals (e.g., power, recognition, wealth) that they will pursue in office. Bureaucrats are regarded as being just as selfish (utility maximizing) as everyone else.

Public-choice theory provides a neat and simple explanation for public-sector decision making. But critics argue that the theory provides a woefully narrow view of public servants. Some people do selflessly pursue larger, "public" goals, such critics argue, and ideas can overwhelm self-interest. Professor Steven Kelman of Harvard, for example, argues that narrow self-interest cannot explain the War on Poverty of the 1960s, the tax revolt of the 1970s, or the deregulation movement of the 1980s. These tidal changes in public policy reflect the power of ideas, not simple self-interest.

Although self-interest cannot provide a complete explanation of public decision making, it adds important perspectives on the policy process. Professor James Buchanan of George Mason University (Virginia) won the 1986 Nobel Prize in economics for helping develop this public-choice perspective. It adds a personal dimension to the faceless mechanics of ballot-box economics, cost–benefit analysis, and other "objective" mechanisms of public-sector decision making.

SUMMARY

- Government intervention in the marketplace is justified by a variety of micro and macro failures.

- The micro failures of the market originate in public goods, externalities, market power, and an inequitable distribution of income. These flaws deter the market from achieving the optimal mix of output or distribution of income.

- The macro failures of the marketplace are reflected in unemployment and inflation. Government intervention is intended to achieve full employment and price stability.

- The public sector grew enormously during World War II but shrank at war's end. Since the 1950s, government purchases of goods and services have accounted for roughly 20 percent of each year's total output. On top of these direct purchases, the public sector redistributes income with tax and income-transfer programs.

- State and local governments outnumber and outspend the federal government. Moreover, their share of the total output has been increasing while the federal share has declined.

- The federal government gets most of its revenue from personal income and Social Security payroll taxes. Corporate, excise, and import taxes account for the rest.

- State governments rely heavily on sales and income taxes; local governments depend primarily on property taxes.

- Government failure occurs when intervention moves us away from rather than toward the optimal mix of output (or income). The elusiveness of public-sector decision making increases the odds of such failure.

Terms to Remember   Define the following terms:

optimal mix of output	transfer payment
market mechanism	unemployment
market failure	inflation
public good	fiscal year (FY)
private good	interest
free rider	opportunity cost
production possibilities	progressive tax
externalities	regressive tax
monopoly	categorical grants
market power	user charge
antitrust	government failure
regulation	public choice

Questions for Discussion

1. Why should taxpayers subsidize public colleges and universities? What benefits do they receive from someone else's education?

2. If you abhor tennis, should you be forced to pay local taxes that are used to build and maintain public tennis courts? If you don't like national defense, should you be able to withhold the part of your taxes that pays for it? What would happen if everyone followed this rationale?

3. Could local fire departments be privately operated, with services sold directly to customers? What problems would be involved in such a system?

4. Identify specific government activities that are justified by different micro failures.

Problems

1. Suppose that the following table describes the spending behavior of individuals at various income levels:

Income	Total spending	Sales tax	Sales tax paid as percentage of income
$ 1,000	$ 1,000	_____	_____
2,000	1,800	_____	_____
3,000	2,400	_____	_____
5,000	3,500	_____	_____
10,000	6,000	_____	_____
100,000	40,000	_____	_____

Assuming that a sales tax of 10 percent is levied on all purchases, calculate:
(a) The amount of taxes paid at each income level
(b) The fraction of income paid in taxes at each income level
Is the sales tax progressive or regressive in relation to income?

2. If a new home can be constructed for $75,000, what is the opportunity cost of federal defense spending, measured in terms of private housing? (Consult Table 3.1 for level of defense spending.)

CHAPTER 4

National-Income Accounting

*T*he economy is so vast that we may be pardoned if we occasionally lose sight of some of the action and forget a few details here and there. But *somebody* has to keep track of all the action in product and factor markets if we are ever going to know what's happening in the economy. How, for example, are we going to know whether we're producing enough goods and services—or, for that matter, the *right* goods and services—unless someone keeps track of our annual output? By the same token, how can we decide whether we can afford another fleet of missiles, more subway systems, or a modernized railroad system unless we know how much output we can produce and how it is now being used? And finally, how would we know when unemployment or inflation was a serious problem unless someone was measuring changes in employment or prices?

To answer these questions, we need to know some basic facts about the macro economy. Specifically,

- How much output do we produce in a year?

- How much income is generated from the production of these goods and services?

- Where does all the output and income go?

It is tempting, of course, to ignore all these measurement questions, especially since they tend to be rather dull. But if we avoid measurement problems, we severely limit our ability to understand how the economy works or how well (or poorly) it is performing. We also limit our ability to design appropriate policies for improving economic performance.

The measurement of aggregate economic activity—**national-income accounting**—serves two basic functions. First, it enables us to identify economic problems. The Great Depression provided an object lesson in how important such information can be. In fact, it was during the depression that our national-income accounting system was first developed, largely through the efforts of Simon Kuznets (who later received a Nobel Prize for his work) and the U.S. Commerce Department.

The second function of national-income accounting is to provide an objective basis for evaluating policy. If national-income accounts allow us to measure the severity of a problem, they can also be used to determine how effective public policy has been in solving it. Elected officials are forever taking

national-income accounting: The measurement of aggregate economic activity, particularly national income and its components.

credit for their alleged success in creating new jobs, holding down prices, and restoring America's standing in the world economy. With national-income accounts, we can put these claims to an objective test.

The national-income accounts also provide a useful perspective on the way the economy works. They show how factor markets relate to product markets, how output relates to income, and how consumer spending and business investment relate to production. They also show how the flow of taxes and government spending may alter economic outcomes. Thus national-income accounts help us not only to measure the economy but also to understand how it functions.

MEASURES OF OUTPUT

National-income accounting focuses on the nation's output of goods and services. The array of goods and services we produce is truly massive, including everything from professional baseball to guided-missile systems. All of these things are part of our total output; the problem is to find a summary measure.

Itemizing the amount of each good or service produced each year will not solve our measurement problems. The resulting list would be so long that it would be both unwieldy and meaningless. We could not even add it up, since it would contain diverse goods measured in a variety of units (e.g., packages, pounds, quarts). Nor could we compare one year's output to another's. Suppose that last year we produced 2 billion oranges, 2 million bicycles, and 700 airplanes, whereas this year we produced 3 billion oranges, 4 million bicycles, and 600 airplanes. Which year's output was larger? Itemizing all our outputs would not only be tedious but would leave a good many questions unanswered as well.

Gross National Product

To facilitate our accounting chores, we need some mechanism for organizing our annual output data into a more manageable summary. The mechanism we use is prices. ***Each good and service produced and brought to market has a price. That price serves as a measure of value for calculating total output.*** Consider again the problem of determining how much output was produced this year and last. There is no obvious way to answer this question in physical terms alone. Once we know the price of each good, however, we can readily calculate the *value* of output produced in a given time period. The total dollar value of final output produced each year is what we refer to as our **gross national product (GNP).** GNP is simply the sum of all final goods and services produced for the market in a given time period, with each good or service valued at its market price.

gross national product (GNP): The total market value of all final goods and services produced in a given time period.

Table 4.1 illustrates the use of prices to value total output in two hypothetical years. If oranges were 20 cents each last year and 2 billion oranges were produced, then the *value* of orange production last year was $400 million ($0.20 × 2 billion). In the same manner, we can determine that the value of bicycle production was $100 million and the value of airplane production was $700 million. By adding up these figures, we can say that the value of last year's production—last year's GNP—was $1,200 million (Table 4.1A).

TABLE 4.1   The Measurement of Output

It is impossible to add up all output when it is counted in *physical* terms. Accordingly, total output is measured in *monetary* terms, with each good or service valued at its market price. GNP refers to the total market value of all goods and services produced in a given time period. According to the numbers in this table, the total *value* of the oranges, bicycles, and airplanes produced last year was $1.2 billion.

Output	Amount
A. Last Year's Output	
In physical terms	
Oranges	2 billion
Bicycles	2 million
Airplanes	700
Total	?
In monetary terms	
2 billion oranges @ $0.20 each	$ 400 million
2 million bicycles @ $50 each	100 million
700 airplanes @ $1 million each	700 million
Total	$1,200 million
B. This Year's Output	
In physical terms	
Oranges	3 billion
Bicycles	4 million
Airplanes	600
Total	?
In monetary terms	
3 billion oranges @ $0.20 each	$ 600 million
4 million bicycles @ $50 each	200 million
600 airplanes @ $1 million each	600 million
Total	$1,400 million

Now we are in a position to compare one year's output to another's. Table 4.1B shows that the use of prices enables us to say that the *value* of this year's output is $1,400 million. Hence *total output* has increased from one year to the next. ***The use of prices to value market output allows us to summarize our output activity and to compare the output of one period with that of another.***

GNP accounting can also provide a basis for comparing one country's economic performance with another's. Suppose you wanted to know how the Soviet economy compared with our own in terms of total annual output. Here again, endless lists of specific outputs would be of little use, as the Russians' production of some goods (e.g., caviar, furs, oil) would certainly be greater than ours, and vice versa. Moreover, differences in the annual outputs of various goods and services would still have to be "added up" somehow. Which leads us back to prices as a common basis for valuation. By adding up the annual *value* of Soviet and American outputs, we can determine which economy is larger.[1] As the accompanying World View indicates, the annual GNP of the United States is nearly twice as large as the Soviet GNP. In fact, our economy is so big that it produces one-fourth of total world output.

[1]International GNP comparisons are complicated by differences in economic structures, price systems, and international exchange rates. Consequently, all such comparisons are rough approximations. Some of the problems of GNP accounting are discussed in the following pages.

W🌐RLD VIEW

GNP COMPARISONS

GNP Around the World

The U.S. economy is the world's largest, as measured by the value of annual output. On a *per capita* basis, we also rank near the top. International comparisons are crude approximations because of differences between countries in the use of prices and markets.

Country	Total GNP (in Billions of Dollars)	GNP per Capita (in Dollars)
United States	$ 4,864	$19,770
Soviet Union	2,535	8,850
Japan	1,758	14,340
Germany (West)	870	14,260
Great Britain	755	13,270
China	350	320
Brazil	325	2,200
Poland	276	7,270
Saudi Arabia	86	6,170
Kuwait	26	13,680
Ethiopia	6	120
World total	$18,600	$ 3,614

Sources: World Bank and Central Intelligence Agency (1988 data).

GNP per capita: Total GNP divided by total population; average GNP.

GNP per capita International comparisons of total output are even more vivid *in per capita terms*. **GNP per capita** relates the total value of annual output to the number of people who share that output; it refers to the average GNP per person. The United States contains only 5 percent of the world's population, yet we produce 25 percent of the world's output. Our production per capita (per person) thus greatly exceeds that of most other countries. The World View box indicates that per capita GNP in the United States is over five times larger than the world average.

GNP per capita is commonly used as a measure of a country's standard of living, because it suggests the amount of annual output available to the average person. Per capita GNP is only a statistical phenomenon, however, and should not be interpreted as a measure of what every citizen is getting. In the United States, for example, millions of individuals have access to far more goods and services than our average per capita GNP. Similarly, millions of others must get by with much less. Although per capita GNP in Kuwait approaches that of the United States (see World View), we cannot conclude that the typical citizen of Kuwait is as well off as the typical American. All these figures tell us is that the average citizen of Kuwait *could* have almost as many goods and services each year as the average American *if* GNP were distributed in the same way in both countries. *Measures of per capita GNP tell us nothing about the way GNP is actually distributed or used; they are only a statistical average.* When countries are quite similar in structure, institutions, and income distribution, however—or when historical comparisons are made within a country—per capita GNP is a rough-and-ready measure of relative standards of living.

Measurement Problems

Nonmarket activities Although the methods for calculating GNP and per capita GNP are straightforward, they do create a few problems. For one thing, our GNP measures exclude most goods and services that are produced but not sold in the market. This may appear to be a trivial point, but it isn't. Vast quantities of output never reach the market. For example, the homemaker who cleans, washes, gardens, shops, and cooks definitely contributes to the output of goods and services. Because she is not paid a market wage for these services, however, her efforts are excluded from the calculation of GNP. At the same time, we do count the efforts of those workers who sell identical homemaking services in the marketplace. This seeming contradiction is explained by the fact that a homemaker's services are not sold in the market and therefore carry no explicit, market-determined value.

The exclusion of homemakers' services from the GNP accounts is particularly troublesome when we want to compare living standards over time or between countries. In the United States, for example, women have demonstrated an increasing tendency to hire domestic help and leave the house to find outside employment. As a result, much housework and child care that was previously excluded from GNP statistics (because it was unpaid family help) is now included (because it is done by paid help). In this respect, our historical GNP figures are not only incomplete but may exaggerate improvements in our standard of living.

Homemaking services are not the only output excluded. If a friend helps you out with your homework, the services never get into the GNP accounts. But if you hire a tutor or engage the services of a term-paper–writing agency, the transaction becomes part of GNP. Here again, the problem is simply that we have no objective way to determine how much output was produced until it enters the market and is purchased.[2]

Unreported income The GNP statistics also fail to capture market activities that are not reported to tax or census authorities. Many people work "off the books," getting paid in unreported cash. This "underground economy" is motivated by tax avoidance and the need to conceal illegal activities. Although illegal activities capture most of the headlines, tax evasion on income earned in otherwise legal pursuits accounts for most of the underground economy. The Internal Revenue Service estimates that over two-thirds of "underground" income comes from legitimate wages, salaries, profits, interest, and pensions that are simply not reported. Relatively little of the unreported income comes from drug dealers, prostitutes, or gambling. Some examples of "underground" transactions are noted in the accompanying In the News box. The accompanying World View suggests that underground activity is more pervasive in other countries.

International activity Another difficulty in computing GNP arises from the international activities of U.S. firms. Multinational firms that operate in many countries may count all sales and profits in their domestic reports. This prac-

---

[2]The Commerce Department does, however, *estimate* the value of some nonmarket activities (e.g., food grown by farmers for their own consumption, the rental value of home ownership) and includes such estimates in GNP calculations.

W🌐RLD VIEW

UNREPORTED INCOME

Underground Economy Keeps Burma Afloat

Government Stores Empty; Vendors Thrive

RANGOON, Burma—At the state-run People's Department Store, sales clerks slouch behind nearly empty shelves. A few eat their lunch, others appear to doze and most stare at a camera-toting foreign tourist—the only customer in a cavernous, dimly lit store. A guard warns the foreigner against photographing the barren shelves.

Outside, the street bustles with vendors hawking books, kitchen utensils, plastic sandals, shirts, rice, dried fruits, colorful textiles, and toys—from China, Thailand and Singapore. Shoppers jostle each other for bargains, some clutching wads of cash equal to the official average annual salary.

The two scenes catch the contrast in Burma's two approaches to commerce, the state-run economy inside and the private vendors outside. "There's a completely parallel economy," said a diplomat. "The country is in a hell of a way, but it's kept up by this . . . underground economy."

Another diplomat said, "The free market is the real one. In the government shops, there is nothing to buy. If you take away the smuggled goods, the government would not survive even a week. They are wholly dependent on it."

Burma's parallel economies are similar to those in Cambodia, and to a lesser extent Vietnam, where communist governments tolerate and lately even encourage a dose of capitalism to boost sagging state-run commerce.

—Keith B. Richburg

The Washington Post, April 30, 1988, p. A16. Copyright © 1988 The Washington Post.

tice exaggerates the amount of productive activity actually occurring in the United States. To remedy this problem, we also compute gross domestic product (GDP), which includes only market transactions originating in the United States.

Value Added   Even when we focus on domestic market activity we encounter problems in calculating GNP. A very basic problem arises from the fact that the production of output typically involves a series of distinct stages. Consider the production of bread, for example. For bread to reach the supermarket, the farmer must grow some wheat, the miller must convert it to flour, and the baker must make bread with it. This chain of production is illustrated in Table 4.2.

TABLE 4.2   Value Added in Various Stages of Production

The value added at each stage of production represents a contribution to total output. Value added equals the market value of a product minus the cost of intermediate goods.

Stages of production	Value of transaction	Value added
1. Farmer grows wheat, sells it to miller	$0.12	$0.12
2. Miller converts wheat to flour, sells it to baker	0.28	0.16
3. Baker bakes bread, sells it to supermarket	0.60	0.32
4. Supermarket sells bread to consumer	0.75	0.15
Total	$1.75	$0.75

In The News

MEASUREMENT PROBLEMS

The Underground Economy

GNP statistics are supposed to measure all market sales of goods and services. But many market transactions escape the notice of national-income accountants. A few examples:

- *Illegal drug trade.* The Drug Enforcement Administration estimates that illegal drug sales in the United States exceed $6 billion per year. None of this market activity is reported to either the Internal Revenue Service or the Commerce Department.

- *Cash income of domestic help.* Babysitters and other domestic help are often paid for their market services in cash. They may prefer cash payments for several reasons. First, cash income may escape both income and Social Security taxes. Second, cash income may escape the notice of public-welfare and unemployment-compensation administrators. Finally, cash payments reduce the paperwork of both employees and employers.

- *Cash income of other self-employed workers.* Other self-employed workers have similar incentives for not reporting cash income. Self-employed carpenters, dentists, electricians, and doctors all have the opportunity to be paid in cash.

- *Tips.* Waiters, waitresses, taxicab drivers, and other service workers typically receive tips in cash. The Internal Revenue Service attempts to estimate the amount of tip income an individual can expect, but the opportunity to evade some taxes remains.

- *Sales revenue of small businesses.* Business firms also have tax incentives for not reporting cash income. Street vendors, bars, sandwich shops, and other small businesses that deal in cash have the opportunity to avoid reporting income.

No one knows how much activity takes place in the "underground economy." Because it deals only in cash, there are no records on which to base GNP estimates. Professor Peter Guttman of New York's Baruch College guesses the underground economy may amount to as much as 12 percent of GNP. Estimates by Professor Edgar Feige of the University of Wisconsin are even higher—as much as 20 percent of GNP. The Internal Revenue Service itself puts the figure at 10 percent of total GNP. Whatever its true dimensions, the underground economy represents a lot of economic activity that is not included in our GNP statistics.

---

intermediate goods: Goods or services purchased for use as input in the production of final goods or services.

value added: The increase in the market value of a product that takes place at each stage of the production process.

Notice that each of the four stages of production depicted in Table 4.2 involves a separate market transaction. Were we simply to add them up, we would come to the conclusion that the value of a loaf of bread was $1.75 and increase GNP accordingly. But that figure is clearly in error. The market value of a loaf of bread—and thus its value to consumers—is only $0.75, as evidenced by the fact that the supermarket sells it to consumers at that price. We cannot simply add up all market transactions if we want to know the value of the economy's output. Instead, we must focus on the value of *final* goods and services and exclude **intermediate goods** from our calculation.

We can arrive at a more accurate measure of *final* output in either of two ways. We could simply include in our calculations only the final transactions in the production process—that is, only sales to consumers. To do this, however, we would have to know who purchased each good or service in order to know when we had reached the end of the process. Such a calculation would also exclude any output produced in stages 1, 2, and 3 of Table 4.2, but not yet reflected in stage 4.

An easier way to calculate GNP is to count only the **value added** at each stage of production. Consider the miller, for example. He does not really contribute $0.28 worth of production to total output, but only $0.16. The other $0.12 reflected in the price of his flour represents the contribution of the farmer who grew the wheat. By the same token, the baker *adds* only $0.32 to the value of output, as part of his output was purchased from the miller. By considering only the value *added* at each stage of production, we eliminate double counting. We do not count twice the *intermediate* goods and services that producers buy from other producers, which are then used as inputs. As Table 4.2 confirms, we can determine that value of final output by summing up the value added at each stage of production. (Note that $0.75 is also the price of bread.)

Real vs. Nominal GNP

Although prices serve as a convenient measure of market value, they can also distort our perceptions of real output. Imagine what would happen to our calculations of GNP if all prices were to double from one year to the next. Suppose, for example, that the price of oranges, as shown in Table 4.1, rose from 20 cents to 40 cents, the price of bicycles to $100, and the price of airplanes to $2 million each. How would such price changes affect this year's GNP? Obviously, the price increases would double the *value* of final output. Measured GNP would rise from $1,400 million to $2,800 million.

Such a rise in GNP does not reflect an increase in the quantity of goods and services available to us. We are still producing the same quantities shown in Table 4.1; only the prices of those goods have changed. Hence changes in GNP brought about by changes in the price level can give us a distorted view of economic reality. Surely we would not want to assert that our standard of living had improved just because price increases raised measured GNP from $1,400 million to $2,800 million.

To distinguish increases in the quantity of goods and services from increases in their prices, we must construct a measure of GNP that takes into account price level changes. We do so by distinguishing between real GNP and nominal GNP. **Nominal GNP** is the value of final output measured in that year's prices, whereas **real GNP** is the value of output measured in constant prices. *To calculate real GNP, we value goods and services at constant prices.*

nominal GNP: The value of final output produced in a given period, measured in the prices of that period (current prices).

real GNP: The value of final output produced in a given period, measured in the prices of a base period (constant prices).

Note, for example, that in Table 4.1 prices are unchanged as we go from last year to this year. In this case, prices in the marketplace are constant, and interyear comparisons of prices are simple. But if all prices double, the comparison becomes more complicated. If all prices doubled from last year to this year, this year's nominal GNP would rise to $2,800 million. But these price increases wouldn't alter the quantity of goods produced. In other words, *real* GNP, valued at constant prices, would remain at $1,400 million. Thus *the distinction between nominal and real GNP is important whenever the level of prices changes.*

Because the price level rarely stays constant, the distinction between nominal and real GNP must be made when the economy's performance is evaluated over time. In calculating real GNP, we can use any year's prices as a base, as long as we consistently value output at the level of prices prevailing in that year. In Table 4.3, we use the average price level of 1933 to compute real GNP in 1990. This allows us to compare today's output to that of the Great Depression.

Figure 4.1 illustrates how nominal and real GNP have changed since 1960. Real GNP is calculated here on the basis of the level of prices prevailing in 1982. (Note that real and nominal GNP are identical in that year.) The dollar

TABLE 4.3 Real vs. Nominal GNP

Suppose that we want to determine how much better off the average American was in 1990, as measured in terms of new goods and services, than people were during the Great Depression. To do this, we would compare GNP per capita in 1990 with GNP per capita in 1933. The following data make that comparison:

	GNP	Population	Per capita GNP
1933	$ 56 billion	126 million	$ 444
1990	5,600 billion	250 million	22,400

In 1933 the nation's GNP of $56 billion was shared by 126 million Americans, yielding a *per capita* GNP of $444. By contrast, 1990's GNP was roughly one hundred times larger, at $5,600 billion. This vastly larger GNP was shared by 250 million people, giving us a per capita GNP of $22,400. Hence it would appear that our standard of living in 1990 was 50 times higher than the standard of 1933.

But this increase in *nominal* GNP vastly exaggerates our material well-being. The average price of goods and services—the *price level*—increased by 800 percent between 1933 and 1990. The goods and services you might have bought for $1 in 1933 cost $9 in 1990. In other words, we needed a lot more dollars in 1990 to buy any given combination of real goods and services.

In order to compare our *real* GNP in 1990 with the real GNP of 1933, we have to adjust for this tremendous jump in prices (inflation). We do so by measuring both years' output in terms of *constant* prices. Since prices went up, on average, ninefold between 1933 and 1990, we simply divide 1990 *nominal* output by nine. The calculation is

$$\begin{matrix} \text{Real GNP} \\ \text{in 1990} \\ \text{(in 1933 prices)} \end{matrix} = \frac{\text{nominal 1990 GNP}}{\dfrac{\text{1990 price level}}{\text{1933 price level}}}$$

By arbitrarily setting the level of prices in 1933 at 100 and noting that prices have increased ninefold since then, we can calculate

$$\begin{matrix} \text{Real GNP} \\ \text{in 1990} \\ \text{(in 1933 prices)} \end{matrix} = \frac{\$5,600 \text{ billion}}{\dfrac{900}{100}}$$

$$= 622 \text{ billion}$$

With a population of 250 million, this left us with real GNP per capita of $2,488 in 1990—as measured in 1933 dollars. This was more than five times the *real* per capita GNP of the depression ($444), but not nearly so great an increase as comparisons of *nominal* GNP suggest.

value of output produced each year has risen considerably faster than the quantity of output, reflecting persistent increases in the price level—that is to say, **inflation.**

Notice in particular that continuing inflation tends to obscure the actual *declines* in real output. Real GNP actually declined in 1970, 1974, 1975, 1980, and 1982, though nominal GNP kept rising. Although the *value* of final output continued to rise in those years, the annual production of goods and services was falling; nominal and real GNP moved in opposite directions.

inflation: An increase in the average level of prices of goods and services.

**FIGURE 4.1
Changes in GNP:
Nominal vs. Real**

Increases in nominal GNP
reflect higher prices as well as
more output. Increases in real
GNP reflect more output only.
To measure these real changes,
we must value each year's
output in terms of common
base prices. In this figure the
base year is 1982. Notice that
real GNP declined in 1974,
1975, 1980, and 1982,
although *nominal* GNP
continued to rise. Nominal
GNP rises faster than real
GNP as a result of inflation.

Source: *Economic Report of the
President,* 1990.

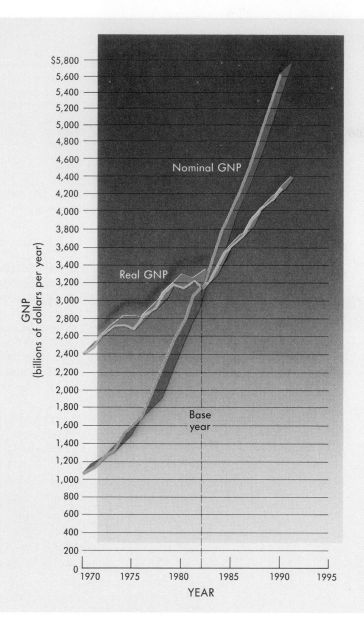

Net National Product

Although changes in real GNP from one year to the next tell us how much
the economy's output has grown, they may exaggerate the growth of **production possibilities.** Recall that our production possibilities depend on the
quantity of land, labor, and capital available and our knowledge of how to
use those factors of production—our technology.

Unfortunately, we use up some of our capital—our plant and equipment—in the process of producing goods and services. As a consequence, it
is possible for GNP to rise at the same time that our production possibilities
are shrinking. Under such circumstances, the higher standards of living we
attain today will be at the expense of our future well-being. Such binges may
provide some temporary enjoyment but are contrary to our long-run interests.

production possibilities: The
alternative combinations of final
goods and services that could be
produced in a given time period
with all available resources and
technology.

depreciation: The consumption of capital in the production process; the wearing out of plant and equipment.

net national product (NNP): GNP less depreciation.

investment: Expenditures on (production of) new plant and equipment (capital) in a given time period, plus changes in business inventories.

gross investment: Total investment expenditure in a given time period.

net investment: Gross investment less depreciation.

What we want to do, then, is to determine how much of our GNP is attributable to the fact that we are using up (consuming) our capital. To do so we subtract from GNP an estimate of our capital consumption, an estimate referred to as **depreciation.**[3] This calculation leaves us with yet another measure of output: **net national product (NNP).** This is the amount of output we could consume without reducing our stock of capital and therewith next year's production possibilities.

The distinction between GNP and NNP has direct implications for our mix of output. To maintain our production possibilities, we must at least replace the capital we consume. This means that at least some of each year's output will have to consist of newly produced plant and equipment—that is, **investment** goods. Indeed, our total production of new plant and equipment—that is, our gross investment—must at least match our depreciation.[4] If we fail to allocate at least that much of our output to investment, our stock of capital and production possibilities will shrink.

The distinction between GNP and NNP is thus mirrored in a distinction between *gross* investment and *net* investment. **Gross investment** is positive as long as some new plant and equipment is being produced. But ***our stock of capital—our total collection of plant and equipment—will not grow unless gross investment exceeds depreciation.*** That is, the *flow* of new capital must exceed depreciation, or our stock of capital will decline. Whenever gross investment exceeds depreciation, **net investment** is positive.

Notice that net investment can be negative as well; in such situations we are wearing out our plant and equipment faster than we are replacing it. If net investment continued to be negative for enough years, our capital stock would diminish to the point where we would be left with very little capital. With less capital, we would be less able to produce goods and services.

THE USES OF OUTPUT

The role of investment in maintaining or expanding our production possibilities helps focus attention on the uses to which GNP is put. It is not just the total value of annual output that matters, but also the use that we make of it. ***The GNP accounts also tell us what mix of output we have selected, that is, society's answer to the question of WHAT to produce.***

Consumption   The major uses of total output conform to the four sets of market participants we encountered in Chapter 2—namely, consumers, business firms, government, and foreigners. Those goods and services received and used by consumers are called *consumption goods.* They range all the way from breakfast cereals to massage parlors and include all goods and services consumers purchase in product markets. By adding up all those expenditures, we can see that consumer spending claims nearly two-thirds of all our annual output (see Figure 4.2).

---

[3]The terms "depreciation" and "capital consumption allowance" are used interchangeably. The depreciation charges firms commonly make, however, are determined in part by income tax regulations, and may thus not accurately reflect the amount of capital consumed.

[4]Investment figures in the GNP accounts also include residential construction and changes in business inventories of final goods and services. Business inventories are discussed in Chapter 8.

FIGURE 4.2
The Uses of GNP

Total GNP amounted to $5.2 trillion in 1989. Nearly two-thirds of this output consisted of private consumer goods and services. The next largest share (20 percent) of output consisted of public-sector goods. Investment goods made up 15 percent of GNP. Finally, because imports exceeded exports, we ended up consuming 1 percent more than we produced.

Source: *Economic Report of the Present*, 1990.

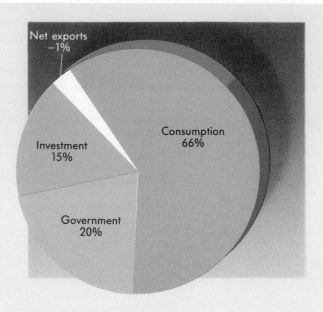

Investment   *Investment goods* represent another use of GNP. Investment goods are the plant, machinery, and equipment that we produce. Like consumption goods, their production entails the use of resources, and thus they compete with consumption goods for our limited resources. Resources used to produce buildings or machinery cannot simultaneously be used to produce television sets or videodiscs (opportunity costs again). Investment spending claims approximately 15 percent of our total output.

Government spending   The third major user of GNP is the *public sector*. Federal, state, and local governments purchase resources to police the streets, teach classes, write laws, and build highways. The resources purchased by the government sector are unavailable for either consumption or investment purposes. At present, government spending claims approximately one-fifth of our annual output.

Net exports   Finally, we should note that some of the goods and services we produce each year are used abroad rather than at home. That is to say, we **export** some of our output to other countries, for whatever use they care to make of it. Thus GNP—the value of output produced—will be larger than the sum of our own consumption, investment, and government purchases to the extent that we succeed in exporting goods and services.

International trade is not a one-way street. While we export some of our own output, we also **import** goods and services from other countries. These imports may be used for consumption (Scotch whiskey, Japanese stereos), investment (German ball bearings), or government (French radar screens). Whatever their use, imports represent purchases of goods and services that were not produced in the United States.

The GNP accounts subtract imports from exports. The difference represents *net* exports. In 1989 the value of exports was $51 billion less than the value of imports. This implies that, on balance, nearly 1 percent of the output

exports: Goods and services sold to foreign buyers.

imports: Goods and services purchased from foreign sources.

we used in 1989 was actually produced in other countries. We subtract this amount from total sales to reflect domestic output levels.

What we end up with, then, is a simple method for computing GNP. This method consists of adding up *expenditures* of market participants. Specifically, we note that

$$\bullet \quad GNP = C + I + G + (X - M)$$

where C = consumption expenditure
I = investment expenditure
G = government expenditure
X = exports
M = imports

This approach to GNP accounting emphasizes the fact that all output is claimed by someone. If we know who is buying our output, we know how much was produced and what uses were made of it.

MEASURES OF INCOME

There is another way of looking at GNP. Instead of looking at who is *buying* our output, we can look at who is *being paid* to produce it. Like markets themselves, ***GNP accounts have two sides: one side focuses on expenditure (the demand side), the other side focuses on income (the supply side).***

We have already observed (Figure 2.2) that every market transaction involves an *exchange* of dollars for a good or resource. Moreover, the *value* of each good or resource is measured by the amount of money exchanged for it (its market price). Hence ***the total value of market incomes must equal the total value of final output, or GNP.*** In other words, one person's expenditure always represents another person's income.

The equivalence of output and income is not dependent on any magical qualities possessed by money. Were we to produce only one product—say, wheat—and pay everyone in bushels and pecks, total income would still equal total output. People could not receive in income more wheat than we produced. On the other hand, all the wheat produced would go to *someone*. Hence one could say that the production possibilities of the economy define the limits to real income. The amount of income actually generated in any year depends on the production and expenditure decisions of consumers, firms, and government agencies.

Table 4.4 shows the actual flow of output and income in the American economy during 1989. Total output is made up of the familiar components of GNP—consumption, investment, government goods and services, and net exports. The figures on the left side of Table 4.4 indicate that consumers spent $3,470 billion, businesses spent $777 billion on plant and equipment, governments spent $1,037 billion, and net imports were $51 billion. Our total output value (GNP) was thus over $5.2 trillion in 1989.

The right-hand side of Table 4.4 indicates who received the income generated from these market transactions. Every dollar spent on goods and services provides income to someone. It may go to a worker (as wage or salary) or to a business firm (as profit and depreciation allowance). It may

TABLE 4.4 The Equivalence of Expenditure and Income
(in billions of dollars)

The value of total expenditure must equal the value of total income. Why? Because every dollar spent on output becomes a dollar of income for someone.

Expenditure		Income	
Consumer goods and services	$3,470	Wages and salaries	$3,145
Investment in plant, equipment, and inventory	777	Corporate profits	298
		Proprietors' income	280
Government goods and services	1,037	Farm income	54
		Rents	63
Exports	624	Interest	461
Imports	(675)	Sales taxes	416
		Depreciation	552
		Adjustments*	(38)
Total value of output	$5,233	Total value of income	$5,233

*Necessary because of sampling, rounding, and other errors in the national accounting system. Such adjustments ensure statistical equivalence of output and income flows.
Source: *Economic Report of the President,* 1990.

go to a landlord (as rent), to a lender (as interest), or to government (as sales or property tax). None of the dollars spent on goods and services disappears into thin air.[5]

National Income Although it may be exciting to know that we collectively received $5.2 trillion of income in 1989, it might be of more interest to know who actually got all that income. After all, there are not only 250 million pairs of outstretched palms among us; millions of businesses and government agencies are also competing for those dollars and the goods and services they represent. By charting the flow of income through the economy, we can see FOR WHOM our output was produced.

Depreciation Our annual income flow originates in product-market sales. Purchases of final goods and services create a flow of income to producers and, through them, to factors of production. But a major diversion of sales revenues occurs immediately, as a result of depreciation charges made by businesses. As we noted earlier, some of our capital resources are used up in the process of production. For the most part, these resources are owned by business firms that expect to be compensated for such investments. Accordingly, they regard some of the sales revenue generated in product markets as reimbursement for wear and tear on capital plant and equipment. They therefore subtract *depreciation charges* from gross revenues in calculating their incomes. Depreciation charges reduce GNP to the level of NNP before any income is available to current factors of production—that is,

- NNP = GNP − depreciation

Indirect business taxes Another major diversion of the income flow occurs at its point of origin. When goods are sold in the marketplace, their purchase price is typically encumbered with some sort of sales tax. Thus some of the

[5]Not all of the national income, however, is accounted for by the U.S. Department of Commerce. The "Adjustments" figure in Table 4.4 includes income that eluded the statisticians at the Commerce Department, as well as miscellaneous transfer payments. For current estimates of national income statistics, consult the annual *Economic Report of the President* or the bimonthly *Survey of Current Business.*

revenue generated in product markets disappears before anyone really gets a chance to touch it. These *indirect business taxes,* as they are called, are not considered part of national income because they do not represent payment for contributions to current output. But they do account for a large part of the income spent in the marketplace.

Once depreciation charges and indirect business taxes are subtracted from GNP, we are left with **national income,** the total income earned by the factors of production that have contributed to current production. Thus

- NI = NNP − indirect business taxes

national income (NI): Total income earned by current factors of production; GNP less depreciation and indirect business taxes.

As Table 4.5 illustrates, our national income in 1989 was $4,265 billion, nearly $1 trillion less than GNP.

Personal Income

National income is the income received not only by households (consumers) but also by corporations. Theoretically, all the income received by corporations represents income for their owners—the households who hold stock in the corporations. But the flow of income through corporations to stockholders is far from complete. First, corporations must pay taxes on their profits. Accordingly, some of the income received on behalf of a corporation's stockholders goes into the public treasury rather than into private bank accounts. Second, corporate managers typically find some urgent need for cash. As a result, part of the profits are retained by the corporation rather than passed on to the stockholders in the form of dividends. Accordingly, both *corporate taxes* and *retained earnings* must be subtracted from national income before we can determine how much income flows into the hands of consumers.

Still another deduction must be made for *Social Security taxes.* Nearly all people who earn a wage or salary are required by law to pay Social Security "contributions." In 1990 the Social Security tax rate for workers was 7.65 percent on the first $51,300 of earnings received in the year (see Chapter 3).

TABLE 4.5   The Flow of Income, 1989

Consumers end up with approximately 70 percent of total income (GNP). The remainder is received by governments and businesses. This table shows how the income flow is distributed.

Income flow	Amount (in billions)
Gross national product (GNP)	$5,233
Less depreciation	(552)
Net national product	4,681
Less indirect business taxes	(416)
National income (*NI*)	4,265
Less corporate taxes	(129)
Less retained earnings*	(57)
Less Social Security taxes	(479)
Plus transfer payments	632
Plus net interest	197
Personal income (*PI*)	4,429
Less personal taxes	(649)
Disposable income (*DI*)	3,780

*Retained earnings are net of inventory valuation changes and depreciation.
Source: *Economic Report of the President,* 1990.

personal income (PI): Income received by households before payment of personal taxes.

Workers never see this income, because it is withheld by employers and sent directly to the U.S. Treasury. Thus the flow of national income is reduced considerably before it becomes **personal income,** the amount of income received by households, before payment of personal taxes.

Not all of our adjustments to national income are negative. Households receive income in the form of transfer payments from the public treasury. More than 40 million people receive monthly Social Security checks, for example, and another 15 million or so receive some form of public welfare. These income transfers represent income for the people who receive them. People also receive interest payments in excess of those they pay (largely because of interest payments on the government debt). This *net* interest is another source of personal income. Accordingly, our calculation of personal income is as follows:

- national income
  less corporate taxes
          retained earnings
          Social Security taxes
  plus transfer payments
          net interest

- *equals* personal income

Disposable Income

disposable income (DI): After-tax income of consumers; personal income less personal taxes.

The total flow of income *generated* in production is significantly reduced before it gets into the hands of individual households. But we have not yet reached the end of the reduction process. We have to set something aside for personal income taxes. To be sure we don't forget about our obligations, Uncle Sam and his state and local affiliates usually arrange to have their share taken off the top. Personal income taxes are withheld by the employer, who thus acts as a tax collector. Accordingly, to calculate **disposable income**—the amount of income consumers may themselves spend (dispose of)—we reduce personal income by the amount of personal taxes:

- Disposable income = personal income − personal taxes

saving: That part of disposable income not spent on current consumption; disposable income less consumption.

Once consumers get some disposable income in their hands, they face two choices. They may choose to *spend* their disposable income on consumer goods and services. Or they may choose to *save* it. These are the only two choices in GNP accounting. **Saving,** in this context, simply refers to disposable income that is not spent on consumption. In the analysis of income and saving flows, we don't care whether savings are hidden under a mattress, deposited in the bank, or otherwise secured. All we want to know is whether disposable income is spent or not. Thus *all disposable income is, by definition, either consumed or saved*—that is,

- Disposable income = consumption + saving

THE FLOW OF INCOME

Figure 4.3 summarizes the relationship between expenditure and income. The essential point again is that every dollar spent on goods and services flows into somebody's hands. Thus *the dollar value of output will always equal*

FIGURE 4.3
The Flow of Expenditure and Income

Consumers, businesses, government, and foreigners lay claim to our output by buying goods and services in the marketplace. This expenditure creates income that flows to consumers (disposable income), businesses (retained earnings and depreciation), and government (taxes). Every dollar spent in the marketplace becomes income for someone.

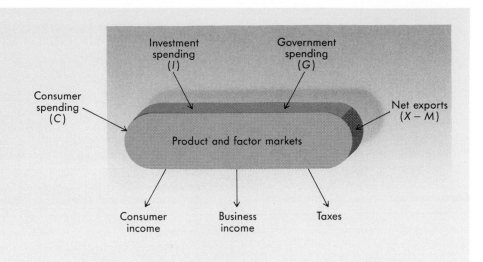

the dollar value of income. Specifically, total income (GNP) ends up distributed in the following way:

- To *consumers,* in the form of disposable income

- To *business,* in the form of retained earnings and depreciation allowances

- To *government,* in the form of taxes

Income and Expenditure

The annual flow of income to households, businesses, and government is part of a continuing process. Households rarely stash their disposable income under the mattress; they spend most of it on consumption. This spending adds to GNP in the next round of activity, thereby helping to keep the flow of income moving.

Business firms also have a lot of purchasing power tied up in retained earnings and depreciation charges. This income, too, may be recycled—returned to the circular flow—in the form of business investment.

Even the income that flows into public treasuries finds its way back into the marketplace, as government agencies hire police officers, soldiers, and clerks, or buy goods and services. Thus *the flow of income that starts with GNP ultimately returns to the market in the form of new consumption (C), investment (I), and government purchases (G).* A new GNP arises, and the flow starts all over again. In Section II of this book we will examine in detail these *expenditure* flows, with particular emphasis on their ability to keep the economy producing at its full potential.

POLICY INSIGHTS:

THE QUALITY OF LIFE

Money, money, money—it seems that's all we talk about. Why don't we talk about important things like beauty, virtue, or the quality of life? Do the GNP accounts—either their expenditure side or their income side—tell us anything about these essential dimensions of existence? If not, why have we spent so much time examining them?

"The way I look at it, there's a price tag
on everything. You want a high standard of living,
you settle for a low quality of life."

The Dig U.S.A. Series: *The Good Life U.S.A.*, New York,
Bantam Books, 1973.

All the economic measures discussed in this chapter are important indexes of individual and collective welfare; they tell us something about how well people are living. They do not, however, capture the completeness of the way in which we view the world or the totality of what makes our lives satisfying. A clear day, a sense of accomplishment, even a smile can do more for a person's sense of well-being than can favorable movements in the GNP accounts. Or, as Professor John Kenneth Galbraith put it, "In a rational lifestyle, some people could find contentment working moderately and then sitting by the street—and talking, thinking, drawing, painting, scribbling, or making love in a suitably discreet way. None of these requires an expanding economy."[6]

The emphasis on economic outcomes arises not from ignorance of life's other meanings but from the visibility of the economic outcomes. We all realize that well-being arises from both material and intangible pleasures, but the intangibles tend to be elusive. It is not easy to gauge individual happiness, much less to ascertain the status of our collective satisfaction. We have to rely on measures we can see, touch, and count. As long as the material components of our environment bear some positive relation to our well-being, they at least serve a useful purpose.

In some situations, however, more physical output may actually worsen our collective welfare. If increased automobile production raises congestion and pollution levels, the rise in GNP occasioned by those additional cars is a misleading index of society's welfare. In such a case, the rise in GNP might actually mask a *decrease* in the well-being of the population. Exclusive emphasis on measurable output would clearly be a mistake in such a situation.

What is true of automobile production might also be true of other outputs. Increased development of urban areas may cause a loss of social welfare if that development occurs at the expense of space, trees, and relative tranquility. Increased mechanization on the farm may raise agricultural output but isolate and uproot farmers. So, too, increased productivity in factories and offices might contribute to a sense of alienation. These ill effects of increased output need not occur; but if they do, indexes of output tell us less about social or individual well-being.

All this does not suggest that the national-income accounts are useless or irrelevant. Rather, these points help to underscore the fact that *social welfare* and *economic welfare* are not synonymous. The GNP accounts tell us whether our economic welfare has increased, as measured by the quantity of goods and services we demanded in the marketplace. What they don't tell us is how highly we value additional goods and services, relative to nonmarket phenomena. Nor do they even tell us whether important social costs were incurred in the process of production. These judgments must be made outside the market; they are social decisions.

SUMMARY

- National-income accounting is the measurement of our annual output and income flows. The national-income accounts provide a basis for assessing our economic performance, for designing public policy, and for understanding how all the parts of the economy interact.

- The most comprehensive measure of our output is gross national product (GNP). This is the total market value of all final goods and services produced during a given time period.

- In calculating GNP, we include only the value added at each stage of production. This procedure eliminates the possibility of the double counting that would result because business firms buy intermediate goods from other firms and include the associated costs in their selling price. For the most part, only marketed goods and services are included in GNP.

[6]Cited in Leonard Silk, *Nixonomics,* 2d ed. (New York: Praeger, 1973), p. 163.

• To distinguish physical changes in output from monetary changes in its value, we compute both nominal and real GNP. Nominal GNP is the value of output expressed in *current* prices. Real GNP is the value of output expressed in *constant* prices (the prices of some *base* year).

• Each year some of our capital equipment is worn out—consumed—in the process of production. Hence GNP is larger than the amount of goods and services we could consume without reducing our production possibilities. The amount of capital used up each year is referred to as "depreciation."

• By subtracting depreciation from GNP, we derive net national product (NNP). The difference between NNP and GNP is also equal to the difference between *gross* investment—the sum of all our current plant and equipment expenditures—and *net* investment—the amount of investment over and above that required to replace worn-out capital.

• All the income generated in market sales (GNP) is received by someone. The sequence of flows involved in this process is:

> GNP
> *less* depreciation
> equals NNP
> *less* indirect business taxes
> equals national income (*NI*)
> *less* corporate taxes,
>   retained earnings, and
>   Social Security taxes
> *plus* transfer payments and
>   net interest
> equals personal income (*PI*)
> *less* personal income taxes
> equals disposable income (*DI*)

• The incomes received by households, business firms, and governments provide the purchasing power required to buy the nation's output. As that purchasing power is spent, further GNP is created and the circular flow continues.

Terms to Remember   Define the following terms:

national-income accounting	net national product (NNP)
gross national product (GNP)	investment
GNP per capita	gross investment
intermediate goods	net investment
value added	exports
nominal GNP	imports
real GNP	national income (NI)
inflation	personal income (PI)
production possibilities	disposable income (DI)
depreciation	saving

Questions for Discussion

1. The manuscript for this text was typed by a friend. Had I hired a secretary to do the same job, GNP would have been higher, even though the amount of output would have been identical. Why is this? Does this make sense?

2. GNP in 1981 was $2.96 trillion. It grew to $3.07 trillion in 1982, yet the quantity of output actually decreased. How is this possible?

3. If gross investment is not large enough to replace the capital that depreciates in a particular year, is net investment greater or less than zero? What happens to our production possibilities?

4. Can we increase consumption in a given year without cutting back on either investment or government services? Under what conditions?

5. What was real per capita GNP in 1933, measured in 1990 prices? (Use data in Table 4.3 on page 93 to compute your answer.)

Problems   1. (a) Calculate national income from the following figures:

Consumption	$200 billion
Depreciation	20 billion
Retained earnings	12 billion
Gross investment	30 billion
Imports	40 billion
Social Security taxes	25 billion
Exports	50 billion
Indirect business taxes	15 billion
Government purchases	60 billion
Personal income taxes	40 billion

(b) If there were 80 million people in this country, what would the GNP per capita be?

(c) If all prices were to double overnight, what would happen to the values of real and nominal GNP per capita?

2. (a) Compute real GNP for 1989 using average prices of 1980 as the base year. (In the front and back endpapers of this book you will find data for GNP and the GNP "price deflator" used to measure inflation.)

(b) By how much did real GNP increase between 1980 and 1989?

(c) By how much did nominal GNP increase between 1980 and 1989?

3. Suppose all of the dollar values in problem 1 were in 1989 dollars. Use the Consumer Price Index shown in the back endpapers of this book to convert the numbers to 1972 dollars. Also, find the value of national income in 1972 dollars. (You will be converting the figures from their nominal to their real values, with 1972 as the base year.)

MACROECONOMICS

MAJOR PROBLEMS

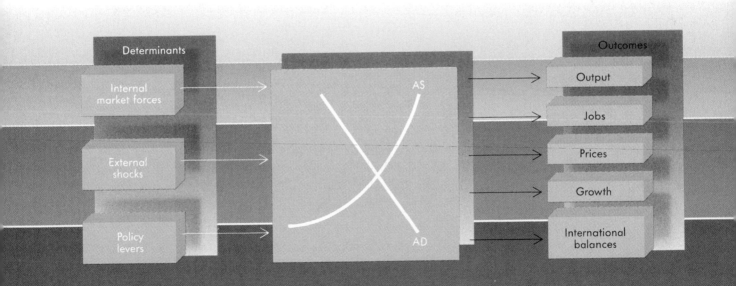

Macro economics focuses on the performance of the entire economy rather than on the behavior of individual participants (a micro concern). The central concerns of macro policy are the rate of output, the level of prices, economic growth, and our trade and payments balances with the rest of the world.

CHAPTER 5

The Business Cycle

*I*n 1929 it looked as though the sun would never set on the American economy. For eight years in a row, the United States economy had been expanding rapidly. During the "Roaring Twenties" the typical American family drove its first car, bought its first radio, and went to the movies for the first time. With factories running at capacity, virtually anyone who wanted to work found a job readily.

Under these circumstances everyone was optimistic. In his Acceptance Address of November 1928, president-elect Herbert Hoover echoed this optimism, by declaring: "We in America today are nearer to the final triumph over poverty than ever before in the history of any land. . . . We shall soon with the help of God be in sight of the day when poverty will be banished from this nation."

The booming stock market seemed to confirm this optimistic outlook. Between 1921 and 1927 the stock market's value more than doubled, adding billions of dollars to the wealth of American households and businesses. The stock-market boom accelerated in 1927, causing stock prices to double again in less than two years. The roaring stock market made it look easy to get rich in America.

The party ended abruptly on October 24, 1929. On what came to be known as Black Thursday, the stock market crashed. In a few short hours, the market value of U.S. corporations fell abruptly, in the most frenzied selling ever seen. The next day President Hoover tried to assure America's stockholders that the economy was "on a sound and prosperous basis." But despite his assurances and the efforts of leading bankers to stem the decline, the stock market continued to plummet. The following Tuesday (October 29) the pace of selling quickened. By the end of the year, over $40 billion of wealth had vanished in the Great Crash. Rich men became paupers overnight; ordinary families lost their savings, their homes, and even their lives.

The devastation was not confined to Wall Street. The financial flames engulfed the farms, the banks, and industry. Between 1930 and 1935, millions of rural families lost their farms. Automobile production fell from 4.5 million cars in 1929 to only 1.1 million in 1932. So many banks were forced to close that newly elected President Roosevelt had to declare a "bank holiday" in March 1933 to stem the outflow of cash to anxious depositors.

111

In The News

THE CRASH OF 1929

Market in Panic as Stocks Are Dumped in 12,894,600 Share Day; Bankers Halt It

Effect Is Felt on the Curb and Throughout Nation—Financial District Goes Wild

The stock markets of the country tottered on the brink of panic yesterday as a prosperous people, gone suddenly hysterical with fear, attempted simultaneously to sell a record-breaking volume of securities for whatever they would bring.

The result was a financial nightmare, comparable to nothing ever before experienced in Wall Street. It rocked the financial district to its foundations, hopelessly overwhelmed its mechanical facilities, chilled its blood with terror.

In a society built largely on confidence, with real wealth expressed more or less inaccurately by pieces of paper, the entire fabric of economic stability threatened to come toppling down.

Into the frantic hands of a thousand brokers on the floor of the New York Stock Exchange poured the selling orders of the world. It was sell, sell, sell—hour after desperate hour until 1:30 p.m.

—Laurence Stern

The World, October 25, 1929.

Throughout these years, the ranks of the unemployed continued to swell. In October 1929 only 3 percent of the work force was unemployed. A year later over 9 percent of the work force was unemployed, and millions of additional workers were getting by on lower wages and shorter hours. Still, things got worse. By 1933 over one-fourth of the labor force was unable to find work. People slept in the streets, scavenged for food, and sold apples on Wall Street.

The Great Depression seemed to last forever. In 1933 President Roosevelt lamented that one-third of the nation was ill-clothed, ill-housed, and ill-fed. Thousands of unemployed workers marched to the Capitol to demand jobs and aid. In 1938, nine years after Black Thursday, nearly 20 percent of the work force was still unemployed.

The Great Depression shook not only the foundations of the world economy but also the assured self-confidence of the economics profession. No one had predicted the Depression and few could explain it. The ensuing search for explanations focused on three central questions:

- How stable is the economy?

- What forces cause instability?

- What, if anything, can the government do to promote steady economic growth?

macroeconomics: The study of aggregate economic behavior, of the economy as a whole.

The basic purpose of **macroeconomics** is to answer these questions—to *explain* the business cycle. These explanations (theories) range from the influence of "sunspots" to money-supply manipulations. In this chapter, some of the more prominent macroeconomic theories are introduced. We examine them more closely in later chapters.

While macroeconomic theories try to explain the business cycle, economic policy tries to *control* it. People don't want to be subjected to recurrent periods of unemployment, inflation, slow growth, or high interest rates. They want the business cycle to be eliminated, or at least dampened. And they expect their elected representatives in Washington to take the necessary action.

What can Congress and the president do? What policy tools might they use to control the business cycle? Is there any reason to believe those tools will do the job? If the tools are adequate, why is the economy still subject to booms and busts?

There is an obvious link between macro theory and macro policy. If macro theory says business cycles are inevitable, then no policy intervention will work. On the other hand, if macro theory can identify a few major causes of the business cycle, there is at least some hope of devising an effective policy to control it.

The major policy options for controlling the business cycle are introduced in this chapter as well. Later chapters examine them more closely, from the perspective of competing macro theories. As we will see, there is a lot of disagreement about what policies, if any, are likely to stem the tides of the business cycle. The theories do provide some clues, however, about what might work at various times.

STABLE OR UNSTABLE?

Classical Theory

Prior to the 1930s, macro economists thought there could never be a Great Depression. The economic thinkers of the time asserted that the economy was inherently stable. During the nineteenth century and the first thirty years of the twentieth century, the U.S. economy had experienced some bad years—years in which the nation's output declined and unemployment increased. But most of these episodes were relatively short-lived. The dominant feature of the Industrial era was growth—an expanding economy, with more output, more jobs, and higher incomes nearly every year.

In this environment, Classical economists, as they later became known, propounded an optimistic view of the macro economy. *According to the Classical view, the economy "self-adjusts" to deviations from its long-term growth trend.* Producers might occasionally reduce their output and throw people out of work. But these dislocations would cause little damage. If output declined and people lost their jobs, the internal forces of the marketplace would quickly restore prosperity. Economic downturns were viewed as temporary setbacks, not permanent problems.

The cornerstones of Classical optimism were flexible prices and flexible wages. If producers were unable to sell all their output at current prices, they had two choices. They could reduce the rate of output and throw some people out of work. Or they could reduce the price of their output, thereby stimulating an increase in the quantity demanded. According to the **law of demand,** price reductions cause an increase in unit sales. If prices fall far enough, all the output produced can be sold. Thus flexible prices—prices that would drop when consumer demand slowed—virtually guaranteed that all output could be sold. No one would have to lose a job because of weak consumer demand.

Flexible prices had their counterpart in factor markets. If some workers were temporarily out of work, they would compete for jobs by offering their services at lower wages. As wage rates declined, producers would find it profitable to hire more workers. Ultimately, flexible wages would ensure that everyone who wanted a job would have a job.

law of demand: The quantity of a good demanded in a given time period increases as its price falls, *ceteris paribus.*

Say's Law: Supply creates its own demand.

These optimistic views of the macro economy were summarized in Say's Law. **Say's Law**—named after the nineteenth-century economist Jean-Baptiste Say—decreed that "supply creates its own demand." Whatever was produced would be sold. All workers who sought employment would be hired. Unsold goods and unemployed labor could emerge in this Classical system. But both would disappear as soon as people had time to adjust prices and wages. There could be no Great Depression—no protracted macro failure—in this Classical view of the world.

The Great Depression was a stunning blow to Classical economists. At the onset of the Depression, Classical economists assured everyone that the setbacks in production and employment were temporary and would soon vanish. Andrew Mellon, Secretary of the U.S. Treasury, expressed this optimistic view in January 1930, just a few months after the stock-market crash. Assessing the prospects for the year ahead, he said: "I see nothing . . . in the present situation that is either menacing or warrants pessimism. . . . I have every confidence that there will be a revival of activity in the spring and that during the coming year the country will make steady progress."[1] Merrill Lynch, one of the nation's largest brokerage houses, was urging people to buy stocks. But the depression deepened. Indeed, unemployment grew and persisted *despite* falling prices and wages (see Figure 5.1). The Classical self-adjustment mechanism simply did not work.

[1]David A. Shannon, *The Great Depression* (Englewood Cliffs, N.J.: Prentice-Hall, 1960), p. 4.

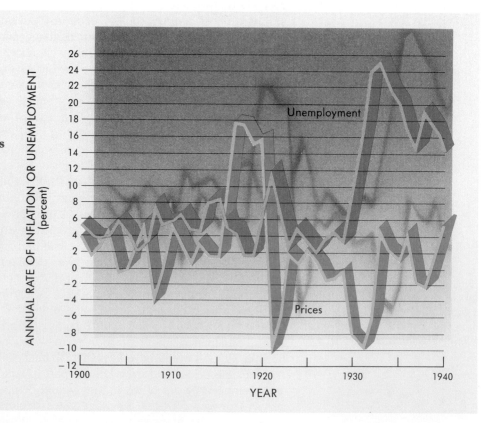

**FIGURE 5.1
Inflation and
Unemployment,
1900-1940**

In the early twentieth century, prices responded to both upward and downward changes in aggregate demand. Periods of high unemployment also tended to be brief. In the 1930s, however, unemployment rates rose to unprecedented heights and stayed high for a decade. Falling wages and prices did not restore full employment. This macro failure prompted calls for new theories and policies to control the business cycle.

Source: U.S. Bureau of the Census, *The Statistics of the United States*, 1957.

The Keynesian Revolution

The Great Depression effectively destroyed the credibility of Classical economic theory. As John Maynard Keynes pointed out in 1935, Classical economists

> were apparently unmoved by the lack of correspondence between the results of their theory and the facts of observation:—a discrepancy which the ordinary man has not failed to observe. . . .
>
> The celebrated optimism of [Classical] economic theory . . . is . . . to be traced, I think, to their having neglected to take account of the drag on prosperity which can be exercised by an insufficiency of effective demand. For there would obviously be a natural tendency towards the optimum employment of resources in a Society which was functioning after the manner of the classical postulates. It may well be that the classical theory represents the way in which we should like our Economy to behave. But to assume that it actually does so is to assume our difficulties away.[2]

Keynes went on to develop an alternative view of the macro economy. Whereas the Classical economists viewed the economy as inherently stable, ***Keynes asserted that the private economy was inherently unstable.*** Small disturbances in output, prices, or unemployment were likely to be magnified, not muted by the invisible hand of the marketplace. The Great Depression was not a unique event, Keynes argued, but a calamity that would recur if we relied on the market mechanism to self-adjust. Macro failure was the rule, not the exception, for a purely private economy.

In Keynes's view, the inherent instability of the marketplace required government intervention. When the economy falters, we cannot afford to wait for some assumed self-adjustment mechanism but must instead intervene to protect jobs and income. The government can do this by "priming the pump"—buying more output, employing more people, providing more income transfers, and making more money available. When the economy overheats, the government must cool it down with higher taxes, spending reductions, and less money.

Keynes's denunciation of Classical theory did not end the macroeconomic debate. On the contrary, economists continue to wage fierce debates about the stability of the economy. Those debates will fill the pages of the next few chapters. Before examining them, however, we will first take a quick look at the economy's actual performance.

HISTORICAL CYCLES

business cycle: Alternating periods of economic growth and contraction.

The central concern of macro economics is the **business cycle**—that is, alternating periods of economic expansion and contraction. These upswings and downswings of the economy are gauged in terms of changes in total output. An economic upswing, or expansion, refers to an increase in the volume of goods and services produced. An economic downswing, or contraction, occurs when the total volume of production declines. Changes in employment typically mirror these changes in production.

[2]John Maynard Keynes, *The General Theory of Employment, Interest and Money* (London: Macmillan, 1936), pp. 33–34.

real GNP: The value of final output produced in a given period, measured in the prices of a base period (constant prices).

Figure 5.2 depicts the basic features of a business cycle. The cycle looks like a roller coaster, climbing steeply, then dropping from its peak. Once the trough is reached, the upswing starts again.

In reality, business cycles are not as regular or as predictable as Figure 5.2 suggests. The U.S. economy has experienced recurrent upswings and downswings, but of widely varying length, intensity, and frequency.

Actual business cycles are measured by changes in **real GNP**—that is, the total market value of all the goods and services produced in one year, with market values measured in *constant* prices (the prices of a specific base year). This allows us to focus on changes in the volume of production, while ignoring changes in the value of production caused by fluctuating prices.

From a distance, America's economic track record looks like a steady growth path. From 1929 to today, real GNP has more than sextupled. That is to say, we are now producing over six times as many goods and services as we did back in 1929. Americans now consume a greater variety of goods and services, and in greater quantities, than earlier generations ever dreamed possible.

This spectacular growth has come in small annual increments. On the average, real GNP has grown by only 3 percent per year. But even 3 percent annual growth adds up to a large sum when continued over decades: in just twenty-four years, 3 percent annual growth will lead to a doubling of GNP. One of our policy objectives is to maintain or increase that growth rate.

Our long-term success in raising living standards is clouded by a spate of short-term macro setbacks. On closer inspection, ***the growth path of the U.S. economy is not a smooth, rising trend, but instead a series of steps, stumbles, and setbacks.*** This short-run instability is evident in Figure 5.3. The dashed line represents the long-term *average* growth rate of the U.S. economy. From 1929 through 1989, the U.S. economy expanded at an average rate of 3 percent per year. Also shown in the figure is the annual growth curve, which indicates *year-to-year* variations in real GNP growth. Clearly, we failed to attain 3 percent growth every year. In some years we even slipped below the zero growth line—that is, output *decreased* from one year to the next.

FIGURE 5.2
The Business Cycle

The model business cycle resembles a roller coaster. Output first climbs to a peak, then decreases. After hitting a trough, the economy recovers, with real GNP again increasing.

A central concern of macroeconomic theory is to determine whether a recurring business cycle exists, and if so, what forces cause it.

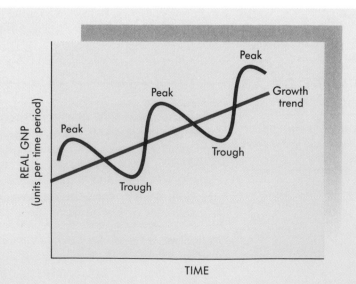

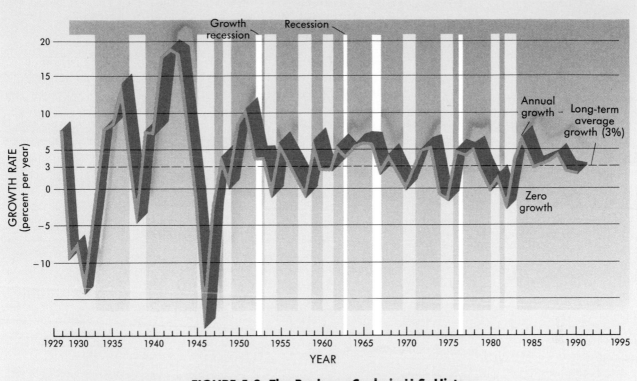

FIGURE 5.3 The Business Cycle in U.S. History

From 1929 to 1990, real GNP increased at an average rate of 3 percent a year. But annual growth rates have departed widely from that average. Years of above-average growth seem to alternate with years of sluggish growth ("growth recessions") and actual decreases in total output ("recessions").

The Great Depression

The most prolonged departure from our long-term growth path occurred during the Great Depression. Between 1929 and 1933, total U.S output steadily declined. Real GNP fell nearly 30 percent in those four years. Investments in new plant and equipment virtually ceased. Economies around the world came to a grinding halt (see World View).

The U.S. economy started to grow again in 1934, but the rate of expansion was modest. Millions of people remained out of work. In 1936–37 the situation worsened again, and total output once more declined. As a consequence, the rate of total output in 1939 was virtually identical to that in 1929. Because of continuing population growth, GNP per capita was actually *lower* in 1939 than it had been in 1929.

World War II

World War II greatly increased the demand for goods and services and ended the Great Depression. During the war years, real GNP grew at unprecedented rates—almost 19 percent in a single year (1942). Virtually everyone was employed, either in the armed forces or in the factories. Throughout the war, our productive capacity was strained to the limit.

W🌐RLD VIEW

COMPARATIVE LOSSES

The Great Depression

The Great Depression was not confined to the U.S. economy. Most other countries suffered substantial losses of output and employment, over a period of many years.

Between 1929 and 1932 industrial production around the world fell 37 percent. The United States and Germany suffered the largest losses, while Spain and the Scandinavian countries lost only modest amounts of output. For specific countries, the decline in output was:

Country	Percentage decline in output
Chile	− 22%
France	− 31
Germany	− 47
Great Britain	− 17
Japan	− 2
Norway	− 7
Spain	− 12
United States	− 46

Some countries escaped the ravages of the Great Depression altogether. The Soviet Union, largely insulated from Western economic structures, was in the midst of Stalin's forced industrialization drive during the 1930s. China and Japan were also relatively isolated from world trade and finance, and so suffered less damage from the Depression.

The Postwar Years

recession: A decline in total output (real GNP) for two or more consecutive quarters.

In the postwar years the U.S. economy resumed a pattern of alternating growth and contraction. The contracting periods are called recessions. Specifically, the term **recession** refers to a decline in real GNP that continues for at least two successive quarters. As Table 5.1 indicates, there have been nine recessions since 1944. The most severe recession occurred immediately after World War II ended. The sudden cutbacks in defense production caused GNP to decline sharply in 1945–46.

The 1980s

growth recession: A period during which real GNP grows, but at a rate below the long-term trend of 3 percent.

The 1980s started with two recessions, the second lasting sixteen months (July 1981–November 1982). Despite the onset of a second recession at mid-year, the economy's total output actually increased in 1981. But the growth rate was so slow (1.9 percent) that few people noticed any improvement in their standard of living. Indeed, because output was growing more slowly than the labor force, the number of unemployed workers actually increased in 1981. These kinds of experiences are called **growth recessions**—that is, the economy grows, but at a slower rate than the long-run (3 percent) average. Thus *a growth recession occurs when the economy expands too slowly. A recession occurs when real GNP actually contracts.* A depression is an extremely deep and long recession.

Whereas 1981 was a year of slow growth, 1982 was a year of actual decline in output. The ensuing recession of 1981–82 threw so many people out of work that the national unemployment rate hit a postwar high of 10.8 percent (Table 5.1).

TABLE 5.1   Eleven Business Slumps

The U.S. economy has experienced eleven business slumps since 1929. In the post–World War II period, these downturns have lasted about ten months each.

Dates	Duration (months)	Percentage decline in real GNP	Peak unemployment rate
Aug. '29–Mar. '33	43	53.4%	24.9%
May '37–June '38	13	32.4	20.0
Feb. '45–Oct. '45	8	38.3	4.3
Nov. '48–Oct. '49	11	9.9	7.9
July '53–May '54	10	10.0	6.1
Aug. '57–Apr. '58	8	14.3	7.5
Apr. '60–Feb. '61	10	7.2	7.1
Dec. '69–Nov. '70	11	8.1	6.1
Nov. '73–Mar. '75	16	14.7	9.0
Jan. '80–July '80	6	8.7	7.6
July '81–Nov. '82	16	12.3	10.8

The economy started to recover in November 1982, then grew very fast in 1983 and 1984. The economic expansion continued through the end of the decade, but at a much slower pace—just below the long-term growth trend of 3 percent. Not until mid-1987 did the unemployment rate fall to its pre-1981 levels.

MODERN VIEWS OF MACRO INSTABILITY

The uneven growth record of the U.S. economy gives some validity to the notion of a recurring business cycle. But the historical record doesn't really answer the key questions we have posed. Are business cycles inevitable? Can we do anything to control them? **Keynes and the Classical economists weren't debating whether business cycles occur, but whether they are an appropriate target for government intervention.** That debate continues.

To determine whether and how the government should try to control the business cycle, we first need to understand its origins. What causes the economy to expand or contract? What forces of the marketplace dampen ("self-adjust") or magnify economic swings?

The bulk of the macro course is devoted to answering these questions. At this early stage, however, we can take a broad view of how the macro economy works. Figure 5.4 offers such a summary view. The primary outcomes of the macroeconomy are arrayed on the right side of the figure. These basic **macro outcomes include**

- **Output:** total volume of goods and services produced
- **Jobs:** levels of employment and unemployment
- **Prices:** average price of goods and services
- **Growth:** year-to-year expansion in production capacity
- **International balances:** international value of the dollar; trade and payments balances with other countries

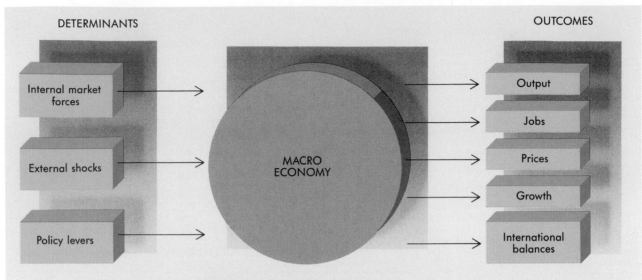

FIGURE 5.4 The Macro Economy

The primary outcomes of the macro economy are output of goods and services, jobs, prices, economic growth, and international balances (trade, currency). These outcomes result from the interplay of internal market forces (e.g., population growth, innovation, spending patterns), external shocks (e.g., wars, weather, trade disruptions), and policy levers (e.g., tax and budget decisions).

These macro outcomes define our economic welfare. That is to say, we measure our economic well-being in terms of the volume of output produced, the number of jobs created, price stability, and the rate of economic expansion. We also seek to maintain a certain balance in our international trade and financial relations. The performance of the economy is rated by the "scores" on these five macro outcomes.

Figure 5.4 also provides an overview of the separate forces that affect macro outcomes. Three very broad forces are depicted. These ***determinants of macro performance include:***

- ***Internal market forces:*** population growth, spending behavior, invention and innovation, and the like

- ***External shocks:*** wars, natural disasters, trade disruptions, and so on

- ***Policy levers:*** tax policy, government spending, changes in the availability of money, and credit regulation, for example

In the absence of external shocks or government policy, an economy would still function—it would still produce output, create jobs, develop prices, and maybe even grow. The U.S. economy operated this way for much of its history. Even today, many less-developed countries and areas operate in relative isolation from government or international events. In these situations, macro outcomes depend exclusively on internal market forces.

Economists continue to debate just how important internal market forces and other influences are for macro (in)stability. Recall that the Classical economists rejected policy levers as an instrument for macro stability. Classical economists argued that the internal forces of the economy were inherently stable. Indeed, internal market forces (e.g., flexible prices and wages) could even provide an automatic adjustment to external shocks (e.g., wars, droughts, trade disruptions) that threatened to destabilize the economy. The Classical economists saw no need for the box labeled "policy levers."

Keynes argued that policy levers were both effective and necessary. Without such intervention, he believed the economy was doomed to bouts of repeated macro failure.

Modern economists hesitate to give policy intervention that great a role. Nearly all economists recognize that policy intervention affects macro outcomes. But there are great arguments about just how effective any policy lever is. A vocal minority of economists even echoes the Classical notion that policy intervention may be either ineffective or, worse still, inherently destabilizing.

These persistent debates can best be understood in the familiar framework of supply and demand—the most commonly used tools in an economist's toolbox. All of the macro outcomes depicted in Figure 5.4 are the result of market transactions—an interaction between supply and demand. Hence *any influence on macro outcomes must be transmitted through supply or demand.* In other words, if the forces depicted on the left side of Figure 5.4 affect neither supply nor demand, they will have no impact on macro outcomes. This makes our job easier. We can resolve the question about macro stability by focusing on the forces that shape supply and demand in the macro economy.

Aggregate Demand

aggregate demand: The total quantity of output demanded at alternative price levels in a given time period, *ceteris paribus.*

Economists use the term "aggregate demand" to refer to the collective behavior of all buyers in the marketplace. Specifically, **aggregate demand** refers to the various quantities of output that all people, taken together, are willing and able to buy at alternative price levels in a given period. Our view here encompasses the collective demand for *all* goods and services, rather than the demand for any single good.

To understand the concept of aggregate demand better, imagine that everyone is paid on the same day. With their income in hand, people then enter the product market. The question becomes: how much will people buy?

To answer this question, we have to know something about prices. If goods and services are cheap, people will be able to buy more with their given income. On the other hand, high prices will limit both the ability and willingness to purchase goods and services. Note that we are talking here about the average price level, not the price of any single good.

This simple relationship between average prices and real spending is illustrated in Figure 5.5. On the horizontal axis we depict the various quantities of (real) output that might be purchased. On the vertical axis we show various price levels that might exist.

The aggregate demand curve illustrates how the volume of purchases varies with prices. The downward slope of the aggregate demand curve suggests that with a given (constant) level of income, people will buy more goods and services at lower prices.

There are several reasons why the aggregate demand curve is downward-sloping. These include:

Real balances effect The most obvious explanation for the downward slope of the aggregate demand curve is that cheaper prices make dollars more valuable. That is to say, *the real value of money is measured by how many*

**FIGURE 5.5
Aggregrate Demand**

Aggregate demand refers to the total output demanded at alternative price levels (*ceteris paribus*). The vertical axis here measures the average level of all prices, rather than the price of a single good. Likewise, the horizontal axis refers to the physical volume of all goods, not the quantity of only one product.

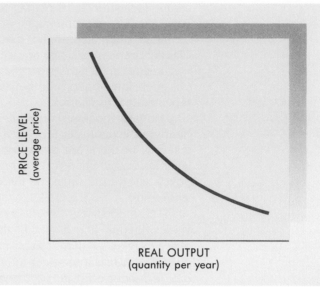

goods and services each dollar will buy. In this respect, lower prices make you "richer": the cash balances you hold in your pocket, in your bank account, or under your pillow are worth more when the price level falls. With a given balance of cash, you can suddenly buy more goods. Lower prices also increase the value of other dollar-denominated assets (e.g., bonds), thus increasing the wealth of consumers. As their wealth increases, consumers feel less need to save and are likely to buy a greater quantity of goods and services. Thus the aggregate demand curve slopes downward to the right.

Foreign trade effect The downward slope of the aggregate demand curve is reinforced by changes in imports and exports. Consumers have the option of buying either domestic or foreign goods. A decisive factor in choosing between imported or domestic goods is their relative price. When the prices of imported goods rise, U.S. consumers tend to buy more American-made products. Conversely, higher prices for domestic output induce U.S. consumers to substitute imports for home-grown products. The quantity of domestic goods demanded will thus decline when the domestic price level rises. Foreign consumers, too, have less incentive to buy American-made products (our exports) when U.S. prices rise. These changes in imports and exports contribute to the downward slope of the aggregate demand curve.

Interest-rate effect Changes in the price level also affect the amount of money people need to borrow, and so tend to affect interest rates. At lower price levels, consumer borrowing needs are smaller. As the demand for loans diminishes, interest rates tend to decline as well. This "cheaper" money stimulates more borrowing and loan-financed purchases.

Aggregate Supply While lower price levels tend to increase the volume of output demanded, they have the opposite effect on the aggregate quantity supplied. Prices determine how much income producers receive for their efforts. If the price level falls, producers as a group are being squeezed. In the short run, producers typically are saddled with some relatively constant costs like rent, interest payments, negotiated wages, and inputs already contracted for. If output prices fall, producers will be hard-pressed to pay these costs, much less earn a profit. Their response will be to reduce the rate of output.

Higher output prices have the opposite effect. Because many costs are relatively constant in the short run, higher prices for goods and services tend to widen profit margins. As profit margins widen, producers will want to produce and sell more goods. Thus *we expect the rate of output to increase when the price level rises.* This expectation is reflected in the upward slope of the aggregate supply curve in Figure 5.6. **Aggregate supply** reflects the various quantities of real output that firms are willing and able to produce at alternative price levels, in a given time period.

The upward slope of the aggregate supply curve is also explained by rising costs. To increase the rate of output, producers must acquire more resources (e.g., labor) and use existing plant and equipment more intensively. These greater strains on our productive capacity tend to raise production costs. Producers must therefore charge higher prices to recover the higher costs that accompany increased capacity utilization. Again, this results in an upward-sloping aggregate supply curve, as seen in Figure 5.6.

aggregate supply: The total quantity of output producers are willing and able to supply at alternative price levels in a given time period, *ceteris paribus.*

Macro Equilibrium

When all is said and done, what we end up with here is two rather conventional-looking supply and demand curves. But these particular curves have special significance. Instead of describing the behavior of buyers and sellers in a single market (e.g., the Clearview College typing market of Chapter 2), *aggregate supply and demand curves summarize the market activity of the whole (macro) economy.* These curves tell us what *total* amount of goods and services will be supplied or demanded at various price levels.

These graphic summaries of buyer and seller behavior provide some initial clues to the business cycle. The most important clue is point *E* in Figure 5.7, where the aggregate demand and supply curves intersect. This is the only point at which the behavior of buyers and sellers is compatible. We know

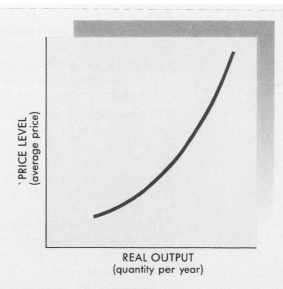

FIGURE 5.6
Aggregrate Supply

Aggregate supply refers to the total volume of output producers are willing and able to bring to the market at alternative price levels (*ceteris paribus*). The upward slope of the aggregate supply curve reflects the fact that profit margins widen when otuput prices rise (especially when short–run costs are constant). Producers respond to wider profit margins by supplying more output.

PRICE LEVEL (average price)

REAL OUTPUT (quantity per year)

FIGURE 5.7
Macro Equilibrium

The aggregate demand and
supply curves intersect at
only one point (*E*). At that
point, the price (*P$_E$*) and output
(*Q$_E$*) combination is compatible
with both buyers' and sellers'
intentions. The economy will
gravitate to those equilibrium
price (*P$_E$*) and output (*Q$_E$*)
levels. At any other price
level (e.g., *P$_1$*), the behavior
of buyers and sellers is
incompatible.

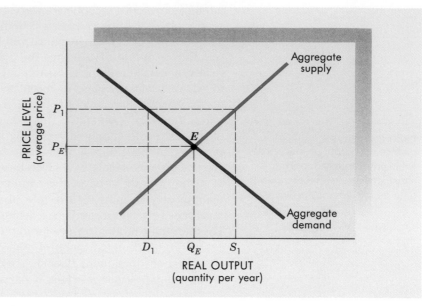

from the aggregate demand curve that people are willing and able to buy the
quantity Q_E when prices are equal to P_E. From the aggregate supply curve we
know that businesses are prepared to sell the quantity Q_E at the price level
P_E. Hence buyers and sellers are willing to trade exactly the same quantity
(Q_E) at that price level. We call this situation **macro equilibrium**—the unique
combination of prices and output that is compatible with both buyers' and
sellers' intentions.

To appreciate the significance of macro equilibrium, suppose that another price or output level existed. Imagine, for example, that prices were
higher, at the level P_1 in Figure 5.7. How much output would people want to
buy at that price level? How much would business want to produce and sell?

The aggregate demand curve tells us that people would want to buy only
the quantity D_1 at the higher price level P_1. In contrast, business firms would
want to sell a larger quantity, S_1. This is a disequilibrium situation, in which
the intentions of buyers and sellers are incompatible. The aggregate quantity
supplied (S_1) exceeds the aggregate quantity demanded (D_1). Accordingly, a
lot of goods will remain unsold at price level P_1.

To sell these goods, producers will have to reduce their prices. As the
prices drop, producers will decrease the volume of goods sent to market. At
the same time, the quantities that consumers seek will increase. This adjustment process will continue until point E is reached and the quantities demanded and supplied are equal. At that point, the lower price level P_E will
prevail.

The same kind of adjustment process would occur if a lower price level
first existed. At lower prices, the aggregate quantity demanded would exceed
the aggregate quantity supplied. The resulting shortages would permit sellers
to raise their prices. As they did so, the aggregate quantity demanded would
decrease, and the aggregate quantity supplied would increase. Eventually, we
would return to point E, where the aggregate quantities demanded and supplied are equal.

***Equilibrium is unique; it is the only price–output combination that
is mutually compatible with aggregate supply and demand.*** In terms of
graphs, it is the only place the aggregate supply and demand curves intersect.

equilibrium (macro): The
combination of price level and
real output that is compatible
with both aggregate demand and
aggregate supply.

At point E there is no reason for the level of output or prices to change. The behavior of buyers and sellers is compatible. By contrast, any other level of output or prices creates a disequilibrium that requires market adjustments. All other price and output combinations, therefore, are unstable. They will not last. Eventually, the economy will return to point E.

Macro Failures

There are two potential problems with the macro equilibrium depicted in Figure 5.7. The ***two potential problems with macro equilibrium are***

- ***Undesirability:*** The price–output relationship at equilibrium may not satisfy our macroeconomic goals.

- ***Instability:*** Even if the designated macro equilibrium is optimal, it may be displaced by macro disturbances.

Undesirability   The macro equilibrium depicted in Figure 5.7 is simply the intersection of two curves. All we know for sure is that people want to buy the same quantity that businesses want to sell at the price level P_E. This quantity (Q_E) may be more or less than our full-employment capacity. This contingency is illustrated in Figure 5.8. The output level Q_F represents our full-employment potential. In this case, the equilibrium rate of output (Q_E) falls far short of capacity production. We have failed to achieve our goal of full employment.

Similar problems may arise from the equilibrium price level. Suppose that P^* represents the most desired price level. In Figure 5.8 we see that the equilibrium price level P_E exceeds P^*. If market behavior determines prices, the price level will rise above the desired level. The resulting increase in average prices is what we call **inflation.**

It could be argued, of course, that our apparent macro failures are simply artificial. We could have drawn our aggregate supply and demand curves to

---

inflation: An increase in the average level of prices of goods and services.

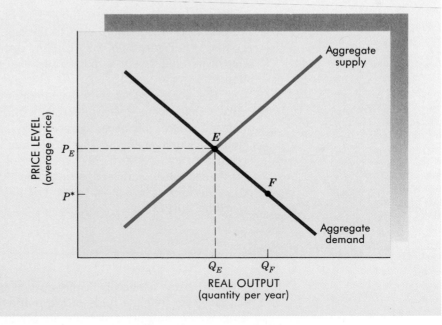

FIGURE 5.8
An Undesired Equilibrium

Equilibrium establishes only the level of prices and output that are compatible with both buyers' and sellers' intentions. These outcomes may not satisfy our policy goals. In this case, the equilibrium price level is too high (above P^*) and the equilibrium output rate falls short of full–employment GNP (Q_F).

intersect at point *F* in Figure 5.8. At that intersection we would be assured of both price stability and full employment. Why didn't we draw them there, rather than intersecting at point *E*?

On the graph we can draw curves anywhere we want. In the real world, however, only one set of curves will correctly express buyers' and sellers' behavior. We must emphasize here that these "correct" curves may *not* intersect at point *F*, thus denying us price stability, full employment, or both. That is the kind of economic outcome illustrated in Figure 5.8.

Instability Figure 5.8 is only the beginning of our macro worries. Suppose, just suppose, that the aggregate supply and demand curves actually intersected in the perfect spot. That is to say, imagine that macro equilibrium yielded the optimal levels of both employment and prices, thus satisfying our two foremost macroeconomic goals. If this happened, could we settle back and stop fretting about the state of the economy?

Unhappily, even a "perfect" macro equilibrium doesn't ensure a happy ending. The aggregate supply and demand curves that momentarily bring us macro bliss are not permanently locked into their respective positions. They can *shift*—and they will, whenever the behavior of buyers and sellers changes.

Suppose the Organization of Petroleum Exporting Countries (OPEC) increased the price of oil. In 1974 they doubled the world price of oil; and they managed to raise the price further in 1979 and again in 1980. These oil price hikes directly increased the cost of production in a wide range of U.S. industries, making producers less willing and able to supply goods at prevailing prices. Thus the aggregate supply curve *shifted to the left,* as in Figure 5.9a.

The impact of a leftward supply shift on the economy is evident. Whereas macro equilibrium was originally located at the optimal point *F*, the new equilibrium is located at point *G*. At point *G*, less output is produced and prices are higher. Full employment and price stability have vanished before our eyes.

A shift of the aggregate demand curve could do similar damage. Suppose American consumers suddenly acquired a greater yen for Japanese products. If they spent more of their income on imports, they would be less able and willing to buy American products. This change in consumer behavior would be reflected in a leftward shift of the aggregate demand curve for domestic goods, as in Figure 5.9b. The resulting disturbance would knock the economy out of its equilibrium at point *F*, leaving us at point *H*, with less output at home.

The situation gets even crazier when the aggregate supply and demand curves shift repeatedly in different directions. A leftward shift of the aggregate demand curve can cause a recession, as the rate of output falls. A later rightward shift of the aggregate demand curve can cause a recovery, with real GNP (and employment) again increasing. Shifts of the aggregate supply curve can cause similar upswings and downswings. Thus ***business cycles are likely to result from recurrent shifts of the aggregate supply and demand curves.***

COMPETING THEORIES

Figures 5.8 and 5.9 hardly inspire optimism about the macro economy. Figure 5.8 suggests that the odds of the market generating an equilibrium at full employment and price stability are about the same as finding a needle in a

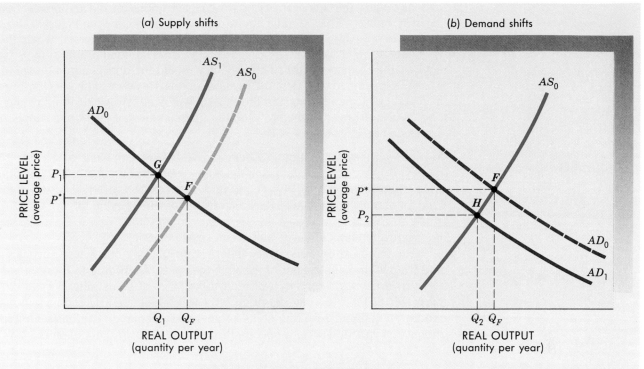

FIGURE 5.9 Macro Disturbances

(a) A decrease (leftward shift) of the aggregate supply (AS) curve tends to reduce real GNP and raise average prices. When supply shifts from AS_0 to AS_1, the equilibrium moves from F to G. Such a supply shift may result from higher import prices, changes in tax policy, or other events.

(b) A decrease (leftward shift) in aggregate demand (AD) tends to reduce output and price levels. A fall in demand may be due to increased taste for imports, changes in expectations, taxes, or other events.

haystack. Figure 5.9 suggests that if we are lucky enough to find the needle, we will probably drop it again. From this perspective, it appears that our worries about the business cycle are well founded.

The Classical economists had no such worries. As we saw earlier, they believed that the economy would gravitate toward full employment. Keynes, on the other hand, worried that the macro equilibrium might start out badly and get worse in the absence of government intervention.

Aggregate supply and demand curves provide a convenient framework for comparing these and other theories on how the economy works. Essentially, ***macro controversies focus on the shape of aggregate supply and demand curves and the potential to shift them.*** With the right shape—or the correct shift—any desired equilibrium could be attained. As we will see, there are differing views as to whether and how this happy outcome might come about. These differing views can be classified as demand-side explanations, supply-side explanations, or some combination of the two.

Demand-Side Theories

Keynesian theory Keynesian theory is the most prominent of the demand-side theories. Keynes argued that a deficiency of spending would tend to depress an economy. This deficiency might originate in consumer saving, inadequate business investment, or insufficient government spending. Whatever its origins, the lack of spending would leave goods unsold and production capacity unused. This contingency is illustrated by point E_1 in Figure 5.10a.

Keynes developed his theory during the Great Depression, when the economy seemed to be stuck at a very low level of equilibrium output, far below full-employment GNP. The only way to end the depression, he argued, was for someone to start demanding more goods. He advocated a big increase in government spending to start the economy moving toward full employment. The details of Keynes's theory—and his unique views of aggregate supply—are examined in Chapters 8–10.

Monetary theories   Another demand-side theory emphasizes the role of money in financing aggregate demand. Money and credit affect the ability and willingness of people to buy goods and services. Accordingly, if the right amount of money is not available, aggregate demand may be too great or too small. In this case, a change in the money supply may be required to shift the aggregate demand curve into the desired position.

The more extreme monetary theories attribute all our macro successes and failures to management of the money supply. According to these *monetarist* theories, the economy will tend to stabilize at something like full-employment GNP. Thus only the price level will be affected by changes in the money supply and resulting shifts of aggregate demand. The basis for this monetarist view and other monetary theories are discussed in Chapters 12–14.

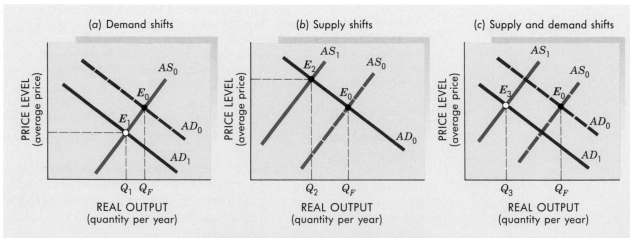

FIGURE 5.10 Origins of a Recession

Unemployment can result from several kinds of market phenomena, including:

(*a*) **Total output will fall if aggregate demand (AD) declines. The shift from AD_0 to AD_1 changes equilibrium from point E_0 to a point E_1.**

(*b*) **Unemployment can also emerge if aggregate supply (AS) declines, as the shift from AS_0 to AS_1 shows.**

(*c*) **If aggregate demand and aggregate supply both decline, output and employment also fall.**

Supply-Side Theories

Figure 5.10*b* illustrates an entirely different explanation of the business cycle. Notice that the aggregate *supply* curve is on the move in Figure 5.10*b*. The initial equilibrium is again at point E_0. This time, however, aggregate demand remains stationary, while aggregate supply shifts. The resulting decline of aggregate supply causes output and employment to decline (to Q_2 from Q_F).

Figure 5.10*b* tells us that aggregate supply may be responsible for downturns as well. Our failure to achieve full employment may result from the unwillingness of producers to provide more goods at existing prices. That unwillingness may originate in simple greed, in rising costs, in resource shortages, or in government taxes and regulation. Whatever the cause, if the aggregate supply curve is AS_1 rather than AS_0, full employment will not be achieved with the demand AD_0. To get more output, the supply curve must shift back to AS_0. The many ways of inducing such a shift are examined in Chapter 15.

Eclectic Explanations

Not everyone blames either the demand side or the supply side exclusively. The various macro theories tell us that both supply and demand can cause us to achieve or miss our policy goals. These theories also demonstrate how various shifts of the aggregate supply and demand curves can achieve any specific output or price level. Figure 5.10*c* illustrates how undesirable macro outcomes can be caused by shifts of both aggregate curves. Eclectic explanations of the business cycle draw from both sides of the market.

Short- vs. Long-Run Aggregate Supply

Another compromise of competing theories is achieved by distinguishing short-term time periods from a long-run time horizon. As we noted earlier, *short-run* price increases tend to widen profit margins. In the *long run*, however, costs are likely to catch up with rising prices. Workers will demand higher wages, landlords will increase rents, and banks will charge higher interest rates as the price level rises. Hence a rising price level will give only a *temporary* boost to profits and supply incentives. In the *long run,* a rising price level will be accompanied by rising costs, giving producers no special incentive to supply more output.

If rising prices don't provide an incentive for more output, then ***the long-run aggregate supply curve is likely to be vertical,*** as in Figure 5.11. The level of output supplied is fixed at the *long-run* equilibrium Q_F. That rate of output is determined by internal market forces like population, technology, and the institutional structure of the economy. The economy will gravitate toward Q_F in the long run.

One of the most startling implications of the long-run AS curve is that changes in aggregate demand have no effect on long-run output. Notice in Figure 5.11 how an upward shift of the AD curve (from AD_1 to AD_2) raises prices but not output on the long-run AS curve. In the long run, changes in demand affect prices but not output and job outcomes of the macro economy.

All of this may well be true. But as John Maynard Keynes pointed out, it is also true that "in the long we are all dead." Whatever the long run may hold, it is in the short run that we must consume, invest, and find a job. However stable and predictable the long run might be, short-run variations in macro outcomes will determine how well we fare in any year. Moreover,

FIGURE 5.11
Short- vs. Long-Run Views

Price increases provide an incentive to supply more output in the short run (when costs are constant) but not in the long run (when costs catch up with prices). Hence the *long–run* AS curve may be vertical, while the *short–run* AS curve is upward–sloping.

An increase in aggregate demand (from AD_1 to AD_2) may increase both output and prices in the short run (point *b*). In the long run, however, only prices will be affected (point *c*).

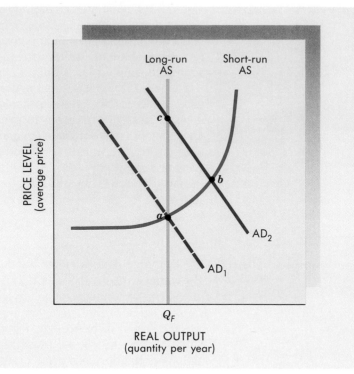

the short-run aggregate supply curve is likely to be upward-sloping, as in Figure 5.11 and our earlier graphs. This implies that both aggregate supply and aggregate demand influence short-run macro outcomes.

By distinguishing between short-run and long-run AS curves, competing economic theories achieve a standoff. Those theories that highlight the necessity of policy intervention emphasize the importance of short-run macro outcomes. On the other hand, theories that emphasize the "natural" stability of the market point to the predictability of long-run outcomes. Even this fragile truce, however, is easily broken when the questions turn to the duration of the "short" run or the effectiveness of any particular policy option.

POLICY OPTIONS

Aggregate supply and demand curves not only help illustrate the causes of the business cycle; they also imply a fairly straightforward set of policy options. Essentially, *we confront three policy options:*

• *Shift the aggregate demand curve.* Find and use policy tools that stimulate or restrain total spending.

• *Shift the aggregate supply curve.* Find and implement policy levers that reduce the costs of production or otherwise stimulate more output at every price level.

• *Do nothing.* If we can't identify or control the determinants of aggregate supply or demand, then we shouldn't interfere with the market.

Historically, all three approaches have been adopted.

The Classical Approach

The "Classical" approach to economic policy embraced the "do nothing" perspective. Prior to the Great Depression, most economists were convinced that the economy would self-adjust to full employment. If the initial equilibrium rate of output was too low, the resulting imbalances would alter prices and wages, inducing changes in market behavior. The aggregate supply and demand curves would "naturally" shift, until they reached the intersection at point E_0 where full employment (Q_F) prevails.

Recent versions of the Classical theory—dubbed the New Classical Economics—stress not only the market's "natural" ability to self-adjust to *long-run* equilibrium, but also the inability of the government to improve *short-run* market outcomes. New Classical Economists point to the increasing ability of market participants to anticipate government policies—and to take defensive actions that thwart them. These and other impediments to macro policy are discussed in Chapter 17.

Fiscal Policy

fiscal policy: The use of government taxes and spending to alter macroeconomic outcomes.

The Great Depression cast serious doubt on the Classical self-adjustment concept. According to Keynes's view, the economy would *not* self-adjust. Rather, it might stagnate at point E_1 until aggregate demand was forcibly shifted. An increase in government spending on goods and services might provide the necessary shift. Or a cut in taxes might be used to stimulate greater consumer and investor spending. These budgetary tools are the hallmark of fiscal policy. Specifically, **fiscal policy** is the use of government tax and spending powers to alter economic outcomes.

Fiscal policy is an integral feature of modern economic policy. Every year the president and the Congress debate the budget. They argue about whether the economy needs to be stimulated or restrained. They then argue about the level of spending or taxes required to ensure the desired outcome. This is the heart of fiscal policy.

Monetary Policy

monetary policy: The use of money and credit controls to influence macroeconomic activity.

The government budget doesn't get all the action. As suggested earlier, the amount of money in circulation may also affect macro equilibrium. If so, then the policy arsenal must include some levers to control the money supply. These are the province of monetary policy. **Monetary policy** refers to the use of money and credit controls to alter economic outcomes.

The Federal Reserve (the "Fed") has direct control over monetary policy. The Fed is an independent regulatory body, charged with maintaining an "appropriate" supply of money. In practice, the Fed increases or decreases the money supply in accordance with its views of macro equilibrium. In Chapter 13 we examine the Fed's structure and its policy levers.

Supply-Side Policy

supply-side policy: The use of tax rates, (de)regulation, and other mechanisms to increase the ability and willingness to produce goods and services.

Fiscal and monetary policies focus on the demand side of the market. Both are motivated by the conviction that appropriate shifts of the aggregate demand curve can bring about desired changes in output or price levels. **Supply-side policies** offer an alternative; they seek to shift the aggregate supply curve.

There are scores of supply-side levers. The most familiar are the tax cuts implemented by the Reagan administration in 1981. These tax cuts were designed to increase *supply,* not just demand (as per traditional fiscal policy). By reducing tax rates on wages and profits, the Reagan tax cuts sought to increase the willingness to supply goods at any given price level. The promise of greater after-tax income was the key incentive for the supply shift.

Other supply-side levers are less well recognized but nevertheless important. Your economics class is an example. Among other things, higher education increases our ability to produce. This implies a greater supply of goods and services at any given price level. Hence government subsidies to higher education might be viewed as part of supply-side policy.

Individual employment and training programs are more explicit about their supply-side objectives. The immediate purpose of government training programs is to increase the skills of unemployed workers. If successful, these programs increase our ability to produce and so shift the aggregate supply curve to the right. Government support of research and innovation has the same effect.

Historical Significance

These various policy options have all commanded center stage at one time or another. The "do nothing" approach prevailed until the Great Depression. Since that devastating experience, more active policy roles have predominated.

Fiscal policy dominated economic debate in the 1960s. When the economy responded vigorously to tax cuts and increased government spending, it appeared that fiscal policy might be the answer to our macro problems. Many economists even began to assert that they could "fine tune" the economy—generate very specific changes in macro equilibrium with appropriate tax and spending policies.

The promise of fiscal policy was tarnished by our failure to control inflation in the late 1960s. It was further compromised by the outbreak of stagflation in the 1970s. Before 1970, the simultaneous occurrence of both inflation and unemployment was rare. During the 1970s, however, it appeared to be chronic, immune to the cures proposed by fiscal policy. Solutions to our macro problems were sought elsewhere.

Monetary policy was next in the limelight. The "flaw" in fiscal policy, it was argued, originated in its neglect of monetary constraints. More government spending, for example, might require so much of the available money supply that private spending would be "crowded out." To ensure a net boost in aggregate demand, more money would be needed, thus requiring action by the Fed.

In the late 1970s the Fed dominated macro policy discussions. It was hoped that appropriate changes in the money supply would foster greater macro stability. Reduced inflation and lower interest rates were the immediate objectives. Both were to be accomplished by placing greater restraints on the supply of money. Full employment was also anticipated, as investment and consumption spending responded positively to lower, and more predictable, interest and inflation rates.

The heavy reliance on monetary policy lated only a short time. When the economy skidded into yet another recession, the search for effective policy tools resumed.

Supply-side policies became important in 1980. In his 1980 presidential campaign, Ronald Reagan asserted that "supply-side" tax cuts, deregulation of markets, and other supply-focused policies would reduce both inflation and unemployment. According to Figure 5.10c such an outcome appeared at least plausible. A rightward shift of the aggregate supply curve does reduce both prices and unemployment. Although the Reagan administration later embraced an eclectic mix of fiscal, monetary, and supply-side policies, its initial supply-side emphasis was very distinctive. A broad range of supply-side policy options will be analyzed in Chapter 15.

President Bush also chose an eclectic mix of fiscal, monetary, and supply-side options for the 1990s. He opposed tax increases that might reduce aggregate demand but acquiesced in monetary policies that kept interest rates high and aggregate demand in check. Some of the more notable successes and failures of the Bush administration will be discussed in Chapter 17.

The Crash of 1987   The whole topic of macroeconomic stability took on a renewed sense of urgency in 1987. From late 1982 to late 1987 the U.S. economy had expanded nicely, with GNP increasing by an average of over 4 percent a year. The stock market, reflecting this prosperity, increased in value more than 200 percent over the same period.

Then, on October 19, 1987, the stock market plummeted (see In the News). The average value of U.S. stocks fell by 23 percent, almost exactly as much as they had fallen on October 28–29, 1929.

The aftermath of the crash of 1987 was very different, however, from that of 1929. The crash of 1929 was followed by ten years of economic depression. After the crash of 1987, however, the economy kept growing. Output and employment kept increasing and even the stock market later recovered.

What was the difference between 1929 and 1987? Were the internal forces of the economy more resilient? Did we have better policies in place? Were our reactions better? These are some of the questions we will ponder as we explore the nature and consequences of the business cycle.

In The News

CRASH OF '87

Stocks Plunge 508 Amid Panicky Selling

Percentage Decline Is Far Steeper than '29; Bond Prices Surge

NEW YORK—The stock market crashed yesterday.

The Dow Jones Industrial Average plummeted an astonishing 508 points, or 22.6%, to 1738.74. The drop far exceeded the 12.8% decline on the notorious day of Oct. 28, 1929, which is generally considered the start of the Great Depression.

Panic-driven trading on the New York Stock Exchange reached 604.3 million shares, nearly double the prior record volume of 338.5 million shares set last Friday, when the Dow plunged a then-record 108.35 points. . . .

Final Slide

The industrial average tumbled 130 points in the final 30 minutes of the session. The decline yesterday and last week totaled 743.47 points, or 30%. By way of comparison, the total drop on Oct. 28 and Oct 29, 1929, was 68.90 points, or 23.1%. . . .

It was "the worst market I've ever seen," said John J. Phelan, the Big Board chairman, and "as close to financial meltdown as I'd ever want to see."

SUMMARY

- The long-term growth rate of the U.S. economy is approximately 3 percent a year. But output doesn't increase 3 percent every year. In some years real GNP grows much faster than that; in other years growth is slower. Sometimes total output actually declines.

- These short-run variations in GNP growth are the focus of macroeconomics. Macro theory tries to explain the alternating periods of growth and contraction that characterize the business cycle; macro policy attempts to control the cycle.

- The primary outcomes of the macro economy are output, prices, jobs, and international balances. The outcomes result from the interplay of internal market forces, external shocks, and policy levers.

- All of the influences on macro outcomes are transmitted through aggregate supply or aggregate demand. Aggregate supply and demand determine the equilibrium rate of output and prices. The economy will gravitate to that unique combination of output and price levels.

- Macro equilibrium may not be consistent with our nation's employment or price goals. Macro failure occurs when the economy's equilibrium is not optimal.

- Macro equilibrium may be disturbed by changes in aggregate supply (*AS*) or aggregate demand (*AD*). Such changes are illustrated by shifts of the *AS* and *AD* curves, and they lead to a new equilibrium.

- Competing economic theories try to explain the shape and shifts of the aggregate supply and demand curves, thereby explaining the business cycle. Specific theories tend to emphasize demand or supply influences.

- In the long run the AS curve tends to be vertical, implying that changes in aggregate demand affect prices but not output. In the short run, however, the AS curve is sloped, making macro outcomes sensitive to both supply and demand.

- Macro policy options range from doing nothing (the Classical approach) to various strategies for shifting either the aggregate demand curve or the aggregate supply curve.

Terms to Remember   Define the following terms:

macroeconomics	aggregate demand
law of demand	aggregate supply
Say's Law	equilibrium (macro)
business cycle	inflation
real GNP	fiscal policy
recession	monetary policy
growth recession	supply-side policy

Questions for Discussion

1. If business cycles were really inevitable, what purpose would macro policy serve?

2. What considerations might prompt consumers to demand fewer goods at current prices?

3. If equilibrium is compatible with both buyers' and sellers' intentions, how can it be undesirable?

4. The stock market crash of October 1987 greatly reduced the wealth of the average American household. How might this have affected aggregate demand? Aggregate supply?

Problems

1. Use the data on the endpapers of this book to compute the average annual growth rate of real GNP for the 1940s, 1950s, 1960s, 1970s, and 1980s. Then compute the average annual unemployment rate for those same five periods. Illustrate both measures on the same graph (rates on the vertical axis, time periods on the horizontal).

2. The following schedule provides information with which to draw both an aggregate demand curve and an aggregate supply curve. Both curves are assumed to be straight lines.

Average price (dollars per unit)	Quantity demanded (units per year)	Quantity supplied (units per year)
$1,000	0	1,000
100	900	100

(a) At what price does equilibrium occur?

(b) What curve would have shifted if a new equilibrium were to occur at an output level of 700 and a price of $700?

(c) What curve would have shifted if a new equilibrium were to occur at an output level of 700 and a price of $500?

(d) What curve would have shifted if a new equilibrium were to occur at an output level of 700 and a price of $300?

(e) Compared to the initial equilibrium (a), how have the outcomes in (b), (c), and (d) changed price levels or output?

Unemployment

George H. had worked at the paper mill for eighteen years. Now he was thirty-seven years old, with a wife and three children. With his base salary of $38,200 and the performance bonus he received nearly every year, he was doing pretty well. He had his own home, two cars, company-paid health insurance for the family, and a growing nest egg in the company's pension plan. The H. family wasn't rich, but it was comfortable and secure.

Or so they thought. Overnight the H. family's comfort was shattered. Without warning, the paper mill was closed in February 1990. George H., along with 2,300 fellow workers, was permanently laid off. The weekly paychecks and the company-paid health insurance stopped immediately; the pension nest egg was in doubt. Within a few weeks, George H. was on the street looking for a new job—an experience he hadn't had since high school. The unemployment benefits provided by the state didn't come close to paying the mortgage payment, groceries, insurance, and other necessities. And even they would soon run out. The H. family quickly used up its savings, including the $5,000 they had set aside for the children's college education. Debts were piling up fast. Unable to find another job after months of trying, George H. wasn't sure they could make it. On July 2, 1990, George H. committed suicide.

Not everyone who loses a job experiences this kind of disaster. But losing a job—or not being able to find one—is a painful experience for just about anyone. Jobless workers also represent a loss for the macro economy. If fewer people are employed, then the total quantity of output will be smaller. We all lose something when workers are without jobs.

The purpose of this chapter is to develop a clearer sense of what unemployment is all about and who suffers from it. Specifically, we seek answers to the following questions:

- When are resources "unemployed"?

- What are the consequences of unemployment for individuals and for the larger economy?

- What causes unemployment?

- What is "full employment"?

As we answer these questions, we shall develop a sense of why full employment is a major goal of macro policy and begin to see some of the obstacles we face in achieving it.

THE LABOR FORCE

To get a sense of what our unemployment problem is all about, we need to clarify the concept of "full employment." *Full employment does not mean that everyone has a job.* On the contrary, we can have "full employment" even when you are going to school, people are in the hospital, children are playing with their toys at home, and older people are enjoying their retirement. We are not concerned that *everybody* be put to work, but only with ensuring jobs for all those persons who are ready and willing to work and who desire and seek jobs.

Our first concern, then, is to distinguish between those individuals who are ready and willing to work and those individuals who, for institutional or personal reasons, are not available for employment. The **labor force** consists of everyone over the age of sixteen who is actually working plus all those who are not working but are actively seeking employment. Individuals are also counted as employed in a particular week if their failure to work is due to vacation, illness, labor dispute (strike), or bad weather. All such persons are regarded as "with a job but not at work." Also, unpaid family members working in a family enterprise (farming, for example) are counted as employed. *People who are neither employed nor actively seeking work are not counted as part of the labor force;* they are referred to as "nonparticipants." As Figure 6.1 shows, only half of our population participates in the labor force.

Note that our definition of labor force participation excludes most household and volunteer activities. A woman who chooses to devote her energies to household responsibilities or to unpaid charity work is not counted as part of the labor force, no matter how hard she works. Because she is neither in paid employment nor seeking such employment in the marketplace, she is

labor force: All persons over age sixteen who are either working for pay or actively seeking paid employment.

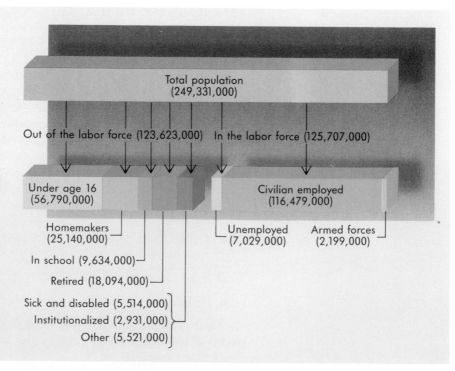

FIGURE 6.1
The Civilian Labor Force, March 1990

Only half of the total U.S. population participates in the civilian labor force. The rest of the population is too young, in school, at home, retired, or otherwise unavailable.

Unemployment statistics count only those participants who are not currently working but are actively seeking paid employment. Nonparticipants are neither employed nor actively seeking employment.

Total population (249,331,000)

Out of the labor force (123,623,000)   In the labor force (125,707,000)

Under age 16 (56,790,000)   Civilian employed (116,479,000)

Homemakers (25,140,000)   Unemployed (7,029,000)   Armed forces (2,199,000)

In school (9,634,000)

Retired (18,094,000)

Sick and disabled (5,514,000)

Institutionalized (2,931,000)

Other (5,521,000)

regarded as outside the labor market (a "nonparticipant"). But if she decides to seek a paid job outside the home and engages in an active job search, we would say that she is "entering the labor force." Students, too, are typically out of the labor force until they leave school and actively look for work, either during summer vacations or after graduation.

Production Possibilities

The distinction between our labor force and our total population can be illustrated by production-possibilities curves. As we first saw in Chapter 1, there is a limit to the quantity of goods and services an economy can produce in any time period. In general, our production possibilities are limited by two factors:

- Resources

- Technology

Figure 6.2 illustrates the limits to our production of any two goods (here called simply "consumption goods" and "investment goods"), given some level of resources and technology. With all our resources devoted to the production of consumption goods, we could produce the amount B of such goods in a year. By devoting all our resources and technology to the production of investment goods, we could produce A of such goods. In the more likely situation that we chose to produce some of both goods, we could have any combination of goods represented by the curve AB.

Although resource availability and technological know-how clearly limit our potential GNP, production has other constraints as well. In particular, the size of our labor force is much smaller than the total number of bodies in the country. In fact, we have imposed very strict limits on the amount of labor that may be used in production. Child-labor laws, for example, prohibit small

FIGURE 6.2
Physical vs. Institutional Production Possibilities

Our physical production possibilities express the maximum output that could be produced if all our resources and technology were employed. We impose limits on the use of resources and technology, however. These limits are reflected in our smaller institutional production possibilities.

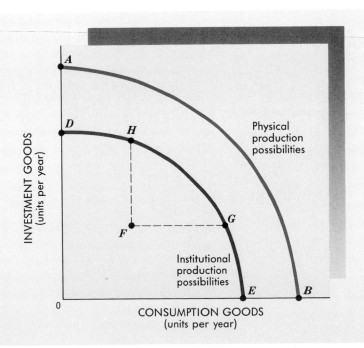

children from working, no matter how much they or their parents yearn to contribute to total output. Yet we could produce more output this year if we put all those little bodies to work. In fact, we could produce a little more output this year if you were to put down this book and get a job. To the extent that small children, students, and others are precluded from working, both the size of our labor force (our *available* labor) and our potential output shrink.

Constraints are also imposed on the use of material resources and technology. We will not cut down all the forests this year and build everybody a wooden palace. We want to preserve a little greenery and save some wood for future years. Therefore, the federal government limits each year's tree harvest on public lands. The federal government also restricts the use of nuclear technology. In both cases, environmental protection constrains the use of resources or technology and limits annual output. For the same reasons, we restrict the use of land, water, and air, and discourage the use of potentially hazardous chemicals and production processes. These are *institutional* constraints on our productive capacity.

In assessing the limits to total output, then, we must consider not only the physical limitations of resources and technology but also the institutional constraints imposed on the use of those inputs. The **physical production possibilities** of society are those that would exist in the absence of institutional constraints. The **institutional production possibilities** are those that incorporate social constraints on the use of resources.

Our institutional and physical production possibilities are illustrated in Figure 6.2. Our physical production possibilities are represented by the curve *AB*, which is based on resource and technology constraints only. Our institutional production possibilities are smaller, because they also reflect restrictions on the use of both resources and technology. Thus the institutional production-possibilities curve (*DE*) always lies *inside* the physical production-possibilities curve (*AB*). The institutional production-possibilities curve is the immediate focus of economic policy.

We cannot move beyond our institutional production-possibilities curve without altering our resources, technology, or social constraints. Any of those things can change, however. New resources are discovered, technology improves, and social constraints change. During World War II, for example, many restraints on labor use were relaxed, and factories were run twenty-four hours a day. Thousands of women entered the labor force to fill positions that men had held before entering the armed forces. These changes in our mode of production shifted the institutional production-possibilities curve outward, permitting us to produce a larger quantity of goods and services.

physical production possibilities: The alternative combinations of final goods and services that could be produced in a given time period within the limits imposed by resources and technology.

institutional production possibilities: The alternative combinations of final goods and services that could be produced in a given time period within the limits imposed by resources, technology, and social constraints on their use.

Unemployment

In the short run (with given resources, technology, and social constraints), our immediate problem is not to expand production possibilities but simply to attain them. We cannot reach points beyond the institutional production-possibilities curve, but we can easily end up somewhere inside that curve. At points inside the curve we end up with fewer goods and services than possible, and some of our available resources are unused. ***To reach a point on the institutional production-possibilities curve, our labor force must be fully employed.*** But there is no guarantee that a job will be available for everyone who is ready and willing to work. On the contrary, the essence of

unemployment: The inability of labor-force participants to find jobs.

unemployment rate: The proportion of the labor force that is unemployed.

our unemployment problem is that we do not make full use of our available labor! Some labor-force participants cannot find jobs and thus remain **unemployed.**

In 1990 an average of 7.0 million persons were counted as unemployed at any time. As Figure 6.1 suggests, these unemployed individuals accounted for 5.6 percent of our total labor force. Accordingly, the average **unemployment rate** in 1990 was 5.6 percent.

$$\bullet \quad \frac{\text{Unemployment}}{\text{rate}} = \frac{\text{number of unemployed people}}{\text{labor force}}$$

MACRO CONSEQUENCES: LOST OUTPUT

The impact of unemployment on our gross national product (GNP) is illustrated in Figure 6.2. If we fail to employ our entire labor force, we will not produce as much output as our institutional production possibilities (curve *DE*) permit. Instead, we will end up somewhere *inside* our institutional production-possibilities curve. In every such case (e.g., point *F*) we are clearly not producing as much output per year as we could, even after institutional constraints are taken into consideration.

Notice in Figure 6.2 that we *could* be at point *G*, producing more consumption goods and no fewer investment goods than are available at point *F*. By not fully employing our labor force, then, we are forsaking an annual flow of consumer goods equal to the distance *FG*. Similarly, we could get more investment goods each year, with no fewer consumption goods, if we were to produce at point *H* rather than at point *F*. Here again, our failure to utilize our entire labor force results in lost output. According to "Okun's Law"—a rule of thumb devised by the economist Arthur Okun—each additional 1 percent of unemployment translates into a loss of 3 percent in real GNP. In 1989 alone, this lost output amounted to roughly $45 billion, or approximately $180 worth of goods and services for every U.S. citizen.

Although the prospect of another $180 worth of goods and services may sound exciting, some people might question whether maximum production is really a desirable goal. After all, what's the difference whether we produce $5.23 trillion or $5.27 trillion? We've already glutted the streets with cars and the air with pollution. Why worry whether or not we are fully utilizing production possibilities?

Resource utilization is of vital concern for two reasons. So long as any private or public needs remain unfilled, we have a social use for unemployed resources. Maybe we do have enough cars on the streets already, but what about other goods and services? Do we have enough parks, schools, and clean rivers? If not, we could use some of our idle resources to produce these things. ***By not using all our resources—not fully utilizing our institutional production possibilities—we are forgoing potential output.*** Even if we felt (and few people do) that all our private and public needs had been met, we could still use our factors of production to aid the rest of the world. The average standard of living on the rest of this planet is only one-fourth as high as our own. Whether we actually use our resources for these purposes is a question of resource allocation and depends on private and public decisions we make in the marketplace. Should those decisions fail to use all our resources, however, we are effectively saying that unmet domestic or international needs are of no value or concern. Few would accept this implication.

MICRO CONSEQUENCES: PEOPLE OUT OF WORK

Society's interest in full employment also has micro roots. The term "labor" refers not simply to another factor of production but to *people*. Not using all our available labor means that somebody is without a job. That may be all right for a day or even a week, but if you need some income to keep body and soul together, prolonged unemployment can hurt. The same is true for plant and equipment or for land. If available machinery or farmland is not used, then somebody's income is going to be in jeopardy. If the company or farm loses a lot of income, it may shut down, throwing still more people out of work. To the extent that society as a whole cares about the welfare of individuals, the full utilization of our productive resources—*full employment*—is a desirable social goal.

The immediate impact of unemployment on individuals is the loss of income associated with working. For workers who have been unemployed for long periods of time, such losses can spell financial disaster. Typically, an unemployed person must rely on a combination of savings, income from other family members, and government unemployment benefits for financial support. After these sources of support are exhausted (see In the News), public welfare is often the only legal support left.

Not all unemployed people experience such a financial disaster, of course. College students who fail to find summer employment, for example, are unlikely to end up on welfare the following semester. Similarly, teenagers and others looking for part-time employment will not suffer great economic losses from unemployment. Nevertheless, the experience of unemployment—of not being able to find a job when you want one—can still be painful. This sensation is not easily forgotten, even after one has finally found employment.

It is difficult to measure the full impact of unemployment on individuals. A study for the U.S. Congress, however, provides some frightening sugges-

In The News

UNEMPLOYMENT BENEFITS

Unemployment Benefits Not for Everyone

In 1990, over 6 million people collected unemployment benefits averaging $160 per week. But don't rush to the state unemployment office yet—not all unemployed people are eligible. To qualify for weekly unemployment benefits you must have worked a substantial length of time and earned some minimum amount of wages, both determined by your state. Furthermore, you must have a "good" reason for having lost your last job. Most states will not provide benefits to students (or their professors!)

during summer vacations, to professional athletes in the off-season, or to individuals who quit their last jobs.

If you qualify for benefits, the amount of benefits you receive each week will depend on your previous wages. In most states the benefits are equal to about one-half of the previous weekly wage, up to a state-determined maximum. The maximum benefit in 1990 ranged from $134 in Nebraska to a high of $323 in Rhode Island.

Unemployment benefits are financed by a tax on employers and can continue for as long as twenty-six weeks. During periods of high unemployment, the duration of benefit eligibility may be extended another thirteen weeks or more.

tions. The author of the study estimated that a prolonged 1-point increase in the national unemployment rate—say, from 6 percent to 7 percent—leads, on average, to

- 920 suicides

- 648 homicides

- 20,240 fatal heart attacks or strokes

- 495 deaths from liver cirrhosis

- 4,227 admissions to mental hospitals

- 3,340 admissions to state prisons[1]

Although these estimates are subject to serious statistical qualifications, they underscore the notion that prolonged unemployment poses a real danger to many individuals. Like George H., many unemployed workers simply cannot cope with the resulting stress (see In the News). Thomas Cottle, a lecturer at Harvard Medical School, stated the case more bluntly: "I'm now convinced that unemployment is *the* killer disease in this country—responsible for wife beating, infertility, and even tooth decay."

German psychiatrists have also observed that unemployment can be hazardous to your health. They estimate that the anxieties and other nervous disorders that accompany one year of unemployment can reduce life expectancy by as much as five years.

[1]Harvey Brenner, "Estimating the Social Costs of National Economic Policy: Implications for Mental and Physical Health, and Criminal Aggression," study prepared for the Joint Economic Committee, U.S. Congress (Washington, D.C., October 1976).

In The News

MICRO LOSSES

Recession Taking Toll in Mental Illness Rate

DETROIT (AP)—In Michigan, perhaps the state hardest hit by recession, the high unemployment rate is triggering increases in "cry for help" calls—increases that mental health experts say may only be just beginning.

Michigan residents are exhibiting symptoms of a problem that is growing nationwide—emotional problems created or aggravated by economic woes.

"It's almost axiomatic that when people are without jobs and their income is down, you're going to see an increase in depression and some overtly dangerous behavior," said James Kipfer, executive director of the Mental Health Association in Michigan. . . .

"The problems that lead people to come to our agencies don't happen the day after one is laid off," said Mel Ravitz, executive director of the Detroit Wayne County Community Mental Health Board.

"It's at some point after people have been out of work a while, after they've experienced the effort to seek reemployment, after creditors are calling their family, when hospitalization coverage ends.

"When all of that ends, and people see no break in the clouds, people begin to yell at each other, abuse each other, experience increasing feelings of pressure and frustration." . . .

In June, police in Detroit and the Port Huron area handled four cases in which unemployed people barricaded themselves with guns inside their homes and threatened neighbors. Two confrontations resulted in suicides.

Washington Star, July 7, 1980, p. A4. Reprinted by permission of The Associated Press.

MEASURING UNEMPLOYMENT

The macro and micro losses resulting from unemployment clearly make it a serious policy concern. To keep policymakers informed of just how serious the problem is at any time, the Census Bureau provides monthly estimates of the number of people unemployed. These estimates are obtained by interviews in 65,000 households across the country each month. All persons interviewed are asked whether they are working that week (*employed* members of the labor force). If they are not working, they are asked if they have been actively seeking employment (*unemployed* members of the labor force).[2] On the basis of these responses, the Census Bureau, together with the U.S. Department of Labor, estimates the size of the labor force, as well as the proportion that is unemployed.

The monthly unemployment figures indicate not only the total amount of unemployment in the economy but also which groups are suffering the greatest unemployment. Typically, teenagers just entering the labor market have the greatest difficulty finding (or keeping) jobs and are most likely to be unemployed. As a result, the average unemployment rate for teenagers is often three times higher than the adult unemployment rate (see Figure 6.3).

[2]Recall that an individual is counted as employed if he or she is on strike, on paid vacation, or absent from work because of illness or bad weather. Among the unemployed are those workers waiting to be recalled from layoff and persons waiting to start a new job within thirty days.

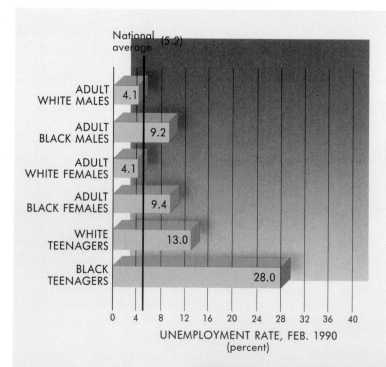

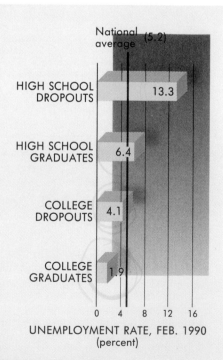

FIGURE 6.3 Unemployment Isn't Experienced Equally Either by Race or by Sex...or by Education

Minority groups, teenagers, and less educated individuals experience high rates of unemployment. Teenage unemployment rates are particularly high, especially for black and other minority youth.

Source: U.S. Department of Labor.

Blacks and other minorities of all ages also suffer a much higher rate of unemployment than do white males. The losses resulting from unemployment are not borne equally.

Discouraged Workers

discouraged worker: An individual who is not actively seeking employment but would look for or accept a job if one were available.

Although the monthly estimates provided by the Census Bureau are an important measure of unemployment, they do not fully capture the dimensions of the problem. When unemployment persists, job seekers become increasingly frustrated in their efforts to secure employment. After repeated rejections, job seekers often get so discouraged that they give up the search and turn to their families, friends, or public welfare for income support. When the census interviewer asks whether they are actively seeking employment, such **discouraged workers** are apt to reply no. Yet they would like to be working, and they would probably be out looking for work if job prospects were better.

Discouraged workers are not counted as part of our unemployment problem because they are technically out of the labor force. The Labor Department estimates that in 1989 roughly 800,000 individuals fell into this uncounted class of discouraged workers.

Underemployment

underemployment: People seeking full-time paid employment work only part-time or are employed at jobs below their capability.

Some people can't afford to be discouraged. Many people who become jobless have family responsibilities and bills to pay: they simply cannot afford to drop out of the labor force. Instead, they are compelled to take some job—any job—just to keep body and soul together. The resultant job may be part-time or full-time and may pay very little. Nevertheless, any paid employment is sufficient to exclude the person from the count of the unemployed, though not from a condition of **underemployment**.

Underemployed workers represent labor resources that are not being fully utilized. They are part of our unemployment problem, even if they are not officially counted as unemployed. In 1989 nearly 4 million workers were underemployed in the U.S. economy.

The Phantom Unemployed

Although discouraged and underemployed workers are not counted in official unemployment statistics, some of the people who are counted probably should not be. Many people report that they are actively seeking a job even when they have little interest in finding employment. To some extent, public policy actually encourages such behavior. For example, most adult welfare recipients are required to look for a job, even though some welfare mothers would prefer to spend all their time raising their children. Their resultant job search is likely to be perfunctory at best, including perhaps only one trip to the state employment office. Similarly, most states require people receiving unemployment benefits to provide evidence that they are looking for a job, even though some recipients may prefer a brief period of joblessness. Here again, reported unemployment may conceal labor force nonparticipation.

THE HISTORICAL RECORD

Figure 6.4 provides a historical summary of unemployment in the United States. The exceptionally high unemployment rates in the middle of the graph are a vivid reminder of the realities of the Great Depression, when as much as one-fourth of the labor force was unemployed. The hard lesson taught by the Great Depression—and enshrined in modern economic theory—is that

Drawing by Brumsic Brandon.

high rates of unemployment can arise and persist in the absence of effective public policy. In recognition of this possibility, Congress has instructed the president to pursue economic policies that will help ensure full employment.

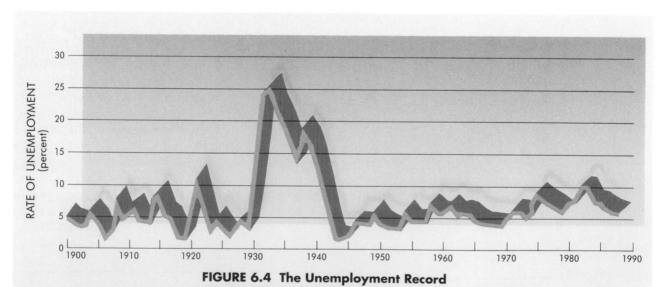

FIGURE 6.4 The Unemployment Record
Unemployment rates reached record heights during the Great Depression. The postwar record is much better than the prewar record, even though "full employment" has been infrequent.

Source: U.S. Department of Labor.

The Full Employment and Balanced Growth Act of 1978 (the Humphrey-Hawkins Act) instructs the president to ensure "fulfillment of the right to full opportunities of all individuals able, willing, and seeking to work."

The means for moving the economy closer to our institutional production possibilities, including a broad array of monetary, fiscal, and other policies, are discussed in detail in Chapters 8–16. Before looking at the potential of economic policy, however, we need to have a clearer notion of what we mean by "full employment."

DEFINING FULL EMPLOYMENT

Our historical record demonstrates that we have never completely eliminated unemployment. Since 1900, the lowest unemployment rate we have attained is 1.2 percent, and that was in 1944, when the economy was mobilized for war production. Some industrialized countries have had somewhat more success in maintaining low unemployment rates (see World View), but none has reached zero unemployment. In view of this record, it has been suggested that "full employment" should not be understood as "zero unemployment," but rather as some *low* (nonzero) level of unemployment.

At first blush, the abandonment of zero unemployment as a national goal might look like an artful attempt to rationalize our historical failures. But there are reasons for believing that zero unemployment is neither possible nor desirable.

Seasonal Unemployment

seasonal unemployment: Unemployment due to seasonal changes in employment or labor supply.

Seasonal variations in employment conditions are one persistent source of unemployment. Some joblessness is virtually inevitable as long as we continue to grow crops, build houses, or go skiing at certain seasons of the year. At the end of each of these "seasons," thousands of workers must go searching for new jobs, experiencing some **seasonal unemployment** in the process.

Seasonal fluctuations also arise on the supply side of the labor market. Teenage unemployment rates, for example, rise sharply in the summer as students look for temporary jobs. To avoid such unemployment completely, we would either have to keep everyone in school or ensure that all students went immediately from the classroom to the workroom. Neither alternative is likely, much less desirable.[3]

Frictional Unemployment

There are other reasons for expecting a certain amount of unemployment. Many workers have sound financial or personal reasons for leaving one job to look for another. In the process of moving from one job to another, a person may well miss a few days or even weeks of work without any serious personal or social consequences. On the contrary, job seekers who end up in more satisfying or higher-paying jobs as a result of their job search will be better off, and so will the economy.

[3]Seasonal variations in employment and labor supply not only create some unemployment in the annual averages but also distort monthly comparisons. Unemployment rates are always higher in February (when farming and housing construction come to a virtual standstill) and June (when a mass of students go looking for summer jobs). The Labor Department adjusts monthly unemployment rates according to this seasonal pattern, and reports "seasonally adjusted" unemployment rates for each month. Seasonal adjustments do not alter *annual* averages, however.

W🌐RLD VIEW

COMPARATIVE UNEMPLOYMENT RATES

Unemployment

U.S. economic growth in the 1980s pushed our unemployment rate down. Economic growth was slower in Europe, so unemployment rates were higher there. Japan and a few other countries have had even more success in reducing unemployment, but no nation achieves zero unemployment.

UNEMPLOYMENT RATE, 1990
(percent)

Source: U.S. Bureau of Labor Statistics (data for January–February 1990).

The same is true of students first entering the labor market. It is not likely that you will find a job the moment you leave school. Nor should you take any job just because it's available. If you spend some time looking for work, you are more likely to find a job you like. The job-search period gives you an opportunity to find out what kinds of jobs are available, what skills they require, and what they pay. Accordingly, a brief period of job search for persons entering the labor market may benefit both the individual involved and the larger economy. The unemployment associated with these kinds of job search is referred to as **frictional unemployment.**

Three things distinguish frictional unemployment from other kinds of unemployment. First, we assume that enough jobs exist for those who are frictionally unemployed—that is, there is adequate demand for labor. Second, we assume that those who are frictionally unemployed can perform the avail-

frictional unemployment: Brief periods of unemployment experienced by people moving between jobs or into the labor market.

able jobs. Third, we assume that the period of job search will be relatively short. Under these conditions, frictional unemployment resembles an unconventional game of musical chairs. There are enough chairs of the right size for everyone, and people dance around them for only a brief period of time.

No one knows for sure just how much of our unemployment problem is frictional. Indeed, many observers have noted that the amount of "friction" in the system is sensitive both to the level of economic activity and to political interest. Most economists agree, however, that friction alone is responsible for an unemployment rate of 2 to 3 percent. Accordingly, our definition of "full employment" should allow for at least this much unemployment.

Structural Unemployment

structural unemployment: Unemployment caused by a mismatch between the skills (or location) of job seekers and the requirements (or location) of available jobs.

For many job seekers, the period between jobs may drag on for months or even years because they do not have the skills that employers require. Imagine, for example, the predicament of coal miners when their mines are mechanized. If they have worked in the mines for ten or fifteen years, they are unlikely to have developed other occupational skills. They may be first-rate miners, but they stand little chance of filling job openings for computer programmers. In this case, there may be as many vacant jobs in the economy as job seekers, but the unemployed coal miners will not be able to fill any of them. Hence we say that the coal miners are **structurally unemployed.**

Teenagers from urban slums also suffer from structural unemployment. Most poor teenagers have an inadequate education, few job-related skills, and little work experience. From their perspective, almost all decent jobs are "out of reach." As a consequence, these teenagers, many of whom are black or from other minority groups, remain unemployed far longer than can be explained by frictional forces.

Structural unemployment violates the second condition for frictional unemployment—that the unemployed can perform the available jobs. Structural unemployment is analogous to a musical chairs game in which there are enough chairs for everyone, but some of them are too small to sit in. It is a more serious concern than frictional unemployment and is incompatible with any notion of "full employment."

Cyclical Unemployment

cyclical unemployment: Unemployment attributable to a lack of job vacancies—i.e., to an inadequate level of aggregate demand.

There are still other forms of unemployment. Of special significance is **cyclical unemployment**—joblessness that occurs when there are simply not enough jobs to go around. Cyclical unemployment exists when the number of workers demanded falls short of the number of persons in the labor force. This is not a case of mobility between jobs (frictional unemployment) or even of job seekers' skills (structural unemployment). Rather, it is simply an inadequate level of demand for goods and services and thus for labor. Cyclical unemployment resembles the most familiar form of musical chairs, in which the number of chairs is always less than the number of players.

The Great Depression is the most striking example of cyclical unemployment. The dramatic increase in unemployment rates that began in 1930 (see Figure 6.4) was not due to any increase in "friction" or sudden decline in workers' skills. Instead, the high rates of unemployment that persisted for a *decade* were due to a sudden decline in the market demand for goods and services. How do we know? Just notice what happened to our unemployment rate when the demand for military goods and services increased in 1941!

W✪RLD VIEW

CYCLICAL UNEMPLOYMENT

Taiwanese Jobless Rate Falls to a Five-Year Low

Taiwanese unemployment fell to 1.7% of the labor force in April, the lowest rate in five years, from 2.3% a year earlier, the government said.

Officials of the Council for Economic Planning and Development attributed the low rate to Taiwan's booming exports, which totaled $15.65 billion in 1987's first four months, up 36% from a year earlier.

Wall Street Journal, June 1, 1987, p. 19. Reprinted by permission of *The Wall Street Journal,* © Dow Jones & Company, Inc. (1987). All Rights Reserved.

West German Jobless Rate Rose to 9.2 Percent in December

NUREMBERG, West Germany—West German unemployment rose to 9.2% of the labor force in December from 8.9% a year earlier and 8.5% in November, the government said.

Though the rate isn't seasonally adjusted, economists said the size of the increase from the prior month was too great to be explained away by seasonal factors. The rate was the highest since March's 9.6%.

"After a long period of stagnation, the labor market worsened slightly at the end of the year," Labor Office President Heinrich Franke said.

Wall Street Journal, January 11, 1988, p. 22. Reprinted by permission of *The Wall Street Journal,* © Dow Jones & Company, Inc. (1988). All Rights Reserved.

THE FULL-EMPLOYMENT GOAL

In later chapters we will examine the causes of cyclical unemployment and explore some potential policy responses. At this point, however, we are just establishing some perspective on the goal of full employment. In general, we can say that our goal is to avoid as much cyclical and structural unemployment as possible, while keeping frictional unemployment within reasonable bounds.

As guidelines for public policy, these perspectives are admittedly vague. It is easier, for example, to define structural and cyclical unemployment than to measure them with precision. As many economists have observed, what appears to be structural (or even frictional) unemployment often vanishes when the demand for labor increases. Similarly, it is easier to advise policymakers to seek the "lowest possible" level of cyclical unemployment than to specify what that level is. As a consequence, we end up agreeing that "full employment" is something more than zero unemployment, but without a more exact numerical goal.

The first attempt to define "full employment" more precisely was undertaken in the early 1960s. At that time the Council of Economic Advisers decided that a 4 percent level of unemployment was tantamount to "full employment." If the unemployment rate dipped below 4 percent, they feared that inflationary pressures would intensify. The optimal balance of employment and price goals (see Chapter 7) seemed to be at 4 percent unemployment.

Rising Structural Unemployment?

During the 1970s and early 1980s, this view of our full-employment potential was considered overly optimistic. Unemployment rates stayed far above 4 percent, even when the economy expanded. Moreover, inflation began to accelerate at higher levels of unemployment. Critics suggested that structural

"I don't <u>like</u> six-per-cent unemployment, either. But I can live with it."

Drawing by Lorenz; © 1974 *The New Yorker Magazine, Inc.*

barriers to full employment had intensified, necessitating a redefinition of our full-employment goal. These structural barriers included

- ***More youth and women.*** Between 1956 and 1979 the proportion of teenagers in the labor force increased from 6 percent to 9 percent, thereby contributing to increased frictional and structural unemployment. During the same period of time, the proportion of adult women in the labor force grew from 29 percent to over 38 percent. Many of these women were entering the labor force for the first time—or reentering it after long periods of homemaking. As a consequence, frictional and structural unemployment increased.

- ***Liberal transfer payments.*** Higher benefits and easier rules for unemployment insurance, food stamps, welfare, and Social Security made unemployment less painful. As a result, critics suggested, more people were willing to stay unemployed rather than work.

- ***Structural changes in demand.*** Changes in consumer demand, technology, and trade shrank the markets in steel, textiles, autos, and other industries. The workers dislocated from these industries could not be absorbed fast enough in new "high-tech" and other service industries.

In view of these factors, the Council of Economic Advisers later raised the level of unemployment thought to be compatible with price stability. In 1983 the Reagan administration concluded that the "inflation-threshold" unemployment rate was between 6 and 7 percent. Most observers pegged a 6 percent unemployment rate as **full employment**.[4]

full employment: The lowest rate of unemployment compatible with price stability; variously estimated at between 4 and 6 percent unemployment.

[4] Full employment is also referred to as the "nonaccelerating inflation rate of unemployment," or NAIRU.

The U.S. Congress provided an alternative definition of "full employment." According to the Full Employment and Balanced Growth Act of 1978 (commonly called the Humphrey-Hawkins Act), our national goal is to attain a 4 percent rate of unemployment. The act also requires a goal of 3 percent inflation. There was an "escape clause," however. In the event that both goals could not be met, the president could set higher, "provisional" definitions of unemployment.

In the 1990s the teenage population has been shrinking (see In the News), and the rate of female labor-force entry has slowed. The structural dislocations of the early 1980s have also faded. Accordingly, it may be possible to achieve lower unemployment rates in the 1990s without risking other policy objectives. These structural changes in the labor force will tend to lower the benchmark for "full employment" below the 5.5 percent standard that prevailed in the late 1980s. President Bush's Council of Economic Advisers pegged the rate closer to 5.0 percent in 1990.

The GNP Gap

full-employment GNP: The total market value of final goods and services that could be produced in a given time period at full employment; potential GNP.

GNP gap: The difference between full-employment GNP and actual GNP.

The standard we use to gauge full employment also provides a measure of how much output we lose due to unemployment. By defining "full employment" as 5 percent unemployment, for example, we imply that only 95 percent of our labor force can be employed without causing other economic problems (particularly inflation). Accordingly, we define **full-employment GNP** as the annual value of final goods and services that could be produced at "full employment"—that is, with 5 percent unemployment. Full-employment GNP is the market value of our institutional production possibilities.

By comparing full-employment GNP with actual GNP, we can calculate the implied loss of goods and services associated with our failure to attain full employment. This loss is referred to as the **GNP gap**. As noted earlier, the GNP gap in 1989 amounted to $45 billion, or approximately $180 per person. Figure 6.5 illustrates the dimensions of the GNP gap for recent years.

In The News

DECLINING UNEMPLOYMENT

Labor Scarcity in the 1990s

In 1980 there were nearly 39 million young people aged 16–24. In 1990 there were only 25 million young people, and the number of 16- to 24-year-olds decreases each year. The cause of this decrease in young people is evident. In the years following World War II, there was a "baby boom" of unprecedented proportions. Twenty years later, those "baby boomers" flooded the labor market, making it difficult for young people to find jobs. Unemployment rates of 15–20 percent were common among teenagers in the 1970s and early 1980s. With the smaller birth cohorts that followed, however, the number of young people seeking jobs began to decline. Fast-food companies, service stations, and retail stores started replacing "No job openings" signs with "Help wanted" signs. Teenage labor became scarce, and youth unemployment rates started falling.

In the 1990s youth labor will become increasingly scarce—the growing U.S. economy will have many more jobs and fewer young workers to fill them. Labor will remain scarce until the next generation—the children of the baby boomers—starts entering the labor market after the year 2000.

FIGURE 6.5
Actual and Potential Gross National Product . . . And How Economists Calculate It

Multiply 95% of the normal labor force (which is considered full-employment) by the normal hours of work per year by normal productivity. The GNP gap is determined by subtracting actual gross national product from potential GNP.

Prior to 1975, full employment was defined as 5% unemployment; from 1975 to 1988 the official rate was increased to 6%; it is now in the range of 5 percent again.

Note: The vertical axis is measured in ratio terms; equal distances indicate equal percentage changes rather than equal absolute changes.

Source: Council of Economic Advisers.

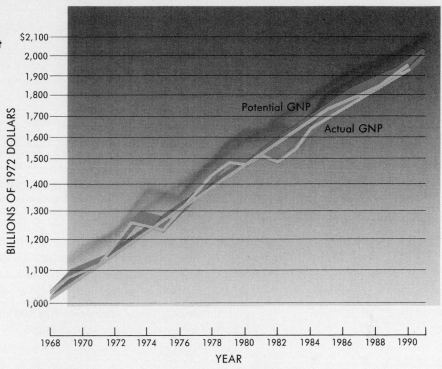

Potential GNP = 95% of normal labor force × normal hours of work per year × normal productivity

GNP gap = potential GNP − actual GNP

SUMMARY

- To understand unemployment, we need to distinguish the labor force from the larger population. Only people who are working (employed) or spend some time looking for a job (unemployed) are participants in the labor force. People who are neither working nor looking for work are outside the labor force.

- The distinction between the labor force and our larger population is mirrored in a distinction between institutional production possibilities and physical production possibilities. Institutional production possibilities express the rate of annual output we could attain if we fully and efficiently employed our entire labor force and heeded social constraints on the use of resources and technology. Physical production possibilities express the maximum output that could be produced if the entire population were put to work and no constraints were imposed on the use of either resources or technology.

- The macroeconomic loss imposed by unemployment is reduced output of goods and services. The microeconomic losses to those individuals actually out of work include lost income, heightened insecurity, and even reduced longevity.

- Unemployment is distributed unevenly; blacks, teenagers, and the less educated have much higher rates of unemployment. Also hurt are discouraged workers—those who have stopped looking for work but still want a job—and underemployed workers—those who are working at part-time or menial jobs because they cannot find full-time jobs equal to their training or potential.

- There are four types of unemployment: seasonal, frictional, structural, and cyclical. Because some seasonal frictional unemployment is inevitable and even desirable, full employment is not defined as zero unemployment. These considerations, plus fear of inflationary consequences, result in full employment being defined as an unemployment rate of 5 percent.

- The GNP gap—the difference between actual output and our potential output at full employment—measures the loss of goods and services implied by our failure to maintain full employment.

Terms to Remember

Define the following terms:

labor force	seasonal unemployment
physical production possibilities	frictional unemployment
institutional production possibilities	structural unemployment
unemployment	cyclical unemployment
unemployment rate	full employment
discouraged worker	full-employment GNP
underemployment	GNP gap

Questions for Discussion

1. Is it possible for unemployment rates to increase at the same time that the number of employed persons is increasing? How?

2. As increasing numbers of women enter the labor force, what happens to (*a*) institutional production possibilities? (*b*) physical production possibilities? (*c*) unemployment rates?

3. Could we now achieve an unemployment rate *below* "full employment" (5 percent)?

4. Can you identify three institutional constraints on the use of resources (factors of production)? What has motivated these constraints?

Problems

1. The unemployment rate in 1982 reached 10 percent.
   (*a*) Determine how far we were from full employment in 1982.
   (*b*) Calculate the GNP gap under the assumption that each unemployed worker could produce $25,000 of goods and services.

2. Suppose the following data describe a nation's population:

	Year 1	Year 2
Population	200 million	203 million
Labor force	120 million	125 million
Unemployment rate	6 percent	6 percent

(*a*) How many people are unemployed in each year?
(*b*) How many people are employed in each year?
(*c*) Compute the employment rate (i.e., number employed ÷ *population*) in each year.
(*d*) How can the employment rate rise when the *un*employment rate is constant?

Inflation

In the 1980s the U.S. inflation rate averaged less than 5 percent per year. In some countries (e.g., Argentina, Brazil, Peru, Nicaragua), prices rose over 5 percent per *week*! In 1989 the inflation rate in Argentina was nearly 5,000 percent; prices rose nearly fiftyfold during that one year. Such hyperinflation also beset Germany in the 1920s and Hungary and China in the late 1940s. In American history, prices never rose so dramatically. The closest we ever came to hyperinflation was during the Revolutionary War when prices doubled in a single year (1777–78). As the World View shows, other countries have much higher rates of inflation even today.

Despite our comparatively mild experiences with inflation, fear of rising prices has had a major influence on U.S. economic policy. According to public-opinion polls, inflation is always one of America's greatest worries

WORLD VIEW

COMPARATIVE INFLATION

Inflation in the 1980s

Many countries continue to grow and prosper despite rates of inflation much higher than those in the United States. What is it, then, that makes inflation so feared?

U.S. prices rose, on average, by 5 percent in the 1980s. This is a comparatively low rate of inflation; in some countries prices double almost every year.

Country	Annual Inflation Rate (average, per year; 1980–89)
Argentina	606.8
Brazil	471.7
Poland	121.6
Israel	118.5
Mexico	97.1
Italy	10.2
Kenya	9.5
Great Britain	6.5
Canada	6.1
South Korea	5.8
Germany (West)	5.3
United States	5.0
Japan	2.0

Source: International Monetary Fund.

(look back to In the News on p. 4). In response to these fears, every American president since Franklin Roosevelt has expressed a determination to keep prices from rising. In 1971 the Nixon administration took drastic action to stop inflation: with prices rising an average of only 3 percent, President Nixon imposed price controls on American producers to keep prices from rising any faster. After the controls were lifted and prices started rising again, his successor, President Gerald Ford, initiated a public-relations campaign to "Whip Inflation Now" (WIN). The anti-inflation fervor continues in the Bush administration. In 1990, Alan Greenspan, chairman of the Federal Reserve, asserted that 5 percent inflation was "unacceptable" and set a goal of zero percent inflation for the 1990s. He also acknowledged that the pursuit of this zero-inflation goal might require us to forsake other macro goals (e.g., full employment), but concluded that such a sacrifice was worthwhile.

The purpose of this chapter is to examine the basis for these policy concerns. Why is inflation so feared? To find out, we confront the following questions:

- What kind of price increases are referred to as "inflation"?

- How does inflation affect individual households and the larger economy?

- How is inflation measured?

- What are the major causes of inflation?

As we will discover, inflation is a serious problem, but not for the reasons most people cite.

WHAT IS INFLATION?

inflation: An increase in the average level of prices of goods and services.

Most people associate **inflation** with price increases on specific goods and services. The economy is not necessarily experiencing an inflation, however, every time the price of a cup of coffee goes up. We must be careful to distinguish the phenomenon of inflation from price increases for specific goods. *Inflation is an increase in the average level of prices, not a change in any specific price.*

Suppose you wanted to know the average price of fruit in the supermarket. Surely you would not have much success in seeking out an average fruit—nobody would be quite sure what you had in mind. You might have some success, however, if you sought out the prices of apples, oranges, cherries, and peaches. Knowing the price of each kind of fruit, you could then compute the average price of fruit. The resultant figure would not refer to any particular product, but would convey a sense of how much a typical basket of fruit might cost. By repeating these calculations every day, you could then determine whether fruit prices, *on average,* were changing. On occasion, you might even notice that apple prices rose while orange prices fell, leaving the *average* price of fruit unchanged.

The same kinds of calculations are made to measure inflation in the entire economy. We first determine the average price of all output—the average price level—then look for changes in that average. A rise in the average price level is referred to as inflation.

deflation: A decrease in the average level of prices of goods and services.

The average price level may fall as well as rise. A decline in average prices—a **deflation**—occurs when price decreases on some goods and services outweigh price increases on all others. Although we have not experienced any general deflation since 1940, general price declines were frequent in earlier periods.

Relative Prices vs. the Price Level

relative price: The price of one good in comparison with the price of other goods.

Because inflation and deflation are measured in terms of average price levels, it is possible for individual prices to rise or fall continuously without changing the average price level. We already noted, for example, that the price of apples can rise without increasing the average price of fruit, so long as the price of some other fruit (e.g., oranges) falls. In such circumstances, **relative prices** are changing, but not average prices. An increase in the relative price of apples, for example, simply means that apples have become more expensive in comparison with other fruits (or any other goods or services).

Changes in relative prices may occur in a period of stable average prices, or in periods of inflation or deflation. In fact, in an economy as vast as ours—where literally millions of goods and services are exchanged in the factor and product markets—relative prices are always changing. Indeed, relative price changes are an essential ingredient of the market mechanism. Recall (from Chapter 2) what happens when the market price of typing services rises relative to other goods and services. This (relative) price rise alerts typists (producers) to increase their output, cutting back on other production or leisure activities. To the extent that the increase in the *relative* price of typing expresses increasing consumer demand for this product, such changes in the mix of output are desirable.

A general inflation—an increase in the average price level—does not perform this same market function. If all prices rise at the same rate, price increases for specific goods are of little value as market signals. In less extreme cases, when most but not all prices are rising, changes in relative prices do occur but are not so immediately apparent. Table 7.1 reminds us that some prices do fall even during periods of general inflation.

TABLE 7.1 Prices That Have Fallen

Inflation refers to an increase in the *average* price level. It does not mean that *all* prices are rising. In fact, many prices fall, even during periods of inflation.

Item	Early price	1990 price
Long-distance telephone call (3-minute rate, coast to coast)	$ 20.70 (1915)	$ 0.46
Pocket electronic calculator	200.00 (1972)	5.90
Digital watch	2,000.00 (1972)	1.99
Polaroid camera (color)	150.00 (1963)	42.75
Pantyhose	2.16 (1967)	1.29
Ballpoint pen	0.89 (1965)	0.29
Transistor radio	55.00 (1967)	5.99
Videocassette recorder	1,500.00 (1977)	196.00
Personal computer (basic 4K)	599.00 (1979)	79.00
Microwave oven	400.00 (1972)	89.00
Contact lenses	275.00 (1972)	39.00
Television (19-inch, color)	469.00 (1980)	299.00
Compact disc player	1,000.00 (1985)	250.00

MICRO CONSEQUENCES OF INFLATION

We must distinguish between average prices and relative prices if we are to understand the true consequences of inflation. Popular opinion notwithstanding, it is simply not true that everyone is worse off when prices rise. Although inflation makes some people worse off, it makes other people better off. Some people even get rich when prices rise! *The micro consequences of inflation are reflected in redistributions of income and wealth, not general declines in either measure of our economic welfare.* These redistributions occur because people buy different combinations of goods and services, own different assets, and sell distinct goods or services (including labor). The impact of inflation on individuals therefore depends on how the prices of the goods and services each person buys or sells actually change. In this sense, *inflation acts just like a tax, taking income or wealth from some people and giving it to others.* This "tax" is levied through changes in prices, changes in incomes, and changes in wealth.

Price Effects   Price changes are the most familiar of inflation's pains. If you have been paying tuition, you know how the pain feels. In the last few years the average cost of tuition has increased rapidly (see In the News). In 1975 the average tuition at public colleges and universities was $400 per year. Today the average tuition exceeds $4,500. At private universities, tuition has increased eightfold in the last ten years, to over $12,000. You don't need a whole course in economics to figure out the implications of these tuition hikes. To stay in college, you (or your parents) must forgo increasing amounts of other goods and services. You end up being worse off, since you cannot buy as many goods and services as you were able to buy before tuition went up.

In The News

PRICE EFFECTS

College Costs Reach as High as $75,000

Tuitions Outstrip Annual Inflation

The cost of a college education is continuing to climb far more rapidly than inflation, according to a new College Board survey. At some of the nation's most prestigious private colleges and universities, the survey indicates, the total four-year cost of a bachelor's degree has reached $75,000. . . .

According to the new College Board data, tuition and required fees will rise an average of 6 percent at four-year public colleges and two-year private schools, and

by 5 percent at two-year community colleges, where tuitions already are relatively low.

It is the seventh straight year in which college costs have outstripped inflation. . . .

The nation's most expensive undergraduate institution is Bennington College, a fine arts school in southern Vermont, whose total annual cost is estimated at $19,400. Other prestigious schools, including the University of Chicago and most Ivy League schools, are charging more than $12,000 in tuition this fall, and estimate their total costs at $18,000 to $19,000.

—Lawrence Feinberg

The Washington Post, August 7, 1987, p. 1. Copyright © 1987 The Washington Post.

nominal income: The amount of money income received in a given time period, measured in current dollars.

real income: Income in constant dollars; nominal income adjusted for inflation.

The effect of tuition increases on your economic welfare is reflected in the distinction between nominal income and real income. **Nominal income** is the amount of money you receive in a particular time period; it is measured in current dollars. **Real income,** by contrast, is the purchasing power of that money, as measured by the quantity of goods and services your dollars will buy. If the number of dollars you receive every year is always the same, your *nominal income* doesn't change—but your *real income* will rise or fall with price changes.

Suppose your parents agree to give you $6,000 a year while you're in school. Out of that $6,000 you must pay for your tuition, room and board, books, and everything else. The budget for your first year at school might look like this:

First year's budget	
Nominal income	$6,000
Consumption	
Tuition	$3,000
Room and board	2,000
Books	300
Everything else	700
Total	$6,000

After paying for all your essential expenses, you have $700 to spend on clothes, entertainment, or anything else you want. That's not exactly living high, but it's not poverty.

Now suppose tuition increases to $3,500 in your second year, while all other prices remain the same. What will happen to your nominal income? Nothing. Unless your parents take pity on you, you will still be getting $6,000 a year. Your nominal income is unchanged. Your *real* income, however, will suffer. This is evident in the second year's budget:

Second year's budget	
Nominal income	$6,000
Consumption	
Tuition	$3,500
Room and board	2,000
Books	300
Everything else	200
Total	$6,000

You now have to use more of your income to pay tuition. This means you have less income to spend on other things. You will have to cut back somewhere. Since room and board and books still cost $2,300 per year, there is only one place to cut—the category of "everything else." After tuition increases, you can spend only $200 per year on movies, clothes, pizzas, and dates—not $700, as in the "good old days." This $500 reduction in purchasing power represents a *real* income loss. Even though your *nominal* income is still $6,000, your *real* income is only $5,500. You have $500 less of "everything else" in your second year than you had in the first.

Although tuition hikes reduce the real income of students and their families, nonstudents are not hurt by such price increases. A nonstudent with $6,000 of nominal income could continue to buy the same goods and services she was buying before tuition went up. In fact, if tuition *doubled,* nonstudents really wouldn't care. They could continue to buy the same bundle of goods and services they had been buying all along. Tuition increases reduce the real incomes only of people who go to college.

There are two basic lessons about inflation to be learned from this sad story:

Not all prices rise at the same rate during an inflation. In our example, tuition increased substantially while other prices remained steady. Hence the "average" rate of price increase was not representative of any particular good or service. Typically, some prices rise very rapidly, others only modestly, and still others not at all. Table 7.2 illustrates some recent variations in price changes.

Not everyone suffers equally from inflation. This follows from our first observation. Those people who consume the goods and services that are rising faster in price bear a greater burden of inflation; their real incomes fall more. Other consumers bear a lesser burden, or even none at all, depending on how fast the prices rise for the goods they enjoy.

We conclude, then, that the price increases associated with inflation redistribute real income. In the example we have discussed, college students end up with fewer goods and services than they had before. Other consumers can continue to purchase at least as many goods as before, perhaps even more. Thus output is effectively *redistributed* from college students to others. Naturally, most college students aren't very happy with this outcome. Fortunately for you, inflation doesn't always work out this way.

TABLE 7.2   Not All Prices Rise at the Same Rate

The average rate of inflation conceals substantial differences in the price changes of specific goods and services. The impact of inflation on individuals depends in part on which goods and services are consumed. People who buy goods whose prices are rising fastest lose more real income. In 1989 college students were particularly hard hit by inflation.

Item	Price change, 1989–90 (percent)	Item	Price change, 1989–90 (percent)
Food		Other	
Potatoes	+ 28.9	College tuition	+ 7.9
Bananas	+ 10.2	Interstate telephone call	− 3.2
Fish	+ 4.5	Women's dresses	0.0
Oranges	+ 1.7	Cigarettes	+12.8
Eggs	+ 26.6	TV sets	− 1.9
Bacon	− 5.1		
Transportation		Average inflation rate	+ 4.8
New cars	+ 2.0		
Gasoline	+ 9.5		
Air fares	+ 6.0		

Source: U.S. Bureau of Labor Statistics.

Income Effects   The redistributive effects of inflation are not limited to changes in prices. Changes in prices automatically influence nominal incomes also.

If the price of tuition does in fact rise faster than all other prices, we can safely make three predictions:

- The *real* income of college students will fall relative to nonstudents (assuming constant nominal incomes).

- The *real* income of nonstudents will rise relative to students (assuming constant nominal incomes).

- The *nominal* income of colleges and universities will rise.

This last prediction simply reminds us that someone always pockets higher prices. ***What looks like a price to a buyer looks like income to a seller.*** If students all pay higher tuition, the university will take in more income. To the extent that the nominal incomes of colleges and universities increase faster than average prices, they actually *benefit* from inflation. That is to say, they end up being able to buy *more* goods and services (including faculty, buildings, and library books) after a period of inflation than they could before. Their real income rises. Whether one likes this outcome depends on whether anyone in the family works for the university or sells it goods and services.

On average, people's incomes do keep pace with inflation. Again, this is a direct consequence of the circular flow: what one person pays out someone else takes in. ***If prices are rising, incomes must be rising, too.*** Notice in Figure 7.1 that average wages have pretty much risen in step with prices. From this perspective, it makes no sense to say that "inflation hurts everybody." On *average,* at least, we are no worse off when prices rise, since our (average) incomes increase at the same time.[1]

No one is exactly "average," of course. In reality, some people's incomes rise faster than inflation while others' increase more slowly. Hence the redistributive effects of inflation also originate in varying rates of growth in nominal income. If everyone's income increased at the rate of inflation, inflation would not have such a large redistributive effect. In reality, however, nominal incomes increase at very different rates.

Wealth Effects   The same kind of redistribution occurs between those who hold some form of wealth and those who do not. Suppose that on January 1 you deposit $100 in a savings account, where it earns 5 percent interest until you withdraw it on December 31. At the end of the year you will have more nominal wealth ($105) than you started with ($100). But what if all prices have doubled in the meantime? In that case, your $105 will buy you no more at the end of the year than $52.50 would have bought you at the beginning. In other words, inflation in this case reduces the *real* value of your savings, and you end up worse off than those individuals who spent all their income earlier in the year!

Inflation also tends to redistribute wealth from people who rent homes or apartments to those who own them. The market prices of homes tend to increase at least as fast as the pace of inflation. Hence the real value of home

---

[1]In fact, average incomes have usually risen even faster than prices, because of increasing output per worker. Thus average real incomes have increased significantly over time. In those years when wages did not keep up with prices, taxes were to blame.

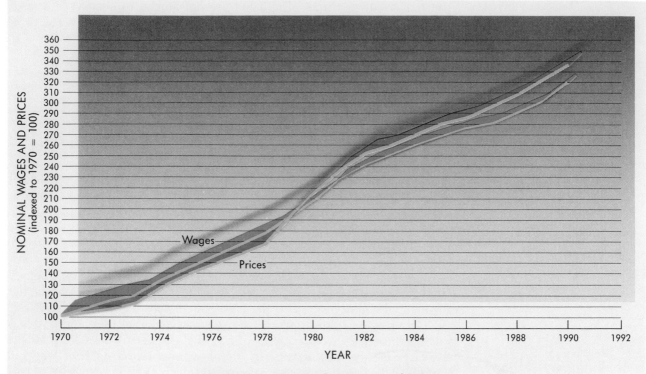

FIGURE 7.1 Nominal Wages and Prices

Inflation implies not only higher prices but higher wages as well. What is a price to one person is income to someone else. Hence inflation cannot make *everyone* worse off. This graph confirms that average wages have risen along with average prices. In most years, wages actually rise a bit faster than prices. These increases in *real wages* reflect higher productivity (more output per worker).

Source: *Economic Report of the President,* 1990.

ownership is not diminished by inflation. By contrast, people who rent homes or apartments usually discover that inflation forces them to spend a larger fraction of their incomes on housing costs (rent); thus their real incomes fall.

By altering relative prices, incomes, and the real value of wealth, then, inflation turns out to be a mechanism for redistributing incomes. ***The redistributive mechanics of inflation include***

- ***Income effects.*** People whose nominal incomes rise faster than the rate of inflation end up with a larger share of total income.

- ***Price effects.*** People who prefer goods and services that are increasing in price least quickly end up with a larger share of real income.

- ***Wealth effects.*** People who own assets that are increasing in real value end up better off than others (see Table 7.3).

On the other hand, people whose nominal incomes do not keep pace with inflation end up with smaller shares of total output. The same thing is true of those who enjoy goods that are rising fastest in price or who hold assets that are declining in real value. In this sense, ***inflation acts just like a tax, taking***

TABLE 7.3   The Real Story of Wealth

Households hold their wealth in many different forms. As the value of various assets changes, so does a person's wealth. Between 1980 and 1990, inflation was very good to people who collected art or held stocks. By contrast, the prices of oil, farmland, and gold and silver fell. The *relative* value of housing fell as well.

Asset	Percentage change in value, 1980–1990
Stocks	393
Bonds	233
Art (old masters)	219
Chinese ceramics	108
U.S. coins	102
Diamonds	86
Housing	58
U.S. farmland	− 1
Oil	− 45
Gold	− 52
Silver	− 64

Source: Salomon Brothers, Inc.

income or wealth from one group and giving it to another. But we have no assurance that this particular tax will behave like Robin Hood, taking from the rich and giving to the poor. Most important, it is a tax that is not subject to sociopolitical controls; it is a capricious tax.

Social Tensions

Because of its redistributive effects, inflation also increases social and economic tensions. Tensions—between labor and management, between government and the people, and among consumers—may overwhelm a society and its institutions. As Gardner Ackley of the University of Michigan observed, "A significant real cost of inflation is what it does to morale, to social coherence, and to people's attitudes toward each other." "This society," added Arthur Okun, "is built on implicit and explicit contracts. . . . They are linked to the idea that the dollar means something. If you cannot depend on the value of the dollar, this system is undermined. People will constantly feel they've been fooled and cheated."[2] This is how the middle class felt in Germany in 1923 and in China in 1948, when the value of their savings was wiped out by sudden and unprecedented inflation. (Table 7.4 illustrates the impact of various rates of inflation on the real value of money, over time.)

Despair

Even in less extreme situations, it's not too hard to see how unsettling inflation can be. With prices changing all the time, a person's comfortable habits are easily upset. People are compelled to cope with a whole new dimension of uncertainty. Should they continue to save part of their incomes, even though the real value of savings is falling? Should they be shopping for different goods and services, at different stores? How can they boost their income to keep up with inflation? All these worries seem to accumulate quickly when prices start to rise rapidly. Psychotherapists report that such "inflation stress" leads to more frequent marital spats, increased pessimism, diminished self-confidence, and even sexual insecurity. In addition, some people turn to crime as a way of solving their inflation stress.

[2]Quoted in *Business Week,* May 22, 1978, p. 118.

TABLE 7.4 Inflation's Impact, 1990–2000

In the 1980s the U.S. rate of inflation ranged from a low of 1 percent to a high of 13 percent. Does a range of 12 percentage points really make much difference? One way to find out is to see how a specific sum of money will shrink in real value in the 1990s.

Here's what would happen to the *real* value of $1,000 from January 1, 1990, to January 1, 2000, at different inflation rates. At 2 percent inflation a thousand dollars held for ten years would be worth $820. At 10 percent inflation that same thousand dollars would buy only $386 worth of goods in the year 2000.

| Year | Annual inflation rate | | | | |
	2 Percent	4 Percent	6 Percent	8 Percent	10 Percent
1990	$1,000	$1,000	$1,000	$1,000	$1,000
1991	980	962	943	926	909
1992	961	925	890	857	826
1993	942	889	840	794	751
1994	924	855	792	735	683
1995	906	822	747	681	621
1996	888	790	705	630	564
1997	871	760	665	584	513
1998	853	731	627	540	467
1999	837	703	592	500	424
2000	820	676	558	463	386

Money Illusion

money illusion: The use of nominal dollars rather than real dollars to gauge changes in one's income or wealth.

Even those people whose nominal incomes "keep up" with inflation often feel oppressed by rising prices. People feel that they *deserve* any increases in wages they receive. When they then discover that their higher (nominal) wages don't buy any additional goods, they feel cheated. They feel worse off, even though they have not suffered any actual loss of real income. This is a phenomenon economists call **money illusion.**

MACRO CONSEQUENCES OF INFLATION

Although redistributions of income and wealth are the primary consequences of inflation, inflation has *macroeconomic* effects as well. Inflation can alter the rate and mix of output by changing consumption, work, saving, investment, and trade behavior.

Uncertainty

One of the most immediate consequences of inflation is uncertainty. When the average price level is changing significantly in either direction, economic decisions become increasingly difficult. Should you commit yourself to four years of college, for example, if you are not certain that you or your parents will be able to afford the full costs? In a period of stable prices you can at least be fairly certain of what a college education will cost over a period of years. But if prices are rising, you can no longer be sure how large the bill will be. Under such circumstances, many individuals may decide not to enter college rather than risk the possibility of being driven out later by rising costs.

The uncertainties created by changing price levels affect production decisions as well. Imagine a firm that is considering building a new factory. Typically the construction of a factory takes two years or more, including

"DO I HAVE YOUR ASSURANCE THAT PRICES WILL NOT BE INCREASED BEFORE WE ARE SERVED?"

Drawing by Dana Fradon; © 1977 *The New Yorker Magazine, Inc.*

From *The Wall Street Journal*—by permission. Cartoon Features Syndicate.

planning, site selection, and actual construction. If construction costs or prices change rapidly during this period, the firm may find that it is unable to complete the factory or to operate it profitably. Confronted with this added uncertainty, the firm may decide to do without a new plant, or at least to postpone its construction until a period of stable prices returns.

Inflation need not always lead to a cutback in consumption and production. On the contrary, the uncertainties generated by inflation may just as easily induce people to buy *more* goods and services now, before prices rise further (see World View). In their haste to beat inflation, however, consumers and producers may make foolish decisions, buying goods or services that they will later decide they don't really need or want.

W**O**RLD VIEW

HOARDING

Yugoslavs Jam Food Stores to Beat Steep Price Boosts

BELGRADE, Yugoslavia (Reuters)—Yugoslavs poured into shops yesterday and began hoarding food supplies after the government announced an anti-inflation package that will initially push up prices of essential goods.

The government, fighting inflation of 135% and trying to reschedule its $20 billion foreign debt, announced price rises of between 30% and 70% Saturday on items ranging from bread and cooking oil to gasoline and rail tickets.

Yugoslavs jammed Belgrade food stores yesterday to buy food before it could be marked up. "This is frightening," said one middle-aged shopper. "People just grab what they can. Nobody even utters a word."

The Wall Street Journal, November 16, 1987, p. 26. Reprinted by permission of *The Wall Street Journal.* © Dow Jones & Company, Inc. (1987). All Rights Reserved.

Whichever response consumers and producers make—decreasing or increasing their rate of expenditure—the economy is likely to suffer in the end. In general, ***people shorten their time horizons in the face of inflation uncertainties.*** If consumers and producers postpone or cancel their expenditure plans, the demand for goods and services will fall. Eventually our production of goods and services will fall as well, and we will end up somewhere inside our (institutional) production-possibilities curve, stuck with a GNP gap and attendant unemployment.

Speculation

Inflation threatens not only to reduce the level of economic activity but to change its very nature. If you really expect prices to rise, it makes sense to buy goods and resources now for resale later. If prices rise fast enough, you can make a handsome profit. These are the kinds of thoughts that motivate people to buy houses, precious metals, commodities, and other assets. But such speculation, if carried too far, can detract from the production process. If speculative profits become too easy, few people will engage in production; instead, everyone will be buying and selling existing goods. People may even be encouraged to withhold resources from the production process, hoping to sell them later at higher prices. As such behavior becomes widespread, production will decline and unemployment will rise.

Shortened Time Horizons

Even people who don't speculate may find their productive activities disrupted by inflation. If prices are rising exceptionally fast, people must buy basic necessities as quickly as possible, while they can still afford them. This phenomenon reached extreme proportions during the German hyperinflation of 1923, when prices doubled every week (see World View). Confronted with these skyrocketing prices, German workers could not afford to wait until the end of the week to do their shopping. Instead, they were paid twice daily and given brief "shopping breaks" to make their essential purchases. In this case, the rate of expenditure on goods and services actually increased as a result of inflation, but the rate of production fell. The same kind of frenzy occurred in China during 1948–49. The Nationalist Chinese yuan declined precipitously in value, and market participants rushed to spend their incomes as fast as they could. No one saved income or even tried to.

Hyperinflation also crippled the Nicaraguan economy in 1987–88. Prices of Nicaraguan goods and services doubled every two months in 1987, creating an annual inflation rate of 1,800 percent! Farmers and merchants, unable to discern the value of their goods, stopped selling goods in the marketplace. In 1988 the Nicaraguan government was forced to issue a new currency and even to compel merchants to resume selling goods.

In general, then, we expect inflation to alter market behavior. The rates of saving and investment will tend to decline when people shorten their time horizons and face the future with less confidence. This reduced level of saving and investment will in turn retard economic growth. People may also cut back on their job-seeking efforts or work, because they conclude that the extra dollars just won't matter much. This cutback in the supply of labor will further retard the economy's growth.

Bracket Creep

Another reason why savings, investment, and work effort decline when prices rise is that taxes go up, too. Federal income tax rates are progressive; that is, tax rates are higher for larger incomes. The intent of these progressive rates

W🌐RLD VIEW

HYPERINFLATION

Inflation and the Weimar Republic

At the beginning of 1921 in Germany, the cost-of-living index was 18 times higher than its 1913 prewar base, while wholesale prices had mushroomed by 4,400%. Neither of these increases are negligible, but inflation and war have always been bedfellows. Normally, however, war ends and inflation recedes. By the end of 1921, it seemed that way; prices rose more modestly. Then, in 1922, inflation erupted.

Zenith of German Hyperinflation

Wholesale prices rose fortyfold, an increase nearly as large as during the prior eight years, while retail prices rose even more rapidly. The hyperinflation reached its zenith during 1923. Between May and June 1923, consumer prices more than quadrupled; between July and August, they rose more than 15 times; in the next month, over 25 times; and between September and October, by ten times the previous month's increase.

The German economy was thoroughly disrupted. Businessmen soon discovered the impossibility of rational economic planning. Profits fell as employees demanded frequent wage adjustments. Workers were often paid daily and sometimes two or three times a day, so that they could buy goods in the morning before the inevitable afternoon price increase. The work ethic suffered; wage earners were both more reluctant to work and less

devoted to their jobs. Bankers were on the phone hour after hour, quoting the value of the mark in dollars, as calls continuously came in from merchants who needed the exchange rate to adjust their mark prices.

In an age that preceded the credit card, businessmen traveling around the country found themselves borrowing funds from their customers each stage of the way. The cash they'd allocated for the entire trip barely sufficed to pay the way to the next stop. Speculation began to dominate production.

As a result of the decline in profitability, in the ability to plan ahead, and the concern with speculation rather than production, unemployment rose, increasing by 600% between Sept. 1 and Dec. 15, 1923. And, as the hyperinflation intensified, people found goods unobtainable.

Hyperinflation crushed the middle class. Those thrifty Germans who had placed their savings in corporate or government bonds saw their lifetime efforts come to naught. Debtors sought out creditors to pay them in valueless currency. The debts of German government and industry disappeared. Farmers, too, profited, for, like farmers elsewhere, they were debtors. Nevertheless, the hyperinflation left a traumatic imprint on the German people, a legacy which colors their governmental policy to this day.

—Jonas Prager

---

bracket creep: The movement of taxpayers into higher tax brackets (rates) as nominal incomes grow.

is to redistribute income from rich to poor. However, inflation tends to increase *everyone's* income. In the process, people are pushed into higher tax brackets, and confront higher tax rates. The process is referred to as **bracket creep.** In recent years bracket creep has been limited by the inflation-indexing of personal income tax rates and a reduction in the number of tax brackets. However, Social Security payroll taxes, and most state and local taxes, are not indexed.

Although the public sector still reaps some gain from inflation, inflation stress tends to create a political backlash. Voters are quick to blame the government for inflation. If the administration does not put a stop to inflation, the voters will turn to someone who promises to do so.

ANTICIPATED INFLATION

Although inflation can have serious consequences for our economic welfare, its impact need not always be so harsh. Modest rates of inflation—particularly if they are constant, and thus predictable—may actually stimulate output. If producers are certain that prices will continue to rise at a moderate rate, they have an incentive to produce output now (at lower costs) for sale later (at higher prices). In effect, a little bit of inflation acts as a guarantee of some profits.

Unfortunately, there is always the danger that prices will not continue to rise at the steady anticipated rate. If the rate of inflation changes, profit and production calculations will be upset. Even if steady inflation were to persist for some time, more and more people would begin to expect rising prices. Those people would then act to protect their own interests through speculation and increased demands for wages and profits. As they did so, the possibility of a little inflation evolving into a big inflation would increase greatly.

Even high rates of inflation are not necessarily disruptive. As we saw earlier (World View on inflation), many other countries do grow and prosper despite much higher inflation rates than ours. Apparently they have adjusted to persistently increasing prices. Indeed, some economists argue that all the costs of inflation result from price increases that are *unanticipated*. If we all knew which prices were going to rise and by how much, we could make appropriate changes in our market behavior. From this perspective, there would be no uncertainty, no profit to speculation, and no cause for despair. Inflation would not even redistribute incomes or wealth, since everyone would foresee changes in relative prices.

Theoretically, there is reason to believe that a fully anticipated inflation would do little real harm. In practice, however, not everyone has the ability or energy to make all the required adjustments in market behavior. Also, there is no way to foresee completely all average and relative price increases. As a consequence, inflation is likely to benefit those who have the best information and the greater ability to adapt their market behavior.

MEASURING INFLATION

In view of the macro and micro consequences of inflation, the measurement of inflation serves two purposes: to gauge the average rate of inflation and to identify its principal victims. Until we know how fast prices are rising and which groups are suffering the greatest loss of real income, we can hardly begin to design appropriate public policies.

Consumer Price Index

Consumer Price Index (CPI): A measure (index) of changes in the average price of consumer goods and services.

inflation rate: The annual rate of increase in the average price level.

The most common measure of inflation is the **Consumer Price Index (CPI).** As its name suggests, the CPI is a mechanism for measuring changes in the average price of consumer goods and services. It is analogous to the fruit price index we discussed earlier. The CPI does not refer to the price of any particular good, but rather to the average price of all consumer goods.

By itself, the "average price" of consumer goods is not a very useful number. Once we know the average price of consumer goods, however, we are able to observe whether that average rises—that is, whether inflation is occurring. By observing the extent to which prices increase, we can calculate the **inflation rate.**

We can get a better sense of how inflation is measured—how it affects the distribution of income—by observing how the CPI is constructed. The process begins by identifying a "market basket" of goods and services the typical consumer buys. For this purpose, the Bureau of Labor Statistics periodically surveys a large sample of families to determine what goods and services consumers actually buy. Figure 7.2 summarizes the results of the most recent survey. The survey reveals that 43 cents out of every consumer dollar is spent on housing (shelter, furnishings, and utilities), 18 cents on food, and another 19 cents on transportation. Only 4.4 cents of every consumer dollar is spent on entertainment. Each of these broad categories contains, of course, a tremendous variety of goods and services, and the survey attempts to identify them as well. The details of the survey show, for example, that private expenditures for reading and education account for only 2.4 percent of the typical consumer's budget, less than is spent on alcoholic beverages and tobacco. It also shows that we spend 10 cents out of every dollar on fuel, to drive our cars (4.8 cents) and to heat and cool our houses (5.2 cents).

Once we know what the typical consumer buys, it is relatively easy to calculate the average price of a market basket. The Bureau of Labor Statistics actually goes shopping in various cities across the country, recording the prices of 184 items that comprise the typical market basket. This shopping survey is undertaken every month, in 85 areas and at a variety of stores in each area.

As a result of its surveys, the Bureau of Labor Statistics can tell us what's happening to consumer prices. Suppose, for example, that the market basket cost $100 in 1990, and that one year later the same basket of goods and services cost $110. On the basis of those two shopping trips, we could conclude that consumer prices had risen by 10 percent in one year—that is, that the rate of inflation was 10 percent per annum.

FIGURE 7.2
The Market Basket

To measure changes in average prices, we must first know what goods and services consumers buy. This diagram, based on consumer surveys, shows how the typical urban consumer spends each dollar.

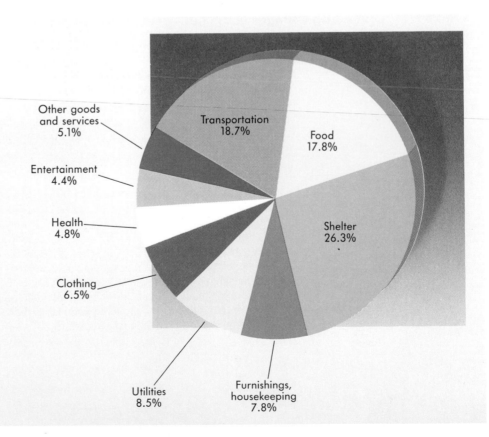

In practice, the CPI is usually expressed in terms of what the market basket cost in 1982–84. For example, the CPI stood at 127 in January 1990. In other words, it cost $127 in 1990 to buy the same market basket that cost only $100 in the base period (1982–84). Thus prices had increased by an average of 27 percent over that period. Each month the Bureau of Labor Statistics updates the CPI, telling us how the current cost of that same basket compares to its cost in 1982–84.[3] The accompanying In the News item shows how a simple "Kidflation" index charts price increases for children's spending. Table 7.5 illustrates how changes in the official CPI are computed.

Producer Price Indexes

In addition to the familiar Consumer Price Index, there are three Producer Price Indexes (PPIs). The PPIs keep track of average prices received by producers. One index includes crude materials, another covers intermediate goods, and the last covers finished goods. The three PPIs do not include all producer prices but primarily those in mining, manufacturing, and agriculture. Like the CPI, changes in the PPIs are identified in monthly surveys.

Over long periods of time, the PPIs and the CPI generally reflect the same rate of inflation. In the short run, however, the PPIs usually increase before the CPI, because it takes time for producers' price increases to be reflected in the prices that consumers pay. For this reason, the PPIs are watched closely as a clue to potential changes in consumer prices.

[3]Since January 1978 the Bureau of Labor Statistics has actually been computing two CPIs, one for urban wage earners and clerical workers and the second and larger one for all urban consumers (about 80 percent of the population). A third index, which uses rent rather than ownership costs of shelter, was introduced in 1983. The "urban/rental" index is most commonly cited.

TABLE 7.5 Computing Changes in the CPI

The Consumer Expenditure Survey of 1982–84 revealed that the average household spends 0.89 cent of every consumer dollar on college tuition. Households without college students don't pay any tuition, of course. And your family probably devotes *more* than 0.89 cent of each consumer dollar to tuition. On *average*, however, 0.89 cent is the proportion of each dollar spent on tuition. This figure is the *item weight* of tuition in computing the CPI.

The impact on the CPI of a price change for a specific good is calculated as follows:

• Item weight × percentage change in price of item = percentage change in CPI

Suppose that tuition prices suddenly go up 20 percent. What impact will this single price increase have on the CPI? In this case, where tuition is the only price that increases, the impact on the CPI will be only 0.178 percent (0.0089 × 20), as illustrated below. Thus a very large increase in the price of tuition (20%) has a tiny impact (0.178%) on the *average* price level.

Housing, on the other hand, accounts for 43 percent of consumer expenditure. Thus if housing prices increase 20 percent, and housing is the only price that increases, the impact on the CPI will be 8.6 percent, as shown below.

The relative importance of an item in consumer budgets—its "item weight"—is a key determinant of its inflationary impact.

Item	Item weight	×	Price increase for the item	=	Impact on the CPI
College tuition	0.0089		20%		0.178%
Housing	0.43		20		8.6

In The News

PRICE INDICES

Allowances Stay Flat, Candy Rises— and Kids Lose Their Innocence

Hurt by Inflation, Children Work, Save and Grumble, Just Like Their Parents

Lauren Krzywkowski is fed up with inflation. She's working as hard as ever, she says, but has less to show for her efforts. To supplement her meager wages, Miss Krzywkowski has begun to seek out odd jobs. "They need it, I do it," she says.

Kelly Collns is feeling the pressure, too. She has been on a fixed income for three years. When asked about inflation, she shakes her head and says glumly, "It's depressing."

Common enough sentiments, these. Except for one thing: The ages of the beleaguered citizens are, respectively, 12 and 14. If schoolyard chatter is any indication, inflation has joined thunderstorms, low grades and neighorhood bullies among kids' most dreaded adversaries.

"It's hard to be a kid today because you've got a lot to worry about, including money, which is one of the biggest problems," explains Miss Krzywkowski, a seventh grader in Cleveland. She says the $1-a-week allowance she usually gets is insufficient to buy the snacks and other things she enjoys. "I wish I was back in the good old days when you could go to the store with 10 cents and have a field day," she says.

No Small Problem

Many parents undoubtedly believe that the problem of "kidflation" is child's play. "In a lot of ways, adults don't give that much import to kids' items going up in price, because the items are discretionary," says Charlotte Baecher, editor of Penny Power, a magazine published by Consumers Union for those aged eight to 12. But many kids themselves feel quite harrassed by increasing prices. So do manufacturers who vie for the estimated $45 billion that children aged six to 16 spend annually.

Discretionary Income

Although the government doesn't keep such statistics and private research is very limited, there are indications that the buying power of children has shrunk significantly over the past five years. Because even dime and quarter increases in the cost of children's items often mean huge leaps in terms of percentages (and weekly allowances), "kidflation" in some cases has outpaced the adult variety.

Based on conversations with over 50 children, this newspaper compiled a "market basket" of 15 items fre-

quently purchased by children, then determined from manufacturers approximately what has happened to the retail prices of those items. While the resulting "Kiddie Consumer Price Index" isn't scientific, and prices may vary from city to city, it offers some insight into what the younger generation is up against.

KIDDIE CONSUMER MARKET BASKET

	1975	1980	1990
1. Chicago White Sox general admission ticket	$2.00	$3.00	$5.00
2. Jack & Jill Soap Bubbles	.29	.45	1.69
3. Wham-O Regular Frisbee	.97	1.29	5.99
4. MAD Magazine	.50	.75	2.50
5. Vending machine 12-oz canned soft drink	.20	.40	.55
6. Wrigley's chewing gum (7-stick pack)	.15	.25	.35
7. Hershey's milk chocolate candy (per 1.05 oz.)	.15	.25	.30
8. Marvel comic book (per 18 editorial pages)	.25	.41	1.00
9. McDonald's hamburger, small fries and 12-oz. soft drink	.80	1.39	2.53
10. Arista record album	6.98	8.98	8.99
11. Crayola crayons (8 crayons)	.25	.45	.83
12. Duncan Imperial Yo-yo	1.29	1.79	2.99
13. Milky Way candy bar (per ounce)	.083	.122	.20
14. Drumstick (ice cream with chocolate and nuts)	.20	.35	.69
15. Topps chewing gum football trading cards (cost per dozen)	.18	.25	.45
Kiddie Consumer Price Index	**14.29**	**20.13**	**34.06**
Consumer Price Index	**166.3**	**258.4**	**380.1**

—Dean Rotbart

The GNP Deflator

The broadest price index is the GNP deflator. The GNP deflator covers all output, including consumer goods, investment goods, and government services. Unlike the CPI and PPIs, the GNP deflator is not based on a fixed "basket" of goods or services. Rather, it allows the contents of the basket to change with people's consumption and investment patterns. The GNP deflator is therefore not a pure measure of price change. Its value reflects both price changes and market responses to those price changes, as reflected in new expenditure patterns. Hence the GNP deflator typcially registers a lower inflation rate than the CPI.

Cost-of-Living Adjustments

For many consumers, changes in a price index are more than a matter of idle curiosity. Many people's incomes depend on changes in the CPI. *Real* income, of course, is always affected by changes in consumer prices. But in a more immediate sense, the size of many paychecks (nominal income) is directly tied to the CPI. Steelworkers, for example, get a raise of $0.01 per hour every time the CPI increases by 0.3 point. In such years as 1980, when the CPI rose by 23.1 points, such raises can be substantial (over $1,000 per year in this case). These raises come about because the workers' wage contracts include a **cost-of-living adjustment (COLA),** which *automatically* adjusts their nominal wages to changing prices.

cost-of-living adjustment (COLA): Automatic adjustments of nominal income to the rate of inflation.

The objective of the COLA is to maintain the workers' *real* wages in an inflationary period. In private industry, those workers with COLA adjustments seldom have full protection against inflation; the adjustments are only partial. Retired workers are even worse off; they seldom get any inflation adjustments in their private pensions.

Federal transfer payments are more completely indexed to inflation. Social Security benefits, for example, go up automatically whenever the rate of inflation exceeds 3 percent. Retired federal employees and veterans get similar protection. As a result of such inflation protection, a 1 percent increase in the CPI triggers $2 billion of additional federal expenditure. All told, the Bureau of Labor Statistics estimates that over half of American families now find some part of their nominal income pegged to the Consumer Price Index.

THE HISTORICAL RECORD

U.S. Inflation Rates

Table 7.6 summarizes our experience with inflation since 1800, as measured by the Consumer Price Index. In this case, the base year for pricing the market basket of goods is again the average price level for 1982–84, and the price index has arbitrarily been set at $100 for that period. Notice that the same market basket cost only $17 in 1800. Consumer prices increased 500 percent in 183 years. But also observe how frequently the price level *fell* in the 1800s and again in the 1930s. These recurrent deflations held down the long-run inflation rate. Because of these periodic deflations, average prices in 1945 were at the same level as in 1800! By contrast, prices have sextupled since 1945.

Figure 7.3 provides a more convenient summary of our recent inflation experience. In this figure we have simply transformed annual changes in the CPI into percentage rates of inflation. The CPI increased from 109.6 to 113.6 during 1987. This four-point jump in the CPI translates into a 3.6 percent rate of inflation ($4 \div 109.6 = 0.036$). This inflation rate is represented by point A in Figure 7.3. The inflation rates for the rest of the years have been calculated in the same way.

TABLE 7.6 The Consumer Price Index, Selected Years 1800–1988
(1982–84 = 100)

Before World War II, the average level of prices rose in some years and fell in others. Since 1945, prices have risen continuously. The Consumer Price Index has more than tripled since 1970.

Year	CPI for all items	Year	CPI for all items	Year	CPI for all items	Year	CPI for all items
1800	17.0	1900	8.3	1940	14.0	1980	82.4
1825	11.3	1915	10.1	1950	24.1	1982–84	100.0
1850	8.3	1920	20.0	1960	29.6	1990	130.5
1875	11.0	1930	16.7	1970	38.8		

Note: Data from 1915 forward reflect the official all-items Consumer Price Index, which used the pre-1983 measure of shelter costs. Estimated indexes for 1800 through 1900 are drawn from several sources.
Source: U.S. Bureau of Labor Statistics.

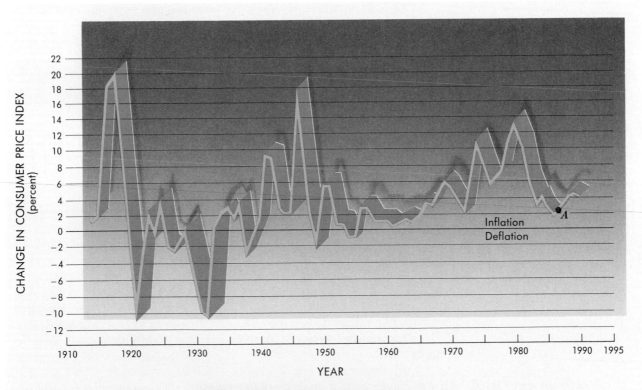

FIGURE 7.3 Historical Price Changes

During the 1920s and 1930s, consumer prices fell significantly, causing a general deflation. Since the Great Depression, however, average prices have risen almost every year. But even during this inflationary period, the annual rate of price increase has varied widely. In 1970 the rate of inflation was 13.5 percent; in 1986 average prices rose only 1.9 percent. Point *A* indicates the inflation rate for 1987.

Source: U.S. Bureau of Labor Statistics.

A quick look at Figure 7.3 confirms that deflations are pretty much a thing of the past; only in the early 1930s did the price level drop substantially. Since that time, prices have risen at least a little nearly every year, and sometimes (1947, 1974, 1979, 1980) by very large amounts. Of particular concern are the generally higher rates of inflation that marked the 1970s and early 1980s. Notice that the price level tripled between 1970 and 1984 (see Table 7.6). This high rate of inflation later subsided, but it left a legacy of fear and pain.

The Resulting Redistributions

As we observed earlier, not everyone suffers equally from high rates of inflation. Insofar as individuals are concerned, it is important to look not only at the *average* increase in consumer prices, but also at the various components of that average. Markedly varying rates of inflation are associated with specific groups of goods and services. In 1989, for example, when the average inflation rate was 4.8 percent, egg prices jumped by 26.6 percent, but bacon prices actually fell. Accordingly, a person who subsisted entirely on coffee and eggs would have experienced an increase in real income in 1989, despite the general inflation taking place. Reading down the list of specific items in Table 7.2 provides further insights into the way inflation redistributed real incomes in 1989. People who ate a lot of fish made out worse than those who ate fruit.

As for transportation expenses, air fares became relatively expensive in 1989, as auto prices rose more slowly. Sadly, tuition and textbook prices increased much faster than the average price level, making students poorer but wiser.

This variation in price changes serves to drive home our basic point: ***inflation redistributes income***. The redistribution occurs as a result of two phenomena:

- Not all prices rise at the same rate in an inflation.

- Not everyone buys (or sells) the same basket of goods and services or holds the same assets.

THE GOAL: PRICE STABILITY

In view of the inequities, anxieties, and real losses caused by inflation, it is not surprising that price stability is a major goal of economic policy. As we observed at the beginning of this chapter, every American president since Franklin Roosevelt has decreed price stability to be a foremost policy goal. Unfortunately, few presidents (or their advisers) have stated exactly what they mean by "price stability." Do they mean *no* change in the average price level? Or is some upward creep in the CPI consistent with the notion of price stability?

A Numerical Goal

price stability: The absence of significant changes in the average price level; officially defined as a rate of inflation of less than 3 percent.

An explicit numerical goal for **price stability** was established for the first time in the Full Employment and Balanced Growth Act of 1978. According to that act, the goal of economic policy is to hold the rate of inflation under 3 percent.

Why did the Congress choose 3 percent inflation rather than zero inflation as the benchmark for price stability? Two considerations were important. First, Congress recognized that efforts to maintain absolutely stable prices (zero inflation) might threaten full employment. Recall that our goal of "full employment" is defined as the lowest rate of unemployment *consistent with stable prices*. The same kind of thinking is apparent here. The amount of inflation regarded as tolerable depends in part on the effect of anti-inflation strategies on unemployment rates. After reviewing our experiences with both unemployment and inflation, Congress concluded that 3 percent inflation was a "safe" target.

Quality Changes

The second argument for setting our price-stability goal above zero inflation relates to our measurement capabilities. Although the Consumer Price Index is very thorough, it is not a perfect measure of inflation. In essence, the CPI simply monitors the price of specific goods over time. Over time, however, the goods themselves change, too. Old products become better as a result of *quality improvements*. A television set costs more today than it did in 1955, but today's TV also delivers a bigger, clearer picture—and in color! Hence increases in the price of television sets tend to exaggerate the true rate of inflation: part of the higher price represents more product.

The same is true of automobile tires. Although tire prices have risen greatly over time, their durability has increased even faster. As a result, the price *per mile* for use of tires has fallen since 1935.

The problem of measuring quality improvements is most apparent in the case of new products. The computers and word processors found in many offices and homes today did not exist when the Census Bureau conducted its 1972–73 survey of consumer expenditure. The 1982–84 survey included these new products, but the CPI itself was not revised until 1987. In the intervening years, the real incomes of consumers were affected by these and other goods the CPI did not include. The same thing is happening now: new products and continuing quality improvements are enriching our consumption, even though they are not reflected in the CPI. Hence there is a significant (though unmeasured) element of error in the CPI insofar as it is intended to gauge changes in the average prices paid by consumers. The goal of 3 percent inflation allows for such errors.

TYPES OF INFLATION

In the last two decades prices have risen less than 3 percent in only one year (1986). Some of the reasons for our failure to attain price stability are discussed at length in later chapters. At this point, however, it is convenient to identify the major types of inflation that occur.

Demand-Side Forces

demand-pull inflation: An increase in the price level initiated by excessive aggregate demand.

The most familiar form of inflation is called **demand-pull inflation.** The name suggests that demand is pulling up the price level, and this is pretty much what happens. If the demand for goods and services increases faster than production, there simply won't be enough goods and services to go around. Prices will rise as consumers try to outbid one another for the available supply. In the process, the price level will move up, and we will be saddled with an inflation.

Consumers are not the only potential villains in a demand-pull story. As we observed in Chapter 2, there are three sets of domestic market participants—consumers, business firms, and government agencies—and all of their dollars look alike. A surge in aggregate demand can come about through increased spending by any of these groups. Even foreigners may contribute to inflation, by bidding up the prices of U.S. exports.

Supply-Side Forces

Increased spending is not the only possible explanation for rising prices. There are two sides to every market, and changes in supply conditions can also raise prices. In 1979, for example, the Organization of Petroleum Exporting Countries (OPEC) sharply increased the price of oil. For domestic producers, this action meant a significant increase in the cost of producing goods and services. Accordingly, domestic producers could no longer afford to sell goods at prevailing prices. They had to raise prices. The result was a **cost-push inflation.**

cost-push inflation: An increase in the price level initiated by an increase in the cost of production.

Not all cost-push inflations have such dramatic beginnings. A more common source of cost-push inflation is an increase in labor costs, often resulting from aggressive labor-union bargaining.

Producers can also contribute to supply-side inflation. If producers decide they want higher incomes, they may try to attain them by raising profit margins. They can increase profit margins by raising product prices faster than costs. The result is a rising price level—that is, inflation.

The distinction between demand-led inflation and supply-led inflation is illustrated in Figure 7.4. Point E_0 is the initial equilibrium and P_0 the initial price level in both cases. In Figure 7.4a prices are pushed up by a *rightward*

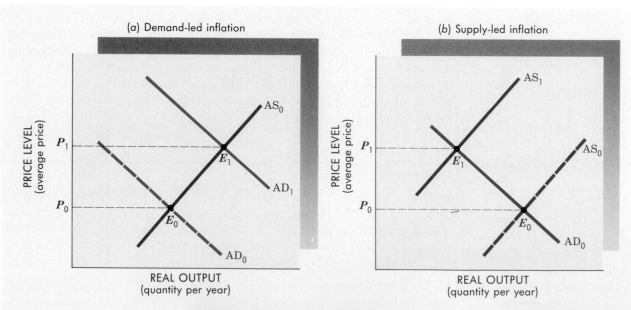

FIGURE 7.4 Sources of Inflation

An increase in average prices may be caused by changes in supply or demand. In part *a*, the price rise from P_0 to P_1 is caused by the rightward shift of the aggregate demand curve (from AD_0 to AD_1). In part *b*, the same price increase (P_0 to P_1) is caused by a leftward shift of the aggregate supply curve (AS_0 to AS_1). The task of economic analysis is to identify the true cause of inflation. Macro policy tries to contain it.

shift of the aggregate *demand* curve. In Figure 7.4*b*, prices are pushed up by a *leftward* shift of the aggregate *supply* curve. Thus an increase in the price level may result from increased aggregate demand, reduced aggregate supply, or a combination of these forces.

In the real world, there are no graphs; all we see are rising prices. By themselves, rising prices don't reveal whether supply or demand forces are at work. Sorting out cause and effect is the objective of macroeconomic analysis (and the subject of the following chapters). At this juncture, an awareness of the different possible causes of inflation will help guide that analysis.

SUMMARY

• Inflation is an increase in the average price level. Typically it is measured by changes in a price index such as the Consumer Price Index (CPI).

• At the micro level, inflation redistributes income by altering relative prices, income, and wealth. Because not all prices rise at the same rate and because not all people buy (and sell) the same goods or hold the same assets, inflation does not affect everyone equally. Some individuals actually gain from inflation, whereas others suffer a drop in real income.

• At the macro level, inflation threatens to reduce total output because it increases uncertainties about the future and thereby inhibits consumption and production decisions. Fear of rising prices can also stimulate spending, forcing the government to take restraining action that threatens full employment. Rising price levels also encourage speculation and hoarding, which detract from productive activity.

• Fully anticipated inflation reduces the anxieties and real losses associated with rising prices. However, few people can foresee actual price patterns or make all the necessary adjustments in their market activity.

• The U.S. goal of price stability is defined as an inflation rate of less than 3 percent per year. This goal recognizes potential conflicts between zero inflation and full employment, as well as the difficulties of measuring quality improvements and new products.

• Inflation may be caused by either demand or supply forces. Demand-pull inflation is caused by an increase in (rightward shift of) aggregate demand. Cost-push inflation is caused by increases in the cost of production or other forces that reduce (shift to the left) aggregate supply.

Terms to Remember   Define the following terms:

inflation	**Consumer Price Index (CPI)**
deflation	**inflation rate**
relative price	**cost-of-living adjustment (COLA)**
nominal income	**price stability**
real income	**demand-pull inflation**
money illusion	**cost-push inflation**
bracket creep	

Questions for Discussion

1. Why is inflation called a "capricious tax"?

2. Can you identify any groups of people who are particularly helped or hurt by inflation? Explain.

3. Does an increase in the price level automatically lower society's real income? Explain.

4. Would it be advantageous to borrow money if you expected prices to rise? Why, or why not? Provide a numerical example.

Problems

1. Between 1985 and 1988, the average household's nominal income increased from $25,000 to $30,000. The following table lists the prices of a small market basket purchased in both of those years. Assuming that this basket of goods is representative of all goods and services, compute the change in real income between 1985 and 1988.

Item	Quantity	Price (per unit) 1985	Price (per unit) 1988
Coffee	20 pounds	$ 3	$ 4
Tuition	1 year	4,000	7,000
Pizza	100 pizzas	8	10
VCR rental	75 days	15	10
Vacation	2 weeks	300	500

2. Use the item weights in Figure 7.2 to determine the percentage change in the CPI that would result from:
   (a) A 10 percent increase in entertainment prices.
   (b) A 6 percent decrease in transportation costs.
   (c) A doubling of clothing prices.
   (Review Table 7.5 for assistance.)

3. Suppose you will have an annual nominal income of $40,000 for the next five years, without any increases. However, the inflation rate is 5 percent.
   (a) Find the real value of your $40,000 salary for each of the next five years.
   (b) Suppose you have a COLA of 5 percent per year in your contract, which raises your $40,000 salary by 5 percent for each of the next five years. Given the 5 percent inflation rate for each of those five years, what is the real value of your salary for each year?
   (c) With inflation and without a COLA, which of the following would you experience, *ceteris paribus*?

      Negative wealth effects
      Negative income effects
      Negative price effects

POLICY OPTIONS:
The
Keynesian
Approach

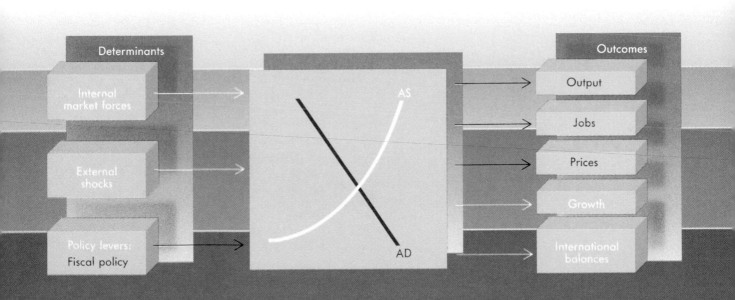

Keynesian theory emphasizes the inherent instability of a market economy. In the Keynesian view, the government must use its tax and spending powers (fiscal policy) to stabilize the macro economy.

CHAPTER 8

Aggregate Spending

*D*uring the Great Depression of the 1930s, as many as 13 million Americans were out of work. They were capable people and eager to work. But no one would hire them. As sympathetic as employers might have been, they simply could not use any more workers. Consumers were not buying the goods and services already being produced. Employers were more likely to cut back production and lay off still more workers than to hire any new ones. As a consequence, an "army of the unemployed" was created in 1929 and continued to grow for nearly a decade. It was not until the outbreak of World War II that enough jobs could be found for the unemployed, and most of these "jobs" were in the armed forces.

As we noted in Chapter 5, the Great Depression was the springboard for the Keynesian approach to economic policy. John Maynard Keynes concluded that the growing ranks of unemployed persons were caused by problems on the *demand* side of product markets. People simply were not able and willing to buy all the goods and services the economy was capable of producing. As a consequence, producers had no incentive to increase output or to hire more labor. So long as the demand for goods and services was inadequate, unemployment was inevitable.

Keynes sought to explain how a deficiency of demand could arise, then to show how and why the government had to intervene. Keynes was convinced that government intervention was necessary to ensure optimal macro outcomes. In this and the next two chapters we examine Keynes's theory in detail. We start with the same questions that Keynes posed:

- What are the components of aggregate demand?

- What determines the level of spending for each component?

- Will there ever be enough demand to maintain full employment?

MACRO EQUILIBRIUM

In Chapter 5 we got a bird's-eye view of how macro equilibrium is established. Producers have some notion of how much output they are willing and able to produce at various price levels. Likewise, consumers, businesses, governments, and the rest of the world have some notion of how much output they

aggregate demand: The total quantity of output demanded at alternative price levels in a given time period, *ceteris paribus.*

aggregate supply: The total quantity of output producers are willing and able to supply at alternative price levels in a given time period, *ceteris paribus.*

equilibrium (macro): The combination of price level and real output that is compatible with both aggregate demand and aggregate supply.

are willing and able to buy at different price levels. These forces of **aggregate demand** and **aggregate supply** confront each other in the marketplace. Eventually, buyers and sellers discover that only one price–output combination is acceptable to *both* sides. This is the price–output combination we designate as **(macro) equilibrium.** At equilibrium, the aggregate quantity of goods demanded exactly equals the aggregate quantity supplied. In the absence of macro disturbances, the economy will gravitate toward equilibrium—and stay there.

Figure 8.1*a* illustrates again this general view of macro equilibrium. It also illustrates the now familiar policy dilemma: equilibrium output (Q_E) falls short of our full-employment goal (Q_F). As we noted earlier, virtually all economists recognize that such a *short-run* macro failure is possible. Keynes, however, offered a unique explanation for the cause and duration of such a failure. ***The Keynesian view of this dilemma is unique in two respects:***

- ***No self-adjustment.*** Keynes rejected the Classical notion that the aggregate supply and demand curves would automatically shift to create a new equilibrium at full employment. In his view, high unemployment could persist indefinitely.

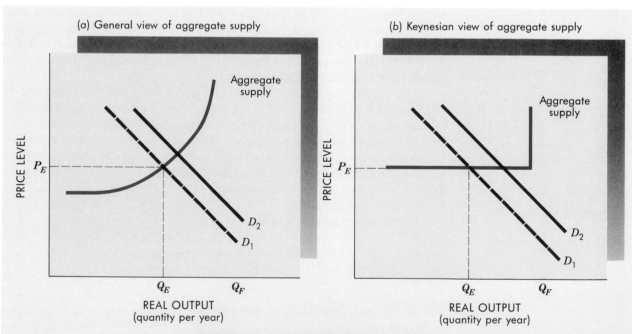

FIGURE 8.1 Contrasting Views of Aggregate Supply

(*a*) In the general view of macro equilibrium, the short–run aggregate supply curve is upward–sloping. Greater output is attainable only if prices rise. Rightward shifts of the demand curve (say, from D_1 to D_2) increase both real output and prices.

(*b*) If excess capacity (unemployment) exists, Keynes assumed producers will be willing and able to supply more output at the prevailing price level. If so, the aggregate supply curve is horizontal, up to capacity. Consequently, increased demand (say, from D_1 to D_2) boosts output but not prices.

• *Horizontal aggregate supply curve.* Keynes believed the aggregate supply curve was horizontal in a recession, making it an ineffective policy lever. Only aggregate demand mattered.

Keynes reached this conclusion by observing that prices are more likely to fall than to rise during a period of high unemployment. Producers don't need the lure of higher prices to increase output at such times. Furthermore, the ample supply of unemployed workers diminishes the chances of cost-push inflation as output is expanded. In view of all this, producers will be more than willing to sell additional output at current prices, if only they can find a buyer.

Keynes's Depression-bred view of aggregate supply is illustrated in Figure 8.1*b*. The aggregate supply curve is horizontal until capacity (Q_F) is reached. As a result, prices do not start to rise until that full-employment rate of output is attained. This Keynesian supply curve differs markedly from the more general perspective expressed by Figure 8.1*a*, in which prices start to rise long before full employment is reached. This does not mean Keynes's view is wrong. The "correctness" of any curve is determined by producer behavior at a given time. Keynes was simply asserting that producer behavior was most likely to look like the horizontal supply curve in Figure 8.1*b*—particularly during periods of high unemployment.

Keynes's view simplifies the macro dilemma in two ways. First, it implies that we have only one curve to worry about rather than two. Rightward shifts of the Keynesian aggregate supply curve (Figure 8.1*b*) will not increase total output. *In the Keynesian model, changes (shifts) in aggregate demand are the only hope for achieving higher employment.* Unemployment results from the position of the aggregate demand curve (too far to the left) and will be eliminated only if the demand curve shifts to the right.

Second, the Keynesian view eliminates any immediate concern about inflation. If we successfully boost (shift) aggregate demand, prices won't rise. Notice, for example in Figure 8.1*b*, how the curve D_2 also intersects aggregate supply at the initial price level P_E. *Increased aggregate demand does not cause inflation in the basic Keynesian model.*

THE CIRCULAR FLOW: INCOME AND SPENDING

In the Keynesian view of the world, then, the primary objective is to shift the aggregate demand curve. If we can shift the curve at will, we can achieve any desired rate of output, including full-employment Q_F.

To shift the aggregate demand curve, we must know what forces determine its position. The most obvious one is *income.* Think back to when we first constructed the aggregate demand curve (Figure 5.5) The curve tells us that *with a given level of income,* people will buy a greater quantity of output at a lower price level. Recall that the lower prices increase the value of money balances (wealth), raise the relative cost of imports, and tend to reduce interest rates. These three phenomena give people the ability and willingness to buy a greater quantity of domestic output as prices fall. They thus explain the *downward slope* of the aggregate demand curve.

But what if people had more income to spend? Then they could buy more output at any given price level. In other words, *an increase in spendable income could shift the aggregate demand curve* to the right. According to Figure 8.1*b*, this is just the kind of boost a depressed economy needs. The other forces that might *shift* the aggregate demand curve are

- Changes in expectations

- Changes in government spending or taxes

- Changes in interest rates

- Changes in wealth

- Changes in international balances

- Changes in population

Keynes was intrigued by these possibilities for *shifting* the aggregate demand curve to cure unemployment. He focused on the relationship between income and spending. Keynes believed that aggregate demand could be shifted to any desired level in two ways:

- by changing the level of income people had to spend

- by changing the proportion of income actually spent

Real vs. Dollar Flows

Keynes's theory of macro instability was developed in *nominal* terms, not the *real* values used in aggregate supply and demand graphs. Keynes focused on how many *dollars* we spend, not on the *quantity* of output we purchase. In Figures 8.1*a* and 8.1*b*, the volume of *real* output is depicted on the horizontal axis. Our concern there is with the quantity of goods and services produced. To determine how many *dollars* people spend on that output we need to look at prices, too. The price level is on the vertical axis of Figures 8.1*a* and 8.1*b*. By multiplying the real output (Q) by the price level (P), we get total *spending*:

$$\bullet \quad \text{Total spending} = P \times Q$$

Total spending is measured in dollars, as is income. Therefore, **Keynes asked how many dollars people will spend and how that rate of expenditure is related to (dollar) income.** This is the Keynesian concept of **aggregate spending.**

aggregate spending: The rate of total expenditure desired at alternative levels of income, *ceteris paribus.*

The dollar flows that commanded Keynes's attention are inherently related to the real flows of output. As we first saw in Chapter 4, there is a circular flow of income in the economy. What one person spends in the marketplace becomes someone else's income. Figure 8.2 illustrates this circular flow again, in both dollar and real terms. Notice that we again have both product markets and factor markets. But we ignore government and foreign trade for the moment, leaving domestic consumers and business firms as the only market participants. In this simplified economy, consumers supply labor to the factor market by going out and looking for jobs; they supply land and capital by offering to sell or rent these factors as well. This supply of resources is illustrated by Step 1 on the inner loop of Figure 8.2.

The role of business firms in factor markets is to hire available workers and other factors of production (Step 2) to produce goods and services (Step 3). The goods and services themselves will later be sold to consumers in product markets (Step 4), thus completing the circular flow.

While the inner loop of Figure 8.2 focuses on the real flow of goods and factors between consumers and businesses, the outer loop summarizes the flow of dollar *income* that accompanies each market transaction. Consumer

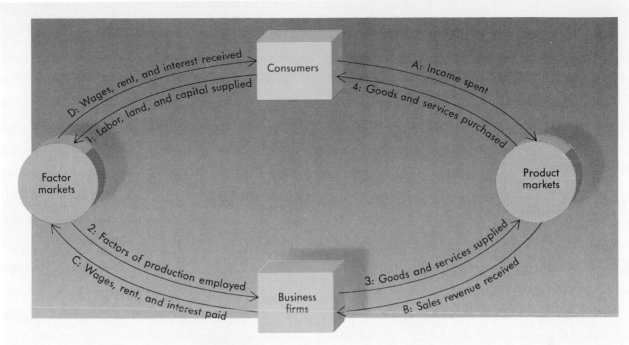

FIGURE 8.2
A Simplified Circular Flow

The circular flow encompasses dollars in one direction, real goods and services in the other. Keynes focused on the dollar flows of income and spending to explain the rate of real output. Producers will produce at full capacity only if people are willing to spend enough income on that output.

expenditures on goods and services (Step A) generate sales revenue (receipts) for business firms. Business firms use their sales revenue (Step B) to hire labor, land, and capital (Step C). The resultant wages, rent, and interest represent income to consumers (D). In fact, all of the income spent in product markets ends up as income for market participants. This recycled income may be used to finance further consumer purchases (A again). And so the flow continues.

Derived Demand

Keynes used the concept of circular flow to illustrate two basic points: first, dollar expenditures (total spending) are directly related to the flow of real goods and services; second, *the level of employment depends on the willingness of people to spend their incomes.* Businesses hire workers only if the goods and services such workers produce can be sold in product markets. Firms will demand more labor only if the demand for the goods and services such labor produces is sufficiently strong. In this sense, we say that employers have a **derived demand** for labor, a demand that is derived from demands for final goods and services.

derived demand: The demand for labor and other factors of production results from (depends on) the demand for final goods and services produced by these factors.

The Keynesian focus on dollar spending and the principle of derived demand provide another view of the causes of unemployment and inflation. In particular,

- If desired spending at full employment equals the value of full-employment output, producers will have enough income and incentive to employ all available workers.

- If desired spending at full employment is less than the value of full-employment output, producers will not have enough income or incentive to employ all available workers. Unemployment will result.

- If desired spending at full employment exceeds the value of full-employment output, producers will seek to hire more labor than is available. Inflation will result.

From a Keynesian perspective, then, we must focus on the rate of desired *spending* at various income levels. With prices assumed constant (the horizontal aggregate supply curve of Figure 8.1*b*), this is equivalent to looking at the rate of real output demanded at different income levels. Keynes was particularly interested in how much spending is desired at the income level corresponding to full employment. If we want to achieve and maintain full employment, desired spending at that level of income must equal the value of total output. Will it?

To answer this question, we must look at the components of total spending. As we saw in Chapter 4, spending on goods and services comes from four different sources:

Total spending = consumption + investment
+ government spending + net exports

That is,

$$\bullet \quad \text{GNP} = C + I + G + (X - M)$$

To determine how much spending will actually occur, we need to look at each one of these components. How much will consumers want to spend on goods and services? How much will businesses want to spend on plant and equipment? How much will government agencies spend? How much will net exports be? How much will all this spending add up to? Will this sum be enough to provide a job for everyone who wants to work? Will total spending exceed our ability to produce?

CONSUMPTION

consumption: Expenditure by consumers on final goods and services.

We begin our analysis of spending behavior by looking at consumers. Consumer expenditures account for two-thirds of total spending in our economy. We need to determine what factors influence the *rate* of **consumption** and thus our potential for achieving full employment.

Consumption decisions are influenced by a variety of forces, including income, prices, interest rates, wealth, and expectations. Keynes, however, asserted that income alone was the most important determinant of consumer spending. Most studies of consumer behavior seem to confirm his view: the rate of consumer spending is directly and closely related to the amount of income consumers have to spend.[1]

---

[1]Recall that in Chapter 2 we simplified the explanation of consumer demand for a specific good by focusing on the two-dimensional relationship between quantity demanded and price. Here we are focusing on the two-dimensional relationship between total consumption and total income.

Disposable income is the key concept here. As noted in Chapter 4, disposable income is the amount of income consumers actually take home. This is the share of total income remaining after all taxes have been paid, transfers (e.g., Social Security benefits) have been received, and depreciation charges and retained earnings have been subtracted (see Figure 4.3). **Disposable income (DI)** represents the amount of income consumers can actually choose to spend or not spend (save) in a given time period; that is,

disposable income (DI): After-tax income of consumers; personal income less personal taxes.

- Disposable income = consumption + saving

Consumption vs. Saving

What interested Keynes is how consumers divide up their disposable income between current consumption and **saving.** In this regard, we ask two separate questions:

saving: That part of disposable income not spent on current consumption; disposable income less consumption.

- What fraction of *total* disposable income is spent on consumer goods and services?

- What fraction of *added* disposable income is spent on consumer goods and services?

The first question reflects an interest in overall patterns of consumption; the second question is concerned with consumer responses to *changes* in income. As we shall discover, this distinction is critical.

The Average Propensity to Consume

The proportion of *total* disposable income spent on consumer goods and services in a given time period is referred to as the **average propensity to consume (APC).** To determine the APC, we simply observe how much consumers spend in a given time period out of that period's disposable income. In 1989, for example, total disposable income amounted to $3,780 billion, out of which consumers spent $3,574 billion and saved only $206 billion.[2] Accordingly, we may calculate the average propensity to consume as

average propensity to consume (APC): Total consumption in a given period divided by total disposable income.

$$\bullet \quad \text{APC} = \frac{\text{total consumption}}{\text{total disposable income}} = \frac{C}{Y_D}$$

For 1989 this works out to

$$\text{APC} = \frac{\$3{,}574 \text{ billion}}{\$3{,}780 \text{ billion}} = 0.946$$

In other words, consumers spent, on average, 95 cents out of every dollar received. The remaining 5 cents of every dollar was saved.

The Marginal Propensity to Consume

The fact that the average propensity to consume was 0.946 in 1989 does not imply that all consumers spent exactly 95 cents out of each dollar received. The APC is simply an *average* that summarizes the behavior of millions of consumers, each responding to his or her own income. With different incomes, consumers might have spent more or less out of each dollar.

It is particularly important to observe how the choice between consumption and saving is affected by *changes* in income. For this purpose, we formulate a second measure of consumption behavior, the marginal pro-

[2]This figure for consumption includes all personal outlays, including net personal transfers to foreigners ($1.5 billion) and interest paid to businesses ($93.5 billion).

marginal propensity to consume (MPC): The fraction of each additional (marginal) dollar of disposable income spent on consumption; the change in consumption divided by the change in disposable income.

pensity to consume. The **marginal propensity to consume (MPC)** tells us how much consumer expenditure will *change* in response to *changes* in income.

$$\bullet \quad \text{MPC} = \frac{\text{change in consumption}}{\text{change in disposable income}} = \frac{\Delta C}{\Delta Y_D}$$

To calculate the marginal propensity to consume, we have to observe how consumers respond to *changes* in income. In the extreme case, we could ask how consumer spending in 1989 was affected by the *last* dollar of disposable income. That is, how did consumer spending change when disposable income increased from \$3,779,999,999 to \$3,780,000,000? If consumer spending increased by \$0.80 when this last \$1.00 was received, we would calculate the *marginal* propensity to consume as

$$\text{MPC} = \frac{\$0.80}{\$1.00} = 0.8$$

marginal propensity to save (MPS): The fraction of each additional (marginal) dollar of disposable income not spent on consumption; $1 - \text{MPC}$.

An MPC of 0.8 implies that consumers are saving 20 cents out of each *additional* dollar. Thus the **marginal propensity to save (MPS)** is the converse of the MPC (see Table 8.1). Since all disposable income is, by definition, either consumed or saved, we have

$$\bullet \quad \text{MPC} + \text{MPS} = 1$$

Notice that the MPC in this particular case (0.8) is lower than the APC (0.95). Suppose we had incorrectly assumed that consumers would always spend 95 cents of every dollar's income. Then we would have expected the rate of consumer spending to rise by 95 cents as the last dollar was received. In fact, however, the rate of spending increased by only 80 cents. In other words, consumers responded to *increases* in their income differently than past averages implied.

TABLE 8.1   Average and Marginal Propensities

MPC vs. APC. The marginal propensity to consume (MPC) is the *change* in consumption that accompanies a *change* in disposable income; that is,

$$\text{MPC} = \frac{\Delta C}{\Delta Y_D}$$

But we may also be interested in the proportion of *total* disposable income that is spent on consumption. This is referred to as the *average* propensity to consume, and it equals $\frac{C}{Y_D}$.

MPS vs. APS. The marginal propensity to *save* (MPS) is the fraction of each additional (marginal) dollar of disposable income *not* spent—that is, saved. This is summarized as

$$\text{MPS} = \frac{\Delta S}{\Delta Y_D}$$

MPS equals $1 - \text{MPC}$, since every additional dollar is either spent (consumed) or not spent (saved). The *average* propensity to save equals $\frac{S}{Y_D}$.

No one would be upset if our failure to distinguish the APC from the MPC led to an error of only 15 cents in forecasts of consumer spending. After all, the rate of consumer spending in the U.S. economy exceeds $3 trillion per year! However, policy decisions are rarely calibrated in single dollars. Typically, they involve billion-dollar changes in income. When we start playing with those sums—the actual focus of economic policymakers—the distinction between APC and MPC is significant.

Like the APC, the MPC may change. The marginal propensity to consume is determined by a variety of social, psychological, and economic factors. People who have very little income often spend every additional dollar they get; their MPC is very close to 1.0. By contrast, people with high incomes may have difficulty finding new ways to spend additional income; their MPC may be low. As a consequence, if we redistributed income from the rich to the poor, our collective MPC might rise. At any time, however, only one MPC prevails, and we use it to characterize the behavior of consumers.

THE CONSUMPTION FUNCTION

The MPC allows us to predict consumer responses to changes in income and thus to predict changes in total spending. Suppose that the rate of consumer spending was *completely* determined by current income and nothing else. In this case, we could say that $C = bY_D$—that is, that the rate of consumer spending (C) depends on the level of disposable income (Y_D) and the marginal propensity to consume (b). Hence the equation $C = bY_D$ would tell us exactly how much consumer spending (C) would take place at various income levels (Y_D).

In reality, consumption is not *completely* determined by current income. In extreme cases, this is evident. People who have no income in a given period continue to consume goods and services. They finance their purchases by dipping into their savings accounts (past income) or using credit (future income), instead of spending current income. More generally, we observe that people's current consumption decisions are influenced by expectations of future income, accumulated savings, the availability of credit, and ingrained habits, as well as current income.

consumption function: A mathematical relationship indicating the rate of desired consumer spending at various income levels.

In recognition of these other determinants of consumption, we generally describe consumer behavior—the **consumption function**—by the equation

$$\bullet \quad C = a + bY_D$$

where a is the rate of consumer spending not dependent on current income and b is again the marginal propensity to consume. The amount of consumption indicated by a is often referred to as *autonomous consumption*. This is the rate of consumer spending determined by forces other than current income. In theory, this amount of consumption would take place even if Y_D equaled zero.

Keynes used this simple equation—with both autonomous and income-dependent consumption—to characterize consumer spending. Because of its unique focus on the relationship of current consumption to current income, it is called the Keynesian consumption function.[3]

[3]The consumption function can be expanded to include other determinants of consumer spending. Keynes focused on disposable income (Y_D) only.

An Individual Function

To see how the consumption function works, imagine an individual who has no monthly income. How much will that person spend? Obviously he must spend *something*, otherwise he will starve to death. At a very low rate of income—in this case zero—consumer spending depends less on current income than on basic survival needs, past savings, and credit. The a in the consumption function expresses this autonomous consumption; we shall assume it is $50 per month. Thus we may say that the monthly rate of consumption expenditure in this case is

$$C = \$50 + bY_D$$

Notice that we have said nothing about how our unlucky consumer is going to pay for his basic consumption of $50 per month. For the moment, all we care about is how much he ends up *spending*. And we know it will be a minimum of $50 per month.

Now suppose that our friend finds a job and begins to earn $100 per month. Will his spending be affected? The $50 per month he had been spending provided very few goods and services. Now that he is earning a little income, our friend will certainly want to improve his life-style. That is to say, *we expect consumption to rise with income.*

But by how much? To predict changes in spending, we have to be more specific about the influence of additional income on consumption. In this case, assume that he increases his consumption $75 per month when his disposable income rises from zero to $100 per month.[4] His *marginal propensity to consume,* then, is 0.75—75 cents of each additional $1.00 of income is spent on consumption.

Knowing how much this consumer spends when his income is zero and also how he responds to increases in income, we can write his consumption function as

$$C = \$50 \text{ per month} + 0.75 \, Y_D$$

With this equation, we can predict exactly how much our friend will spend per month at various income levels. According to this equation, our friend's *total* consumption will be $125 per month when his income is $100 per month. This is indicated in row B of the table in Figure 8.3. This consumption consists of his basic survival package ($50 per month) plus the added $75 of goods and services each month that are financed by his sudden prosperity.

Our friend's rate of consumption still exceeds his income. According to row B of Figure 8.3, he is now spending $125 per month but taking in only $100 of income. The other $25 is still being begged, borrowed, or withdrawn from savings. Without peering further into our friend's personal finances, we may simply conclude that he is **dissaving** $25 per month. Dissaving occurs whenever current consumption exceeds current income (see In the News).

If our friend's monthly income continues to rise, he will stop dissaving at some point. Perhaps he will even start saving enough to pay back all the people who have sustained him throughout these difficult months. Figure 8.3 shows just how and when this will occur.

The black line in Figure 8.3, with a 45-degree angle, represents all points where consumption and income are exactly equal ($C = Y_D$). Recall that our hapless friend currently has an income of $100 per month. By moving up

dissaving: Consumption expenditure in excess of disposable income; a negative saving flow.

---

[4]We are assuming that the $100 he "earns" is equal to his disposable income. We will confront the government and its inevitable taxes a bit later.

FIGURE 8.3
A Hypothetical Consumption Function

The rate of consumer spending (C) is directly related to current disposable income (Y_D). As income rises, so does consumption. The marginal propensity to consume indicates how much consumption will increase with each added dollar of income. In the table, consumption increases by $75 whenever income increases by $100 (e.g., from row B to row C). The marginal propensity to consume equals 0.75.

The consumption function can be expressed in an equation, a table, or a graph. The graph conveys the same information as the table. Point B, for example, corresponds to row B of the table. Both indicate that this consumer will desire to spend $125 per month when his income is only $100 per month. The difference between income and consumption equals (dis)saving.

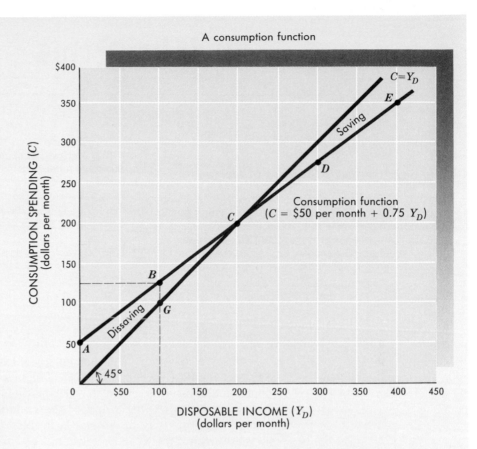

A consumption function

Consumption (C = $50 + 0.75 Y_D)

	Disposable income (Y_D)	Consumption at zero income	+	Additional spending	=	Total consumption
A	$ 0	$50		$ 0		$ 50
B	100	50		75		125
C	200	50		150		200
D	300	50		225		275
E	400	50		300		350
F	500	50		375		425

from the horizontal axis at Y_D = $100, we see all the consumption possibilities he confronts. Were he to spend exactly $100 on consumption, he would end up on the 45-degree line, at point G. But we already know he doesn't stop there. Instead, he proceeds further, to point B. At point B the consumption function lies above the 45-degree line, so consumption exceeds income; dissaving is occurring.

In The News

DISSAVING

Consumer Spending Rises 0.9 Percent

July Gain Outpaces Increase in Income

Consumer spending, bolstered by brisk auto sales and heavy use of air conditioning, rose 0.9 percent in July for the second month in a row, more than twice as fast as incomes grew, the government reported yesterday.

The Commerce Department said that personal income rose at a slightly faster rate in July, 0.4 percent compared with 0.3 percent in both May and June.

With the growth of spending far outpacing the growth of incomes, Americans dipped deeper into their savings to make up the difference.

Personal savings, the ratio of savings to after-tax income, fell to 2.8 percent in July from 3.3 percent in June and 4.3 percent for all of 1986.

—Tom Raum

The Washington Post, August 25, 1987, p. E1. Reprinted by permission of The Associated Press.

Observe, however, what happens when his disposable income rises to $200 per month (row *C* in the table of Figure 8.3). The upward slope of the consumption function (Figure 8.3) tells us that consumption spending will rise with income. In fact, *the slope of the consumption function equals the marginal propensity to consume.* In this case, we see that when income increases from $100 to $200, consumption rises from $125 (point *B*) to $200 (point *C*). Thus the *change* in consumption ($75) equals three-fourths of the *change* in income. The *MPC* is still 0.75.

Point *C* has further significance. At an income of $200 per month our modest consumer is no longer dissaving but is now breaking even—that is, disposable income equals consumption, so saving equals zero. In Figure 8.3, we see that point *C* lies on the 45-degree line, indicating that current consumption equals current income. Should he be so fortunate as to experience still further increases in income, he will actually begin saving (not spending all his income). To the right of point *C*, the consumption function always lies below the 45-degree line.

Our friend's experiences can be summarized in an equation (as before), a schedule, or a graph; all of them tell the same story. Take another look at the equation. It says that a consumer will spend something each month (the amount *a*) even when disposable income (Y_D) equals zero. This is confirmed in Figure 8.3, where the consumption function crosses the vertical axis; at that point (*A*), monthly income equals zero, yet consumption equals $50 per month.

Now recall what happens when income rises. We have observed that our friend's marginal propensity to consume is 0.75. Thus if disposable income equals $100 per month, consumption (*C*) equals $50 + 0.75 ($100) = $125 per month. This is confirmed in row *B* of the table of Figure 8.3 as well as by point *B* on the graph. Thus all versions of the consumption function tell the same story. Any one of them can be used to predict how much consumers will spend out of any given income. We will make most use of the graphic consumption function, as drawn in Figure 8.3.

The Aggregate Function

We need not dwell any longer on the perils and hardships of this one consumer. Our immediate interest is not in the eating and spending habits of any particular consumer (a micro issue) but in the behavior of consumers as a class (a macro issue).

Repeated studies of consumers suggest that there is nothing very remarkable about the individual we have been studying, except perhaps for his ingenuity during hard times. The consumption function we have constructed for him can be used for the total of all consumers simply by changing the numbers involved. Instead of dealing in hundreds of dollars per month, we now play with trillions of dollars per year. But the basic relationship is the same. That is to say, we still assume (and can observe) that the rate of consumption spending depends on disposable income, as in Figure 8.3.

The actual relationship of U.S. consumer spending to disposable income is depicted in Figure 8.4. Notice the use of the 45-degree line again. ***At all points on the 45-degree line, consumption and income are equal.*** Actual consumer spending lies below the 45-degree line, however, indicating that American families tend to save some fraction of their income.

Expectations and Shifts

Although consumption generally depends on current income, we should not conclude that all individual consumption functions are identical or that the aggregate consumption function never changes. Most consumption functions are of the form $C = a + bY_D$. But the values of a and b may change. When

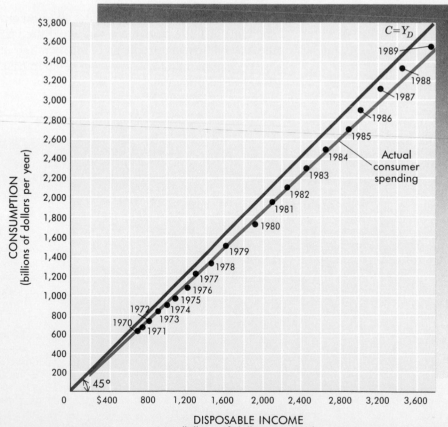

FIGURE 8.4
U.S. Consumption and Income

The points on the graph indicate the actual rates of U.S. disposable income and consumption for the years 1970—89. By connecting these dots, we can approximate the long–term consumption function. Over time, the average propensity to consume has been around 0.9.

consumers are optimistic about the future, they tend to spend more, often by borrowing or using credit (apparently in the belief that the proverbial rainy day will never come). Thus increased optimism can lead to more autonomous spending, as reflected in a larger value for a. The size of a may also increase if consumers expect higher prices later and rush to the stores to "beat inflation" (see Chapter 7).

Notice what happens to the consumption function when these things happen. In Figure 8.5, the consumption function is initially at $C = a_1 + bY_D$. When consumer confidence increases, autonomous consumption rises to a_2. The new consumption function is therefore $C = a_2 + bY_D$. The consumption function has *shifted* upward; more consumption will occur at every rate of income.

Were consumers to become more pessimistic, the consumption function would shift downward rather than upward. When the stock market plummeted in 1987, for example, consumers lost considerable wealth and became fearful about the state of the economy. Their reduced confidence caused a cutback in consumption plans (see In the News). Thus a ***surge in consumer confidence will shift the consumption function upward; a bout of pessimism will knock it down.*** The *slope* of the consumption function may also change if the MPC responds to changes in consumer confidence.

LEAKAGE FROM THE CIRCULAR FLOW

Our basic objective in this chapter is to determine whether the rate of total spending at full employment will equal the value of full-employment output, thereby minimizing problems of inflation and unemployment. With the aid of the consumption function, we can begin to assess the difficulties of achieving this desired outcome.

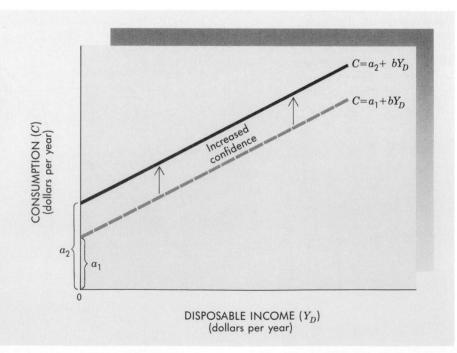

FIGURE 8.5
Shifts in the Consumption Function

The willingness of consumers to spend their current income is affected by their confidence in the future. If consumers become more optimistic, autonomous consumption may increase from a_1 to a_2. This change will shift the entire consumption function upward. It is also possible for b to change, thus changing the slope of the consumption function as well.

In The News

SHIFT OF CONSUMPTION

Crash Makes Many Fearful About Future

One out of three Americans plans to postpone or reduce a major purchase such as a house, car or vacation because of the recent stock market crash, the Los Angeles times Poll has found, a prospect that economists fear could lead to a recession.

The market plunge also has made many Americans doubtful about the future and concerned about a possible recession, regardless of whether they own stock or not, the poll found. In fact, Americans who do not own stock are more inclined to cut back on spending as a result of the crash than those who lost money in the collapse. . . .

Consumer spending—which accounts for about two-thirds of gross national product and thus is critical to the nation's economic health—had already been expected to slow down even before the market crash, in part because consumers appear to have worn themselves out from their high level of spending during earlier stages of the current economic expansion.

But the high level (31%) of Americans indicating they would cut back purchases because of the market crash came as a surprise to some economists who said they did not expect that its effects would be felt as wide and as fast, particularly among those who do not own stock.

—Bill Sing

Los Angeles Times, November 4, 1987, p. 1. Copyright © 1987 *Los Angeles times.* Reprinted by permission.

---

full-employment GNP: The total market value of final goods and services that could be produced in a given time period at full employment; potential GNP.

Suppose for the moment that we were fortunate enough to be producing at the rate of **full-employment GNP**—that is, the value of all final goods and services produced at full employment. For convenience, we shall assume that full-employment GNP adds up to $2 trillion per year. At this rate of output, we would be generating an equivalent amount of income, as every dollar spent on production ends up in someone's pocket (see Chapter 4). In Figure 8.6 we designate this level of annual income Y_F (income at full employment). For simplicity, we shall continue to assume that there is no government—and thus no taxes—and that *all* income is received by consumers. Under these assumptions, disposable income (Y_D) and GNP are identical. Thus we can relate the rate of consumer spending directly to total output.[5]

Some inkling of potential problems in maintaining full employment should already be evident. We have observed that consumers do not spend all of their income; instead, they save some fraction of it. If all income is not spent, the movement of income around the circular flow (Figure 8.2) is not continuous; on the contrary, the circular flow leaks. Saving is a primary cause of such leakage.

Total Output at Full Employment

If we are receiving $2 trillion worth of income at full employment (Y_F), then $2 trillion worth of output is being produced. Thus the horizontal axis of Figure 8.6 tells us not only how much income will be available for spending, but also the value of goods and services that will be for sale in product markets.

As before, *we use the 45-degree line to illustrate all points where spending equals income.* All points on this line are equidistant from the vertical and horizontal axes. Point Z_F on that line reminds us how much output

---

[5]Notice that we are also ignoring depreciation, retained earnings, and transfer payments. Taxes and other complications will be introduced in Chapter 9; in the meantime, these assumptions simplify the analysis without changing our basic conclusions.

FIGURE 8.6
The Aggregate Consumption Function

To determine how much output consumers will demand at full–employment output (Y_F), we refer to the aggregate consumption function. First locate full-employment GNP on the horizontal axis (at Y_F). Then move up until you reach the consumption function. In this case, the amount C_F (equal to $1,600 billion per year) will be demanded at full-employment output ($2,000 billion per year).

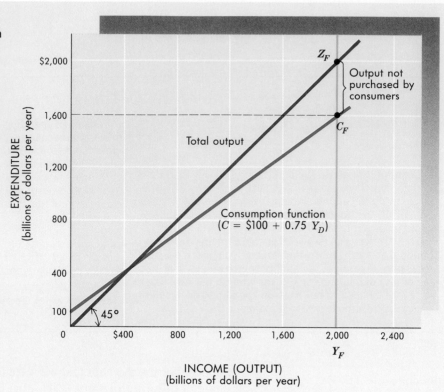

is being supplied to the market at full employment; it has the same dollar value as Y_F. Were consumers to spend that much income, all output would be sold.

Consumer Spending at Full Employment

To find out how much output will actually be demanded at Y_F, we need to look at spending behavior, as reflected in the consumption function. The consumption function tells us how much consumers will wish to spend at different income levels, including full-employment GNP.

Suppose that the aggregate consumption function is $100 billion per year + $0.75Y_D$, as illustrated in Figure 8.6. Using this function, we can determine the rate of expenditure that consumers desire to maintain when total income equals Y_F. When we substitute $2,000 billion for Y_D, we observe what the annual rate of consumer spending at full employment (C_F) is:

$$C_F = \$100 \text{ billion } + 0.75 \, (\$2,000 \text{ billion})$$

$$= \$1,600 \text{ billion}$$

We find the same conclusion in Figure 8.6 by moving up from point Y_F on the horizontal (income) axis to the consumption function and noting the value of consumer spending ($1,600 billion) at that juncture.

The message relayed by the consumption function is straightforward. If business firms produce goods and services at the rate of $2 trillion per year (and that much income), consumers will demand only $1,600 billion per year. In short, the rate of production at Y_F ($2,000 billion per year) will exceed the

W🌐RLD VIEW

CONSUMPTION

Japan's Consumers Go on a Spending Spree, and Economy Booms

TOKYO—Japanese consumers are on a buying and building binge in their own country.

"Using old things is old-fashioned, so you have to keep buying," says 40-year-old Tatsuo Saito, as he and his wife eye an American-size Japanese refrigerator to replace their two-year-old model. Mr. Saito, a small-business man, has recently bought a new color-television set, a new videocassette recorder, home lighting and a Mercedes-Benz.

Many Japanese, young and old, are giving up the self-sacrificing ways of the past. Though few are going into debt the way American consumers do, they clearly want to enjoy their own affluence. "We are on the threshold of a new age of consumer behavior," says Ryosuke Shibata, a consumer-behavior expert at Dentsu Inc., Japan's giant advertising agency.

The result: a booming economy at a time when its major trading partners are struggling to achieve growth. The Japanese built 1.6 million new homes last year, the most since 1973. That, in turn, has triggered a surge in domestic demand that is crowding stores and forcing factories to increase production.

—Damon Darlin and Masayoshi Kanabayashi

The Wall Street Journal, January 5, 1988, p. 1. Reprinted by permission of *The Wall Street Journal,* © Dow Jones & Company, Inc. (1988). All Rights Reserved.

rate of consumer expenditure ($1,600 billion per year). Unless someone else purchases the remaining output ($400 billion per year), producers will start cutting back on production. As production is cut back, people will be thrown out of work.

Consumer Saving at Full Employment

leakage: Income not spent directly on domestic output, but instead diverted from the circular flow, e.g., saving, imports, taxes.

The failure of consumers to maintain a rate of expenditure equal to the rate of full-employment output is attributable to their desire to save. People want to put aside some fraction of their current income for future use. What we want to emphasize here is that *consumer saving represents income that does not return directly to product markets as expenditure on final goods and services.* In this sense, consumer saving represents **leakage** from the circular flow (see Figure 8.7).

In our example, this leakage is substantial: at full-employment GNP, consumers desire to save $400 billion per year (recall that $S = Y_D - C$). This saving reduces the rate of expenditure below the rate of production and raises the specter of increasing unemployment. Unless other market participants (e.g., investors, the government, or foreigners) offset this leakage with purchases of their own, the shortfall in consumer spending will be reflected in growing stocks of unsold goods and services. This accumulation of unwanted inventories in stores and warehouses will ultimately lead to job layoffs.

Imports and taxes   Notice that imports as well as savings represent leakage from the circular flow. If consumers buy imported goods rather than domestic goods, some current income flows out of the domestic economy. As a consequence, domestic producers may end up with unsold output. The consequences of such leakage are potentially the same as those that occur as a result of consumer saving. Income taxes are another form of leakage, as we shall demonstrate in Chapter 10.

FIGURE 8.7
Leakage

Income saved or spent on imports does not return directly to the circular flow. As a consequence, the total value of goods demanded in a given time period may be less than the value of goods produced. If no other source of spending replaces this leakage, some goods will remain unsold and undesired inventories will accumulate.

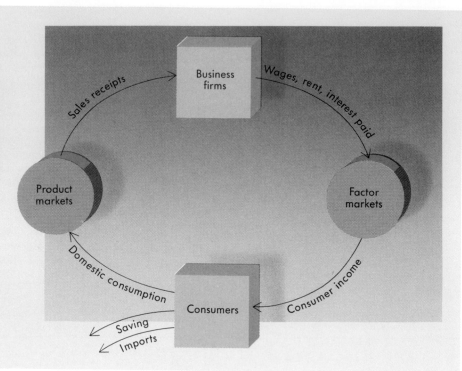

INVESTMENT

Although leakage from the circular flow is obviously a potential source of unemployment problems, we should not conclude that the economy will sink as soon as consumers start saving some of their income. Consumers are not, after all, the only ones who buy goods and services in product markets; business firms and government agencies also contribute to total spending. So do foreigners who buy our exports. So before we run out in the streets screaming, "The circular flow is leaking!" we need to take a look at what other market participants are doing.

Business firms purchase new plant and equipment for the purpose of expanding or improving their output capabilities; such purchases are called *fixed investment*. Firms also acquire inventories of goods that can be used to satisfy consumer demands; such expenditures are called *inventory investment*. Both forms of **investment** represent a demand for output and are therefore counted as part of aggregate spending.[6]

Because investment spending represents a demand for current output, it might compensate for the leakage created by consumer saving. ***Investment represents an injection into the circular flow that may offset the leakage caused by consumer saving.*** But how much investment will take place? Will it be large enough to offset the leakage due to consumer saving? Or will leakages exceed injections, thus causing the circular flow of spending and income to fall below the level of full-employment GNP? To answer these questions, we need to look at how investment decisions are made.

investment: Expenditures on (production of) new plant and equipment (capital) in a given time period, plus changes in business inventories.

[6]Residential construction is also counted in investment statistics, even though houses are a consumer good. The durability of housing motivates this accounting decision.

Expectations   There are several theories about what determines the rate of desired investment spending, but two explanations are most common. First, we recognize that a firm's desire to invest reflects its *expectations* of future sales and profits. Investment decisions are influenced less by *current* income levels than by expectations of *future* income and sales. Surely no firm would want to purchase new plant and equipment unless its managers were convinced that people would later buy the output produced by that plant and that equipment. Nor would producers want to accumulate larger inventories of goods if they thought sales were going to decline. Thus favorable expectations of future sales are a necessary condition for investment spending.

No one is entirely sure what shapes investors' expectations. Essentially, it is a question of confidence in the future course of economic events. Whatever raises investor hopes for economic growth and increased sales will stimulate additional investment (see In the News). Favorable tax or budget policy, new inventions, or unanticipated sales increases can all raise investor expectations. On the other hand, an unwelcome event—a coal strike or an oil shortage, for example—may shake investors' faith in the course of economic events. Whatever the reasons, expectations are as uncertain as the future itself and are not easy to predict.

Interest Rates   The second major determinant of desired investment spending is the rate of interest. Business firms often borrow money in order to purchase plant and equipment. Naturally, they will be concerned about the cost of such borrowing, as reflected in the rate of interest they have to pay. The higher the rate of interest, the costlier it is to invest. Accordingly, we anticipate a lower rate of investment spending at higher interest rates, more investment at lower rates (*ceteris paribus*).

Figure 8.8 summarizes the influence of expectations and interest rates on investment demand. The curve I_1 tells us how much investment spending business firms will want to undertake at various interest rates, given some

In The News

EXPECTATIONS

Capital Outlays To Grow 7.8% At U.S. Firms

Commerce Survey Shows Higher Spending in '90 Than Earlier Forecasts

WASHINGTON—U.S. businesses, showing unexpected optimism about the economy, plan to increase capital spending 7.8% this year, the Commerce Department reported.

Despite evidence that business activity remains sluggish, companies told the department in a survey taken in January and February that they plan to spend $512.82 billion on new plant and equipment this year.

Two Years of Booming Spending

This year's expected growth would follow two years of booming capital spending, and could keep the eight-year economic expansion alive. The survey suggests higher spending than econometric models have been forecasting, said Gordon Richards, an economist for the National Association of Manufacturers. Many analysts didn't anticipate companies would increase capital spending as much because economic growth has been slow because of high interest rates.

—Katherine Walsh

The Wall Street Journal, April 12, 1990, p. A2. Reprinted by permission of *The Wall Street Journal* © Dow Jones & Company, Inc. (1990). All rights reserved.

FIGURE 8.8
Investment Demand

The rate of desired investment depends on expectations, the rate of interest, and innovation. A *change* in expectations will *shift* the investment-demand curve. With given expectations, a change in the rate of interest will lead to *movements* along the existing investment-demand curve. In this case, an increase in investment beyond $300 billion per year (point *A*) may be caused by lower interest rates (point *B*) or improved expectations (point *C*). Keynes emphasized the role of investor expectations in maintaining full-employment spending.

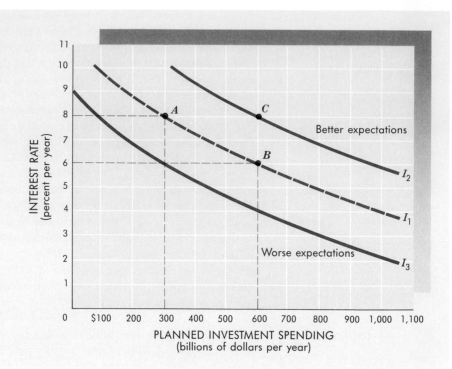

fixed set of expectations about future sales and profits. Within this context, we see that lower rates of interest lead to higher rates of investment (compare points *A* and *B*).

Curves I_2 and I_3 illustrate the impact on investment demand of a *change* in expectations. If investors suddenly foresee improved prospects for sales and profits, they will be more eager to invest. They will borrow more money at any given interest rate and use it to buy plant and equipment. This increased willingness to borrow is illustrated by a rightward *shift* of the investment curve to I_2 (that is, greater investment at any given interest rate). On the other hand, should investors' faith in the future be shaken, expectations will worsen and the investment curve will shift to the left (I_3).

Technology and Innovation

The demand for investment goods may shift for other reasons as well. When scientists learned how to miniaturize electronic circuitry, an entire new industry of electronic calculators, watches, and other goods sprang to life. In this case, the demand for investment goods shifted to the right as a result of improved miniaturized circuits and imaginative innovation (the use of the new technology in pocket calculators). More recently, technological advances and cost reductions have stimulated an investment spree in lap-top computers (see Chapter 22), compact-disc players, fax machines, and lifesaving medical equipment.

Investment at Full Employment

Because the demand for investment goods is so heavily influenced by expectations, interest rates, technology, and innovation, Keynes concluded that it is *not* very sensitive to current levels of income. This is in marked contrast to the demand for consumer goods, which Keynes asserted was directly determined by the level of current income.

As long as investment spending is *not* sensitive to the rate of current income, the investment function may be drawn as a horizontal line in Figure 8.9, which has current income on the horizontal axis. Notice that the assumed rate of investment spending is $300 billion per year, regardless of the level of total income. Remember our assumption that *the rate of desired investment spending depends on expectations, the rate of interest, and technology, but **not** on the current level of income.*

To determine the desired rate of investment at full employment (or any other rate of output), we must refer back to Figure 8.8, check the current rate of interest, and see how much investment businesses desire to undertake.[7] For the moment we will assume that the rate of interest is 8 percent and thus that the desired rate of investment spending is $300 billion per year (point *A* in Figure 8.8).

TOTAL SPENDING AT FULL EMPLOYMENT ────────────

Consumption and Investment

Figure 8.9 also tells us how much *combined* consumer and investor spending will occur at every rate of output. Consider the rate of full-employment GNP again. From the consumption function, we know that consumers will want to spend the amount C_F ($1,600 billion per year) at the output level Y_F ($2,000 billion per year). Now we know that investors will want to spend the additional amount I_F ($300 billion per year). By simply adding these two quantities, we can determine the total spending of consumers and investors at full employ-

[7]This is a turn that real-world policymakers often miss, since they seldom have such a detailed map to follow. More on this in Chapter 17.

FIGURE 8.9
A Spending Shortfall

Desired consumer and investor expenditure at full-employment output (Y_F) may not equal total output. In this case, C_F equals $1,600 billion and I_F equals $300 billion. Thus total spending ($C_F + I_F$) is $100 billion per year less than full-employment output. As a consequence, producers will accumulate unwanted inventories ($100 billion) if they maintain full–employment output.

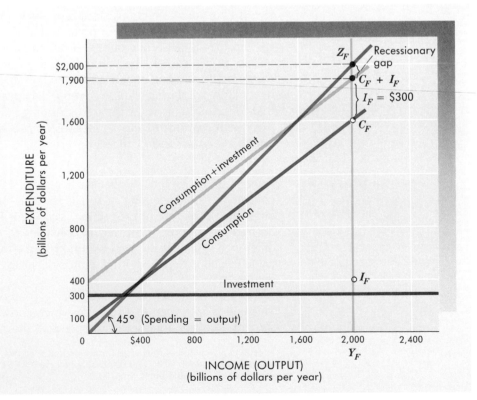

ment. It is C_F plus I_F, or $1,900 billion per year. If we perform the same kind of addition at other income levels, we can quickly confirm that the "consumption plus investment" line expresses the total value of goods and services demanded by consumers and investors at alternative rates of output (income). This line—the Keynesian *aggregate spending function*—reflects the rate of desired spending at different levels of income.

Government Spending and Exports

Consumption and investment are not the only forms of spending, as any taxpayer or traveler knows. As we observed in Chapter 3, government expenditures on goods and services represent over 20 percent of total spending. Purchases by foreigners of the goods and services we produce (exports) also represent a significant fraction of total demand (see World View). Hence our analysis of spending behavior will not be complete until we have examined the determinants of these additional sources of demand. But we can simplify our analysis by ignoring government expenditure and exports for the moment. We will simply pretend that domestic consumers and investors are the only participants in the product market. This has the advantage of illustrating how a completely *private* economy would function, without government purchases or foreign trade.[8] We shall reconsider the expenditure decisions of government and foreigners in the next chapter.

POTENTIAL INSTABILITY

Assuming for the moment that consumers and business firms are the only purchasers of the goods and services produced—that government agencies and foreigners do not exist—we may say that the combined expenditure desires of consumers and investors represent (private) *aggregate spending* for goods and services. The question now is how these spending intentions compare to the value of total output at full employment.

As noted earlier, the 45-degree line in Figure 8.9 represents all points where total spending equals total income. This line doesn't tell us, however, how much people will want to spend at any given income level. To determine that, we must look at the desired spending $(C + I)$ curve. ***Only where the aggregate spending curve intersects the 45-degree line will desired spending equal total output.***

A Recessionary Gap

recessionary gap: The amount by which desired spending at full employment falls short of full-employment output.

Figure 8.9 tells us that this is clearly not the case at full employment. On the contrary, desired spending at Y_F falls short of total output. At full-employment output (Y_F), the rate of production is S_F ($2,000 billion per year); the rate of desired expenditure, however, is only $C_F + I_F$ ($1,900 billion per year). The difference is called the **recessionary gap**—the amount by which the total value of goods supplied at full employment exceeds the total value of goods demanded.

In our example, the recessionary gap amounts to $100 billion per year. This gap is also seen in Table 8.2, which shows the amount of income consumers and investors desire to spend at alternative income (output) levels.

[8]A second advantage of this simplification is that it allows us to ignore the distinction between net national product (NNP) and disposable income (DI), since the two concepts differ primarily as a result of taxes and public transfers.

W🌐RLD VIEW

EXPORT DEMAND

Exports Boost U.S. Industrial Capacity Usage

America's factories, mines and utilities operated at 80.5 percent of capacity in July, the highest rate in 18 months, as manufacturers continued to benefit from larger export sales, the government reported yesterday.

The Federal Reserve said that the July operating rate was 1.3 percentage points higher than a year ago and that steel and other primary metal manufacturers were operating at the highest rate in almost six years.

"Manufacturing is coming back. There is no doubt about it," said Tom Megan, an economist with Evans Economics in Washington.

Analysts credited the rebound to the 40 percent decrease in the value of the dollar over the past two years, which has made U.S. products more competitive overseas.

John Hagens, an economist with Wharton Economics of Bala Cynwyd, Pa., said that the turnaround has been concentrated in nondurable-goods industries such as paper, textiles, plastics and chemicals.

High export sales in these industries have left them with exceptionally high operating rates. Paper factories were operating at 96 percent of capacity, the highest level of any industry. . . .

—Martin Crutsinger

The Washington Post, August 18, 1987, p. £1. Reprinted by permission of The Associated Press.

At the full-employment rate of production Y_F, consumers desire to spend $1,600 billion per year and investors desire to spend $300 billion, leaving $100 billion worth of goods unsold.

An Inflationary Gap

inflationary gap: The amount by which desired spending at full employment exceeds full-employment output.

We will not always be burdened with a recessionary gap. Under some circumstances, total desired spending at full employment might actually exceed full-employment output. This would create an **inflationary gap,** in which people want to buy more at full-employment output than the economy can produce. The resulting pressure is likely to push prices higher.

TABLE 8.2   A Recessionary Gap
(all figures in billions of dollars per year)

The recessionary gap is measured at the full-employment level of income. At this level (Y_F), consumers and investors desire to spend less than the economy produces. This difference ($100 billion) between full-employment output and expenditure is called the "recessionary gap." It is illustrated in Figure 8.9.

At income (output) of:	Consumers desire to spend:	+	Investors desire to spend:	=	Total private spending
$ 400	$ 400		$300		$ 700
800	700		300		1,000
1,200	1,000		300		1,300
1,600	1,300		300		1,600
Y_F = 2,000	1,600		300		1,900

Desired vs. Actual Investment

Our purpose here is not to show that an imbalance will necessarily exist between the desired spending at full employment and the rate of production. We wish to show only that such an imbalance is possible. We also want to observe what happens when such an imbalance does exist.

Consider first the imbalance created when supply exceeds demand at full employment. When such a recessionary gap emerges, producers are unable to sell all the goods that they had hoped to. The goods don't disappear, however. As we have emphasized before, all output produced must go to someone. In this case, the unsold goods pile up on producers' shelves as additional inventory. In the auto industry, the unsold goods accumulate on dealers' lots (see In the News). Producers don't want this added inventory, but they are stuck with it if consumer spending is too low. Ironically, this additional inventory is counted as part of investment spending. (Recall that

In The News

UNDESIRED INVENTORY

Inventory Buildup Could Pose Threat for Some Big Companies

Heard on the Street

NEW YORK—It *is* possible to have too much of a good thing.

Especially inventory. When business inventories are on the rise while sales are slackening, it's a classic harbinger of recession—and it's exactly what happened in September.

Autos, metals and even a big retailer here and there are already showing signs of inventory problems, analysts say—and a bulge of unsold goods won't be helpful to stock prices. It isn't clear, of course, whether the now-spotty distress will ripple through large parts of the economy. Business stockpiles for the nation as a whole remain roughly on a par with those of recent months.

Yet inventory problems are already at hand for some of the nation's biggest companies, notably General Motors and K mart, analysts say.

GM has the fattest inventories of the Big Three U.S. auto makers, as the nearby table shows. . . .

Government numbers also showed rising inventories at retailers in September. The most serious buildup is probably at K mart, according to Linda Kristiansen, retail analyst for Dean Witter, a unit of Sears Roebuck.

K mart's inventory is up 17% from year-ago levels, but sales have risen only 5.5%, she says. "It's a problem that's been developing all year. A lot of it is in hard goods, not apparel." The result, she says, is that K mart will have to reduce prices to get inventories down to better proportions. . . .

Acres of Unsold Cars
Dealer inventories on Oct. 31, as calculated by Ronald A. Glantz of Montgomery Securities. He uses a year-to-date selling rate to gauge supplies on dealer lots.

	Unsold days' supply		Percent above normal*
	Cars	Trucks	
General Motors	70 days	87 days	18%
Chrysler	69	88	17
Ford	63	76	5

*Normal defined as a 20-year average for cars and trucks combined.

Other industries where inventory problems are starting to crop up include appliances and building materials, plus some segments of the paper, chemicals and capital-equipment industries, says A. Gary Shilling, a New York economist.

With the economy slowing, inventories of the nation's manufacturers, retailers and wholesalers in September edged up 0.2% from August to $791.82 billion, as sales slipped 0.3% to $524.58 billion. So far, business inventories are holding at a respectable ratio of 1.51 times sales. But if sales keep declining while inventories rise further, the pattern would be a recessionary one.

—John R. Dorfman

The Wall Street Journal, November 28, 1989, p. C1. Reprinted by permission of *The Wall Street Journal,* © Dow Jones & Company, Inc. (1989). All Rights Reserved.

our definition of investment spending includes changes in business inventories.) This additional inventory is clearly undesired, however, as producers had planned on selling these goods.

To keep track of these unwanted changes in investment, we **distinguish desired *(or planned)* investment from** actual **investment.** *Desired* investment represents purchases of new plant and equipment plus any desired changes in business inventories. By contrast, *actual* investment represents purchases of new plant and equipment plus *actual* changes in business inventories, desired or otherwise. In other words,

$$\bullet \quad \frac{\text{Actual}}{\text{investment}} = \frac{\text{desired}}{\text{investment}} + \frac{\text{undesired}}{\text{investment}}$$

If actual investment at full employment equals desired investment, producers' plans have been fulfilled. No imbalance exists between the rates of expenditure and production at full employment. By contrast, *a recessionary gap implies that producers' expectations have not been fulfilled: actual investment exceeds desired investment and excess (undesired) inventories are piling up.* An inflationary gap, on the other hand, implies that desired investment at full employment exceeds actual investment and that inventories are being depleted faster than producers desire. By observing changes in producer inventories, then, we may detect potential imbalances in product markets.

Desired Investment vs. Desired Saving

Imbalances between desired spending and production are also reflected in differences between desired saving by consumers and desired investment by producers. In particular, a recessionary gap implies that desired saving exceeds desired investment. In our illustration of Keynesian demand, we observed (Figure 8.6) that consumers desire to spend only $1,600 billion per year at full-employment output ($2,000 billion). By implication, then, they desire to save (not spend) $400 billion per year. This $400 billion represents leakage from the circular flow.

We also observed that desired producer investment spending in this case amounts to only $300 billion per year, not enough to compensate for the leakage represented by consumer saving. From this perspective, *a recessionary gap emerges because desired investment is less than desired saving at full employment.* The leakage caused by saving is not being fully replaced by injections of investment spending. As a consequence, producers will be unable to sell all the goods they have produced at the prices they expected. The relationship between desired investment and desired saving is illustrated in Figure 8.10. The consumption function is identical to the one used in previous graphs—that is,

$$C = \$100 \text{ billion} + 0.75\,Y$$

What is new to this graph is the savings function. Because saving equals unspent income, we have the following savings function:

$$\bullet \quad S = Y - C$$

Thus

$$S = Y - (\$100 \text{ billion} + 0.75\,Y)$$
$$= -\$100 \text{ billion} + 0.25\,Y$$

FIGURE 8.10
Desired Saving and Investment

The savings function indicates desired saving at each income level. By definition, desired saving equals $Y - C$.

In this case, desired saving at full employment equals $400 (point F). This exceeds desired investment (point G). Because leakage exceeds injections, the level of income will fall.

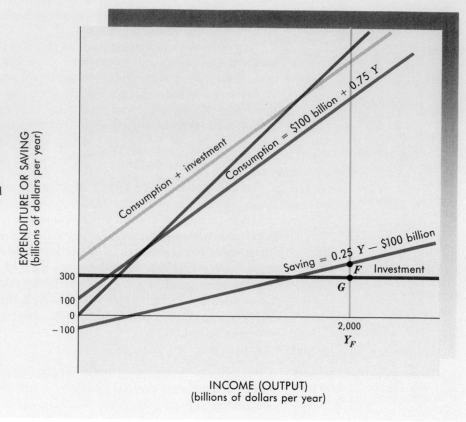

Consumption + investment

Consumption = $100 billion + 0.75 Y

Saving = 0.25 Y − $100 billion

F Investment

G

EXPENDITURE OR SAVING (billions of dollars per year)

300
100
0
−100

2,000

Y_F

INCOME (OUTPUT)
(billions of dollars per year)

W🌐RLD VIEW

UNDESIRED INVENTORY

High Inventories Force Cuts on Japanese Carmakers

April may be one of the kinder months for watchers of the U.S. trade deficit. For the past several years auto imports slackened in the first quarter, after Japanese carmakers had used up their export quotas. Then, with the Apr. 1 start of Japan's fiscal year and new quotas, car imports would surge. But this year may be different.

Over the past 12 months higher prices have dampened sales, even as Japanese car companies worried that quotas might be cut if each failed to ship all the cars it was allotted. Hence, they continued to export more cars even as sales lagged and inventories rose. As of Feb. 1, Nissan had 133 days' worth of cars on hand in the U.S., up from 76 days a year earlier, according to *Automotive News*, and Isuzu's inventories jumped to 168 days from 71 on Jan. 1.

So the Japanese are cutting back. Even though car and truck sales in Japan are booming, production in January dropped 2%. That at least implies that there could be fewer cars clearing U.S. customs come April than last year, and it foreshadows even fewer imports during the summer months.

—James B. Treece

Reprinted from March 14, 1988, issue of *Business Week* by special permission, copyright © 1988 by McGraw-Hill, Inc.

This savings function is drawn in Figure 8.10. Notice that consumers *dissave* $100 billion per year when they have no income. They continue to dissave until they have $400 billion of income. At still higher income levels, saving continues to increase by 25 cents for every additional dollar of income (the marginal propensity to save equals 0.25, as the preceding equation reveals).

The most important thing about Figure 8.10 is the relationship between desired saving and desired investment. Recall our earlier assumption that businesses desire to invest $300 billion (the horizontal investment function). What Figure 8.10 illustrates is the gap between saving and investment plans. At full employment, consumers desire to save $400 billion, more than investors desire to spend. Hence leakage (saving) exceeds injections (investment) at full employment. As undesired inventories accumulate, producers are likely to reduce the rate of production and lay off workers, sending us down the long road to unemployment.

POLICY INSIGHTS:

MACRO FAILURE

The emergence of an imbalance between desired spending and full-employment production threatens our economic goals. If desired spending at full employment is less than the rate of production, some workers will not be needed and unemployment will spread. Such an imbalance—a recessionary gap—is the origin of **cyclical unemployment.**

cyclical unemployment: Unemployment attributable to a lack of job vacancies, i.e., to an inadequate level of aggregate demand.

When desired spending at full employment exceeds production, a different problem emerges. In this case, consumers and investors begin to compete with each other for the goods and services available. Production cannot be expanded beyond full-employment GNP without exerting upward pressure on prices. As a consequence, competition for available goods and services drives prices upward, setting in motion a **demand-pull inflation.**

demand-pull inflation: An increase in the price level initiated by excessive aggregate demand.

Although unemployment and inflation may arise from other causes (to be examined later), the potential imbalances we have described here go a long way toward explaining many of our economic problems. How serious these problems become depends on how producers, workers, and consumers respond to the initial imbalance between desired spending at full employment and the rate of production. Classical economists thought the economy would adjust quickly to a recessionary gap, setting in motion forces that would close it. Keynesian economists, however, drawing from the lessons of the 1930s, have suggested that a recessionary gap may cripple the economy so severely that it cannot recover on its own. In Chapter 9 we shall examine how the economy responds to both recessionary and inflationary gaps. If Keynes was right—if the economy does not adjust automatically to these macro failures— then the government may have strong grounds for intervening in the macro economy.

SUMMARY

- The Keynesian model of the business cycle is unique in its assumptions of (1) no automatic "self-adjustment" to full employment and (2) a horizontal aggregate supply curve.

• Keynes emphasized the role of aggregate demand (especially shifts thereof) in determining the equilibrium rate of output. With the price level assumed constant (a horizontal aggregate supply curve), the rate of dollar spending directly reflects the (real) demand for goods and services.

• Macro failure occurs when the desired rate of spending at full employment is not equal to the value of output (full-employment GNP). To determine whether unemployment or inflation might occur, we must assess the spending plans of consumers (C), investors (I), the government (G), and foreign buyers (net exports $= X - M$).

• The rate of desired consumer spending (C) at any income level can be calculated from the consumption function $C = a + bY_D$. The marginal propensity to consume (b) in this function tells us what fraction of added disposable income will be spent on goods and services. What is not spent is saved.

• A potential imbalance between total spending and total output first arises because consumers save some of their income, creating a leak in the circular flow. To offset this leak, we need additional spending from somewhere else.

• Business-investment expenditures represent an injection into the circular flow that might offset saving leakage. Business firms purchase new plant and equipment and accumulate inventories of goods and services; all such investments augment total spending.

• We have no assurance that desired investment at full-employment GNP will equal desired consumer saving. On the contrary, the rate of desired investment spending depends on sales expectations, interest rates, and technology and may differ from the rate of desired saving.

• A recessionary gap emerges whenever the level of desired spending at full employment is less than full-employment GNP. In a completely private and closed economy (no government or foreign trade), a recessionary gap will appear whenever desired saving at full employment exceeds desired investment. The gap will appear as an increase in unsold goods and services (undesired inventories) and may lead to cutbacks in production and employment.

• An inflationary gap emerges when the rate of desired expenditure at full employment exceeds the rate of output, setting the stage for demand-pull inflation.

Terms to Remember Define the following terms:

aggregate demand	**marginal propensity to save**
aggregate supply	**(MPS)**
equilibrium (macro)	**consumption function**
aggregate spending	**dissaving**
derived demand	**full-employment GNP**
consumption	**leakage**
disposable income (DI)	**investment**
saving	**recessionary gap**
average propensity to consume	**inflationary gap**
(APC)	**cyclical unemployment**
marginal propensity to consume	**demand-pull inflation**
(MPC)	

Questions for Discussion

1. What factors other than current income might influence consumer spending? How would changes in these factors affect the consumption function?

2. Are current sales really ignored in investment decisions? How might changes in current sales affect expectations or the rate of desired investment? Illustrate graphically.

3. Why do imbalances in the rates of expenditure and production at full employment arise? How might they be avoided?

4. If the price level were not constant (Keynes assumed it was), how would changes in total spending affect the quantity of goods and services demanded (aggregate demand)?

Problems

1. Assume that the consumption function is $C = \$150 + 0.8Y$, that desired investment is $500, and that no other forms of expenditure exist.
   (a) Complete the following table (all numbers in billions of dollars per year):

At Income of:	C	+	I	=	Desired Private Spending
$ 500	$550		$500		$1,050
700	___		___		___
1,000	___		___		___
1,200	___		___		___
1,500	___		___		___
2,000	___		___		___

   (b) If full employment is $2,000, how large is the recessionary or inflationary gap?
   (c) Illustrate the gap on a graph.

2. From the information in the table in problem 1 compute the amount of saving at each rate of income shown. At what rate of income would consumer saving equal desired investment?

3. For each of the following situations, decide whether there will be a shift of or a movement along the consumption function.
   (a) Disposable income increases.
   (b) Consumers switch their purchases from domestically produced goods to imports.
   (c) The government increases taxes.
   (d) The stock market crashes; people become scared that they are holding too much debt and therefore begin to use more of their income to repay their debts.
   (e) People become fearful that the Social Security system will go bankrupt, so they decide to save more of their income for old age.
   (f) A depression lowers disposable incomes.

4. Using the consumption and investment functions of Figure 8.9, determine how much income is needed to generate total spending equal to full-employment output.

CHAPTER 9

Potential Instability

An imbalance between desired spending and desired production can lead to economic instability. As we observed in Chapter 8, if the rate of desired spending at full employment is not equal to the rate of production, we may confront macro failure. But the amount of unemployment or inflation that results and the length of time it lasts depend on the way the economy responds to recessionary and inflationary gaps. If the gaps are closed quickly, the resulting unemployment or inflation will be of little lasting significance. But if such gaps persist, the resulting unemployment or inflation may do real damage.

Our objective in this chapter is to examine the economy's response to imbalances between desired spending and output. Specifically,

- How do producers respond to an imbalance between output and sales?

- How do consumers respond to changes in output and income?

- What macro outcomes will these responses create?

As noted in Chapter 5, the Classical theory of the adjustment process concluded that recessionary gaps and their resulting unemployment would be short-lived. The Keynesian theory of the adjustment process, on the other hand, suggests that a recessionary gap will lead to prolonged periods of unemployment unless deliberate steps are taken to close it. Keynesian perspectives on the adjustment to an inflationary gap are equally pessimistic about the prospects for a "natural" return to a more desired equilibrium.

ADJUSTMENT TO A RECESSIONARY GAP

A **recessionary gap** emerges when desired spending at full employment falls short of full-employment output. In a completely closed (no foreign trade) and private (no government) economy, *a recessionary gap occurs when desired saving exceeds desired investment.* In Chapter 8, this situation arose when consumers desired to spend only $1,600 billion per year at the full-employment rate of income ($2,000 billion per year). This left $400 billion earmarked for desired saving (see Table 9.1). Because this saving exceeded the rate of desired investment ($300 billion per year), a recessionary gap of $100 billion emerged. The critical question is how the economy adjusts to this imbalance between desired saving and desired investment.

recessionary gap: The amount by which desired spending at full employment falls short of full-employment output.

TABLE 9.1   An Initial Recessionary Gap
(in billions of dollars per year)

The consumption and investment schedules tell us how much people desire to spend at various rates of income (output). In this case, consumption and investment desires at full employment (Y_F) fall short of full-employment output. Desired consumption and investment spending at Y_F amounts to only $1,900 per year, $100 short of full-employment output.

At output (income) level of:	Consumers' desire to spend	Consumers' desire to save	Investors' desire to invest	Recessionary gap*
$ 400	$ 400	$ 0	$300	—
800	700	100	300	—
1,200	1,000	200	300	—
1,600	1,300	300	300	—
$Y_F = 2,000$	1,600	400	300	100

*Measured only at full employment.

Classical Adjustment: A Recap

Classical economists believed that desired investment would increase and so close the recessionary gap. Their optimism was based on the assumption that interest rates would fall in a recession, inducing business to buy more plant and equipment.

The excess of desired saving that causes a recessionary gap will tend to reduce interest rates. As consumer savings pile up in banks, lenders will lower the rate of interest in the hope of attracting additional borrowers.

But will lower interest rates stimulate additional investment? Classical economists thought so. As we observed in Chapter 8, the rate of desired investment spending is influenced by the rate of interest. In the specific example we used, producers' desire to invest $300 billion was determined by the investment-demand function and an assumed 8 percent rate of interest. This intention is illustrated again by point *A* in Figure 9.1*a*.

Figure 9.1*a* suggests that a lower interest rate would stimulate more investment. Indeed, it appears that if interest rates were to drop to 7 percent, desired investment would increase to $400 billion per year (point *D*). Such an increase in investment would be enough to close the recessionary gap of Table 9.1, thus averting the pains of unemployment.

Keynes: Changing Expectations

Keynes accepted the Classical argument that an excess of desired saving would tend to lower the rate of interest. But he suggested that a lower interest rate would not be an adequate incentive for additional investment. Businesses buy new plant and equipment and accumulate desired inventories only if they expect increased sales. Yet a recessionary gap implies that they are not even able to sell their current output. Why, then, should business firms want to *expand* their production or sales capacity? Keynes argued that it was more reasonable to anticipate that sales expectations will drop when a recessionary gap emerges. Further, this loss of confidence might overwhelm any investment stimulus resulting from lower interest rates.

Keynes's view of investment decisions is reflected in our earlier distinction between *shifts* of the investment function and movements along any particular investment-demand curve. **If expectations worsen, the entire investment function may shift to the left**, implying a *lower* rate of investment at any given rate of interest. Notice in Figure 9.1*b*, for example, that worsened

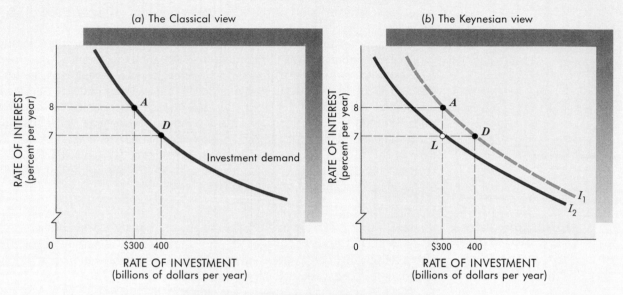

FIGURE 9.1 Contrasting Views of Investment

(*a*) **Classical economists emphasized the influence of interest rates on investment. If interest rates fall far enough, any desired rate of investment can be attained. In this case, a drop in interest rates from 8 percent to 7 percent stimulates an additional $100 billion in investment. This additional investment closes the recessionary gap.**

(*b*) **Keynes stressed that worsened expectations shift the entire investment demand curve (*I*₁) to the left (to *I*₂). Thus lower interest rates may not result in more investment. In this case, we move from point *A* to point *L* rather than point *D*. The recessionary gap may persist—or even widen.**

expectations shift the investment function from I_1 to I_2. As a result of this shift, the rate of desired investment spending remains at $300 billion per year (point L) despite a reduced interest rate. In other words, the Classical as-

In The News

REDUCED EXPECTATIONS

Businessmen Cut Back on Investment

Plagued by high interest rates, collapsing markets and fast declining profits, businessmen are slashing their plans to invest in new plants and equipment, jeopardizing a key element of the Reagan economic program.

A Commerce Department survey released yesterday showed businesses plan to invest 2.4 percent less this year than they did in 1981, after adjustment for inflation. The new survey indicates a sharp reversal in business spending plans since the start of the year.

Most private forecasters expect the actual cutbacks in investment will turn out to be even larger than shown by the survey.

—John M. Berry

The Washington Post, June 11, 1982. Copyright © 1982 The Washington Post.

sumption that lower interest rates will drive us from point A to point D is upset by a leftward shift of the investment function. This shift leaves us at point L.

The Keynesian emphasis on expectations suggests that the Classical economists' optimism was ill-founded. If expectations worsen in response to recessionary gap, we have no assurance that desired investment spending will rise to the level of desired saving at full employment. Indeed, the rate of investment may actually *decline* once sales start dropping. Even if interest rates continue to fall, expectations may continue to worsen as well, constantly frustrating the effort to close the recessionary gap. This was evidently the case in the Great Depression. Total U.S. investment fell from $16 billion in 1929 to only $1.4 billion in 1933, despite a steep decline in interest rates (to a low of 1.5 percent!).

Inflexible Prices and Wages

It appears that a flexible interest rate might not equalize desired saving and investment. But what about flexible prices and wages? Classical economists also asserted that falling prices and wages would stimulate enough additional spending to close a recessionary gap.

Keynes rejected this view of the adjustment process as well. To begin with, prices and wages are not easily reduced. Many producers are unwilling to lower product prices in the face of a short-run decline in sales. Moreover, they have no assurance that wages and other factor costs can be reduced to compensate for lower product prices. On the contrary, not only do workers typically respond angrily to any suggestion of wage reductions, but labor unions and other employee organizations have often secured contracts that prohibit such reductions.

Keynes argued that even if prices and wages did fall in response to a recessionary gap, such wage and price reductions would not restore full employment. On the contrary, such price and wage reductions might actually aggravate the unemployment problem by reducing disposable income. This was the conclusion that made Keynesian theory so revolutionary.

THE MULTIPLIER PROCESS

Suppose for the moment that the economy is chugging merrily along at full employment when a recessionary gap of $100 billion per year suddenly appears (Table 9.1). The gap itself may be due to a downward shift of the consumption function (Figure 8.5) or a sudden drop in other spending (e.g., investment, exports, or government purchases). Whatever its origins, confirmation of the recession will be evident in growing piles of undesired inventory.

As undesired inventory begins to accumulate, producers will respond either by reducing wages and prices or by cutting back on production (laying off workers). The buildup of undesired auto inventories led to layoffs in that industry in early 1990 (see In the News). Such layoffs reduce disposable income. Wage reductions have the same effect. Those consumers who end up with less income will not be able to purchase as many goods and services as they did before. As a consequence, the total value of goods and services demanded will fall further, leading to still larger stocks of unsold goods, more

In The News

PRODUCTION CUTBACKS

Layoffs at Big Three Spreading

DETROIT — Robert Stempel came to the North American International Auto Show to talk about electric cars, supercharged engines and sleek styling.

Instead, the General Motors Corp. president got question after question this week about the health of the auto industry, which is caught in its biggest spasm of layoffs since the early 1980s. Finally, Stempel grew exasperated. The Big Three will emerge from their latest slump, he said summarily, "when the customers come back to the showrooms."

Tell that to the quarter of the nation's autoworkers—133,500—who have been getting layoff notices since December from automakers struggling to cut production to meet falling demand. Some of those workers are being idled for as little as a week, but several thousand at GM will be out of work "indefinitely," along with 1,700 Chrysler workers. Auto executives refuse to rule out more "down weeks" in the near future. Meantime, sales continue to drag: On Thursday GM reported that its December car sales were off 27.6% from December 1988; Ford's fell 28.4%; and Chrysler's were down 31.2%.

The layoffs touch almost every corner of the country.

—James Cox and James R. Healey

USA Today, January 5, 1990, p. 1B. Copyright © 1990 USA TODAY. Reprinted with permission.

---

job layoffs, and further reductions in income. It is this sequence of events—called the *multiplier process*—that makes a recessionary gap so frightening.

We can see the multiplier process at work by watching what happens to the $100 billion gap as it makes its way around the circular flow (Figure 9.2). At first (Step 1), the only thing that happens is that unsold goods appear (in the form of undesired inventories). Producers adjust to this problem by cutting back on production and laying off workers or reducing wages and prices (Step 2). In either case, consumer income falls $100 billion per year shortly after the recessionary gap emerges (Step 3).

How will consumers respond to this drop in disposable income? Keynes asserted that consumer spending depends on consumers' disposable incomes. Hence *if disposable income falls, we expect consumer spending to drop as well*. In fact, the **consumption function** tells us just how much spending will drop.

The general form of the consumption function is

$$\bullet \quad C = a + bY_D$$

According to the specific function we examined in Chapter 8

Annual consumption = $100 billion + (0.75) income

The **marginal propensity to consume (MPC)** in this function equals 0.75. Therefore, we anticipate that consumers will reduce their spending by 75 cents for every dollar of lost income. In the present example, the loss of $100 billion of annual income will force consumers to reduce their rate of spending by $75 billion per year ($0.75 \times \$100$ billion). This drop in spending is illustrated by Step 4 in Figure 9.2.

consumption function: A mathematical relationship indicating the rate of desired consumer spending at various income levels.

marginal propensity to consume (MPC): The fraction of each additonal (marginal) dollar of disposable income spent on consumption; the change in consumption divided by the change in disposable income.

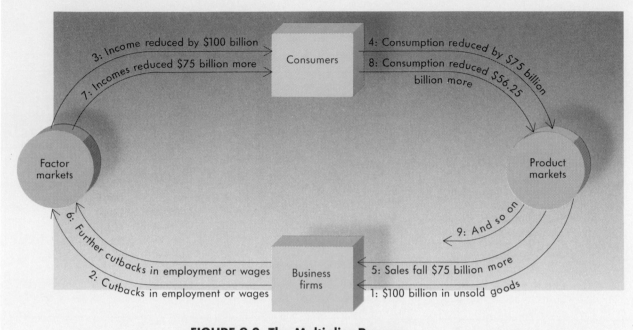

FIGURE 9.2 The Multiplier Process

A recessionary gap may lead to a cutback in production and income. A reduction in total income will in turn lead to a reduction in consumer spending. These additional cuts in spending cause a further decrease in income, leading to additional spending reductions, and so on. This sequence of adjustments is referred to as the "multiplier process."

The multiplier process does not stop here. A reduction in consumer spending quickly translates into more unsold output (Step 5). As additional goods pile up on producers' shelves, we anticipate further cutbacks in production, employment, and wages (Step 6), in accordance with the principle of derived demand.

As consumer incomes are further reduced by job layoffs and wage cuts (Step 7), more reductions in consumer spending are sure to follow (Step 8). Again the marginal propensity to consume (MPC) tells us how large such reductions will be. With an MPC of 0.75, we may expect spending to fall by another $56.25 billion per year (0.75 × $75 billion).

The Multiplier   The multiplier process continues to work until the reductions in income and sales become so small that no one's market behavior is significantly affected. We need not examine each step along the way, because all the steps begin to look alike once you've gone around the circular flow a few times. We can foresee how large an impact the multiplier process will ultimately have. Each time the multiplier process works its way around the circular flow, the reduction in spending equals the previous drop in income multiplied by the MPC. Accordingly, by pressing a few keys on an electronic calculator, we can produce a sequence of events like that depicted in Table 9.2.

TABLE 9.2   The Multiplier Cycles

The circular flow of income implies that an initial change in income will lead to cumulative changes in consumer spending and income. Here, an initial income loss of $100 billion (first cycle) causes a cutback in consumer spending in the amount of $75 billion (second cycle). At each subsequent cycle, consumer spending drops by the amount MPC × prior change in income. Ultimately, total spending (and income) falls by $400 billion, or 1/(1 − MPC) × initial change in spending:

Spending cycles	Change in this cycle's spending and income (billions per year)	Cumulative decrease in spending and income (billions per year)
First cycle: recessionary gap emerges	$100.00	$100.00
Second cycle: consumption drops by MPC × $100	75.00	175.00
Third cycle: consumption drops by MPC × $75	56.25	231.25
Fourth cycle: consumption drops by MPC × $56.25	42.19	273.44
Fifth cycle: consumption drops by MPC × $42.19	31.64	305.08
Sixth cycle: consumption drops by MPC × $31.64	23.73	328.81
Seventh cycle: consumption drops by MPC × $23.73	17.80	346.61
Eighth cycle: consumption drops by MPC × $17.80	13.35	359.95
.	.	.
.	.	.
.	.	.
Nth cycle and beyond		400.00

The impact of the multiplier is devastating. The ultimate reduction in total spending and output resulting from the initial recessionary gap is not $100 billion per year but $400 billion! Even if one is accustomed to thinking in terms of billions and trillions, this is a huge drop in demand, and thus in GNP. What the multiplier process demonstrates is that the dimensions of an initial recessionary gap greatly understate the severity of the economic dislocations that will follow in its wake. *The decline in equilibrium GNP will be much larger than the initial recessionary gap.* This was evident in the recession of 1981–82, when layoffs snowballed from industry to industry (see In the News), ultimately leaving over 10 million people unemployed.

The ultimate impact of a recessionary gap on GNP can be determined by computing the change in income and consumption at each cycle of the circular flow, for an infinite number of cycles. This is the approach summarized in Table 9.2. The entire computation can be simplified considerably, however, by use of a single figure, the multiplier. The **multiplier** tells us the extent to which the rate of total spending will change in response to an initial change in the flow of expenditure. The multiplier summarizes the sequence of steps described in Table 9.2.[1]

In our example, the initial change in spending occurs with the appearance of the recessionary gap ($100 billion per year) at full-employment GNP ($2,000 billion per year). Table 9.2 indicates that this gap will lead to a $400 billion

multiplier: The multiple by which an initial change in aggregate spending will alter total expenditure after an infinite number of spending cycles; 1/(1 − MPC).

---

[1]The multiplier summarizes the geometric progression $1 + MPC + MPC^2 + MPC^3 + \cdots + MPC^n$, which equals 1/(1 − MPC) when n becomes infinite.

In The News

THE MULTIPLIER

Plants Plan December Shutdowns as the Recession Spreads Rapidly

It looks as if 1981 will end with a whimper.

From the iron ore mines around Lake Superior to the furniture plants at the southern Appalachians, there will be a lot of shutdowns and short workweeks this month as companies adjust to the rapidly spreading recession. Some plants won't run at all in December, and many will be open only 10 or 15 days.

"It's been a tough year for durable consumer goods, and orders have slowed even more lately," says Henry Timnick, chairman and chief executive of Stanley Interiors Corp., Stanleytown, Va., a producer of furniture and draperies. "All over the United States, manufacturers are waiting for interest rates to come down some more and for consumer confidence to return." While they wait, they're curtailing production.

Spreading Rapidly

The shutdowns indicate that the recession is spreading very rapidly, but not necessarily that it will be exceptionally deep or prolonged. Prompt action to halt or even avoid inventory buildup could shorten any downturn—if consumers start buying again.

No government statistics measure how many mines, mills and factories will close extra days during December, but a check by The Wall Street Journal shows that the shutdowns will be widespread. The hard-hit auto, truck, farm equipment and construction machinery industries, which ordinarily close plants for the final week of the year, will take a lot of extra time off this year, as will a number of their suppliers. Other businesses, from lumber mills to appliance makers, will lock their doors for additional days or weeks, too.

. . . The plant closings also are evidence of how fast the slump has spread since it began in September. . . .

"We adjusted production to lower levels but before we could react, our inventories were too high," says Ronald Fountain, treasurer of White Consolidated Industries Inc., a producer of household appliances and industrial equipment. "As a result, we're taking an additional week of downtime in December at many of our appliance plants," he says, shutting down two weeks instead of the usual one week. General Electric Co., hit even harder, has halted major appliance production at its Appliance Park facility in Louisville for all of December.

—Ralph E. Winter

reduction in the rate of total spending. Using the multiplier, we arrive at the same conclusion by observing that

$$\text{Total change in spending} = \text{multiplier} \times \text{initial change in aggregate spending}$$

$$= \frac{1}{1 - \text{MPC}} \times \$100 \text{ billion per year}$$

$$= \frac{1}{1 - 0.75} \times \$100 \text{ billion per year}$$

$$= 4 \times \$100 \text{ billion per year}$$

$$= \$400 \text{ billion per year}$$

In other words, ***the cumulative decrease in total spending ($400 billion per year) resulting from the appearance of a recessionary gap at full employment is equal to the gap ($100 billion per year) multiplied by the multiplier (4).*** More generally, we may observe that the larger the fraction (MPC) of income respent in each round of the circular flow, the greater the impact of any change in spending on cumulative aggregate demand.

The Period Multiplier The actual impact of a recessionary gap depends on two basic things: (1) the size of the MPC and (2) the amount of time that elapses. The larger the MPC, the larger the multiplier. But the full impact of the multiplier will not be felt until we have gone around the circular flow an infinite number of times. In a short period of time—say, one year—we will not travel that far but will go through only two or three spending cycles. Hence the shorter the period of time (the fewer the number of spending cycles) or the smaller the MPC, the smaller the cumulative change in total spending. For policymakers who are more concerned about next year's election than about the millennium, such a distinction is critical. The *period multiplier* is the value of the multiplier over a finite period of time. It tells us how large multiplier effects will be in a finite period of time. From Table 9.2 we can see how multiplier effects grow with the passage of time and accumulation of spending cycles.

EQUILIBRIUM GNP

The key features of the Keynesian adjustment process are

- Producers reduce output and employment when output exceeds desired spending.

- The resulting loss of income causes a decline in consumer spending.

- Declines in consumer spending lead to further production cutbacks, more lost income, and still less consumption.

This adjustment process is illustrated again in Figure 9.3. The problem starts at full employment (Y_F), with the emergence of a recessionary gap. Suddenly, consumption plus investment spending at full employment ($C_F + I_F$) was less than full-employment income (point Z_F). A gap existed between the value of total output and the value of goods *demanded*. As a consequence of that gap, production cutbacks began, and the recessionary process got under way.

We now know that such reductions will continue until GNP has fallen $400 billion per year (the multiplier times the initial gap). That is to say, GNP will fall from its initial full-employment level of $2,000 billion per year ($Y_F$) to $1,600 billion ($Y_e$). Notice the unique character of this particular level of income. At Y_e, desired consumption and investment spending are exactly equal

W🌐RLD VIEW

ADJUSTMENT

Porsche Cutbacks

West German auto maker Porsche yesterday put 6,100 workers on short shifts to make up for a sharp decline in U.S. sales of its cars.

Porsche announced in November that it would cut pro-

duction after its October U.S. sales dropped 30 percent in the aftermath of the Oct. 19 stock market collapse and the sharp decline in the dollar.

The Washington Post, January 12, 1988, p. C1. Copyright © 1988 The Washington Post.

FIGURE 9.3
Adjustment to Equilibrium

A recessionary gap indicates that desired spending at full-employment ($C_F + I_F$) falls short of full-employment output ($Z_F = Y_F$). The resulting excess output leads producers to reduce the rate of production. The rate of production continues to fall until desired spending is in balance with the rate of output. The equilibrium rate of output occurs at point E—the output rate Y_e.

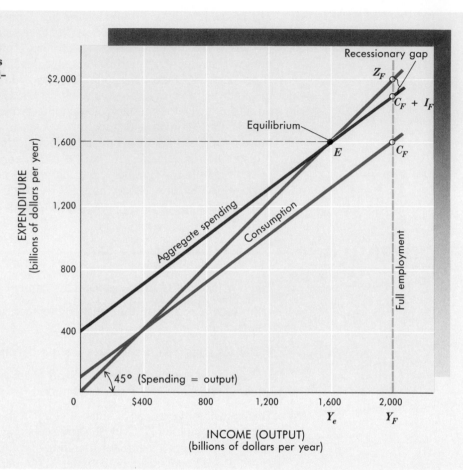

to total income (point E). In other words, the rate of desired expenditure equals the rate of production at Y_e. ***At the equilibrium rate of income there is no longer any cause for further changes in output, because everything produced is being sold.*** This is also illustrated in Table 9.3. At an income level of $1,600 billion per year, desired consumer and investor expenditures total $1,600 exactly.

There is only one rate of **equilibrium GNP,** and it occurs where the aggregate spending curve ($C + I$ in this case) intersects the total output curve (the 45-degree line). In Figure 9.3 that intersection occurs at point E. The rate of output at point E (Y_e) is the only rate of output at which the total value of goods demanded equals the total value of goods supplied.

What brings supply and demand into harmony at this rate of output is the fact that desired investment by producers exactly equals desired saving by consumers. At an income level of $1,600 billion per year, consumers desire to spend $1,300 billion and to save the remaining $300 billion (see Table 9.3). We also noted that business firms desire to invest $300 billion per year. Hence, ***in equilibrium, desired investment exactly equals desired saving.*** As a consequence, no excess (undesired) inventories accumulate, and producers have no incentive to reduce output further.[2]

equilibrium GNP: Output at which the rate of desired spending equals the rate of production.

---
[2]We are assuming here that desired investment remains at $300 billion, despite falling sales. This may be wishful thinking. If investors' expectations worsen greatly, both desired investment and equilibrium GNP will decline.

TABLE 9.3   Equilibrium GNP
(in billions of dollars per year)

There is only one rate of output at which desired spending equals total output. That equilibrium (Y_e) occurs at an output rate of $1,600 billion per year in this case. At equilibrium, desired saving equals desired investment. At all other rates of output, desired spending and output are not balanced, and the economy will expand or contract.

Output (income) level	Consumers' desire to spend	Consumers' desire to save	Investors' desire to invest	Economy
$ 400	$ 400	$ 0	300	expands
800	700	100	300	expands
1,200	1,000	200	300	expands
Y_e = 1,600	1,300	300	300	stabilizes
Y_F = 2,000	1,600	400	300	contracts

At equilibrium (Y_e), producers have no incentive to expand production either, because they are selling only as much as they produce, without depleting desired inventories. By contrast, if GNP were less than $1,600 billion per year, desired investment would exceed desired saving (see Table 9.3). In this case, inventories would drop below desired levels, and producers would want to increase output up to the equilibrium level.

Equilibrium GNP vs. Full-Employment GNP

Although equilibrium GNP implies a certain measure of stability in the rate of output, it is not necessarily a *desirable* rate of output. Indeed, the equilibrium output we end up with in this case is considerably smaller than our full-employment potential. At Y_e we are producing only $1,600 billion of output per year, rather than $2,000 billion. We are stuck at some point *inside* our production-possibilities curve, with a high rate of unemployment. Moreover, there is no obvious relief in sight, as the equilibrium at Y_e equates the desires of consumers and producers. There is no incentive for producers to hire more labor or to increase output. ***This is the dilemma that Keynes emphasized; there is no "natural" adjustment back to full employment.***

Equilibrium GNP will not always be less than full-employment GNP. If the consumption and investment functions were to shift upward, equilibrium GNP would move closer to full-employment GNP and possibly even exceed it (in which case we would confront an inflationary gap). It is evident, however, that equilibrium GNP *might* be less than full-employment GNP, resulting in persisent **cyclical unemployment.**

cyclical unemployment: Unemployment attributable to a lack of job vacancies, i.e., to an inadequate level of aggregate demand.

ADJUSTMENT TO AN INFLATIONARY GAP

Imagine for the moment that consumers desire to spend $1,600 billion per year at full-employment GNP ($2,000 billion per year), but that business firms now desire to invest $500 billion rather than only $300 billion per year, as before (Table 9.3). As a result, the rate of desired spending at full employment ($2,100 billion per year) exceeds the rate of full-employment production by $100 billion (see Figure 9.4). This excess of spending over output at full employment represents an **inflationary gap.** How will the economy adjust to this gap?

inflationary gap: The amount by which desired spending at full employment exceeds full-employment output.

**FIGURE 9.4
An Inflationary Gap**

An inflationary gap indicates that desired spending at full employment $(C_F + I_F)$ exceeds full-employment output (Y_F). This excessive demand at full employment leads to an equilibrium rate of output (Y_e^*) that exceeds the economy's productive capacity (Y_F). As a consequence, the higher nominal income at Y_e^* ($2,400 billion per year) implies inflation rather than higher *real* income.

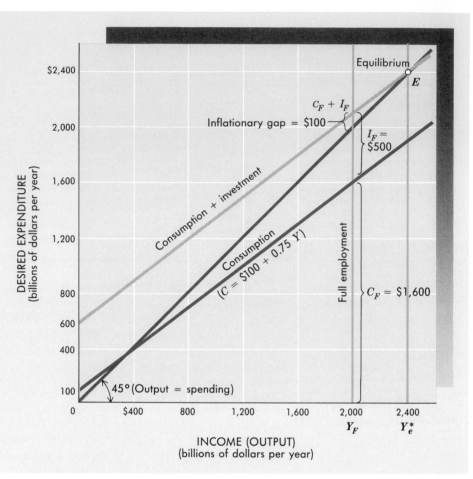

The Classical View

Classical economists recognized that the economy could not produce output in excess of its production possibilities; hence an inflationary gap cannot be closed by an increased rate of production. If an inflationary gap is to be closed, the rate of desired spending at full employment will have to be reduced. But what mechanisms will lower the rate of spending?

Rising interest rates   The Classical economists argued that a flexible rate of interest could discourage investment spending as well as encourage it. In particular, a higher rate of interest, by raising the cost of investment, would discourage businesses from buying new plant and equipment or adding to inventories. If the rate of interest increased sufficiently, the rate of desired investment would fall to a level compatible with desired saving.

Will the rate of interest rise as required? The Classical economists said it would. *The existence of an inflationary gap implies that desired investment exceeds desired saving* (see Figure 9.4). Thus the flow of income into capital markets (banks and other financial institutions) will not be large enough to satisfy the desires of would-be investors. As investors start competing for scarce savings, they will bid up the interest rate. Hence the expenditure desires that initially created the inflationary gap will force interest rates up, thereby altering investment plans and closing the gap.[3]

---

[3]Higher interest rates may also discourage consumer expenditures (especially on new houses and other large purchases). The impact of higher interest rates on the mix of output is discussed in Chapter 14.

Rising prices and wages   The Classical economists also noted that the existence of an inflationary gap implies upward pressure on prices—that is, **demand-pull inflation.** Such inflation will itself set in motion forces to reduce the rate of expenditure and therefore close the gap.

The Classical economists argued that higher prices for goods and services would dampen consumer enthusiasm and lead to less spending. In addition, higher wage rates, if attained, would raise production costs and therefore make continued production less profitable. The Classical economists argued that this combination of higher prices and wage rates, together with higher interest rates, would lower the rate of expenditure and close the inflationary gap. Inflation, therefore, would soon disappear as the economy "self-corrected."

demand-pull inflation: An increase in the price level initiated by excessive aggregate demand.

The Keynesian Response

Keynes's response to the Classical view is predictable. It emphasizes the effect of expectations on investment and the impact of higher prices and wages on disposable income. According to Keynes, the economy might not "self-adjust" to an inflationary gap; instead, inflation might persist.

Higher expectations   If desired spending exceeds the rate of production, firms are selling everything they produce and some of their desired inventory as well. Such buoyant sales tend to raise producers' expectations for *future* sales and thus shift the investment demand curve to the right (see Figure 9.5). With higher expectations, businesses will not so easily be deterred from their investment plans by a higher rate of interest. Indeed, if expectations improve significantly, the rate of desired investment may even *increase,* despite rising interest rates. Notice in Figure 9.5 that the rate of desired investment expenditures rises from $500 billion (point *M*) to $600 billion per year (point *N*) despite an increase in the interest rate. Here again, ***Keynes emphasized that changes in expectations may overwhelm changes in the interest rate as a determinant of desired investment.*** As a consequence, interest-rate changes may not lead the economy back to full-employment equilibrium.

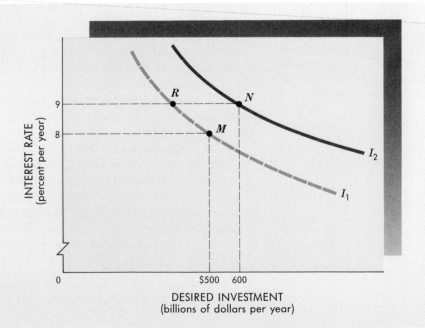

**FIGURE 9.5
Keynesian Emphasis
on Expectations**

Classical economists assumed that higher interest rates would reduce the rate of investment. This assumption is illustrated by the move from point *M* to point *R*. Keynes argued, however, that improved sales expectations might shift the investment demand curve to the right. At point *N*, the rate of investment is higher, despite a rise in interest rates.

Higher incomes The second line of the Classical defense against continuing inflation must be abandoned, too. Higher prices and wage rates increase disposable income and thus encourage more consumer spending, not less. As illustrated in Figure 9.4, the excessive rate of expenditure at full employment (Y_F) amounts to $100 billion per year. As this expenditure enters the circular flow, it creates an equivalent amount of income. Consumers, in turn, will use this added income to purchase additional goods and services, as indicated by the marginal propensity to consume (MPC). This process is repeated until the multiplier finally propels the economy to the new equilibrium at Y_e^* in Figure 9.4. At Y_e^* the rate of desired spending is $2,400 billion per year, far in excess of the economy's output capability ($2,000 billion per year). But there is no incentive to reduce the rate of desired spending, because everyone is spending as much as he or she desires at that income level; Y_e^* represents an *equilibrium* situation.

Notice that this new equilibrium rate of output (Y_e^*) exceeds full-employment output (Y_F). By definition, however, *real* output, valued at constant prices, cannot exceed full-employment output. Hence the higher *nominal* value of Y_e^* must reflect increased prices. Indeed, the inflationary gap implies that people want to spend more than the economy can produce. As consumers compete against each other for available goods and services, they push prices up, resulting in demand-pull inflation and higher nominal incomes.

LEAKAGES AND INJECTIONS

Figure 9.6 summarizes the imbalances that cause either inflation or unemployment. The essential characteristic of a market economy is the circular flow of spending and income. Spending on goods and services creates income that fuels further spending.

What worried Keynes is that some income leaks out of the circular flow. The primary source of leakage is consumer saving. Consumers tend to save (not spend) some fraction of each additional dollar of income. So long as this **marginal propensity to save (MPS)** exceeds zero, leakage occurs (see Figure 9.6). In the real world, leakage includes not only consumer saving but also taxes and spending on imports.

marginal propensity to save (MPS): The fraction of each additional (marginal) dollar of disposable income not spent on consumption; $1 - MPC$.

The leakage caused by saving, imports, and taxes may be offset by injections of spending. Such injections come not only from business investment but also from government spending and exports (spending by foreigners on American products).

If leakages equal injections, the circular flow will be in equilibrium. That is to say, when leakages equal injections, the circular flow of income will be constant. Keynes worried, however, that the flow of equilibrium income, though constant, might not be sufficient to provide jobs for everyone who sought work. Indeed, he thought it highly unlikely that equilibrium GNP would "naturally" equal full-employment GNP.

The economy contracts or expands whenever injections and leakages are not equal. In particular:

- *If leakages exceed injections, the economy contracts* until it stabilizes at a lower level of (equilibrium) GNP and employment (see Figure 9.7).

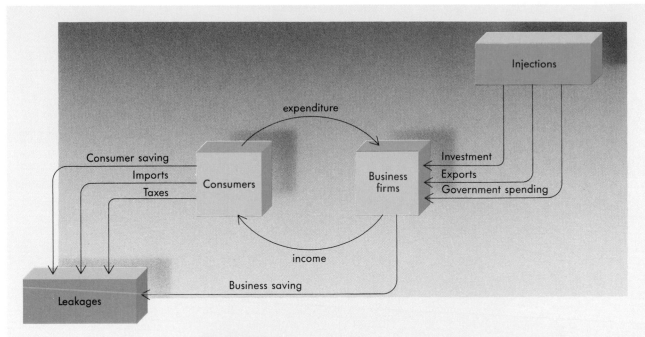

FIGURE 9.6
Leakages and Injections

The circular flow of income has several leaks in it. Income diverted into consumer saving, business saving (retained earnings and depreciation), taxes, or imports reduces the value of the circular flow.

Other autonomous spending injects income into the circular flow. These injections come from investment, export sales, and government spending.

When leakages equal injections, the economy is in equilibrium. If leakages exceed injections, the economy will contract. When injections exceed leakages, total spending will increase.

- *If injections exceed leakages, the economy expands* and employment increases. If too much income is injected into the circular flow, however, prices may also rise.

POLICY INSIGHTS:

MACRO INTERVENTION

The Keynesian theory of adjustment was formulated by John Maynard Keynes in the 1930s. As noted earlier, the Classical economists believed that the economy would always rebound to full employment, at least as long as interest rates or prices and wages were flexible. Keynes's major contribution was to demonstrate that the economy might not self-adjust, even when interest rates, prices, and wages were all (downwardly) flexible. Rather than self-adjust to a recessionary gap, an economy might flounder in a high-unemployment equilibrium. Keynes's insights were well timed. His theory of stagnation was published during the Great Depression, when unemployment rates not only were exceptionally high but persisted for a much longer time than anyone had previously thought possible.

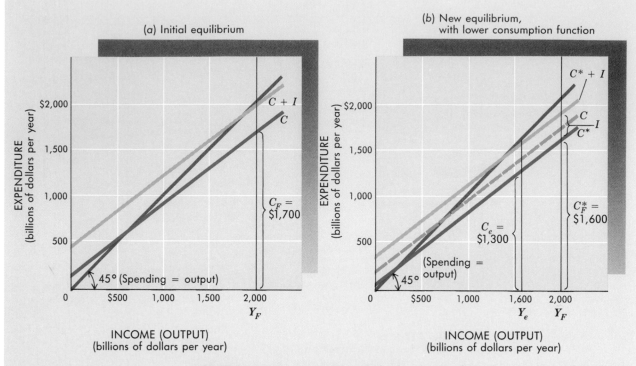

FIGURE 9.7 The Paradox of Thrift: Desired Saving vs. Actual Saving

Thrift was always thought to be a virtue. As Ben Franklin advised us, "A penny saved is a penny earned."

Keynes, however, warned that thrift (saving) might not be such a good thing. In fact, he showed how the attempt to save more could result in *less* income and no more saving. To visualize this "paradox of thrift," suppose that the economy is in full-employment equilibrium. Consumers are spending $1,700 billion per year and saving $300 billion while investors are spending $300 billion per year (see part *a*).

Suddenly, consumers decide they want to save a larger fraction of their incomes. This greater desire to save results in a downward shift of the consumption function. Specifically, if consumers decide to save $100 billion more at full employment, consumption at full employment must drop from $1,700 billion per year to only $1,600 billion. This is illustrated in part *b*.

If consumption drops, unwanted inventories accumulate and producers cut back on production and lay off workers. Consumer incomes fall, and the economy contracts until a new and lower equilibrium is reached. At the new equilibrium, we observe that (1) income has been reduced (from $2,000 billion per year [$Y_F$] to $1,600 billion per year [$Y_e$]); (2) consumption has been reduced (from $1,600 billion per year [$C_F^*$]) to $1,300 billion per year [$C_e$]); and (3) desired saving has been reduced (from $400 billion per year [$Y_F - C_F^*$] to $300 billion per year [$Y_e - C_e$]).

Desired saving is once again equal to desired investment (unchanged at $300 billion per year), as it must be in equilibrium.

What has happened here? An attempt by consumers to save more creates a recessionary gap. The gap leads to a lower equilibrium output, less income, and a resumption of the initial rate of saving. Hence *an attempt to save more results in less income and no more saving!* This "paradox of thrift" is explained by the impact of reduced consumer demand on production decisions and income, as illustrated by the multiplier process.

The principal implication of the Keynesian message is that public policy must be used to alter the rate of aggregate demand. Once the aggregate demand curve shifts to the left (Figure 8.1) there is no guarantee that it will shift rightward again. Whereas the Classical economists advised policymakers to maintain a wait-and-see posture in the face of cyclical unemployment, Keynes argued that policymakers would have to take explicit action to restore the nation's economic health. They would have to find ways to increase aggregate spending, and thereby to increase aggregate demand.

Even if the economy might eventually self-adjust in a Classical manner, Keynes argued, the costs of waiting for the adjustment were too great. *At best,* Keynes felt, self-adjustment was a long-run phenomenon. Such a long-term horizon was inappropriate for public policy, however. As he bluntly put it: "In the long run we are all dead."

Keynes's prescription for ending the Great Depression was simple: increase the rate of government spending. Without such an increase, Keynes argued, the rate of production would remain low, leaving millions of workers unemployed. Keynes's advice was largely ignored, and the Great Depression persisted until the outbreak of World War II, when aggregate demand surged and the depression ended.

The policy implications of Keynes's recessionary-gap analysis also apply to inflationary gaps. In this case, a wait-and-see attitude on the part of policymakers might leave the economy burdened with persistent demand-pull inflation. The alternative? To force reductions in the rate of desired expenditure, either by cutting government spending or by increasing taxes on consumers and businesses.

The Keynesian call for increased government participation in product markets has been heeded. In Chapter 3 we saw that government expenditures on goods and services absorb one-fifth of annual output. In Chapter 10 we shall examine the impact of changes in government spending and taxes on output, employment, and prices—key outcomes of the macro economy.

SUMMARY

- The seriousness of a recessionary or inflationary gap depends on the way the economy responds to an imbalance between desired spending at full employment and the rate of full-employment production.

- Classical economists argued that the economy would self-adjust to an imbalance between desired spending and output. The two mechanisms of Classical self-adjustment were thought to be (*a*) flexible interest rates (to equate desired saving and investment); and (*b*) flexible prices and wages (to equate the quantity demanded and the quantity supplied)

- Keynes argued that these mechanisms might not work, because (*a*) changes in expectations have more influence on investment spending than changes in interest rates; (*b*) prices and wages rarely fall; and (*c*) changes in prices or wages alter disposable incomes and therefore the rate of consumer spending. As a consequence, the economy would not self-adjust to full employment but might instead end up at an equilibrium GNP lower or higher than the rate of full-employment production (with stable prices).

• The multiplier indicates the cumulative change in total spending that follows an initial change in the flow of expenditure; it equals $1/(1 - MPC)$. The multiplier reflects the fact that a reduction in the rate of expenditure will reduce disposable income, leading to further reductions in consumer spending, which further reduce income, and so on.

• The Keynesian theory of the adjustment process suggests that the economy may not self-adjust to either inflation or unemployment. On the contrary, if persistent cyclical unemployment or demand-pull inflation is to be avoided, the government may have to intervene to alter the rate of desired expenditure.

Terms to Remember   Define the following terms:

recessionary gap
consumption function
marginal propensity to consume
    (MPC)
multiplier
equilibrium GNP

cyclical unemployment
inflationary gap
demand-pull inflation
marginal propensity to save
    (MPS)

Questions for Discussion

1. Suppose that the rate of interest were to fall to zero. Can you think of any reasons business firms might have for *not* increasing the rate of investment at such a low rate of interest?

2. Why might consumers continue to buy a great many goods and services when prices are rising?

3. In 1982 auto workers accepted reduced wages, hoping thereby to increase employment. Is such a strategy likely to succeed? What would happen if all workers did the same thing?

4. How can an economy escape an equilibrium that is above or below full-employment GNP?

Problems

1. Assume that the economy is in a depression and that the government increases expenditures by $100 billion to stimulate the economy. Assume further that the economy has a marginal propensity to consume of 90 percent.
   (a) Compute eight rounds of multiplier effects and the cumulative increase in spending, as in Table 9.2.
   (b) What will be the final cumulative impact on aggregate spending?
   (c) Compare your results with those in Table 9.2. With a higher marginal propensity to consume, does the cumulative change in expenditure become larger or smaller?

2. Assume that all expenditure is summarized in the following consumption and investment functions:

$$C = \$200 \text{ billion per year } + 0.80Y_D$$

$$I = \$300 \text{ billion per year}$$

Use this information to complete this problem.
(a) Identify the equilibrium rate of output.
(b) Compute the size of the recessionary gap when full-employment GNP equals $2,800 billion.
(c) What is the value of the multiplier?
(d) What would happen to equilibrium GNP if the rate of investment increased to $350 billion per year?
(e) Illustrate your answers on a graph.

3. Suppose the consumers in the economy in problem 2 were suddenly to increase their saving by $100 billion per year. Their new consumption function would become

$$C = \$100 \text{ billion per year} + 0.80Y_D$$

Investment continues to be $300 billion per year. Use this information to repeat problem 2. On the basis of comparisons between your answers in problem 2 and your answers in this problem, answer the following questions:
(a) What paradox is illustrated by the differences between this problem and problem 2?
(b) What relationship does the change in the recessionary gap have to the change in the rate of saving?
(c) Does the marginal propensity to consume change with increased saving?
(d) Does the impact of increased investment change with more saving?

Fiscal Policy

*T*he Keynesian theory of instability leads directly to a mandate for government policy. From a Keynesian perspective, an insufficiency of aggregate spending causes unemployment; an excess of aggregate spending causes inflation. Since the market itself will not correct these imbalances, the federal government must. This implies increasing aggregate spending when it is too low and decreasing aggregate spending when it is excessive. By balancing desired spending and full-employment GNP in this way, the federal government can achieve our macro goals of full employment and price stability.

In this chapter we examine some of the Keynesian tools the federal government *can* use to alter economic outcomes. The questions we confront are

- Can government spending and tax policies help stabilize the economy?
- What kinds of policy will produce desired macro outcomes?
- How do these policies affect the government's budget balance?

THE NATURE OF FISCAL POLICY

The First Article of the U.S. Constitution empowers Congress "to lay and collect taxes, duties, imposts and excises, to pay the debts and provide for the common defense and general welfare of the United States." It was not until 1915, however, that the Sixteenth Amendment to the Constitution extended that power to include income taxes. And it was not until the 1930s that the use of income taxes to achieve macroeconomic goals was seriously considered.

Today things are different. In exercising its tax powers, the federal government now collects and spends more than $1 trillion each year. About half of that spending takes the form of income transfers, interest, and intergovernmental grants. The rest represents a demand for goods and services (see Chapter 3). When we speak of **fiscal policy**, we are referring to these public tax and expenditure activities. More particularly, fiscal policy is the use of the government's tax and spending powers to alter macroeconomic outcomes.[1]

fiscal policy: The use of government taxes and spending to alter macroeconomic outcomes.

[1] Recall that state and local governments also impose taxes and purchase goods and services (see Chapter 3). Their role in fiscal policy will be examined later in this chapter and in Chapter 17.

Although fiscal policy can be used to pursue any of our economic goals, we begin our study by exploring its potential to ensure full employment. We then look at its impact on inflation. Along the way we also observe the potential of fiscal policy to alter the mix of output and the distribution of income.

FISCAL POLICY TO ACHIEVE FULL EMPLOYMENT

recessionary gap: The amount by which desired spending at full employment falls short of full-employment output.

As we observed in Chapters 8 and 9, the circular flow of income leaks. The most important form of such leakage in a completely private economy (with no government) is consumer saving. Consumers do not return all of their income directly to the circular flow, but instead save some fraction of it. Unless additional expenditure is injected into the circular flow to make up the shortfall in consumer spending at full employment, a **recessionary gap** will emerge.

Maintaining Full Employment

The potential for closing a recessionary gap is evident in the components of aggregate spending; that is,

$$\bullet \quad GNP = C + I + G + (X - M)$$

aggregate spending: The rate of total expenditure desired at alternative levels of income, *ceteris paribus.*

If a recessionary gap results from a deficiency of consumer spending, then the logical thing to do is to increase consumption or any other component of **aggregate spending.** The government can do this by purchasing available goods and services, that is, by increasing its own rate of expenditure. The potential of such expenditures to fill the gap is illustrated in Figure 10.1.

**FIGURE 10.1
The Fiscal Policy Objective**

In this case, a recessionary gap of $100 billion exists in the absence of government spending. (The gap equals Y_F minus [$C_F + I_F$].) In the absence of any other changes, this gap would push the economy into the recessionary equilibrium Y_e. By spending $100 billion, however, the government eliminates the recessionary gap. Notice that total spending at full employment ($C_F + I_F + G$) now intersects the 45-degree line (the output = spending curve) at full employment (Y_F).

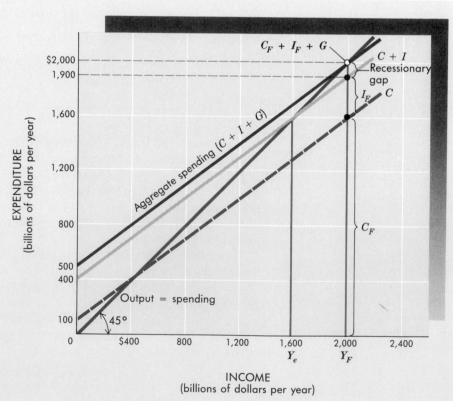

The consumption and investment functions of Figure 10.1 are identical to those we used in Chapters 8 and 9. The economy is assumed to be at full employment (Y_F) initially, with a GNP of $2 trillion ($2,000 billion). Consumer spending is determined by the function

$$C = \$100 \text{ billion per year } + 0.75Y$$

Thus desired consumption at full employment (C_F) equals $1,600 billion per year. Investments of $300 billion per year ($I_F$) are dictated by producers' expectations of sales and profits, as well as by the prevailing rate of interest. For convenience, we will assume that net exports ($X - M$) are zero, thus allowing us to focus on domestic consumers and investors. In sum, aggregate private spending at full employment ($C_F + I_F$) totals $1,900 billion per year, leaving a recessionary gap of $100 billion per year.

To close the recessionary gap, we need to boost total spending at full employment by $100 billion per year. The government can do this by entering the market to purchase airplanes, highways, schools, courthouses, public toilets, or whatever else we deem useful—that is, by "priming the pump" (see World View). We can illustrate such expenditures by adding a third layer to the aggregate spending function, as in Figure 10.1.

The line $C + I + G$ represents *total* domestic spending at different rates of output. At full employment, aggregate spending includes $1,600 billion of annual consumption (C_F), $300 billion in annual investment (I_F), and an added $100 billion per year in government purchases of goods and services (G). Since that rate of expenditure equals the rate of full-employment production, no recessionary gap will emerge, and the economy will chug merrily along at full employment. (Y_F is now the equilibrium rate of output.)

This view of fiscal policy is a simple extension of the leakage–injection model we discussed in Chapter 9 (Figure 9.6). Government spending repre-

W🌐RLD VIEW

PUMP-PRIMING

Japan Adopts Package to Prime Economy

TOKYO, Sept. 19—The Japanese Cabinet, reacting to pressure from both the United States and its own business leaders, today adopted a nearly $24 billion package of pump-priming measures to prop up its sagging economy.

Heading the spending list is about $20 billion for public works and new housing construction.

Many business leaders and private economists were skeptical today that the measures will be sufficient to keep Japan at its officially projected real growth of 4 percent in the year that began April 1.

Prime Minister Yasuhiro Nakasone told reporters, however, that "we are going to make steady efforts toward that target." . . .

The Japanese have been devising domestic demand packages for years. But officials call this one the largest so far. . . . The program's major elements:

- $9.2 billion of new or accelerated public works spending by the central government, with $5.3 billion in such spending by local governments.

- $4.6 billion of new housing investment, stimulated by expanded loans from the government.

- Accelerated investment by major utility companies and telecommunications service companies, including the mammoth Nippon Telegraph and Telephone Corp. . . .

—John Burgess

The Washington Post, September 20, 1986, p. D1. Copyright © 1987 The Washington Post.

sents an injection into the circular flow. If a recessionary gap is caused by insufficient spending, then such an injection can eliminate the gap. In other words, *an injection of government spending helps offset the leakage created by consumer saving* (or imports and taxes), thus maintaining aggregate expenditure at the rate of full-employment output.

Paying for government expenditure   Notice that we haven't said anything about how the government is going to finance this spending. If the government gets the required $100 billion by imposing taxes on consumers and investors, the added leakage may offset the intended injection. In that case, the stimulus of government spending will be offset in part by reduced consumption and investment. If, on the other hand, the government *borrows* the money from the private sector, less credit may be available to finance consumption and investment, again creating an offsetting reduction in private demand. In either case, government spending may **"crowd out"** some private expenditure. For the moment, however, we will ignore these problems and assume that the government's expenditure of $100 billion per year does not reduce private consumer or business spending. Keynes made the same assumption. We shall reconsider this assumption in Chapters 12–14, when we look at the way money markets work. As we shall see there, the degree of assumed "crowding out" is a focal point of macroeconomic controversy.

crowding out: A reduction in private-sector borrowing (and spending) necessitated by increased government borrowing.

Attaining Full Employment

If an increase in government spending will not reduce private spending, then the potential of increased government expenditure to close a recessionary gap is evident. Unfortunately, we have no assurance that such spending will take place or that it will get there in time. Economic policy might not come to our timely rescue for many reasons. We might not realize that a recessionary gap is forming until it is too late. Or perhaps Congress will be on vacation ("in recess") when we need authorization to spend the money. Maybe a presidential election is approaching, and no one is keeping an eye on the economy. Whatever the reason—and we shall discuss the reasons in greater detail in Chapter 17—it is surely possible that the economy will slide into a recession before effective action is taken. Indeed, our experience with unemployment problems (Chapter 6) provides convincing evidence of that possibility.

Let us imagine a different economic dilemma. Suppose now that the economy has already contracted and that we are stuck in a recessionary equilibrium (Y_e in Figure 10.1). In that case, **equilibrium GNP** is simply too low. Such a situation was typified by the Great Depression but also resembles more recent recessions. The problem then becomes one of *achieving* full employment rather than just maintaining it.

equilibrium GNP: The rate of output at which desired spending equals the rate of production.

Recall our assumption that total output (and income) at Y_e is only $1,600 billion per year, or $400 billion less than our full-employment potential (see Figure 10.1). In such a situation what should the government do? Should it go into the market and buy $400 billion worth of goods and services per year?

The multiplier   In this situation the government does *not* need to purchase $400 billion of goods and services. A much smaller increase in the rate of expenditure is all that is required, thanks to the **multiplier.**

multiplier: The multiple by which an initial change in aggregate spending will alter total expenditure after an infinite number of spending cycles; $1/(1 - MPC)$.

Recall that *an increase in autonomous spending (an injection) implies an increase in disposable income* (see Figure 10.2). In this case, suppose that the government decided to spend $100 billion per year on a new fleet of cruise missiles. How would this decision affect total spending? In the

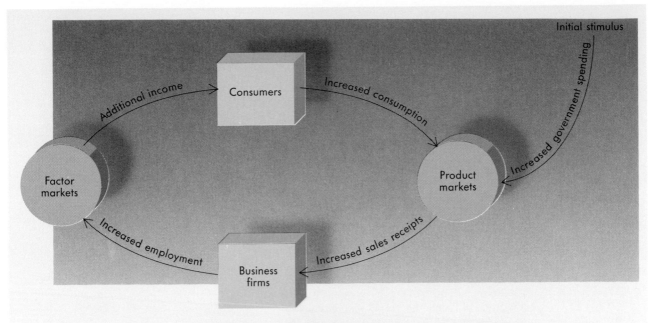

FIGURE 10.2 Stimulus to the Circular Flow of Income

An increase in government spending has a *multiplied* impact on total spending. The additional government expenditures in product markets are an injection into the circular flow of income. This added income finances increased consumption. These income and spending cycles continue until total income (spending) has increased by $\Delta G \times 1/(1 - \text{MPC})$.

first instance, such an expenditure would clearly increase aggregate spending by $100 billion. This is only the beginning of a very long story, however, as Table 10.1 reminds us. The people who build cruise missiles will be on the receiving end of a lot of income and will be in a position to increase *their* spending accordingly.

If aerospace workers have a marginal propensity to consume (MPC) of 0.75, we expect their collective spending to increase by $75 billion (three-fourths of $100 billion per year). Now we have $100 billion of government spending *plus* $75 billion of additional consumption. This brings the *cumulative* increase in total spending to $175 billion per year, already much larger than the initial increase in government spending.

Table 10.1 summarizes the rest of the multiplier story; in each cycle, someone's income and spending increase. When the story is over, the cumulative increase in total spending will be $400 billion per year. Thus the multiplier effects generated by the increased government spending are large enough to propel the economy from the recessionary equilibrium at Y_e ($1,600 billion per year) to the economy's full-employment potential at Y_F ($2,000 billion per year).

Figure 10.3 provides a graphic summary of the multiplier process. When we introduce $100 billion of government expenditure at Y_e, the aggregate spending curve shifts upward by that amount. In other words, *a new injection of spending shifts the aggregate spending curve upward.* Desired spending is suddenly much larger than the current rate of production (compare points D and Z). Producers respond to this imbalance by hiring more workers and producing more missiles. In so doing, they set off a chain of

TABLE 10.1 The Multiplier Process at Work

Purchasing power is passed from hand to hand in the circular flow. The *cumulative* change in total expenditure that results from a new injection of spending into the circular flow depends on the MPC and the number of spending cycles that occur. The limit to multiplier effects is established by the ratio $1/(1 - MPC)$. In this case, MPC = 0.75, so the multiplier equals 4. That is to say, total spending will ultimately rise by $400 billion per year as a result of an increase in G of $100 billion per year.

Hypothetical spending cycles	Change in this cycle's spending (billions per year)	Cumulative increase in spending (billions per year)
First cycle: government buys $100 billion worth of missiles	$100.00	$100.00
Second cycle: missile workers have more income, buy new boats (MPC = 0.75).	75.00	175.00
Third cycle: boat builders have more income, spend it on beer (0.75 × $75)	56.25	231.25
Fourth cycle: bartenders and brewery workers have more income ($56.25 billion), spend it on new cars (0.75 × $56.25)	42.19	273.44
Fifth cycle: auto workers have more income, spend it on clothes (0.75 × $42.19)	31.64	305.08
Sixth cycle: apparel workers have more income, spend it on movies and entertainment (0.75 × $31.64)	23.73	328.81
⋮	⋮	⋮
Nth cycle and beyond		400.00

multiplier effects that includes repeated increases in consumption. This new consumption keeps the economy expanding. By the time we reach full employment, consumption has increased from $1,300 billion per year at Y_e to $1,600 billion per year at Y_F. Thus the *cumulative* increase in total spending includes $100 billion per year in increased government expenditure *plus* $300 billion per year in additional consumption.

The desired stimulus   The multiplier adds a lot of punch to fiscal policy. *Every new dollar of expenditure injected into the circular flow has a multidollar impact on equilibrium income.* Specifically,

$$\text{Total change in spending} = \text{new injection} \times \text{multiplier}$$

While such leverage is often desirable, it also suggests that fiscal-policy mistakes tend to be magnified. For instance, a small stimulus to spending may leave the economy in a deep recession; a large stimulus can rapidly lead to excessive spending and inflation.

If we knew the exact dimensions of aggregate expenditure, as in Figure 10.3, we could easily calculate the required increase in the rate of government spending. At our recessionary equilibrium (Y_e) the economy is $400 billion short of full-employment GNP. But we require an initial stimulus of only $100 billion per year to get to full employment. This amount is exactly equal to the recessionary gap that would exist at full employment with our initial aggregate-spending function. Thus to determine the appropriate size of a needed

FIGURE 10.3
An Expansionary Stimulus

An injection of government spending (Step 1) shifts aggregate spending upward. This creates an imbalance between the rate of expenditure (D) and the rate of output (Z). As producers expand the rate of output (hire additional factors of production), they create additional income. This additional income finances increased consumption (Step 2). Total output and spending continue to increase until a new equilibrium (E) is attained at Y_F (Step 3).

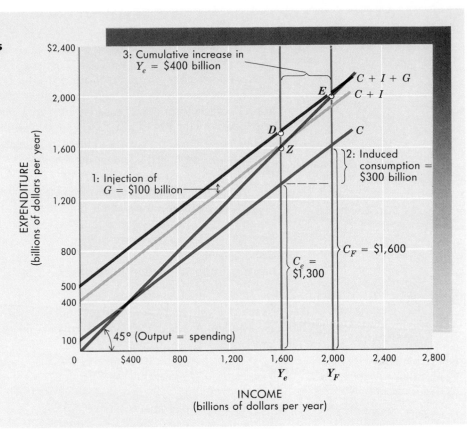

injection (increased government spending in this case), we simply look at the consumption and investment functions. At full employment (Y_F), they show how large a recessionary gap exists. Once we increase spending by that amount, the economy will follow our lead, propelled by the multiplier process.

In the first case we looked at, the problem was to keep a recessionary gap from emerging. We maintained full employment by increasing government spending by the amount of the *anticipated* gap. No change in the aggregate level of spending actually occurred. Increased G compensated for an *expected* shortfall in C and I.

In the second case, a gap had already emerged, and the economy was in a recession at Y_e. In this case, the injection of additional government spending shifted the aggregate spending curve upward. This injection set the multiplier in action. Total output grew by $1/(1 - \text{MPC}) \times$ recessionary gap. Hence ***the initial injection required to restore full employment is always equal to the size of the recessionary gap*** — that is,

- Desired new injection = $\dfrac{\text{size of}}{\text{recessionary gap}}$

Unfortunately, our knowledge of aggregate spending is rarely so perfect. As a consequence, we often end up guessing the size of the recessionary gap (anticipated or actual) and hoping our guesses are not too far off. This is another reason economic policy is not always on target. We'll discover other reasons in Chapter 17.

ALTERNATIVES TO GOVERNMENT SPENDING ─────────

Although government spending is capable of moving the economy to its full-employment potential, increased G is not the only way to get there. The increased spending required to raise output and employment levels from Y_e to Y_F could emerge from C and I as well as from G. It could also come from abroad, in the form of increased demand for our exports. In other words, any Big Spender would help, whether from the public sector or the private sector. Of course, the reason we are initially at Y_e, instead of Y_F, in Figure 10.3 is that consumers and investors have chosen not to spend as much as is required for full employment.

Consumer and investor decisions are subject to change. Moreover, fiscal policy can help stimulate such changes. On the outlay side of the budget, Congress not only buys goods and services, but also distributes income transfers. By increasing or decreasing such transfers, Congress directly affects the disposable income of consumers. On the revenue side of the budget, Congress has the power to raise or lower taxes.

Transfers and Consumption

transfer payment: Payments to individuals for which no current goods or services are exchanged, e.g., Social Security, welfare, unemployment benefits.

marginal propensity to save (MPS): The fraction of each additional dollar of disposable income not spent on consumption: 1 − MPC.

Nearly half of the federal budget consists of **transfer payments.** The fiscal 1991 budget, for example, included over $264 billion in Social Security benefits and billions more in unemployment, welfare, and veterans' benefits (Table 3.1). All of these benefits add to the disposable income of consumers. By increasing disposable income, transfer payments induce a change in consumer spending.

Injections of transfer payments aren't as powerful as injections of government purchases, however. When the government spends an additional dollar on weapons, that entire dollar becomes part of aggregate expenditure. On the other hand, when government increases income transfers by a dollar, only *part* of that dollar gets spent on goods and services. Some fraction of the transfer dollar—the **marginal propensity to save (MPS)**—remains unspent by the transfer recipient. This initial leakage from transfer payments reduces the impact of income transfers on GNP. Nevertheless, changes in income transfers remain an alternative to government purchases as a means for shifting the aggregate expenditure curve upward or downward.

Taxes and Consumption

disposable income: After-tax income of consumers; personal income less personal taxes.

Changes in tax policy also have the potential to shift the aggregate expenditure curve. The primary impact of taxes is to reduce disposable income at any given rate of output. Up to now, we have ignored the distinction between disposable income and GNP, implicitly assuming that neither government nor business saving (depreciation and retained earnings) existed (see Chapter 4). Now the government has entered the picture, however, and with it have come taxes on income, property, sales, and many other things (see Chapter 3). As a consequence, we now have to distinguish more carefully between the amount of income we produce (total output) and the amount available to consumers to spend **(disposable income).**

It remains true that the rate of consumer spending is directly related to disposable income, that is,

$$\bullet \quad C = a + bY_D$$

But disposable income (Y_D) is no longer equal to total income (Y). Instead, the government taxes total income, leaving consumers with less than they had before. As a consequence, consumers spend less at every rate of *total* income. Hence ***taxes lower the amount of consumer spending that takes place at any given rate of output (GNP).***[2]

The general impact of taxes can be illustrated with a downward shift of the consumption function, as in Figure 10.4. Before the introduction of taxes, consumers desired to spend $1,600 billion per year at full employment, as indicated by point *M*. Once they start paying taxes, however, consumers can no longer afford to spend so much: the rate of consumption at full employment drops to $1,300 billion per year (point *N*). Similar reductions in consumer spending occur at all other levels of output, shifting the consumption function downward.[3]

The government's power to tax us gives it another instrument for manipulating aggregate spending. As we have just observed, an increase in taxes reduces disposable income and consumer spending. By the same token, ***a reduction in taxes—a tax cut—can be used to increase disposable income and consumer spending.***

Suppose again that the economy has contracted to the recessionary equilibrium represented by Y_e in Figure 10.3. At Y_e, total output is only $1,600 billion per year, $400 billion short of full-employment output. To achieve full employment, aggregate spending must be increased. Earlier we had increased government spending (G) or income transfers to achieve this objective; now we want to increase consumer spending (C) via changes in taxes.

[2]We are still ignoring business taxes, retained earnings, and depreciation here (see Chapter 4). Our purpose is to assess the impact of taxes on consumer spending.

[3]In practice, income taxes may also change the slope of the consumption function. The example used here ignores this added complication, without misrepresenting the general impact of taxes.

FIGURE 10.4
Taxes and Consumption

Taxes lower disposable income and consumer spending at all levels of output. In this case, consumer spending at full employment (Y_F) drops from $1,600 billion per year (point *M*, before the introduction of taxes) to $1,300 billion per year (point *N*, after taxes are imposed). Taxes shift the consumption function downward.

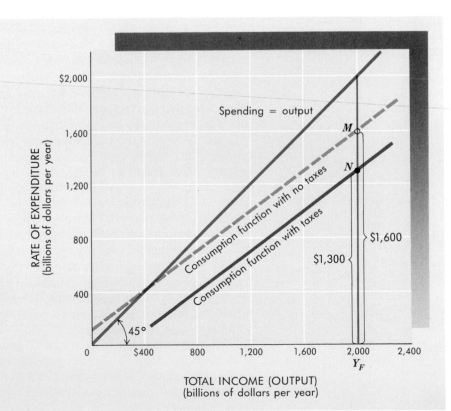

RATE OF EXPENDITURE (billions of dollars per year)

TOTAL INCOME (OUTPUT) (billions of dollars per year)

We have already demonstrated that an additional injection of $100 billion per year (at Y_e) is sufficient to propel the economy to full employment, thanks to the multiplier process. Hence we want to encourage consumers to increase their spending at Y_e by this amount. How large a tax cut is required to stimulate $100 billion more of consumer spending?

If your answer is $100 billion, you have forgotten the marginal propensity to consume. ***Changes in consumer spending (C) are smaller than changes in disposable income (Y_D)*** because consumers save some of their income. Accordingly, if we reduce taxes by $100 billion, disposable income will increase by the same amount. But consumption will rise by *less* than $100 billion. If MPC = 0.75, consumer spending will initially rise by only $75 billion in response to a $100 billion tax cut, and our policy objective will not be attained. Therefore, we must reduce taxes *more* than $100 billion.

The appropriate size of the tax cut can be calculated directly from the formula

$$\bullet \quad \frac{\text{Desired}}{\text{tax cut}} = \frac{\text{desired injection}}{\text{MPC}}$$

We have assumed that MPC = 0.75 and that we need an additional injection of $100 billion. Therefore,

$$\frac{\text{Desired}}{\text{tax cut}} = \frac{\$100 \text{ billion}}{0.75} = \$133 \text{ billion}$$

By cutting taxes $133 billion, we directly increase disposable income by the same amount. Consumers then increase their rate of spending $100 billion (0.75 × $133 billion); they save the remaining $33 billion. As the added spending enters the circular flow, it will start the multiplier process, ultimately increasing total spending (income) by $400 billion per year.

Notice that tax policy suffers from the same shortcomings that afflict transfer policy. A dollar of tax cuts does not result in a dollar of spending. Some part of the tax cut—the marginal propensity to save—will remain unspent. As a result, ***a dollar of tax cuts is less stimulative than a dollar of government purchases.*** This doesn't mean that tax cuts are undesirable, just that they need to be larger than the desired injection of spending.

Another implication of the evident leakage from tax cuts is that tax increases don't "offset" government spending of equal value. This unexpected result is described in Table 10.2.

Taxes and Investment
A tax cut may also be an effective mechanism for increasing investment spending. As we observed in Chapter 8, investment decisions are guided by expectations of future profit, particularly after-tax profits. If a cut in corporate taxes raises potential after-tax profits, it should encourage additional investment. Once an increase in the rate of investment spending enters the circular flow, it has a multiplier effect on total spending like that which follows an initial change in consumer spending. Thus tax cuts for consumers or investors provide an alternative to increased government spending as a mechanism for stimulating aggregate spending.

Tax cuts designed to stimulate C and I have been used frequently. In 1963 President John F. Kennedy announced his intention to reduce taxes in order to stimulate the economy, citing the fact that the marginal propensity to consume for the average American family at that time appeared to be

---

TABLE 10.2   The Balanced Budget Multiplier

Many taxpayers and politicians demand that any new government spending be "balanced" with new taxes. Such balancing "at the margin," it is asserted, will keep the budget deficit from rising, while avoiding further economic stimulus.

We have shown, however, that changes in government spending (G) are more powerful than changes in taxes (T) or transfers. This implies that a budget balanced at the margin will shift aggregate expenditure. An increase in G apparently "offset" with an equal rise in T will increase aggregate expenditure.

To see how this curious result comes about, suppose that the government decided to spend $50 billion per year on a new fleet of space shuttles and to pay for them by raising income taxes by the same amount. Thus

Change in G = +$50 billion per year
Change in T = +$50 billion per year
Change in budget balance = 0

How will these decisions affect total spending?

The increase in the rate of government spending directly boosts aggregate spending by $50 billion per year. But what about the increased taxes? How will consumer spending respond to the resultant drop in disposable income? According to the consumption function, consumer spending will decrease when taxes go up, but not dollar for dollar. Instead, the rate of consumption will diminish by a *fraction* of the tax increase, that fraction being equal to the marginal propensity to consume (MPC). Thus the initial reduction in annual consumer spending equals MPC × $50 billion.

The reduction in consumption is therefore less than the increase in government spending, implying a net increase in *aggregate* spending. The *initial* change in aggregate spending brought about by this balanced-budget expenditure is

Initial increase in government spending = $50 billion
Initial reduction in consumer spending = MPC × $50 billion
Net initial change in total spending   = (1 − MPC) $50 billion

Like any other changes in the rate of spending, this initial increase in aggregate spending will start a multiplier process in motion. The *cumulative* change in expenditure will be much larger, as indicated by the multiplier. In this case, the cumulative (ultimate) change in total spending is

$$\frac{\text{The}}{\text{multiplier}} \times \frac{\text{initial change}}{\text{in spending per year}} = \frac{\text{cumulative change}}{\text{in total spending}}$$

$$\frac{1}{1-\text{MPC}} \times (1-\text{MPC})\$50 \text{ billion} = \$50 \text{ billion}$$

Thus the balanced-budget multiplier is equal to 1. In this case, a $50 billion increase in annual government expenditure combined with an equivalent increase in taxes increases equilibrium income (ultimately) $50 billion per year.

exceptionally high. His successor, Lyndon Johnson, concurred with Kennedy's reasoning. Johnson agreed to "shift emphasis sharply from expanding federal expenditure to boosting private consumer demand and business investment." He proceeded to cut personal and corporate taxes $11 billion. President Johnson proclaimed that "the $11 billion tax cut will challenge American businessmen, investors, and consumers to put their enlarged incomes to work in the private economy to expand output, investment, and jobs." He added, "I am confident that our private decision makers will rise to this challenge."[4] They apparently did, because $C + I$ increased $33 billion in 1963 and another $46 billion in 1965 (in part as a result of multiplier effects, of course).

The largest tax cut in history was initiated by President Ronald Reagan in 1981. The Reagan administration persuaded Congress to cut personal taxes $250 billion over a three-year period and to cut business taxes another $70 billion. The resulting increase in disposable income stimulated consumer spending and helped push the economy out of the 1981–82 recession. When the economy slowed down at the end of the 1980s, President George Bush proposed to cut the capital gains tax. His principal argument for this tax cut was its potential to stimulate investment (i.e., to shift the investment function in an upward direction).

FISCAL POLICY TO ACHIEVE PRICE STABILITY

Fiscal policy will not always be used to *increase* aggregate spending. Just as the expenditure decisions made by consumers and investors may result in deficient aggregate spending, so too may they result in *excessive* aggregate spending. The potential for such an occurrence is illustrated here by Figure 10.5a. Note that aggregate private expenditure $(C + I)$ at full employment (Y_F) is now larger than total output. The excess demand represented by the difference between desired spending and total output at full employment is an **inflationary gap.**

inflationary gap: The amount by which desired spending at full employment exceeds full-employment output.

Figure 10.5b also illustrates an inflationary gap, but one to which government spending has contributed as well. In fact, excessive aggregate spending could have surfaced because we earlier overestimated the size of a recessionaryy gap and introduced too much government spending and/or overly large tax cuts!

Whatever its source, an inflationary gap implies that goods and services are selling faster than they can be produced at full employment. The existence of inventories makes such selling possible, at least for a while. But as inventories are depleted, there is no longer any way to satisfy the excessive demand with goods and services. Accordingly, prices will start to rise as market participants try to outbid each other for available goods.

The objective of fiscal policy in an inflationary environment is to decrease total spending rather than increase it. In this sense, fiscal policy is a two-edged sword, which may be used either to stimulate or to suppress aggregate spending.

Government Cutbacks

The means available to the federal government for restraining total spending emerge again from both sides of the budget. The difference here is that we use the tools in reverse. We now want to reduce injections or increase leakage in order to curb total expenditure.

As before, we can gauge the dimensions of the desired intervention by the size of the imbalance between desired spending and output at full employment. On the outlay side of the budget, this implies

$$\text{Desired reduction in injections} = \text{amount of inflationary gap}$$

[4]*Economic Report of the President,* 1964, p. 6.

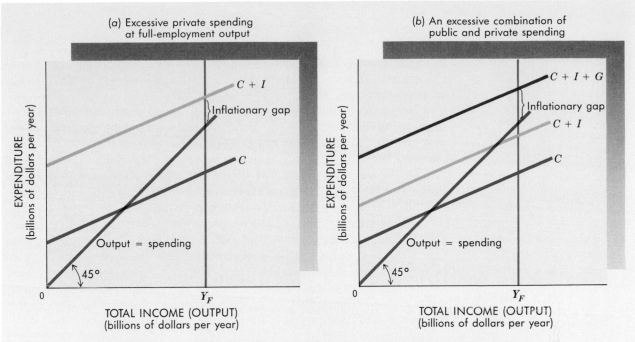

(a) Excessive private spending at full-employment output

(b) An excessive combination of public and private spending

FIGURE 10.5 An Inflationary Gap May Result From...

An inflationary gap will arise in a completely private economy if $C + I$ at full-employment exceeds total output (part a). In a mixed economy, the combination of public (G) and private ($C + I$) spending may exceed full-employment output (part b). In either case, the objective of fiscal policy is to restrain aggregate spending by raising taxes or cutting government expenditure.

Cutbacks in government purchases (G) directly reduce aggregate spending. Thus the desired cut in government purchases is equal to the inflationary gap. Such cutbacks will shift the aggregate expenditure curve downward and ultimately reduce total income and spending by the initial cutback multiplied by the multiplier. If we cut G by $10 billion per year, for example, sales and income will drop initially by exactly $10 billion. But the income and spending reductions will accumulate as the cut in G makes its way around the circular flow. Ultimately, income and expenditure will drop $10 billion times the multiplier (see Table 10.1).

Reductions in transfer payments have similar but less powerful effects. If income transfers are reduced $10 billion, consumer spending will initially fall less than that amount, specifically, by MPC $\times$ $10 billion. As before, we note that *changes in transfers are less powerful than changes in government spending.*

Tax Increases Tax increases are another mechanism for closing an inflationary gap. Our objective here is to increase the leakage from the circular flow, bringing total spending down to the level of our productive capacity. Once again, however, we confront a potential problem. Consumers do not reduce their spending by the same amount that taxes rise. Some of the additional taxes are paid with reduced saving. Hence *taxes must be increased more than a dollar to reduce spending by a dollar.* This leads us to the following guideline:

$$\text{Desired increase} \atop \text{in taxes} = \frac{\text{desired increase} \atop \text{in leakage}}{\text{MPC}}$$

In other words, changes in taxes must always be larger than the desired change in leakages or injections. How much larger depends on the marginal propensity to consume.

Tax increases have been used to "cool" the economy on several occasions. In 1968, for example, the economy was rapidly approaching full employment and Vietnam War expenditures were helping to drive up prices. Congress responded by imposing a 10 percent surtax (temporary additional tax) on income, which took more than $10 billion in purchasing power away from consumers. Resultant multiplier effects reduced spending in 1969 over $20 billion and thus helped restrain price pressures.

In 1982 there was great concern that the 1981 tax cuts had been excessive and that an inflationary gap was emerging. To reduce that inflationary pressure, Congress withdrew some of its earlier tax cuts, especially those designed to increase investment spending. The net effect of the Tax Equity and Fiscal Responsibility Act of 1982 was to increase taxes roughly $90 billion for the years 1983–85. This shifted the aggregate spending function downward, thus narrowing the projected gap.

Fiscal Guidelines   Table 10.3 summarizes the basic objectives of fiscal policy. The primary goal is to make equilibrium GNP equal to full-employment GNP. The fiscal mechanism for attaining that goal is the government budget. By changing taxes, transfers, or government spending, the government can alter the rate of leakage or injection. These changes, in turn, may increase or decrease aggregate spending.

TABLE 10.3   Fiscal Policy Primer

Leakages: Saving, taxes, imports
Injections: Investment, government spending, exports
Equilibrium GNP: The rate of output at which desired spending equals the rate of production. In equilibrium, injections and leakage are exactly equal. This implies:

In a closed, private economy: desired I = desired S
In a closed, mixed economy: desired $I + G$ = desired $S + T$
In an open economy: desired $I + G + X$ = desired $S + T + M$

Full-employment GNP: The total value of final goods and services that could be produced in a given time period at full employment; potential GNP.

The policy objective: To make equilibrium GNP equal to full-employment GNP.
Fiscal strategy:
Desired new injection = recessionary gap
Desired new leakage = inflationary gap

THE CONCERN FOR CONTENT

The guidelines for fiscal policy don't say anything about how the government spends its revenue or whom it taxes. The important thing is that the right amount of spending take place at the right time. In other words, insofar as our stabilization objectives are concerned, the content of total spending is of secondary interest; the level of spending is the only thing that counts.

But it does matter, of course, whether federal expenditures are devoted to military hardware, urban transit systems, or tennis courts. Our economic goals include not only full employment and price stability but also a desirable mix of output, an equitable distribution of income, and adequate economic growth. These other goals are directly affected by the content of total spending. The relative emphasis on and sometimes exclusive concern for, stabilization objectives—to the neglect of related GNP content—has been designated by Joan Robinson as the "second crisis of economic theory." She explains:

> The first crisis arose from the breakdown of a theory which could not account for the *level* of employment. The second crisis arises from a theory that cannot account for the *content* of employment.
>
> Keynes was arguing against the dominant orthodoxy which held that government expenditure could not increase employment. He had to prove, first of all, that it could. He had to show that an increase in investment will increase consumption—that more wages will be spent on more beer and boots whether the investment is useful or not. He had to show that the secondary increase in real income [the multiplier effect] is quite independent of the object of the primary outlay. Pay men to dig holes in the ground and fill them up again if you cannot do anything else.
>
> There was an enormous orthodox resistance to this idea. The whole weight of the argument had to be on this one obvious point.
>
> The war was a sharp lesson in Keynesism. Orthodoxy could not stand up any longer. Governments accepted the responsibility to maintain a high and stable level of employment. Then economists took over Keynes and erected the new orthodoxy. Once the point had been established, the question should have changed. Now that we all agree that government expenditure can maintain employment, we should argue about what the expenditure should be for. Keynes did not *want* anyone to dig holes and fill them.[5]

The alternatives to paying people for digging and filling holes in the ground are enormous in scope and are only suggested by the summary of federal expenditures provided in Table 3.1. It is abundantly clear that with over $1 trillion to spend each year, the federal government has great influence not only on prices and employment, but also on the degree to which our other goals are fulfilled.

The kinds of expenditures and taxes that are appropriate at any given time depend on the values and perceived needs of society, and no structured blueprint can be provided in an economics textbook. We can, however, highlight two major issues.

[5]Joan Robinson, "The Second Crisis of Economic Theory," *American Economic Review*, May 1972, p. 6.

Public vs. Private Spending

Fiscal policy can be directed toward private expenditure ($C + I$) or toward public expenditure (G). If G is increased, the public sector grows relative to the private sector. In this case, the government increases its influence over the dimensions of our economic and social welfare. If C and I are stimulated, the result will be exactly the opposite. The share of government purchases in total expenditure has actually risen dramatically over time, from only 2 percent in 1902 to 20 percent in the 1990s.

We have no objective standard for determining how large the public sector should be. Ultimately it boils down to a question of whether specific public-sector goods are more desired than specific private goods (see the discussion of "government waste" in Chapter 3). And the question of desirability is inherently subjective. We might also note, however, that some people believe individual freedom and big government are inherently inconsistent. They attach a low or even negative benefit to public-sector activity. Milton Friedman, for one, believes that as the government increases its control over the economy, individuals lose their freedom to pursue their own economic and political goals.[6]

Output Mixes Within Each Sector

In addition to choosing whether to increase public or private spending, fiscal policy must also consider the specific content of spending within each sector. Suppose we determine that stimulation of the private sector is preferable to additional government spending as a means of promoting full employment. We still have many choices. We could, for example, cut corporate taxes, cut individual taxes, reduce excise taxes, or increase Social Security benefits. Each alternative implies a different mix of consumption and investment and a different distribution of income. When President Bush proposed to cut the capital gains tax, for example, congressional Democrats objected that such a cut would unfairly benefit wealthy taxpayers. They preferred a payroll tax cut that would benefit the average worker. As they saw it, the same amount of economic stimulus could be achieved with very different distributional consequences.

The same is obviously true of public-sector expenditures. Once an appropriate level of government spending is chosen, we still have to decide what to spend it on. Many people argue that defense spending should be reduced sharply in recognition of the thaw in East–West relations. That needn't reduce government expenditure, however. On the contrary, a long list of alternative uses of the so-called "peace dividend" has been proposed (see In the News). Any such changes in the mix of output will affect our collective well-being.

WHO SETS FISCAL POLICY?

The general outlines of fiscal policy are reasonably easy to describe. When it comes to specific choices about the level, direction, or content of taxes and expenditures, however, the going gets pretty rough. Fiscal planners must pursue a variety of goals and take into account the probable consequences of

---

[6]Milton Friedman, *Capitalism and Freedom* (Chicago: University of Chicago Press, 1962). George Gilder echoes these thoughts in *The Spirit of Enterprise* (New York: Simon and Schuster, 1984). For a very different view, read John Kenneth Galbraith's *The Affluent Society* (Boston: Houghton Mifflin, 1958) or his *Economics and the Public Purpose* (Boston: Houghton Mifflin, 1973).

In The News

CONCERN FOR CONTENT

Political Wars Loom Over the Peace Dividend

First Casualty May Be Will to Cut Budget Deficit

A mad scramble is underway on Capitol Hill to grab a share of any "peace dividend" produced by defense spending cuts, and the political will to reduce the federal budget deficit may get trampled in the process.

The first official word of what the Bush administration thinks the dividend should be will come tomorrow, when the White House releases its fiscal 1991 budget. It is expected to be no more than $4 billion to $6 billion in the first year.

But the very idea of a peace dividend—plus an apparently exaggerated sense of how large it might be—has eroded the budget-cutting discipline on the Hill, lawmakers say.

Calls are being heard to use defense savings to pay for increased education and child care assistance, nuclear plant cleanups, highway construction and more. Other members of Congress want to deploy the peace dividend to cut taxes. . . .

The peace dividend is hardly likely to satisfy all of those ambitions. In the 1991 budget coming out tomorrow, the administration is expected to propose lowering military appropriations by about 2 percent or so a year, after adjustment for inflation. . . .

Whatever its size, the peace dividend should prove a plus for the American economy and living standards, according to most economists.

Military spending does provide jobs, but the same amount of money spent on something else would provide other jobs. The purpose of military spending, of course, is to provide national security. If that security can be purchased for less money because the Soviet threat has diminished, then that money can be directed elsewhere.

—John M. Berry and Paul Blustein

The Washington Post, January 28, 1990, p. H1. Copyright © 1990 The Washington Post.

any action (or inaction) on each one. They must then weigh the alternatives in terms of values and opportunity costs and design the optimal set of policy actions.

Discretionary Fiscal Spending

fiscal year (FY): The twelve-month period used for accounting purposes; begins October 1 for federal government.

As we saw in Chapter 3, the president and Congress jointly make our basic fiscal-policy decisions. Each year they put together the federal budget, which details anticipated revenues and expenditures for the following **fiscal year (FY).** The entire budget is not re-created each year, however. As the Brookings Institution staff has noted, "To pretend that a trillion-dollar federal budget is freshly put together each year is an exercise in self-delusion. From one year to the next, most of the changes that occur in budget expenditures are 'built-in'; that is, they result from decisions made in previous years."[7] The fiscal 1991 budget (Table 3.1), for example, contained provisions for $264 billion for Social Security benefits to retired and disabled persons. These benefits represented a commitment first established in 1935 and reaffirmed every few years since. It also contained provisions for $16 billion in veterans' benefits, $173 billion for interest payments on the national debt, and many billions more for completion of projects begun in previous years. Short of repudiating all prior commitments, there is little that Congress or the president can do to alter these expenditures in any given year. ***To a large extent,***

[7]Charles L. Schultze et al., *Setting National Priorities: The 1973 Budget* (Washington, D.C.: Brookings Institution, 1972), p. 464; figures have been updated.

current revenues and expenditures are the results of prior decisions. Those portions of the budget that are subject to current decision making are referred to as *discretionary spending* (or *nonspending*). Expenditures that are built into the annual budget process are called "uncontrollables."

That is not to say that the ability of fiscal policy to alter economic outcomes in a given year is negligible. It is much smaller, however, than one might infer from the size of the federal budget. Most observers of the budget process conclude that less than one-fifth of the budget in any year represents **discretionary fiscal spending.** Moreover, the discretionary share has been shrinking as interest payments and entitlements (e.g., Social Security, Medicare) have absorbed more and more of the federal budget.

discretionary fiscal spending: Those elements of the federal budget not determined by past legislative or executive commitments.

Automatic Stabilizers

Although the existence of uncontrollable expenditures in the budget limits the range of current fiscal policy, such expenditures often contribute to increased economic stability. Consider unemployment insurance benefits. The unemployment insurance program, established in 1935, provides that persons who lose their jobs will receive some income (an average of $160 per week) from the government (see Chapter 6). In 1982 total unemployment insurance benefits nearly doubled, not because Congress consciously redirected federal expenditures, but simply because more people were unemployed in 1982 than in 1981. Hence these benefits provided an **automatic stabilizer** by increasing federal outlays at a time when aggregate spending was too low to employ our available resources fully. Welfare benefits, which also increased in 1982, constitute a similar kind of stabilizer. Neither change in outlays required congressional or executive action; they occurred *automatically* in response to changing economic conditions.

automatic stabilizer: Federal expenditure or revenue item that automatically responds counter-cyclically to changes in national income, e.g., unemployment benefits, income taxes.

Automatic stabilizers also exist on the revenue side of the federal budget. Income taxes, in particular, constitute an important stabilizer, because they move up and down with the value of spending and output. When total spending increases and incomes rise, income taxes siphon off some of the increased purchasing power. This helps to counteract inflationary pressures that might emerge. Progressive income taxes are particularly effective stabilizers, as they siphon off increasing proportions of purchasing power when incomes are rising and decreasing proportions when demand and output are falling.

POLICY INSIGHTS:

AN UNBALANCED BUDGET

Keynesian theory offers us some fairly straightforward guidelines for combating macro failure: when aggregate spending at full employment is too low, boost it with tax cuts or increased government spending; if aggregate demand is too high, curb it with tax hikes and cutbacks in government spending. From this perspective, the federal budget is a key policy lever for controlling the economy.

Budget Surpluses and Deficits

Use of the budget to stabilize the economy implies that federal expenditures and receipts will not always be equal. In the face of a recessionary gap, for example, the government has sound reasons both to cut taxes and to increase its own spending. By reducing tax revenues and increasing expenditures si-

deficit spending: A situation wherein government expenditures exceed government revenues.

multaneously, however, the federal government will throw its budget out of balance. This will lead to **deficit spending,** a situation in which government spending exceeds tax revenues. The size of the deficit is equal to the difference between expenditures and receipts:

$$\bullet \quad \frac{\text{Budget}}{\text{balance}} = \frac{\text{government}}{\text{revenue}} - \frac{\text{government}}{\text{spending}}$$

To pay for deficit spending, the government must borrow money, either directly from the private sector or from the banking system. In either case, the U.S. Treasury issues (sells) bonds that increase the public debt.[8]

budget surplus: An excess of government revenues over government expenditures in a given time period.

There are also occasions when government revenues will exceed government expenditures, thereby giving rise to a **budget surplus.** Such a surplus might arise as a result of tax increases coupled with reductions in government spending.

To Balance or Not to Balance?

From a Keynesian perspective, budget deficits and surpluses are a routine feature of fiscal policy. The appropriateness of any given deficit or surplus depends on the need for more or less spending injections. *In Keynes's view, a balanced budget would be appropriate only if all other injections and leakages were in balance and the economy was in full-employment equilibrium.* If either of these conditions was not met, an unbalanced budget would be appropriate.

Whatever the merits of Keynes's theory, the practice of fiscal policy has produced few budget surpluses. As Figure 10.6 confirms, the federal budget has been in deficit every year of your life. Although our deficits haven't been particularly high by international standards (see World View), this string of deficits has raised a chorus of protests about both the practice and the principles of fiscal policy.

Cyclical Deficits

The string of deficits illustrated in Figure 10.6 is not wholly attributable to discretionary fiscal policy. As powerful as fiscal policy might be, it does not fully control the size of the deficit. On the contrary, *the size of the federal deficit is sensitive to cyclical conditions of the macro economy.*

The cyclical sensitivity of the federal budget is rooted in the automatic stabilizers we noted earlier. In a recession, tax receipts fall automatically, while government spending increases. Table 10.4, page 254, shows the consequences of these automatic stabilizers for the federal budget. Notice that when the unemployment rate rises 1 percent, tax revenues decline $21 billion. As the economy slows, people also turn to the government for additional income support: unemployment benefits and other transfer payments increase by $7 billion. As a consequence, the budget deficit widens by $28 billion. Inflation also affects the budget deficit by automatically increasing both revenues and spending.

The most important implication of Table 10.4 is that neither the president nor the Congress has complete control of the federal deficit. *Actual budget deficits and surpluses may arise from economic conditions as well as policy.* Perhaps no one learned this better than President Reagan. In 1980 he

---

[8]Recall that such borrowing may "crowd out" private consumption or investment. The mechanics of government borrowing and its potential impact on the private sector are discussed in Chapters 12, 13, and 14.

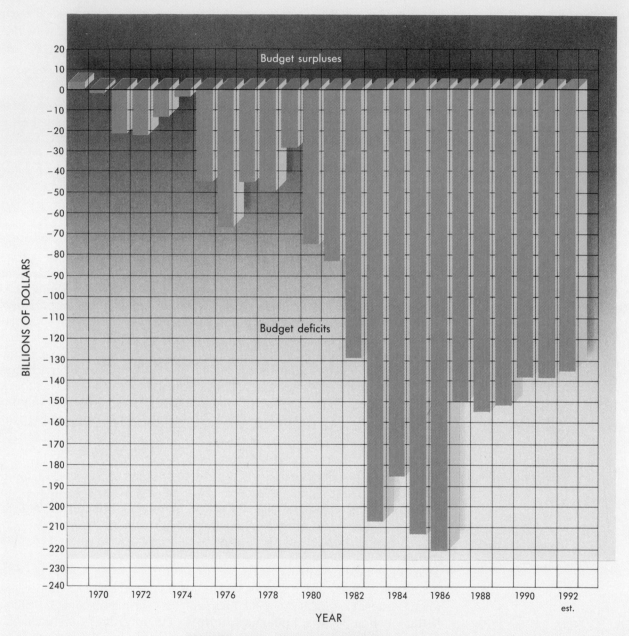

FIGURE 10.6 A String of Deficits

The federal government has not achieved an annual budget surplus since 1969. In the early 1980s, federal deficits increased dramatically. Since then, they have declined substantially but still fall far short of a balanced budget.

campaigned on a promise to balance the budget. The 1981–82 recession, however, caused the actual deficit to soar. The president later had to admit that actual deficits are not solely the product of "big spenders" in Washington.

W🌐RLD VIEW

DEFICIT SPENDING

U.S. Deficits Not Unusually Large

Although the U.S. budget deficits receive the most attention, deficit spending is a common feature of fiscal policy. As the figures below reveal, few Western governments had budget surpluses in 1988; most had budget deficits that were at least as large, in relation to GNP, as that of the United States.

Country	Budget deficit (−) or surplus (+) as percentage of GNP
Australia	−2.0
Austria	−3.6
Belgium	−6.9
Canada	−4.6
Denmark	+0.9
Finland	0.0
France	−2.5
Germany (West)	−2.0
Greece	−10.1
Italy	−12.2
Japan	−0.2
Norway	+1.1
Spain	−4.8
United Kingdom	−2.7
United States	−2.6

Source: Organization for Economic Cooperation and Development, 1988 estimates.

Structural Deficits

structural deficit: Federal revenues at full employment minus expenditures at full employment under prevailing fiscal policy.

If actual deficits don't necessarily reflect fiscal-policy decisions, how are we to know whether fiscal policy is stimulative or restrictive? Clearly, some other policy measure is needed.

To isolate the effects of fiscal policy, economists break down the actual deficit into *cyclical* and *structural* components. The cyclical portion of the deficit reflects the impact of the business cycle on federal tax revenues and spending. The **structural deficit** reflects fiscal-policy decisions. Rather than comparing actual outlays to actual receipts, the structural deficit compares the outlays and receipts that would occur if the economy were at full employment.[9]

The structural-deficit concept excludes from consideration reductions in revenue or increases in spending brought about by less than full levels of output and (taxable) income. Those reductions are the result of economic conditions, not fiscal policy. Consider what happened to the federal budget in 1980. In 1979 the federal deficit amounted to $28 billion. In 1980 it more than doubled, to nearly $60 billion. At first glance it would appear that the government was desperately trying to stimulate economic activity with expansionary fiscal policies. But this was not the case. The primary reason for the larger 1980 deficit was increased unemployment. The rate of unemployment jumped from 5.8 percent in 1979 to 7.1 percent in 1980. As a result, government outlays increased, and revenues fell.

[9]The structural deficit is also referred to as the "full-employment" or "high-employment" deficit.

TABLE 10.4   The Budget Impact of Increased Unemployment and Inflation
(in 1990 dollars)

Changes in economic conditions alter the federal budget balance. When unemployment increases, the budget deficit grows. When inflation accelerates, the budget deficit shrinks. To discern the true intentions of fiscal policy, we must abstract from these effects. The structural deficit serves this purpose.

A. *When the unemployment rate increases by 1 percentage point:*
  1. Government spending (G) automatically increases for:
     - Unemployment insurance benefits
     - Food stamps
     - Welfare benefits
     - Social Security benefits
     - Medicaid
     Total increase in outlays: + $7 billion
  2. Government tax revenues (T) automatically decline for:
     - Individual income taxes
     - Corporate income taxes
     - Social Security payroll taxes
     Total decline in revenues: − $21 billion
  3. The deficit widens by $28 billion

B. *When the inflation rate increases by 1 percentage point:*
  1. Government spending (G) automatically increases for:
     - Indexed retirement and Social Security benefits
     - Higher interest payments
     Total increase in outlays: + $15 billion
  2. Government tax revenues (T) automatically increase for:
     - Corporate income taxes
     - Social Security payroll taxes
     Total increase in revenues: + $18 billion
  3. The deficit shrinks by $3 billion

Source: Office of Management and Budget.

Fiscal policy in 1980 was expansionary, but not to nearly as great a degree as the actual change in the deficit indicates. The structural deficit increased only $16 billion (rather than $32 billion, as in the actual budget). This increase represented explicit expansionary policies. Table 10.5 shows how the actual, structural, and cyclical deficits have behaved in recent years.

Fiscal Policy in the Great Depression

The structural-deficit concept also sheds new light on the Great Depression. During the 1930s, the federal budget was in a deficit position each year. Many observers have regarded those deficits as the results of good Keynesian economics. But this was far from the case. In 1931 President Herbert Hoover observed, "Business depressions have been recurrent in the life of our country and are but transitory." Rather than proposing fiscal stimulus, Hoover complained that expansion of public-works programs had unbalanced the federal budget. In 1932 he proposed *cutbacks* in government spending and *higher* taxes. In his view, the "unquestioned balancing of the federal budget . . . is the first necessity of national stability and is the foundation of further recovery."

Franklin Roosevelt, Hoover's successor in the White House, shared this Classical view of fiscal policy. He criticized Hoover for not balancing the budget, and in 1933 he warned Congress that "all public works must be con-

TABLE 10.5 Cyclical vs. Structural Deficits
(in billions of dollars)

The actual (observed) budget deficit includes both cyclical and structural components. Changes in the structural component result from policy changes; changes in the cyclical component result from changes in the economy. Between FY 1983 and FY 1984 the structural deficit grew by $25 billion due to tax cuts and increased defense spending. The cyclical deficit shrank by $46 billion, however, as the economy grew. As a result, the federal deficit shrank by $21 billion.

Fiscal year	Actual deficit	=	Cyclical deficit	+	Structural deficit
1980	60		4		55
1981	58		19		39
1982	111		62		48
1983	196		95		101
1984	175		49		126
1985	210		46		163
1986	221		34		187
1987	150		32		118
1988	157		27		130
1989	176		30		146
1990	167		27		140

Source: Congressional Budget Office.

sidered from the point of view of the ability of the government treasury to pay for them."

As Figure 10.7 shows, the budget deficit persisted throughout the Great Depression. But these deficits were the result of a declining economy, not stimulative fiscal policy.

Between 1929 and 1932, federal expenditures rose only $200 million. As a result, the structural deficit actually *decreased* from 1931 to 1933 (see Figure 10.7), thereby restraining aggregate spending at a time when producers were

FIGURE 10.7
The Impact of Fiscal Policy in the 1930s
(all figures in 1947 prices)

During the Great Depression the federal budget was in deficit. But those deficits were the consequence of reduced tax revenues caused by high unemployment rates and low incomes. Fiscal policy was not expansionary. On the contrary, the structural deficit was decreasing in 1932, 1933, and 1937.

Source: Adapted from E. Cary Brown, "Fiscal Policy in the Thirties: A Reappraisal," *American Economic Review*, December 1956, Table 1.

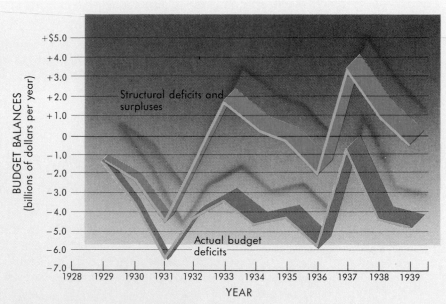

desperate for increased sales. Only when the deficit was expanded tremendously by spending during World War II did fiscal policy have a decidedly positive effect. Federal defense expenditures jumped from $2.2 billion in 1940 to $87.4 billion in 1944!

By distinguishing between the structural budget and the actual budget, we can evaluate fiscal policy more accurately. If the structural budget has a growing deficit (or declining surplus), the government is stimulating total expenditure. Whenever the structural deficit is shrinking (or surplus is growing), the government is trying to restrain total spending and output. The size of any changes in the structural budget measures the intensity of such efforts.

Accordingly, **changes in the structural deficit are the basic measure of fiscal policy.** Using this simple test and the data in Table 10.5, you can determine whether fiscal policy was stimulative or restrictive in the 1980s.

SUMMARY

• The Keynesian explanation of macro instability requires government intervention to shift the aggregate demand curve to the desired rate of output. The government can do this by balancing aggregate spending with the economy's full-employment potential. Fiscal policy is used to increase aggregate spending in the face of a recessionary gap and to restrain aggregate spending when an inflationary gap appears.

• To stimulate total expenditure, the government may choose to increase its own rate of spending. Alternatively, it may increase transfer payments or reduce taxes on consumers and businesses, leaving them with more income to spend.

• To restrain total expenditure, the government may reduce its own rate of spending. Or it may reduce income transfers and increase taxes, thereby reducing the income and spending of the private sector.

• Injections into the circular flow have a multiplied impact on total spending and output. An increase in the annual rate of government spending, for example, will result in more disposable income, which will be used to finance further consumer spending.

• Changes in government spending are more powerful than changes in transfer payments or taxes. Changes in G directly alter aggregate expenditure.

• Changes in government spending and taxes will also alter the content of GNP, and thus influence *what* to produce. Fiscal policy affects the relative size of the public and private sectors, as well as the mix of output in each sector.

• Fiscal policy is formulated annually by the president and Congress. Each year's receipts and expenditures, however, are substantially determined by uncontrollables that reflect policy decisions of earlier years. Only a fraction of any year's budget represents discretionary spending that results from current decisions.

• An important feature of some uncontrollable receipts and expenditures is that they respond countercyclically to changing economic conditions and thus operate as automatic stabilizers. Income taxes and unemployment benefits are examples.

• The federal budget is the primary vehicle for implementing fiscal policy. Actual budget deficits, however, reflect both cyclical and structural (policy) conditions. Only changes in the structural deficit reflect discretionary fiscal policy.

Terms to Remember

Define the following terms:

fiscal policy	disposable income
recessionary gap	inflationary gap
aggregate spending	fiscal year (FY)
crowding out	discretionary fiscal spending
equilibrium GNP	automatic stabilizer
multiplier	deficit spending
transfer payments	budget surplus
marginal propensity to save (MPS)	structural deficit

Questions for Discussion

1. Would a constitutional amendment that would require the federal government to balance its budget (incur no deficits) be desirable? Explain.

2. Will $20 billion per year spent on housing have the same impact on the economy as $20 billion spent on interstate highways? Explain.

3. Do fiscal-policy makers really need to know the magnitudes of the MPC and multipliers? Could they get along as well without such information?

4. "Zero-based budgeting" refers to a situation wherein each year's budget starts from zero—that is, all spending is discretionary. Is this possible? Give some examples.

5. Why might policies intended to reduce the deficit actually increase it?

Problems

1. Suppose the economy's full-employment potential is $2,000 billion per year and that the spending desires of market participants are

   $C = \$400$ billion per year $+ 0.5Y$
   $I = \$300$ billion per year
   $G = \$400$ billion per year

   There is no foreign trade (imports or exports).
   (a) What macro problem does this economy confront?
   (b) How could the government eliminate the problem with
      (i) a change in taxes
     (ii) a change in government spending
    (iii) a combination of tax and spending changes?
       Be specific as to amounts of each change.
   (c) Draw an aggregate expenditure curve to illustrate the equilibrium and full-employment levels of this economy.

2. Assume the existence of the same economy as in problem 1 and that the economy is at full employment. The government decides to make two fiscal policy changes: to lower both government expenditures and taxes by $200 billion each.

   (*a*) How does this change alter the consumption function?

   (*b*) Find the new equilibrium for the economy and illustrate it graphically.

   (*c*) Compared to problem 1, how has equilibrium changed?

   (*d*) How has the government's budget deficit changed?

3. Suppose Congress decides to increase Social Security benefits by $20 billion per year.

   (*a*) How will this single budget outlay affect equilibrium GNP?

   (*b*) What if Congress "pays" for these increased transfers by reducing defense spending by $20 billion. What will be the net effect on equilibrium GNP? Assume that the marginal propensity to save is 0.2.

The National Debt

*T*he Continental Congress needed to borrow money in 1777 to continue fighting the Revolutionary War. The Congress tried to raise tax revenues and even printed new money (the Continental dollar) in order to buy needed food, tents, guns, and ammunition. But by the winter of 1777, these mechanisms for financing the war were failing. To acquire needed supplies, the Continental Congress plunged the new nation into debt.

The U.S. government has been borrowing money ever since. Every year that federal spending exceeds tax revenues, the government borrows money to cover the resulting deficit. As a result of those deficits, the accumulated national debt now exceeds $3 trillion. That works out to roughly $12,000 of debt for every man, woman, and child in the United States.

Most taxpayers recoil at the notion of being so deeply in debt. In fact, nine out of ten American adults believe that the federal budget should be balanced. Over 80 percent of the electorate is even willing to support legislation that would *require* Congress to balance the budget every year. Moreover, virtually every congressional and presidential candidate since Calvin Coolidge has promised to eliminate the deficit and reduce the national debt.

What accounts for this startling contradiction between the clamor for balanced budgets and the long record of unbalanced budgets? Does this contradiction reflect a breakdown of the political system? A triumph of Keynesian economics over politics? Or are we simply unable or unwilling to exercise the kind of budget restraint that many economists and politicians say is required for our economic health?

This chapter takes a closer look at annual budget deficits and the national debt they create. Three core questions motivate this discussion:

- How did we get so far in debt?

- Who bears the burden of our national debt?

- Should we require balanced budgets and gradual elimination of the debt?

ACCUMULATED DEBT

Debt Creation

budget deficit: The amount by which government expenditures exceed government revenues in a given time period.

Treasury bonds: Promissory notes (IOUs) issued by the U.S. Treasury.

national debt: Accumulated debt of the federal government.

All of our national debt originates in the **budget deficits** of the federal government. In any year that federal outlays exceed revenues, the U.S. Treasury must finance the deficit by borrowing money. To do so, it sells U.S. Treasury bonds. The **Treasury bonds** are IOUs of the federal government, and they stipulate a date of repayment (typically between 5 and 30 years in the future) and an annual interest payment. People buy bonds—lend money to the U.S. Treasury—because bonds pay interest and are a relatively safe haven for idle funds.

The total stock of all outstanding bonds represents the **national debt.** It is equal to the sum total of our accumulated deficits, less net repayments in years when a budget surplus existed. In other words, *the national debt is a stock of IOUs created by annual deficit flows.*

Early History, 1776–1900

The United States began accumulating debt as soon as independence was declared. By 1783, the United States had borrowed over $8 million from France and $250,000 from Spain. Most of these funds were secretly obtained to help finance the Revolutionary War. After the war, France and the United States argued whether these funds were indeed loans or were grants requiring no repayment. After years of negotiation—and prompting by Treasury Secretary Alexander Hamilton, who wanted to establish the creditworthiness of the new nation—the loans were settled (with partial repayment) in 1835.

During the period 1790–1812, the United States often incurred debt but typically repaid it quickly. The War of 1812, however, caused a massive increase in the national debt. With neither a standing army nor an adequate source of tax revenues to acquire one, the U.S. government had to borrow money to repel the British. By 1816 the national debt was over $129 million. Although that figure seems exceedingly small by today's standards, it amounted to 13 percent of national income in 1816.

After the War of 1812, the U.S. government used recurrent budget surpluses to repay the debt. By 1835 all of the government's debt had been repaid, and the federal government distributed its revenue surplus to the states.

The same pattern of explosive, war-induced increases in the national debt, followed by gradual repayment, prevailed throughout the nineteenth century. The Mexican-American War (1846–48) was accompanied by a fourfold increase in the debt. That debt was pared down the following decade. Then the Civil War (1861–65) broke out, and both sides needed debt financing. By the end of the Civil War the North owed over $2.6 billion, or approximately half of its national income. The South depended more heavily on newly printed Confederate currency to finance its side of the Civil War, relying on bond issues for only one-third of its financial needs. When the South lost, however, neither Confederate currency nor Confederate bonds had any value.[1]

The Twentieth Century: Wars and Depression

The Spanish-American War (1898) also increased the national debt. But all prior debt was dwarfed by World War I, which increased the national debt from 3 percent of national income in 1917 to 41 percent at the war's end.

---

[1]In anticipation of this situation, European lenders had forced the South to guarantee most of its loans with cotton. When the South was unable to repay its debts, these creditors could sell the cotton they had held as collateral. But most holders of Confederate bonds or currency received nothing.

The national debt declined during the 1920s because the federal government was consistently spending less revenue than it took in. Budget surpluses disappeared quickly when the economy fell into the Great Depression, however. The Depression reduced incomes and profits, and thus the amount of taxes people had to pay. Prohibitive tariffs on imported goods virtually eliminated international trade and so depleted another source of government revenue (tariff revenues). At the same time, widespread hunger and joblessness increased the need for government expenditures on welfare, public works, and other relief. Although President Herbert Hoover and his successor, President Franklin Roosevelt, promised to balance the federal budget (Chapter 10), they could not prevent a growing budget deficit.

The most explosive debt occurred during World War II, when the government had to mobilize all available resources. Rather than raising taxes to the fullest, the U.S. government restricted the availability of consumer goods. With consumer goods rationed, consumers had little choice but to increase their saving. Uncle Sam encouraged people to lend their idle funds to the U.S. Treasury by buying U.S. war bonds. The resulting bond purchases raised the national debt from 45 percent of GNP in 1940 to over 125 percent of GNP in 1946!

The Korean War (1950–53) added little to the national debt. The Vietnam War (1965–72), however, increased the debt by over $100 billion, largely owing to the refusal of President Lyndon Johnson or Congress to raise taxes to pay for that war (see Chapter 17).

The 1980s   During the 1980s the national debt jumped again—by nearly $2 trillion. This ten-year increase in the debt exceeded all of the net debt accumulation since the country was founded. This time, however, the debt increase was not war-related. Instead, the debt explosion originated in the recessions of 1980 and 1981–82 and the massive tax cuts of 1981–84.

In summary, *the historical accumulation of the national debt reflects three distinct phenomena:*

- *Wars*

- *Recessions*

- *Tax cuts*

In absolute terms, the recessions and tax cuts of the 1980s account for most of our accumulated debt (see Table 11.1). As a percentage of GNP, however, earlier debt accumulations were far more significant. As Figure 11.1 shows, the *relative* size of the debt has actually shrunk since World War II, despite its growing absolute size. This trend reflects the fact that GNP has been growing faster than the national debt since that time.

WHO OWNS THE DEBT?

To the average citizen, the accumulated national debt is both incomprehensible and frightening. Who can understand debts that are measured in *trillions* of dollars? Who can ever be expected to pay them? The burden of the debt seems larger than anyone could possibly bear. It is this burden that arouses calls for a balanced budget—a halt to debt accumulation. The fears that prompt this call, however, may be exaggerated.

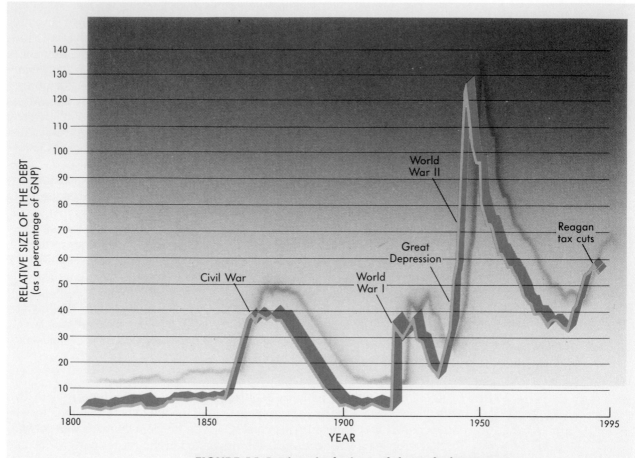

FIGURE 11.1 Historical View of the Debt/GNP Ratio

From 1790 to 1917, the national debt exceeded 10 percent of GNP only during the Civil War years. After 1917, however, the relative size of the debt grew sharply. World War I, the Great Depression, and World War II all caused major increases in the debt ratio. The tax cuts of 1981—84 caused a further increase in the debt/GNP ratio.

Source: U.S. Department of Commerce, and Office of Management and Budget.

Liabilities = Assets

liability: An obligation to make future payment; debt.

asset: Anything having exchange value in the marketplace; wealth.

The first thing to note about the national debt is that it represents not only a liability but an asset as well. When the U.S. Treasury borrows money, it issues bonds. Those bonds are a **liability** for the federal government, since it then has a later obligation to repay. But those same bonds are an **asset** to the people who hold them. Bondholders have a claim to future repayment and can even convert that claim into cash by selling their asset in the bond market. Therefore, ***national debt creates as much wealth (for bondholders) as liabilities (for the U.S. Treasury).*** Neither money nor any other form of wealth disappears when the government borrows money.

The fact that total bond assets equal total bond liabilities is of little consolation to taxpayers who are confronted with $3 trillion of national debt and worry when, if ever, they will be able to repay it. The fear that either the U.S. government or its taxpayers will be "bankrupted" by the national debt always lurks in the shadows. How legitimate is that fear?

TABLE 11.1   The Mounting Debt

It took nearly a century for the national debt to reach $1 trillion. Then the debt tripled in a mere decade. The *ratio* of debt to GNP, however, has fluctuated greatly (see Figure 11.1).

Year	Total debt outstanding (millions of dollars)
1791	75
1800	83
1810	53
1816	127
1820	91
1835	0
1850	63
1865	2,678
1890	1,122
1900	1,263
1915	1,191
1920	24,299
1930	16,185
1940	42,967
1945	258,682
1960	286,331
1970	370,919
1980	914,300
1985	1,827,500
1990	3,163,000

Source: Office of Management and Budget.

**FIGURE 11.2
The Deficit/GNP Ratio**

Although the absolute size of deficits has increased greatly, their relative size has not. The $135 billion budget deficit in fiscal 1990 was 2.9 percent of GNP, about the same relative size as the $53 billion deficit in 1977. In recent years the deficit has shrunk while GNP has continued to increase. The declining deficit/GNP ratio diminished the debt/GNP ratio as well.

Source: Congressional Budget Office.

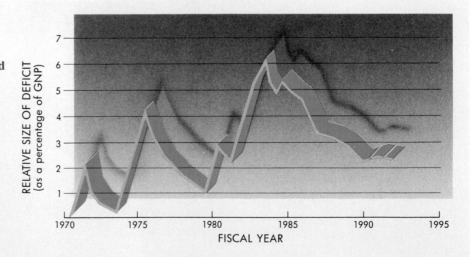

Ownership of the Debt

Figure 11.3 shows who owns the bonds the U.S. Treasury has issued. One of the largest bondholders is the U.S. government itself, with over 31 percent of all outstanding Treasury bonds. The Federal Reserve System, an independent agency of the U.S. government, acquires Treasury bonds in its conduct of monetary policy (Chapters 13 and 14). Other agencies of the U.S. government also purchase bonds. The Social Security Administration, for example, maintains a trust fund balance to cover any shortfall between monthly payroll tax receipts and retirement benefits. Most of that balance is held in the form of interest-bearing Treasury bonds. Thus one arm of the federal government (the U.S. Treasury) owes another arm (the U.S. Social Security Administration) a significant part of the national debt. During the 1990s the Social Security Trust Fund is accumulating huge reserves because payroll tax receipts exceed Social Security benefits every year. These annual surpluses are used to purchase Treasury bonds. As a result, the Social Security Trust Fund is becoming the largest owner of U.S. debt.[2]

Another 11 percent of the national debt is held by state and local governments. This debt, too, arises when state and local governments use their own budget surpluses to purchase interest-bearing Treasury bonds.

The general public owns *directly* only about 7 percent of the national debt. This private wealth is in the form of familiar U.S. savings bonds or other types of Treasury bonds. Even more private wealth is held *indirectly*. As Figure 11.3 shows, over 35 percent of the national debt is held by banks, insurance companies, money-market funds, corporations, and other institutions. All of

[2]Beginning in the year 2013, the flow of Social Security funds will reverse, with annual benefit outlays exceeding payroll tax revenues. This will require the U.S. Treasury to start repaying the debt held by the Social Security Trust Fund. To do that, the federal government will have to increase other taxes or reduce other spending.

FIGURE 11.3
Debt Ownership

The bonds that create the national debt represent wealth that is owned by bondholders. Nearly one-third of that wealth is held by the U.S. government itself. The private sector in the United States holds nearly half of the debt, and foreigners own about one-seventh.

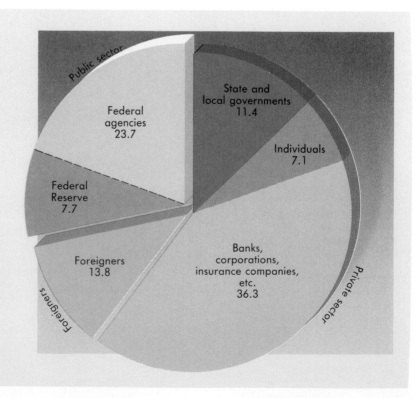

Public sector

Federal agencies
23.7

State and local governments
11.4

Individuals
7.1

Federal Reserve
7.7

Banks, corporations, insurance companies, etc.
36.3

Foreigners
13.8

Private sector

this wealth is ultimately owned by the people who have deposits at the bank or in money-market funds, who own stock in corporations, or who are insured by the insurance companies that hold Treasury bonds. Thus U.S. households hold almost half of the national debt, either directly or indirectly.

All of the debt held by U.S. households, institutions, and government entities is referred to as **internal debt.** As Figure 11.3 illustrates, approximately 86 percent of the national debt is internal.

The last major group of bondholders is foreign. Foreign governments, banks, corporations, and investors include U.S. Treasury bonds in their asset portfolios. U.S. Treasury bonds are attractive to foreigners because of their relative security, the interest they pay, and the general acceptability of dollar-denominated assets in world trade. All of the bonds held by foreign households and institutions is referred to as **external debt.** At present, external debt accounts for about 14 percent of total U.S. debt.

internal debt: U.S. government debt (Treasury bonds) held by American households and institutions.

external debt: U.S. government debt (Treasury bonds) held by foreign households and institutions.

BURDEN OF THE DEBT

It may be comforting to know that most of our national debt is owned internally, and much of it by the government itself. Figure 11.3 will not still the fears of most taxpayers, however, especially those who don't hold any Treasury bonds. From their perspective, the total debt still looks frightening.

Refinancing

How much of a "burden" the debt really represents is not so evident, however. None of the debt has been repaid since you were born. As we have observed, the federal government has borrowed *more* money each year to finance deficits, adding to accumulated debt. The last year in which the federal government reduced the national debt—that is, paid some of it off—was 1957, and that lone repayment reduced the total debt by less than a billion dollars. Since then, as debts have become due, the federal government has simply borrowed new funds to pay them off. New bonds have been issued to replace old bonds. This **refinancing** of the debt is a routine feature of the U.S. Treasury's debt management (see In the News).

refinancing: The issuance of new debt in payment of debt issued earlier.

In The News

REFINANCING

Treasury Plans to Borrow $27 Billion

The Treasury Department announced yesterday that it will borrow $27 billion to replenish government coffers at a series of debt auctions next week. . . .

The auctions, known as quarterly refundings, are the main process by which the government finances the $2.4 trillion national debt.

The Treasury's auctions next week call for:

- $9.25 billion in three-year notes in minimum denominations of $5,000 to be auctioned Tuesday.

- $9 billion in 10-year notes in minimum denominations of $1,000 to be auctioned on Wednesday.

- $8.75 billion in 30-year bonds in minimum denominations of $1,000 to be auctioned on Thursday.

The $27 billion to be raised includes $14.9 billion in new cash and $12.1 billion to pay off maturing securities.

The Washington Post, January 28, 1988, p. E2. Reprinted by permission of the Associated Press.

The ability of the U.S. Treasury to refinance its debt raises an intriguing question. What if the debt could be eternally refinanced? What if no one *ever* demanded to be "paid off" more than others were willing to lend Uncle Sam? Then the national debt would truly accumulate forever, to infinity.

Two things are worrisome about this scenario. First of all, eternal refinancing seems like a chain letter that promises to make everyone rich. In this case, the chain requires that people hold ever-larger portions of their wealth in the form of Treasury bonds. People worry that the chain will be broken and they will be forced to repay all the outstanding debt. Parents worry that the scheme might break down in the next generation, unfairly burdening their own children or grandchildren.

Aside from its seeming implausibility, the notion of eternal refinancing seems to defy a basic maxim of economics, namely that "there ain't no free lunch." Eternal refinancing makes it look as though government borrowing has no cost, as though federal spending financed by the national debt is really a "free lunch."

There are two flaws in this way of thinking. The first relates to the interest charges that accompany debt. The second and more important oversight relates to the real economic costs of government activity.

Debt Servicing

debt servicing: The interest required to be paid each year on outstanding debt.

Interest payments must be made on outstanding debts. With $3 trillion in accumulated debt, the U.S. government must make enormous interest payments each year. **Debt servicing** refers to these annual interest payments. In FY 1991 the U.S. Treasury paid over $173 billion in interest charges (see Table 3.1) Figure 11.4 illustrates how debt-servicing requirements have consumed an increasing share of the federal budget in recent years.

Interest payments are a large and "uncontrollable" component of the federal budget. As such, they force the government to reduce outlays for other purposes or to finance a larger budget each year. In this respect, *interest*

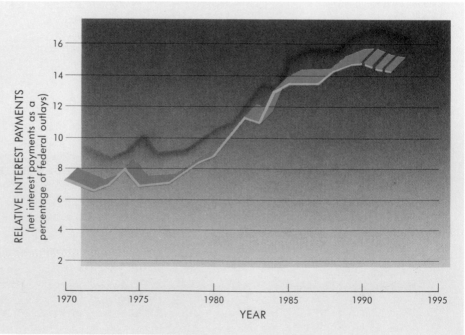

**FIGURE 11.4
Relative Interest Payments**

During the last twenty years the relative cost of debt servicing increased sharply. The increase was caused by both rising interest rates and rapidly mounting debt. The increasing requirements of debt servicing make it more difficult to balance the federal budget or to fund public-sector activities.

Source: Congressional Budget Office.

RELATIVE INTEREST PAYMENTS
(net interest payments as a percentage of federal outlays)

YEAR

payments restrict the government's ability to balance the budget or fund other public-sector activities.

Although the debt-servicing requirements may pinch Uncle Sam's spending purse, the real economic consequences of interest payments are less evident. Who gets the interest payments? What economic resources are absorbed by those payments?

As noted, most of the nation's outstanding debt is internal—that is, owned by domestic households and institutions. Therefore, most interest payments are made to people and institutions within the United States. *Most debt servicing is simply a redistribution of income from taxpayers to bondholders.* In many cases, the taxpayer and bondholder are the same person. In all cases, however, the income that leaks from the circular flow in the form of taxes to pay for debt servicing returns as interest payments. Total income is unchanged. Thus debt servicing may not have any direct effect on aggregate demand.[3]

Debt servicing also has little impact on the real resources of the economy. The collection of additional taxes and the processing of interest payments require the use of some land, labor, and capital. But the value of the resources used for the processing of debt service is trivial—a tiny fraction of the interest payments themselves. This means that *interest payments themselves have virtually no opportunity cost.* The amount of goods and services available for other purposes is virtually unchanged as a result of debt servicing.

Opportunity Costs

opportunity cost: The most desired goods or services that are forgone in order to obtain something else.

If debt servicing absorbs few economic resources, can we conclude that the national debt really does represent a "free lunch"? Unfortunately not. But the concept of **opportunity cost** does provide a major clue about the true burden of the debt and who bears it.

Opportunity costs are incurred only when real resources (factors of production) are used. The amount of that cost is measured by the other goods and services that could have been produced with those resources, but weren't. As we noted earlier, the *process* of debt servicing absorbs few resources and so has negligible opportunity cost. To understand the true burden of the national debt we have to look at what that debt financed. *The true burden of the debt is the opportunity cost of the activities financed by the debt.* To assess that burden, we need to ask what the government did with the borrowed funds.

Government purchases Suppose that Congress decided to upgrade our naval forces and borrowed $10 billion for that purpose. What is the implied opportunity cost of that decision? The economic cost of the fleet upgrade is measured by the goods and services forgone in order to build more ships. The labor, land, and capital used to upgrade the fleet cannot be used to produce something else. We give up the opportunity to produce another $10 billion worth of private goods and services when Congress upgrades the fleet.

The economic cost of the naval buildup is unaffected by the method of government finance. Whether the government borrows $10 billion or increases taxes by that amount, the forgone civilian output will still be $10 billion. *The opportunity cost of government purchases is the true burden of government activity, however financed.* The decision to finance such activity with debt rather than taxes doesn't materially alter that cost.

[3]The rate and composition of aggregate demand will be affected by debt servicing if bondholders and taxpayers have different marginal propensities to consume and different tastes.

Notice also *when* that cost is incurred. If the fleet is upgraded this year, then the opportunity cost is incurred this year. It is only while resources are actually being used by the Navy that we give up the opportunity to use them elsewhere. Opportunity costs are incurred at the time a government activity takes place, not when the resultant debt is paid. In other words, ***the burden of the debt is incurred when the debt-financed activity takes place.***

If the entire naval construction program is completed this year, what costs are borne next year? None. The land, labor, and capital available next year can be used for whatever purposes are then desired. Once the new ships are built, no further resources are allocated to their construction. The real costs of ship construction cannot be postponed until a later year. In other words, the real burden of the debt cannot be passed on to future generations. On the contrary, future generations will benefit from the sacrifices made today to build ships, parks, highways, dams, and other public-sector projects. Future taxpayers will be able to *use* these projects without incurring the opportunity costs of their construction.

Somehow this still doesn't sound right. Don't future generations get stuck with the debt that financed the government purchases? Don't they still end up paying the bill? No. If and when the debt is paid, income will simply be transferred from one set of taxpayers to another (bondholders). If this repayment occurs in a later generation, it is still income redistrubition, *not* a reduction in real resources.

transfer payment: Payments to individuals for which no current goods or services are exchanged, e.g., Social Security, welfare, unemployment benefits.

Transfer payments   Suppose that the government uses debt financing to pay for increased **transfer payments** rather than the purchase of real goods and services. That is, suppose a sudden contraction in the economy triggers a demand for more unemployment and welfare benefits. To pay those higher benefits, the federal government would prefer to borrow additional funds rather than raise taxes in a recession. The resultant increase in the deficit would add to the national debt. What would be the burden of the debt in this case, and who would have to bear it?

The first thing to note is that transfer payments entail few real costs. Income transfers entail a redistribution of income from the taxpayer to the transfer recipient. The only direct costs of those transfer payments are the land, labor, and capital involved in the administrative process of making that transfer.[4] As pointed out earlier, those costs tend to be so trivial that they can be ignored. This means that ***there is no direct real burden for the debt that originates in deficit-financed income transfers.*** Virtually no economic resources are used for those transfers.

Since debt-financed income transfers create no real burden, there is no burden to pass on to future generations. If and when the debts that financed the transfers are repaid, income will again be redistributed. If the resulting distribution is not appealing, it can be changed with new tax and transfer initiatives.

The Real Tradeoffs   Although the national debt poses no special burden to the economy, the transactions it finances have a substantial impact on the basic questions of WHAT, HOW, and FOR WHOM to produce. The core issue of what mix of

---

[4]Income transfers may also have indirect effects on the labor supply of both taxpayers and beneficiaries. These "supply-side" effects are discussed in Chapter 15.

output to produce is influenced by how much deficit spending the government undertakes. The purchasing power created by the national debt allows the federal government to bid for scarce resources. The larger the deficit, the more spending power the government has. With that spending power, the government reallocates resources to the public sector, changing the mix of output. In general, *deficit financing tends to change the mix of output in the direction of more public-sector goods.* Higher taxes could bring about the same result but are more visible and always less popular. By borrowing rather than taxing, the federal government has a better chance of expanding.

The shift in output toward public-sector production is the essence of the **crowding out** problem mentioned in Chapter 10. The borrowing necessitated by deficit financing makes it more difficult for investors and consumers to obtain loans. With fewer funds available, they are less able to acquire output. Their share of the nation's output is thus "crowded out" by an expanding public sector.

crowding out: A reduction in private-sector borrowing (and spending) necessitated by increased government borrowing.

Economic growth   Of particular concern is the potential of the national debt to retard investment. Investment spending is essential to enlarging our production possibilities and attaining increased living standards in the future. If federal deficits and debt-servicing requirements crowd out private investment, they will curtail the rate of economic growth. This will leave future generations with less productive capacity. Thus *if debt-financed government spending crowds out private investment, future generations will bear some of the debt burden.* Their burden will take the form of smaller-than-anticipated productive capacity.

There is no certainty that such crowding out will occur. Also, any reduction in private investment may be offset by public works (e.g., highways, schools, defense systems) that benefit future generations. So future generations may not suffer a net loss in welfare even if the national debt slows private investment and economic growth. From this perspective, *the whole debate about the burden of the debt is really an argument over the optimal mix of output.* If we permit more deficit spending, we are promoting more public-sector activity. On the other hand, limits on deficit financing curtail growth of the public sector. Battles over deficits and debts are a proxy for the more fundamental issue of private versus public spending.

optimal mix of output: The most desirable combination of output attainable with existing resources, technology, and social values.

EXTERNAL DEBT

We observed earlier that most of America's national debt is *internal*—that is, held by U.S. households, institutions, and government agencies. Everything we have said about the burden of the debt and income redistributions applies fully to this internal debt.

External debt, however, poses some special problems and can be a more legitimate worry. In particular,

- External debt can eliminate the initial opportunity of debt-financed spending.

- External debt can impose a real burden on future taxpayers.

When we borrow funds from abroad, we increase our ability to consume, invest, and finance government activity. In effect, foreign nations are lending us the income necessary for *importing* more goods. If we can buy more

RELATIVE DEBT

National Debt

The United States is not alone in using debt to finance government spending. Most countries use a combination of debt, taxes, and newly created money to pay for the expenditures of the central government. The accompa-

nying figure indicates the size of accumulated national debt in relation to GNP for industrialized countries. Less-developed countries have comparable debt ratios but a higher proportion of external debt. The ratios here refer to total debt, whether internal or external.

Source: Organization for Economic Cooperation and Development, 1988 estimates.

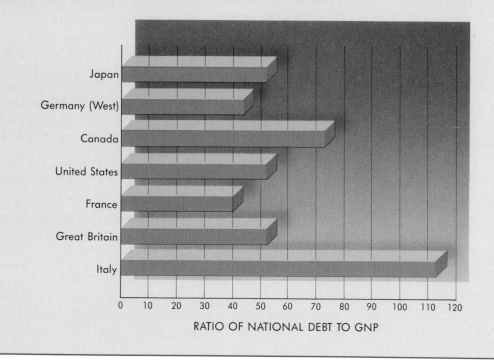

RATIO OF NATIONAL DEBT TO GNP

---

production possibilities: The alternative combinations of final goods and services that could be produced in a given time period with all available resources and technology.

imports with borrowed funds (without offsetting exports), then our real income will exceed our **production possibilities.** As Figure 11.5 illustrates, external borrowing allows us to enjoy a mix of output that lies *outside* our production-possibilities curve. Specifically, ***external financing allows us to get more public-sector goods without cutting back on private-sector production.*** As we use external debt to increase government spending, we move from point A to point C in Figure 11.5. Imported goods and services eliminate the need to cut back on private-sector activity, a cutback that would otherwise force us to point B. The additional imports financed by external debt eliminate this opportunity cost of increased government spending. The initial burden of that spending is relieved by foreign lenders. The move from point A to point C reflects the additional imports financed by external debt.[5]

[5]The imports need not be public-sector goods. If enough consumer goods are imported to maintain private-sector activity at the rate g_1, the domestic resources idled by imports can be used to increase public-sector production.

FIGURE 11.5
External Financing

A closed economy must forsake some private-sector output in order to increase public-sector output. The opportunity cost of increasing public-sector output from g_1 to g_2, for example, is the cutback in private-sector output from f_1 to f_2.

External financing eliminates that opportunity cost. Instead of having to move from A to B, external borrowing allows us to move from A to C. At point C we have more public output and no less private output.

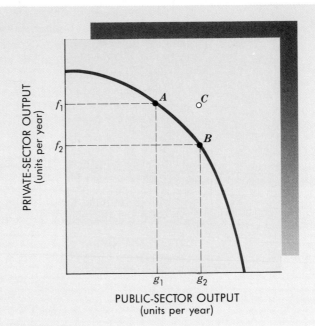

External financing not only lifts the burden of government spending off present taxpayers but also puts it on future taxpayers. At some later date, foreign bondholders may want to collect the IOUs they hold. If at that time they use the dollars they receive to buy American goods (our exports), there will be less output available for our domestic use. This *exported future output represents the real cost of government activity initially financed by external debt.*

There is no certainty that foreign lenders (bondholders) will ever want to redeem their bonds for U.S. products. They, too, may choose to accept refinancing, thus postponing any debt collection. Even if they cash in their bonds, they may choose to save or invest in the United States rather than spend their dollars on our exports. Finally, as inflation drives the average U.S. price level up, foreign bondholders will discover that their bonds have less and less purchasing power. Over time, then, inflation reduces the potential cost of external debt.

POLICY INSIGHTS:

DEBT LIMITS

Although external and internal debts pose very different problems, most policy discussions overlook these distinctions. In policy debates, the aggregate size of the national debt is the focal concern. The key policy questions are whether and how to limit or reduce the national debt.

Deficit Ceilings

deficit ceiling: An explicit, legislated limitation on the size of the budget deficit.

The only way to limit or reduce the national debt is to eliminate the budget deficits that create debt. The first step in debt reduction, therefore, is a balanced annual budget. A balanced budget will at least stop the debt from growing further. **Deficit ceilings** are explicit limitations on the size of the annual budget deficit. A deficit ceiling of zero compels a balanced budget.

As discussed in Chapter 10, it may not be desirable or even possible to balance the federal budget every year. However, it is possible to strive for a balance between *projected* revenues and outlays. Essentially, this requires Congress to be less optimistic about projected revenues and more tightfisted about spending plans.

The Balanced Budget and Emergency Deficit Control Act of 1985—popularly referred to as the Gramm-Rudman-Hollings Act—was an explicit attempt to force the federal budget into balance. The essence of the Gramm-Rudman Act is simple:

- First, it set a lower ceiling on each year's deficit, until budget balance is achieved.

- Second, it called for automatic cutbacks in spending if Congress failed to keep the deficit below the ceiling.

The original Gramm-Rudman law required Contress to pare the deficit from over $200 billion in FY1985 to zero (a balanced budget) by 1991. But Congress was unwilling to cut spending and increase taxes enough to meet those targets. And the Supreme Court declared that the "automatic" mechanism for spending cuts was unconstitutional. So Congress paid only lip service to the deficit ceilings while continuing to exceed them.

Congress amended the Gramm-Rudman Act in 1987. The immediate effect of the revision was to postpone the balanced-budget ceiling for a couple of years, until 1993. This extension was to give Congress and the president more time to agree on a deficit-cutting strategy. President Reagan was opposed to tax hikes or cuts in defense spending. The Democrat-controlled Congress was opposed to cuts in nondefense spending. These opposing views left little room

In The News

GRAMM-RUDMAN-HOLLINGS

The Federal Budget Process

Here is a look at how the federal budget is debated and how spending bills are passed.

1. In January, the president proposes a budget for the year beginning the following Oct. 1.

2. Congress holds hearings on the president's budget (winter and spring).

3. In the spring, Congress passes a broad outline of the budget called the "budget resolution" of how money will be spent. This sets the overall spending tax and deficit targets (Not subject to presidential veto).

4. By the beginning of the new fiscal year, Congress must pass 13 individual spending or "appropriation" bills, to cover various programs in the government like agriculture, education, defense. President can veto spending bills.

If some of the appropriation bills do not pass by Oct. 1, a continuing resolution—emergency funding—can be enacted to provide money for a few weeks until the appropriation bill is approved.

5. In the fall, Congress passes a reconciliation bill specifying which spending cuts or tax increases are needed to meet that year's deficit target. President can veto this.

6. By Oct. 15, automatic spending cutbacks under the Gramm-Rudman law take effect if Congress hasn't reached the deficit target. The automatic cuts can be rescinded or halted if Congress takes action to cut the deficit.

The Boston Globe, January 30, 1990, p. 12.

for deficit reduction. To help force a compromise, Congress strengthened the provisions for automatic spending cuts in the event that acceptable budget compromises were not reached.

In the end, however, the Democratic Congress and President Reagan were unable to reach a deficit-cutting compromise. The only thing they could agree on was to ignore the newly voted rule for "automatic" spending cuts. President Bush surprised Congress in his first year by permitting some automatic spending cuts ("sequestering") to occur. Although the automatic cuts were small, they aroused fears that the Gramm-Rudman rules had become too restrictive. Both the Bush administration and Congress proposed to make the deficit limits more realistic by again extending the legislative deadline for a balanced budget.

Although Gramm-Rudman has failed to balance the budget, such deficit-limitation measures do have some impact. First and foremost, they increase the *visibility* of the tradeoffs inherent in budget decisions. Deficit ceilings force legislators to ask how new programs are to be financed. Should other programs be cut back? Should taxes be raised? Or should Congress publicly disavow the deficit ceiling?

Because deficit ceilings push these financing questions into the spotlight, they also tend to restrain government spending. Congress is less likely to propose new programs when it must also describe how new initiatives will be financed. This increased caution slows government spending and so changes the mix of output. If taxpayers prefer a relatively smaller government, then deficit limitations serve some real purpose, even if they are not completely enforced.

Debt Ceilings

debt ceiling: An explicit, legislated limit on the amount of outstanding national debt.

Explicit **debt ceilings** are another mechanism for curbing the national debt. They are at best a substitute for deficit ceilings, however. If a limit is set on the national debt, the only way to stay within that limit is to reduce or eliminate the annual federal deficit.

Despite this evident shortcoming, debt ceilings are frequently invoked in Congress. If a debt ceiling is in place, the U.S. government must cease activity when that ceiling is reached. This causes an immediate operational crisis, with government workers suspended, income transfers withheld, and all but critical federal functions disrupted. This disruption typically lasts less than twenty-four hours and is often averted completely at the last minute when Congress raises the debt ceiling a bit further. Like deficit ceilings, debt ceilings are intended to force congressional compromise on specific issues. Often as not, the issue has little if anything to do with the budget.

SUMMARY

- Annual deficits create national debt. The national debt grew sporadically until World War II, then skyrocketed. A strong of huge deficits in the 1980s increased the national debt to $3 trillion.

- Although the absolute size of the deficits and the debt has grown, the relative size of both has declined in recent years. The deficits equaled 6.3 percent of GNP in 1983 and only 2.3 percent of GNP in 1990.

• Every dollar of national debt represents a dollar of assets to the people who hold U.S. Treasury bonds. Most U.S. bonds are held by government agencies, American households, and U.S. banks, insurance companies, and other institutions.

• The real burden of the debt is the opportunity cost of the activities financed by the debt. That cost is borne at the time the deficit-financed activity takes place.

• The potential for government deficits and debt servicing to crowd out private investment is a major concern. If investment becomes the opportunity cost of increased government spending, economic growth may slow.

• External debt permits the public sector to expand without reducing private-sector output. External debt also makes it possible to shift some of the real debt burden on to future generations.

• Deficit and debt ceilings are largely symbolic efforts to force consideration of real tradeoffs, restrain government spending, and change the mix of output.

Terms to Remember   Define the following terms:

budget deficit	**debt servicing**
Treasury bonds	**opportunity cost**
national debt	**transfer payments**
liability	**crowding out**
asset	**optimal mix of output**
internal debt	**production possibilities**
external debt	**deficit ceilng**
refinancing	**debt ceiling**

Questions for Discussion

1. Who paid for the Revolutionary War? Did the deficit financing initiated by the Continental Congress pass the cost of the war on to future generations?

2. In what ways do future generations benefit from this generation's deficit spending? Cite three examples.

3. What is "too much" debt or "too large" a deficit? Can you provide any guidelines for deficit or debt ceilings?

4. If deficit spending "crowds out" some private investment, could future generations be worse off? If external financing eliminates crowding out, are future generations thereby protected?

Problem

1. Suppose a government has no debt and a balanced budget. Suddenly it decides to spend $10 billion while raising only $8 billion worth of taxes.
   (*a*) What will be the government's deficit?
   (*b*) If the government decides to finance the deficit by issuing bonds, what amount of bonds will it issue?
   (*c*) At a 10 percent rate of interest, what debt-servicing requirement will the government incur on the newly issued bonds?
   (*d*) Add the interest payment to the government's $10 billion expenditure for the next year, and assume that taxes remain at $8 billion. In the second year, compute the deficit, the amount of new debt (bonds) issued, and the new debt-service requirement.

(e) Repeat these calculations for the third, fourth, and fifth years, assuming that the government taxes at a rate of $8 billion each year and has noninterest expenditures of $10 billion annually.

(f) What will happen to the size of interest payments, relative to the deficit, with each passing year?

(g) What will happen to the ratio of government debt to government expenditure with each passing year?

POLICY OPTIONS:
Monetary Approaches

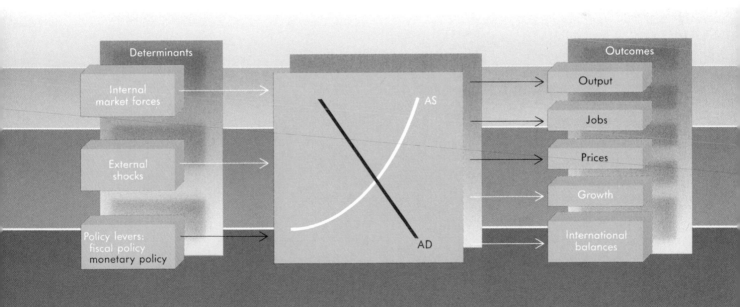

Monetary policy tries to alter macro outcomes by managing the amount of money available in the economy. By changing the money supply and/or interest rates, monetary policy seeks to shift aggregate demand.

Money and Banks

Sophocles, the ancient Greek playwright, had very strong opinions about the role of money. As he saw it, "Of evils upon earth, the worst is money. It is money that sacks cities, and drives men forth from hearth and home; warps and seduces native intelligence, and breeds a habit of dishonesty."

In modern times, people may still be seduced by the lure of money and fashion their lives around its pursuit. Nevertheless, it is hard to imagine an economy functioning without money. Money affects not only morals and ideals, but also the way an economy works.

The purpose of this and the following two chapters is to examine the role of money in the economy today. We begin with a very simple question:

- What is money?

As we shall discover, money isn't exactly what you think it is. Once we have established the characteristics of money, we go on to ask:

- How is money created?
- What role do banks play in the circular flow of income and spending?

In the next chapter we look at how the Federal Reserve System controls the amount of money created. Finally, in Chapter 14 we look at the implications for monetary policy, another policy lever in our basic macro model.

THE USES OF MONEY

To appreciate the significance of money for a modern economy, imagine for a moment that there were no such thing as money. How would you get something for breakfast? If you wanted eggs for breakfast, you would have to tend your own chickens or go see Farmer Brown. But how would you pay Farmer Brown for his eggs? Without money, you would have to offer him goods or services that he could use. In other words, you would have to engage in primitive **barter**—the direct exchange of one good for another—in order to get eggs for breakfast. You would get those eggs only if Farmer Brown happened to want the particular goods or services you had to offer and if the two of you could agree on the terms of the exchange.

The use of money greatly simplifies market transactions. It's a lot easier to exchange money for eggs at the supermarket than to go into the country and cut hay or lay sod every time you crave some eggs. Our ability to use

barter: The direct exchange of one good for another, without the use of money.

money in market transactions, however, depends on the grocer's willingness to accept money as a *medium of exchange.* The grocer sells eggs for money only because he can use the same money to pay his help and buy the goods he himself desires. He, too, can exchange money for goods and services. Accordingly, money plays an essential role in facilitating the continuous series of exchanges that characterize a market economy.

Money has other desirable features. The grocer who accepts your money in exchange for a carton of eggs doesn't have to spend his income immediately. On the contrary, he can hold onto the money for a few days or months, without worrying about its spoiling. Hence money is also a useful *store of value,* that is, a mechanism for transforming current income into future purchases.[1] Finally, common use of money serves as a *standard of value* for comparing the market worth of different goods. A dozen eggs is more valuable than a dozen onions if it costs more at the supermarket.

The great virtue of money is that it facilitates market exchanges and specialization in production. In fact, efficient division of labor requires a system whereby people can exchange the things they produce for the things they desire. Money makes this system of exchange possible.

THE MONEY SUPPLY

Before trying to answer a lot of complicated questions about the role of money, we should first decide what money is. ***Anything that serves all of the following purposes can be thought of as money:***

- ***Medium of exchange:*** is accepted as payment for goods and services (and debts)

- ***Store of value:*** can be held for future purchases

- ***Standard of value:*** serves as a yardstick for measuring the prices of goods and services

Items that have actually been used as money have included beads, shells, stones, furs, fishhooks, grain, cattle, and cigarettes. In the early days of colonial America, first Indian wampum, then tobacco, grain, fish, and furs were used as money. Throughout the colonies, gunpowder and bullets were frequently used for small change. The first paper money issued by the federal government consisted of $10 million worth of "greenbacks," printed in 1861 to finance the Civil War. The accompanying World View describes how Polish consumers used cigarettes and vodka as means of exchange when conventional money became worthless. (Poland has since changed its monetary system; as part of its basic economic reform program; see Chapter 38.)

In the U.S. economy today, such unusual forms of money are rarely used. Nevertheless, the concept of money includes more than the dollar bills and coins in your pocket or purse. Most people realize this when they offer to pay for goods with a check rather than cash. People do distinguish between "cash" and "money," and for good reason. The "money" you have in a checking account can be used to buy goods and services or to pay debts, or it can be retained for future use. In these respects, your checking account balance is as much a part of your "money" as are the coins and dollars in your pocket

---

[1]Recall, however, that the purchasing power of money will diminish if prices rise. In other words, inflation reduces the desirability of money as a store of value (see Chapter 7).

W🌐RLD VIEW

BARTER

Poles Survive Collapse of Currency by Using Own System of Barter

KARTUZY, Poland—Marietta Dzoitek will wake up long before dawn at least one day this week and wrap herself in three thick layers of clothing. She will slip quietly out the front door, so as not to disturb her sick mother, and go out into the bitter cold to wait in line for hours outside the neighborhood newspaper kiosk.

Miss Dzoitek—a frail, 31-year-old hospital switchboard operator—will say little or nothing to those around her as she waits for the shop to open: Conversations in lines these days too often end in arguments.

She complains but endures the tedium for the reward at the end—cigarettes to use as barter. If she is lucky, she'll be able to buy four of the 12 packs her ration coupons entitle her to each month. She'll go through the same sort of ritual later in the week to buy her monthly half liter of vodka.

Miss Dzoitek herself rarely smokes or drinks, but such goods have taken on special significance in Polish society. "Tobacco and alcohol are the best currencies nowadays," Miss Dzoitek says wanly. "Money no longer matters."

Stock in Trade

This small northern town of 15,000, just 20 miles from the Baltic coast and 70 miles from the Soviet border, is surviving on barter. So, indeed, is all of Poland. If one has the right item to trade, he can bypass some of the other exasperating and ubiquitous lines and the frequently empty shop shelves.

This month, Miss Dzoitek wants to use her vodka and cigarettes to buy toothpaste, washing powder, and coffee. She also hopes to persuade a nurse to help find medicine, otherwise unobtainable, to treat her mother's asthma.

Finance minister Marian Krzak has warned: "The devolution of Poland into a barter society is our greatest problem. We must stop cigarettes from becoming money and money from becoming nothing."

The Worthless Zloty

Indeed, the Zloty, Poland's monetary unit, is one of the few things in Kartuzy that isn't in short supply. More than one-third of Polish wages aren't matched by goods in shops, and that gap grows every day. Incomes have increased more than 25% in the past year, but the supply of consumer goods has dropped by nearly as much. A general flight from money is taking place, and as a result the most desired and least available products—spirits, cigarettes, sugar, meat, washing powder, to name a few—have become the means of exchange.

—Frederick Kempe

---

or purse. In fact, if everyone accepted your checks (and if the checks could also operate vending machines and pay telephones), there would be no need to carry cash.

There is nothing unique about cash, then, insofar as the market is concerned. ***Checking accounts can and do perform the same market functions as cash.*** Accordingly, we must include checking account balances in our concept of **money**. The essence of money is not its taste, color, or feel, but rather its ability to purchase goods and services.

money: Anything generally accepted as a medium of exchange.

Transactions Accounts

To determine how much money is available to purchase goods and services, we need to do more than count up all our coins and currency—we must also include our checking account balances. Traditionally, checking accounts were maintained only at large commercial ("full-service") banks. However, the Monetary Control Act of 1980 made it possible for many kinds of banks to offer "checking" accounts. Many people hold deposits, for example, in Negotiable Order of Withdrawal (NOW) accounts or Automatic Transfer of Savings (ATS) accounts. Both types of account serve the same basic function as regular checking accounts. They permit depositors to spend their deposit balances easily, without making a special trip to the bank to withdraw funds.

Credit unions and savings banks also offer the convenience of traditional checking accounts. A depositor may now "spend" funds maintained in a credit union by writing a credit-union "share draft," a piece of paper that looks just like a check. The same is true of many deposits held at mutual savings banks.

At first, the advantage of NOW, ATS, credit union, and savings accounts was that they paid interest on deposit balances—which regular checking accounts were not permitted to do. The Monetary Control Act of 1980 called for an end to such regulations, however. This deregulation eliminated the competitive advantage of saving and loan associations, pushing them toward extinction (see In the News). Today all banks offer a variety of "checking accounts," paying various interest rates, with sundry check-writing privileges, charges, and minimum-balance requirements.

These many different types of "checking accounts" are confusing. More important than their differences, however, is their one common feature—their easy accessibility. You can spend all such deposits directly in the marketplace, simply by writing a check.

transactions account: A bank account that permits direct payment to a third party (e.g., with a check).

Because all such deposits can be used directly in market transactions (without a trip to the bank), they are collectively referred to as "transactions accounts." The distinguishing feature of all **transactions accounts** is that they permit direct payment to a third party, without requiring a trip to the bank to make a special withdrawal.

Basic Money Supply

money supply (M1): Currency held by the public, plus balances in transactions accounts.

Because all transactions accounts can be spent as readily as cash, they are counted as part of our money supply. Adding transactions-account balances to the quantity of coins and currency held by the public gives us one measure of the amount of money available—that is, the basic **money supply.** The basic money supply is typically referred to by the abbreviation **M1.**

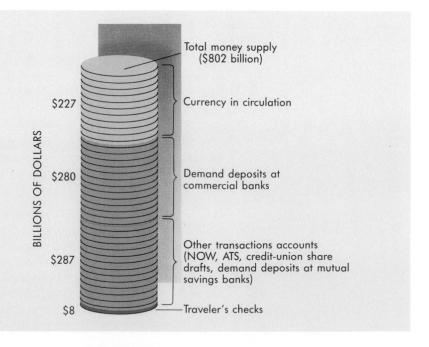

**FIGURE 12.1
Composition of the
Basic Money Supply (M1)**

The money supply (M1) includes all cash held by the public plus balances people hold in transactions accounts (e.g., checking, NOW, ATS, and credit–union share–draft accounts). Cash is a relatively small part of our money supply.

Source: *Federal Reserve,*
February 1990.

Total money supply
($802 billion)

$227 — Currency in circulation

$280 — Demand deposits at commercial banks

$287 — Other transactions accounts (NOW, ATS, credit-union share drafts, demand deposits at mutual savings banks)

$8 — Traveler's checks

BILLIONS OF DOLLARS

In The News

S & L FAILURES

The Thrift Bailout

On August 9, 1989, President Bush signed the Financial Institutions Reform, Recovery and Enforcement Act, better known as the Thrift Bailout Bill. The new law reorganizes regulation of the S&Ls, while providing funds for bailing out failed institutions.

The Problem

Historically, savings and loan associations have been the primary source of mortgage lending for American homeowners. They attracted deposits by offering interest rates on savings accounts that were higher than those permitted in commercial (full-service) banks. The Monetary Control Act of 1980 eliminated this advantage by permitting all banks to provide essentially identical services and interest rates. As a result, S&Ls had to compete more aggressively for deposits. This meant paying higher interest rates to attract and keep deposits. To offset these higher interest costs, the S&Ls made riskier loans, both within and outside their traditional housing market.

Shortly after deregulation of the banking industry got under way, interest rates skyrocketed. The prime rate hit a high of $21\frac{1}{2}$ percent in 1981. The S&Ls were squeezed. They had portfolios of long-term mortgages, fixed at low interest rates. To keep their deposit base, however, they had to offer ever higher interest rates to savers.

The death knell for the S&Ls was sounded by the recessions of 1980–81 and 1981–82. A combination of high interest rates and a contracting economy dried up sales of new houses and buildings. At the same time, the failing price of oil was bankrupting oil producers in Texas, Louisiana, and Oklahoma. Suddenly, S&Ls were burdened with the foreclosed properties of builders and oil drillers which no one wanted to buy.

Most of the failing S&Ls were insured by the Federal Savings and Loan Insurance Corporation (FSLIC). But the tide of S&L failures soon threatened to overwhelm the FSLIC. From 1980 to 1987 a total of 631 FDIC-insured banks failed. In 1988 more banks failed (200) than in any year since the Great Depression.

The Response

The centerpiece of the new regulatory structure is the Regulatory Trust Corporation (RTC). The RTC buys the assets and deposits of a failed S&L, then seeks to sell the assets and/or the entire bank.

The new law also created a new insurance fund for S&Ls and put stricter limits on their lending activity. Owners of S&Ls must also keep more of their own wealth invested in their banks.

The Outlook

The basic problem is that S&Ls are obsolete. Deregulation has permitted a variety of financial institutions to offer identical services. There is no special niche for S&Ls. Over 1,000 S&Ls have disappeared since 1985 and most of the remaining 3,000 S&Ls will fade away over time. In fact, Congress has facilitated this transformation by now permitting commercial banks to acquire healthy as well as sick S&Ls. In a few years, S&Ls will be indistinguishable from the other 14,000 financial institutions that comprise the banking system.

Figure 12.1 illustrates the actual composition of our money supply. The first component of M1 is the cash people hold (currency in circulation outside of commercial banks). Clearly the cash we carry around in our pockets is a small part of our money supply; most money consists of transactions deposits. This is not so surprising. People generally prefer to use checks or credit cards rather than cash for large market transactions (see In the News). The credit card purchases are themselves later paid for by check, typically through the mail. Checks turn out to be more convenient than cash, because they eliminate trips to the bank. Checks are also safer: lost or stolen cash is gone forever; checkbooks and credit cards are easily replaced, at little or no cost.

Figure 12.1 indicates that the largest type of transactions account in M1 consists of conventional checking accounts at commercial banks. Balances held in regular checking accounts are often called **demand deposits,** be-

demand deposit: Checking-account balance.

In The News

MEDIUMS OF EXCHANGE

Purchase Plans

When asked what method of payment they use for purchases of selected sizes, these percentages of surveyed adults said:

	Cash	Check	Credit card	Other
$1–$50	70%	24%	5%	1%
$51–$100	35	42	21	2
$101–$250	22	43	32	2
Above $250	18	42	34	3

Note: Numbers may not total 100% because of no response or rounding.

Source: *The Wall Street Journal*, November 23, 1987, p. 29. Reprinted by permission of *The Wall Street Journal*, © Dow Jones & Company, Inc. (1987). All Rights Reserved.

cause they can be converted into cash "on demand" or used to pay for goods and services directly. Typically, such accounts pay little or no interest and permit maximum check-writing privileges. Although other transactions accounts offer similar services, they are usually referred to by their specific names (e.g., NOW accounts).

The last component of our basic money supply consists of traveler's checks issued by nonbank firms (e.g., American Express). These, too, can be used directly in market transactions, just like good old-fashioned cash.

Other Money Measures   Transactions accounts are not the only substitute for cash. Even a conventional savings account can be used to finance market purchases. This use of a savings account may require a trip to the bank for a special withdrawal. But that is not too great a barrier to consumer spending. Many savings banks make that trip unnecessary by offering computerized withdrawals and transfers from their savings accounts, some even at supermarket service desks or cash machines. Others offer to pay your bills if you phone in instructions.

Not all savings accounts are so easily spendable. Many savings accounts require a minimum balance to be kept in the bank for a specified number of months or years; early withdrawal results in a loss of interest. Such accounts are called "certificates of deposit" rather than passbook savings. Funds held in certificates of deposit cannot be transferred automatically to a checking account (like passbook savings balances) or to a third party (like NOW-account balances). As a result, certificates of deposit are seldom used for everyday market purchases. Nevertheless, such accounts still function like "near money" in the sense that savers can go to the bank and withdraw cash if they really want to buy something.

Another popular way of holding money is to buy shares of money-market mutual funds. Deposits into money-market mutual funds are pooled and used to purchase interest-bearing securities (e.g., Treasury bills). The resultant interest payments are typically higher than those paid by banks. Moreover, the deposits made into the funds can often be withdrawn immediately, just like those in transactions accounts. When interest rates are high, deposits move out of regular transactions accounts into these money-market mutual funds in order to earn a higher return.

Additional measures of the money supply have been constructed to account for the possibility of using money-market mutual funds and various other deposits to finance everyday spending. These other money-supply measures are noted in Table 12.1.

aggregate spending: The rate of total expenditure desired at alternative levels of income, *ceteris paribus*.

Our concern about the specific nature of money stems from our broader interest in **aggregate spending.** What we want to know is how much purchasing power consumers have, since this will affect their ability to purchase goods and services. What we have observed, however, is that money is not so easily defined. How much spending power people have depends not only on the number of coins in their pockets, but also on their willingness to make frequent trips to the bank or to convert other assets into cash. For the time being, however, we shall focus on M1, since it is the most spendable form of money and is the core of all other money-supply definitions. We shall also refer to all depository institutions as "banks," even though there are important distinctions among them (see Table 12.2).

CREATION OF MONEY

Once we have decided what money is, we still have to explain where it comes from. Part of the explanation is simple. The currency in circulation comes from the Bureau of Engraving and Printing in Washington, D.C. Coins come

TABLE 12.1   Alternative Measures of the Money Supply

Measures of the money supply are intended to gauge the extent of purchasing power held by consumers. But the extent of purchasing power depends on how accessible assets are and how often people use them. The various money-supply measures reflect variations in the liquidity and accessibility of assets.

Measure	Components
M1	Currency in circulation outside of commercial banks
	Demand deposits at commercial banks
	NOW and ATS accounts
	Credit-union share drafts
	Demand deposits at mutual savings banks
	Traveler's checks (nonbank)
M2	M1 plus:
	Savings accounts
	Time deposits of less than $100,000
	Money-market mutual funds
	Overnight Eurodollars
M3	M2 plus:
	Time deposits larger than $100,000
	Repurchase agreements
L	M3 plus other liquid assets, for example:
	Treasury bills
	U.S. savings bonds
	Bankers' acceptances
	Term Eurodollars
	Commercial paper

TABLE 12.2   What Is a Bank?

The essential functions of a bank are to:	Type of bank	Characteristics
• **Accept deposits** • **Offer drafts (check-writing privileges)** • **Make loans** **In the United States, roughly 40,000 "depository institutions" fulfill these functions. These "banks" are typically classified into four general categories, even though most "banks" (and many other financial institutions) now offer similar services.**	Commercial banks	Provide a full range of banking services, including savings ("time") and checking accounts and loans for all purposes. Hold nearly all demand deposits and nearly half of total savings deposits. There are nearly 15,000 commercial banks in the United States.
	Savings and loan associations	Begun in 1831 as a mechanism for pooling the savings of a neighborhood in order to provide funds for home purchases, which is still the basic function of such banks. The nearly 3,000 S&Ls channel virtually all of their savings deposits into home mortgages.
	Mutual savings banks	Originally intended to serve very small savers (e.g., the Boston Five Cents Savings Bank). Can use their deposits for a wider variety of purposes, including investment in bonds and "blue chip" stocks. Almost all of the 575 mutual savings banks are located in only five states (New York, Massachusetts, Connecticut, Pennsylvania, and New Jersey).
	Credit unions	A cooperative society formed by individuals bound together by some common tie, such as a common employer or labor union. Typically credit-union members hold members' savings accounts and enjoy access to the pooled savings of all members. Most credit-union loans are for consumer purchases. Although there are close to 22,000 credit unions in the United States, they hold less than 5 percent of total savings deposits.

from the U.S. mints located in Philadelphia and Denver. In both cases, most of this new money just replaces old bills and coins that have been lost or worn out.

As we observed in Figure 12.1, currency is a small fraction of our total money supply (M1). So we need to look elsewhere for the origins of money. Specifically, where do all the transactions accounts come from? How do people acquire transactions deposits (checking-account balances, NOW balances, etc.)? How does the total amount of such deposits—and therefore the money supply of the economy—change?

Deposit Creation   Most people assume that all transactions-account balances come from cash deposits. But this is not the case. There are other, perfectly legal ways to achieve a positive balance. The easiest way is simply to *borrow* money from your bank. If the bank thinks there is a good chance you will repay the loan, it will lend you money. That is, it will create a transactions deposit for you that you would not otherwise have. ***In making a loan, a bank effectively creates money, because transactions-account balances are counted as part of the money supply.*** And you are free to spend that money, just as if you had earned it yourself.

To understand the origins of our money supply, then, we must recognize two basic principles:

- Transactions-account balances are the largest portion of our money supply.

- Banks can create transactions-account balances by making loans.

deposit creation: The creation of transactions deposits by bank lending.

In the following two sections we shall examine this process of **deposit creation** more closely. What we want to determine is how banks actually create deposits and what forces might limit the process of deposit creation.

Bank regulation   The deposit-creation activities of banks are regulated by the government. The most important agency in this regard is the Federal Reserve System. The Fed puts limits on the amount of bank lending, thereby controlling the basic money supply. These limits take the form of reserve requirements that force banks to hold reserves rather than use them to support loans. The structure and functions of the Fed are discussed at length in Chapter 13. In this chapter we focus on the process of deposit creation itself.

A Monopoly Bank   Suppose, to keep things simple, that there is only one bank in town, University Bank. Imagine also that you have been saving some of your income by putting loose change into a piggy bank. Now, after months of saving, you break the bank and discover that your thrift has yielded $100. You immediately deposit this money in a new checking account at University Bank. How will this deposit affect the money supply?

Your initial deposit will have no immediate effect on the money supply (M1). The coins in your piggy bank were already counted as part of the money supply, because they represented cash held by the public. ***When you deposit cash or coins in a bank, you are simply changing the composition of***

W🌐RLD VIEW

MULTINATIONAL MONEY

A Euro Currency?

In 1967 twelve European nations pledged to create a European community. To achieve this goal, they agreed to adopt policies that would permit the free flow of labor, capital, and products across their borders. National barriers were to give way to the common interest of greater trade and economic growth.

After twenty-five years of negotiation, the European Community (EC) has become a reality. Goods and resources move freely between the twelve member nations and common trade policies with the rest of the world have been established. One vexing problem remains,

however. Each member nation maintains its own national currency. Although these currencies are exchanged easily, the existence of twelve different monies makes trade cumbersome. Each nation also retains the ability to pursue its own money and loan policies, with the potential for economic tension. To achieve a truly integrated union, the EC must have a single currency.

EC members have pledged to create a single Euro currency, with a common central bank. But negotiations over the details of a common monetary unit, begun in April 1989, have been difficult. Adoption of a Euro currency implies that each country gives up control of its own money supply—a difficult step to take.

the money supply. The public (you) now holds $100 less of coins but $100 more of transactions deposits. Accordingly, no money is created by the demise of your piggy bank (the initial deposit).

University Bank is not in business just for your convenience, however. On the contrary, it is in business to earn a profit. To earn a profit on your deposit, University Bank will have to put your money to work. This means using your deposit as the basis for making a loan to someone who is willing to pay the bank interest for use of money. If the function of banks was merely to store money, they would not pay interest on their accounts or offer free checking services. Instead, you would have to pay them for these services. Banks pay you interest and offer free (or inexpensive) checking because they can use your money to make loans that themselves earn interest.

Typically, a bank does not have much difficulty finding someone who wants to borrow money. Many firms and individuals have expenditure desires that exceed their current money balances and are eager to borrow money. The question is, how much money can a bank lend? Can it lend your entire deposit? Or must University Bank keep some of your coins in reserve, in case you want to withdraw them?

To answer this question, suppose that University Bank decided to lend the entire $100 to Campus Radio. Campus Radio wants to buy a new antenna but doesn't have any money in its own checking account. To acquire the antenna, Campus Radio must take out a loan. It finds a willing creditor at University Bank.

When University Bank agrees to lend Campus Radio $100, it does so by crediting the account of Campus Radio. Instead of giving Campus Radio $100 cash, University Bank simply adds $100 to Campus Radio's checking-account balance. That is to say, the loan is made with a simple bookkeeping entry.

This simple bookkeeping procedure has important implications. When University Bank lends $100 to the Campus Radio account, it "creates" money. Keep in mind that transactions deposits are counted as part of the money supply. Moreover, Campus Radio can use this new money to purchase its desired antenna, without worrying that its check will bounce.

bank reserves: Assets held by a bank to fulfill its deposit obligations.

Or can it? Once University Bank grants a loan to Campus Radio, both you and Campus Radio have $100 in your checking accounts to spend. But the bank is holding only $100 of **reserves** (your coins). In other words, the increased checking-account balance obtained by Campus Radio does not limit your ability to write checks. There has been a net *increase* in the value of transactions deposits, but no increase in bank reserves.

What happens if Campus Radio actually spends the $100 on a new antenna? Won't this "use up" all the reserves held by the bank, and endanger your check-writing privileges? The answer is no.

Consider what happens when Atlas Antenna receives the check from Campus Radio. What will Atlas do with the check? Atlas could go to University Bank and exchange the check for $100 of cash (your coins). But Atlas probably doesn't have any immediate need for cash. Atlas may prefer to deposit the check in its own checking account at University Bank (still the only bank in town). In this way, Atlas not only avoids the necessity of going to the bank (it can deposit the check by mail), but also keeps its money in a safe place. Should Atlas later want to spend the money, it can simply write a check. In the meantime, the bank continues to hold its entire reserves (your coins) and both you and Atlas have $100 to spend.

Fractional reserves   Notice what has happened here. The money supply has increased by $100 as a result of deposit creation (the loan to Campus Radio). Moreover, the bank has been able to support $200 of transaction deposits (your account and either the Campus Radio or Atlas account) with only $100 of reserves (your coins). In other words, ***bank reserves are only a fraction of total transactions deposits.*** In this case, University Bank's reserves (your $100 in coins) are only 50 percent of total deposits. Thus the bank's **reserve ratio** is 50 percent, rather than 100 percent—that is,

reserve ratio: The ratio of a bank's reserves to its total transactions deposits.

$$\bullet \quad \frac{\text{Reserve}}{\text{ratio}} = \frac{\text{bank reserves}}{\text{total deposits}}$$

The ability of University Bank to hold reserves that are only a fraction of total deposits results from two facts: people use checks for most transactions and there is no other bank. Accordingly, reserves are rarely withdrawn from this monopoly bank. In fact, if people *never* withdrew their deposits and *all* transactions accounts were held at University Bank, University Bank would not really need any reserves. In this most unusual case, University Bank could continue to make as many loans as it wanted.

A Multibank World

In reality, many banks are available, and people both withdraw cash from their accounts and write checks to people who have accounts in other banks. In addition, bank lending practices are regulated by the Federal Reserve System. ***The Federal Reserve System requires banks to maintain some minimum reserve ratio.*** This reserve requirement directly limits the ability of banks to grant new loans.[2]

The potential impact of Federal Reserve requirements on bank lending can be readily seen. Suppose that the Federal Reserve had imposed a minimum reserve requirement of 75 percent on University Bank. Such a requirement would have prohibited University Bank from lending $100 to Campus Radio. That loan would have resulted in $200 of deposits, supported by only $100 of reserves. The actual ratio of reserves to deposits would have been 50 percent ($100 of reserves ÷ $200 of deposits). That would have violated the Fed's assumed 75 percent reserve requirement. A 75 percent reserve requirement means that University Bank must hold **required reserves** equal to 75 percent of *total* deposits, including those created through loans.

required reserves: The minimum amount of reserves a bank is required to hold by government regulation; equal to required reserve ratio times transactions deposits.

The bank's dilemma is evident in the following equation:

$$\bullet \quad \frac{\text{Required}}{\text{reserves}} = \frac{\text{minimum reserve}}{\text{ratio}} \times \frac{\text{total}}{\text{deposits}}$$

To support $200 of total deposits, University Bank would need to satisfy this equation:

$$\frac{\text{Required}}{\text{reserves}} = 0.75 \times \$200 = \$150$$

But the bank has only $100 of reserves (your coins) and so would violate the reserve requirement if it increased total deposits to $200 by lending $100 to Campus Radio.

[2]The role of the Federal Reserve System in regulating banks and their reserves is discussed in Chapter 13.

University Bank can still issue a loan to Campus Radio. But the loan must be less than $100 in order to keep the bank within the limits of the required reserve formula. Thus *a minimum reserve requirement directly limits deposit-creation possibilities.* It is still true, however, as we shall now illustrate, that the banking system, taken as a whole, can create multiple loans (money) from a single deposit.

An illustration   The process of deposit creation in a multibank world with a required reserve ratio is illustrated in Table 12.3. In this case, we assume that legally required reserves must equal at least 20 percent of transactions deposits. Now when you deposit $100 in your checking account, University Bank must hold at least $20 as required reserves.[3]

[3]The reserves themselves may be held in the form of cash in the bank's vault but are usually held as credits with one of the regional Federal Reserve banks.

TABLE 12.3   Deposit Creation

Excess reserves (Step 1) are the basis of bank loans. When a bank uses its excess reserves to make a loan, it creates a transactions deposit (Step 2). When the loan is spent, a deposit will be made somewhere else (Step 3). This new deposit creates additional excess reserves (Step 3) that can be used for further loans (Steps 4, etc.). The process of deposit creation continues until the money supply has increased by a multiple of the initial deposit.

Step 1: You deposit cash at University Bank

University Bank

Assets		Liabilities		Change in transactions deposits	Change in M1
Required reserves	$ 20	Your demand deposit	$100	+$100	$ 0
Excess reserves	80				
Total	$100		$100		

Step 2: Bank makes a loan to Campus Radio

University Bank

Assets		Liabilities			
Required reserves	$ 36	Your account	$100	+$ 80	+$ 80
Excess reserves	64	Campus Radio account	80		
Loans	80				
Total	$180		$180		

Step 3: Campus Radio buys an antenna

University Bank				Eternal Savings					
Assets		Liabilities		Assets		Liabilities			
Required reserves	$ 20	Your account	$100	Required reserves	$16	Atlas Antenna account	$80	$ 0	$ 0
Excess reserves	0	Campus Radio account	0	Excess reserves	64				
Loan	80								
Total	$100		$100		$80		$80		

TABLE 12.3 *(continued)*

Step 4: Eternal Savings lends money to Herman's Hardware

University Bank		Eternal Savings		Change in transaction deposits	Change in M1
Assets	Liabilities	Assets	Liabilities		
Required reserves $ 20	Your account $100	Required reserves $ 29	Atlas Antenna account $ 80	+$ 64	+$ 64
Excess reserves 0	Campus Radio account 0	Excess reserves 51	Herman's Hardware account 64		
Loan 80		Loans 64			
Total $100	$100	$144	$144		
⋮ ⋮	⋮ ⋮	⋮	⋮	⋮	⋮
*N*th step: Some bank lends $1.00				+ 1	+ 1
Cumulative change					
Bank reserves	Transactions deposits				Money supply
+$100	+$500				+$400

excess reserves: Bank reserves in excess of required reserves.

The remaining $80 the bank obtains from your deposit is regarded as **excess reserves.** These reserves are "excess" in that your bank is *required* to hold in reserve only $20 (equal to 20 percent of your initial $100 deposit).

$$\text{Excess reserves} = \text{total reserves} - \text{required reserves}$$

The $80 of excess reserves is not required and may be used to support additional loans. Hence the bank can now lend $80. In view of the fact that banks earn profits (interest) by making loans, we assume that University Bank will try to use these excess reserves as soon as possible.

To keep track of the changes in reserves, transactions deposits, and loans that occur in a multibank world we shall have to do some bookkeeping. For this purpose we will use the same balance sheet, or "T-account," that banks themselves use. On the left side of the balance sheet, a bank lists all its assets. *Assets* are things the bank owns or is owed by others. These assets include cash held in a bank's vaults, IOUs (loan obligations) from bank customers, reserve credits at the Federal Reserve (essentially the bank's own deposits at the central bank), and securities (bonds) the bank has purchased.

On the right side of the balance sheet a bank lists all its liabilities. *Liabilities* are things the bank owes to others. The largest liability is represented by the transactions deposits of the bank's customers. The bank owes these deposits to its customers and must return them "on demand."

The use of balance sheets is illustrated in Table 12.3. Notice how the balance of University Bank looks immediately after it receives your initial deposit (Step 1 of Table 12.3). Your deposit of coins is entered on both sides of University's balance sheet. On the left side, your deposit is regarded as an asset, because your piggy bank's coins have an immediate market value and can be used to pay off the bank's liabilities. The reserves these coins represent are divided into required reserves ($20, or 20 percent of your deposit) and excess reserves ($80).

On the right side of the balance sheet, the bank reminds itself that it has an obligation (liability) to return your deposit when you so demand. Thus the bank's accounts balance, with assets and liabilities being equal. In fact, *a bank's books must always balance, because all of the bank's assets must belong to someone (its depositors or its owners).*

University Bank wants to do more than balance its books, however; it wants to earn profits. To do so, it will have to make loans—that is, put its excess reserves to work. Suppose that it lends $80 to Campus Radio.[4] As Step 2 in Table 12.3 illustrates, this loan alters both sides of University Bank's balance sheet. On the right-hand side, the bank creates a new transactions deposit for (credits the account of) Campus Radio; this item represents an additional liability (promise to pay). On the left-hand side of the balance sheet, two things happen. First, the bank notes that Campus Radio owes it $80 ("loans"). Second, the bank recognizes that it is now required to hold $36 in *required* reserves, in accordance with its higher level of transactions deposits ($180). (Recall we are assuming that required reserves are 20 percent of total transactions deposits.) Since its total reserves are still $100, $64 is left as *excess* reserves. Note again that *excess reserves are reserves a bank is not required to hold.*

Changes in the money supply   Before examining further changes in the balance sheet of University Bank, consider what has happened to the economy's money supply during these first two steps. In the first step, you deposited $100 of cash in your checking account. This initial transaction did not change the value of the money supply. Only the composition of M1 was affected ($100 less cash held by the public, $100 more in transactions accounts).

It is not until Step 2—when the bank makes a loan—that all the excitement begins. In making a loan, the bank automatically increases the total money supply by $80. Why? Because someone (Campus Radio) now has more money (a transactions deposit) than it did before, and no one else has any less. And Campus Radio can use its money to buy goods and services, just like anybody else.

This second step is the heart of money creation. Money effectively appears out of thin air when a bank makes a loan. To understand how this works, you have to keep reminding yourself that money is more than the coins and currency we carry around. Transactions deposits are money too. Hence *the creation of transactions deposits via new loans is the same thing as creating money.*

More deposit creation   Suppose again that Campus Radio actually uses its $80 loan to buy an antenna. The rest of Table 12.3 illustrates how this additional transaction leads to further changes in balance sheets and the money supply.

In Step 3, we see that when Campus Radio buys the $80 antenna, the balance in its checking account at University Bank drops to zero, because it has spent all its money. As University Bank's liabilities fall (from $180 to $100), so does the level of its required reserves (from $36 to $20). (Note that required reserves are still 20 percent of its remaining transactions deposits.) But University Bank's excess reserves have disappeared completely! This disappear-

---

[4]Because of the Fed's assumed minimum reserve requirement (20 percent), University Bank can now lend only $80 rather than $100, as before.

ance reflects the fact that Atlas Antenna keeps *its* transactions account at another bank (Eternal Savings). When Atlas deposits the check it received from Campus Radio, Eternal Savings does two things. First it credits Atlas's account by $80. Second, it goes to University Bank to get the reserves that support that deposit.[5] The reserves later appear on the balance sheet of Eternal Savings as both required ($16) and excess ($64) reserves.

Observe that the money supply has not changed during Step 3. The increase in the value of Atlas Antenna's transactions-account balance exactly offsets the drop in the value of Campus Radio's transactions account. Ownership of the money supply is the only thing that has changed.

In Step 4, Eternal Savings takes advantage of its newly acquired excess reserves by making a loan to Herman's Hardware. As before, the loan itself has two primary effects. First, it creates a transactions deposit of $64 for Herman's Hardware and thereby increases the money supply by the same amount. Second, it increases the required level of reserves at Eternal Savings. (To how much? Why?)

THE MONEY MULTIPLIER

money multiplier: The number of deposit (loan) dollars that the banking system can create from $1 of excess reserves; equal to 1 ÷ required reserve ratio.

By now it is perhaps obvious that the process of deposit creation will not come to an end quickly. On the contrary, it can continue indefinitely, just like the income multiplier process of Chapter 9. Indeed, people often refer to deposit creation as the money-multiplier process, with the **money multiplier** expressed as the reciprocal of the required reserve ratio.[6] That is,

$$\bullet \quad \frac{\text{Money}}{\text{multiplier}} = \frac{1}{\substack{\text{required} \\ \text{reserve ratio}}}$$

The money-multiplier process is illustrated in Figure 12.2. When a new deposit enters the banking system, it creates both excess and required reserves. The required reserves represent leakage from the flow of money, since they cannot be used to create new loans. Excess reserves, on the other hand, can be used for new loans. Once those loans are made, they typically become transactions deposits elsewhere in the banking system. Then some additional leakage into required reserves occurs, and further loans are made. The process continues until all excess reserves have leaked into required reserves. Once excess reserves have completely disappeared, the total value of new loans will equal initial excess reserves multiplied by the money multiplier.

The potential of the money multiplier to create loans is summarized by the equation

$$\bullet \quad \substack{\text{Excess} \\ \text{reserves} \\ \text{of banking} \\ \text{system}} \times \substack{\text{money} \\ \text{multiplier}} = \substack{\text{potential} \\ \text{deposit creation}}$$

Notice how the money multiplier worked in our previous example. The value of the money multiplier was equal to 5, since we assumed that the required

[5]In actuality, banks rarely "go" anywhere; such interbank reserve movements are handled by bank clearinghouses and regional Federal Reserve banks. The effect is the same, however. The nature and use of bank reserves are discussed more fully in Chapter 13.

[6]The money multiplier ($1/r$) is the sum of the infinite geometric progression $1 + (1 - r) + (1 - r)^2 + (1 - r)^3 + \cdots + (1 - r)^\infty$.

FIGURE 12.2
The Money-Multiplier Process

Part of every new bank deposit leaks into required reserves. The rest—excess reserves—can be used to make loans. These loans, in turn, become deposits elsewhere. The process of money creation continues until all available reserves are required.

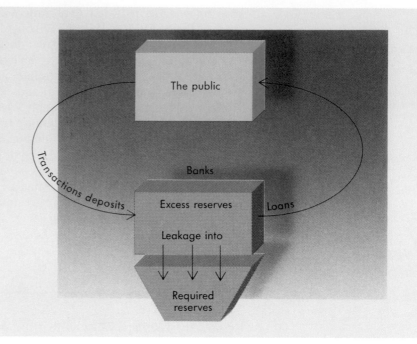

reserve ratio was 0.20. Moreover, the initial level of excess reserves was $80, as a consequence of your original deposit (Step 1). According to the money multiplier, then, the deposit-creation potential of the banking system was

$$\underset{(\$80)}{\text{Excess reserves}} \times \underset{(5)}{\text{money multiplier}} = \underset{\text{creation (\$400)}}{\text{potential deposit}}$$

When all the banks fully utilized their excess reserves at each step of the money-multiplier process, the ultimate increase in the money supply was in fact $400 (see the last row of Table 12.3).

Excess Reserves as Lending Power

While you are struggling through Table 12.3, notice the critical role that excess reserves play in the process of deposit creation. A bank can make loans only if it has excess reserves. Without excess reserves, all of a bank's reserves are required, and no further liabilities (transactions deposits) can be created with new loans. On the other hand, a bank with excess reserves can make additional loans. In fact,

• *Each bank may lend an amount equal to its excess reserves and no more.*

As such loans enter the circular flow and become deposits elsewhere, they create new excess reserves and further lending capacity. As a consequence,

• *The entire banking system can increase the volume of loans by the amount of excess reserves multiplied by the money multiplier.*

By keeping track of excess reserves, then, we can gauge the lending capacity of any bank or, with the aid of the money multiplier, the entire banking system.

TABLE 12.4   The Money Multiplier at Work

The process of deposit creation continues as money passes through different banks in the form of multiple deposits and loans. At each step, excess reserves and new loans are created. The lending capacity of this system equals the money multiplier times excess reserves. In this case, initial excess reserves of $80 create the possibility for $400 of new loans.

	Change in transactions deposits	Change in total reserves	Change in required reserves	Change in excess reserves	Change in lending capacity
If $100 in cash is deposited in Bank A, Bank A acquires	$100.00	$100.00	$ 20.00	$80.00	$ 80.00
If loan made and deposited elsewhere, Bank B acquires	80.00	80.00	16.00	64.00	64.00
If loan made and deposited elsewhere, Bank C acquires	64.00	64.00	12.80	51.20	51.20
If loan made and deposited elsewhere, Bank D acquires	51.20	51.20	10.10	41.00	41.00
If loan made and deposited elsewhere, Bank E acquires	41.00	41.00	8.20	32.80	32.80
If loan made and deposited elsewhere, Bank F acquires	32.80	32.80	6.60	26.20	26.20
If loan made and deposited elsewhere, Bank G acquires	26.20	26.20	5.20	21.00	21.00
$\vdots$					
If loan made and deposited elsewhere, Bank Z acquires	0.40	0.40	0.08	0.32	0.32
Cumulative, through Bank Z	$498.80	$100.00	$ 99.76	$ 0.24	$398.80
$\vdots$	$\vdots$	$\vdots$	$\vdots$	$\vdots$	$\vdots$
And if the process continues indefinitely	$500.00	$100.00	$100.00	$ 0.00	$400.00

A **$100 cash deposit creates $400 of new lending capacity when the required reserve ratio is 0.20. Initial excess reserves are $80 (= $100 deposit − $20 required reserves). The money multiplier is 5 (= 1 ÷ 0.20). New lending potential equals $400 (= $80 excess reserves × 5).**

Table 12.4 summarizes the entire money-multiplier process. In this case, we assume that all banks are initially "loaned up"—that is, without any excess reserves. The money-multiplier process begins when someone deposits $100 in cash into a transactions account at Bank A. If the required reserve ratio is 20 percent, this initial deposit creates $80 of excess reserves at Bank A, while adding $100 to total transactions deposits.

If Bank A uses its newly acquired excess reserves to make a loan that ultimately ends up in Bank B, two things happen. Bank B acquires $64 in excess reserves (0.80 × $80), and total transactions deposits increase by another $80.

The money-multiplier process continues with a series of loans and deposits. When the twenty-sixth loan is made (by bank Z), total loans grow by only $0.32 and transactions deposits by an equal amount. Should the process continue further, the *cumulative* change in loans will ultimately equal $400, that is, the money multiplier times initial excess reserves. The money supply will increase by the same amount.

POLICY INSIGHTS:

THE IMPORTANCE OF BANKS

The bookkeeping details of bank deposits and loans are rarely exciting and often confusing. But they do demonstrate convincingly that banks can create money. This implies that banks must have some direct influence on economic activity, because all of our market transactions involve the use of money. The purpose of this final section is to determine the role of the banking system in the circular flow of income and expenditure.

Banks and the Circular Flow

What we have demonstrated in this chapter is that banks perform two essential functions:

- Banks transfer money from savers to spenders by lending funds (reserves) held on deposit.

- The banking system creates additional money by making loans in excess of total reserves.

In performing these two functions, banks change the size of the money supply—that is, the amount of purchasing power available for buying goods and services. Market participants may alter their spending behavior in response to these money-supply changes and so shift the aggregate spending and demand curves.

Figure 12.3 provides a simplified perspective on the role of banks in the circular flow. As before, income flows from product markets through business firms to factor markets and returns to consumers in the form of disposable income. Consumers spend most of their income but also save (don't spend) some of it.

The leakage represented by consumer saving is a potential source of stabilization problems, particularly unemployment. If additional spending by business firms, foreigners, or governments does not compensate for consumer saving at full employment, a recessionary gap will emerge, creating unemployment (see Chapters 8 and 9). Our interest here is in the role the banking system can play in encouraging such additional spending.

Suppose for the moment that *all* consumer saving was deposited in piggy banks rather than depository institutions (banks) and that no one used checks. Under these circumstances, banks could not transfer money from savers to spenders by holding deposits and making loans.

In reality, a substantial portion of consumer saving *is* deposited in banks. These and other bank deposits can be used as the basis of loans, thereby returning purchasing power to the circular flow.[7] In fact, the primary economic function of banks is not to store money but to transfer purchasing power from savers to spenders. They do so by lending money to businesses for new plant and equipment, to consumers for new homes or cars, and to government entities that desire greater purchasing power. Moreover, because the banking system can make *multiple* loans from available reserves, banks don't have to receive all consumer saving in order to carry out their function. On the contrary, ***the banking system can create any desired level of money supply if allowed to expand or reduce loan activity at will.***

[7]Business savings and government deposits also enter the banking system and become sources of bank lending, but we will ignore these complications here, at no loss to the principles of deposit creation.

FIGURE 12.3
Banks in the Circular Flow

Banks help to transfer income from savers to spenders. They do this by using their deposits to make loans to business firms and consumers who desire to spend more money than they have. By lending money, banks help to maintain any desired rate of aggregate spending.

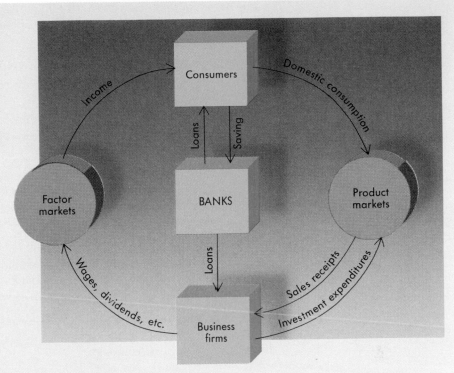

Constraints on Deposit Creation

There are three major constraints on the deposit creation of the banking system. The first of these constraints is the willingness of consumers and businesses to continue using and accepting checks rather than cash in the marketplace. If people preferred to hold cash rather than checkbooks, banks would not be able to acquire or maintain the reserves that are the foundation of bank lending activity.

The second constraint on deposit creation is the willingness of consumers, businesses, and governments to borrow the money that banks make available. The chain of events we have observed in deposit creation depends on the willingness of Campus Radio to borrow $80, of Herman's Hardware to borrow $64, and so on. If no one wanted to borrow any money, deposit creation would never begin. By the same reasoning, if all excess reserves are not borrowed (lent), deposit creation will not live up to its theoretical potential.

The third major constraint on deposit creation is the Federal Reserve System. As we have observed, the Fed may limit deposit creation by imposing reserve requirements. These and other tools of monetary policy will be discussed in Chapter 13.

SUMMARY

- In a market economy, money serves a critical function in facilitating exchanges and specialization, thus permitting increased output. "Money" in this context may refer to any medium that is generally accepted in exchange.

• The most common measure of the money supply (M1) includes both cash and balances people hold in transactions accounts (e.g., checking, NOW, and ATS accounts).

• Banks have the power to create money simply by making loans. In making loans, banks create new transactions deposits, which become part of the money supply.

• The ability of banks to make loans—create money—depends on their reserves. Only if a bank has excess reserves—reserves greater than those required by federal regulation—can it make new loans.

• As loans are spent, they create deposits elsewhere, making it possible for other banks to make additional loans. The money multiplier (1 ÷ required reserve ratio) indicates the total value of deposits that can be created by the banking system from excess reserves.

• The role of banks in creating money includes the transfer of money from savers to spenders as well as deposit creation in excess of deposit balances. Taken together, these two functions give banks direct control over the amount of purchasing power available in the marketplace.

• The deposit-creation potential of the banking system is limited by government regulation. It is also limited by the willingness of market participants to hold deposits or borrow money.

Terms to Remember   Define the following terms:

barter	deposit creation
money	bank reserves
transactions account	reserve ratio
money supply (M1)	required reserves
demand deposit	excess reserves
aggregate spending	money multiplier

Questions for Discussion

1. Does money have any intrinsic value? If not, why are people willing to accept money in exchange for goods and services?

2. Does the fact that your bank keeps only a fraction of your account balance in reserve make you uncomfortable? Why don't people rush to the bank and retrieve their money? What would happen if they did?

3. If people never withdrew cash from banks, how much money could the banking system potentially create? Could this really happen? What might limit deposit creation in this case?

4. If all banks heeded Shakespeare's admonition "Neither a borrower nor a lender be," what would happen to the circular flow?

Problems

1. Suppose that an Irish Sweepstakes winner deposits $10 million in cash into her transactions account at the Bank of America. Assume a reserve requirement of 25 percent and no excess reserves in the banking system prior to this deposit.

   (a) Show the changes on the Bank of America balance sheet when the $10 million is initially deposited.

    (b) Show the balance sheet changes after the Bank of America has used its added lending capacity.

    (c) How much has the money supply changed due to the lending by the Bank of America?

    (d) After all banks in the entire banking system have used their lending capacity, show the total changes to reserves and demand deposits resulting from the $10 million deposit.

    (e) How much is the money supply of the total banking system changed due to the $10 million deposit?

2. In Table 12.4, the effect of a $100 cash deposit is followed through the banking system, which has a 20 percent reserve requirement. Now suppose that the reserve requirement was only 10 percent. Follow the $100 cash deposit through the banking system in a similar way.

    (a) What will be the cumulative change in transactions deposits, total reserves, and lending capacity?

    (b) When the reserve requirement changes, which of the following will change for the first bank that receives the initial deposit (Bank A): transactions deposits, total reserves, required reserves, excess reserves, or lending capacity?

    (c) When the reserve requirement changes, which of the following will experience a cumulative change in the total banking system: transactions deposits, total reserves, required reserves, excess reserves, or lending capacity?

CHAPTER 13

The Federal Reserve System

We have seen how money is created. We have also gotten a few clues about how the government limits money creation and thus influences aggregate spending. The intent of this chapter is to examine the mechanics of government control more closely. The basic issues to be addressed are

- How does the government control the amount of money in the economy?

- Which government agency is responsible for exercising this control?

- How are banks and bond markets affected by the government's policies?

Most people have a ready answer for the first question. The popular view is that the government controls the amount of money in the economy by printing more or fewer dollar bills. But we have already observed that the concept of "money" is not so simple. In Chapter 12 we demonstrated that banks, not the printing presses, create most of our money. In making loans, banks create transactions deposits that are counted as part of the money supply (M1).

Because bank lending activities are the primary source of money, the government must regulate bank lending if it wants to control the amount of money in the economy. That is exactly what the Federal Reserve System does. The Federal Reserve System—the "Fed"—not only limits the volume of loans that the banking system can get from any given level of reserves, it can also alter the amount of reserves in the banking system.

The Federal Reserve System's control over the supply of money is the key mechanism of **monetary policy.** The potential of this policy lever to alter macro outcomes will be examined in Chapter 14. There we shall look at the way changes in the supply of money can alter the rate of unemployment, the rate of inflation, or both. We shall also look at the arguments between Keynesians and Monetarists about whether and how monetary policy is an effective tool for stabilizing aggregate demand. For the time being, however, we focus on the tools available for implementing monetary policy.

monetary policy: The use of money and credit controls to influence macroeconomic activity.

STRUCTURE OF THE FED

In the absence of any government regulation, the supply of money would be determined by individual banks. Moreover, individual depositors would bear all the risks of bank failures. In fact, this is the way the banking system

301

operated until 1914. The money supply was subject to abrupt changes, and consumers frequently lost their savings in recurrent bank failures.

A series of bank failures resulted in a severe financial panic in 1907. Millions of depositors lost their savings, and the economy was thrown into a tailspin. In the wake of this panic, a National Monetary Commission was established to examine ways of restructuring the banking system. The mandate of the commission was to find ways to avert recurrent financial crises. After five years of study, the commission recommended the creation of a Federal Reserve System. Congress accepted the commission's recommendations, and President Wilson signed the Federal Reserve Act in December 1913.

Federal Reserve Banks

The core of the Federal Reserve System consists of twelve Federal Reserve banks, located in the various regions of the country. Each of these banks acts as a central banker for the private banks in its region. In this role, the Fed banks perform many critical services, including the following:

- *Clearing checks between private banks.* Suppose the Bank of America in San Francisco receives a deposit from one of its customers in the form of a share draft written on the New York State Employees Credit Union. The Bank of America doesn't have to go to New York to collect the cash or other reserves that support that draft. Instead, the Bank of America can deposit the draft (check) at its account with the Federal Reserve Bank of San Francisco. The Fed then collects from the Credit Union. This vital clearinghouse service saves the Bank of America and other private banks a great deal of time and expense. In view of the fact that over 50 billion checks are written every year, this clearinghouse service is an important feature of the Federal Reserve System.

- *Holding bank reserves.* Notice that the clearinghouse service of the Fed was facilitated by the fact that the Bank of America (and the New York Employees Credit Union) had their own accounts at the Fed. As we have noted before, banks are *required* to hold some minimum fraction of their transactions deposits in reserve. Nearly all of these reserves are held in accounts at the Federal Reserve banks. Only a small amount of reserves is held as cash in a bank's vaults. These accounts at the Fed provide greater security and convenience for bank reserves. They also enable the Fed to monitor the actual level of bank reserves.

- *Providing currency.* Before every major holiday there is a great demand for cash. People want some "pocket money" during holidays and know that it is difficult to cash checks on weekends or holidays, especially if they are going out of town. After the holiday is over, most of this cash is returned to the banks, typically by the stores, gas stations, and restaurants that benefited from holiday spending. Because banks hold very little cash in their vaults, they turn to the Fed to meet these sporadic cash demands. A private bank can simply call the regional Federal Reserve bank and order a supply of cash, to be delivered (by armored truck) before a weekend or holiday. The cash will be deducted from the bank's own account at the Fed. When all the cash comes back in after the holiday, the bank can reverse the process, sending the unneeded cash back to the Fed.

- *Providing loans.* The Federal Reserve banks may also loan reserves to private banks. This practice, called "discounting," will be examined more closely in a moment.

Member Banks

Before the Monetary Control Act of 1980, only those banks that were "members" of the Federal Reserve System were subject to its regulations and services. Of the nearly 15,000 banks in the United States, only 5,700 were member banks. Now, however, all depository institutions (banks, credit unions, and so on) are subject to reserve requirements established by the Fed. All banks can also use the services the Fed offers. Although the distinction between member banks and nonmember banks still exists, it is of little significance for monetary policy.[1]

The Board of Governors

At the top of the Federal Reserve System's organization chart (Figure 13.1) is the Board of Governors. The Board of Governors has broad responsibility for the behavior of the regional Federal Reserve banks, as well as for the formulation of general Fed policy. The Board, located in Washington, D.C., consists of seven members appointed by the president of the United States and confirmed by Congress. Board members are appointed for fourteen-year terms and cannot be reappointed. Because of their exceptionally long appointments, the Fed's governors tend to be relatively immune to short-term political considerations. Many people regard this immunity as desirable, as it keeps control of the nation's money supply beyond the immediate reach of politicians (especially members of Congress, elected for two-year terms). The political independence of the Fed, however, has been subject to intense controversy, as we shall see.

The president selects one of the governors to serve as chairman of the Board for four years. In July 1979 President Carter appointed Paul Volcker to the Board and designated him chairman. That assured Volcker of fourteen years of Board membership and four years as chairman. President Reagan reappointed Volcker for another four-year chairman's term in 1983. But Volcker resigned from the Board in mid-1987, after a further reappointment as chairman by President Reagan became uncertain.[2] Volcker was replaced by Alan Greenspan, an economic consultant who had earlier served as chairman of President Ford's Council of Economic Advisers.

The Federal Open Market Committee

The fourth major component of the Fed is the Federal Open Market Committee (FOMC). The FOMC is responsible for the Fed's daily activity in financial markets. As we shall see, it plays a critical role in determining the level of reserves held by private banks. The membership of the FOMC includes all seven governors and five of the twelve regional Reserve bank presidents. The FOMC meets in Washington, D.C., every four or five weeks throughout the year.

MONETARY TOOLS

money supply (M1): Currency held by the public, plus balances in transactions accounts.

Our immediate interest is not in the structure of the Federal Reserve System but in the way the Fed can use its powers to alter the **money supply (M1).** The levers of the Fed's power include

[1]The nominal distinction continues because only member banks can vote in the elections of regional Federal Reserve bank directors. This distinction has more political than economic significance.

[2]It is expected that a chairman will resign if demoted by the president. However, Marriner Eccles refused to do so when demoted by President Harry Truman and remained a constant critic of subsequent Fed policy.

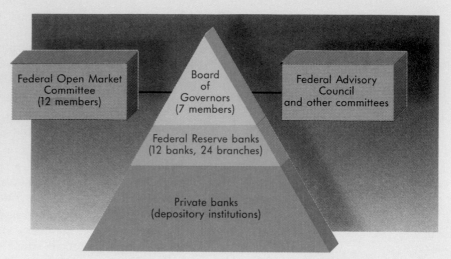

FIGURE 13.1
Structure of the Federal Reserve System

The broad policies of the Fed are determined by the seven-member Board of Governors. The twelve Reserve banks provide central-banking services to individual banks. The Federal Open Market Committee directs Federal Reserve transactions in the money market. Various committees offer formal and informal advice to the Board of Governors.

- Reserve requirements
- Discount rates
- Open-market operations

Reserve Requirements

required reserves: The minimum amount of reserves a bank is required to hold by government regulation; equal to required reserve ratio times transactions deposits.

We have already emphasized the need for banks to maintain some minimal level of reserves. As noted in Chapter 12, the Fed requires private banks to keep some stated fraction of their deposits "in reserve." **Reserves** are held either in the form of actual vault cash or, more commonly, as credits (deposits) in the bank's "reserve account" at a regional Federal Reserve bank. ***By changing the reserve requirement, the Fed can directly alter the lending capacity of the banking system.***

Recall that the ability of the banking system to make additional loans—create deposits—is determined by two factors: (1) the amount of excess reserves banks hold and (2) the money multiplier. Both of these factors are directly influenced by the Fed's required reserve ratio.

Suppose, for example, that banks hold $100 billion of transactions deposits and total reserves of $30 billion. Assume, too, that the minimum reserve requirement is 20 percent. Under these circumstances, banks are holding more reserves than they have to. Recall that

$$\bullet \quad \text{Required reserves} = \text{required reserve ratio} \times \text{total deposits}$$

so that, in this case

$$\text{Required reserves} = 0.20 \times \$100 \text{ billion}$$

$$= \$20 \text{ billion}$$

excess reserves: Bank reserves in excess of required reserves.

Banks are *required* to hold $20 billion in reserve to meet Federal Reserve regulations. They are actually holding $30 billion, however. The $10 billion difference between actual and required reserves is **excess reserves**—that is,

- $$\frac{\text{Excess}}{\text{reserves}} = \frac{\text{total}}{\text{reserves}} - \frac{\text{required}}{\text{reserves}}$$

The existence of excess reserves implies that banks are not fully utilizing their lending powers. With $10 billion of excess reserves and the help of the **money multiplier** the banks *could* lend an additional $50 billion.

The potential for additional loans is calculated as

money multiplier: The number of deposit (loan) dollars that the banking system can create from $1 of excess reserves; equal to 1 ÷ required reserve ratio.

- $$\frac{\text{Available lending capacity}}{\text{of banking system}} = \text{excess reserves} \times \text{money multiplier}$$

or, in this case,

$$\$10 \text{ billion} \times \frac{1}{0.20} = \$50 \text{ billion of unused lending capacity}$$

That is to say, the banking system could create another $50 billion of money (transactions-account balances) without any additional reserves.

A simple way to confirm this—and thereby check your arithmetic—is to note what would happen to total deposits if the banks actually made further loans. Total deposits would increase to $150 billion in this case (the initial $100 billion plus the new $50 billion), an amount that could be supported with $30 billion in reserves (20 percent of $150 billion).

But what if the Fed doesn't want the money supply (M1) to increase this much? Maybe prices are rising and the Fed wants to restrain rather than stimulate total spending in the economy. Under such circumstances, the Fed would want to restrict the availability of credit (loans). Does it have the power to do so? Can the Fed reduce the lending capacity of the banking system?

The answer is clearly yes. ***By raising the required reserve ratio, the Fed can immediately reduce the lending capacity of the banking system.***

The impact of an increase in the required reserve ratio is summarized in Table 13.1. In this case, the required reserve ratio is increased from 20 to 25 percent. Notice that this change in the reserve requirement has no effect on the amount of initial transactions deposits in the banking system (row 1 of Table 13.1) or the amount of total reserves (row 2). They remain at $100 billion and $30 billion respectively. What the increased reserve requirement *does* affect is the way those reserves can be used. Before the increase, only $20 billion in reserves was *required,* leaving $10 billion of *excess* reserves. Now, however, banks are required to hold $25 billion (0.25 × $100 billion) in reserves, leaving them with only $5 billion in excess reserves. Thus an increase in the reserve requirement immediately reduces excess reserves, as illustrated in row 4 of Table 13.1.

TABLE 13.1 The Impact of an Increased Reserve Requirement

An increase in the required reserve ratio reduces both excess reserves (row 4) and the money multiplier (row 5). As a consequence, changes in the reserve requirement have a substantial impact on the lending capacity of the banking system.

	Required reserve ratio	
	20 percent	25 percent
1. Total deposits	$100 billion	$100 billion
2. Total reserves	30 billion	30 billion
3. Required reserves	20 billion	25 billion
4. Excess reserves	10 billion	5 billion
5. Money multiplier	5	4
6. Unused lending capacity	$ 50 billion	$ 20 billion

In The News

BANK REGULATION

Other Bank Regulators

The Federal Reserve System is not the only public institution that regulates banks. Other important regulatory institutions include the following:

- *State banking commissions.* Long before the Federal Reserve System was established (1914), individual states regulated banks. Even today these commissions determine who may open a bank within a state's borders. They also establish rules for lending, other services, and accounting for state-chartered banks.

- *Comptroller of the Currency.* Permission to open a national bank (rather than a state-chartered bank) must be received from the Comptroller of the Currency. The comptroller not only controls national bank charters, but also polices the behavior of national banks.

- *Federal Deposit Insurance Corporation (FDIC).* The FDIC insures individual depositors against the loss of their funds. Should a bank fail, the FDIC stands ready to repay the bank's customers for their losses up to a maximum of $100,000 per account. The FDIC administers two separate insurance funds; (1) the Savings Association Insurance Fund (SAIF) for S&Ls and (2) the Bank Insurance Fund (BIF) for commercial banks.

- *Office of Thrift Supervision (OTS).* The OTS regulates savings banks, S&Ls, and other depository institutions not formerly members of the Federal Reserve System.

- *National Credit Union Administration (NCUA).* The NCUA regulates credit unions much the same way the OTS regulates savings banks. A subsidiary unit provides the same insurance for credit union members as does the FDIC.

There is a second effect also. Notice what happens to the money multiplier (1 ÷ reserve ratio). Previously it was 5 (1 ÷ 0.20); now it is only 4 (1 ÷ 0.25). Consequently, a higher reserve requirement not only reduces excess reserves, but diminishes their lending power as well.

A change in the reserve requirement, therefore, hits banks with a double whammy. *A change in the reserve requirement causes*

- *A change in excess reserves*

- *A change in the money multiplier*

These changes lead to a sharp reduction in bank lending power. Whereas the banking system initially had the power to increase the volume of loans by $50 billion ($10 billion of excess reserves × 5), it now has only $20 billion ($5 billion × 4) of unused lending capacity, as noted in the last row of Table 13.1.

Changes in reserve requirements are a powerful weapon for altering the lending capacity of the banking system. The Fed uses this power sparingly, so as not to cause abrupt changes in the money supply and severe disruptions of banking activity. From 1970 to 1980, for example, reserve requirements were changed only twice, and then only by half a percentage point each time (for example, from 12.0 to 12.5 percent). The reserve requirements effective in 1990 are described in Table 13.2. Note that reserve requirements increase with the size of a bank's deposits. These different reserve requirements reflect a desire to give smaller banks a competitive advantage by providing them with a higher ratio of loan capacity to deposits.

TABLE 13.2   Federal Reserve Requirements, 1990

The Fed's reserve requirements vary with bank size. Smaller banks are allowed to maintain lower reserve ratios. Smaller banks thus have a competitive advantage; they enjoy a larger lending capacity per dollar of deposits.

Value of transactions accounts	Reserve requirement (percent)
$0–40.4 million	3
Over $40.4 million	12

Source: Federal Reserve System.
Note: The amount of deposits subject to a 3 percent reserve ratio automatically increases each year by 80 percent of the growth in total transactions deposits.

The Discount Rate

Banks have a tremendous incentive to maintain their reserves at or close to the minimum established by the Fed. Money held in reserve earns no interest, but loans and bonds do.[3] Hence a profit-maximizing bank seeks to keep its excess reserves as low as possible, preferring to put its reserves to work. In fact, banks have demonstrated an uncanny ability to keep their reserves close to the minimum federal requirement (see Figure 13.2).

Because banks continually seek to keep excess reserves at a minimum, they run the risk of falling below reserve requirements. A large borrower may be a little slow in repaying a loan, or the rate of deposit withdrawals and transfers may exceed expectations. At such times a bank may find that it doesn't have enough reserves to satisfy Fed requirements.

Banks could ensure continual compliance with reserve requirements by maintaining large amounts of excess reserves. But that is an unprofitable procedure, as we have noted. Fortunately, at least from a profit-seeking banker's point of view, there are alternatives.

The federal funds market   A bank that finds itself short of reserves can turn to other banks for help. If a reserve-poor bank can borrow some reserves from a reserve-rich bank, it may be able to bridge its temporary deficit and satisfy the Fed. Reserves borrowed by one bank from another are referred to as "federal funds" and are lent for short periods, usually overnight. Although trips to the federal funds market—via telephone and computer—will usually satisfy Federal Reserve requirements, such trips are not free. The lending bank will charge interest (the "federal funds rate") on its interbank loan.[4] The use of the federal funds market to satisfy Federal Reserve requirements also depends on other banks having excess reserves to lend.

Sale of securities   Another option available to reserve-poor banks is the sale of securities. Banks use some of their excess reserves to buy government bonds, which pay interest. If a bank needs more reserves to satisfy federal regulations, it may sell these securities and deposit the proceeds at the re-

---

[3]Legislation that would require the Fed to pay interest on bank reserves is frequently proposed. Like all other activities of the Federal Reserve System, the practice of not paying interest on reserves can be ended by Congress.

[4]An overnight loan of $1 million at 12 percent interest (per year) costs $329 in interest charges plus any service fees that might be added. Banks make multimillion-dollar loans in the federal funds market.

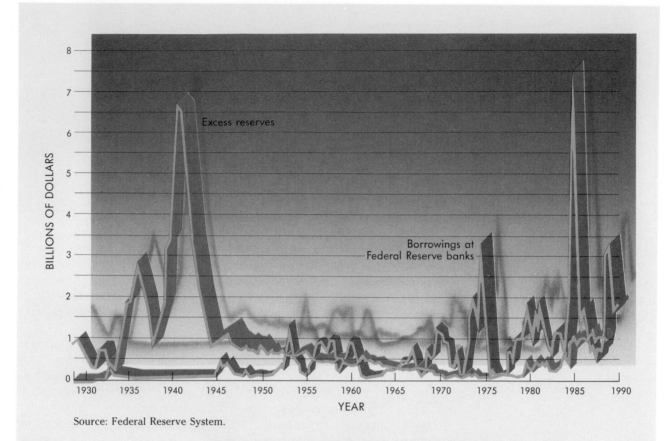

Source: Federal Reserve System.

FIGURE 13.2 Excess Reserves and Borrowings

Excess reserves represent unused lending capacity. Hence banks
strive to keep excess reserves at a minimum. The one exception to
this practice occurred in the Great Depression, when banks were
hesitant to make any loans.

In trying to minimize excess reserves, banks occasionally fall
short of required reserves. At such times they may borrow from
other banks (the federal funds market) or they may borrow reserves
from the Fed. Borrowing from the Fed is called "discounting."

gional Federal Reserve bank. Its reserve position is thereby increased. This
option also involves distinct costs, however, both in forgone interest-earning
opportunities and in the possibility of capital losses when the bond is offered
for quick sale.

Discounting   A third option for avoiding a reserve shortage lies in the structure of the Federal Reserve System itself. The Fed not only establishes certain
rules of behavior for banks but also functions as a central bank, or banker's
bank. Banks maintain accounts with the regional Federal Reserve banks, much
the way you and I maintain accounts with a local bank. Individual banks
deposit and withdraw "reserve credits" from these accounts, just as we deposit and withdraw dollars. Should a bank find itself short of reserves, it can

discounting: Federal Reserve lending of reserves to private banks.

discount rate: The rate of interest charged by the Federal Reserve banks for lending re- serves to private banks.

go to the Fed's "discount window" and borrow some reserves. This process is called **discounting.** Discounting means the Fed is lending reserves directly to private banks.[5]

The discounting operation of the Fed provides private banks with an important source of reserves, but not without cost. The Fed, too, charges interest on the reserves it lends to banks, a rate of interest referred to as the **discount rate.**

The discount window provides a mechanism for directly influencing the size of bank reserves. ***By raising or lowering the discount rate, the Fed changes the cost of money for banks and therewith the incentive to borrow reserves.*** At high discount rates, borrowing from the Fed is expensive. High discount rates also signal the Fed's desire to restrain the money supply and an accompanying reluctance to lend reserves. Low discount rates, on the other hand, make it profitable to acquire additional reserves and to exploit one's lending capacity to the fullest. Low discount rates also indicate the Fed's willingness to support credit expansion. The accompanying news clipping illustrates the Fed's use of this policy lever.

Open-Market Operations

Reserve requirements and discount-window operations are important tools of monetary policy. But they do not come close to open-market operations in day-to-day impact on the money supply. ***Open-market operations are the principal mechanism for directly altering the reserves of the bank- ing system.*** Since reserves are the lifeblood of the banking system, open- market operations are of immediate and critical interest to private banks and the larger economy.

Portfolio decisions   To appreciate the impact of open-market operations, you have to think about the alternative uses for idle funds. Just about every- body has some idle funds, even if they amount to just a few dollars in your

---

[5]In the past, the banks had to present loan notes to the Fed in order to borrow reserves. The Fed "discounted" the notes by lending an amount equal to only a fraction of their face value. Although banks no longer have to present loans as collateral, the term "discounting" endures.

In The News

DISCOUNT RATE

Fed, Banks Increase Key Interest Rates

Moves Expected to Boost Cost of Borrowing

The Federal Reserve Board, concerned about the slide in the dollar and potential inflationary pressures in the economy, yesterday raised the discount rate from $5\frac{1}{2}$ percent to 6 percent, its first increase in three years. . . .

In an immediate reaction to the rise in the discount rate, most of the nation's major banks raised their prime rates from $8\frac{1}{4}$ percent to $8\frac{3}{4}$ percent. The prime rate is used by commercial banks as the basis for determining interest rates on business and consumer loans.

As a result of yesterday's Federal Reserve action, in- creased interest rates are expected for personal, small business, home equity and some home mortgage loans.

—Cindy Skrzycki

The Washington Post, September 5, 1987, p. 1. Copyright © 1987 The Washington Post.

pocket or a minimal balance in your checking account. Other consumers and corporations have great amounts of idle funds, even millions of dollars at any time. What we're concerned with here is what people decide to do with such funds.

People (and corporations) do not hold all their idle funds in transactions accounts or cash. Idle funds are also used to purchase stocks, build up savings-account balances, and purchase bonds. These alternative uses of idle funds are attractive because they promise some additional income in the form of interest, dividends, or capital appreciation (e.g., higher stock prices). Table 13.3 provides a sampling of the ways idle funds can be used to earn interest and the different interest rates paid on each. Idle funds placed in other forms of wealth (e.g., stocks) entail still other rates of return and accessibility. Deciding where, among all these choices, to place idle funds is referred to as the **portfolio decision.**

portfolio decision: The choice of how (where) to hold idle funds.

Hold money or bonds? The open-market operations of the Federal Reserve focus on one of the portfolio choices people make—whether to deposit idle funds in transactions accounts or to purchase government bonds. In essence, the Fed attempts to influence this choice by making bonds more or less attractive, as circumstances warrant. It thereby induces people to move funds from banks to bond markets or vice versa. In the process, reserves either enter or leave the banking system, thereby altering the lending capacity of banks.

Figure 13.3 depicts the general nature of Federal Reserve open-market operations. As we first observed in Chapter 12 (Figure 12.2) the process of deposit creation begins when people deposit money in the banking system. But people may also hold their assets in the form of bonds. The Fed's objective is to alter this portfolio decision by buying or selling bonds. ***When the Fed buys bonds from the public, it increases the flow of deposits (reserves) to the banking system. Bond sales by the Fed reduce the flow.***

The bond market To understand how open-market operations work, we have to take a closer look at the bond market. Not all of us buy and sell bonds, but a lot of consumers and corporations do: daily volume in bond

W☾RLD VIEW

MONETARY RESTRAINT

Bank of Canada Increases Rate on Loans to 12.59%

OTTAWA—Bank of Canada, the nation's central bank, boosted its bank rate to the highest level in nine months, increasing fears that high interest rates will push Canada into a recession, if it isn't in one already.

The bank rate, the levy charged on central bank loans to financial institutions, was set yesterday at 12.59%, up from 12.29%. . . .

High interest rates and the elevated level of the Canadian dollar have "exerted a strong drag on the Canadian economy," Royal Bank of Canada said in an economic report yesterday. It estimated that gross domestic product declined in the 1989 fourth quarter at an annual rate of 0.5%, and it predicted a further 0.5% decline in the first three months of 1990.

The Wall Street Journal, February 2, 1990, p. A2. Reprinted by permission of *The Wall Street Journal,* © Dow Jones & Company, Inc. (1990). All Rights Reserved.

TABLE 13.3 A Variety of Interest Rates

The interest rates paid on bonds vary with the creditworthiness of the borrower. A corporation or government agency with an impeccable record of repaying debts and bright prospects for the future (a "triple-A" borrower) will be able to borrow money at a relatively low rate of interest. By contrast, New York City and Fly-by-Nite Corp. must often pay high interest rates.

Banks, too, offer a variety of interest rates, rather than only one. The basic *prime rate* is the rate of interest charged by commercial banks for short-term loans to their most creditworthy corporate customers. Above the prime rate is a multitude of others, reflecting the purposes of loans (automobile, mortgage, personal, commercial), their duration (one week, one year, several decades), and the risk of nonpayment (default) associated with a particular customer.

When we speak of "the" interest rate, we are referring to an average of the many rates charged. Some of the more frequently cited rates are listed here. Rates shown are for February 1990.

Source: Federal Reserve Board.

Type of security	Interest rate (percent)
Long-term rates	
Tax-exempt bonds (an index of yields for long-term A-rated general-obligation bonds compiled weekly by *The Bond Buyer*)	7.27
Aa utility bonds (for new long-term issues)	9.94
Treasury bonds (weekly average yield of outstanding thirty-year Treasury issues)	8.61
Short-term rates	
Federal funds (the rate for overnight loans among financial institutions)	8.25
Treasury bills (discount rate for six-month Treasury bills traded in the secondary market)	7.77
Commercial paper (discount rate for unsecured six-month notes of high-quality corporate borrowers)	8.05
Prime rate (the rate posted by large banks as a base rate for loans to corporations)	10.00
Discount rate (the interest rate charged by Federal Reserve banks on loans to depository institutions)	7.00
Broker call loans (the rate charged on bank loans to securities dealers, with stocks as collateral)	9.25
Bankers acceptances (discount rate in the secondary market for bank credits created to finance trade)	8.05
Certificates of deposit (offering yield in the secondary market for six-month certificates of large banks in blocks of $1 million or more)	8.29
Eurodollar time deposits (rates paid on one-month dollar deposits outside the United States)	8.19
London interbank offered rate (the rate paid in London on three-month dollar deposits from other banks, used as a base rate in international lending)	10.18

markets exceeds $80 billion. What is being exchanged in this market, and what influences decisions to buy or sell?

In our discussion thus far, we have portrayed banks as intermediaries between savers and spenders. Banks are not the only mechanism available for transferring purchasing power from nonspenders to spenders. Funds are

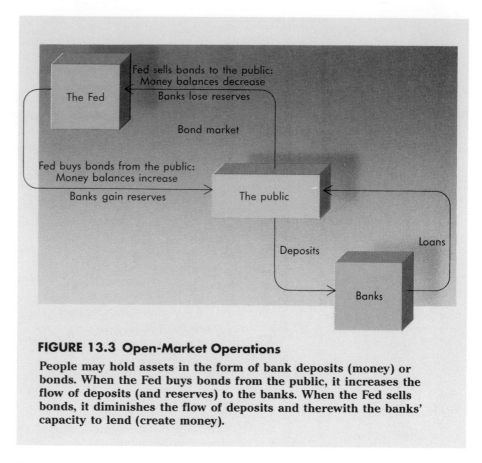

FIGURE 13.3 Open-Market Operations

People may hold assets in the form of bank deposits (money) or bonds. When the Fed buys bonds from the public, it increases the flow of deposits (and reserves) to the banks. When the Fed sells bonds, it diminishes the flow of deposits and therewith the banks' capacity to lend (create money).

bond: A certificate acknowledging a debt and the amount of interest to be paid each year until repayment; an IOU.

lent and borrowed in bond markets as well. In this case, a corporation may borrow money directly from consumers or other institutions. When it does so, it issues a bond as proof of its promise to repay the loan. A **bond** is simply a piece of paper certifying that someone has borrowed money and promises to pay it back at some future date. In other words, a bond is nothing more than an IOU. In the case of bond markets, however, the IOU is typically signed by a giant corporation or a government agency, rather than a friend. It is therefore more widely accepted by lenders.

Because most of the corporations and government agencies that borrow money in the bond market are well known and able to repay their debts, their bonds are actively traded. If I lend $1,000 to General Motors on a ten-year bond, for example, I don't have to wait ten years to get my money back. I can resell the bond to someone else at any time, and that person will collect the face value of the bond (plus interest) from GM when it is due. The actual purchase and sale of bonds takes place in the bond market. Although a good deal of the action occurs on Wall Street in New York, the bond market has no unique location. Like other markets we have discussed, the bond market exists whenever and however bond buyers and sellers get together.

Bond yields   People buy bonds because bonds pay interest. If you buy a General Motors bond, GM is obliged to pay you interest during the period of the loan. For example, an 8 percent 2005 GM bond in the amount of $1,000

yield: The rate of return on a bond; the annual interest payment divided by the bond's price.

states that GM will pay the bondholder $80 interest annually (8 percent of $1,000) until 2005. At that point the initial $1,000 loan will be repaid.

The current **yield** paid on a bond depends on the promised interest rate (8 percent in this case) and the actual purchase price of the bond. Specifically,

$$\bullet \quad \text{Yield} = \frac{\text{annual interest payment}}{\text{price paid for bond}}$$

If you pay $1,000 for the bond, then the current yield is

$$\text{Yield} = \frac{\$80}{\$1,000} = 0.08, \text{ or 8 percent}$$

which is the same as the interest rate printed on the face of the bond. But what if you pay only $900 for the bond? In this case, the promised interest rate remains at 8 percent, but the *yield* jumps to

$$\text{Yield} = \frac{\$80}{\$900} = 0.089, \text{ or 8.9 percent}$$

Buying a $1,000 bond for only $900 might seem like too good a bargain to be true. But bonds are often bought and sold at prices other than their face value. In fact, ***a principal objective of Federal Reserve open-market activity is to alter the price of bonds, and therewith their yields.*** By doing so, the Fed makes bonds a more or less attractive alternative to holding money.

Open-market activity   The basic premise of open-market activity is that participants in the bond market will respond to changes in bond prices and yields. As we have observed, the less you pay for a bond, the higher its yield. Accordingly, the Fed can induce people to buy bonds by offering to sell them at a lower price (e.g., a $1,000, 8 percent bond for only $900). Similarly, the Fed can induce people to sell bonds by offering to buy them at high prices. In either case, the Fed hopes to move reserves into or out of the banking

In The News

YIELDS

Zero-Coupon Bonds

Conventional bonds make interest payments each year, often quarterly. However, some bonds pay no current interest. Because so-called zero-coupon bonds make no interest payments, they have a *current* yield of zero. In effect, a zero-coupon bond accumulates interest pay-

ments, paying them all at once when the bond comes due. The *yield to maturity* on such bonds is implied by the difference between the purchase price and the face value of the bond. A $1,000 "zero" due in ten years, for example, might cost only $400 today. You lend $400 now and get back $1,000 in ten years. The implied yield to maturity is approximately 9 percent.

open-market operations: Federal Reserve purchases and sales of government bonds for the purpose of altering bank reserves.

system. In other words, **open-market operations** entail the purchase and sale of government securities (bonds) for the purpose of altering the flow of reserves into and out of the banking system.

Suppose that the Fed wants to increase the money supply and therefore desires to provide the banking system with additional reserves. To do so, it must persuade people to deposit a larger share of their financial assets in banks and hold less in other forms, particularly government bonds. If the Fed offers to pay a high price for bonds, it will effectively lower bond yields. The lower yields will reduce the attractiveness of holding bonds. If the price offered by the Fed is high enough, people will sell some of their bonds to the Fed and deposit some or all of the proceeds of the sale in their bank accounts. This influx of money into bank accounts will directly increase bank reserves.

Figure 13.4 illustrates the dynamics of open-market operations in more detail. Notice that when the Fed buys a bond from the public, it pays with a check written on itself. The bond seller must deposit the Fed's check in his bank account if he wants to use part of the proceeds or simply to hold the money for safekeeping. The bank, in turn, deposits the check at a regional Federal Reserve bank, in exchange for a reserve credit. The bank's reserves are directly increased by the amount of the check. Thus *by buying bonds, the Fed increases bank reserves.* These reserves can be used to expand the money supply still further, as banks put their newly acquired reserves to work making loans.

Should the Fed desire to slow the growth in the money supply, it can reverse the whole process. Instead of offering to *buy* bonds, the Fed in this case will try to *sell* bonds. If it sets the price sufficiently low—so that bond yields are sufficiently high—individuals, corporations, and government agencies will convert some of their transactions deposits into bonds. When they do so, they write a check, paying the Fed for the bonds.[6] The Fed then returns

[6] In actuality, the Fed deals directly with only thirty-six "primary" bond dealers. These intermediaries then trade with other, "secondary" dealers, financial institutions, and individuals. These additional steps do not significantly alter the flow of funds depicted here.

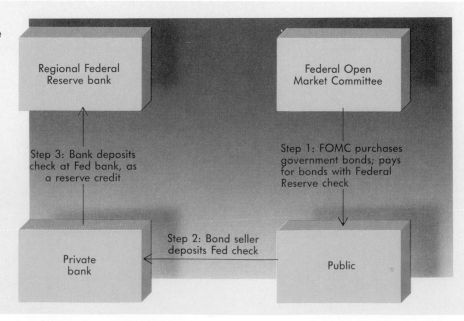

**FIGURE 13.4
An Open-Market Purchase**

The Fed can increase bank reserves by buying government securities from the public. The Fed check used to buy securities (Step 1) gets deposited in a private bank (Step 2). The bank returns the check to the Fed (Step 3), thereby obtaining additional reserves. To decrease bank reserves, the Fed would sell securities, thus reversing the flow of reserves.

Regional Federal Reserve bank

Federal Open Market Committee

Step 3: Bank deposits check at Fed bank, as a reserve credit

Step 1: FOMC purchases government bonds; pays for bonds with Federal Reserve check

Step 2: Bond seller deposits Fed check

Private bank

Public

the check to the depositor's bank, taking payment through a reduction in the bank's reserve account. The reserves of the banking system are thereby diminished. So is the capacity to make loans. Thus **by selling bonds, the Fed reduces bank reserves.**

To appreciate the significance of open-market operations, one must have a sense of the magnitudes involved. The volume of trading in U.S. government securities exceeds seventy billion dollars per day. The Fed alone owned two-hundred fifty billion dollars worth of government securities at the beginning of 1990 and bought or sold enormous sums daily. Thus open-market operations involve tremendous amounts of money and, by implication, potential bank reserves. Each $1 of reserves represents something like $8 of potential lending capacity (via the money multiplier). Thus open-market operations can have a profound impact on the money supply.

INCREASING THE MONEY SUPPLY

The three major levers of monetary policy are reserve requirements, discount rates, and open-market operations. The Fed can use these levers individually or in combination to change the money supply. In this section, the use of each tool to attain a specific policy goal is illustrated.

Suppose the policy goal is to increase the money supply from an assumed level of $340 billion to $400 billion. In surveying the nation's banks, the Fed discovers the facts shown in Table 13.4. On the basis of the facts presented in Table 13.4, it is evident that

- The banking system is "loaned up." Because excess reserves are zero, there is no additional lending capacity.

- The required reserve ratio must be equal to 25 percent, because this is the current ratio of required reserves ($60 billion) to total deposits ($240 billion).

Accordingly, *if the Fed wants to increase the money supply, it will have to pump additional reserves into the banking system or lower the reserve requirement.*

Lowering Reserve Requirements

Lowering the reserve requirement is an expedient way of increasing the lending capacity of the banking system. But by how much should the reserve requirement be reduced?

TABLE 13.4 How to Increase M1

The accompanying data depict a banking system that has $340 billion of money (M1) and no further lending capacity (excess reserves = 0). To enlarge M1 to $400 billion, the Fed can (1) lower the required reserve ratio, (2) reduce the discount rate, or (3) buy bonds held by the public.

Item	Amount
Cash held by public	$100 billion
Transactions deposits	240 billion
Total money supply (M1)	$340 billion
Required reserves	$ 60 billion
Excess reserves	0
Total reserves of banks	$ 60 billion
U.S. bonds held by public	$460 billion
Discount rate	7 percent

Recall that the Fed's policy objective is to increase the money supply from $340 billion to $400 billion, an increase of $60 billion. If the public is not willing to hold any additional cash, this entire increase in the money supply will have to take the form of added transactions deposits. In other words, total deposits will have to increase from $240 billion to $300 billion. These additional deposits will have to be *created* by the banks, in the form of new loans to consumers or business firms.

If the banking system is going to support $300 billion in transactions deposits with its *existing* reserves, the reserve requirement will have to be reduced from 25 percent; thus

$$\frac{\text{Total reserves}}{\text{Desired level of deposits}} = \frac{\$60\text{ billion}}{\$300\text{ billion}} = 0.20$$

At the moment the Fed lowers the minimum reserve ratio to 0.20, *total* reserves will not change. The banks' potential lending power will change, however. Required reserves will drop to $48 billion (0.20 × $240 billion), and excess reserves will jump from zero to $12 billion. These added excess reserves imply an additional lending capacity:

$$\begin{matrix}\text{Excess reserves} \\ (\$12\text{ billion})\end{matrix} \times \begin{matrix}\text{money multiplier} \\ (5)\end{matrix} = \begin{matrix}\text{unused} \\ \text{lending} \\ \text{capacity} \\ (\$60\text{ billion})\end{matrix}$$

If the banks succeed in putting all this new lending power to work—actually make $60 billion in new loans—the Fed's objective of increasing the money supply will be attained.

Lowering the Discount Rate

The second monetary tool available to the Fed is the discount rate. We assumed it was 7 percent initially (see Table 13.4). If the Fed lowers this rate, it will become cheaper for banks to borrow reserves from the Fed. The banks will be more willing to borrow (cheaper) reserves so long as they can make additional loans to their own customers at higher interest rates. The profitability of discounting depends on the *difference* between the discount rate and the interest rate the bank charges its loan customers. The Fed increases this difference when it lowers the discount rate.

There is no way to calculate the appropriate discount rate without more detailed knowledge of the banking system's willingness to borrow reserves from the Fed. Nevertheless, we can determine how much reserves the banks *must* borrow if the Fed's money-supply target is to be attained. The Fed's objective is to increase transactions deposits by $60 billion. If these deposits are to be created by the banks—and the reserve requirement is unchanged at 0.25—the banks will have to borrow an additional $15 billion of reserves ($60 billion divided by 4, the money multiplier).

Buying Bonds

The Fed can also get additional reserves into the banking system by buying U.S. bonds in the open market. As Table 13.4 indicates, the public holds $460 billion in U.S. bonds, none of which are counted as part of the money supply. If the Fed can persuade people to sell some of these bonds, bank reserves will surely rise.

To achieve its money-supply target, the Fed will offer to buy $15 billion of U.S. bonds. It will pay for these bonds with checks written on its own account at the Fed. The people who sold the bonds will deposit these checks in their own transactions accounts. As they do so, they will directly increase bank deposits and reserves by $15 billion.

Is $15 billion of open-market purchases enough? Yes. Note that the $15 billion is a direct addition to transactions deposits, and therefore to the money supply (M1). The additional deposits bring in $15 billion of reserves, only $3.75 billion of which is required (0.25 × $15 billion). Hence the new deposits bring in $11.25 billion of excess reserves, which themselves create an additional lending capacity:

$$\begin{matrix} \text{Excess reserves} \\ (\$11.25 \text{ billion}) \end{matrix} \times \begin{matrix} \text{money multiplier} \\ (4) \end{matrix} = \begin{matrix} \text{unused} \\ \text{lending} \\ \text{capacity} \\ (\$45 \text{ billion}) \end{matrix}$$

Thus the $15 billion of open-market purchases will eventually lead to a $60 billion increase in M1 as a consequence of both direct deposits ($15 billion) and subsequent loan activity ($45 billion).

DECREASING THE MONEY SUPPLY

All of the tools used to increase the money supply can also be used to decrease it. *To reduce the money supply, the Fed can*

- *Raise reserve requirements*

- *Increase the discount rate*

- *Sell bonds*

On a week-to-week basis the Fed does occasionally seek to reduce the total amount of cash and transactions deposits held by the public. These are minor adjustments, however, to broader policies. A growing economy needs a steadily increasing supply of money to finance market exchanges. Hence the Fed rarely seeks an outright reduction in the size of the money supply. What it does do is regulate the *rate of growth* in the money supply. When the Fed wants to slow the rate of consumer and investor spending, it restrains the *growth* of money and credit. Although many people talk about "reducing" the money supply, they are really talking about slowing its rate of growth.

POLICY INSIGHTS:

GLOBAL AND "NONBANK" MONEY

The policy tools at the Fed's disposal imply tight control of the nation's money supply. By altering reserve requirements, discount rates, or open-market purchases, the Fed apparently has the ability to increase or decrease the money supply at will. But the Fed's control is far from complete. The nature of "money," as well as our notion of what a "bank" is, keeps changing. As a result, the Fed has to run pretty fast just to stay in place.

Declining Control in the 1970s

Before 1980 the Fed's control of the money supply was not only incomplete but actually weakening. The Fed did not have authority over all banks. Only one-third of all commercial banks were members of the Federal Reserve System and subject to its regulations. In addition, all savings and loan associations and other savings banks remained outside the Federal Reserve System. These banks were subject to regulations of state banking commissions and other federal agencies but not to Federal Reserve requirements. As a consequence, a substantial quantity of money and near-money lay beyond the control of the Fed.

The limits to Federal Reserve authority became more significant when nonmember banks began to offer automatic transfers, NOW accounts, and other new transactions accounts (see Chapter 12). These changes in bank behavior made it easier for people to spend funds that lay outside the Fed's regulatory authority. As a result, the Fed's control over the money supply diminished.

New Power in the 1980s

To increase the Fed's control of the money supply, Congress passed the Depository Institutions Deregulation and Monetary Control Act of 1980. Commonly referred to simply as the Monetary Control Act, the new legislation called for a complete restructuring of the U.S. banking system. Its principal objectives were (1) to extend the Fed's control of the money supply and (2) to encourage greater competition in the banking industry.

The Monetary Control Act subjects *all* commercial banks, S&Ls, savings banks, and most credit unions to Fed regulation. All such banks now have to satisfy new (and lower) Fed reserve requirements. All banks also enjoy access to the Fed's discount window. These reforms (phased in over a period of seven years) obliterated the distinction between member and nonmember banks and greatly strengthened the Fed's control of the money supply.

Escape Clauses

The Fed's greater control of the money supply triggered a search for escape clauses. Banks don't welcome regulation. Many banks would prefer to manage their own reserves, without worrying about Fed requirements or reports. Also, new data-processing technology makes it far easier for banks and other institutions to move assets across the country or the world in seconds, while changing the form of "money" at the same time (see World View). These capabilities give banks the means to circumvent regulation.

The official definition of a "bank" provided one loophole for circumventing regulation. Federal law defines a bank as an institution that both takes in public deposits *and* makes commercial loans. This left open the possibility of creating "banks" that offered one of these services, but not both. Specifically, a "bank" could take in deposits but *not* make commercial loans and thus exempt itself from Fed regulation. These "nonbank banks," as they came to be known, would instead confine their lending activities to consumer loans (vs. commercial loans). Also called "consumer banks," these nonbank banks behave like other depository institutions, but they offer fewer services.

Nonbanks elude federal prohibitions against interstate banking. The McFadden Act of 1927 prohibits banks from crossing state lines. The intent was to prevent the outflow of savings from one state to another and to prevent the largest "big-city" banks from taking over the banking industry. Nonbank banks are not subject to this prohibition, however, and so can engage in nationwide banking. In so doing, they have the potential to transform even more "money" from one form to another. Nonbank banks also circumvent

W🌐RLD VIEW

REGULATORY PROBLEMS

The Globalization of Money

The movement of money is not confined by national boundaries. Money moves as easily from a domestic bank to a foreign bank as it does between two domestic banks. In either case, all it takes is a couple of entries on a computer and some electronic bookkeeping.

Over $1.2 trillion of money is transmitted by bank wire every day, in billions of separate transactions. Most of these transactions go through one of two clearinghouses, either the Fed's "Fedwire" system, or CHIPS (the Clearing House Interbank Payments System), which specializes in international finance. These clearinghouses move money so efficiently that the same dollar can be used seven times in a day—in seven different countries!

The network of international wire transfers has globalized money. "Eurodollars" are dollar deposits kept in European banks. These dollars may be used in Europe—perhaps to finance a British purchase of French champagne. Or American corporations may borrow Eurodollars to finance investments at home or abroad. In either case, a couple of electronic signals is all it takes to move the money across international borders.

The globalization of money markets increased in January 1990, when U.S. banks received permission to accept deposits in foreign currency. On top of that, international credit cards provide worldwide access to cash and credit.

The globalization of money makes it more difficult for the Fed to control the money supply. If "tight" money policies make domestic credit less available, U.S. firms can turn to Eurodollars or other foreign markets. Electronic outflows can similarly frustrate the Fed's attempts to increase the domestic money supply.

federal regulations that prevent nonfinancial companies (e.g., securities firms, insurance companies) from owning banks.

Once the "nonbank" loophole was discovered, financial institutions rushed to squeeze through it. Early in 1984, U.S. Trust Company was the first national bank to win approval to operate a nonbank. When Congress failed to pass legislation closing this loophole, the Comptroller of the Currency approved hundreds of additional applications, over the objections of the Federal Reserve. The nonbanks still faced stiff political and judicial opposition, however, because of their potential to siphon local funds into major money centers in New York and California. In 1985 the Supreme Court neutralized this threat by permitting *regional* banking—that is, interstate banking confined to a few states, rather than nationwide. In 1987 Congress banned the creation of additional nonbank banks and limited the growth of the 168 existing ones to 7 percent annually.

Other institutions also started acting more and more like banks, however. Many brokerage houses began offering not only to buy and sell stocks, but also to pay interest on idle funds and to permit third-party withdrawals. Many credit-card, insurance, and retail companies now offer similar services. The existence of all of these regional, "nonbank," and other creative financial services implies that controlling the money supply is still a tough job. The concept of "money" is still elusive, and it will remain so as long as people can devise new ways of gaining access to purchasing power. The "globalization" of money represents a further challenge to the Fed's power to control the money supply. Control of the money supply will thus remain incomplete, despite the much stronger regulations of the Monetary Control Act.

SUMMARY

- The Federal Reserve System controls the nation's money supply by regulating the loan activity (deposit creation) of private banks (depository institutions).

- The core of the Federal Reserve System is the twelve regional Federal Reserve banks, which provide check-clearance, reserve deposit, and loan ("discounting") services to individual banks. Private banks are required to maintain minimum reserves on deposit at one of the regional Federal Reserve banks.

- The general policies of the Fed are set by its Board of Governors. The Board's chairman is selected by the U.S. president and confirmed by Congress. The chairman serves as the chief spokesman for monetary policy. The general policies of the Fed are carried out by the Federal Open Market Committee (FOMC), which directs open-market sales and purchases of U.S. bonds.

- The Fed has three basic tools for changing the money supply. By altering the reserve requirement, the Fed can immediately change both the quantity of excess reserves in the banking system and the money multiplier that limits banks' lending capacity. By altering discount rates (the rate of interest charged by the Fed for reserve borrowing), the Fed can also influence the amount of reserves maintained by banks. Finally, and most important, the Fed can increase or decrease the reserves of the banking system by buying or selling government bonds, that is, by engaging in open-market operations.

- When the Fed buys bonds, it causes an increase in bank reserves (and lending capacity). When the Fed sells bonds, it induces a reduction in reserves (and lending capacity).

- The ability of the Fed to control the money supply was strengthened by the Monetary Control Act of 1980. That act subjects all banks to the reserve requirements of the Fed and permits them to offer more banking services. Changing financial practices continually challenge the Fed's control of the money supply, however.

Terms to Remember   Define the following terms:

monetary policy	**discount rate**
money supply (M1)	**portfolio decision**
required reserves	**bond**
excess reserves	**yield**
money multiplier	**open-market operations**
discounting	

Questions for Discussion

1. Why do banks want to maintain as little excess reserves as possible? Under what circumstances might banks desire to hold excess reserves? (Hint: see Figure 13.2.)

2. Why do people hold bonds rather than larger savings-account or checking-account balances? Under what circumstances might they change their portfolios, moving their funds out of bonds into bank accounts?

3. What is the current price and yield of U.S. Treasury bonds? Of General Motors bonds? (Check the financial section of your daily newspaper.) What accounts for the difference?

4. Why might the Fed want to increase the money supply?

Problems 1. Assume that the following data describe the condition of the commercial banking system:

Total reserves:	$200 billion
Transactions deposits:	$800 billion
Cash held by public:	$100 billion
Reserve requirement:	0.20

(a) How large is the money supply (M1)?
(b) Are the banks fully utilizing their lending capacity? Explain.
(c) What would happen to the money supply *initially* if the public deposited another $50 billion of cash in transactions accounts? Explain.
(d) What would the lending capacity of the banking system be after such a portfolio switch?
(e) How large would the money supply be if the banks fully utilized their lending capacity?
(f) What three steps could the Fed take to offset that potential growth in M1?

2. Suppose a banking system with the following balance sheet has no excess reserves. Assume that banks will make loans in the full amount of any excess reserves that they acquire and will immediately be able to eliminate loans from their portfolio to cover inadequate reserves.

Assets (in billions)		Liabilities (in billions)	
Total reserves	$30	Transactions accounts	$300
Securities	90		
Loans	180		
Total	$300		$300

(a) What is the reserve requirement?
(b) Suppose the reserve requirement is changed to 5 percent. Reconstruct the balance sheet of the total banking system after all banks have fully utilized their lending capacity.
(c) Suppose the Federal Open Market Committee buys $10 billion of securities from the commercial banking system. Reconstruct the balance sheet to show the changes and new totals after this transaction but before any new loans are made or called in. Assume the reserve requirement is still 5 percent.
(d) Suppose the banking system now expands its loans and transactions accounts by the maximum amount it can on the basis of its excess reserves. Reconstruct the balance sheet showing the new totals after the loans have been made.
(e) As a result of both the reserve requirement change and the open-market operations,

The money supply has expanded by a total of $_____ billion.
Total reserves have gone up by $_____ billion.
Loans have increased by $_____ billion.

CHAPTER 14

Monetary Policy

With minor exceptions, the Federal Reserve System can control the nation's money supply. But why is this significant? Does it matter how much money is available? Will the money supply affect our ability to achieve full employment, price stability, or any other macroeconomic goal?

Vladimir Lenin thought so. The first communist leader of the Soviet Union once remarked that the best way to destroy a society is to destroy its money. If a society's money became valueless, it would no longer be accepted in exchange for goods and services in product markets. As a consequence, people would resort to barter, and the economy's efficiency would be severely impaired. Adolf Hitler tried unsuccessfully to use this weapon against Great Britain during World War II. His plan was to counterfeit British currency, then drop it from planes flying over England. He believed that the sudden increase in the quantity of money, together with its suspect origins, would render the British pound valueless.

Even in peacetime, the quantity of money in circulation will influence its value in the marketplace. Moreover, access to credit (bank loans) is a basic determinant of spending behavior. Consequently, control over the money supply implies an ability to influence our macroeconomic performance.

But how much influence does the money supply have on macro performance? Specifically,

- What is the relationship between the amount of money and aggregate expenditure?

- How can the Fed use its control of the money supply to alter macro outcomes?

- How effective is monetary policy, compared to fiscal policy?

Economists offer very different answers to these questions. John Maynard Keynes, for one, was primarily concerned about aggregate spending in the economy. Money was a secondary concern: it mattered only if it could alter desired investment, consumption, government spending, or net exports. As a consequence, Keynesians regard **monetary policy** as less important than fiscal policy. They concede that changes in the money supply may affect

monetary policy: The use of money and credit controls to influence macroeconomic activity.

prices and output (employment), but they would rather use tax and budget policies to influence the macro economy.

Not everyone shares the Keynesian view of money. Monetarists think money has direct and powerful effects, particularly on the price level. From their perspective, neither fiscal policy nor monetary policy significantly affects real output levels. But monetary policy at least has a direct influence on prices (inflation).

In this chapter we examine these different views of money. We start with the Keynesian view of money, then look at the monetarist view. The chapter ends with a comparison of these two views and their implications for fiscal and monetary policy.

THE KEYNESIAN VIEW

From Keynes's perspective, the supply of money has a potentially important but indirect impact on the macro economy. A change in the money supply has an immediate effect on interest rates. Aggregate demand and therefore GNP are affected, however, only to the extent that interest rates alter spending plans. To see how this chain of events might occur, we start in money markets, then proceed to product markets.

Money Markets

interest rate: The price paid for the use of money.

The Keynesian view of money starts with a simple proposition: money is simply a commodity that is traded in the marketplace. Like other goods, there is a supply of money and a demand for money. Together they determine the "price" of money, or the **interest rate.**

At first glance, it may appear strange to call interest rates the price of money. But when you borrow money, the "price" you pay is measured by the interest rate you are charged. When interest rates are high, money is "expensive." When interest rates are low, money is "cheap."

Even people who don't borrow must contend with the price of money. We all make a basic portfolio choice: we either hold our money or put it to work. *People hold (demand) money (M1) by keeping cash in their wallets or maintaining positive balances in their transactions accounts.* Money held in this form earns little or no interest. By contrast, money used to buy bonds or simply lent to someone else is likely to earn a higher rate of interest. The choice, then, is to hold (demand) money or to use it. This is the basic **portfolio decision** we first encountered in Chapter 13.

portfolio decision: The choice of how (where) to hold idle funds.

The nature of the "price" of money should be apparent: people who hold *cash* are forgoing an opportunity to earn interest. So are people who hold money in checking accounts that pay no interest. In either case, forgone interest is the opportunity cost (price) of money people choose to hold. How high is that price? It is equal to the market rate of interest.

Money held in interest-paying transactions accounts (e.g., NOW accounts) does earn some interest. The rate of interest paid, however, is typically quite low. In this case, the opportunity cost of holding money (M1) is the *difference* between the prevailing rate of interest and the rate paid on transactions-account balances. As is the case with cash and regular checking accounts, opportunity cost is measured by the forgone interest.

The Demand for Money

demand for money: The quantities of money people are willing and able to hold at alternative interest rates, *ceteris paribus*.

transactions demand for money: Money held for the purpose of making everyday market purchases.

precautionary demand for money: Money held for unexpected market transactions or for emergencies.

speculative demand for money: Money held for speculative purposes, for later financial opportunities.

Once we recognize that money does have a price, we can easily formulate a demand for money. As is the case with all goods, the **demand for money** is simply a schedule (or curve) showing the quantity of money demanded at alternative prices (interest rates).

Why would people ever want to hold money and thereby forgo the opportunity to earn interest? Why do you carry cash around? Why do you keep a positive balance in your checking account? Are you missing an opportunity to amass a small fortune in interest payments? Are there any good reasons for doing so?

Transactions demand Even people who have mastered the principles of economics do hold money, and for several good reasons. The most obvious is the desire to buy goods and services. In order to transact business in product or factor markets, we need money, in the form of either cash or a positive checking-account balance. Even when we use credit cards, we are only postponing the date of payment by a few weeks or so. Accordingly, we recognize a basic **transactions demand for money.**

Precautionary demand Another reason people hold money is their fear of the proverbial rainy day. A sudden emergency may require money purchases over and above normal transactions needs. Moreover, such needs may arise when the banks are closed or in a community where one's checks are not accepted. Also, future income is uncertain and may diminish unexpectedly. Therefore, people hold a bit more money (cash or transactions deposits) than they anticipate spending. This **precautionary demand for money** is the extra money being held as a safeguard against the unexpected.

Speculative demand People also hold money for speculative purposes, so they can respond to financially attractive opportunities. This represents a **speculative demand for money.** Suppose you were interested in buying stocks or bonds but had not yet picked the right ones, or regarded their present prices as too high. In such circumstances, you might want to hold some money so that you could later buy a "hot" stock or bond at a price you think attractive. Thus you would be holding money in the hope that a better financial opportunity would later appear. In this sense, you would be *speculating* with your money, forgoing present opportunities to earn interest in the hope of hitting a real jackpot later.

The market-demand curve These three motivations for holding money combine to create a *market demand* for money. The question is, what shape does this demand curve take? Does the quantity of money demanded decrease sharply as the rate of interest rises? Or do people tend to hold the same amount of money, regardless of its price?

People do cut down on their money balances when interest rates rise. At such times, the opportunity cost of holding money is simply too high. This explains why so many people move their money out of transactions deposits (M1) and into money-market mutual funds when interest rates are extraordinarily high (e.g., in 1980–82). Corporations are even more careful about managing their money when interest rates rise. Better money management requires watching checking-account balances more closely and even making more frequent trips to the bank, but the opportunity costs are worth it.

The total market demand for money is illustrated in Figure 14.1. Like nearly all demand curves, the market demand curve for money slopes downward. The downward slope indicates that *the quantity of money people are willing and able to hold (demand) increases as interest rates fall (ceteris paribus).*

Equilibrium

Once a money-demand curve and a money-supply curve are available, the action in money markets is easy to follow. This action is summarized in Figure 14.1. The money-demand curve in Figure 14.1 is assumed to reflect existing demands for holding money. The money-supply curve has been drawn at an arbitrary level of g_1. In practice, its position depends on Federal Reserve policy (Chapter 13), the lending behavior of private banks, and the willingness of consumers and investors to borrow money.

The intersection of the money-demand and money-supply curves (E_1) establishes an **equilibrium rate of interest.** Only at this interest rate is the quantity of money supplied equal to the quantity demanded. In this case, we observe that an interest rate of 7 percent equates the desires of suppliers and demanders.

At any rate of interest other than 7 percent, the quantity of money demanded would not equal the quantity supplied. Look at the imbalance that exists, for example, when the interest rate is 9 percent. At that rate, the quantity of money supplied (g_1) exceeds the quantity demanded (g_2). All the money (g_1) must be held by someone, of course. But the demand curve indicates that people are not *willing* to hold so much money at that interest rate (9 percent). People will adjust their portfolios by moving money out of cash and transactions deposits into bonds, money-market mutual funds, or other interest-earning assets. This will tend to lower interest rates (recall that buying bonds tends to lower their yields). As interest rates drop, people will be willing to hold more money. Ultimately we will get to E_1, where the quantity of money demanded equals the quantity supplied. At that equilibrium, people will be content with their portfolio choices.

equilibrium rate of interest: The interest rate at which the quantity of money demanded in a given time period equals the quantity of money supplied.

FIGURE 14.1
Money-Market Equilibrium

All points on the market–demand curve represent the quantity of money people are willing to hold at a specific interest rate. The equilibrium interest rate occurs at the intersection (E_1) of the money–supply and money–demand curves. At that rate of interest, people are willing to hold as much money as is available. At any other interest rate (e.g., 9 percent), the quantity of money people are *willing* to hold will not equal the quantity available, and people will adjust their portfolios.

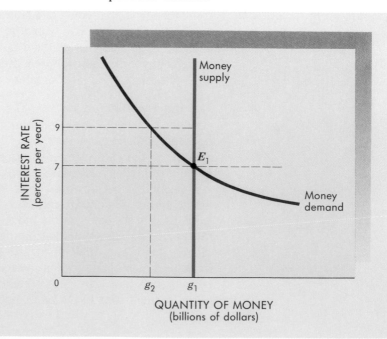

KEYNESIAN STIMULUS

Money and Interest Rates

The equilibrium rate of interest is subject to change, of course. In fact, Keynesian economists assert that the principal effect of monetary policy is to alter the equilibrium rate of interest. As we saw in Chapter 13, the Federal Reserve System can alter the money supply through changes in reserve requirements, changes in the discount rate, or open-market operations. By implication, then, the Fed can alter the equilibrium rate of interest.

Figure 14.2 illustrates the potential impact of monetary policy on the equilibrium rate of interest. Assume that the money supply is initially at g_1 and the equilibrium interest rate is 7 percent. The Fed then increases the money supply to g_2 by lowering the reserve requirement, reducing the discount rate, or, most likely, purchasing additional bonds in the open market. The impact of this expansionary monetary policy is evident. If the market demand for money is unchanged, the larger money supply will bring about a new equilibrium, at E_2. At this intersection, the market rate of interest is only 6 percent. Hence by increasing the money supply, the Fed tends to lower the equilibrium rate of interest. Or, to put the matter differently, people are *willing* to hold larger money balances only at lower interest rates.

Were the Fed to reverse its policy and reduce the money supply, interest rates would rise. You can see this result in Figure 14.2 also, by observing the change in the rate of interest that occurs when the money supply shrinks from g_2 to g_1.

Interest Rates and Spending

A change in the interest rate is not the end of this story. The ultimate objective of monetary policy is to alter macroeconomic outcomes—prices, output, employment. In the Keynesian model, this requires a change in the rate of aggregate spending. Hence the next question is how changes in interest rates affect consumer, investor, government, and net export spending.

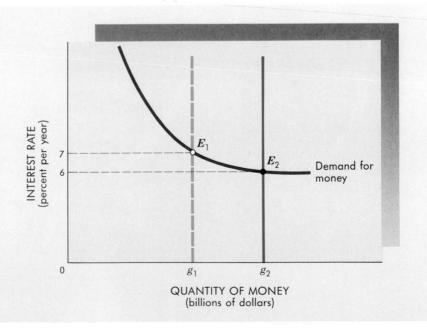

FIGURE 14.2
Changing the Rate of Interest

Changes in the money supply tend to alter the equilibrium rate of interest. In this case, an increase in the money supply (from g_1 to g_2) lowers the equilibrium rate of interest (from 7 percent to 6 percent).

INTEREST RATE (percent per year)

E_1

E_2

Demand for money

0   g_1 g_2

QUANTITY OF MONEY
(billions of dollars)

In The News

KEYNESIAN APPROACH TO MONEY

Looser Reins

Signs of a Slowdown Suggest Fed Will Ease Its Grip on Credit

Move to Trim Interest Rates Could Help Avert Slump

With signs of a slowing economy on the horizon, interest rates are headed down.

In the credit markets yesterday, yields on long-term bonds dropped again, and signals from the Federal Re-

serve suggest the central bank may soon ease its grip on credit. That would allow a broader retreat in interest rates, with widespread effects. A further mortgage-rate decline, to cite just one of them, could help to resuscitate housing construction, possibly helping head off any recession.

—Alan Murray and Tom Herman

Will lower interest rates encourage spending? In Chapter 8 we observed that investment decisions are sensitive to the rate of interest. Specifically, we demonstrated that lower rates of interest reduce the cost of buying plant and equipment, making investment more profitable. Accordingly, a lower rate of interest should result in a higher rate of desired investment spending, as shown in Figure 14.3*b*.

The increased investment brought about by lower interest rates represents an increase in total spending. This increase is illustrated in Figure 14.3*c* by an upward *shift* of the aggregate spending function. If the shift is large enough, it will close the assumed recessionary gap and bring the economy closer to full employment. Thus *from a Keynesian perspective, the Fed's objective of stimulating the economy is achieved in three distinct steps:*

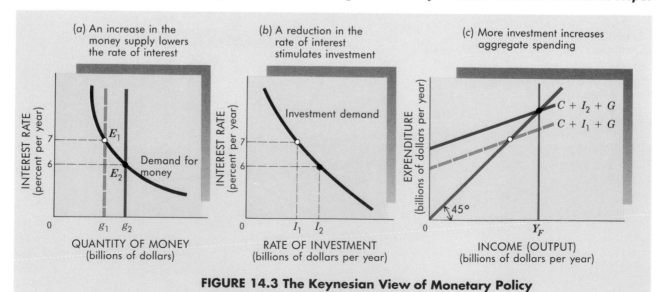

FIGURE 14.3 The Keynesian View of Monetary Policy

- *An increase in the money supply*

- *A reduction in the interest rate*

- *An increase in aggregate spending*

If the price level remains constant (as Keynes assumed), the increased spending implies an increased quantity of goods and services demanded—that is, a shift of **aggregate demand** as well.

aggregate demand: The total quantity of output demanded at alternative price levels in a given time period, *ceteris paribus*.

Lower interest rates might also stimulate consumer spending. Household appliances, cars, and other expensive goods are often purchased with borrowed money. Accordingly, both the availability and the cost of loanable funds may influence consumer expenditures.

Even government spending may be affected by changes in the rate of interest. State and local governments are particularly sensitive to money-market conditions and may postpone planned expenditures when interest rates are too high. When the supply of money is expanded, however, both the availability of loanable funds and their cost improve.

Policy Constraints

Figure 14.3 demonstrates how monetary policy might change the rate of aggregate spending. Monetary policy does not always succeed as easily as Figure 14.3 implies, however. From a Keynesian viewpoint, the effectiveness of monetary policy depends on two distinct phenomena:

- The sensitivity of interest rates to changes in the money supply (Figure 14.3*a*)

- The sensitivity of spending decisions to changes in interest rates (Figure 14.3*b*)

liquidity trap: The portion of the money-demand curve that is horizontal; people are willing to hold unlimited amounts of money at some (low) interest rate.

The liquidity trap   The possibility that interest rates may not respond to changes in the money supply is illustrated by the liquidity trap. When interest rates are low, the opportunity cost of holding money is cheap. At such times people may decide to hold all the money they can get, waiting for income-earning opportunities to improve. Further increases in the money supply will be absorbed readily, without reducing interest rates. At this juncture—a phenomenon Keynes called the **liquidity trap**—further expansion of the money supply has no effect on the rate of interest. This situation is portrayed by the horizontal section of the money-demand curve in Figure 14.4.

What happens to interest rates when the initial equilibrium falls into this trap? Nothing at all. Notice that the equilibrium rate of interest does not fall when the money supply is increased from g_1 to g_2 (Figure 14.4). People are willing to hold all that additional money without a reduction in the rate of interest.

Expectations   Even if we are able to avoid a liquidity trap, we have no assurance that desired spending will increase as expected. Keynes put great emphasis on *expectations*. Recall that investment decisions are motivated not only by interest rates but by expectations as well. During a recession—when unemployment is high and the rate of spending low—corporations have little incentive to expand production capacity. With little expectation of future profit, investors are likely to be unimpressed by "cheap money" (low interest rates) and may decline to use the lending capacity that banks make available.

FIGURE 14.4
A Liquidity Trap Can Stop Interest Rates from Falling

If people are willing to hold unlimited amounts of money at the prevailing interest rate, increases in the money supply will not push interest rates lower. A liquidity trap—the horizontal segment of the money-demand curve—prevents interest rates from falling. If interest rates do not fall, monetary policy may not be able to close a recessionary gap (see Figure 14.3).

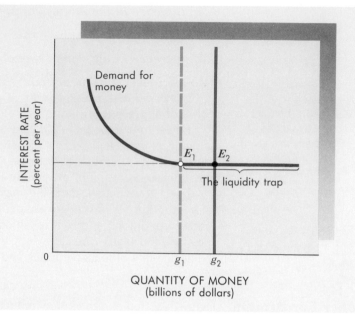

Investment demand that is slow to respond to the stimulus of cheap money is said to be *inelastic,* because it will not expand. Consumers, too, are reluctant to borrow when current and future income prospects are uncertain or distinctly unfavorable. Accordingly, even if the Fed is successful in lowering interest rates, there is no assurance that lower interest rates will stimulate borrowing and spending.

The possibility that investment spending may not respond to changes in the rate of interest is illustrated in Figure 14.5 by the vertical portion of the investment demand curve. Notice that a reduction in the rate of interest from 7 percent to 6 percent does *not* increase investment spending. In this case, businesses are simply unwilling to invest any more funds. As a consequence,

FIGURE 14.5
Inelastic Investment Demand Can also Impede Monetary Policy

A lower interest rate will not always stimulate investment. If investors have unfavorable expectations for future sales, small reductions in interest rates may not alter their investment decisions. Here the rate of investment remains constant when the interest rate drops from 7 to 6 percent. This kind of situation blocks the second step in the Keynesian approach to monetary policy (see Figure 14.3b).

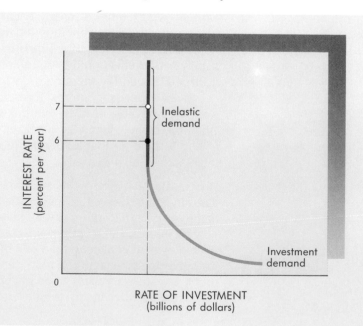

aggregate spending does not rise. The Fed's policy objective remains unfulfilled, even though the Fed has successfully lowered the rate of interest. Recall that the investment-demand curve may also *shift* if expectations change. If expectations worsened, the investment-demand curve would shift to the left and might result in even *less* investment at 6 percent interest (see Figure 9.1*b*).

KEYNESIAN RESTRAINT

Like fiscal policy, monetary policy is a two-edged sword. At times it will seek to increase aggregate demand; at other times it will try to restrain it. When an inflationary gap threatens, the objective of monetary policy is to reduce the rate of total spending at full employment. This puts the Fed in the position of "walking against the wind" (see In the News). If successful, the resulting reduction in spending will keep aggregate demand within the dimensions of our production possibilities.

Money and Interest Rates

The mechanics of monetary policy designed to combat inflation are similar to those used to fight unemployment; only the direction is reversed. In this case, we seek to discourage spending by increasing the rate of interest. The Federal Reserve can push the rate of interest up by selling bonds, increasing

In The News

FIGHTING INFLATION

The Fed Walks Against the Wind

Everywhere Alan Greenspan looks these days, the Federal Reserve chairman sees pressure for lower interest rates. The economy is slowing sharply from its summer surge. . . .

Presidential Pressure
The Bush Administration keeps issuing pointed suggestions that monetary policy is too tight. . . .

Reluctant Response
The Fed is responding—on its own terms. . . .

The ever-cautious Greenspan is not about to abandon the gradualism that has guided monetary policy for the past 19 months. By yearend, short rates should be lower—but only enough to take the prime rate from its current 10.5% to perhaps 10%.

The Fed feels comfortable enough to resist all outside pressures for now. Officials are pleased with the economic "soft landing" they have engineered, and they're confident that they can steer the economy right along the fine line between slow growth and no growth. . . .

Zero-Inflation Target
This self-assurance stems in large part from the Fed's new emphasis on "price stability." During his two years at the helm, Greenspan has succeeded in focusing the central bank's sights on the single long-term goal of reducing inflation to a negligible level by the mid-1990s. The chairman and his colleagues believe that zero inflation will ultimately let the economy grow faster—even though getting from the current 4.3% rate of price increases to zero will require subpar growth for several years. The Fed is willing to put the economy through that trial, Greenspan told the House Banking Committee on Oct. 25, because "whatever losses are incurred in the pursuit of price stability would surely be more than made up in increased output thereafter."

But others in Washington aren't so willing to suffer now to achieve zero inflation later. President Bush and a chorus of top Administration officials believe that the central bank's commitment to an economic ideal is putting the economy at risk.

Business Week, November 6, 1989, p. 40.

the discount rate, or increasing the reserve requirement. All of these actions reduce the money supply and thus establish a new and higher equilibrium rate of interest.

Interest Rates and Spending

The ultimate objective of a restrictive monetary policy is to reduce the rate of aggregate spending, not just to raise interest rates. Will it succeed?

The effects of an expansionary policy were illustrated in Figure 14.3. When the Fed's monetary policy is restrictive, we expect higher interest rates to curb investment and consumer spending. At higher rates of interest, many marginal investments will no longer be profitable. Likewise, many consumers will decide that they cannot afford the higher monthly payments associated with increased interest rates; purchases of homes, cars, and other consumer durables will be postponed. As a result, the aggregate spending curve will shift downward to close the inflationary gap, and a more desirable equilibrium will be established.

Policy Constraints

Although the potential impact of restrictive monetary policy is evident, its success is not assured either. We have seen that low sales and profit expectations may overwhelm low interest rates in the investment decision during recessionary periods. Similarly, high sales and profit expectations may negate the impact of high interest rates during an expansionary period.

The expectations that may frustrate restrictive monetary policy are of two sorts. First, there are the expectations of future sales and profits. If sales expectations are high, higher interest rates alone may not discourage continued investment. Second there are expectations of inflation. If people think prices (and interest rates) will continue to rise in the future, then "high" interest rates now will not deter borrowing or spending.

The Keynesian Conclusion

Liquidity traps, shifting expectations, and unresponsive investment demands all appear to dim any hopes for monetary policy. Indeed, these obstacles suggest that monetary policy doesn't really matter much. Modern Keynesians don't draw quite such a hard conclusion, however, They concede that money does indeed matter. But, they believe, the effects of monetary policy are indirect and subject to substantial limitations. *In the Keynesian model, changes in the money supply affect macroeconomic outcomes only through the intermediary of interest rates.* Moreover, the impact of interest rate changes may be muted by expectations. In the Keynesian view, these forces limit but do not negate the potential of monetary policy. The effectiveness of monetary policy may also be constrained by international capital flows (see World View). All of these considerations imply that fiscal policy might be a more dependable policy lever for altering macro outcomes.

THE MONETARIST PERSPECTIVE

Not everyone accepts these Keynesian views of monetary policy. Members of another school of economists, the Monetarists, claim that Keynes's explanation of monetary policy is unduly complex. They also claim that Keynes misjudged the power of monetary policy. In their view monetary policy has little impact on real output and employment levels but has a far more powerful and certain impact on the price level than Keynes surmised.

W🌐RLD VIEW

POLICY OBSTACLES

International Constraints on Monetary Policy

Money is an international commodity that moves across continents almost as fast as it moves across the street (see Chapter 13 World View on The Globalization of Money, p. 319). One of the things that lures money across international borders is the rate of interest. If interest rates are higher abroad than at home, American businesses and investors will move their money out of the United States and into countries with higher interest rates. When domestic interest rates are higher, the flow of money will reverse.

These international money flows are another constraint on monetary policy. Suppose the Fed wants to slow the economy by limiting money-supply growth. Such tight-money policies will tend to raise interest rates in the United States. A higher interest rate is supposed to curb domestic investment and consumer spending. But those higher U.S. interest rates will also be an attraction for foreign money. People holding dollars abroad will want to move more money to the United States, where it can earn higher interest rates. Foreigners will also want to exchange their currencies for dollars, again in order to earn higher interest rates.

As international money flows into the United States, the money supply will expand more quickly than the Fed desired. This will frustrate the Fed's policy objectives and may force it to tighten the money supply even more. Capital inflows will also tend to increase the international value of the dollar, making it more difficult to sell U.S. exports. In sum, the internationalization of money is one more problem the Fed has to worry about when it conducts monetary policy.

The Equation of Exchange

equation of exchange: Money supply (M) times velocity of circulation (V) equals level of aggregate spending (P × Q).

income velocity of money (V): The number of times per year, on average, a dollar is used to purchase final goods and services; $PQ \div M$.

Monetarists assert that the potential of monetary policy can be expressed in a simple equation called the **equation of exchange.** It is written as

$$\bullet \quad MV = PQ$$

where M refers to the quantity of money in circulation and V to its **velocity** of circulation. Total spending in the economy is equal to the average price (P) of goods times the quantity (Q) of goods sold in a period. This spending is financed by the supply of money (M) times the velocity of its circulation (V).

Suppose, for example, that there are only two participants in the market and that the money supply consists of one crisp $20 bill. What is the limit to total spending in this case? If you answer "$20," you have not yet grasped the nature of the circular flow. Suppose I begin the circular flow by spending $20 on eggs, bacon, and a gallon of milk. The money I spend ends up in Farmer Brown's pocket, because he is the only other market participant. Once in possession of the money, Farmer Brown may decide to satisfy his long-smoldering desire to learn something about economics and buy one of my books. If he acts on that decision, the $20 will return to me. At that point, both Farmer Brown and I have sold $20 worth of goods, Hence $40 of total spending has been financed with one $20 bill.

As long as we keep using this $20 bill to buy goods and services from each other, we can continue to do business. Moreover, the faster we pass the money from hand to hand during any period of time, the greater the value of sales each of us can register. If the money is passed from hand to hand eight times, then I will be able to sell $80 worth of textbooks and Farmer Brown will be able to sell $80 worth of produce during that period, for a total nominal output of $160. The quantity of money in circulation and the velocity with which it travels (changes hands) in product markets will always be equal to the value of total spending and income. The relationship is summarized as

$$\bullet \quad M \times V = P \times Q$$

In this case, the *equation of exchange* confirms that

$$\$20 \times 8 = \$160$$

The value of total sales for the year is $160.

Notice that the identity of *MV* and *PQ* says nothing about which dimensions of the economy will change. All we can say with certainty is that if either the velocity of money (*V*) increases or the money supply (*M*) increases, we may anticipate an increase in total sales (*PQ*). But we don't know whether prices (*P*) or the quantity of output (*Q*) or both will increase. That will depend on how the supply side of the economy responds to a change in spending. In our illustration, an increase in *V* or *M* could stimulate Farmer Brown and me to produce more output, raise our produce and textbook prices, or some combination of these responses.

Monetarists use the equation of exchange to simplify the explanation of how monetary policy works. There is no need, they argue, to follow the effects of changes in *M* through the money markets to interest rates and further to changes in aggregate spending. The basic consequences of monetary policy are evident in the equation of exchange. The two sides of the equation of exchange must always be in balance. Hence we can be absolutely certain that **If M increases, prices (P) or output (Q) must rise, or V must fall.**

Stable Velocity

Monetarists assert that the velocity of money (*V*) is unlikely to fall when *M* increases. How fast people use their money balances depends on the institutional structure of money markets and people's habits. Neither the structure of money markets nor people's habits are likely to change when *M* is increased. Indeed, Monetarists assert that *V* tends to be very stable (predictable) over long periods of time. Accordingly, an increase in *M* will not be offset by a reduction in *V*. Instead, the impact of an increased money supply will be transmitted to the right-hand side of the equation of exchange. That means that **total spending must rise if the money supply (M) grows and V is stable.**

Money-Supply Focus

From a monetarist perspective, there is no need to trace the impacts of monetary policy through interest rate movements. Indeed, interest rate changes and the response of consumers and investors to interest rates are irrelevant

to the monetarist perspective. This perspective leads to a fundamentally stronger role for monetary policy.

From a Keynesian perspective, the Federal Reserve must manipulate interest rates to increase or decrease total spending. Changes in the money supply are appropriate only insofar as the desired interest rates are achieved.

A monetarist perspective leads to a wholly different strategy for the Fed. Because interest rates are not part of the monetarist explanation of how monetary policy works, the Fed should not try to manipulate interest rates (see In the News). The Fed should instead focus on the money supply itself. Monetarists also argue that the Fed cannot really control interest rates well, since they depend on both the supply of and the demand for money. What the Fed *can* control is the supply of money, and the equation of exchange clearly shows that money matters.

"Natural" Unemployment

Some Monetarists add yet another perspective to the equation of exchange. They assert that not only V but Q as well is stable. If this is true, then changes in the money supply (M) would affect only prices (P). But the link between monetary policy and inflation would be direct and unambiguous.

What does it mean for Q to be stable? The argument here is that the quantity of goods produced is primarily dependent on production capacity, labor-market efficiency, and other "structural" forces. These structural forces establish a **"natural" rate of unemployment** that is fairly immune to short-run policy intervention. This is the *long-run* aggregate supply curve we first encountered in Chapter 5. From this perspective, there is no reason for producers to depart from this "natural" rate of output when the money supply increases. Producers are smart enough to know that both prices and costs will rise when spending increases. Hence rising prices will not create any new profit incentives for increasing output. Firms will just continue producing at the "natural" rate, with higher (nominal) prices and costs. As a result, increases in aggregate spending—whether financed by more M or faster V—are not likely to alter real output levels. Q will stay constant.

natural rate of unemployment: Long-term rate of unemployment determined by structural forces in labor and product markets.

In The News

MONETARISM

Monetarists Reject Focus on Lowering Rates

A group of monetarist economists urged the Reagan administration and the Federal Reserve yesterday to stop trying to encourage faster economic growth by insisting on lower interest rates.

The group, known as the Shadow Open Market Committee, said that the gross national product, adjusted for inflation, has grown during the past two years at a 2½ percent annual rate, only slightly less than its average for the last 100 years.

"Efforts to force interest rates lower, to depreciate the dollar and to stimulate the economy to head off protectionist (trade) legislation are based on the mistaken belief that we have learned how to stimulate now and prevent inflation later," the committee said in a statement issued after one of its semiannual meetings in New York. . . .

The Shadow Committee, headed by economists Allan H. Meltzer of Carnegie-Mellon University and Karl Brunner of the University of Rochester, was formed more than a decade ago to provide economic analysis and policy recommendations from a monetarist point of view.

—John M. Berry

The Washington Post, September 23, 1986, p. C1. Copyright © 1986 The Washington Post.

If the quantity of real output is in fact stable, then P is the only thing that can change. Thus *the most extreme monetarist perspective concludes that changes in the money supply affect prices only.* When M increases, total spending rises, but the higher nominal value of spending is completely absorbed by higher prices. In this view, monetary policy affects only the rate of inflation.

Figure 14.6 illustrates the extreme monetarist argument in the context of aggregate supply and demand. The assertion that real output is fixed at the natural rate of unemployment is reflected in the vertical aggregate supply curve. With real output stuck at Q^*, any increase in aggregate demand directly raises the price level.

Monetarist Policies

At first glance, the monetarist argument looks pretty slick. Keynesians worry about how the money supply affects interest rates, how interest rates affect spending, and how spending affects output. By contrast, Monetarists point to a simple equation ($MV = PQ$) that produces straightforward responses to monetary policy.

There are fundamental differences between the two schools here, not only about how the economy works, but also about how successful macro policy might be. To appreciate those differences, consider monetarist responses to inflationary and recessionary gaps.

Closing an Inflationary Gap

Consider again the options for controlling demand-pull inflation. This is a situation where the value of goods and services demanded at full employment exceeds the economy's full-employment capacity. The objective of policy is to reduce aggregate spending.

From a Keynesian perspective, the way to do this is to shrink the money supply and drive up interest rates. But Monetarists argue that nominal interest rates are already likely to be high. Furthermore, if an effective anti-inflation policy is adopted, interest rates will come *down,* not go up.

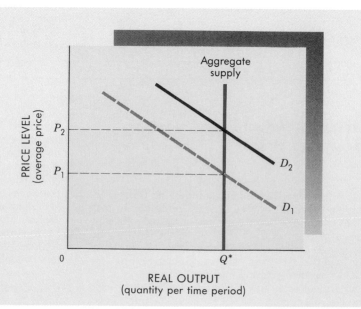

FIGURE 14.6
The Monetarist View

Monetarists argue that the rate of real output is set by structural factors. Furthermore, firms are not likely to be fooled into producing more just because prices are rising if costs are rising just as much. Hence aggregate supply remains at the "natural" level Q^*. Any increases in demand, therefore, raise the price level (inflation) but not output.

Real vs. nominal interest   To understand this monetarist conclusion, we have to distinguish between *nominal* interest rates and *real* ones. Nominal interest rates are the ones we actually see and pay. When a bank pays 5½ percent interest on your bank account, it is quoting (and paying) a nominal rate.

Real interest rates are never actually seen and rarely quoted. These are "inflation-adjusted" rates. Specifically, the **real rate of interest** equals the nominal rate *minus* the anticipated rate of inflation.

Recall what inflation does to the purchasing power of the dollar: as inflation continues, each dollar purchases fewer goods and services. As a consequence, dollars borrowed today are of less real value when they are paid back later. The real rate of interest reflects this inflation adjustment.

Suppose you lend someone $100 at the beginning of the year, at 8 percent interest. You expect to get more back at the end of the year than you start with. That "more" you expect refers to real goods and services, not just dollar bills. Specifically, you anticipate that when the loan is repaid with interest at the end of the year, you will be able to buy more goods and services than you could at the beginning. This expectation of a *real* gain is at least part of the reason for making a loan.

Your expected gain will not materialize, however, if all prices rise by 8 percent during the year. If the inflation rate is 8 percent, you will discover that $108 buys you no more at the end of the year than $100 would have bought you at the beginning. Hence you would have given up the use of your

real rate of interest: The nominal rate of interest minus anticipated inflation rate.

In The News

TOO MUCH MONEY

"Not Worth a Continental": The U.S. Experience with Hyperinflation

The government of the United States had no means to pay for the Revolutionary War. Specifically, the federal government had no power to levy taxes that might transfer resources from the private sector to the public sector. Instead, it could only request the states to levy taxes of their own and contribute them to the war effort. The states were not very responsive, however: state contributions accounted for only 6 percent of federal revenues during the war years.

To pay for needed weapons and soldiers, the federal government had only two other options, either (1) borrow money or (2) create new money. When loans proved to be inadequate, the Continental Congress started issuing new paper money—the "Continental" dollar—in 1775. By the end of 1779, Congress had authorized issuance of over $250 million in Continental dollars.

At first the paper money enabled George Washington's troops to acquire needed supplies, ammunition, and vol-

unteers. But soon the flood of paper money inundated product markets. Wholesale prices of key commodities skyrocketed. Commodity prices *doubled* in 1776, in 1777, and again in 1778. Then prices increased *tenfold* in the next two years.

Many farmers and storekeepers refused to sell goods to the army in exchange for Continental dollars. Rapid inflation had taught them that the paper money George Washington's troops offered was nearly worthless. The expression "not worth a Continental" became a popular reference to things of little value.

The states tried price controls and even empowered themselves to seize needed war supplies. But nothing could stop the inflation fueled by the explosive increase in the money supply. Fortunately, the war ended before the economy collapsed. After the war, the U.S. Congress established a new form of money, and in 1787 it empowered the federal government to levy taxes and mint gold and silver coins.

The Evolution of the American Economy, Sidney Ratner, copyright © 1979, Basic Books, Inc.

money for an entire year without any real compensation. In such circumstances, the *real* rate of interest turns out to be zero.

The nominal rate of interest, then, really has two components. The first component is the real rate of interest. The second is an inflation adjustment. If the real rate of interest was 4 percent and an inflation rate of 9 percent was expected, the nominal rate of interest would be 13 percent. If inflationary expectations worsened to, say, 10 percent, the nominal rate would climb to 14 percent. Thus

$$\bullet \quad \frac{\text{Nominal}}{\text{interest rate}} = \frac{\text{real}}{\text{interest rate}} + \frac{\text{anticipated rate}}{\text{of inflation}}$$

Monetarists argue that the real rate of interest is low and fairly stable. If the nominal rate of interest is high, this is likely to reflect bad inflationary expectations. That is to say, ***Monetarists see high nominal rates of interest as a symptom of inflation, not a cure.*** Indeed, high nominal rates may even look cheap if inflationary expectations are worsening faster than interest rates are rising (see In the News).

Consider the implications of all this for monetary policy. Suppose we want to close an inflationary gap. Monetarists and Keynesians alike agree that a reduced *M* will deflate total spending. But Keynesians rely on a "quick attack" of high interest rates to slow consumption and investment spending. Monetarists, by contrast, assert that consumers and investors need to be convinced that the Fed will continue a tight money policy long enough to really slow the rate of inflation. Then and only then will inflationary expectations recede. When inflationary expectations diminish, nominal interest rates will begin to fall. Therefore, ***Monetarists emphasize steady and predictable changes in the money supply.***

Closing a Recessionary Gap

The link between anticipated inflation and nominal interest rates also constrains expansionary monetary policy. The Keynesian cure for a recession is to expand *M* and lower interest rates. But Monetarists fear that an increase

In The News

REAL INTEREST RATES

Money Is Free!

"Money's not tight, it's cheap. It's free!"

So says one of our most articulate friends along Wall Street. The point is that short-term interest rates, horrendous as they are, are below the short-term inflation rate, horrendous as it is. The August numbers showed a six-month inflation rate of 9.4%, for example, while six months earlier the prime interest rate was 8.0%. If you borrowed and paid back in cheaper dollars, you got your money for free.

We relate the quote because we have the impression a lot of folks in Washington don't realize how those of us out here in the real world look at these matters. In particular, the observation ought to be of interest to the Federal Reserve's Open Market Committee, which meets today to set money growth targets for both the next two months and the next year.

Out here in the real world, folks know free money when they see it. That is why interest rates will not go down, nor the dollar recover meaningfully, until inflation is reduced. And the longer the Fed delays in starting to curb money growth, the higher price the nation will have to pay before inflation is ultimately brought under control.

Reprinted by permission of *The Wall Street Journal,* © Dow Jones & Company, Inc. (1978). All Rights Reserved.

in M will lead—via the equation of exchange—to higher P. If everyone believed this would happen, then an unexpectedly large increase in M would immediately raise people's inflationary expectations. Nominal interest rates would go up, not down, when the money supply was increased!

From a monetarist perspective, expansionary monetary policies are not likely to lead us out of a recession. On the contrary, such policies might double our burden by heaping inflation on top of our unemployment woes. The rate of real output and employment is more dependent on structural characteristics of the economy than on changes in the money supply. All monetary policy should do is ensure a stable and predictable rate of growth in the money supply. Then people could concentrate on real production decisions without worrying so much about fluctuating prices.

THE CONCERN FOR CONTENT

Monetary policy, like fiscal policy, can affect more than just the *level* of total spending. We must give some consideration to the impact of Federal Reserve actions on the *content* of GNP if we are going to be responsive to the "second crisis" of economic theory.[1] Both Keynesians and Monetarists agree that monetary policy will affect nominal interest rates. When interest rates change, not all spending decisions will be affected equally. Investment decisions that are highly sensitive to interest rates are obviously more susceptible to monetary policy than others. The construction industry, especially the residential housing market, stands out in this respect. The sensitivity of housing costs to interest-rate changes forces the construction industry to bear a disproportionate burden of restrictive monetary policy. Accordingly, when the Fed pursues a policy of tight money—high interest rates and limited lending capacity—it not only restrains total spending but reduces the share of housing in that spending. Utility industries, public-works projects, and state and local finances are also disproportionately affected by monetary policy.

In addition to altering the content of demand and output, monetary policy affects the competitive structure of the market. When money is tight, banks must ration available credit among loan applicants. Large and powerful corporations are not likely to run out of credit, because banks will be hesitant to incur their displeasure and lose their business. Thus General Motors and IBM stand a much better chance of obtaining tight money than does the corner grocery store. Moreover, if bank lending capacity becomes excessively small, GM and IBM can always resort to the bond market and borrow money directly from the public. Small businesses seldom have such an alternative.

POLICY INSIGHTS:

FISCAL VS. MONETARY POLICY

Keynesians and Monetarists clearly have very different views about the efficacy of monetary policy. They also disagree about the effectiveness of fiscal policy. Indeed, ardent Monetarists contend that changes in government spending or taxes—the basic levers of fiscal policy—have no impact on prices, output, or total spending! From their perspective, *only* money matters. At the

[1]See the quotation from Joan Robinson in Chapter 10, calling attention to the exclusive focus of economists on the *level* of economic activity (the "first crisis"), to the neglect of content (the "second crisis").

other extreme, ardent Keynesians assert that changes in the money supply—the basic levers of monetary policy—don't really matter, that only fiscal policy can solve our macroeconomic problems.

At this juncture, any further argument between the Keynesian and monetarist perspectives might seem hopelessly confusing. By examining these extreme positions, however, we may find a good way of summarizing all that we have learned about both monetary and fiscal policy. This summary also highlights the key issues that concern actual policymakers.

The Policy Levers

The equation of exchange provides a convenient summary of the differences between Keynesian and monetarist perspectives. There is no disagreement about the equation itself: aggregate spending ($M \times V$) *must* equal the value of total sales ($P \times Q$). ***What Keynesians and Monetarists argue about is which of the policy levers—M or V—is likely to be effective in altering aggregate spending.***

- ***Monetarists*** point to changes in the money supply (M) as the principal lever of macroeconomic policy. They assume V is reasonably stable

- ***Keynesian*** fiscal policy *must* rely on changes in the velocity of money (V), because tax and expenditure policies have no direct impact on the money supply.

Crowding Out

The extreme monetarist position that *only* money matters is based on the assumption that the velocity of money (V) is constant. ***If V is constant, changes in total spending can come about only through changes in the money supply.*** There are no other policy levers on the left side of the equation of exchange.

Think about an increase in government spending designed to stimulate the economy. How does the government pay for this fiscal-policy initiative? Monetarists argue that there are only two ways to pay for this increased expenditure (G). The government must either raise additional taxes or borrow more money. If the government raises taxes, the disposable income of consumers will be reduced, and private spending will fall. On the other hand, if the government borrows more money to pay for its expenditures, there will be less money available for loans to private consumers and investors. In either case, more government spending (G) implies less private spending (C or I). Thus *increased G* effectively **"crowds out"** some C or I, leaving total spending unchanged. From this viewpoint, fiscal policy is ineffective; it can't even shift the aggregate spending curve. At best, fiscal policy can change the composition of demand and thus the mix of output. Only changes in M (monetary policy) can shift the aggregate spending curve.

Milton Friedman, formerly of the University of Chicago, champions the monetarist view with this argument:

crowding out: A reduction in private-sector borrowing (and spending) caused by increased government borrowing.

> I believe that the state of the government budget matters; matters a great deal—for some things. The state of the government budget determines what fraction of the nation's income is spent through the government and what fraction is spent by individuals privately. The state of the government budget determines what the level of our taxes is, how much of our income we turn over to the government. The state of the government budget has a considerable effect on

interest rates. If the federal government runs a large deficit, that means the government has to borrow in the market, which raises the demand for loanable funds and so tends to raise interest rates.

If the government budget shifts to a surplus, that adds to the supply of loanable funds, which tends to lower interest rates. It was no surprise to those of us who stress money that enactment of the surtax was followed by a decline in interest rates. That's precisely what we had predicted and what our analysis leads us to predict. But—and I come to the main point—in my opinion, the state of the budget by itself has no significant effect on the course of nominal income, on inflation, on deflation, or on cyclical fluctuations.[2]

Keynesians reply that the alleged constant velocity of money is a monetarist's pipe dream. Some even argue that the velocity of money is so volatile that changes in V can completely offset changes in M, leaving us with the proposition that money doesn't matter.

The liquidity trap illustrates the potential for V to change. Keynes argued that people tend to accumulate money balances—slow their rate of spending—during recessions. A slowdown in spending implies a reduction in the velocity of money. Indeed, in the extreme case of the liquidity trap, the velocity of money falls toward zero. Under these circumstances, changes in M (monetary policy) will not influence total spending. The velocity of money falls as rapidly as M increases. On the other hand, increased government spending (fiscal policy) can stimulate aggregate spending by putting idle money balances to work (thereby increasing V). Changes in fiscal policy will also influence consumer and investor expectations, and thereby further alter the rate of aggregate spending.

[2]Milton Friedman and Walter W. Heller, *Monetary vs. Fiscal Policy* (New York: Norton, 1969), pp. 50–51.

In The News

CROWDING OUT

U.S. Share of Borrowing Expected to Hit 56 Percent

More than half the money raised in U.S. credit markets this year will be borrowed by the federal government, as the private sector draws in its horns and the government's borrowing needs swell, according to new estimates from the Office of Management and Budget.

This will be the first year in which the government's share of the total funds raised in U.S. credit markets tops the 50 percent level—56 percent, according to the estimates. In fiscal 1981 it totaled 34.8 percent, the OMB said, and the new estimates show it dropping back to 46 percent for fiscal 1983. However, that figure assumes that Congress cuts next year's deficit to just over $100 billion.

A major reason for the large anticipated jump in the government's share of credit-markets is that the budget office forecasts a big drop in total funds raised in the U.S. markets, from $408 billion in fiscal 1981 to $368 billion in the current fiscal year. This is presumably a result of today's deep recession, which discourages individuals and businesses from borrowing more than they have to.

Another is the sharp rise in the federal deficit, which the administration says has come largely because of unforeseen developments in the economy.

—Caroline Atkinson

The Washington Post, June 5, 1982. Copyright © 1982 The Washington Post.

How Fiscal Policy Works: Two Views

These different perspectives on fiscal and monetary policy are summarized in Tables 14.1 and 14.2. The first table evaluates fiscal policy from both Keynesian and monetarist viewpoints. The central issue is whether and how a change in government spending (G) or taxes (T) will alter macroeconomic outcomes. Keynesians assert that aggregate spending will be affected as the velocity of money (V) changes. Monetarists say no, because they anticipate an unchanged V.

If aggregate spending isn't affected by a change in G or T, then fiscal policy won't affect prices (P) or real output (Q). Thus Monetarists conclude that fiscal policy is not a viable tool for combating either inflation or unemployment. By contrast, Keynesians believe V will change and that output and prices will respond accordingly.

Insofar as interest rates are concerned, Monetarists recognize that nominal interest rates will be affected (read Friedman's quote again) but *real* rates won't be. This is because real interest rates depend on real output and growth, both of which are seen as immune to fiscal policy. Keynesians see less impact on nominal interest rates and more on real interest rates.

What all this boils down to is this: fiscal policy, by itself, will be effective only if it can alter the velocity of money. ***How well fiscal policy works depends on how much the velocity of money can be changed by government tax and spending decisions.***

How Monetary Policy Works: Two Views

Table 14.2 provides a similar summary of monetary policy. This time the positions of Monetarists and Keynesians are reversed, or nearly so. Monetarists say a change in M must alter total spending ($P \times Q$) because V is stable. Keynesians assert that V may vary, so they aren't convinced that monetary policy will always work. The heart of the controversy is again the velocity of money. Monetary policy works so long as V is stable, or at least predictable. ***How well monetary policy works depends on how stable or predictable V is.***

TABLE 14.1 How Fiscal Policy Matters: Monetarist vs. Keynesian Views

Monetarists and Keynesians have very different views on the impact of fiscal policy. Monetarists assert that changes in government spending (G) and taxes (T) do not alter the velocity of money (V). As a result, fiscal policy alone cannot alter total spending. Keynesians reject this view, arguing that V is changeable. They claim that tax cuts and increased government spending increase the velocity of money and so alter total spending.	Do changes in G or T affect:	Monetarist view	Keynesian view
	1. Aggregate spending?	No (stable V causes crowding out)	Yes (V changes)
	2. Prices?	No (aggregate spending not affected)	Maybe (if at capacity)
	3. Real output?	No (aggregate spending not affected)	Yes (output responds to demand)
	4. Nominal interest rates?	Yes (crowding out)	Maybe (may alter demand for money)
	5. Real interest rates?	No (determined by real growth)	Yes (real growth and expectations may vary)

TABLE 14.2   How Money Matters: Monetarist vs. Keynesian Views

Because Monetarists believe that V is stable, they assert that changes in the money supply (M) must alter total spending. But all of the monetary impact is reflected in prices and nominal interest rates; *real* output and interest rates are unaffected.

Keynesians think that V is variable and thus that changes in M might *not* alter total spending. If monetary policy does alter aggregate spending, however, Keynesians expect all outcomes to be affected.

Do changes in M affect:	Monetarist view	Keynesian view
1. Aggregate spending?	Yes (V stable)	Maybe (V may change)
2. Prices?	Yes (V and Q stable)	Maybe (V and Q may change)
3. Real output?	No (rate of unemployment determined by structural forces)	Maybe (output responds to demand)
4. Nominal interest rates?	Yes (but direction unknown)	Maybe (liquidity trap)
5. Real interest rates?	No (depends on real growth)	Maybe (real growth may vary)

Once the central role of velocity is understood, everything else falls into place. Monetarists assert that prices but not output will be directly affected by a change in M. This is because the right-hand side of the equation of exchange contains only two variables (P and Q), and one of them (Q) is assumed to be unaffected by monetary policy. Keynesians, by contrast, are not so sure prices will be affected by M, or that real output won't be. It all depends on V and the responsiveness of P and Q to changes in aggregate spending.

Finally, Monetarists predict that nominal interest rates will respond to changes in M, although they are not sure in what direction. It depends on how inflationary expectations adapt to changes in the money supply. Keynesian economists are not so sure nominal interest rates will change but are sure about the direction if they do.

Is Velocity Stable?

Tables 14.1 and 14.2 provide many insights into how fiscal and monetary policies work. As we have emphasized, the velocity of money plays a key role in the debate over the relative effectiveness of these two policy levers. The critical question appears to be whether V is stable or not. Why hasn't someone answered this simple question and resolved the debate over fiscal versus monetary policy?

Long-run vs. short-run views   To understand the persistence of the debate over V and thus over the question of whether fiscal or monetary policy "works"—we must distinguish between the long run and the short run. The velocity of money (V) turns out, in fact, to be quite stable over long periods of time. Since World War II, the velocity of money has grown at the rate of roughly 3 percent per year. This appears to be a fairly predictable long-run pattern. Accordingly, Monetarists conclude that the many changes in fiscal policy that have occurred in the postwar period have been inconsequential. With V persistently growing at 3 percent per year, only changes in M have been of any significance.

Keynesians reply, however, that Monetarists are nearsighted and don't see all the short-run variations in V that surround its long-term growth rate. In some years, V grew much faster than 3 percent; in others, it hardly increased at all; and in the early 1980s, velocity actually declined (see Figure 14.7). Keynesians argue that these short-run changes in V are important for economic welfare—that is, that people care about what happens to their jobs, income, and prices *this* year. Moreover, government tax and spending policies can help counteract any undesirable changes in V.

Policy risks   The Monetarists offer one last argument. They concede that velocity just *might* fluctuate in the short run. But they argue that short-run changes in the velocity of money are *unpredictable.* Accordingly, both fiscal and monetary policies are subject to considerable uncertainty. Under these circumstances, Monetarists argue, policymakers are just as likely to fail as to succeed if they attempt to alter aggregate spending in the short run.

As Monetarists see it, the private sector of the economy (consumption and investment spending) is inherently stable. What upsets the economy is the unpredictable nature of public-sector intervention. Since the Fed cannot foresee the future much better than anyone else, it is likely to intervene too often and in the wrong way. These "quick-fix" interventions tend to increase instability and raise the level of uncertainty. Investors and consumers then have to anticipate not only "natural" changes in economic activity but also ever-changing monetary policy.

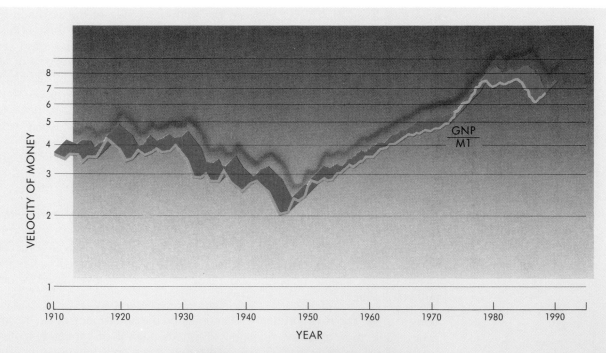

FIGURE 14.7 Income Velocity of Money

(annually, 1910–60; seasonally adjusted, quarterly, 1960–90)

The income velocity of money (V) equals GNP divided by the supply of money. During the Great Depression the velocity of money fell sharply. From 1945 to 1981, however, V increased at a fairly predictable rate. In the 1980s V became less predictable, rendering monetary policy's impact less certain.

Money-Supply Targets In view of the risks and uncertainties inherent in discretionary monetary policy, Monetarists conclude that there is only one safe course to follow. The safe course, Monetarists argue, is to maintain a stable and predictable monetary policy. This means expanding the money supply at a steady rate of roughly 3 percent per year. This would permit real GNP to grow at 3 percent, while allowing for inflation of roughly the same magnitude (recall that V is growing at 3 percent also). This steady, predictable monetary policy would reduce market uncertainties and policy risks.

The Monetarists' policy advice to the Fed is straightforward. ***Monetarists favor fixed money-supply targets.*** All the Fed has to do is announce its intention to increase the money supply by some fixed amount (e.g., 3 percent), then use its central-banking powers to hit that money-growth target.

Keynesians reject fixed money-supply targets, favoring more flexibility in control of the money supply. In their view, a fixed money-supply target would render monetary policy useless in combating cyclical swings of the economy. Keynesians prefer the risks of occasional policy errors to the "straitjacket" of a fixed money-supply target. ***Keynesians advocate targeting interest rates, not the money supply.***

The Fed's Eclecticism For a brief period (1979–82) the Fed adopted the monetarist's policy of fixed money-supply targets. On October 6, 1979, the chairman of the Fed (Paul Volcker) announced that the Fed would begin focusing on the money supply exclusively, without worrying about interest rates. The Fed's primary goal was to reduce inflation, which was then running at close to 14 percent a year. To slow the inflationary spiral, the Fed decided to limit sharply growth of the money supply.

The Fed succeeded in reducing money-supply growth and the inflationary spiral. But its tight-money policies sent interest rates soaring and pushed the economy into a deep recession (1981–82). Exactly three years after adopting the monetarist approach, the Fed abandoned it.

In place of a strict monetarist approach,[3] the Fed has adopted an eclectic mixture of monetarist and Keynesian policies. Each year the Fed announces targets for money-supply growth. But the targets are very broad, and not very stable. At the beginning of 1986, for example, the Fed set a target of 3 to 8 percent growth for M1. That wide target gave it plenty of room to adjust to changing interest rates and cyclical changes. But the Fed actually missed the target by a mile—M1 increased by 15 percent in 1986. In explaining this mile-wide miss to Congress, Chairman Volcker emphasized pragmatism. "Success in my mind," he asserted, "will not be measured by whether or not we meet some preordained, arbitrary target" but by our macroeconomic performance. Since the economy was growing steadily in 1987, and inflation was not increasing, he concluded that monetary policy had been a success. He concluded his testimony by telling Congress that the Fed would no longer set targets for M1 but would instead keep an eye on broader money-supply measures (M2 and M3; see Table 12.1) and interest rates. In other words, the Fed would do whatever it thought necessary to promote price stability and economic growth. Volcker's successor, Alan Greenspan, appears committed to the same brand of eclecticism. In early 1990 he refused to set a target for growth of the narrowly defined money supply (M1) and set very wide targets

---

[3]The Fed's policy of 1979–82 was not strict monetarism. Although the Fed emphasized money-supply targets, it allowed the money supply to fluctuate much more than strict Monetarists prescribed.

In The News

POLICY COMPROMISES

Among Economists, Eclecticism Is All the Rage

When E. Gerald Corrigan was chosen to head the Federal Reserve Bank of New York, he was asked whether it was true that he did not consider himself a monetarist.

"That is very correct," he replied, adding that he opposed such "economic rules." But he went on to muddy the water by saying that he does believe in controlling money-supply growth "over time."

It isn't easy to sort that out, but it would appear that Mr. Corrigan belongs to the growing ranks of economic eclectics. . . .

An eclectic, according to the dictionary, is someone who selects his ideas "from various systems, doctrines or sources." Somehow it has come to be seen as a virtue that a person is unable to make up his mind.

Monetarist Karl Brunner suggests that an eclectic is someone who on Monday thinks the earth revolves around the sun, while on Tuesday it's the other way around.

Even the hard-core eclectics don't reject monetarism in its entirety. Like Mr. Corrigan, they have come to accept the notion that it's a good idea to control money growth over some usually undefined long run.

The analytic portions of monetarism, in fact, have become quite widely accepted. . . .

It's when you get to the policy prescription that you begin to run into trouble. Mr. Poole puts it simply: "The monetary authorities ought simply to maintain a constant rate of growth of the money stock."

Some of the eclectics believe that monetarists want the growth rate fixed over the short term, which is ridiculous. It would suit most monetarists if the average growth rates gradually declined to a level compatible with stable prices.

Mr. Poole would like to see a money-growth rule written into law. I have some trouble with that idea, but Mr. Poole's description of the legislative proposal surely stresses flexibility.

"A rule should not be interpreted as providing for every detail of monetary management for all time," Mr. Poole writes. "Legislated rules can and ought to be changed from time to time as conditions change and knowledge accumulates. The most important part of the argument for rules is that pertaining to a known legislated provision for a specific rate of money growth; the damage is done by permitting the monetary authorities to muddle along, making day-to-day decisions that generate an unpredictable rate of money growth.

"A legislated rule might be changed annually, or even more often, though the available evidence strongly suggests that stability of money growth over much longer periods of time would be desirable." . . .

Mr. Poole says the prime argument against discretionary monetary policy is subtle and difficult to understand, but give it a try:

"For discretionary policy adjustments to be effective, the policy makers must be able to predict the responses of households and firms to policy adjustments. But households and firms, in making their plans, must form predictions as to what the policy makers are going to do. Each side may, so to speak, end up playing a game: Side one is guessing what side two is guessing side one will do, and vice versa."

Monetarists want to adjust money targets when past experience shows they are wrong. Hard-core eclectics want to adjust monetary targets to accord with their guesses about the future. . . .

—Lindley H. Clark, Jr.

(3–7 percent) for broader measures of the money supply (M2). He, too, has proclaimed that the Fed cannot be bound to any one theory but must instead use a mix of money-supply and interest-rate adjustments to attain desired macro outcomes.

SUMMARY

- The essence of monetary policy lies in the Federal Reserve's control over the money supply. By altering the money supply, the Fed can determine the amount of purchasing power available.

• There are sharp disagreements about how monetary policy works. Keynesians argue that monetary policy works indirectly, through its effects on interest rates and spending. Monetarists assert that monetary policy has more direct and more certain impacts, particularly on price levels.

• In the Keynesian view, the demand for money is important. This demand reflects desires to hold money (in cash or transactions deposits) for transactions, precautionary, and speculative purposes. The interaction of money supply and money demand determines the equilibrium rate of interest.

• From a Keynesian perspective, the impact of monetary policy on the economy occurs in three distinct steps. First, changes in the money supply alter the equilibrium rate of interest. Second, changes in the interest rate alter the rate of investment expenditure. Third, the increase in desired investment enhances aggregate spending.

• For Keynesian monetary policy to be fully effective, interest rates must be responsive to changes in the money supply, and investment spending must be responsive to changes in interest rates. Neither condition is assured. In a liquidity trap, people are willing to hold unlimited amounts of money at some low rate of interest. The interest rate will not fall below this level as the money supply increases. Also, investor expectations of sales and profits may override interest-rate considerations in the investment decision.

• The monetarist view of monetary policy is simpler, and it builds on the equation of exchange ($MV = PQ$). Monetarists assert that the velocity of money (V) is stable, so that changes in M must influence ($P \times Q$). Monetarists focus on the money supply; Keynesians, on interest rates.

• Some Monetarists also argue that the level of real output (Q) is set by structural forces, as illustrated by the vertical, long-run aggregate supply curve. Q is therefore insensitive to changes in aggregate spending. If both V and Q are constant, changes in M directly affect P.

• Monetary policy attempts to influence total expenditure by changing M and will be fully effective only if V is constant. Fiscal policy attempts to influence total expenditure by changing V and will be fully effective only if M does not change in the opposite direction. The controversy over the effectiveness of fiscal versus monetary policy depends on whether the velocity of money (V) is stable or instead is subject to policy influence.

• The velocity of money is more stable over long periods of time than over short periods. Keynesians conclude that this makes fiscal policy more powerful in the short run. Monetarists conclude that the unpredictability of short-run velocity makes *any* short-run policy risky.

Terms to Remember   Define the following terms:

monetary policy	aggregate demand
interest rate	liquidity trap
portfolio decision	equation of exchange
demand for money	income velocity of money (*V*)
transactions demand for money	natural rate of unemployment
precautionary demand for money	real rate of interest
speculative demand for money	crowding out
equilibrium rate of interest	

Questions for Discussion

1. What proportions of your money balance are held for transactions, precautionary, and speculative purposes? Can you think of any other purposes for holding money?

2. Why do high interest rates so adversely affect the demand for housing and yet have so little influence on the demand for strawberries?

3. If the Federal Reserve banks mailed everyone a brand-new $100 bill, what would happen to prices, output, and income? Illustrate with the equation of exchange.

4. Suppose that the Fed wanted to reduce aggregate spending (to fight inflation) and the president wanted to increase total expenditure (to fight unemployment). What kind of action would each take? What effects would their combined actions have on GNP?

5. Monetarists argue that the money supply may grow too fast if the Fed focuses on interest rates as a mechanism for stimulating demand. What problems do they see?

Problems

1. Suppose the Federal Reserve decided to purchase $10 billion worth of government securities in the open market. What impact would this action have on the economy? Specifically, answer the following questions, using graphs where appropriate. Note and explain any differences in the answers of Monetarists and Keynesians.
   (a) How will M1 be affected initially?
   (b) How will the lending capacity of the banking system be affected if the reserve requirement is 25 percent?
   (c) How will banks induce investors to utilize this expanded lending capacity?
   (d) How will aggregate spending be affected if investors borrow and spend all the newly available credit?
   (e) Under what circumstances would the Fed be pursuing such an open-market policy?
   (f) How could those same objectives be achieved through changes in the discount rate or reserve requirement?

2. Following is a demand and supply schedule for money. Assume that for every 1 percentage point decline in the interest rate, the aggregate spending schedule shifts upward by $5 billion and that the marginal propensity to consume is 0.8. Assume further that there is a recessionary gap of $20 billion.

Interest rate (percent)	Total demand for money (in billions)	Total supply of money (in billions)
0%	$400	$280
2	360	280
4	320	280
6	280	280
8	240	280
10	200	280

   (a) Graph the demand and supply curves for money, based on the schedule.

(*b*) What is the equilibrium rate of interest? What is the quantity of money?

(*c*) Suppose the Fed increases the money supply by $40 billion. What will be the new interest rate, the increase in investment, and the ultimate increase in income after all multiplier effects have been worked through?

(*d*) How much would the Fed have to increase the money supply to eliminate the recessionary gap?

POLICY OPTIONS:
Supply-Side Approaches

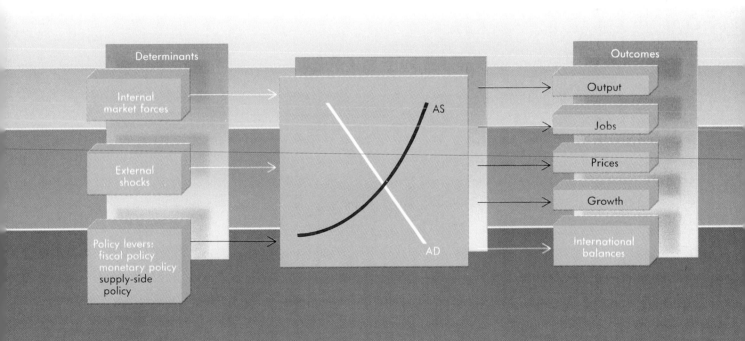

Fiscal and monetary levers attempt to alter macro outcomes by managing aggregate demand.
Supply-side policies focus on possibilities for shifting the aggregate *supply* curve instead. They also tend to emphasize
the importance of long-run economic growth instead of focusing exclusively on short-run stability.

Supply-Side Policies

*A*lthough Keynesian and monetarist economists seem to disagree on most aspects of macroeconomic policy, they have one basic trait in common: they both focus on the *demand* side of the economy. As Keynesians see it, changes in taxes or government spending shift the aggregate demand curve, triggering more or less production. As Monetarists see it, changes in the money supply also shift aggregate demand, but they affect prices rather than real output. In either view, all of the action in the macro economy lies on the demand side; aggregate supply plays a passive role.

Supply-siders have a very different view of the world. They start on the supply side of markets, rather than on the demand side. They emphasize that an assortment of government policies *directly* affect the ability and willingness of business firms to produce goods and services. Government policies also affect the ability and willingness of individuals to participate in the production process. In other words, the **aggregate supply** curve can also be shifted. Demand-side policies are neither necessary nor sufficient to attain our macro goals.

aggregate supply: The total quantity of output that producers are willing and able to supply at alternative price levels in a given time period, *ceteris paribus*.

The so-called supply-side tax cuts of 1981–83 are the most familiar supply-side initiative. The supply-side perspective has a much longer history, however, and covers a much broader array of policy options. Many of these options are designed to reduce structural barriers to increased output and employment. These structural policies include deregulation, education and training, and reduction of discriminatory barriers. Also legitimately part of the supply-side perspective are controls that limit the ability of workers and firms to increase wages and prices. Some Supply-siders reject some or all of these policy options. Nevertheless, ***the common element in all supply-side policy options is the attempt to alter supply behavior independently of changes in demand.***

Our objective in this chapter is to evaluate the potential of these many supply-side policies. In particular,

- How can the aggregate supply curve be shifted?

- How do shifts of the aggregate supply curve affect macro outcomes?

SUPPLY-SIDE RESPONSES

equation of exchange: Money supply (M) times velocity of circulation (V) equals level of aggregate spending ($P \times Q$).

The origins of supply-side theory are reflected in the **equation of exchange.** As noted in Chapter 14, the equation

$$\bullet \quad \underset{\substack{\text{(money} \\ \text{supply)}}}{M} \quad \times \quad \underset{\substack{\text{(velocity} \\ \text{of money)}}}{V} \quad = \quad \underset{\text{(prices)}}{P} \quad \times \quad \underset{\substack{\text{(quantity} \\ \text{of output)}}}{Q}$$

relates aggregate spending to prices and output.

Demand-Side Options

In Chapter 14 we used the equation of exchange to illustrate how fiscal and monetary policies work. Both operate on the demand side of the equation—that is, the left side. Monetary policy attempts to change the money supply (M), while fiscal policy focuses on changes in the velocity of money (V). In either case, the objective of policy is to alter the rate of inflation (P) or the rate of output (Q). In other words, *the tools of demand-side macroeconomic policy are on the left side of the equation of exchange; the targets of macroeconomic policy are on the right side.*

Although fiscal and monetary policies can alter the level of aggregate spending, they have no direct influence on P (prices) or Q (the rate of output). Price and output outcomes depend on producer responses to changes in aggregate spending.

Suppose, for example, that we want to stimulate aggregate demand to reduce unemployment. By increasing M and/or V we can increase total spending. But we do not know whether prices (P), real output (Q), or both will go up. Our objective, of course, is to increase output (Q) and thus reduce unemployment. All we can guarantee, however, is that the value of the right-hand side of the equation of exchange will rise; we cannot guarantee which component will increase. It could happen that prices (P) would increase rather than output (Q). We would then be left with our original unemployment problem *plus* a new inflation problem.

The same kind of dilemma could confront efforts to stop inflation. Suppose we were experiencing significant inflation at full employment. The appropriate macro response would be to restrain aggregate spending by reducing the rate of growth in M or V. Such efforts, however, ensure only that the value of the right-hand side of the equation will fall; they don't tell us whether prices, real output, or both will decline. We hope that average prices (P) will rise more slowly, bringing a halt to inflation. But it is at least *possible* that the rate of output (Q) may fall instead, leaving us with our original inflation *plus* a new unemployment problem.

The various responses of the economy to demand-side policies are illustrated in Figure 15.1. Figure 15.1*a* depicts the Keynesian view. By cutting taxes or increasing public spending, the government can increase the rate of aggregate demand at any given price level. But what happens to prices (P) and real output (Q) as demand expands? According to Keynes, producers will respond automatically to increased demand by increasing output. Prices will not be raised until capacity (Q^*) is reached. Accordingly, the aggregate supply curve is horizontal until capacity; then it rises abruptly. Below capacity production, increased demand raises output (Q) only, not prices (P).

The monetarist view of supply behavior is very different. In the most extreme monetarist view, real output remains at its "natural" rate, regardless of fiscal or monetary interventions. Hence only prices can respond to changes

**FIGURE 15.1
Contrasting Views
of Aggregate Supply**

(*a*) In the simple
Keynesian model, the
rate of output responds
fully and automatically
to increases in demand
until full employment (Q^*)
is reached. If demand
increases from D_1 to D_2,
equilibrium GNP will
expand from Q_1 to Q^*,
without any inflation.
Inflation becomes a
problem only if demand
increases beyond capacity—
to D_3, for example.

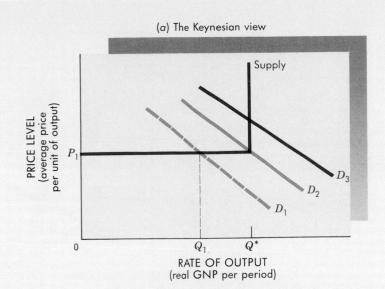

(*b*) Monetarists assert that
changes in the money
supply affect prices but
not output. They regard
aggregate supply as a
fixed quantum, at the long-
run, "natural" rate of
unemployment (here noted
as Q_N). Accordingly, a shift
of demand (from D_4 to D_5)
can affect only the price
level (from P_4 to P_5).

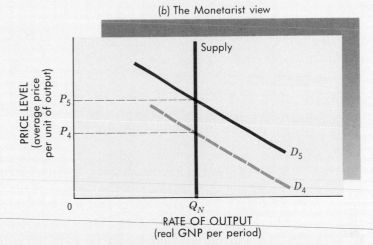

(*c*) Supply-side economists
emphasize that the rate
of output responds to
economic incentives,
including prices. At higher
prices, the incentive to
produce is greater, *ceteris
paribus*. Also, the cost
of production tends to
increase as the economy
approaches capacity. For
both these reasons, the
aggregate supply curve
slopes upward to the right.
When demand increases,
both prices and output
increase.

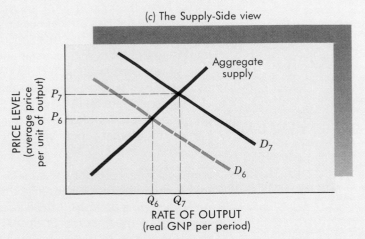

The Great Divide

Copyright © *Houston Chronicle*.

Courtesy of C. P. Houston in the *Houston Chronicle*.

in aggregate demand. From a monetarist perspective, the aggregate supply curve is vertical at the natural rate of unemployment (here assumed to be Q_N). This view is illustrated in Figure 15.1*b*.

Supply-siders take a more moderate position. They contend that both prices and output may be affected by changes in aggregate demand. They envision the aggregate supply curve as being upward-sloping, as in Figure 15.1*c*. From their perspective, supply behavior is variable. How successful demand-side policies are depends on the exact slope (response) of aggregate supply. In this view, the position of the aggregate supply curve is just as important as that of the aggregate demand curve.

As we noted in Chapter 5, modern Keynesians and Monetarists concede that at least the *short-run* aggregate supply curve is likely to be upward-sloping (see Figure 5.11). What sets Supply-siders apart, however, is the focus on policy levers for altering the shape and position of the aggregate supply curve. This is what supply-side policy is all about.

The Phillips Curve Tradeoff

Supply-side theorists use Figure 15.1*c* to illustrate some of the undesirable effects demand-side policies might have. Notice that ***all rightward shifts of the aggregate demand curve increase both prices and output if the aggregate supply curve is upward-sloping.*** This implies that fiscal and monetary efforts to reduce unemployment will always cause some inflation.

Similarly, demand-side attempts to control inflation will always increase unemployment. In Figure 15.1*c* ***all leftward shifts of the aggregate demand curve cause both prices and output to fall.*** In theory, then, demand-side policies alone can never succeed; they will always cause some unwanted inflation or unemployment.

Supply-side theorists point to our macro track record to support their view. Consider, for example, our experience with unemployment and inflation during the 1960s, as shown in Figure 15.2. This figure shows a ***Phillips curve*** indicating that prices (*P*) generally started rising before the objective of expanded output (*Q*) had been completely attained. In other words, inflation struck before full employment was reached.

The Phillips curve was developed by an English economist, A. W. Phillips, to summarize the relationship between unemployment and inflation in England for the years 1826–1957.[1] The Phillips curve was raised from the status of an obscure graph to that of a policy issue by the discovery that the same kind of relationship apparently existed in other countries and at other times. Professors Paul Samuelson and Robert Solow of the Massachusetts Institute of Technology (M.I.T.) were among the first to observe that the Phillips curve was a reasonable description of U.S. economic performance for the years 1900–60. For the post–World War II years in particular, Samuelson and Solow noted that an unemployment rate of 4 percent was likely to be accompanied by an inflation rate of approximately 2 percent. This relationship is expressed by point *A* in Figure 15.2. By contrast, lower rates of unemployment were associated with higher rates of inflation, as at point *B*. Alternatively, complete price stability appeared attainable only at the cost of an unemployment rate of 5.5 percent (point *C*). Such observations led many economists to conclude that a seesaw kind of relationship existed between inflation and unemployment: when one went up, the other fell. Full employment with price stability looked unattainable.

Phillips curve: A historical (inverse) relationship between the rate of unemployment and the rate of inflation; commonly expresses a tradeoff between the two.

[1]A. W. Phillips, "The Relationship Between Unemployment and the Rate of Change of Money Wage Rates in the United Kingdom, 1826–1957." *Economica,* November 1958. Phillips's paper studied the relationship between unemployment and *wage* changes, rather than *price* changes; most later formulations (and public policy) focus on prices.

**FIGURE 15.2
The Phillips Curve
for the 1960s**

In the 1960s it appeared that efforts to reduce unemployment rates below 5.5 percent (point *C*) led to increasing rates of inflation (points *A* and *B*). Inflation threatened to reach unacceptable heights long before everyone was employed.

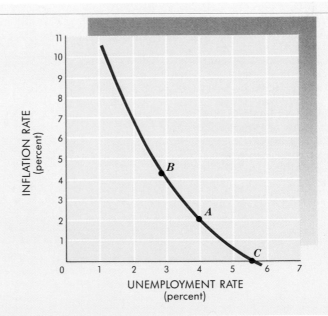

Stagflation: Phillips Curve Shifts

stagflation: The simultaneous occurrence of substantial unemployment and inflation.

If the Phillips curve shown in Figure 15.2 was a bad dream, later experiences were a real nightmare. Notice in Figure 15.3 that our unemployment and inflation experiences in the 1970s and early 1980s all lie above and to the right of the earlier Phillips curve (PC_1). These experiences suggest that the Phillips curve *shifted* to the right—first to PC_2, then to PC_3, and further to PC_4. These shifts left us with a new and more ominous problem, **stagflation,** the simultaneous occurrence of both inflation and unemployment. Movement along a Phillips curve implies a tradeoff between unemployment and inflation—that is, one good outcome, one bad one. Rightward *shifts* of the Phillips curve, however, imply that *both* outcomes get worse. Such shifts are bound to make us more miserable (see In the News).

According to Figure 15.3, these shifts of the Phillips curve were substantial. In the 1960s it seemed possible to achieve 4 percent unemployment with relatively little (2 percent) inflation (point A). By 1970 it appeared that the inflation rate would increase to 7 percent (point A^*) before unemployment could fall to 4 percent. By 1980, a 4 percent unemployment rate looked unattainable, no matter how high prices rose.

Our experience with stagflation in the 1970s and early 1980s hardly invites optimism about the prospects of achieving full employment and price stability at the same time. On the contrary, the worst Phillips curve (PC_4) appears to offer us only three alternatives, none of which is desirable. According to curve PC_4, we must either (1) accept very high unemployment rates in return for relative price stability, (2) accept very high inflation rates in return for full employment, or (3) learn to live with "moderate" amounts of both unemployment and inflation.

FIGURE 15.3
Shifts of the Phillips Curve

In the 1960s it appeared that 4 percent unemployment was compatible with 2 percent inflation (point A). In the early 1970s a much higher rate of inflation (point A^*) appeared to be consistent with 4 percent unemployment. In the late 1970s and early 1980s a 4 percent unemployment rate looked completely unattainable at tolerable rates of inflation. The worsening tradeoff is expressed by the rightward shifts of the Phillips curve, from PC_1 to PC_4.

Source: *Economic Report of the President,* 1990.

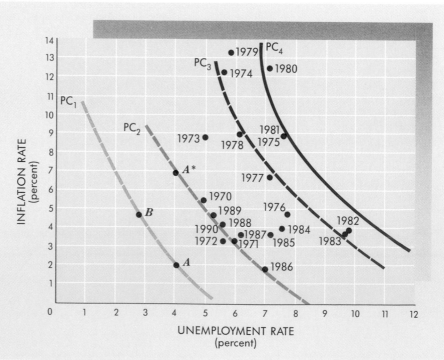

In The News

STAGFLATION

The Discomfort Index: A Measure of Stagflation

Stagflation is a situation in which both unemployment and inflation are "too high." But how should the extent of stagflation be measured? And how can we determine whether our stagflation problem is getting better or worse?

The measurement problem results from the fact that we are interested in *two* separate ills: inflation and unemployment. If one goes up while the other goes down, is our economic welfare unchanged? If government pol-

icies succeed in bringing down the rate of inflation but not the rate of unemployment, are we better off?

To answer these questions, Arthur Okun proposed a *single* measure of stagflation. He called it the "discomfort index." The discomfort index is simply the *sum* of our inflation and unemployment rates. If the rate of inflation is 9 percent and unemployment is at 7 percent, the discomfort index is 16. Lower values indicate an improvement in our economic welfare; higher values, a worse situation. The accompanying graph shows that we suffered increasing levels of discomfort in the 1970s, then enjoyed a marked improvement in the 1980s.

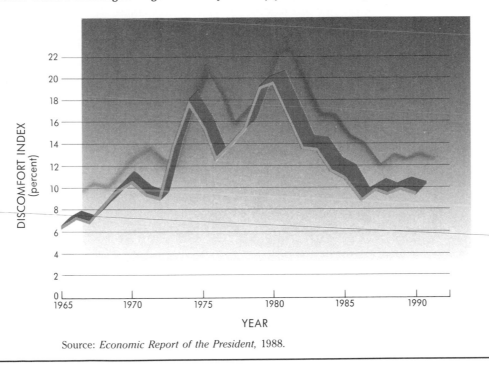

Source: *Economic Report of the President,* 1988.

A leftward shift? In the later 1980s the tradeoff looked a bit better. Notice in Figure 15.3 how the unemployment–inflation experiences for 1985–89 cluster around the curve PC₂. In those years it looked as though inflation could be controlled with a far smaller sacrifice of jobs.

The experience with unemployment and inflation during the period 1960–90 raises some basic questions. Do Phillips curves really shift so often? If so, what causes the unemployment–inflation tradeoff, or changes in its terms? Critics are quick to suggest that the apparent instability (constant shifting) of the Phillips curve makes it an unreliable policy tool.

Supply-siders reject such a suggestion. They emphasize that the Phillips curve tradeoff between inflation and unemployment is a natural extension of demand-side perspectives. Figure 15.4 illustrates this point. Suppose the economy is initially at equilibrium A, with fairly stable prices but high unemployment (low output). When aggregate demand expands to D_2, prices rise along with output. So we end up with higher inflation but less unemployment. This is also shown in Figure 15.4b by the move from point A to point B on the Phillips curve. As demand is increased again, to D_3, a still lower unemployment rate is achieved, but at the cost of higher inflation (point C).

Supply Shifts The upward slope of the aggregate supply curve explains why prices rise before full employment is reached. It also helps explain the more general tradeoff between unemployment and inflation, as reflected in the Phillips curve. But that is not the end of the story. Having demonstrated the existence of an aggregate supply curve, supply-side economists are quick to point out that its position is not permanent. On the contrary, aggregate supply—like aggregate demand—can be *shifted.* These shifts don't invalidate the concept of the Phillips curve. On the contrary, they demonstrate the potential for improving our macroeconomic performance.

The potential of supply shifts to improve macro outcomes is illustrated in Figure 15.5. Suppose we are initially at the equilibrium E_1, with too much unemployment and too much inflation. What can we do? Demand-side economists would have us meddle with the aggregate demand curve. But a right-

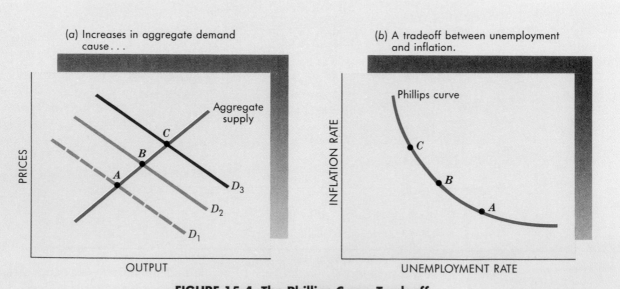

FIGURE 15.4 The Phillips Curve Tradeoff

If the aggregate supply curve slopes upward, increases in aggregate demand always cause both prices and output to rise. Thus higher inflation becomes a cost of achieving lower unemployment. In (*a*), increased demand moves the economy from point *A* to point *B*. At *B*, unemployment is lower, but prices are higher. This tradeoff is illustrated on the Phillips curve in (*b*).

**FIGURE 15.5
Shifts of Aggregate
Supply**

The objective of supply-side
policies is to shift the
aggregate supply curve to
the right. Such shifts imply
less inflation and lower
unemployment for any given
state of aggregate demand.
Thus supply-side economists
see the possibility of
overcoming stagflation.

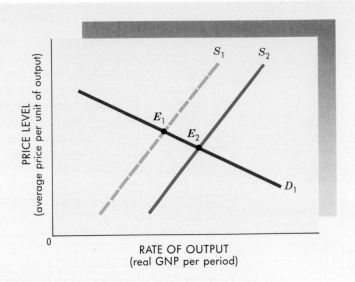

ward shift of the aggregate demand curve would aggravate inflation and a
leftward shift would increase unemployment. On the other hand, *a rightward
shift of the aggregate supply curve both reduces inflationary pressures
and increases employment (output).* Note in Figure 15.5 that the new equilibrium E_2 offers more output and lower prices than E_1. Rightward shifts of
the aggregate supply curve thus have the potential to overcome stagflation.

Policy Levers   The next question, of course, is how to shift the aggregate supply curve. The
supply-side economists look for clues on the right-hand side of the equation
of exchange. That is to say, they focus directly on the targets of macro policy—price and output behavior. They look for forces that influence the supply-
side response to changes in demand. Why doesn't output (Q) respond quickly
and fully to a change in demand? Why does inflation (P) rather than output
often increase when demand is increased? What role do government policies
play in these response patterns? What kinds of new policies would improve
the supply-side response?

To answer these questions, supply-side economists have developed a
small laundry list of alternative policy options. They include

- Supply-side tax cuts
- Deregulation
- Elimination of structural bottlenecks
- Wage and price controls

All of these policies have the potential to change supply decisions *independently* of any changes in aggregate demand. If they are effective, they will
result in a rightward shift of the aggregate supply curve. They hold out the
promise of an *improved* tradeoff between unemployment and inflation. If Supply-siders are right, then the Phillips curve depicted in Figure 15.4 can be
shifted to the left, giving us both lower inflation and lower unemployment.

SUPPLY-SIDE TAX CUTS

The most renowned supply-side policy option for improving the unemployment–inflation tradeoff was the supply-side tax cuts of the early 1980s. Tax cuts, of course, are a staple of Keynesian economics. But Supply-siders view tax cuts in a wholly different way. *In Keynesian economics, tax cuts are used to increase aggregate demand.* By putting more disposable income in the hands of consumers, Keynesian economists seek to increase expenditure on goods and services. The rate of output is expected to increase in response. From a Keynesian perspective, the form of the tax cut is not very important, so long as disposable income increases.

Supply-side economists have a different view of taxes. Taxes not only determine disposable income but also affect the incentives to work and produce. High tax rates destroy the incentives to work and produce, so they end up reducing total output. Low tax rates, by contrast, allow people to keep more of what they earn and so stimulate greater output. *The direct effects of taxes on the supply of goods are the concern of supply-side economists.* The difference between demand-side and supply-side perspectives on tax policy is illustrated in Figure 15.6.

Marginal Tax Rates

marginal tax rate: The tax rate imposed on the last (marginal) dollar of income.

Supply-siders are particularly interested in marginal tax rates. The **marginal tax rate** is the tax rate imposed on the last (marginal) dollar of income received. In our progressive income-tax system, marginal tax rates increase as more income is received. Hence Uncle Sam takes a larger share out of each additional dollar earned.

Labor supply   The marginal tax rate influences the financial incentive to *increase* one's work or production. *If the marginal tax rate is high, there is little incentive to work more or expand production:* Uncle Sam will get most of the added income. Low marginal tax rates, on the other hand, permit people to keep most of the income that results from additional output. Hence people are likely to work more when marginal tax rates are low.

investment: Expenditures on (production of) new plant and equipment (capital) in a given time period, plus changes in business inventories.

Investment   High marginal tax rates discourage not only work effort but **investment** as well. Business investment is motivated by the desire for profits. Firms buy new plant and equipment only if they think the resulting output will be profitable. But the profitability of an investment depends in part on taxes. If Uncle Sam imposes a high tax rate on business profits, the payoff to investors will be diminished. Consequently, *high business taxes also discourage investment.* With less new investment the economy's productive capacity will be smaller—and more costly.

Tax-Induced Supply Shifts

tax rebate: A lump-sum refund of taxes paid.

If tax rates affect supply decisions, then changes in tax rates will shift aggregate supply. Specifically, Supply-siders conclude that *a reduction in marginal tax rates will shift the aggregate supply curve to the right,* as in Figure 15.5. The increased supply will come from two sources: more work effort and more investment. This increased willingness to produce will reduce the rate of unemployment. The additional output will also help reduce inflationary pressures. Thus we end up with less unemployment *and* less inflation.

From a supply-side perspective, the form of the tax cut is critical. For example, **tax rebates** are not advocated by Supply-siders. Rebates are a one-time windfall to consumers and have no effect on marginal tax rates. As a

FIGURE 15.6
Two Theories
for Getting the
Economy Moving
Keynesians and Supply-siders both advocate cutting taxes to reduce unemployment. But they have very different views on the kind of tax cuts required and the impact of any cuts enacted.

Source: Adapted from *U.S. News & World Report*, February 23, 1981. Copyright © 1981 U.S. News & World Report.

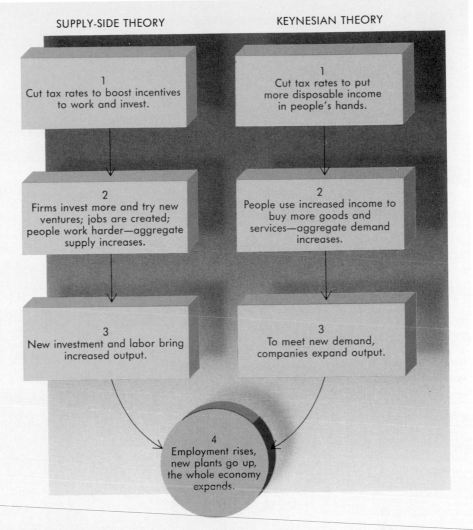

SUPPLY-SIDE THEORY

KEYNESIAN THEORY

1
Cut tax rates to boost incentives to work and invest.

1
Cut tax rates to put more disposable income in people's hands.

2
Firms invest more and try new ventures; jobs are created; people work harder—aggregate supply increases.

2
People use increased income to buy more goods and services—aggregate demand increases.

3
New investment and labor bring increased output.

3
To meet new demand, companies expand output.

4
Employment rises, new plants go up, the whole economy expands.

consequence, disposable income rises, but not the incentives for work or production. Rebates directly affect only the demand side of the economy.

To stimulate aggregate *supply,* tax *rates* must be reduced, particularly at the margin. These cuts can take the form of reductions in personal income tax rates or reductions in the marginal tax rates imposed on businesses. In either case, the lower tax rates will give people a greater incentive to work, invest, and produce.

The distinction between Keynesian and supply-side tax cuts is illustrated in Table 15.1. Under both tax systems (*A* and *B*) a person earning $200 pays $80 in taxes before the tax cut and $60 after the tax cut. But under system *A,* the marginal tax rate is always 50 percent. This means that Uncle Sam is getting half of every dollar earned above $100. By contrast, system *B* imposes a marginal tax rate of only 30 percent—30 cents of every dollar above $100 goes to the government. Under system *B,* people have a greater incentive to earn more than $100.

TABLE 15.1   Average vs. Marginal Tax Rates

The same amount of taxes can be raised with two very different systems. In the initial example, a person earning $200 pays $80 in taxes under either system, A or B, so the *average* tax rate (total tax ÷ total income) is the same in both cases ($80 ÷ $200 = 40%). But the *marginal* tax rates are very different. System A has a high marginal tax rate (50%), whereas system B has a low marginal tax rate (30%). Thus system B provides a greater incentive for people to earn over $100.

The lower panel shows that the average tax rate could be cut to 30 percent under either system. Under both systems, the revised tax would be $60 and disposable income would be increased to $140. Keynesians would be happy with either form of tax cut. But Supply-siders would favor system B, because the lower marginal tax rate gives people more incentive to earn higher incomes.

Initial Alternatives

Tax system	Initial tax schedule	Tax on income of $200	Tax rate Average	Tax rate Marginal	Disposable income
A	$30 + 50% of income over $100	$80	40%	50%	$120
B	$50 + 30% of income over $100	$80	40%	30%	$120

Alternative Forms of Tax Cut

Tax system	Revised tax schedule	Tax on income of $200	Tax rate Average	Tax rate Marginal	Disposable income
A	$10 + 50% of income over $100	$60	30%	50%	$140
B	$30 + 30% of income over $100	$60	30%	30%	$140

The Laffer Curve

Virtually all economists agree that tax rates influence people's decisions to work, invest, and produce. But the policy-relevant question is, how much influence do taxes have? Do reductions in the marginal tax rate shift the aggregate supply curve far to the right? Or are the resultant shifts quite small?

Arthur Laffer argued that cuts in marginal tax rates were likely to induce substantial shifts of the aggregate supply curve. Indeed, the resultant increases would be so large that tax revenues would actually *increase* when marginal tax rates were *cut!*

Laffer's extreme supply-side argument is illustrated in Figure 15.7. The **Laffer curve** is the relationship between tax *rates* and total tax *revenues*. If tax rates were zero, no tax revenues would be collected. Similarly, if the tax rate was 100 percent, no one would want to work or report his or her income. Hence there are two very different tax *rates* (0 and 100 percent) that generate the same *level* of total tax revenues (zero). These two possibilities are illustrated by points *A* and *B* in Figure 15.7.

Laffer curve: A graph depicting the relationship of tax rates to total tax revenues.

FIGURE 15.7
The Laffer Curve

The Laffer curve illustrates the relationship between tax rates and total tax revenues. High tax rates (e.g., point *B*) discourage output and yield minimal tax revenue. As tax rates are reduced (point *D*), work effort increases so much that tax revenues actually increase. This response continues until point *F*, where total revenue is maximized. Below that point, further tax cuts lower tax revenues. Because *two* different tax rates will generate any desired level of tax revenue, rates above *F* are regarded as "prohibitive."

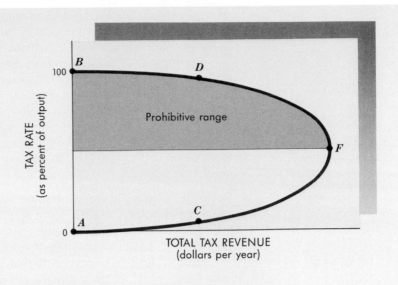

Points *A* and *B* also imply very different rates of output. At point *B*, output of goods and services is at a minimum, since all (reported) output is confiscated by the tax authorities. Output at point *A* is much greater, since no taxes are collected.

The focus of the Laffer curve is on the response of output and tax revenues to changes in tax rates. Suppose, for example, that the tax rate was lowered from 100 percent (point *B*) to something less (point *D*). How would workers and investors respond? With a 100 percent tax rate, there was no incentive to work or invest because all output was confiscated. At lower rates, people are permitted to keep some part of what they produce. Hence there is a greater incentive to work and invest at point *D* than at point *B*. We therefore expect more output to be produced at *D*. In this case, a *reduction* in tax rates leads to an *increase* in output. Tax revenues rise, too, since the increase in output is larger than the decline in tax rates.

Tax elasticity of supply   The expected response of labor and capital to a change in tax rates is summarized by the **tax elasticity of supply.** Like other elasticities, this one measures the proportional response of supplies to a change in price (in this case, a tax rate). Specifically, the tax elasticity of supply is the percentage change in quantity supplied divided by the percentage change in tax rates—that is,

tax elasticity of supply: The percentage change in quantity supplied divided by the percentage change in tax rates.

$$\bullet \quad \begin{array}{c} \text{Tax elasticity} \\ \text{of supply} \end{array} = \dfrac{\begin{array}{c}\text{percentage change} \\ \text{in quantity supplied}\end{array}}{\begin{array}{c}\text{percentage change} \\ \text{in tax rate}\end{array}}$$

Normally we expect quantity supplied to go up when tax rates go down. Elasticity (*E*) is therefore negative, although it is usually expressed in absolute terms (without the minus sign). The (absolute) value of *E* is typically greater than zero, since we expect *some* response to a tax cut. (A zero value for E would imply no increase in quantity supplied.) The policy issue boils down to the question of how large E actually is.

The top half of the Laffer curve assumes very high tax elasticities. As we lower tax rates from point B (100 percent) to point D, tax revenues actually increase in Figure 15.7. *A reduction in tax rates will yield larger tax revenues only if the tax elasticity of supply is greater than 1.* If E is greater than 1 ("relatively elastic"), the loss in tax revenues implied by a lower tax rate will be more than made up by increases in taxable output. This expectation is illustrated by the move from point B to point D and again from point D to point F.

Revenue maximization   The lower and upper portions of the Laffer curve converge at point F. Point F has a special significance. At this tax rate, total tax revenues are *maximized* (there are no points to the right of F). A government that sought to maximize its own revenues would choose this tax rate.

Another feature of point F is that it clearly separates "good" tax rates from "bad" ones. All rates above F are undesirable because some lower rate would generate just as much tax revenue and more output. (If the high tax rate at D generates no more revenue than the low rate at C, then less output must be produced [and taxed] at D.) Because of this, Laffer labeled all tax rates above F as "prohibitive." No government would want to depress total output unnecessarily.

Laffer and others used Figure 15.7 to help convince President Ronald Reagan to cut taxes in 1981. Tax cuts, they argued, would not only increase output and reduce inflation but would also reduce the budget deficit. By implication, the Supply-siders were assuming that 1981 tax rates were in the prohibitive range of the Laffer curve, above F in Figure 15.7. Only in this range does output (supply) increase faster than tax rates fall. Below F output continues to increase but at a slower pace than tax rates fall.

Demand-side economists and even other Supply-siders scoffed at the notion that 1981 tax rates were in the "prohibitive range" of the Laffer curve. If tax rates were in that range, the tax elasticity of supply (E) would have to be greater than 1. There simply wasn't any empirical support for such a claim. On the contrary, Professor Don Fullerton of Princeton University argued that 0.15 is a more reasonable estimate of labor-supply elasticity in the United

W🌐RLD VIEW

MARGINAL TAX RATES

Supply-Side Tax Cuts

On Tuesday, two widely different countries, Sweden and Tunisia, announced massive cuts in their top marginal tax rates. Swedish officials say they will cut the top rate from 72% to 50% by 1991 and then index tax brackets to inflation. Unfortunately, increases in gasoline and other taxes will wipe out some of the savings. Tunisia, which

is liberalizing its government and economy at a dizzying pace, is going even further and lowering its top rate from 65% to 35% as of January. This leaves only certain isolated regions on Capitol Hill inalterably opposed to cutting taxes.

The Wall Street Journal, November 9, 1989, p. A16. Reprinted by permission of *The Wall Street Journal,* © Dow Jones & Company, Inc. (1989). All Rights Reserved.

States.[2] In other words, the supply-side increase in output is only a fraction of the percentage cut in taxes. The aggregate supply curve shifts to the right—but not very far—when tax rates are cut.

Depite all the evidence to the contrary, President Reagan used the Laffer argument to help "sell" his 1981 tax-cut proposals. Congress responded by reducing personal income taxes by 30 percent over a period of three years (1981–83). According to estimates by Lawrence Lindsey, these tax cuts boosted real GNP about 0.5 percent a year during the period 1981–85. This implies that 2.5 million more people had jobs in 1989 as a result of the tax-induced shift of the aggregate supply curve. Although this was an impressive increase in aggregate supply, it fell far short of Laffer's claims. Instead of shrinking, the budget deficit widened sharply after Reagan's tax cuts were implemented.

Encouraging Saving

Supply-side economists respond that their tax-cut proposals have important long-run effects that are not immediately apparent. On the demand side, an increase in income translates very quickly into increased spending. On the supply side, things don't happen so fast. It takes time to construct new plants and equipment. People are also slow to respond to new work and investment incentives. Hence the full benefits of supply-side tax cuts will not be immediately visible.

Of particular concern to supply-side economists is the rate of saving in the economy. Demand-side economists emphasize spending and tend to treat **saving** as a leakage problem. Supply-siders, by contrast, emphasize the importance of saving for financing investment and economic growth. New investment competes directly with consumption for scarce factors of production. At full employment, a greater volume of investment is possible only if the rate of consumption is cut back. In other words, additional investment requires additional saving. Hence *supply-side economists favor tax incentives that encourage saving as well as greater tax incentives for investment.* This kind of perspective contrasts sharply with the Keynesian emphasis on stimulating consumption.

saving: That part of disposable income not spent on current consumption; disposable income less consumption.

In the early 1980s Congress greatly increased the incentives for saving. First, banks were permitted to increase the rate of interest paid on various types of savings accounts. Second, the tax on earned interest was reduced. And finally, new forms of tax-free saving were created (e.g., Individual Retirement Accounts [IRAs]).

Despite these incentives, the U.S. savings rate declined during the 1980s. Household saving dropped from 6.2 percent of disposable income in 1981 to a low of 2.5 percent in 1987. Neither the tax incentive nor the high interest rates that prevailed in the early 1980s convinced Americans to save more. As a result, the U.S. saving rate fell considerably below that of other nations (see World View).

Most of the special tax incentives for saving were eliminated by the Tax Reform Act of 1986. In 1990, however, President Bush attempted to restore some of those incentives (see In the News). He proposed that interest and other income earned in "Family Savings Accounts" be tax free if the savings were held for at least seven years. Critics observed, however, that such incentives had failed to boost saving rates before and weren't likely to stimulate either saving or investment in the 1990s.

[2]Don Fullerton, "Can Tax Revenues Go Up When Tax Rates Go Down?" Office of Tax Analysis, U.S. Department of the Treasury, September 1980.

W🌐RLD VIEW

SAVING RATES

Americans Save Little

American households save very little. On average, Americans spend roughly 96 cents out of every dollar of disposable income, leaving only 4 cents for saving. This saving rate is far below that in most other countries. As shown here, the United States ranked near the bottom of the savers' list in 1988.

Supply-siders are especially concerned about low saving rates. They argue that Americans must save more, to finance increased investment and economic growth. Otherwise, they fear, the United States will fall behind other countries in the progression toward higher productivity levels and living standards.

Country	Saving rate (1988)
Italy	21.3%
Japan	16.8
Germany (West)	13.2
France	12.0
Canada	8.9
United States	**4.0**
Great Britain	3.7

Note: Saving rate equals household saving divided by disposable income.
Source: Central Intelligence Agency.

DEREGULATION

Tax policy is not the only available tool for shifting the aggregate supply curve. The government also intervenes directly in supply decisions by *regulating* employment and output behavior. In general, such regulations limit the flexibility of producers to respond to changes in demand. Government regulation

In The News

TAX INCENTIVES

Administration Is Considering New "Family Savings Account"

Interest, Dividends Would Be Tax-Free

The Bush administration, seeking ways to boost the U.S. savings rate, is strongly considering a proposal that would allow people to earn interest and dividends tax-free on money that is saved for a number of years, according to administration officials.

Under one option being considered, a taxpayer could deposit up to $5,000 a year in what is being called a "Family Savings Account" and avoid paying taxes on the interest and dividends as long as the money was left untouched for at least 7 years. Unlike individual retirement accounts (IRAs), the taxpayer would not be allowed to deduct the annual contribution. . . .

But the proposal is a major departure from earlier savings proposals because it suggests that taxpayers may be allowed a tax advantage on savings without requiring them to hold the money until retirement. Both IRAs and employer-sponsored savings plans set stiff penalties on money that is withdrawn prior to retirement.

—Paul Blustein

The Washington Post, December 16, 1989 p. C1. Copyright © 1989 The Washington Post.

also tends to raise production costs. The higher costs result not only from required changes in the production process but also from the expense of monitoring government regulations and filling out endless government forms. These added costs of production shift the aggregate supply curve to the left. The net result is to increase the rate of inflation and reduce the rate of output.

Regulation of Factor Markets

Minimum wages Minimum-wage laws are one of the most familiar forms of factor-market regulation. The Fair Labor Standards Act of 1938 required employers to pay workers a minimum of 25 cents per hour. Over time, Congress has increased the coverage of that act and the minimum wage itself repeatedly. In 1990 the minimum wage was increased to $3.80 per hour, and then to $4.25 in 1991.

The goal of the minimum-wage law is to ensure workers a decent standard of living. But the law has other effects as well. By prohibiting employers from using lower-paid workers, it limits the ability of employers to hire additional workers. As a consequence, the principle of **derived demand** cannot be exploited fully. Firms faced with increased demand for their products cannot hire labor below the minimum wage, so they must use more expensive labor and raise prices instead.

derived demand: The demand for labor and other factors of production results from (depends on) the demand for final goods and services produced by these factors.

The minimum-wage law focuses on decisions in factor markets. The wage and employment decisions that result, however, affect product markets as well. With labor less available and more expensive, firms are not so able or willing to produce. Hence the minimum-wage law shifts the aggregate supply curve to the left, as in Figure 15.8.

Occupational health and safety Government regulation of factor markets extends beyond minimum-wage laws. The government also sets standards for workplace safety and health. The Occupational Safety and Health Administration (OSHA), for example, sets limits on the noise levels at work sites. OSHA's Noise Exposure Standard limits the average sound level to 90 decibels for eight hours, 92 decibels for six hours, 95 decibels for three hours, and so forth, up to a maximum of 115 decibels for fifteen minutes or less. If noise levels exceed these limits, the employer is required to adopt administrative or engineering controls to reduce the noise level. Personal protection of work-

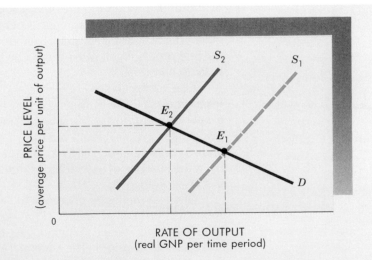

**FIGURE 15.8
Leftward Shifts
of Aggregate Supply**

Leftward shifts of the aggregate supply curve result from higher marginal tax rates, government regulation, structural bottlenecks, excessive wage and price demands, and other forces. All such shifts tend to worsen stagflation, by increasing both inflation and unemployment. Compare equilibrium points E_1 and E_2.

ers (e.g., earplugs or earmuffs), though much less costly, will suffice only if source controls are not feasible. All such regulations are intended to improve the welfare of workers. In the process, however, these regulations raise the costs of production and inhibit supply responses.

Regulation of Product Markets

The government's regulation of factor markets tends to raise production costs and inhibit supply. The same is true of regulations imposed directly on product markets. A few examples illustrate the impact.

Transportation costs At the federal level, various agencies regulate the output and prices of transportation services. Until 1984 the Civil Aeronautics Board (CAB) determined which routes airlines could fly and how much they could charge. The Interstate Commerce Commission (ICC) has had the same kind of power over trucking, interstate bus lines, and railroads. The routes, services, and prices for ships (in U.S. coastal waters and foreign commerce) have been established by the Federal Maritime Commission. In all these cases, the regulations constrained the ability of producers to respond to increases in demand. Existing producers could not increase output at will, and new producers were excluded from the market. Hence the rate of output was kept too low and prices too high.

Food and drug standards The Food and Drug Administration (FDA) has a broad mandate to protect consumers from dangerous products. In fulfilling this responsibility, the FDA sets health standards for the content of specific foods. A hot dog, for example, can be labeled as such only if it contains specific mixtures of skeletal meat, pig lips, snouts, and ears. By the same token, a milk-chocolate bar is a milk-chocolate bar, according to the FDA, only if it

> contains not less than 3.66 percent by weight of milk fat, not less than 12 percent by weight of milk solids, and not less than 10 percent by weight of chocolate liquor as calculated by subtracting from the weight of chocolate liquor used the weight of cacao fat therein and the weights therein of alkali and seasoning ingredients, if any, multiplying the remainder by 2.2, dividing the result by the weight of the finished milk chocolate, and multiplying the quotient by 100.

In addition, the FDA requires that chocolate bars must contain no more than 60 microscopic insect fragments (including rat feces) per 100 grams of chocolate. The FDA also sets standards for the testing of new drugs and evaluates the test results. In all three cases, the goal of regulation is to minimize health risks to consumers.

Like all regulation, however, the FDA standards entail real costs. The tests required for new drugs are very expensive and time-consuming. Getting a new drug approved for sale can take years of effort and require a huge investment. The net results are that (1) fewer new drugs are brought to market and (2) those that do reach the market are more expensive than they would be in the absence of regulation. In other words, the aggregate supply of goods is shifted to the left.

Other examples of government regulation are commonplace. The Environmental Protection Agency (EPA) regulates auto emissions, the discharges of industry, and water pollution. The U.S. Congress restricts foreign imports and raises their prices. The Federal Trade Commission (FTC) limits the freedom of firms to increase their output or advertise their products.

Deregulation

Many—perhaps most—of these regulatory activities are beneficial. In fact, all were originally designed to serve specific public purposes. As a result of such regulation, we do get safer drugs, cleaner air, and less deceptive advertising. We must also consider the costs involved, however. All regulatory activities impose direct and indirect costs. These costs must be compared to the benefits received. ***The basic contention of supply-side economists is that regulatory costs are now too high.*** To improve our economic performance, they assert, we must *deregulate* the production process, thereby shifting the aggregate supply curve to the right again.

During the last few years, serious efforts to deregulate sectors of the private economy have taken place. As noted in Chapter 13, the Monetary Control Act of 1980 permitted much greater flexibility in the prices and services offered by domestic banks. Before that, the Securities and Exchange Commission had granted stockbrokers the same kind of flexibility. The Airline Deregulation Act of 1978 put an end to regulation of airline routes and fares as of 1983. The trucking and oil and gas industries were also substantially deregulated in the 1980s.

ELIMINATING STRUCTURAL BOTTLENECKS

It is tempting to blame the government for all of our stagflation problems. And most Americans apparently do. A Gallup survey asked people who was to blame for our continuing inflation. Eighty-four percent of the respondents singled out the government, either by itself (33 percent) or in conjunction with business, labor, and consumers (51 percent).

This tendency to blame the government for all our stagflation problems not only is unfair but also focuses all our attention on tax rates and deregulation. There are other supply-side causes of stagflation and other policy levers as well.

Structural Unemployment

Another major cause of stagflation originates from a mismatch between available workers and the requirements of production. When aggregate spending ($M \times V$) increases, we want output (Q) to increase, not prices (P). For this

"*I blame government, labor, business, and my ex-wife.*"

Drawing by C. Barsotti. Copyright © 1978 The New Yorker Magazine, Inc.

to happen, the required factors of production must be available at the right time and place. If they are not, we will not be able to increase output (Q) as we desire but will instead end up watching prices (P) rise.

A decision to stimulate aggregate spending is usually prompted by excessive unemployment, so it seems reasonable to assume that labor will be available. But we can't be sure that the right kind of labor will be available at the right price (wage rate), or that the desired labor will be available where it is needed. Recall our earlier discussion of structural unemployment (Chapter 6). The basic message of **structural unemployment** is that the workers we demand may not be there when we need them. If they are not, output (Q) cannot expand; instead, prices will rise as demand increases.

Table 15.2 provides some evidence on structural unemployment. The aggregate rate of unemployment of 5.8 percent that prevailed in early 1990 was not representative of all workers. Unemployed managers, administrators, and technicians were very hard to find. Nonfarm laborers were readily available, however, and even operators (people who operate production machinery) and service workers were not hard to locate. Unemployment also varied greatly across industries and regions. Unemployment in the auto, construction, and lumber industries was high. At the same time, relatively few people were unemployed in the office-machines industry, financial services, or even government. Accordingly, some groups were in a position to secure wage increases, while other groups remained unemployed.

Experience is also an important determinant of employability. The more experience a worker has had, the higher his or her productivity is likely to be. Hence employers will prefer such workers. This preference is often expressed in terms of age, particularly in a reluctance to hire teenagers. The impact of this barrier is evident in unemployment statistics. In early 1990 the unemployment rate for teenagers was nearly 15 percent, about three times higher than for the rest of the **labor force.** Had employers been more willing and able to fill their job vacancies with younger workers, more employment might have been attained with less inflation than actually occurred.

structural unemployment: Unemployment caused by a mismatch between the skills (or location) of job seekers and the requirements (or location) of available jobs.

labor force: All persons over age sixteen who are either working for pay or actively seeking paid employment.

TABLE 15.2   Unemployment Rates by Occupation

Unemployment rates vary markedly across occupations. As a result, a shortage of more skilled workers (e.g., professional and technical workers) may emerge long before other occupational groups are fully employed.

Occupational category	Unemployment rate (percent)
Professional	1.6
Managers and administrators	2.2
Sales workers	5.1
Clerical workers	3.9
Craftsmen	5.7
Operatives	8.5
Nonfarm laborers	11.5
Service workers	7.5
Farmers and farm workers	8.4
All occupations	5.8

Source: U.S. Bureau of Labor Statistics, February 1990 (not seasonally adjusted).

During the 1970s a far greater proportion of women also began to enter the labor force, many with little job experience. They, too, contributed to structural unemployment. As a result, it became more difficult to reach full employment before prices started to rise. In other words, *the aggregate supply curve shifted to the left as the labor force became less skilled.* These trends began to reverse in the late 1980s as the relative size of the teenage labor force fell and women gained more job experience.

Employment and training   Two possibilities for overcoming structural unemployment problems are fairly obvious. First, the government could provide or encourage training for those unemployed people whose skills fail to match available job openings. Such training would reduce the mismatch of skills and job openings that characterizes structural unemployment and would thus speed the flow of unemployed workers into jobs.

Job-search assistance   Another supply-side policy option is to bring job seekers and jobs together more efficiently. Want ads in the newspapers list only a fraction of all potential job openings. As a consequence, people with the required skills may remain unemployed simply because they don't know about available jobs. They don't find jobs because they don't know where to look.

The most important public agency for bringing employers and job seekers together is the U.S. Employment Service, more commonly referred to as the "state unemployment office," because it also has the responsibility for disbursing unemployment-insurance checks. The Employment Service acts as a clearinghouse for prospective employers and job seekers, conveying information from one to the other. The government can also provide less direct job-search assistance. Tax credits for job relocation and other job-search expenses reduce the costs of finding and accepting new jobs and thus speed up the matching of job seekers with jobs.

Discrimination   Lack of skills and experience are not the only reason it's sometimes hard to find the "right" workers. The mismatch between unemployed workers and jobs is often less a matter of skills than of race, gender, or age. In other words, discrimination can create an artificial barrier between job seekers and available job openings. Employers (and unions) who are convinced that women and blacks or other minority groups are inherently less capable are unlikely to look at these groups when job vacancies occur. In overlooking such workers, producers create an artificial shortage of skilled labor and push production costs up. The consequences are by now predictable—a leftward shift of the aggregate supply curve.

Equal opportunity programs   If discrimination tends to shift the aggregate supply curve leftward, then reducing discriminatory barriers should shift it to the right. Equal opportunity programs are thus a natural extension of a supply-side approach to macro policy. However, Supply-siders are also quick to point out the risks inherent in government regulation of hiring decisions. From a supply-side perspective, laws that forbid discrimination are welcome and should be enforced. But aggressive "affirmative action" programs that require employers to hire specific numbers of women or minority workers limit productive capabilities and can lead to excessive costs.

Transfer Payments

transfer payment: Payments to individuals for which no current goods or services are exchanged, e.g., Social Security, welfare, unemployment benefits.

Supply-siders also point to welfare programs that discourage workers from taking available jobs. Unemployment and welfare benefits provide a source of income when a person is not working. Although these **transfer payments** are motivated by humanitarian goals, they also inhibit labor supply. Transfer recipients must give up some or all of their welfare payments when they take a job. This makes working seem less attractive and therefore reduces the number of available workers. The net result is a leftward shift of the aggregate supply curve. Supply-siders advocate reductions in such labor-supply disincentives.

Trade Restrictions

A final supply bottleneck is international in scope. Goods imported from abroad are a potential substitute for domestically produced goods. If domestic producers are unable or unwilling to increase output at prevailing prices, foreign producers can step in and keep the aggregate supply curve from rising. In reality, however, the government imposes various limitations on the price or quantity of imported goods. These trade restrictions effectively shift the aggregate supply curve to the left. Supply-siders urge freer trade, with fewer import restrictions.

WAGE AND PRICE CONTROLS

Suppose the supply side of the economy contained no structural bottlenecks, was unfettered by government regulations, and confronted low marginal tax rates. In such a supply-side utopia, producers could respond quickly and fully to increases in aggregate demand. But what assurance do we have that they would? *Producers might find it more profitable to raise prices rather than output when aggregate demand increased. Likewise, workers might respond to increased demand for labor by increasing wages rather than employment.* In either case, we could end up with more inflation rather than more output when demand increases.

Profit-Push Inflation

profit-push inflation: An increase in the price level initiated by attempts of producers to raise profit margins.

market power: The ability to alter the market price of a good or service.

The option of increasing prices rather than output when demand increases looks very tempting. If production costs don't rise, higher prices imply more profits for any given rate of production. Surely there are more than a few producers who would want to increase their profits in this way. By demanding higher prices and profits for a given rate of output, however, they would shift the aggregate supply curve to the left. This process is often referred to as **profit-push inflation.**

Market power   As tempting as profit-push inflation might look, not all producers can do it. The extent to which a producer can increase prices and profits unilaterally depends on the amount of market power he possesses. The essence of **market power** is the ability to change market prices without suffering a substantial decline in unit sales. Individual fishermen, for example, seldom have the power to change the market price of fish; they have no market power. General Motors, however, can directly alter the price at which Chevrolets are sold; GM has market power. In this case, market power exists because GM produces over one-third of the cars made in the United States. As a result, GM can exercise significant control over the market supply curve (and thereby the market price). By contrast, our lone fisherman accounts for a tiny fraction of all the fish brought to market and thus has no significant control over the market supply curve.

Producers who have significant market power are in a unique position to determine whether prices or output responds to an increase in aggregate demand. Should those producers decide to increase their prices and profit margins, they would contribute to inflation while slowing progress toward full employment. In other words, the exercise of market power can cause stagflation.

The potential of market power to aggravate a stagflation problem is equally apparent when the government is trying to close an inflationary gap. The objective of restrictive fiscal and monetary policies is to reduce the rate of inflation (changes in P) while maintaining output (Q). But it is producers who must ultimately decide to cut back on P or Q. Should producers decide to cut back output rather than prices, we could end up with both high unemployment and high inflation—that is, stagflation.

Inflationary Wage Demands

Profit-push is not, of course, the source of all price increases, even in a supply-side utopia. We must take care to avoid what Reuben Kessel of the University of Chicago calls "the simplicity of an old Western," in which the bad guys (the big corporations) are responsible for all price increases.[3] Prices may go up simply because costs have risen. If producers are to maintain (not increase) their profit margins, they must raise product prices when the costs of production increase. In these cases, however, it is a change in costs, not profit margins, that fuels **cost-push inflation.**

cost-push inflation: An increase in the price level initiated by an increase in the cost of production.

Costs may be forced up by any number of events. A drought in the Midwest, for example, can sharply reduce agricultural output and drive up prices, thereby contributing to stagflation. Likewise, a decision by foreign oil producers (who have market power) to cut off oil supplies can curtail domestic production and set off an inflationary spiral at the same time. These kinds of external shocks, which suddenly and unexpectedly reduce aggregate supply, played a major role in the stagflations of the 1970s.

labor productivity: Amount of output produced by a worker in a given period of time; output per hour (or day, etc.).

unit labor cost: Hourly wage rate divided by output per labor-hour.

Labor costs Costs may also go up because workers demand and receive wage increases. The labor cost of producing a product depends on two things: the wage rate paid and the worker's **productivity.**

Not all wage increases are inflationary. On the contrary, *only wage increases that exceed productivity improvements are truly inflationary.* When wages increase faster than output per hour, **unit labor costs** rise. As unit labor costs go up, producers respond by increasing prices, and a cost-push inflation is under way.

The relationship among wage rates, productivity, and unit labor cost is illustrated in Table 15.3. If workers become more productive—produce more output per hour—and wage rates are unchanged, unit labor costs will fall. The employer ends up getting more output for the same wage. Such a drop in unit labor costs would enhance profits, of course, and be welcomed by an employer. The important point here, though, is that wage increases equal to productivity gains simply maintain unit labor costs; they do not increase them. Such wage increases do not cut into profits or contribute to cost-push inflation. Indeed, were wages to keep pace with productivity improvements, both employers and workers would benefit (by the same percentage) from productivity advances (see Table 15.3).

[3]Reuben A. Kessel, "Inflation and Controls," *American Economic Review,* September 1972, p. 528.

TABLE 15.3 Productivity, Wages, and Profits

While profits increase most when wage rates do not rise, profits also increase when wages rise in line with productivity improvements. In fact, when wage increases equal to productivity improvements are allowed, both wages and profits rise by the same percentage (without price increases). In this sense, stable prices and productivity-based wage-rate increases fix the income shares of capital and labor.

Suppose we are producing 50 art posters and selling them for $2 each. Our revenues and costs initially consist of:

A. Gross revenues:

50 posters @ $2.00 each =		$100.00
Costs:		
Labor: 10 labor hours @ $6.00 an hour		
or $1.20 per poster =	$60	
Materials: $0.40 per poster × 50 =	$20	−80.00
Profits:		$ 20.00

Owing to increased experience, our artists become more productive and can now turn out 20 percent more posters; that is, *productivity* increases by 20 percent. If we did *not* increase wage rates, profits would become:

B. Gross revenues:

60 posters @ $2.00 each =		$120.00
Costs:		
Labor: 10 labor hours @ $6.00 an hour		
or $1.00 per poster =	$60	
Materials: $0.40 per poster × 60 =	$24	−84.00
Profits:		$ 36.00

On the other hand, if we *increase wage rates in line with productivity improvements*—that is, by 20 percent, from $6.00 to $7.20 an hour—profits would be:

C. Gross revenues:

60 posters @ $2.00 each =		$120.00
Costs:		
Labor: 10 labor hours @ $7.20 an hour		
or $1.20 per poster =	$72	
Materials: $0.40 per poster × 60 =	$24	−96.00
Profits:		$ 24.00

Labor unions One force that might drive wage rates up faster than productivity gains is labor unions. To the extent that a labor union controls the supply of a particular type of labor (bricklayers, say, or fire fighters), it has power in that labor market. With such market power, a union can push up market wage rates, just as corporations with market power can push up product prices. Indeed, a major objective of labor unions is to increase the wage rates of their members.

Limits on Wages and Prices

wage–price controls: Direct governmental restraints on the wage and price decisions of market participants.

To the extent that powerful producers and unions can shift the aggregate supply curve to the left, they aggravate our stagflation problems. For this reason, many economists have advocated explicit limits on wage and price increases. The essence of **wage–price controls** is some form of direct governmental restraint on the wage and price decisions of market participants.

The Kennedy guideposts The wage–price "guideposts" issued by President John F. Kennedy in 1961 illustrate one form of wage–price controls. In general, the guideposts decreed that wage rates should not rise faster than productivity improvements. If output per labor-hour increased by 3.2 percent—as it had been doing over the preceding five years—wage rates could also increase by

3.2 percent without fueling inflation. The reasoning was identical to that which we used earlier. If wages increased no faster than productivity, unit labor costs would not rise, and there would be no cost-push pressure on prices.

The Nixon freeze   The Nixon administration introduced more explicit controls on wage and price behavior. In 1971 President Richard Nixon proclaimed a general wage and price freeze—a prohibition of *any* wage or price increases. The freeze lasted 90 days and was succeeded by a comprehensive set of wage and price controls.

A unique feature of the Nixon wage–price program was its explicit recognition of market power. Rather than trying to police millions of individual firms, the administration classified all business and labor unions in three tiers, on the basis of size. The 1,500 largest firms were watched most closely and were required to get prior approval for any price increase. They were also required to submit quarterly price, cost, and profit reports.

The Carter wage–price standards   President Gerald Ford did not ask Congress to renew the power to impose wage–price controls, and President Jimmy Carter likewise disavowed their use. Instead, President Carter outlined a voluntary wage and price program designed to slow the rate of inflation. According to these guideposts, wage rates (including fringe benefits) were not to rise by more than 7 percent per year, and prices were not to increase by more than 5.75 percent.[4] In explaining these standards, the president noted the need for collective action. When wages and prices are rising rapidly, no single individual or group can risk the loss of real income implied by a more modest wage or price demand. "It is like a crowd standing at a football stadium," he noted. "No one is willing to be the first one to sit down" and miss the action.

Do Controls Work?   Assessment of the impact of wage and price controls is difficult. It requires us to compare actual wage and price behavior with the behavior that would have occurred in the absence of controls. We know, for example, that the price level rose hardly at all during Nixon's wage–price freeze. We also know that the price level increased by less than 3 percent during the subsequent period of controls. Since we don't know how fast prices would have risen during the period without controls, however, we can't be sure how effective the controls were in *reducing* the rate of inflation. We do know, though, that prices increased more rapidly (by over 5 percent) right after controls were eliminated. Hence it is possible that controls only *postponed* price increases rather than prevent them.

We should not conclude that wage–price controls have been ineffective in reducing inflation; all we are saying is that their effectiveness is difficult to measure. In fact, most economists who have tried to measure the effectiveness of wage and price controls have concluded that controls were at least somewhat successful in reducing the rate of inflation.

The costs of controls   Those who regard wage–price controls as a failure are less concerned with the impact of these controls on the rate of inflation than with their impact on market efficiency. Indeed, many economists argue that the apparent effectiveness of wage–price controls is proof of their failure!

---

[4]The actual price guidelines asked firms to "decelerate" the rate of inflation by limiting price increases to one-half of a percentage point below the firm's average annual rate of price increase during 1976–77. On average, this increase would have amounted to 5.75 percent.

W🌐RLD VIEW

WAGE–PRICE CONTROLS

Mexico Freezes Peso, Prices to Slow Rampant Inflation

MEXICO CITY, Feb. 29—The Mexican government, trying to curb the nation's high inflation rate, said today it will freeze the peso's exchange rate and the prices of all state-controlled goods and services during March, while allowing moderate wage increases.

The month-long economic program, outlined in government decrees published today and going into effect Tuesday, is being portrayed as the second and final phase of a new inflation-fighting plan begun in mid-December by the administration of President Miguel De la Madrid. . . .

The price freeze will affect items ranging from gasoline,

water and electricity to air fares and refined sugar. The prices of basic household products produced privately but subject to government controls also will be frozen through March. Merchants and manufacturers are being pressed to keep other prices down.

The government is also ordering an immediate 3 percent across-the-board payhike for all wage earners. Though far below the 10 percent raise demanded by government-affiliated unions, the settlement was reluctantly endorsed by the official labor movement. Veteran labor boss Fidel Velazquez warned today, however, that if business does not keep its promise to hold down prices "it will have to pay the consequences" with higher wages.

—William A. Orme, Jr.

The Washington Post, March 1, 1988, p. C2. Copyright © 1988 The Washington Post.

Because such controls suspend normal market functioning to some degree, they tend to distort resource allocation over time. Market prices, it will be recalled, operate as signals to direct product distribution and resource allocation. If demand shifts from product X to product Y, the resulting increase in Y's relative price constitutes a signal and incentive for resources to move in the same direction. Changes in wage rates (the price of labor) perform the same function, motivating workers to enter industries or companies that offer higher relative wages. The changing structure of (relative) prices is thus a basic motivating force in a market economy.

Wage–price controls constitute a threat to economic efficiency to the extent that they constrain movements in relative prices. A general price freeze freezes not only the *level* of prices but the *structure* of prices as well. If demand were to shift from product X to product Y during a price freeze, prices would not be allowed to emit the required signals to producers and workers. Although the mix of output might still respond to changes in demand, the response would be less certain and less timely. These kinds of inefficiencies grow in importance the longer wage–price controls are continued and the more broadly and severely they are applied. Such inefficiencies have the effect of shifting the aggregate supply curve in the wrong direction.

POLICY INSIGHTS:

AN ECLECTIC AGGREGATE SUPPLY CURVE

Experience with stagflation has taught us the futility of trying to achieve macro goals with demand-side policies alone. By focusing exclusively on only one side of the market, we have effectively tied one hand behind our backs. That handicap has not left us helpless, but it has turned out to be costly. The basic implication of supply-side economics is that we would fare much better if we pursued macroeconomic goals from *both* sides of the marketplace—demand *and* supply.

The Costs of Demand-Side Dependence

The costs of fighting macro failures with demand-side policies alone are illustrated by the Phillips curve. Basically, such policies encourage a tradeoff between unemployment and inflation. To reduce inflation, for example, restrictive monetary and fiscal policies discourage aggregate demand. But those same policies tend to increase unemployment.

The costs of this demand-side dependence can be high. In 1979 the Congressional Budget Office (CBO) evaluated the prospects for reducing the rate of inflation in the 1980s with restrictive monetary and fiscal policies. The CBO assumed a goal of 4 percent inflation, to be reached in 1984. To reach this goal, the CBO figured the unemployment rate would have to stay up around 7 percent for five years. This persistently high rate of unemployment would have reduced GNP in 1984 by roughly $250 billion. That works out to roughly $1,000 less GNP per person. The cost of fighting inflation would not have been distributed equally, of course. Much of the impact would have fallen on the additional 1.5 million workers who would have been without jobs in 1984 as a result of reduced output. Figure 15.3 suggests that these CBO estimates were not far off the mark: the unemployment rate soared in the early 1980s, while the inflation rate fell to 4 percent.

Supply-Side Options

It should be apparent from our review of supply-side options that we need not pay such a high cost to control inflation. To the extent that demand-side policies cannot cope with stagflation, we may use supply-side policies that directly influence prices and output. This does not mean that full employment and price stability are assured, only that no particular combination of inflation and unemployment is inevitable. We have observed that policymakers have a variety of policy levers for shifting the aggregate supply curve to the right (and the Phillips curve to the left), thereby improving macro outcomes.

The Eclectic AS Curve

To guide policy choices, many economists have proposed an "eclectic" aggregate supply curve—one that draws on the insights of both demand- and supply-side theories. Rather than accepting an aggregate supply curve that is completely Keynesian (horizontal), monetarist (vertical), or supply-side oriented (upward-sloping), many economists prefer to use an eclectic curve. As shown in Figure 15.9, the eclectic aggregate supply curve contains segments from each of the three theories.

The horizontal (Keynesian) segment applies to the lowest levels of output. At low levels of output, unemployment and excess production capacity are rampant. At such times, it seems likely that output can be increased without the risk of inflation.

The vertical (monetarist) segment reflects an entirely different situation. As full employment (Q^*) is approached, further increases in demand are likely to raise price levels, not output. So the aggregate supply curve turns sharply upward, approaching its vertical limit.

Between the horizontal Keynesian segment and the vertical monetarist segment, the aggregate supply curve is bent. This (supply-side) bend reflects

**FIGURE 15.9
An Eclectic
Aggregate Supply Curve**

Keynesians, Monetarists, and Supply-siders have very different views of the aggregate supply curve, as Figure 15.1 indicates. These three perspectives are not completely irreconcilable, however. Perhaps each theory is relevant at a different level of economic activity.

The short-run aggregate supply curve shown here incorporates this eclectic view. The aggregate supply curve is horizontal (Keynesian) at low levels of output, is curved (supply-side) in the middle, and becomes vertical (monetarist) as full employment is approached. Note how inflation accelerates as full employment is approached.

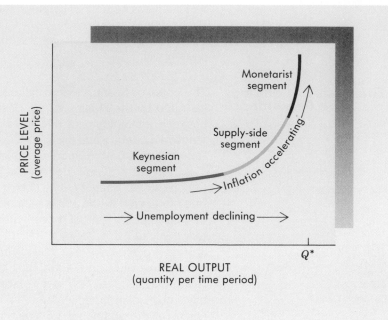

the likelihood that both prices and output are responsive to changes in the region between recession and full employment.

Because the eclectic curve is a compromise of competing theories, it appeals to none of them. As a practical guide to short-run policy, however, the eclectic aggregate supply curve has gained a large following.

SUMMARY

• Fiscal and monetary policies seek to attain full employment and price stability by altering the level of aggregate demand. Their success, however, depends on microeconomic responses, as reflected in the price and output decisions of market participants.

• The market's response to shifts in demand is reflected in the shape and position of the aggregate supply curve. If the curve slopes upward, a tradeoff between unemployment and inflation exists. This tradeoff is illustrated by the Phillips curve.

• If the aggregate supply curve shifts to the left, the tradeoff between unemployment and inflation worsens. Stagflation—a combination of substantial inflation and unemployment—results. This is illustrated by rightward shifts of the Phillips curve.

• Supply-side policies attempt to alter price and output decisions directly. If successful, they will shift the aggregate supply curve to the right. Such a shift implies less inflation *and* less unemployment.

• Marginal tax rates are a major concern of supply-side economists. High tax rates discourage extra work, investment, and saving. A reduction in marginal tax rates should shift aggregate supply to the right.

• The tax elasticity of supply measures the response of quantity supplied to changes in tax rates. Empirical evidence suggests that tax elasticity is low and that shifts of the aggregate supply curve are therefore small.

• Deregulation is intended to reduce costly restrictions on price and output behavior. Again the goal is to shift aggregate supply to the right.

• Structural bottlenecks also contribute to sluggish and costly output responses. To alleviate such bottlenecks, the government can facilitate training, job search, equal opportunity in labor markets, and free trade in product markets.

• Wage–price controls represent an attempt to limit inflationary abuses of market power. Large firms and unions often have considerable discretion to raise wages and prices. Wage–price controls are often viewed as a mechanism for limiting such supply decisions. Controls also foster inefficiency, however, by constraining relative prices.

• Supply-side theory enlarges the range of policy options. The eclectic aggregate supply curve reflects the insights of Keynesian, monetarist, and supply-side theories.

Terms to Remember

aggregate supply	derived demand
equation of exchange	structural unemployment
Phillips curve	labor force
stagflation	transfer payments
marginal tax rate	profit-push inflation
investment	market power
tax rebate	cost-push inflation
Laffer curve	labor productivity
tax elasticity of supply	unit labor cost
saving	wage–price controls

Questions for Discussion

1. What were the rates of unemployment and inflation last year? Where would they lie on Figure 15.3? Can you explain the implied shift from curve PC_4?

2. If you were suddenly to start earning $20,000 per year, how much of that income would you have to pay in taxes? Include not only federal income taxes but Social Security and any state and local taxes as well. At what tax rate would you stop working?

3. Can you give specific examples of government regulations that significantly increase production costs?

4. How can job vacancies exist when people are unemployed (that is, looking for work)? What forces in the labor market contribute to this apparent inconsistency?

Problems 1. The following table depicts the rate of output people would be willing and able to produce at different price levels, under different tax structures (tax systems *A* and *B*).

Price level	100	110	120	130	140	150	160
Rate of output							
Tax system *A*	100	125	150	175	200	225	250
Tax system *B*	120	150	180	210	240	270	300

(*a*) Graph the relevant aggregate supply curves for each tax system.
(*b*) Which tax system is likely to have higher tax rates?
(*c*) How do tax rates affect supply decisions?

2. Suppose taxpayers are required to pay a base tax of $50 plus 30 percent on any income over $100, as in the initial tax system *B* of Table 15.1. Suppose further that the taxing authority wishes to raise by $20 the taxes of people with incomes of $200.
(*a*) If marginal tax rates are to remain unchanged, what will the new base tax have to be?
(*b*) If the base tax of $50 is to remain unchanged, what will the marginal tax rate have to be?

Economic Growth:
Sources and Limits

*I*n dismissing Classical claims for the economy's "natural" long-term equilibrium, Keynes observed that "in the long run we are all dead." In Keynes's view, *short-term* macro instability is the legitimate focus of economic policy. Keynes's rebuke of long-run horizons was neither fair nor entirely accurate, however. A society lives longer than the individuals in it. New generations are being born every minute. In the long run *we* may be dead, but the next generation will be alive and kicking. Moreover, if history is any guide, later generations are likely to be living much better than we are.

Even those of us who will be dead in the long run have an interest in the future. If the economy's capacity increases each year, we, too, may enjoy higher living standards long before we die. Indeed, we could *double* our material well-being in less than thirty years if our output per capita increased by just 3 percent a year.

The purpose of this chapter is to take a longer-term view of U.S. economic performance. Chapters 5–15 have been concerned with the business cycle—that is, *short-run* variations in output and prices. This chapter looks at the prospects for *long-run* growth. In this chapter we consider three questions:

- How important is economic growth?

- How does an economy grow?

- Is continued economic growth either possible or desirable?

We develop answers to these questions by first examining the nature of economic growth and then examining its sources and potential.

THE NATURE OF GROWTH

Economic growth refers to increases in the output of the economy. But there are two distinct ways in which output increases, and they have very different implications for our economic welfare.

Short-Run Changes in Capacity Utilization

production possibilities: The alternative combinations of final goods and services that could be produced in a given time period with all available resources and technology.

The easiest kind of growth comes from increased use of our productive capabilities. At any given moment there is a limit to an economy's potential output. This limit is determined by the quantity of resources available and our technological know-how. We previously illustrated these short-run limits with a **production-possibilities** curve, as in Figure 16.1*a*. By using all of our (institutionally) available resources and our best expertise, we can produce any combination of goods on our production-possibilities curve.

We do not always take full advantage of our productive capacity, however. The economy often produces a mix of output that lies *inside* our production possibilities, like point *A* in Figure 16.1*a*. A major short-run goal of macroeconomics is to achieve full employment—to move us from point *A* to some point on the production-possibilities curve (e.g., point *B*). In the process, we produce more output.

Long-Run Changes in Capacity

economic growth: An increase in output (real GNP); an expansion of production possibilities.

As desirable as full employment is, there is an obvious limit to how much additional output we can obtain in this way. Once we are fully utilizing our productive capacity, further increases in output are attainable only if we *expand* that capacity. To do so we have to *shift* the production possibilities outward, as in Figure 16.1*b*. Such shifts imply an increase in *potential* GNP—that is, our productive capacity.

Over time, increases in capacity are critical. Short-run increases in the utilization of existing capacity can generate only modest increases in output. Even "high" unemployment rates (e.g., 7 percent) leave little room for increased output. ***To achieve large and lasting increases in output we must push our production possibilities outward.*** For this reason, economists tend to define **economic growth** in terms of changes in *potential* GNP.

FIGURE 16.1
Two Types of Growth

Increases in output may result from increased use of existing productive capacity or from increases in that capacity itself. In part *a* the initial mix of output at point *A* does not make full use of our production possibilities. Hence we can grow—get more output—by employing more of our available resources or using them more efficiently. This is illustrated by point *B* (or any other point on the curve). Once we are on the production-possibilities curve, we can increase our output further only by *increasing* our productive capacity. This is illustrated by the *shift* of the production-possibilities curve in part *b*.

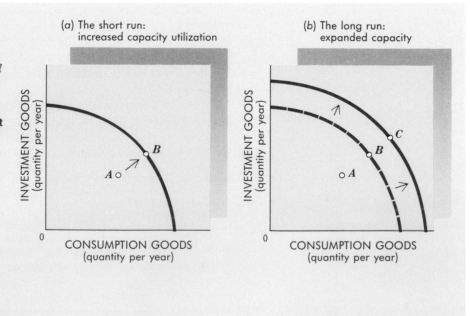

(a) The short run: increased capacity utilization

(b) The long run: expanded capacity

The unique character of economic growth can also be illustrated with aggregate supply and demand curves. Figure 16.2 depicts both a sloped, short-run AS curve and a vertical, long-run AS curve. In the short run, macro stabilization policies try to shift the AD curve to a more desirable price–output equilibrium. Such demand-side policies are unlikely to change the country's long-run capacity to produce, however.

Our productive capacity may increase nevertheless. If it does, the "natural" long-run AS curve will also shift. In this framework, ***economic growth implies a rightward shift of the long-run aggregate supply curve.***

Nominal vs. Real GNP

nominal GNP: The value of final output produced in a given period, measured in the prices of that period (current prices).

real GNP: The value of final output produced in a given period, measured in the prices of a base period (constant prices).

Notice that we refer to *real* GNP, not *nominal* GNP, in our concept of economic growth. **Nominal GNP** is the current dollar value of output—that is, the average price level (P) multiplied by the quantity of goods and services produced (Q). Accordingly, increases in nominal GNP can result from either increases in the price level or increases in the quantity of output. In fact, nominal GNP can rise even when the quantity of goods and services falls. This was the case in 1982, for example. The total quantity of goods and services produced in 1982 was less than the quantity produced in 1981. Nevertheless, prices rose enough in 1982 to keep nominal GNP growing.

Real GNP refers to the actual quantity of goods and services produced. Real GNP avoids the distortions of inflation by valuing output in *constant* prices. By using 1972 prices as a standard, we observe that real GNP fell from $1,512 billion in 1981 to only $1,480 billion in 1982.

GROWTH INDEXES

The Growth Rate

growth rate: Percentage change in real GNP from one period to another.

Typically, changes in real GNP are expressed in percentage terms, as a growth *rate*. The **growth rate** is simply the change in real output between two periods divided by total output in the base period. The percentage decline in real output during 1982 was thus $32 billion ÷ $1,512 billion, or 2.1 percent. By contrast, real output grew in 1983 by 3.7 percent.

**FIGURE 16.2
Shifts of Long-Run Supply**

Macro stabilization policies try to shift the aggregate demand curve (e.g., from AD_1 to AD_2) to achieve greater output and employment. The vertical long–run AS curve implies that these efforts will have no lasting impact on the "natural" rate of output, however. To achieve economic growth, the long-run aggregate supply curve must be shifted to the right (e.g., from $LRAS_1$ to $LRAS_2$).

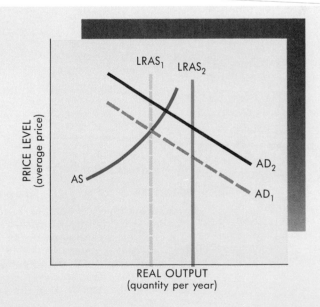

Figure 16.3 illustrates the recent growth experience of the U.S. economy. During the 1970s we enjoyed a growth rate that averaged 3.2 percent per year. In the 1960s we did even better, averaging 4.2 percent per year. The 1980s got off to a bad start but turned in above-average growth in 1983–84. Then growth slowed again. The challenge of the 1990s is to resume the higher rates of economic growth we enjoyed in the past.

The exponential process   At first blush, the "challenge" of raising the growth rate from 1 or 2 percent to 3 percent may appear neither difficult nor important. Indeed, the whole subject of economic growth looks rather dull when you discover that "big" gains in economic growth are measured in fractions of a percent. However, this initial impression is not fair. First of all, even one year's "low" growth implies lost output. If we had just *maintained* the rate of total output in 1982—that is, "achieved" a *zero* growth rate rather than a 2.5 percent decline—we would have had $32 billion more worth of goods and services. That works out to $136 worth of goods and services per person. Lots of people would have liked that extra output.

Second, economic growth is a *continuing* process. Gains made in one year accumulate in future years. It's like interest you earn at the bank. If you leave your money in the bank for several years, you begin to earn interest on your interest. Eventually you accumulate a nice little bankroll.

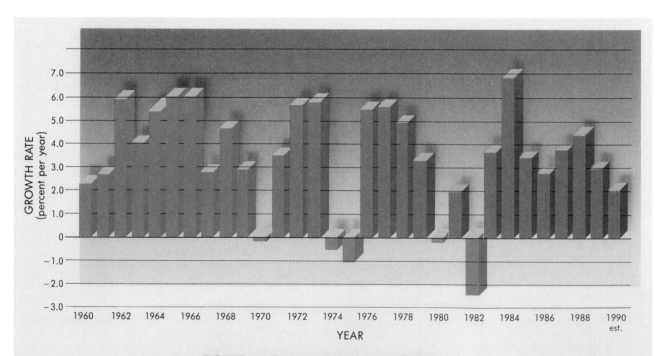

FIGURE 16.3 Recent U.S. Growth Rates

Total output typically increases from one year to another. The focus of policy is on the growth *rate*—that is, how fast real GNP increases from one year to the next. In the 1960s real GNP grew an average of 4.2 percent per year. In the 1970s the growth rate declined to 3.2 percent, and total output actually fell in two years (1970 and 1975). Growth in the 1980s was even slower, largely due to two recessions at the start of the decade. Will the 1990s be better?

The process of economic growth works the same way. Each little shift of the production-possibilities curve broadens the base for future GNP. As shifts accumulate over many years, the economy's productive capacity is greatly expanded. Ultimately we discover that those "little" differences in annual growth rates generate tremendous gains in GNP.

This cumulative process, whereby interest or growth is compounded from one year to the next, is called an "exponential process." To get a feel for its impact, consider the longer-run difference between annual growth rates of 3 and 5 percent. In thirty years, a 3 percent growth rate will raise our GNP to $13 trillion (in 1990 dollars). But a 5 percent growth rate would give us $24 trillion of goods and services in the same amount of time. Thus in a single generation, 5 percent growth translates into a standard of living that is 80 percent higher than 3 percent growth. From this longer-term perspective, the difference between 3 percent and 5 percent growth begins to look very meaningful.

GNP per Capita: A Measure of Living Standards

GNP per capita: Total GNP divided by total population; average GNP.

The exponential process might look even more meaningful if we translated it into *per capita* terms. We can do this by looking at *GNP per capita* rather than total GNP. **GNP per capita** is simply total output divided by total population. In 1989 the total output of the U.S. economy was $5.2 trillion. Since there were 250 million of us to share that output, GNP per capita was

$$1989 \text{ GNP per capita} = \frac{\$5.2 \text{ trillion of output}}{250 \text{ million people}} = \$20,800$$

This does not mean that every man, woman, and child in the United States received $20,800 worth of goods and services in 1989. Rather, it simply indicates how much output was potentially available to the "average" person.

GNP per capita is often used as a basic measure of our standard of living. It tells us a lot about the material well-being of the population. The higher the GNP per capita, the greater the volume of goods and services likely to be available to the average citizen.

Growth in GNP per capita is attained only when the growth of output exceeds population growth. In the United States, this condition is usually achieved. In the 1970s our population grew by an average of only 1 percent a year. Hence our average economic growth rate of 3.2 percent was more than sufficient to ensure steadily rising living standards. This is illustrated in Figure 16.4 by the widening gap between real GNP growth and population growth. Faster growth of GNP—or slower population growth—would have generated even larger gains in GNP per capita.

Less developed countries do not enjoy such rapid growth. Most of these countries suffer from both slower growth of GNP and faster rates of population growth. Ethiopia, for example, is one of the poorest countries in the world, with GNP per capita of less than $200. Yet its population continues to grow more rapidly (2.7 percent per year) than GNP (2.2 percent growth), further depressing living standards. The population of Zambia grew by more than 3 percent per year in the 1980s, while GNP grew at a slower rate of only 0.5 percent. As a consequence, GNP per capita *declined* more than 2 percent per year.

By comparison with these countries, the United States has been most fortunate. Our GNP per capita has more than doubled since World War II. This means that the average person today has twice as many goods and services as the average person had only forty-five years ago.

**FIGURE 16.4
U.S. Output and
Population Growth,
1900–1990**

Over time, the growth of
output in the United States
has greatly exceeded
population growth. As
a consequence, GNP
per capita has grown
tremendously. GNP per
capita was three times
higher in 1990 than in
1900.

Source: U.S. Department of Labor.

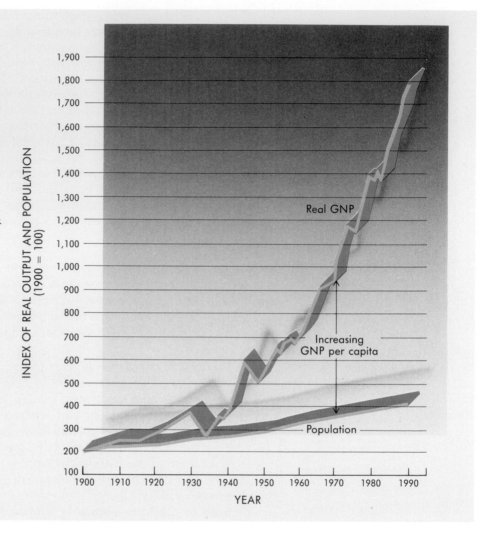

What about the future? Will we continue to enjoy substantial gains in living standards? It all depends on how fast output continues to grow in relation to population. Table 16.1 indicates some of the possibilities. If GNP per capita continues to grow at 1.8 percent per year—as it did in the 1980s—our average income will double again in thirty-nine years. If GNP per capita grows just half a percent faster, say, by 2.3 percent per year, our standard of living will double in only thirty-one years.

GNP per Worker: A Measure of Productivity

labor force: All persons over age sixteen who are either working for pay or actively seeking paid employment.

The increases in living standards depicted in Table 16.1 will not occur automatically. Someone is going to have to produce more output if we want GNP per capita to rise. One reason our living standard rose in the 1980s is that the labor force grew faster than the population. Those in the World War II baby boom had reached maturity and were entering the **labor force** in droves. At the same time, more women took jobs outside the home. As a consequence, the number of workers grew faster than the population. This

TABLE 16.1   The Rule of 72

Small differences in annual growth rates cumulate into large differences in GNP. Shown here are the number of years it would take to double GNP per capita at various net growth rates. "Net" growth refers to GNP growth rate minus the population growth rate. Doubling times can be approximated by the "rule of 72." Seventy-two divided by the growth rate equals the number of years it takes to double.	Net growth rate (percent)	Doubling time (years)
	0.0	Never
	0.5	140
	1.0	70
	1.5	47
	2.0	35
	2.5	30
	3.0	24
	3.5	20
	4.0	18

increase in the proportion of workers in the economy helped to increase GNP per capita.

The percentage of people who participate in the labor market cannot increase forever. At the limit, everyone would be in the labor market, and no further workers could be found. Sustained increases in GNP per capita are more likely to come from increases in output *per worker*. The total quantity of output produced depends not only on how many workers are employed but also on how productive each worker is. If **productivity** is increasing, then GNP per capita is likely to rise as well.

productivity: Output per unit of input, e.g., output per labor hour.

The most common measure of productivity is output per labor hour. This is simply the ratio of total output to the number of hours worked. As noted earlier, total GNP in 1989 was $5.2 trillion. In that same year the labor force was employed for a total of 212 billion hours. Hence the average worker's productivity was $24.62 of output per hour.

The increase in our GNP per capita in recent decades is directly related to the higher productivity of the average American worker. As Figure 16.5 reveals, the average worker today produces 75 percent more goods and services than the average worker did in 1960.

The productivity slowdown   For economic growth to continue, the productivity of the average American worker must continue to rise. In the 1970s and early 1980s, however, productivity growth slowed considerably (see Figure 16.5). The annual increase in productivity averaged 3.4 percent from 1947 to 1966, then fell to 2.15 percent for the years 1966–73. From 1973 to 1982, the growth of productivity was even slower, averaging less than 1 percent a year. This productivity slowdown pushed the U.S. economy to the bottom of international comparisons (see World View). It also caused people to wonder if the American "growth machine" was wearing out. To address this concern, we need to identify the sources of past productivity growth.

FIGURE 16.5
U.S. Productivity Gains,
1960–1990

Economic growth originates in an increased number of workers and increases in output per worker. In recent years, improvements in productivity have been the primary source of growth. Since 1960 productivity has increased 75 percent. Note, however, that this gain has been uneven and has included some slowdowns (e.g., 1974, 1979, 1982).

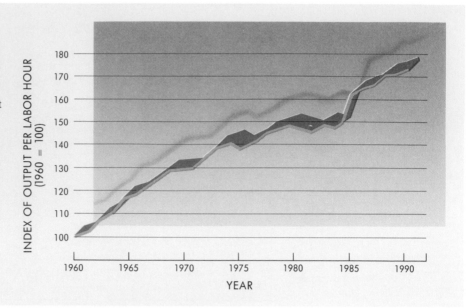

W🌐RLD VIEW

COMPARATIVE PRODUCTIVITY

Productivity Gains

From 1960 to 1986 U.S. productivity improvements fell significantly behind those of other industrial nations. During that 26-year period, output per worker in U.S. manufacturing increased only 2.8 percent per year. The average productivity gain in Japan, Italy, and Belgium was more than double that. Below are some examples of productivity growth during this period.

The relatively slow productivity gains in the United States reflect several factors, including changes in labor-force composition, recessions, a shift from manufacturing to services, and low saving and investment rates. In the mid-1980s these negative forces abated and U.S. productivity growth again exceeded that of most other countries.

Country	Average yearly gain in productivity, 1960–84
Japan	7.9%
Belgium	6.3
Italy	5.7
France	5.2
Germany (West)	4.6
Sweden	4.6
Great Britain	3.6
Canada	3.3
United States	**2.8**

Source: U.S. Bureau of Labor Statistics.

SOURCES OF PRODUCTIVITY GROWTH

The key to economic growth is increasing output per worker. Such *productivity gains may come from*

- *Higher skills*—an increase in labor skills
- *More capital*—an increase in the ratio of capital to labor
- *Technological advance*—the development and use of better capital equipment
- *Improved management*—better use of available resources in the production process

Labor Quality

The skills of the labor force change over time. In general, continuing advances in education and skill training have increased the quality of labor. In 1950 less than 8 percent of all U.S. workers had completed college. Today over 20 percent of the work force has completed four years of college. In addition to this advance in general education, there has been a substantial increase in vocational training, both in the public sector and by private firms.

In the 1970s these improvements in the quality of individual workers were offset by a change in the composition of the labor force. As we observed in Chapters 6 and 15, the proportion of teenagers and women in the labor force grew tremendously in the 1960s and 1970s. These additional workers contributed to higher output. Because teenagers and women (re)entering the labor market generally have less job experience than adult men, however, *average* productivity fell. This phenomenon is reversing itself in the 1990s, as the baby boomers enter their prime working years. This aging of the baby boomers is significantly increasing the average skills of the work force and therewith the productivity of the U.S. economy.

Capital Investment

A worker's productivity is not determined entirely by age and experience. On the contrary, a worker's productivity depends to a large extent on the quantity and quality of other inputs in the production process. A worker with no tools or equipment will not be very productive. Similarly, a worker with outmoded equipment will not produce as much as an equally capable worker who is equipped with the newest machines and the best technology. From this perspective, *a primary determinant of labor productivity is the rate of capital investment.* In other words, improvements in output per labor hour depend in large part on increases in the quantity and quality of capital equipment.

While labor-force growth accelerated in the 1970s, the growth of capital slowed. As Table 16.2 indicates, the capital stock increased by 4.1 percent per year in the late 1960s. In the 1970s, however, the growth of capital slowed to only 2.5 percent per year; and in the early 1980s it slowed even further. The stock of capital was still growing faster than the labor force (compare columns 1 and 2), but the difference was getting smaller. This means that although the average worker was continuing to get more and better machines, the rate at which he was getting them was slower. As a consequence, productivity growth declined (see column 3).

TABLE 16.2 Average Annual Growth Rate of Labor, Capital, and Productivity, 1959–1985

In the 1970s the rate of capital growth slowed while the rate of labor growth increased. As a consequence, productivity gains declined. These trends were reversed in the late 1980s.

| Period | Average annual percentage change in: | | |
	Labor stock	Capital stock	Output per labor hour
1959–65	0.9	3.8	3.3
1965–69	1.2	4.1	2.2
1969–73	0.4	3.5	2.6
1973–79	1.6	2.5	0.8
1979–85	1.6	2.2	0.9

Source: *Economic Report of the President*, 1988.

Saving and investment rates   The dependence of productivity gains on capital investment puts a new perspective on consumption and saving. In the short run, the primary concern of macroeconomic policy is to balance aggregate demand and aggregate supply. In this context, savings are a form of leakage that requires offsetting injections of investment or government spending. To this end, fiscal and monetary policies seek to manipulate the rate of total spending. Success is measured by how close equilibrium GNP comes to full-employment GNP.

From the longer-run perspective of economic growth, saving and investment take on added importance. ***Savings are not just a form of leakage, but a basic source of investment financing.*** Our limited production possibilities force us to choose among consumption, government spending, exports, and investment. If we use all our resources to produce consumer, export, and public-sector goods, there won't be any investment. In that case, we might not face a short-run stabilization problem—our productive capacity might be fully utilized—but we would confront a *growth* problem. By consuming everything we produced at full employment, we would be leaving nothing for investment and further growth. Indeed, if we consumed our entire output, our productive capacity would actually shrink, since we wouldn't even be replacing worn-out plant and equipment. We must have at least enough saving to finance **net investment**.

net investment: Gross investment less depreciation.

Actual saving and investment rates have been quite low in the United States. In the 1960s and 1970s, consumers saved 7–8 percent of their disposable income. Consumer saving rates then dropped in the 1980s, hitting a low of 3.2 percent in 1987. During this period, federal budget deficits also widened, absorbing much of the available saving. An investment rate of close to 16 percent was maintained only by an increase in business saving (depreciation plus retained earnings) and an inflow of foreign saving. These added sources of investment financing permitted the U.S. economy to continue growing at above-average rates in the 1980s (see World View). To maintain or increase that rate of economic growth, we have to allocate a larger share of output to saving and investment.

Management   The quantity and quality of factor inputs do not completely determine the rate of economic growth. Resources, however good and abundant, must be organized into a production process and managed. Hence entrepreneurship

W🌐RLD VIEW

COMPARATIVE INVESTMENT

Investment and Growth

Investment in new plant and equipment is essential for economic growth. In general, countries that allocate a larger share of output to investment will grow more rapidly. In the 1970s and 1980s Japan had the highest investment and growth rates.

Country	Investment as percentage of GNP (average, 1975–87)	Growth rate of GNP (average, 1976–87)
Japan	21	4.1
Canada	20	3.4
United States	**16**	**3.1**
Germany (West)	17	2.4
France	18	2.3
Great Britain	15	2.3

Source: *Economic Report of the President*, 1990, and Organization for Economic Cooperation and Development.

and the quality of continuing management are major determinants of economic growth.

It is difficult to characterize differences in management techniques or to measure their effectiveness. However, much attention has been focused in recent years on the alleged shortsightedness of American managers. U.S. firms, it is said, focus too narrowly on short-term profits, neglecting long-term gains in productivity. They also emphasize quantity over quality of output. And they fail to include workers in key decisions, thus depriving themselves of important insights and good will. By contrast, firms in Japan and elsewhere concentrate on longer-term gains, quality control, and strong bonds between labor and management. As a consequence, Japanese firms enjoy remarkably good labor and customer relations, intense worker loyalty, and faster productivity gains.

No single management style can be characterized as "best." The recent critiques of traditional management styles, however, have led to some new approaches. American labor unions and managers have experimented with some new cooperative approaches. These include "quality-of-work" circles and other collective efforts to improve relationships and productivity. In some cases workers have even assumed a direct role in management or ownership. At the same time, U.S. firms have put renewed emphasis on product quality, as exemplified by the recent offering of multiyear warranties on American-made cars and other products.

In many industries, labor unions play a critical, if indirect, role in management. Unions bargain not only for wages but also for working conditions. These conditions include the nature of the tasks to be performed on the job, the number of workers assigned to each task, the frequency and duration of breaks (e.g., lunchtime), and even seniority rights to specific jobs. Such work rules tend to limit management's ability to alter production processes and to increase productivity. Increased productivity often requires explicit work-rule concessions by labor unions, and in all cases union–management cooperation.

Research and Development

A fourth and vital source of productivity advance is research and development (R&D). R&D is a broad concept that includes scientific research, product development, innovations in production technique, and the development of management improvements. R&D activity may be a specific, identifiable activity (e.g., in a research lab) or it may be part of the process of "learning by doing." In either case, the insights developed from R&D generally lead to new products and cheaper ways of producing them. Over time, R&D is credited with the greatest contributions to economic growth. In his study of U.S. growth during the period 1929–82, Edward Denison concluded that 26 percent of *total* growth was due to "advances in knowledge." The relative contribution of R&D to productivity (output per worker) was probably twice that much. There is some concern, however, that America's R&D effort is falling behind that of other nations (see World View).

There is an important link between R&D and capital investment. As noted earlier, part of each year's gross investment compensates for the depreciation of existing plant and equipment. However, new machines are rarely identical to the ones they replace. Instead, new capital equipment tends to embody improved technology. Indeed, the availability of improved technology is often a major motivation for new investment, long before old machines have literally worn out. From this perspective, R&D and capital investment make a joint contribution to productivity advance.

W◉RLD VIEW

COMPARATIVE R&D

Research and Development Spending to Rise 4.8% in 1990, Battelle Predicts

Research and development spending in the U.S. is expected to increase 4.8% next year to $138.7 billion, according to a study by Battelle Memorial Institute.

Next year's spending will rise 2.1% in inflation-adjusted terms, Battelle estimates, which is well below the 3.1% average rate over the past 10 years. . . .

Battelle, a Columbus, Ohio, technology organization that performs research on a contract basis for industry and government agencies, doesn't forecast 1990 R&D spending outside the U.S. But other studies indicate that the U.S. is lagging its toughest foreign competitors. Latest figures from the National Science Foundation show that in 1987 the U.S. spent 2.6% of its gross national product on R&D, slightly below 2.8% for West Germany and 2.9% for Japan.

However, the U.S. spent only 1.8% of GNP, which is the total value of a nation's output of goods and services, on nondefense R&D in 1987, far below 2.6% for West Germany and 2.8% for Japan, the government agency said. France and the U.K. invested about the same share of GNP in nondefense R&D as the U.S. did.

And some experts are concerned that the U.S. may fall further behind in the years ahead. For one thing, spending on weapons research is almost certain to slow as Congress cuts the defense budget in response to the peace initiatives of the Soviet Union. Also, companies may be spending more carefully, partly because the economy isn't booming and earnings may be pinched.

—Ralph E. Winter

The Wall Street Journal, December 28, 1989, p. A2. Reprinted by permission of *The Wall Street Journal* © Dow Jones & Company, Inc. (1989). All Rights Reserved.

Policy Levers To a large extent, the pace of economic growth is set by market forces. The government plays an important role as well, however. Supply-side policies are particularly relevant to economic growth since they focus on shifts of the aggregate supply curve. Many of the same policies that increase the *short*-run supply potential also increase the economy's *long*-run capacity to produce. Government support of education, training, and R&D activity enhances both short- and long-run capacity. Tax incentives for saving and investment may also have a continuing effect on the ability and willingness to produce.

Government regulation of business is also relevant here. Indeed, many business executives blame excessive government regulation for most of their productivity problems. Although this charge is vastly exaggerated, government regulation undoubtedly has raised costs and restrained innovation in many industries. From this perspective, deregulation may contribute to increased productivity and growth. The recent deregulation of the airline, trucking, oil, banking, and securities industries illustrates how deregulation can spur growth. Deregulation—particularly the adoption of uniform regulations in its twelve member nations—has also contributed to the economic growth of the European Community (see World View).

The goals of increased productivity and growth do not require abrupt rejections of all government intervention in product and factor markets. However, these goals do add an important consideration in evaluating public policy. Policies must be evaluated not only in terms of their own narrow objectives (e.g., cleaner air), but also in terms of their impact on productivity and growth.

The dependence of economic growth on capital investment also adds an important dimension to the debate about government deficits and debt. To the extent deficit-financed government spending **crowds out** private invest-

crowding out: A reduction in private-sector borrowing (and spending) caused by increased government borrowing.

W🌐RLD VIEW

SOURCES OF GROWTH

The 1990s Euro Boom

Analysts expect economic growth in Western Europe to accelerate sharply in the 1990s. The expectations for this "Euro boom" are based on the emerging reality of a unified European Community (EC). After twenty-six years of negotiation, the twelve member nations of the EC are finally moving toward a true common market. Their goal: a fully integrated EC by the end of 1992.

Even if they do not achieve complete integration, the EC economies will benefit from

• *Market expansion:* The free flow of goods and resources across EC borders will permit greater specialization and economies of scale.

• *More competition:* New cross-border competition will force industries to cut costs, innovate, and deliver better products.

• *Uniform regulation:* Common regulations on product quality, taxes, mergers, and other business practices will eliminate a major barrier to the cross-border flow of resources and products.

• *More resources:* The expanded potential for business will attract capital investment as well as labor from outside the EC. Japanese and American companies have been rushing to increase their Euro investments.

The Euro boom will draw additional strength from the opening of Eastern Europe to free trade and labor mobility.

ment, it may curtail economic growth. Hence fiscal and monetary policies must be evaluated in terms of their impact not only on (short-run) aggregate demand but also on long-run aggregate supply.

The availability of labor is also subject to policy intervention. In addition to education and training activities, the government affects the supply of labor through its immigration policies. During the 1980s nearly 10 million legal immigrants settled in America. The federal government estimates that as many as 5 million more may have entered the country illegally. All of these immigrants add to the potential supply of labor and thus our long-run growth prospects (see World View).

Sources of Past Growth

The contributions of capital investment and other forces to the past growth of the American economy are depicted in Table 16.3. Increases in the labor force and capital investment explain only half of our past growth. Productivity advances attributable to education, new technology, and improved management have been equally important "engines" of growth. Those productivity advances account for an even larger share of our rising GNP per capita.

THE LIMITS TO GROWTH

Continued economic growth is neither assured nor easy. At a minimum, further increases in our living standards will require more research and development, additional investment, continuing skill development, improved management, and supportive government policies. Even if all these things happen, however, success is not assured. On the contrary, some people assert that there are insurmountable limits to growth, and even our best efforts will ultimately prove futile.

TABLE 16.3 The Sources of U.S. Growth

From 1929 to 1982 total output grew by 3.2 percent annually. More than half of this growth was due to improvements in our technological and managerial capabilities. In the 1980s productivity advances were even more important in increasing output. Such productivity improvements have shifted our production-possibilities curve outward, increasing GNP per capita as well.

Source	Percentage contribution to output growth
More inputs	
Additional labor	34
Additional capital	17
	51
Productivity advances	
Education of labor	13
Advances in knowledge	26
Improved resource allocation	8
Economies of scale	8
	55
Miscellaneous	−6
	100

Source: Edward F. Denison, *Trends in American Economic Growth, 1929–1982* (Washington, D.C.: Brookings Institution, 1985).

W🌐RLD VIEW

LABOR SUPPLY

Let's Change the Immigration Law—Now

Millions of Eastern Europeans and Soviets—educated and talented for the most part—are likely to try to start fresh lives in the West as barriers to free emigration continue to tumble. The U.S. sorely needs immigrant talent as a way to compensate for the shrinking birthrate common to the West and to replenish the stagnating pool of skilled labor. But to get that talent, America will have to change its immigration policies and open her doors to those with proven skills.

America's outdated immigration law simply is not geared to admit the very ones the country needs most. Following a principle that has remained unchanged since 1952, the law offers the right of immigration based on family preference. As a result, the vast majority of new arrivals are spouses, children, and siblings of earlier immigrants—and the system self-perpetuates: Once they become citizens, they in turn bring in *their* families. Since these immigrants' skills are never a factor in whether or not they are admitted, any benefits that they bring to the U.S. economy are coincidental. Of last year's 650,000 new immigrants, just 54,000 qualified solely on the basis of their education or ability.

A more sensible policy would be to expand opportunities for those immigrants who possess skills in short supply, as Canada and Australia have recently done.

Some anti-immigrant sentiment has already boiled up in various communities around America. If the U.S. government doesn't bring the law into line with the nation's needs, that sentiment could spread while the country loses the chance to welcome newcomers who could bring with them the skills that are in critically short supply.

—Louis S. Richman

Fortune, January 29, 1990, p. 12. Copyright © 1990 The Time Inc. Magazine Company. All rights reserved.

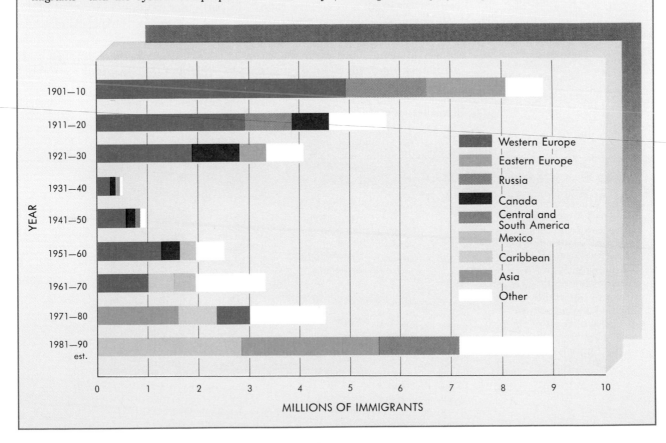

The Malthusian Formula for Destruction

The prospect of an eventual limit to economic growth originated in the eighteenth-century warnings of the Reverend Thomas Malthus. Malthus argued that continued economic growth was impossible because food production could not keep pace with population growth. His dire projections earned the economics profession its characterization as the "dismal science."

When Malthus first issued his warnings, in 1798, the population of England (including Wales) was about 9 million. Annual production of barley, oats, and related grains was approximately 162 million bushels, and wheat production was around 50 million bushels, just about enough to feed the English population (a little had to be imported from other countries). Although the relationship between food and population was satisfactory in 1798, Malthus reasoned that starvation was not far off. First of all, he observed that "population, when unchecked, goes on doubling itself every twenty-five years, or increases in a geometrical ratio."[1] Thus he foresaw the English population increasing to 36 million people by 1850, 144 million by 1900, and more than 1 billion by 1975, unless some social or natural restraints were imposed on population growth.

One natural population check that Malthus foresaw was a scarcity of food. England had only a limited amount of land available for cultivation and was already farming the most fertile tracts. Before long, all available land would be in use and only improvements in agricultural productivity (output per acre) could increase food supplies. Some productivity increases were possible, Malthus concluded, but "the means of subsistence, under circumstances the most favorable to human industry, could not possibly be made to increase faster than in an arithmetical ratio."[2] In particular, he concluded that barley and oat production could increase by only 162 million bushels and wheat production by 50 million bushels every 25 years.

With population increasing at a *geometric* rate and food supplies at an *arithmetic* rate, the eventual outcome is evident. Table 16.4 and Figure 16.6

[1]Thomas Malthus, *An Essay on the Principle of Population* (1798; reprint ed., Homewood, Ill.: Richard D. Irwin, 1963), p. 4.
[2]Ibid., p. 5.

TABLE 16.4 Malthusian Projections, Circa 1798

In the nineteenth century, the English population appeared to be doubling every 25 years (geometric growth). Yet the output of food was growing by a constant amount each year (arithmetic growth). This implied a diminishing quantity of food per capita and, ultimately, starvation of the English population.

Year	English population (millions)	Output of barley and oats (millions of bushels)	Output of wheat (millions of bushels)	Barley and oats output per capita (bushels)	Wheat output per capita (bushels)
1800	9	162	50	18.0	5.5
1825	18	324	100	18.0	5.5
1850	36	486	150	13.5	4.2
1875	72	648	200	9.0	2.8
1900	144	810	250	5.6	1.7
1925	288	972	300	3.4	1.0
1950	576	1,134	350	2.0	0.6
1975	1,152	1,296	400	1.1	0.3
2000	2,304	1,458	450	0.6	0.2

Source: Malthus's arithmetic applied to actual data for 1800 (see text.)

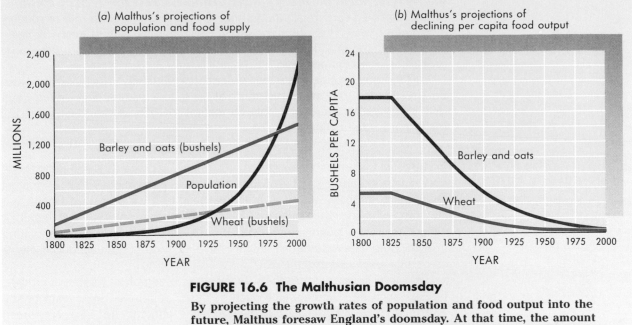

FIGURE 16.6 The Malthusian Doomsday

By projecting the growth rates of population and food output into the future, Malthus foresaw England's doomsday. At that time, the amount of available food per capita would be too small to sustain human life. Fortunately, Malthus overestimated population growth and underestimated productivity growth.

Source: Malthus's arithmetic applied to actual data for 1800 (see text).

geometric growth: An increase in quantity by a constant proportion each year.

arithmetic growth: An increase in quantity by a constant amount each year.

illustrate Malthus's projections. In Figure 16.6*a* the difference between a **geometric growth** path and an **arithmetic growth** path is obvious.

Figure 16.6*b* simply translates this growing imbalance between population size and food supplies into per capita terms. From Malthus's time on, the amount of barley, oats, and wheat available to the average Englishman declines rapidly. Even if we assume that the average Englishman was well fed in 1800 (an erroneous assumption, according to nutrition experts), he could have expected to experience hunger pains before 1850. As Malthus calculated it, per capita wheat output would decline from 5.5 bushels in 1800 to only 1.7 bushels in 1900 (Table 16.4). This was not enough food to feed the English people. According to Malthus's projections, either England died off about 100 years ago, or it has been maintained at the brink of starvation for more than a century. Its continued survival can be explained only by recurrent plagues, wars, or the kind of "moral restraint" commonly associated with Victorian preachments.

Malthus's logic was impeccable. As long as population increased at a geometric rate while output increased at an arithmetic rate, England's doomsday was as certain as two plus two equals four. Malthus's error was not in his logic but in his empirical assumptions. He did not know how fast output would increase over time, any more than we know whether people will be wearing electronic wings in the year 2203. He had to make an educated guess about future productivity trends. He based his estimates on his own experiences at the very beginning of the Industrial Revolution. As is turned out (fortunately), he grossly underestimated the rate at which productivity would increase. ***Output, including agricultural products, has increased at a geo-***

metric rate, not at the much slower arithmetic rate foreseen by Malthus. As we observed earlier, U.S. output has grown at a long-term rate of roughly 3 percent a year. This *geometric* growth has doubled output every 25 years or so. Even the productivity slowdown in the 1970s left us with geometric growth of 1 percent per year.

In addition to underestimating potential productivity growth, Malthus also underestimated the "moral restraint" of his fellow Britons. The United Kingdom's population numbered only 60 million in 1975, far short of the 1,152 million projected by Malthus.

The Modern Doomsday Formula

In retrospect, Malthus's projections look absurd. The earth is still finite, however, and population is still growing—by 150 people a minute! Hence we must *continue* to increase output at a geometric rate if we wish to maintain our standard of living. In particular, the rate of output growth must equal or exceed the rate of population growth. If output growth falls behind population growth, output per capita will decline. If that trend continues, doomsday is as certain as simple arithmetic.

Modern doomsday prophets, working with complex, computer models, foresee such an outcome. One such analysis, conducted by a team of scientists from the Massachusetts Institute of Technology (M.I.T.), concluded that "under the assumption of no major change in the present system, population and industrial growth will certainly stop within the next century, at the latest."[3] Most of the M.I.T. calculations indicated that the world's growth would come to a halt around the year 2050 and be followed by rapidly deteriorating standards of living.

Resource constraints   Like Malthus, the M.I.T. scientists were particularly worried about an ultimate shortage of land. The earth has only 7.86 billion acres of land potentially suitable for agriculture, and we are already farming half that total. We can boost agricultural production only by bringing the rest of the land into cultivation or by increasing the output per acre. Using these Malthusian observations as a benchmark, the M.I.T. scientists estimated how much land we would "require" to feed ourselves over time. Their results are presented in Figure 16.7. With no improvements in productivity, the world's growing population will run out of arable land around the year 2010.

The M.I.T. team recognized that we will probably increase agricultural productivity (output per acre) over time. Therefore, they also estimated our land requirements under the assumption that our productivity will double or even quadruple over the next 50 to 100 years. As is evident in Figure 16.7, even such large increases in productivity only postpone the day of reckoning a few years. The M.I.T. team's most optimistic assumptions carry us only to the year 2070.

As impressively detailed as the M.I.T. calculations are, they still suffer from the same flaw that upset Malthus's projections. They reflect good logic and arithmetic, but faulty assumptions. The M.I.T. team concedes that productivity increases are possible, but they still perceive such possibilities as being unduly limited. Note that their "most optimistic" projection calls for a quadrupling of current crop yields. Admittedly, a fourfold increase in productivity sounds heroic, but it amounts to no more than a 3 percent *annual* productivity increase compounded over a period of 47 years. The United States and other countries have maintained even higher rates of productivity

---

[3]Dennis L. Meadows et al., *The Limits to Growth* (New York: Universe Books, 1972), p. 126.

FIGURE 16.7
The Land Constraint

The amount of arable land is limited. Hence increases in food output will depend on productivity advances. But how fast will productivity grow? The M.I.T. model projected low rates of productivity growth, and thus a foreseeable doomsday.

Source: *The Limits to Growth,* by Donella H. Meadows, Dennis L. Meadows, Jorgen Randers, William W. Behrens III. A Potomac Associates book published by Universe Books, New York, 1972.

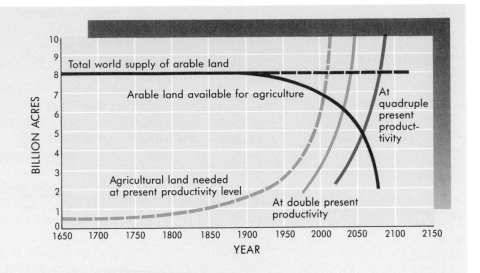

increase, and less developed countries may soon exceed them. Thus the M.I.T. team's "most optimistic" productivity projections may be unduly pessimistic.

Moreover, productivity changes are a *continuing* phenomenon. There is no reason to believe that productivity improvements will cease after we have quadrupled present crop yields. Accordingly, it is difficult to accept the M.I.T. projections. It is equally difficult to accept the dire warnings of Stanford demographer Paul Ehrlich that "no conceivable increase in food supply can keep up with the current population growth rates over the long term."[4] It is actually quite conceivable: ***as long as the rate of productivity growth exceeds the rate of population growth, per capita output will continue to increase.***

The price mechanism   There are some good *economic* reasons for assuming that food production will continue to grow faster than the population. If food production slows significantly, food prices will rise. The higher food prices will have two important effects. On the demand side, higher prices will induce people to buy and consume less food. In view of our present consumption habits, this might not be a wholly undesirable consequence. Such a solution to the food problem has biologically limited potential, however. It could not even be applied in many areas of the world, where undernourishment (inadequate calorie intake) and malnutrition (inadequate intake of nutrients) are common.

An increase in the price of food would affect the supply side of the market as well. Higher food prices would create greater incentives for productivity research. Farmers and nonfarmers alike would begin to see the enhanced value of agricultural innovation and would try to improve crop yields. Suffice it to observe here that if potatoes were suddenly worth their weight in gold, everyone and his brother would be devising methods to grow potatoes faster and cheaper. Thus ***the market mechanism helps both to signal impending shortages (via higher prices) and to alleviate them (via the profit motive).***

[4]Paul R. Ehrlich and Anne H. Ehrlich, *Population, Resources, Environment: Issues in Human Ecology,* 2nd ed. (San Francisco: W. H. Freeman, 1972), p. 138. Copyright © 1970, 1972 by W. H. Freeman and Company. Reprinted with permission.

substitution effect: The replacement of one resource (or good) with another in response to changing relative prices.

Even if we make the totally unfounded assumption that all agricultural productivity improvements will cease tomorrow, we need not starve to death as quickly as the M.I.T. computer predicts. Another essential economic phenomenon neglected by the computer is the potential for **substitution effects** in food consumption.

The M.I.T. computer projected our current consumption habits 100 years into the future, thereby assuming that we would continue to eat the same foods we do today. One hundred years from today, however, people may not even know what a hamburger is, much less a Big Mac. If land does become scarce, the price of those foods that require more land to produce will rise relative to those that require less. The Japanese, who have about as little land per person as anybody, learned this lesson long ago. The relative price of beef in Japan is about three times as high as it is in the United States, primarily because beef production requires a lot of land. The Japanese thus end up *substituting* fish and other foods for the red meat we tend to regard as essential. Chemists claim we may even be able to make do on entirely synthetic foods. Whether or not these diets appeal to you is beside the point. The essential observation is that we *can* survive with less land per capita and a different diet. The price mechanism will encourage us to make the required adjustments.

The same economic forces that tend to avert universal starvation also help overcome other resource constraints. In future generations, we can expect to substitute more plentiful (and thus cheaper) resources for less plentiful (and thus more expensive) resources (see In the News). Recycling also becomes attractive from an economic perspective as "natural" resources become more expensive to obtain. Thus changing prices should help us overcome future resource "crises."

In The News

SUBSTITUTION EFFECTS

Are the Great Plains Drying Up?

Fifty years ago the Great Plains region was bone dry, and Depression-era farmers were leaving the area in droves. Today, however, the Great Plains is one of the richest agricultural areas in the world. Water is the resource that transformed the farmlands of Nebraska, South Dakota, Kansas, Oklahoma, and northern Texas into such a fertile region. Below the ground in these states lies the Ogallala aquifer, a gigantic deposit of water-laden sand, silt, and gravel. The aquifer is 1,000 feet thick in parts of Nebraska, although only a few inches thick in parts of Texas. The Ogallala holds a quadrillion gallons of water, the equivalent of Lake Huron.

The Ogallala was first tapped in the 1930s. However, not until the 1950s were high-capacity pumps used to exploit it. Now the region's farmers use water extensively, oftentimes with the aid of massive sprinklers. In the process, the Ogallala water supply is being depleted. The annual net drainage (overdraft) is now almost equal to the annual flow of the Colorado River. Gradually built up over a period of millions of years, the Ogallala is being depleted in a few decades.

To irrigate their farms, many Great Plains farmers must dig new and deeper wells to replace those that have dried up. But this does not solve the problem. Ultimately, the water will become so expensive to pump that farmers will have to alter their production processes. This will require a change in crops (e.g., to wheat and sorghum from corn) as well as new water-saving technologies. The Great Plains will dry up only if the farmers who live there ignore economics completely and are willing to pay any price to get the last drop of the Ogallala's water.

Environmental Destruction

The market's ability to circumvent resource constraints would seem to augur well for our future. Doomsayers warn, though, that other limits to growth will emerge, even in a world of "unlimited" resources. The villain this time is pollution. As Professor Ehrlich sees it:

> Attempts to increase food production further will tend to accelerate the deterioration of our environment, which in turn will eventually *reduce* the capacity of the Earth to produce food. It is not clear whether environmental decay has now gone so far as to be essentially irreversible; it is possible that the capacity of the planet to support human life has been permanently impaired. Such technological "successes" as automobiles, pesticides, and inorganic nitrogen fertilizers are major contributors to environmental deterioration.[5]

Because of the pollution problem, Professor G. Evelyn Hutchinson gauges the remaining time of habitable existence on earth "in decades."[6]

It is not difficult for anyone with the basic five senses to comprehend the pollution problem. Pollution is as close these days as the air we breathe. Moreover, we cannot fail to observe a distinct tendency for pollution levels to rise along with GNP and population expansion. If one projects such pollution trends into the future, things are bound to look pretty ugly.

Although pollution is universally acknowledged to be an important and annoying problem, we cannot assume that the *rate* of pollution will continue unabated. On the contrary, the growing awareness of the pollution problem has already led to significant abatement-policy efforts. The Environmental Protection Agency (EPA), for example, is unquestionably a force working for cleaner air and water. Indeed, active policies to curb pollution are as familiar as auto-exhaust controls and DDT bans. A computer programmed ten or twenty years ago to project present pollution levels would not have foreseen these abatement efforts and would thus have overestimated current pollution levels.

This is not to say that we have in any final way "solved" the pollution problem or that we are even doing the best job we possibly can. It simply says that geometric increases in pollution are not inevitable. There is simply no compelling reason why we have to continue polluting the environment; if we stop, another doomsday can be averted.

FUTURE GROWTH

The Possibility of Growth

These considerations suggest that there are no limits to growth, at least none emanating from resource constraints or pollution thresholds. As Professor Robert Solow summed up the issue:

> My real complaint about the Doomsday school [is that] it diverts attention from the really important things that can actually be done, step by step, to make things better. The end of the world *is* at hand—the earth, if you take the long view, will fall into the sun in a few billion years anyway, unless some other disaster happens first. In the meantime, I think we'd be better off passing a strong sulfur-emissions tax, or getting some Highway Trust Fund money allocated to mass transit, or

---

[5]Ibid., p. 442.
[6]G. Evelyn Hutchinson, "The Biosphere," *Scientific American,* September 1970, p. 53; Meadows et al., *Limits to Growth,* Chapter 4.

"*And so, extrapolating from the best figures available, we see that current trends, unless dramatically reversed, will inevitably lead to a situation in which the sky will fall.*"

Drawing by Lorenz; © 1972 The New Yorker Magazine, Inc.

building a humane and decent floor under family incomes, or overriding President Nixon's veto of a strong Water Quality Act, or reforming the tax system, or fending off starvation in Bengal—instead of worrying about the generalized "predicament of mankind."[7]

Karl Marx expressed these same thoughts nearly a century earlier. Marx chastised "the contemptible Malthus" for turning the attention of the working class away from what he regarded as the immediate problem of capitalist exploitation to some distant and ill-founded anxiety about "natural" disaster.[8]

Finally, the Club of Rome, the group of eminent scientists that had supported and adopted the M.I.T. doomsday projections in 1972, later decided that perhaps growth was possible. In 1976 the Club of Rome concluded that the real issue was not whether the world economy would continue to grow, but how the benefits of growth would be distributed.

The Desirability of Growth

Let us concede, then, that continued, perhaps even "limitless" growth is *possible*. Can we also agree that it is *desirable*? Those of us who commute on congested highways, breathe foul air, and can't find a secluded camping site may raise a loud chorus of no's. But before reaching a conclusion let us at least determine what it is people don't like about the prospect of continued growth. Is it really economic growth per se that people object to, or instead the specific ways GNP has grown in the past? To state the question this way may provoke a few second thoughts.

First of all, let us distinguish very clearly between economic growth and population growth. Congested neighborhoods, dining halls, and highways are the consequence of too many people, not of too many goods and services.

[7]Robert M. Solow, "Is the End of the World at Hand?" *Challenge*, March 1973, p. 50.
[8]Cited by John Maddox in *The Doomsday Syndrome* (New York: McGraw-Hill, 1972), pp. 40 and 45.

Indeed, if we had *more* goods and services—if we had more houses and transit systems—much of the population congestion we now experience might be relieved. Maybe if we had enough resources to meet our existing demands *and* to build a solar-generated "new town" in the middle of Montana, people might move out of the crowded neighborhoods of Chicago and St. Louis. Well, probably not, but at least one thing is certain: with fewer goods and services, more people will have to share any given quantity of output.

Which brings us back to the really essential measure of growth, GNP per capita. Are there any serious grounds for desiring less GNP per capita, a reduced standard of living? And don't say yes just because you think we already have too many cars on our roads or calories in our bellies. That argument refers to the *mix* of output again and does not answer the question of whether or not we want *any* more goods or services per person. As noted in Chapter 4, increasing GNP per capita can take a million forms, including the educational services you are now consuming. The rejection of economic growth per se implies that none of those forms is desirable.

We could, of course, acquire more of the goods and services we consider beneficial simply by cutting back on the production of the things we consider unnecessary. But who is to say which mix of output is "best," and how are we going to bring about the desired shift? The present mix of output may be considered bad because it is based on a maldistribution of income, deceptive advertising, or failure of the market mechanism to account for external costs. If so, it would seem more efficient (and politically more feasible) to address those problems directly rather than to attempt to lower our standard of living.

SUMMARY

- Economic growth refers to increases in real GNP. Short-run growth may result from increases in capacity utilization (e.g., less unemployment). In the long run, however, growth requires increases in capacity itself—rightward shifts of the long-run aggregate supply curve.

- GNP per capita is a basic measure of living standards. By contrast, GNP per worker gauges our productivity. Over time, increases in productivity have been the primary cause of rising living standards.

- Productivity gains can originate in a variety of ways. These sources include better labor quality, increased capital investment, research and development, improved management, and supportive government policies.

- Supply-side policies increase both the short- and long-run capacity to produce. Monetary and fiscal policies may also affect capital investment and thus the rate of economic growth.

- The productivity slowdown of the late 1970s resulted from lower investment, a shift in the composition of the labor force, increases in government taxes and regulation, and other factors. Many of these forces were reversed in the 1980s and early 1990s.

- The argument that there are identifiable and imminent limits to growth— perhaps even a cataclysmic doomsday—are founded on one of two concerns: (1) the depletion of resources and (2) pollution of the ecosystem.

• The general weakness of doomsday arguments is that they regard existing patterns of resource use or pollution as unalterable. As a consequence, they consistently underestimate the possibilities for technological advance or adaptation. Even "optimistic" projections of technological possibilities turn out to be pessimistic.

• Continued economic growth is desirable as long as it brings a higher standard of living for people and an increased ability to produce and consume socially desirable goods and services.

Terms to Remember   Define the following terms:

production possibilities	**productivity**
economic growth	**net investment**
nominal GNP	**crowding out**
real GNP	**geometric growth**
growth rate	**arithmetic growth**
GNP per capita	**substitution effect**
labor force	

Questions for Discussion

1. In what specific ways (if any) does a college education increase a worker's productivity?

2. Why don't we consume all of our current output instead of sacrificing some present consumption for investment?

3. In 1866 Stanley Jevons predicted that economic growth would come to a halt when England ran out of coal, a doomsday that he reckoned would occur in the mid-1970s. How have we managed to avert that projection?

4. Fertility rates in the United States have dropped so low that we are approaching zero population growth, a condition that France has maintained for decades. How will this affect our economic growth? Our standard of living?

5. Is limitless growth really possible? What forces do you think will be most important in slowing or halting economic growth?

Problems

1. What is the current rate of population growth in the United States? In the world? At these rates, how many years will it take for the United States and world populations to double?

2. How fast is productivity growing in the United States? In the world?

3. On the basis of problems 1 and 2, how fast is per capita output growing? How long will it be before it doubles?

4. What factors might improve the rate of productivity increase or lower the rate of population growth?

(*Note:* For information on population and productivity, you may want to consult an almanac, the *Economic Report of the President, The Statistical Abstract of the United States*, or the end covers of this book.)

CURRENT POLICIES

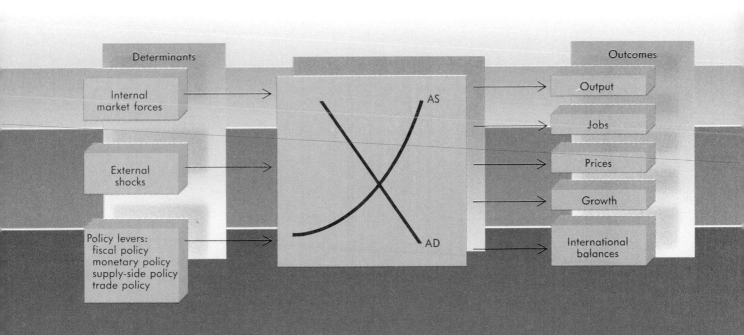

Macro theories often provide conflicting advice about whether and how to intervene. To make matters worse, the information needed to make a decision is typically incomplete. Politics muddies the waters, too, by changing priorities and restricting the use of policy levers. Finally, there is the inescapable reality that everything changes at once —there is no *ceteris paribus* in the real world.

CHAPTER 17

Theory and Reality

There is no one solution. It isn't just a question of the budget. It isn't just the question of inflationary labor rates. It isn't just the question of sticky prices. It isn't just the question of what the Government does to keep prices up or to make regulations that tend to be inflationary. It isn't just the weather or just the drought.
It is all these things. The interaction of these various factors is what is so terribly difficult for us to understand and, of course, what is so terribly difficult for us to deal with.

—Former Secretary of the Treasury W. Michael Blumenthal

*M*acroeconomic theory is supposed to explain the business cycle and show policymakers how to control it. But something is obviously wrong. As first observed in Chapter 5, we have repeatedly failed to achieve our goals of full employment, price stability, and vigorous economic growth. No matter how hard we try, the business cycle seems to persist.

What accounts for this discrepancy between economic theory and economic performance? Are our theories no good? Or is sound economic advice being ignored?

Many people blame the economists. They point to the conflicting theories and advice of Keynesians, Monetarists, and Supply-siders and wonder what theory is supposed to be followed. If economists themselves can't agree, it is asked, why should anyone else listen to them?

Not surprisingly, economists see things a bit differently. First of all, they point out, the **business cycle** isn't as bad as it used to be. Since World War II, the economy has had many ups and downs, but none has been as severe as the Great Depression or earlier catastrophes. Second, economists place most of the responsibility for continuing business-cycle problems on the real world, not on their theories. They complain that "politics" takes precedence over good economic advice. Politicians are reluctant, for example, to raise taxes, cut spending, or slow money growth in order to control inflation. Their concern is winning the next election, not solving the country's economic problems.

In his 1978 Economic Report, President Jimmy Carter pointed to another problem—the complexity of economic decision making. In the real world, neither theory nor politics can keep up with all our economic goals. As President Carter observed: "We cannot concentrate just on inflation or just on unemployment or just on deficits in the federal budget or our international payments. Nor can we act in isolation from other countries. We must deal with all of these problems simultaneously and on a worldwide basis."

business cycle: Alternating periods of economic growth and contraction.

As if the burdens of a continuously changing world were not enough, the president must also contend with sharply differing economic theories and advice, a slow and frequently hostile Congress, a massive and often unresponsive bureaucracy, and a complete lack of knowledge about the future.

The purpose of this chapter is to confront these and other frustrations of the real world. In so doing, we will try to provide answers to the following questions:

- What is the ideal "package" of macro policies?

- How well does our macro performance live up to the promises of that package?

- What kinds of obstacles prevent us from achieving all of our economic goals?

The answers to these questions may shed some light on a broader concern that has long troubled students and policymakers alike, namely, "If economists are so smart, why is the economy always in such a mess?"

POLICY LEVERS

The macroeconomic tools available to policymakers are summarized in Table 17.1. Although this list is brief, we hardly need a reminder at this point of how powerful each instrument can be. Every one of these major policy instruments can significantly alter the dimensions of the economy. Their use may not only affect inflation and unemployment rates but may also change our answers to the basic economic questions of WHAT, HOW, and FOR WHOM to produce.

Fiscal Policy

fiscal policy: The use of government taxes and spending to alter macroeconomic outcomes.

The basic tools of **fiscal policy** are taxes and the budget. Tax cuts are supposed to stimulate spending by putting more income in the hands of consumers and businesses. Tax increases are intended to curtail spending and thus reduce inflationary pressures. Some of the major tax changes implemented in recent years are summarized in Table 17.2.

The expenditure side of the federal budget provides another fiscal-policy tool. From a Keynesian perspective, increases in government spending raise aggregate demand and so encourage more production. A slowdown in gov-

TABLE 17.1   The Policy Levers

Economic policymakers have access to a variety of policy instruments. The challenge is to choose the right tools at the right time. The mix of tools required may vary from problem to problem.

Type of policy	Policy instruments
Fiscal	Tax cuts and increases
	Changes in government spending
Monetary	Open-market operations
	Reserve requirements
	Discount rates
Supply-side	Tax incentives
	Deregulation
	Skill training and other labor-market aid
	Wage and price controls
	Free trade

TABLE 17.2 Fiscal-Policy Milestones

1981	Economic Recovery Tax Act	Three-year consumer tax cut of $213 billion plus $59 billion of business tax cuts
1982	Tax Equity and Fiscal Responsibility Act	Raised business, excise, and income taxes by $100 billion over three years
1983	Social Security Act Amendments	Increased payroll taxes and cut future retirement benefits
1984	Deficit Reduction Act	Increased income, business, and excise taxes by $50 billion over three years
1985	Gramm-Rudman-Hollings Act	Required a balanced budget by 1991 and authorized automatic spending cuts to achieve it
	FY86 budget passed by Congress	First budget to include outlays of $1 trillion
1986	Tax Reform Act	Major reduction in tax rates coupled with broadening of tax base
1987	Gramm-Rudman-Hollings Reaffirmation	Postponed balanced-budget target until 1993
1989	President Bush uses sequester power of Gramm-Rudman-Hollings	Spending cuts of $5.7 billion imposed
1990	National debt surpasses $3 trillion	National debt tripled in 1980s

ernment spending is supposed to restrain aggregate demand the thus lessen any inflationary pressures that might exist. With government spending well above $1 trillion a year, changes in the federal budget could influence aggregate demand significantly.

Who makes fiscal policy?   As we first observed in Chapter 10, changes in taxes and government spending originate both in economic events and in explicit policy decisions. When the economy slows, for example, tax revenues decline, and government spending increases automatically. Likewise, when real GNP grows, tax revenues automatically rise, and government transfer payments decline. These **automatic stabilizers** are a basic countercyclical feature of the federal budget. They do not represent active fiscal policy. On the contrary, *fiscal policy refers to deliberate changes in tax or spending legislation.* These changes can be made only by the U.S. Congress. Every year the president proposes specific budget and tax changes, negotiates with Congress, then accepts or vetoes specific acts that Congress has passed. The resulting policy decisions represent "discretionary" fiscal policy. Those policy decisions expand or shrink the **structural deficit** and thus give the economy a Keynesian boost or restraint.

automatic stabilizer: Federal expenditure or revenue item that automatically responds counter-cyclically to changes in national income—e.g., unemployment benefits, income taxes.

structural deficit: Federal revenues at full employment minus expenditures at full employment under prevailing fiscal policy.

Monetary Policy

The policy arsenal described in Table 17.1 also contains monetary tools. The tools of **monetary policy** include open-market operations, discount-rate changes, and reserve requirements.

As we saw in Chapter 14, there are disagreements over how these monetary tools should be used. Keynesians believe that interest rates are the critical monetary variable. In their view, the money supply should be expanded or curtailed in order to achieve whatever interest rate is needed to attain the

monetary policy: The use of money and credit controls to influence macroeconomic activity.

proper level of aggregate demand. Monetarists, on the other hand, contend that the money supply itself is the critical variable and that it should be expanded at a steady and predictable rate. This, they believe, will ensure price stability and a **natural rate of unemployment.**

Who makes monetary policy? Actual monetary-policy decisions are made by the Federal Reserve's Board of Governors. Each year the Fed sets a broad target for money-supply growth, based on its expectations for economic growth, inflation, and the velocity of money. The Federal Open Market Committee meets every month to assess the economy and to make policy adjustments that will achieve its intended outcomes.

Table 17.3 depicts some milestones in recent monetary policy. Of particular interest is the October 1979 decision to adopt a pure monetarist approach. This involved an exclusive focus on the money supply, without regard for interest rates. After interest rates soared and the economy appeared to be on the brink of a depression, the Fed abandoned the monetarist approach and again began keeping an eye on interest rates (the Keynesian focus) as well as on the money supply.

Monetarists contend that the Fed never fully embraced their policy. The money supply grew at a very uneven pace in 1980, they argue, not at the steady, predictable rate that they demanded. Nevertheless, the policy shifts of 1979 and 1982 were distinctive and had dramatic effects.

Also of interest in Table 17.3 is the Fed's brief imposition of credit controls in 1980. After the Fed tightened the money supply, it attempted to ensure that

natural rate of unemployment: Long-term rate of unemployment determined by structural forces in labor and product markets.

TABLE 17.3 Monetary-Policy Milestones

August 1979	Paul Volcker becomes Fed chairman
October 1979	Fed adopts monetarist approach, focusing exclusively on money supply; interest rates soar
March 1980	Fed imposes direct credit controls
July 1982	Deep into recession, Fed votes to ease monetary restraint
October 1982	Volcker abandons pure monetarist approach and expands money supply rapidly
May 1983	Fed reverses policy and begins slowing money-supply growth
June 1983	Reagan reappoints Volcker
January–November 1984	Reagan administration and Fed criticize each other's policies: Fed criticized for being too tight; Reagan criticized for being too stimulative
January–May 1985	Fed relaxes money-supply grip with cuts in discount rate and more open-market purchases
1986	Money supply increases by 15 percent; velocity declines
May 1987	Volcker abandons money-supply targets as policy guides
June 1987	Volcker resigns; replaced by Alan Greenspan
September–December 1987	Money-supply growth decreases; discount rate increased
1989	Greenspan announces goal of "zero inflation"
1990	Greenspan defends Fed's cautious policy against administration's demands for faster money-supply growth

the available money would be allocated to the "right" uses, particularly business investment. It tried to ensure this outcome by restricting consumer credit. The credit controls restrained borrowing so much, however, that they further threatened the economy. The controls were lifted a few months later.

The Fed permitted the money supply to grow by 15 percent in 1986. In defending this unprecedented increase in the money supply, the Fed pointed to declining velocity. Deregulation of the banking system, the availability of interest-bearing checking accounts, and a low inflation rate all encouraged people to hold larger money balances.

In 1987 the Fed discarded M1 as a reliable policy target, arguing that changing banking practices (deregulation) had made it too volatile. Shortly thereafter Alan Greenspan replaced Paul Volcker as chairman of the Fed and began to reduce money-supply growth. Greenspan vowed to keep a tight rein on money-supply growth in order to eliminate inflation. He also hoped that his public commitment to "zero inflation" (see In the News) would reduce inflationary expectations.

Supply-Side Policy

supply-side policy: The use of tax rates, (de)regulation, and other mechanisms to increase the ability and willingness to produce goods and services.

Supply-side theory offers the third major set of policy tools. The focus of **supply-side policy** is to provide incentives to work, invest, and produce. Of particular concern are high tax rates and regulations that reduce supply incentives. Supply-siders argue that marginal tax rates and government regulation must be reduced in order to get more output without added inflation.

In the 1980s tax rates were reduced dramatically. The maximum marginal tax rate on individuals was cut from 70 percent to 50 percent in 1981, and then still further, to 28 percent, in 1987. The 1980s also witnessed major milestones in the deregulation of airlines, trucking, telephone service, and other industries (see Table 17.4).

In The News

MONETARY POLICY

Fed Chief Supports Zero-Inflation Resolution

Federal Reserve Chairman Alan Greenspan yesterday endorsed a congressional resolution calling for eliminating inflation within five years, but he turned thumbs down on every part of a bill that would give the executive branch greater opportunities to influence monetary policy decisions.

Greenspan said a formal target for ending inflation might make it easier to achieve by lowering the public's expectations about what future inflation levels will be.

He cautioned, however, that there would be "costs" in getting from today's inflation rate, which he put at about 4.5 percent, to a rate low enough that people would no longer bother to take it into account in making private economic decisions—the resolution's definition of zero inflation.

"During this transition period, growth could be reduced for a while from what it otherwise would have been," the Fed chairman told the House subcommittee on domestic monetary policy.

Greenspan agreed, however, with subcommittee Chairman Rep. Stephen L. Neal (D-N.C.), sponsor of the resolution, that price stability ought to be the Fed's goal.

"In the longer run," Greenspan said, "whatever losses are incurred in the pursuit of price stability would surely be more than made up in increased output thereafter."

—John M. Berry

The Washington Post, October 26, 1989, p. E3. Copyright © 1989 The Washington Post.

TABLE 17.4   Supply-Side Milestones

1978	Airline Deregulation Act	Phased out federal regulations of airline routes, fares, and entry
1980	Motor Carrier Act	Eliminated federal restrictions on entry, routes, and fares in the trucking industry
1981	Economic Recovery Tax Act	Decreased marginal tax rates by 30 percent
1982	AT&T breakup	AT&T monopoly on local phone service ended via antitrust action
1986	Tax Reform Act	Eliminated most tax preferences for investment and saving, but sharply reduced marginal tax rates
1989	Fair Labor Standards Act amended	Congress increases minimum wage to $3.80 in 1990 and $4.25 in 1991
1990	Social Security Act amendments implemented	Payroll tax increased to 7.65 percent

Who makes supply-side policy?   Because tax rates are a basic tool of supply-side policy, fiscal and supply-side policies are often intertwined. When Congress changes the tax laws, it almost always alters marginal tax rates and thus changes production incentives. Notice, for example, that tax legislation appears in Table 17.4 as well as in Table 17.2. The Tax Reform Act of 1986 not only changed total tax revenues (fiscal policy) but also restructured production and investment incentives (supply-side policy). Congress also has broad authority over regulatory policies, although the president and his executive agencies make day-to-day decisions on how to interpret and enforce these policies.

IDEALIZED USES

These fiscal, monetary, and supply-side tools are potentially powerful levers for controlling the economy. In principle, they can cure the excesses of the business cycle. To see how, let us review their use in three distinct macroeconomic settings.

Case 1: Depression or Serious Recession

recessionary gap: The amount by which desired spending at full employment falls short of full-employment output.

multiplier: The multiple by which an initial change in aggregate spending will alter total expenditure after an infinite number of spending cycles; $1/(1 - MPC)$.

When output and employment levels fall far short of the economy's full-employment potential, the mandate for public policy is clear. Total spending must be increased so that producers can sell more goods, hire more workers, and move the economy toward its productive capacity. At such times the most urgent need is to put people to work, and relatively little concern is expressed for other, possibly conflicting economic goals.

How should people be put to work? Pure Keynesians emphasize the need to stimulate aggregate spending. They seek to close the **recessionary gap** by cutting taxes or boosting government spending. The resulting stimulus will set off a **multiplier** reaction, propelling the economy to full employment.

Modern Keynesians acknowledge that monetary policy might also help. Specifically, increases in the money supply may lower interest rates and thus give investment spending a further boost. All of these actions can be taken simultaneously. To give the economy a really powerful stimulus, we might want to cut taxes, increase government spending, and expand the money supply all at the same time. By taking such convincing action, we might also increase consumer confidence, raise investor expectations, and induce still greater spending and output.

Monetarists would proceed differently. To begin with, they would see no point in toying with the federal budget. In the pure monetarist model, changes in taxes or government spending alter the mix of output, but not its level. So long as the **velocity of money (V)** is constant, fiscal policy doesn't matter. In this view, the appropriate policy response to a recession is patience. As sales and output slow, interest rates will decline, and new investment will be stimulated.

Supply-siders would emphasize the need to improve production incentives. They would urge cuts in marginal tax rates on investment and labor. They would also look for ways to reduce government regulation.

Whatever actions are taken to push the economy out of a slump can also help to fulfill other economic goals. If we want our full-employment economy to reflect an improved distribution of income or a different mix of output, we can push fiscal, monetary, and supply-side levers more selectively. Recall also the choice we face between stimulating the private sector and expanding public employment and output. The policy choices are never easy, but they must be made.

velocity of money (V): The number of times per year, on average, that a dollar is used to purchase final goods and services; $PQ \div M$.

Case 2: Excessive Demand and Inflation

An overheated economy provides as clear a policy mandate as does a sluggish one. In this case, the task of policy is to restrain aggregate spending until the rate of total expenditure is compatible with the productive capacity of the economy. This entails shifting the aggregate demand curve to the left. Keynesians would do this by raising taxes and cutting government spending. Their objective would be to close the **inflationary gap,** again relying on the multiplier to cool down the economy. Keynesians would also see the desirability of reducing the growth of the money supply so as to raise interest rates and curb investment spending.

inflationary gap: The amount by which desired spending at full employment exceeds full employment output.

Monetarists would simply cut the money supply. In their view, the short-run aggregate supply curve is unknown and unstable. The only predictable response is reflected in the vertical, long-run aggregate supply curve. According to this view, changes in the money supply alter prices, not output. Therefore, inflation must reflect excessive money-supply growth or the anticipation of such growth. The role of public policy, Monetarists would assert, is not only to reduce money supply growth but to convince market participants that a more cautious monetary policy will be continued. This was the intent of Chairman Greenspan's public commitment to zero inflation (see preceding In the News).

Supply-siders would point out that inflation implies both "too much money" and "not enough goods." They would look at the supply side of the market for ways to expand productive capacity. In a highly inflationary setting, they would propose more incentives to save. The additional savings would automatically reduce consumption while creating a larger pool of investable funds. Supply-siders would also cut taxes and regulations that raise production costs, and lower import barriers that keep out cheaper foreign goods. Finally, some Supply-siders might propose wage–price controls to diminish inflationary expectations while giving other macro policies time to work.

Copyright © 1986 The Philadelphia Inquirer.

When cooling the economy, the government also influences other dimensions of our economic well-being. Cutbacks in government spending shrink the size of the public sector, whereas tax increases tend to have the opposite effect: either action will cut aggregate demand. Likewise, the government may choose to raise everyone's taxes equally, thus maintaining the current distribution of income. Or it might choose to increase taxes on the rich only, making the distribution of income more equal. Here again, the essential message is that *any* action taken to alter the rate of total spending will influence other economic outcomes as well.

Case 3: Stagflation

Although serious inflations and depressions provide clear mandates for economic policy, simultaneous inflation and unemployment complicate policy decisions. If aggregate demand were stimulated to reduce unemployment, the resultant pressure on prices might fuel the existing inflation. And if fiscal and monetary restraints were used to reduce inflationary pressures, unemployment might worsen. In such a situation—the most familiar one for modern economies—there are no simple solutions. More often than not, a variety of forces created stagflation, and policy actions to combat it have to be equally complex.

If prices are rising before full employment is reached, there is likely to be some degree of structural unemployment. Prices may be rising in the telecommunications industry, for example, while unemployed workers are abundant in the housing industry. The higher prices and wages in telecommunications function as a signal to transfer resources from the housing industry into telecommunications. Such resource shifts, however, may not occur smoothly or quickly. In the interim, public policy can be developed to alter the structure of supply or demand.

On the demand side, the government could decrease the demand for telecommunications by increasing excise taxes on phone and other transmission services, buying fewer terminals for government use, or raising installment-loan interest rates. It could increase the demand for houses by providing housing subsidies to poor people, greater home-related tax deductions for everyone, or lower interest rates in the mortgage market. On the supply side, the government could offer tax credits for housing construction, teach construction workers how to install and operate telecommunications equipment, or speed up the job-search process.

High tax rates or costly regulations might also contribute to stagflation. If either of these constraints exists, high prices (inflation) may not be a sufficient incentive for increased output. In this case, reductions in tax rates and regulation might help reduce both unemployment and inflation. This is the basic goal of supply-side policies.

Finally, we have noted that stagflation may be aggravated by noncompetitive market structures. As we saw in Chapter 15, powerful corporations may respond to increasing product demand with higher prices, even if they have excess production capacity. In competitive markets, output would increase faster and prices more slowly in response to an expansion of demand that occurred at a time of significant unemployment and excess capacity. The same is true in labor markets; the less competitive they are, the more wages will rise as demand expands. Accordingly, the simultaneous reduction of both unemployment and inflation in an economy with concentrations of market power may require more than conventional fiscal, monetary, and supply-side policies.

Stagflation may also arise from a temporary contraction of aggregate supply that both reduces output and drives up prices. In this case, neither structural unemployment nor excessive demand is the culprit. Rather, an "external shock" (such as a natural disaster) or an abrupt change in world trade (such as an oil embargo) is likely to be the cause of the policy dilemma. Accordingly, none of our familiar policy tools is likely to provide a complete "cure." In most cases the economy simply has to adjust to a temporary setback. In the short run, economic policy must educate the public about the nature of the sudden dislocation and thereby restrain unfounded inflationary fears. In the long run, policymakers may also try to avoid a repetition of the events that caused the dislocation, thus reducing the chances of future stagflation.

Fine-Tuning

The apparently inexhaustible potential of public policy to alter the economy's performance has often generated optimistic expectations about the efficacy of fiscal, monetary, and supply-side tools. In the early 1960s such optimism pervaded even the highest levels of government. People frequently spoke of the ability of economic policy not only to solve major economic problems, but also to fulfill a broad spectrum of lesser objectives. Those were the days when prices were relatively stable, unemployment rates were falling, the economy was growing rapidly, and preparations were being made for man's first trip into space. The potential of economic policy looked great indeed. It was also during the 1960s that a lot of people (mostly economists) spoke of the potential for **fine-tuning,** or altering economic outcomes to fit very exacting specifications. Flexible responses to changing market conditions, it was argued, could ensure fulfillment of our economic goals. As far as stabilization was concerned, the prescription was simple. When unemployment is the problem, simply give the economy a jolt of fiscal or monetary stimulus; when inflation is worrisome, simply apply the fiscal or monetary brakes. To fulfill our goals for content and distribution, we simply pick the right target for stimulus or restraint. With a little attention and experience, the right speed could be found and the economy guided successfully down the road to prosperity.

fine-tuning: Adjustments in economic policy designed to counteract small changes in economic outcomes; continuous responses to changing economic conditions.

THE ECONOMIC RECORD

In view of the much-heralded potential of economic policy to fulfull our goals, the actual record is disappointing. To be sure, the economy has continued to grow and we have attained an impressive standard of living. We cannot lose sight of the fact that our per capita income greatly exceeds the realities and even the expectations in most other countries of the world. Nevertheless, we must also recognize that our economic history is punctuated by periods of recession, high unemployment, inflation, and recurring concern for the distribution of income and mix of output. We have witnessed a significant gap between the potential and the reality of economic policy.

The graphs in Figure 17.1 provide a quick summary of our experiences since 1946, the year the Employment Act committed the federal govenment

FIGURE 17.1
The Economic Record

The Full Employment and Balanced Growth Act of 1978 established specific goals for unemployment (4 percent), inflation (3 percent), and economic growth (4 percent). We have rarely attained those goals, however, as these graphs illustrate. Measurement, design, and policy implementation problems help explain these shortcomings.

Source: Economic Report of the President, 1990.

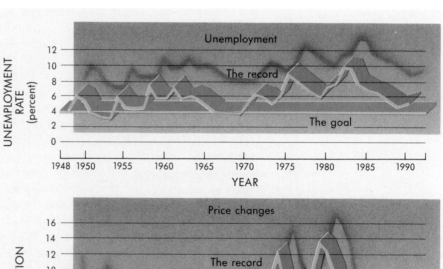

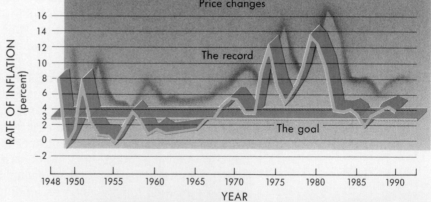

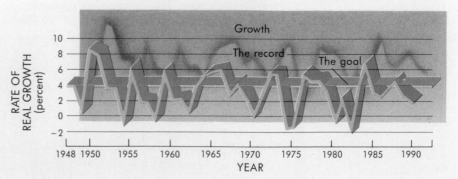

to macro stability. It is evident that we have not successfully fulfilled our major economic goals during this period. In the 1970s we rarely came close. Although we approached our inflation and growth goals in the 1980s, our economic performance was far from perfect. Two recessions sent unemployment to post–World War II heights in the early 1980s. Then inflation accelerated at the end of the 1980s, despite the fact that we were still a long way from the avowed goal of 4 percent unemployment.

growth recession: A period during which real GNP grows, but at a rate below the long-term trend of 3 percent.

In terms of real economic growth, the record is equally spotty. Output actually declined (i.e., recessions) in eight years and grew less than 3 percent (i.e., **growth recessions**) in another thirteen. The 1990s got underway with virtually zero growth as the seven-year expansion of the 1980s petered out. Moreover, the distribution of income in 1990 looked virtually identical to that of 1946, and nearly 30 million people were still officially counted as poor in the later year. Accordingly, we must acknowledge that the potential of economic policy to fulfill our goals has not yet been fully realized.

The economic performance of the United States is similar to that of other Western nations. The economies of most countries did not grow as fast as the U.S. economy in the 1980s. But, as the accompanying World View shows, some countries did a better job of restraining prices or reducing unemployment.

When one looks at the specific policy initiatives of various administrations, the gap between theory and practice looks even larger. The decision of the Federal Reserve System to reduce the money supply on repeated occasions during the Great Depression was colossally perverse. Only slightly less so was the Fed's decision to expand the money supply rapidly in 1978, despite evidence that inflationary pressures were already building up. In 1980–81 the Fed slowed money-supply growth much more and far longer than was justified. As a consequence, the economy suffered two consecutive recessions (in 1980 and 1981–82).

W RLD VIEW

COMPARATIVE PERFORMANCE

Macro Performance in the 1980s

The performance of the U.S. economy in the 1980s was similar to that of other developed economies. Germany had the greatest success in restraining inflation (2.6 per-cent), but suffered from very slow growth. The Japanese economy grew rapidly (3.7 percent) and kept unemployment low (2.5 percent), but had a relatively high rate of inflation (6.1 percent). The U.S. inflation rate was less (4.6 percent), but growth (2.9 percent) and unemployment (7.2 percent) performance was above average.

Performance (annual average percentage)	U.S.	Japan	Germany	United Kingdom	France	Italy	Canada
Real growth	2.9	3.7	1.1	2.1	0.8	1.2	3.3
Inflation	4.6	6.1	2.6	6.2	6.5	10.1	6.1
Unemployment	7.2	2.5	6.1	9.9	9.3	6.5	9.3

Source: *Economic Report of the President*, 1990.

On the fiscal side of the ledger, we must note President Roosevelt's timid efforts to expand aggregate demand during the Great Depression. Also worth remembering is President Johnson's refusal to "pay" for the Vietnam War by either raising taxes or cutting nonmilitary expenditures. The resulting strain on the economy's capacity kindled inflationary pressures that lasted for years. For his part, President Carter increased labor costs (higher payroll taxes and minimum wages), farm prices, and government spending at a time when inflation was a foremost policy concern, President Reagan made his share of mistakes, too, including the pursuit of deep budget cuts in the early stages of a recession.

WHY THINGS DON'T ALWAYS WORK

We have already noted the readiness of economists and politicians to blame each other for the continuing gap between our economic goals and performance. Rather than taking sides, however, we may note some general constraints on successful policy making. In this regard, we can distinguish *four obstacles to policy success*:

- *Goal conflicts*
- *Measurement problems*
- *Design problems*
- *Implementation problems*

Goal Conflicts   The first factor to take note of is potential conflicts in policy priorities. Suppose for the moment that the economy was suffering from stagflation and, further, that all macro policies involved some tradeoff between unemployment and inflation. Should we try to cure inflation, unemployment, or just a bit of both? Answers are likely to vary. Unemployed people will put the highest priority on attaining full employment. Bankers, creditors, and people on fixed incomes will demand an end to inflation. There is no "right" solution to this goal conflict. As a result, we cannot completely succeed.

In practice, these goal conflicts are often institutionalized in the decision-making process. The Fed is traditionally viewed as the guardian of price stability and so tends to place the highest priority on fighting inflation. The president and Congress worry more about people's jobs and government programs, so they are less willing to raise taxes or cut spending. Thus a basic policy conflict is likely to arise.

Distributional goals may also conflict with macro objectives. Anti-inflationary policies may require cutbacks in programs for the poor, the elderly, or needy students. These cutbacks may be politically impossible. Likewise, tight-money policies may be viewed as too great a burden for small businesses. In either case, policy decisions will be constrained by basic goal conflicts.

Although the policy levers listed in Table 17.1 are powerful, they cannot grant all our wishes. Since we still live in a world of scarce resources, *all policy decisions entail opportunity costs.* This means that we will always be confronted with tradeoffs; the best we can hope for is a set of compromises that yields optimal outcomes, not ideal ones. This means getting as much collective satisfaction as possible from our available resources. It also means that we're always likely to fall a little shorter of one goal or another.

Even if we all agreed on policy priorities, success would not be assured. We would still have to confront the more mundane problems of measurement, design, and implementation.

Measurement Problems

The measurement problems that plague economic policy have little to do with economic theory. Although our theoretical perspectives are by no means complete, they are adequately developed to deal with most economic situations. As long as we can diagnose the major dimensions of a problem, economic theory is equipped to provide a fairly reliable set of policy guidelines.

A good many of our problems arise in the diagnosis stage, however. One reason fire fighters are pretty successful in putting out fires before whole cities burn down is that fires are highly visible phenomena. Such visibility is not characteristic of economic problems, at least not in their more moderate manifestations. An increase in the unemployment rate from 5 to 6 percent, for example, is not the kind of thing you notice while crossing the street. Unless you work in the unemployment-insurance office or lose your own job, the increase in unemployment is not likely to attract your attention. The same is true of prices; small increases in product prices are unlikely to ring many alarms. Hence both inflation and unemployment may worsen considerably before anyone takes serious notice. Were we as slow and ill equipped to notice fires, whole neighborhoods would burn before someone rang the alarm.

Measurement problems are a very basic policy constraint. To formulate appropriate economic policy, we must first determine the nature of our problems. To do so we must measure employment changes, output changes, price changes, and other macro outcomes. The old adage that governments are willing and able to solve only those problems they can measure is relevant here. Indeed, before the Great Depression, one of the fundamental barriers to public policy was the lack of statistics on what was happening in the economy. One of the lasting benefits of that experience is that we now try to keep informed on changing economic conditions.

The massive data collections we now maintain—in the Bureau of Labor Statistics, the Census Bureau, the National Center for Social Statistics, the Federal Reserve Board, and elsewhere—have substantially improved the basis for policy formulation. The information at hand, however, is always dated and incomplete. ***At best, we know what was happening in the economy last month or last week.*** The processes of data collection, assembly, and presentation take time, even in this age of high-speed computers. The average recession lasts about eleven months, but official data generally do not even confirm the existence of a recession until eight months after a downturn starts! In the absence of more timely information, policy prescriptions are by necessity based on yesterday's perceptions. Even those perceptions may be faulty, since yesterday's data are often revised later.

Forecasts   In an ideal world, policymakers would not only respond to economic problems that occur but also anticipate their occurrence and act to avoid them. If we foresee an inflationary gap emerging, for example, we want to take immediate action to keep aggregate spending from increasing. That is to say, the successful fire fighter not only responds to fires but also looks for hazards that might start one.

Unfortunately, economic policymakers are again at a disadvantage. Their knowledge of future problems is even worse than their knowledge of current problems. *In designing policy, policymakers must depend on economic forecasts*, that is, informed guesses about what the economy will look like in future periods.

Macro models   Those guesses are often based on complex computer models of how the economy works. These models—referred to as *econometric macro models*—are mathematical summaries of the economy's performance. The models try to identify the key determinants of macro performance then show what happens to macro outcomes when they change.

An economist "feeds" the computer two essential inputs. One is a model of how the economy allegedly works. Such models are quantitative summaries of one or more macro theories. A Keynesian model, for example, will include equations that show multiplier spending responses to tax cuts. A Monetarist model will show that tax cuts raise interest rates ("crowding out"), not total spending: And a Supply-side model stipulates labor-supply and production responses. The computer can't tell which theory is right; it just predicts what it is programmed to see. In other words, the computer sees the world through the eyes of its economic master.

The second essential input in a computer forecast is the assumed values for critical economic variables. A Keynesian model, for example, must specify how large a multiplier to expect. All the computer does is carry out the required mathematical routines, once it is told that the multiplier is relevant and what its value is. It cannot discern the true multiplier any better than it can pick the right theory.

Given the dependence of computers on the theories and perceptions of their economic masters, it is not surprising that computer forecasts often differ greatly. It's also not surprising that they are often wrong. To generate an accurate forecast, the computer's economic masters must not only hold the right theories of how the world works but also be able to foresee changes in all the critical variables that drive the model. Despite frequent claims to the contrary, few economists possess such clairvoyance.

Leading indicators   Given the complexity of macro models, many people prefer to use simpler tools for divining the future. One of the most popular is the Index of Leading Economic Indicators. The Leading Indicators are things we can observe today that are frequently related to future events. One of the eleven leading indicators, for example, is orders for new equipment. Those orders should trigger future production. Hence today's orders are said to presage tomorrow's output.

Unfortunately, equipment orders and the other leading indicators (see Table 17.5) are not wholly reliable forecasting tools, either. Equipment orders might be canceled, for example. Or producers might be unwilling or unable to fill those orders quickly. In either event, today's orders would *not* result in tomorrow's output.

Crystal balls   In view of the fragile foundations and spotty record of computer and index-based forecasts, many people shun them altogether, preferring to use their own "crystal balls." In a Gallup survey of corporate chief executives, most respondents said economists' forecasts had litle or no influence on company plans or policies. The head of one large company said, "I go out of my way to ignore them." The general public apparently shares this

---

TABLE 17.5   The Leading Economic Indicators

Everyone wants a crystal ball to foresee future economic events. In reality, forecasters must reckon with very crude predictors of the future. One of the most widely used predictors is the Index of Leading Economic Indicators compiled by the U.S. Department of Commerce. This index includes eleven factors that are believed to predict economic activity three to six months in advance. Changes in the leading indicators are therefore used to forecast changes in GNP.

The leading indicators rarely move in the same direction at the same time. They are weighted together to create the index. Up-and-down movements of the index are reported each month.

Indicator	Expected impact
1. Average workweek	Hours worked per week typically increase when greater output and sales are expected.
2. Unemployment claims	Initial claims for unemployment benefits reflect changes in industry layoffs.
3. Delivery times	The longer it takes to deliver ordered goods, the greater the ratio of demand to supply.
4. Credit	Changes in business and consumer borrowing indicate potential purchasing power.
5. Materials prices	When producers step up production they buy more raw materials, pushing their prices higher.
6. Equipment orders	Orders for new equipment imply increased production capacity and higher anticipated sales.
7. Stock prices	Higher stock prices reflect expectations of greater sales and profits.
8. Money supply	Faster growth of the money supply implies a pickup in aggregate demand.
9. New orders	New orders for consumer goods trigger increases in production and employment.
10. Building permits	A permit represents the first step in housing construction.
11. Inventories	Companies build up inventory when they anticipate higher sales.

---

view, giving higher marks to the forecasts of sportswriters and weathermen than to those of economists (see In the News). Donald Regan, secretary of the Treasury and later President Reagan's chief of White House staff, echoed these feelings in testimony to the U.S. Congress. Regan blasted "the obsession that people have with economic forecasts in spite of their consistent failure." These failed forecasts, he noted, have contributed greatly to failed economic policies.

In The News

CREDIBILITY

How They Rate

A survey by R. H. Bruskin Associates, New Brunswick, N.J., finds adults give high grades for accuracy in forecasts to sportswriters, sports announcers and weather-men. Who get low marks? Economists, stockbrokers and people who prepare horoscopes.

Economic forecasters defend themselves in two ways. First, they note that economic-policy decisions are inevitably based on anticipated changes in the economy's performance. The decision to stimulate or restrain the economy cannot be made by a flip of a coin; *someone* must try to foresee the future course of the economy. Second, forecasters claim that their quantitative approach is the only honest one. Because forecasting models require specific behavioral assumptions and estimates, they force people to spell out their versions of the future. Less rigorous ("gut feeling") approaches are too ambiguous and often inconsistent.

These are valid arguments. Still, one must be careful to distinguish the precision of a computer from the inevitable uncertainties of their spoon-fed models. The basic law of the computer is GIGO: garbage in, garbage out. If the underlying models and assumptions are no good, the computer's forecasts won't be any better.

Policy and forecasts   The task of forecasting the economic future is made still more complex by today's policy options. As we observed in previous chapters, policy decisions affect the course of economic events. Accordingly, forecasts of the future are dependent on current policy decisions, and vice versa. Figure 17.2 illustrates this mutual dependence. First a forecast is made, based on current economic conditions, likely disturbances to the economy, and anticipated economic policy. These forecasts are then used to project likely budget deficits and other policy variables. Congress and the president react to these forecasts and projections by revising fiscal, monetary, or supply-side policies. These changes, in turn, alter the basis for the initial forecasts.

In The News

POLITICAL FORECASTING

Wishful Thinking? The Rosy Forecasts of CBO and OMB

Congress and the president need forecasts of future GNP and future budget deficits to make informed decisions on fiscal policy. Those forecasts are prepared by the Office of Management and Budget (OMB) for the president and by the Congressional Budget Office (CBO) for the Congress.

Like private forecasters, the CBO and OMB have dismal track records in divining the future. The accompanying table shows by how far OMB and CBO missed the mark on forecasts of GNP growth and the federal budget deficit for the period 1977–89. On average, they erred by 1.2 percentage points for annual growth—an error margin of 40 percent. They also erred by $29–30 billion on annual deficit projections.

CBO and OMB errors do not appear to be random. On the contrary, both offices tend to overstate economic growth and underestimate budget deficits about 75 percent of the time. These rosy outlooks are always welcomed by the president and Congress, since they make budget decisions appear easier. Wishful thinking, in other words, may be part of the job.

Economic growth forecasts 1977–89			Budget deficit forecasts 1977–89		
Average error	Frequency of underestimates	Frequency of overestimates	Average error	Frequency of underestimates	Frequency of overestimates
CBO 1.16%	28%	72%	$29 billion	67%	33%
OMB 1.19%	28%	72%	$40 billion	80%	20%

**FIGURE 17.2
The Mutual Dependence
of Forecasts and Policy**

Because tax revenues
and government spending
are sensitive to economic
conditions, budget projections
must rely on economic
forecasts. The budget
projections may alter policy
decisions, however, and so
change the basis for the
initial forecasts. This
interdependence between
macro forecasts, budget
projections, and policy
decisions is virtually
inevitable.

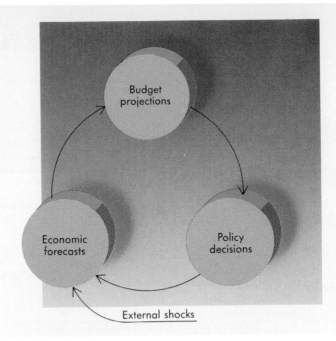

This interdependence among forecasts, budget projections, and policy decisions was superbly illustrated in the early months of President Reagan's first term. One of the principal themes of Ronald Reagan's 1980 election campaign was the need to balance the federal budget. When he took office, his plan for balancing the budget included big cuts in both taxes and government spending. Congress resisted this approach, however, for fear that the tax cuts would greatly increase the federal budget deficit and aggravate inflation. The Congressional Budget Office and others foresaw a strong economy in 1981 and urged Congress to reject massive tax cuts.

By the time Congress finally approved a scaled-down tax cut and the spending cuts, the economy had actually entered a recession. No one knew it, though. Indeed, President Reagan was still demanding further spending cuts in November 1981. Only a few weeks later the president and Congress belatedly realized that the country was in a deep recession. They then began talking about the need to postpone further spending cuts and accelerate planned tax reductions.

The saga of the 1981 budget debate illustrates two major points about fine-tuning. First, it may be possible to fine-tune an economy if we know what problems exist and how serious they are likely to become. Second, it reminds us that we seldom have such good information. Thus, we are likely to fail as often as we succeed. Moreover, our fine-tuning mistakes are not always so easily remedied. The "mistakes" of 1981 turned out to be well timed. But what if the economy had overheated? Could the president have gone on TV and asked people not to spend their tax cuts? Could he have quickly raised taxes again, as some of his advisers actually suggested?

Design Problems   Once the existence of a problem is clearly established, the designed of policy initiatives can proceed. We still confront significant obstacles, however. What action should we take? Which theory of macro behavior should guide us? How will the marketplace respond to any specific action we take?

In The News

FORECASTING

Who Was Right?

Successful policy design depends on accurate forecasts of future economic performance. But forecasts vary widely—and all of them, may be wrong. Notice in particular the different forecasts of the president, Congress, and the Federal Reserve, each of whom formulates economic policy. Did anyone forecast 1990 performance correctly?

Economic Forecasts for 1990

	Real growth in GNP (percent)	Inflation rate (percent)	Average unemployment (percent)
Private forecasts			
U.S. Chamber of Commerce	5.2	3.3	6.6
Data Resources, Inc.	1.8	4.3	5.6
University of Michigan	3.1	4.3	5.5
Georgia State University	2.0	4.7	5.5
University of California, L.A.	2.0	3.6	5.7
A. Gary Shilling	−3.2	2.5	8.8
Public forecasts			
Bush administration	2.6	4.1	5.4
Congressional Budget Office	1.8	4.1	5.6
Federal Reserve Board	1.8	4.2	5.6
The actual record	?	?	?

Source: Forecasts published in late 1989 or January/February 1990: Federal Reserve forecast is midpoint of Federal Open Market Committee projections.

Suppose, for example, that we adopt a Keynesian approach to ending a recession. Specifically, we cut income taxes to stimulate consumer spending, with the hope of closing a recessionary gap. How do we know that consumers will respond as anticipated? Perhaps the marginal propensity to consume has changed. Or the velocity of money may have slowed. Maybe the level of consumer confidence has dropped. Any of these changes could frustrate even the best-intentioned policy. The successful policymaker needs a very good crystal ball—one that will also foretell how market participants are going to respond to any specific actions taken.

Implementation Problems   Measurement and design problems can break the spirit of even the best policymaker (or his economic advisers). Yet measurement and design problems are only part of the story. A good idea is of little value unless someone puts it to use. Accordingly, to understand why things often go wrong, we must also consider the difficulties of implementing a well-designed (and credible) policy initiative.

Congressional deliberations   Suppose that the president and his Council of Economic Advisers (perhaps in conjunction with the secretary of the Treasury and the director of the Office of Management and Budget) decide that the rate of aggregate spending is slowing down. A tax cut, they believe, is necessary to stimulate demand for goods and services. Can they simply go ahead and cut tax rates? No, because all tax changes must be legislated by Congress. Once the president decides on the appropriate policy initiative, he must ask Congress for authority to take the required action. This means a delay in implementing policy, and possibly no policy at all.

At the very least, the president must convince Congress of the accuracy of his own perspectives and the appropriateness of his suggested action. The tax proposal must work its way through separate committees of both the House of Representatives and the Senate, get on the congressional calendar, and be approved in each chamber. If there are important differences in Senate and House versions of the tax-cut legislation, they must be compromised in a joint conference. The modified proposal must then be returned to each chamber for approval.

The same kind of process applies to the outlay size of the budget. Once the president has submitted his budget proposals (in January), Congress reviews them, then sets its own spending goals. After that, the budget is broken into thirteen different categories, and a separate appropriations bill is written for each one. These bills spell out in detail how much can be spent and for what purposes. Once Congress passes them, they go to the president for acceptance or veto.

In theory, all of these budget deliberations are to be completed in nine months. The Gramm-Rudman-Hollings Act of 1985 requires Congress to finish the process by October 1 (the beginning of the federal fiscal year) and to keep the budget within the deficit limits of that act. In fact, however, Congress never completes the budget process in time. In 1988 and 1989 Congress didn't pass any of the required appropriations bills on time. Instead, Congress used a so-called Omnibus Budget Reconciliation Act to get spending authority. The FY 1990 budget legislation was nearly 1,000 pages long and passed in the wee hours of the morning on the day before Thanksgiving. By then, one-sixth of the fiscal year was already over. Worse still, the massive size of the bill, together with the rush to pass it, virtually ensured that no one knew how the $700 billion included in the act was actually being spent.

This description of congressional activity is not an outline for a civics course; rather, it is an important explanation of why economic policy is not fully effective. ***Even if the right policy is formulated to solve an emerging economic problem, there is no assurance that it will be implemented. And if it is implemented, there is no assurance that it will take effect at the right time***. One of the most frightening prospects for economic policy is that a policy design intended to serve a specific problem will be implemented much later, when economic conditions have changed. The policy's effect on the economy may then be the opposite of what was intended.

Figure 17.3 is a schematic view of why things don't always work out as well as economic theory suggests they might. There are always delays between the time a problem emerges and the time it is recognized. There are additional delays between recognition and response design, between design and implementation, and finally between implementation and impact. Not only may mistakes be made at each juncture, but even correct decisions may be overcome by changing economic conditions.

We can illustrate the processes of Figure 17.3 by considering how the income surtax of 1968 came about. The expansion of the Vietnam War in July

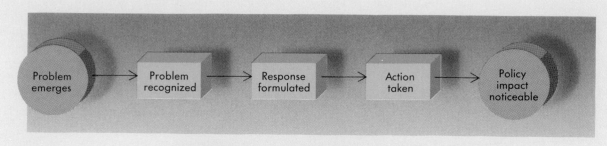

FIGURE 17.3 Policy Response: A Series of Time Lags

Even the best-intentioned economic policy can be frustrated by time lags. It takes time for a problem to be recognized, time to formulate a policy response, and still more time to implement that policy. By the time the policy begins to affect the economy, the underlying problem may have changed.

1965 added something like $15 billion to aggregate demand.[1] At that time the economy was already buoyant, and the unemployment rate was moving down to 4 percent. To offset resulting inflationary pressures, the president and Congress took limited fiscal action, including the restoration of excise taxes on cars and telephones. Much stronger action was necessary, however, if the higher rate of Vietnam spending was to be maintained. But President Lyndon Johnson insisted that the escalation of the war was temporary and that hostilities would soon end. From his perspective, the imposition of stronger fiscal restraints was tantamount to an admission that the war would not be won quickly. Only after the expanded war effort continued for eighteen months did the administration propose further action. In January 1967 President Johnson called for a 6 percent surtax to correct the "imbalances created by the special pressures of Vietnam procurement."[2] Thus the problem that emerged in July 1965 was not recognized until 1966, and a response was not formulated until January 1967. Compounding these delays was the reluctance of Congress to help finance an undeclared war. Congress did not take the requested action until June 1968. Thus there was a three-year lag between the time the problem emerged and the implementation of a responsive action. In the interim, of course, inflationary pressures worsened.

Politics vs. economics　The delayed fiscal response to accelerated Vietnam expenditures also illustrates the very first barrier to policy implementation: *goal conflicts*. Just as the design of policy is compromised by conflicting interests and objectives, so too is the implementation of those designs. Especially noteworthy in this regard is the potential conflict of economic policy with political objectives. The conflict that existed between President Johnson's war objectives and his economic objectives is obvious. More generally, observers have noted that the president and Congress are reluctant to impose fiscal restraints (tax increases or budget cutbacks) in election years, regardless of economic circumstances.

　　This reluctance was evident in the fiscal policies of the 1980s. When he first convinced Congress to cut taxes in 1981, President Reagan projected strong economic growth and a shrinking budget deficit. Although his budget

[1]This figure includes multiplier effects through the first quarter of 1966.
[2]*Economic Report of the President,* 1967, pp. 5 and 9.

projections were notoriously optimistic, even critics were surprised at the economy's slow growth and the huge deficits that followed. By 1984 the need for greater fiscal restraint was apparent. But when Walter Mondale, Reagan's opponent in the 1984 presidential election, proposed a tax increase, he was soundly beaten. After that experience, neither party was willing to propose a tax increase. In the 1988 elections George Bush picked up votes by telling voters to "read my lips" and repeatedly promising not to raise taxes. During his first two years, both Bush and the Congress also avoided budget cuts that might have reduced the federal deficit. They were more willing to risk slow growth and higher real interest rates than voter wrath.

The tendency of Congress to hold fiscal policy hostage to electoral concerns has created a pattern of short-run stops and starts—a kind of policy-induced business cycle. Indeed, some argue that the business cycle has been replaced with the political cycle: the economy is stimulated in the year of an election, then restrained in the postelection year (see In the News). The conflict between the urgent need to get reelected and the necessity to manage the economy results in a seesaw kind of instability.

In theory, the political independence of the Fed's Board of Governors provides some protection from ill-advised but politically advantageous policy initiatives. In practice, however, the Fed's relative obscurity and independence may backfire. The president and the Congress know that if they don't take effective action against inflation—by raising taxes or cutting government spending—the Fed can and will take stronger action to restrain aggregate demand. This is a classic case of having one's cake and eating it too. Elected officials win votes for not raising taxes or cutting some constituent's favorite spending program. They also take credit for any reduction in the rate of inflation brought about by Federal Reserve policies. To top it off, Congress and the president can also blame the Fed for driving up interest rates or starting a recession if monetary policy becomes too restrictive.

The conflict between political reality and economic reality often arises out of ignorance. For example, nearly 90 percent of the people in this country

In The News

POLICY-INDUCED CYCLES

Political Parties and the Business Cycle

Since World War II, Democratic administrations have favored short-run economic expansions at the risk of higher inflation whereas Republican administrations have favored fighting inflation at the risk of short-run unemployment. Democratic presidents begin their terms by stimulating the economy, whereas Republican presidents begin by restraining inflation.

During the second year of each Democratic term, when the new policies begin to take effect, there has been an economic expansion, with real GNP growing 6.4 percent on average. In contrast, during the second year of each Republican term, real GNP has fallen 0.9 percent on average.

By the second half of each presidential term, there is very little difference in economic growth. Both parties have averaged about 4 percent growth in real GNP, lower growth than during the first half of Democratic terms but higher growth than in the first half of Republican terms. In other words, politics tends to create short-run cycles, but the economy returns to its long-run trend regardless of which party occupies the White House.

From Jeffrey Sachs and Alberto Alesina, *Political Parties and the Business Cycle in the United States, 1948–1984.* NBER Working Paper 1940, 1986.

In The News

POLITICAL CONSTRAINTS

The Politics of Fighting Unemployment and Inflation

"I can't think of anything you can do to keep inflation down that is popular," lamented one frustrated Cabinet official. "It's completely different from fighting unem-

ployment. There, you pump money into programs and people feel they benefit. When you fight inflation, people feel you're taking something away from them. You are always goring somebody's ox."

—Hedrick Smith

The New York Times, March 8, 1978. Copyright © 1978 by The New York Times Company. Reprinted by permission.

believe a balanced federal budget is "important," regardless of economic circumstances. As noted in Chapter 11, there is even a growing call for a constitutional amendment that would require balanced federal budgets. Yet economic theory suggests that budget deficits or surpluses are typically required to achieve our economic goals. Under such circumstances, should a president promise to balance the budget—thereby winning votes but risking greater economic instability—or unbalance it, as economic conditions require?[3]

Finally, we must recognize that policy design is obstructed by a certain lack of will. Neither the man in the street nor the elected public official is constantly attuned to economic goals and activities. Even students enrolled in economics courses have a hard time keeping their minds on the economy and its problems. The executive and legislative branches of government, for their part, are likely to focus on economic concerns only when economic problems become serious or voters demand action. Otherwise, policymakers are apt to be complacent about economic policy as long as economic performance is within a "tolerable" range of desired outcomes.

POLICY INSIGHTS:

RULES VS. DISCRETION

In view of the goal conflicts and the measurement, design, and implementation problems that policymakers confront, it is less surprising that things sometimes go wrong than that things often work out right. The maze of obstacles through which theory must pass before it becomes policy explains a great many of our collective shortcomings. On this basis alone, we may conclude that ***consistent fine-tuning of the economy is not compatible with either our design capabilities or our decision-making procedures.*** We have exhibited a strong capability to avoid major economic disruptions in the last four decades. We have not, however, been able to make all the minor adjustments necessary to fulfill our goals completely. As Arthur Burns, former chairman of the Fed's Board of Governors, said:

[3]A successful politician might do both, of course—that is, *promise* to balance the budget, but unbalance it at the same time. President Reagan had considerable success with this approach and President Bush has employed the same strategy.

There has been much loose talk of "fine-tuning" when the state of knowledge permits us to predict only within a fairly broad level the course of economic development and the results of policy actions.[4]

The Need for Rules

Some critics of economic policy take this argument a few steps further. If fine-tuning isn't really possible, they say, we should abandon discretionary policies altogether. Typically, policymakers seek minor adjustments in interest rates, unemployment, inflation, and growth. The pressure to "do something" is particularly irresistible in election years. In so doing, however, policymakers are as likely to worsen the economic situation as to improve it. Moreover, the potential for such short-term discretion undermines people's confidence in the economy's future.

Critics of discretionary policies say we would be better off with fixed policy rules. As we saw in Chapter 14, pure monetarism would require the Fed to increase the money supply at a constant rate. Critics of fiscal policy would require the government to maintain balanced budgets, or at least to offset deficits in sluggish years with surpluses in years of high growth. Such rules would prevent policymakers from over- or understimulating the economy, and the risks of economic instability would be reduced.

Milton Friedman has been one of the most persistent advocates of fixed policy rules instead of discretionary policies. With discretionary authority, Friedman argues,

> the wrong decision is likely to be made in a large fraction of cases because the decision-makers are examining only a limited area and not taking into account the cumulative consequences of the policy as a whole. On the other hand, if a general rule is adopted for a group of cases as a bundle, the existence of that rule has favorable effects on people's attitudes and beliefs and expectations that would not follow even from the discretionary adoption of precisely the same policy on a series of separate occasions.[5]

The case for nondiscretionary monetary authority is based on practical, not theoretical, arguments. Everyone agrees that flexible, discretionary policies *could* result in better economic performance. But Friedman and others argue that the practical requirements of monetary and fiscal management are too demanding and thus prone to failure. Moreover, required policies may be compromised by political pressures.

New Classical Economics

Monetarist critiques of discretionary policy are echoed by a new perspective referred to as New Classical Economics. Classical economists saw no need for discretionary macro policy. In their view, the private sector is inherently stable and government intervention serves no purpose. New Classical Economics (NCE) reaches the same conclusion, but for different reasons. At the core of NCE is a belief in **rational expectations.** This notion contends that people make decisions on the basis of all available information, including the future effects of government policy.

Suppose, for example, that the Fed decided to increase the money supply in order to boost output. If people had rational expectations, they would anticipate that this money-supply growth will fuel inflation. To protect them-

rational expectations: Hypothesis that people's spending decisions are based on all available information, including the anticipated effects of government intervention.

[4]*Newsweek,* August 27, 1973, p. 4.

[5]Milton Friedman, *Capitalism and Freedom* (Chicago: University of Chicago Press, 1962), p. 53. Copyright © 1962 The University of Chicago Press.

selves, they would immediately demand higher prices and wages. As a result, the stimulative monetary policy would fail to boost real output. (Monetarists reach the same conclusion but for different reasons; for Monetarists, the countervailing forces are technological and institutional, rather than rational expectations.)

Discretionary fiscal policy could be equally ineffective. Suppose Congress accelerated government spending in an effort to boost aggregate demand. Monetarists contend that the accompanying increase in the deficit would push interest rates up and crowd out private investment and consumption. New Classical economists again reach the same conclusion via a different route. They contend that people with rational expectations would anticipate that a larger deficit will necessitate later tax increases. To prepare for later tax bills, consumers will reduce spending now, thereby saving more. This "rational" reduction in consumption will offset the increased government expenditure, thus rendering fiscal policy ineffective.

If the New Classical economists are right, then the only policy that works is one that surprises people—one that consumers and investors don't anticipate. But a policy that surprises isn't very practical. Accordingly, New Classical economists conclude that minimal policy intervention is best. This conclusion provides yet another guideline for policy decisions (see Table 17.6 for a roster of competing theories).

TABLE 17.6 Who's on First? Labeling Economists

It's sometimes hard to tell who's on what side in economic debates. Although some economists are proud to wear the colors of Monetarists, Keynesians, or other teams, many economists shun such allegiances. Indeed, economists are often accused of playing on one team one day and on another team the next. This makes it hard to tell which team is at bat. To simplify matters, the following guide may be used for quick identification of the players. Closer observation is advised, however, before choosing up teams.

Keynesians	Keynesians believe that the private sector is inherently unstable and likely to stagnate at low levels of output and employment. They want the government to use tax cuts and government spending to increase demand and output.
Modern ("neo") Keynesians	Post–World War II followers of Keynes worry about inflation as well as recession. They urge budgetary restraint to cool an overheated economy. They also use monetary policy to change interest rates.
Monetarists	The money supply is their only heavy hitter. By changing the money supply, they can raise or lower the price level. Pure Monetarists shun active policy, believing that it destabilizes the otherwise stable private sector. Output and employment gravitate to their "natural" levels.
Supply-siders	Incentives to work, invest, and produce are the key to their plays. Cuts in marginal tax rates and government regulation are used to expand production capacity, thereby increasing output and reducing inflationary pressures.
New Classical economists	They say fine-tuning won't work, because once the private sector realizes what the government is doing, it will act to offset it. They also question the credibility of "quick-fix" promises. They favor steady, predictable policies.
Marxists	Marxists contend that the failures of the economy are inherent in its capitalist structure. The owners of capital will not strive for full employment or a more equitable income distribution. Workers, without any capital, have little incentive to excel. This team proposes starting a new game, with entirely different rules.

The Bush administration embraced the general perspective of New Classical Economics. In its 1990 Economic Report, Bush's Council of Economic Advisers noted that the many lags and uncertainties in economic policymaking severely limit the potential of discretionary macro policies. The council urged more *systematic* policies, focused on *long-term* goals. As they see it, the *credibility* of announced policy plans is the key to macro success. If market participants believe that systematic, long-run policy plans are appropriate—and will be implemented consistently—they will adjust their expectations accordingly. If, for example, people *believe* that fiscal policy will systematically reduce inflationary pressure, they will anticipate less inflation. These lowered inflationary expectations will restrain wage and price demands, thereby reinforcing the policy objective.

The Need for Flexibility

Bush's advisers conceded, however, that "even the most carefully designed systematic policies may need to be revised occasionally in view of significant changes in economic structure."[6] In other words, some flexibility is essential; long-run rules may need to be broken on occasion. Other critics of fixed policy rules go even further, questioning the very foundation of rational expectations. They argue that few people understand, much less anticipate, the consequences of monetary, fiscal, and supply-side policies. The emphasis on the *credibility* of long-run policies may be exaggerated in the context of the short-term horizons of market participants.

Critics of fixed rules acknowledge occasional policy blunders but emphasize that the historical record of prices, employment, and growth has improved since active fiscal and monetary policies were adopted. Without flexibility in the money supply and the budget, they argue, the economy would be less stable and our economic goals would remain unfulfilled.

When we assess the arguments for and against discretionary policy, it is important to note that historical evidence is ambiguous at best. Victor Zarnowitz showed that the U.S. economy has been much more stable since 1946 than it was in earlier periods (1875–1918 and 1919–45).[7] Recessions have gotten shorter and economic expansions longer. But a variety of factors—including a shift from manufacturing to services, a larger government sector, and automatic stabilizers—have contributed to this improved macro performance. The contribution of discretionary macro policy is less clear. It is easy to observe what actually happened but almost impossible to determine what would have occurred in other circumstances. It is also evident that there have been noteworthy occasions—World War II, for example—when something more than fixed rules for monetary and fiscal policy was called for, a contingency even Professor Friedman acknowledges. Thus occasional flexibility is required, even if a nondiscretionary policy is appropriate in most situations.

Finally, one must contend with the difficulties inherent in adhering to any fixed rules. How is the Fed, for example, supposed to maintain a steady rate of growth in M1? As we observed in Chapter 12, people move their funds back and forth between different kinds of "money." Also, the demand for money is subject to unpredictable shifts. To maintain a steady rare of M1 growth in this environment would require superhuman foresight and responses. As

[6]*Economic Report of the President,* 1990 (Washington D.C.: Government Printing Office, 1990), p. 65.

[7]Victor Zarnowitz, *Facts and Factors in the Recent Evolution of the Business Cycle in the United States* (Cambridge, Mass.: National Bureau of Economic Research, 1989).

former Fed chairman Paul Volcker told Congress, it would be "exceedingly dangerous and in fact practically impossible to eliminate substantial elements of discretion in the conduct of Federal Reserve policy."

The same is true of fiscal policy. Government spending and taxes are directly influenced by changes in unemployment, inflation, interest rates, and growth. These automatic stabilizers make it virtually impossible to maintain any fixed rule for budget balancing. Moreoever, if we eliminated the automatic stabilizers, we would risk greater instability.

Modest Expectations   The clamor for fixed policy rules is more a rebuke of past policy than a viable policy alternative. We really have no choice but to pursue discretionary policies. Recognition of measurement, design, and implementation problems is important for an understanding of the way the economy functions. But even though it is difficult or even impossible to reach all our goals, we cannot abandon conscientious attempts to get as close as possible to goal fulfillment. If public policy can create a few more jobs, a better mix of output, a little more growth and price stability, or an improved distribution of income, those initiatives are worthwhile. Modest improvements in our economic performance are important even if perfection is not attained. More restrained expectations about the potential of public policy need not and should not constrain our efforts to improve economic performance.

SUMMARY

- The basic principles of economics engender optimism about the potential of policy to fulfill our economic goals. The government possesses an array of policy levers, each of which can significantly alter economic outcomes. To end a recession, we can cut taxes, expand the money supply, or increase government spending. To curb inflation, we can reverse each of these policy levers. To overcome stagflation, we can combine fiscal and monetary levers with improved supply-side incentives.

- Although the potential of economic theory seems impressive, the economic record does not look so good. Persistent unemployment, recurring economic slowdowns, and nagging inflation suggest that the realities of policymaking are more difficult than theory implies.

- To a large extent, the "failures" of economic policy are a reflection of scarce resources and competing goals. Even when consensus exists, however, serious obstacles to effective economic policy remain. These obstacles include:

  (*a*) Measurement problems. Our knowledge of economic performance is always dated and incomplete. We must rely on forecasts of future problems.
  (*b*) Design problems. We don't know exactly how the economy will respond to specific policies.
  (*c*) Implementation problems. It takes time for Congress and the president to agree on an appropriate plan of action. Moreover, the agreements reached may respond more to political needs than to economic needs.

For all these reasons, the fine-tuning of economic performance rarely lives up to its theoretical potential.

• Monetarists and New Classical economists favor rules rather than discretionary macro policies. They argue that discretionary policies are unlikely to work and risk being wrong. Critics respond that discretionary policies are needed to cope with ever-changing economic circumstances.

Terms to Remember

Define the following terms:

business cycle	recessionary gap
fiscal policy	multiplier
automatic stabilizer	velocity of money (*V*)
structural deficit	inflationary gap
monetary policy	fine-tuning
natural rate of unemployment	growth recession
supply-side policy	rational expectations

Questions for Discussion

1. Should economic policies respond immediately to any changes in reported unemployment or inflation rates? When should a response be undertaken?

2. Suppose that it is an election year and that aggregate demand is growing so fast that it threatens to set off an inflationary movement. Why might Congress and the president hesitate to cut back on government spending or raise taxes, as economic theory suggests is appropriate?

3. In his fiscal 1991 budget, President Bush proposed increases in defense spending while arguing for cutbacks in total spending. Should military spending be subject to macroeconomic constraints? What programs should be expanded or contracted to bring about needed changes in the budget? Is this feasible?

4. Suppose that the president proposes mandatory wage–price controls to slow the rate of inflation. What is likely to happen to wages and prices in the interval between the time the proposal is made and the time Congress acts to impose controls?

5. Suppose the government proposes to cut taxes while maintaining the current level of government expenditures. To finance this deficit, it may either (1) sell bonds to the public or (2) print new money (via Federal Reserve cooperation). What are the likely effects of each of these alternatives on each of the following? Would Keynesians, Monetarists, and Supply-siders give the same answers?
   (*a*) Interest rates
   (*b*) Consumer spending
   (*c*) Business investment
   (*d*) Aggregate demand

Problems

1. (*a*) Outline a macro policy package for attaining full employment and price stability in the next twelve months.
   (*b*) What obstacles, if any, will impede attainment of these goals?

2. The following table presents hypothetical data on government expenditure, taxes, exports, imports, the GNP deflator, unemployment, and pollution for three levels of equilibrium income (GNP). A government decision maker is trying to determine the optimal level of government expenditures, with each of the three columns being a possible choice. At the time of the choice the GNP deflator is 1.0. Dollar amounts are in billions per year.

	Nominal GNP		
	$7,000	$8,000	$9,000
Government expenditure	$700	$800	$900
Taxes	$600	$800	$1,000
Exports	$300	$300	$300
Imports	$100	$300	$500
GNP deflator (index)	1.00	1.04	1.15
Unemployment rate	10%	4%	3.5%
Pollution index	1.00	1.80	2.00

(a) Compute the federal budget balance, balance of trade, and real GNP for each level of nominal GNP.

(b) What government expenditure level would best accomplish each of the following goals?

　　Lowest taxes
　　Largest trade surplus
　　Lowest pollution
　　Lowest inflation rate
　　Lowest unemployment rate
　　Highest amount of public goods and services
　　Highest real income
　　Balancing the federal budget
　　Achieving a balance of trade
　　Maintaining price stability
　　Achieving full employment

(c) What government expenditure levels would most flagrantly violate each of the preceding goals?

(d) Which policy would be in the best interests of the country?

(e) What policies, in addition to changes in government expenditures, might the government use to attain more of its desired goals?

CHAPTER 18

Global Macro

*I*n 1990 the Fed wanted to stimulate the U.S. economy with faster money-supply growth and lower interest rates. But it worried that lower interest rates in U.S. capital markets would discourage foreigners from buying U.S. bonds (see World View). Foreign buying was needed to maintain the value of the U.S. dollar in world markets and to help finance America's import imbalance.

This is the kind of global policy dilemma the real world imposes. The United States now exports over 10 percent of total domestic output and imports an even higher percentage. And money flows across international borders nearly as fast as across state lines. All such transactions make the U.S. economy highly interdependent with the rest of the world. When economic growth in the rest of the world slows, the U.S. economy suffers as well. Likewise, when the U.S. economy stumbles, other world economies feel pain. From this perspective, the world economy is like a mobile—if one piece moves, every other piece jiggles.

W⬤RLD VIEW

GLOBAL MACRO

Boxed in at the Fed

Will the Rate Runup Bring on Recession?

Oh, the aching economy. Corporate profits are falling, borrowers are struggling to meet interest payments, and lenders are choking on their own loans. Auto sales remain stuck in low gear, real estate is moribund, and the financial markets are swooning. The prescription for the ailment is a familiar one: lower interest rates. The problem is, that option just isn't available. . . .

Why can't America lower interest rates? As the central bank to the world's largest debtor nation, the Federal Reserve is boxed in. Interest rates are rising abroad, so the Fed has to support yields on U.S. debt to keep foreign capital flowing in and prevent what's here from fleeing. And Congress is acting as if it might cut taxes in the face of a $150 billion budget deficit even as corporate tax payments are declining. That leaves the Fed no choice but to keep money tight—and rates up. It's the nation's only defense in the battle against inflation. "The easing of monetary policy is over," says Stefan Abrams, investment strategist for Kidder, Peabody & Co.

Business Week, February 5, 1990, p. 22.

This chapter explores this global interdependence. Of particular concern are the following questions:

- How does the U.S. economy interact with the rest of the world?
- How does the rest of the world affect U.S. macro outcomes?
- How does global interdependence limit macro policy options?

As we shall see, international transactions significantly affect U.S. economic performance and policy.

INTERNATIONAL TRADE

Japanese cars are the most visible reminders of America's global interdependence. American consumers purchase over a million cars from Japan each year and buy another million or so Toyotas, Nissans, Hondas, Mazdas, and Subarus produced in the United States. On the other side of the Pacific Ocean, Japanese auto workers are apt to wear Levis, sip Coca-Cola, and grab a quick meal at McDonald's.

The motivations for international trade are explained at length in Chapter 35. Also discussed in Chapter 35 are the *microeconomic* demands for greater protection from "unfair" imports. What concerns us here is how such trade affects our domestic *macro* performance. Does trade help or hinder our efforts to attain full employment, price stability, and economic growth?

Imports as Leakage

imports: Goods and services purchased from foreign sources.

leakage: Income not spent directly on domestic output, but instead diverted from the circular flow, e.g., saving, imports, taxes.

multiplier: The multiple by which an initial change in aggregate spending will alter total expenditure after an infinite number of spending cycles.

marginal propensity to import (MPM): The fraction of each additional (marginal) dollar of disposable income spent on imports.

marginal propensity to save (MPS): The fraction of each additional (marginal) dollar of disposable income not spent on consumption: 1 − MPC.

We first noticed in Chapter 8 that **imports** are a source of **leakage** in the circular flow. The income that American consumers spend on Japanese cars *could* be spent in America. When that income instead leaks out of the circular flow, it limits domestic spending and related **multiplier** effects.

The traditional Keynesian model can be expanded easily to include this additional leakage. In a closed (no-trade) economy, total income and domestic spending are always equal—that is,

$$\bullet \quad \text{Closed economy}: C + I + G = Y$$

When some goods are sold as exports and others can be purchased from abroad, however, this equality no longer holds. In an open economy, we have to take account of imports and exports—that is,

$$\bullet \quad \text{Open economy}: C + I + G + X = Y + M$$

where X refers to exports and M to imports. In an open economy, the combined spending of consumers, investors, and the government may not equal domestic output. Total spending is augmented by the demand for exports, and the supply of goods is increased by imports.

Although imported goods may be desired, their availability complicates macro policy. In the Keynesian model, increases in aggregate spending are supposed to boost domestic output and employment. With imports, however, the link between spending and output is weakened. ***Part of any increase in income will be spent on imports.*** This fraction is called the **marginal propensity to import (MPM).** Like its cousin, the **marginal propensity to save (MPS),** the marginal propensity to import:

- Reduces the initial impact of any autonomous income change

- Reduces the size of the income multiplier

Table 18.1 illustrates the impact of imports on the Keynesian multiplier process. The process starts with an increase (upward shift) of $10 billion in government spending. This directly adds $10 billion to consumer income (assuming an economy with no taxes).

The successive panels of Table 18.1 illustrate the sequence of events that the new government spending sets in motion. In the closed economy, consumers have only two uses for their income: They may spend it on domestic consumption (B1) or save it (B2). In this case we assume the marginal propensity to save is 0.10. Hence consumers save $1 billion and spend the remaining $9 billion on domestic consumption.

In an open economy, consumers have more choices. They may spend their income on domestic goods (B1), save it (B2), or spend it on imported goods (B3). In Table 18.1 we assume that the marginal propensity to import is 0.10. Hence consumers use their additional $10 billion of income in the following way:

$8 billion spent on domestic consumption

$1 billion saved

$1 billion spent on imports

In the open economy only $8 billion rather than $9 billion is initially spent on domestic consumption. Thus *imports reduce the initial spending impact of added income.*

Import leakage continues through every round of the circular flow. As a consequence, *imports also reduce the value of the income multiplier.* In this case, the multiplier is reduced from 10 to 5.

To see how this change in the multiplier comes about, note that *the value of the multiplier depends on the extent of leakage.* The most general form of the multiplier is

TABLE 18.1   Imports as Leakage

Import leakage reduces the initial spending impact of autonomous changes in consumer income. Continuing import leakage reduces the size of the multiplier as well. In this case, the ultimate impact of added government spending is cut in half by import leakage: GNP rises by $50 billion rather than $100 billion in response to a $10 billion increase in government spending.

Action	Impact on equilibrium GNP	
	Closed economy	Open economy
A. Government spends additional $10 billion	+ $10 billion	+ $10 billion
B. Consumers used added $10 billion of income for:		
1. Domestic consumption	+ $9 billion	+ $8 billion
2. Saving (MPS = 0.1)	($1 billion)	($1 billion)
3. Imports (MPM = 0.1)	N/A	($1 billion)
C. Multiplier	$\dfrac{1}{\text{MPS}} = 10$	$\dfrac{1}{\text{MPS} + \text{MPM}} = 5$
D. Additional multiplier-induced consumption = $C \times B1$	+ $90 billion	+ $40 billion
E. Cumulative change in GNP = $A + D$	+ $100 billion	+ $50 billion

$$\bullet \quad \begin{array}{c} \text{Generalized} \\ \text{multiplier} \end{array} = \frac{1}{\text{leakage fraction}}$$

In a closed (no-trade) and private (no-taxes) economy, the multiplier takes the familiar Keynesian form:

$$\bullet \quad \begin{array}{c} \text{Closed-economy} \\ \text{multiplier} \\ \text{(without taxes)} \end{array} = \frac{1}{\text{MPS}}$$

In this case, consumer saving is the only form of leakage. Therefore, the marginal propensity to save (MPS) is the entire leakage fraction. In Table 18.1 the closed economy multiplier is equal to 10 (see panel C).

Once we open the economy to trade, we have to contend with additional leakage. In an open economy, leakage results from the MPS *and* the MPM. Thus the generalized multiplier must be transformed to

$$\bullet \quad \begin{array}{c} \text{Open-economy} \\ \text{multiplier} \\ \text{(without taxes)} \end{array} = \frac{1}{\text{MPS} + \text{MPM}}$$

Imports act just like saving leakage, decreasing the multiplier bang of each consumer buck. In Table 18.1 (panel C),

$$\bullet \quad \text{Open-economy multiplier} = \frac{1}{\text{MPS} + \text{MPM}} = \frac{1}{0.1 + 0.1} = \frac{1}{0.2} = 5$$

The consequences of these different multipliers are striking. Panel D shows that additional consumption of \$90 billion is induced in the closed economy. By comparison, the open economy generates only \$40 billion of additional consumption.

The last panel of Table 18.1 summarizes the consequences for equilibrium GNP. The ultimate change in equilibrium GNP is computed as

$$\bullet \quad \begin{array}{c} \text{Ultimate change} \\ \text{in equilibrium GNP} \end{array} = \begin{array}{c} \text{initial change} \\ \text{in spending} \end{array} \times \begin{array}{c} \text{income} \\ \text{multiplier} \end{array}$$

In this example, the initial injection of spending is the \$10 billion spent by the government. In the closed economy, this injection leads to a \$100 billion increase in GNP (panel E). In the open economy, the same injection increases equilibrium GNP only \$50 billion! This end result is also illustrated in Figure 18.1, which shows how ***imports reduce the slope of the (domestic) consumption function.*** This reduced slope leads to a lower equilibrium GNP.

Exports as Injections

exports: Goods and services sold to foreign buyers.

Were imports our only link to the rest of the world, we might be tempted to erect a wall around "Fortress America" to preserve our output and employment levels. But international trade is a two-way street. While we import goods and services from the rest of the world, other countries buy our **exports.** Thus foreigners *inject* spending into the circular flow at the same time that imports cause leakage. Figure 18.2 reminds us of these offsetting effects.

Exports are simply a fourth component of aggregate demand. Like other components, ***changes in exports will shift the aggregate spending function up or down.*** These shifts can cause changes in equilibrium output and price levels, just as would other autonomous changes in spending.

Figure 18.3 illustrates the impact of increased export sales. When exports increase, the aggregate spending function shifts upward. The added income

FIGURE 18.1
Imports and Consumption

Imports reduce the slope of the domestic consumption function, as some consumer spending goes abroad. This leakage reduces equilibrium GNP; in this case from Y_a to Y_b.

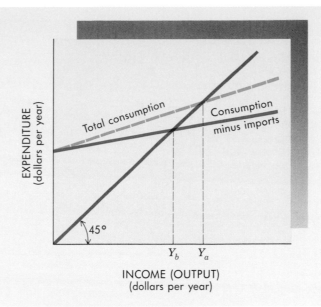

generated by export sales induces consumers to spend more. Multiplier effects then push the equilibrium GNP from Y_1 to Y_2.

TRADE IMBALANCES

With exports adding to aggregate spending, and imports subtracting from the circular flow, the net impact of international trade on the domestic economy comes down to a question of balance. ***What counts is the difference between exports (injections) and imports (leakages).*** If exports and imports

FIGURE 18.2
Exports as Injections

Exports represent foreign spending on domestic output. Exports thus inject additional spending and income into the circular flow. By increasing aggregate spending, injections help offset the leakage caused by imports.

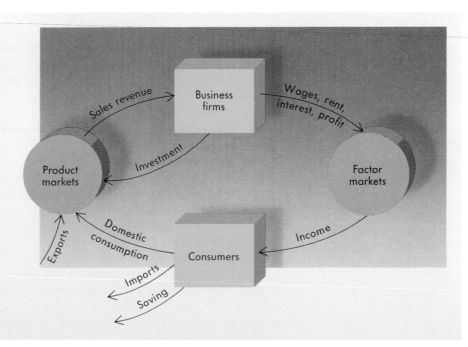

FIGURE 18.3
Exports Boost Total Spending

Exports add a fifth component to aggregate spending, and so shift the aggregate spending function upward. This added spending tends to increase equilibrium GNP; e.g., from Y_1 to Y_2. Net exports $(X - M)$ represent the international contribution to aggregate spending.

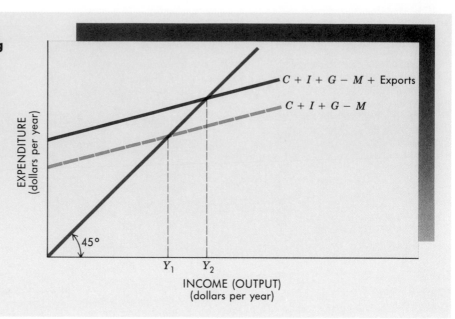

were exactly equal, there would be no net stimulus or leakage from the rest of the world.

A convenient way of emphasizing the offsetting effects of exports and imports is to rearrange the income identity to

$$\bullet \quad C + I + G + (X - M) = Y$$

net exports: Exports minus imports: $(X - M)$.

where $(X - M)$ equals **net exports.**

If exports and imports were always equal, the term $(X - M)$ would disappear and we could focus on domestic spending behavior. But there is no more reason to expect imports and exports to be equal than there is to expect domestic saving (leakage) and investment (injection) to be equal. Indeed, the core macro stability problem arises because investment and saving decisions are made by different people and for very different reasons. There is no *a priori* reason to expect those outcomes to be identical.

The same problem affects international trade. Foreign decisions about how much to spend on American exports are made outside U.S. borders. U.S. decisions about how much to spend on foreign imports are made by American consumers, investors, and government agencies. Because these sets of shoppers are so isolated from each other, it seems unlikely that exports will always equal imports. Instead, we have to expect a trade imbalance.

trade surplus: The amount by which the value of exports exceeds the value of imports in a given time period.

trade deficit: The amount by which the value of imports exceeds the value of exports in a given time period.

There are specific terms for characterizing trade imbalances. A **trade surplus** exists when America is exporting more goods and services than it is importing—that is, when net exports $(X - M)$ are positive. When net exports are negative, imports have exceeded exports and the United States has incurred a **trade deficit.** In 1989 the United States had a trade deficit of $92 billion. That deficit implies that U.S. consumers, investors, and government agencies were buying $92 billion more output in 1989 than American factories and offices were producing.[1]

[1]The trade deficit of $92 billion resulted from a merchandise (goods) deficit of $113 billion and a services surplus of $21 billion.

Macro Effects   A trade deficit isn't all bad. After all, when imports exceed exports, we end up consuming more than we are producing. In effect, *a trade deficit permits domestic living standards to exceed domestic output.* It's almost like getting something for nothing—the proverbial "free lunch."

Although the additional consumption a trade deficit permits may be enjoyed, a negative trade flow may have unwelcome effects as well. A trade deficit represents net leakage. That leakage may frustrate attempts to attain full employment.

The central policy concern is still the relationship between equilibrium GNP and full-employment GNP. In an open economy, the condition for equilibrium GNP is

- $\dfrac{\text{Equilibrium GNP}}{\text{(open economy)}}$: desired $S + T + M =$ desired $I + G + X$

where T refers to tax revenues. In other words, desired leakage $(S + T + M)$ must be equal to desired injections $(I + G + X)$ for equilibrium to be attained.

As noted in Chapter 10, however, equilibrium GNP may not be equal to full-employment GNP or any other policy target. Suppose that the economy is sluggish and that the policy goal is to stimulate spending, output, and employment. The fiscal policy agenda may include tax cuts or increased government spending. With import leakage, however, any given fiscal action will have less impact (see Table 18.1). Thus a trade deficit during a recessionary period tends to make fiscal policy more difficult. A larger tax cut or spending increase will be required to attain any particular target for domestic spending.

The dilemma worsens when we look again at the trade gap (deficit). The fiscal stimulus intended to boost domestic output will also *worsen* the trade deficit! Consumers will spend some fraction of their additional income—the marginal propensity to import (MPM)—on imports. These added imports will widen the trade gap. Thus the *objective of reducing the trade deficit may conflict with the goal of attaining full employment.*

At other times our trade and domestic goals might be more compatible. Suppose that we were approaching full employment and were more concerned about inflation than about unemployment. In this context, we might welcome some net import leakage. In this case, import leakage would act as a "safety valve" to help keep the economy from overheating. In this situation, restrictive fiscal policies would help close both the domestic inflationary gap and the trade gap (deficit).

A trade surplus can create similar problems. The additional spending implied by positive net exports may fuel inflationary pressures. If the economy is overheating, the policy objective is to restrain aggregate spending. But fiscal and monetary policies do not directly affect the incomes, expectations, or tastes of foreign consumers. Foreign spending on U.S. goods may continue unabated, even as domestic monetary and fiscal restraint "squeezes" domestic consumers and investors. Indeed, domestic monetary and fiscal restraint will have to be harder, just to offset continuing export demand.

Worse yet, the trade surplus may grow in response to restrictive macro policies. Domestic consumers, squeezed by monetary and fiscal restraint, will reduce purchases of imported goods. On the other hand, if fiscal and monetary restraint reduces domestic inflation, foreigners may increase their export purchases. Here again, *trade goals and domestic macro goals may conflict.*

Foreign Perspectives

Who cares if our trade balance worsens? Why don't we just focus on our domestic macro equilibrium and ignore any trade imbalances that result? If we ignored trade imbalances, we wouldn't have a goal conflict and could achieve our domestic policy goals.

Unfortunately, our trading partners have their own policy objectives and may not be content to ignore our trade imbalances. ***If the U.S. has a trade deficit, other countries must have a trade surplus.*** This is simple arithmetic. Its implications are potentially worrisome, however. The rest of the world might not be happy about shipping us more goods then they are getting in return. In real economic terms, they would be paying for our "free lunch." Their exports would be financing a higher standard of living for us than our output alone permitted. At the same time, their living standards would be less than their output made possible. These disparities could cause tension. In addition, foreign nations might also be concerned about inflationary pressures of their own, and so resist additional demand for their exports (our imports).

The whole notion of macro equilibrium gets much more complicated when we adopt these global views. From a global perspective, ***we cannot focus exclusively on domestic macro goals and ignore international repercussions.*** If our trade balance upsets other economies, foreign nations may respond with their own macro and trade initiatives. These responses, in turn, would affect America's trade flows and so alter domestic outcomes. A *global* macro equilibrium would be attained only when no trading partner had reason to change macro or trade policy.

A Policy Constraint

We conclude, then, that trade imbalances are inherently neither good nor bad. From a macro perspective, our basic objective remains the same—to find the optimal balance of aggregate demand and aggregate supply. Trade flows may help or hinder this effort, depending on the timing, size, and source of the trade imbalance. All we know for certain is

- Imports and exports alter the rate and composition of aggregate spending.

- Trade flows may help or impede domestic macro policy attain its objectives.

- Macro policy decisions need to take account of international trade repercussions.

Thus international trade adds an important new wrinkle to macro policy decision making.

W RLD VIEW

EXTERNAL SHOCKS

Oil Shocks

In 1973 and again in 1979 the Organization of Petroleum Exporting Countries (OPEC) sharply increased crude oil prices. The price of oil quadrupled in 1973 and doubled again in 1979. The resulting "shock" to macro equilibrium caused both higher unemployment and more inflation in oil-importing nations.

Inflationary Impact

In mid-1973 the world price of OPEC oil was about $3.30 per barrel. OPEC pushed the price up to $12 a barrel almost overnight and ultimately to over $30 a barrel. The increase in the price of oil set the stage for cost-push inflation. Industries using oil to fuel their machines or heat their furnaces were hit with an increase in production costs. These higher costs shifted the aggregate *supply* curve to the left, as in the accompanying figure.

Recessionary Impact

The leftward shift of the aggregate supply curve not only pushed the average price level up (to P_2) but also reduced output (to Q_2). In the United States, the reduction in total domestic output was aggravated by price controls on domestic oil and gas. As a consequence, many manufacturers were forced to shut down, because they could not get the oil they were willing and able to purchase. Others shut down because higher fuel costs made continued production unprofitable.

Decreased Consumption

Although the most visible effects of the 1973 and 1979 oil shocks were inflation and shortages, the greatest threat lay on the demand side of product and factor markets. The OPEC price boosts forced consumers to spend more of their income on foreign oil imports. In 1973 the United States was spending approximately $10 billion a year on imported oil. After the OPEC price increase, however, our annual import bill suddenly jumped to $25 billion. This sudden increase in import leakage left consumers with less income to spend on domestic output. Thus the aggregate *demand* curve also shifted to the left.

Policy Options

The oil shocks of 1973 and 1979 underscored America's interdependence with the rest of the world. In this case the external shocks contributed to stagflation and forced macro policymakers to respond. During the 1973–74 shock, the Nixon administration focused on the inflationary threat. It pursued restrictive fiscal policies and encouraged the Fed to reduce money-supply growth. These policies shifted aggregate demand further to the left and pushed the economy into a severe recession. The economy suffered from similar policies in the wake of the 1979 oil price hikes.

Declining Oil Prices

Since 1980, the price of imported oil has declined. In 1986–87 the price cuts were particularly sharp, with the price of oil hitting a low of $10 per barrel. This oil price decline again altered trade and capital flows, to the general benefit of oil-importing nations. Lower oil prices reduced production costs, shifting the aggregate supply curve to the right. Reduced import leakage also left more income in consumers' pockets and thus boosted spending on domestic output.

The higher prices of imported oil increased production costs. As a consequence, producers were less able or willing to sell output at any given price. The domestic aggregate supply curve shifted to the left (from S_1 to S_2).

The increased leakage caused by higher oil–import prices also curtailed demand for domestic goods. Aggregate demand shifted from D_1 to D_2. The U.S. economy ended up with higher prices and less employment.

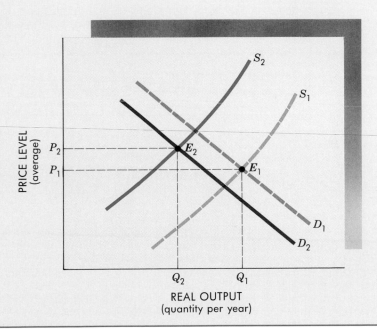

INTERNATIONAL FINANCE

Our global interactions with the rest of the world are further complicated by international money flows. Money flows across international borders as easily as goods and services. In fact, money *must* move across borders to pay for imports and exports. In addition, people move money across borders to get bigger profits, higher interest rates, or more security. Like trade in goods and services, these international money flows alter macro outcomes and complicate macro decision making.

Capital Inflows   In 1989 over $200 billion of foreign capital flowed into the United States. A lot of this capital inflow was used to purchase U.S. bonds. U.S. Treasury bonds were attractive to foreigners for two reasons. First, real interest rates in the U.S. economy were relatively high, making them a more attractive investment than foreign bonds. Second, the U.S. economy looked more prosperous and more politically stable than many other places, making U.S. Treasury bonds appear more secure. Corporate bonds, stocks, and other U.S. investments also looked attractive, for much the same reasons. So people and institutions around the world moved some of their funds into U.S. markets, creating a tremendous capital inflow.

The profits of U.S. corporations operating abroad added to that capital inflow. When U.S. firms build plants abroad, they anticipate earning profits they can bring home. Over time, U.S. multinational firms have accumulated a sizable share of world markets, giving them a regular inflow of international profits.

Capital Outflows   Money flows out of the United States to the rest of the world for the same purposes. Most of the outflow is used to finance American imports. Additional *capital* flows, however, are motivated by a variety of purposes. American investors may seek to invest in foreign countries and so need to buy foreign land, labor, and capital. In addition, U.S. households and institutions may be attracted to overseas *financial* investments—for example, foreign bonds or

W🌐RLD VIEW

CAPITAL INFLOWS

U.S. a Magnet for Foreign Investment

TOKYO—On the top floor of one of the swankiest department stores in Tokyo, salesmen are doing brisk business in a popular new product: United States real estate.

With ever-increasing frequency, doctors, businessmen and others leaf through glossy photos and floor plans on display at Seibu department store and then spend hundreds of thousands of dollars, or more, to buy Hawaiian beach-front properties and Manhattan high-rise apartments.

According to sales manager Kazuo Saito, these affluent Japanese are eager to "buy American" for the same reasons that investors—especially corporate ones—from Europe and elsewhere are buying up some of the United States' best-known landmarks, along with its clothing stores, book publishers, country clubs, and stocks and bonds. Viewed from abroad, the United States is a huge, wonderfully stocked discount store, overflowing with bargains because of the depressed value of the dollar.

While Americans fret about the "hollowing out" of their industrial base, and runaway budget and trade deficits, foreigners see a stable political system, an unfettered economy with inflation more or less under control and a huge, open marketplace up for grabs. "It basically comes down to faith in America," said Walter Buytaert, vice president of Prudential-Bache Securities Inc. in Frankfurt, West Germany. "With good solid (corporate) earnings growth, it's the place to go."

Across the Pacific, Shigeru Kobayashi, head of Shuwa Corp., one of the major purchasers of prime U.S. real estate, echoed the sentiments: "No other country in the world can accept foreign people and investment as freely as the U.S.," he said recently.

—Margaret Shapiro

The Washington Post, October 13, 1987, p. E1. Copyright © 1987 The Washington Post.

stocks. Some people simply want to keep their money in Swiss banks to avoid scrutiny, taxes, or the risks of international currency revaluations. Finally, the U.S. government spends money in foreign countries to maintain American defenses, operate embassies, encourage economic development, and provide emergency relief. All of these motivations prompt Americans to spend money in foreign countries.

Part of the dollar outflow is also prompted by foreign investors and institutions. We have already noted that a motivation for capital *inflows* is the desire for investments and profits. As interest and profits accumulate, foreigners may want to retrieve some of their assets. Those repatriated interest and profit payments are part of the capital *outflows.* If the relative attractiveness of investments in the United States diminishes, even more foreign capital will flow out. When the U.S. stock market crashed in October 1987, many foreign investors took their money and ran.

CAPITAL IMBALANCES

capital deficit: The amount by which the capital outflow exceeds the capital inflow in a given time period.

capital surplus: The amount by which the capital inflow exceeds the capital outflow in a given time period.

Like trade flows, capital flows will not always be balanced. There are times when the outflow of dollars will exceed the inflow, and the United States will have a **capital deficit.** At other times, the balance may be reversed, leaving the United States with a **capital surplus.** In 1989 the United States had a capital surplus of $71 billion.

The huge capital surplus of 1989 is directly related to the huge trade deficit in that same year. When we import more than we export, we are effectively buying foreign goods and services on credit. The bulk of that "credit" is derived from the net inflow of foreign capital. The net inflow of money prompted by foreign investors creates a pool of funds that can be used to purchase foreign goods and services. If the capital inflow were smaller, our ability to purchase imports would be less, too. The reverse of this is true as well. If Americans weren't buying so many imports, foreigners wouldn't have as many dollars to invest in American banks, corporations, and property. Thus *capital imbalances are directly related to trade imbalances.*

Macro Effects

The inherent relationship between capital imbalances and trade imbalances resembles the dilemma of whether the chicken or the egg came first. Do capital surpluses cause trade deficits? Or does the causation run in the opposite direction? The answer depends largely on the circumstances that motivate changes in trade and capital flows. These motivations are discussed at length in Chapters 35 and 36. What concerns us here is how the capital imbalances alter macro outcomes and policy options.

Capital imbalances pose an obvious problem for monetary policy. The essence of monetary policy is control of the money supply. When money is able to move across international borders at will, control of the money supply becomes much more difficult.

Suppose inflationary forces are building and the Federal Reserve wants to reduce money-supply growth. To do so, it might engage in open-market operations, with the objective of net selling. By selling bonds, the Fed would seek to draw reserves out of the banking system and so slow money-supply growth. The bond sales will also tend to raise interest rates and thus dampen both consumer and investor spending. This relatively straightforward sequence of events is illustrated on the left side of Figure 18.4.

The figure also illustrates how an open economy complicates monetary policy. The higher interest rates caused by the Fed's bond sales attract foreign-held assets. As the return on U.S. bonds increases, the inflow of foreign capital will accelerate. This will frustrate the Fed's goal of reducing money-supply growth and tend to put downward pressure on domestic interest rates. The Fed will have to work harder (e.g., sell more bonds) to achieve any desired money-supply target.

Exchange Rates

An important feature of Figure 18.4 is the box marked "Higher value of dollar." When we purchase goods and services from foreign countries, we must exchange our dollars for foreign currency. The Japanese workers who make Toyotas, for example, are paid in yen. Their willingness to supply cars is based on how many yen, not dollars, they will receive. Thus we must first exchange dollars for yen before we can import Toyotas. When you travel abroad, you do these exchanges yourself, typically at banks, hotels, or special foreign-exchange offices. When you stay at home and buy imported goods, someone else handles the exchange for you.

Whether you or some middleman does the exchange is irrelevant. What matters is how many yen you get for your dollar. The more yen you get, the more Toyotas and other Japanese goods you are able to buy. In other words, *if the dollar's value in the world markets is high, imports are cheap.*

The dollar's value in international trade is reflected in the **exchange rate.** The exchange rate is simply the price (value) of one currency, measured in terms of another. The exchange rate prevailing at any time reflects the interplay of trade and capital flows and all their determinants. (Foreign exchange

exchange rate: The price of one country's currency, expressed in terms of another's; the domestic price of a foreign currency.

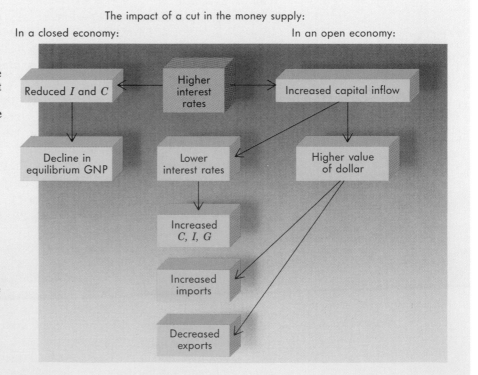

FIGURE 18.4
International Constraints on Monetary Policy

A reduction in the money supply is intended to reduce consumption and investment spending and so relieve inflationary pressures. If the money–supply reduction increases domestic interest rates, however, it may trigger additional capital inflow. That increased capital inflow will frustrate monetary policy by increasing the money supply and holding down interest rates. The capital inflow will also tend to increase the value of the U.S. dollar and so widen the trade deficit.

The impact of a cut in the money supply:

In a closed economy:

In an open economy:

Reduced *I* and *C*

Higher interest rates

Increased capital inflow

Decline in equilibrium GNP

Lower interest rates

Higher value of dollar

Increased *C, I, G*

Increased imports

Decreased exports

markets are examined in Chapter 36.) What matters here is that exchange rates *change,* often in response to monetary and fiscal policy.

In Figure 18.4, restrictive monetary policy causes domestic interest rates to rise. These higher interest rates make U.S. bonds more attractive and so increase capital inflow from the rest of the world. To buy Treasury bonds, however, foreigners need dollars. As they clamor to exchange their yen, marks, francs, and pounds for dollars, the value (price) of the dollar will increase. A higher dollar means that you can get more yen for every dollar. Imports thus become cheaper, and so Americans buy more of them. On the other hand, a stronger (more expensive) dollar makes U.S. exports costlier for foreigners, and so foreigners buy less of them. The end result is a widening trade gap.

Capital Flows—Another Policy Constraint

International capital flows add yet another complication to macro policy. The very existence of international capital flows weakens the ability of the Fed to control the money supply. Furthermore, the goals of domestic monetary policy may conflict with international finance objectives (see World View on Japan's goal conflict).

In addition to all our other macro worries we now have to be concerned about

- The flow of capital in and out of the country

- The effect of capital imbalances on domestic macro performance

- How macro policy initiatives will affect international capital flows, exchange rates, and trade balances, and how these in turn will affect domestic policy goals

W RLD VIEW

COMPETING GOALS

Japan Raises Discount Rate to Bolster Yen

TOKYO, May 30—The Bank of Japan, reacting to incipient signs of inflation and worried about the weakening of the yen against the dollar, today announced an increase in its key interest rate, the first such hike in more than nine years. . . .

Bank officials, led by governor Satoshi Sumita, had warned that the economy was overheating and that the decline in the yen's value was putting upward pressure on prices. Last Friday's release of figures showing a 3.3 percent increase in Tokyo area consumer prices apparently triggered today's action.

Japan had resisted international pressure to raise its discount rate, and its action is likely to cause other central banks to reassess their rates, Tokyo economists said today.

The Bank of Japan last raised its rate in March 1980 and has gradually reduced it since, holding to a generally expansionary monetary policy.

Some here worried that the increase will dampen consumption, slow the recent growth in imports and thus postpone any reduction in Japan's trade surplus with the United States.

—Margaret Shapiro

The Wall Street Journal, May 31, 1989, p. F1.

PRODUCTIVITY AND COMPETITIVENESS ————————————

At this juncture, a global view may look rather unsettling. International trade and capital add new complexities to the economy. They clearly make it more difficult to attain our macro policy goals. One might reasonably wonder whether international trade and finance is really worth all the trouble. Couldn't we get along just as well without the rest of the world?

Specialization

Perhaps. But we wouldn't be able to drink much coffee. Or spend summer vacations in Europe. Or buy Japanese cars and Mexican beer.

To decide whether international trade and finance is worth all the trouble, we have to consider how international exchanges affect our standard of living. One obvious advantage of trade is that it gives us access to goods and services we don't or can't produce at home—such as coffee, vacations abroad, bananas, and Italian shoes. These *imported goods and services broaden our consumption possibilities.*

Most of the goods and services we import *could* be produced at home. Cars and shoes are made in America as well as abroad. Even coffee and bananas *could* be produced in the United States if we invested enough in greenhouses that duplicated tropical conditions. Home-grown coffee and bananas would turn out to be terribly expensive, however, so we are better off importing them. This leaves domestic resources available for the production of other goods that we can more easily grow (corn), manufacture (computers), or build (houses). In other words, we are better off *specializing* in the production of things we do relatively well and *trading* with other nations for the rest of the goods and services we desire. *Specialization among countries increases world efficiency and output, making all nations richer.*

A demonstration of the benefits of international specialization (the theory of comparative advantage) is provided in Chapter 35. At this juncture we may note that the same principles that motivate *individuals* to specialize and then exchange their goods and services (Chapters 1 and 2) also motivate *nations* to specialize and then exchange their goods and services in international trade. In both cases, **productivity** and total output increase.

productivity: Output per unit of input, e.g., output per labor hour.

Competitiveness

The increased output and productivity that specialization makes possible is not the only benefit of international trade. *Trade stimulates improvements in productivity.* The presence of foreign producers keeps domestic producers on their toes. To compete in international markets, domestic producers must reduce costs and increase efficiency. Likewise, foreign producers must maintain a competitive position in the face of improvements in American productivity. This mutual competitiveness tends to improve efficiency, shifting the production-possibilities curve outward.

In recent years America's huge trade deficits have provoked questions about the competitiveness of U.S. producers. The excess of imports over exports has suggested to many people that America is not producing goods of the quality and value that consumers demand. Productivity may have lagged in some U.S. industries. And other nations inevitably become more efficient in producing certain goods and services. But the trade gap is not a general indictment of U.S. competitiveness.

As we have observed, international trade and capital flows are interrelated, and both are directly influenced by exchange rates. In the early 1980s, the relative attractiveness of America's capital markets led to a surge of capital inflows and a higher exchange rate for the U.S. dollar. Between 1981 and 1985 the world value of the U.S. dollar rose 50 percent. This made all American goods more expensive in international markets. To *maintain* their prices in international markets, American producers would have had to cut costs enough to offset that increase in the dollar's value. Although American productivity increased faster than foreign productivity in those years, few U.S. producers could stay ahead of the rising dollar. The resulting increase in the trade deficit was a product of the rising dollar, not of a decline in U.S. productivity.

Although a trade gap is not necessarily evidence of declining competitiveness, it does draw policy attention to productivity issues. Productivity improvements are essential to economic growth and rising living standards. If a trade gap stimulates fiscal, monetary, and supply-side policies that foster productivity advances, then the economy may be better off as a result. By the same token, trade gaps remind us that policies that restrain productivity improvements (research, innovation, and investment) also have international consequences.

GLOBAL COORDINATION

As all countries begin to acknowledge the international dimensions of their economies, the desire for coordination grows. We have observed, for example, that restrictive monetary policies in the United States may spark a capital inflow. That capital inflow may create a predicament for domestic monetary policy. The Fed may be forced to choose between high interest rates that attract foreign capital (and thereby increase the value of the dollar) or low interest rates that stimulate the domestic economy. This is exactly the kind of dilemma the Fed confronted in 1990 (see World View, page 437). It wanted to help stimulate domestic spending with faster money-supply growth, yet it also needed to keep interest rates high enough to attract foreign capital.

The Fed need not shoulder this burden alone, however. The motivation for a capital inflow into the United States is the *difference* between domestic and foreign interest rates. If foreign interest rates were to fall, then the Fed's job would be easier. It could then let domestic interest rates decline without worrying about a sudden capital outflow.

But the Fed has no direct power over foreign interest rates. Other nations have their own central banks, which establish their own money-supply and interest-rate targets. Declining interest rates may not be part of their domestic policy agendas.

There is some basis for seeking cooperation here, however. Recall that a capital *inflow* into the United States represents a capital *outflow* for other nations. Similarly, a trade *deficit* for the United States means that other nations must have a trade *surplus*. In a global market, **any imbalances in capital or trade flows affect all trading partners.** Thus the U.S. trade deficits and capital surpluses are really *global* problems, not just domestic headaches.

The same community of interests applies to other nations' macro performance. In the late 1980s Germany's economy grew very slowly. This sluggish growth caused high unemployment and stagnant living standards for

In The News

Stock-Price Collapse Is Confronting Fed with Policy Dilemma

A Loss of Economic Control

WASHINGTON—The stock market's collapse is propelling the Federal Reserve toward a perilous policy choice: to defend the U.S. dollar by keeping interest rates up or to defend U.S. economic growth by keeping interest rates down.

The stakes are enormous. If the Fed keeps rates too high, it risks repeating the mistakes of the 1930s and turning the market's drop into an economic slump. But if it lets rates fall too low, it may cause a free fall of the dollar, reignite fears of inflation and set off a renewed flight from the U.S. by foreign investors.

"There are no favorable choices," says David Jones of Aubrey G. Lanston & Co. "This shows the extent to which we've lost control of our economic destiny by borrowing too much, spending too much and importing too much."

—Walter S. Mossberg and Alan Murray

The Wall Street Journal, October 29, 1987, p. 1. Reprinted by permission of *The Wall Street Journal,* © Dow Jones & Company, Inc. (1987). All Rights Reserved.

German citizens. Germany's slow growth had international repercussions as well. With their incomes stagnating, German consumers were less able to buy imported goods. The resulting decline in export sales for other countries made foreign producers and consumers bear some of the pain of Germany's growth recession. Consequently, other nations had a direct interest in Germany's faster economic growth.

The dismantling of the Berlin Wall had the opposite effect. The sudden availability of more resources and an increase in demand from East Germany, Poland, and other Eastern European countries stimulated the (West) German economy. This economic boon increased the international value of the German mark and enabled Germans to buy more imported goods. Hence, the U.S. economy received a positive external shock from the fall of the Berlin Wall.

This global interdependence has sparked efforts to coordinate the macro policies of national economies. Such global coordination takes many forms. It includes explicit agreements to encourage or limit trade, joint efforts to "stabilize" exchange rates, and "understandings" about appropriate monetary and fiscal policies. Such global coordination ultimately reduces the likelihood of severe external shocks that would disrupt many nations. The stock-market crash of 1987 (see In the News) illustrates this benefit. Although the "Black Monday" of 1987 was more severe than the "Black Thursday" of 1929, it did not spark a worldwide calamity. Instead, the industrial nations of the world worked quickly and collectively to coordinate their monetary and market policies, thus helping to contain the damage of the stock-market crash.

Global interests will never fully displace national policy priorities. However, even limited global coordination helps smooth out some of the rough spots of macro performance in an increasingly interdependent world.

SUMMARY

- The United States exports about 10 percent of total output, and imports an even larger percentage. This international trade ties our macro performance to that of the rest of the world.

• Imports represent leakage from the circular flow and so tend to reduce equilibrium GNP. The marginal propensity to import also diminishes the impact of stimulative fiscal and monetary policies.

• Exports represent added spending on domestic output and so tend to increase equilibrium GNP. This added spending may conflict with restrictive macro policy objectives.

• Trade imbalances occur when exports and imports are unequal. Trade deficits imply that we are consuming more output than we are producing. Trade surpluses indicate the opposite.

• Capital imbalances occur when the inflow of capital does not equal the outflow of capital. Capital surpluses help finance trade deficits but may also conflict with macro policy goals at home or abroad.

• International trade and capital flows place additional constraints on macro policy. Macro policy must both anticipate and respond to changes in trade and capital flows.

• The benefits of international trade and capital markets are the broadening of consumption possibilities and the enhanced productivity they promote. Productivity advances arise from specialization in production and from the competitive pressure of foreign producers and markets.

Terms to Remember Define the following terms:

imports	trade surplus
leakage	trade deficit
multiplier	capital deficit
marginal propensity to import (MPM)	capital surplus
marginal propensity to save (MPS)	exchange rate
exports	productivity
net exports	

Questions for Discussion

1. Suppose investors in other countries increased their purchases of U.S. corporate stock. How would this influx of capital affect the U.S. economy?

2. Why is it unrealistic to expect trade flows to be balanced?

3. U.S. farmers export about one-third of their major crops. What would happen to America's farmers if foreigners stopped buying American food? What would happen to our macro equilibrium?

4. Japan imports most of the raw materials it uses in the production of finished goods. If the international prices of raw materials rose sharply, how would Japan's economy be affected? Would Japanese exports be affected?

5. How would a tax cut in the United States affect international capital and trade flows?

Problems

1. Suppose that the expenditure patterns of a country are as follows:

$C = \$60$ billion per year $+ 0.8Y$
$I = \$100$ billion per year
$G = 0$ (no taxes either)
Exports = imports = \$10 billion per year

As a result of higher oil prices, this country must now spend an additional $10 billion per year on imported oil. Assuming that prices of other goods do not change, what impact will the higher oil prices have on equilibrium GNP?

2. Recompute the answer to problem 1 by assuming that the marginal propensity to import equals 0.1 (and thus that the MPC for domestic goods is 0.7).

MICROECONOMICS

PRODUCT MARKETS:
Basic Theory

The prices and products we see every day emerge from decisions made by millions of individual consumers and firms. A primary objective of microeconomic theory is to explain how those decisions are made. How do consumers decide which products to buy and in what quantities? How do business firms decide how much to produce? How are market outcomes affected by the *structure* of markets, i.e., the number and size of producers? These are the issues addressed in Chapters 19–24.

The Demand for Goods

*A*mericans love to go shopping. Consumer purchases of goods and services now exceed *$3 trillion* annually. This works out to about $12,000 of consumption for every man, woman, and child in the United States. On a per capita basis, this is five times as much as we consumed in 1929 and also about five times as much as the rest of the world spends today.

A major concern of microeconomics is to explain all of this activity. What drives us to department stores, grocery stores, and every Big Sale in town? More specifically,

- Why do we buy certain goods and not others?

- How do we decide how much of any good to buy?

- What factors change our consumption patterns?

The Law of Demand first encountered in Chapter 2 gives us some clues for answering these questions. But we need to look beyond that law to fashion more complete answers. We need to know what forces give demand curves their particular shape. We also need to know more about using demand curves to predict consumer behavior.

The motivations and behavior of consumers are of interest not only to economists, but also to sociologists, psychologists, advertisers, and just about everyone who owns or manages a business. Economists hope their theories of consumer demand will produce reliable forecasts of consumer behavior. People in business hope to use the principles of consumer demand to increase their sales and profits.

PATTERNS OF CONSUMPTION

Figure 19.1 provides a quick summary of how the average consumer dollar is spent. Nearly two-thirds of all consumer spending is for food and shelter. Out of the typical consumer dollar, 43 cents is devoted to housing—including everything from rent and repairs to utility bills and grass seed—and another 18 cents is spent on food.

The other large items in our shopping bag are transportation (car purchases and maintenance, gasoline, bus fares) and clothing. These items are followed by medical care, entertainment, and an assortment of other goods and services.

459

**FIGURE 19.1
How the Consumer
Dollar is Spent**

Consumers spend their
incomes on a vast array
of goods and services. This
figure summarizes those
consumption decisions by
showing how the average
consumer dollar is spent.
The goal of economic theory
is to explain and predict these
consumption choices.

Source: 1982—84 Consumer
Expenditure Survey.

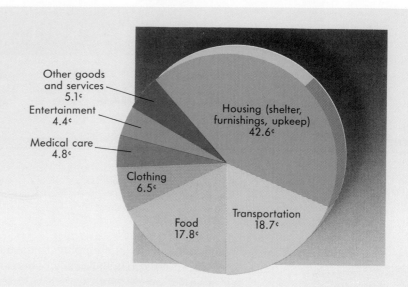

Other goods
and services
5.1¢

Entertainment
4.4¢

Medical care
4.8¢

Clothing
6.5¢

Food
17.8¢

Housing (shelter,
furnishings, upkeep)
42.6¢

Transportation
18.7¢

A closer look inside the average shopping bag reveals the specific items that we consume. For example, we observe that the average U.S. consumer purchases 298 eggs a year—slightly less than 1 per day. We also consume, on average, 220 pounds of meat each year, 121 pounds of potatoes, and 15 quarts of ice cream. Indeed, when all our food consumption is added up, it comes to 1,500 pounds of food per year for the average person! Small wonder that diet plans and health spas are so popular. In addition, we consume, on average, nearly 37 gallons of alcohol a year, while trying to maintain a sense of sobriety with 9.4 pounds of coffee.

Not all our consumer expenditures are related to food, of course. Food expenditures account for less than one-fifth of our total purchases. The variety of consumer items ranges from the practical to the useless, from the familiar to the bizarre. The list of consumer goods also grows longer daily, with over 100 new products introduced each week.

DETERMINANTS OF DEMAND

Why do we buy and consume so many goods and services year in and year out? Do our materialistic appetites know any limits? What leads us to buy some goods while rejecting others?

**The Sociopsychiatric
Explanation**

As one might expect, psychiatrists and psychologists have had a virtual field day formulating explanations of our behavior in the supermarket. Sigmund Freud was among the first to describe us poor mortals as bundles of subconscious (and unconscious) fears, complexes, and anxieties. From a Freudian perspective, we strive for ever higher levels of consumption to satisfy basic drives for security, sex, and ego gratification. Like the most primitive of people, we seek to clothe and adorn ourselves in ways that assert our identity and worth. We eat and smoke too much because we need the oral gratifications and security associated with mother's breast. Self-indulgence, in general, creates in our minds the safety and satisfactions of childhood. Oversized homes and cars provide us with a source of warmth and security remembered from the womb. On the other hand, we often buy and consume some things we expressly don't desire, just to assert our rebellious feelings against our parents (or parent substitutes). In Freud's view, it is the constant interplay of these id, ego, and superego drives that motivates us to buy, buy, buy.

Sociologists have provided still more explanations for our consumption behavior. Lloyd Warner and David Riesman, for example, have noted our yearning to stand above the crowd, to receive recognition from the masses. For those of truly exceptional talents, such recognition may come easily. But for the ordinary person, recognition may depend on conspicuous consumption. A larger car, a newer fashion, a more exotic vacation become expressions of identity that provoke recognition, even social acceptance. Thus, we strive for ever higher levels of consumption—so as to *surpass* the Joneses, not just to keep up with them.

Not *all* consumption is motivated by ego or status concerns, of course. Some food is consumed for the sake of self-preservation, some clothing for warmth, and some housing for shelter. Once our incomes exceed minimum subsistence levels, however, the potential for discretionary spending grows. Spending on nonnecessities is obviously more susceptible to the dictates of personality and social interaction. This helps explain why women have different spending preferences than men (see In the News) and affluent teenagers have their own unique tastes (Figure 19.2).

The Economic Explanation   Sociopsychiatric theories help explain why consumers *desire* certain goods. They don't explain which goods will actually be purchased, however. Desire is only the first step in the consumption process. To acquire goods and

In The News

CONSUMPTION PATTERNS

Men vs. Women: How They Spend

Now that so many men live on their own or share shopping chores in two-earner households, two Harvard economists ask: Do men really spend money differently from women?

Based on an analysis of 2,443 households from the Bureau of Labor Statistics' Consumer Expenditure Survey, David E. Bloom and Sanders D. Korenman found significant differences in the way men and women spend money. Women age 18 to 64 who live alone spend more than twice as much as men on medical services, including prescription drugs and health insurance. Single women also allocate a bigger share of their budgets to gifts and make three times the cash contributions to charitable activities that men do.

Men, on the other hand, spend more on entertainment, food, and drink. Five percent of men's budgets go to en-

tertainment compared with 3% of women's. Because they eat away from home more often, men outspend women in that area almost 2 to 1. (Women spend 13% of their budgets on food for the home; men spend 11%.) Men spend 5% of their budgets on alcohol while women spend only 2%.

Although some of the differences appear small, in the aggregate, they amount to billions of dollars. Providers of goods and services can't assume that just because single men and women lead similar work lives, their spending patterns will be the same. Advertising for medical services and gifts may find a more receptive audience among women, whereas some restaurants may want to target men.

**FIGURE 19.2
Affluent Teenagers**

The following percentages of U.S. teenagers own these items:

Source: Rand Youth Poll.

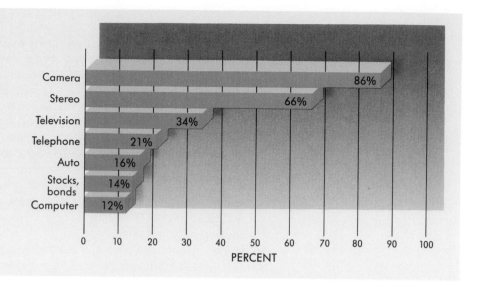

Camera 86%
Stereo 66%
Television 34%
Telephone 21%
Auto 16%
Stocks, bonds 14%
Computer 12%

0 10 20 30 40 50 60 70 80 90 100
PERCENT

services, one must be willing and able to *pay* for one's wants. Producers won't give you their goods just because you want to satisfy your Freudian desires. They want money in exchange for their goods. Hence prices and income are just as relevant to the consumption decision as are more basic desires and preferences.

In explaining consumer behavior, then, economists focus on the demand for goods and services. **Demand** entails the *willingness and ability to pay* for goods and services. Many people with a strong desire for a Rolls-Royce have neither the ability nor the willingness actually to buy it; they do not *demand* Rolls-Royces. Similarly, there are many rich people who are willing and able to buy goods they only remotely desire; they *demand* all kinds of goods and services.

demand: The ability and willingness to buy specific quantities of a good at alternative prices in a given time period, *ceteris paribus.*

To say that someone *demands* a particular good means that he or she is able and willing to buy it at some price(s). ***An individual's demand for a specific product is determined by:***

• ***Tastes*** (desire for this and other goods)

• ***Income*** (of the consumer)

• ***Expectations*** (for income, prices, tastes)

• ***Other goods*** (their availability and prices)

Note again that desire (tastes) is only one determinant of demand. Other determinants of demand (income, expectations, and other goods) also influence whether a person will be willing and able to buy a certain good at a specific price.

In the remainder of this chapter we shall examine these determinants of demand. Our objective is not only to explain consumer behavior but also to see (and predict) how consumption patterns change in response to *changes* in the price of a good, or to *changes* in underlying tastes, income, prices or availability of other goods, or expectations.

THE DEMAND CURVE

Utility Theory

The starting point for an economic analysis of demand is quite simple. Economists take consumers' tastes as given, then see how those tastes affect consumption decisions. We assume that the more additional pleasure a product gives us, the higher the price we would be willing to pay for it. If the oral sensation of buttered popcorn at the movies really turns you on, you're likely to be willing to pay dearly for it. If you have no great taste or desire for popcorn, the theater might have to give it away before you'd eat it.

utility: The pleasure or satisfaction obtained from a good or service.

total utility: The amount of satisfaction obtained from entire consumption of a product.

marginal utility: The change in total utility obtained from an additional (marginal) unit of a good or service consumed.

Total vs. marginal utility Economists use the term **utility** to refer to the expected pleasure, or satisfaction, obtained from goods and services. We also make an important distinction between total utility and marginal utility. **Total utility** refers to the amount of satisfaction obtained from your *entire* consumption of a product. By contrast, **marginal utility** refers to the amount of satisfaction you get from consuming the *last* (i.e., "marginal") unit of a product. More generally, note that

$$\text{Marginal utility} = \frac{\text{change in total utility}}{\text{change in quantity}}$$

Diminishing marginal utility The concepts of total and marginal utility explain not only why we buy popcorn at the movies but also why we stop eating it at some point. Even people who love popcorn (i.e., derive great utility from it), and can afford it, don't eat endless quantities of popcorn. Why not? Presumably because the thrill diminishes with each mouthful. The first box of popcorn may bring sensual gratification, but the second or third box is likely to bring a stomachache. We express this change in perceptions by noting that the marginal utility of the first box of popcorn is higher than the additional or marginal utility derived from the second box.

The behavior of popcorn connoisseurs is not abnormal. Generally speaking, the amount of additional utility we obtain from a product declines as we continue to consume it. The third pizza is not so desirable as the first, the sixth beer not so satisfying as the fifth, and so forth. Indeed, this phenomenon of diminishing marginal utility is so nearly universal that economists have fashioned a law around it. This **law of diminishing marginal utility** states that each successive unit of a good consumed yields less *additional* utility.

law of diminishing marginal utility: The marginal utility of a good declines as more of it is consumed in a given time period.

The law of diminishing marginal utility does *not* say that we won't like the third box of popcorn, the second pizza, or the sixth beer; it just says we won't like them as much as the ones we've already consumed.[1] This expectation is illustrated in Figure 19.3, in which total utility is related to varying levels of consumption. Notice that total utility continues to rise as we consume the first five boxes (ugh!) of popcorn. But total utility increases by smaller and smaller increments. Each successive step of the total utility curve in Figure 19.3 is a little smaller.

The height of each step of the total utility curve in Figure 19.3 represents *marginal* utility—the increments to total utility. *Marginal* utility is clearly diminishing. Nevertheless, because marginal utility is still positive, total utility

[1]Note also that time is important here: if the first pizza was eaten last year, the second pizza may now taste just as good. The law of diminishing marginal utility is most relevant to short time periods.

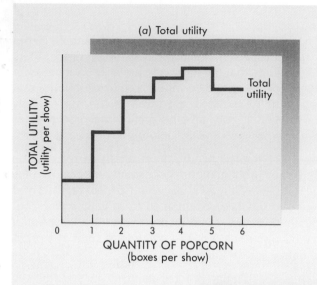

(a) Total utility

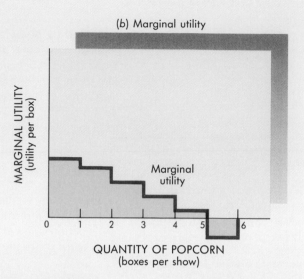

(b) Marginal utility

FIGURE 19.3 Total vs. Marginal Utility

The *total* utility derived from consuming a product comes from the *marginal* utilities of each successive unit. The total utility curve shows how each of the first five boxes of popcorn contributes to total utility. Note that each successive step is smaller. This reflects the law of diminishing marginal utility.

The sixth box of popcorn causes the steps to descend; the sixth box actually *reduces* total utility. This means that the sixth box has *negative* marginal utility.

The marginal utility curve (*b*) shows the change in total utility with each additional unit. It is derived from the total utility curve. Marginal utility here is positive but diminishing for the first five boxes.

must be increasing. The *total* utility curve keeps rising. ***So long as marginal utility is positive, total utility must be increasing*** (note that the total utility curve is still rising for the fifth box of popcorn).

The situation changes with the sixth box of popcorn. According to Figure 19.3, the good sensations associated with popcorn consumption are completely forgotten by the time the sixth box arrives. Nausea and stomach cramps dominate. Indeed, the sixth box is absolutely *distasteful*, as reflected in the downturn of total utility and the negative value for marginal utility. We were happier—in possession of more total utility—with only five boxes of popcorn. The sixth box—yielding negative marginal utility—has reduced total satisfaction.

Not every good ultimately reaches negative marginal utility. And it's clear that people won't desire those increments of a good that detract from total satisfaction. Yet the more general principle of diminishing marginal utility is experienced daily. That is to say, ***additional quantities of a good tend to yield increasingly smaller increments of satisfaction.*** Total utility continues to rise, but at an ever slower rate as more of a good is consumed. For our purposes, it does not matter whether marginal utility can be measured (it cannot), just so long as it declines with continued consumption of a good. There are exceptions to the law of diminishing marginal utility, but not many. (Can you think of any?)

Price and Quantity

How much of a certain good we are willing to buy at any particular price depends not only on its marginal utility (a measure of our "taste"), but also on our income, our expectations, and the prices of alternative goods and services. Rather than try to explain all these forces at once, however, let us focus on the relationship between the *price* of the good and the amount of it we are willing to buy. This simplification is common to economic analysis. If we want to focus on the relationship between any two phenomena (e.g., price and consumption), we momentarily ignore everything else. This doesn't mean that other forces are unimportant, just that we want to proceed one step at a time. In effect, we are assuming that everything else is constant, or unchanging. This is the **ceteris paribus** assumption first encountered in Chapter 2.

ceteris paribus: The assumption of nothing else changing.

With the aid of *ceteris paribus,* the transition from utility theory to the law of demand is simple. Recall our earlier observation that the willingness to pay is directly related to marginal utility; the more marginal utility a product delivers, the more a consumer will be willing to pay for it. But we have also noted that marginal utility *diminishes* as increasing quantities of a product

**FIGURE 19.4
A Demand
Schedule and Curve**

Consumers are generally willing to buy larger quantities of a good at lower prices. This demand schedule illustrates the specific quantities demanded at alternative prices. If popcorn sold for 25 cents per ounce, this consumer would buy 12 ounces per show (row *F*). At higher prices, less popcorn would be purchased.

A downward–sloping demand curve expresses the law of demand: the quantity of a good demanded increases as its price falls. People buy more popcorn at low prices than at high prices. Notice that points *A* through *J* on the curve correspond to the rows of the demand schedule.

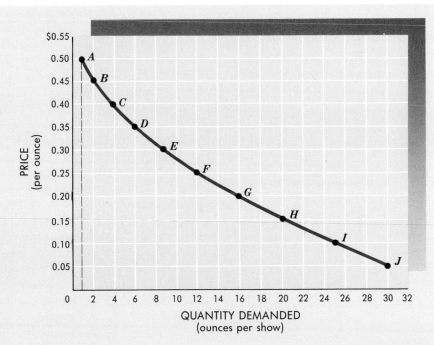

	Price (per ounce)	Quantity demanded (ounces per show)
A	$0.50	1
B	0.45	2
C	0.40	4
D	0.35	6
E	0.30	9
F	0.25	12
G	0.20	16
H	0.15	20
I	0.10	25
J	0.05	30

are consumed. This suggests that consumers will be willing to pay progressively less for additional quantities of a product. The moviegoer who is willing to pay 50 cents for that first mouth-watering ounce of buttered popcorn may not be willing to pay so much for a second or third ounce. The same is true for the second pizza, the sixth beer, and so forth. *With given income, taste, expectations, and prices of other goods and services, **people are willing to buy additional quantities of a good only if its price falls.*** In other words, as the marginal utility of a good diminishes, so does our willingness to pay. This inverse relationship between the quantity demanded of a good and its price is referred to as the **law of demand.** Figure 19.4 illustrates this relationship again, for the case of popcorn. Notice that the **demand curve** slopes downward.

law of demand: The quantity of a good demanded in a given time period increases as its price falls, *ceteris paribus.*

demand curve: A curve describing the quantities of a good a consumer is willing and able to buy at alternative prices in a given time period, *ceteris paribus.*

The law of demand and the law of diminishing marginal utility tell us nothing about why we crave popcorn or why our cravings subside. They simply describe our market behavior.

PRICE ELASTICITY

The theory of demand gives us some general insights into consumer behavior. Often, however, much more specific information is desired. Imagine you owned a theater and were actually worried about popcorn prices and sales. The general observation that popcorn sales decline when prices increase would be of little use. What you would really want to know is *by how much* the quantity demanded fell when the price was raised. And you'd want to know how total revenues—the dollar value of total sales—were affected.

Such concerns are not unique to profit-hungry theater managers. In 1982 President Reagan's advisers urged him to raise excise taxes on cigarettes, liquor, and gasoline. The objective of the proposed tax increases was to raise government revenues. In the process, however, the prices of these products would have gone up and their sales would have declined. The resulting decline in quantity demanded would have diminished output and employment in those industries. Because unemployment rates were already quite high, President Reagan decided against such tax hikes. (He later changed his mind, however, and raised taxes on all three products in 1983 and 1984.)

Even communists have to worry about the law of demand. In the Soviet Union and China, the prices of most goods are still set by central planners. In setting prices, the central planners must consider how consumption will vary with different prices. If the price of wheat is set too low, the quantity demanded may exceed available supplies, and consumer demand will not be met. On the other hand, if the price of wheat is raised too high, the quantity demanded may fall so far that the nutritional well-being of the population will be threatened.

The central question in all these decisions is the response of quantity demanded to a change in price. ***The response of consumers to a change in price is measured by the price elasticity of demand.*** Specifically, the **price elasticity of demand** refers to the percentage change in quantity demanded divided by the percentage change in price—that is,

price elasticity of demand: The percentage change in quantity demanded divided by the percentage change in price.

$$\bullet \quad \text{Price elasticity} \atop (E) = \frac{\text{percentage change in quantity demanded}}{\text{percentage change in price}}$$

W🌐RLD VIEW

CHANGING CONSUMPTION

Curbing Smoking

Nations around the world have tried to curb cigarette smoking. Consumption theory has provided some useful ideas, about how this might be done.

Changing Tastes

The cigarette industry has spent billions of dollars on advertising to convince consumers that smoking is smart, elegant, and pleasurable. To counter this effort, governments have restricted cigarette advertising, forced manufacturers to issue health warnings, and undertaken antismoking campaigns in the media. All such efforts attempt to *shift the demand curve to the left.* Some examples:

USA. Television advertising was prohibited in 1971. Health warnings are required on cigarette packs, printed advertising, and billboards.

Sweden. Print advertisements may portray only a cigarette pack against a plain background; no billboard or poster advertising is permitted.

Sudan. All cigarette advertising is prohibited.

Cuba. Fidel Castro gave up smoking in 1985 and urged his countrymen to follow his example.

Raising Prices

Higher prices also can deter people from smoking, by *changing the quantity demanded.* Some examples:

USA. Between 1981 and 1987, the price of cigarettes in the United States increased from 67 cents to $1.10 a pack. This large price increase reduced the quantity demanded, especially among young teenagers. According to Professor Jeffery Harris of M.I.T., the price increase induced 2 million Americans to quit smoking and 600,000 teenagers not to start.

Great Britain. The British government imposes an extra tax on high-tar and high-nicotine cigarettes.

Poland. In Poland cigarettes cost only 22 zlotys, or about 65 cents a pack. With the world's lowest prices, Poland also has one of the highest levels of consumption. Per capita cigarette consumption exceeds 3,500 in Poland, versus roughly 2,500 in the United States.

Bans on Smoking

Outright bans on smoking represent an effort to *circumvent the market,* preventing smokers from consuming as many cigarettes as they are willing and able to buy. Some examples:

USA. Smoking is prohibited or restricted in federal offices and military facilities. In 37 states and 400 cities smoking is limited in public places.

Spain. Smoking is prohibited on public transportation; segregated smoking areas are designated in public buildings and large commercial establishments.

East Germany. Smoking is not permitted on public transportation or at railway stations; smoking is restricted in restaurants.

According to the law of demand, when price increases (decreases), the quantity demanded decreases (increases). Since price and quantity demanded always move in opposite directions, the price elasticity of demand (E) is always negative. However, E is typically expressed in absolute terms (without the minus sign).

Computing Price Elasticity

To get a feel for the concept of elasticity, let us return to the popcorn counter at the movies. We have already observed that consumers respond to reductions in the price of popcorn by demanding larger quantities of it. At a price of 45 cents an ounce (point B in Figure 19.4), the average moviegoer demands 2 ounces of popcorn per show. At the lower price of 40 cents per ounce (point C), the quantity demanded jumps to 4 ounces per show.

We can summarize this response with the price elasticity of demand. To do so, we have to calculate the *percentage* changes in quantity and price. Consider the percentage change in quantity first. In this case, the change in quantity demanded is 4 ounces − 2 ounces = 2 ounces. The *percentage* change in quantity is therefore

$$\text{Percentage change in quantity} = \frac{2}{q}$$

The problem is to transform the denominator q into a number. Should we use the quantity of popcorn purchased *before* the price reduction, that is, $q_1 = 2$? Or should we use the quantity purchased *after* the price reduction, that is, $q_2 = 4$? The choice of denominator will have a marked impact on our calculation of the percentage change. To ensure consistency, economists prefer to use the *average* quantity in the denominator.[2] The average quantity is simply

$$\text{Average quantity} = \frac{q_1 + q_2}{2} = \frac{2 + 4}{2} = 3 \text{ ounces}$$

We can now complete the calculation of the percentage change in quantity demanded. It is

- $$\text{Percentage change in quantity demanded} = \frac{\text{change in quantity}}{\text{average quantity}} = \frac{q_1 - q_2}{\frac{q_1 + q_2}{2}} = \frac{2}{3} = 0.667$$

Popcorn sales increased by an average of 67 percent when the price of popcorn was reduced from 45 cents to 40 cents per ounce.

The computation of the percentage change in price is similar. We first note that the price of popcorn fell by 5 cents (45¢ − 40¢) when we move from point B to point C on the demand curve (Figure 19.4). We then compute the *average* price of popcorn in this range of the demand curve as

$$\text{Average price of popcorn} = \frac{p_1 + p_2}{2} = \frac{45 + 40}{2} = 42.5 \text{ cents}$$

This is our denominator in calculating the percentage price change. Using these numbers, we see that

- $$\text{Percentage change in price} = \frac{\text{change in price}}{\text{average price}} = \frac{p_1 - p_2}{\frac{p_1 + p_2}{2}} = \frac{5}{42.5} = 0.118$$

The price of popcorn fell by 11.8 percent.

Now we have all the information required to compute the price elasticity of demand. In this case,

- $$E = \frac{\text{percentage change in quantity}}{\text{percentage change in price}} = \frac{q_1 - q_2}{\frac{q_1 + q_2}{2}} \div \frac{p_1 - p_2}{\frac{p_1 + p_2}{2}} = \frac{0.667}{0.118} = 5.65$$

What have we learned from all these calculations? Have we gotten anything useful? Fortunately, the answer is yes. The computed elasticity of demand is a very useful number. It says that the consumer response to a price reduction will be extremely large. Specifically, the quantity of popcorn consumed will increase 5.65 times as fast as price falls. A 1 percent reduction in price brings about a 5.65 percent increase in purchases. The theater manager

[2]This procedure is referred to as the *arc* (midpoint) elasticity of demand. If a single quantity (price) is used in the denominator, we refer to the *point* elasticity of demand.

can therefore boost popcorn sales greatly by lowering price a little. Central planners would view such a high elasticity of demand as signaling the need for great caution in abruptly changing the price of wheat.

Elastic vs. inelastic   In general, we categorize goods according to their relative elasticity—whether E is larger or smaller than 1. If E is larger than 1, demand is *relatively elastic* in the immediate price range. If E is less than 1, we say demand is *relatively inelastic*. In that case, the percentage change in quantity demanded is less than the percentage change in price; that is, consumers are not very responsive to price changes. Notice in Table 19.1, for example, the relatively low elasticity of demand for coffee and cigarettes. When the prices of these products increase, consumers don't reduce their consumption very much. In the extreme case, when quantity demanded does not respond at all to a change in price—people are willing and able to buy the same (unchanged) quantity of a good no matter how high its price goes—the price elasticity of demand is zero. Varying degrees of elasticity are illustrated in Figure 19.5.

Price Elasticity and Total Revenue

total revenue: The price of a product multiplied by the quantity sold in a given time period: $p \times q$.

The concept of price elasticity is useful for destroying the popular misconception that producers often charge the "highest price possible." Except in the very rare case of completely inelastic demand, this notion makes no sense. Indeed, higher prices may actually *lower* total sales revenue.

The **total revenue** of a seller is the amount of money received from product sales. It is determined by the quantity of the product sold and the price at which it is sold. Specifically,

$$\bullet \quad \frac{\text{Total}}{\text{revenue}} = \text{price} \times \frac{\text{quantity}}{\text{sold}}$$

If the price of popcorn is 40 cents per ounce and only 4 ounces are sold, total revenue equals $1.60 per show. This total revenue is illustrated by the shaded

---

TABLE 19.1   Elasticity Estimates

Price elasticities vary greatly. When the price of gasoline increases, consumers reduce their consumption only slightly. When the price of fish increases, however, consumers cut back their consumption substantially. These differences reflect the availability of immediate substitutes, the prices of the goods, and the amount of time available for changing behavior.

Type of elasticity	Estimate
Relatively elastic (E > 1)	
Airline travel, long run	2.4
Fresh fish	2.2
New cars, short run	1.2–1.5
Unitary elastic (E = 1)	
Private education	1.1
Radios and televisions	1.2
Shoes	0.9
Relatively inelastic (E < 1)	
Cigarettes	0.4
Coffee	0.3
Gasoline, short run	0.2

Source: Compiled from Hendrick S. Houthakker and Lester D. Taylor, *Consumer Demand in the United States, 1929–1970* (Cambridge: Harvard University Press, 1966); and F. W. Bell, "The Pope and Price of Fish," *American Economic Review,* December 1968.

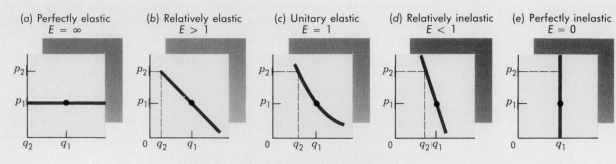

FIGURE 19.5 Degrees of Elasticity

These various demand curves illustrate different responses to a price increase from p_1 to p_2. In each case, the initial quantity demanded at price p_1 is q_1. In part *a* when price rises to p_2, no output is sold (quantity demanded drops to zero); the demand curve is perfectly elastic. In part *e* quantity demanded does not change at all; people continue to buy the quantity q_1 even when price goes up. In that case, demand is completely inelastic. Between these two extremes, consumer response may be relatively elastic (part *b*), unitary elastic (part *c*), or relatively inelastic (part *d*).

rectangle in Figure 19.6. (Recall that the area of a rectangle is equal to its height [p] times its width [q].)

Now consider what happens to total revenue when the price of popcorn is increased. From the law of demand, we know that an increase in price will lead to a decrease in quantity demanded. Without Figure 19.6 it is not apparent whether total revenue will rise or fall. The change in total revenue depends on *how much* quantity demanded falls when price goes up. This brings us back to the concept of elasticity.

**FIGURE 19.6
Elasticity and
Total Revenue**

Total revenue is equal to the price of the product times the quantity sold. It is illustrated by the area of the rectangle formed by $p \times q$. The shaded rectangle illustrates total revenue ($1.60) at a price of 40 cents and a quantity demanded of 4 ounces. When price is increased to 45 cents, the rectangle and total revenue shrink (see dashed lines) because demand is relatively elastic in that price range. Price hikes increase total revenue only if demand is relatively inelastic.

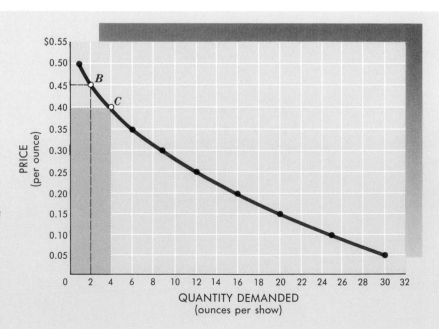

Suppose we raise popcorn prices again, from 40 cents back to 45 cents. What happens to total revenue? At 40 cents per box, 4 ounces are sold (see Figure 19.6) and total revenue equals $1.60. If we increase the price to 45 cents, only 2 ounces are sold and total revenue drops to 90 cents. In this case, an increase in price leads to a decrease in total revenue. This new and smaller total revenue is illustrated by the dashed rectangle in Figure 19.6.

Price increases don't always lower total revenue. If demand were relatively *inelastic* ($E < 1$), a price increase would lead to higher total revenue. Thus we conclude that

- *A price hike increases total revenue only if demand is relatively inelastic (E < 1).*

- *A price hike reduces total revenue if demand is relatively elastic (E > 1).*

- *A price hike does not change total revenue if demand is unitary elastic (E = 1).*

Table 19.2 summarizes these and other responses to price changes.

Once we know the price elasticity of demand, we can predict quite accurately how consumers will respond to changing prices. By the same token, we can also predict what will happen to the total revenue of the seller. However, *the elasticity of demand applies to a specific range of prices only.* The demand for popcorn or any other product may be highly elastic at one price level but relatively inelastic at other prices. Figure 19.7 illustrates how E varies along a linear demand curve.[3] Finally, elasticity, like the demand curve itself, is subject to the vagaries of changing tastes, changing incomes, and changes in the prices or availability of alternative goods. All of these potential changes are ignored when we calculate elasticity along a given demand curve.

Determinants of Elasticity

The price elasticity of demand is influenced by all of the determinants of the demand curve. Table 19.1 indicated the actual price elasticity for a variety of familiar goods and services. These large differences in elasticity are explained by several factors. One of them is *price* relative to income. If the price of an item is very high in relation to one's income, then price changes

---

[3]Thus elasticity is not equal to the slope of the demand curve. A linear demand curve has a constant slope but a changing elasticity.

TABLE 19.2   Price Elasticity of Demand and Total Revenue

The impact of higher prices on total revenue depends on the price elasticity of demand. Higher prices result in higher total revenue only if demand is relatively inelastic. If demand is relatively elastic, *lower* prices result in *higher* revenues.	If demand is:	and price increases, total revenue will:	and price decreases, total revenue will:
	Elastic ($E > 1$)	decrease	increase
	Inelastic ($E < 1$)	increase	decrease
	Unitary elastic ($E = 1$)	not change	not change

FIGURE 19.7
The Changing Price Elasticity of Demand

The concept of price elasticity can be used to determine whether kids will spend more money on bubble gum when its price rises, an issue of continuing concern to bubble gum producers. The answer to this question is yes and no, depending on how high the price goes.

Notice in the table and the graphs that total revenue rises when the price of bubble gum increases from 1 cent to 2 cents, and again to 3 cents. At low prices, the demand for bubble gum is relatively inelastic: price and total revenue move in the same direction.

As the price of bubble gum continues to increase, however, total revenue starts to fall. As the price is increased from 3 cents to 4 cents, total revenue drops. At higher prices, the demand for bubble gum is relatively elastic: price and total revenue move in opposite directions. Hence the price elasticity of demand depends on where one is on the demand curve; that is, at which price–quantity combination one starts.

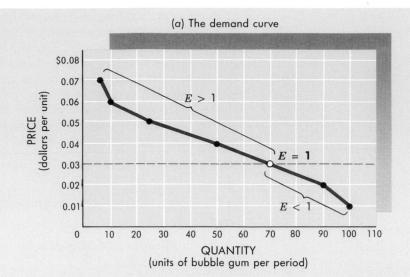

(a) The demand curve

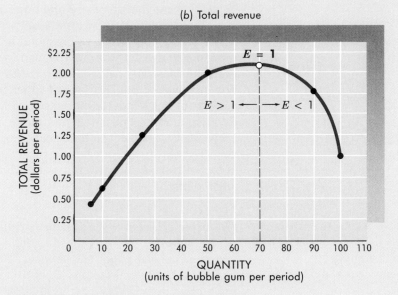

(b) Total revenue

Price of bubble gum	×	Quantity demanded	=	Total revenue	
$0.01		100		$1.00	⎱ Low elasticity
0.02		90		1.80	⎰ (total revenue rising
0.03		70		2.10	as price increases)
0.04		50		2.00	⎱
0.05		25		1.25	⎰ High elasticity
0.06		10		0.60	⎰ (total revenue falling
0.07		6		0.42	as price increases)

will be important. Airline travel and new cars, for example, are quite expensive, so even a small percentage change in their prices could have a big impact on a consumer's budget (and consumption decisions). By contrast, coffee is so cheap for most people that even a large percentage change in price is of little real significance.

A second determinant of elasticity is the *availability of substitutes*. The high elasticity of demand for fish reflects the fact that consumers can always eat chicken, beef, or pork if fish prices rise. On the other hand, most cigarette smokers cannot imagine any other product that could substitute for a cigarette. As a consequence, when cigarette prices rise, smokers do not reduce their purchases very much at all. The price elasticity of demand for cigarettes is very low.

Finally, *time* affects the price elasticity of demand. Car owners cannot switch to coal-fired autos every time the price of gasoline goes up. In the short run, consumers are stuck with their gasoline-drinking automobiles and can only vary the amount of driving they do. Even that can't be varied much, however, unless one relocates one's home or job. Hence the quantity of gasoline demanded doesn't drop much immediately when gasoline prices increase. In the short run, the elasticity of demand for gasoline is quite low. With more time to adjust, however, consumers can buy more fuel-efficient cars, relocate homes or jobs, and even switch fuels. As a consequence, ***the long-run price elasticity of demand is higher than the short-run elasticity.***

OTHER ELASTICITIES

The price elasticity of demand tells us how consumers will respond to a change in the price of a good under the assumption of *ceteris paribus*. But other things do change, and consumption behavior may respond to those changes as well.

Shifts vs. Movements   We recognized this problem back in Chapter 2 when we first distinguished *movements* along a demand curve from *shifts* of the demand curve. A movement along an unchanged demand curve represents consumer response to a change in the price of that specific good. The magnitude of that movement is expressed in the price elasticity of demand.

When the underlying determinants of demand change, the entire demand curve shifts. These shifts also alter consumer behavior. The price elasticity of demand is of no use in gauging these behavioral responses, since it refers to price changes (movements along a constant demand curve) for that good only.

Income Elasticity   A change in any determinant of demand will shift the demand curve. Consider a change in consumer income. As we observed earlier, the demand for popcorn depends not only on taste, but also on income (as well as other determinants). If income were to change, we would expect popcorn consumption to change as well.

Suppose consumer incomes were to increase. How would popcorn consumption be affected? Figure 19.8 provides an answer. Before the change in income, consumers demanded 12 ounces of popcorn at a price of 25 cents per ounce. With more income to spend, they could munch even more popcorn. Indeed, the new demand curve (D_2) suggests that consumers will now purchase a greater quantity of popcorn at every price. The increase in income has caused a rightward *shift in demand*. If popcorn continues to sell for 25 cents per ounce, consumers will now purchase 16 ounces per show (point N) rather than only 12 ounces (point F).

In The News

PRICE ELASTICITY

Raising the D.C. Gas Tax: A Lesson in Elasticity

Like many local governments, the District of Columbia is perennially short of revenues. In an effort to raise additional revenue, Mayor Marion Barry of Washington, D.C., decided in early 1980 to increase the city's tax on gasoline. On August 6, 1980, the city government raised the gas tax to 18 cents per gallon, from the previous level of only 10 cents per gallon. The higher tax raised the retail price of gasoline by 8 cents, to $1.60 per gallon.

The mayor and city council thought the higher gas tax would be an easy way to increase city revenue. The difference of a few pennies a gallon would hardly be noticed, they reasoned, since gasoline prices were already so high. Furthermore, much of the increased tax would be paid by tourists and suburbanites rather than city residents (i.e., voters). Finally, a few pennies a gallon would generate lots of revenue, since District gas stations were then selling 16 million gallons a month.

The D.C. Department of Finance and Revenue know about the law of demand. But it thought the reduction in quantity demanded (gasoline sales) would be very small in relation to the gas-tax increase. Economists had consistently estimated the price elasticity of demand for gasoline to be very low (see Table 19.1).

Unfortunately, the District's projections were grossly in error. In August 1980, gasoline sales in the nation's capital fell from 16 million gallons per month to only 11 million. Ten gas stations closed down, and more than 300 service-station workers were laid off. Realizing his mistake, Mayor Barry asked the city council to repeal the higher gas tax in November, just four months after it was introduced.

The price elasticity of demand for D.C. gasoline obviously turned out to be much higher than the city had thought. How did the city make such a mistake? Evidently the leaders forgot about the *price and availability of other goods.* True, the price elasticity for gasoline is generally quite low. But motorists in the D.C. area can buy gasoline in the District itself or in the neighboring states of Virginia and Maryland. Hence there are readily available substitutes for D.C. gasoline. By driving just another mile or so, a motorist can buy gasoline not subject to D.C. taxes. When the price of D.C. gasoline went up, motorists responded by doing just that. The ready availability of cheaper gasoline in Maryland and Virginia doomed the hopes of the D.C. government for increased revenues.

**FIGURE 19.8
Income Elasticity**

If income changes, the demand curve *shifts.* In this case, an increase in income enables consumers to buy more popcorn at every price. At a price of 25 cents, the quantity demanded increases from 12 ounces (point *F*) to 16 ounces (point *N*). The *income elasticity of demand* measure this response of demand to a change in income.

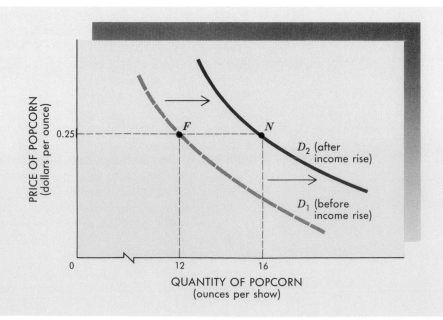

It appears that changes in income have a substantial impact on consumer demand for popcorn. The graph in Figure 19.8 does not tell us, however, how large the change in income was. The observed increase in popcorn consumption would be impressive if it resulted from a small increase in income. On the other hand, the observed sensitivity of popcorn consumption to income would be less impressive if it required a doubling of income to induce a small increase in popcorn purchases.

A simple calculation provides a more convenient measure of consumer responses to changes in income. The **income elasticity of demand** relates the *percentage* change in quantity demanded to the *percentage* change in income—that is,

income elasticity of demand: Percentage change in quantity demanded divided by percentage change in income.

$$\text{Income elasticity of demand} = \frac{\text{percentage change in quantity demanded}}{\text{percentage change in income}}$$

The similarity to the price elasticity of demand is apparent. In this case, however, the denominator refers to a change in one of the underlying determinants of demand.

Computing income elasticity As was the case with price elasticity, we compute income elasticity with *average* values for the changes in quantity and income. Suppose that the shift illustrated in Figure 19.8 occurred when income increased from $100 per week to $110 per week. We would then compute

$$\text{Income elasticity} = \frac{\dfrac{\text{change in quantity demanded}}{\text{average quantity}}}{\dfrac{\text{change in income}}{\text{average income}}}$$

$$= \frac{\dfrac{16 \text{ ounces} - 12 \text{ ounces}}{14 \text{ ounces}}}{\dfrac{\$110 - \$100}{\$115}}$$

$$= \frac{4}{14} \div \frac{10}{115}$$

$$= \frac{0.286}{0.087} = 3.29$$

Popcorn purchases are *very* sensitive to changes in income. When incomes rise by 8.7 percent, popcorn sales increase by a whopping 28.6 percent (i.e., 8.7 percent × 3.29)! The computed elasticity of 3.29 summarizes this relationship.

Normal vs. inferior goods Demand and income do not always move in the same direction. Popcorn is a **normal good** because consumers buy more of it when their incomes rise. People actually buy *less* of some goods, however, when they have more income. People tend to buy fewer discount clothes and less cheap beer when their incomes rise. With more money to spend, they switch to designer clothes and premium beers. The former items are called

normal good: Good for which demand increases when income rises.

inferior good: Good for which demand decreases when income rises.

inferior goods because the quantity demanded falls when income rises. For inferior goods, the income elasticity of demand is negative; for normal goods, it is positive.[4]

Cross-Price Elasticity

Changes in income are only one of the forces that shift demand curves. Consumers also alter their consumption patterns when other determinants of demand change.

If popcorn were the only snack offered in movie theaters, people would undoubtedly eat more of it. In reality, people have other choices: candy, soda, ice cream, and more. Thus the decision to buy popcorn depends not only on its price, but also on the price and availability of other goods.

Suppose for the moment that the prices of these other goods were to fall. Imagine that candy bars were put on sale at a quarter, rather than the usual dollar. Would this price reduction on candy affect the consumption of popcorn?

According to Figure 19.9, the demand for popcorn would *decrease* if the price of candy fell. The leftward shift of the demand curve tells us that consumers now demand less popcorn at every price. At 25 cents per ounce, consumers now demand only 8 ounces of popcorn (point *R*) rather than the previous 12 ounces (point *F*). In other words, a decline in the price of *candy* has caused a reduction in the demand for *popcorn*. We conclude that candy and popcorn are **substitute goods**—when the price of one declines, demand for the other falls.

substitute goods: Goods that substitute for each other; when the price of good *X* rises, the demand for good *Y* increases, *ceteris paribus*.

Popcorn sales would follow a very different path if the price of soda fell. People like to wash down their popcorn with soda. When soda prices fall, moviegoers actually buy *more* popcorn. Here again, *a change in the price*

[4]All goods have a negative *price* elasticity of demand, because of the law of demand. Income elasticities are usually positive but can also be negative, as noted.

FIGURE 19.9
Substitutes and Complements

The curve D_1 represents the initial demand for popcorn, given the prices of other goods. Other prices may change, however. If a reduction in the price of another good (candy) causes a *reduction* in the demand for this good (popcorn), the two goods are substitutes. Popcorn demand shifts to the left (to D_2) when the price of a substitute good falls.

If a reduction in the price of another good (e.g., Pepsi) leads to an *increase* in the demand for this good (popcorn), the two goods are complements. Popcorn demand shifts to the right (to D_3) when the price of a complementary good falls.

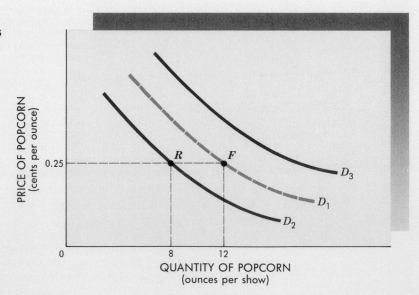

complementary goods: Goods frequently consumed in combination; when the price of good X rises, the demand for good Y falls, *ceteris paribus*.

of one good affects the demand for another good. In this case, however, we are dealing with **complementary goods** since a decline in the price of one good causes an increase in the demand for the other good.

The distinction between substitute goods and complementary goods is illustrated in Figure 19.9. Note that in the case of substitute goods, the price of one good and the demand for the other move in the *same* direction. (A *decrease* in candy prices causes a *decrease* in popcorn demand.) Likewise, as the price of compact discs *declined,* the demand for long-playing vinyl discs declined (see In the News); CDs and LPs are *substitute* goods.

In the case of complementary goods (e.g., Pepsi and popcorn, cream and coffee), the price of one good and the demand for the other move in opposite directions. This helps explain why American consumers cut back on car purchases when the price of gasoline jumped in 1979 and 1980 and demanded more cars in 1984–85 when the price of gasoline fell.

Calculating cross-price elasticity   The relationship between the price of one good and demand for another is summarized in yet another elasticity concept. The **cross-price elasticity of demand** is the *percentage* change in the quantity demanded on one good divided by the *percentage* change in the price of another good, that is,

cross-price elasticity: Percentage change in the quantity demanded of X divided by percentage change in price of Y.

$$\text{Cross-price elasticity of demand} = \frac{\text{percentage change in quantity demanded of good } X}{\text{percentage change in price of good } Y}$$

If the cross-price elasticity is positive, the two goods are *substitutes;* if the cross-price elasticity is negative, the two goods are *complements.* Pepsi and popcorn are complements because a fall $(-)$ in the price of one leads to an increase $(+)$ in the demand for the other; in other words, the cross-price elasticity is negative.

CHOOSING AMONG PRODUCTS

Our analysis of demand thus far has focused on the decision to buy a single product, at varying prices. Actual consumer behavior is multidimensional, however, and therefore more complex. When we go shopping, our concern

In The News

SUBSTITUTE GOODS

CDs Displace LPs

In 1984 the record industry sold 205 million LPs (long-playing vinyl discs) and only 6 million CDs (compact discs). The times, they have changed. In 1990 about 200 million CDs and fewer than 100 million LPs were sold.

Fueling the change in consumer buying is the steep decline in the price of CDs and their players. In 1984 CD players sold for nearly $1,000. By 1990 they retailed for less than $200. During those same years the price of a CD declined from an average of $12 to only $9. Industry observers foresee the LP becoming the dinosaur of the record industry when the price of a CD drops to $5 or less.

Source: Recording Industry Association of America.

is not limited to how much of one good to buy. Rather, we must decide *which* of many available goods to buy, at their respective prices.

The presence of so many goods complicates consumption decisions. Our basic objective remains the same, however; we want to get as much satisfaction as possible from our available income. In striving to reach that objective, we now have to recognize that the purchase of any single good means giving up the opportunity to buy more of other goods. In other words, consuming popcorn (or any other good) entails distinct **opportunity costs.** When we purchase popcorn, we are not only giving up income for popcorn but also relinquishing the opportunity to buy something else with that same income. On what basis do we make such choices? How can we be confident of achieving maximum satisfaction from our choices?

opportunity cost: The most desired goods or services that are forgone in order to obtain something else.

Marginal Utility vs. Price

The economic explanation for consumer choice builds on the theory of marginal utility and the law of demand. Suppose you have a choice between buying a Coke and playing a video game. The first proposition of consumer choice simply states that if you think a Coke will be more satisfying than playing a video game, you will prefer to buy the Coke. Hardly a revolutionary proposition.

The second postulate of consumer-choice theory takes into account the market prices of the goods we desire. Although you may prefer to drink a Coke rather than play a video game, one play of a video game is cheaper than a Coke. Under these circumstances, your budget may win out over your desires, and you may forgo the Coke. There is nothing irrational about playing a video game instead of buying a Coke when you have a limited amount of income to spend. On the contrary, *rational behavior requires one to compare the anticipated utility of each expenditure with its cost* and to choose those products that promise to provide the most pleasure for the amount of income available.

Suppose your desire for a Coke is one-and-a-half times as great as your desire to play a video game. In economic terms, this means that the marginal utility of the first Coke is 1.5 times as high as the marginal utility of the first video game. Which one should you consume? Before reaching for the Coke, you'd better look at prices. What if a Coke costs 50 cents, while one play on a video game costs only 25 cents? In this case, you must pay *two* times as much for a Coke that gives only 1.5 times as much pleasure. This is not a good deal. You could get more utility per dollar by playing video games.

The same kind of principle explains why some rich people drive around in Fords rather than shiny new Mercedeses. The marginal utility (MU) of driving a Mercedes is substantially higher than the MU of driving a Ford. A nice Mercedes, however, costs about four times as much as a basic Ford. A rich person who drives a Ford must feel that driving a Mercedes is not four times as satisfying as driving a Ford. For such people, a Ford yields more *marginal utility* per dollar spent.

The key to utility maximization, then, is not simply to buy the things you like best. Instead, you must compare goods on the basis of their marginal utility *and* price. *To maximize utility, the consumer should choose that good which delivers the most marginal utility per dollar.*

Utility Maximization

This basic principle of consumer choice is easily illustrated. Suppose you have $1.50 to spend on a combination of Cokes and video games, the only consumer goods available. Your objective, as always, is to get the greatest satisfaction possible from this limited income. That is to say, you want to maximize the *total* utility attainable from the expenditure of your income. The question is how to do it. What combination of Cokes and games will maximize the utility you get from $1.50?

We have already assumed that the marginal utility of the first Coke is 1.5 times as high as the MU of the first video game. This is reflected in the second row of Table 19.3. The MU of the first video game has been set arbitrarily at 10 utils (units of utility). We don't need to know whether 10 utils is a real thrill or just a bit of amusement. Indeed, the concept of "utils" has little meaning by itself; it is only a useful basis for comparison. In this case, we want to compare the MU of the first game with the MU of the first Coke. Hence we set the MU of the first game at 10 utils and the MU of the first Coke at 15 utils. The first Coke is 1.5 times as satisfying as the first video game ($MU_{Coke} = 1.5 \ MU_{game}$).

The remainder of Table 19.3 indicates how marginal utility diminishes with increasing consumption of a product. Look at what happens to the good taste of Coke. The marginal utility of the first Coke is 15; but the MU of the second Coke is only 8 utils. Once you've quenched your initial thirst, a second Coke still tastes good but is not nearly so satisfying as the first one. A third Coke yields even less marginal utility, and a fourth one none at all ($MU = 0$). A fifth or sixth Coke would make your teeth rattle and cause other discomforts—its marginal utility is actually negative.

Video games also conform to the law of diminishing marginal utility. However, marginal utility doesn't decline quite so rapidly in the consumption of video games. The second game is almost as much fun ($MU = 9$) as the first ($MU = 10$). It's not until you have played several games that you begin to feel the tension and enjoy the game less. By the sixth game, marginal utility is fast approaching zero.

With these psychological insights to guide us, we can now determine how best to spend $1.50. What we are looking for is that combination of Cokes and video games which *maximizes* the total utility attainable from an expenditure of $1.50. We call this combination **optimal consumption**—that is, the mix of goods that yields the most utility for the available income.

We can start looking for the optimal mix of consumer purchases by assessing the utility of spending the entire $1.50 on video games. At 25 cents

optimal consumption: The mix of consumer purchases that maximizes the utility attainable from available income.

TABLE 19.3   Maximizing Utility

Q. How can you get the most satisfaction (utility) from $1.50 if you must choose between buying Cokes that cost 50 cents each and video games that cost 25 cents each?

A: By drinking one Coke and playing four video games. See text for explanation.

| Quantity consumed | Amount of utility (in units of utility, or utils) | | | |
| | From Cokes | | From video games | |
	Total	Marginal	Total	Marginal
0	0	0	0	0
1	15	15	10	10
2	23	8	19	9
3	25	2	26	7
4	25	0	31	5
5	22	-3	34	3
6	12	-10	35	1

per play, we could buy 6 games. This would give us *total* utility of 35 utils (see Table 19.3).

You might also want to consider spending all your income on Cokes. With $1.50 to spend, you could buy 3 Cokes. However, this would generate only 25 utils of total utility. Hence if you were forced to choose between 3 Cokes and 6 games, you would pick the games.

Fortunately, we do not have to make such awful choices. In reality, we can buy a *combination* of Cokes and video games. This complicates our decision making (with more choices) but also permits us to attain still higher levels of total satisfaction.

To reach the peak of satisfaction, consider spending your $1.50 in three 50-cent increments. How should you spend the first 50 cents? If you spend it on 1 Coke, you will get 15 utils of satisfaction. On the other hand, 50 cents will buy your first 2 video games. The first game has an MU of 10 and the second game adds another 9 utils to your happiness. Hence by spending the first 50 cents on games, you reap 19 utils of total utility. This is superior to the pleasures of a first Coke and is therefore your first purchase.

Having played 2 video games, you now can spend the second 50 cents. How should it be spent? Your choice now is that first Coke or a third and fourth video game. That first unconsumed Coke still promises 15 utils of real pleasure. By contrast, the MU of a third video game is 7 utils and the MU of a fourth game only 5 utils. Together, then, the third and fourth games will increase your total utility by 12 utils, whereas a first Coke will give you 15 utils. You should spend the second 50 cents on a Coke.

The decision on how to spend the remaining half dollar is made the same way. The final choice is either a second Coke (MU = 8) or the third (MU = 7) and fourth (MU = 5) video games. The two games together offer more marginal utility and are thus the correct decision.

After working your way through these calculations, you will end up drinking 1 Coke and playing 4 video games. Was it worth it? Do you end up with more total utility than you could have gotten from any other combination? The answer is yes. The *total* utility of 1 Coke (15 utils) and 4 games (31 utils) amounts to 46 units of utility. This is significantly better than the alternatives of spending your $1.50 on Cokes alone (total utility = 25) or games alone (total utility = 35). In fact, the combination of 1 Coke and 4 games is the *best* one you can find. Because this combination maximizes the total utility of your income ($1.50), it represents *optimal consumption*.

Utility-Maximizing Rule

Optimal consumption refers to the mix of output that maximizes total utility for the limited amount of income you have to spend. The basic approach to utility maximization is to purchase that good next which delivers the most *marginal utility per dollar*. Marginal utility per dollar is simply the MU of the good divided by its price: MU ÷ P.

From Table 19.3 we know that a first Coke has an MU of 15 and a price of 50 cents. It thus delivers a marginal utility per dollar of

$$\frac{MU_{\text{first Coke}}}{P_{\text{Coke}}} = \frac{15}{0.50} = 30 \text{ utils per dollar}$$

On the other hand, the first video game has a marginal utility of 10 and a price of 25 cents. It offers a marginal utility per dollar of

$$\frac{MU_{first\ game}}{P_{game}} = \frac{10}{0.25} = 40 \text{ utils per dollar}$$

From this perspective, the first video game is a better deal than the first Coke and should be purchased.

Optimal consumption implies that the utility-maximizing combination of goods has been found. If this is true, you cannot increase your total utility by trading one good for another. There is no unpurchased good that offers a higher marginal utility per dollar. Moreover, there is no good in your shopping bag that offers less MU per price. If there were, you would trade it in for a preferred good. Hence we conclude that all goods included in the optimal consumption mix yield the *same* marginal utility per dollar. We know we have reached maximum utility when we have satisfied the following rule:

- Utility-maximizing rule: $\dfrac{MU_x}{P_x} = \dfrac{MU_y}{P_y}$

where x and y represent any two goods included in our consumption.

The essence of utility maximization, then, lies in comparisons of marginal utilities and prices. If a dollar spent on product X yields more marginal utility than a dollar spent on product Y, we should buy product X. To use this principle, of course, we have to know the amounts of utility obtainable from various goods and be able to perform a little arithmetic. By doing so, however, we can be assured of getting the greatest satisfaction from our limited income.

POLICY INSIGHTS:

CAVEAT EMPTOR

No discussion of consumer demand would be complete without considering the role that advertising plays in shaping our consumer behavior. As noted earlier, psychiatrists see us as complex bundles of basic drives, anxieties, and layers of consciousness. They presume that we enter the market with confused senses of guilt, insecurity, and ambition. Economists, on the other hand, regard the consumer as the rational *homo economicus,* aware of his or her wants and knowledgeable about how to satisfy them. In reality, however, we do not always know what we want or which products will satisfy us. This uncertainty creates a vacuum into which the advertising industry has eagerly stepped.

The efforts of producers to persuade us to buy, buy, buy are as close as the nearest television, radio, magazine, or billboard. American producers now spend over $100 *billion* per year to change our tastes. This spending works out to over $450 per consumer, one of the highest per capita advertising rates in the world (see World View). Much of this advertising (including product labeling) is intended to provide information about existing products or to bring new products to our attention. A great deal of advertising, however, is also designed to exploit our senses and lack of knowledge. Recognizing that we are guilt-ridden, insecure, and sex-hungry, advertisers offer us pictures and promises of exoneration, recognition, and love; all we have to do is buy the right product.

One of the favorite targets of advertisers is our sense of insecurity. Thousands of products are marketed in ways that appeal to our need for identity, most often by creating a specific identity image for each product. Thousands

W🌐RLD VIEW

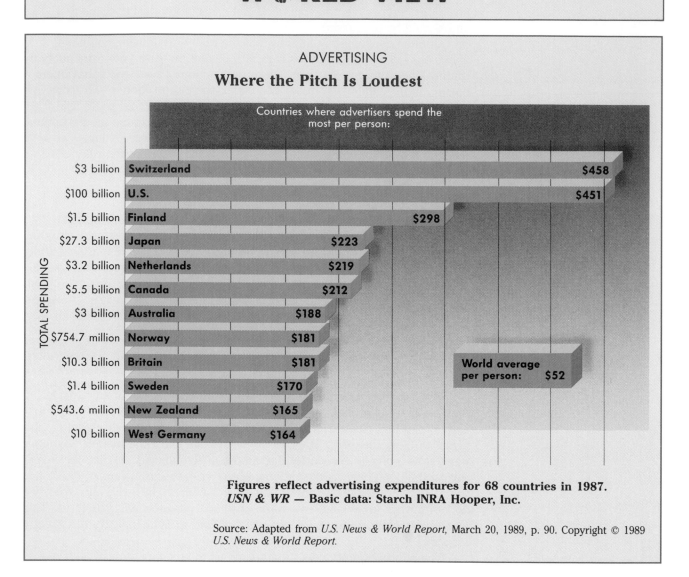

ADVERTISING
Where the Pitch Is Loudest

Countries where advertisers spend the most per person:

TOTAL SPENDING	Country	Per person
$3 billion	Switzerland	$458
$100 billion	U.S.	$451
$1.5 billion	Finland	$298
$27.3 billion	Japan	$223
$3.2 billion	Netherlands	$219
$5.5 billion	Canada	$212
$3 billion	Australia	$188
$754.7 million	Norway	$181
$10.3 billion	Britain	$181
$1.4 billion	Sweden	$170
$543.6 million	New Zealand	$165
$10 billion	West Germany	$164

World average per person: $52

Figures reflect advertising expenditures for 68 countries in 1987.
USN & WR **— Basic data: Starch INRA Hooper, Inc.**

Source: Adapted from *U.S. News & World Report,* March 20, 1989, p. 90. Copyright © 1989 *U.S. News & World Report.*

of brand images are designed to help the consumer answer the nagging question "Who am I?" The answers, of course, vary. *Playboy* magazine says I'm a virile man of the world; Marlboro cigarettes say I'm a rugged individualist who enjoys "man-sized flavor." Users of Tide detergent are worthy homemakers, whereas Virginia Slims cigarette smokers are liberated women. The right bourbon or scotch is reserved for the successes among us, of either sex.

Other needs and drives are equally susceptible to the blandishments of promoters. Those who fear rejection can find solace and confidence in the right mouth freshener or deodorant; exhibitionist urges can be sublimated with the right bra (or no bra). A measure of immortality may be achieved through insurance plans that will exercise our wishes and control in our absence. On the other hand, eternal youth can be preserved with a proper mix of vitamin supplements, face lotions, and laxatives.

In The News

CHANGING TASTES

Miller Lite: An Advertising Success

In January 1975 Miller Brewing Company set out to change the tastes of U.S. beer drinkers. It introduced Miller Lite, a low-calorie beer. Many other companies had produced low-calorie beers and failed. But Miller was convinced it could succeed. Other companies had directed their sales pitches to diet-conscious people and had ignored the mass of beer drinkers. In introducing its new beer, Miller emphasized that Lite tasted as good as regular beer but simply contained fewer calories. In its advertising, Miller used macho sports figures and other celebrities to emphasize that Lite was *real* beer, not a diet drink for sissies. As one analyst noted, "The typical

beer drinker is not dietetically oriented, but when he sees a football player drinking this low-calorie beer, he figures he shouldn't be ashamed to drink it." Miller spent nearly $10 million per year to get this message across.

The results of the advertising campaign were phenomenal. Sales of Miller Lite skyrocketed and Miller Brewing moved up from fifth place to second place in total U.S. beer sales. In the wake of Miller's success, all other brewers were forced to introduce their own low-calorie beers to satisfy the new tastes of American drinkers. In the process, the demand for regular beer shifted to the left, while the demand for light beer shifted to the right. In 1990 light beers accounted for 24 percent of all beer sales.

Are Wants Created? Advertising cannot be blamed for all of our "foolish" consumption. The dynamics of personality structure and social interaction give rise to drives and needs that operate in any economic context. Even members of the most primitive tribes, uncontaminated by the seductions of advertising, adorned themselves with rings, bracelets, and pendants. Furthermore, advertising has grown to massive proportions only in the last three decades, but regular increases in consumption spending have taken place throughout recorded history. Accordingly, it is a mistake to attribute the growth of consumption to the persuasions of advertisers.

This is not to say that advertising has necessarily made us happier or directed consumption into preferred channels. Although advertising cannot be charged with creating our needs, it does provide specific (if not necessarily correct) outlets for satisfying those needs. The objective of all advertising is

In The News

UNCHANGED TASTES

The New Coke: An Advertising Flop

In April 1985 the Coca-Cola Company announced that it was changing the 99-year-old formula of its world-famous product. Coca-Cola spent millions of advertising dollars trying to convince consumers that the new, sweeter Coke was better. But consumer tastes didn't budge. The Coca-Cola Company was besieged with letters and phone calls from consumers demanding a return to the old formula.

The cries of protest did not diminish with time: in June the company said it was still receiving 1,500 calls a day. In July the company succumbed to consumer pressure, announcing that it would revive the original formula and market it under the name Coca-Cola Classic. By 1990, Coca-Cola Classic was the best-selling soft drink, outselling "New Coke" by a margin of eight to one. In early 1990 the company renamed ("Coke II") and packaged the "new" Coke in an effort to bolster lagging sales.

FIGURE 19.10
The Impact of Advertising on a Demand Curve

Advertising seeks to increase our taste for a particular product. If our taste (the product's perceived utility) increases, so will our willingness to buy. The resulting change in demand is reflected in a rightward shift of the demand curve, often accompanied by diminished elasticity.

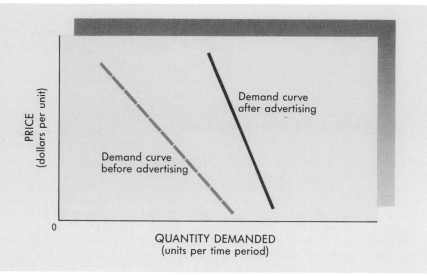

to alter the choices we make. Just as product images are used to attract us to particular commodities, so are pictures of hungry, ill-clothed children used to persuade us to give money to charity. In the same way, public-relations gimmicks are employed to sway our votes for public servants. In the case of consumer products, advertising seeks to increase tastes for particular goods and services and therewith our willingness to pay. *A successful advertising campaign is one that shifts the demand curve to the right,* inducing consumers to increase their purchases of a product at every price (see Figure 19.10). Advertising may also make the demand curve less elastic, thus reducing consumer responses to price increases. By influencing our choices in this way, advertising alters the distribution of our consumption expenditures, if not their level.

SUMMARY

- Our desires for goods and services originate in the structure of personality and social dynamics and are not explained by economic theory. Economic theory focuses on *demand*—that is, our ability and willingness to buy specific quantities of a good at various prices.

- Marginal utility measures the additional satisfaction obtained from consuming one more unit of a good. The law of diminishing marginal utility says that the more of a product we consume, the smaller the increments of pleasure we tend to derive from additional units of it. This provides a basis for the law of demand.

- The price elasticity of demand is a numerical measure of consumer response to a change in price (*ceteris paribus*). It equals the percentage change in quantity demanded divided by the percentage change in price. Elasticity depends on the relative price of a good, the availability of substitutes, and time.

• The shape and position of any particular demand curve depend on a consumer's income, tastes, expectations, and the price and availability of other goods. Should any of these things change, the assumption of *ceteris paribus* will no longer hold, and the demand curve will *shift*.

• The income elasticity of demand measures the response of demand to a change in income. If demand increases with income, the product being considered is a normal good. If the demand falls when income rises, it is an inferior good.

• Cross-price elasticity measures the response of demand for one good to a change in the price of another. The cross-price elasticity of demand is positive for substitute goods and negative for complementary goods.

• In choosing among alternative goods and services, a consumer compares the prices and anticipated satisfactions that they offer. To maximize utility with one's available income—to achieve an optimal mix of goods and services—one has to get the most utility for every dollar spent. To do so, one must compare the relative prices and pleasures and choose those goods that offer the most additional pleasure per dollar.

• Advertising seeks to change consumer tastes and thus the willingness to buy. If tastes do change, the demand curve will shift.

Terms to Remember   Define the following terms:

demand	total revenue
utility	income elasticity of demand
total utility	normal good
marginal utility	inferior good
law of diminishing marginal utility	substitute goods
ceteris paribus	complementary goods
law of demand	cross-price elasticity
demand curve	opportunity cost
price elasticity of demand	optimal consumption

Questions for Discussion

1. Is it possible to have a great taste for French cooking and still eat at McDonald's? What is the relationship of tastes, income, prices, and consumer behavior in this case?

2. Identify three of each of the following: (*a*) substitute goods; (*b*) complementary goods; (*c*) normal goods; (*d*) inferior goods. Why would anyone consume inferior goods?

3. It has been suggested that a consumer can get the most satisfaction from expenditures by buying a mix of goods such that the marginal utility of the last dollar spent on each good is equal to the marginal utility of the last dollar spent on every other good. Is this suggestion correct? Can you prove it?

4. What is the effect of Schlitz beer advertisements on your total consumption of beer? On your demand for Budweiser?

5. What is the price elasticity of demand for gasoline in Washington, D.C. (see In the News on p. 474)? What accounts for this elasticity?

Problems   **1.** The following is a demand schedule for shoes:

Price (per pair)	$100	$80	$60	$40	$20
Quantity demanded (in pairs per day)	10	14	18	22	26

(*a*) Graph the demand curve.
(*b*) Determine how much money will be spent on shoes (the seller's total revenue) at prices of $30, $50, and $70.

2. From Figure 19.4,
(*a*) Compute the price elasticity of demand between points *D* and *E*, *E* and *F*, *F* and *G*, and *G* and *H*.
(*b*) Show what happens to total revenue as you move from point to point.
(*c*) Explain the likely cause of the varying elasticity.

3. Suppose the following table reflects the total satisfaction derived from consumption of pizza slices and Pepsis. Assume that pizza costs $1 per slice and a large Pepsi costs $2. With $20 to spend, what consumption mix will maximize satisfaction?

Quantity consumed	1	2	3	4	5	6	7	8	9	10	11	12	13	14
Total units of pleasure from pizza slices	47	92	132	166	196	224	251	271	288	303	313	315	312	300
Total units of pleasure from Pepsis	111	200	272	336	386	426	452	456	444	408	340	217	92	−17

4. The following table shows how many vacations by air the average family will take at different income levels:

Income (per year)	Vacations (per year)
$ 20,000	0
50,000	1
100,000	3
200,000	5
500,000	8

What is the income elasticity of demand at different incomes? Why does the income elasticity change?

APPENDIX

Indifference Curves

A consumer's demand for any specific product is an expression of many forces. As we have observed, the actual quantity of a product demanded by a consumer varies inversely with its price. The price–quantity relationship is determined by

- *Tastes* (desire for this and other goods)
- *Income* (of the consumer)
- *Expectations* (for income, prices, tastes)
- *Other goods* (their availability and price)

Economic theory attempts to show how each of these forces affects consumer demand. Thus far, we have used two-dimensional demand curves to illustrate the basic principles of demand. We saw that, in general, a change in the price of a good causes a movement along the demand curve, while a change in tastes, income, expectations, or other goods shifts the entire demand curve to a new position.

We have not looked closely at the origins of demand curves, however. We assumed that a demand curve could be developed from observations of consumer behavior, such as the number of boxes of popcorn that were purchased at various prices (Figure 19.4). Likewise, we observed how the demand curve shifts in response to changes in tastes, income, expectations, or other goods (Figures 19.8 and 19.9).

It is possible, however, to derive a demand curve without actually observing consumer behavior. In theory we can identify consumer *preferences* (tastes), then use those preferences to construct a demand curve. In this case the demand curve is developed explicitly from known preferences rather than on the basis of market observations. The end result—the demand curve—is the same, at least so long as consumers' behavior in product markets is consistent with their preferences.

Indifference curves are a mechanism for illustrating consumer tastes. We shall examine their construction and use in this appendix. As suggested above, indifference curves provide an explicit basis for constructing a demand curve. In addition, they provide another view of the way consumption is affected by price, tastes, and income. Indifference curves are also a useful tool for illustrating explicitly consumer *choice*— that is, the decision to purchase one good rather than another.

CONSTRUCTING AN INDIFFERENCE CURVE

marginal utility: The change in total utility obtained from an additional (marginal) unit of a good or service consumed.

optimal consumption: The mix of consumer purchases that maximizes the utility attainable from available income.

Recall the dilemma that arises when you want Coke and video games but don't have enough money to buy enough of each to satisfy yourself. The income constraint compels you to make hard decisions. You have to consider the **marginal utility** each additional Coke or video game will provide, compare their respective prices, then make a selection. With careful introspection and good arithmetic you can select the optimal mix of Cokes and video games—that is, the combination that yields the most satisfaction (utility) for the income available. This process of identifying your **optimal consumption** was illustrated in Table 19.3.

The difficult thing about finding your optimal consumption is the necessity of assessing the marginal utility of each prospective purchase. In Table 19.3 we assumed that the marginal utility of the first Coke was 15 utils, while the first video game had a marginal utility of 10. Then we had to specify the marginal utility of every additional Coke and video game. Can we really be so specific about our tastes?

Indifference curves require a bit less arithmetic. ***Instead of trying to measure the marginal utility of each prospective purchase, we now look for combinations of goods that yield equal satisfaction.*** All we need to do is determine that one particular combination of Cokes and video games is as satisfying as another. We don't have to say how many "units of pleasure" both combinations provide—it is sufficient that they are both equally satisfying.

The initial combination of 1 Coke and 8 video games is designated as combination *A* in Table A.1. This combination of goods yields a certain, but unspecified, level of total utility. What we want to do now is to find another combination of Cokes and games that is just as satisfying as combination *A*. Finding other combinations of equal satisfaction isn't easy, but it's at least possible. After careful deliberation and a lot of

TABLE A.1   Equally Satisfying Combinations

Different combinations of two goods may be equally satisfying. In this case we assume that the combinations A, B, and C all yield equal total utility. Hence the consumer will be indifferent about which of the three combinations he receives.

Combination	Cokes	Video games
A	1	8
B	2	5
C	3	4

soul searching, we decide that 2 Cokes and 5 video games would be just as satisfying as 1 Coke and 8 games.[1] This combination is designated as B in Table A.1.

Table A.1 also depicts a third combination of Cokes and video games that is as satisfying as the first. Combination C includes 3 Cokes and 4 games, a mix of consumption assumed to yield the same total utility as 1 Coke and 8 games (combination A).

Notice that we have not said anything about how much pleasure combinations A, B, and C provide. We are simply asserting that these three combinations are *equally* satisfying.

Figure A.1 illustrates the information about tastes that we have assembled. Points A, B, and C represent the three equally satisfying combinations of Cokes and video games we have identified. By connecting these points we create an **indifference curve.** The indifference curve illustrates all combinations of two goods that are equally satisfying. A consumer would be just as happy with any combination represented on the curve, so a choice among them would be a matter of indifference.

indifference curve: A curve depicting alternative combinations of goods that yield equal satisfaction.

An Indifference Map

Not all combinations of Coke and video games are as satisfying as combination A, of course. Surely, 2 Cokes and 8 games would be preferred to only 1 Coke and 8 games. Indeed, any combination that provided more of one good and no less of the other

[1]The utility computations used here are not based on Table 19.3; a different set of tastes is assumed.

FIGURE A.1
An Indifference Curve

An indifference curve illustrates the various combinations of two goods that would provide equal satisfaction. The consumer is assumed to be indifferent to a choice between combinations A, B, and C (and all other points on the curve), as they all yield the same total utility.

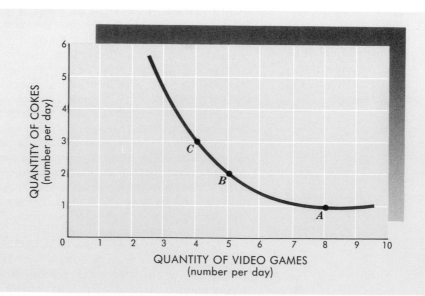

would be preferred. Point *D* in Figure A.2 illustrates just one such combination. Combination *D* must yield more total utility than combination *A* because it includes one more Coke and no fewer games. A consumer would not be indifferent to a choice between *A* and *D;* on the contrary, combination *D* would be preferred.

Combination *D* is also preferred to combinations *B* and *C.* How do we know? Recall that combinations *A*, *B*, and *C* are all equally satisfying. Hence if combination *D* is better than *A*, it must also be better than *B* and *C.* Given a choice, a consumer would select combination *D* (2 Cokes, 8 games) in preference to *any* combination depicted on indifference curve I_1.

There are also combinations that are as satisfying as *D*, of course. These possibilities are illustrated on indifference curve I_2. All of these combinations are equally satisfying, and must therefore be preferred to any points on indifference curve I_1. In general, *the farther the indifference curve is from the origin, the more total utility it yields.*

The curve I_3 illustrates various combinations that are less satisfying. Combination *F*, for example, includes 3 Cokes and 3 games. This is 1 game less than the number available in combination *C.* Therefore, *F* yields less total utility than *C* and is not preferred: a consumer would rather have combination *C* than *F.* By the same logic we used above, all points on indifference curve I_3 are less satisfying than combinations on curve I_2 or I_1.

Curves 1, 2, and 3 in Figure A.2 are the beginnings of an **indifference map.** An indifference map depicts all the combinations of goods that would yield various levels of satisfaction. A single indifference curve, in contrast, illustrates all combinations that provide a single (equal) level of total utility.

indifference map: The set of indifference curves that depicts all possible levels of utility attainable from various combinations of goods.

UTILITY MAXIMIZATION

We assume that all consumers strive to maximize their utility. They want as much satisfaction as they can get. In the terminology of indifference curves, this means getting to the indifference curve that is farthest from the origin. The farther one is from the origin, the greater the total utility.

Although the goal of consumers is evident, the means of achieving it is not so clear. Higher indifference curves are not only more satisfying but also more expensive. We are confronted again with the basic conflict between preferences and prices. With

**FIGURE A.2
An Indifference Map**

All combinations of goods depicted on any given indifference curve (e.g., I_1) are equally satisfying. Other combinations are more or less satisfying, however, and thus lie on higher (I_2) or lower (I_3) indifference curves. An indifference map shows all possible levels of total utility (e.g., $I_1, I_2, I_3, \ldots, I_n$) and their respective consumption combinations.

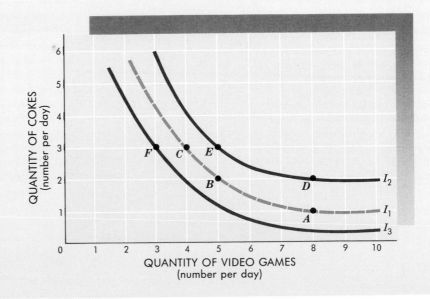

a limited amount of income to spend, we cannot attain infinite satisfaction (the farthest indifference curve). We have to settle for less (an indifference curve closer to the origin). The question is: how do we maximize the utility attainable with our limited income?

The Budget Constraint

The first thing to do is to determine how much we have to spend. Suppose for the moment that we can spend $2 per day and that Cokes and video games are still the only objects of our consumption desires. The price of Coke is 50 cents; the price of a game is 25 cents. Accordingly, the maximum number of Cokes we could buy is 4 per day, if we didn't play any video games. On the other hand, we could play as many as 8 games if we were to forsake Coke.

The limitations placed on our consumption possibilities by a finite income are depicted in Figure A.3. The **budget constraint** illustrates all combinations of goods affordable with a given income. In this case, the outermost budget line illustrates the combinations of Cokes and video games that can be purchased with $2.

The budget line is easily drawn. The end points of the budget constraint are found by dividing one's income by the price of the good on the corresponding axis. Thus the outermost curve begins at 4 Cokes (= $2 ÷ 50 cents) and ends at 8 games (= $2 ÷ 25 cents). All the other points on the budget constraint represent other combinations of Cokes and video games that could be purchased with $2.

A smaller income is also illustrated in Figure A.3. If we had only $1 to spend, we could afford fewer Cokes and fewer games. Hence a smaller income is represented by a budget constraint that lies closer to the origin.

budget constraint: A line depicting all combinations of goods that are affordable with a given income and given prices.

Optimal Consumption

With a budget constraint looming before us, the limitation on utility maximization is evident. We want to reach the highest indifference curve possible. Our limited income, however, restricts our grasp. We can go only as far as our budget constraint allows. In this context, ***the objective is to reach the highest indifference curve that is compatible with our budget constraint.***

Figure A.4 illustrates the process of achieving optimal consumption. We start with an indifference map depicting all utility levels and product combinations. Then we impose a budget line that reflects our income. In this case, we continue to assume that Coke costs 50 cents, video games cost 25 cents, and we have $2 to spend. Hence we can afford only those consumption combinations that are on or inside the budget line.

FIGURE A.3
The Budget Constraint

Consumption possibilities are limited by available income. The budget constraint illustrates this limitation. The end points of the budget constraint are equal to income divided by the price of each good. All points on the budget constraint represent affordable combinations of goods.

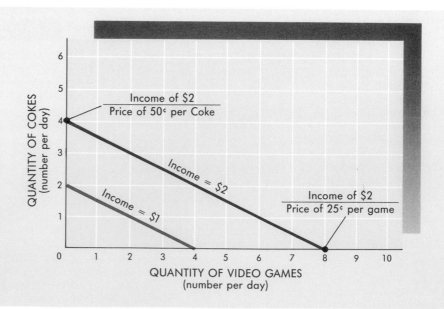

FIGURE A.4
Optimal Consumption

The optimal consumption combination—the one that maximizes the utility of spendable income—lies at the point where the budget line is tangent to (just touches) an indifference curve. In this case, point *M* represents the optimal mix of Cokes and video games, since no other affordable combination lies on a higher indifference curve than I_c.

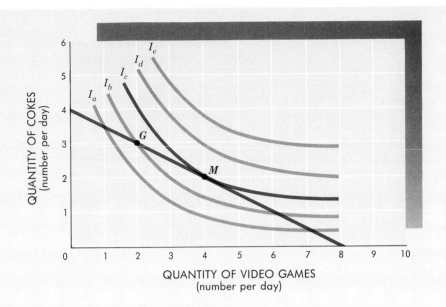

Which particular combination of Cokes and video games maximizes the utility of our $2? It must be 2 Cokes and 4 video games, as reflected in point *M*. Notice that point *M* is not only on the budget line but also touches indifference curve I_c. No other point on the budget line touches I_c or any higher indifference curve. Accordingly, I_c represents the most utility we can get for $2 and is attainable only if we consume 2 Cokes and 4 video games. Any other affordable combination yields less total utility—that is, falls on a lower indifference curve. Point *G*, for example, which offers 3 Cokes and 5 video games for $2, lies on the indifference curve I_b. Because I_b lies closer to the origin then I_c, point *G* must be less satisfying than point *M*. We conclude, then, that ***the point of tangency between the budget constraint and an indifference curve represents optimal consumption.*** It is the combination we should buy if we want to maximize the utility of our limited income.

Marginal Utility and Price: A Digression

We earlier illustrated the utility-maximizing rule. This rule required a comparison of the ratios of marginal utilities to prices. Specifically, optimal consumption was represented as that combination of Cokes and video games that yielded

$$\frac{MU \text{ Coke}}{P \text{ Coke}} = \frac{MU \text{ games}}{P \text{ games}}$$

Does point *M* in Figure A.4 conform to this rule?

To answer this question, first rearrange the preceding equation as follows:

$$\frac{MU \text{ Coke}}{MU \text{ games}} = \frac{P \text{ Coke}}{P \text{ games}}$$

In this form, the equation says that the relative marginal utilities of Cokes and video games should equal their relative prices when consumption is optimal. In other words, if a Coke costs twice as much as a video game, then it must yield twice as much marginal utility if the consumer is to be in an optimal state. Otherwise, some substitution of Cokes for video games (or vice versa) would be desirable.

With this foundation, we can show that point *M* conforms to our earlier rule. Consider first the slope of the budget constraint. It is determined by the relative prices of Cokes and video games. In fact, *the (absolute) slope of the budget constraint equals the relative price of the two goods.* In Figure A.4 the slope equals the price of video games divided by the price of Cokes (= 25 cents ÷ 50 cents = ½). It tells us the rate at which video games can be exchanged for Cokes in the market. In this case, one video game is "worth" half a Coke.

The relative marginal utilities of the two goods are reflected in the slope of the indifference curve. Recall that the curve tells at what rate a consumer is willing to substitute one good for another, with no change in total utility. In fact, the slope of the indifference curve is called the **marginal rate of substitution.** It is equal to the relative marginal utilities of the two goods. Presumably one would be indifferent to a choice between 2 Cokes + 5 games and 3 Cokes + 4 games—as suggested in Table A.1—only if the third Coke were as satisfying as the fifth video game.

At the point of optimal consumption (M) in Figure A.4 the budget constraint is tangent to the indifference curve I_c. This means that the two curves must have the same slope at the point. In other words,

$$\frac{P \text{ games}}{P \text{ Cokes}} = \frac{MU \text{ games}}{MU \text{ Cokes}}$$

marginal rate of substitution: The rate at which a consumer is willing to exchange one good for another; the relative marginal utilities of two goods.

or, alternatively,

$$\text{Rate of market exchange} = \text{marginal rate of substitution}$$

Both indifference curves and marginal utility comparisons lead us to the same optimal mix of consumption.

DERIVING THE DEMAND CURVE

We noted at the beginning of this appendix that indifference curves not only give us an alternative path to optimal consumption but also can be used to derive a demand curve. To do this, we need to consider how the optimal consumption combination changes when the price of one good is altered. We can see what happens in Figure A.5.

Figure A.5 starts with the optimal consumption attained at point M, with income of $2 and prices of 50 cents for a Coke and 25 cents for a video game. Now we are going to change the price of video games and observe how consumption changes.

**FIGURE A.5
Changing Prices**

When the price of a good changes, the budget constraint shifts, and a new consumption combination must be sought. In this case, the price of video games is changing. When the price of games increases from 25 cents to 50 cents, the budget constraint shifts inward and optimal consumption moves from point M to point N.

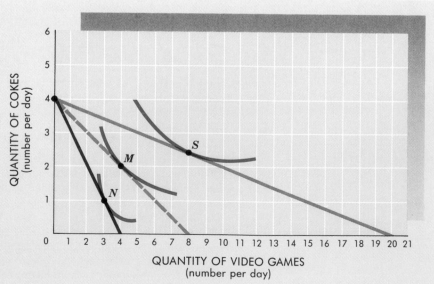

Suppose that the price of a video game doubles, from 25 cents to 50 cents. This change will shift the budget constraint inward: our income of $2 now buys a maximum of 4 games rather than 8. Hence the lower end point of the budget constraint moves from 8 games to 4 games. *Whenever the price of a good changes, the budget constraint shifts.*

Only one end of the budget constraint is changed in Figure A.5. The budget line still begins at 4 Cokes, because the price of Coke is unchanged. If only one price is changed, then only one end of the budget constraint is shifted.

Because the budget constraint has shifted inward, the combination *M* is no longer attainable. Two Cokes (at 50 cents each) and 4 games (at 50 cents each) now cost more than $2. We are forced to accept a lower level of total utility. According to Figure A.5, optimal consumption is now located at point *N*. This is the point of tangency between the new budget constraint and a lower indifference curve. At point *N* we consume 1 Coke and 3 video games.

Consider what has happened here. The price of video games has increased (from 25 cents to 50 cents), and the quantity of games demanded has decreased. This is the kind of relationship that demand curves describe. **Demand curves** indicate how the quantity demanded of a good changes in response to a change in its price, given a fixed income and all other things held constant. Not only does Figure A.5 provide the same information; it also conforms to the **law of demand:** as the price of games increases, the quantity demanded falls.

Suppose the price of video games were to fall rather than increase. Specifically, assume that the price of a game fell to 10 cents. This price reduction would shift the budget constraint farther out on the horizontal axis, since as many as 20 games could then be purchased with $2. As a result of the price reduction, we can now buy more goods and thus attain a higher level of satisfaction.

Point *S* in Figure A.5 indicates the optimal combination of Cokes and video games at the new video-game price. At these prices we consume 8 video games and 2.4 Cokes (we may have to share with a friend). The law of demand is again evident: when the price of video games declines, the quantity demanded increases.

demand curve: A curve describing the quantities of a good a consumer is willing and able to buy at alternative prices in a given time period, *ceteris paribus.*

law of demand: The quantity of a good demanded in a given time period increases as its price falls, *ceteris paribus.*

**FIGURE A.6
The Demand
for Video Games**

Figure A.5 shows how optimal consumption is altered when the price of video games changes. From that figure we can determine the quantity of video games demanded at alternative prices, *ceteris paribus.* That information is summarized here in the demand schedule (below) and the demand curve (above).

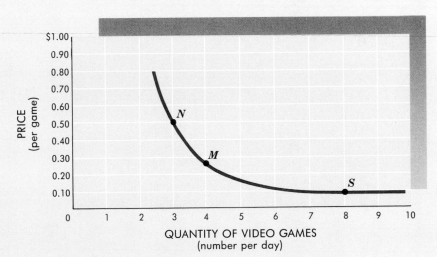

Point	Price (per game)	Quantity demanded (games per day)
N	50 cents	3
M	25 cents	4
S	10 cents	8

The Demand Schedule and Curve

Figure A.6 summarizes the information we have acquired about the demand for video games. The demand schedule depicts the price–quantity relationships prevailing at optimal consumption points *N, M,* and *S* (from Figure A.5). The demand curve generalizes these observations to encompass other prices. What we end up with is a demand curve explicitly derived from our (assumed) knowledge of consumer tastes.

CHAPTER 20

The Costs of Production

*L*ast year American consumers bought over $600 billion of imported goods, including Korean VCRs, Japanese cars, Italian shoes, and clothes from Hong Kong. As you might expect, this angers domestic producers, who frequently end up with unsold goods, half-empty factories, and unemployed workers. They lament the "unfair" competition from abroad, asserting that producers in Korea, Brazil, and Taiwan can pay much lower wages and thus consistently undersell American producers.

But lower wages don't necessarily imply lower costs. You could pay me $2 per hour to type and still end up paying a lot for typing. Truth is, I type only about ten words a minute, with a lot of misteaks. The cost of producing goods depends not only on the price of inputs (e.g., labor) but also on the productivity of those inputs.

In this chapter, we begin to look at the costs of producing the goods and services that consumers demand. Specifically, we confront the following questions:

- What are the costs of producing a good or a service?

- How do costs change as the rate of output varies?

- How do company size and productivity affect production costs?

The answers to these questions are important not only to producers faced with foreign competition but to consumers as well. As we will see, the costs of producing a good have a direct impact on the prices we pay and on the availability of specific goods and services.

THE PRODUCTION FUNCTION

No matter how large a business is or who owns it, all businesses confront one central fact: it costs something to produce goods. To produce corn, a farmer needs land, water, seed, equipment, and labor. To produce fillings, a dentist needs a chair, a drill, some space, and labor. Even the "production" of educational services (e.g., this economics class) requires the use of labor (your teacher), land (on which the school is built), and some capital (the building and blackboard). In short, unless you are producing unrefined, unpackaged air, you need **factors of production**—that is, resources that can be used to produce a good or service.

factors of production: Resource inputs used to produce goods and services, e.g., land, labor, capital.

The factors of production used to produce a good or service provide the basic measure of economic cost. The costs of your economics class, for example, are measured by the amounts of land, labor, and capital it requires. These are *resource* costs of production.

An essential question for production is how many resources are actually needed to produce a given product. The answer depends on our technological know-how and how we organize the production process. At any moment, however, there is sure to be some minimum amount of resources needed to produce a good. Alternatively, there will always be some *maximum* amount of output attainable from a given quantity of resources. These limits to our production of any good are reflected in the **production function.** The production function tells us the maximum amount of good X producible from various combinations of factor inputs. With one chair and one drill, a dentist can fill a maximum of 32 cavities per day. With two chairs, a drill, and an assistant, a dentist can fill up to 55 cavities per day.

A production function is a technological summary of our ability to produce a particular good.[1] Table 20.1 provides a partial glimpse of one such function. In this case, the desired output is designer jeans, as produced by Tight Jeans Corporation. The essential inputs in the production of jeans are land, labor (garment workers), and capital (a factory and sewing machines). With these inputs, Tight Jeans Corp. can produce and sell fancy jeans to status-conscious consumers.

As in all production endeavors, we want to know how many pairs of jeans we can produce with available resources. To make things easy, we shall assume that the factory is already built, with fixed space dimensions. The

production function: A technological relationship expressing the maximum quantity of a good attainable from different combinations of factor inputs.

---

[1]By contrast, the production possibilities curve discussed in Chapter 1 expresses our ability to produce various *combinations* of goods, given the use of *all* our resources. The production-possibilities curve summarizes the output capacity of the entire economy. A production function describes the capacity of a single firm.

TABLE 20.1   A Production Function
(pairs of jeans per day)

A production function tells us the maximum amount of output attainable from alternative combinations of factor inputs. This particular function tells us how many pairs of jeans we can produce in a day with a given factory and varying quantities of capital and labor. With one sewing machine, and one operator, we can produce a maximum of 15 pairs of jeans per day, as indicated in the second column of the second row. To produce more jeans, we need more labor or more capital.

Capital input (sewing machines per day)	Labor input (workers per day)							
	0	1	2	3	4	5	6	7
0	0	0	0	0	0	0	0	0
1	0	15	34	44	48	50	51	47
2	0	20	46	64	72	78	81	80
3	0	21	50	73	83	92	99	102

only inputs we can vary are labor (the number of garment workers per day) and additional capital (the number of sewing machines we lease per day).

As you would expect, the quantity of jeans we can produce depends on the amount of labor and capital we employ. ***The purpose of a production function is to tell us just how much output we can produce with varying amounts of factor inputs.*** Table 20.1 provides such information for jeans production.

Consider the simplest option, that of employing no labor or capital (the upper left corner of Table 20.1). An empty factory cannot produce any jeans; maximum output is zero per day. The lesson here is quite simple: no inputs, no outputs. Even though land, capital (an empty factory), and even denim are available, some essential labor and capital inputs are missing, and jeans production is impossible.

Suppose now we employ some labor (a machine operator) but do not lease any sewing machines. Will output increase? Not according to the production function. The first row of Table 20.1 illustrates the consequences of employing labor without any capital equipment. Without sewing machines, the operators cannot make jeans out of denim. Maximum output remains at zero, no matter how much labor is employed in this case.

The dilemma of machine operators without sewing machines illustrates a more general principle of production. ***The productivity of any factor of production depends on the amount of other resources available to it.*** Industrious, hard-working machine operators cannot make designer jeans without sewing machines.

productivity: Output per unit of input, e.g., output per labor hour.

We can increase the productivity of garment workers by providing them with machines. The production function again tell us by *how much* jeans output could increase if we leased some sewing machines. Suppose we leased just one machine per day. Now the second row of Table 20.1 is the relevant one. It says jeans output will remain at zero if we lease one machine but employ no labor. If we employ one machine *and* one worker, however, the jeans will start rolling out the front door. Maximum output under these circumstances (row 2, column 2) is 15 pairs of jeans per day. Now we're in business!

The remaining columns of row 2 tell us how many additional jeans we can produce if we hire more workers, still leasing only one sewing machine. With one machine and two workers, maximum output rises to 34 pairs per day. If a third worker is hired, output could increase to 44 pairs.

Table 20.1 also indicates how production would increase with additional sewing machines (capital). By reading down any column of the table, you can see how more machines increase potential jeans output.

Efficiency

The production function summarized in Table 20.1 underscores the essential relationship between resource *inputs* and product *outputs*. It also provides a basic introduction to economic costs. To produce 15 pairs of jeans per day, we need one sewing machine, an operator, a factory, and some denim. All of these inputs comprise the *resource cost* of producing jeans.

Another essential feature of Table 20.1 is that it conveys the *maximum* output of jeans producible from particular input combinations. The standard garment worker and sewing machine, when brought together at Tight Jeans Corporation, can produce *at most* 15 pairs of jeans per day. They could also produce a lot less. Indeed, a careless cutter can waste a lot of denim. A lazy

efficiency (technical): Maximum output of a good from the resources used in production.

or inattentive one will not keep the sewing machines humming. As many a producer has learned, actual sales (output) can fall far short of the limits described in the production function. Indeed, jeans output will reach the levels of Table 20.1 only if the jeans factory operates with relative **efficiency.** This requires getting maximum output from the resources used in the production process. ***The production function represents maximum technical efficiency—that is, the most output attainable from any given level of factory inputs.***

We can always be inefficient, of course. This merely means getting less output than possible for the inputs we use. But this is not a desirable situation. To a factory manager, it means less output for a given amount of input (cost). To society as a whole, inefficiency implies a waste of resources. If Tight Jeans isn't producing efficiently, we are being denied some potential output. It's not only a question of having fewer jeans. We could use some of the labor and capital now employed by Tight Jeans to produce something else. We give up the opportunity to produce something else when Tight Jeans employs our scarce resources. Those forsaken opportunities are a basic measure of the cost of production. Specifically, the **opportunity cost** of a product is measured by the most desired goods and services that could have been produced with the same resources. Hence if jeans production is not up to par, society is either (1) getting fewer jeans than it should for the resources devoted to jeans production or (2) giving up too many other goods and services in order to get a desired quantity of jeans.[2]

opportunity cost: The most desired goods or services that are forgone in order to obtain something else.

Although we can always do worse than the production function suggests, we cannot do better, at least in the short run. The production function represents the best we can do with our current technological know-how. For the moment, at least, there is no better way to produce a specific good. As our technological and managerial capabilities increase, however, we will attain higher levels of productivity. These advances in our productive capability will be represented by new production functions.[3] These new functions will then define the new and higher limits of efficiency, at least until new technologies are discovered.

Short-Run Constraints

Let us step back from the threshold of scientific advance for a moment and return to Tight Jeans. Forget about possible technological breakthroughs in jeans production (e.g., electronic sewing machines or robot operators) and concentrate on the economic realities of our modest endeavor. For the present time, we are stuck with existing technology. In fact, all of the output figures in Table 20.1 are based on the use of a specific factory. Once we have purchased or leased that factory, it sets a limit to current jeans production. When such commitments to fixed inputs (e.g., the factory) exist, we are dealing with a **short-run** production problem. If no land or capital were in place—if we could build or lease any sized factory—we would be dealing with a *long-run* decision.

short run: The period in which the quantity (and quality) of some inputs cannot be changed.

Our short-run objective is to make the best possible use of the factory we have acquired. This entails selecting the right combination of labor and capital inputs to produce jeans. To simplify the decision, we will limit the number of sewing machines in use. Each row of Table 20.1 is based on a

[2]Inefficiency in the production of any good implies that the economy is operating inside our production-possibilities frontier, rather than on it; see pp. 13–14.

[3]From an economy-wide perspective, technological advances are illustrated by outward shifts of the production-possibilities curve; see pp. 14–15.

different number of machines in place. If we lease only one sewing machine, then the second row of Table 20.1 is the only one we have to consider. In this case, the single sewing machine (capital) becomes another short-run constraint on the production of jeans. That leaves us with only one decision to make: namely, how many workers to employ in jeans production.

Figure 20.1 illustrates the short-run production function applicable to the factory with one sewing machine. As noted before, a factory with a sewing machine but no machine operators produces no jeans. This was observed in Table 20.1 (row 1, column 0) and is now illustrated by point *A* in Figure 20.1. To get any jeans output, we need to hire some labor. In this simplified example, *labor is the variable input that determines how much output we get from our fixed inputs (land and capital).* By placing one worker in the factory, we can produce 15 pairs of jeans per day. This possibility is represented by point *B*. At this point, total output is 15 pairs per day. The remainder of the production function shows how jeans output changes as we employ more workers in our single-machine factory.

MARGINAL PRODUCTIVITY

marginal physical product (MPP): The change in total output associated with one additional unit of input.

The production function provides a critical measure of each worker's contribution to output. Notice again that jeans output increases from zero (point *A* in Figure 20.2). to 15 pairs (point *B*) when the first machine operator is hired. Another way of viewing this situation is to note that total output *increased* by 15 pairs when we employed the first worker. This is called the **marginal physical product (MPP)** of that first worker—that is, the *change* in total

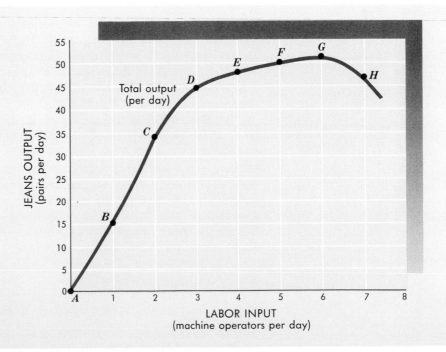

**FIGURE 20.1
Short-Run
Production Function**

In the short run some inputs (e.g., land, capital) are fixed in quantity. Output then depends on how much of a variable input (e.g., labor) is used. The short-run production function shows how output changes when more labor is used. This figure is based on the second (one-machine) row of Table 20.1.

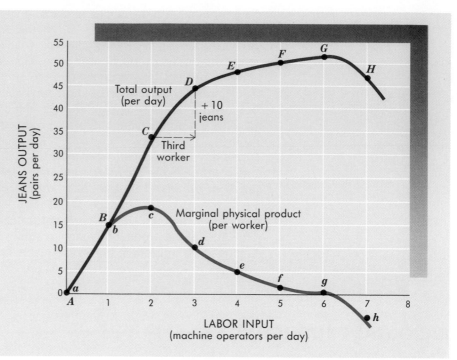

FIGURE 20.2
Marginal Physical Product

Marginal physical product is the *change* in total output that results from employing one more unit of input. The *third* unit of labor, for example, increases *total* output from 34 (point *C*) to 44 (point *D*). Hence the *marginal* output (MPP) of the third worker is 10 pairs of jeans (point *d*). What is the MPP of the fourth worker? What happens to *total* output when this worker is hired?

output that results from employment of one more unit of (labor) input; or

$$\text{Marginal physical product (MPP)} = \frac{\text{change in total output}}{\text{change in input quantity}}$$

With zero workers, total output was zero. With the first worker, total output increases to 15 pairs of jeans per day. The MPP of the first worker is 15 pairs of jeans.

If we employ a second operator, jeans output more than doubles, to 34 pairs per day (point *C*). Whereas the marginal physical product of the first worker was only 15 pairs, a second worker increases total output by 19 pairs.

The higher MPP of the second worker raises a question about the first. Why was the first's MPP lower? Laziness? Is the second worker faster, less distracted, or harder working?

The higher MPP of the second worker is not explained by superior talents or effort. We assume, in fact, that all "units of labor" are equal—that is, one worker is just as good as another.[4] Their different marginal products are explained by the structure of the production process, not by their respective abilities. The first garment worker had not only to sew jeans but also to unfold bolts of denim, measure the jeans, sketch out the patterns, and cut them to approximate size. A lot of time was spent going from one task to another. Despite the worker's best efforts (and assuming perfect efficiency), this person simply could not do everything at once.

A second worker alleviates this situation. With two workers, less time is spent running from one task to another. While one is measuring and cutting, the other can continue sewing. This improved ratio of labor to other factors of production results in the large jump in total output. The superior MPP of

[4]In reality, garment workers do differ greatly in energy, talent, and diligence. These differences can be eliminated by measuring units of labor in *constant-quality* units. A person who works twice as hard as everyone else would count as two *quality-adjusted* units of labor.

the second worker is not unique to this person: it would have occurred even if we had hired the workers in the reverse order. What matters is the amount of other factors of production each unit of labor must work with.

Diminishing Returns

Unfortunately, these large increases in output cannot be maintained as still more workers are hired. Look what happens when a third worker is hired. Total jeans production continues to increase. But the increase from point *C* to point *D* in Figure 20.2 is only 10 pairs per day. Hence the MPP of the third worker (10 pairs) is *less* than that of the second (19 pairs). Marginal physical product is *diminishing*. This is illustrated by point *d* in Figure 20.2.

What accounts for this decline in MPP? The answer again lies in the ratio of labor to other factors of production. A third worker begins to crowd our facilities. We still have only one sewing machine. Two people cannot sew at the same time. As a result, some time is wasted as the operators wait for their turns at the machine. Even if they split up the various jobs, there will still be some "downtime," since measuring and cutting are not as time-consuming as sewing. In this sense, we cannot make full use of a third worker. The relative scarcity of other inputs (capital and land) constrains the marginal physical product of labor.

Resource constraints are even more evident when a fourth worker is hired. Total output increases again, but the increase this time is very small. With three workers, we got 44 pairs of jeans per day (point *D*); with four workers, we get a maximum of 48 pairs (point *E*). Thus the marginal physical product of the fourth worker is only 4 pairs of jeans. A fourth worker really begins to strain our productive capacity to the limit. There simply aren't enough machines to make productive use of so much labor.

If a seventh worker is hired, the operators get in each other's way, argue, and waste denim. Total output actually falls when a seventh person is hired! In other words, the MPP of the seventh worker is *negative*, as reflected in point *h* of Figure 20.2 and the downturn in the total output curve after point *G* (from 51 to 47 pairs of jeans).

Law of diminishing returns   The problems of crowded facilities applies to most production processes. In the short run, a production process is characterized by a fixed amount of available land and capital. Typically, the only factor that can be varied in the short run is labor. Yet **as more labor is hired, each unit of labor has less capital and land to work with.** This is simple division: the available facilities are being shared by more and more workers. At some point, this constraint begins to pinch. When it does, marginal physical product starts to decline. This situation is so common that it is the basis for the **law of diminishing returns.** This law says that the marginal physical product of any factor of production (e.g., labor) will begin to diminish at some point, as more of it is used in a given production setting.

law of diminishing returns: The marginal physical product of a variable input declines as more of it is employed with a given quantity of other (fixed) inputs.

RESOURCE COSTS

The law of diminishing returns has important implications for the costs of production. The economic cost of a product is measured by the value of the resources needed to produce it. What we have seen here is that those resource requirements eventually increase. Each additional sewing machine operator produces fewer and fewer jeans. In effect, then, each additional pair of jeans produced uses more and more labor.

Suppose that we are employing one sewing machine and one operator again, for a total output of 15 pairs of jeans per day. How much labor are we using *per pair?* The answer is one-fifteenth of a worker's day, that is, 0.067 unit of labor. This is illustrated by point 1/*b* in Figure 20.3*b*.

Marginal Cost

In order to increase total output, we need more labor—that is, a second garment worker. When we employ that second worker, output increases by 19 pairs. This is illustrated by point *c* in Figure 20.3*a*. To get these additional 19 pairs, we did not lease more space or machines, but instead just hired one more unit of labor. Hence an increase in labor and denim costs is the only extra, or marginal, cost of those additional jeans. **Marginal cost (MC)** refers to the increase in total costs required to get one additional unit of output. More generally, we may note that

marginal cost (MC): The increase in total cost associated with a one-unit increase in production.

$$\text{Marginal cost (MC)} = \frac{\text{change in total cost}}{\text{change in output}}$$

In this case, only labor and denim costs change, since no additional land or capital is required to increase output.

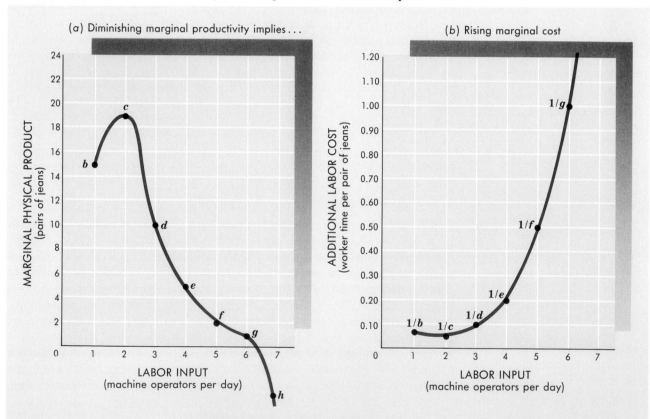

(a) Diminishing marginal productivity implies . . .

(b) Rising marginal cost

FIGURE 20.3 Falling MPP Implies Rising Marginal Cost

Marginal physical product (MPP) is the additional output obtained by employing one more unit of input. If MPP is falling, each additional unit of input is producing less additional output. This means that the input cost of each unit of output is rising. The MPP of the third worker is 10 pairs (point *d* in part *a*). Therefore, the labor cost of these additional jeans is approximately 1/10 unit of labor per pair (point 1/*d* in part *b*).

Since we need one more unit of labor to get 19 additional pairs of jeans, the amount of labor input required to produce *one* more pair of jeans must be $1 \div 19$, or 0.053 unit of labor. That labor cost plus the price of the denim itself constitute the marginal cost of additional jeans. These represent the *change* in total cost, as we increase jeans output.

Notice that the marginal labor cost of jeans production declines when the second worker is hired. Marginal cost falls from 0.067 unit of labor (plus denim) per pair to only 0.053 unit of labor per pair. It costs less labor *per pair* to use two workers rather than only one. This is a reflection of the increased *MPP* of the second worker. **Whenever MPP is increasing, the marginal cost of producing a good must be falling.** This is illustrated in Figure 20.3 by the move from *b* to *c* in part (*a*) and the corresponding move from 1/*b* to 1/*c* in part (*b*).

Unfortunately, marginal physical product typically declines at some point. As it does, the marginal costs of production rise. In this sense, each additional pair of jeans becomes more expensive—it uses up more and more labor per pair. This inverse relationship between MPP and marginal cost is illustrated in Figure 20.3. The third worker has an MPP of 10 pairs, as illustrated by point *d*. The marginal labor input of these extra 10 pairs is thus $1 \div 10$, or 0.10 unit of labor. In other words, one-tenth of a third worker's daily effort goes into each pair of jeans. This additional labor cost *per unit* is illustrated by 1/*d* in part (*b*) of the figure.

Note in Figure 20.3 how marginal physical product declines after point *c* and how marginal costs rise after point 1/*c*. This is no accident. *If marginal physical product declines, marginal cost increases.* Thus increasing marginal cost is as common as—and the direct result of—diminishing returns. These increasing marginal costs are not the fault of any person or factor, but simply a reflection of the resource constraints found in any established production setting (i.e., existing and limited plant and equipment). Nevertheless, they imply that increased output of any good from existing facilities will drive up the economic cost of that good. To keep costs from rising, we would have to discover new and improved production technologies or build better production facilities. These are *long-run* possibilities, however, and not available for short-run cost savings. In the *short run,* the quantity and quality of land and capital are fixed, and we can vary only their intensity of use (e.g., with more or fewer workers). It is in this short-run context that we keep running into diminishing marginal returns and rising marginal costs.

DOLLAR COSTS

This entire discussion of diminishing returns and marginal costs may seem a bit alien. After all, we are interested in the costs of production, and costs are typically measured in *dollars,* not such technical notions as MPP. Jeans producers need to know how many dollars it costs to keep jeans flowing; they don't want a lecture on marginal physical product. Can't we provide any useful answers?

Jeans manufacturers need not study marginal physical products, or even the production function. They can confine their attention to dollar costs. The dollar costs observed, however, are directly related to the underlying production function. To understand *why* costs rise—and how they might be reduced—some understanding of the production function is necessary. In this section we shall translate production functions into dollar costs.

Total Cost

total cost: The market value of all resources used to produce a good or service.

The **total cost** of producing a product includes the market value of all the resources used in its production. To determine this cost we simply identify all the resources used in production, determine their value, then add everything up.

In the production of jeans, these resources included land, labor, and capital. Table 20.2 identifies these resources, their unit values, and the total costs associated with their use. This table is based on maximum output of 15 pairs of jeans per day, with the use of one machine operator and one sewing machine. The rent on the factory is $100 per day, a sewing machine costs $20 per day, the wages of a garment worker are $80 per day. We shall assume Tight Jeans Corporation can purchase bolts of denim for $30 apiece, each of which provides enough denim for 10 pairs of jeans. In other words, one-tenth of a bolt ($3 worth of material) is required for one pair of jeans. We shall ignore any other potential expenses.[5] With these assumptions, the total cost of producing 15 pairs of jeans per day amounts to $245, as shown in Table 20.2.

Total costs will change, of course, as we alter the rate of production. But not all costs increase. In the short run, some costs don't increase at all when output is increased. These are **fixed costs,** in the sense that they do not vary with the rate of output. The factory lease is an example. Once you lease a factory, you are obligated to pay for it, whether you use it or not. The person who owns the factory wants $100 per day, whether you produce any jeans or not. Even if you produce no jeans, you still have to pay the rent. That is the essence of fixed costs.

fixed costs: Costs of production that do not change when the rate of output is altered, e.g., the cost of basic plant and equipment.

The leased sewing machine is another fixed cost. When you rent a sewing machine, you must pay the rental charge. It doesn't matter whether you use it for a few minutes or all day long—the rental charge is fixed at $20 per day.

Labor costs are another story altogether. The amount of labor employed in jeans production can be varied easily. If we decide not to open the factory tomorrow, we can just tell our worker to take the day off. We will still have to pay rent, but we can cut back on wages. On the other hand, if we want to increase daily output, we can also get additional workers easily and quickly. Labor is regarded as a **variable cost** in this line of work—that is, a cost that *varies* with the rate of output.

variable costs: Costs of production that change when the rate of output is altered, e.g., labor and material costs.

The denim itself is another variable cost. Denim not used today can be saved for tomorrow. Hence how much we "spend" on denim today is directly

[5]One cost we are ignoring is profit. Traditionally, "normal" profits are counted as a cost of production. The concept of profit is explored in Chapter 21.

TABLE 20.2   The Total Costs of Production
(total cost of producing 15 pairs of jeans per day)

The total cost of producing a good equals the market value of all the resources used in its production. In this case, we have assumed that the production of 15 pairs of jeans per day requires resources worth $245.	Resource	Price	Total cost
	1 factory	$100 per day	$100
	1 sewing machine	20 per day	20
	1 operator	80 per day	80
	1.5 bolts of denim	30 per bolt	45
	Total cost		$245

related to how many jeans we produce. In this sense, the cost of denim input varies with the rate of jeans output.

Figure 20.4 illustrates how these various costs are affected by the rate of production. On the vertical axis are the costs of production, in dollars per day. Notice that the total cost of producing 15 pairs per day is still $245, as indicated by point B. This figure consists of $120 of fixed costs (factory and sewing machine rents) and $125 of variable costs ($80 in wages and $45 for denim). If we increase the rate of output, total costs will rise. ***How fast total costs rise depends on variable costs only,*** however, since fixed costs remain at $120 per day. (Notice the horizontal fixed cost curve in Figure 20.4.)

With one sewing machine and one factory, there is an absolute limit to daily jeans production. The capacity of a factory with one machine is roughly 51 pairs of jeans per day. If we try to produce more jeans than this by hiring additional workers, our total costs will rise, but our output will not. Recall that the seventh worker had a *negative* marginal physical product (Figure 20.2), actually reducing total output. In fact, we could fill the factory with garment workers and drive total costs sky-high. But the limits of space and one sewing machine do not permit output in excess of 51 pairs per day. This limit to productive capacity is represented by point G on the total cost curve. Further expenditure on inputs will increase production costs but *reduce* output.

Although there is no upper limit to costs, there is a lower limit. If output is reduced to zero, total costs fall only to $120 per day, the level of fixed costs. This is illustrated by point A in Figure 20.4. As before, ***there is no way to avoid fixed costs in the short run.***

**FIGURE 20.4
The Costs of
Jeans Production**

Total cost includes both fixed and variable costs. Fixed costs must be paid even if no output is produced (point A). Variable costs start at zero and increase with the rate of output. The total cost of producing 15 pairs of jeans (point B) includes $120 in fixed costs (rent on the factory and sewing machines) and $125 in variable costs (denim and wages). Total cost rises as output increases, because additional variable costs must be incurred.

In this example, the short-run capacity is equal to 51 pairs (point G). If still more inputs are employed, costs will rise but not total output.

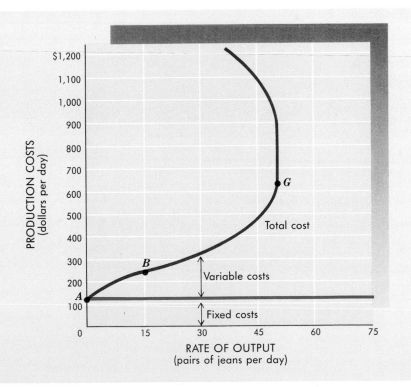

Average Costs

average total cost (ATC): Total cost divided by the quantity produced in a given time period.

Once we know the total costs of production, we can compute a lot of other cost measures. One of the most common measures of cost is average, or per-unit, cost. **Average total cost (ATC)** is simply total cost divided by the rate of output; that is,

$$\text{Average total cost (ATC)} = \frac{\text{total cost}}{\text{total output}}$$

At an output of 15 pairs of jeans per day, total costs are $245. The average cost of production is thus $16.33 per pair ($245 ÷ 15) at this rate of output.

Figure 20.5 shows how average costs change as the rate of output varies. Row *J* of the cost schedule, for example, again indicates the fixed, variable, and total costs of producing 15 pairs of jeans per day. Fixed costs are still $120; variable costs are $125. Thus the total cost of producing 15 pairs per day is $245.

average fixed cost (AFC): Total fixed cost divided by the quantity produced in a given time period.

average variable cost (AVC): Total variable cost divided by the quantity produced in a given time period.

The rest of row *J* shows the average costs of jeans production. These figures are obtained by dividing each total (columns 2, 3, and 4) by the rate of output (column 1). At an output rate of 15 pairs per day, **average fixed cost (AFC)** is $8 per pair, **average variable cost (AVC)** is $8.33, and *average total cost* (ATC) is $16.33. ATC, then, is simply the sum of AFC and AVC; that is,

$$\text{ATC} = \text{AFC} + \text{AVC}$$

Falling AFC   At this relatively low rate of output, fixed costs are a large portion of total costs. The rent paid for the factory and sewing machine works out to $8 per pair ($120 ÷ 15). This high average fixed cost accounts for

W RLD VIEW

COMPETITIVENESS

Unit Labor Costs

Foreign producers typically enjoy the advantage of low wage rates. Whereas U.S. manufacturers must pay at least $8–$10 per hour for labor, foreign manufacturers may pay as little as a few dollars per day.

However, the relative cost of labor also depends on productivity—on the amount of output the average worker produces. American workers are typically more productive than foreign workers, thanks to higher levels of capital investment, better technology, and higher education and skill levels.

Unit labor costs take into account both wage rates and physical productivity. They are computed as

$$\text{Unit labor costs} = \frac{\text{total labor cost}}{\text{quantity of output}}$$

In essence, unit labor costs are the average *labor* cost of output.

In the 1970s unit labor costs in the United States increased by 8 percent per year. In the 1980s, however,

productivity advances and lower wage growth reduced the escalation of unit labor costs to only 2.3 percent per year. This moderation of unit labor costs gave American producers a cost advantage over most foreign producers, as the following figures reveal.

Country	Average increase in unit labor costs, 1979–88 (percent per year)
Italy	8.5
France	6.7
Korea	7.6
Norway	7.6
Sweden	5.8
Great Britain	4.8
Canada	5.2
Germany (West)	2.7
United States	**2.3**
Belgium	1.1
Japan	−1.1

FIGURE 20.5
Average Costs

Average total cost (ATC) in column 7 equals total cost (column 4) divided by the rate of output (column 1). Since total cost includes both fixed (column 2) and variable (column 3) costs, ATC also equals AFC (column 5) plus AVC (column 6). This relationship is illustrated in the graph. The ATC of producing 20 pairs per day (point *K*) equals $13.50, the sum of AFC ($6.00) and AVC ($7.50).

	(1) Rate of output	(2) Fixed costs	+	(3) Variable costs	=	(4) Total cost	(5) Average fixed cost	+	(6) Average variable cost	=	(7) Average total cost
H	0	$120		$ 0		$120	—		—		—
I	10	120		85		205	$12.00		$ 8.50		$20.50
J	15	120		125		245	8.00		8.33		16.33
K	20	120		150		270	6.00		7.50		13.50
L	30	120		240		360	4.00		8.00		12.00
M	40	120		350		470	3.00		8.75		11.75
N	50	120		550		670	2.40		11.00		13.40
O	51	120		633		753	2.35		12.41		14.76

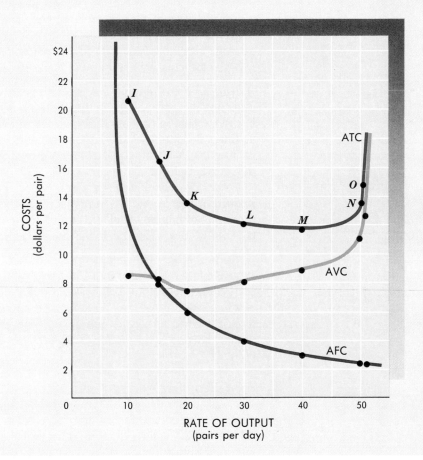

nearly one-half of total average costs. This suggests that it is quite expensive to lease a factory and sewing machine to produce only 15 pairs of jeans per day. To reduce average costs, we must make fuller use of our leased plant and equipment.

Notice what happens to average costs when the rate of output is increased to 20 pairs per day (row *K* in Figure 20.5). Average fixed costs are cut by a fourth, to only $6 per pair. This sharp decline in AFC results from the fact that total fixed costs ($120) are now spread over much more output. Even though our rent has not dropped, the *average* fixed cost of producing jeans has.

If we increase production beyond 20 pairs of jeans per day, AFC will continue to fall. Recall that

$$\bullet \quad \text{AFC} = \frac{\text{total fixed cost}}{\text{total output}}$$

The numerator is fixed (at $120 in this case). Increases in output enlarge the denominator. Hence *any increase in output will lower average fixed cost.* This is reflected in Figure 20.5 by the constantly declining AFC curve.

As jeans output is increased from 15 to 20 pairs per day, AVC falls as well. AVC includes the price of denim purchased and labor costs. The price of denim is unchanged, at $3 per pair ($30 per bolt). But per-unit *labor* costs have fallen, from $5.33 to $4.50 per pair. Thus the reduction in AVC is completely due to the greater productivity of a second worker. To get 20 pairs of jeans, we had to employ a second worker part-time.[6] In the process, the marginal physical product of labor rose and AVC fell.

With both AFC and AVC falling, ATC must decline as well. In this case, *average* total cost falls from $16.33 per pair to $13.50. This is reflected in row *K* of the table as well as in point *K* on the ATC curve in Figure 20.5.

Rising AVC   Although AFC continues to decline as output expands, AVC does not keep dropping. On the contrary, AVC tends to start rising quite early in the expansion process. Look at column 6 of the table in Figure 20.5. After an initial decline, AVC starts to increase. At an output of 20 pairs, AVC is $7.50. At 30 pairs, AVC is $8.00. By the time the rate of output reaches 51 pairs per day, AVC is $12.41.

Average variable cost rises because of diminishing returns in the production process. We have discussed this before. As output expands, each unit of labor has less land and capital to work with. Marginal physical product falls. As it does, labor costs *per pair of jeans* rise, pushing up AVC.

U-shaped ATC   The steady decline of AFC, when combined with the typical increase in AVC, results in a U-shaped pattern for average total costs. In the early stages of output expansion, the large declines in AFC tend to outweigh any increases in AVC. As a result, ATC tends to fall. Notice that ATC declines from $20.50 to $11.75 as output increases from 10 to 40 pairs per day. This is also illustrated in Figure 20.5 with the downward move from point *I* to point *M*.

The battle between falling AFC and rising AVC takes an irreversible turn soon thereafter. When output is increased from 40 to 50 pairs of jeans per day, AFC continues to fall (row *N* in the table). But the decline in AFC (-60 cents) is overshadowed by the increase in AVC ($+$2.25). Once rising AVC dominates, ATC starts to increase as well. ATC increases from $11.75 to $13.40 when jeans production expands from 40 to 50 pairs per day.

This and further increases in average total costs cause the ATC curve in Figure 20.5 to start rising. *The initial dominance of falling AFC, combined with the later resurgence of rising AVC, is what gives the ATC curve its characteristic U shape.*

Minimum average cost   The bottom of the U is an important point. Point *M* in Figure 20.5 represents *minimum* average total costs. Any other rate of production alters the balance between AFC and AVC and increases average

---

[6]We are assuming a worker can be hired for less than a full day, that is, worker-time is divisible.

total costs. By producing exactly 40 pairs per day, we minimize the amount of land, labor, and capital used per pair of jeans. For Tight Jeans Corporation, point *M* represents least-cost production—the lowest-cost jeans. For society as a whole, point *M* also represents the lowest possible opportunity cost; that is, we are minimizing the sacrifice of resources implied by the production of a pair of jeans. We are maximizing the amount of resources left over for the production of other goods and services.

As attractive as point *M* is, you should not conclude that it is everyone's dream. The primary objective of producers is to maximize their *profits*. This is not necessarily the same thing as minimizing average *costs*. In fact, the two objectives rarely coincide, as we shall see in the next chapter.

Marginal Cost

One final cost concept is important. Indeed, this last concept is probably the most important one for production. It is *marginal cost*. We have already encountered this concept in our discussion of resource costs. There we noted that marginal cost refers to the value of the resources needed to produce one more unit of a good. To produce *one* more pair of jeans, we need the denim itself and a very small amount of additional labor. These are the extra or added costs of increasing output by one pair of jeans per day. To compute the dollar value of these marginal costs, we could determine the market price of denim and labor, then add them up. Table 20.3 provides an example. In this case, we calculate that the additional or *marginal cost* of producing a sixteenth pair of jeans is $7.24. This is how much *total* costs will increase if we decide to expand jeans output by only one pair per day (from 15 to 16).

Table 20.3 emphasizes the link between resource costs and dollar costs. However, there is a much easier way to compute marginal cost. **Marginal cost refers to the change in total costs associated with one more unit of output.** Accordingly, we can simply observe *total* dollar costs before and after the rate of output is increased. The difference between the two totals equals the *marginal cost* of increasing the rate of output. This technique is obviously much easier for jeans manufacturers who don't know much about marginal resource utilization but have a sharp eye for dollar costs. It's also a lot easier for economics students, of course. But they have an obligation to understand the resource origins of marginal costs and what causes marginal costs to rise or fall. As we noted before, diminishing returns in production cause marginal costs to increase as the rate of output is expanded. Hence the marginal cost curve eventually slopes upward, as in Figure 20.6.

TABLE 20.3   Resource Computation of Marginal Cost

Marginal cost refers to the value of the additional inputs needed to produce one more unit of output. To increase daily jeans output from 15 to 16 pairs, we need 0.053 unit of labor and one-tenth of a bolt of denim. These extra inputs cost $7.24.	Resources used to produce 16th pair of jeans	Market value	Marginal cost
	0.053 unit of labor	0.053 × $80 unit of labor	$4.24
	0.1 bolt of denim	0.1 × $30	3.00
			$7.24

FIGURE 20.6
The Marginal Cost Curve

Marginal cost (MC) is the increase in *total* cost resulting from a one–unit increase in the rate of production. MC is the additional cost of producing one more unit. These hypothetical numbers indicate that total cost increases from $25 to $34 when a fifth unit is produced (compare rows *u* and *t*). Hence the MC of the fifth unit is $9, as illustrated by point *u* on the marginal cost curve. The MC curve generally rises (as a consequence of the law of diminishing returns).

	Rate of output	Total cost		Marginal cost
p	0	$10	>	
q	1	13	>	3
r	2	15	>	2
s	3	19	>	4
t	4	25	>	6
u	5	34	>	9
v	6	48	>	14
w	7	68	>	20
x	8	98	>	30

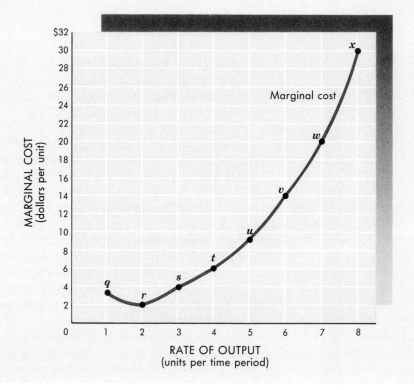

MARGINAL COST (dollars per unit)

RATE OF OUTPUT (units per time period)

A Cost Summary

A quick review of the key cost concepts is provided in Table 20.4. The relationship between them is illustrated in Figure 20.7. As before, we are concentrating on a short-run production process, with fixed quantities of land and capital. In this case, however, we have abandoned the Tight Jeans Corporation and provided hypothetical costs for an idealized production process. The purpose of these figures is to provide a more general view of how the various cost concepts relate to each other. Note that MC, ATC, AFC, and AVC can all be computed from total costs. All we need, then, is the first two columns of the table in Figure 20.7 and we can compute and graph all the rest of the cost figures.

The centerpiece of Figure 20.7 is the U-shaped ATC curve. What is of special significance is its relationship to marginal costs. Notice that ***the MC curve intersects the ATC curve at its lowest point*** (point *m*). This will always be the case. So long as the marginal cost of producing one more unit

TABLE 20.4   A Guide to Costs

Total costs of production include **fixed costs** and **variable costs:**

- $TC = FC + VC$

Dividing these costs by the quantity of output yields the **average total cost,** which includes **average fixed cost** and **average variable cost:**

- $ATC = AFC + AVC$

The most important measure of changes in cost is **marginal cost,** which equals the increase in total costs when one additional unit of output is produced:

- $MC = \dfrac{\text{change in total cost}}{\text{change in output}}$

**FIGURE 20.7
Basic Cost Curves**

With total cost and the rate of output, all other cost concepts can be computed. The resulting cost curves have several distinct features. The AFC curve always slopes downward. The MC curve typically rises, sometimes after a brief decline. The ATC curve has a U shape. And the MC curve will always intersect both the ATC and AVC curves at their lowest points (*m* and *n*, respectively).

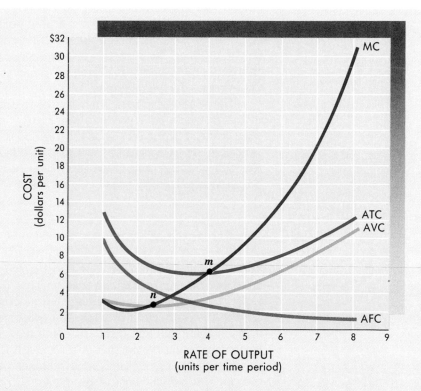

Rate of output	TC	MC	ATC	AFC	AVC
0	$10.00	—	—	—	—
1	13.00	$ 3.00	$13.00	$10.00	$ 3.00
2	15.00	2.00	7.50	5.00	2.50
3	19.00	4.00	6.33	3.33	3.00
4	25.00	6.00	6.25	2.50	3.75
5	34.00	9.00	6.80	2.00	4.80
6	48.00	14.00	8.00	1.67	6.33
7	68.00	20.00	9.71	1.43	8.28
8	98.00	30.00	12.25	1.25	11.00

is less than the previous average cost, average costs must fall. Thus average costs decline as long as the marginal cost curve lies below the average cost curve, as to the left of point *m* in Figure 20.7.

We have already observed, however, that marginal costs themselves tend to rise as output expands, largely because additional workers reduce the amount of land and capital available to each worker (in the short run, the size of plant and equipment is fixed). Consequently, at some point (*m* in Figure 20.7) marginal costs will rise to the level of average costs.

As marginal costs continue to rise beyond point *m*, they begin to pull average costs up, giving the average cost curve its U shape. Average costs increase whenever marginal costs exceed average costs. This is the case to the right of point *m*, since the marginal cost curve always lies above the average cost curve in that part of Figure 20.7.

To visualize the relationship between marginal cost and average cost, imagine computing the average height of people entering a room. If the first person who comes through the door is 6 feet tall, then the average height of people entering the room is 6 feet at that point. But what happens to average height if the second person entering the room is only 3 feet tall? *Average height declines because the last (marginal) person entering the room is shorter than the previous average.* Whenever the last entrant is shorter than the average, the average must fall.

The relationship between marginal costs and average costs is also similar to that between your grade in this course and your grade-point average. If your grade in economics is better (higher) than your other grades, then your overall grade-point average will rise. In other words, a high *marginal* grade will pull your *average* grade up. If you don't understand this, your grade-point average is likely to fall.

ECONOMIC VS. ACCOUNTING COSTS

An essential characteristic of the cost curves we have observed is that they are based on *real* production relationships. The dollar costs we compute are a direct reflection of underlying resource costs—the land, labor, and capital used in the production process. Not everyone counts this way. On the contrary, accountants and businesspeople typically count dollar costs only and ignore any resource use that doesn't result in an explicit dollar cost.

Return to Tight Jeans for a moment to see the difference. When we computed the dollar cost of producing 15 pairs of jeans per day, we noted the following resource inputs:

INPUTS	COST
1 factory rent	@ $100
1 machine rent	@ 20
1 machine operator	@ 80
1.5 bolts of denim	@ 45
Total cost	$245

The total value of the resources used in the production of 15 pairs of jeans was thus $245 per day. But this figure need not conform to *actual* dollar costs. Suppose the owners of Tight Jeans decided to sew jeans. Then they would not have to hire a worker or pay $80 per day in wages. *Dollar* costs would drop to $165 per day. The producers and their accountant would consider this to be a remarkable achievement. They would assert that the cost of producing jeans had fallen.

Economic Cost

An economist would draw no such conclusions. ***The essential economic question is how many resources are used in production.*** This has not changed. One unit of labor is still being employed at the factory; now it's simply the owners, not a hired worker. In either case, one unit of labor is not available for the production of other goods and services. Hence society is still paying $245 for jeans, whether the owners of Tight Jeans write checks in that amount or not. We really don't care who sews jeans—the essential point is that someone (i.e., a unit of labor) does.

The same would be true if Tight Jeans owned its own factory rather than rented it. If the factory was owned rather than rented, the owners probably would not write any rent checks. Hence accounting costs would drop by $100 per day. But society would not be saving any resources. The factory would still be in use for jeans production and therefore unavailable for the production of other goods and services. The economic (resource) cost of producing 15 pairs of jeans would still be $245.

The distinction between an economic cost and an accounting cost is essentially one between resource and dollar costs. *Dollar cost* refers to the actual dollar outlays made by a producer; it is the lifeblood of accountants. **Economic cost,** in contrast, refers to the dollar *value* of all resources used in the production process; it is the lifeblood of economists. In other words, economists count costs as:

economic cost: The value of all resources used to produce a good or service; opportunity cost.

- Economic cost = Explicit costs + Implicit costs.

As this formula suggests, ***economic and accounting costs will diverge whenever any factor of production is not paid an explicit wage (or rent, etc.).***[7]

The cost of homework   These distinctions between economic and accounting costs apply also to the "production" of homework. You can pay people to write term papers for you, and at large schools you can often buy lecture notes. But most students end up doing their own homework, so that they will learn something and not just turn in required assignments.

Doing homework is expensive, however, even if you don't pay someone to do it. The time you spend reading this chapter is valuable. You could be doing something else if you weren't reading right now. What would you be doing? The forgone activity—the best alternative use of your time—represents the economic cost of doing homework. Even if you don't pay yourself for reading this chapter, you'll still incur that *economic* cost.

LONG-RUN COSTS

All of our discussion thus far has been confined to short-run production costs. ***The short run is characterized by fixed costs***—a commitment to plant and equipment. A factory, an office building, or some other plant and equipment have been leased or purchased: we are stuck with *fixed* costs. In the short

[7]The distinction between economic and accounting costs is also referred to as the difference between implicit costs (all costs) and explicit costs (only those paid).

run, our objective is to make the best use of those fixed costs by choosing the appropriate rate of production.

The long run opens up a whole new range of options. In the **long run,** we have no lease or purchase commitments. We are free to start all over again, with whatever scale of plant and equipment we desire. *There are no fixed costs in the long run.*

long run: A period of time long enough for all inputs to be varied (no fixed costs).

Long-Run Average Costs

The opportunities available in the long run include building a plant of any desired size. Suppose we still wanted to go into the jeans business. In the long run, we could build or lease any size factory we wanted and could lease as many sewing machines as we desired. Figure 20.8 illustrates three choices: a small factory (ATC_1), a medium-sized factory (ATC_2), and a large factory (ATC_3). As we observed earlier, it is very expensive to produce lots of jeans with a small factory. The ATC curve for a small factory (ATC_1) starts to head straight up at relatively low rates of output. In the long run, we would lease or build such a factory only if we anticipated a continuing low rate of output.

The ATC_2 curve illustrates how costs might fall if we leased or built a medium-sized factory. With a small-sized factory, ATC becomes prohibitive at an output of 50 to 60 pairs of jeans per day. A medium-sized factory can produce these quantities at lower cost. Moreover, ATC continues to drop as jeans production increases in the medium-sized factory—at least for a while. Even a medium-sized factory must contend with resource constraints and therefore rising average costs: its ATC curve is U-shaped also.

If we expected to sell really large quantities of jeans, we would want to build or lease a large factory. Beyond the rate of output *b*, the largest factory offers the lowest average total cost. There's a risk in leasing such a large factory, of course. If our sales don't live up to our high expectations, we will end up with very high fixed costs and thus very expensive jeans. Look at the high average cost of producing only 60 pairs of jeans per day with the large factory (ATC_3).

In choosing an appropriate factory, then, we need to know how many jeans we expect to sell. Once we know our expected output, we can easily pick the right-sized factory. It will be the one that offers the lowest ATC for

FIGURE 20.8
Long-Run Costs
with Three Options

Long-run cost possibilities are determined by all possible short-run options. In this case, there are three options of varying size (ATC_1, ATC_2, and ATC_3). In the long run we would choose that option which yielded the lowest average cost for any desired rate of output. The solid portion of the curves (LATC) represents these choices. The smallest factory (ATC_1) is best for output levels below *a*; the largest (ATC_3), for output rates in excess of *b*.

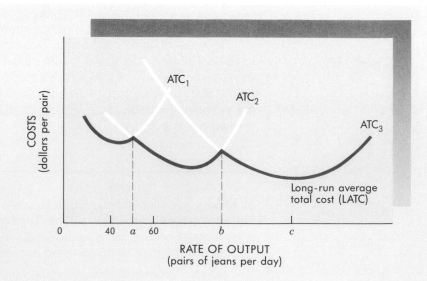

that rate of output. In this case, the decision is pretty easy. If we expect to sell fewer jeans than *a*, we will choose the small factory. If we expect to sell jeans at a rate between *a* and *b*, we will select a medium-sized factory. Beyond rate *b*, we will want the largest factory. These choices are reflected in the solid part of the three ATC curves. The "curve" created by these three segments constitutes our long-run cost possibilities. ***The long-run cost curve is just a summary of our best short-run cost possibilities***.

We might confront more than three choices, of course. There is really no reason we couldn't build a factory to any desired size. In the long run we face an infinite number of scale choices, not just three. The effect of all these choices is to smooth out the long-run cost curve. Figure 20.9 depicts the long-run curve that results. Each rate of output is most efficiently produced by some size (scale) of plant. That sized plant indicates the minimum cost of producing a particular rate of output. Its corresponding short-run ATC curve provides one point on the long-run ATC curve.

Long-Run Marginal Costs

Like all average cost curves, the long-run (LATC) curve has its own marginal cost curve. The long-run marginal cost (LMC) curve is not a composite of short-run marginal cost curves. Rather, it is computed on the basis of the costs reflected in the long-run ATC curve itself. We won't bother to compute those costs here. We will note, however, that the long-run MC curve—like all MC curves—intersects its associated average cost curve at its lowest point.

ECONOMIES OF SCALE

In reality, a producer is not confined to the choice of only one plant. A producer can use either one large plant or several smaller ones to produce the same output. Suppose the output level *c* was desired in Figure 20.8. The producer would never try to produce such a high rate of output with a single small plant (ATC_1). But it might be desirable to produce that rate of output with *several* small plants rather than one large one (ATC_3). In this case, the producer must compare the *minimum ATC* associated with different plant sizes.

**FIGURE 20.9
Long-Run Costs
with Unlimited Options**

If plants of all sizes can be built, short–run options are infinite. In this case, the LATC curve becomes a smooth U–shaped curve. Each point on the curve represents lowest-cost production for a plant size best suited to one rate of output. The long–run ATC curve has its own MC curve.

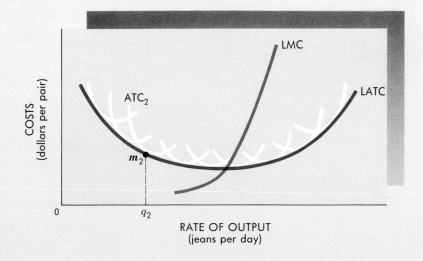

economies of scale: Reductions in minimum average costs that come about through increases in the size (scale) of plant and equipment.

Notice what happens to *minimum ATC* in Figure 20.8 when the size (scale) of the factory changes. When a medium-sized factory (ATC_2) replaces a small factory (ATC_1), minimum average cost drops (the bottom of ATC_2 is below the bottom of ATC_1). This implies that a jeans producer who wants to minimize costs should build one medium-sized factory rather than try to produce the same quantity with two small ones. **Economies of scale** exist in this situation: larger facilities reduce minimum average costs.

Larger production facilities do not always result in cost reductions. Suppose a firm has the choice of producing the quantity Q_m from several small factories or from one large, centralized facility. Centralization may have three different impacts on costs. These are illustrated in Figure 20.10. In each of the three illustrations, we see the average total cost (ATC) curve for a typical small firm or plant and the ATC curve for a much larger plant producing the same product.

Figure 20.10*a* depicts a situation in which there is no economic advantage to centralization of manufacturing operations, becuse a large plant is no more efficient than a multitude of small plants. The critical focus here is on the *minimum* average costs attainable for a given rate of output. Note that the lowest point on the smaller plant's ATC curve (point *c*) is no higher or lower than the lowest point on the larger firm's ATC curve (point m_1). Hence it would be just as cheap to produce the quantity Q_m from a multitude of small plants as it would be to produce Q_m from one large plant. Thus increasing the size (or *scale*) of individual plants will not reduce minimum average costs: this is a situation of **constant returns to scale**.

constant returns to scale: Increases in plant size do not affect minimum average cost; minimum per-unit costs are identical for small plants and large plants.

Figure 20.10*b* illustrates the situation in which a larger plant is able to attain a lower minimum average cost than a smaller plant. That is, economies of scale (or *increasing returns to scale*) exist. This is evident from the fact that the larger firm's ATC curve falls *below* the dotted line in the graph (m_2 is less than *c*). The greater efficiency of the large factory might come from any of several sources. A large factory, for example, might be able to

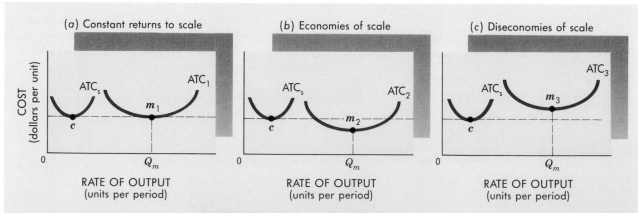

FIGURE 20.10 Economies of Scale

In choosing to produce a given rate of output (Q_m) from one large plant or many small ones, a producer must consider the impact of plant size (scale) on costs. Here we contrast the average total costs associated with one small plant (ATC_s) and three large plants (ATC_1, ATC_2, and ATC_3). If a large plant attains the same minimum average costs (point m_1 in part *a*) as a smaller plant (point *c*), there is no advantage to large size. Many small plants can produce the same output just as cheaply. However, either economies (part *b*) or diseconomies (part *c*) of scale may exist.

enjoy greater specialization of labor, with each worker becoming expert in a particular skill. By contrast, a smaller establishment might have to use the same individual(s) to perform several functions, thereby reducing productivity at each task. Also, some kinds of machinery may be economical only if they are used to produce massive volumes,[8] an opportunity only very large factories have. Finally, a large plant might acquire a persistent cost advantage through the process of learning by doing. That is, its longer experience and greater volume of output may translate into improved organization and efficiency.

Even though large plants may be able to achieve greater efficiencies than smaller plants, there is no assurance that they actually will. In fact, increasing the size (scale) of a plant may actually *reduce* operating efficiency, as depicted in Figure 20.10*c*. Workers may feel alienated in a plant of massive proportions and feel little commitment to productivity. Moreover, a large plant may offer greater opportunities to slack off without getting caught. For these reasons and others, a large plant may require more intensive managerial supervision, which would raise production costs. Indeed, even a decentralized supercorporation may find that the managerial efforts required to coordinate a multitude of separate plants raise average costs above those of the smaller firm.

[8]That is to say, the machinery itself may be subject to economies of scale.

In The News

DISECONOMIES OF SCALE

Some Firms Fight Ills of Bigness by Keeping Employee Units Small

At 3M Plants, Workers Have Flexibility, Involvement—and Their Own Radios

St. Paul, Minn.—For a company with some 87,000 employees and annual sales in excess of $6 billion. Minnesota Mining & Manufacturing Co. spends a lot of time "thinking small."

"We are keenly aware of the disadvantages of large size," says Gordon W. Engdahl, the company's vice president for human resources and its top personnel officer. "We made a conscious effort to keep our units as small as possible because we think it helps keep them flexible and vital," he says. "When one gets too large, we break it apart. We like to say that our success in recent years amounts to multiplication by division."

Mr. Engdahl's comment is no conceit. 3M's average U.S. manufacturing plant employs just 270 people, and management groups as small as five guide the fortunes of the company's numerous household, industrial and scientific products. In the 1970s, its sales and earnings grew almost fourfold, while its U.S. work force increased by 40%.

3M's record stands in sharp contrast to a mostly overlooked trend developing over the past 15 years or so: the declining role of large companies in this country's employment picture. . . .

The Inefficiencies of Size
Not all of the mechanisms behind these developments are clear, and some surely are complex. Observers note that many of the biggest companies of the 1970s were manufacturers that suffered from heightened foreign competition and the related swing of the U.S. economy toward "service" functions. . . .

Increasingly, however, blame for the laggard performance of many large corporations is focusing on their structures and entrenched ways of doing things. A growing body of opinion has it that the "economies of scale" made possible by bigness often are more than nullified by organizational rigidities and bottlenecks.

"More companies seem to be showing concern that their neat organization charts don't always reflect reality and certainty don't, in themselves, overcome the tensions between autonomy and control that get worse with size," says Larry E. Grejner, a professor of organizational behavior at the University of Southern California's School of Business Administration.

—Frederick C. Klein

These kinds of situations, wherein minimum average costs rise as the scale of operations increases, are *diseconomies of scale* (see In the News).

In evaluating long-run options, then, we must be careful to recognize that **efficiency and size do not necessarily go hand in hand**. Some firms and industries may be subject to economies of scale, but others may not be. Bigger is not always better.

POLICY INSIGHTS:

PRODUCTIVITY IMPROVEMENTS

All of the cost concepts discussed in this chapter have been derived from the production function. That function, describing our productive capabilities, has been taken as a technological fact of life. It represents the best we can do, given our state of technological and managerial knowledge. In the real world, however, the best is always getting better. Science and technology are continuously advancing. So is our knowledge of how to organize and manage our resources. These advances keep *shifting* our production functions upward: more can be produced with any given quantity of inputs. In the process, the costs of production shift downward. This is illustrated in Figure 20.11 by the downward shifts of the MC and ATC curves. These downward shifts imply that we can get more of the goods and services we desire with available resources.

Productivity advances have been critical in raising American living standards. From 1948 to 1973, total output grew at nearly 4 percent per year. Less than half of this growth was due to increased use of labor and capital—that is, more inputs. The rest of our growth came from improvements in technology, management, and the quality of our labor. In the 1980s productivity improvements were even more critical to our economic growth.

The implication of this historical experience is that rising living standards depend on continuing advances in productivity. Government policy can and does play an important role in this regard. At present, the federal government pays for 49 percent of all basic research (see In the News). The public sector is also responsible for most of our educational system. Finally, the government

**FIGURE 20.11
Improvements in
Productivity Reduce Costs**

**Advances in technological
or managerial knowledge
increase our productive
capability. This is reflected
in upward shifts of the
production function (part *a*)
and downward shifts of
production cost curves
(part *b*).**

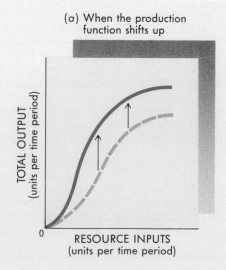

(*a*) When the production function shifts up

TOTAL OUTPUT (units per time period)

RESOURCE INPUTS (units per time period)

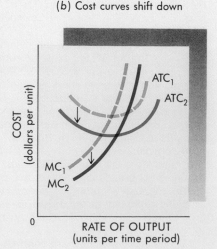

(*b*) Cost curves shift down

COST (dollars per unit)

ATC_1
ATC_2
MC_1
MC_2

RATE OF OUTPUT (units per time period)

In The News

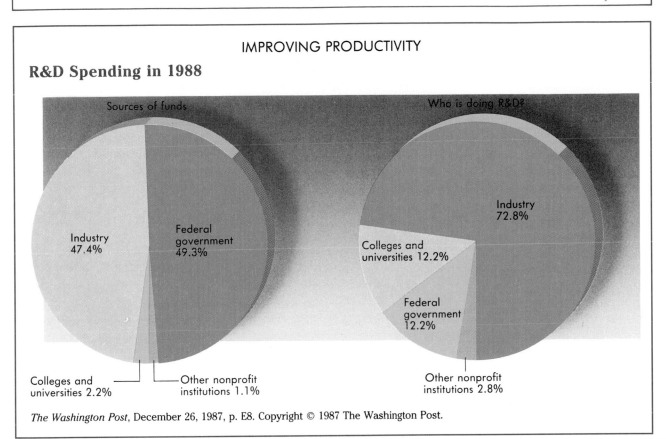

IMPROVING PRODUCTIVITY

R&D Spending in 1988

Sources of funds

Industry 47.4%

Federal government 49.3%

Colleges and universities 2.2%

Other nonprofit institutions 1.1%

Who is doing R&D?

Industry 72.8%

Colleges and universities 12.2%

Federal government 12.2%

Other nonprofit institutions 2.8%

The Washington Post, December 26, 1987, p. E8. Copyright © 1987 The Washington Post.

helps establish the institutional climate (e.g., regulations, standards) for U.S. businesses. How fast productivity advances thus depends not only on the persistent inquiries of lone scientists and managers, but also on how well the public sector encourages or impedes research and development.

SUMMARY

- A production function indicates the maximum amount of output that can be produced with different combinations of inputs. It is a technological relationship and changes (shifts) when new technology or management techniques are discovered.

- In the short run, some inputs (e.g., land and capital) are fixed in quantity. Increases in (short-run) output result from more use of variable inputs (e.g., labor).

- The contribution of a variable input to total output is measured by its marginal physical product (MPP). This is the amount by which *total* output increases when one more unit of the input is employed.

- The MPP of a factor tends to decline as more of it is used in a given production facility. Diminishing returns result from "crowding" more of a variable input into a production process, reducing the amount of fixed inputs *per unit* of variable input.

• Marginal cost is the increase in total cost that results when output is increased by one unit. Marginal cost increases whenever marginal physical product diminishes.

• Not all costs go up when the rate of output is increased. Fixed costs (e.g., space and equipment leases) do not vary with the rate of output. Only variable costs (e.g., labor and material) go up when output is increased.

• Average total cost (ATC) equals total cost divided by the quantity of output produced. ATC declines whenever marginal cost (MC) is less than average cost and rises when MC exceeds it. The MC and ATC curves intersect at minimum ATC (the bottom of the U). That intersection represents least-cost production.

• The economic costs of production include the value of *all* resources used. Accounting costs typically include only those dollar costs actually paid (explicit costs).

• In the long run there are no fixed costs; the size (scale) of production can be varied. The long-run ATC curve indicates the lowest cost of producing output with facilities of appropriate size.

• Economies of scale refer to reductions in minimum average cost attained with large plant size (scale). If minimum ATC rises with plant size, diseconomies exist.

• Historically, advances in technology and the quality of our inputs have been the major source of economic growth. These advances have shifted production functions up and pushed cost curves down.

Terms to Remember   Define the following terms:

factors of production	fixed costs
production function	variable costs
productivity	average total cost (ATC)
efficiency (technical)	average fixed cost (AFC)
opportunity cost	average variable cost (AVC)
short run	economic cost
marginal physical product (MPP)	long run
law of diminishing returns	economies of scale
marginal cost (MC)	constant returns to scale
total cost	

Questions for Discussion

1. What is the marginal cost of enrolling one more student in your class? What are the fixed and variable costs associated with "production" of students?

2. Suppose all your friends offered to help wash your car. Would marginal physical product decline as more friends helped? Why or why not?

3. Owner-operators of small gas stations rarely pay themselves an hourly wage. Does this practice reduce the economic cost of dispensing gasoline?

4. Supermarkets have replaced small grocery stores in many areas, in large part because of the lower costs they achieve. What kind of economies of scale exist in supermarkets? Why doesn't someone build one colossal supermarket and drive costs down further?

Problems 1. Complete the following table, then plot the marginal cost and average total cost curves on the same graph. Identify the lowest per-unit cost on the graph.

Rate of output	Total cost	Marginal cost	Average fixed cost	Average variable cost	Average total cost
0	$100	____	____	____	____
1	110	____	____	____	____
2	130	____	____	____	____
3	165	____	____	____	____
4	220	____	____	____	____
5	300	____	____	____	____

2. Refer to the production table for jeans (Table 20.1). Suppose a firm had three sewing machines and could vary only the amount of labor input.
   (a) Graph the total output curve for jeans given the three sewing machines.
   (b) Compute the marginal physical product of jeans for 1, 2, 3, 4, 5, 6, and 7 workers used with the three sewing machines.
   (c) Graph the marginal physical product curve if there are three sewing machines.
   (d) At what amount of labor input does the law of diminishing returns first become apparent in your graph of marginal physical product?
   (e) What is the relationship between the slope of the total output curve and marginal physical product?

3. The following table indicates the average total cost of producing varying quantities of output from three different plants:

Rate of output	Average total cost for:		
	Small firm	Medium firm	Large firm
10	$ 600	$800	$1,000
20	500	650	900
30	400	500	800
40	500	350	700
50	600	200	600
60	700	300	500
70	800	400	400
80	900	500	300
90	1,000	600	400
100	1,100	700	500

   (a) Plot the ATC curves for all three firms on the same graph.
   (b) Which plant(s) should be used to produce 40 units?
   (c) Which plant(s) should be used to produce 100 units?
   (d) Are there economies of scale in these plant-size choices?

The Competitive Firm

*P*eople are in business to make a profit. To supply the goods and services consumers demand, producers have to incur real costs. They have to employ land, labor, and capital in the production process. In return, they want to be paid enough for their goods to at least recover the production costs. And they want more than that—they want profits. Indeed, the pursuit of profits is what keeps the supply side of product markets humming. Without the prospect of profits, few producers would be willing to supply the goods and services we demand.

Not all firms have the same opportunities for earning profits. Huge corporations often have the power to raise prices, change consumer tastes (through advertising), or use other strategies for increasing profits. Small competitive firms have fewer options, as we will discover. Nevertheless, the quest for profits is the common motivation for virtually all supply activity.

In this chapter we examine how the profit motive affects the decision to produce goods and services. We focus on the behavior of competitive firms, postponing a discussion of larger, more powerful firms until later. We first want to observe how the pursuit of profit determines how much output a competitive firm will produce. In answering this question, we confront the following issues:

- What are profits?

- What are the unique characteristics of competitive firms?

- How can a competitive firm maximize profits?

After answering these questions, we also observe how various types of taxes alter production decisions.

THE PROFIT MOTIVE

The market mechanism answers a basic question—FOR WHOM to produce—by distributing goods and services on the basis of ability to pay. To the extent that people who own a business want a share of total output, they must generate an income that can be used to buy consumer goods they desire. *Owning* plant and equipment is not enough. To generate a current flow of income, one must *use* that plant and equipment to produce goods. When sold,

523

those goods generate the income business owners need for their own consumption desires. ***The basic incentive to produce is the expectation of income.***

Whereas the monetary incentives for motivating workers are usually expressed in terms of wages and salaries, returns to the efforts of a business are commonly referred to as profits. **Profit** is the difference between the total revenues of a firm and its total costs. It is the "residual" that the owners of a business receive. The recipient of the residual may be the single owner of a corner grocery store or it may be the group of stockholders who collectively own a large corporation. In either case, it is the hope of some residual profit that motivates people to own and operate a business.

profit: The difference between total revenue and total cost.

Other Motivations

Profit is not the only thing that motivates producers. Like the rest of us, producers also worry about social status and crave recognition. They are generally more willing to produce those products or services that enjoy high social acceptance or prestige. Producers will also be more willing to make the leisure and consumption sacrifices required by production if they are generally held in high regard by the rest of society. That is to say, producers will work for less profit if we reward them with high status.

Psychological influences are also important in motivating producers. People who have a need to feel important, to control others, or to demonstrate achievement are likely candidates for the job of producing goods. Other people are lured into business by a relentless need to "be their own person," to confirm their independence and freedom. As the accompanying survey reveals (see In the News) owners of small businesses are especially prey to such motivations. Many small businesses are maintained by people who gave up 40-hour weeks, $30,000 incomes, and a sense of alienation in exchange for 80-hour weeks, $25,000 incomes, and a sense of identity.

Additional motivations for producing arise from the structure of many production units. The ownership of large corporations tends to be fragmented among thousands of individual stockholders, most of whom have never even seen corporate headquarters. The people who manage the corporation's business on a day-to-day basis may have little or no stock in the company. As a consequence, the self-interests of owners and of managers may conflict. Corporate managers who have little or no ownership rights are likely to be at least as interested in their own jobs, salaries, and self-preservation as in the profits that accrue to the owners. Such "technocrats," as John Kenneth Galbraith of Harvard University labeled them, may seek to mollify owners with a steady flow of profits rather than maximum profits at any given point in time. To the extent that their salaries depend on corporate size or sales—as they usually do—corporate managers may show more interest in corporate growth than in corporate profits. If these efforts reduce the flow of profits below some minimum acceptable to owners, however, the corporation may start looking for new managers. Hence the level of profits must still be an object of concern.

ECONOMIC VS. ACCOUNTING PROFITS

Although profits might be a necessary inducement for producers, most consumers feel that profits are too high. And they may be in many cases. But most consumers do not have any idea how much profit U.S. businesses actually make. Public *perceptions* of profit are seven or eight times higher than

In The News

MOTIVATION

Are Money and Status Losing Their Allure?

What do owners find most satisfying about their businesses? Not money or status, concludes a survey of 198 owners by Cicco & Associates Inc., a Murrysville, Pa., management-consulting concern.

The owners ranked the pride of offering a product or service tops in a list of 12 possible sources of satisfaction. Income ranked No. 7; status, dead last.

"In contrast to the capitalist stereotype, owners of small businesses appear to enjoy the satisfactions traditionally associated more with the craftsman than the financier," says Mary Del Brady, director of Cicco's Small Business Market Task Force.

Women indicated greater overall satisfaction than men in owning a business, noting higher satisfaction levels in nine of the 12 categories, including customer contact and self-reliance. Men derived more satisfaction in only one area: employee contact.

The Wall Street Journal, January 12, 1988, p. 39. Reprinted by permission of *The Wall Street Journal,* © Dow Jones & Company, Inc. (1988). All Rights Reserved.

Small-Business Benefits

Surveyed small-business owners rank pride in product as their most important source of satisfaction. The rankings:

1	Pride in product/service
2	Control
3	Freedom
4	Flexibility
5	Self-reliance
6	Customer contact
7	Income
8	Employee contact
9	Recognition
10	Privacy
11	Security
12	Status

Source: Cicco and Associates.

"You know what I think, folks? Improving technology isn't important. Increased profits aren't important. What's important is to be warm, decent human beings."

Drawing by Handelsman; © 1987 The New Yorker Magazine, Inc.

actual profits. The typical consumer believes that 35 to 40 cents of every sales dollar goes to profits. In reality, average profit per sales dollar is closer to 5 cents.

Faulty perceptions of profits are not confined to the general public. As surprising as it might seem, most businesses also measure their profits incorrectly. This misuse of the term "profits" is directly related to our earlier discussion of economic costs.

Economic Profits

economic cost: The value of all resources used to produce a good or service; opportunity cost.

economic profit: The difference between total revenues and total economic costs.

Everyone agrees with the general notion that profit represents the difference between total revenues and total costs. Where people part ways is over the decision of what to include in total costs. Recall from Chapter 20 how economists compute costs. **Economic cost** refers to the value of *all* resources used in production, whether or not they are paid an explicit wage. By contrast, most businesses count only explicit costs—that is, those they actually write checks for.

Because economists and businesspeople compute costs differently, their calculations of profits differ as well. If businesses (and their accountants) count only *paid* (explicit) costs, they will understate true costs. This incomplete accounting of costs leads to an overstatement of profits. Part of the accounting "profit" will really be compensation to unpaid land, labor, or capital used in the production process. ***Whenever economic costs exceed explicit costs, observed (accounting) profits will exceed true (economic) profits.*** To determine the **economic profit** of a business, we must subtract all implicit factor costs from observed "net returns"; profits, if any, are the residual. That is,

$$\text{Economic profit} = \text{total revenue} - \text{total economic cost}$$

Suppose, for example, that Table 21.1 accurately summarizes the revenues and costs associated with a local drugstore. Monthly sales revenues amount to $27,000. Explicit costs paid by the owner-manager include the cost

TABLE 21.1   The Computation of Economic Profit
(per month)

To calculate economic profit, we must take account of *all* costs of production. The economic costs of production include the implicit (opportunity) costs of the labor and capital a producer contributes to the production process. The accounting profits of a business take into account only explicit costs paid by the owner. Reported (accounting) profits will exceed economic profits whenever implicit costs are ignored.

Total (gross) revenues	$27,000
less explicit costs:	
Cost of merchandise sold	$17,000
Wages to cashier, stock, and delivery help	2,500
Rent and utilities	800
Taxes	700
Total explicit costs	$21,000
Accounting profit (revenue minus explicit costs)	$ 6,000
less implicit costs:	
Wages of owner-manager, 300 hrs. @ $10 per hour	$ 3,000
Return on inventory investment, 10% per year on $120,000	1,000
Total implicit costs	$ 4,000
Economic profit (revenue minus *all* costs)	$ 2,000

of merchandise bought from producers for resale to consumers ($17,000), wages to the employees of the drugstore, rent and utilities paid to the landlord, and local sales and business taxes. When all of these explicit costs are subtracted from total revenue, we are left with an *accounting profit* of $6,000 per month.

The owner-manager of the drugstore may be quite pleased with an accounting profit of $6,000 per month. He is working hard for this income, however. To keep his store running, the owner-manager is working 10 hours per day, 7 days a week. This adds up to 300 hours of labor per month. Were he to work this hard for someone else, his labor would be compensated explicitly, with a paycheck. Although he doesn't choose to pay himself in this way, his labor still represents a real resource cost. To compute economic profits, we must subtract this additional cost from the accounting profits of the drugstore. To do this, we need to know the owner-manager's implicit wage rate—that is, how much he could earn if he worked elsewhere. Suppose he could earn $10 per hour in the best alternative job. Multiplying this wage rate ($10) by the number of hours he works in the drugstore (300), we see that the implicit return for his labor is $3,000 per month. This is a real cost for the drugstore, and for society as well.

We also observe that the owner has used his savings to purchase inventory for the store. He purchased the goods on his shelves for $120,000. This amount represent his investment in the business. If he had invested his savings in some other business, he could have earned a return of 10 percent per year. This forgone return represents a real cost. In this case, the implicit return (opportunity cost) on his capital investment amounts to $12,000 per year (10 percent × $120,000), or $1,000 per month.

To calculate the "economic profit" generated by this drugstore, we must count both explicit and implicit costs (i.e., total opportunity costs). Hence we must subtract all implicit factor payments (costs) from reported profits. The residual in this case amounts to $2,000 per month. That is the drugstore's *economic* profit.

Note that when we computed the drugstore's economic profits, we included a measure of the opportunity costs of the owner's capital. Specifically, we assumed that his funds would have reaped a 10 percent return somewhere else. In effect, we have assumed that a standard, or "normal," rate of return is 10 percent. This **normal profit** (average rate of return) is an economic cost. Rather than investing in a drugstore, the owner could have earned a 10 percent return on his funds by investing in a fast-food franchise, video games, a steel plant, or some other production activity. By choosing to invest in a drugstore instead, the owner was seeking a *higher* return on his funds—an *above-average* return. Had he not succeeded, he would have had no *economic* profits. In other words, ***economic profits represent an above-average return—something over and above "normal profits."***

Our treatment of "normal" returns as an economic cost leads to a startling conclusion: on average, economic profits are zero. Only firms that reap *above-average* returns can claim economic profits. If some firms are above the average, other firms must be below the average. In other words, the economic profits (above-average returns) of some firms are offset by the economic losses (below-average returns) of other firms. This seemingly strange perspective on profits emphasizes the opportunity costs of all economic activities. ***A productive activity is "profitable" only if it earns more than its opportunity cost.***

normal profit: The opportunity cost of capital; the average rate of return.

Entrepreneurship Naturally, everyone in business wants to earn an economic profit. But relatively few people can stay ahead of the pack. To earn economic profits, a business must see opportunities that others have missed, discover new products, find new and better methods of production, or take above-average risks. In fact, economic profits are often regarded as a reward to entrepreneurship, the ability and willingness to take risks, to organize factors of production, and to produce something society desires. From this perspective, profit represents a return to an intangible but vitally important "fourth factor of production."

Consider the local drugstore again. People in the neighborhood clearly desire such a drugstore, as evidenced by its substantial sales revenue. But why should anyone go to the trouble and risk of starting and maintaining one? In calculating the profits of the drugstore, we noted that the owner-manager *could* earn $3,000 in wages by accepting a regular job plus $1,000 per month in returns on capital by investing in an "average" business. Why should he take on the added responsibilities and risk of owning and operating his own drugstore?

The inducement to take on the added responsibilities of owning and operating a business is the potential for profit, the "extra" income over and above nominal factor payments. In the case of the drugstore owner, this "extra" income is the economic profit of $2,000 (Table 21.1). In the absence of such additional compensation, few people would want to make the extra effort required. From this perspective, the potential for profit is a major source of economic activity and growth.

Risk It is also important to observe that the *potential* for profit is not a *guarantee* of profit. Quite the contrary. Substantial risks are attached to starting and operating a business. Thousands of businesses fail every year (see Table 21.2), and still more suffer economic losses. From this perspective, profit also represents compensation for risks incurred.

TABLE 21.2 Business Failures

Entrepreneurship entails risks as well as potential rewards. Each year tens of thousands of firms fail. Their owners typically lose all or most of their capital investment and the opportunity cost of their labor. The chance to earn economic profit is the incentive for taking such risks.

Industry	Number of firms failing in 1989
Services	17,399
Retail trade	10,803
Construction	6,829
Manufacturing	3,840
Wholesale trade	3,534
Finance, insurance, and real estate	2,770
Transportation and public utilities	2,023
Farming and fishing	1,444
Mining	344
Other	733
Total	49,719

Source: Dun & Bradstreet Corp.

THE NATURE OF COMPETITION

As noted earlier, all businesses do not have an equal opportunity to earn an economic profit. The opportunity for profit may be limited by the *structure* of the industry in which the firm is engaged. An industry dominated by one large firm has different profit possibilities from an industry composed of thousands of small firms.

Price Takers

market power: The ability to alter the market price of a good or service.

The most distinctive characteristic of a competitive industry is that the many individual firms that make up the industry are all price takers. A competitive firm can sell all its output at the prevailing market price. If it tries to charge a higher price, it will not sell anything, because consumers will shop elsewhere. In this sense, a perfectly competitive firm has no **market power**—no ability to control the market price for the good it sells.

At first glance, it might appear that all firms have market power. After all, who is to stop a producer from raising prices? The important concept here, however, is *market* price, that is, the price at which goods are actually sold. You might want to resell this textbook for $50. But you will discover that the bookstore will not buy it at that price. Anyone can change the *asking* price of a good, but actual sales will occur only at the market price. With so many other students offering to sell their books, the bookstore knows it does not have to pay the $50 you are asking. Because you do not have any market power, you have to accept the "going price" for used texts if you want to sell this book.

The same kind of powerlessness is characteristic of the small wheat farmer. Like any producer, the lone wheat farmer can increase or reduce his rate of output by making alternative production decisions. But his decision will not affect the market price of wheat.

market supply: The total quantities of a good that sellers are willing and able to sell at alternative prices in a given time period, *ceteris paribus*.

Even a larger farmer who can alter his harvest by as much as 10,000 bushels of wheat per year will not influence the market price of wheat. Why not? Because nearly *2 billion* bushels of wheat are brought to market every year, and another 10,000 bushels simply isn't going to be noticed. in other words, *the output of the lone farmer is so small relative to the* **market supply** *that it has no significant effect on the total quantity or price in the market.*

competitive firm: A firm without market power, with no ability to alter the market price of the goods it produces.

A distinguishing characteristic of *powerless* firms is that, individually, they can sell as much output as they can produce at the prevailing market price. We call all such producers **competitive firms;** they have no independent influence on market prices. *A perfectly competitive firm is one whose output is so small in relation to market volume that its output decisions have no perceptible impact on price.* The complete and sudden demise of such a firm would not be noticed in the market. By contrast, the demise of a large and powerful firm would visibly reduce market supplies and disrupt the previous market equilibrium.

One can visualize the difference between competitive firms and firms with market power by considering what would happen to U.S. egg supplies and prices if Farmer Kitt's thirty-seven hens were to die. Then contrast this with the likely consequences for U.S. auto supplies and prices if the Ford Motor Company were to close down suddenly. The one event would go unnoticed by the public; the impact of the other would be dramatic.

The same kind of contrast is evident when an expansion of output is contemplated. Were Farmer Kitt to double his production capacity (buy another thirty-seven hens), the added output would not show up in commerce statistics. U.S. egg production is calibrated in the billions, and no one is going to notice another thirty-seven hens. Were Ford, on the other hand, to double its production, the added output would not only be noted but would tend to depress automobile prices as Ford tried to unload its heavy inventories.

The critical distinction between Ford and Farmer Kitt is not in their motivation but in their ability to alter market outcomes. Both are out to make a buck and thus seek to produce the rate of output that maximizes profit. What makes Farmer Kitt's situation different is the fact that his output decisions do not influence egg prices. In this sense, he has one less problem to worry about. *A perfectly competitive firm confronts a horizontal demand curve for its own output.* However much Farmer Kitt stimulates his hens to produce, he will have no influence on the price of eggs. All eggs look alike, so Farmer Kitt's eggs will fetch the same price as everyone else's eggs. To maximize his profits, Farmer Kitt can only strive to run an efficient operation, producing up to the point where his marginal cost of production equals the going market price for eggs. In this sense, he is a *price taker,* taking the market price of eggs as a fact of life and doing the best he can within that constraint. Were he to attempt to enlarge his profits by raising his egg prices above market levels, he would find himself without customers, because the consumers would go elsewhere to buy their eggs.

Ford Motor Company, on the other hand, can behave like a *price setter.* Instead of waiting to find out what the market price is and making appropriate output adjustments, Ford has the discretion to "announce" prices at the beginning of every model year. Fords are not exactly like Chevrolets or Chryslers in the minds of consumers. Because Fords are *differentiated,* Ford knows that sales will not fall to zero if its car prices are set a little higher than those of other car manufacturers. Ford confronts a downward-sloping rather than a perfectly horizontal demand curve.

Market Demand Curves vs. Firm Demand Curves

It is important to distinguish between the market demand curve and the demand curve confronting a particular firm. Farmer Kitt's small operation does not contradict the law of demand. The quantity of eggs purchased in the supermarket still depends on egg prices. That is to say, the *market* demand curve for eggs is still downward-sloping, just as the market demand for cars is downward-sloping. Farmer Kitt himself faces a horizontal demand curve only because his share of the market is so infinitesimal that changes in his output do not disturb the market equilibrium.

Collectively, though, individual farmers do count. If 10,000 small, competitive farmers were to expand their egg production at the same time as Farmer Kitt, the market equilibrium would be disturbed. That is to say, a competitive market composed of 10,000 individually powerless producers still sees a lot of action. The power here resides in the collective action of all the producers, however, and not in the individual action of any one. Were egg production to increase so abruptly, the eggs could be sold only at lower prices, in accordance with the downward-sloping nature of the *market* demand curve. The distinction between the actions of a single producer and those of the market are illustrated in Figure 21.1. Notice that

- *The market demand curve for a product is always downward sloping.*

- *The demand curve confronting a perfectly competitive firm is horizontal.*

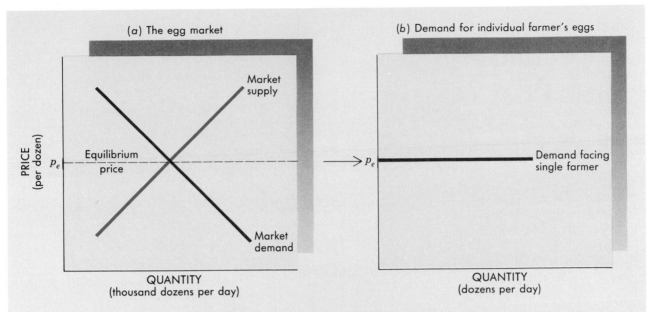

FIGURE 21.1 Market vs. Firm Demand

Consumer demand for any product is downward-sloping, as in the egg market. The equilibrium price (p_e) of eggs is established by the intersection of *market* demand and *market* supply. This market-established price is the only one at which an individual farmer can sell eggs. If the farmer asks a higher price, no one will buy his eggs, since they can buy identical eggs from other farmers at p_e. But he can sell all of his eggs at the equilibrium price. The lone farmer thus confronts a horizontal demand curve for his own output. (Notice the difference in market and individual farmer quantities.)

THE PRODUCTION DECISION

production decision: The selection of the short-run rate of output (with existing plant and equipment).

In view of the fact that a competitive firm can sell all of its output at the market price, it has only one decision to make—that is, how much to produce. Choosing a rate of output is a firm's **production decision.** Should it produce all the output it can? Or should it produce at less than its capacity output?

Output and Revenues

total revenue: The price of a product multiplied by the quantity sold in a given time period, $p \times q$.

The more output a competitive firm produces, the greater its revenues will be. **Total revenue** is simply the price of the good multiplied by the quantity sold:

- Total revenue = price × quantity

Since a competitive firm can sell all of its output at the market price (p_e), total revenue is a simple multiple of p_e. The total revenue of Farmer Kitt, for example, is the price of eggs (p_e) multiplied by the quantity sold. Graphically, the total revenue curve is a straight line, with a slope equal to p_e. This unique total revenue curve is illustrated in Figure 21.2.

If a competitive firm wants to maximize its total revenue, its strategy is clear. Since revenues are a simple multiple of output, more output always

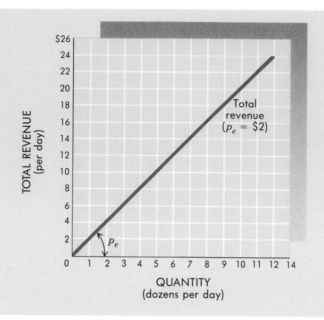

FIGURE 21.2
Total Revenue

Because a competitive firm can sell all of its output at the prevailing price, its revenue curve is linear. In this case, the market (equilibrium) price of eggs is assumed to be $2 per dozen. Hence the farmer's total revenue is equal to $2 multiplied by quantity sold.

leads to more revenue. Hence a competitive firm that seeks to maximize total revenue should always produce at capacity. In reality, however, the objective of all firms is to maximize profits, not revenues. Hence a firm must consider how additional output affects costs as well as revenues.

Output and Costs

fixed costs: Costs of production that do not change when the rate of output is altered, e.g., the cost of basic plant and equipment.

short run: The period in which the quantity (and quality) of some inputs cannot be changed.

variable costs: Costs of production that change when the rate of output is altered, e.g., labor and material costs.

marginal cost: The increase in total costs associated with a one-unit increase in production.

We have already examined the nature of production costs. As we observed in Chapter 20, producers are saddled with certain **fixed costs** in the **short run.** An egg farmer has to pay the mortgage on the farm and the leases on equipment. The Tight Jeans Corporation of Chapter 20 had to pay the fixed costs of its factory and leased sewing machine. These fixed costs are incurred even if no output is produced.

Once a firm starts producing output it incurs **variable costs** as well. Since profits depend on the *difference* between revenues and costs, the costs of added output will determine how much profit a producer can make. Figure 21.3 illustrates a fairly conventional total cost curve. Total costs increase as output expands. But the rate of cost increase varies. At first total costs rise slowly (notice the gradually declining slope until point z), then they start to increase more quickly (the rising slope after point z). This S-shaped curve reflects the *law of diminishing returns.* As we first observed in Chapter 20, **marginal costs** (MC) often decline in the early stages of production and then increase as the available plant and equipment are used more intensively. These changes in marginal cost cause *total* costs to rise slowly at first, then to accelerate as output increases.

It may be evident by now that the road to profits is not an easy one. ***Maximizing output is not the way to maximize profits.*** Notice in Figure 21.4 how total costs exceed total revenues at high rates of output (beyond point g). As production capacity is approached, costs tend to skyrocket, offsetting any gain in sales revenue.

Total profit in Figure 21.4 is represented by the vertical distance between the two curves. Notice that total costs in this case exceed total revenue at

FIGURE 21.3
Total Cost

Total cost increases with output. The rate of increase is not steady, however. Typically, the rate of cost increase slows initially, then speeds up. After point *z*, diminishing returns (rising marginal costs) cause accelerating costs. These accelerating costs limit the profit potential of increased output.

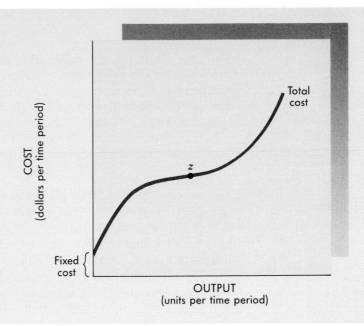

low rates of output as well. The firm incurs a loss at output levels below *f*. The firm is profitable only at output rates between *f* and *g*.

The primary objective of the producer is to find that rate of output that maximizes profits. In Figure 21.4 that profit-maximizing rate of output must occur between output *f* and *g*. With a ruler, one could find it by measuring the distance between the revenue and cost curves at all rates of output. In the real world, most producers operate without graphs and rulers, however, and so need more practical guides to profit maximization. Those are the guides we will now develop.

FIGURE 21.4
Total Profit

Profit is the *difference* between total revenue and total cost. It is represented as the vertical distance between the total revenue curve and the total cost curve. At output *h*, profit equals *r* minus *s*. The objective is to find that rate of output that *maximizes* profit.

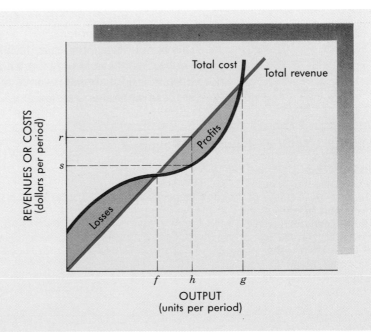

PROFIT-MAXIMIZING RULE

The best single rule for maximizing profits in the short run is this: never produce a unit of output that costs more than it brings in. By following this simple rule, a producer is likely to make the right production decision. We shall see how this rule works, first by looking at the revenue side of production ("what it brings in"), then at the cost side ("what it costs").

Marginal Revenue = Price

In making a production decision, we are searching for the most profitable rate of output from existing plant and equipment. This implies looking at all possible short-run rates of output. In each case, we want to know if *one more* unit of output would increase our profits. In making this decision, we need to know what that additional unit of output will bring in—that is, how much it adds to the total revenue of the firm.

marginal revenue: The change in total revenue that results from a one-unit increase in the quantity sold.

The contribution to total revenue of an additional unit of output is called **marginal revenue (MR)**. Marginal revenue is the *change* in total revenue that occurs when the rate of output is increased by one unit; that is,

$$\bullet \quad \text{Marginal revenue} = \frac{\text{change in total revenue}}{\text{change in output}}$$

To calculate marginal revenue, we compare the total revenues received before and after a one-unit increase in the rate of production; the *difference* between the two totals equals marginal revenue.

When the price of a product is constant, it is even simpler to compute marginal revenue. Suppose we are actually selling eggs at a constant price of $2 a dozen. In this case, a one-unit increase in sales (one more dozen) increases total revenue by $2. This is illustrated in Table 21.3. Notice that as long as the price of a product is constant, price and marginal revenue are one and the same thing. Hence **for perfectly competitive firms, price equals marginal revenue.**

This is not always the case. In imperfectly competitive situations, additional output can be sold only if price is reduced. In these situations, price is not constant, and marginal revenue and price are no longer equal. We shall look at these situations a bit later.

TABLE 21.3 Total and Marginal Revenue

Marginal revenue (MR) is the *change* in total revenue associated with the sale of one more unit of output. A third dozen eggs increases total revenue from $4 to $6; MR equals $2. If the price is constant (at $2 here), marginal revenue equals price.	Quantity sold (dozens per day)	×	Price (per unit)	=	Total revenue (per day)	Marginal revenue (per dozen)
	0	×	$2	=	$ 0	
	1	×	2	=	2	$2
	2	×	2	=	4	$2
	3	×	2	=	6	$2
	4	×	2	=	8	$2
	5	×	2	=	10	$2

Marginal Cost   Knowing what marginal revenue is leaves us just one step away from applying the simple rule for profit maximization: never produce anything that costs more than it brings in. We already know what one more unit brings in (its price); all we need to do now is look at its cost.

To acquire a closer perspective on costs, we will leave the egg farm and take up jewelry manufacture. In jewelry manufacture or any other production process, the added cost of producing one more unit of a good is its *marginal cost*. Figure 21.5 summarizes the marginal costs associated with the production of silver bracelets.

The production of silver bracelets requires a certain set of tools and equipment that can be leased for $10 a day on a long-term basis. Once leased, these tools and equipment become part of fixed costs; they must be paid for no matter how many bracelets are produced. In addition, labor and material (primarily silver) must be purchased to produce the bracelets. Obviously, the quantity of labor and silver varies with the number of bracelets produced. These are *variable costs. Marginal costs* in this case are the cost of the added labor and silver needed to produce *each* additional bracelet.

According to Figure 21.5 marginal costs tend to increase when bracelet production is increased. Like most production processes, bracelet manufac-

FIGURE 21.5
The Costs of
Bracelet Production

Marginal cost is the increase
in total cost associated
with a one–unit increase in
production. When production
expands from 2 to 3 units per
day, total costs increase by
$9 (from $22 to $31 per day).
The marginal cost of the
third bracelet is therefore
$9, as illustrated by point *D*
in the graph.

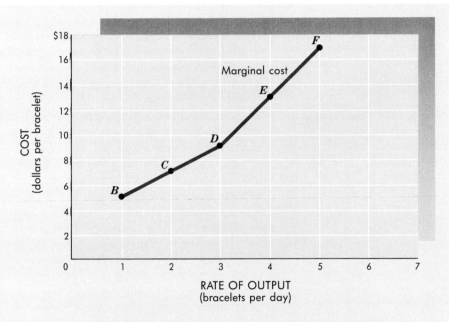

	Rate of output (bracelets per day)	Total cost (per day)	Marginal cost (per unit)	Average cost (per unit)
A	0	$10	—	—
B	1	15	$ 5	$15.00
C	2	22	7	11.00
D	3	31	9	10.33
E	4	44	13	11.00
F	5	61	17	12.20

ture takes place in an existing plant that is equipped with a certain amount of tools and machinery. To increase output in the short run, more labor is hired to use that (fixed) plant and equipment. As we crowd more workers into the plant, however, each worker has fewer tools and machines to work with. In other words, the existing (fixed) plant and equipment must be shared by an ever larger (variable) number of workers. Eventually, this situation reflects the law of diminishing returns. As marginal product diminishes, marginal cost increases. The upward-sloping MC curve of Figure 21.5 illustrates this phenomenon.

Profit-Maximizing Rate of Output

We are now in a position to make a production decision. The rule about never producing anything that costs more than it brings in can now be stated in more technical terms. What an additional unit of output brings in is its marginal revenue (MR); what it costs is its marginal cost (MC). Since price equals marginal revenue for competitive firms, we can base the production decision on a comparison of *price* and marginal cost. We do not want to produce an additional unit of output if its MC exceeds its price. If MC exceeds price, we are spending more to produce that extra unit than we are getting back: total profits will decline if we produce it.

The opposite is true when price exceeds MC. If an extra unit brings in more revenue than it costs to produce, it is adding to total profit. Total profits must increase in this case. Hence a competitive firm wants to expand the rate of production whenever price exceed MC.

Since we want to expand output when price exceeds MC and contract output if price is less than MC, the profit-maximizing rate of output is easily found. *Short-run profits are maximized at that rate of output where* MR = MC. For competitive firms this implies that **profits are maximized at the rate of output where price equals marginal cost**. The **profit-maximization rule** is summarized in Table 21.4.

profit-maximization rule: Produce at that rate of output where marginal revenue equals marginal cost.

Figure 21.6 illustrates the application of our profit-maximization rule in the production of silver bracelets. We shall assume that the prevailing price of silver bracelets is $13 apiece. At this price we can sell all the silver bracelets we can produce, up to our short-run capacity. The bracelets cannot be sold at a higher price, because lots of producers make bracelets and sell them for $13. If we try to charge a higher price, consumers will buy their bracelets from other producers. Hence the demand curve facing this one firm is horizontal at the price of $13.

The costs of producing silver bracelets were already examined in Figure 21.5. The key concept illustrated here is marginal cost. The MC curve slopes upward, in conventional fashion.

TABLE 21.4 Short-Run Profit-Maximization Rules for Competitive Firm

The relationship between marginal revenue and marginal cost dictates short-run production decisions. For competitive firms, profits are maximized at that rate of output where price = MC. (See Table 22.2 for long-run rules.)	If	Then
	price $> MC$	increase output rate
	price $= MC$	maintain output rate (profits maximized)
	price $< MC$	decrease output rate

FIGURE 21.6
Maximization of
Profits for Competitive Firm

A competitive firm maximizes
total profit at the output
rate where MC = *p*. If MC
is less than price, the firm can
increase profits by producing
more. If MC exceeds price, the
firm should reduce output. In
this case, profit maximization
occurs at an output of 4
bracelets per day.

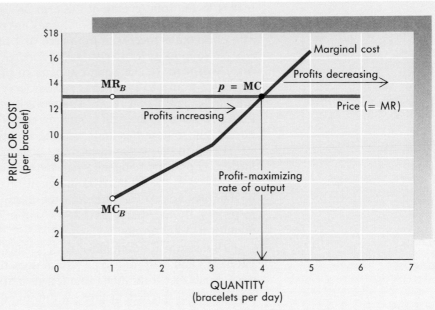

	(1) Number of bracelets (per day)	(2) Price	(3) Total revenue	(4) Total cost	(5) Total profit	(6) Marginal revenue	(7) Marginal cost
A	0	—	0	$10.00	− 10.00	—	—
B	1	$13.00	$13.00	15.00	− 2.00	$13.00	$ 5.00
C	2	13.00	26.00	22.00	+ 4.00	13.00	7.00
D	3	13.00	39.00	31.00	+ 8.00	13.00	9.00
E	4	13.00	52.00	44.00	+ 8.00	13.00	13.00
F	5	13.00	65.00	61.00	+ 4.00	13.00	17.00

Also depicted in Figure 21.6 are the total revenues, costs, and profits of
alternative production rates. Study the table first. Notice that the firm loses
$10 per day if it produces no bracelets (row *A*). At zero output, total revenue
is zero ($p \times q = 0$). However, the firm must still contend with fixed costs of
$10 per day. Total profit—total revenue minus total cost—is therefore *minus*
$10; the firm incurs a loss.

Row *B* of the table shows how this loss is reduced when 1 bracelet is
produced per day. The production and sale of 1 bracelet per day brings in
$13 of total revenue (column 3). The total cost of producing 1 bracelet per
days is $15 (column 4). Hence the total loss associated with an output rate
of 1 bracelet per day is $2 (column 5). This may not be what we hoped for,
but it is certainly better than the $10 loss incurred at zero output.

The superiority of producing 1 bracelet per day rather than none is also
evident in columns 6 and 7 of row *B*. The first bracelet produced has a
marginal revenue of $13. Its *marginal cost* is only $5. Hence it brings in more
added revenue than it costs to produce. Under these circumstances—whenever price exceeds MC—output should definitely be expanded.

The excess of price over MC for the first unit of output is also illustrated
by the graph in Figure 21.6. Point MR_B ($13) lies above MC_B ($5); the *difference*
between these two points measures the contribution that the first bracelet

makes to the total profits of the firm. In this case, that contribution equals $13 − $5 = $8, and production losses are reduced by that amount when the rate of output is increased from zero to 1 bracelet per day.

So long as price exceeds MC, further increases in the rate of output are desirable. Notice what happens to profits when the rate of output is increased from 1 to 2 bracelets per day (row *C*). The price (MR) of the second bracelet is $13; its MC is $7. Therefore it *adds* $6 to total profits. Instead of losing $2 per day, the firm is now making a profit of $4 per day. The second unit of daily output has improved the situation considerably.

The firm can make even more profits by expanding the rate of output further. Look what happens when the rate of output reaches 3 bracelets per day (row *D* of the table). The marginal revenue of the third bracelet is $13; its marginal cost is $9. Therefore the third bracelet makes a $4 contribution to profits. By increasing its rate of output to 3 bracelets per day, the firm doubles its total profits.

This firm will never make huge profits. The fourth unit of output has a MR of $13 and a MC of $13 as well. It does not contribute to total profits, nor does it subtract from them. The fourth unit of output represents the highest rate of output the firm desires. At the rate of output when price = MC, total profits of the firm are maximized.[1]

Notice what happens if we expand output beyond 4 bracelets per day. The price of the fifth bracelet is still $13; its MC is $17. The fifth bracelet costs more than it brings in. If we produce that fifth bracelet, total profit will decline by $4. The fifth unit of output makes us worse off. This eventuality is evident in the graph of Figure 21.6; at the output rate of 5 bracelets per day, the MC curve lies above the MR curve. The lesson here is clear: ***output should not be increased if MC exceeds price.***

The outcome of the production decision is illustrated in Figure 21.6 by the intersection of the price and MC curves. At this intersection, price equals MC and profits are maximized. If we produced less, we would be giving up potential profits. If we produced more, total profits would also fall.

Adding Up Profits   To reach the right production decision, we have relied on *marginal* revenues and costs. Having found the desired rate of output, however, we may want to take a closer look at the profits we are accumulating. We could, of course, content ourselves with the statistics in the table of Figure 21.6. But a picture would be nice, too, especially if it reflected our success in production. To draw that picture, we can use either *total* revenue and cost curves or *average* revenue and cost curves. Figure 21.7 illustrates both approaches.

Figure 21.7*a* depicts *total* revenues and costs at various rates of output. Recall that all silver bracelets are sold at the prevailing price of $13 each. Hence total revenue equals $q \times \$13$. The resulting total revenue (TR) curve is a straight line. The total cost (TC) curve in Figure 21.7*a* starts above the total revenue line (fixed costs at zero output), dips below it, then rapidly overtakes it again. This is a reflection of the fact that marginal costs are initially low but rise quite rapidly as output expands.

---

[1]In this case, profits are the same at output levels of three and four. Given the choice between the two levels, most firms will choose the higher level. By producing the extra unit of output, the firm increases its customer base. This not only denies rival firms an additional sale but also provides some additional "cushion" when the economy slumps. Also, corporate size may connote both prestige and power (more on this later). In any case, the higher output level defines the limit to maximum-profit production.

FIGURE 21.7
Illustrating Total Profit with...

Total profits can be computed as TR – TC, as in part *a*. Or they can be computed as profit *per unit* (*p* – ATC) multiplied by the quantity sold. This is illustrated in part *b* by the shaded rectangle. To find the profit–maximizing rate of output, we could use either of these graphs or the MR and MC curves of Figure 21.6.

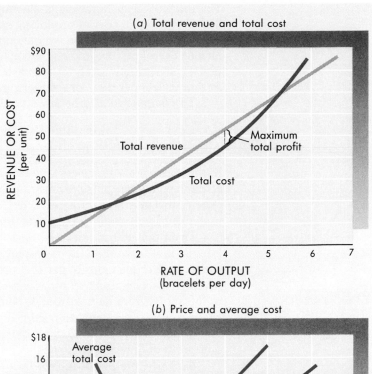

(a) Total revenue and total cost

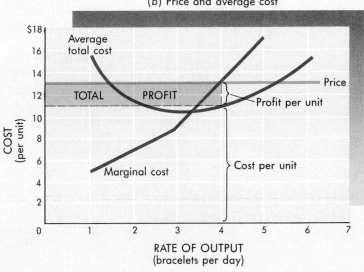

(b) Price and average cost

Total profits are represented in Figure 21.7*a* by the vertical distance between the total revenue and total cost curves. This is a straightforward interpretation of our definition of total profits—that is,

- Total profits = TR – TC

The vertical distance between the TR and TC curves is maximized at the output of 4 bracelets per day.

Our success in producing silver bracelets can also be illustrated by *average* revenue and costs. Total profit is equal to *average* profit per unit multiplied by the number of units produced. Profit *per unit*, in turn, is equal to price *minus* average total cost—that is,

- Profit per unit = *p* – ATC

The price of silver bracelets is illustrated in Figure 21.7b by the price line at $13. The average cost of producing silver bracelets is illustrated by the ATC curve. Like the ATC curve we encountered in Chapter 20, this one has a U shape. Therefore, the *difference* between price and average cost—profit per unit—is illustrated by the vertical distance between the price and ATC curves. At 4 bracelets per day, for example, profit per unit equals $13 − $11 = $2.

To compute *total* profits, we note that

- Total profits = profit per unit × quantity

$$= (p - \text{ATC}) \times q$$

In this case, the 4 bracelets generate a profit of $2 each, for a *total* profit of $8 per day. *Total* profits are illustrated in Figure 21.7b by the shaded rectangle. (Recall that the area of a rectangle is equal to its height [profit per unit] multiplied by its width [quantity sold].)

Profit per unit is not only used to compute total profits but is often of interest in its own right. Businesspeople like to cite statistics on "mark-ups," which are a crude index to per-unit profits. However, *the profit-maximizing producer never seeks to maximize per-unit profits.* What counts is *total* profits, not the amount of profit per unit. This is the old $4 ice cream problem again. You might be able to maximize profit per unit if you could sell 1 cone for $4, but you would make a lot more money if you sold 100 cones at a per-unit profit of only 50 cents each.

Similarly, *the profit-maximizing producer has no desire to produce at that rate of output where ATC is at a minimum.* Minimum ATC does represent least-cost production. But additional units of output, even though they raise average costs, will increase total profits. This is evident in Figure 21.7; price exceeds MC for some output to the right of minimum ATC (the bottom of the U). Therefore, total profits are increasing as we increase the rate of output beyond the point of minimum average costs.

THE SHUTDOWN DECISION

The rule established for short-run profit maximization provides no guarantee of profits. By equating price and marginal cost, the competitive producer is only assured of achieving the *optimal* rate of output. This is the best possible rate of output for the firm, given the existing market price and the (short-run) costs of production.

But what if the best possible rate of output generates a loss? It is quite possible that the total costs of producing the optimal output will exceed total revenues. What should a producer do in this case? Keep producing output? Or shut down the factory and find something else to do?

The first instinct may be to shut down the factory to stop the flow of red ink. But this is not necessarily the wisest course of action. It may, in fact, be smarter to keep operating a money-losing operation than to shut it down.

The rationale for this seemingly ill-advised course of action resides in the fixed costs of production. *Fixed costs must be paid even if all output ceases.* The firm is still obligated to pay rent on the factory and equipment even if it does not use these inputs. This is why we call such costs "fixed."

The persistence of fixed costs casts an entirely different light on the shutdown decision. Since fixed costs will have to be paid in any case, the question becomes: Which option creates greater losses? Does the firm lose more money by continuing to operate (and incurring a loss) or by shutting down (and incurring a loss equal to fixed costs)? In these terms, the answer becomes clear: *a firm should shut down only if total revenues are less than total variable costs.* If this is the case, the losses from continuing production would exceed fixed costs.

Price vs. AVC   The shutdown decision can be made without a detailed accounting of fixed costs. Figure 21.8 shows how. The relationship to focus on is between the price of a good and its average *variable* cost.

The curves in Figure 21.8 represent the short-run costs and potential demand curves associated with production of bracelets. As long as the price of bracelets is $13, the typical firm will produce 4 a day, as determined by the intersection of the MC and MR (= price) curves (point X). In this case, price ($13) exceeds average total cost ($11) and bracelet production is profitable.

The situation would not look so good, however, if the market price of bracelets fell to $9. Following the short-run rule for profit maximization, the firm would be led to point Y, where MC intersects the new demand (MR) curve. At this intersection, the firm would produce 3 bracelets per day. But total revenues would no longer cover total costs, as can be seen from the fact that the ATC curve now lies above the demand curve. The ATC of producing 3 bracelets is $10.33 (Figure 21.5); price is $9. Hence the firm is incurring a loss of $4 per day (3 bracelets at a loss of $1.33 each).

Should the firm stay in business under the circumstances? The answer is yes. Recall that the producer has already leased the plant and equipment required for bracelet production, at a (fixed) cost of $10 per day. The producer will have to pay these fixed costs whether the machinery is used or not. Stopping production would result in a loss amounting to $10 per day. Staying in business, even when bracelet prices fall to $9 each, generates a loss of

FIGURE 21.8
The Firm's Shutdown Point

A firm should cease production only if total revenue is less than total variable cost. The shutdown decision may be based on a comparison of price and *AVC*. If the price of bracelets was $13, a firm would want to produce at point X. At that rate of output, price exceeds average variable cost and production should continue. The same is true when price equals $9 (point Y). At point Y, the firm is losing money (p is less than *ATC*) but more than covering all variable costs (p is greater than *AVC*). If the price falls to $4 per bracelet, output should cease (p is less than *AVC*).

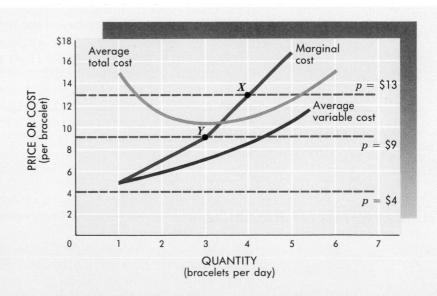

W✷RLD VIEW

SHUTDOWN DECISION

Volkswagen to Close Only U.S. Plant

Shutdown Will Eliminate 2,500 Jobs at Pa. Facility

Volkswagenwerk AG,the first foreign auto maker in modern history to build passenger cars in the United States, yesterday announced plans to close its only vehicle assembly plant in this country in mid-1988.

The shutdown of Volkswagen's sprawling facility in New Stanton, Pa., will eliminate 2,500 jobs—2,100 assembly and 400 administrative positions. The closing also is expected to cause layoffs at Volkswagen's U.S. headquarters offices in Troy, Mich.

The New Stanton plant produced Volkswagen Golf subcompacts and Jetta compact cars, both of which have been under withering competition from comparable, and often less expensive, models sold by Japanese, American,

and South Korean auto makers.

The plant, operated by Volkswagen since 1978, has been running at less than half of its 200,000-unit annual production capacity in the last five years.

At present volumes, the New Stanton plant simply is not cost effective. Jay Amestoy, a Volkswagen spokesman, said. And because of the proliferation of cars in the U.S. small-car market—at least 34 models competing against the Golf, for example—sales of Volkswagen's New Stanton cars are not likely to increase in the future, he added.

"It's not that Volkswagen is giving up its U.S. franchise. It's just that they can't possibly continue to operate that plant on the amount of volume they're building there," said Donald DeScenza, auto industry analyst with Nomura Securities Inc. in New York.

—Warren Brown

The Washington Post, November 21, 1987, p. C1. Copyright © 1987 The Washington Post.

only $4 a day. In this case, ***where price exceeds average variable costs but not average total costs, the profit-maximization rule minimizes losses.***

The Shutdown Point

If the price of bracelets falls far enough, however, the producer may be better off to cease production altogether. Suppose the price of bracelets fell to $4 each (Figure 21.8). A price this low does not even cover the marginal cost of producing 1 bracelet per day ($5). Continued production of even 1 bracelet per day would imply a total loss of $11 per day ($10 of fixed costs plus $1 of variable costs). Higher rates of output would lead to still greater losses. Hence the firm would be well advised to shut down production, even though that action implies a loss of $10 per day. In all cases ***where price does not cover average variable costs at any rate of output, production should cease.*** Thus the **shutdown point** occurs where price is equal to minimum average variable cost. Any lower price will result in losses that are larger than fixed costs.

shutdown point: That rate of output where price equals minimum AVC.

THE INVESTMENT DECISION

The shutdown decision is a short-run response. It is based on the fixed costs of an established plant and the variable costs of operating it. Obviously, the producer who built or leased the plant never expected to end up in such a bad situation. The only reason this producer got into the business was to make a profit—not to face the miserable choice of taking either a big loss or a small loss, depending on how operating losses compare to fixed costs.

investment decision: The decision to build, buy, or lease plant and equipment; to enter or exit an industry.

long run: A period of time long enough for all inputs to be varied (no fixed costs).

Ideally, this producer would never have gotten into business in the first place. Entry was based on an **investment decision** that the producer now regrets. *Investment decisions are inherently* **long-run** *decisions,* however, and the firm now must pay for its bad luck or judgment. The investment decision entails the assumption of fixed costs (e.g., the lease of the factory); once the investment is made, the short-run production decision is designed to make the best possible use of those fixed inputs. The short-run profit-maximizing rule we have discussed applies only to this second decision; it assumes that a production unit exists.

To producers, of course, the investment decision is of enormous importance. The fixed costs that we have ignored in the production decision represent the producers' (or the stockholders') investment in the business. If they are going to avoid an economic loss, they have to generate at least enough revenue to recoup their investment, i.e., the cost of (fixed) plant and equipment. Failure to do so will result in a net loss, despite allegiance to our profit-maximizing rule.

Whether or not fixed costs count, then, depends on the decision being made. For producers trying to decide how best to utilize the resources they have purchased or leased, fixed costs no longer enter the decision-making process. For producers deciding whether to enter business, sign a lease, or replace existing machinery and plant, fixed costs count very much. Businesspeople will proceed with an investment only if the anticipated profits are adequate to compensate for the effort and risk undertaken.

Long-Run Costs

In contemplating an investment decision, businesspeople confront not one set of cost figures, but many. A plant not yet built can be designed for various rates of production. Producers expecting to sell large quantities of a good may want to build a large plant. In making long-run decisions, a given producer is not bound to one size of plant or to a particular mix of tools and machinery. In the long run, one can be flexible. In general, *a producer will want to build, buy, or lease a plant that is most efficient for the anticipated rate of output.*[2] Once such a plant is selected, the producer may proceed with the problem of short-run profit maximization. Once production is started, he can only hope that his choice was a good one and that a shutdown can be avoided.

DETERMINANTS OF SUPPLY

Whether the time frame is the short run or the long run, the one central force in production decisions is the quest for profits. Producers will go into production—incur fixed costs—only if they see the potential for economic profits (above-average returns). Once in business, they will expand the rate of output so long as profits are increasing. They will get out of business—cease production—when economic losses exceed the fixed costs of production.

Nearly anyone could make money with these principles if he or she had complete information on costs and revenues. What renders the road to fortune less congested is the general absence of such complete information. In the real world, production decisions involve considerably more risk. People often don't know how much profit or loss they will incur until it's too late to

---

[2]The choice of long-run plant size (and related cost curves) was illustrated in Chapter 20.

alter production decisions. Consequently, businesspeople are compelled to make a reasoned guess about prices and costs, then proceed. By way of summary, we can identify the major influences that will shape their short- and long-run decisions on how much output to supply to the market.

Short-Run Determinants

The short-run production decisions of a competitive firm are dominated by marginal costs. Hence the quantity of a good supplied will be affected by all forces that alter MC. Specifically, the determinants of supply include:

- *The price of factor inputs*

- *Technology* (the available production function)

- *Expectations* (for costs, sales, technology)

- *Taxes*

Each of these determinants affects the ability and willingness of a producer to supply output at any particular price.

The price of factor inputs determines how much the producer must pay for resources used in production. Technology determines how much output the producer will get from each unit of input. Expectations are critical because they express producers' perceptions of what future costs, prices, sales, and profits are likely to be. And finally, taxes may alter costs or the amount of profit a firm gets to keep.

The short-run supply curve By using the familiar *ceteris paribus* assumption, we can predict quite accurately how the quantity supplied in the short run will respond to a change in price. In other words, we can draw a short-run **supply curve** in the same way that we earlier constructed consumer demand curves. In this case, the forces we assume to be constant are input prices, technology, expectations, and taxes. The only thing we allow to change is the price of the product itself. Under these circumstances, how will the quantity supplied change when the price of the product rises or falls?

Figure 21.9 illustrates the response of quantity supplied to a change in price. Notice the critical role of marginal costs: ***the marginal cost curve is the short-run supply curve for a competitive firm.*** Recall our basic profit-maximization rule. A competitive producer wants to supply a good only if its price exceeds its marginal cost. Hence marginal cost defines the lower limit for an "acceptable" price. A producer of bracelets is willing and able to produce 4 bracelets per day only if the price of bracelets is $13 (point *X*). If the price of bracelets dropped to $9, the *quantity* supplied would fall to 3 (point *Y*). The marginal cost curve tells us what the quantity supplied would be at all other prices as well. So long as price exceeds minimum AVC (the shutdown point), the MC curve summarizes the response of a producer to price changes: it *is* the short-run supply curve.[3]

The shape of the marginal cost curve provides a basic foundation for the **law of supply.** Because marginal costs tend to rise as output expands, an increase in output makes sense only if the price of that output rises. If the price does rise, it is profitable to increase the quantity supplied.

supply curve: A curve describing the quantities of a good a producer is willing and able to sell (produce) at alternative prices in a given time period, *ceteris paribus.*

law of supply: The quantity of a good supplied in a given time period increases as its price increases, *ceteris paribus.*

---

[3]In imperfectly competitive situations—where the demand curve facing the firm is downward-sloping rather than horizontal—the marginal cost curve does not represent the short-run supply curve. Such firms are discussed in Chapters 23–25.

FIGURE 21.9
The Short-Run Supply Curve

A profit–maximizing producer will not supply additional quantities of output unless marginal revenue at least equals marginal cost. For competitive firms, price and marginal revenue are identical. Hence marginal cost defines the lowest price a firm will accept for a given quantity of output. In this sense, the marginal cost curve is the supply curve: it tells us how quantity supplied will respond to price. At $p = \$13$, the quantity supplied is 4; at $p = \$9$, the quantity supplied is 3.

Recall, however, that the firm will shut down if price falls below minimum average variable cost. The supply curve does not exist below minimum average cost ($5 in this case).

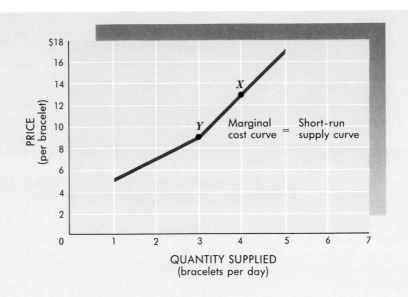

Supply Shifts All of the forces that shape the short-run supply curve are subject to change. Factor prices change; technology changes; expectations change; and tax laws get revised. *If any determinant of supply changes, the supply curve shifts.*

A reduction in silver prices, for example, would reduce the marginal cost of producing bracelets. This would make it possible for producers to supply larger quantities at any given price.

An improvement in technology would have the same effect. By increasing productivity, new technology would lower the marginal cost of producing a good. The supply curve would shift.

POLICY INSIGHTS:

TAXING BUSINESS

In 1989 the Exxon Corporation threatened to move out of New York City. The taxes in New York were so high, the company argued, that it could not make enough profit there. Exxon began shutting down its New York operations and moving to New Jersey.

Businesses, like most individuals, are always complaining about high taxes. But actions like those of Exxon raise fundamental questions about the impact of taxes on the supply of goods and services. Do taxes alter the production decisions of competitive firms? Can tax increases actually induce a firm to shut down its operations? Are investment decisions affected by taxes? If the answer to any of these questions is yes, then tax policy will alter the flow of goods and services supplied to the market.

There are three distinct kinds of taxes to consider: property taxes, payroll taxes, and profits taxes. The issue in each case is whether and how taxes alter the behavior of a competitive firm.

Property Taxes

Property taxes are levied by local governments on land and buildings. The tax is based on the value of the property. The tax rate is typically some small fraction (e.g., 1 percent) of total value. Hence the owner of a $10 million factory might have to pay $100,000 per year in property taxes.

Property taxes have to be paid regardless of whether the factory is used. Hence *property taxes are a fixed cost* for the firm. These additional fixed costs increase total costs and so shift the average total cost (ATC) upward, as in Figure 21.10a.

Notice that the MC curve does not move when property taxes are imposed. Property taxes are not based on the quantity of output produced. Accordingly, the production decision of the firm is not affected by property taxes. The quantity q_1 in Figure 21.10a remains the optimal rate of output even after a property tax is introduced.

Although the optimal output remains at q_1, the profitability of the firm is reduced by the property tax. Profit per unit has been reduced by the upward

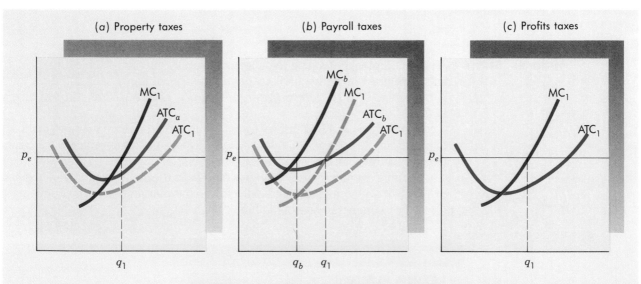

FIGURE 21.10 Impact of Taxes on Business Decisions

(*a*) Property taxes are a fixed cost for the firm. Since they do not affect marginal costs, they leave the optimal rate of output (q_1) unchanged. Property taxes raise average costs, however, and so reduce profits. Lower profits may alter investment decisions.

(*b*) Payroll taxes add directly to marginal costs and so reduce the optimal rate of output (to q_b). Payroll taxes also increase average costs and lower total and per–unit profits.

(*c*) Taxes on profits are neither a fixed cost nor a variable cost since they depend on the existence of profits. They do not affect marginal costs or price so leave the optimal rate of output (q_1) unchanged. By reducing after–tax profits, however, such taxes lessen incentives to invest.

shift of the ATC curve. If property taxes reduce profits too much, the firm's investment decision may be affected. Like Exxon, the firm may move its facilities to another city where property taxes are lower.

Payroll Taxes   Payroll taxes have very different effects on business decisions. Payroll taxes are levied on the wages paid by the firm. Employers must pay, for example, a 7.65 percent Social Security tax on the wages they pay (employees pay an identical amount). This tax is used to help finance federal retirement benefits. Other payroll taxes are levied by federal and state governments to finance unemployment and disability benefits.

All payroll taxes add to the cost of hiring labor. In the absence of a tax a worker might cost the firm $8 per hour. Once Social Security and other taxes are levied, the cost of labor increases to $8 plus the tax rate. Hence $8-per-hour labor might end up costing the firm $9 or more. In other words, *payroll taxes increase marginal costs.* This is illustrated in Figure 21.10*b* by the upward shift of the MC curve.

Notice how payroll taxes change the production decision. The new MC curve (MC_b) intersects the price line at a lower rate of output (q_b). Thus payroll taxes tend to reduce output and employment.[4]

Payroll taxes also shift the ATC curve upward and so reduce profits. In fact, *any time the MC curve shifts ATC must shift as well,* since marginal costs are part of total costs. (The opposite is *not* true, however. Can you explain?)

Profit Taxes   Taxes are also levied on the profits of a business. Uncle Sam and most state governments impose some form of income (profits) tax on businesses. Such taxes are very different from either property or payroll taxes since profit taxes are paid only when profits are made. Thus they are neither a fixed cost nor a variable cost! As Figure 21.10*c* indicates, neither the MC nor the ATC curve moves when a profits tax is imposed. The only difference is that the firm now gets to keep less of its profits, instead "sharing" its profits with the government. Uncle Sam takes 34 percent of total corporate profits, and most state and local governments also grab a small share.

Although a profits tax has no direct effect on marginal or average costs, it does reduce the "take-home" (after-tax) profits of a business. This reduction in after-tax profits diminishes the rewards of running a business and so may alter investment decisions. These concerns were at the forefront of the "supply-side" tax reforms of 1981 and 1986 (see Chapter 32).

SUMMARY

• Economic profit is the difference between total revenue and total cost. Total economic cost includes the value of *all* inputs used in the production, not just those for which an explicit payment is made.

• A competitive firm has no control over the price of its output. It effectively confronts a horizontal demand for its output.

[4]These and other taxes also alter market prices, thus causing additional changes in equilibrium outcomes. The effects illustrated here are most noticeable when neighboring jurisdictions impose differing tax rates.

• The short-run objective of a firm is to maximize profits from the use of its existing facilities (fixed costs). For a competitive firm, the profit-maximizing output occurs where marginal cost equals price (marginal revenue).

• A firm may incur a loss even at the optimal rate of output. It should not shut down, however, so long as price exceeds average variable cost. If fixed costs exceed operating losses, the firm incurs a smaller loss by continuing to produce.

• In the long run there are no fixed costs and the firm may choose any sized plant it wants. The decision to incur fixed costs (i.e., build or lease a plant) is an investment decision.

• A competitive firm's supply curve is identical to its marginal cost curve. In the short run, the quantity supplied will rise or fall with price.

• The determinants of supply include the price of inputs, technology, and expectations. If any of these determinants change, the firm's supply curve will shift.

• Business taxes alter business behavior. Property taxes raise fixed costs; payroll taxes increase marginal costs. Profit taxes raise neither but diminish the take-home (after-tax) profits of a business.

Terms to Remember Define the following terms:

profit	**short run**
economic cost	**variable cost**
economic profit	**marginal cost**
normal profit	**marginal revenue**
market power	**profit-maximization rule**
market supply	**shutdown point**
competitive firm	**investment decision**
production decision	**long run**
total revenue	**supply curve**
fixed cost	**law of supply**

Questions for Discussion

1. What economic costs is a large corporation likely to overlook when computing its "profits"? How about the owner of a family-run business or farm?

2. How many fish should a commercial fisherman try to catch in a day? Should he catch as many as possible or return to dock before filling the boat with fish? Under what economic circumstances should he not even take the boat out?

3. If a firm is incurring an economic loss, would society be better off if the firm shut down? Would the firm want to shut down? Explain.

4. Why wouldn't a profit-maximizing firm want to produce at the rate of output that minimizes average total cost? Illustrate your answer with graphs.

5. What rate of output is appropriate for a "nonprofit" corporation (e.g., a university or hospital)?

Problems
1. Use the data in Figure 21.6 to find
   (*a*) The rate of output that minimizes ATC
   (*b*) The rate of output that maximizes profit per unit
   (*c*) The rate of output that maximizes total profit

   What are total profits at each of these rates of output?

2. A firm has leased plant and equipment to produce video-game cartridges, which can be sold in unlimited quantities at $21 each. The following figures describe the associated costs of production:

Rate of output (per day)	0	1	2	3	4	5	6	7	8
Total cost (per day)	$50	$55	$62	$75	$96	$125	$162	$203	$248

   Using these figures:
   (*a*) Draw total revenue and total cost curves on the same graph. How much are fixed costs?
   (*b*) On a separate graph, draw the average total cost (ATC), marginal cost (MC), and price curves.
   (*c*) What is the profit-maximizing rate of output?
   (*d*) Should the producer stay in business? Why or why not?

3. Suppose a local government were to tax the video game business described in problem 2. How would the production and investment decisions be affected by:
   (*a*) A property tax of $10 per day?
   (*b*) A payroll tax that added $8 of cost to every unit of output?
   (*c*) A 50 percent profits tax?

4. How would the video game business described in problem 2 be affected by:
   (*a*) A public subsidy of $10 per day?
   (*b*) A tax credit that paid the business $8 for every unit of output produced?

CHAPTER 22

Competitive Markets

Catfish farmers in Mississippi are upset. During the last few years they have invested millions of dollars in converting cotton farms into breeding ponds for catfish. They now have 90,000 acres of ponds and supply over 80 percent of the nation's catfish. Unfortunately, catfish prices are dropping. In 1989 alone, catfish prices fell 15 percent. Price declines have killed any hopes of making huge profits. Indeed, catfish prices are so low that many farmers are getting out of the business.

The dilemma the catfish farmers find themselves in is a familiar occurrence in competitive markets. When the profit prospects look good, everybody wants to get in on the act. As more and more firms start producing the good, however, prices and profits tumble. This helps explain why over 200,000 new firms are formed each year as well as why 50,000 others fail.

This chapter focuses on the behavior of competitive markets. We have three principal questions:

- How are prices determined in competitive markets?
- How does competition affect the profits of a firm or industry?
- What does society gain from market competition?

As we discover in this and the following chapters, market outcomes are significantly influenced by the number, size, and power of producers. In this chapter we observe how markets work when all producers are relatively small and lack market power. In subsequent chapters we turn to imperfectly competitive markets—that is, those dominated by large and powerful firms.

FIRM VS. MARKET SUPPLY

In the previous chapter we examined the supply behavior of a competitive firm. As we observed, the production decision of a competitive firm is based on a comparison of price and the marginal cost of producing its output. The perfectly competitive firm has no power over the price at which its product sells; instead, the competitive firm is a price taker. It *responds* to the market price by producing that rate of output where marginal cost equals price.

551

This profit-maximizing rule implies that the short-run supply curve of the competitive firm is its marginal cost curve. Accordingly, whatever determines marginal cost also determines the competitive firm's supply response. We thus concluded that *a competitive firm's supply is determined by*

- *The price of factor inputs*
- *Technology*
- *Expectations*

A catfish farmer will supply more fish at any given price if the price of feed declines, fish can be bred faster because of advances in genetic engineering, or prices are expected to decline later.

But what about the *market* supply of catfish? We need a market supply curve to determine the **equilibrium price** the individual farmer will confront. In the previous chapter we simply drew a market supply curve arbitrarily, in order to establish a market price. Now, however, our objective is to find out where that **market supply** curve comes from.

Like the market supply curves we first encountered in Chapter 2, the market supply of catfish is obtained by simple addition. All we have to do is add up the quantities each farmer stands ready to supply at a given price and we will know the total number of fish to be supplied to the market at that price. Figure 22.1 illustrates this summation. Notice that *the market supply curve is the sum of the marginal cost curves of all the firms.* Hence whatever determines the marginal cost of a typical firm will also determine industry supply. Specifically, the *market supply of a competitive industry is determined by*

- *The price of factor inputs*
- *Technology*
- *Expectations*
- *The number of firms in the industry*

equilibrium price: The price at which the quantity of a good demanded in a given time period equals the quantity supplied.

market supply: The total quantities of a good that sellers are willing and able to sell at alternative prices in a given time period, *ceteris paribus.*

Entry and Exit

If the number of firms in an industry increases, the market supply curve will shift to the right. This is the problem confronting the catfish farmers in Mississippi. It is fairly inexpensive to get into the catfish business. You can start with a pond, some breeding stock, and relatively little capital equipment. Accordingly, when catfish prices are high, lots of cotton farmers are ready and willing to bulldoze a couple of ponds and get into the catfish business (see In the News). These **investment decisions** shift the market supply curve to the right and drive down catfish prices. This process is illustrated in Figure 22.2.

If prices fall too far, some catfish farmers will drain their ponds and plant cotton again. As they leave (exit) the industry the market supply curve will shift to the left.

investment decision: The decision to build, buy, or lease plant and equipment; to enter or exit an industry.

Tendency toward Zero Profits

Whether or not more cotton farmers enter the catfish industry depends on the profit outlook they perceive. If the relationship between price and cost in catfish farming looks better than that in cotton, more farmers will flood their cotton fields. As they do, the market supply curve will continue shifting to the right, driving catfish prices down.

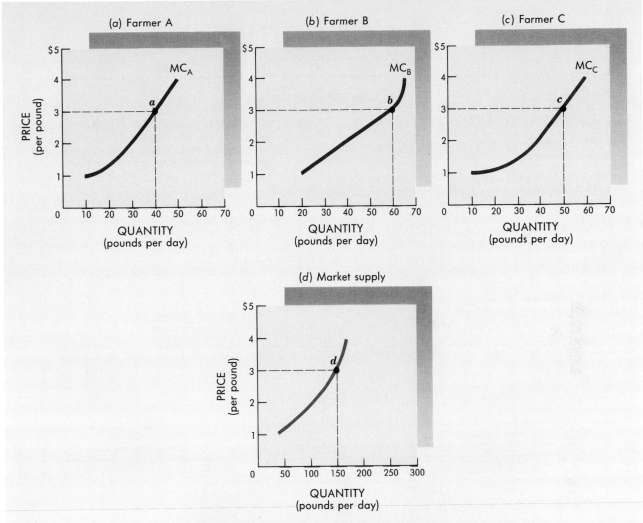

FIGURE 22.1 Competitive Market Supply

The portion of the MC curve that lies above AVC is a competitive firm's short-run supply curve. The curve MC$_A$ tells us that Farmer A will produce 40 pounds of catfish per day if the market price is $3 per pound.

To determine the *market* supply, we add up the quantities supplied by each farmer. The total quantity supplied to the market here is 150 pounds per day (= *a* + *b* + *c*). Market supply depends on the number of firms and their respective marginal costs.

---

economic profit: The difference between total revenues and total economic costs.

At some point, the **economic profits** in catfish farming will disappear. The declining market price will squeeze profit margins until the returns in catfish farming are no better than those in cotton farming. When that happens, cotton farmers will stop building fish ponds and resume planting cotton. *Once entry ceases, the market price will stabilize.* At that new equilibrium, economic profits will no longer exist.

Catfish farmers would be happier, of course, if the price of catfish did not decline to the point where economic profits disappear. But how are they going to prevent it? Bo Smith knows all about the law of demand and would

In The News

COMPETITIVE MARKETS

Southern Farmers Hooked on New Cash Crop

Catfish are replacing crops and dairy farming as a cash industry in much of the South, particularly in Mississippi's Delta region, where 80 percent of farm-bred catfish are grown.

Production has skyrocketed in the USA from 16 million pounds in 1975 to an expected 340 million pounds this year.

The business is growing among farmers in Alabama, Arkansas and Louisiana.

Catfish farming is similar to other agriculture, experts say. One thing is the same: It takes money to get started.

"If you have a good row-crop farmer, you have a good catfish farmer," says James Hoffman of Farm Fresh Catfish Co. in Hollandale, Miss. "But you can't take a poor row-crop farmer and make him a good catfish farmer."

Greensboro, Ala., catfish farmer Steve Hollingsworth says he spends $18,000 a week on feed for the 1 million catfish in his ponds.

"Each of the ponds has about 100,000 fish," he says. "You get about 60 cents per fish, so that's about $60,000."

The investment can be lost very quickly "if something's wrong in that pond," like an inadequate oxygen level, Hollingsworth says.

"You can be 15 minutes too late getting here, and all your fish are gone," he says.

—Mark Mayfield

USA Today, December 5, 1989, p. 3A. Copyright © 1989 USA TODAY. Reprinted with permission.

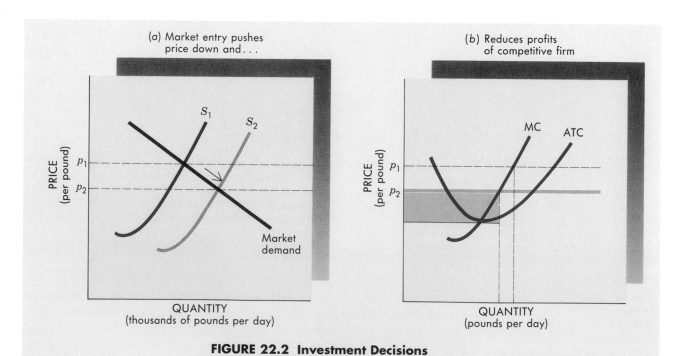

FIGURE 22.2 Investment Decisions

If economic profits exist in an industry, more firms will want to enter it. As they do, the market supply curve will shift to the right and cause a drop in the market price (part *a*). The lower market price, in turn, will reduce the output and profits of the typical firm (part *b*).

competitive market: A market in which no buyer or seller has market power.

like to get other farmers to slow production a little before all the profits disappear. But Bo is powerless to stop the forces of a **competitive market.** He cannot afford to reduce his own catfish production. Nobody would notice the resulting drop in market supplies, and catfish prices would continue to slide. The only one affected would be Bo Smith, who would be denying himself the opportunity to share in the good fortunes of the catfish market while they lasted. As long as others are willing and able to enter the industry and increase output, Bo Smith must do the same or deny himself even a small share of the available profits. Others will be willing to expand catfish production so long as catfish breed economic profits—that is, so long as the rate of return in catfish production is superior to that available elsewhere. They will be able to do so as long as it is easy to get into catfish production.

Bo Smith's dilemma goes a long way toward explaining why catfish farming is not highly profitable. Every time the profit picture looks good, everybody tries to get in on the action, a phenomenon that keeps catfish prices down close to the costs of production. This kind of pressure on prices and profits is a fundamental characteristic of competitive markets. *As long as it is easy for existing producers to expand production or for new firms to enter an industry, economic profits will not last long.* Industry output will expand, market prices will fall, and rates of profit will diminish. Thus the rate of profits in catfish farming is kept down by the fact that anyone with a pond and a couple of catfish can get into the business fairly easily. People will be tempted to enter the catfish business whenever profits are attractive.

Low Barriers to Entry

barriers to entry: Obstacles that make it difficult or impossible for would-be producers to enter a particular market, e.g., patents.

New producers will be able to enter a profitable industry and help drive down prices and profits as long as there are no significant **barriers to entry.** Such barriers may include patents, control of essential factors of production, long-established consumer acceptance, and various forms of price control. All such barriers make it expensive, risky, or impossible for new firms to enter into production. In the absence of such barriers, new firms can enter an industry more readily and at less risk. Not surprisingly, firms already entrenched in a profitable industry do their best to keep newcomers out, by erecting barriers to entry. As we saw, there are few barriers to entering the catfish business.

Market Characteristics

This brief review of catfish economics illustrates a few general observations about the structure, behavior, and outcomes of a competitive market:

- *Many firms.* A competitive market will include a great many firms, none of which has a significant share of total output.

- *Identical products.* Products are homogeneous. One firm's product is virtually indistinguishable from any other firm's product.

- *MC = p.* All competitive firms will seek to expand output until marginal cost equals price, inasmuch as price and marginal revenue are identical for such firms.

- *Low barriers.* Barriers to enter the industry are low. If economic profits are available, more firms will enter the industry.

- *Zero economic profit.* The tendency of production and market supplies to expand when profit is high puts heavy pressure on prices and profits in competitive industries. Economic profit will approach zero in the long run as prices are driven down to the level of average production costs.

COMPETITION AT WORK: MICROCOMPUTERS

Few, if any, product markets are perfectly competitive. However, many industries function much like the competitive model we have sketched out. In addition to catfish farming, most other agricultural product markets are characterized by highly competitive market structures, with hundreds of thousands of producers supplying the market.[1] Other highly competitive, and hence not very profitable, businesses are retail food, printing, clothing manufacturing and retailing, dry-cleaning establishments, and furniture. Other markets exhibit competitive structures as well, and even more behave as the competitive model suggests. In these markets, prices and profits are always under the threat of expanded supplies brought to market by existing or new producers. Prices and profits both decline over time as market sales expand.

The electronics industry offers numerous examples of how competition reduces prices and profits. Between 1972 and 1983, the price of small, hand-held calculators fell from $200 to under $10. The price of digital watches fell even more dramatically, from roughly $2,000 in 1975 to under $7 in 1990. Videocassette recorders (VCRs) that sold for $2,000 in 1979 now sell for under $200. CD players that sold for $1,000 in 1984 are now priced below $200 as well. Movies that rented for $3 a night in 1986 now rent for 99 cents.

What accounts for these tremendous price reductions? Did producers lose their profit-maximizing ambitions? Did they decide that society needed more calculators, watches, and VCRs and generously offer them at lower prices? Did the government set price limits? Did consumers revolt and refuse to pay higher prices? Or did competitive market pressures force producers to reduce prices and improve quality?

Competitive market forces deserve credit for most of these price reductions. To get a better feel for how these forces work, we will look closely at one market—microcomputers. The microcomputer industry never had a perfectly competitive structure and today is dominated by a relatively few firms (IBM, Apple, Compaq, Tandy). But in its early stages of development, the industry exhibited many of the essential behavioral characteristics of a highly competitive market. Hundreds of firms entered and exited the industry in the span of only a few years (1977–83). Microcomputers improved greatly in power, design, and features, while at the same time their prices fell steadily. The driving force for these advances was the lure of profits. The high profits obtained by the early microcomputer producers attracted swarms of imitators. Over 250 firms entered the microcomputer industry between 1976 and 1983 in search of high profits. These upstart companies pushed prices downward and improved the product. When prices and profits tumbled, scores of companies went bankrupt. They left a legacy, however, of a vastly larger market, much-improved computers, and sharply lower prices.

We will use the early experiences of the microcomputer industry to illustrate the key behavioral features of a competitive market.

---

[1] In some of these markets, the independent producers may try to exercise market power by establishing some form of producer association that can influence market supplies (e.g., the dairy associations). Even catfish farmers have organized a Catfish Institute for industry marketing and are developing "bargaining associations" to affect catfish prices. More on this subject in Chapter 25.

Initial Conditions: The Apple I

The microcomputer industry really got started in 1977. Prior to that time, microcomputers were essentially a hobby item for engineers and programmers, who bought circuits, keyboards, monitors, and tape recorders, then assembled their own basic computers. Steve Jobs, then working at Atari, and Steven Wozniak, then working at Hewlett-Packard, were among these early computer enthusiasts. They spent their days working on large systems and their nights and weekends trying to put together small computers from mail-order parts. They were active members of the local Homebrew Computer Club.

Eventually, Jobs and Wozniak decided they had the capability to build commercially attractive small computers. They ordered the parts necessary for building 100 computers and set up shop in the garage of Jobs's parents. Their finished product—the Apple I—was nothing more than a circuit board with a simple, built-in operating system. Nevertheless, it sold out immediately. This quick success convinced Jobs and Wozniak to package their computers more fully—by enclosing them in plastic housing—and to offer more of them for sale. Shortly thereafter, in January 1977, the Apple Computer Corporation was established.

Apple revolutionized the market by offering a preassembled desktop computer with attractive features and an accessible price. The impact on the marketplace was much like that of Henry Ford's early Model T—suddenly a newfangled piece of technology came into reach of the average American household, and everybody, it seemed, wanted one. The first mass-produced Apple computer—the Apple II—was just a basic keyboard with an operating system that permitted users to write their own programs. It had no disc drive, no monitor, and only 4K of random access memory (RAM). Consumers had to use their television sets as screens and audiocassettes for data storage. This primitive Apple II was priced at just under $1,300 when it debuted in June 1977. Apple was producing them at the rate of 500 per month.

Apple did not engineer or manufacture chips or semiconductor components. Instead, it simply packaged existing components purchased from outside suppliers. Hence it was easy for other companies to follow Apple's lead. Within a very brief time, other firms, such as Tandy (Radio Shack), also started to assemble computers. By the middle of 1978, the basic small computer was selling for $1,000, and industry sales were about 2,000 a month (or 24,000 a year).

Figure 22.3 depicts the initial (1978) equilibrium in the computer market and the approximate costs of production for the typical computer manufacturer at that time. Note that the market demand curve (part *a*) slopes downward, just as the law of demand requires. Note also that the market supply curve intersects the demand curve at a price of $1,000, which thereby becomes the market *equilibrium price*. That same intersection tells us that 2,000 computers a month were bought and sold at that price. Individual producers never see these market curves, of course. All they see are their own cost curves and the price at which computers are selling. That price ($1,000) has been determined by market forces.

The Production Decision

The short-run goal of every producer is to find the rate of output that maximizes profits. In the long run, a producer can decide to enter or leave the computer industry or to alter the firm's scale of operation. In this analysis,

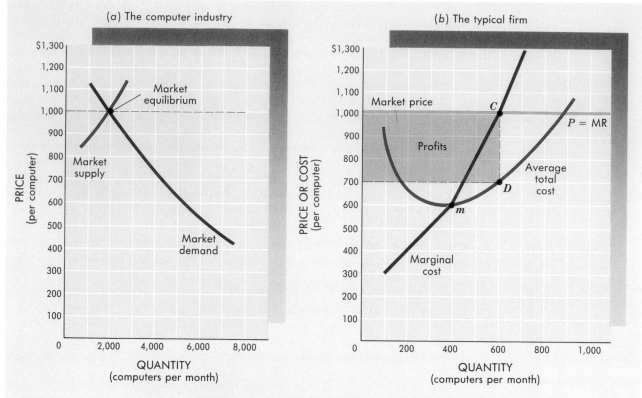

FIGURE 22.3 Initial Equilibrium in the Computer Market

(*a*) In 1978, the market price of microcomputers was $1,000. This price was established by the intersection of the market supply and demand curves.

(*b*) Each competitive producer in the market sought to produce computers at that rate (600 per month) where marginal cost equaled price (point *C*). Profit per computer was equal to price (point *C*) minus average total cost (point *D*). Total profits for the typical firm are indicated by the shaded rectangle.

production decision: The selection of the short-run rate of output (with existing plant and equipment).

marginal cost (MC): The increase in total cost associated with a one-unit increase in production.

however, we shall assume that affirmative investment decisions have been made, and we shall focus on the **production decision.** In this short-run context, *each firm seeks the rate of output at which marginal cost equals marginal revenue.* For a competitive firm, this means finding the point at which **marginal cost (MC)** equals price.

Figure 22.3*b* illustrates the cost and price curves the typical computer producer confronted in 1978. As in most lines of production, the marginal costs of computer production tend to rise with the rate of output, as reflected in the rising MC curve. Marginal costs rose in part because output could be increased in the short run (with existing plant and equipment) only by crowding additional workers onto the assembly line. In 1978, Apple had only 10,000 square feet of manufacturing space. As more workers were hired, each worker had less capital and land to work with, and marginal physical product fell. The law of diminishing returns thus pushed marginal costs up. Moreover, additional labor could be obtained only by paying overtime wages, and even the price of microprocessors and other materials tended to rise as increased quantities were ordered.

For all these reasons, marginal costs rose quite sharply, intersecting the price line at an output level of 600 computers per month (point C in Figure 22.3b).[2] That was the profit-maximizing rate of output (MC = MR = p) for the typical manufacturer. To manufacture any more than 600 computers per month would entail an excess of marginal costs over price and would reduce total profits. To manufacture any less would be to pass up an opportunity to make another buck.

Profit Calculations

To figure out how much *profit* a typical computer manufacturer was making at the output rate of 600 per month, we need to look at something besides marginal cost and price. We can calculate those profits quickly by looking at Table 22.1. As the profit column indicates, the typical computer manufacturer could make a real killing in the computer market, reaping a monthly profit of $180,000 by producing and selling 600 microcomputers.

We could also calculate the computer manufacturers' profits by asking how much they make on *each* computer and multiplying that figure by total output. Clearly,

$$\bullet \quad \frac{\text{Total}}{\text{profit}} = \frac{\text{profit}}{\text{per unit}} \times \frac{\text{quantity}}{\text{sold}}$$

We can compute these profits by studying the first and last columns of Table 22.1 or by using a little geometry on Figure 22.3b. In the figure, average costs

[2]The marginal cost curves depicted here rise more steeply than they did in reality, but the general shape of the curves is our primary concern at this point.

TABLE 22.1 Computer Revenues, Costs, and Profits

Producers seek that rate of output where total profit is maximized. This table illustrates the alternatives the typical computer producer faced in 1978. The profit-maximizing rate of output occurred at 600 computers per month. At that rate of output, marginal cost was equal to price ($1,000) and profits were $180,000 per month.

Output per month	Price	Total revenue	Total cost	Profit	Marginal revenue*	Marginal cost*	Average cost	Profit per unit (price minus average cost)
0	—	—	$ 60,000	– $ 60,000	—	—	—	—
100	$1,000	$100,000	90,000	10,000	$1,000	$ 300	$ 900	$100
200	1,000	200,000	130,000	70,000	1,000	400	650	350
300	1,000	300,000	180,000	120,000	1,000	500	600	400
400	1,000	400,000	240,000	160,000	1,000	600	600	400
500	1,000	500,000	320,000	180,000	1,000	800	640	360
600	1,000	600,000	420,000	180,000	1,000	1,000	700	300
700	1,000	700,000	546,000	154,000	1,000	1,260	780	220
800	1,000	800,000	720,000	80,000	1,000	1,740	900	100
900	1,000	900,000	919,800	– 19,800	1,000	1,998	1,022	– 22

*Note that output levels are calibrated in hundreds in this example; therefore, we have divided the *change* in total costs and revenues from one output level to another by 100 to calculate marginal revenue and marginal cost. Very few manufacturers deal in units of one. The additional revenue associated with a multiple-unit increase in sales is often called *incremental revenue* to distinguish it from the *marginal revenue* generated by one additional sale; we ignore this distinction here.

average total cost (ATC): Total cost divided by the quantity produced in a given time period.

profit per unit: Total profit divided by the quantity produced in a given time period; price minus average total cost.

(total costs divided by the rate of output) are portrayed by the **average total cost (ATC)** curve. At the output rate of 600 (the row in white in Table 22.1), the distance between the price line ($1,000 at point *C*) and the ATC curve ($700 at point *D*) is $300. This represents the average **profit per unit.** Multiplying this figure by the number of units sold (600 per month) gives us *total* profit per month. Total profits are represented by the shaded rectangle in Figure 22.3*b* and are equal, of course, to our earlier profit figure of $180,000 per month.

While gaping at the computer manufacturer's enormous profits, we should note two things about the average cost curve. First is its familiar shape. Average costs fall initially as output is expanded because (1) fixed costs are spread over an increasingly large number of microcomputers,[3] and (2) marginal costs are lower than average costs at low rates of output. At some point, however, marginal costs begin to exceed average costs and exert an upward pull on the ATC curve. Beyond point *m*, the minimum average cost point, the higher marginal costs begin to raise average costs. There is nothing very tricky about these relationships; they only reflect a little arithmetic.

A more interesting observation about the ATC curve depicted in Figure 22.3*b* is the fact that maximum profits are not attained at the point where average costs are at a minimum (point *m*). On the contrary, the most profitable rate of output is considerably to the right of point *m*. As we observed in Chapter 21, *a profit-maximizing producer seeks to maximize total profits, and this is not necessarily or even very frequently the same thing as maximizing profits per unit.*

The Lure of Profits

We could discuss the computer manufacturers' profits at length, but we should not lose sight of the fundamental fact that they are enormous. Indeed, the more quick-witted among us will already have seen and heard enough to know they've discovered a good thing. And in fact, the kind of profits attained by the early microcomputer manufacturers attracted a lot of entrepreneurial interest. *In competitive markets, economic profits attract new entrants.* Within a very short time, a whole crowd of profit maximizers entered the microcomputer industry in hot pursuit of its fabulous profits (see In the News).

Low Entry Barriers

A critical feature of the microcomputer market was its lack of barriers to entry. A microcomputer is little more than a box containing a microprocessor "brain," which connects to a keyboard (to enter data), a memory (to store data), and a screen (to display data). The microprocessors are fingernail-sized chips of silicon on which the computer's "instructions" have been etched. These instructions tell the computer what to do with the data (or words) it receives. Additional routines are fed in by "software" packages that supplement the computer's "brain." Although the microprocessors that guide the computer are extremely sophisticated, they can be purchased on the open market. Thus to enter the computer industry, all one needs is some space, some money to buy components, and some dexterity in putting parts together. Such *low entry barriers permit new firms to enter competitive markets.* According to Table 22.1, the "typical" producer needed only $60,000 of plant

[3]That is, the tendency for $60,000/x$ to get smaller as x gets larger. As Table 22.1 confirms, $60,000 is the *fixed cost* of microcomputer production, as that much expense is incurred even when output is zero. In this case, fixed costs are the costs of rent, utilities, and equipment leases.

In The News

and equipment (fixed costs) to get started in the microcomputer market. Jobs and Wozniak had even less when they started making Apples. Thousands of other people thought they had the necessary qualifications, and they, too, sought entry into the microcomputer market. There were no significant barriers to entry and thus no mechanism for preventing these entrepreneurial upstarts from elbowing in to share the spoils.

A Shift of Market Supply

Figure 22.4 shows what happened to the computer market and the profits of the typical firm once the word got out. As more and more entrepreneurs heard how profitable computer manufacturing could be, they quickly got hold of a book on electronic circuitry, rushed to the bank, got a little financing, and set up shop. Before many months had passed, scores of new firms had started producing small computers. *The entry of new firms shifts the market supply curve to the right.* In Figure 22.4a, the supply curve shifted from S_1 to S_2. Almost as fast as a computer can calculate a profit (loss) statement, the willingness to supply increased abruptly.

The new computer companies were in for a bit of disappointment, however. With so many new firms hawking microcomputers, it became increasingly difficult to make a fast buck. The downward-sloping market demand curve confirms that a greater quantity of microcomputers could be sold only if the price of computers dropped. And drop it did. The price slide began as computer manufacturers found their inventories growing and so offered price discounts to maintain sales volume. The price fell rapidly, from $1,000 in mid-1978 to $800 in early 1980.

The lower market price changed the profit picture and production decisions for the typical firm. The sliding market price squeezed the profits of each firm, causing the profit rectangle to shrink (compare Figure 22.3b to Figure 22.4b). Although the typical firm's cost structure hadn't changed, its sales opportunities had been drastically reduced. It now found that marginal cost was equal to marginal revenue (the new price) at an output of 500 computers per month. As Table 22.1 confirms, in 1978 the typical firm could

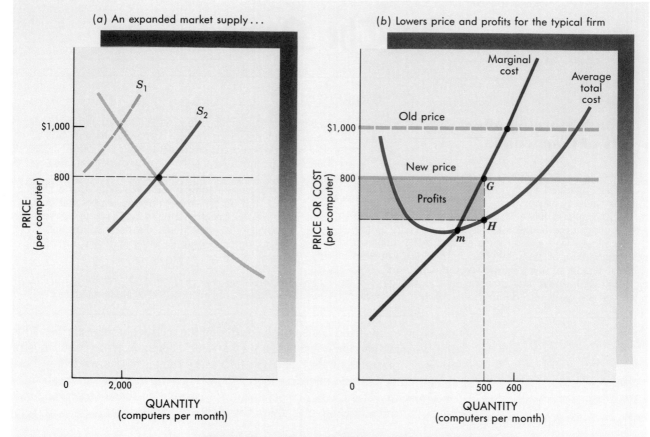

(a) An expanded market supply...

(b) Lowers price and profits for the typical firm

FIGURE 22.4 The Competitive Price and Profit Squeeze

(*a*) The availability of substantial economic profits in the computer industry encouraged new firms to enter the industry. As they did so, the market supply curve shifted from S_1 to S_2. This rightward shift of the supply curve lowered the equilibrium price of computers.

(*b*) The lower market price, in turn, forced the typical producer to cut back the rate of output to the point where MC and price were equal again (point *G*). At this reduced rate of output, the typical firm earned less total profit than it had earned before.

produce 500 computers a month at a marginal cost of $800 and an average cost of $640. But the prices, revenues, and profits depicted in Table 22.1 no longer applied at the beginning of 1980, owing to the changed market situation. By 1980, the typical firm could earn only $80,000 a month (500 × [price of $800 − average total cost of $640])—not a paltry sum, to be sure, but nothing like the fantastic fortunes pocketed earlier. Output of 500 computers per month represented the new **short-run equilibrium** for the typical firm in 1980. In other words, 500 computers per month was the rate of output that maximized profits, given prevailing cost and market prices.

That short-run equilibrium was not destined to last, however. *As long as an economic profit is available, it will continue to attract new entrants.* Those entrepreneurs who were a little slow to digest the implications of Figure 22.3 eventually perceived what was going on and tried to get in on the action, too. Even though they were a little late, they did not wish to bypass

short-run competitive equilibrium: p = MC.

the opportunity to make the $80,000 in monthly profits still available to the typical firm. Hence the market supply curve continued to shift, and computer prices slid further, as in Figure 22.5. This process squeezed the profits of the typical firm still more, further shrinking the profit rectangle.

The competitive pressure on market suppliers, prices, and profits will continue as long as the rate of profit obtainable in computer production is higher than that available in other industries. Profit-maximizing entrepreneurs have a special place in their hearts for economic profits, not for computers. When that profit looks no better than the profit obtainable elsewhere, computer manufacturers may move on to other ventures, and would-be suppliers will lose their fervor to enter the industry.

Price and profit decline will cease when the price of computers is equal to the minimum average cost of production. At that price (point *m* in Figure 22.5*b*), there is no longer any economic profit to be squeezed out. Firms no longer have an incentive to enter the industry and the supply curve stops

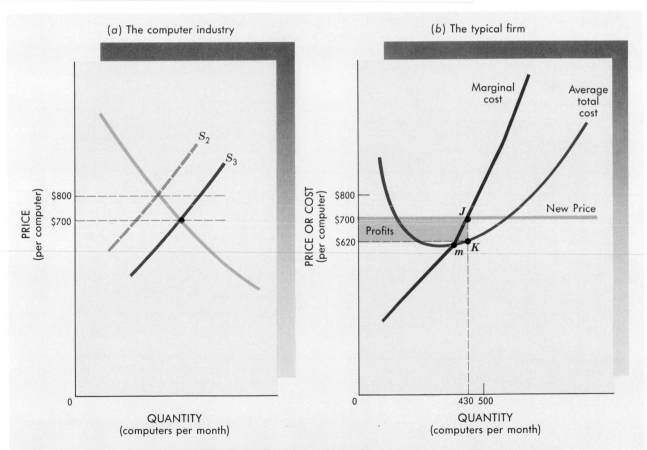

FIGURE 22.5 The Competitive Squeeze Approaching Its Limit

(*a*) Even at a price of $800 per computer, economic profit was available in the computer industry. Such profit attracted still more entrepreneurs, shifting the market supply curve further (*S₃*). The resultant equilibrium occurred at a price of $700 per computer.

(*b*) At this reduced market price, the typical manufacturer wanted to supply only 430 computers per month (point *J*). Total profits were much less than they had been earlier, with fewer producers and higher prices.

long-run competitive equilibrium: p = MC = minimum ATC.

shifting. This situation represents the **long-run equilibrium** for the firm and for the industry. Entry and exit cease, and zero economic profit (i.e., normal profit) prevails (see Figure 22.6). Table 22.2 summarizes the profit-maximizing rules that bring about this long-run equilibrium.

Once a long-run equilibrium is established, it will continue until market demand shifts or technological progress reduces the cost of computer production. In fact, both of these things happened in the computer market.

Home Computers vs. Personal Computers

As profit margins narrowed to the levels shown in Figure 22.5, quick-thinking entrepreneurs realized that future profits would have to come from product improvements or cost reductions. Product improvements would permit firms to continue selling microcomputers at higher prices. By adding features to the basic microcomputer, firms could expect to increase the demand for microcomputers and so broaden their market.

On the other hand, cost reductions would permit firms to widen their profit margins at existing prices or to reduce prices and increase sales. This strategy would not require assembling more complex computers or risking consumer rejection of an upgraded product.

In late 1979 and early 1980, producers of small computers had to choose one of these strategies. In doing so, they effectively created two distinct mar-

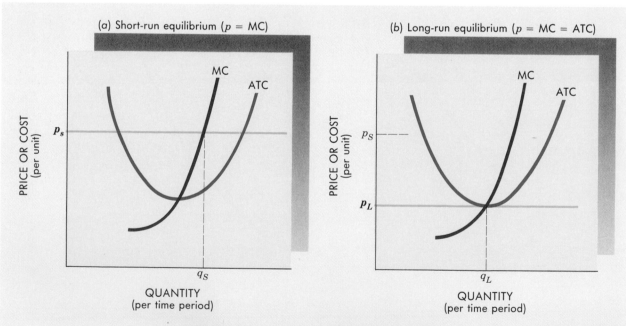

FIGURE 22.6 Short vs. Long-Run Equilibrium for the Competitive Firm

(*a*) Competitive firms strive for the rate of output at which marginal cost (MC) equals price (MR). When they achieve that rate of output, they are in *short–run equilibrium,* in the sense that they have no incentive to alter the rate of output produced with existing (fixed) plant and equipment.

(*b*) If the short–run equilibrium is profitable (p > ATC), other firms will want to enter the industry. As they do, market price will fall until it reaches the level of minimum average total costs, and economic profits are eliminated. In this *long–run equilibrium,* economic profits are zero and there is no further incentive to enter the industry.

TABLE 22.2 Long-Run Rules for Entry and Exit

The relationship between price and average total cost dictates long-term investment decisions. Firms will enter an industry if economic profits exist ($P >$ ATC). They will exit if economic losses ($P <$ ATC) prevail. Entry and exit cease in long-run equilibrium ($P =$ ATC). (See Table 21.4 for short-run profit-maximization rules.)

Market situation	Result for a typical firm	Correct investment decision
$P >$ ATC	Profits	Enter industry (or expand capacity)
$P <$ ATC	Loss	Exit industry (or reduce capacity)
$P =$ ATC	Break even	Maintain existing capacity (no entry or exit)

kets. Microcomputers that were upgraded with new features came to be known as "personal" computers, or PCs. The basic unadorned computer first introduced by Apple came to be known as a "home" computer. The limited capabilities of that basic home computer greatly restricted its usefulness to simple household record keeping, games, and elementary programming. These limited functions had little use outside the home. By contrast, personal computers, with the capacity to perform more complex functions, could be used for professional and business purposes as well as household activities.

Apple chose the personal computer route. It started enlarging the memory of the Apple II in late 1978 (from 4K to as much as 48K). It offered a monitor (produced by Sanyo) for the first time in May 1979. Shortly thereafter, Apple ceased making the basic Apple II and instead produced only upgraded versions (the Apple IIe, the IIc, and III). Hundreds of other companies followed Apple's lead, offering increasingly sophisticated personal computers.

While one pack of entrepreneurs was chasing PC profits, another pack was chasing the profits still available in home computers. They chose to continue producing the basic Apple II look-alike, hoping to profit from greater efficiency, lower costs, and increasing sales.

Price Competition in Home Computers

The home computer market confronted the fiercest form of price competition. With prices continually sliding, the only way to make an extra buck was to push the cost curve down.

As noted earlier, a basic home computer has very few parts, the most important of which are the microprocessor chips that function as its brain. A basic determinant of computer manufacturing costs is the number of chips required to make the computer work. Fewer chips not only mean a reduction in direct materials costs but, more important, significantly reduce the amount of labor required for computer assembly. The key to lower manufacturing costs was more powerful chips.

More powerful chips appeared when Intel, Motorola, and Texas Instruments developed 16-bit chips. The first generation of personal computers could process only 8 bits of information at a time—a "bit" being a 1 or a 0 in the binary language of a computer. The 16-bit chips—the "computers on a chip"—doubled the computer's "brain" capabilities. This meant that faster, more powerful computers could be built at lower costs.

Further Supply Shifts

The impact of the improved chips on computer production costs and profits is illustrated in Figure 22.7, which takes over where Figure 22.5 left off. Recall that the market price of computers had been driven down to $700 by the beginning of 1980. At this price the typical firm maximized profits by producing 430 computers per month, as determined by the intersection of the prevailing price and MC curves (point *J* in Figure 22.7).

The only way for the firm to improve profitability at this point was to reduce costs. The new chips facilitated such cost reductions. Such ***technological improvements are illustrated by a downward shift of the ATC and MC curves.*** Notice, for example, that the new technology permits 430 home computers to be produced for a lower marginal cost (about $500) than previously (point *J*).

The lower cost structure increases the profitability of computer production and stimulates a further increase in production. Note in particular that the new MC curve intersects the price ($700) line at an output of 600 computers per month (point *N*). By contrast, the old, higher MC curve dictated a production rate of only 430 computers per month for the typical firm (point *J*) at that price. Thus existing producers suddenly had an incentive to expand production, and new firms had a greater incentive to enter the industry. The great rush into computer production was on again.

The market implications of another entrepreneurial stampede should now be obvious. As more and more firms tried to get in on the action, the market supply curve again shifted to the right. As output increased, computer prices slid further down the market demand curve. The rightward shift of the market

**FIGURE 22.7
A Downward Shift of
Costs Improves Profits
and Stimulates Output**

The quest for profits encouraged producers to discover cheaper ways to manufacture computers. The resultant improvements lowered costs and encouraged further increases in the rate of output. The typical computer producer increased output from point *J* to point *N*.

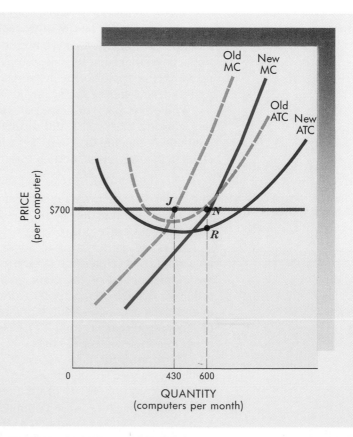

supply curve also diminished the profitability of production, squeezing the profit potential once again.

Table 22.3 illustrates how steeply home computer prices fell after 1980. Texas Instruments (TI) was one of the largest firms producing home computers in 1980. The lower costs made possible by improved microprocessors enabled TI to sell its basic home computer for $650 in 1980. Despite modest improvements in the TI machine, TI had to reduce its price to $525 in early 1981 in order to maintain unit sales. Shortly thereafter, the additional output of new entrants and existing companies—including Tandy (Radio Shack), Atari, and Commodore—pushed market prices to around $400, and TI was forced to accept that lower price.

Even at $400, TI and other home computer manufacturers were making handsome profits. In the fourth quarter of 1981, total industry sales were in excess of 200,000 per month—light-years removed from the 2,000 units per month sold just three years earlier. Profits were good, too. Just one company, Atari, recorded total profits of $137 million in the fourth quarter of 1981, far more profit than Apple Computer had made during its first five *years* of production. The profits of the home computer market appeared boundless.

The remainder of Table 22.3 shows the consequences of the continued competition for those "boundless" profits. Between December 1981 and January 1983, the retail price of home computers fell from $400 to $149. Profit margins became razor-thin. Fourth-quarter profits at Atari, for example, fell from $137 million in 1981 to only $1.2 million in 1983.

Shutdowns
That didn't stop the competitive process, however. At Texas Instruments, minimum variable costs were roughly $100 per computer. So TI and other manufacturers could afford to keep producing even at lower prices. And they had little choice but to do so, since if they did not, other companies would quickly take up the slack. Industry output kept increasing, pushing computer prices ever lower.

By the time computer prices reached $99, TI was losing $300 million per year. In September 1983, the company recognized that the price would no longer even cover average variable costs. ***Once a firm is no longer able to***

TABLE 22.3   Plummeting Prices

Improved technology and fierce competition forced home computer prices down. In the span of only a few years, the price of a basic home computer fell from just under $1,000 to only $49. In the process, price fell below average variable cost, and many firms were forced to shut down.

Date	Price of Texas Instruments Model 99/4A
December 1979	$950
February 1980	700
June 1980	650
April 1981	525
December 1981	400
April 1982	249
September 1982	199
January 1983	149
September 1983	99
November 1983	49

shutdown point: The rate of output at which price equals minimum AVC.

cover variable costs, it should shut down production. When the price of home computers dipped below minimum average variable costs, TI had reached the **shutdown point,** and the company ceased production. At the time TI made the shutdown decision, the company had an inventory of nearly 500,000 unsold computers. To unload them, TI reduced its price to $49, forcing lower prices and losses on other computer firms.

Exits

Shortly after Texas Instruments shut down its production, it got out of the home computer business altogether. Mattel, Atari, and scores of smaller companies also withdrew from the home computer market. The exit rate in 1983–85 matched the entry rate of 1979–82.

The Personal Computer Market

The same kind of price competition that characterized the home computer market eventually hit the personal computer market too. As noted earlier, the microcomputer industry split into two segments around 1980, with most firms pursuing the "upgraded" personal computer (PC) market.

At first, competition in the PC market was largely confined to product improvements. Firms added more memory, faster microprocessors, better monitors, expanded operating systems, new applications software, and other features.

The stampede of new firms and products into the PC market soon led to outright price competition too. As firms discovered that they couldn't sell all the PCs they were producing at prevailing prices, they offered price discounts. These discounts soon spread, and the slide down the demand curve accelerated.

Firms that couldn't keep up with the dual pace of improving technology and falling prices soon fell by the wayside. Scores of firms ceased production and withdrew from the industry once price fell below minimum average variable cost. The president of one small firm (Archives Corporation of Davenport, Iowa) summed up the situation nicely: "The price competition is terrible. Everyone praised our computers for their reliability, but nobody wanted to pay for them." Another company, Osborne Computer, which had pioneered portable PCs, provided one of the most spectacular exits, going from an industry leader to bankruptcy in less than two years. Even Apple Computer, which had taken the "high road" to avoid price competition in home computers, was slowed by price competition. And IBM, which had entered the industry late, was forced to shut down after realizing that steep price cuts would be required to sell its small PCs (the "PCjr") to household users (see In the News).

REFLECTIONS ON THE COMPETITIVE PROCESS

In view of the sudden demise of so many firms, one may wonder whether all this frenzy in the computer market really benefited anyone. Did consumers benefit? Did any producers make a profit? Was there a net gain for society?

That consumers reaped substantial benefit from competition in the computer market is by now evident. Over 100 million home and personal computers have been sold. Along the way, technology has made personal computers 50 times faster than the first Apple IIs, with 500 times more memory. A lot of consumers have found that computers are great for doing accounting chores, keeping records, writing papers, and playing games. Perhaps

In The News

SHUTDOWN DECISION

IBM to Halt PCjr Output Next Month

Computer's Sales Dried Up After Steep Price Cuts Ended Earlier This Year

NEW YORK—International Business Machines Corp. ended its up-and-down struggle to revive its PCjr home computer by announcing it would stop making the product next month.

The surprise move marks IBM's most visible product failure since its enormously successful entry into the personal-computer business four years ago. IBM announced the PCjr in late 1983 and began selling it early last year with an advertising campaign believed to exceed $40 million. IBM's efforts to make Junior a hit ranged from technical changes to steep price cuts. But while aggressive IBM price cuts before Christmas increased PCjr sales substantially, sales dried up after the promotions ended in January. . . .

With the PCjr decision, more questions surfaced as to whether any company could do well in the home-computer market.

At the time of its introduction, the PCjr had a list price of $699 or $1,269, depending on the model. The prices later were cut to $599 and $999, and the more powerful model's price dropped below the $800 level during the Christmas promotion.

—Dennis Kneale

it is true that an abundance of inexpensive computers would have been produced in other market (or nonmarket) situations as well. But we cannot ignore the fact that competitive market pressures were a driving force in the growth of the industry (see In the News on next page).

The Relentless Profit Squeeze

market mechanism: The use of market prices and sales to signal desired outputs (or resource allocations).

The unrelenting squeeze on prices and profits that we have observed in the computer market is a fundamental characteristic of the competitive process. Indeed, the **market mechanism** works best under such circumstances. The existence of economic profits is an indication that consumers place a high value on a particular product and are willing to pay a comparatively high price to get it. The high price and profits signal this information to profit-hungry entrepreneurs, who eagerly come forward to satisfy consumer demands. Thus *high profits in a particular industry indicate that consumers want a different mix of output* (more of that industry's goods). The competitive squeeze on those same profits indicates that resources are being reallocated to produce that desired mix. In a competitive market, consumers get more of the goods they desire, and at a lower price.

When the competitive pressure on prices is carried to the limit, the products in question are also produced at the least possible cost, another dimension of economic efficiency. This was illustrated by the tendency of computer prices to be driven down to the level of minimum average costs. Figure 22.8 summarizes this competitive process, showing how the industry moves from short-run to long-run equilibrium. Once the long-run equilibrium has been established, society is getting the most it can from its available (scarce) resources.

At the limit of long-run equilibrium, all economic profit is eliminated. This doesn't mean that producers are left empty-handed, however. To begin with, the zero-profit limit is rarely, if ever, reached, because new products are continually being introduced, consumer demands change, and more efficient production processes are discovered. In fact, the competitive process creates

In The News

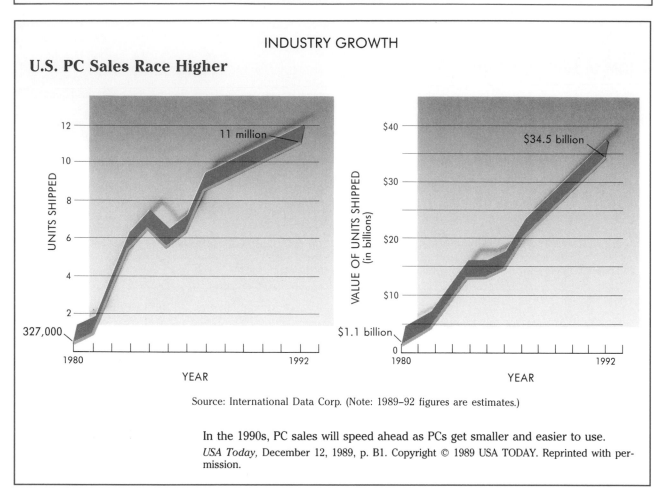

INDUSTRY GROWTH

U.S. PC Sales Race Higher

Source: International Data Corp. (Note: 1989–92 figures are estimates.)

In the 1990s, PC sales will speed ahead as PCs get smaller and easier to use.
USA Today, December 12, 1989, p. B1. Copyright © 1989 USA TODAY. Reprinted with permission.

strong pressures to pursue product and technological innovation. In a competitive market, the adage about the early bird getting the worm is particularly apt. As we observed in the computer market, the first ones to perceive and respond to the potential profitability of computer production were the ones who made the greatest profits.

The sequence of events common to a competitive market situation includes:

- High prices and profits signal consumers' demand for more output.

- Economic profit attracts new suppliers.

- The market supply curve shifts to the right.

- Prices slide down the market demand curve.

- A new equilibrium is reached at which increased quantities of the desired product are produced and its price is lower. Average costs of production are at or near a minimum, much more of the product is supplied and consumed, and economic profit approaches zero.

FIGURE 22.8
Summary of Competitive Process

All competitive firms seek to produce at that output rate where MC = *p*. Hence a competitive *industry* will produce at that rate of output where *industry* MC (the sum of all firms' MC curves) intersects market demand (point *a*).

If economic profits exist in the industry (as they do here), more firms will enter the industry. As they do, the *industry* MC (supply) curve will shift to the right. The shifting MC curve will pull the industry ATC curve along with it. As the industry MC curve continues to shift rightward, the intersection of MC and ATC (point *b*) eventually will reach the demand curve at point *c*. At point *c*, MC still equals price, but no economic profits exist and entry (shifts) will cease. Point *c* will be the *long–term* equilibrium of the industry.

If competitive pressures reduce costs (i.e., improve technology), the supply (MC) curve will shift further to the right, reducing long-term prices even more.

Note that MC = *p* in both short- and long–run equilibrium. Notice also that equilibrium must occur on the market demand curve.

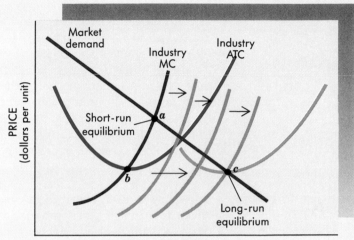

- Throughout the process producers experience great pressure to keep ahead of the profit squeeze by reducing costs, a pressure that frequently results in product and technological innovation.

What is essential to note about the competitive process is that the potential threat of other firms to expand production or new firms to enter the industry keeps existing firms on their toes. Even the most successful firm cannot rest on its laurels for long. To stay in the game, competitive firms must continually improve technology, improve their product, and reduce costs.

The Social Value of Losses   As we have observed, not all firms can maintain a competitive pace. Throughout the competitive process, many firms incur economic losses, shut down production, and exit the industry. These losses are a critical part of the market mechanism. ***Economic losses are a signal to producers that they are not using society's scarce resources in the best way.*** Consumers want those resources reallocated to other firms or industries that can better satisfy consumer demands.

The demise of the home computer industry illustrates this essential dimension of the competitive process. In 1982, consumers bought $3 billion worth of video games. By 1985, diminishing marginal utility had become apparent, and consumers spent only $100 million on video games. The decline in demand forced game producers to reduce prices sharply. The lower prices, in turn, transformed profits into losses. Atari, the largest video-game producer, lost over $80 million in 1984–85. Such huge losses compelled Atari and other video-game manufacturers to reduce output, thus freeing up resources for use in other industries. When consumers stopped buying video games, they started spending more on other goods. This increased the demand for other goods and raised prices and profits elsewhere, giving non–video producers an incentive to expand output. Thus the factors of production released from the video-game industry moved to other industries. In the process, the mix of output changed, in accordance with changing consumer demands.

Competitive Efficiency

In seeking to keep ahead of the game, competitive firms collectively move closer to society's goals, producing the level and mix of output consumers desire with the most efficient combination of resources. In this sense, a market composed of hundreds or even thousands of individually powerless firms is capable of maximizing consumer welfare. Two specific dimensions of competitive efficiency are noteworthy.

Minimum average cost of production   Because competitive pressures squeeze profit margins, the price of a competitively produced good is driven down to its minimum average cost of production (Figure 22.8). This means that society is devoting the minimal amount of resources necessary to produce that good. In deciding how to produce, a competitive market tends, therefore, to promote maximum **efficiency.**

efficiency (technical): Maximum output of a good from the resources used in production.

Marginal cost pricing   The second dimension of competitive efficiency relates to the *mix* of output. In choosing WHAT to produce, we know that the production of one good must be cut back if we are to get more of another good (as long as we are operating on or near the production-possibilities curve). The goods given up are, of course, the **opportunity cost** of getting what we want.

Rational choices about the mix of output require that we know how many resources are required to get one more computer (or anything else). The labor and materials used up in the production of computers cannot be used to produce harmonicas. Our measure of the amount of resources used to produce one more computer is its *marginal cost.* Thus rational decision making requires that we be able to choose among alternative goods and services on the basis of our desires and each good's marginal cost.

opportunity cost: The most desired goods or services that are forgone in order to obtain something else.

A competitive market provides us with the information necessary for making such choices. Why? Because competitive firms offer their goods for sale at the level of marginal costs. That is, they always strive to produce at the rate of output at which price equals marginal cost. Hence the price signal the consumer gets in the marketplace is an accurate reflection of opportunity cost. As such, it offers a reliable basis for making choices about the mix of

marginal cost pricing: The offer (supply) of goods at prices equal to their marginal cost.

output and attendant allocation of resources. In this sense, the **marginal cost pricing** characteristic of competitive markets permits society to fulfill its economic goals. The amount consumers are willing to pay for a good (its price) equals its opportunity cost (marginal cost).

POLICY INSIGHTS:

COMPETITIVE MARKET EFFICIENCY

In Chapter 2 we noted that there is a comparatively strong case to be made for the market mechanism. In particular, we observed that the market mechanism permits individual consumers and producers to express their views about WHAT to produce, HOW to produce, and FOR WHOM to produce by "voting" for particular goods and services by way of market purchases and sales. If a great many people want and are willing to pay for a particular good, the market mechanism will assist in bringing about more of the desired production. If little of a particular good or service is desired, the market mechanism will signal this fact to producers and stimulate a reallocation of the economy's resources in another direction. Even communist countries have come to recognize and respect the power of competitive markets to allocate resources (see World View). Many of the recent reforms in Eastern Europe are designed to harness this power.

As powerful and productive as competition is, however, government intervention may still be desired—even where markets are perfectly competitive. A laissez-faire view of the world must be tempered by at least three qualifications. The appropriateness or fairness of consumer "voting" patterns

W🌐RLD VIEW

MARKET vs. CENTRAL CONTROL

No Competition = No Soap in Russia

Communist countries have learned about competitive markets the hard way—by doing without them. The soap industry in the Soviet Union illustrates their experience.

Like most Soviet goods, the amount of soap produced each year is determined by central planners. They then assign to each soap factory a production quota and the resources needed to produce the soap. The responsibility of the factory manager is to fulfill or "over-fulfill" the quota. Up until 1985, domestic production was supplemented by over 100,000 tons of imported soap.

In 1985 the Soviet Union was awash in soap. The central planners had overestimated consumption and underestimated production. To remedy the surplus, they cut off imports and allocated lower quotas and fewer resources to domestic soap factories.

In 1985–1986 the demand for soap increased along with consumer incomes. The supply of soap, however,

was constrained by a lack of imports and a cutback in the output of sulphanol (a key ingredient in soap) from the nation's only sulphanol plant. A market shortage emerged in 1988. Panic buying of soap led to empty shelves in 1989. Soviet consumers had to line up for hours outside of state-owned stores to buy soap, detergent, washing powder, or toothpaste. On the black market, such items fetched prices three to four times the official price. The official price of soap did not change, however. Moreover, factory managers had neither the incentive nor the resources to increase output. As a result, the government had to start rationing soap and to resume importing soap. In 1989 over 200,000 tons of soap were imported to relieve the market shortage.

One of the objectives of perestroika—Mikhail Gorbachev's restructuring of the Soviet economy—is to introduce more market-oriented incentives and flexibility. If successful, these reforms will help avert future shortages of basic consumer goods.

depends on how equitably voting power is distributed. If some consumers have little opportunity to acquire income or wealth, they will be unable to participate fully in the collective decision making in resource and product markets. We also noted that some goods and services cannot be peddled efficiency in the market because their consumption cannot be confined to those who pay for them. These *public goods* are an important exception to laissez-faire economics. Finally, we have observed that the concept of public goods applies more generally to externalities—benefits or harm that cannot be communicated efficiently through the marketplace. In the presence of externalities, government intervention may be required to reallocate resources.

In view of these three major qualifications to market efficiency, the argument for a completely laissez-faire policy must be met with some skepticism. Nevertheless, we cannot disregard the fact that the market mechanism is an efficient tool for communicating and fulfilling society's wishes. It is particularly important to note that markets tend to be most efficient when competitive forces are at work. As we observed in our microcomputer illustration, competitive firms and industries tend to respond quickly and efficiently to consumer desires. In this sense, competitive markets do best what markets are supposed to do, and it is in society's interest to maintain competitive market structures. In the following chapters we shall look more closely at our successes and failures in this regard.

SUMMARY

- A perfectly competitive firm has no power to alter the market price of the goods it sells. The perfectly competitive firm confronts a horizontal demand curve for its own output even though the relevant *market* demand curve is negatively sloped.

- Profit maximization induces the competitive firm to produce at that rate of output where marginal cost equals price. This represents the short-term equilibrium of the firm.

- If short-term profits exist in a competitive industry, new firms will enter the market. The resulting shift of supply will drive market prices down the market demand curve. As prices fall, the profit of the industry and its constituent firms will be squeezed.

- The limit to the competitive price and profit squeeze is reached when price is driven down to the level of minimum average cost. At this point (long-run equilibrium) additional output and profit will be attained only if technology is improved (lowering costs) or if demand increases.

- Firms will shut down production if price falls below average variable cost. Firms will exit the industry if they foresee continued economic losses.

- The most distinctive thing about competitive markets is the persistent pressure they exert on prices and profits. The threat of competition is a tremendous incentive for producers to respond quickly to consumer demands and to seek more efficient means of production. In this sense, competitive markets do best what markets are supposed to do—efficiently allocate resources.

Terms to Remember   Define the following terms:

equilibrium price	profit per unit
market supply	short-run competitive equilibrium
investment decision	long-run competitive equilibrium
economic profit	shutdown point
competitive market	market mechanism
barriers to entry	efficiency (technical)
production decision	opportunity cost
marginal cost (MC)	marginal cost pricing
marginal revenue (MR)	
average total cost (ATC)	

Questions for Discussion

1. Why would anyone want to enter a profitable industry knowing that profits would eventually be eliminated by competition?

2. Why wouldn't producers necessarily want to produce output at the lowest average cost? Under what conditions would they end up doing so?

3. What industries do you regard as being highly competitive? Can you identify any barriers to entry in those industries?

4. How did the computer industry end up being dominated by only a few firms?

5. How would competitive markets have helped avoid or relieve the Soviet soap crisis described in the preceding World View?

Problems

1. Suppose that the monthly market demand schedule for Frisbees is:

Price	$8	$7	$6	$5	$4	$3	$2	$1
Quantity demanded	1,000	2,000	4,000	8,000	16,000	32,000	64,000	150,000

Suppose further that the marginal and average costs of Frisbee production for every competitive firm are

Rate of output	100	200	300	400	500	600
Marginal cost	$2.00	$3.00	$4.00	$5.00	$6.00	$7.00
Average cost	2.00	2.50	3.00	3.50	4.00	4.50

Finally, assume that the equilibrium market price is $6 per Frisbee.
(a) Draw the cost curves of the typical firm and identify its profit-maximizing rate of output and its total profits.
(b) Draw the market demand curve and identify market equilibrium.
(c) How many (identical) firms are initially producing Frisbees?
(d How much profit is the typical firm making?
(e) In view of the profits being made, more firms will want to get into Frisbee production. In the long run, these new firms will shift the market supply curve to the right and push price down to average total cost, thereby eliminating profits. At what equilibrium price are all profits eliminated? How many firms will be producing Frisbees at this price?

2. Suppose the typical catfish farmer was incurring an economic loss at the prevailing price p_1. What forces would raise the price? What price would prevail in long-term equilibrium? Illustrate your answers with graphs for the catfish market and the typical farmer.

Monopoly

*I*n 1908 Ford produced the Model T, the car "designed for the common man." It was cheap, reliable, and as easy to drive as the horse and buggy it was replacing. Ford sold 10,000 Model T's in its first full year of production (1909). After that, sales more than doubled every year. In 1913, nearly 200,000 Model T's were sold and Ford was fast changing American patterns of consumption, travel, and living standards.

During this early development of the U.S. auto industry, Henry Ford dominated the field. There were other producers, but the Ford Motor Company was the only producer of an inexpensive "motorcar for the multitudes." In this situation, Henry Ford could dictate the price and the features of his cars. When he opened his new assembly line factory at Highland Park, he abruptly raised the Model T's price by $100—an increase of 12 percent—to help pay for the new plant. Then he decided to paint all Model T's black. When told of consumer complaints about the lack of colors, Ford advised one of his executives in 1913: "Give them any color they want so long as it's black."[1]

market power: The ability to alter the market price of a good or service.

Henry Ford had **market power.** He could dictate what color car Americans would buy. And he could raise the price of Model T's without fear of losing all his customers. Such power is alien to competitive firms. Competitive firms are always under pressure to reduce costs, improve quality, and cater to consumer preferences.

In this chapter we will examine how market structure influences market outcomes. Specifically, we examine how a market controlled by a single producer—a monopoly—behaves. We are particularly interested in the following questions:

- What price will a monopolist charge for his output?

- How much will he produce?

- Are consumers better or worse off when only one firm controls an entire market?

[1]Charles E. Sorensen, *My Forty Years with Ford* (New York: W. W. Norton & Co., 1956), p. 127.

MARKET POWER

The essence of market power is the ability to alter the price of a product. The catfish farmers of Chapter 22 had no such power. Because many other farms were producing and selling the same good, each catfish producer had to act as a *price taker*. Each producer could sell all it wanted at the prevailing price but would lose all of its customers if it tried to charge a higher price. This inability to raise the price of their own output is the most distinguishing characteristic of perfectly competitive firms.

The total absence of market power is illustrated by a horizontal demand curve. Although the demand for the product itself always slopes downward, the demand curve confronting a single competitive firm is horizontal. *Horizontal demand curves are the hallmark of perfectly competitive firms.*

The Downward-Sloping Demand Curve

Firms that have market power *can* alter the price of their output without losing all their customers. Sales volume may drop when price is increased, but the quantity demanded will not drop to zero. In other words, *firms with market power confront downward-sloping demand curves for their own output.*

The distinction between perfectly competitive (powerless) and imperfectly competitive (powerful) firms is illustrated again in Figure 23.1. Figure 23.1a re-creates the market situation that confronts a single producer of bracelets. In Chapter 21 we assumed that the prevailing price of silver bracelets was $13 and that a small, competitive firm could sell its entire output at this price. Hence each individual firm effectively confronted a horizontal demand curve.

We also noted earlier that silver bracelets don't violate the law of demand. As nice as silver bracelets are, people are not willing to buy unlimited quantities of them at $13 each. The marginal utility of extra bracelets, in fact, diminishes very rapidly. To induce consumers to buy more bracelets, the price of bracelets must be reduced.

This seeming contradiction between the law of demand and the situation of the competitive firm is resolved in Figure 23.1. There are *two* relevant

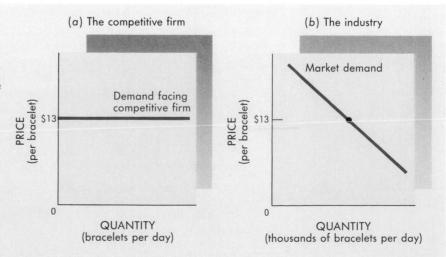

FIGURE 23.1
Firm vs. Industry Demand

A competitive firm can sell its entire output at the prevailing market price. In this sense, the firm confronts a horizontal demand curve, as in part *a*. Nevertheless, market demand for the product still slopes downward. The demand curve confronting the industry is illustrated in part *b*. Note the difference in the units of measurement (single bracelets vs. thousands).

(a) The competitive firm

PRICE (per bracelet)

$13

Demand facing competitive firm

0

QUANTITY (bracelets per day)

(b) The industry

PRICE (per bracelet)

Market demand

$13

0

QUANTITY (thousands of bracelets per day)

demand curves. The one on the left, which appears to contradict the law of demand, refers to a single competitive producer. The one on the right refers to the entire *industry,* of which the competitive producer is one very tiny part. The industry or market demand curve *does* slope downward, even though individual competitive firms are able to sell their output at the going price.

Monopoly

monopoly: A firm that produces the entire market supply of a particular good or service.

An industry need not be composed of many small firms, however. The entire output of bracelets could be produced by a single large producer. Such a firm would be a **monopoly**—that is, a single firm that produces the entire market supply of a good.

The emergence of a monopoly obliterates the distinction between industry demand and the demand curve facing the firm. A monopoly *is* the industry. Hence there is only *one* demand curve to worry about, and that is the market (industry) demand curve, as illustrated in Figure 23.1*b*. *In monopoly situations the demand curve facing the firm is identical to the market demand curve for the product.*

Price and Marginal Revenue

profit-maximization rule: Produce at that rate of output where marginal revenue equals marginal cost.

Although monopolies simplify the geometry, they complicate the arithmetic of **profit maximization.** The basic rule for maximizing profits is unchanged—that is, produce the rate of output where marginal revenue equals marginal cost. This rule applies to *all* firms. In a competitive industry, however, this general rule for profit maximization takes on a unique interpretation. For competitive firms, marginal revenue is equal to price. Because the demand curve facing a competitive firm is horizontal, a competitive firm can maximize profits by producing at that rate of output where marginal cost equals *price.*

This special adaptation of the profit-maximizing rule does not work for a monopolist. The demand curve facing a monopolist is downward-sloping. Because of this, *marginal revenue is not equal to price for a monopolist.* On the contrary, marginal revenue is always *less* than price in a monopoly, as we shall see. This makes it just a bit more difficult to find the profit-maximizing rate of output.

Figure 23.2 provides a simple illustration of the relationship between price and marginal revenue. The monopolist can sell one bracelet per day at a price of $13. If he wants to sell a larger quantity of bracelets, however, he has to reduce his price. According to the demand curve shown here, the price must be lowered to $12 to sell two bracelets per day. This reduction in price is shown by a movement along the demand curve from point *A* to point *B*.

Our primary interest here is marginal revenue. We want to show what happens to total revenue when sales increase by 1 bracelet per day. To do this, we simply compute the total revenue associated with each rate of output. **Marginal revenue (MR)** represents the *change* in total revenue that results from a one-unit increase in the rate of output. More generally, we use the formula:

marginal revenue (MR): The change in total revenue that results from a one-unit increase in the quantity sold.

$$\text{Marginal revenue} = \frac{\text{change in total revenue}}{\text{change in quantity sold}} = \frac{\Delta TR}{\Delta q}$$

where the delta symbol (Δ) denotes "change in."

The calculations necessary for computing MR are summarized in Figure 23.2. Row *A* of the table indicates that the total revenue resulting from one sale per day is $13. To increase sales, price must be reduced. Row *B* indicates

FIGURE 23.2
Price Exceeds Marginal Revenue in Monopoly

If a firm must lower its price to sell additional output, marginal revenue is less than price. If the firm wants to increase its sales from 1 to 2 bracelets per day, for example, price must be reduced from $13 to $12. The marginal revenue of the second bracelet is therefore only $11. This is indicated in row *B* of the table and by point *b* on the graph.

	(1) Quantity	×	(2) Price	=	(3) Total revenue	(4) Marginal revenue
A	1		$13		$13	
B	2		12		24	$11
C	3		11		33	9
D	4		10		40	7
E	5		9		45	5
F	6		8		48	3
G	7		7		49	1

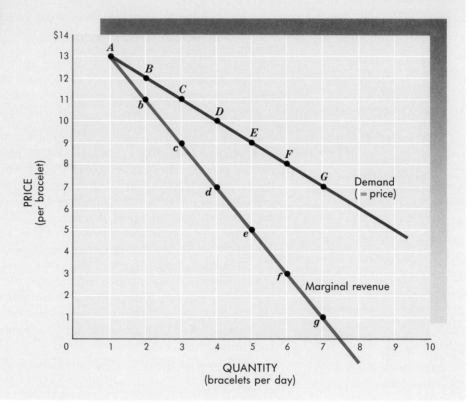

that total revenues rise to only $24 per day when bracelet sales double. The *increase* in total revenues resulting from the added sales is thus $11. The marginal revenue of the second bracelet is therefore $11. This is illustrated in the last column of the table and by point *b* on the marginal revenue curve.

Notice that the MR of the second bracelet ($11) is *less* than its price ($12). This is because both bracelets are being sold for $12 apiece. In effect, the firm is giving up the opportunity to sell only 1 bracelet per day at $13 in order to sell a larger quantity at a lower price. In this sense, the firm is sacrificing $1 of potential revenue on the first bracelet in order to increase *total* revenue. Marginal revenue measures the change in total revenue that results.

So long as the demand curve is downward-sloping, MR will always be less than price. Compare columns 2 and 4 of the table in Figure 23.2. At each rate of output in excess of one bracelet, marginal revenue is less than price. This is also evident in the graph: *the MR curve lies below the demand (price) curve at every point but the first.*

Profit Maximization

The most immediate consequence of market power, then, is an extra curve— one for marginal revenue. The rules of profit maximization remain the same, however. Now instead of looking for an intersection of marginal cost and price, we look for the intersection of marginal cost and marginal revenue. This is illustrated in Figure 23.3 by the intersection of the MR and MC curves (point *d*). Looking down from that intersection, we see that the associated rate of output is 4 bracelets per day. Thus 4 bracelets is the profit-maximizing rate of output.

How much should the monopolist charge for these 4 bracelets? Naturally, the monopolist would like to charge a very high price. But his ability to charge a high price is limited by the demand curve. If he charges $13, consumers will buy only 1 bracelet, leaving him with 3 unsold bracelets. As the monopolist will soon learn, *only one price is compatible with the profit-maximizing rate of output.* In this case, the price is $10. This price is found in Figure 23.3 by moving up from the quantity 4 until reaching the demand curve at point *D*. Point *D* tells us that consumers are able and willing to buy 4 bracelets per day only at the price of $10 each. A monopolist who tries to charge more than $10 will not be able to sell all 4 bracelets.

Also illustrated in Figure 23.3 are the total profits of the bracelet monopoly. To compute total profits we can first calculate profit per unit, that is,

FIGURE 23.3
Profit Maximization

The most profitable rate of output is indicated by the intersection of marginal revenue and marginal cost (point *d*). In this case, marginal revenue and marginal cost intersect at an output of 4 bracelets per day. Point *D* indicates that consumers will pay $10 per bracelet for this much output. Total profits equal price ($10) minus average total cost ($8), multiplied by the quantity sold (4).

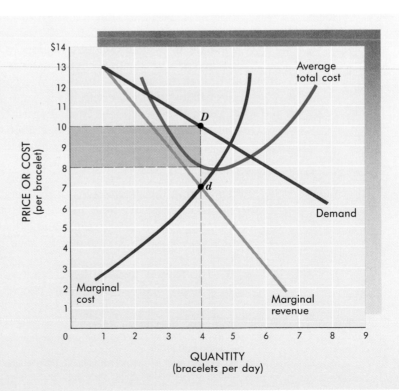

price minus *average* total cost. In this case, profit per unit is $2. Multiplying profit per unit by the quantity sold (4) gives us total profits of $8 per day, as illustrated by the shaded rectangle.

MARKET POWER AT WORK: THE COMPUTER MARKET REVISITED ───────

barriers to entry: Obstacles that make it difficult or impossible for would-be producers to enter a particular market; e.g., patents.

To develop a keener appreciation for the nature of market power, we can return to the microcomputer market of Chapter 22. This time we will make some different assumptions about market structure. In particular, assume that a single firm, Universal Electronics, acquires an exclusive patent on the production of the microprocessors that function as the computer's "brain."[2] This one firm is now in a position to deny potential competitors access to the basic ingredient of computers. The patent thus functions as a **barrier to entry,** to be erected or set aside at the will of Universal Electronics.[3]

The management of Universal is familiar enough with the principles of economics (including W. C. Fields's advice about never giving a sucker an even break) to know when it's onto a good thing. It is not about to let every would-be Horatio Alger have a slice of the profit pie. So we shall assume that Universal decides not to sell or give away any rights to its patent or the chips it produces and thus establishes itself as the sole producer of home computers. That is to say, Universal Electronics sets itself up as a computer monopoly.

economies of scale: Reductions in minimum average costs that come about through increases in the size (scale) of plant and equipment.

Let us also assume that Universal has a multitude of manufacturing plants, each of which is identical to the typical competitive firm of Chapter 22. This is an unlikely situation, because a monopolist would probably be able to achieve **economies of scale** by closing at least a few plants and consolidating production in larger plants. Universal would maintain a multitude of small plants only if constant returns to scale or actual diseconomies of scale were rampant. Nevertheless, by assuming that multiple plants are maintained, we can compare monopoly behavior with competitive behavior on the basis of identical cost structures. In particular, if Universal continues to operate the many plants that once comprised the competitive home computer industry, it will confront the same short-run marginal and average cost curves already encountered in Chapter 22. Later in this chapter we shall relax this assumption of multiplant operations to determine whether, in the long run, a monopolist may actually lower the costs of production below those attained by a competitive industry.

Figure 23.4*a* re-creates the marginal costs faced by the typical competitive firm in the early stages of the microcomputer boom (from Figure 22.3 and Table 22.1). We now assume that this MC curve expresses the costs of operating one of Universal's many (identical) plants. Thus the extension of monopoly control is assumed to have no immediate effect on production costs.

The market demand for computers is also assumed to be unchanged. There is no obvious reason why people should be less willing to buy com-

─────────────

[2]In actuality, several firms attempted to obtain such patents, but their applications were rejected by the U.S. Patent Office on the grounds that the microprocessors did not constitute a new technological process.

[3]At least as long as the patent is valid; patents expire at the end of 17 years (although they can usually be extended with product improvements). Other barriers to entry are discussed in Chapter 25.

puters now than they were when the market was competitive. Thus Figure 23.4*b* expresses an unchanged demand for computers.

Our immediate concern is to determine how Universal Electronics, as a monopolist, will respond to these demand and cost curves. Will it produce as many computers as a competitive industry in the same situation? Can it squeeze out more profits? Will it achieve comparable cost reductions? Will it improve the product as much or as fast?

The Production Decision

production decision: The selection of the short-run rate of output (with existing plant and equipment).

Like any producer, Universal Electronics will strive to produce its output at the rate that maximizes total profits. But unlike competitive firms, Universal will explicitly take account of the fact that an expansion of its output will put downward pressure on computer prices. This may threaten corporate profits.

The implications of Universal's market position for the **production decision** of its many plants can be seen clearly in the new price and marginal

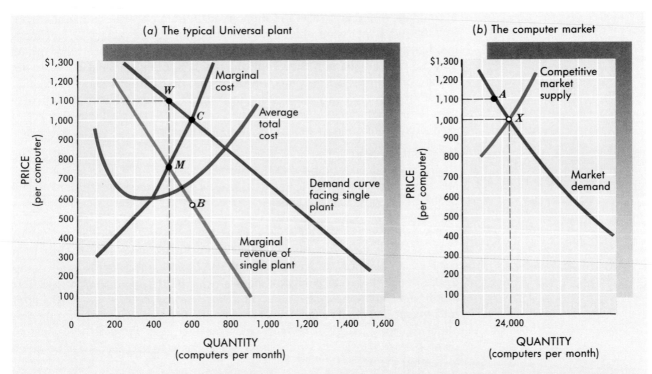

FIGURE 23.4 Initial Conditions in the Monopolized Computer Market

We assume that a monopoly firm (Universal Electronics) would confront the same costs (MC and ATC) and demand as would the competitive industry of Chapter 22. In the initial short-run equilibrium, the competitive price was $1,000 (point *C*). However, the monopolist is not bound by the competitive market price. Instead, the monopolist must contend with downward-sloping demand and marginal revenue curves. If each monopoly plant produced where MC = $1,000 (point *C* in part *a*), marginal cost (point *C*) would exceed marginal revenue (point *B*). To maximize profits, the monopolist must find that rate of output where MC = MR (point *M* in part *a*). That rate of output can be sold at the monopoly price of $1,100 (point *W* in part *a*). Part *b* illustrates the market implications of the monopolist's production decision: a reduced quantity is sold at a higher price (point *A*).

revenue curves imposed on each of its manufacturing plants. Universal cannot afford to let each of its plants compete with the others, expanding output and driving down prices. That is the kind of folly reserved for truly competitive firms. Instead, Universal will seek to *coordinate* the production decisions of its plants, instructing all plant managers to expand or contract output simultaneously, to achieve the corporate goal of profit maximization.

A simultaneous reduction of output by each Universal plant will lead to a significant reduction in the quantity of computers supplied to the market. This reduced supply will cause a move up the market demand curve to higher prices. By the same token, an expansion of output by all Universal plants will lead to an increase in the quantity supplied to the market and a slide down the market demand curve. As a consequence, each of the monopolist's plants effectively confronts a downward-sloping demand curve. These downward-sloping demand curves are illustrated in Figure 23.4a.[4]

Notice that in Figure 23.4b the market demand for computers is unchanged; only the demand curve confronting each plant (firm) has changed. A competitive *industry*, like a monopoly, also must obey the law of demand. But the individual firms that comprise a competitive industry all act independently, *as if* they could sell unlimited quantities at the prevailing price. That is, they all act as if they confronted a horizontal demand curve at the market price of $1,000. A competitive firm that doesn't behave in this fashion will simply lose sales to other firms. In contrast, a monopolist not only foresees the impact of increased production on market price but can also act to stop such production increases by its separate plants.

Marginal revenue   The downward-sloping demand curve now confronting each Universal plant implies that marginal revenue no longer equals price. Marginal revenue will fall faster than price because the additional revenues generated by increased computer sales are offset by the price reductions necessary to increase sales volume.

Notice that the marginal revenue curve in Figure 23.4a lies *below* the demand curve at every rate of output. Because marginal revenue is less than price for a monopoly, Universal's plants would no longer wish to produce up to the point where marginal cost equals price. ***Only firms that confront a horizontal demand curve (perfect competitors) equate marginal cost and price.*** Universal's plants must stick to the generic profit-maximizing rule about equating marginal revenue and marginal cost. Should the individual plant managers forget this rule, Universal's central management will be quick to remind them.

The output and price implications of Universal's monopoly position become apparent as we examine the new revenue and cost relationships of Figure 23.4. Recall that the equilibrium price of computers in the early stages of the home computer boom was $1,000. This equilibrium price is indicated in Figure 23.4b by the intersection of the competitive market supply curve with the market demand curve (point X). Each competitive *firm* produced up to the point where marginal cost (MC) equaled that price. This rate of output is indicated by the intersection of the firm's MC curve and the industry's price line (point C in Figure 23.4a). At that point, each competitive firm was producing 600 computers a month.

---

[4]The demand and marginal revenue curves in Figure 23.4a are illustrative; they are not derived from earlier tables. As discussed above, we are assuming that the central management of Universal determines the profit-maximizing rate of output, then instructs all individual plants to produce equal shares of that output.

The emergence of Universal as a monopolist alters these production decisions. Now each plant has to recognize that marginal revenue is less than price. Each Universal plant *does* have an impact on market price because its behavior is imitated simultaneously by all Universal plants. In fact, the marginal revenue associated with the 600th computer is only $575, as indicated by point *B* in Figure 23.4*a*. At this rate of output, the typical Universal plant would be operating with marginal costs ($1,000) far in excess of marginal revenues ($575). Such behavior is inconsistent with profit maximization and requires another look at the production decision.

The enlightened Universal plant manager will soon discover that the profit-maximizing rate of output is less than 600 computers per month. In Figure 23.4*a* we see that the marginal revenue and marginal cost curves intersect at point *M*. This intersection, which identifies the profit-maximizing rate of output, occurs at an output level of only 475 computers per month. Accordingly, the typical Universal plant will want to produce fewer computers than were produced by the typical competitive firm in the early stages of the home computer boom. Individual competitive firms, you will recall, had no incentive to engage in such production cutbacks. They could not alter the market supply curve or price on their own and were not coordinated by a central management. Thus the first consequence of Universal's monopoly position is a reduction in the rate of industry output.

The Monopoly Price

The reduction in output at each of Universal's plants translates automatically into a decrease in the *quantity supplied* to the market. As consumers compete for this reduced market supply, they will bid computer prices up. We can observe the increased prices in Figure 23.4 by looking at either the typical Universal plant or the computer market. Notice that in Figure 23.4*a* the price is determined by moving directly up from point *M* to the demand curve confronting the typical Universal plant. The demand curve always tells how much consumers are willing to pay for any given quantity. Hence once we have determined the quantity that is going to be supplied (475 computers per month), we can look at the demand curve to determine the price ($1,100 at point *W*) that consumers will pay for these computers. That is to say,

- *the intersection of the marginal revenue and marginal cost curves (point M) establishes the profit-maximizing rate of output.*

- *The demand curve tells us how much consumers are willing to pay for that quantity of output.*

Figure 23.4*a* thus confirms that Universal's monopoly position results in both reduced output and increased prices. This result is also evident in Figure 23.4*b*. Here we see that a smaller quantity supplied to the market will force a move up the demand curve to the higher price of $1,100 per computer (point *A*).

Monopoly Profits

Universal is not going through all this effort to establish a new market equilibrium simply to exercise our minds. Its objective was and remains the maximization of profits. That it has succeeded in its effort can be confirmed by a scrutiny of Figure 23.5. As you can see, the typical Universal plant ends up selling 475 computers a month at a price of $1,100 each (point *W*). The **average total cost (ATC)** of production at this rate of output is only $630 (point *K*), as we can see also in Table 22.1.

average total cost (ATC): Total cost divided by the quantity produced in a given time period.

FIGURE 23.5
Monopoly Profits:
The Typical Universal
Plant

The profit–maximizing rate of output occurs where the marginal cost and marginal revenue curves intersect (point *M*). The demand curve indicates the price (point *W*) that consumers will pay for this output. Total profit equals price (*W*) minus average total cost (*K*) multiplied by the quantity sold (475). Total profits are represented by the shaded rectangle.

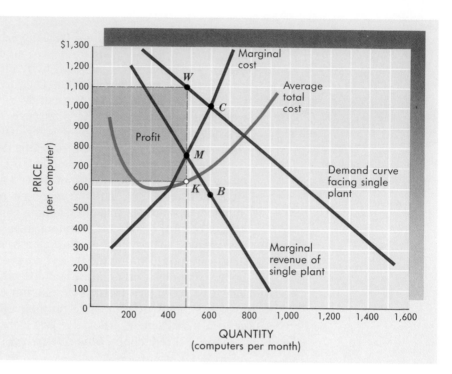

As always, we can compute total profit as

$$\text{Total profit} = \frac{\text{profit}}{\text{per unit}} \times \frac{\text{quantity}}{\text{sold}}$$

In this case, we see that

$$\text{Total profit} = (\$1{,}100 - \$630) \times 475$$
$$= \$223{,}250$$

This figure may be compared with the monthly profit of $180,000 earned by the typical competitive firm in the early stages of the computer boom (see Table 22.1).

It is apparent from these profit figures that Universal management has learned its economic principles well. By reducing the output of each plant and raising prices a little, it has managed to enlarge the size of the profit pie, while keeping it all to itself, of course. This can be seen again in Figure 23.6, which is an enlarged illustration of the *market* situations for the home computer industry. The figure translates the economics of our single-plant and competitive-firm comparison into the dimensions of the whole industry. Figure 23.6 reaffirms that the competitive industry of Chapter 22 initially produces the quantity q_c and sells it at a price of $1,000 each. Its profits are denoted by the rectangle formed by the points *R, X, U, T.* The monopolist, on the other hand, produces the smaller q_m and charges a higher price, $1,100. The monopoly firm's profits are indicated by the larger profit rectangle that is shaded in the figure. We see that *a monopoly receives larger profits than a comparable competitive industry by reducing the quantity supplied and pushing prices up.* The larger profits make Universal very happy and make consumers a little sadder and wiser. Consumers are now paying

**FIGURE 23.6
Monopoly Profit:
The Entire Company**

Total profits of the monopolist (including all plants) are illustrated by the shaded rectangle. The monopolist's total output (q_m) is determined by the intersection of the (industry) MR and MC curves. The price of his output is determined by the market demand curve (point A). In contrast, a competitive industry would produce q_c computers in the short run and sell them at a lower price (X) and profit per unit ($X - U$). Those profits would attract new entrants until long-run equilibrium (point V) was reached. (See Figure 22.8 for a summary of competitive market equilibrium.)

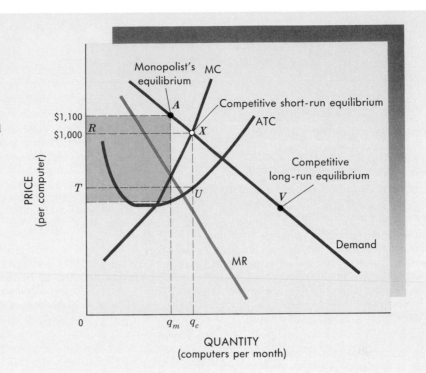

more and getting less, in effect, transferring additional income to Universal. Indeed, this kind of income redistribution is the primary objective of those who seek to establish and exploit market power.

Barriers to Entry   The higher profits attained by Universal Electronics as a result of its monopoly position are not the end of the story. As we observed earlier, the existence of economic profit tends to bring profit-hungry entrepreneurs swarming like locusts. Indeed, in the competitive home computer industry of Chapter 22, the lure of high profits brought about an enormous expansion of home computer output and a steep decline in home computer prices. In Figure 23.6 the long-run equilibrium of a competitive industry is indicated by point V. What, then, can we expect to happen in the home computer market now that Universal has a monopoly position and is enjoying huge profits?

Remember that Universal is now assumed to have an exclusive patent on microprocessor chips and can use this patent as an impassable barrier to entry. Consequently, would-be competitors can swarm around Universal's profits until their wings drop off; Universal is not about to let them in on the spoils. According to the accompanying In the News, Nintendo was similarly protected from competition. The Soviet Union used even more Draconian methods to protect its sable monopoly (see World View). In all of these cases, the competitive forces that earlier led to such a dramatic boom in computer sales are prohibited from going to work. As long as Universal is able to keep the competition out, only the more affluent consumers will be able to use computers. A monopoly has no incentive to move from point A in Figure 23.6, and there is no competitive pressure to force such a move. Universal may discover ways to reduce the costs of production and thus lower prices, but there is no *pressure* on it to do so, as there was in the competitive situation.

In The News

BARRIERS TO ENTRY

Congressman Seeks Antitrust Probe of Nintendo Marketing

Company Accused of Intimidating Retailers

The chairman of a House antitrust panel yesterday charged there is "strong evidence" that unfair marketing practices by Nintendo of America Inc. have monopolized the home video game industry and kept the prices of Super Mario and his buddies artificially high.

Rep. Dennis Eckart (D-Ohio) asked the Justice Department's antitrust division to investigate Nintendo, the U.S. subsidiary of a Japanese manufacturer that revived the domestic electronic game industry and now controls 80 percent or more of the $3.4 billion market.

Nintendo officials angrily disputed the charges and ac-cused Eckart of denying them an opportunity to defend themselves. "This guy is just grandstanding," said Howard C. Lincoln, senior vice president of Nintendo.

Eckart, chairman of the House Small Business subcommittee on antitrust, accused Nintendo of intimidating retailers to keep competitors' games off toy store shelves.

He said Nintendo has used exclusive software arrangements and physical computer-chip barriers to control the market, and he charged Nintendo had created artificial shortages of some games.

He said the result of Nintendo's marketing practices is that only games licensed or sold by Nintendo can be played on the Nintendo players, blocking independent software publishers and inflating the cost of games to consumers by an estimated 20 percent to 30 percent.

—William M. Welch

The Washington Post, December 8, 1989, p. D12. Reprinted by permission of The Associated Press.

W✪RLD VIEW

MONOPOLY

Foxy Soviets Pelt the West

Sable Monopoly Traps Hard Currency, Coats Capitalists

LENINGRAD—Crown sable from the eastern Siberian region of Barguzin, star of the Soviet fur collection, went on sale just as a deep freeze gripped this former imperial city.

It was a good day to sell furs and on that day late last month, the first in the 99th Leningrad fur auction, the Soviet Union collected a cool $30 million from merchants of high fashion gathered from around the capitalist world.

Fur is one of the Soviet Union's best known consumer goods exports. It is also bait for a country eager to trap hard currency: last year, the Soviet Union earned $100 million in fur sales.

In the case of sable, the Soviet Union has something no one else has—in capitalist lingo, a monopoly.

Ivan the Terrible is said to have made the sale of live sables abroad a crime punishable by death. Peter the Great on his travels in the West is said to have carried along trunks of sable skins to use as currency.

In the best-selling novel Gorky Park, popular among fur traders, it was the Soviet sable monopoly that was the key to the tangled tale of murderous intrigue.

There is another story, origin and veracity unknown, that an American once traded a rare North American species to the Soviets in exchange for two live Russian sables—only to find when he got home that they had been sterilized.

This year Neiman-Marcus bought about 3,000 sable skins, the highest priced at $560 for a pelt that could fit on a big cat. The skins must be carefully matched for texture and colors to make a coat. At least 50 pelts go into a street-length coat.

David Wolfe, Neiman-Marcus senior vice president, estimated that this year, the firm bought enough for about 10 top-quality coats, after the mixing and matching is done. The rest will go into sable jackets and trimmings, and any small pieces left on the cutting room floor will be swept up and sold in bags to be patched together elsewhere.

The careful selection process explains the final price for a sable coat: about $100,000 and up for the best.

—Celestine Bohlen

The Washington Post, Feb. 5, 1985, p. A10. Copyright © 1985 The Washington Post.

A COMPARATIVE PERSPECTIVE ON MARKET POWER

The different behavior of the microcomputer market under competitive and monopoly conditions illustrates basic features of industrial structures. We may summarize the sequence of events that occurs in each type of market structure as follows:

COMPETITIVE INDUSTRY

- High prices and profits signal consumers' demand for more output.
- The high profits attract new suppliers.
- Production and supplies expand.

- Prices slide down the market demand curve.
- A new equilibrium is established wherein more of the desired product is produced, its price falls, average costs of production approach their minimum, and economic profits approach zero.
- Price equals marginal cost throughout the process.
- Throughout the process, there is great pressure to keep ahead of the profit squeeze by reducing costs or improving product quality.

MONOPOLY INDUSTRY

- High prices and profits signal consumers' demand for more output.
- Barriers to entry are erected to exclude potential competition.
- Production and supplies are constrained.
- Prices don't move down the market demand curve.
- No new equilibrium is established; average costs are not necessarily at or near a minimum, and economic profits are at a maximum.

- Price exceeds marginal cost at all times.
- There is no squeeze on profits and thus no pressure to reduce costs or improve product quality.

In our discussion, we have assumed that both the competitive industry and the monopoly adjust their production schedules from some given point of departure—a fixed equilibrium in which the price of computers is $1,000. In reality, of course, an industry may manifest concentrations of market power *before* such an equilibrium is established. That is to say, the sequence of events we have depicted may be altered (with step 3 occurring first, for example). Nevertheless, the basic distinctions between competitive and monopolistic market behavior are evident.

To the extent that monopolies behave as we have discussed, they alter our output of goods and services in two specific ways. You remember that competitive industries tend, in the long run, to produce at minimum average costs. Competitive industries also pursue cost reductions and product improvements relentlessly. These pressures tend to expand our production possibilities. No such forces are at work in the monopoly we have discussed here. Hence there is a basic tendency for monopolies to inhibit economic growth.

Another important feature of competitive markets is their tendency toward **marginal cost pricing.** Marginal cost pricing is important to consumers because it permits rational choices among alternative goods and services. In particular, it informs consumers of the true opportunity costs of various goods, thereby allowing them to choose the mix of output that delivers the most utility with available resources. In our monopoly example, however, consumers end up getting fewer computers than they would like, while the economy continues to produce other goods that are less desired. Thus the mix of output shifted away from computers when Universal took over the industry.

marginal cost pricing: The offer (supply) of goods at prices equal to their marginal cost.

The power to influence prices and product flows may have far-reaching consequences for our economic welfare. Changes in prices and product flows directly influence the level and composition of output, employment and resource allocation, the level and distribution of income, and, of course, the level and structure of prices. Hence firms that wield significant market power affect all dimensions of economic welfare.

Market power is not the only kind of power wielded in society, of course. Political power, for example, is obviously a different kind of power and important in its own right. Indeed, the power to influence an election or to sway a Senate committee vote may ultimately be more important than the power to increase the price of laundry soap. Nevertheless, market power is a force that influences the way we live, the incomes we earn, and our relationships with other countries. Moreoever, market power may provide the basis for other forms of power. The individual or firm with considerable market power is likely to have the necessary resources to influence an election or sway a vote on a congressional committee. Hence market power is a critical dimension of both economic and social welfare.

The Limits to Power

Even though market power does permit a producer or supplier to manipulate market outcomes, there is a clear limit to the exercise of power. Even a monopolist cannot get everything it wants. Universal, for example, would really like to sell q_m computers at a price of $1,500 each, because that kind of price would bring it even greater profits. Yet, despite its monopoly position, Universal is constrained to sell that quantity of computers at the much lower price of $1,100 each. Even monopolists have their little disappointments.

The limitations to a monopolist's exercise of power are evident in Figure 23.6. Universal's attainment of a monopoly position allows it only one prerogative: the ability to alter the quantity of output *supplied* to the market. This is no small prerogative, but it is far from absolute power. Universal, and every other monopolist, must still contend with the market *demand* curve. Note again that the new equilibrium in Figure 23.6 occurs at a point on the *unchanged* demand curve. In effect, a monopolist has the opportunity to pick any point on the market demand curve and designate it as the new market equilibrium. The point it selects will depend on its own perceptions of effort, profit, and risk (in this case point *A,* determined by the intersection of marginal revenue and marginal cost).

The limitation to monopoly power arises from the fact that the monopolist has no direct control over consumer behavior. As a supplier, the monopolist can alter the choices available to consumers, but he cannot force them to pick any combination he desires. Universal could set the price of computers at $1,500 each, for example, but it could not compel consumers to purchase the number of computers it wished to sell at that price. Were the company to set such an exorbitant price, even the more affluent among us would go back to counting on their fingers.

price elasticity of demand: The percentage change in quantity demanded divided by the percentage change in price.

The ultimate constraint on the exercise of market power, then, resides in the market demand curve.[5] The greater the **price elasticity of demand** by consumers, the more a monopolist will be frustrated in its attempts to establish both high prices and high volume. Consumers will simply reduce

---

[5]Government regulation can also be used to constrain monopolistic behavior, but we are concerned here with market constraints.

their purchases if price is increased. If, however, consumer demand is highly inelastic—if consumers need or want that product badly and few viable substitutes are available—the monopolist can reap tremendous profits from market power.

Price Discrimination

price discrimination: The sale of an identical good at different prices to different consumers by a single seller.

Even in situations where the *market* demand is relatively elastic, a monopolist may be able to extract high prices. A monopolist has the power not only to raise the market price of a good (by reducing the quantity supplied), but also to charge various prices for the same good. Recall that the market demand curve reflects the combined willingness of many individuals to buy. Some of those individuals are willing to buy the good at prices higher than the market price, just as other individuals will buy only at lower prices. A monopolist may be able to increase total profits by selling each unit of the good separately, at a price each *individual* consumer is willing to pay. This practice is called **price discrimination.**

The airline industry has practiced price discrimination for many years. Basically, there are two distinct groups of travelers, business and nonbusiness travelers. Business executives generally must fly from one city to another on a certain day and at a particular time. They typically must make flight arrangements on short notice and may have no other way to get to their destination. Nonbusiness travelers (for example, people on vacation and students going home during semester break) usually have more flexible schedules. They may plan their trips weeks or months in advance and often have the option of traveling by car, bus, or train.

The different travel needs and opportunities of business and vacation travelers are reflected in their respective demand curves. Business demand for air travel tends to be less price-elastic than the demand of nonbusiness travelers for the same service. Few business executives would stop flying if air fares increased. Higher air fares would, however, discourage air travel by nonbusiness travelers.

What should airlines do in this case? Should they *raise* air fares to take advantage of the relative price inelasticity of business demand, or should they *lower* air fares to attract more nonbusiness travelers?

They should do both. In fact, they have done both. The airlines offer a "full fare" ride, available at any time, and a "discount fare" ride, available only by purchasing one's ticket in advance and agreeing to some restrictions on time of departure. The advance-purchase and other restrictions on discount fares effectively exclude most business travelers, who end up paying full fare. The higher "full" fare does not, however, discourage most nonbusiness travelers, who can fly at a discount. Consequently, the airlines are able to sell essentially identical units of the same good (an airplane ride) at substantially different prices to different customers. Indeed, by experimenting with various discount fares and travel restrictions, airlines can discriminate even more thoroughly among passengers, thereby reaping the highest possible average price for the quantity supplied. The same type of price discrimination is commonly practiced by doctors, lawyers, and new- and used-car dealers. In all of these cases, the seller may "adjust" the price to the income and taste of each individual consumer. In effect, the seller is able to "divide and conquer" the individual consumers who are positioned along the length of the market demand curve. A monopolist is best positioned to engage in price discrimination, since consumers have no competitive alternatives.

PROS AND CONS OF MARKET POWER —————————

Despite the strong and general case to be made against market power, it is conceivable that it could also yield some benefit to society. One of the arguments made for concentrations of market power is that monopolies have greater ability to pursue research and development. Another is that the lure of market power creates a tremendous incentive for invention and innovation. A third argument in defense of monopoly is that large companies can produce goods more efficiently than smaller firms. Finally, it is argued that even monopolies have to worry about *potential* competition and will behave accordingly. We must pause to reflect, then, on whether and how market power might be of some benefit.

Research and Development

The argument that monopolies are in a position to undertake valuable research and development rests on two facts. First, such firms are sheltered from the constant pressure of competition. Second, they have the resources (monopoly profits) with which to carry out expensive R&D functions. The manager of a perfectly competitive firm, by contrast, has to worry about day-to-day production decisions and profit margins. As a result, she is unable to take the longer view necessary for significant research and development and could not afford to pursue such a view even if she could see it. Thus, it is contended, market power is desirable because of the research and development opportunities it creates.

The basic problem with the R&D argument is that it says nothing about *incentives*. Although monopolists have a clear advantage in pursuing research and development activities, they have no clear incentive to do so. They can continue to make substantial profits just by maintaining market power. Research and development are not necessarily required for profitable survival. In fact, research and development that tend to make existing plant and equipment technologically obsolete run counter to a monopolist's vested interest and so may actually be suppressed (see In the News). In contrast, a perfectly competitive firm cannot continue to make significant profits unless it stays ahead of the competition. This pressure constitutes a significant incentive to discover new products or new and cheaper ways of producing old products.

A very limited but suggestive perspective on the intensity of R&D efforts in competitive environments can be gained by comparing different industries. The highly competitive semiconductor industry spends less on research and development than the much less competitive automobile industry. But the semiconductor industry is also much smaller. When relative size is considered, the semiconductor industry spends three times as much on R&D as the automobile industry does. In 1989, the semiconductor industry spent 9.3 percent of sales on R&D efforts; the auto industry spent only 3.4 percent.

The commitment of electronics firms to R&D has had dramatic effects on consumer products and prices. Cheap personal computers are just one example of the benefits of that competitive R&D. Had technology in the auto industry advanced as rapidly as it did in semiconductors—and had prices fallen as costs were reduced—the 1990 Cadillac would have been priced at less than $100 rather than over $25,000.

It is also important to observe that the R&D efforts that a monopolist does pursue will tend to serve his own interests and will probably enhance his market power. The result will be greater redistribution of income and welfare in his direction. Accordingly, if we wish to create research opportu-

𝔍𝔫 𝔗𝔥𝔢 𝔑𝔢𝔴𝔰

SUPPRESSING R&D

Jury Rules Magnetek Unit Is Liable For Keeping Technology Off Market

SAN FRANCISCO—Is a company liable if it deliberately keeps a technology off the market? Apparently so, judging from an unusual ruling by a California jury.

A county superior court jury in Oakland ordered a unit of Magnetek Inc. to pay $25.8 million to two California entrepreneurs and their companies. They charged that the unit had failed to bring the pair's energy-saving fluorescent-light technology to market in a profitable manner, suppressing it in favor of an outmoded technology.

The lawsuit reads like familiar legends of big business quashing inventions that threaten its interests.

"It's deeply ingrained in American folklore that this kind of thing goes on," said Roger Cook, a patent-litigation attorney at the San Francisco law firm of Townsend & Townsend. "But the provable instances have been few and far between."

In 1984, the two entrepreneurs, C.R. Stevens and William R. Alling, charged that Universal Manufacturing Corp., now a unit of Los Angeles-based Magnetek, buried a technology through which fluorescent lights use 70% less energy. The two said they sold Universal the technology, called a solid-state ballast, in 1981 after the company promised to market it aggressively.

Instead, they charged, Universal suppressed the technology to protect its less-efficient existing ballast models. "They told us they were going to be first on the market with our tech, yet they planned otherwise," said Mr. Alling. Mr. Alling said a study showed that the plaintiffs lost $54 million to $70 million in patent royalties that should have come from the sales of their solid-state ballast.

The jury award, he said, "Sends a message that you can't acquire a technology promising to put it out and not do anything with it." The jury awarded $18.3 million in compensatory damages and $7.5 million in punitive damages.

—Stephen Kreider Yoder

The Wall Street Journal, January 10, 1990, p. B2.

---

nities unattainable by the typical competitive firm, we need not embrace monopolies. A stronger case can be made for directly subsidizing R&D efforts (for instance, through tax credits or research grants) than for indirectly subsidizing them through the mechanism of monopoly profits. In that way, we could achieve our goals of innovation and growth without sacrificing our income-distribution goals.

To some extent, of course, all firms are capable of improving their productive efficiency as they acquire experience. That is to say, firms can develop improved techniques via the process of "learning by doing," a process that may not necessitate any research expenditures. Hence large firms may learn to cut costs as they grow larger. Small firms, too, however, can profit from experience and increase their efficiency. The critical question is whether experience-based improvements in efficiency are intrinsically related to output volume. We shall return to this argument—and potential economies of scale—in a moment.

Entrepreneurial Incentives

The second defense of market power is that monopoly profits act as a tremendous incentive for entrepreneurial activity. As we observed in Chapter 21, every business is out to make a buck, and it is the quest for profits that keeps industries running. Thus, it is argued, even greater profit prizes will stimulate more entrepreneurial activity. Little Horatio Algers will work harder and longer if they can dream of one day possessing a whole monopoly.

The incentive argument for market power is enticing but not entirely convincing. After all, an innovator can make substantial profits in a competitive market, as it typically takes a considerable amount of time for the competition to catch up. Recall that the early birds did get the worm in the competitive computer industry in Chapter 22, even though profit margins were later squeezed. Hence it is not evident that the profit incentives available in a competitive industry are at all inadequate.

We must also recall the arguments about research and development efforts. A monopolist has little incentive to pursue R&D and may have a vested interest in discouraging such efforts. Furthermore, those who might pursue product innovation or technological improvements for a particular industry may be dissuaded by their inability to penetrate the market. The barriers to entry that surround market power may not only keep out potential competitors but also lock out promising ideas. These impediments to entrepreneurship must be balanced against any unique incentives flowing from the promise of market power.

Economies of Scale

A third defense of market power is the most convincing and also the simplest. A large firm, it is argued, can produce goods at a lower unit (average) cost than a small firm. That is, there are economies of scale. Thus if we desire to produce goods in the most efficient way—with the least amount of resources per unit of output—we should encourage and maintain large firms. By increasing efficiency through economies of scale, large firms expand society's production possibilities.

Consider once again the comparison we made earlier between Universal Electronics and the competitive computer industry. We explicitly assumed that Universal confronted the same production costs as the competitive industry. We simply converted each typical competitive firm into a separate plant owned and operated by Universal. Thus Universal was not able to produce computers any more cheaply than the competitive counterpart, and we concerned ourselves only with the different production decisions made by competitive and monopolistic firms.

investment decision: The decision to build, buy, or lease plant and equipment, to enter or exit an industry.

As time passes, however, firms have an opportunity to make different **investment decisions** as well. In this long-run context, there is no compelling reason why we should assume that Universal will construct or maintain a multitude of separate plants. Why wouldn't it instead construct one large plant and centralize its manufacturing operations? One potential advantage to centralization would be an increase in efficiency and an attendant reduction in unit costs.

Even though large firms may be able to achieve greater efficiencies than smaller firms, there is no assurance that they actually will. As we observed in Chapter 20, increasing the size (scale) of a plant may actually reduce operating efficiency (see Figure 20.10). In evaluating the economies-of-scale argument for market power, then, we must recognize that efficiency and size do not necessarily go hand in hand. Some firms and industries may be subject to economies of scale, but others will not be. Therefore, each market-power situation must be examined separately.

natural monopoly: An industry in which one firm can achieve economies of scale over the entire range of market supply.

Natural monopolies Industries that exhibit economies of scale over the entire range of market output are often referred to as **natural monopolies.** In these cases, one single firm can produce the entire market supply more efficiently than any large number of (smaller) firms. As the size (scale) of the one firm increases, its minimum average costs continue to fall. These economies of scale give the one large producer a decided advantage over would-be rivals. Hence economies of scale act as a "natural" barrier to entry.

Telephone and utility services are classic examples of natural monopoly. A single telephone or utility company can supply the market more efficiently than a large number of competing firms.

Although natural monopolies are economically desirable, they may be abused. We must ask whether and to what extent consumers are reaping some benefit from the efficiency a natural monopoly makes possible. Do consumers end up with lower prices, expanded output, and better service? Or does the monopoly tend to keep much of the benefits for itself, in the form of higher profits, wages, and more comfortable offices? Typically, federal, state, and local governments are responsible for regulating natural monopolies to ensure that the benefits of increased efficiency are shared with consumers.

Contestable Markets

contestable market: An imperfectly competitive industry subject to potential entry if prices or profits increase.

Governmental regulators are not necessarily the only force keeping monopolists in line. Even though a firm may produce the entire supply of a particular product at present, it may face *potential* competition from other firms. Potential rivals may be sitting on the sidelines, watching how well the monopoly fares. If it does too well, these rivals may enter the industry, undermining the monopoly structure and profits. In such **contestable markets,** monopoly behavior may be restrained by potential competition.

How "contestable" a market is depends not so much on its structure as on entry barriers. If entry barriers are insurmountable, would-be competitors are locked out of the market. But if entry barriers are modest, they will be surmounted when the lure of monopoly profits is irresistible. Foreign rivals already producing the same goods are particularly likely to enter domestic markets when monopoly prices and profits are high (see accompanying World View).

Structure vs. behavior From the perspective of contestable markets, the whole case against monopoly is misconceived. Market *structure* per se is not a problem; what counts is market *behavior*. If potential rivals force a monopolist to behave like a competitive firm, then monopoly imposes no cost on consumers or on society at large.

The experience with the Model T Ford illustrates the basic notion of contestable markets. At the time Henry Ford decided to increase the price of the Model T and paint them all black, the Ford Motor Company enjoyed a virtual monopoly on mass-produced cars. But potential rivals saw the profitability of offering additional colors and features (e.g., self-starter, left-hand drive). When they began producing cars in volume, Ford's market power was greatly reduced. In 1926 the Ford Motor Company tried to regain its dominant position by again supplying cars in colors other than black. By that time, however, consumers had more choices. Ford ceased production of the Model T in May 1927.

The experience with the Model T suggests that potential competition can force a monopoly to change its ways. Critics point out, however, that even contestable markets don't force a monopolist to act exactly like a competitive firm. There will always be a gap between competitive outcomes and those monopoly outcomes likely to entice new entry. That gap can cost consumers

W🌐RLD VIEW

POTENTIAL COMPETITION

Contestable Markets

In 1983, the "Big Three" U.S. car makers, although technically not a monopoly, together produced over 95 percent of all American-made cars. But General Motors, Ford, and Chrysler still faced stiff competition. Foreign producers were selling over 2 million cars to U.S. consumers and millions more in foreign markets coveted by the Big Three. Competition accelerated even further when foreign producers started building factories in the United States (1978) and confronted the Big Three in their own backyard.

The experience of the auto industry underscores the importance of global markets in restraining monopoly power. As long as foreign producers are able to supply products to U.S. consumers—and even to build factories in the United States—domestic monopolies are unable to exploit their market power to the fullest. Attempts to in-

crease monopoly prices or profits may attract more foreign rivals. This potential competition may force monopolies to behave more like competitive producers—holding prices and costs down and seeking technological improvements.

From this perspective, the question for antitrust policy is not whether a monopoly exists but whether the market power is "contestable." Can potential producers (foreign or domestic) enter the industry if prices or profits increase? In other words, are the barriers to entry surmountable? If so, monopoly *structure* may not necessarily result in monopoly *behavior*.

As a practical matter, antitrust experts have tried to measure how "contestable" markets are. The basic measuring rod is the size of the monopoly price increase that would lure rival producers into the market. If only a small price increase would prompt new entrants into the market, then that monopoly market is highly "contestable."

a lot. The absence of *existing* rivals is also likely to inhibit product and productivity improvements. From 1913 to 1926, all Model Ts were black, and consumers had few alternatives. Ford changed its behavior only after *potential* competition became *actual* competition. Even after 1927, when the Ford Motor Company could no longer act like a monopolist, it still didn't price its cars at marginal cost.

POLICY INSIGHTS:

AT&T AND IBM

Antitrust Laws

antitrust: Government intervention to alter market structure or prevent abuse of market power.

Monopolies may have adverse effects on prices, output, technological advance, and the distribution of income. For this reason, federal, state, and even local governments have been empowered to prevent or regulate concentrations of market power. The legal foundations of federal **antitrust** activity are contained in three laws:

- *The Sherman Act (1890).* The Sherman Act prohibits "conspiracies in restraint of trade," including mergers, contracts, or acquisitions that threaten to monopolize an industry. Firms that violate the Sherman Act are subject to fines of up to $1 million, and their executives may be subject to imprisonment. In addition, consumers who are damaged—for example, via high prices—by a "conspiracy in restraint of trade" may recover treble damages. With this act as its principal "trust-busting" weapon, the U.S. Department of Justice has blocked attempted mergers and acquisitions, forced changes in price or output behavior, required large companies to sell some of their assets, and even sent corporate executives to jail for "conspiracies in restraint of trade."

- *The Clayton Act (1914).* The Clayton Act of 1914 was passed to outlaw specific antitrust behavior not covered by the Sherman Act. The principal aim of the act was to prevent the development of monopolies. To this end, the Clayton Act prohibited price discrimination, exclusive dealing agreements, certain types of mergers, and interlocking boards of directors among competing firms.

- *The Federal Trade Commission Act (1914).* The increased antitrust responsibilities of the federal government created the need for an agency that could study industry structures and behavior so as to identify anticompetitive practices. The Federal Trade Commission was created for this purpose in 1914.

Although the Sherman, Clayton, and FTC acts create a legal basis for government antitrust activity, they leave some basic implementation issues unanswered. What, for example, constitutes a "monopoly" in the real world? Must a company produce 100 percent of a particular good to be a threat to consumer welfare? How about 99 percent? Or even 75 percent?

And what specific monopolistic practices should be prohibited? Should we be looking for specific evidence of "price gouging"? Or should we focus on barriers to entry and unfair market practices?

These kinds of questions determine how and when antitrust laws will be enforced. The first question relates to the *structure* of markets, the second to their *behavior.* Both questions were the center of attention in two historic cases—against IBM and AT&T. The two cases were ended on the same day (January 8, 1982) but for very different reasons. Together they illustrate the central concerns of public antitrust policy.

AT&T: Extending a Natural Monopoly

The American Telephone and Telegraph (AT&T) Company long held a virtual monopoly on domestic phone service. As recently as 1981, AT&T provided 96 percent of all long-distance phone service and over 80 percent of local phone service. AT&T had total revenues of roughly $60 billion in 1981 (equal to 2 percent of GNP!) and profits of $7 billion.

The dominant position of AT&T in the telephone industry was widely viewed as inevitable. As noted earlier, telephone service tends to be a natural monopoly. One large firm can supply the market more cheaply than a multitude of small, competitive firms. The source of this natural monopoly lies in the economies of scale associated with transmission networks. Once the networks are in place, the marginal costs of increasing output are negligible. In recognition of this situation, the government permitted development of a monopolistic structure in the telephone industry.

While permitting monopoly structure, the government regulated AT&T's behavior. In particular, state utility commissions and the Federal Communications Commission (FCC) regulated the price and quantity of phone service while setting a limit on AT&T's monopoly profits. The objective of this regulation was to ensure that consumers reaped the advantages of a natural monopoly.

What got AT&T into trouble was its attempt to extend its monopoly beyond its "natural" limits. AT&T established a subsidiary, Western Electric, to manufacture phones and other equipment that could be connected to the transmission network. Because it controlled all telephone service, AT&T could effectively dictate whose phones would be used. By establishing Western Electric, AT&T was essentially proclaiming a monopoly in phone manufacturing and sales, as well as in the telephone service. There are no inherent economies of scale in phones themselves, so AT&T's move could not be defended as a "natural" extension of telephone service. Instead, the creation of Western Electric looked like a mechanism for transferring monopoly profits out of a regulated market (phone service) into an unregulated one (phone manufacture).

As the electronics revolution progressed, other firms wanted to produce and sell not only telephones but also more sophisticated long-distance services, including satellite transmissions. To do so, however, they had to have access to local AT&T transmission networks (including the users' phones). AT&T resisted all such attempts, arguing that the hooking up of non-AT&T equipment would harm the transmission network. When pressed by lawsuits or regulatory actions to permit such hookups, AT&T required costly and cumbersome connection devices.

As a result of such behavior, the U.S. Department of Justice filed suit against AT&T in 1978, arguing that AT&T and "their co-conspirators have used their positions of dominance in long-distance transmission, equipment manufacturing, and local franchise monopolies, and the leverage derived therefrom, to suppress this new competition and to maintain and enhance their monopoly power."[6]

As the federal suit against AT&T made its way through the courts, some of AT&T's competitors filed antitrust suits of their own. Two of these suits, by MCI, Inc., and Litton Industries, ended with huge fines against AT&T. The Federal Trade Commission and the U.S. Congress also increased the pace of their own investigations. By 1982 it was fairly clear that AT&T would not be able to defend itself successfully against the Justice Department's charges. Accordingly, AT&T agreed—without admitting to monopoly practices—to give up its monopoly position in local phone service.

The court-ordered split of AT&T's local and long-distance services created a new structure for the phone industry (see In the News). Local phone service is now provided by new and independent local telephone-service companies ("Baby Bells"), all of which remain under government regulation. The rest of AT&T ("Ma Bell")—including its long-distance service, Western Electric, and other subsidiaries—must stay out of local telephone service but is free to compete on an equal and unregulated basis in all other segments of the communications industry. The divestiture was completed on January 1, 1984. Now consumers can reap the advantages of enhanced competition in long-distance service and phone manufacturing, while continuing to enjoy the advantages of a natural monopoly in local transmission networks.

IBM: Big Is Not Necessarily Bad

The federal government's antitrust case against IBM was very different. Like AT&T, IBM dominated its industry. At the time the suit was filed in 1969, IBM was producing roughly 70 percent of all computers. The Justice Department argued that there was no "natural" basis for such dominance and thus that

---

[6]This was the third major antitrust case filed by the Justice Department against AT&T; the second one was settled by consent decree in 1956. That consent decree required AT&T to stay out of all new unregulated markets.

In The News

ANTITRUST

A New Era of Hot Competition

The game is monopoly. The board is the telecommunications industry, one of the fastest growing markets in the world.

For the past 50 years, nearly all the spaces on the board have been occupied by American Telephone & Telegraph Co., whose $66 billion in revenues this year will probably exceed all of the 1983 federal tax payments by all of the businesses in the United States.

On Jan. 1, the rules of the game will suddenly change, when a court-ordered split of AT&T's local and long-distance businesses takes effect.

Thousands of companies will grapple for chunks of the old AT&T empire and the outcome will affect how Americans communicate in a new age of information. It will decide the fate of AT&T, the largest corporation in the world and a unique American institution.

The stakes are great for millions of employees in the industry and its millions of shareholders. And the money on the table comes ultimately from the savings and spending of consumers.

The separation of AT&T's former local phone companies from the rest of the Bell System represents a gamble that consumers will benefit more from competition than from a continuation of AT&T's telephone monopoly.

"The whole basis of the antitrust law is that competition will drive prices down and will ultimately benefit the consumer," says U.S. District Judge Harold H. Greene, who is overseeing the AT&T divestiture. "Nobody has given any good reason why that shouldn't be true in the telephone industry." . . .

With increased competition, the long-distance business should boom, growing from about $45 billion to $100 billion by 1990, says Stephen Chrust, a financial analyst with Sanford C. Bernstein.

If the competition is strong, consumers could benefit from sharply lower long-distance charges, which could fall by 40 percent or more by 1990, says Robert LaBlanc, a telecommunications consultant.

—Caroline E. Mayer and Merrill Brown

The Washington Post, December 12, 1983, p. A1. Copyright © 1983 The Washington Post.

the structure of the computer market was considered to be anticompetitive.

It was further asserted that IBM's *behavior* stifled increased competition. Three specific practices were cited. First, it was alleged that IBM intimidated customers who wanted to connect non-IBM equipment (e.g., disk drives, add-on memories) to IBM systems (a charge like the one leveled at AT&T). Second, IBM was said to discourage prospective buyers of competing computers by "preannouncing" new IBM models. By hinting that a newer and better IBM computer was just around the corner, IBM could persuade customers to withhold orders from competitors. Finally, IBM was alleged to engage in aggressive price cutting whenever competition increased.

The IBM suit dragged on for thirteen years. During that time, over 66 *million* pages of documents were filed. Both the structure of the industry and IBM's behavior were contested. With respect to structure, IBM claimed the computer market was larger than the government alleged and growing enormously. Although IBM was dominant in one segment of the industry (large mainframe computers), it was a relatively small force in other segments (see Figure 23.7). Furthermore, IBM had to contend with aggressive competitors even in the one market segment it dominated. Hence, IBM argued, the charge of monopoly was baseless.

IBM also denied engaging in monopolistic behavior. IBM pointed out that it had no barriers to entry (unlike AT&T) and therefore had no power to create or maintain a monopoly. On the contrary, competitors were continually swarming like flies into the computer industry. All IBM was "guilty" of, it

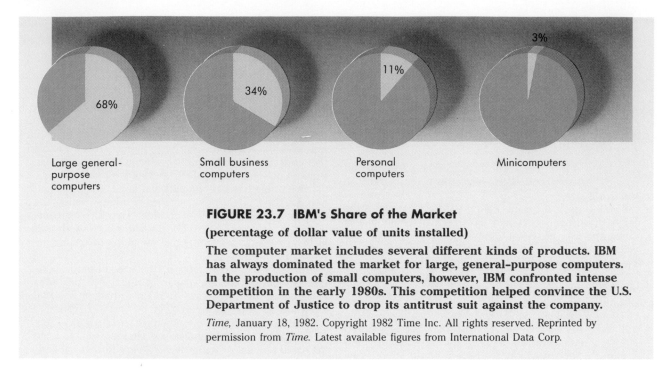

Large general-purpose computers   Small business computers   Personal computers   Minicomputers

FIGURE 23.7 IBM's Share of the Market

(percentage of dollar value of units installed)

The computer market includes several different kinds of products. IBM has always dominated the market for large, general-purpose computers. In the production of small computers, however, IBM confronted intense competition in the early 1980s. This competition helped convince the U.S. Department of Justice to drop its antitrust suit against the company.

Time, January 18, 1982. Copyright 1982 Time Inc. All rights reserved. Reprinted by permission from *Time*. Latest available figures from International Data Corp.

argued, was reducing prices, improving its products, and competing aggressively. In the process, consumers had benefited enormously from dramatic technological improvements in computer design and service and markedly lower prices.

On January 8, 1982, the Justice Department accepted these arguments and dropped the suit against IBM. In explaining his decision, Assistant Attorney General William Baxter said: "What we learned today is that a company that is large and has a large market share should be allowed to compete aggressively. Period." With those remarks, the government acknowledged that monopoly powers can either harm (AT&T) or benefit (IBM) consumers, depending on how that power is obtained and used.

SUMMARY

• Market power is the ability to influence the market price of goods and services. In product markets, such power usually resides on the supply side of the market, as consumers are too numerous and too independent to have any individual influence on the shape of the market demand curve.

• The extreme case of market power is monopoly, a situation in which only one firm produces the entire supply of a particular product, and thus has an immediate impact on the quantity supplied to the market and the market price.

• The distinguishing feature of any firm with market power is the fact that the demand curve it faces is downward-sloping. In the case of monopoly, the demand curve facing the firm and the market demand curve are identical.

- The downward-sloping demand curve facing a monopolist creates a divergence between marginal revenue and price. To sell larger quantities of output, the monopolist must lower product prices. A firm without market power has no such problem.

- Like other producers, a monopolist will produce at the rate of output at which marginal revenue equals marginal cost. Because marginal revenue is always less than price for an imperfectly competitive firm, the monopolist will produce less output than will a competitive industry confronting the same market demand and cost opportunities. That reduced rate of output will be sold at higher prices, in accordance with the (downward-sloping) market demand curve.

- A monopoly will attain a higher level of profit than a competitive industry because of its ability to equate industry (i.e., its own) marginal revenues and costs. By contrast, a competitive industry ends up equating marginal costs and price, because its individual firms have no control over the market supply curve.

- Because the higher profits attained by a monopoly will attract envious entrepreneurs, barriers to entry are needed to prohibit other firms from expanding market supplies. Patents are one such barrier to entry.

- The defense of market power rests on (1) the alleged ability of large firms to pursue long-term research and development, (2) the incentives implicit in the chance to attain market power, (3) the efficiency that larger firms may attain, and (4) the contestability of even monopolized markets. The first two arguments are weakened by the fact that competitive firms are under much greater pressure to innovate and can stay ahead of the profit game if they do so. The contestability defense at best concedes some amount of monopoly exploitation.

- A natural monopoly exists when one firm can produce the output of the entire industry more efficiently than can a number of smaller firms. This advantage is attained from economies of scale. Large firms are not necessarily more efficient, however, because either constant returns to scale or diseconomies of scale may prevail.

Terms to Remember

Define the following terms:

market power	**marginal cost pricing**
monopoly	**price elasticity of demand**
profit-maximization rule	**price discrimination**
marginal revenue (MR)	**investment decision**
barriers to entry	**natural monopoly**
economies of scale	**contestable market**
production decision	**antitrust**
average total cost (ATC)	

Questions for Discussion

1. The objective in the game of Monopoly is to get all the property and then raise the rents. Can this power be explained with market supply and demand curves?

2. Is single ownership of a whole industry necessary to exercise monopoly power? How might an industry with many firms achieve the same result? Can you think of any examples?

3. In addition to higher profits, what other benefits accrue to a firm with market power?

4. Why don't monopolists try to establish "the highest price possible," as many people allege? What would happen to sales? to profits?

5. Do consumers have any market power? Explain.

Problems

1. Use Figure 23.2 to answer the following questions:
   (a) What rate of output maximizes total revenue?
   (b) What is marginal revenue at that rate of output? What is price?
   (c) What rate of output maximizes total profit?
   (d) What is MR at that rate of output? What is price?

2. The following table summarizes the weekly sale and cost situation confronting a monopolist:

Price	Quantity demanded	Total revenue	Marginal revenue	Total cost	Marginal cost	Average total cost
$45.00	10			$160		
44.50	11			186		
44.00	12	$528.00	$38.50	214	$28.00	$17.83
43.50	13			244		
43.00	14			276		
42.50	15			310		
42.00	16			346		
41.50	17			384		
41.00	18			424		
40.50	19			466		
40.00	20			510		

   (a) Complete the table.
   (b) Graph the demand, MR, MC, and ATC curves.
   (c) At what rate of output is total revenue maximized?
   (d) What are the values of MR and MC at the revenue-maximizing rate of output?
   (e) At what rate of output are profits maximized?
   (f) What are the values of MR and MC at the profit-maximizing rate of output?
   (g) What are total profits at that output rate?
   (h) If a competitive industry confronted the same demand and costs, what price and output levels would emerge?
   (i) Suppose many competitors were to enter the market, bringing an end to the monopoly. What would be the lowest price that a firm with the foregoing costs could tolerate without being forced to exit from the market?

3. The following table indicates the prices various buyers are willing to pay for a Miata sports car:

Buyer	Maximum price
Buyer A	$50,000
Buyer B	40,000
Buyer C	30,000
Buyer D	20,000
Buyer E	10,000

The cost of producing the cars includes $50,000 of fixed costs and a constant marginal cost of $10,000.

(*a*) Graph the demand, marginal revenue, and marginal cost curves.

(*b*) What is the profit-maximizing rate of output and price for a monopolist? How much profit does the monopolist make?

(*c*) If the monopolist can price discriminate, how many cars will he sell? How much profit will he make?

(*d*) What techniques could the monopolist use to employ price discrimination?

Imperfect Competition

Although it is convenient to think of the economy as composed of the powerful and the powerless, market realities do not always provide such clear distinctions. There are very few perfectly competitive markets in the world, and few monopolies. But market power is an important phenomenon nonetheless. It's just that it is typically shared by several firms rather than monopolized by one. In the automobile industry, for example, General Motors, Ford, and Chrysler share tremendous market power, even though none qualifies as a pure monopoly. The same kind of power is shared by Coca-Cola, Pepsi, and Dr Pepper in the soft-drink market, and by Kellogg, General Mills, and General Foods in the breakfast-cereals market.

These kinds of situations, which fall between the extremes of perfect competition and pure monopoly, fall into the category of *imperfect competition*. They contain some elements of competitive rivalry but also exhibit traces of monopoly. In many cases, imperfect competitors behave much like a monopoly, restricting output, charging higher prices, and reaping greater profits than firms in a competitive market. But behavior in imperfectly competitive markets is more complicated than in a monopoly, because it involves a number of decision makers (firms) rather than only one.

In this chapter we shall focus on two major forms of imperfect competition: *oligopoly* and *monopolistic competition*. We shall examine the nature of decision making in each of these market structures and the likely impacts on prices, production, and profits. What we want to know is:

- What determines how much market power a firm has?

- How do firms with some but not total (monopoly) power set prices and output?

- How do imperfectly competitive firms "compete" for sales?

- What impact does imperfect competition have on prices, costs, and the mix of output?

After answering these questions, we shall look (in Chapter 25) at the actual behavior of some familiar firms that possess market power.

DEGREES OF POWER

Some individuals and firms have virtually no influence over the prices or the products they buy and sell, and thus no market power. They are constrained to reacting to market prices and are unable to change them by withholding production or purchases. Other individuals and firms do have some influence over prices and thus some degree of market power. The degree of power they possess, however, varies tremendously. As we saw in Chapter 23, AT&T was the sole supplier of telephone services in most urban areas of the United States for decades. As a result, it had tremendous market power. The corner grocery store, on the other hand, must compete with other stores and has less control over prices. But even the corner grocery is not completely powerless. If it is the only grocery within walking distance, or the only one open on Sunday—it, too, exerts *some* influence on prices and product flows. The amount of power it possess depends on the proximity and convenience of alternative retail outlets.

The same kind of gradations in power can be seen in thousands of products and market situations. Take the case of Coca-Cola. The Coca-Cola Company has an exclusive license to use that particular brand name. As a result, it is the sole supplier of Coca-Cola and can exert considerable influence on the price of that product. Coca-Cola's market power is diluted, however, by the availability and price of other thirst quenchers. If Coca-Cola's price rises too far, more and more people will switch to Pepsi, cold beer, or, as a last resort, water. Consequently, the ability of the Coca-Cola Company to alter prices—its market power—is far from absolute.

Market Structures

perfect competition: A market in which no buyer or seller has market power.

monopoly: A firm that produces the entire market supply of a particular good or service.

The many gradations of market power are summarized by several market structures. The case of absolute powerlessness is referred to as **perfect competition.** *Perfect competition is perfect in the sense that no buyer or seller of a particular product has any direct influence on the market price of that good.* Of course, the interactions of all buyers and sellers together still determine the market price. Each buyer and seller functions independently, however, and with no discernible effect on the market price. Were any single buyer or seller to change his or her behavior, the market price would remain the same. Such a situation exists when I sell my two shares of IBM stock or when Farmer Evans decides not to harvest his 30 acres of wheat. In each case, the dimensions of individual action are so small in relation to the size of the market that the action has no impact.

At the other extreme of market power is perfect **monopoly.** A perfect monopoly exists when only one individual or firm is the exclusive supplier of a particular product. In such a case, any change in the quantity supplied to the market by the monopolist is immediately reflected in the price and quantity sold of that good. Our illustration of Universal Electronics (the imaginary computer monopolist of Chapter 23) exemplifies such a firm. The amount of power a "perfect" monopoly can wield still depends on the availability of substitute goods, however. Even as perfect a monopoly as AT&T once was must take into consideration the prices of alternative communications media: Western Union, communications satellites, and the mail.

Between the two extremes of perfect competition and perfect monopoly lies most of the real world, which is imperfectly competitive. *In imperfect competition, individual firms have some power in a particular product market.* Two forms of imperfect competition are particularly noteworthy: oligopoly and monopolistic competition.

Oligopoly is a situation in which only a few firms have a great deal of power in a product market. An oligopoly may exist because only a few firms produce a particular product or because a few firms account for most, though not all, of a product's output. In either case, firms in an oligopoly are highly *interdependent*, because of their very small number. Changes in the price or output of one oligopolist immediately affect the others.

A more limited degree of market power is possessed by firms engaged in **monopolistic competition.** In this case, there are many firms supplying the market, not just a few. Because of the larger number of sellers, the individual firms are less interdependent than oligopolistic firms. An individual firm can alter its own price or output without directly affecting the other firms in the industry. At the same time, each firm has its own identity (brand name and image) in the market and can increase the price of its own output without losing most of its customers to its rivals.

Table 24.1 summarizes the characteristics of these market structures.

oligopoly: A market in which a few firms produce all or most of the market supply of a particular good or service.

monopolistic competition: A market in which many firms produce similar goods or services but each maintains some independent control of its own price.

TABLE 24.1 Types of Market Structure

Market structure varies, depending on the number of producers, their size, barriers to entry, and the availability of substitute goods.

Market structure	Characteristics
Perfect competition	A market consisting of many powerless firms. The production decisions of any single firm have no effect on other firms or the market price of the product it sells. Barriers to entry are minimal. Individual farmers are classic examples of perfect competitors.
Monopolistic competition	A situation in which many firms sell similar products, each of which is perceived by consumers as being in some way unique. Although each firm has some influence over the price at which its own output (brand) is sold, the production decisions of any single firm do not directly affect the sales or selling price of other firms (brands). Examples include gas stations, restaurant fast-food chains (McDonald's, Ponderosa, Burger King), supermarkets, and most apparel manufacturers.
Oligopoly	A market in which a few firms control such a large share of total industry output that they can influence market price. In *pure (perfect) oligopoly,* all firms produce an identical good (e.g., cement, steel rods, paper clips). In a *differentiated (imperfect) oligopoly,* each firm's product has a unique identity (e.g., cigarettes, breakfast cereals), although all are basically the same. In either kind of oligopoly, the production decisions of any single firm affect all other firms and the market price of the product sold.
Duopoly	A market in which two firms produce the entire market supply.
Monopoly	A market with only one supplier, who therefore controls the quantity supplied to the market and its price.

Determinants of Market Power

The amount of market power that exists in any given situation depends on several factors. ***The determinants of market power include***

- ***Number of producers***

- ***Size of each firm***

- ***Barriers to entry***

- ***Availability of substitute goods***

The most obvious determinant of power is the number of producers or sellers. When only one or a few producers or suppliers exist, market power is automatically conferred. In addition to the number of producers, however, the size of each firm is also important. One large producer competing with seventeen small ones may possess more market power than it would if it had to compete with only six relatively large firms. Other firms of comparable size at least have some ability to withstand pressures and threats to change prices or product flows.

A third and critical determinant of market power is the extent of barriers to entry for potential competitors. A highly successful monopoly or oligopoly arouses the envy of other profit maximizers. If it is a **contestable market,** potential rivals will seek to enter the market and share in the spoils. Should they succeed, the power of the former monopolist or oligopolists would be reduced. Accordingly, the ease of entry into an industry limits the ability of a powerful firm to dictate prices and product flows for any substantial period of time. In Chapter 23 we observed how a patent can be used to block entry. In Chapter 25 we shall examine other barriers to entry employed by powerful firms.

A fourth factor that defines the dimensions of market power is the availability of substitute products. If a monopolist or other power baron sets the price of a product too high, consumers may decide to switch to other products. Thus the price of Coors is kept in check by the price of Coke, and the price of sirloin steak is restrained by the price of chicken and pork. By the same token, a lack of available substitute products keeps the price of insulin high.

The absence of readily available substitutes may confer very great market power, as reflected in a very low price elasticity of demand for the product in question. Those who possess market power often attempt to extend and reinforce it by using advertising to create the impression that their product has no substitutes. If 10 million beer drinkers refuse to quench their thirst with anything but Coors beer, then the Adolph Coors Company will possess considerable market power. For loyal Coors drinkers, it simply doesn't matter how many other beer producers exist or how large they are. The same is true for Tide detergent, Maxwell House coffee, Coca-Cola, and Marlboro cigarettes. As long as each consumer identifies with and purchases only one brand, it doesn't matter how many other firms produce basically identical products: each consumer will have effectively imposed a monopoly on him- or herself.

contestable market: An imperfectly competitive industry subject to potential entry if prices or profits increase.

OLIGOPOLY BEHAVIOR

We can illustrate the behavior of a typical oligopoly by assuming a different market structure for the microcomputer market. In Chapter 22 we observed that the computer market was highly competitive in its early stages, when entry barriers were low and hundreds of firms were producing similar products. In Chapter 23 we created an impassable barrier to entry (a patent on the electronic brain of the computer) that transformed the computer industry into a monopoly of Universal Electronics. Now we shall transform the industry again, this time assuming that three separate firms (Universal, World, and International) all possess patent rights. The patent rights permit each firm to produce and sell all the computers it desires and to exclude all other would-be producers from the market.

The Initial Equilibrium

market share: The percentage of total market output produced by a single firm.

As before, we shall assume that the initial conditions in the microcomputer market are represented by a market price of $1,000 and market sales of 2,000 computers per month, as illustrated in Figure 24.1.

We shall also assume that the **market share** of each producer is accurately depicted in Table 24.2. Thus Universal Electronics is assumed to be producing 800 computers per month, or 40 percent of total market supply. World Computers has a market share of 32.5 percent, while International Semiconductor has only a 27.5 percent share.

The Battle for Market Shares

The first thing to note about the computer oligopoly is that it is likely to exhibit great internal tension. Neither World Computers nor International Semiconductor is really happy playing second or third fiddle to Universal Electronics. Each company would like to be Number One in this market. On the other hand, Universal, too, would like a larger market share, particularly in view of the huge profits being made on computers. As we observed in Chapter 22, the initial equilibrium in the computer industry yielded an *average* profit of $300 per computer, and total *industry* profits of $600,000 per month (2,000 × $300). Universal would be all too happy to take over the market shares of its fellow oligopolists, thereby grabbing all this industry profit for itself.

But how does an oligopolist acquire a larger market share? In a truly competitive market, a single producer could expand production at will, with no discernible impact on market supply. But *in an oligopoly, increased*

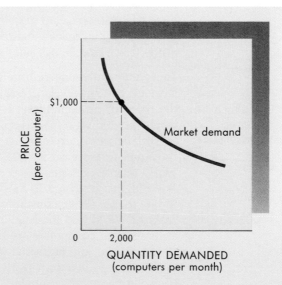

FIGURE 24.1
Initial Conditions in the Computer Market

As in Chapters 22 and 23, we assume that the initial equilibrium in the home computer market occurs at a price of $1,000 and a quantity of 2,000 per month. How will an oligopoly alter these outcomes?

TABLE 24.2 Initial Market Shares of Microcomputer Producers

The market share of a firm is the percentage of total market output it produces. These are hypothetical market shares of three fictional oligopolists.

Producer	Output (computers per month)	Market share (percent)
Universal Electronics	800	40.0
World Computers	650	32.5
International Semiconductor	550	27.5
Total industry output	2,000	100.0

sales on the part of one firm will be noticed immediately by the other firms.

How do we know that increased sales will be noticed so quickly? Because increased sales by one firm will have to take place either at the existing market price ($1,000) or at a lower price. Either of these two events will ring an alarm at the corporate headquarters of the other two firms.

Increased sales at the prevailing market price   Consider first the possibility of Universal Electronics increasing its sales at the going price of $1,000 per computer. We know from the demand curve of Figure 24.1 that consumers are *willing to buy* only 2,000 microcomputers per month at that price. Hence any increase in computer sales by Universal must be immediately reflected in *lower* sales by World or International. That is to say, increases in the market share of one oligopolist necessarily reduce the shares of the remaining oligopolists. If Universal were to increase its sales from 800 to 900 computers per month, the combined monthly sales of World and International would have to fall from 1,200 to 1,100 (see Table 24.2). The **quantity demanded** at $1,000 remains 2,000 computers per month (see Figure 24.1). Thus any increased sales at that price by Universal will have to be offset by reduced sales by its rivals.

This interaction among the market shares of the three oligopolists ensures us that Universal's sales success will be noticed. Moreover, it won't be necessary for World Computers or International Semiconductor to engage in industrial espionage to acquire the necessary information about Universal. These firms can quickly figure out what Universal is doing simply by looking at their own (declining) sales figures.

Increased sales at reduced prices   Universal could pursue a different strategy. Specifically, Universal could attempt to increase its sales by lowering the price of its computers. Following the **law of demand,** reduced prices would expand total market sales, as demonstrated by the downward-sloping market demand curve of Figure 24.1. Hence price reductions could enable Universal to increase its sales without directly reducing the sales of either World or International.

But this outcome is most unlikely. If Universal lowered its price from $1,000 to, say, $900, consumers would flock to Universal Computers, and the sales of World and International would plummet. After all, we have always assumed that consumers are rational enough to want to pay the lowest possible price for any particular good. It is unlikely that consumers would continue to pay $1,000 for a World or International machine when they could get basically the same computer from Universal for only $900. If there were no

quantity demanded: The amount of a product a consumer is willing and able to buy at a specific price in a given time period, *ceteris paribus.*

law of demand: The quantity of a good demanded in a given time period increases as its price falls, *ceteris paribus.*

difference, either perceived or real, in the computers of the three firms, a *pure* oligopoly would exist. In that case, Universal would capture the *entire* market if it lowered its price below that of its rivals.

More often, consumers perceive differences in the products of rival oligopolists, even when the products are essentially identical. These perceptions (or any real differences that may exist) create a *differentiated* oligopoly. In this case, Universal would gain many but not all customers if it reduced the price of its computers. That is the outcome we will assume here. In either case, there simply isn't any way that Universal can increase its sales at reduced prices without causing all the alarms to go off at World and International.

Retaliation

So what if all the alarms do go off at World Computers and International Semiconductor? As long as Universal Electronics is able to enlarge its share of the market and grab more profits, why should it care if World and International find out? Indeed, Universal might even get some added satisfaction knowing that World and International are upset by its marketing success.

Universal *does* have something to worry about, though. World and International may not be content to stand by and watch their market shares and profits diminish. On the contrary, World and International are likely to take some action of their own once they discover what is going on.

There are two things World and International can do once they decide to act. In the first case, where Universal is expanding its market share at prevailing prices ($1,000), World and International can retaliate by

- Stepping up their own marketing efforts

- Cutting prices on their computers

To step up their marketing efforts, World and International might increase their advertising expenditures, repackage their computers, put more sales representatives on the street, or sponsor a college homecoming week. This is the kind of behavior engaged in by rival beer companies and producers of aspirin (see In the News). Such attempts at **product differentiation** are designed to make one firm's products appear different and superior to those produced by other firms. If successful, such marketing efforts will increase the sales and market shares of World and International, or at least stop Universal from grabbing a larger share for itself. In either case, Universal's initial sales initiative will fail. To make matters worse, Universal may have to incur higher advertising or other marketing costs just to combat the efforts of World and International.

An even quicker way to stop Universal from enlarging its market share is for World and International to lower the price of their computers. Such price reductions will destroy Universal's hopes of increasing its market share at the old price. In fact, this is the other side of a story we have already told. If the price of World and International computers drops to, say, $900, it is preposterous to assume that Universal will be able to expand its market share at a price of $1,000. Instead, we assume that Universal's market share will drop substantially if it maintains a price of $1,000 per computer after World and International drop their prices to $900. Hence the threat to Universal's market-share grab is that the other two oligopolists will retaliate by reducing their prices. Should they carry out this threat, Universal would be forced to cut computer prices, too, or accept a greatly reduced market share.

product differentiation: Features that make one product appear different from competing products in the same market.

In The News

Marketing: Cold Cures Spread Like Flu as Companies Fight for Sales

Everyone knows the standard prescription for a bad cold: Take two aspirins and go to bed. That's still as good a remedy as most, but it hasn't deterred drug companies from bringing out product after product to stop sniffles, quiet coughs and dry runny noses.

Competition this year is fiercer than ever: More than a dozen new cold cures have hit pharmacy and supermarket shelves, with more on the way. The prize is a piece of the $1.2 billion cold-remedy market, among the largest in the nonprescription drug industry. The problem: Unit sales of cold medicines have been growing only about 3% a year.

"Because the market isn't very dynamic, brands succeed at the expense of others," says Emma W. Hill, a securities analyst with Wertheim & Co. "Companies therefore must maintain a steady flow of new products, enter new segments of the market, do anything to increase their shelf space."

Coming out with new products isn't easy. The ingredients available and levels that can be used are strictly limited by the Food and Drug Administration. A product's success often depends on a company's inventiveness in using these limited ingredients and on its marketing ability. . . .

The company to beat in this business is Richardson-Vicks, which markets 20 different lozenges, syrups, ointments, nasal sprays and other products for the treatment of coughs and colds. It claims to have 30% of the entire market "because we know the cold-remedy consumer and we gear our message to get a response," according to Ronald A. Ahrens, president of the company's health-care division. "Frankly, our products are no better or worse than anybody else's."

—Michael Waldholz

The Wall Street Journal, reprinted by permission of *The Wall Street Journal,* © Dow Jones & Company, Inc. (1982). All Rights Reserved.

The same kind of threat exists in the second case, where we assumed that Universal Electronics expands its sales by initiating a price reduction. As we noted earlier, World and International are not going to just sit by and applaud Universal's marketing success. They will have to respond with price cuts of their own. Hence ***an attempt by one oligopolist to increase its market share by cutting prices will lead to a general reduction in the market price.*** The three oligopolists will end up using price reductions as weapons in the battle for market shares, the kind of behavior normally associated with competitive firms. Should this behavior continue, not only will oligopoly become less fun, but it will also become less profitable as prices slide down the market demand curve (Figure 24.2).

THE KINKED DEMAND CURVE

The close interdependence of oligopolists—and the limitations it imposes on individual price and output decisions—is the principal moral of this story about Universal Electronics, World Computers, and International Semiconductor. We can summarize this story with the aid of the kinked demand curve in Figure 24.3.

Recall that at the beginning of this oligopoly story Universal Electronics had a market share of 40 percent and was selling 800 computers per month at a price of $1,000 each. This output is represented by point *A* in Figure 24.3. The rest of the demand curve illustrates what would happen to Universal's sales if it changed its selling price. What we have to figure out is why this particular demand curve has such a strange, "kinked" shape.

FIGURE 24.2
Rivalry for Market Shares Threatens an Oligopoly

If oligopolists start cutting prices to capture larger market shares, they will be behaving much like truly competitive firms. The result will be slide down the market demand curve to lower prices, increased output, and smaller profits. In this case, the market price and quantity would move from point *F* to point *G* if rival oligopolists cut prices to gain market shares.

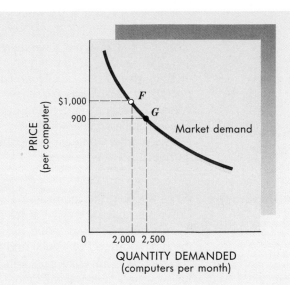

Price Reductions

Consider first what would happen to Universal's sales if it lowered the price of its computers to $900. In general, we expect a price reduction to increase sales. However, *the degree to which sales increase when the price is reduced depends on the response of rival oligopolists.* Suppose World and International did not match Universal's price reduction. In this case, Universal would have the only low-priced computer in the market. Consumers would flock to Universal, and sales would increase dramatically, to point *D*. But point *D* is little more than a dream, as we have observed. World and International are sure to cut their prices to $900, too, in order to maintain their market shares. As a consequence, Universal's sales will expand only slightly, to point *C*, rather than to point *D*. Universal's increased sales at point

FIGURE 24.3
The Kinked Demand Curve Confronting an Oligopolist

The shape of the demand curve facing an oligopolist depends on the responses of its rivals to its price and output decisions. If rival oligopolists match price reductions but not price increases, the demand curve will be kinked.

Initially, the oligopolist is at point *A*. If it raises its price to $1,100 and its rivals do not raise their prices, it will be driven to point *B*. If its rivals match a price reduction (to $900), the oligopolist will end up at point *C*.

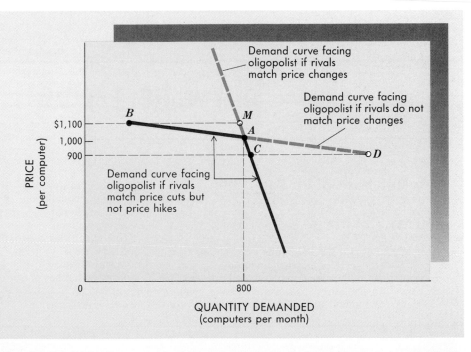

C reflect the fact that the total quantity demanded in the market has risen as the market price has fallen to $900 (see Figure 24.2). Thus although Universal's *market share* may not have increased, its monthly sales have.

The section of the demand curve that runs from point *A* to point *D* is unlikely to exist in an oligopolistic market. Instead, **we expect rival oligopolists to match any price reductions** that Universal initiates, forcing Universal to accept the demand curve that runs from point *A* through point *C*. The accompanying news clipping (below) illustrates such behavior in the auto industry, where one car company is forced to match the price reductions of its rivals.

Price Increases

What about price increases? How will World and International respond if Universal raises the price of its computers to $1,100?

Recall that the demand for computers is assumed to be price-elastic in the neighborhood of $1,000 and that all computers are basically similar. Accordingly, if Universal raises its price and neither World nor International follows suit, Universal will be out there alone with a higher price and reduced sales. **Rival oligopolists may not match price increases.** In terms of Figure 24.3, a price increase that it not matched by rival oligopolists will drive Universal from point *A* to point *B*. At point *B*, Universal is selling very few computers at its price of $1,100 each.[1]

Is this a likely outcome? Suffice it to say that World Computers and International Semiconductor would not be unhappy about enlarging their own market shares. Unless they see the desirability of an industry-wide price increase, they are not likely to come to Universal's rescue with price increases of their own.

Anything is possible, however, and World and International might match Universal's price increase. In this case, the *market price* would rise to $1,100 and the total quantity of computers demanded would diminish. Under such

---

[1]Notice again that we are assuming that Universal is able to sell some at a higher price (point *B*) than its rivals. The kinked demand curve applies only to differentiated oligopolies. As we shall discuss later, such differentiation may result from slight product variations, advertising, customer habits, location, friendly service, or any number of other factors. Most oligopolies exhibit some differentiation.

In The News

RESPONSE TO PRICE CUTS

Ford Matches GM on Rate Cuts

DETROIT, Aug. 6—Ford Motor Co. followed General Motors Corp.'s lead today by offering financing on car loans as low as 1.9 percent for 24 months, or cash allowances of up to $700 for most of its small and mid-size cars. . . .

Despite "extremely strong demand for Ford and Mercury cars" and a relatively low average dealer inventory of 63 days. "We intend to continue responding to these programs because we want to keep our dealers competitive and maintain our strong sales momentum," said Louis Lataif, Ford's vice president of North American Sales Operations.

GM, which has been suffering from large inventories and slow sales, yesterday announced its lowest rates in company history, with 1.9 percent financing for 24 months or rebates of up to $1,000. . . .

Reprinted with permission, Knight-Ridder Newspapers. Excerpt of article, 1987.

In The News

Texas Air Corp. Carriers Refuse to Boost Fares

Continental, Eastern Move Forces United to Cancel Increases It Had Initiated

HOUSTON—Texas Air Corp.'s Continental and Eastern airline units announced they wouldn't follow a fare increase initiated by United Airlines, forcing United and American Airlines to back down on the increase.

Industry analysts discounted the financial effect of the action by Texas Air's units explaining that the proposed fare increases were small and would affect only a small number of seats. Analysts also said, however, the quick reaction of United and American demonstrated the extent of the pricing power now wielded by the units of Texas Air, which has recently become the nation's largest airline-holding company.

—Paulette Thomas

circumstances Universal's sales would diminish, too, in accordance with its (constant) share of a smaller market. This would lead us to point *M* in Figure 24.3.

Gamesmanship We may draw two conclusions from Figure 24.3:

- The shape of the demand curve facing an oligopolist depends on the responses of its rivals to a change in the price of its own output.

- That demand curve will be kinked if rival oligopolists match price reductions but not price increases.

An interesting thing about oligopolies is the potential they create for gamesmanship. The appropriateness of an oligopolist's pricing decision depends on the expected response of its rivals. But this response is normally not known in advance; it must be guessed. For example, Universal *would* want to lower its prices *if* it thought its rivals would not retaliate with similar price cuts. It probably won't lower its prices, however, since it fears retaliation. Universal might be tempted to experiment a bit, though. It might offer a few large customers a discount, hoping World and International Would not notice or would not react to modest reductions of their market shares.

The potential cost of such experimentation is high, however. Selective price cutting may lead to an all-out price war over market shares. In this sense, oligopolistic behavior is not unlike the kind of Cold War games that the world's great powers play. Neither side is certain of the enemy's next move but knows it could bring total destruction. As a consequence, the United States and the Soviet Union are continually probing each other's responses but are quick to retreat from the brink whenever all-out retaliation is imminent. Oligopolists play the same kind of game on a much smaller scale, using price discounts and advertising, rather than nuclear warheads, as their principal weapons. The reward they receive for coexistence is the oligopoly profits that they continue to share. This reward, together with the threat of mutual destruction, leads oligopolists to limit their price rivalry.

Industry Price: The Monopoly Target

Thus far we have focused on a single oligopolist's decision about whether to change the price of its output. But how was the initial (market) price determined? In this example, we assumed that the initial price was $1,000 per computer, the price that prevailed initially in a *competitive* market. But the market is no longer competitive. As we saw in the previous chapter, a change in industry structure will affect market outcomes. A monopolist, for example, would try to maximize *industry* profits, all of which it would keep. To do this, it would select that one rate of output where marginal revenue equals marginal cost. And it would charge whatever price consumers were willing and able to pay for that rate of output (see Figure 23.3).

An oligopoly would seek similar profits. *The collective interest of oligopolists is to maximize industry profits.* To do so, an oligopoly must charge the same price as a monopolist would. Since the monopoly price *maximizes* industry profits, no other price will generate higher total profits for the oligopoly. The challenge for an oligopoly is to find that price and maintain it. This requires a common view of the industry demand curve, satisfaction with respective market shares, and precise coordination.

Sticky Prices

An oligopoly may not be coordinated enough to set the price that maximizes industry profits. Whatever price is established, however, will tend to be stable. This price stability is a direct consequence of the kinked demand curve and an even stranger-looking marginal revenue curve.

The kinked demand curve is really a composite of two separate demand curves (Figure 24.4). One curve is predicated on the assumption that rival oligopolists do not respond to price increases (d_1). The other curve is predicated on the assumption that rivals do respond to price cuts (d_2). Each of these demand curves has its own marginal revenue curve, as shown in Figure 24.4. The demand curve d_1 has **marginal revenue (MR)** curve mr_1, for example, while demand curve d_2 has marginal revenue curve mr_2.

---

marginal revenue (MR): The change in total revenue that results from a one-unit increase in the quantity sold.

FIGURE 24.4
An Oligopolist's Marginal Revenue Curve

A kinked demand curve incorporates portions of two different demand curves (d_1 and d_2). Hence a kinked demand curve also has portions of two distinct marginal revenue curves (mr_1 and mr_2). Below the kink in the demand curve (point *A*), a gap exists between the two marginal revenue curves. The segment *SF* comes from marginal revenue curve mr_1; the segment *GH* comes from mr_2.

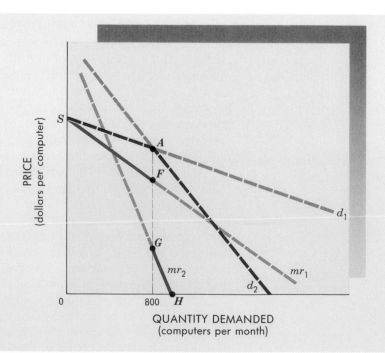

To the extent that oligopolists behave in accordance with the kinked demand curve, each firm confronts the possibility of starting down the demand curve d_1 and switching to d_2 at point A. Hence from point S to point A the curve mr_1 depicts the relevant marginal revenues. At point A (the quantity of 800 computers per month), however, we suddenly switch demand curves (to d_2). Hence we must seek out a new marginal revenue curve corresponding to d_2. To the right of point A, the marginal revenue curve mr_2 is operational.

The oligopolist's marginal revenue curve thus contains two distinct segments. In Figure 24.4, the first segment runs from point S to point F. The second segment runs from point G down to point H (below the horizontal axis MR is negative and so of no interest here).

Between points F and G *there is a gap in the oligopolist's marginal revenue curve.* Notice that *this gap occurs just below the kink in the demand curve.* This gap turns out to be an important explanation of an oligopolist's behavior.

profit-maximization rule: Produce at that rate of output where marginal revenue equals marginal cost.

Recall that *all* producers **maximize profits** by producing at the rate of output at which marginal revenue equals marginal cost. As a consequence, most producers alter their production decision when the costs of production change. In general, a reduction in production costs (a downward shift of the marginal cost curve) will lead to an increase in the rate of output. An upward shift of the marginal cost curve will lead to a cutback in production.

These expectations are not always fulfilled in an oligopoly. Look at the marginal cost curves in Figure 24.5. If the marginal cost curve passes through the gap in the marginal revenue curve, *modest shifts of the cost curve will have no impact on the production decision of an oligopolist.* That is to say, an oligopolist need not reduce its rate of output when costs rise somewhat or increase its rate of output when costs fall. As a consequence, an

**FIGURE 24.5
Sticky Prices**

The kinked demand curve confronting an oligopolist creates a gap in its marginal revenue curve. As a consequence, a change in cost may not have any impact on the production decision. In this case, higher (MC_2) or lower (MC_3) marginal costs do not change the profit–maximizing rate of output.

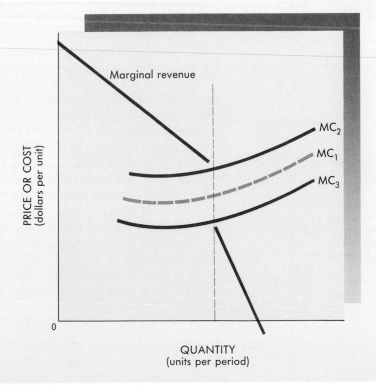

oligopolist's output does not fluctuate as much as either a competitive firm's or a profit-maximizing monopolist's. An oligopolist has a cost cushion around its production decision. This cushion allows the oligopolist to maintain a given price for longer periods and to incur higher marketing costs (such as advertising) if the need arises. In other words, the kinked demand curve results in "sticky" prices.

OLIGOPOLY VS. COMPETITION

Our examination of the demand and marginal revenue curves confronting an oligopolist reveals the close interdependence of rival oligopolists. Specifically, we have seen that *an individual oligopolist must consider rivals' responses before altering its own rate of output or price.* Now it is time to take a broader view of an oligopoly and compare its behavior with that of a perfectly competitive market.

Price Rigidity   A basic lesson to be learned from the kinked demand curve is that *oligopoly prices tend to be "sticky":* they will not fluctuate much. This stickiness arises from the fact that individual oligopolists cannot lower their prices without inviting retaliation and cannot raise them without risking sales losses.

The price behavior of an oligopoly stands in vivid contrast to that of a firm in a competitive market. A competitive market typically has thousands of individual producers. The survival of any individual firm depends on its ability to hold down costs. To increase profits, individual firms must reduce costs. Consequently, competitive firms are under constant pressure to lower their costs (and prices), knowing that some other firm is going to do so eventually. Competitive firms are not restrained by fears of "retaliation"; on the contrary, they are constantly being pushed toward price reductions.

The tendency toward price rigidity in oligopolistic markets is reinforced by the nature of the marginal revenue curves facing individual oligopolists. The gap we saw in oligopoly marginal revenue curves allows oligopolists to withstand modest changes in costs. No such flexibility exists in a perfectly competitive industry. Should a competitive firm experience a cost reduction, it will expand production to the point where marginal cost again matches marginal revenue (price). As other firms react in the same way, an increased market supply will drive prices downward. By the same token, a competitive firm cannot afford to absorb cost increases; it will have to cut back output until marginal cost again matches marginal revenue (price). As all firms respond similarly to cost increases, the market supply will diminish and prices will rise. Thus market prices will tend to rise and fall with costs in a competitive market but may not respond to cost changes in an oligopoly.

The greater size of the typical oligopolist also permits it to withstand changes in costs or demand. An oligopolist with profits in excess of $100 million a year is obviously in a better position to ignore small changes in costs or sales than the competitive firm with typical profits of less than $100,000.

Price and Output   The joint objective of an oligopoly is to establish a price that maximizes total industry profits. To do that, *an oligopoly will want to behave like a monopoly, choosing a rate of industry output that maximizes total indus-*

try profit. As we saw in Chapter 23, a monopoly will produce less and charge a higher price than a competitive industry with similar costs.

Clearly, both competitive industries and oligopolies desire to make as much profit as consumer demand and production costs will allow. But competitive industries experience relentless pressure on profits, as individual firms expand output, reduce costs, and lower prices. To maximize *industry* profits, competitive firms would have to band together and agree to restrict output and raise prices. If they did, though, the industry would no longer be competitive.

The potential for maximizing *industry* profits is clearly greater in an oligopoly, because very few firms are involved and each is aware of its dependence on the behavior of the others.

Coordination

The biggest problem oligopolists confront is how to coordinate their production decisions and so limit the quantity supplied to the market. ***There is an inherent conflict in the joint and individual interests of oligopolists.*** Their joint, or collective, interest is in maximizing industry profit. The individual interest of each oligopolist, however, is to maximize its own share of sales and profit. This conflict creates great internal tension within an oligopoly. Recall that each firm desires as large a market share as possible, at prevailing prices. But encroachments in the market shares of rival oligopolists threaten to bring retaliation, price reductions, and reduced industry profits. To avoid such self-destructive behavior oligopolists have a mutual interest in accommodation. Specifically, they have a mutual interest in coordinating their production decisions so that

- Industry profits are maximized.

- Each oligopolistic firm is content with its market share.

To bring about this happy outcome, the rival oligopolists could discuss their common interests and attempt to iron out an agreement on both issues. Identifying the profit-maximizing rate of industry output would be comparatively simple, as Figure 24.6 illustrates. The difficult issue would be the division of this output among the oligopolists—that is, the assignment of market shares. The outcome would depend on the relative strength of each firm and its negotiating skills.

collusion: Explicit agreements among producers to limit competition among them.

Unfortunately for oligopolists, all such explicit discussions, or **collusion,** are, according to the Sherman Act of 1890, "conspiracies in restraint of trade" and thus illegal. Corporations found to have colluded in this way are subject to stiff financial penalties and their executives may be sent to prison.

Because collusion is illegal (although not extinct, as we shall see in Chapter 25), oligopolistic firms must reach a consensus on total output and market shares in less explicit ways. One firm may "signal" its desire to reduce total output and raise prices by publicly announcing that it is studying the need for a price increase. This announcement gives rival oligopolists the opportunity to assess the implications of a move up the market demand curve. Should they agree that such a move is desirable, they may themselves announce similar "studies" of potential price increases, or they may simply increase their prices. This process, by which one oligopolistic firm "leads" its rivals to a change in price, is referred to as **price leadership.**

price leadership: An oligopolistic pricing pattern that allows one firm to establish the (market) price for all firms in the industry.

The firm that first expresses concern about potential price increases may be called the *price leader,* although leadership may also be retained by the

FIGURE 24.6
Maximizing Oligopoly Profits

An oligopoly strives to behave like a monopoly, maximizing total industry profits. Industry profits are maximized at the rate of output at which the industry's marginal cost equals its marginal revenue (point *J*). In a monopoly, this profit all goes to one firm; in an oligopoly, it must be shared among a few firms.

In an oligopoly, the MC and ATC curves represent the combined production capabilities of several firms, rather than only one. The industry MC curve is derived by horizontally summing the MC curves of the individual firms.

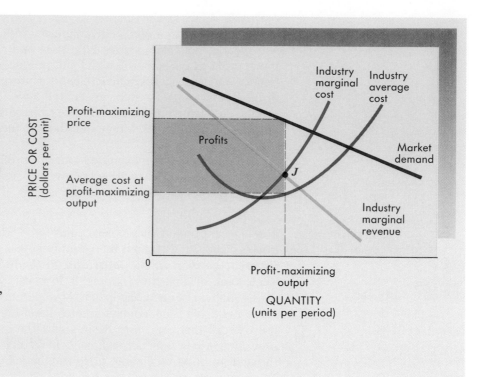

firm that casts the decisive vote on the size of the ultimate price increase. Typically, the firm with the greatest market share will have the most influence on the oligopoly's final price decision, even if it is not the first one to announce a price increase. Price leadership is a matter less of who raises prices first than of whose decision has the greatest influence on the oligopoly.

Some form of industry-wide coordination—be it explicit price fixing, price leadership, or informal experimentation—is required to establish the profit-maximizing price and rate of output for the industry. Once this price is established, the dynamics of the kinked demand curve ensure that it will be maintained—for a while, anyway. When the market demand curve or the cost curve shifts substantially, or when the rival oligopolists become dissatisfied with their respective market shares, a new price will be established. The accompanying World View discusses the problems OPEC has had in establishing and maintaining an industry-wide oil price acceptable to all participating oligopolists.

MONOPOLISTIC COMPETITION

However harmoniously an oligopoly may function, its existence is always threatened. On the inside, there is persistent tension for larger market share and the attendant threat of self-destructive price cuts. From the outside, there is the persistent threat that high profits will attract new firms into the industry. If the barriers to entry are not formidable enough, sooner or later the oligopoly will be destroyed.

The demise of an oligopoly does not necessarily lead to perfect competition, however. On the contrary, it is at least as likely that each of the many firms that enter the industry will establish its own identity ("brand image"),

W RLD VIEW

OLIGOPOLY TENSIONS

OPEC Prices

In 1979, the Organization of Petroleum Exporting Countries (OPEC) was selling the rest of the world about 31 million barrels of oil a day. At a price of nearly $34 dollars a barrel, the thirteen OPEC countries were reaping enormous oligopoly profits.

But then things began to unravel. The United States and other Western nations suffered serious recessions in 1980–82. These economic contractions reduced the demand for oil. The demand for oil was reduced further by changes in consumption patterns (e.g., smaller, more fuel-efficient cars; better home insulation). And the demand for OPEC oil was diminished by the increased availability of oil from non-OPEC countries (e.g., Norway, Great Britain, and Mexico).

These market forces doomed OPEC's oligopoly price. In a desperate attempt to maintain that price ($34), the OPEC countries agreed in 1986 to slash their production by over 40 percent, to only 17.5 million barrels a day.

Each member country agreed to cut back its own production to ensure that the quantity supplied to the market would stay at that level.

But cheating was rife. Ecuador complained that it needed to sell at least 283,000 barrels a day, not the measly 183,000 barrels assigned as its production quota. In order to finance its costly war with Iraq, Iran produced nearly three times its assigned quota of 1.2 million barrels. Nigeria offered oil at discount prices, further eroding the oligopoly pact. Ultimately, the price of oil collapsed, hitting a low of $10 a barrel in early 1987. OPEC members later agreed to new production quotas and set a new oligopoly price of $18 a barrel. The maintenance of that price depended on each OPEC member's accepting its designated market share. Individual members, however, tried repeatedly to increase their revenues by producing more oil than agreed. This caused oil prices to drop and intensified market-share disputes. Those disputes erupted into military aggression in 1990 when Iraq invaded Kuwait and threatened Saudi Arabia.

---

giving it some modest amount of market power. In this case, the industry will manifest *monopolistic competition.* Note that product differentiation (brand image) exists in either a differentiated oligopoly or monopolistic competition. The difference here is the number of producers; ***there are many firms in monopolistic competition, but only a few in an oligopoly.***

How will a monopolistically competitive industry behave? Will each firm act like an oligopolist? Or will the many firms that constitute the industry behave more competitively?

Independent Production Decisions

Once many firms enter an industry, each firm's market share will decline. Ultimately, there may be twenty-five firms in the industry, each with a market share of close to 4 percent. ***In monopolistic competition, modest changes in the output or price of any single firm will have no perceptible influence on the sales of any other firm.*** This relative independence results from the fact that the effects of any one firm's behavior will be spread over many other firms (rather than only two or three other firms, as in an oligopoly).

The relative independence of monopolistic competitors means that they don't have to worry about retaliatory responses to every price or output change. As a result, they confront more traditional demand curves, with no kinks. The kink in the oligopolist's curve resulted from the likelihood that rival oligopolists would match any price reduction (to preserve market shares) but not a price increase (to increase their shares). In monopolistic competition, the market shares of rival firms are not perceptibly altered by one firm's price changes.

Product Differentiation
A monopolistically competitive firm is distinguished from a purely competitive firm by its downward-sloping demand curve. Individual firms in a perfectly competitive market confront horizontal demand curves because consumers view their respective products as interchangeable ("homogeneous"). As a result, an attempt by one firm to raise its price will drive its customers to other firms. In monopolistic competition, each firm has a distinct identity—a "brand image." Its output is perceived by consumers as being somewhat different from the output of all other firms in the industry. As a consequence, *a monopolistically competitive firm faces a downward-sloping demand curve*—it can raise its own price without losing all of its customers to rival firms.

At first blush, the demand curve facing a monopolistically competitive firm looks like the demand curve confronting a monopolist. There is a profound difference, however. In a monopoly, there are no other firms. In monopolistic competition, *each firm has a monopoly only on its brand image; it still competes with other firms offering close substitutes.* The number and performance of such rivals will affect the position of the demand curve confronting any particular firm.

The In the News box shows the degree of brand loyalty associated with various products. A small price increase is not likely to cause a Marlboro smoker to switch to Kent cigarettes. Brand loyalty is less strong for paper towels, however, and virtually nonexistent for tomatoes.

In the microcomputer industry, product differentiation has been used to establish brand loyalty. Although virtually all microcomputers use identical

In The News

BRAND LOYALTY

Who Can Be Loyal to a Trash Bag?

When generic products were coming on strong a few years ago, J. Walter Thompson, the New York–based ad agency, gauged consumers' loyalty to brands in 80 product categories. It found that the leader in market share was not necessarily the brand-loyalty leader. At that time, Bayer aspirin was the market share leader among headache remedies, but Tylenol had the most loyal following.

Thompson measured the degree of loyalty by asking people whether they'd switch for a 50% discount. Cigarette smokers most often said no, making them the most brand-loyal of consumers (see table). Film is the only one of the top five products that the user doesn't put in his mouth—so why such loyalty? According to Edith Gilson, Thompson's senior vice president of research, 35-mm film is used by photography buffs, who are not your average snapshooter: "It's for long-lasting, emotionally valued pictures, taken by someone who has invested a lot of money in his camera." Plenty of shoppers will try a different cola for 50% off, and most consumers think one plastic garbage bag or facial tissue is much like another.

Fortune, August 5, 1985, p. 46. © 1985 by Time Inc. All rights reserved.

High-loyalty products	Medium-loyalty products	Low-loyalty products
Cigarettes	Cola drinks	Paper towels
Laxatives	Margarine	Crackers
Cold remedies	Shampoo	Scouring powder
35-mm film	Hand lotion	Plastic trash bags
Toothpaste	Furniture polish	Facial tissues

Brand names matter more in some products than in others, researchers find.

microprocessor "brains," the particular mix of functions performed on any computer can be varied, as can its appearance ("packaging"). Effective advertising can convince consumers that one computer is "smarter," more efficient, or more versatile than another. Also, a single firm may differentiate itself by providing faster or more courteous repair service. If successful in any of these efforts, ***each monopolistically competitive firm will establish some consumer loyalty.*** Thus it is able to alter its own price somewhat, without fear of great changes in unit sales (quantity demanded). In other words, the demand curve facing each firm will slope downward, as in Figure 24.7*a*.

Inefficiency

marginal cost pricing: The offer (supply) of goods at prices equal to their marginal cost.

Because the demand curve facing a firm in monopolistic competition slopes downward, such a firm will violate the principle of **marginal cost pricing.** Specifically, it will always price its output *above* the level of marginal costs, just like firms in an oligopoly or monopoly (see Figure 24.7*a*). As a consequence, monopolistically competitive industries will tend to restrict output and misallocate society's resources.

No long-run profit The long-run profit outlook in monopolistically competitive industries, however, is very different from monopoly or oligopoly. In oligopoly or monopoly, an above-normal rate of profit can be maintained indefinitely, because only one or a few firms ever participate in the market. In monopolistic competition, however, new firms can and do enter the market,

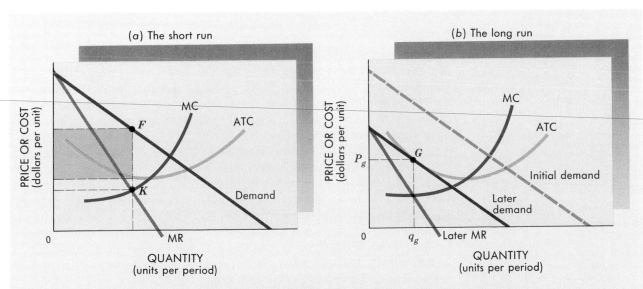

FIGURE 24.7 Equilibrium in Monopolistic Competition

(*a*) In the short run, a monopolistically competitive firm equates marginal revenue and marginal cost (point *K*). It sells the resulting output at a price (point *F*) above marginal cost. Total profits are represented by the shaded rectangle.

(*b*) In the long run, more firms enter the industry. As they do so, the demand curve facing each firm *shifts* to the left, as all market shares decline. Ultimately, the demand curve will be tangent to the ATC curve (point *G*), at which point price equals average total cost and no economic profits exist.

depressing average prices and profits. In the absence of significant barriers to entry, new firms will continue to enter a monopolistically competitive industry until its profit potential is no higher than that of alternative pursuits. Point G in Figure 24.7b illustrates the absence of **economic profit** in long-run equilibrium. At the profit-maximizing rate of output (q_g), price (p_g) equals average total cost. There are no economic profits.

Above-minimum cost   The zero-profit equilibrium of firms in monopolistic competition, as illustrated in Figure 24.7b, differs from the perfectly competitive equilibrium. In the long run, a competitive industry produces at the *lowest* point on the average total cost (ATC) curve and thus maximizes efficiency. In monopolistic competition, however, the demand curve facing each firm slopes downward. Hence it cannot be tangent to the ATC curve at its lowest point (the bottom of the U), as in perfect competition. Instead, the demand curve of a monopolistically competitive firm must touch the ATC curve on the left side of the U. Note in Figure 24.7b how point G lies above and to the left of the bottom of the ATC curve. This long-run equilibrium occurs at an output rate that is less than the minimum-cost rate of production. In long-run equilibrium, the monopolistically competitive industry is *not* producing at minimum average cost. As a consequence, monopolistic competition tends to be less efficient in the long run than a perfectly competitive industry.

economic profit: The difference between total revenues and total economic costs.

POLICY INSIGHTS:

NONPRICE COMPETITION

These models of oligopoly and monopolistic competition suggest that industry structure does affect market behavior. Of particular interest is the way in which different kinds of firms "compete" for sales and profits. ***In truly (perfectly) competitive industries, firms compete on the basis of price.*** Competitive firms "win" by achieving greater efficiency and offering their products at the lowest possible price.

Firms in imperfectly competitive markets do not "compete" in the same way. In oligopolies, the kink commonly found in the demand curve facing each firm inhibits price reductions, even when cost reductions might otherwise justify a lower price. In monopolistic competition, there is also a tendency toward reduced price competition. Because each firm has its own "captive" market—consumers who prefer its particular brand over competing brands—price reductions by one firm will not induce many consumers to switch brands. Thus price reductions are not a very effective way to increase sales or market share in monopolistic competition.

If imperfectly competitive firms do not compete on the basis of price, do they really compete at all? The answer is evident to anyone who listens to the radio, watches television, reads magazines or newspapers, or drives on the highway: ***imperfectly competitive firms engage in nonprice competition.***

The most prominent form of *nonprice competition* is advertising. An imperfectly competitive firm typically uses advertising to enhance its own product's image, thereby increasing the size of its "captive market" (consumers who identify with a particular brand). The Coca-Cola Company hires rock stars to create the image that Coke is superior to other soft drinks (see In the

In The News

The Cola Wars: It's Not All Taste

American consumers gulp nearly 40 million soft drinks per day. The Coca-Cola Company produces about 40 percent of those soft drinks, while Pepsi-Cola produces about 30 percent of the market supply. With nearly 70 percent of the market between them, Pepsi and Coke wage fierce battles for market share.

The major weapon in these "cola wars" is advertising. Coke spends over $100 million a year to convince consumers that its products are superior. Pepsi spends almost as much to win the hearts and taste buds of American consumers. The advertisements not only tout the superior taste of their respective products but also try to create a particular image for each cola.

The advertising apparently works. Half of all soft-drink consumers profess loyalty to either Coke or Pepsi. In their view, there is only one "real" cola, and that's the one they will buy every time. Few of these loyalists can be persuaded to switch cola brands, even when offered lower prices for the "other" cola.

Ironically, few people can identify their favorite cola in blind taste tests. Seventy percent of the people who swore loyalty to either Coke or Pepsi picked the wrong cola in a 1987 taste test.

The moral of the story? That in imperfectly competitive markets, product *image* and *perceptions* may be as important as product quality and price in winning market shares.

News), thereby creating brand loyalty. In 1990 oligopolies and monopolistically competitive firms spent over $100 *billion* on advertising for such purposes. Through advertising, an imperfectly competitive firm seeks to shift its own demand curve to the right, while perhaps making it less price elastic as well (see Figure 19.10). By contrast, **competitive firms have no incentive to advertise because they can individually sell their entire output at the current market price.**

Advertising is not the only form of nonprice competition. Before the airline industry was deregulated (1978), individual airlines were compelled to charge the same price for any given trip; hence price competition was prohibited. But airlines did compete—not only by advertising, but also by offering "special" meals, movies, more frequent or convenient departures, and "faster" ticketing and baggage services.

Is there anything wrong with nonprice competition? Surely airline passengers enjoyed their "special" meals, "extra" services, and "more convenient" departure times. But these services were not free. As always, there were opportunity costs. From an air traveler's perspective, the "special" services stimulated by nonprice competition substituted for cheaper fares. With more price competition, customers could have chosen to travel more cheaply *or* in greater comfort. From society's perspective, the resources used in advertising and other forms of nonprice competition could be used instead to produce larger quantities of desired goods and services (including airplane trips). Unless consumers are given the chance to *choose* between "more" service and lower prices, there is a presumption that nonprice competition leads to an undesirable use of our scarce resources. Hence there is a presumption that imperfectly competitive structures will result in higher costs of production and suboptimal allocation of resources. These considerations reinforce the justification for government antitrust activity (to prevent noncompetitive *structures*) as well as regulation of market *behavior* (e.g., deceptive advertising, price setting).

SUMMARY

- Imperfect competition refers to markets in which individual suppliers (firms) have some independent influence on the price at which their output is sold. Two prominent forms of imperfect competition are oligopoly and monopolistic competition.

- An oligopoly is a market structure in which a few firms produce all or most of a particular good or service; it is essentially a shared monopoly. Because oligopolies involve several firms rather than only one, each firm must consider the effect of its price and output decisions on the behavior of its rivals. Such firms are highly interdependent.

- A basic conflict exists between the desire of each individual oligopolist to expand its market share and the *mutual* interest of all the oligopolists in restricting total output so as to maximize industry profits. This conflict must be resolved in some way, via either collusion or some less explicit form of agreement (e.g., price leadership).

- Once a common oligopoly price is established, it trends to be fairly rigid, as illustrated by the kinked demand curve. The kink results from the threat of rival oligopolists to match price reductions but not price increases.

- The basic "stickiness" of oligopoly output and prices is reinforced by the gap that occurs in an oligopolist's marginal revenue curve. The gap itself occurs just below the kink in the demand curve and results from the switch from one marginal revenue (and demand) curve to another. Because marginal cost may not equal marginal revenue in this gap, small changes in cost need not alter the production decision.

- In monopolistic competition, many producers supply the market but each retains some independent control of its own price. The demand curve facing each firm is downward-sloping but not kinked. Firms in monopolistic competition engage in product differentiation, seeking to maintain and expand "captive" markets.

- In the long run, economic profits are eliminated in monopolistic competition by the entry of additional firms, even though minimum average costs are never attained.

- Oligopoly and monopolistic competition encourage nonprice competition instead of price competition. Because the resources used in nonprice competition (advertising, packaging, service, etc.) may have more desirable uses, these industry structures lead to resource misallocation.

Terms to Remember   Define the following terms:

perfect competition	product differentiation
monopoly	marginal revenue (MR)
oligopoly	profit-maximization rule
monopolistic competition	collusion
contestable market	price leadership
market share	marginal cost pricing
quantity demanded	economic profit
law of demand	

Questions for Discussion

1. Can an oligopolist ever increase its market share? How?

2. What is the function of advertising in monopolistic competition? Provide specific examples.

3. What prevents other firms from entering an oligopolistic industry and sharing in the profits? Give some examples.

4. The personal computer industry came to be dominated by IBM and Apple. Given this oligopolistic structure, what has kept computer prices so low?

Problems

1. By drawing a linear industry demand curve, a corresponding marginal revenue curve, and standard average and marginal cost curves, depict each of the following situations on the same graph:
   (a) Short-run equilibrium output in competition
   (b) Long-run equilibrium output in competition
   (c) Long-run equilibrium output in monopoly
   (d) Long-run equilibrium output in monopolistic competition

   (Note the relationship between industry entry and shifts of the industry cost curves.)

2. Suppose that the following schedule summarizes the sales (demand) situation confronting an oligopolist:

Price (per unit)	$8	$10	$12	$14	$16	$17	$18	$19	$20
Quantity demanded (units per period)	9	8	7	6	5	4	3	2	1

   Using the figures provided:
   (a) Draw the demand and marginal revenue curves facing the firm.
   (b) Identify the profit-maximizing rate of output in a situation where marginal cost is constant at $10 per unit.

3. Suppose the initial demand (D_1) confronting a monopolistically competitive firm is summarized by

   $$D_1: \text{quantity demanded} = 30 - (3 \times \text{price})$$

   Thus at a price of $5, the quantity demanded is equal to 15.
   (a) Complete a demand schedule and draw the demand and marginal revenue curves.
   (b) If the marginal cost is constant at $7, what is the optimal rate of output?
   Now suppose the firm starts advertising, spending $2 on every unit of output for that purpose. As a result of its advertising campaign, demand shifts to

   $$D_2: \text{quantity demanded} = 36 - (2 \times \text{price})$$

   (c) Graph the new demand and marginal revenue curves on the graph drawn in part a.
   (d) What has happened to the optimal rate of output?

PART B
CHAPTERS 25, 26, 27, 28

PRODUCT MARKETS:
Issues

Microeconomic theory provides insights into how prices and product flows are determined. Sometimes those market outcomes may not be optimal. In such cases, we may seek government intervention to alter market structure or behavior. In Chapters 25–28 we examine this possibility in the areas of antitrust, regulation, environmental protection, and farm policy.

Market Power and Antitrust

*C*hapters 22–24 examined the potential of market power to restrict output, raise prices, and command above-normal profits. But we have not yet demonstrated how much market power actually exists in American product markets or how it is used. In this chapter we attempt to measure the extent of market power in U.S. product markets and assess its impact on the economy. We are specifically concerned with the following questions:

- How is market power measured?

- How do firms use their market power?

- What should the government do about it?

In seeking to answer these questions, we must remain mindful of the warning given by Adam Smith in 1776: "People of the same trade seldom meet together, but the conversation ends in a conspiracy against the public, or in some diversion to raise prices."

BUSINESS ORGANIZATION

More than *17 million* business firms produce goods and services in the United States. Among these firms are 218,000 grocery stores, 216,000 gas stations, 40,000 pizza parlors, and over 50,000 movie-rental outlets. Among them also are a handful of giant computer firms that provide the machinery for counting and classifying the millions of other firms.

Business Types   Most people think all U.S. business firms are corporations. This is far from the truth. As Table 25.1 shows, corporations account for only 19 percent of all business firms. Much more common are the other two forms of business enterprise, proprietorships and partnerships. The primary distinction among these three forms lies in their ownership characteristics. A single proprietorship is a firm owned by one individual. A partnership is owned by a small number of individuals. A corporation is typically owned by many—even hundreds of thousands—individuals (stockholders).

631

TABLE 25.1 Number and Types of Business Firms, by Industry

Millions of business firms supply goods and service to U.S. product markets. They are organized as proprietorships, partnerships, or corporations. Most proprietorships are found in agriculture, services, and retail trade.

Industry	Proprietorship		Partnership		Corporation		Total	
	Number (thousands)	Percentage of industry	Number (thousands)	Percentage of industry	Number (thousands)	Percentage of industry	Number (thousands)	Percentage of industry
Agriculture	1,809	87	200	10	67	3	2,088	100
Mining	160	63	53	21	40	16	253	100
Construction	1,577	80	61	3	342	17	1,980	100
Manufacturing	329	51	28	4	285	45	642	100
Transportation, public utilities	576	78	21	3	138	19	735	100
Wholesale trade	304	47	23	4	314	49	641	100
Retail trade	1,886	71	151	6	621	23	2,658	100
Financial, insurance, real estate	1,129	45	853	34	537	21	2,519	100
Services	5,738	81	325	5	1,012	14	7,095	100
Total, all industries	12,394*	71	1,703*	10	3,429*	19	17,526*	100

*Sums do not total because business not allocable to individual industries are included.
Source: U.S. Department of Commerce, *Statistical Abstract of the United States,* 1990.

One consequence of different ownership structures is reflected in the disparate size of proprietorships, partnerships, and corporations. In general, the more people you can get to invest in a firm, the larger its potential size. As a rule, corporations tend to be much larger than the other two forms, because they bring together the financial resources of more individuals. Single proprietorships are typically quite small, because few individuals have vast sources of wealth or credit. The typical proprietorship has less than $10,000 in assets, whereas the average corporation has assets in excess of $1 million. As a result of their size, corporations dominate market transactions, accounting for 87 percent of all business sales.

We can describe who's who in the business community, then, in two very different ways. In terms of numbers, the single proprietorship is the most common type of business firm in America. Proprietorships are particularly dominant in agriculture (the family farm), retail trade (the corner grocery store), and services (your dentist). In terms of size, however, the corporation is the dominant force in the economy (see Figure 25.1). The four largest nonfinancial corporations in the country (GM, Exxon, Ford, IBM) alone have more assets than *all* the 12 million proprietorships represented in Table 25.1. Just one of the four, General Motors, commands over $170 billion in assets and $130 billion in sales and employs more than 500,000 workers (and pays its president ten times as much as we pay the president of the country). Even in agriculture, where corporate entities are still comparatively rare, the few "agribusiness" corporations are so large as to dominate many thousands of small farms.

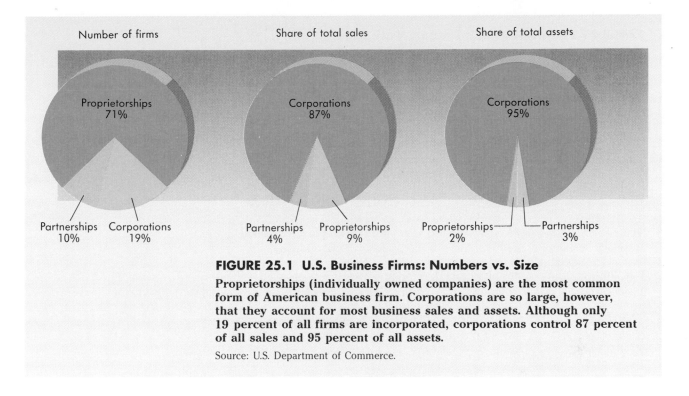

Number of firms — Share of total sales — Share of total assets

Proprietorships 71% / Partnerships 10% / Corporations 19%

Corporations 87% / Partnerships 4% / Proprietorships 9%

Corporations 95% / Proprietorships 2% / Partnerships 3%

FIGURE 25.1 U.S. Business Firms: Numbers vs. Size

Proprietorships (individually owned companies) are the most common form of American business firm. Corporations are so large, however, that they account for most business sales and assets. Although only 19 percent of all firms are incorporated, corporations control 87 percent of all sales and 95 percent of all assets.

Source: U.S. Department of Commerce.

Market Power

market power: The ability to alter the market price of a good or service.

Although corporations control the lion's share of U.S. business, we should not conclude that all corporations are powerful. As noted in Chapters 22–24, **market power** is bestowed by many different factors. The degree of market power possessed by any single firm is determined by

• The number of producers in the market

• Their relative size

• The extent of barriers to entry

• The availability of substitute products

All of these factors are important in both theory and fact. Nevertheless, it is useful—and far simpler—to focus on just one measure of market power to attain some perspective on the structure of U.S. product markets.

Concentration Ratio

concentration ratio: The proportion of total industry output produced by the largest firms (usually the four largest).

The standard measure of market power is the **concentration ratio.** This ratio tells the share of output (or combined market share) accounted for by the largest firms in an industry. Using this ratio, one can readily distinguish between an industry composed of hundreds of small, relatively powerless firms and another industry also composed of hundreds of firms but dominated by a few that are large and powerful. Thus *the concentration ratio is a measure of market power that relates the size of firms to the size of the product market.*

Table 25.2 gives the concentration ratios for selected products in the United States. The standard measure used here depicts the proportion of domestic production accounted for by the largest firms, usually the four larg-

TABLE 25.2   Power in U.S. Product Markets

The domestic production of many familiar products is concentrated among a few firms. These firms have substantial control over the quantity supplied to the market and thus over market price. The concentration ratio measures the share of total domestic output produced by the largest producers in a given market.

Product	Largest firms	Concentration ratio (percent)
Automobiles	General Motors, Ford, Chrysler, Honda	97
Telephone service (long distance)	**AT&T**, MCI, U.S. Sprint	89
Chewing gum	**Wm. Wrigley**, Warner-Lambert, Squibb, Philip Morris	97
Toothpaste	**Procter & Gamble,** Colgate-Palmolive, Lever Bros., Beecham	85
Tennis balls	**Pepsico** (Wilson), Gen Corp (Penn), Dunlop, Spalding	100
Breakfast cereals	**Kellogg,** General Mills, General Foods, Quaker Oats	85
Instant breakfast	**Carnation,** Pillsbury, Dean Foods	100
Cigarettes	**Philip Morris,** RJR Nabisco, Brown & Williamson, Lorillard	90
Razor blades	**Gillette**, Warner-Lambert (Schick), Procter & Gamble (Wilkinson), Philip Morris (American Safety)	98
Electric razors	**Norelco,** Remington, Warner-Lambert, Sunbeam	96
Sanitary napkins	**Johnson & Johnson,** Kimberly-Clark, Procter & Gamble	96
Handguns	**Smith & Wesson,** Sturm, Ruger, Colt, Harrington & Richardson	76
Car rentals	Hertz, Avis, National, Budget	94
Canned soup	**Campbell,** Heinz, Progresso	85
Cameras and film	**Eastman Kodak,** Polaroid, Bell & Howell, Berkey Photo	98
Perfume	Estée Lauder, Cosmair, Unilever, Revlon	67
Pet food	Ralston Purina, Carnation, Quaker Oats, Heinz	63
Contact lens care	Bausch & Lomb, Allergan Optical, Alcon, Coopervision	90
Aspirin	Johnson & Johnson, Bristol-Myers, American Home Products, Sterling Drug	78
Disposable diapers	**Procter & Gamble,** Kimberly-Clark, Curity, Romar Tissue Mills	99
Detergents	**Procter & Gamble,** Lever Bros., Colgate-Palmolive	86
Soft drinks	**Coca-Cola,** Pepsico, Hicks and Haas (7-Up, Dr Pepper, A&W)	81
Office typewriters	**IBM,** Royal, SCM, Olivetti	85
Portable typewriters	**SCM,** Royal, Brother, Olivetti	86
Records and tapes	Warner Bros., Sony, Capitol, General Electric (RCA)	54
Tires and tubes	Goodyear, Firestone, Uniroyal, B. F. Goodrich	85
Coffee	Philip Morris, Procter & Gamble, Hills Bros., Chock Full o' Nuts	75
Chocolate candy	**Mars**, Hershey, Peter Paul, Cadbury, Nestlé	85
Beer	**Anheuser-Busch,** Philip Morris (Miller), Stroh, Coors	86
Jeans	Levi Strauss, VF Industries (Lee, Wrangler, Blue Bell)	52
Home computers	**Commodore,** Atari, Tandy	85
Sports shoes	Reebok, Nike, Converse, L.A. Gear	61
Telephones	**Western Electric,** General Telephone, United Telecommunications, Continental Telephone	95
Air travel	American, United Air Lines, Delta, Northwest	58
Bicycles	**Huffy,** Murray Ohio, Schwinn, AMF	67
Greeting cards	**Hallmark,** American Greetings, Gibson	86
Cable TV (for-pay)	Time-Warner (HBO), Viacom (Showtime), Cinemax, Movie Channel	83

Sources: Data from Federal Trade Commission, *The Wall Street Journal, Advertising Age, Financial World, Standard & Poor's, Fortune,* and industry sources.
Note: Individual corporations with a market share of at least 40 percent are designated in boldface type. Market shares based on selected years, 1985–1990.

est. In some cases, however, the concentration ratio refers to the combined market share of even fewer firms—for example, the home computer market, which is now dominated by only three firms.

As is apparent from the table, the supply of some of the most familiar consumer products is dominated by a very few firms. In most of the examples cited here, producer concentration is so great as to be tantamount to a monopoly shared among a few corporations. The supply side of these product markets can be described as **oligopolies.** Indeed, in some markets, one single firm is so large than an outright monopoly is nearly attained. Seventy percent of all canned soup, for example, is produced by Campbell. Eastman Kodak supplies two-thirds of all still cameras and film. Procter & Gamble makes 62 percent of this country's disposable diapers. All firms that have a market share of at least 40 percent are printed in boldface type in the table.

oligopoly: A market in which a few firms produce all or most of the market supply of a particular good or service.

Any one of the firms listed in Table 25.2 can significantly affect the quantity of a particular good supplied to the market and thus its market price. If William Wrigley decides to supply Spearmint gum only at prices higher than those of its rivals, gum chewers will have to pay more for Spearmint or switch to another brand. If Wrigley, Squibb (Beech-Nut), and Warner-Lambert (Chiclets) all raise their prices at the same time (see In the News), gum chewers will have to choose between paying higher prices and biting their nails. This is the essential feature of market power. In a more competitive market, with a large number of small firms, the likelihood of an across-the-board price increase would be much smaller.

Firm Size

We noted before that market power is not necessarily associated with firm size—in other words, a small firm could possess a lot of power in a relatively small market. Table 25.2, however, should be convincing testimony that we are not talking about small product markets here. Every one of the products listed enjoys a broad-based market. Even the greeting card market rings up annual sales of over $4 billion. Sales of autos exceed $200 billion per year. Accordingly, for most of the firms listed in the table, market power and firm size go hand in hand. Indeed, the largest of the firms listed here (General Motors and Ford) enjoy sales volumes that exceed the entire output of most

In The News

MARKET POWER

Wm. Wrigley Boosts Gum Prices in U.S. Except Orbit Brand

CHICAGO—Wm. Wrigley Jr. Co. said it increased the wholesale price of all its chewing gum brands in the U.S. except the recently introduced Orbit sugar-free brand. The new schedule brings the price for a regular 20-package box to $2.25, up from $1.72.

Graham Morgan, Wrigley's vice president, sales, said a factor in the price move was a recent similar increase by American Chiclet, Co., a Morristown, N.J.–based division of Warner-Lambert Co.

of the *countries* in the world (see World View). That kind of size and market concentration constitutes undeniable power.

Although concentration ratios are a neat summary of power in a particular product market, they do not fully convey the extent to which particular firms can influence the production and consumption of goods and services. The vast size of the corporations listed in Table 25.2 creates the potential for extending market power beyond the confines of a particular product market. Firms whose sales and assets are measured in billions of dollars have the power to extend their influences into other production areas. The most striking example of such an extension is AT&T, which until 1984 not only supplied

W RLD VIEW

FIRM SIZE

Market Power

The largest firms in the United States are also the dominant forces in global markets. They export products to foreign markets and produce goods abroad for sale there or to import back into the United States. In terms of size

alone, these business giants rival most of the world's nations. GM's gross sales, for example, would make it the twenty-fourth largest "country" in terms of national GNP.

American corporations are not the only giants in the global markets. Toyota (Japan) and Shell Oil (Netherlands) are among the foreign giants that contest global markets.

Corporate Sales and World GNP, by Rank
(1990 data, in billions of dollars)

Rank	Country or corporation	Sales or GNP	Rank	Country or corporation	Sales or GNP
1	United States	$4,864	26	Switzerland	$117
2	USSR	2,535	27	Austria	111
3	Japan	1,758	28	Denmark	95
4	West Germany	870	29	Finland	92
5	France	762	30	Hungary	92
6	United Kingdom	755	31	**Ford Motor**	**92**
7	Italy	754	32	Saudi Arabia	86
8	Canada	475	33	Norway	84
9	Spain	365	34	Argentina	83
10	China	350	35	**Exxon**	**80**
11	Brazil	325	36	**Royal Dutch/Shell**	**78**
12	Poland	276	37	South Africa	77
13	India	271	38	Indonesia	72
14	Australia	218	39	Bulgaria	68
15	East Germany	207	40	Turkey	68
16	The Netherlands	191	41	**IBM**	**60**
17	Mexico	176	42	Algeria	58
18	South Korea	169	43	Venezuela	57
19	Sweden	160	44	Thailand	54
20	Czechoslovakia	158	45	Hong Kong	52
21	Yugoslavia	154	46	**Toyota**	**51**
22	Romania	126	47	**General Electric**	**49**
23	Belgium	125	48	**Mobil**	**48**
24	**General Motors**	**121**	49	Greece	47
25	Taiwan	118	50	**British Petroleum**	**46**

Sources: U.S. Central Intelligence Agency, World Bank, and *Fortune* magazine.

nearly all telephone services, but also owned Western Electric, the firm that manufactured most telephone hardware. Thus the sixth largest corporation in the country owned the tenth largest manufacturing corporation.[1]

Other corporations, too, have considerable power in more than one product market. Procter & Gamble, for example, shows up in six of the markets listed in Table 25.2, producing not only 62 percent of all disposable diapers, but also 52 percent of all detergents, 40 percent of all toothpaste, 10 percent of all razor blades, and 20 percent of all coffee. Warner-Lambert and Philip Morris also appear in many of the product markets listed here.

Table 25.2 indicates the market power possessed by corporations in specific product markets. But because concentration ratios refer to only one product or industry, they tend to understate the power of many corporations to influence economic outcomes. Obviously, a firm that can affect the supplies (and prices) of many products may have at least as much economic power as those that wield control over a single product. Procter & Gamble, Warner-Lambert, and Philip Morris are clear examples. In fact, many other corporations control some of the action in many product markets, although not necessarily a large share of the action in any single market. Such heterogeneous firms even have a special name: **conglomerates.**

conglomerate: A firm that produces significant quantities of output in several industries.

Although rarely observed in concentration ratio lists, conglomerates (such as ITT, LTV, Litton Industries, Tenneco, Textron, Rockwell International) are among the largest corporations in the country. International Telephone & Telegraph, for example, with annual sales in excess of $8 billion, has supplied such familiar products as Avis Rent-A-Cars, Levitt housing, Sheraton hotels, Hartford Life Insurance, and Hostess Twinkies.[2] Litton Industries, with sales in the $5 billion range, has supplied S&H Green Stamps, Stouffer foods, missile guidance systems, and nuclear attack submarines. Such conglomerate firms enjoy many of the prerogatives otherwise reserved for those with extensive power in a single market. Even General Motors, which already dominates one market, has acquired companies in aerospace (Hughes Aircraft), financial services (Core States Financial), and electronics (Electronic Data Systems).

Measurement Difficulties

A high concentration ratio is not the only way to achieve market power. The supply and price of a product can be altered by the actions of many firms acting in unison. Even a thousand small producers can band together to change the quantity supplied to the market, thus exercising market power. Recall how our mythical Universal Electronics exercised market power by coordinating the production decisions of its many separate plants. Those plants could have attempted such coordination on their own even if they had not all been owned by the same corporation. Lawyers and doctors possess and exercise this kind of power by maintaining uniform fee schedules for members of the American Bar Association (ABA) and the American Medical Association (AMA).[3] Similarly, dairy farmers act jointly through three large cooperatives (the American Milk Producers, Mid-America Dairies, and Dairymen, Inc.), which together control 50 percent of all milk production.

[1]As noted in Chapter 23, AT&T was required to divest its local phone service as of January 1, 1984.

[2]ITT agreed to sell Avis and Levitt after threat of antitrust action.

[3]In recent years, the courts have ruled that uniform fee schedules are illegal and that individual lawyers and doctors have the right to advertise their prices (fees). Nevertheless, a combination of inertia and self-interest has effectively maintained high fee schedules and inhibited advertising.

Finally, all the figures and corporations cited here refer to *national* markets. They do not convey the extent to which market power may be concentrated in a *local* market. Yet local concentrations of market power are of immediate concern to every consumer, even if the firms and stores that possess such power have little national impact. In fact, many industries with low concentration ratios nationally tend to be represented by just one or a few firms locally. Prime examples include milk, newspapers, and transportation (both public and private). For example, fewer than sixty cities in the United States have two or more independently owned daily newspapers, and nearly all of those newspapers rely on only two news services (Associated Press and United Press International).

We may conclude, then, that market power is real and pervasive in the U.S. economy. The corporations listed in Table 25.2 only suggest the dimensions of that power. These firms have combined sales of well over $600 billion and employ over 7 million people. The 200 largest manufacturing companies—only 0.06 percent of the total—account for almost one-half of all manufacturing output, assets, and employment. Accordingly, although many product markets can also be characterized as highly competitive (furniture, fashions, computer software, printing, motels, produce), concentration and market power characterize a broad spectrum of American industry.

MARKET BEHAVIOR

With so much market power concentrated in so few hands, evidence of power at work should be easy to find. Indeed, it would be surprising to find many product markets unaffected by the concentration ratios we have surveyed. As we review examples of market power at work in some of these markets, the ultimate objective of those who wield the power must be kept in view. Power in product markets is sought and exercised for the primary purpose of increasing the profits of those who wield the power.[4] In pursuit of higher profits, monopolies and oligopolies may seek to restrict market supplies, raise product prices, lower product quality, or reduce direct costs. In all of these cases, they rely on their ability to control market supply. Where possible, they attempt to extend such power by influencing market demand as well.

Successful use of market power will, of course, attract the interest and envy of other profit maximizers. Should these would-be rivals ever enter the market, market power would be lost. Thus market power has the potential to self-destruct. To avert that disaster, monopolies and oligopolies must erect **barriers to entry** to protect their market control. ***Above-normal profits cannot be maintained over the long run unless barriers to entry exist.*** In the following pages we will focus on both the exercise of market power and the kinds of barriers to entry that establish and preserve such power.

barriers to entry: Obstacles that make it difficult or impossible for would-be producers to enter a particular market, e.g., patents.

Price Fixing
A basic focus of market power is the price at which particular goods and services are sold. In general, we expect firms with market power to raise prices whenever it is profitable to do so and to maintain prices at levels higher than a more competitive market would sustain.

[4]The profits accrue not just to the faceless corporations, of course, but also to the stockholders who own them. In this regard, it is well to remember that 5 percent of the population owns 83 percent of all corporate stock. In addition, the executives and employees of powerful corporations are themselves paid above-average wages.

price fixing: Explicit agreements among producers regarding the price(s) at which a good is to be sold.

In oligopolies, the establishment and maintenance of a high market price require some form of coordination among the rival firms. The most explicit form of coordination among oligopolies involves **price fixing**: the oligopolists explicitly agree to charge a uniformly high price. Consumers are compelled to pay that high price or do without.

Price-fixing agreements are particularly successful when market demand for the product is highly inelastic, as high prices will not significantly reduce the quantity demanded. Although price fixing is outlawed by the Sherman Antitrust Act—and therefore often difficult to document—a few examples may serve to convey the nature of such agreements:

- In 1961 General Electric, Westinghouse, and other electrical-products firms were convicted of fixing prices on equipment that they had been selling to the Tennessee Valley Authority and commercial customers. Their price-fixing conspiracy had raised product prices on sales totaling nearly $2 billion per year. Seven corporate executives went to prison and twenty-three others were put on probation. In addition, the companies were fined a total of $1.8 million and compelled to pay triple damages in excess of $500 million to their victimized customers. Nevertheless, another suit was filed against General Electric and Westinghouse in 1972, charging these same companies—still the only two U.S. manufacturers of turbine generators—with continued price fixing.

- In January 1982 three major dairies in Arkansas pleaded no contest to federal charges of price fixing. State officials had discovered that the three firms (Borden, Inc.; Coleman Dairy, Inc.; and Dean Foods) had been submitting identical bids to provide milk for schools in Little Rock and other cities in central Arkansas. They were also said to be fixing the price of milk sold to the public. The state attorney general estimated that the price fixing, which had begun as far back as 1963, had boosted prices by $3 million per year. Convictions for fixing milk prices were also obtained in Florida, Georgia, and Kentucky. In 1990 the attorney general of Virginia launched a similar investigation.

- In 1981 the three largest supermarket operators in Cleveland agreed to give consumers $21.5 million worth of free groceries to settle price-fixing charges. Suits against the companies (Fisher Foods, First National Supermarkets, and Association of Stop-N-Shop Supermarkets) asserted that officers of the three supermarkets had secretly met in parking lots, hotels, and an apartment to fix meat and grocery prices.

- Control of the supply of quinine was achieved by a group of international firms in the early 1960s. The firms then raised the price of quinine from $0.37 an ounce to $2.13. The demand for quinine (in the form of the drug quinidine) is highly inelastic; the drug is taken primarily by the elderly to restore natural heart rhythm. Profits of the quinine suppliers and their distributors skyrocketed, the profits of one company quintupling in a period of six months.

- The price of tetracycline (a common antibiotic) was allegedly inflated by an illegal conspiracy involving five leading drug companies (American Cyanamid, Pfizer, Bristol-Myers, Upjohn, and Squibb Beech-Nut). Although the drug cost only $1.52 per 100 capsules to manufacture, the companies sold it to druggists at a price of $30.60. The druggists, in turn, sold it to the public at $51. After the government began to prosecute the companies for a price-fixing conspiracy, the retail price fell to $6. The five companies agreed to pay over $120 million to settle claims resulting from their pricing behavior.

- In 1990 the U.S. Justice Department filed suit against Manischewitz Company, the leading maker of kosher foods and wines. The suit alleged that the company had fixed artificially high prices on $25 million worth of matzo—unleavened bread consumed during the Jewish Passover holiday.

- In 1987 the Los Angeles district attorney filed price-fixing charges against local trash-hauling firms. The trash firms were accused of operating a covert cartel that divided the market among three firms, fixing high prices for trash-removal services, and quoting even higher prices ("high balling") to any customer wanting to switch to another cartel member.

Similar price-fixing agreements have been discovered in the markets for soft drinks (see In the News), plumbing fixtures, cigarettes, drugs, and newspaper advertising. One of the most widespread price-fixing schemes occurred in road construction. Federal prosecutors discovered that paving contractors were rigging bids (fixing prices) on road projects around the country. Between 1979 and 1984 over 400 criminal convictions were obtained, along with $50 million in fines and over 150 jail sentences. In Chicago, Atlanta, and many other areas, highway paving prices fell 10 to 20 percent after some paving contractors were indicted.

Price Leadership Although price-fixing agreements are undoubtedly still a reality in many product markets, oligopolies have discovered that they do not necessarily need *explicit* agreements to arrive at uniform prices. If all oligopolists in a particular product market follow the lead of one firm in raising prices, the result is the same as if they had all agreed to raise prices simultaneously. Instead of conspiring in motel rooms (as in the electrical products and soft drink cases),

In The News

PRICE FIXING

Price Fixing Charged on Soft Drinks

A former president and general manager of Allegheny Pepsi-Cola Bottling Co. was charged yesterday with conspiring to fix prices of soft drinks sold in the Norfolk and Richmond areas.

The one-count felony charge against James P. Sheridan was filed in U.S. District Court in Norfolk as part of the Justice Department's investigation into price fixing in the soft-drink industry.

Sheridan conspired during meetings and telephone conversations with unnamed coconspirators to set promotional prices for soft drinks and decided when to raise or lower them, according to court papers filed in the case.

Those actions, which occurred between February 1983 and the end of 1984, deprived customers of the opportunity to purchase certain soft drinks in an open and competitive market, a violation of the Sherman Act, court documents said.

—Sharon Warren Walsh

The Washington Post, June 26, 1987, p. C1. Copyright © 1987 The Washington Post.

MARKET POWER AND ANTITRUST

price leadership: An oligopolistic pricing pattern that allows one firm to establish the (market) price for all firms in the industry.

the firms can achieve their objective simply by reading the *Wall Street Journal* or industry publications and responding appropriately. Such **price leadership** is common in the automobile and airline industries and frequently characterizes other product markets (television, cigarettes, detergents).

What happens in these cases is that one firm announces a price increase of *x* percent. In a highly competitive market, other companies would exploit this price differential by continuing to sell their products at lower prices. The more expensive firm would thus be driven out of business or forced to rescind its price increases. In a highly concentrated industry, however, the remaining oligopolists may decide to match the price increase. Often the price followers raise their prices a bit less than *x* percent, compelling the price leader to shave its initial price increase. These actions often give the impression of intense competition. These minor "adjustments," however, do not alter the fact that in highly concentrated industries a price increase by one firm often signals price increases by all firms.[5]

Allocation of Market Shares

Whenever oligopolists successfully raise the price of a product, the law of demand tells us that unit sales will decline. Even in markets with highly inelastic demand curves (such as those for tetracycline and quinine), *some* decrease in sales always accompanies an increase in price. When this happens in a monopolistic industry, the monopolist simply cuts back his rate of output to adjust to the reduced sales. In an oligopolistic industry, however, it is not obvious which of the oligopoly firms will confront diminished sales. A reduction in sales and output will occur; how will that reduction be spread around? Clearly, no single firm will wish to incur the whole weight of that cutback while the other oligopolists maintain their previous output; some form of accommodation is required.

The adjustment to the reduced sales volume can take many forms. Once again, the firms may engage in an explicit agreement on dividing up the sales reduction. If market sales drop 10 percent, each firm may agree to reduce its rate of output by that same proportion. Such an agreement would preserve the **market share** previously enjoyed by the separate companies.

market share: The percentage of total market output produced by a single firm.

A particularly novel method of allocating market shares occurred in the price-fixing case involving General Electric and Westinghouse. Agreeing to establish high prices on electrical equipment was not particularly difficult. But how would the companies decide who was to get the sales? General Electric, Westinghouse, Allis-Chalmers, and a few other companies agreed that each firm would be designated as the "low" bidder for a particular phase of the moon. The "low" bidder would charge the previously agreed-upon (high) price, with the other firms offering their products for sale at even higher prices. The "low" bidder would naturally get the sale. Each time the moon entered a new phase, the order of "low" and "high" bidders would change. Hence each firm got a share of the business, and the price-fixing scheme was hidden behind a façade of "competitive" bidding.[6]

Such intricate plans for allocating market shares are more the exception than the rule. More often the oligopolists let the sales and output reduction be divided up according to consumer demands, intervening only when market

[5]As the kinked demand curve of Chapter 24 illustrated, no single oligopolistic firm will raise its price unless it is convinced that rivals will follow suit. When they do, a new market price is established, from which the rival firms are not expected to deviate.

[6]For a detailed description of this price-fixing arrangement, see Richard Austin Smith, "The Incredible Electrical Conspiracy," *Fortune,* May 1961.

predatory price cutting: Temporary price reductions designed to alter market shares or drive out competition.

shares are thrown markedly out of balance. At such times an oligopolist may take drastic action, such as **predatory price cutting.** Predatory price cuts are temporary price reductions that are intended to drive out new competition or reestablish market shares. The sophisticated use of price cutting can also function as a significant barrier to entry, inhibiting potential competitors from trying to gain a foothold in the price cutter's market.

Gasoline station "price wars" are a familiar manifestation of predatory price cutting. The cigarette industry provides another example. Liggett Group, one of the six major cigarette producers, had seen its market share tumble from 21 percent in 1947 to only 2.3 percent in 1980. To increase its sales, it introduced "generic" cigarettes—sold in plain packages at prices 35 percent lower than branded cigarettes. Sales zoomed. Threatened by Liggett's expanding market share, Brown and Williamson counterattacked. It offered low-priced cigarettes in packs designed just like Liggett's. B & W also offered wholesalers huge rebates to purchase from B & W rather than Liggett. The rebates were so large that B & W was incurring a loss on each pack of cigarettes sold. Liggett tried to match the rebates but did not have the financial strength to continue the battle. Liggett's share of the generic market fell from 90 percent in 1983 to 14 percent in 1989. In the process, the price of generics increased, and the rebates decreased, making generics profitable to produce again. In 1990 a federal jury ordered Brown and Williamson to pay Liggett $149 million for damages caused by Brown's predatory pricing.

Another example of price cutting to enforce market power suggests elements of both collusion and price fixing. The automobile manufacturers sell a substantial number of cars to fleet owners—firms or agencies that purchase at least ten vehicles. General Motors and Ford had always dominated fleet sales. Chrysler's share of the market, however, grew from 4 to 25 percent after it offered price reductions. As a result, Ford and GM were compelled to lower their prices in order to maintain sales. The price reductions, however, lowered profits, a most unwelcome result. According to government complaints, GM and Ford then conspired to cut prices so low that they actually fell below cost. These severe price cuts caused Chrysler to lose money and rethink its pricing policy. When GM and Ford eliminated all price concessions on 1971 models, Chrysler followed suit the following week. As *Business Week* reported, "GM let it be known that it planned to retaliate, presumably by further price cutting, if Chrysler did not go along."[7]

Patents

Price cutting, either real or threatened, can be an effective weapon for excluding competition. It is by no means the only available weapon, however. Patents, control of distribution outlets, acquisitions, government regulation, and product differentiation can also be used to limit competition.

Patents are intended to encourage research and innovation by prohibiting others from copying a newly developed product. In the process, however, patents also stifle competition. A patent endows the holder with exclusive use of her technology for seventeen years. A potential competitor cannot set up shop until he either develops an alternative method for producing a product or receives permission from the patent holder to use the patented process. Such permission, when given, will cost something, of course. Moreover, the larger, more powerful firm will always have more resources available to pur-

[7]*Business Week,* January 27, 1973, p. 24. In December 1973, GM and Ford were acquitted of criminal charges by a federal district court in Detroit; civil suits against these companies were dismissed in 1977 on the basis of inadequate evidence of collusion.

sue further research and development, thus increasing the comparative disadvantage of the would-be rival. Patents were the primary source of market power for the hypothetical Universal Electronics case of Chapter 22. In the real world, they also provide a substantial explanation for the market power of such firms as Xerox and Polaroid.

Even tennis rackets are now patented. In 1976 the Prince Manufacturing Company convinced the U.S. Patent Office that its oversized rackets were a unique product. The racket's design, it was claimed, provided more power and stability than conventionally sized (70-square-inch) rackets. The Patent Office agreed and gave Prince the exclusive right to produce rackets with surface areas of 85–130 square inches. With that patent, Prince has been able to monopolize sales of oversized rackets and reap extraordinary profits.[8]

Distribution Control

Another way to control the supply of a product is to take control of distribution outlets. A firm will usually sell wares in a variety of retail outlets. If it can persuade those outlets not to peddle anyone else's competitive wares, it will increase its market power. This control of distribution outlets can be accomplished through many means, including price concessions, long-term supply contracts, and expensive gifts at Christmas. The automobile industry provides an even more effective option.

Nearly all new cars in the United States are sold through dealerships franchised by car manufacturers. The individual dealers are beholden to the manufacturer for the "'right" to buy and sell cars. As a condition of their franchises, dealers are prohibited from selling cars produced by a competitor. Although the clause detailing this prohibition was ruled illegal by the Supreme Court in 1949, few dealers have taken it on themselves to defy the wishes of GM, Ford, and Chrysler. As a result, the supply of new cars sold to the public is effectively governed by a few manufacturers who exercise control over approximately 26,000 dealerships (GM alone has over 10,000). As the accompanying news clipping suggests, unauthorized dealers—especially those who want to sell cars at discounted prices—have difficulty getting a supply of cars to sell.

To tighten their control over distribution networks, auto manufacturers have also entered the parts-replacement industries. Although most auto parts could easily be designed to be interchangeable, only "authorized" parts and services, provided by franchised dealers, may be used to maintain the warranty. Hence the Big Three effectively fragment the independent parts and service market. They force auto purchasers to pay higher prices for such services, and they compel would-be entrants to the auto industry to establish their own parts and service networks. As a result of these many barriers to entry, it has been estimated that a potential competitor would need at least $1 *billion* to establish a foothold in the automobile industry. Few entrepreneurs are prepared for that kind of investment.

The breakfast cereal industry has discovered an easier way to limit competition. Sales of breakfast cereals are heavily influenced not only by product advertising but also by shelf displays at the local supermarket. The package with the most prominent display (shelf height, space, and position) is most likely to catch the attention of the shopper (or child in tow). One might think that the grocer takes responsibility for such displays, but the Federal Trade

---

[8]Prince later sold Wilson a license to manufacture oversized rackets. Such licenses permit a patent holder to profit from the production of its rivals without forsaking its primary monopoly.

In The News

CONTROLLING SUPPLY

Car Buyers Caught in the Middle of GM's Battle with Discounters

Richard Whittaker was intrigued when Porter Chevrolet, a discount dealer in Cambridge, Mass., offered to sell him a 1985 Chevy Blazer for $14,500. Chevrolet dealers all over Boston had quoted him prices between $18,000 and $19,000.

Mr. Whittaker ordered from Porter—and then his trouble began. When the vehicle didn't arrive within two months he called General Motors Corp. GM told him, he claims, that "the price I was paying was ridiculously low and ... I should shop someplace other than Porter."

Eight months and scores of angry phone calls later, GM finally delivered Mr. Whittaker's Blazer. The GM manager with whom Mr. Whittaker says he spoke doesn't recall the incident and insists he wouldn't have said such a thing.

Caught in the Middle

Mr. Whittaker and thousands of other buyers have been caught since 1983 in the middle of a scrap between the new discount dealers on one side and GM and its conventional dealers on the other. The discounters scream that GM won't give them enough cars to fill the flood of orders they have received. They say that placates conventional dealers because they can maintain price levels.

Although some buyers have managed to snag GM cars at deep discounts in reasonable time, others have waited for a year and more before canceling orders. Now the issue may be coming to a boil in Minnesota, where a discount dealer, John Peterson, is suing GM, charging antitrust violations. Mr. Peterson claims GM and dealers in the Minneapolis area conspired to put him out of business. The Federal Trade Commission is investigating.

GM staunchly denies holding back cars to discounters in an attempting to put them out of business. It calls the suit meritless. But GM does say that its distribution policies attempt to protect the investments of the vase majority of its 10,000 conventional dealers, many of whom have been hurt by the appearance of these few dozen deep discounters.

The impact of the discounters has been much greater than their numbers would imply. GM dealers in major U.S. car markets acknowledge they have been forced in many cases to lower prices in response to discounters, cutting profit margins. Edward Powell, a Buick dealer form Shreveport, La., grouses: "These guys (discounters) are like cockroaches. It's more what they louse up than what they eat." ...

Although they can't produce hard evidence, most discounters suspect competitors' complaints have helped influence GM to allegedly squeeze competitors' deliveries. ...

GM blames the shortage of gas in part of its inability to manufacture enough of the hotter-selling models to meet demand. Moreover, the car-maker says it isn't obliged to fill a particular order from a dealer. ...

—Doron P. Levin

Commission claimed that is often not the case. In particular, the FTC discovered that

> Kellogg is the principal supplier of shelf space services for the RTE (ready-to-eat) cereal sections of retail grocery outlets. Such services include the selection, placement and removal of RTE cereals to each respondent and to other RTE cereal producers.
>
> Through such services respondents have interfered with and now interfere with the marketing efforts of other producers of RTE and other breakfast cereals and producers of other breakfast foods. Through such services respondents restrict the shelf positions and the number of facings for Nabisco and Ralston RTE cereals, and remove the RTE cereals of small regional producers.
>
> All respondents [Kellogg, General Mills, General Food, Quaker Oats] acquiesce in and benefit from the Kellogg shelf space program which protects and perpetuates their respective market shares through the removal or controlled exposure of other breakfast food products including, but not limited to, RTE cereal products.[9]

[9]Complaint, *Kellogg Company et al.,* FTC Dkt. 8883 (1972). The FTC dropped the case in 1982 after ten years of litigation.

According to the FTC complaint, this control over shelf space gave the cereal makers control of the market supply curve and cost consumers over $100 million per year in the form of higher grocery prices.

Mergers and Acquisition

Large and powerful firms can restrain competition and attain control of product supply by a number of means, by none quite so direct as outright *acquisition*. When one firm buys another, the effect on its market share, and thus its market power, is fairly obvious. A *merger* between two firms amounts to the same thing, although mergers often entail the creation of new corporate identities. The new identity, however, does not alter the fact that a single firm has attained increased market power.

Perhaps the single most dramatic case of acquisition for this purpose occurred in the breakfast-cereals industry. In 1946 General Foods acquired the cereal-manufacturing facilities of Campbell Cereal Company, a substantial competitor. Following this acquisition, General Foods dismantled the production facilities of Campbell Cereal and shipped them off to South Africa!

Although the General Foods acquisition was more dramatic than most, acquisitions have been the most popular route to increased market power. General Motors, for example, attained a dominant share of the auto market largely by its success in merging with and acquiring two dozen independent manufacturers. In the cigarette industry, the American Tobacco Company attained monopoly powers by absorbing some 250 independent companies. Each acquisition increased the company's market control and ability to acquire additional companies. Later antitrust action (1911) split up the resultant tobacco monopoly into an oligopoly consisting of four companies (R. J. Reynolds, Liggett & Myers, Lorillard, and American Tobacco), which continue to dominate the cigarette market. Other companies that came to dominate their product markets through mergers and acquisitions include U.S. Steel, U.S. Rubber, General Electric, United Fruit, National Biscuit Company, and International Salt. In addition, all the conglomerates discussed earlier attained their size and power via the acquisition route. ITT alone purchased an average of ten companies per year in the period 1964–69. The biggest mergers and acquisitions of the 1980s are noted in Chapter 34.

In The News

ELIMINATING COMPETITION

Business Journal to Buy, Then Close, Business Review

Owners of the Washington Business Journal said yesterday that they will buy and close down their competitor, The Business Review, a nine-year-old weekly business newspaper distributed in the Washington area.

James Bergfalk, executive vice president of development for the American City Business Journals Inc., which owns the Washington Business Journal, said yesterday that the company was in the process of buying The Business Review. . . .

With the purchase of The Business Review, American City eliminates the major competitor to its Washington publication.

"It becomes confusing to readers when there is more than one paper doing the same thing," Bergfalk said. . . .

—Sandra Sugawara

The Washington Post, May 27, 1987, p. F3. Copyright © 1987 The Washington Post.

Government Regulation

The government often helps companies to acquire and maintain control of market supply. Patents are issued by and enforced by the federal government and so represent one form of supply-restricting regulation. Barriers to international trade are another government-imposed barrier to entry. By limiting imports of everything from Chinese mushrooms to Japanese cars (see Chapter 35), the federal government reduces potential competition in U.S. product markets. Government regulation also limits *domestic* competition in many industries. From 1984 to 1990, the Federal Communications Commission (FCC) allowed only one company (GTE Corporation) to provide telephone service on airlines. When the FCC ended the monopoly in 1990, phone charges were expected to decline sharply.

New York City also limits competition—in this case, the number of taxicabs on the streets. In 1990, exactly 11,787 taxicabs were licensed—far fewer than the public wants. As a result, taxi fares are exceptionally high in New York City, and license holders reap substantial profits. A good measure of those profits is the price of the medallions that the city sells as taxi licenses. The market price of a New York City taxi medallion—and thus the price of entry into the industry—is $110,000. By contrast, a Washington, D.C., taxi license costs only $35, and fares are about half those in New York.

Nonprice Competition

Producers who have control over market supply are in a position to alter prices and thereby increase their share of economic welfare. They can enhance their power and income even further by establishing some influence over market demand. The primary mechanism of control is *advertising*. To the extent that a firm can convince you that its product is essential to your well-being and happiness, it has effectively shifted your demand curve. If the firm can convince millions of other consumers in the same way, it will have acquired some degree of direct control over the *market* demand curve. With such control, the producer can attain a still more profitable price–quantity equilibrium. Accordingly, we may anticipate that firms with large amounts of market power will tend to advertise most heavily.[10]

Advertising not only strengthens brand loyalty, but also makes it expensive for new producers to enter the market. A new entrant must buy not only production facilities but advertising outlets as well. In addition, the proliferation of brand names—all produced by a few companies—tends to mask the concentration of power that exists. Thus **product differentiation** both increases profits (and prices) and camouflages the true extent of market power.

product differentiation: Features that make one product appear different from competing products in the same market.

The cigarette industry is a classic case of high concentration and product differentiation. As Table 25.2 shows, the top four cigarette companies produce 90 percent of all domestic output; two more firms produce the rest. Yet you would never guess that such high concentration exists in the industry if you glanced at the cigarette shelves at the local supermarket. Together, the six cigarette companies produce well over 100 brands. To solidify brand loyalties, the cigarette industry spent over $2 billion in 1990 for advertisements in newspapers and magazines, on radio, and at sports events (televised cigarette ads were banned after 1971).

Another highly concentrated industry that advertises heavily is the breakfast cereal industry. Although the Federal Trade Commission has suggested that "a corn flake is a corn flake no matter who makes it," the four firms

[10]Next time you watch television, note which companies sponsor the programs. Then check to see if they, or their parent corporations, are included in our list of powerful firms (Table 25.2).

(Kellogg, General Foods, General Mills, and Quaker Oats) that supply more than 90 percent of all ready-to-eat breakfast cereals spend over $400 million a year to convince consumers otherwise. During the last 20 years, more than 150 brands of cereals have been marketed by these companies. As the FTC has documented, the four companies "produce basically similar RTE [ready-to-eat] cereals, and then emphasize and exaggerate trivial variations such as color and shape. . . . [They] employ trademarks to conceal such basic similarities and to differentiate cereal brands."[11] Makers of designer jeans do the same thing with a little extra stitching or a fancy label (see in the News).

The detergent industry provides a final example of product differentiation. Only three firms (Procter & Gamble, Lever Brothers, and Colgate-Palmolive) account for 86 percent of all detergent output. These firms, however, package detergents under twenty trademarked brands and a host of private labels for supermarket chains. Procter & Gamble alone, with over 50 percent of the market, produces nine trademarked bands (including Tide, which accounts for nearly one-fourth of all detergent sales). To create and maintain brand loyalty (and less elastic demand), Procter & Gamble spends more on advertising than any company in the world, with one exception (see Table 25.3).

Other Barriers to Entry   Predatory price cutting, patents, control of distribution outlets, acquisitions, and product differentiation are all effective barriers to entry. These barriers enable powerful producers to maintain high prices and profits without fear of attracting too much competition. As important as these barriers are, however, market power may be solidified in other ways as well.

Training   In today's technology-driven markets, early market entry can create an important barrier to later competition. Customers of computer hardware and software, for example, often become familiar with a particular system or computer package. To switch to a new product may entail significant

[11]Complaint, *Kellogg Company et al.,* FTC Dkt. 8883 (1972).

In The News

NONPRICE COMPETITION

Designer Jeans: Product Differentiation Is Everything

The Levi Strauss Company first produced jeans in the 1850s and has dominated the industry ever since. In the late 1970s, however, a whole new mini-industry evolved: the "designer jeans" market. It all started when Puritan Corporation came up with the idea of selling jeans emblazoned with the label of fashion designer Calvin Klein. Calvin Klein jeans sold like hotcakes, at about twice the price of traditional jeans. Within only a few years' time, Puritan was selling over $30 million worth of Calvin Klein jeans.

Other companies were quick to follow Puritan's lead. Murjani Industries was the next big success story. In 1978 Murjani put the Gloria Vanderbilt label on its jeans and started advertising heavily. Sales in 1979 reached $150 million. Jordache came next, also in 1978. In its second year, sales of Jordache jeans reached $75 million.

By 1981 the status jeans industry looked like a classic case of monopolistic competition. There were over 200 different labels available. Yet all of the jeans were basically identical, their only difference residing in the designer's name and the color or pattern of the stitching. To make their own jeans seem different, the makers of designer jeans advertise extensively.

TABLE 25.3   Advertising Expenditures of the Top Ten Advertisers

Firms with market power attempt to preserve and extend that power through advertising. A successful advertising campaign alters the demand curve facing the firm, thus increasing potential profits. Shown here are the 1988 advertising outlays of the biggest advertisers.

Company	Advertising expenditure (in millions)
Philip Morris	$ 2,058
Procter & Gamble	1,507
General Motors	1,294
Sears, Roebuck	1,045
RJR Nabisco	815
Eastman Kodak	736
McDonald's Corp.	728
Pepsico Inc.	712
Kellogg	683
Anheuser-Busch	635
Total	$10,213

Source: *Advertising Age,* September 27, 1989. Copyright © 1989 Crain Communications, Inc. Reprinted with permission of the publisher.

cost, including the retraining of user staff. As a consequence, would-be competitors will find it difficult to sell their products even if they offer better quality and lower prices.

The popular Lotus 1-2-3 spreadsheet program illustrates this market barrier. Lotus Development Corporation introduced Lotus 1-2-3 in 1982 as one of the first spreadsheets for the IBM personal computer. By 1988, Lotus had 3.5 million copies of its program in use—82 percent of all spreadsheet sales. Although other software firms offered comparable (and even better) products at much lower prices, users were reluctant to try new software that would require retraining.

IBM has enjoyed the same kind of user-based entry barrier. IBM continues to sell over 70 percent of large business computers. In 1990 Digital Equipment introduced comparable machines at half the price of IBM machines (costing $2 million to $7 million apiece). But IBM users were reluctant to switch, because they had accumulated so much IBM-compatible software and expertise.

Firm size   The very size of a powerful oligopoly may preclude effective competition. Once a firm or group of firms attains tremendous size, potential competitors may be kept at bay by the capital-investment requirements necessary to attain competitive status. IBM's dominance of the mainframe computer market is reinforced by the billion-dollar cost of developing new mainframe technology. Few companies can afford to make—or risk—that kind of initial investment. Even in disposable diapers, initial capital investment and advertising expenses are so high that only one new entrant—Johnson & Johnson, already a large corporation—joined this highly concentrated industry in the 1970s, despite the potential profits available. Smaller firms were reluctant to enter, for fear that the existing firms could use their control over prices, supply, and demand to destroy competitive possibilities. Johnson & Johnson itself pulled out of the industry after only a few years.

A single firm or group of firms with considerable market power can also extend and solidify that power by exacting concessions from resource suppliers. Powerful firms can erect protective entry barriers by winning price concessions or distribution guarantees from those who supply them with labor, capital, or other productive inputs. Firms with market power may also get preferential treatment from government agencies that enhances their profits or protects their market share.

ANTITRUST GUIDELINES

Examples of market power at work in U.S. product markets could be extended to the closing pages of this book. The few cases cited here, however, are testimony enough to the fact that market power has some influence on our lives. Market power *does* exist; market power *is* used. In general, power in U.S. product markets has contributed to **market failure**—to resource misallocations, higher prices, restricted output, higher levels of unemployment, and greater inequality of income and wealth.

market failure: An imperfection in the market mechanism that prevents optimal outcomes.

What should we do about these abuses? Should we leave it to market forces to find ways of changing industry structure and behavior? Or should the government step in to curb noncompetitive practices? How much can the government really do?

Industry Behavior

Our primary concern is the *behavior* of market participants. What ultimately counts is the quantity of goods supplied to the market, their quality, and their price. Few consumers care about the underlying *structure* of markets; what we seek are good market *outcomes*.

In principle, the government could change industry behavior without changing industry structure. We could, for example, explicitly outlaw collusive agreements and cast a jaundiced eye on industries that regularly exhibit price leadership. We could also dismantle barriers to entry and thereby promote **contestable markets.** We might also prohibit oligopolists from extending their market power via such mechanisms as acquisitions, excessive or deceptive advertising, and, alas, the financing of political campaigns. In fact, the existing **antitrust** laws—the Sherman Act, the Clayton Act, and the Federal Trade Commission Act (see pp. 596–597)—explicitly forbid most of these practices.

contestable market: An imperfectly competitive industry subject to potential entry if prices or profits increase.

antitrust: Government intervention to alter market structure or prevent abuse of market power.

There are several problems with this behavioral approach, however. The first limitation is scarce resources. Policing the markets and penalizing noncompetitive conduct require more resources than the public sector can muster. Indeed, the firms being investigated often have more resources than the public watchdogs. The advertising expenditures of just one oligopolist, Procter & Gamble, are more than ten times as large as the *combined* budgets of both the Justice Department's Antitrust Division and the Federal Trade Commission. As Ralph Nader has suggested, "The posture of two agencies with a combined budget of $20 million and 550 lawyers and economists trying to deal with anticompetitive abuses in a trillion-dollar economy, not to mention an economy where the 200 largest corporations control two-thirds of all manufacturing assets, is truly a charade."[12] The dimensions of this charade were strikingly demonstrated in 1969, when the Justice Department filed suit against IBM for monopoly practices. In the subsequent thirteen years, IBM submitted 66 million pages of documents in its own defense, effectively stymieing the

[12]Mark J. Green et al., *The Closed Enterprise System: The Report on Antitrust Enforcement* (New York: Grossman, 1972), p. x.

prosecution. By the time the case was dropped (see Chapter 23), all of the Antitrust Division lawyers who had originally prepared the IBM case had left the Justice Department.

The paucity of antitrust resources is partly a reflection of public apathy. Consumers are generally insensitive to the relationship between market structure and their own economic welfare. They (and you) rarely think about the connection between market power and the price of the goods they buy, the wages they receive, or the way they live. As Ralph Nader sadly discovered, "Antitrust violations are part of a phenomenon which, to the public is too complex, too abstract, and supremely dull."[13] As a result, there is little political pressure to regulate market behavior—much less to increase antitrust budgets. On the other hand, the vested interest of oligopolists creates an active lobby to constrain government regulation.

The behavioral approach also suffers from the "burden of proof" requirement. How often will "trust-busters" catch colluding executives in the act? More often than not, the case for collusion rests on such circumstantial evidence as simultaneous price hikes, identical bids, or other market outcomes. The charge of explicit collusion is hard to prove. Even in the absence of explicit collusion, however, consumers suffer. If an oligopoly price is higher than what a competitive industry would charge, consumers get stuck with the bill whether or not the price was "rigged" by explicit collusion. The U.S. Supreme Court recognized that consumers may suffer from *tacit* collusion, even where no *explicit* collusion is proven or occurs.

Industry Structure

The concept of tacit collusion directs attention to the very *structure* of an industry. It essentially says that oligopolists and monopolists will act in their own best interest. As former Supreme Court Chief Justice Earl Warren observed, "An industry which does not have a competitive structure will not have competitive behavior."[14] To expect an oligopolist to disavow profit op-

[13]Ibid., p. ix.
[14]Ibid., p. 7.

In The News

ANTITRUST

Topps Gum Strikes Out on Baseball Card Game

PHILADELPHIA (UPI)—Topps Chewing Gum Inc. lost its 14-year monopoly of the bubblegum baseball card industry this week and was ordered to pay triple damages of $3 to a Philadelphia competitor.

Fleer Corp. of Philadelphia filed a lawsuit in 1975 against Topps of Brooklyn, which since 1966 signed exclusive contracts with virtually every major and minor league baseball player to appear on 2½-by-3½ cards tucked in with a sheet of pink bubble gum.

U.S. District Judge Clarence Newcomer rules that Topps and the Major League Baseball Players' Association unfairly edged Fleer out of the market.

But he balked at what he called "guesswork" at determining the extent of Fleer's losses. Newcomer awarded Fleer a nominal $1 damage award, which under antitrust laws is tripled to $3. . . .

Topps is the nation's largest manufacturer and seller of baseball cards, selling $6.6 million worth in 1978.

The Washington Post, July 5, 1980. Copyright © 1980 United Press International, Inc. Reprinted with permission.

portunities or to ignore its interdependence with fellow oligopolists is naive. It also violates the basic motivations imputed to a market economy. As long as markets are highly concentrated, we must expect to observe oligopolistic behavior.

Judge Learned Hand used these arguments to dismantle the Aluminum Company of America (Alcoa) in 1945. Alcoa was not charged with any illegal *behavior*. Nevertheless, the company controlled over 90 percent of the aluminum supplied to the market. This monopoly structure, the Supreme Court concluded, was itself a threat to the public interest.

Public efforts to alter market structure have been even less frequent than efforts to alter market behavior. With the exception of the AT&T case (Chapter 23) and Alcoa, the few really concerted efforts to break up market concentration occurred at the beginning of the century, when Standard Oil and the Tobacco Trust were partially dismantled. The prevalent feeling today, even among antitrust practitioners, is that the oligopolies are too big and too powerful to make deconcentration a viable policy alternative. At most, antitrust activity tries to limit further concentration of specific industries. This is the approach currently being used in the European Community as well (see World View).

Objections to Antitrust Even a limited policy of preventing further concentration raises objections. The companies challenged by the public "trust-busters" protest that they are being penalized for their success. Alcoa, for example, attained a monopoly by investing heavily into a new product before anyone else recognized its value. Other firms, too, have captured dominant market shares by being first, best, or most efficient. Having "won" the game fairly, why should they have

W RLD VIEW

ANTITRUST GUIDELINES

European Antitrust Agreement

Big Mergers to Face Community Review

PARIS, Dec. 21—After a 16-year struggle, European Community ministers adopted a far-reaching plan today to give the community powers to review corporate mergers. They unanimously adopted a compromise plan after a bitter tug-of-war in which Britain's and West Germany's powerful antitrust bodies fought against ceding any of their powers to the bureaucracy in Brussels.

Under the plan, the European Commission, the community's executive branch, will be empowered to review mergers within the community—including those involving American or Japanese companies—in which the resulting company has revenues of more than five billion European Currency Units, equivalent to $5.85 billion.

The community's 12 member nations would effectively give up their power to review large mergers, but could continue to scrutinize deals in which the resulting company would have revenues of less than five billion E.C.U.'s. . . .

Sir Leon estimated that the commission would examine 40 to 50 mergers a year after the plan takes effect on Sept. 21, 1990.

Community officials said the commission would examine various factors in a planned merger including the structure of the markets concerned; actual and potential competition, both inside and outside the community; the market position of the parties concerned; freedom of choice for third parties; barriers to entry; the interest of consumers, and technological and economic progress.
—Steven Greenhouse

The New York Times, December 22, 1989, p. D1. Copyright © 1989 The New York Times Company. Reprinted by permission.

to give up their prize? They contend that noncompetitive *behavior,* not industry *structure,* should be the only concern of antitrust.

Essentially the same argument is made for proposed mergers and acquisitions. The firms involved claim that the increased concentration will enhance productive efficiency (e.g., via economies of scale). Antitrust critics also argue that big firms are needed to maintain America's competitive position in international markets (which are themselves often dominated by foreign monopolies and oligopolies). Those same global markets, they contend, ensure that even highly concentrated domestic markets will be contested by international rivals.

Finally, critics suggest that market forces themselves assure competitive behavior. Not only foreign firms, but domestic entrepreneurs as well will stalk a monopolist's preserve. People will always be looking for ways to enter a profitable market. Monopoly or oligopoly power may slow entry but is unlikely to stop it forever. Eventually, competitive forces will prevail.

The Herfindahl–Hirshman Index

There are no easy answers. In theory, competition is valuable, but some mergers and acquisitions undoubtedly increase efficiency. Moreover, some international markets may require a minimum firm size not consistent with perfect competition. Finally, our regulatory resources are limited; not every acquisition or merger is worthy of public scrutiny.

Where should we draw the line? Can a firm hold a 22 percent market share, but not 30 percent? Are five firms too few, but six firms in an industry enough? Someone has to make those decisions. That is to say, ***the broad mandates of the antitrust laws must be transformed into specific guidelines for government intervention.***

In 1982 the Antitrust Division of the U.S. Department of Justice adopted specific guidelines for intervention. Those guidelines are based on industry *structure* alone. They are based on a concentration ratio that takes into account the size of *each* firm, however, rather than just the *combined* market share of the top four firms. Specifically, the **Herfindahl–Hirshman Index** (HHI) of market concentration is calculated as

Herfindahl–Hirshman Index: Measure of industry concentration that accounts for number of firms and size of each.

$$\bullet \quad HHI = \sum_{i=1}^{n} S_i^2$$

$$= \left(\begin{array}{c}\text{share of}\\\text{firm 1}\end{array}\right)^2 + \left(\begin{array}{c}\text{share of}\\\text{firm 2}\end{array}\right)^2 + \cdots \left(\begin{array}{c}\text{share of}\\\text{firm } n\end{array}\right)^2$$

Thus a three-firm oligopoly like that described in Chapter 24 (Table 24.2) would have an HHI value of

$$HHI = (40.0)^2 + (32.5)^2 + (27.5)^2 = 3{,}412.5$$

where the numbers in parentheses indicate the market shares of the three fictional computer companies. The calculation yields an HHI value of 3,412.5.

For policy purposes, the Justice Department decided it would draw the line at 1,800. Any merger that creates an HHI value over 1,800 will be challenged by the Justice Department. If an industry has an HHI value between 1,000 and 1,800, the Justice Department will challenge any merger that *increases* the HHI by 100 points or more. Mergers and acquisitions in industries with an HHI value of less than 1,000 will not be challenged.

The HHI provides an arbitrary but workable tool for deciding when the government should intervene to challenge mergers and acquisitions. Drawing the line at 1,800 is a compromise based on available antitrust resources and the perceived threat of concentration.

Even when intervention is signaled, however, there are still decisions to make. Should a challenged merger be allowed? The same old questions arise. Will the proposed merger enhance efficiency in domestic and global markets? Or will it tend to constrain competitive forces and optimal outcomes? Each case requires scrutiny. On balance, however, antitrust must be based on the presumption that more competition is better. The case for mergers and acquisitions must be proven with demonstrations of increased efficiency. Even then, the threat of antitrust action must be credible enough to assure more competitive behavior.

SUMMARY

- Nearly three-fourths of all U.S. firms are small proprietorships. Large corporations, however, control roughly 90 percent of all sales, assets, and profits.

- The concentration ratio is a measure of the extent of market power in a particular product market. It equals the share of total industry output accounted for by the largest firms, usually the top four.

- In addition to those firms with a large market share in one product market, many others have large market shares in several markets. Also, conglomerates have a little power in each of many markets. Finally, regional and local markets create still further opportunities for market power.

- The primary mechanism for the exercise of market power is control over prices, particularly price fixing and price leadership.

- To maintain and exercise market power, firms must be sheltered from potential competition by barriers to entry. Patents are one form of barrier. Other barriers include predatory price cutting ("price wars"), control of distribution outlets, high capital-investment requirements, government regulation, advertising and product differentiation, and resource control. Outright acquisition and merger offer additional means to eliminate competition.

- Market power causes market failure. The symptoms of that failure include increased prices, reduced output, and a transfer of income from the consuming public to a relatively few powerful corporations and the people who own them.

- Government intervention may focus on either market structure or market behavior. In either case, difficult decisions must be made about when and how to intervene. Some market concentrations may increase efficiency; others may be too small to matter. International trade and a credible antitrust threat are minimum safeguards against abuse of market power.

- The Herfindahl–Hirshman Index is a measure of industry concentration that takes into account the number of firms and the size of each. It is used to identify cases worthy of antitrust concern.

Terms to Remember

market power	market share
concentration ratio	predatory price cutting
oligopoly	product differentiation
conglomerate	market failure
barriers to entry	contestable market
price fixing	antitrust
price leadership	Herfindahl–Hirshman Index

Questions for Discussion

1. Market power usually results in high profits. Why, then, don't more firms enter an oligopolistic industry to share in the high profits and thereby increase competition? Why don't more firms enter the auto industry? the photocopying industry?

2. In 1977 Laker Airways, then a three-plane airline, introduced a "Skytrain" air fare between New York and London that was less than half the fare previously charged by TWA, Pan Am, and other large airlines. Why didn't some other firm lower the fare sooner? Why did Laker eventually go bankrupt (in 1982)?

3. For many years videocassette recorders were produced by only two firms (Sony and Matsushita). Yet VCR prices fell dramatically, while the quality of VCRs improved. How did this happen in such an imperfectly competitive industry structure?

4. What would be the advantages of breaking up the market power depicted in Table 25.2? Why problems would such "trust busting" create?

Problem

1. The following table indicates the respective market shares of firms in three different industries:

Firms	Industry A	Industry B	Industry C
Alpha	40	20	70
Beta	20	20	5
Kappa	10	20	5
Sigma	10	20	5
Lambda	10	10	5
Delta	5	5	5
Zeta	5	5	5

Based on this information,
(a) Compute the four-firm concentration ratio in all three industries.
(b) Compute the Herfindahl–Hirshman Index for all three industries.
(c) In which industry would the Justice Department permit additional mergers?
(d) Which firms would be permitted to merge in that industry?

(De)Regulation of Business

*I*n his successful presidential election campaign of 1980, Ronald Reagan promised to "get government off your back and out of your pocket." As he saw it, excessive government regulation and high taxes were stifling private-sector entrepreneurship and productivity. The only way to restore U.S. productivity and profits, he argued, was to deregulate American business and to cut taxes.

The deregulation movement did not originate with President Reagan. The Nixon, Ford, and Carter administrations also took steps to deregulate major industries. The Reagan administration accelerated the deregulation movement, however, and gave it greater prominence. In the last decade or so, the airline, trucking, gas, telephone, banking, and railroad industries have all been substantially deregulated.

The recent surge of deregulation raises several basic questions about the government's role in the marketplace:

- When is government regulation necessary?

- What form should that regulation take?

- When is it appropriate to deregulate an industry?

In answering these questions we will draw on economic principles as well as recent experience. This will permit us to contrast the theory of (de)regulation with the reality of (de)regulation.

ANTITRUST VS. REGULATION

A perfectly competitive market provides a model for economic efficiency. As we first observed in Chapter 2, the market mechanism can answer the basic economic questions of WHAT to produce, HOW to produce it, and FOR WHOM. Under ideal conditions, the market's answers may also be optimal—that is, they may represent the best possible mix of output. To achieve this **laissez-faire** ideal, all producers must be perfect competitors; people must have full information about tastes, costs, and prices; all costs and benefits must be reflected in market prices; and pervasive economies of scale must be absent.

laissez faire: The doctrine of "leave it alone," of nonintervention by government in the market mechanism.

market failure: An imperfection in the market mechanism that prevents optimal outcomes.

In reality, these ideal conditions are rarely if ever fully attained. Markets may be dominated by large and powerful producers. In wielding their power, these producers may restrict output, raise prices, stifle competition, and inhibit innovation. In other words, market power may cause **market failure**, leaving us with suboptimal market outcomes.

Sanctions vs. Rules

antitrust: Government intervention to alter market structure or prevent abuse of market power.

regulation: Government intervention to alter the behavior of firms, e.g., in pricing, output, or advertising.

Government intervention may be appropriate in industries where market power prevails. As we observed in the previous chapter, the government has two options for intervention. It may focus on the *structure* of an industry or on its *behavior*. **Antitrust** laws cover both options: they prohibit mergers and acquisitions that reduce potential competition (structures) and forbid market practices (behavior) that are anticompetitive.

Government **regulation** has a different focus. Regulation pretty much takes industry structure as a given. In fact, government regulation often makes industries *less* rather than *more* competitive, as we will see.

Rather than worrying about industry structure, regulation focuses almost exclusively on *behavior*. In general, regulation seeks to change market outcomes directly, by imposing specific limitations on price, output, and investment decisions. Whereas antitrust statutes *forbid* some kinds of behavior, regulation mandates specific behavior. Regulation is thus a more activist form of intervention.

Social vs. Economic Regulation

As Table 26.1 indicates, government regulations range widely. Two types of regulation are distinguished in the table. The first, *social* regulation, is concerned with such issues as workplace safety, health, environmental protection, and highway safety. According to the table, over 80,000 federal employees police these issues.

Economic regulation is more directly focused on prices, production, and the conditions for industry entry or exit. Although both social and economic regulation affect market outcomes, economic regulation tends to focus more closely on business behavior.

Market Failure

The scope of regulatory activity is a response to market failure. As we first observed in Chapter 3, market power is only one source of market failure. *The specific sources of market failure include*

- *Externalities.* Externalities are benefits or costs of a market activity that are imposed on parties other than the buyer or seller. If external costs (e.g., pollution) exist, private production costs and prices understate actual resource use. As a consequence, the good tends to be produced and consumed in greater quantity than society really desires.

- *Public goods.* Goods and services that are nonexclusive in consumption are called *public goods*. Everybody can enjoy (consume) them simultaneously, even if only one person pays. As we observed in Chapter 3, there is simply no way to exclude nonpayers ("free riders") from consuming such public goods as national defense, flood control, or cloud seeding.

- *Market power.* Where one or more producers have some direct control over industry prices or output, market outcomes may be suboptimal. As we observed in Chapters 23–25, powerful firms may produce less of a prod-

TABLE 26.1 Empolyment in 51 Federal Regulatory Agencies (FY 1990 estimates)

The human and capital resources employed by the bureaucracy represent a real opportunity cost. The 107,194 people employed in these 51 federal agencies—and tens of thousands more employed in state and local bureaucracies—could be producing other goods and services. These and other costs must be compared to the benefits of regulation.

Agency	Number of employees	Agency	Number of employees
SOCIAL REGULATION		Office of Surface Mining Reclamation	
Consumer Safety and Health		and Enforcement	1,116
Consumer Product Safety Commission	498	Environmental Protection Agency	14,417
Agriculture Marketing Service	2,747	Nuclear Regulatory Commission	3,041
Animal and Plant Health Inspection	4,848	Office of the Federal Inspector for the	
Federal Grain Inspection Service	800	Alaska Natural Gas Pipeline	1
Food Safety and Inspection Service	9,100	Subtotal—Environment and Energy	21,496
Packers and Stockyards Administration	193	ECONOMIC REGULATION	
Food and Drug Administration	7,363	*General Business*	
Drug Enforcement Administration	310	International Trade Administration	282
Coast Guard	7,361	Export Administration	553
Federal Aviation Administration	5,828	Patent and Trademark Office	3,898
Federal Highway Administration	633	Dept. of Justice Antitrust Division	544
Federal Railroad Administration	501	Federal Election Commission	238
National Highway Traffic Safety		Federal Trade Commission	872
Administration	656	International Trade Commission	497
Bureau of Alcohol, Tobacco,		Library of Congress: Copyright Office	564
and Firearms	3,828	Securities and Exchange Commission	2,451
National Transportation Safety Board	314	Subtotal—General Business	9,899
Subtotal—Consumer Safety		*Finance and Banking*	
and Health	44,980	Comptroller of the Currency	3,730
Job Safety and Working Conditions		Farm Credit Administration	580
Employment Standards Administration	2,469	Federal Deposit Insurance Corporation	3,641
Labor–Management Administration	991	Federal Reserve Banks	2,250
Mine Safety and Health Administration	2,729	Federal Reserve System Board	
Occupational Safety and Health		of Governors	429
Administration	2,403	National Credit Union Administration	619
Equal Employment Opportunity		Subtotal—Finance and Banking	11,249
Commission	2,948	*Industry-Specific Regulation*	
National Labor Relations Board	3,000	Commodity Futures Trading Commission	562
Occupational Safety and Health Review		Federal Communications Commission	1,894
Commission	88	Federal Energy Regulatory Commission	1,578
Subtotal—Job Safety and Working		Federal Maritime Commission	233
Conditions	14,628	Interstate Commerce Commission	675
Environment and Energy		Subtotal—Industry-Specific	
Council on Environmental Quality	13	Regulation	4,942
Army Corps of Engineers	1,122	TOTALS	
Economic Regulatory Administration	210	*Social regulation*	81,104
Petroleum Regulation	76	*Economic regulation*	26,090
Fish and Wildlife Service	1,500	GRAND TOTAL	107,194

Source: Melinda Warren and Kenneth Chilton, *An Analysis of 1990 Federal Regulatory Budget and Staffing*, Washington University, Center for the Study of American Business, 1989, Table A-2.

uct than consumers desire and charge a higher price for it. Monopolists, oligopolists, and monopolistically competitive firms may also waste resources and retard technology and innovation.

- *Natural monopoly.* In some circumstances, a concentration of market power may actually be efficient. Where one large firm can produce total industry output at a lower average cost than several smaller (competitive) firms, a natural monopoly exists. As we observed in Chapter 23, a natural monopoly originates in pervasive economies of scale.

- *Inequities.* In addition to generating the wrong mix of output (a less than optimal allocation of resources), the market may also dictate an undesired distribution of income. In other words, the distribution of income generated by the market may not correspond with society's view of equity. Some people may not be able to afford basic necessities; others may have too many goods.

If any of these conditions are present, the market will not provide satisfactory answers to our basic WHAT, HOW, and FOR WHOM questions. This raises the possibility that government intervention *might* improve the mix of output or distribution of income.

Antitrust is a potential intervention strategy only in the case of market power. Regulation, on the other hand, is a potential form of intervention in all cases of market failure.

Government Failure

The core issure here is whether we need or want so much regulation. Although regulation is a *potential* response to all forms of market failure, it is not necessarily a *desirable* response. Everyone acknowledges that markets are imperfect and that government intervention might improve the mix of output. But the heavy hand of government might be worse than the "invisible hand" of the market. Government intervention might *worsen* the mix of output or the distribution of income. In the real world **the choice is not between imperfect markets and flawless government intervention but rather between imperfect markets and imperfect intervention.**

The argument for *deregulation* rests on the observation that government regulation sometimes worsens market outcomes. **Government failure** may be worse than market failure. Specifically, regulation may lead to price, cost, or production outcomes that are inferior to those of an unregulated market. Or the regulations themselves may be more costly to implement and enforce than the benefits of the intervention are worth. In either case, an inferior allocation of resources results.

government failure: Government intervention that fails to improve economic outcomes.

NATURAL MONOPOLY

Market failure originating in natural monopoly provides the most convincing case for government regulation. To see this, we can compare the behavior of an *unregulated* natural monopoly to the optimal outcomes we desire.

Declining ATC

natural monopoly: An industry in which one firm can achieve economies of scale over the entire range of market supply.

Figure 26.1 illustrates the unique characteristics of a **natural monopoly**. *The distinctive characteristic of a natural monopoly is its downward-sloping average total cost (ATC) curve.* Because unit costs keep falling as the rate of production increases, a single large firm can underprice any smaller firm. Ultimately, it can produce all of the market supply at the lowest attainable cost. In an unregulated market, such a firm will "naturally" come to dominate the industry.

The force that pulls down the ATC curve in a natural monopoly is low marginal costs. Notice that the marginal cost (MC) curve in Figure 26.1 lies below the ATC curve at all rates of output. The ATC curve never rises into its conventional U shape because marginal costs never exceed average costs.

Subway systems, local telephone and utility companies, and cable TV operators are examples of natural monopoly. In all of these cases, huge fixed costs are required to establish production facilities (e.g., subway tunnels, transmission cables). The marginal costs of producing another rider, call, or program are negligible, however. As a result, average total costs start high but continuously decline until capacity is reached.

economies of scale: Reductions in minimum average costs that come about through increases in the size (scale) of plant and equipment.

The declining costs of a natural monopoly are of potential benefit to society. The **economies of scale** offered by a natural monopoly imply that no other market structure can supply the good as cheaply. Hence there is no reason to break up a natural monopoly with antitrust statutes.

Although the *structure* of a natural monopoly may be beneficial, its *behavior* may leave something to be desired. Natural monopolists have the same

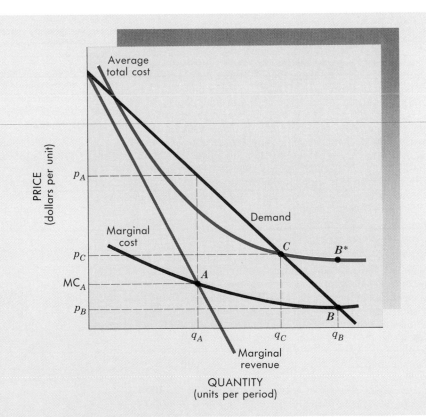

FIGURE 26.1
Natural Monopoly: Price Regulation

A natural monopoly confronts a downward–sloping ATC curve; MC is always less than ATC. If unregulated, a natural monopoly will produce q_A and charge p_A, as determined by the intersection of the marginal cost and marginal revenue curves (point A).

Regulation designed to achieve efficient prices will seek point B, where $p = $ MC. Still lower average costs (production efficiency) are attainable at higher rates of output, however. On the other hand, a zero-profit, zero-subsidy outcome exists only at point C.

Which price—output combination should be sought?

profit-maximizing motivations as other producers. Moreover, they have the monopoly power to achieve and maintain economic profits. Hence there is no guarantee that consumers will reap the benefits of a natural monopoly. Critics charge that the monopolist tends to keep most of the benefits (see In the News).

marginal cost pricing: The offer (supply) of goods at prices equal to their marginal cost.

Suboptimal outcomes Figure 26.1 illustrates the profit-maximizing behavior of a natural monopolist. An unregulated natural monopoly will seek the intersection of the marginal cost and marginal revenue curves (point A) and end up producing the quantity q_A and charging the price p_A

The natural monopolist's preferred outcome is not the most desirable one for society. This price–output combination violates the competitive principle of **marginal cost pricing.** The monopoly price p_A greatly exceeds the marginal cost of producing q_A of output, as represented by MC_A in Figure

In The News

NATURAL MONOPOLY

Prying Open the Cable-TV Monopolies

Prices, Lawsuits Place Pressure on the Industry

LOS ANGELES—The city of Los Angeles has spent roughly $1 million so far to keep some local entrepreneurs from competing against a cable-TV monopoly controlled out of Boston.

With a handful of exceptions, the roughly 9,000 cable franchises in the U.S. are monopolies, granted by local governments to a favored company, one usually partly owned by politically well-connected people. Governments pass out such monopolies and fiercely defend them, yet don't regulate prices charged to customers. The "franchise fees" that local governments charge cable operators rise with the revenues, and total hundreds of millions of dollars annually.

Soaring Prices

But the winds of competition are rustling in the cable business. Two or three dozen communities now allow second cable companies to compete, estimates John Mansell, a senior analyst with Paul Kagan Associates, a media research firm. Public unhappiness over service and rising prices is fueling the push for competition. Just last week, the General Accounting Office released a study saying rates charge by cable operators for basic service jumped 29% between December 1986 and October 1988. . . .

Defenders argue that cable television is one of those businesses, like a utility, that works best as a monopoly. Given the expense and street disruption required to lay cable to every home in an area, putting in more than one system is simply a waste of resources and an annoyance for residents in the area, they say.

Operators argue that in some places competition was tried, but it failed, leaving a monopoly anyway. "It's simply not viable to have two franchises in one area," says Marc Nathanson, chairman of Los Angeles-based Falcon Cable TV, which operates cable franchises nationwide.

Nor is price regulation necessary, cable operators say, because cable prices are held down by competition with regular, free broadcasters and other media. Recent price surges were simply a "catch-up" for prior years when cable rates were regulated and artificially depressed, operators contend.

Cable Television's Growing Reach

	Average monthly price of basic cable (in dollars)	Cable revenue from basic services (in millions of dollars)
1980	$ 7.85	$1,648.5
1981	8.14	2,100.1
1982	8.46	2,678.6
1983	8.76	3,101.0
1984	9.20	3,632.2
1985	10.25	4,366.5
1986	11.09	5,083.7
1987	13.27	6,552.7
1988	14.40	7,724.7

Source: Paul Kagan Associates Inc., Cable TV Investor.

—John R. Emshwiller

The Wall Street Journal, August 10, 1989, p. B1. Reprinted by permission of *The Wall Street Journal,* © Dow Jones & Company, Inc. (1989). All Rights Reserved.

In The News (continued)

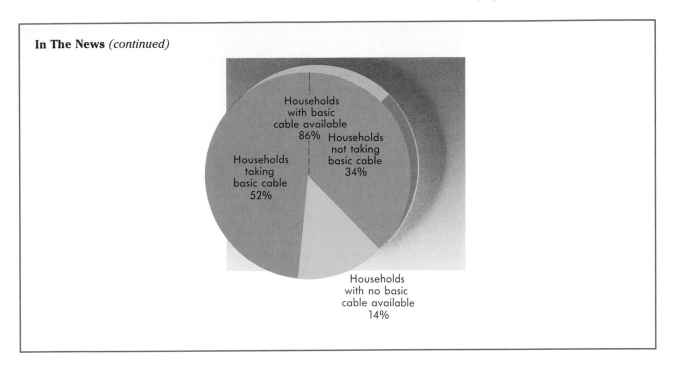

Households with basic cable available 86%

Households not taking basic cable 34%

Households taking basic cable 52%

Households with no basic cable available 14%

---

opportunity cost: The most desired goods or services that are forgone in order to obtain something else.

26.1. As a result of this gap, consumers are not getting accurate information about the **opportunity cost** of this product. This flawed price signal is the cause of market failure. The consequence of market failure is a suboptimal mix of output. We end up consuming less of this product (and more of other goods) than we would if charged its true opportunity cost.

The natural monopolist's profit-maximizing output (q_A) also fails to minimize average total cost. In a competitive industry, ATC is driven down to its minimum by relentless competition. In this case, however, reductions in ATC cease when the monopolist achieves his preferred output (q_A). Were he to increase output further, average total costs would fall.

economic profit: The difference between total revenues and total economic costs.

Finally, notice that the higher price (p_A) associated with the monopolist's preferred output (q_A) assures a fat profit. The **economic profit** may violate our visions of equity.

The suboptimal outcomes likely to emerge from a free-swinging natural monopoly create the basis for government intervention. The market alone cannot overcome the natural advantage of pervasive economies of scale. But the government could compel different outcomes. The question is, Which outcomes do we want?

Price Regulation

The first option we might consider is price regulation. The natural monopolist's preferred price (p_A) is, after all, the cause of our market failure. By regulating his behavior, we could compel a more appropriate price.

Price efficiency   Our case against the unregulated natural monopolist is based on his flawed price signal. By charging a price in excess of marginal cost, the monopolist causes a suboptimal allocation of resources. We could improve market outcomes, therefore, by compelling the monopolist to set the price equal to marginal cost. Such an efficient price would lead us to point B in Figure 26.1, where the demand curve and the marginal cost curve intersect. To achieve this objective, we simply set the regulated price at p_B.

Unfortunately, the price p_B will bankrupt the producer. In a natural monopoly, MC is always less than ATC. Hence *marginal cost pricing by a natural monopolist implies a loss on every unit of output produced.* In this case, the loss per unit is equal to $B^* - B$. If confronted with the price p_B, the firm will ultimately shut down and exit from the market.

If we want efficient pricing, we must provide a subsidy to the natural monopoly. In Figure 26.1 the amount of the subsidy would have to equal the anticipated loss at q_B, that is, the quantity q_B multiplied by the per-unit loss $(B^* - B)$. Such subsidies are provided to subway systems, thus helping maintain efficient fares and optimal ridership. However, taxpayers always complain about such subsidies and are loath to provide them for private companies. Hence political considerations typically preclude efficient (marginal cost) pricing, despite their economic benefits.

Production efficiency   Even if it were possible to impose marginal cost pricing, we still wouldn't achieve production efficiency. Production efficiency is attained at the lowest possible average total cost. At q_B we are producing a lot of output but still have some unused capacity. Since ATC falls continuously, we could achieve still lower average costs if we increased output beyond q_B. In a natural monopoly, production efficiency is achieved at capacity production.

Increasing output beyond q_B raises the same problems we encountered at that rate of output. At production rates in excess of q_B, ATC is always higher than price. Even MC is higher than price to the right of point B. Thus no regulated price can induce the monopolist to achieve minimum average cost. Some sort of subsidy would be required to offset the market losses.

Profit Regulation   An alternative to price regulation is profit regulation. If we choose not to subsidize a natural monopolist, we must permit it to charge a price high enough to cover all its costs, including a normal profit. We can achieve this result while eliminating any economic profit by compelling a price equal to average total cost. In Figure 26.1 this regulatory objective is achieved at point C. In this case, the rate of output is q_C and the regulated price is p_C.

Profit regulation looks appealing for two reasons. First, it eliminates the need to subsidize the monopolist. Second, it allows us to focus on profits only, thus removing the need to develop demand and cost curves. In theory, all we have to do is check the firm's annual profit-and-loss statement to confirm that it is earning a normal (average) profit. If its profits are too high, we can force the firm to reduce its price; if profits are too low, we may permit a price increase.

In practice, though, profit regulation can lead to bloated costs and dynamic inefficiency. *If a firm is permitted a specific profit rate (or "rate of return"), it has no incentive to limit costs.* On the contrary, higher costs imply higher profits if the profit *rate* is the focus of regulation. If permitted to charge 10 percent over unit costs, a monopolist may be better off with average costs of $6 rather than only $5. That translates into 60 cents of profit per unit, rather than only 50 cents. Hence there is an incentive to "pad costs." (See In the News for the way in which this relates to the regulation of AT&T.) If those costs actually represent improvements in wages and salaries, fringe benefits, or the work environment, then cost increases are doubly attractive to the firm and its employees. Cost efficiency is as welcome as the plague under such circumstances.

In The News

PRICE OR PROFIT REGULATION?

FCC Hopes New Regulations Will Cut Phone Rates— but Others Aren't So Sure

Since the breakup of the Bell System $3\frac{1}{2}$ years ago, federal regulators have forced American Telephone & Telegraph Co. to cut long-distance rates a whopping 33.5%. But whether phone bills will go even lower under newly proposed regulation is a matter of heated debate.

Earlier this week, the Federal Communications Commission proposed removing its limit on AT&T's profits and replacing it with a price cap. FCC Chairman Dennis Patrick and AT&T executives contend that the company would have more incentive to cut costs, passing part of the savings to consumers, with the rest fattening AT&T's bottom line. Moreover, says Larry Garfinkel, an AT&T vice president, the company would be more inclined to put new technology in its network, which would generate new services.

But consumer groups are skeptical. "Based on what we know, rates go down more under profit regulation," says Fred Goldberg, the Washington counsel to the National Association of State Utility Consumer Advocates.

Monitoring Costs

Currently, AT&T's interstate rates are set by limiting how much it can earn on its $9.1 billion investment in interstate plant and equipment. The allowed rate of return is now 12.2%. Under price regulation, the FCC would instead set a ceiling on what AT&T can charge. The ceiling would rise or fall depending on inflation, taxes, the industry's productivity, and AT&T's costs to connect to local phone companies.

The debate over which system is best centers in large part on how good the FCC is at monitoring AT&T's costs. Under profit regulation, prices should drop as technological advances reduce the company's costs. But if AT&T can keep its costs artificially high—and many people think it has—prices won't drop as fast as they could. One analyst estimates that AT&T could easily cut $2 billion of costs without affecting service.

AT&T denies it pads its costs, but acknowledges it doesn't have any incentive to cut them under profit regulation. "With price-cap regulation instead of rate-of-return, prices will go down more because we'll have the incentive to really try to be more efficient. We would pass some of that (savings) on to customers," says Wendell Lind, administrator of rates and tariffs for AT&T.

But Mr. Goldberg says that even if AT&T does pad its costs, the current regulatory system still does a better job of ensuring that the industry's declining costs are reflected in lower rates than a price-cap approach would....

—Janet Guyon

Output Regulation   Given the difficulties in regulating prices and profits, regulators may choose to regulate output instead. The natural monopolist's preferred output rate is q_A, as illustrated in Figure 26.2. We could compel this monopolist to provide a minimum level of service in excess of q_A. This regulated minimum is designated q_D in Figure 26.2. At q_D consumers get the benefit not only of more output but also of a lower price (p_D). At q_D total monopoly profit must also be less than at q_A, since q_A was the profit-maximizing rate of output.

It appears, then, that compelling any rate of output in excess of q_A can only benefit consumers. Moreover, output regulation is an easy rule to enforce.

Unfortunately, minimum service regulation can cause lots of problems. If forced to produce at the rate of q_D, the monopolist may seek to increase profits by cutting cost corners. This can be accomplished by deferring plant and equipment maintenance, reducing quality control, or otherwise lowering the quality of service. ***Regulation of the quantity produced may induce a decline in quality.*** Since a monopolist has no direct competition, consumers pretty much have to accept whatever quality the monopolist offers.

FIGURE 26.2
Minimum Service Regulation

Regulation may seek to ensure some minimal level of service. In this case, the required rate of output is arbitrarily set at q_D. Consumers are willing to pay p_D per unit for that output.

Regulated output q_D is preferable to the unregulated outcome (q_A, p_A) but may induce a decline in quality. Cost cutting is the only way to increase profits when the rate of output is fixed and price is on the demand curve.

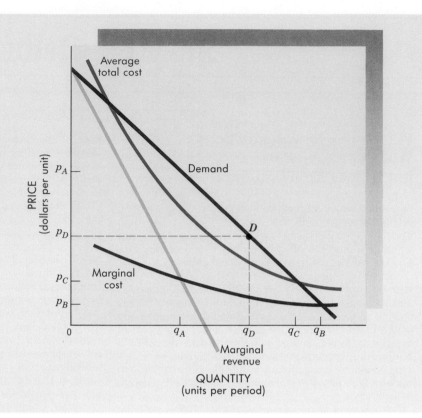

In addition to encouraging quality deterioration, output regulation at q_D also violates the principle of marginal cost pricing. Because an economic profit exists at q_D, equity goals may be jeopardized as well. Hence minimum service (output) regulation is not a panacea for the regulatory dilemma. Goal conflicts are inescapable, and any regulatory rule may induce undesired producer responses.

Second-Best Solutions

The call for public regulation of natural monopolies is based on the recognition that profit-maximizing behavior does not maximize social welfare in such circumstances. The starting point for our analysis is the recognition that a natural monopolist's unregulated price is too high and its rate of output is too low. However, the appropriate strategy for correcting these problems is not evident. Regulators can compel efficient prices or least-cost production only by offering a subsidy. Profit regulation is likely to induce cost-inflating responses. Output regulation provides an incentive for quality deterioration. No matter which way we turn, regulatory problems result.

The problems associated with regulation of natural monopolies will constrain regulatory outcomes. There is not much hope for transforming unregulated market failure into "perfect" regulated outcomes. In reality, regulators will have to choose a strategy that balances competing objectives (e.g., price efficiency, equity). A realistic goal for regulation is to *improve* market outcomes, not to *perfect* them.

THE COSTS OF REGULATION

Perhaps the problems and pitfalls of regulation are becoming clear. Once an industry has been targeted for regulation, a variety of choices must be made. What should be regulated—prices, profits, output, or the production process itself (e.g., workplace safety)? Typically, alternative forms of regulation lead to different prices, output, or costs, and they thus entail different answers to the questions of WHAT, HOW, and FOR WHOM to produce. Our choice is not just between an imperfect market outcome and a single regulated outcome but between a market outcome and *several* regulated alternatives. Each entails a distinct tradeoff between economic goals.

Administrative Costs Someone must sit down and assess these tradeoffs. To make a sound decision, a regulatory administration must have access to lots of information. At a minimum, the regulator must have some clue as to the actual shape and position of the demand and cost curves depicted in Figures 26.1 and 26.2. Crude illustrations won't suffice when decisions on the prices, output, or costs of a multibillion-dollar industry are being made. The regulatory commission needs volumes of details about actual costs and demand, and a platoon of experts must collect and analyze the needed production and market data. All of this labor represents a real cost to society, since the commission's lawyers, accountants, and economists could be employed elsewhere.

Table 26.1 illustrates the scope of opportunity costs associated with federal regulation. In fiscal year 1990, an estimated 107,194 people were employed in 51 regulatory agencies of the federal government. Thousands more had regulatory responsibilities in smaller agencies and the major executive departments. In addition to these federal workers, tens of thousands more were employed by state and local regulatory agencies.

Compliance Costs The administrative costs of regulation focus on resources used in the public sector. By its very nature, however, regulation also changes resource use in the private sector. Regulated industries must expend resources to educate themselves about the regulations, to change their production behavior, and often to file reports with the regulatory authorities. The human and capital resources used for these purposes represent the compliance cost of regulation.

Efficiency Costs Finally, we have to consider the potential costs of changes in output. Most regulation alters the mix of output, either directly or indirectly. Ideally, regulation will always improve the mix of output. But it is possible that bad decisions, incomplete information, or faulty implementation may actually *worsen* the mix of output. If this occurs, then the loss of utility associated with an inferior mix of output imposes a further cost on society, over and above administrative and compliance costs.

Efficiency costs may increase significantly over time. Over time, consumer tastes change, demand and marginal revenue curves shift, costs change, and new technologies emerge. Can regulatory commissions respond to these changes as fast as the market mechanism does? If not, even optimal regulations may soon become obsolete and counterproductive. Worse still, the regulatory process itself may impede new technology, new marketing approaches, or improved production processes. In these circumstances, regulation becomes a drag on economic growth, limiting outward shifts of the production-possibilities curve while perpetuating an increasingly undesired mix of output.

Balancing Benefits and Costs

The economic costs of regulation are a reminder of the "no free lunch" maxim. Although regulatory intervention may improve market outcomes, that intervention is not without cost. The real resources used in the regulatory process (and responses thereto) could be used for other purposes. Hence even if we could achieve "perfect" outcomes with enough regulation, the cost of achieving perfection might outweigh the benefits. ***Regulatory intervention must balance the anticipated improvements in market outcomes against the economic cost of regulation.*** In principle, the marginal benefit of regulation must exceed its marginal cost. If this is not the case, then additional regulation is not desirable, even if it would improve market outcomes.

The calculus of balancing regulatory benefits and costs is seldom simple. It is particularly difficult when the market failure results from externalities, where the market price of benefits and costs may not be apparent (pollution regulation is discussed in Chapter 27). Moreover, the two sides in every regulatory debate offer conflicting advice and information.

DEREGULATION IN PRACTICE

In recent years, the balance between costs and benefits has tipped in the direction of less regulation for some industries. The push to deregulate was prompted by two concerns. The first concern focused on the dynamic inefficiencies that regulation imposes. It appeared that these inefficiencies had accumulated over time, rendering the regulated industries less productive than desired. The other push for deregulation came from advancing technology, which destroyed the basis for natural monopoly. A brief review of the resulting deregulation illustrates the impact of these forces.

Railroads

The railroad industry was the first broad regulatory target of the federal government. Railroads are an example of natural monopoly, with high fixed costs and negligible marginal costs. And in 1887, when Congress created the Interstate Commerce Commission (ICC) to resolve disputes between the railroads and shippers, there were no airports or interstate highways to compete with the railroads. The ICC was established to limit monopolistic exploitation of this situation while assuring a "fair" profit to railroad owners. The ICC established rates and routes for the railroads while limiting both entry to and exit from the industry.

With the advent of buses, trucks, subways, airplanes, and pipelines as alternative modes of transportation, railroad regulation became increasingly obsolete and counterproductive. Regulated cargoes, routes, and prices prevented railroads from adapting their prices or services to meet changing consumer demands. With regulation-protected routes, they also had little incentive to invest in new technologies or equipment. As a result, railroad traffic and profits declined, while other transportation industries flourished. Many railroads, including the giant Penn Central, fell into bankruptcy.

In The News

DEREGULATION

The Milking of New York City

During the Great Depression the New York state legislature started regulating the milk industry. To prevent "destructive competition," it limited the number of firms permitted to distribute milk in the state. Eventually, five firms acquired oligopoly control over milk sales in New York City.

The harm to consumers was substantial. In the early 1980s the price of milk in New York City was 36 cents more per gallon than in adjacent New Jersey. In response to this higher price, New York City residents consumed 15 percent less milk. One state official estimated that the regulatory barriers to competition cost downstate milk consumers $100 million per year.

The first crack in the regulated milk cartel came in 1985 when Farmland Dairies was granted access to the Staten Island market. Milk prices on Staten Island dropped by 40 cents a gallon in the ensuing competition.

Farmland then applied for access to the rest of New York City's market. The state's commissioner of agriculture denied the application, fearing "deterioration in the quality and level of service to the market." That decision earned the commissioner the Federal Trade Commission's "National Consumer Fleece Award." Subsequently, that decision was overturned by the courts. On January 9, 1987, Farmland Dairies became the first new entrant into New York City's milk distribution market. Milk prices in the city fell by 20 percent overnight.

Adapted from *Regulation.* 1987, No. 1. Copyright 1987, The American Enterprise Institute, reprinted with permission.

The Railroad Revitalization and Regulatory Reform Act of 1976 was a response to this crisis. Its major goal was to reduce the scope of government regulation. Additional deregulation was included in the Staggers Act of 1980. Since then, railroads have had much greater freedom to adapt their prices and service to market demands.

Starting in 1979 whole classes of freight were exempted from rate regulation. Railroad companies have used that flexibility to increase their share of total freight traffic. Fresh fruits and vegetables, for example, were exempted

WORLD VIEW

DEREGULATION

London's "Big Bang"

On October 27, 1986, London's financial markets were deregulated. The British refer to that event as the "Big Bang."

Before the Big Bang, entry into London's stock and bond markets was highly restricted. Only a handful of firms traded government bonds, and foreign firms were prohibited from owning brokerage companies. Trading commissions—the price of service in financial markets—were fixed by regulation. The clubbish members of London's regulated financial markets enjoyed six-hour days, long lunches, and economic profits.

Deregulation transformed London's financial markets overnight. American, Japanese, and Swiss firms franti-

cally entered the London markets, via acquisitions, mergers, and the development of new firms. The new competition forced drastic cuts in trading commissions and stimulated a massive increase in trading volume. The average daily volume in the London stock market quadrupled in less than six months.

The Big Bang generated immediate benefits for investors, who now pay much lower commissions. Deregulation also strengthened London's position in global financial markets and generated thousands of new jobs. Not everyone was happy with deregulation, however. Many established firms could not keep up with the new competitive pace and so suffered losses and even had to shut down.

from ICC rate regulation in 1979. Railroads responded by *reducing* their rates and improving service. In the first year of deregulated rates, fruit and vegetable shipments increased over 30 percent. As Table 26.2 shows, this was a dramatic reversal of earlier trends. Deregulation of coal traffic (in 1980) and piggyback (trucks on railroad flatcars) traffic (in 1982) prompted similar turnarounds.

Not all rail rates have fallen. Railroads now have more flexibility to raise rates as well. The ICC still sets limits, however, on railroad prices (rates) where "market dominance" exists, to prevent abuse of monopoly powers. The ICC also continues to restrict route abandonment to assure at least minimal service in low-traffic areas.

Trucking

In the 1930s the ICC intervened in the trucking industry. In the depths of the Great Depression freight business was scarce and truckers had to slash their rates to attract customers. Trucking companies were incurring losses, and many were going broke. Congress feared that further competition would jeopardize this vital industry. To prevent this, Congress broadened the powers of the ICC to regulate interstate trucking. Minimum freight rates were established, routes were fixed, and barriers were erected to keep out new competition.

For a long while, the trucking industry flourished. Traffic grew nicely, profits increased regularly, and truck drivers became one of the nation's largest and best-paid unions (the Teamsters). The value of the established monopoly routes was reflected in the sale price of trucking licenses. In 1976–77, the average price of a trucking license exceeded $500,000 (see Table 26.3). People were willing to pay that much just to enter the industry and share in the regulation-protected profits.

Entry regulations were relaxed in 1978, and major reforms were instituted by 1979. These changes greatly diminished the value of existing licenses. Finally, Congress passed the Motor Carrier Act of 1980, which dismantled most remaining entry barriers. One thousand firms entered the trucking industry in 1980 alone. Within five years, the number of firms increased from 18,000 to over 30,000. The new entrants, most of them small owner-operated firms, put great pressure on prices and profits. Between 1977 and 1982 real truck rates (prices) fell 25 percent, and the rate of return on invested capital fell 50 percent. As Table 26.3 shows, the value of existing trucking licenses plummeted from $171,000 in 1980 to only $13,000 in 1981. Deregulation eliminated monopoly profits while greatly increasing the quantity and variety of service.

TABLE 26.2   Railroad Traffic, Selected Years, 1969–82

Deregulation enabled railroads to offer more competitive prices and services. When fruit and vegetable freight rates were deregulated in 1979, for example, railroads reduced their prices and reversed a serious decline in traffic.

Traffic	Index of rail carloadings (1978 = 100)						
	1969	1975	1978	1979	1980	1981	1982
Fruit	632	274	100	104	136	196	232
Vegetables	538	284	100	92	140	203	232
Coal	116	106	100	119	129	130	128
Grain	96	100	100	107	117	101	95
Piggyback traffic	84	71	100	101	90	95	105

Source: Center for the Study of American Business.

TABLE 26.3   Value of Trucking Licenses, 1975–82

To prevent "excessive' competition, the ICC limited entry into the trucking industry. This barrier to entry enabled established trucking firms to earn an economic profit. The value of these profits was reflected in the sales price of operating licenses. When entry barriers were lowered in 1978, more firms entered the industry, profits were squeezed, and the value of an operating license plummeted.

Year	Average, sale price
1975	$398,000
1976	579,000
1977	531,000
1978	370,000
1979	55,000
1980	171,000
1981	13,000
1982	15,000

Source: Thomas Gale Moore, "Rail and Truck Reform—The Record So Far," *Regulation,* November/December 1983.

Telephone Service

The telephone industry has long been the classic example of natural monopoly. Although enormous fixed costs are necessary to establish a telephone network, the marginal cost of an additional telephone call approaches zero. As we discussed in Chapter 23, AT&T long held the monopoly on both long-distance and most local telephone service. Once again, however, technology outpaced regulation. Communications satellites made it much easier and less costly for new firms to provide long-distance telephone service. The rate structure established by AT&T and the Federal Communications Commission also made long-distance service highly profitable. Accordingly, start-up firms clamored to get into the industry, and consumers petitioned for lower rates.

In 1982 the courts put an end to AT&T's monopoly, transforming long-distance telecommunications into a more competitive industry with more firms and less regulation. Since then, over 400 firms have entered the industry, and long-distance telephone rates have dropped sharply. Between 1983 and 1990, long-distance telephone rates fell more than 40 percent. The quality of service has also been improved with fiber optic cable, advanced switching systems, push-button phones, and a myriad of new phone-line services (e.g., Fax data transmission). All of these changes have contributed to a doubling of long-distance telephone use in the United States. The same kinds of changes have occurred around the world as other telephone monopolies have crumbled (see World View).

The new competition in long-distance services destroyed the "profit umbrella" AT&T had used to subsidize local phone services. Without that cross-subsidization, local telephone companies (the "Baby Bells") have had to increase prices for local service. These changes effectively redistributed resources and income from local users to long-distance users, thereby altering the market's response to WHAT and FOR WHOM. The HOW outcome was also changed by new technology.

Even after the breakup of AT&T, the Federal Communications Commission continued to regulate AT&T's profits. In 1987, however, the FCC proposed to adopt price regulation rather than profit regulation. As illustrated earlier, the FCC confronted one of the basic regulatory dilemmas (see In the News, p. 663).

W🌐RLD VIEW

DEREGULATION

Demise of Telephone Monopolies

The breakup of AT&T was spurred by new technology that undercut the basis for natural monopoly. The same technological advances have transformed the telecommunications industry around the world:

Japan: In 1984 the Japanese government ended the monopoly long held by Nippon Telegraph & Telephone (NTT). More than 500 companies have now entered the industry, chipping away at NTT's market share.

Great Britain: The British government has "privatized" British Telecommunications and licensed another company to build a second, competing network.
France: The French government has retained a single, state-owned network but opened the door to competition in equipment and services.
European Community: As the member nations of the European community remove trade barriers, competition between state monopolies (e.g., France and Germany) is increasing. A German citizen can call New York by using the Bundespost to call London, then switching to a cheaper service for the transmission to the United States.

Airlines

The Civil Aeronautics Board (CAB) was created in 1938 to regulate airline routes and fares. From its inception, the primary concern of the CAB was to ensure a viable system of air transportation for both large and small communities. Such a system would be assured, the CAB believed, only if a "fair" level of profits was maintained by entry and price regulations. So the focus of the CAB was on *profit* regulation.

Initially, the CAB set airline fares at roughly the levels of Pullman rates for train travel. This implied that air fares would be proportional to distance, as they were for train travel. In the late 1930s this fare structure was not unreasonable, as most flights were relatively short and planes were small.

As the airline industry grew, the CAB abandoned fare comparisons with trains but maintained the basic distance-based fare structure. To ensure "fair" profits, the CAB set fares in accordance with airline costs. This required the CAB to undertake intensive cost studies, based on accounting data provided by the airlines. Once the average cost of service and capital equipment was established, the CAB then set an average price that would assure a fair rate of return (profit). This approach was illustrated in Figure 26.1

A secondary objective of the CAB was to ensure air service to smaller, less-traveled communities. Short hauls entail higher average costs and therefore justify higher fares. To avoid high fares on such routes, the CAB permitted airlines to charge prices well in excess of average costs on longer, more efficient routes so long as they maintained service on shorter, unprofitable routes. This **cross-subsidization** was similar to that of the telephone industry, in which long-distance profits helped to keep local telephone charges low.

cross-subsidization: Use of high prices and profits on one product to subsidize low prices on another product.

To maintain this price and profit structure, the CAB had to regulate routes and limit entry into the airline industry. Otherwise, established carriers would abandon short, unprofitable routes, and new carriers would offer service only on more profitable routes. Unregulated entry thus threatened both cross-subsidization and the CAB's vision of a "fair" profit.

The CAB was extremely effective in restricting entry into the industry. Would-be entrants had to demonstrate to the CAB that their proposed service was required by "public convenience and necessity" and was superior to that of established carriers. Established carriers could oppose a new application for operating authority by demonstrating sufficient service, offering to expand their service, or claiming superior service. In view of the fact that new applicants had no airline experience, established carriers easily won the argument. From 1938 until 1977 the CAB *never* awarded a major route to a new entrant. Over the years the CAB rejected scores of applications to start new airlines.

The CAB also eliminated price competition between established carriers. The CAB fixed air fares on all routes. Airlines could reduce fares no more than 5 percent, and could not increase them more than 10 percent without CAB approval.

The absence of new entrants and price competition kept interstate air fares high, even while larger planes and more efficient engines were reducing marginal costs. The behavior of *intrastate* airlines—which were not regulated by the ICC—provided a yardstick for measuring the inefficiency of regulation. Studies showed that regulated interstate fares were as much as 60 percent higher than those on comparable intrastate routes that lay beyond CAB's regulatory authority.

Ironically, the established airlines failed to reap as much profit as possible from these high fares. Unable to compete on the basis of price, the established carriers had to engage in nonprice competition.

The most costly form of nonprice competition was frequency of service. Once the CAB authorized service between any two cities, a regulated carrier could provide as many flights as desired. This enticed the regulated carriers to purchase huge fleets of planes and provide frequent departures. In the process, however, load factors (the percentage of seats filled with passengers) fell and average costs rose.

product differentiation: Features that make one product appear different from competing products in the same market.

The regulated carriers also pursued **product differentiation** by offering various amenities, including special meals, first-run movies, free drinks, better service, and wider seats. This nonprice competition further inflated average costs and reduced profits.

Profit regulation ultimately came to be regarded as a failure. The regulated airline industry was not as profitable as anticipated. And consumers were not being offered very many price–service combinations. The CAB started to change its regulatory approach in 1977. The first step was approval of "Super Saver" fares that entailed discounts of up to 70 percent from regulated fare levels. This permitted regulated carriers to reduce prices on long-distance routes and thereby increase load factors.

The Airline Deregulation Act of 1978 (see Table 26.4) changed the structure and behavior of the airline industry even more dramatically. Entry regulation was effectively abandoned. New firms are now permitted entry into the industry if they can show that they are "fit, willing, and able" to provide the service they propose. The showing of public "necessity" or superior service is no longer required. With the elimination of this **barrier to entry,** the number of carriers increased greatly. Between 1978 and 1985 the number of airline companies increased from 37 to 174! The new entrants intensified competition on nearly all routes. The share of domestic markets with four or more carriers grew from 13 percent in May 1978 to 73 percent in May 1981.

barriers to entry: Obstacles that make it difficult or impossible for would-be producers to enter a particular market, e.g., patents.

The new entrants into the airline industry brought not only more service possibilities but also sharply lower cost. In the era of regulation, airlines had had little incentive to control costs. Wages and salaries had increased continually, while productivity had declined. By contrast, new entrants were able to offer lower wages and experiment with new management systems. This

TABLE 26.4 The History of Airline (De)Regulation)

Year	Event
1938	Civil Aeronautics Authority and the Air Safety Board established by Congress under the Civil Aeronautics Act.
1940	Independent status given to CAB, including rule-making, licensing, adjudicatory, and accident-investigating powers.
1958	Federal Aviation Act establishes CAB as an independent agency responsible for the promotion and regulation of the U.S. air transportation system; safety aspects of CAB (including accident-investigating power) transferred to Federal Aviation Administration (FAA).
1978	Airline Deregulation Act of 1978 is passed by Congress and signed into law by President Carter.
1979	Barriers to entry relaxed; entry permitted to firms that prove that they are "fit, willing, and able."
1982	CAB's authority over route regulation ceased; airlines able to add or delete routes at will.
1983	CAB's authority for fare approval ceased; discount fares flourish.
1984	CAB eliminated (December 31).

greatly reduced the average cost of providing service. In 1985, for example, People Express had average costs of 5.2 cents per available seat-mile, while United Airlines had an average cost of 7.2 cents and Delta had 8.2 cents. This cost advantage enabled the new entrants to offer significantly lower fares. The resulting price competition reduced average fares as much as 40 percent below regulated levels (see Table 26.5). The most dramatic fare reductions came on long-distance travel, triggered by a variety of discount fares. In 1978, some 46 percent of all passengers flew at discount fares; in 1985, over 80 percent flew at reduced fares. At the same time, however, fares on shorter, less-traveled routes increased as cross-subsidization ended.

On January 1, 1982, the CAB's authority over route regulation ended (see Table 26.4). Since then, airlines have been able to add or delete routes at will. The only constraint on new routes into busy airports is the availability of "slots"—that is, takeoff and landing rights for specific times. This is a problem for local airports, however, not an issue for federal regulation.

The CAB's authority over air fares ended on January 1, 1983. Since then, airlines have been able to adapt their fares to market supply and demand. The CAB itself was eliminated at the end of 1984. Its remaining responsibilities—for foreign travel, mail service, mergers, and operating authority—were transferred to the U.S. Department of Transportation.

Deregulation of the airline industry greatly increased market entry and price competition. According to a 1988 study by the Federal Trade Commission, deregulation saved consumers $100 billion in air fares and enabled millions of Americans to fly who otherwise couldn't afford it. The massive increase in airline use even had an unforeseen externality. As air traffic increased from 250 million to 455 million trips per year, highways became less congested. According to Professor Richard McKenzie, airline deregulation resulted in 600,000 fewer *auto* accidents a year and reduced traffic fatalities

TABLE 26.5   Prices After Deregulation, 1983
(deregulated fares as percentage of regulated levels)

Air fares have risen since 1978. But the fare increases have been much smaller than they would have been under the CAB's previous pricing formula. In 1983 average fares on heavily used long-distance routes were only 60 percent of those dictated by the CAB's pricing formula. Rates on previously subsidized short hauls were higher, however.

Market distance	Market density (passengers per day)			
	10–50	51–200	201–500	500+
1–400 miles	114	112	95	71
401–1,500 miles	110	97	87	80
1,501+ miles	N/A	75	65	60

Source: Civil Aeronautics Board, *Implementation of the Provisions of the Airline Deregulation Act of 1978,* January 1984.

by nearly 1,700 per year! At the same time, *air* traffic safety also improved, as evidenced by a decline in the rate of air accidents and fatalities.

Increasing concentration   The tremendous growth in airline traffic since deregulation has been hailed as one of the greatest policy achievements of the 1980s. The changing character of the industry has spurred criticism as well, however. Of particular concern is the increasing concentration of the industry. In the competitive fray spawned by deregulation, lots of new entrants and even some established airlines went broke. Unable to match lower fares and increased service, scores of airline companies exited the industry in the period 1985–90. In the process, a handful of major carriers increased their market share and gained near monopoly power in specific "hub" airports (e.g., USAir provides 80 percent of the flights departing Pittsburgh; TWA in St. Louis and Northwest Airlines in Minneapolis have comparable power). In 1990 just eight carriers accounted for over 90 percent of all scheduled airline traffic. Moreover, these dominant firms had erected high barriers to entry, including frequent-flier programs, computerized load-control programs, centralized reservation systems, long-term leases of scarce airport landing rights (slots), and hub connections. This consolidation of power raises fears of oligopoly pricing and spurs calls for "reregulation." As Senator John Danforth said, "We cannot have a system that is both deregulated and uncompetitive."

Defenders of deregulation are quick to point out that despite increasing *industry* concentration, there is more competition in most airline markets. In 1979 some 22 percent of all traffic was in monopoly markets, where a single carrier supplied at least 90 percent of all traffic. By 1989 only 11 percent of all traffic was in such monopoly markets. Furthermore, entry is still easier today than it was before deregulation. Hence the airline industry is more of a **contestable market,** even if not a perfectly competitive one. Finally, supporters of deregulation point to the precipitous drop in air fares, the growth of traffic, and the improvement of safety. Why, they ask, would anyone want to reregulate an industry whose deregulation has generated so many benefits? Public policy should instead focus on keeping entry barriers low, thus maximizing the contestability of airline markets.

contestable market: An imperfectly competitive industry subject to potential entry if prices or profits increase.

DEREGULATE EVERYTHING?

Deregulation of the railroad, trucking, telephone, and airline industries has yielded substantial benefits. In general, deregulation has resulted in more competition, lower prices, and increased and more varied service. Such experiences bolster the case for less government intervention in the marketplace. Nevertheless, we should not jump to the conclusion that all regulation of business should be dismantled. All we know from experience is that the regulation of these specific industries had become outmoded. Changing consumer demands, new technologies, and substitute goods had simply made existing regulations obsolete and counterproductive. A combination of economic and political forces doomed them to extinction.

But were these regulations ever necessary? In the 1880s there were no viable alternatives to railroads for overland transportation. The forces of natural monopoly could easily have exploited consumers and retarded economic growth. The same was largely true for long-distance telephone service prior to the launching of communications satellites. Even the limitations on competition in trucking and banking made some sense in the depths of the Great Depression. One should not conclude that regulatory intervention never made sense just because the regulations themselves later became obsolete.

Even today, most people recognize the need for regulation of many industries. Local telephone and utility companies, for example, are still natural monopolies. In the absence of government regulation, their prices and profits would undoubtedly be higher. The regulated price–output combinations may not be optimal, but they are probably superior to those of unregulated monopoly.

Likewise, few people seriously propose relying on competition and the good judgment of consumers to determine the variety or quality of drugs on the market. Regulations imposed by the Food and Drug Administration restrain competition in the drug industry, raise production costs, and inhibit new technology. But they also make drugs safer. Here, as in other industries, there is a tradeoff between the virtues of competition and those of regulation. The basic policy issue, as always, is whether the benefits of regulation exceed their administrative, compliance, and efficiency costs. The persistent challenge for public policy is to adapt regulations—or to discard them (i.e., deregulate)—as market conditions, consumer demands, or technology changes.

SUMMARY

- Government intervention is justified when the market fails to generate the optimal (best possible) mix of output or distribution of income.

- Sources of market failure (suboptimal outcomes) include externalities, public goods, and market power. In addition, an undesirable income distribution may prompt government intervention.

- Antitrust and regulation are alternative intervention options for dealing with market power. Antitrust focuses on market structure and anticompetitive practices. Regulation stipulates specific market behavior.

- Natural monopolies offer pervasive economies of scale. Because of this potential efficiency antitrust may be inappropriate.

• Regulation of natural monopoly can focus on price, profit, or output. Price regulation may require subsidies; profit regulation may induce cost escalation; and output regulation may lead to quality deterioration. These problems compel compromises and acceptance of second-best solutions in meeting goals.

• The demand for deregulation rests on the argument that the costs of regulation exceed the benefits. These costs include the opportunity costs associated with regulatory administration and compliance as well as the (dynamic) efficiency losses that result from inflexible pricing and production rules.

• Deregulation of the railroad, trucking, telephone, and airline industries has been a success. In all these industries, regulation had been outmoded by changing consumer demands, products, and technology. As regulation was relaxed, these industries became more competitive, output increased, and prices fell.

• Recent experiences with deregulation do not imply that all regulation should end. Regulation is appropriate if market failure exists *and* if the benefits of regulation exceed the costs. As benefits and costs change, decisions about what and how to regulate must be reevaluated.

Terms to Remember   Define the following terms:

laissez faire	marginal cost pricing
market failure	opportunity cost
antitrust	economic profit
regulation	cross-subsidization
government failure	product differentiation
natural monopoly	barriers to entry
economies of scale	contestable market

Questions for Discussion

1. How do restrictions on route abandonment (e.g., in the railroad and airline industries) affect the distribution of income?

2. What would happen to railroad shipping rates if the ICC eliminated price ceilings? Would any new competition emerge?

3. Prior to 1982, AT&T kept local phone rates low by subsidizing them from long-distance profits. Was such cross-subsidization in the public interest? Explain.

4. In most cities local taxi fares are regulated. Should such regulation end? Who would gain or lose?

Problems

1. Suppose a natural monopolist has fixed costs of $30 and a constant marginal cost of $2. The demand for the product is as follows:

Price (per unit)	$10	$9	$8	$7	$6	$5	$4	$3	$2	$1
Quantity demanded (units per day)	0	2	4	6	8	10	12	14	16	18

Under these conditions,
(*a*) What price and quantity will prevail if the monopolist is not regulated?
(*b*) What price–output combination would be appropriate for regulation that seeks to duplicate competitive outcomes?

(*c*) What price–output combination would be appropriate for regulation that seeks to eliminate economic profits?
Illustrate your answers with a graph.

2. In the long-distance telephone industry, three new transmission technologies—microwaves, satellites, and fiber optic cable—have replaced the traditional coaxial cable made of copper. The following schedule indicates the costs of the different technologies. (Although similar to the actual figures, the data have been altered to ease calculation and graphing.) Voice circuits indicate the number of phone conversations that can be carried simultaneously. Costs are given in thousands of dollars per month.

Number of voice circuits	50	100	500	1,000	1,500
Total cost of:					
Fiber optic cable	$60	$100	$250	$300	$337
Microwave	$40	$45	$150	$250	$375
Satellite	$35	$50	$200	$350	$525

(*a*) Compute and graph (in a single diagram) the average total costs of each technology.
(*b*) Draw the long-run average cost curve facing a long-distance telecommunication company that is deciding what transmission technology to use.
(*c*) Are there economies, diseconomies, or constant returns to scale?
(*d*) In the long run, how many firms would you expect to provide long-distance service over any given route between two cities? (Base your answer on the long-run average cost curve you drew.)
(*e*) With microwave technology, what would be the smallest number of voice circuits that a company could provide and still achieve minimum average cost?
(*f*) What kind of technology would be most appropriate if only 50 voice circuits were needed between two towns? If between 100 and 1,000 voice circuits were needed? If more than 1,000 voice circuits were needed?
(*g*) Currently there is a national debate about whether or not long-distance telephone service should be deregulated. Do you think the long-distance market should be regulated? Why or why not?

Environmental Protection

Progress in environmental problems is impossible without a clear understanding of how the economic system works in the environment and what alternatives are available to take away the many roadblocks to environmental quality.

–Council on Environmental Quality, First Annual Report

What good is a clean river if you've got no jobs?

–Steelworkers' Union Official in Youngstown, Ohio

A hole in the ozone layer is allowing increased ultraviolet radiation to reach the earth's surface. The hole is the result of excessive release of chlorine gases (chlorofluorocarbons, or CFCs) from air conditioners, plastic-foam manufacture, industrial solvents, and aerosol spray cans (e.g., deodorants, insecticides). The resulting damage to the stratosphere is causing skin cancer, cataracts, and immune disorders.

Skin cancer may turn out to be one of our less serious problems. As carbon dioxide builds up in the atmosphere, it creates a gaseous blanket around the earth that is trapping radiation and thus heating the atmosphere. Scientists predict that the rising temperature will melt the polar ice caps, raise sea levels, flood coastal areas, and turn rich croplands into deserts. Environmentalists warn that if we don't stop dumping so much carbon dioxide into the atmosphere, we may confront this environmental calamity within sixty years.

Everyone wants a cleaner and safer environment. So why don't we just stop polluting the environment with CFCs, carbon dioxide, toxic chemicals, and other waste? If we won't do it ourselves, why doesn't the government step in and force people to stop polluting?

Economics is part of the answer. To reduce pollution, we have to change our patterns of production and consumption. This will entail economic costs, in terms of both restricted opportunities and more expensive ways of producing or consuming goods. This suggests that we have to weigh the benefits of a cleaner, safer environment against the costs of environmental protection.

Instinctively, most people don't like the idea of measuring the value of a cleaner environment in dollars and cents. But most people might also agree that spending $2 trillion to avoid a few cataracts is awfully expensive. There has to be *some* balance between the benefits of a cleaner environment and the cost of cleaning it up. The **optimal rate of pollution** is the one that achieves the desired balance between the benefits and costs of environmental protection.

optimal rate of pollution: The rate of pollution that occurs when the marginal social benefit of pollution control equals its marginal social cost.

677

In this chapter we assess our environmental problems from this economic perspective. We have four primary concerns:

- How do (unregulated) markets encourage pollution?
- What are the costs of greater environmental protection?
- How much of our (scarce) resources should be allocated to environmental protection?
- How can government policy best ensure an "optimal" environment?

To answer these questions, we first survey the major types and sources of pollution. Then we examine the benefits and costs of environmental protection, highlighting the economic incentives that shape market behavior. The chapter ends with a review of President Bush's sweeping 1990 proposals for environmental cleanup.

THE ENVIRONMENTAL THREAT

The hole in the ozone layer and the earth's rising temperature are at the top of the list of environmental concerns. The list is much longer, however, and very old as well. As early as A.D. 61, the statesman and philosopher Seneca was complaining about the smoky air emitted from household chimneys in Rome. And historians are quick to remind us that open sewers running down the street were once the principal mode of urban waste disposal and that typhoid epidemics were a recurrent penalty for water pollution. So we cannot say that environmental damage is a new phenomenon, or that it is now worse than ever before.

But we do know more about the sources of environmental damage than our ancestors did, and we can better afford to do something about it. After all, it was centuries before people discovered the scientific relationship between open sewers and periodic epidemics. And it took nearly a century for us to discern the chemical link between auto exhaust and air pollution.

Our understanding of the economics of pollution has increased as well. We have come to recognize that pollution imposes direct costs on the economy. Pollution impairs health and thus reduces labor-force activity and output (see In the News). Pollution also destroys capital (e.g., the effects of air pollution on steel structures) and diverts resources to undesired activities (e.g., car washes, laundry, and cleaning). Not least of all, pollution directly reduces our social welfare by denying us access to clean air, water, and beaches.

Air Pollution

Air pollution is as familiar as a smoggy horizon. But smog is only one form of air pollution. There are five major air pollutants: carbon monoxide (CO), total suspended particulates (TSP), sulfur dioxide (SO_2), volatile organic compounds (VOC), and nitrogen oxides (NO_x). Each of these pollutants has a unique effect on the environment.

Carbon monoxide (CO) is the colorless, odorless, and poisonous gas that is produced by incomplete burning of the carbon in fuels. In general, carbon monoxide slows reaction speeds and contributes to a wide variety of heart and lung problems. The primary source of CO pollution is the automobile. Another familiar source of carbon monoxide is cigarette smoking, which accounts for a tiny fraction of total air pollution but for most of the CO in the lungs of smokers.

In The News

AIR POLLUTION

Is Breathing Hazardous to Your Health?

A New Report Says the Air Is Full of Poisons

Data collected by the Environmental Protection Agency show that the air may be far more poisonous than expected. Ozone, a lung irritant and precursor of smog, was up 5 percent from 1986 to 1987 and another 15 percent last year. And in 1987 industry routinely released 2.4 billion pounds of toxic substances into the air—which suggests that air should carry a warning from the surgeon general.

In the EPA's first national inventory of toxic releases, the chemical industry headed the list with 886.6 million pounds. Emissions in eight states exceeded 100 million pounds (table). Kansas's total was smaller, but had a surprise ingredient: 69,000 pounds of the nerve gas phosgene, which killed thousands of soldiers in World War I. Indiana air got 143,097 pounds of methyl isocyanate, which killed over 3,000 Indians in Bhopal. Though the Chemical Manufacturers Association (CMA) insists that its members have reduced emissions since 1987, the survey may understate the problem. It omits vapors from waste dumps, small sources such as dry cleaners and cars, and releases into soil or water that enter the air after evaporating. In fact, toxics may exceed 4.8 billion pounds annually, says EPA spokesman Chris Rice.

The health effects of the emissions remain unclear. Industry argues that the chemicals become so diluted in the air that they're innocuous. But the brew is hardly health food for lungs. It includes 235 million pounds of carcinogens such as benzene and formaldehyde, and 527 million pounds of such neurotoxins as toluene and trichloroethylene (TCE). Although no one has estimated how much of the toxics people actually breathe, the EPA calculates that air toxics cause more than 2,000 cases of cancer every year—based on only 20 chemicals, not the 329 in the survey.

The Toxic 10
Of 2.4 billion pounds of toxics emitted in 1987, more than half came from 10 states.

States	Millions of pounds of toxic pollutants released into the air
Texas	229.9
Louisiana	134.5
Tennessee	132.5
Virginia	131.4
Ohio	122.5
Michigan	106.2
Indiana	103.5
Illinois	103.1
Georgia	94.3
North Carolina	92.3

Source: EPA.

—Sharon Begley *with* Mary Hager *in Washington and* Harry Hurt III *in Los Angeles*

Particulates, such as industrial soot and smoke, contribute to respiratory problems and are a major factor in the reduction of visibility. Some specific particulates, such as asbestos (from construction materials and brake linings) and lead (from car exhausts), have also been identified as particularly dangerous to health.

Sulfur dioxide (SO_2) is an acrid, corrosive, and poisonous gas that is created whenever fuels containing high levels of sulfur are burned. Electric utilities and industrial plants that burn high-sulfur coal or fuel oil are the prime sources of SO_2. Coal burning alone accounts for about 60 percent of all emissions of sulfur oxides. Sulfur oxides have been identified as the primary villain in air-pollution disasters. During one such disaster, in Donora, Pennsylvania, in 1948, half of the town's 14,000 inhabitants fell ill, and 20 died. In 1952 a "killer smog" in London accounted for 1,600 deaths.

Acid rain Sulfur dioxide is also a big ingredient in the formation of acid rain. Acid rain destroys vegetation and has been held responsible for the destruction of forests in West Germany, Canada, and the United States. Canada claims that the acid rain destroying its forests and lakes comes from coal-burning power plants in the American Midwest.

Smog Nitrogen oxides (NO_x), another ingredient in the formation of acid rain, are also a principal ingredient in the formation of smog. Smog not only irritates the eyes and spoils the view, but it also damages plants, trees, and human lungs. Automobile emissions account for 40 percent of urban smog. Bakeries, dry cleaners, and production of other consumer goods account for an equal amount of smog. The rest comes from electrical power plants and industrial boilers.

The greenhouse effect The greenhouse effect noted at the outset of this chapter is caused by many of the air pollutants just mentioned. The prime "villain" in the greenhouse effect, however, is the otherwise harmless carbon dioxide (CO_2) that we exhale. Unfortunately, we and nature now release so much CO_2 that the earth's oceans and vegetation can no longer absorb it all. The "excess" CO_2 is creating a gaseous blanket around the earth.

Although the buildup of CO_2 and other gases in the atmosphere is undisputed, the scope of the resulting environmental threat is intensely debated (see World View). Everyone agrees, however, that the burning of fossil fuels is a significant source of CO_2 buildup. The destruction of rain forests, which absorb CO_2, also contributes to the greenhouse effect.

Water Pollution Water pollution is another environmental threat. Its effects are apparent in the contamination of drinking water, restrictions on swimming and boating, foul-smelling waterways, and swarms of dead fish and floating debris. The

W♦RLD VIEW

AIR POLLUTION

The Greenhouse Controversy

Worldwide pollution is causing a buildup of gases in the atmosphere. These gases act as a blanket, trapping radiation and warming the earth. But how much danger does the greenhouse effect pose?

Some scientists argue that the greenhouse effect is already evident. They say the earth's temperature has risen by 0.6 degree centigrade in the last century and that the warming trend is accelerating. They foresee a further temperature increase of 3–5 degrees by the year 2030. That would be enough to raise the ocean levels 4 feet and radically alter global weather. Moreover, because the gas buildup is continuous, they assert that we must reduce carbon dioxide emissions sharply just to hold temperatures steady.

Other scientists are skeptical about both the temperature change and its causes. A 1988 study by the National Oceanic and Atmospheric Administration concluded that there has been no ocean warming in the past century.

Therefore, the observed increase in land temperature must be due to other phenomena (e.g., increasing urbanization). Furthermore, the amount of CO_2 emitted into the atmosphere by human activity (about 7 billion tons per year) is a tiny fraction of natural emissions (200 billion tons per year) from volcanoes, fires, and lightning. Skeptics also point out that the same computer models predicting global warming in the next generation also "predict" a much larger increase in temperature for the previous century than actually occurred.

In view of these scientific disputes, there is no consensus on what steps to take. At a global conference in 1989 the Dutch government proposed a freeze on the level of greenhouse emissions and a 20 percent reduction in emissions by 2005. Fewer than half of the sixty-eight nations in attendance supported that proposal. The Bush administration chose instead to spend $250 million on the additional climate research in 1990 while endorsing continued multilateral negotiations on global responses to the greenhouse problem.

In The News

WATER POLLUTION

Dangerous Amounts of Lead in Drinking Water

Nearly one of every five Americans served by public water systems consumes levels of lead in drinking water higher than the government considers safe, according to preliminary findings of the Environmental Protection Agency.

The excess lead found in the drinking water of 38 million people nationwide accounts for slightly lower intelligence among 143,500 children every year, according to a draft copy of a new EPA report. It also accounts for 118,400 cases of hypertension, 75 strokes and 370 heart attacks among middle-aged white males, and higher risk of pregnancy complications among 622,000 women of child-bearing age, according to the EPA analysis.

In financial terms, the lead contamination problem costs more than $1 billion a year in medical care, plumbing repairs and specialized education and reduced future earnings among children with learning disabilities, the report said.

—Michael Weisskopf

The Washington Post, November 6, 1986, p. 1. Copyright © 1986 The Washington Post.

Environmental Protection Agency (EPA) estimates that one-third of U.S. water characteristically is polluted, in the sense that it violates federal water-quality standards. Nearly 80 percent of all water basins suffer measurable pollution, though not necessarily enough to make the water unsafe.

Organic pollution   The most common form of water pollution occurs in the disposal of organic wastes. These not only are unsightly and foul smelling, but also strain the biological capacity of water to sustain life.[1]

The most familiar sources of organic waste are the bathroom toilet and the kitchen garbage disposal. The wastes that originate there are collected in sewer systems and ultimately discharged into the nearest waterway. The key question is whether the wastes are treated (separated and decomposed) before ultimate discharge. Sophisticated waste-treatment plants can reduce organic pollution up to 99 percent.[2] Unfortunately, only 70 percent of the U.S. population is served by a system of sewers and adequate (secondary) treatment plants.

In addition to household wastes, our waterways must also contend with industrial wastes. Over half the volume of industrial discharge comes from just a few industries—principally paper, organic chemicals, petroleum, and steel. And within these industries, a relatively small number of very large firms account for most of the discharge. In a study of industrial pollution in the Southeast, the EPA found that only 1 percent of the 1,920 operating plants were responsible for more than 50 percent of the total untreated waste discharged.

Finally, there are all those herds of cattle and other farm animals. Organic waste from livestock enters waterways directly, particularly after heavy rains. Animal wastes don't cause too great a problem in such places as Boston and New York, but they can wreak havoc on the water supplies of towns in California, Texas, and Kansas.

[1]The standard measure of such pollution is *biochemical oxygen demand* (BOD), the amount of oxygen used in five days to decompose organic wastes. Waste-treatment plants help reduce BOD by separating out and decomposing some of the waste before it is discharged into the water.

[2]But that doesn't mean that all our pollution problems will be solved. On the contrary, the treatment of sewage creates new disposal problems, as we shall discuss shortly.

Thermal pollution *Thermal pollution* is an increase in the temperature of waterways brought about by the discharge of steam or heated water. Heat discharges can kill fish, upset marine reproductive cycles, and accelerate biological and chemical processes in water, thereby reducing its ability to retain oxygen.

The sources of thermal pollution are very few and quite specific. Heat discharges are the result of using water to cool an industrial process, just as radiator water is used to cool a car's engine. Electric power plants account for over 80 percent of all thermal discharges, with primary metal, chemical, and petroleum-refining plants accounting for nearly all the rest.

Eutrophication Another common form of water pollution results from the discharge of sediments and nutrients into waterways. The sediments tend to make the water shallower, while the nutrients increase algae growth. During this process, called *eutrophication*, the character of the waterway is altered, with fish populations changing and eventually disappearing. If eutrophication continues long enough, a lake will "die," ultimately turning into marshland and swamp.

Phosphates in household detergents, which reach waterways via municipal sewage systems, account for approximately half the phosphate volume. Chemical fertilizers are another major source of eutrophication.

Solid-Waste Pollution

Solid waste represents yet another environmental threat. Solid-waste pollution is apparent everywhere, from the garbage can to litter on the streets and beaches, to debris in the water, to open dumps. Although we tend to think of consumption as the end of the line for economic activity, a great deal of solid waste is generated in the process of consumption. Indeed, from a physical point of view, all we do in production and consumption is change the form of the earth's fixed stock of resources. Our world environment contains as many atoms now as it did 10,000 years ago. During those years, however, we (and nature) have continually changed the physical form of our resources. Virgin timber is converted into pulp, the pulp into newsprint, the newsprint into a newspaper; the newspaper is read (thereby "consumed") and discarded; the discarded newspaper ends up at the dump. No material is lost, it just takes on several different forms. This is what environmentalists refer to as the "materials-balance problem." Resources will not disappear once we have used them but must instead be shuffled around into a new use or hidden from view.[3]

Empty cans and bottles, discarded packaging, paper bags, old tires, and steak bones are everyday reminders of the materials-balance problem. According to EPA estimates, we generate over 5 billion tons of solid waste each year (see Table 27.1). This figure includes more than 30 billion bottles, 60 billion cans, 100 million tires, and millions of discarded automobiles and major appliances. Where do you think all this refuse goes?

As Table 27.1 indicates, most solid wastes originate in agriculture (slaughter wastes, orchard prunings, harvest residues) and mining (slag heaps, mill tailings). The much smaller amount of solid waste originating in residential and commercial use is considered more dangerous, however, simply because it accumulates where people live. In fact, most large cities are simply running

---

[3]This is true even of wastes that are treated in an attempt to eliminate water pollution. The treated (removed) wastes are referred to as "sludge," which, alas, transforms the water-pollution problem into a waste-disposal problem. If we choose to burn the solid waste, we create an air-pollution problem.

TABLE 27.1 What Makes Solid Wastes?

Over 5 billion tons of solid waste (paper, glass, scraps, etc.) are generated each year. Where does it all go?

Source	Tonnage (millions)
Municipal trash and garbage	173
Sewage sludge	5
Industrial wastes	340
Mineral wastes	2,100
Agricultural wastes	2,600
Total	5,218

Source: Environmental Protection Agency.

out of places to dump their garbage. New York City alone generates 24,000 tons of trash a day. Because it has neither the land area nor the incinerators needed for disposal, it must ship its garbage to other states. Philadelphia ships its garbage all the way to Panama.

THE COST OF POLLUTION

Shipping garbage to Panama is an expensive answer to our waste-disposal problem. But even those costs are only a small fraction of the total cost of environmental damage. Much greater costs are associated with the damage to our health (labor), buildings (capital), and land. Even the little things count, like being able to enjoy a clear sunset or take a deep breath.

Although many people don't like to put a price on the environment, some monetary measure of environmental damage is important in decision making. Unless we value the environment above everything else, we have to establish some method of ranking the importance of environmental damage. Although it's tempting to say, for example, that clean air is "priceless," *we won't get clean air unless we spend resources to get it*. This economic reality suggests that we begin by determining how much clean(er) air is worth to us.

Assigning Prices   In some cases, it is fairly easy to put a price on environmental damage. Scientists can measure the increase in cancer, heart attacks, and other disorders attributable to air pollution. Engineers can also measure the rate at which buildings decay or forests and lakes "die." Economists can then estimate the dollar value of this damage by assessing the economic value of lives, forests, lakes, and other resources. If, for example, people are willing to pay $5,000 for a cataract operation, then we could assert that the avoidance of such eye damage is worth at least $5,000. Saving a tree is worth whatever the marketplace is willing to pay for the "products" of that tree. Using such computations, the U.S. Environmental Protection Agency estimates that air pollution alone costs us over $40 billion a year in health, property, and vegetation damage.

The job of pricing environmental damage is much more difficult with intangible losses like sunsets. Nevertheless, when governmental agencies and courts are asked to assess the damages of oil spills and other accidents, they must try to inventory *all* costs, including polluted sunsets, reduced wildlife, and lost recreation opportunities. Such computations were a critical consideration in determining the multi-billion-dollar damages caused by the 1989 Exxon oil spill in Prince William Sound off the town of Valdez, Alaska.

The "science" of computing environmental damage is a very inexact one. The primary problem is that much of the damage is due to intangibles that have no market price. Nevertheless, crude but reasonable procedures generate damage estimates measured in hundreds of billions of dollars per year.

Cleanup Possibilities

One of the most frustrating things about all of this environmental damage is that it could be avoided. The EPA estimates that *95 percent of current air and water pollution could be eliminated by known and available technology*. Nothing very exotic is needed; just simple things like auto-emission controls, smokestack cleaners, improved sewage and waste-treatment facilities, and cooling towers for electric power plants. Even solid-waste pollution could be reduced by comparable proportions if we made the necessary effort. Approximately half of our municipal and commercial wastes respresent salvageable materials (paper, glass, metal) that can be recycled for further use. Or we could compact and burn the whole mess under controlled conditions, thereby transforming our garbage into a useful (relatively low-polluting) energy source. That would still leave us with some noncombustible residuals and hydrocarbons to contend with, but we would at least be getting some cheap energy.

MARKET INCENTIVES

During the last decade, public policy has been increasingly forceful in combating pollution. In many cases (as in that of auto emissions), the results have been dramatic. The question remains, however, why we continue to pollute so much. Why do individual consumers and business firms pollute the air, water, and land?

Previous chapters have placed great stress on the market forces that influence the economic behavior of individual consumers, firms, and government agencies. A persistent theme running through those discussions was the role that various kinds of incentives can play in altering behavior. Incentives in the form of price reductions can be used to change consumer buying habits. Incentives in the form of high profit margins encourage production of desired goods and services. And market incentives in the form of cost differentials help to allocate resources efficiently. Accordingly, we should not be too surprised to learn that market incentives play a major role in pollution behavior.

The Production Decision

Imagine that you are the majority stockholder and manager of an electric power plant. As we have observed, such plants are responsible for a significant amount of air pollution (especially sulfur dioxide and particulates) and nearly all thermal water pollution. Hence your position immediately puts you on the most-wanted list of pollution offenders. But suppose you bear society no grudges and would truly like to help to eliminate pollution. Let's consider the alternatives.

As the owner-manager of an electric power plant, you will strive to make a profit-maximizing **production decision**. That is to say, you will seek the rate of output at which marginal revenue equals marginal cost. We shall

---

production decision: The selection of the short-run rate of output (with existing plant and equipment).

assume that the electric power industry is regulated by the state power commission so that the price of electricity is fixed, at least in the short run. The effect of this assumption is to render marginal revenue equal to price, thus giving us a horizontal price line, as in Figure 27.1a.

Figure 27.1a also depicts the marginal and average total costs (MC and ATC) associated with the production of electricity. By equating marginal cost (MC) to price (marginal revenue, MR), we observe (point A) that profit maximization occurs at an output of 1,000 kilowatt hours per day. Total profits are illustrated by the shaded rectangle between the price line and the average total cost (ATC) curve.

FIGURE 27.1 Profit Maximization in Electric Power Production

Production processes that control pollution may be more expensive than those that do not. If they are, the MC and ATC curves will shift upward (to MC_2 and ATC_2). At the new profit–maximizing rate of output (point B), output and total profit shrink. Hence a producer has an incentive to continue polluting, using cheaper technology.

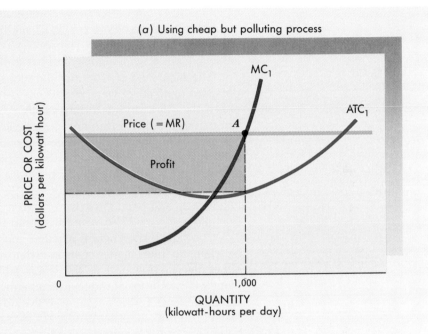

(a) Using cheap but polluting process

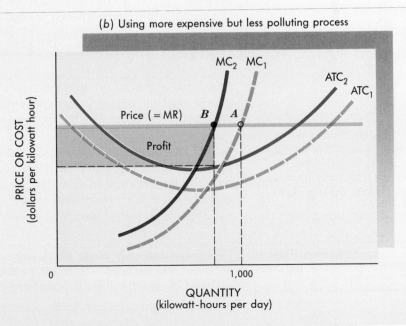

(b) Using more expensive but less polluting process

The Efficiency Decision

---

efficiency decision: The choice of a production process for any given rate of output.

The profits illustrated in Figure 27.1*a* are achieved in part by use of the cheapest available fuel under the boilers (which create the steam that rotates the generators). Recall that the construction of a marginal cost curve presumes some knowledge of alternative production processes. Recall, too, that the **efficiency decision** requires a producer to choose that production process (and its associated cost curve) that minimizes costs for any particular rate of output.

Unfortunately, the efficiency decision in this case leads to the use of high-sulfur coal, the prime villain in SO_2 and particulate pollution. Other fuels, such as low-sulfur coal, fuel oil, and nuclear reactors, cost considerably more. Were you to switch to one of them, the ATC and MC curves would both shift upward, as in Figure 27.1*b*. Under these conditions, the most profitable rate of output would be less than before (point *B*), and total profits would decline (note the smaller profit rectangle in Figure 27.1*b*). Thus pollution abatement can be achieved, but only at significant cost to the plant.

The same kind of cost considerations lead the plant to engage in thermal pollution of adjacent waterways. Cool water must be run through an electric utility plant to keep the turbines from overheating. And once the water runs through the plant, it is too hot to recirculate. Hence it must be either dumped back into the adjacent river or cooled off by being circulated through cooling towers. As you might expect, it is cheaper simply to dump the hot water in the river. The fish don't like it, but they don't have to pay the construction costs associated with cooling towers. Were you to get on the environmental bandwagon and build those towers, your production costs would rise, just as they did in Figure 27.1*b*. The fish would benefit, but at your expense.

The big question here is whether you and your fellow stockholders would be willing to incur higher costs in order to cut down on pollution. Eliminating either the air pollution or the water pollution emanating from the electric plant will cost a lot of money; eliminating both will cost much more. And to whose benefit? To the people who live downstream and downwind? We don't expect profit-maximizing producers to take such concerns into account. The behavior of profit maximizers is guided by comparisons of revenues and costs, not by philanthropy, aesthetic concerns, or the welfare of fish.

MARKET FAILURE: EXTERNALITIES ———————————————

---

externalities: Costs (or benefits) of a market activity borne by a third party; the difference between the social and private costs (benefits) of a market activity.

The moral of this story—and the critical factor in pollution behavior—is that people tend to maximize their personal welfare, balancing private benefits against private costs. For the electric power plant, this means making production decisions on the basis of revenues received and costs incurred. The fact that the power plant imposes costs on others, in the form of air and water pollution, is irrelevant to its profit-maximizing decision. Those costs are *external* to the firm and do not appear on its profit-and-loss statement. Those external costs—or **externalities**—are no less real, but they are incurred by society at large rather than by the firm.[4]

Externalities in Production

Whenever external costs exist, a private firm will not allocate its resources and operate its plant in such a way as to maximize social welfare. In effect, society is permitting the power plant the free use of valued

---

[4]The term "externalities" may be used to refer to either external costs or external benefits; here we are dealing only with external costs.

"Where there's smoke, there's money."

Drawing by Joe Mirachi; © 1985 The New Yorker Magazine, Inc.

resources—clean air and clean water. Thus the power plant has a tremendous incentive to substitute those resources for others (such as high-priced fuel or cooling towers) in the production process. The inefficiency of such an arrangement is obvious when we recall that the function of markets is to allocate scarce resources in accordance with consumers' expressed demands. Yet here we are, proclaiming a high value for clean air and clean water and encouraging the power plant to use up both resources by offering them at zero cost to the firm.

social costs: The full resource costs of an economic activity, including externalities.

private costs: The costs of an economic activity directly borne by the immediate producer or consumer (excluding externalities).

The inefficiency of this market arrangement can be expressed in terms of a distinction between social costs and private costs. **Social costs** are the total costs of all the resources that are used in a particular production activity. On the other hand, **private costs** are the resource costs that are incurred by the specific producer.

Ideally, a producer's private costs will encompass all the attendant social costs, and production decisions will be consistent with our social welfare. Unfortunately, this happy identity does not always exist, as our experience with the power plant illustrates. ***When social costs differ from private costs, external costs exist. In fact, external costs are equal to the difference between the social and private costs***—that is,

- External costs = social costs − private costs

market failure: An imperfection in the market mechanism that prevents optimal outcomes.

When external costs are present, the market mechanism will not allocate resources efficiently. This is a case of **market failure**. The price signal confronting producers is flawed. By not conveying the full (social) cost of scarce resources, the market encourages excessive pollution. We end up with a suboptimal mix of output and the wrong production processes. Our collective social welfare would be greater with different market behavior and a cleaner environment.

**FIGURE 27.2
Market Failure**

Social costs exceed private costs by the amount of external costs (externalities). Production decisions based on private costs alone will lead us to point B, where private MC = MR. At point B, the rate of output is q_p.

To maximize social welfare, we equate *social* MC and MR, as at point A. Only q_s of output is socially desirable. The failure of the market to convey the full costs of production keeps us from attaining this outcome.

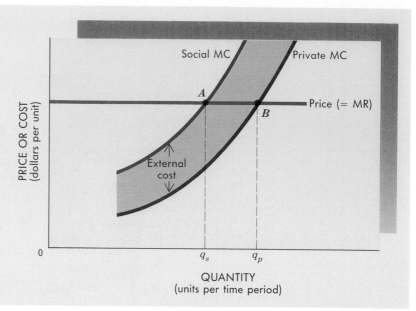

The nature and consequences of this market failure are illustrated in Figure 27.2, which again depicts the cost situation confronting the electric power plant. Notice that we use two different marginal cost curves this time. The lower one, the *private* MC curve, reflects the private costs incurred by the power plant when it operates on a profit-maximization basis, using high-sulfur coal and no cooling towers. It is identical to the MC curve of Figure 27.1a. We now know, however, that such operations impose external costs on others in the form of air and water pollution. Hence social costs are higher than private costs, as reflected in the *social* MC curve. To maximize social welfare, we would equate social marginal costs with marginal revenue (point A in Figure 27.2) and thus produce at the output level q_s. The private profit maximizer, however, equates *private* marginal costs and marginal revenue (point B) and thus ends up producing at q_p, making more profit but also causing more pollution. As a general rule, *if pollution costs are external, firms will produce too much of a polluting good*.

Externalities in Consumption

The divergence between private and social costs that is apparent in the case of electric power plants can also be observed in many consumption activities. A consumer, like a producer, tends to maximize personal welfare. We buy and use more of those goods and services that yield the highest satisfaction (marginal utility) per dollar expended. By implication (and the law of demand), we tend to use more of a product if we can get it at a discount—that is, pay less than the full price. Unfortunately, the "discount" often takes the form of an external cost imposed on neighbors and friends.

Automobile driving illustrates the problem. The amount of driving one does is influenced by the price of a car and the marginal costs of driving it. As was convincingly illustrated during the energy crisis of the 1970s, people buy smaller cars and drive less when the attendant marginal costs (for instance, gasoline prices) increase substantially. But automobile use involves not only *private costs* but *external costs* as well. As observed earlier, auto emissions (carbon monoxide, hydrocarbons, and nitrogen oxides) have long been a principal cause of air pollution. In effect, automobile drivers have been

W🌐RLD VIEW

EXTERNALITIES

Cleaning Up the West's Dirtiest Nation

Environment: Green Power Has Arrived in the Land of the Tulip

Off the port of Rotterdam, there is a half-mile-wide chasm in the North Sea, sealed off from the waves by dikes. The Dutch are clever with water. They have contrived this latest wonder as the final destination for what none of Europe wants. Into it goes the poisoned sediment of waste dumped by the industries and cities that crowd the banks of the Rhine. Peering into the hole from atop a breezy dike, a marine engineer says, "It'll take 20 years to fill it. Then what?"

You could ask the same question of Holland. The land of tulips, windmills, scrubbed doorsteps and creamy cows is in reality the dirtiest nation in the West, and its poisoned air and water have put the Dutch in the vanguard of a broad political change sweeping across Europe. . . .

Pigs, Cows and Cars

Being the sump of Europe makes Holland particularly sensitive. Three of the continent's industry-choked rivers—the Rhine, the Meuse and the Schelde—all converge on the tiny country. But the 14.7 million Hollanders are also their own worst ecological enemies. They are crowded into the most densely populated country in Europe—14 times more tightly packed than are Americans—but they drive the most cars per square kilometer, they burn the most fossil fuel per person in Europe, and their busy farmers are among the most intensive users of chemical fertilizers. On top of that, Holland's human population is outnumbered by its pigs and cows, whose manure is too fulsome for their fragile land to bear. And heavily concentrated Dutch industry is no less prolific a producer of toxic waste and noxious fumes than are its neighbors.

—David Lawday

U.S. News & World Report, September 11, 1989, p. 68. Copyright © 1989 U.S. News & World Report.

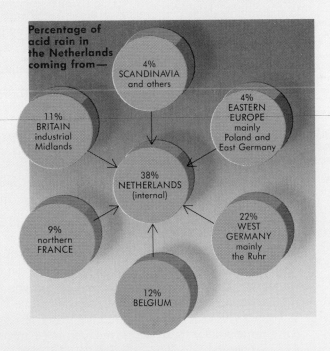

Percentage of acid rain in the Netherlands coming from—

4% SCANDINAVIA and others

11% BRITAIN industrial Midlands

4% EASTERN EUROPE mainly Poland and East Germany

38% NETHERLANDS (internal)

9% northern FRANCE

22% WEST GERMANY mainly the Ruhr

12% BELGIUM

The Sump of Europe

About half the pollution in the Netherlands comes from other countries, including roughly 80 percent of the country's surface water pollution, 50 percent of its smog, and 60 percent of its acid rain.

able to use a valued resource, clean air, at no cost to themselves. Naturally, they tended to use more of that resource than they otherwise would, thus lowering their private marginal costs and driving and polluting more. Few motorists saw any personal benefit in installing exhaust-control devices, because the quality of the air they breathed would be little affected by their efforts. Hence low private costs led to excessive pollution when high social costs were dictating cleaner air.

A divergence between social and private costs can be observed even in the simplest of consumer activities, such as throwing an empty beer can out the window of your car. To hang onto the beer can and later dispose of it in a trash barrel involves personal effort and thus private marginal costs. To throw it out the window not only is more exciting but effectively transfers the burden of disposal costs to someone else. Thus private costs can be distinguished from social costs. The resulting externality ends up as roadside litter.

The same kind of divergence between private and social costs helps to explain why people abandon old cars in the street rather than haul them to scrapyards. It also explains why people use vacant lots as open dumps. In all of these cases, *the polluter benefits by substituting external costs for private costs.* In other words, market incentives encourage environmental damage.

REGULATORY OPTIONS

The failure of the market to include environmental costs in production and consumption decisions creates a basis for government intervention. As always, however, we confront a variety of policy options. We may define these options in terms of *two general strategies for environmental protection:*

- *Alter market incentives* in such a way that they discourage pollution.

- *Bypass market incentives* with some form of regulatory intervention.

Altering Market Incentives

Insofar as market incentives are concerned, the key to environmental protection is to eliminate the divergence between private costs and social costs. The opportunity to shift some costs onto others lies at the heart of the pollution problem. If we could somehow compel producers to *internalize* all costs—pay for both private and previously external costs—the divergence would disappear, along with the incentive to pollute. Thus we have to find a way to make polluters pay for their pollution.

emission charge: A fee imposed on polluters, based on the quantity of pollution.

Emission charges   One possibility is to establish a system of **emission** (or effluent) **charges,** direct costs attached to the act of polluting. Suppose that we let you keep your power plant and permit you to operate it according to profit-maximizing principles. The only difference is that we no longer agree to supply you with clean air and cool water at zero cost. From now on, we will charge you for these scarce resources. We might, say, charge you 2 cents for every gram of noxious emission you discharge into the air. In addition we might charge you 3 cents for every gallon of water you use, heat, and discharge back into the river.

Confronted with such emission charges, you would have to alter your production decision. *An emission charge increases private marginal cost and thus encourages lower output.* Figure 27.3 illustrates this effect.

FIGURE 27.3
Emission Fees

Emission charges can be used to close the gap between marginal social costs and marginal private costs. Faced with an emission charge of t, a private producer will reduce output from q_0 to q_1. Emission charges may also induce different investment and efficiency decisions.

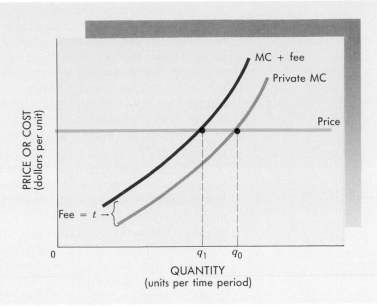

Once an emission fee is in place, a producer may also reevaluate the efficiency decision. Consider again the choice of fuels to be used in our fictional power plant. We earlier chose high-sulfur coal, for the very good reason that it was the cheapest fuel available. Now, however, there is an additional cost attached to burning such fuel, in the form of an emission charge on noxious pollutants. This cost may change the efficiency decision in one of two ways. The increased cost of using high-sulfur coal may encourage you to switch to other, cleaner sources of energy. This would increase the private marginal costs but substitute for the payment of emission fees. A fee-induced change in fuels would also reduce pollution per unit of output.

An emission charge might also persuade a firm to incur higher fixed costs. Rather than pay emission charges, it may prove more economical to install "scrubbers" and other smokestack controls that reduce the volume of emissions from the burning of high-sulfur coal. This would entail additional capital outlays for the necessary abatement equipment but might not alter marginal costs. In this case, the fee-induced change in fixed costs might reduce pollution without any reduction in output.

The actual response of producers will depend on the relative costs involved. If emission charges are too low, it may be more profitable to continue burning and polluting with high-sulfur coal and simply pay a nominal fee. This is a simple pricing problem. We could set the emission price higher, prompting the behavioral responses we desire.

The same kind of relative cost considerations would apply to the thermal pollution associated with the power plant. The choice heretofore has been between building expensive cooling towers (and not polluting) and not incurring such capital costs (and simply discharging the heated water into the river). The profit-maximizing choice was fairly obvious. Now, however, the choice is between building cooling towers or paying out a steady flow of emission charges; the profit-maximizing decision is not so evident. The decisive factor will be how high we set the emission charges. If the emission charges are set high enough, the producer will find it unprofitable to pollute.

What works on producers will also sway consumers. Surely you've heard of deposits on returnable bottles. At one time the deposits were imposed by the beverage producer to encourage you to bring the bottle back so it could be used again. But producers discovered that such deposits discouraged sales and yielded very little cost savings. The economics of returnable bottles were further undermined by the advent of metal cans and, later, plastic bottles. Thirty years ago, virtually all soft drinks and most beer came in returnable bottles. Today, returnable bottles are rarely used. One result is the inclusion of over 30 billion bottles and 60 billion cans in our solid-waste-disposal problem.

We could reduce this solid-waste problem by imposing a deposit on all beverage containers. This would internalize pollution costs for the consumer and render the throwing of a beer can out the window equivalent to throwing away money. Some people would still find the thrill worthwhile, but they would be followed around by others who attached more value to money. The state of Oregon imposed a 5 cent deposit on beverage containers in 1972 and soon thereafter discovered that beverage-container litter in Oregon declined by 81 percent! Since that time, other states and communities have also imposed mandatory deposits as a mechanism for eliminating the distinction between social and private costs.

Recycling materials An important bonus that emission charges offer is an increased incentive for the recycling of materials, and thus a reduction in our solid-waste problem. The glass and metal in used bottles and cans can be recycled to produce new bottles and cans. Such recycling not only eliminates a lot of unsightly litter, but also diminishes the need to mine new resources from the earth, a process that often involves its own environmental problems. The critical issues are once again relative costs and market incentives. A container producer has no incentive to use recycled materials unless they offer superior cost efficiency and thus greater profits. The largest component in the costs of recycled materials is usually the associated costs of collection and transportation. In this regard, an emission charge such as the 5-cent container deposit lowers collection costs because it motivates consumers to return all their bottles and cans to a central location.

Higher user fees Another market alternative is to raise the price consumers pay for scarce resources. If people used less water, we wouldn't have to build so many sewage treatment plants. In most communities, however, the price of water is so low that people use it indiscriminately. Higher water fees would encourage water conservation.

A similar logic applies to auto pollution. The cheapest way to cut down on auto pollution is to drive less. Higher gasoline prices would encourage people to use alternative transportation and drive more fuel-efficient cars.

Pollution fines Not far removed from the concept of emission and user charges is the imposition of fines or liability for cleanup costs. In some situations, such as an oil spill, the pollution is so sudden and concentrated that society has little choice but to clean it up quickly. The costs for such cleanup can be imposed on the polluter, however, through appropriate fines. Such fines place the cost burden where it belongs. In addition, they serve as an incentive for greater safety, for such things as double-hulled oil tankers and more efficient safety mechanisms on offshore oil wells. In the absence of pollution penalties, a producer has an incentive to avoid safety costs and take greater risks. The Water Quality Improvement Act of 1970 established financial liability for the cleanup costs involved in oil spills. It also required the producer to notify the government whenever such spills occurred.

The EPA acquired still greater authority to control oil and chemical spills with passage of the Comprehensive Environmental Response, Compensation, and Liability Act of 1980. That act established a tax on crude oil and an assortment of chemical products. The resulting revenues have created a "superfund" to be used to monitor and clean up hazardous oil and chemical spills. The act also allows the EPA to recoup *treble* damages from a firm that causes a spill but fails to help clean it up. In 1989 alone the federal government levied over $15 billion in pollution fines.

Privatization Another mechanism for establishing and enforcing fines is to *privatize* the environment. In England, for example, individuals can purchase fishing rights along stretches of a stream. As owners of the environment, they are quick to identify any pollution and sue the polluter for damages. This threat of quick response and financial liability discourages would-be polluters. When streams are in the public domain, by contrast, no individual has enough of a direct interest to monitor and enforce environmental protection.

Privatization of parks, beaches, and waterways would undoubtedly create a strong market for environmental protection. There are two objections to this market approach, however. Privatization is not a viable option for some of our worst environmental threats, like the greenhouse effect or the ozone thinning. Moreover, where privatization might be an effective deterrent to environmental damage, questions of equity arise. Privatized beaches, parks, and lakes would be accessible only to those who were willing and able to pay the price of admission. Although such a pricing policy makes economic sense, it conflicts with firmly held views about equal access to these natural resources.

Bypassing the Market Although the potential of altered market incentives to encourage environmental protection are substantial, they are not the only or always the best intervention strategy. Consider again the case of automobile emissions. Were we to rely on emission charges as a mechanism for abating auto pollution, we might have to measure the amount of pollutants discharged by each vehicle and levy appropriate charges. But such a program would require tremendous effort and cost, because there are over 100 million cars on the road. In this case, the costs of monitoring emissions and levying charges might outweigh the benefits of reduced pollution. An alternative control mechanism might be more appropriate.

Regulatory standards Direct regulation has been a frequently used alternative. The federal government began regulating auto emissions in 1968 and got tough under the provisions of the Clean Air Act of 1970. The act required auto manufacturers to reduce hydrocarbon, carbon monoxide, and nitrogen oxide emissions by 90 percent within six years of the act's passage. Although the timetable for reducing pollutants was later extended, the act did stimulate auto manufacturers to reduce auto emissions dramatically: by 1990, new cars were emitting only 4 percent as much pollution as 1970 models. (The greater number of cars on the street and their extended use kept air pollution levels high, however.)

Regulatory standards may specify not only the required reduction in emissions, but also the *process* by which those reductions are to be achieved. Clean air legislation mandated not only fewer auto emissions but also specific processes (e.g., catalytic converters, lead-free gasoline) for attaining them. Specific processes and technologies are also required for toxic waste disposal and water treatment. Laws requiring the sorting and recycling of trash (see In the News) are also examples of process regulation.

Although such hands-on regulation can be effective, this policy option also entails risks. By requiring all market participants to follow specific rules, the regulations may impose excessive costs on some activities and too low a constraint on others. Some communities may not need the level of sewage treatment the federal government prescribes. Individual households may not generate enough trash to make sorting and separate pickups economically sound. Some producers may have better or cheaper ways of attaining environmental standards. *Excessive process regulation may raise the costs of environmental protection* and discourage cost-saving innovation. There is also the risk of regulated processes becoming entrenched long after they are obsolete. When that happens we may end up with worse outcomes than a less regulated market would have generated—that is to say, a situation of **government failure.**

government failure: Government intervention that fails to improve economic outcomes.

Central Planning

Some of the worst evidence of government failure exists in the most regulated economies—the countries of Eastern Europe. Prior to 1990, Eastern Europe relied on central planning to make production and investment decisions. There was no *market* incentive to pollute, since there was no opportunity for private profit. On the other hand, the central planners had to set priorities. Their choice was to maximize production. Environmental concerns had lower priority. This set of priorities created an environmental catastrophe: polluted air and water, dying forests, poisoned food, and deteriorating human health. Poland, for example, produces six times more air pollution per unit of output than does Western Europe. Europe's largest coal-burning power plant, located in Belchatow, burns soft brown coal and covers the countryside with sulfur and soot. In East Germany, the state-produced car, the Trabant, burns a mix of gasoline and fuel oil that leaves city centers coated in greasy soot. A third of East Germany's rivers are biologically dead because of toxic waste from state-owned chemical plants. As Eastern Europe has learned, government-directed production is not necessarily cleaner than market-directed production.

In The News

BYPASSING THE MARKET

Los Angeles Requires Recycling, Trash Separation

LOS ANGELES—The City Council has unanimously approved mandatory trash separation and recycling in a $160 million program to halve the amount of garbage deposited in the city's rapidly filling landfills.

While about 1,000 U.S. cities, including Washington, D.C., have some kind of recycling program, the Los Angeles effort will be among the nation's largest, along with those in New York City and statewide in New Jersey.

The plan will require all 720,000 single-family households in the city to separate glass and plastic bottles, aluminum cans and newspaper into different containers for collection. The city eventually will sell reusable materials to recyclers.

The Washington Post, December 22, 1989, p. A14.

W🌐RLD VIEW

CENTRAL PLANNING

Darkness at Noon: As Shroud of Secrecy Lifts in East Europe, Smog Shroud Emerges

Old Technology, Dirty Fuels Lower Life Expectancies, Turn the Danube Brown

Getting One's Fix of Clean Air

BUDAPEST—Heavy breathing and wheezing resonate in the somber corridor outside a lung clinic here. Dozens of people, from tiny children to the elderly, wait patiently for their 15-minute turns in one of the five "inhalitoriums," telephone-booth-size closets where they can breathe clean air.

"It's just like being at the ocean," says Kornelia Lanyi, a doctor at the clinic, who assists a young mother and her two-year-old asthmatic son as they emerge from the cool, white mist.

On days when the pollution is heaviest, this clinic treats more than 180 people, all seeking a brief respite from the greasy brown Budapest air outside. Other Hungarians retreat into one of the underground caves scattered across the country, to breathe natural steam.

Scientists and doctors here think that as many as 10% of the deaths in Hungary are directly related to pollution.

And ghastly though the problem is here, they believe it is even worse in parts of Czechoslovakia, Poland and East Germany.

Dark Side

As political reform has swept across Eastern Europe, lifting the secrecy that shrouded so many aspects of life, one of the most disturbing revelations has been the extent to which the Communist regimes ravaged the environment. The new access to government data has brought disclosures suggesting that outmoded technologies and a dependence on the cheapest fuels caused pollution at levels almost unimaginable in the West.

Eastern European countries spew more than 17 million tons of sulfur into the air each year, the equivalent of five million loaded dump trucks. Emission levels per square mile are almost seven times as high as in the U.S. Then there are the huge quantities of nitrogen oxide—the poisonous reddish-brown gas emitted in auto exhausts—and such heavy metals as lead, mercury, cadmium, zinc and copper, which have been linked to forest decline, genetic defects and cancer.

As Olga Banlaky, a 75-year-old pensioner waiting in the Budapest clinic, puts it, "In this part of the world, nobody takes breathing for granted."

—Mark M. Nelson

BALANCING BENEFITS AND COSTS

Even if a "perfect" regulatory strategy could be designed, it still might not be desirable. Protecting the environment entails costs as well as benefits. Installing smokestack scrubbers on factory chimneys and catalytic converters on cars requires the use of scarce resources. Taking the lead out of gasoline wears out engines faster and requires expensive changes in technology. Switching to "clean" fuels requires enormous investments in technology, plant, and equipment. The EPA estimates that a ten-year program to achieve national air and water standards would cost close to $1 trillion. Reducing carbon dioxide emissions to a level that would forestall the greenhouse effect would cost another $1 trillion to $4 trillion, according to the Bush administration.

Opportunity Costs   Whatever the exact costs of environmental protection, it is apparent that we are talking about an enormous reallocation of productive resources. Although cleaning up the environment is a universally acknowledged goal, we must remind ourselves that those resources could be used to fulfill other goals as well. The multi–trillion-dollar tab would buy a lot of subways and parks or build decent homes for the poor. If we choose to devote those resources

opportunity cost: The most desired goods or services that are forgone in order to obtain something else.

instead to environmental efforts, we shall have to forgo some other goods and services. This is not to say that environmental goals don't deserve that kind of priority, but simply to remind us that any use of our scarce resources involves an **opportunity cost.**

Fortunately, the amount of additional resources required to clean up the environment is relatively modest in comparison to our productive capacity. Over a ten-year period we will produce well over $70 trillion of goods and services (GNP). On this basis, the environmental expenditures contemplated by present environmental policies and goals represent only 1–3 percent of total output.

The Optimal Rate of Pollution

Whether a small percentage of GNP is too much or too little to spend on environmental protection depends on the value we assign to other goods and services and to a cleaner environment. That is to say, the optimal rate of pollution occurs at the point at which the opportunity costs of further pollution control equal the benefits of further reductions in pollution. To determine the optimal rate of pollution, we need to compare the marginal social benefits of additional pollution control with the marginal social costs of additional pollution-control expenditure. ***The optimal rate of pollution is achieved when***

- Optimal rate of pollution : marginal benefit of pollution abatement = marginal cost of pollution abatement

This formulation is analogous to the utility-maximizing rule in consumption. If another dollar spent on pollution control yields no more than a dollar of social benefits, then additional pollution-control expenditure is not desirable. In such a situation, the goods and services that would be forsaken for additional pollution control are more valued than the environmental improvements that would result.

The formula for the optimal rate of pollution implies that ***a totally clean environment is not economically desirable.*** The marginal benefit of achieving zero pollution may be infinitesimal. But the marginal cost of eliminating that last particle of pollution may be very high. As we weigh the marginal benefits and costs, we will conclude that some pollution is cost-effective.

Who Will Pay?

Because clean air, water, and land are not market goods, the calculation of the marginal social benefits of pollution control is a formidable task. It is far easier to determine who will pay for the associated costs. Pollution-abatement efforts will not affect all producers and consumers equally. A relatively small number of economic activities account for the bulk of emissions and effluents. These activities will have to bear a disproportionate share of the cleanup burden (see In the News).

To ascertain how the burden of environmental protection will be distributed, consider first the electric power plant discussed earlier. As we observed (Figure 27.2), the plant's output will decrease if production decisions are based on social rather than private marginal costs—that is, if environmental consequences are considered. If the plant itself is compelled to pay full social costs, in the form of either compulsory investment or emission charges, its profits will be reduced. Were no other changes to take place, the burden of environmental improvements would be borne primarily by the producer.

In The News

BENEFITS VS. COSTS

Breathing Easier: Clean-Air Legislation Will Cost Americans $21.5 Billion a Year

Industries, Workers, Regions Debate Who Should Pay How Much for Clear Skies

WASHINGTON—How much are Americans willing to pay to make the Blue Ridge Mountains look bluer, to save brook trout from acid rain, or to make living next door to a chemical plant no riskier than smoking six cigarettes a year?

To achieve air that pure, U.S. industry is on the verge of being socked with a bill for at least $21.5 billion *annually*—more than General Motors, General Electric, Ford Motor, IBM and Exxon collectively earned last year. Ultimately, many of the staggering costs of coming clean will be paid by consumers and workers.

The wallop will be delivered by Congress in legislation proposed by President Bush that will have a wider impact on American business than anything since the 1986 tax-reform law. The Senate is poised to pass its version next week, and then the House will vote on the bill, perhaps in May.

But passage of the legislation, the first national clean-air bill since 1977, is considered so likely that the battle now is over high-stakes tradeoffs: Who will be the winners and the losers?

Touching Ordinary Lives

Utility customers in the heavily industrialized Midwest may stagger under double-digit electricity rate increases. And in Appalachia, the loss of thousands of coal-mining jobs could create ghost towns.

The legislation will touch the lives of average American families, adding perhaps $600 to the cost of a new car. It will also require new anti-pollution gadgets for cars and maybe even a totally new fuel. And it will mean changes in products from aerosol air fresheners to windshield fluid.

The payoff will be fewer smog-alert days in some major urban areas, perhaps by the mid-1990s. Within 20 years, motorists stalled in big-city traffic may never again have to choke on the fumes of diesel buses. And eventually, lives and money should be saved by sharply reducing air pollution that now contributes to the premature deaths of more than 50,000 people a year and costs the nation $10 billion to $25 billion annually in health bills, according to Bailus Walker Jr., past president of the American Public Health Association.

—Barbara Rosewicz and Rose Gutfeld

The Wall Street Journal, March 28, 1990, p. 1.

Such a scenario is unlikely, however. Rather than absorb all of the costs of pollution controls themselves, producers will seek to pass some of this burden on to their customers in the form of higher prices. Their ability to do so will depend on the extent of competition in their industry, their relative cost position in it, and the price elasticity of consumer demand. In reality, the electric power industry is not very competitive, and its prices are subject to government regulation. In addition, consumer demand is relatively price-inelastic. Accordingly, the profit-maximizing producer will appeal to the state or local power commission for an increase in electricity prices based on the costs of pollution control. Electric power consumers are likely to end up footing part or all of the environmental bill. This distribution of costs may be regarded as equitable because the increased prices will more fully reflect the social costs associated with electricity use.

In addition to the electric power industry, the automobile, paper, steel, and chemical industries will be adversely affected by pollution controls. In all of these cases, the prices of the related products will increase, in some instances by significant percentages. These price increases will help to reduce pollution in two ways. First, they will help to pay for pollution-control equipment. Second, they will encourage consumers to change their expenditure patterns in the direction of less polluting goods.

The same kinds of arguments apply to public-sector expenditures for pollution control. If a municipality wants to clean up the water, it will have to invest in better sewage and treatment facilities. If it finances these investments out of its existing budget, it will have to cut back on expenditures in other areas—schools, roads, public welfare. If it wants to maintain existing levels of those services, it will have to finance its pollution-control investments out of increased taxes, higher emission charges, or aid from Washington. All of these financing mechanisms entail opportunity costs. The only issue is who will pay them.

Local impacts   Even though the resource requirements for environmental protection are relatively modest and the means for allocating them known, we should not conclude that our cleanup efforts will proceed painlessly. As already noted, some producers and consumers will end up paying a disproportionate share of the costs. In some cases, the added costs of environmental protection may be so great as to force a plant to shut down. According to surveys by the EPA and the U.S. Department of Commerce, 107 plants were closed in the period 1971–77 as a result of pollution-control regulations and costs. Over 20,000 workers lost their jobs. Although these plant closings involved a very tiny proportion of the labor force, the affected workers and producers hardly welcomed their role in environmental progress. In general, affected firms and workers seek to postpone or avoid their losses through legal and political action. To reduce political friction and ease the transition to a cleaner environment, public policy has to respond to such microeconomic costs. The response may entail phasing out plants, retraining and relocating workers, or rebuilding a community's economic base.

1990 Clean Air Act Amendments

Legislative strategies affecting the environment are found in a dozen or so congressional acts. The most important of these is the Clean Air Act, first passed in 1970 and amended in 1977. President Bush proposed to amend the act again in 1990 with sweeping changes in environmental goals and strategies. Promising to make "the 1990s the era for clean air," Bush proposed

- A 50 percent cut in sulfur dioxide emissions by the year 2000.

- A cut of 2 million tons in nitrogen oxide emissions.

- The attainment of ozone health standards in all cities by 2000.

- A 75 percent reduction in emissions of toxic compounds.

To meet these ambitious goals, President Bush proposed to "harness" the power of the marketplace to protect the environment. To do this, the amendments give firms and cities substantial flexibility in choosing the most cost-effective methods of attaining the new goals.

Marketable pollution rights   One of the most important features of the plan is the creation of marketable pollution rights. A firm that would have to spend a lot on pollution control can buy the right to pollute from another firm with lower control costs. The second firm would then assume the job of additional cleanup.

Suppose the policy objective is to reduce sulfur dioxide emissions by two tons. There are only two major polluters in the community—a copper smelter and an electric utility. Should each company be required to reduce its SO_2

emissions by one ton? Or can the same SO_2 reduction be achieved more cheaply with marketable pollution rights?

Assume that the copper smelter would have to spend $2 million to reduce SO_2 emissions by one ton. The electric utility can achieve the same SO_2 reduction for only $1 million. Rather than spending $2 million of resources on its own pollution control, the smelter can pay the electric utility to reduce *its* SO_2 emissions by an additional ton. The price of this trade would be somewhere between $1 million (the utility's cost) and $2 million (the smelter's cost). The smelter would continue to pollute, but total SO_2 emissions would still drop by 2 tons. Both firms—and society—would be better off. By permitting firms to trade pollution permits, society achieves the desired level of environmental protection at the lowest possible cost.

The 1990 clean-air amendments seek to use market incentives in this way to achieve a cleaner environment. The amendments contain sticks as well as carrots, however: stiff financial penalties and process regulations are also included.

SUMMARY

- Air, water, and solid-waste pollution impose social and economic costs. The costs of pollution include the direct damages inflicted on our health and resources, the expense of cleaning up, and the general aesthetic deterioration of the environment.

- Pollution is an externality, a cost of a market activity imposed on someone (a third party) other than the immediate producer or consumer.

- Producers and consumers generally operate on the basis of private benefits and costs. Accordingly, a private producer or consumer has an incentive to minimize his own costs by transforming private costs into external costs. One way of making such a substitution is to pollute—to use "free" air and water rather than install pollution-control equipment, or to leave the job of waste disposal to others.

- Social costs are the total amount of resources used in a production or consumption process. When social costs are greater than private costs, the market's price signals are flawed. This market failure will induce people to harm the environment by using suboptimal processes and products.

- One way to correct the market inefficiency created by externalities would be to compel producers and consumers to internalize all (social) costs. This result could be attained by the imposition of emission charges and higher user fees. Such charges would create an incentive to invest in pollution-abatement equipment, recycle reusable materials, and conserve scarce elements of the environment.

- Privatizing public property would also create a market force to protect the environment. Privatization is impossible for some elements of the environment, however, and resisted on equity grounds in other cases.

- An alternative approach to cleaning up the environment is to require specific pollution controls or to prohibit specific kinds of activities. Direct regulation runs the risk of higher cost and discouraging innovations in environmental protection.

- The opportunity costs of environmental protection are the most desired goods and services given up when factors of production are used to control pollution. The optimal rate of pollution is reached when the marginal social benefits of further pollution control equal associated marginal social costs.

• In addition to diverting resources, pollution-control efforts alter relative prices, change the mix of output, and redistribute incomes. These outcomes cause losses for particular groups and may thus require special economic or political attention.

• The proposed 1990 Amendments to the Clean Air Act create marketable pollution permits. By allowing firms to trade pollution rights, the cost of achieving environmental protection is minimized.

Terms to Remember   Define the following terms:

optimal rate of pollution	private costs
production decision	market failure
efficiency decision	emission charge
externalities	government failure
social costs	opportunity cost

Questions for Discussion

1. Should we try to eliminate *all* pollution? What economic considerations might favor permitting some pollution?

2. Why would auto manufacturers resist exhaust-control devices? How would their costs, sales, and profits be affected?

3. Does anyone have an incentive to maintain auto exhaust-control devices in good working order? How can we ensure that they will be maintained?

4. Suppose we established a $10,000 fine for water pollution. Would some companies still find that polluting was economical? Under what conditions?

5. What economic costs are imposed by mandatory sorting of trash?

6. How would the privatization of beaches help the environment? Who would benefit? Who would pay?

Problems

1. The following cost schedule depicts the private and social costs associated with the daily production of apacum, a highly toxic fertilizer. The sales price of apacum is $18 per ton.

Output (in tons)	0	1	2	3	4	5	6	7	8
Total private cost	$5	7	13	23	37	55	77	103	133
Total social cost	$7	13	31	61	103	157	223	301	391

Using the schedule:
(a) Graph the private and social marginal costs associated with apacum production.
(b) Identify the profit-maximizing private and social rates of output and associated profits.
(c) On the basis of these curves, identify the pollution fee (fine) we would have to charge per unit in order to persuade the producer to produce the socially optimal rate of output.

2. In some states, mining for coal leaves large mounds of rubble. This poses flooding problems, causes land damage, and is unsightly. The following table shows the estimated annual social benefits and costs of restoring various amounts of such land.

Land restored (in acres)	0	100	200	300	400	500
Social benefits of restoring land	0	$70	$120	$160	$190	$220
Social costs of restoring land	0	$10	$40	$80	$140	$230

(a) Compute the marginal social benefits and the marginal social costs for each restoration level.

(b) What is the optimal rate of restoration?

3. Suppose three firms confront the following costs for pollution control:

Emissions reduction (tons per year)	Total costs of control		
	Firm A	Firm B	Firm C
1	$ 50	$ 60	$ 40
2	100	140	150
3	180	230	300
4	300	350	600

(a) If each firm must reduce emissions by 1 ton, how much will be spent?

(b) If the firms can trade pollution rights, what would be the cheapest way of attaining a net 3-ton reduction?

(c) How much would a pollution permit trade for?

(d) Repeat parts a, b, and c for a net reduction of 6 tons.

The Farm Problem

*I*n the 1980s the federal government spent over $250 billion on farm subsidies. With that much money, Uncle Sam could have bought every farm, barn, and tractor in thirty-four states. And the subsidies are continuing—at a rate of $15 billion to $25 billion a year. For the same cost the federal government could buy every full-time subsidized farmer two new Mercedeses every year.

Taxpayers are not happy about these massive income transfers. Nor do they like the idea of paying farmers *not* to produce crops—a common feature of many government programs. Moreover, it appears that many of the programs simply do not work. Farms in the United States continue to produce more food than people eat, even as the number of farmers continues to shrink. Farm incomes continue to be unstable, with recurring booms and busts.

In view of these developments, people wonder what the farm problem is all about. Why is the government so entrenched in the farm industry? Would we be better off with different policies or less intervention? Could an unregulated farm sector work at least as well?

In this chapter we look more closely at the forces that determine farm prices, output, and income. In doing so, we explore these questions:

- Why are farm prices and profits so unstable?

- Why has the farm sector shrunk so much?

- How do government farm programs affect farm output, prices, and income?

DESTABILIZING FORCES

Competition in Agriculture

market power: The ability to alter the market price of a good or service.

The agriculture industry is one of the most competitive of all U.S. industries. To begin with, there are over 2 million farms in the United States. Although some of these farms are immense in size—with tens of thousands of acres— no single farm has the power to affect the market supply or price of farm products. That is to say, individual farmers have no **market power.**

CHAPTER 28

barriers to entry: Obstacles that make it difficult or impossible for would-be producers to enter a particular market; e.g., patents.

economic profit: The difference between total revenues and total economic costs.

Competition in agriculture is maintained by low **barriers to entry.** Although farmers need large acreages, expensive farm equipment, substantial credit, hard work, and hired labor, all of these resources become affordable when farming is generating **economic profits.** When farming is profitable, existing farmers expand their farms, farmers' children are able to start new farms, and new farmers can obtain enough credit to start farming on a large enough scale to survive. It would be much harder to enter the automobile industry, air service, or even the farm-machinery market than it would be to enter farming. Because of these low barriers to entry, economic profits don't last long in agriculture.

Given the competitive structure of U.S. agriculture, *individual farmers tend to behave like perfect competitors.*[1] Individual farmers seek to expand their rate of output until marginal cost equals price. By following this rule, each farmer makes as much profit as possible from existing resources, prices, and technology.

Like other competitive firms, U.S. farmers can maintain economic profits only if they achieve continuing cost reductions. Above-normal profits obtained from current production techniques and prices are not likely to last. Such economic profits will entice more people into agriculture and will stimulate greater output from existing farmers. This is exactly the kind of dilemma that confronted the early producers of microcomputers. To stay ahead, individual firms (farms) must continue to improve their productivity.

Technological Advance

The rate of technological advance in agriculture has, in fact, been spectacular. Since 1929, the farm labor force has shrunk by two-thirds, yet farm output has increased by 60 percent. Between the early 1950s and today:

- Annual egg production has jumped from 183 to 243 eggs per laying chicken.

- Milk output has increased from 5,400 to 12,100 pounds per cow.

- Wheat output has increased from 17.3 to 35.3 bushels per acre.

- Corn output has jumped from 39.4 to 102 bushels per acre.

Farm output per labor hour has grown even faster, having increased by 700 percent in the same time period. Such high rates of productivity advance rival those of our most "technological" industries. These technological advances have come about in countless ways, including development of higher yielding seeds (the "green revolution"), advanced machinery (e.g., mechanical feeders and milkers), improved animal breeding (e.g., crossbreeding), improved plants (e.g., rust-resistant wheat), better land-use practices (e.g., crop rotation and fertilizers), and computer-based management systems. These improvements have been discovered and developed by individual farmers, by the companies that sell products to them, and by research supported by the U.S. Department of Agriculture.

Inelastic Demand

In most industries, continuous increases in technology and output would be most welcome. The agricultural industry, however, confronts a long-term problem. Simply put, there is a limit to the amount of food people want to eat. Hence more and more output threatens to satiate our collective hunger.

---

[1]There are exceptions, including a variety of production and marketing associations. These are discussed in Chapter 25.

price elasticity of demand:
The percentage change in quantity demanded divided by the percentage change in price.

income elasticity of demand:
The percentage change in quantity demanded divided by the percentage change in income.

This constraint on the demand for agricultural output is reflected in the relatively inelastic demand for food. Typically, consumers do not increase their food purchases very much when farm prices fall. The **price elasticity** of food demand is low. As a consequence, abundant harvests (rightward shifts of the supply curve) can lead to sharply lower prices and a decline in total revenue.

The **income elasticity** of food demand is also low. The income elasticity of demand for food refers to the responsiveness of food demand to changes in income. Specifically,

$$\bullet \quad \begin{array}{c} \text{Income elasticity} \\ \text{of demand} \end{array} = \frac{\begin{array}{c}\text{percentage change in quantity demanded}\\ \text{(at constant price)}\end{array}}{\text{percentage change in income}}$$

Since 1929, per capita income has risen 175 percent. But per capita food consumption has increased only 85 percent. Hence neither lower prices nor higher incomes significantly increase the quantity of food demanded.

In the long run, then, the increasing ability of U.S. agriculture to produce food must be reconciled with very slow growth of U.S. demand for food. Over time, this implies that farm prices will fall, relative to nonfarm prices. And they have. Between the years 1910–14 and 1990, the ratio of farm prices to nonfarm prices fell 50 percent. In the absence of government price-support programs and foreign demand for U.S. farm products, farm prices would have fallen still further.

Abrupt Shifts of Supply

The long-term downtrend in (relative) farm prices is only one of the major problems confronting U.S. agriculture. The second major problem is short-run in nature. Prices of farm products are subject to abrupt short-term swings. If the weather is good, harvests are abundant. Abundant harvests imply a severe drop in prices, however, particularly when food demand is relatively price inelastic. On the other hand, a late or early freeze, a drought, or an infestation by disease or insect pests can reduce harvests substantially and push prices sharply higher. So long as agricultural harvests are subject to the whims of nature, farm prices will be highly unstable from year to year. These natural price swings are illustrated in Figure 28.1.

Natural forces are not the only cause of short-term price instability. Time lags between the production decision and the resultant harvest also contribute to price instability. If prices are high one year, farmers have an incentive to increase their rate of output. In this sense, prices serve the same signaling function in agriculture as they do in nonfarm industries. What distinguishes the farmers' response is the lack of inventories and the fixed duration of the production process. In the auto and electronics industries, a larger quantity of output can be supplied to the market fairly quickly. Some additional supplies can be marketed immediately by reducing available inventories. A further increase in the quantity supplied can be obtained by increasing the rate of output, perhaps with periods of overtime. In farming, supply cannot respond so quickly. In the very short run, the farmer can only till more land, plant additional seed, or breed more livestock. No additional food supplies will be available until a new crop or herd grows. Hence the agricultural supply response to a change in prices is always one harvest (or breeding period) later.

The natural lag in responses of agricultural supplies intensifies short-term price swings. Suppose corn prices are exceptionally high at the end of a year, due to a reduced harvest. High prices will make corn farming appear

FIGURE 28.1
Short-Term Instability

Changes in weather cause abrupt shifts of the food supply curve. When combined with the relatively inelastic demand for food, these supply shifts result in wide price swings. Notice how the price of grain jumps from p_1 to p_2 when bad weather reduces the harvest. If good weather follows, prices may fall to p_3.

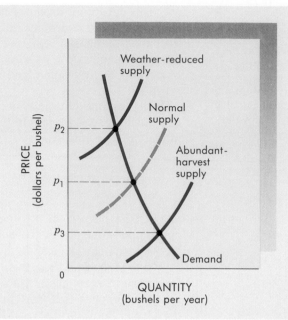

unusually profitable. Farmers will want to expand their rate of output—plant more corn acreage—to share in these high profits. But the corn will not appear on the market until the following year. By that time, there is likely to be an abundance of corn on the market, as a result of both better weather and increased corn acreage. Hence corn prices are likely to plummet (look again at Figure 28.1).

No single farmer can avoid the boom-or-bust movement of prices. Even a corn farmer who has mastered the principles of economics has little choice but to plant more corn when prices are high. If he does not plant additional corn, prices will fall anyway, because his own production decisions do not affect market prices. By not planting additional corn, he only denies himself a share of corn market sales. *In a highly competitive market, each producer acts independently.*

The historical instability of corn prices is illustrated in Figure 28.2. Notice how corn prices repeatedly rise, then abruptly fall. This kind of price swing is particularly evident in 1915–20, 1935–37, 1946–48, 1973–76, and 1980–84.

THE FIRST FARM DEPRESSION, 1920–40

The U.S. agricultural industry operated without substantial government intervention until the 1930s. In earlier decades, an expanding population, recurrent wars, and less advanced technology had helped to maintain a favorable supply–demand relationship for farm products. There were frequent short-term swings in farm prices, but these were absorbed by a generally healthy farm sector. The period 1910–19 was particularly prosperous for farmers, largely because of the expanded foreign demand for U.S. farm products by countries engaged in World War I.

The two basic problems of U.S. agriculture grew to crisis proportions after 1920. In 1919, most farm prices were at historical highs (see Figures 28.2 and 28.3). After World War I ended, however, European countries no longer

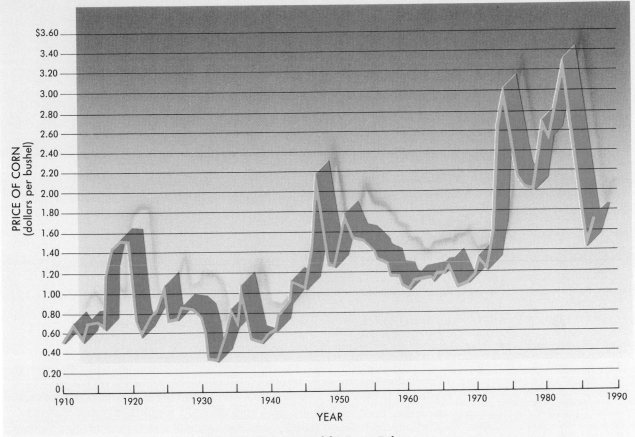

FIGURE 28.2 Unstable Corn Prices

Most agricultural prices are subject to abrupt short-term changes. Notice how corn prices rose dramatically during World Wars I and II, then fell sharply. Poor harvests in the rest of the world increased demand for U.S. food in 1973—74.

Source: U.S. Department of Agriculture.

demanded as much American food. U.S. exports of farm products fell from nearly $4 billion in 1919 to $1.9 billion in 1921. Farm exports were further reduced in the following years by increasing restrictions on international trade. At home, the end of the war implied an increased availability of factors of production and continuing technological improvement.

The impact of reduced demand and steadily increasing supply is evident in Figure 28.3. In 1919 farm prices were more than double their levels of the period 1910–14. Prices then fell abruptly, however. In 1921 alone, average farm prices fell nearly 40 percent.

Farm prices rose somewhat in the mid-1920s but resumed a steep decline in 1930. In 1932 average farm prices were 75 percent lower than they had been in 1919 and were only 65 percent of their prewar levels. At the same time, the average income per farmer from farming fell from $2,651 in 1919 to $855 in 1932.

The Great Depression hit small farmers particularly hard. They had fewer resources to withstand consecutive years of declining prices and income.

**FIGURE 28.3
Farm Prices, 1910–40
(1910–14 = 100)**

Farm prices are less
stable than nonfarm prices.
During the 1930s, relative
farm prices fell 50 percent.
This experience was the
catalyst for government
price supports and other
agricultural assistance
programs.

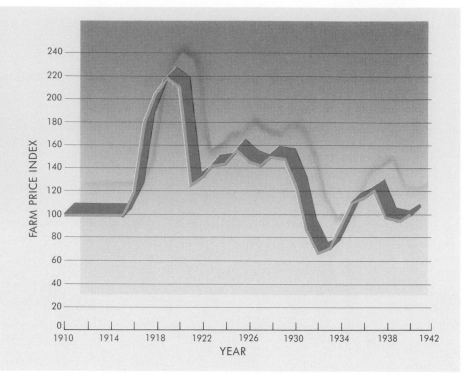

Even in good times, small farmers must continually expand output and reduce costs just to maintain their incomes. Hence the Great Depression accelerated an exodus of small farmers from agriculture, a trend that continues today.

Table 28.1 shows that the number of small farms has declined dramatically. In 1910 there were 3.7 million farms under 100 acres in size. Today, there are fewer than 1 million small farms. During the same period, the number of large farms (500 acres or more) has more than doubled. This loss of small farmers, together with the increased mechanization of larger farms, has reduced the farm population by 23 million people since 1910.[2]

[2]The Census Bureau defines a farm as property that produces at least $1,000 worth of agricultural products for the market in a year.

TABLE 28.1   Size Distribution of U.S. Farms, 1910 and 1990

Inelastic food demand, combined with increasing agricultural productivity, implies a declining number of farmers. Small farmers are particularly vulnerable because they do not have the resources to maintain a high rate of technological improvement. As a result, the number of small farms has declined dramatically, while the number of large farms has grown.

Size of farm	Number, 1910	Percent	Number, 1990	Percent
Under 100 acres	3,691,611	58.0	897,449	41.3
100–499 acres	2,494,461	39.2	921,352	42.4
500–999 acres	125,295	2.0	197,743	9.1
1,000 acres and over	50,135	0.8	156,456	7.2
Total	6,361,502	100.0	2,173,000	100.0

Source: U.S. Department of Agriculture.

U.S. FARM POLICY

The U.S. Congress has responded to these agricultural problems with a variety of programs. Most seek to raise and stabilize the price of farm products. Other programs seek to reduce the costs of production. When all else fails, the federal government also provides direct income support to farmers.

Price Supports and Supply Restrictions

market surplus: The amount by which the quantity supplied exceeds the quantity demanded at a given price; excess supply.

Price supports have always been the primary focus of U.S. farm policy. As early as 1926, Congress decreed that farm products should sell at a "fair" price. By "fair," Congress meant a price higher than the market equilibrium. Unfortunately, *a price floor creates a* **market surplus** (see Figure 28.4). Hence by setting an above-equilibrium price for food, Congress had to find some way of disposing of the resultant food surplus. Initially, Congress proposed to get rid of this surplus by selling it abroad at world market prices. President Calvin Coolidge vetoed this legislation both times Congress passed it.

The notion of "fair" prices resurfaced in the Agricultural Adjustment Act of 1933. The basic objective of the act was to restore the purchasing power of farm products to the 1909–14 level. The farm–nonfarm price relationships of 1909–14 were regarded by Congress as "fair" and came to be known as **parity** prices. The objective of the 1933 act was to restore that parity by raising farm prices.

parity: The relative price of farm products in the period 1910–14.

Set-asides The easiest way to increase farm prices without creating a surplus is to reduce the production of food. Congress did this by paying farmers for voluntary reductions in crop acreage. These **acreage set-asides** shifted the food supply curve to the left.

acreage set-aside: Land withdrawn from production as part of policy to increase crop prices.

In 1983 the Reagan administration offered to pay farmers in kind rather than in cash for their set aside acreage. The Payment-in-Kind (PIK) program paid farmers with surplus grain and crops. The farmers were then free to sell those surplus crops on the market. In that one year, the government paid out

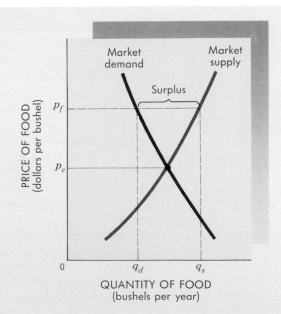

**FIGURE 28.4
"Fair" Prices
and Market Surplus**

The interaction of market supply and demand establishes an equilibrium price (p_e) for any product, including food. If a higher price (p_f) is set, the quantity of food supplied (q_s) will be larger than the quantity demanded (q_d). Hence attempts to establish a "fair" (higher) price for farm products must cope with resultant market surpluses.

more than $70 billion in surplus grain and corn in return for the set-aside of 80 million acres of farmland—nearly one-third of the country's eligible cropland for wheat, corn, sorghum, rice, and cotton. In 1983 U.S. farmers idled more acreage than all of Western Europe planted. These acreage set-asides are still a mainstay of U.S. farm policy.

Dairy termination program   To prop up dairy prices, the federal government also started a Dairy Termination Program in 1985. This is analogous to a set-aside program. In this case, however, the government pays dairy farmers to slaughter or export dairy cattle. Between 1985 and 1987 the government paid dairy farmers over a billion dollars to "terminate" 1.6 million cows. The reduction in dairy herds boosted prices for milk and other dairy products.

Marketing orders   The federal government also permits industry groups to limit the quantity of output brought to market. By themselves, individual farmers can't raise the market price by withholding output. If they act collectively, however, they can do so by agreeing not to sell more than a specified quantity. If a quantity greater than authorized is actually grown, the "surplus" is disposed of by individual farmers. In the 1980s these "marketing orders" forced farmers to waste each year roughly 500 million lemons, 1 billion (!) oranges, 70 million pounds of raisins, 70 million pounds of almonds, and millions of plums, nectarines, and other fruits. This wholesale destruction of crops gave growers market power and kept farm prices artificially high.

Import quotas   The market supply of farm products is also limited by import restrictions. Imports of sugar, dairy products, cotton, and peanuts are severely limited by import quotas. Imports of beef are limited by "voluntary" export limits in foreign countries. Import taxes (duties) limit the foreign supply of other farm products.

Government stockpiles   Another mechanism for reducing market supply was introduced by an executive order of President Franklin Roosevelt. In October 1933 he established the Commodity Credit Corporation (CCC). Its function is ostensibly to lend money to farmers. But farmers may use their crops as collateral. If a farmer does not repay the loan, the CCC simply keeps the crops held as collateral. Hence the farmer effectively "sells" his crops to the CCC whenever he defaults on a loan. The "price" for these crops is equal to the crop loan rate, that is, the amount of money lent for each bushel of grain. Whenever market prices exceed CCC loan rates, the farmer can repay the loan, retrieve the crops, and sell them in the open market.

The effect of CCC price supports on individual farmers and the agricultural market is illustrated in Figure 28.5. In the absence of price supports, competitive farmers would confront a horizontal demand curve at price p_1, itself determined by the intersection of market supply and demand (in part b). The CCC's offer to buy ("loan") unlimited quantities at a higher price shifts the demand curve facing each farmer upward, to the guaranteed price p_2. This higher price induces individual farmers to increase their rate of output, from q_1 to q_2.

As all farmers respond to price supports, the agriculture market is pushed out of equilibrium. At the support level p_2, more output is supplied than demanded. The market surplus created by government price supports creates an additional policy dilemma. ***The market surplus induced by price supports must be eliminated in one of three ways:***

(a) On the individual farmer

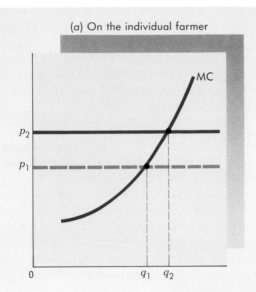

(b) On the agricultural market

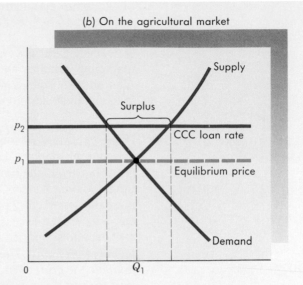

FIGURE 28.5 The Impact of Price Supports

In the absence of price supports, the price of farm products would be determined by the intersection of market supply and demand. In this case, the equilibrium price would be p_1, as shown in part *b*. All individual farmers would confront this price and produce up to the point where MC = p_1, as in part *a*.

Government price supports raise the price to p_2. By offering to buy (or "loan") unlimited quantities at this price, the government shifts the demand curve facing each farmer upward. Individual farmers respond by increasing their output to q_2. As farmers increase their output, a market surplus develops (part *b*).

- *Government purchases* and stockpiling of surplus food

- *Export sales*

- *Restrictions on supply*

Government purchases of surplus crops have led to massive stockpiles of wheat, cotton, corn, and dairy products. Excess wheat no longer fits in silos; much of it is stored in old ammunition bunkers in Nebraska and scrubbed-out oil tanks in Texas. Surplus nonfat dry milk is stored in caverns near Kansas City, and surplus cotton fills warehouses in the South.

Because farm prices are artificially high in the United States, export sales are difficult. As a result, the federal government must give away lots of food to poor nations and even subsidize exports to developed nations. In 1987 the U.S. government went so far as to subsidize wheat exports to the Soviet Union and China.

Cost Subsidies   The market surplus induced by price supports is exacerbated by cost subsidies. Irrigation water, for example, is delivered to many farmers by federally funded reclamation projects. The price paid by farmers for the water is substantially below the cost of delivering it; the difference amounts to a subsidy. In 1986 this water subsidy cost taxpayers over $500 million. The Department of Agriculture has distributed an additional $150 million to $200 million a year to farmers to help defray the costs of fertilizer and drainage and other production costs.

The federal government has also provided basic research, insurance, marketing, grading, and inspection services to farmers at subsidized prices. All of these subsidies serve to lower fixed or variable costs. Their net impact is to stimulate additional output, as illustrated in Figure 28.6.

Direct Income Support

Price supports, cost subsidies, and supply restrictions are designed to stabilize agricultural markets and assure farmers an adequate income. As we have seen, however, they entail significant distortions of market outcomes. The Congressional Budget Office estimates that the milk price supports alone have increased retail dairy prices 3–6 percent, reduced consumption 1–5 percent, and encouraged excessive dairy production. Because of such distortions, direct income supports were authorized by the Agriculture and Consumer Protection Act of 1973. ***The advantage of direct income supports is that they achieve the goal of income security without distortions of market prices and output.***

deficiency payment: Income transfer paid to farmers for difference between target and support prices.

The principal form of direct income support are so-called **deficiency payments.** Producers of wheat, feed grains, rice, cotton, and other commodities receive direct payments from the federal government when crop prices are low (below stipulated "target prices"). These payments are designed to make up the deficiency in income that results from low prices. Deficiency payments are made to farmers who agree to reduce their output (acreage) of certain crops.

W RLD VIEW

FARM POLICY

EC Farm Subsidies

In Europe, believe it or not, the subsidy for every cow is greater than the personal income of half the people in the world.

–British Prime Minister Margaret Thatcher

United States farm policy is not unique. On the contrary, most industrialized countries go to even greater lengths to protect domestic agriculture. France, Germany, and Switzerland all shield their farmers from international competition while subsidizing their exports. Japan protects its inefficient rice producers, while the Netherlands subsidizes greenhouse vegetable farmers.

The motivations for farm subsidies are pretty much the same in every country. First, every country wants a secure source of food in the event of war. Second, most nations want to maintain a viable farm sector, which is viewed as a source of social stability. Finally, politicians in every country must be responsive to a well-established and vocal political constituency.

The crazy quilt of farm subsidies in Europe has created a formidable challenge to the European Community (EC). The reduction in trade barriers between EC nations has facilitated the flow of food across national borders. This has forced the member governments to adjust their subsidy programs. Italy and Spain wanted protection for their fruits (especially olives) and vegetables. The Germans, Dutch, and British wanted to protect their dairy and grain farmers. The resulting compromise was greater subsidies for all EC food production.

The EC imposes high tariffs on imported food, thus keeping domestic prices high. The member governments also agree to purchase any surplus production. To get rid of the surplus, the governments then subsidize exports. All of this protection costs the average EC consumer over $200 a year.

The EC's farm policies also affect world markets. Until 1974, the EC was a net importer of wheat, for example. The increased subsidies, however, have transformed the EC into a net exporter of wheat. This has depressed worldwide wheat prices and deprived more efficient foreign producers of wheat sales.

FIGURE 28.6
The Impact of Cost Subsidies

Cost subsidies lower the marginal cost of producing at any given rate of output, thereby shifting the marginal cost curve downward. The lower marginal costs make higher rates of output more profitable and thus increase output. At price p_2, lower marginal costs increase the desired rate of output from q_2 to q_3.

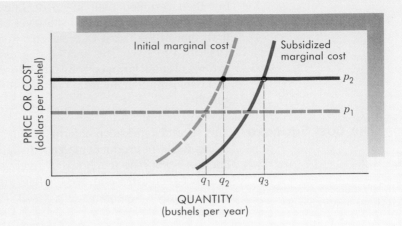

In principle, direct income payments are a more efficient mechanism for subsidizing farm incomes. But farmers don't like them. Five thousand angry farmers drove their tractors to Washington, D.C., in February 1979 to protest this policy approach. Their rallying cry was "parity, not charity." They wanted higher price supports (an indirect subsidy) rather than more deficiency payments (a direct subsidy). They got higher price supports in 1981.

THE SECOND FARM DEPRESSION, 1980–86

With so many price supports, supply restrictions, cost subsidies, and income transfers, one would think that farming should be a riskless and profitable business. But this has not been the case. Incomes remain low and unstable, especially for small farmers. In fact, the entire agricultural sector experienced another setback in the 1980s. In 1980 the net income of U.S. farmers fell 42 percent. As Figure 28.7 shows, farm incomes recovered somewhat in 1981

FIGURE 28.7
Net Farm Income, 1977–90

Between 1979 and 1983 net farm income fell 64 percent. This decline was steeper than the income slide that occurred during the Great Depression (when net farm income fell 45 percent between 1929 and 1933). Farm incomes have risen sharply since 1983. Total farm income in 1990 was the highest in 15 years.

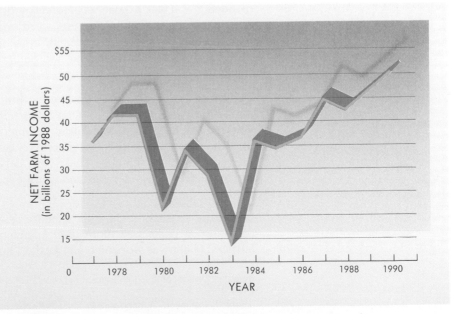

but then resumed their steep decline in 1982. In 1983 the net income of farmers was only one-third the level of 1979. This income loss was steeper than that of the Great Depression.[3] Real farm income was actually lower in 1983 than in 1933. This second depression of farm incomes accelerated the exodus of small farmers from agriculture, severely weakened rural economies, and bankrupted many farm banks and manufacturers of farm equipment and supplies.

The Cost Squeeze

profit: The difference between total revenue and total cost.

This second depression of farm incomes was not due to abrupt price declines. Prices for farm products increased slightly between 1979 and 1983—but production costs rose much faster. Average farm production costs rose 30 percent between 1979 and 1983, while the average price of farm products increased only 1.5 percent. As a result, the **profit** (net income) of farmers fell abruptly.

Fuel costs   The cost squeeze on farm incomes started with an abrupt increase in fuel prices. In 1979 the OPEC nations raised crude oil prices 50 percent. This action pushed up the price of gasoline and related fuels 37 percent in 1980 alone, making it more expensive to operate farm equipment.

Fertilizer costs   The increase in crude oil prices also pushed up the price of fertilizer. Most fertilizers are manufactured from a petroleum base. As a consequence, fertilizer prices rose in tandem with fuel prices, increasing 24 percent in 1980 and another 7 percent in 1981.

Interest rates   The third, and perhaps most devastating, source of the farmers' cost squeeze was an increase in interest rates. Farming is extremely land- and capital-intensive. The value of U.S. farmers' assets is roughly $1 trillion. Many of these assets (such as land and machinery) are purchased with borrowed funds, often at variable interest rates. Farmers also borrow money for planting and harvesting. All of this debt renders farmers vulnerable to abrupt changes in interest rates. When interest rates skyrocketed—the prime rate rose from 9 percent in 1978 to over 20 percent in 1980—the debt burden of farmers mounted. As Harold Breimyer of the University of Missouri at Columbia summed it up: "A farmer who had borrowed money on the expectation of paying $50,000 a year as interest suddenly was billed for as much as $150,000."[4] Thousands of farmers were unable to make these unexpectedly high interest payments. As a result, more than 100,000 farmers were forced out of business, with their land and equipment often auctioned off by their creditors.

Declining land values   High interest rates and declining incomes also reduced the value of farmers' most important asset—their land. The value of land reflects its present and future income-generating potential (see Chapter 31). The cost squeeze reduced potential income, and high interest rates made future income less valuable. These twin forces sent land values into a tailspin, which made it more difficult and more expensive for farmers to get needed credit.

Declining exports   The cost squeeze resulting from higher fuel, fertilizer, and interest costs was more than sufficient to choke off farm profits. The farmers' plight was worsened still further, however, by declining export sales.

[3]Real net farm income fell 45 percent between 1929 and 1933 and 64 percent between 1979 and 1983.

[4]Harold F. Breimyer, "Agriculture's Problem Is Rooted in Washington," *Challenge,* May–June 1985.

In 1980 President Jimmy Carter imposed an embargo on grain sales to the Soviet Union. This directly reduced wheat sales by 15,000–20,000 tons per year and indirectly encouraged foreign competition.

Export sales were reduced even further by the strong value of the U.S. dollar. Between 1980 and 1984, the international value of the dollar rose a staggering 50 percent. This made it much more expensive for foreigners to buy American farm output. As a result, the quantity of exports declined.

POLICY OPTIONS FOR THE 1990s

To a large extent, the farm crisis of the 1980s had nothing to do with federal farm policy. The increase in oil prices was initiated by OPEC. Higher interest rates were a reflection of macroeconomic conditions. Likewise, the high value of the dollar was a response to U.S. interest rates and the economic recovery, and its effects were not confined to the farm sector. All these adverse forces were reversed in the mid-1980s, and farm incomes rose sharply from their 1983 lows (see Figure 28.7).

Despite the dominance of macroeconomic forces in the recent farm crisis, inconsistent farm policies still played a significant role. High support and target prices encouraged farmers to keep increasing output, despite stagnant sales. The resulting surpluses not only kept a lid on farm prices but also became a costly source of embarrassment for the makers of farm policy. In the early 1980s the U.S. government "bought" up to one-fourth of all corn and wheat output and substantial quantities of other farm products.

By the mid-1980s, virtually everyone was unhappy with U.S. farm policies. Taxpayers were upset with ballooning farm subsidies and disgusted with overflowing crop surpluses. And farmers were unhappy about declining export sales and uneasy about accepting so much government "welfare." These rising frustrations reflected the impossibility of fulfilling two irreconcilable goals, namely:

- Preserving the family farm

- Permitting the market to determine farm prices and income

In The News

GOVERNMENT SUBSIDIES

Milk Taxpayers Instead of Cows?

Less than a year after deciding to pay farmers not to grow crops, President Reagan signed legislation to pay dairy producers not to produce milk.

For the next 15 months, the government will give dairy farmers $10 for every 100 pounds—about 12.5 gallons—cut from their normal production. Producers can trim output by as much as 30 percent and get paid for not producing.

The law also directs the government to keep dairy prices propped up by buying the milk, cheese and butter that farmers cannot sell. Costs of buying and storing surplus milk soared to 2.7 billion dollars in the past fiscal year, and surpluses remained as big as ever. The Congressional Budget Office concluded that paying farmers not to produce milk would be cheaper, saving 1.7 billion dollars over four years. . . .

U.S. News & World Report, December 12, 1983, p. 12. Copyright © 1983, U.S. News & World Report.

Nearly two-thirds of the nation's farmers need income from nonfarm sources to support themselves. If farm prices and incomes were determined solely by market forces, many if not most of these farmers would be forced to shut down operation. Government supports keep these farmers in business and thus preserve an American tradition (and a political constituency).

On the other hand, American taxpayers rebel at the thought of massive farm subsidies and the lunacy of encouraging more production every year than consumers demand. If the marketplace were the sole determinant of farm prices and output, government subsidies and overproduction would cease.

Market Pricing The conflict between propping up farm incomes and letting the market mechanism work has been the central dilemma of farm policy since Herbert Hoover first tried to raise crop prices in 1929. The Farm Security Act of 1985 edged policy a little closer to the market mechanism. The core feature of the act was a gradual reduction in government support prices. For example, the support price ("loan rate") for wheat was reduced from $3.30 per bushel in 1986 to $2.40 in 1987 and to $2.28 per bushel in 1988. By reducing the support price, the government hoped to bring it closer to market realities.

Another feature of the 1985 act was to limit the government purchase of market surpluses. Rather than buying surpluses at the guaranteed loan price, the government now encourages farmers to sell their surpluses at market prices. The government then reimburses the farmers for the difference between the guaranteed (support) price and the market price.

Income Support The reduction in support prices threatened the livelihood of American farmers, however. To maintain their incomes, the Food Security Act continued a separate set of target prices. The target price represents the price Congress feels farmers need to ensure them an adequate living standard. The federal government pays farmers a "deficiency payment" for the difference between the target price and the guaranteed support price.

The support and target prices represent two different guarantee levels. However, Congress intended that deficiency payments triggered by the target price would be limited. No more than $50,000 in deficiency payments is permitted for any farm. In principle, then, deficiency payments do not encourage excess production, especially by large farms. In practice, however, large farms have been subdivided into many smaller farms and farmers have thus gained access to multiple deficiency payments.

To be eligible for any government price supports, farmers must still agree to acreage set-asides. Farmers can also idle additional land for "soil-conserving" purposes. If a farmer agrees to idle erosion-prone soil for ten years, the federal government will rent the idle land. In 1987 alone, corn farmers idled for ten years land equal to the total area of South Carolina. All these acreage set-asides restrict the supply and help prop up market prices.

Despite these efforts, government support and target prices are still far in excess of market prices (see Figure 28.8). As a result, government payments to farmers account for over 30 percent of net farm income. To bring farm prices closer to market realities, the government must either let the farm sector shrink still further or "decouple" farm payments from farm production. In other words, the government must accept one of three options:

FIGURE 28.8
Corn: Target Price,
Loan Rate,
and Market Price

American farmers
confront three distinct
prices: market price,
government guarantee
price ("loan rate"), and
target price. Farmers who
idle some acreage are
guaranteed a minimum
support price for their
output. They may also
receive a deficiency
payment of up to $50,000
for the difference between
congressionally mandated
target prices and support
prices. These above-market
prices induce farmers to
produce a market surplus.

Source: U.S. Department of
Agriculture.

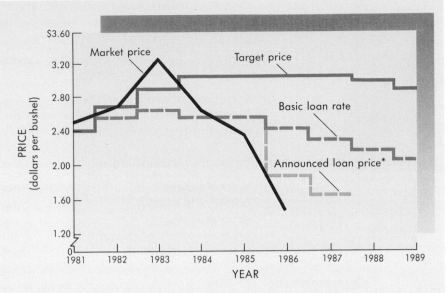

*Set by the Secretary of Agriculture within mandated limits.

- Reduce the number of farmers (by allowing more to go broke)

- Transform farm subsidies into explicit welfare payments based on need ("decoupling" from production)

- Accept continuing market distortions and huge farm subsidies

In negotiating the Farm Act of 1990, both the Bush administration and the Congress recognized the need for a clearer decoupling of price supports from income support. By bringing price supports closer to market prices, they sought to reduce the persistent surpluses in U.S. agriculture.

SUMMARY

- The agricultural sector has a highly competitive structure, with over 2 million farms.

- In a free market, farm prices tend to decline over time because of increasing productivity and low elasticity of demand. The same forces, plus the weather, make farm prices unstable.

- Most of today's farm policies originated during the Great Depression, in response to low farm prices and incomes.

- The government uses price supports and cost subsidies to raise farm prices and profits. These policies also create market surpluses that must be disposed of via government purchases, increased exports, or supply restrictions.

- Direct income support to farmers would ensure income stability without creating market surpluses, and might be less expensive as well. Farm groups oppose such visible subsidies and argue that the replacement of existing programs would threaten the stability of food supplies.

• Farm incomes declined sharply between 1979 and 1983, causing a second depression in the farm sector. The drop was caused by sharp increases in fuel, fertilizer, and interest costs.

• The goal of current farm policy is to reduce market surpluses by gradually lowering price supports. At the same time, high target prices and related deficiency payments guarantee income support.

Terms to Remember   Define the following terms:

market power	market surplus
barriers to entry	parity
economic profit	acreage set-aside
price elasticity of demand	deficiency payment
income elasticity of demand	profit

Questions for Discussion

1. Would the U.S. economy be better off without government intervention in agriculture? Who would benefit? Who would lose?

2. Are large price movements inevitable in agricultural markets? What other mechanisms might be used to limit such movement?

3. Why doesn't the United States just give its crop surpluses to poor countries? What problems might such an approach create?

Problems

1. Suppose that there are 100 grain farmers, each with identical cost structures as shown in the following table:

Production costs (per farm)		Demand	
Output (bushels per day)	Total cost (per day)	Price (per bushel)	Quantity demanded (bushels per day)
0	$ 5	$1	600
1	7	2	500
2	10	3	400
3	14	4	300
4	19	5	200
5	25	6	100
6	33	7	50

Under these circumstances,
(a) What is the equilibrium price for grain?
(b) How much grain will be produced at the equilibrium price?
(c) How much profit will each farmer earn at that price?
(d) What will happen to grain output, price, and profit if the government gives farmers a cost subsidy equal to $1 per bushel?
(e) What will happen to total output if the government additionally guarantees a price of $5 per bushel?
(f) What price is required to sell this output?
(g) What is the cost to the government in (d) and (f)?
(h) Graph your answers.

2. Suppose that consumers' incomes fall 20 percent, which results in a 2 percent drop in consumption of farm goods without any change in prices. Compute the income elasticity of demand for farm goods.

3. Reread the article about paying farmers not to produce milk (p. 715). Assume that the supply schedule for milk prior to the government's action is the following:

Price (per pound)	5¢	7¢	8¢	10¢	14¢
Quantity supplied (billions of pounds per year)	42	53	63	76	103

(a) Draw the supply and demand curves for milk, assuming that the demand for milk is perfectly inelastic and consumers will buy 53 billion pounds of it. What is the equilibrium price?

(b) Suppose that the farmers' response to the government's offer to pay them for not producing milk results in the following supply schedule:

Price (per pound)	5¢	7¢	8¢	10¢	14¢
Quantity supplied (billions of pounds per year)	19	30	40	53	80

(c) Draw this new supply curve on the same set of axes as the supply curve prior to the government's action. What is the equilibrium price following the government's action?

(d) How much more money would consumers pay for the 53 billion pounds of milk because of the higher equilibrium price?

(e) Shade in the area in your diagram that represents how much more consumers will pay because of the government-sponsored cutbacks.

FACTOR MARKETS:
Basic
Theory

Factor markets operate like product markets, with supply and demand interacting to determine prices and quantities. In factor markets, however, resource inputs rather than products are exchanged. Those exchanges determine the wages paid to workers and the rent, interest, and profits paid to other inputs. The micro theories presented in Chapters 29–31 explain how those factor payments are determined.

The Labor Market

In 1990 the chairman of General Motors was paid over $2 million for his services. The president of the United States was paid $200,000. And the secretary who typed the manuscript of this book was paid $17,000. What accounts for these tremendous disparities in earnings?

And why is it that the average college graduate was earning over $35,000 in 1990 while the average high school graduate earned less than $25,000? Do such disparities simply reflect a reward for enduring the rigors of four years of college, or do they reflect real differences in talent? Are you really learning anything that makes you that much more valuable than a high school graduate?

Surely we cannot hope to explain these earnings disparities on the basis of the willingness to work. After all, my secretary would be more than willing to work day and night for $2 million per year. For that matter, so would I. Accordingly, the earnings disparities cannot be attributed to differences in the quantity of labor supplied. If we are to explain why some people earn a great deal of income while others earn very little, we will have to consider both the *supply* and the *demand* for labor. In this regard, the following questions arise:

- How do people decide how much time to spend working?

- What determines the wage rate an employer is willing to pay?

- Why are some workers paid so much and others so little?

To answer these questions, we need to examine the behavior of labor *markets*.

LABOR SUPPLY

The following two ads recently appeared in the campus newspaper of a well-known university:

Will do ANYTHING for money: able-bodied liberal-minded male needs money, will work to get it. Have car. Call Tom 765-3210.

Computer Programmer: Computer sciences graduate, fluent in FORTRAN, COBOL, APL; experience with UNIVAC, IBM and CDC systems. Looking for part-time position on or off campus. Please call Judy, ext. 4120, 9–5.

Although placed by individuals of very different talents, the ads clearly expressed Tom's and Judy's willingness to work. Although we don't know how much money they were asking for their respective talents, or whether they ever found jobs, we can be sure that they were prepared to take a job at some wage rate. Otherwise, they would not have paid for the ads in the "Jobs Wanted" column of their campus newspaper.

The advertised willingness to work expressed by Tom and Judy represents a **supply of labor.** They are offering to sell their time and talents to anyone who is willing to pay the right price. Their explicit offers are similar to those of anyone who looks for a job. Job seekers who check the current job openings at the student employment office or send résumés to potential employers are demonstrating a willingness to accept employment—that is, to supply labor. The 25,000 Muscovites who applied for jobs at the Soviet Union's first McDonald's were also offering to supply labor (see World View).

Our first concern in this chapter is to explain these labor supply decisions. In general, we expect that the quantity of labor supplied depends on the wage rate. Specifically, we anticipate that the quantity of labor supplied—the number of hours people are willing to work—will increase as wage rates rise (see Figure 29.1).

But how do people decide how many hours to supply at any given wage rate? Do people try to maximize their total wages? If they did, we would all be holding three jobs and sleeping on the commuter bus. Since most of us don't behave this way, other motives must be present. What are these other motivations, and how do they affect the quantity of labor supplied at various wage rates?

labor supply: The willingness and ability to work specific amounts of time at alternative wage rates in a given time period, *ceteris paribus.*

Income vs. Leisure

The reward for working consists of the intrinsic satisfaction of working plus the income derived from a job. The more hours you work, the more income you are likely to receive. Hence there is a substantial incentive to work more hours (i.e., supply a greater quantity of labor).

W RLD VIEW

LABOR SUPPLY

In Moscow, 25,000 Apply for 630 Jobs at McDonald's

More than 25,000 Muscovites have dreams of flipping burgers beneath the golden arches as a member of the worldwide Big Mac and French fry brigade, eager to share in the West's most greasy rite of passage.

The flood of job-seekers started almost immediately after a Moscow newspaper advertisement was published last month. More than 1,000 applications for the 630 available crew spots came the first day, said George Cohon, deputy chairman of Moscow McDonald's. More than 3,100 interviews have been conducted, seven days a week, with such criteria as whether applicants are legal Moscow residents.

Many job seekers are housewives and students from the prestigious Moscow University, and more than 20 percent speak two languages. Hiring is almost complete now, said Cohon, with only a few spots left to be filled. . . .

The Pushkin Square outlet, the biggest McDonald's in the world, will serve 15,000 diners a day, with 700 seats inside and 200 outside. . . .

Part-time Soviet workers make about $1\frac{1}{2}$ rubles per hour, said Cohon, which is $2.50 at the commercial rate. But workers will also be rewarded every few months for productivity.

—Kara Swisher

The Washington Post, December 14, 1989, p. E1. Copyright © 1989 The Washington Post.

FIGURE 29.1
The Supply of Labor

The quantity of any good or service offered for sale typically increases as its price rises. Labor supply responds in the same way. At the wage rate w_1, the quantity of labor supplied is q_1 (point A). At the higher wage w_2, workers are willing to work more hours per week, that is, to supply a larger quantity of labor (q_2).

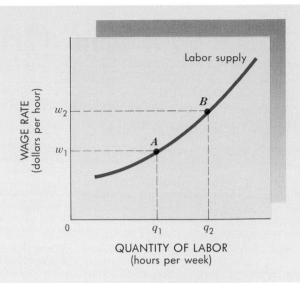

Not working obviously has some value, too. In part, we need some non-work time just to recuperate from working. We also want some time to watch TV, go to a soccer game, or otherwise enjoy the goods and services we have purchased.

Our conflicting desires for income and leisure create an obvious dilemma: the more time we spend working, the less time we have to enjoy our incomes, or simply to relax. Working, like all activities, involves an opportunity cost. Generally, we say that ***the opportunity cost of working is the amount of leisure time that must be given up in the process.***

The inevitable tradeoff between labor and leisure explains the shape of individual labor-supply curves. As we work more hours, our leisure time becomes more scarce—and thus more valuable.[1] Hence ***higher wage rates are required to compensate for the increasing opportunity cost of labor.*** We will supply a larger quantity of labor only if offered a higher wage rate.

The upward slope of the labor-supply curve is reinforced with the changing value of income. Our primary motive for working is the income a job provides. Those first few dollars are really precious, especially if you have bills to pay and no other source of support. As you work and earn more, however, you discover that your most urgent needs have been satisfied. You have food, shelter, some new clothes and perhaps even a little entertainment. You may still want more things, but the urgency of your consumption desires is likely to be diminished. In other words, ***the marginal utility of income declines as you earn more.*** Accordingly, the wages offered for more work lose some of their allure. You may not be willing to work more hours unless offered a higher wage rate.

The upward slope of an individual's labor supply curve is thus a reflection of two phenomena:

- The increasing opportunity cost of labor

- The decreasing marginal utility of income as a person works more hours.

[1]In other words, as leisure becomes more scarce, its marginal utility increases. This is consistent with the more general law of diminishing marginal utility.

In The News

NONMONETARY INCENTIVES

MBA Grads Seek Challenge at Work, Not Just Big Bucks

Cynics might argue, but money apparently isn't what drives most graduate business students, *Inc.* magazine says.

But that doesn't mean they expect to be poor. In its June issue, on sale today, *Inc.* says the average MBA graduate expects to earn $42,797 annually in his or her first job.

Stanford University's MBAs have the loftiest goals. *Inc.* says they expect to pull down $65,756. Students at the University of Miami had the most modest expectations. The average starting pay they're looking for: $33,732.

Inc. talked to 907 graduating MBA students at 10 schools this spring. Just 12% of those questioned said they went into graduate school primarily because of big salaries down the road. Only 24% rated a high salary as one of the most important considerations in choosing their next job.

Those answers don't surprise Teresa Miles, 23, who just earned her MBA at Duke University's Fuqua School of Business. "There are definitely some students who fit that greedy mold," says Miles, a native of Greenwich, Conn. "But it's such a stereotype I have to laugh at it."

Miles, who starts work June 15 at the Bank of New York's commercial lending department, will earn about $44,000 annually. But it was "a challenging experience and something that will do something for me" that led her to accept the bank's offer.

Most students think along those lines, says Associate Dean Dennis Weidenear at Purdue University's Krannert School of Management. "I don't think you should dis-count the pay they'll be getting because it is important," he says. "But they're not willing to walk over their grandmothers just to get a better salary."

Other poll results:

- Challenging work was rated a "most important" job characteristic by 75% of the students; 44% ranked atmosphere first; 40%, location. . . .

What MBAs at Some Top Schools Expect to Earn

School	Expected earnings	
	First job	In 1992
Carnegie-Mellon	$45,189	$87,703
Duke University	$43,071	$94,547
Indiana University	$36,784	$71,195
University of Miami	$33,732	$68,901
University of Minnesota	$39,453	$67,973
Northwestern University	$48,067	$121,036
University of Pennsylvania	$52,548	$131,065
University of Southern California	$38,795	$94,895
Stanford University	$65,756	$185,276
University of Texas	$37,037	$84,004
Average	*$42,797*	*$97,136*

Source: *Inc.* magazine.

—Mark Memmott

USA Today, May 28, 1987, p. 6B. Copyright © 1987 USA TODAY. Excerpted with permission.

A Backward Bend?

substitution effect of wages: An increased wage rate encourages people to work more hours (to substitute labor for leisure).

The force that drives people up the labor-supply curve is the marginal utility of income, as represented by the goods and services that wages can buy. Higher wages represent more goods and services and thus induce people to **substitute** labor for leisure.

At some point, however, additional goods and services will be of little value. Individuals with extremely high incomes already have a multitude of goods and services to enjoy. If offered a higher wage rate, they may *reduce* the number of hours they work, thereby maintaining a high income *and* increasing their leisure. While you might do cartwheels for $15 an hour, a Rockefeller or Du Pont might not lift an eyelash for such a paltry sum. Muhammad Ali once announced that he would not spend an hour in the ring for less than $1 million and would box *less,* not more, as the pay for his fights exceeded $3 million. For him, the added income obtainable from one championship fight was so great that he felt he did not have to fight more to satisfy

income effect of wages: An increased wage rate allows a person to reduce hours worked without losing income.

his income and consumption desires. This negative response to increased wage rates is referred to as the **income effect** of a wage increase.

A utility-maximizing individual will respond to these income and substitution effects by offering different quantities of labor at alternative wage rates. The *substitution effect* of high wages encourages people to work more hours. The *income effect,* on the other hand, allows them to reduce work hours without losing income. If substitution effects dominate, the labor supply curve will be upward-sloping. ***If income effects outweigh substitution effects, an individual will supply*** **less** ***labor at higher wages.*** This kind of reaction is illustrated by the backward-bending portion of the supply curve in Figure 29.2.[2]

MARKET SUPPLY

market supply of labor: The total quantity of labor that workers are willing and able to supply at alternative wage rates in a given time period, *ceteris paribus.*

The **market supply of labor** represents the sum of all individual labor-supply decisions. Although it is true that many high-income individuals have backward-bending supply curves, these negative responses to higher wages are swamped by the positive responses of over 120 million workers. At any point in time, therefore, the market supply curve is most likely to be upward-sloping.

Over time, however, the market supply curve may shift, as incomes rise and more workers choose leisure over labor. This has evidently happened. In 1890 the average worker was employed 60 hours a week at a wage rate of 20 cents an hour. In 1990 the average worker worked only 35 hours per week at a wage rate of close to $9.00 an hour.

[2]Income effects are relevant at low incomes also. A person paid very low wage rates (e.g., migrant workers, babysitters, household workers) may end up working more hours at low wages in order to maintain some minimum level of income. The higher income made possible by higher wage rates may induce some cutback in hours of work. These are the kinds of situations Karl Marx had in mind when he said that capitalists would strive to keep wage rates low to induce people to work. The modern version of this problem is discussed in Chapter 33, where the welfare system is considered.

**FIGURE 29.2
The Backward-Bending
Supply Curve**

Increases in wage rates make additional hours of work more valuable, but also less necessary. Higher wage rates increase the quantity of labor supplied as long as substitution effects outweigh income effects. At the point where income effects begin to outweigh substitution effects, the labor–supply curve starts to bend backward.

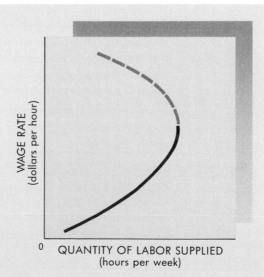

Elasticity of Labor Supply

elasticity of labor supply: The percentage change in the quantity of labor supplied divided by the percentage change in wage rate.

Despite the evident long-run shifts of the labor-supply curve, workers still respond positively to higher wage rates in the short run. To measure the resulting movements along the labor-supply curve, we use the concept of elasticity. Specifically, **elasticity of labor supply** is the percentage change in the quantity of labor supplied divided by the percentage change in the wage rate—that is,

$$\bullet \quad \text{Elasticity of} \atop \text{labor supply} = \frac{\text{percentage change in quantity of labor supplied}}{\text{percentage change in wage rate}}$$

The elasticity of labor tells us how much more labor will be available if a higher wage is offered. If the elasticity of labor is 0.2, a 10 percent increase in wage rates will induce a 2 percent increase in the quantity of labor supplied.[3]

The actual responsiveness of workers to a change in wage rates depends on a variety of factors. *These determinants of labor-supply elasticity include*

* *Tastes* (for leisure, income, and work)

* *Income and wealth*

* *Expectations* (e.g., for income or consumption)

* *Prices* of consumer goods

* *Taxes*

Institutional Constraints

The labor-supply curve and its related elasticities tell us how much time people would like to allocate to work. We must recognize, however, that people seldom have the opportunity to adjust their hours of employment at will. True, a Bo Jackson, a Whitney Houston, a Mike Tyson, or a Stephen King can alter almost at will the amount of labor supplied. Most workers, however, face more rigid choices. They must usually choose to work at a regular eight-hours-a-day, five-days-a-week job or not to work at all. Very few firms are flexible enough to accommodate a desire to work only between the hours of 11 A.M. and 3 P.M. on alternate Thursdays. Adjustments in work hours are more commonly confined to choices about overtime work or secondary jobs ("moonlighting") and vacation and retirement decisions. Insofar as families make collective decisions about the labor they supply, adjustments in work effort may also be reflected in decisions about the number of family members to send into the labor force at any given time.

LABOR DEMAND

demand for labor: The quantities of labor employers are willing and able to hire at alternative wage rates in a given time period, *ceteris paribus.*

Regardless of how many people are *willing* to work, it is up to employers to decide how many people will *actually* work. Employers must be willing and able to hire workers if people are going to hold jobs and earn some income. That is to say, there must be a **demand for labor.** What determines the number of workers employers are willing to hire at various wage rates?

[3]See Chapter 19 for further discussion of elasticity computations.

Derived Demand

derived demand: The demand for labor and other factors of production results from (depends on) the demand for final goods and services produced by these factors.

In earlier chapters we emphasized that employers are profit maximizers. Their primary motivation for going into business is to make as much income as possible. In their quest for maximum profits, firms attempt to identify the rate of output at which marginal revenue equals marginal cost. Once they have identified the profit-maximizing rate of output, firms enter factor markets to purchase the required amounts of labor, equipment, and other resources. Thus *the quantity of resources purchased by a business depends on the firm's expected sales and output.* In this sense, we say that the demand for factors of production, including labor, is a **derived demand;** it is derived from the demand for goods and services.

Consider the plight of strawberry pickers. Strawberry pickers are paid very low wages and are employed only part of the year. But their plight cannot be blamed on the greed of the strawberry growers. Strawberry growers, like most producers, would love to sell more strawberries at higher prices. If they did, there is a strong possibility that the growers would hire more pickers and even pay them at a higher wage rate. But the growers must contend with the market demand for strawberries. Growers have discovered that consumers are not willing to buy more strawberries at higher prices. As a consequence, the growers cannot afford to hire more pickers or pay them higher wages. In contrast, producers of computers are always looking for more workers and offer very high wages to get them. Table 29.1 lists other occupations likely to experience unusually high or low demand in the next few years.

The principle of derived demand suggests that if consumers really want to improve the lot of strawberry pickers, they should eat more strawberries. An increase in the demand for strawberries will motivate growers to plant more berries and hire more labor to pick them. Until then, the plight of the pickers is not likely to improve.

TABLE 29.1 Shifting Demands for Labor

Wages and job prospects in future years will depend on changes in the demand for labor. The U.S. Department of Labor foresees major increases in the demand for computer technicians, medical aides, and paralegals, as consumer demands for computer, medical, and legal services continue to increase. Conversely, an actual decline in the demand for college professors is anticipated, as college enrollments decline. Things look even worse for railroad conductors and farmers. These figures show projected job growth for the fastest and slowest growing occupations.

Occupation	Projected growth of jobs, 1988–2000
In increasing demand	
Paralegals	75%
Medical assistants	70
Home-health aides	68
Office machine technicians	61
Travel agents	54
Computer systems analysts	53
Computer programmers	48
Corrections officers and jailers	41
In decreasing demand	
Electronic assemblers	−44
Stenographers	−23
Farmers	−23
Directory assistance operators	−21
Railroad conductors	−20
Sewing machine operators	−14

Source: U.S. Bureau of Labor Statistics.

The Labor-Demand Curve

The number of strawberry pickers hired by the growers is not completely determined by the demand for strawberries. On the contrary, the number of pickers will also depend on the wage rate of pickers. That is to say, **the quantity of labor demanded will depend on its price (the wage rate).** In general, we expect that strawberry growers will be *willing to hire* more pickers at low wages than at high wages. Hence the demand for labor looks very much like the demand for any good or service (see Figure 29.3).

Marginal Physical Product

The fact that the demand curve for labor slopes downward does not tell us what quantity of labor will be hired. Nor does it tell us what wage rate will be paid. To answer such questions, we need to know what determines the particular shape and position of the labor-demand curve.

A strawberry grower will be willing to hire another picker only if that picker contributes more to output than he or she costs. Growers, as rational businesspeople, recognize that *every* sale, *every* expenditure has some impact on total profits. Hence the truly profit-maximizing grower will want to evaluate each picker's job application in terms of the applicant's potential contribution to profits.

Fortunately, a strawberry picker's contribution to output is easy to measure; it is the number of boxes of strawberries he or she picks. Suppose for the moment that Marvin, a college dropout with three summers of experience as a canoe instructor, can pick 5 boxes per hour. These 5 boxes represent Marvin's **marginal physical product (MPP),** in other words, the *addition* to total output that will occur if the grower hires Marvin for an hour—that is,

$$\bullet \quad \frac{\text{Marginal}}{\text{physical product}} = \frac{\text{change in total output}}{\text{change in quantity of labor}}$$

marginal physical product (MPP): The change in total output associated with one additional unit of input.

Marginal physical product establishes an *upper limit* to the grower's willingness to pay. Clearly the grower can't afford to pay Marvin more than 5 boxes of strawberries for an hour's work; the grower will not pay Marvin more than he produces.

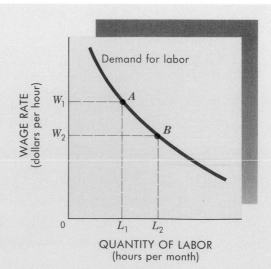

FIGURE 29.3
The Demand for Labor

The higher the wage rate, the smaller the quantity of labor demanded (*ceteris paribus*). At the wage rate W_1, only L_1 of labor is demanded. If the wage rate falls to W_2, a larger quantity of labor (L_2) will be demanded. The labor–demand curve obeys the law of demand.

In The News

MARGINAL PRODUCTIVITY

Merit Pay for Priests

The Episcopal Diocese of Newark, N.J., next year starts paying priests according to performance. Under the merit-pay plan, priests can qualify for salary rises based on goals that could include parish growth, education and choir programs, and quality of sermons.

The Wall Street Journal, March 5, 1985, p. 1. Reprinted by permission of *The Wall Street Journal,* © Dow Jones & Company, Inc. (1985). All Rights Reserved.

Marginal Revenue Product

marginal revenue product (MRP): The change in total revenue associated with one additional unit of input.

Most strawberry pickers don't want to be paid in strawberries, of course. At the end of a day in the fields, the last thing a picker wants to see is another strawberry. Marvin, like the rest of the pickers, wants to be paid in cash. To find out how much cash he might be paid, all we need to know is what a box of strawberries is worth. This is easy to determine. The market value of a box of strawberries is simply the price at which the grower can sell it. Thus Marvin's contribution to output can be measured in either marginal physical product (5 boxes per hour) or the dollar value of that product.

The dollar value of a worker's contribution to output is called **marginal revenue product (MRP).** Marginal revenue product is the change in total revenue that occurs when more labor is hired—that is,

$$\bullet \quad \frac{\text{Marginal}}{\text{revenue product}} = \frac{\text{change in total revenue}}{\text{change in quantity of labor}}$$

If the grower can sell strawberries for $2 a box, Marvin's marginal revenue product is simply 5 boxes per hour × $2 per box, or $10 per hour. In compliance with the rule about not paying anybody more than he or she contributes, the profit-maximizing grower should be willing to pay Marvin up to $10 an hour. Thus *marginal revenue product sets an upper limit to the wage rate an employer will pay.*

But what about a lower limit? Suppose that the pickers aren't organized and that Marvin is desperate for money. Under such circumstances, he might be willing to work—to supply labor—for only $3 an hour.

Should the grower hire Marvin for such a low wage? The profit-maximizing answer is obvious. If Marvin's marginal revenue product is $10 an hour and his wages are only $3 an hour, the grower will be eager to hire him. The difference between Marvin's marginal revenue product ($10) and his wage ($3) implies additional profits of $7 an hour. In fact, the grower will be so elated by the economics of this situation that he will want to hire everybody he can find who is willing to work for $3 an hour. After all, if the grower can make $7 an hour by hiring Marvin, why not hire 1,000 pickers and accumulate profits at an even faster rate?

The Law of Diminishing Returns

The exploitive possibilities suggested by Marvin's picking are clearly attractive; however, they merit some careful consideration. It isn't at all clear, for example, how the grower could squeeze 1,000 workers onto one acre of land

and have any room left over for strawberry plants. There must be some limit to the profit-making potential of this situation.

A few moments' reflection on the absurdity of trying to employ 1,000 people to pick one acre of strawberries should be convincing evidence of the limits to profits here. You don't need two years of business school to recognize this. But some economics may help explain exactly why the grower's eagerness to hire additional pickers will begin to fade long before 1,000 are hired. The magic concept here is *marginal productivity.*

Diminishing MPP   The decision to hire Marvin originated in his marginal physical product—that is, the 5 boxes of strawberries he can pick in an hour's time. To assess the profitability of hiring additional pickers, we again have to consider what will happen to total output as additional labor is employed. To do so we need to keep track of marginal physical product.

Figure 29.4 provides a summary of the increases in strawberry output as additional pickers are hired. We start with Marvin, who picks 5 boxes of strawberries per hour. Total output and his marginal physical product are identical, because he is initially the only picker employed. When the grower hires George, Marvin's old college roommate, we observe the total output increases to 10 boxes per hour. This figure represents another increase of 5 boxes per hour. Accordingly, we may conclude that George's *marginal physical product* is 5 boxes per hour, the same as Marvin's. Naturally, the grower will want to hire George and continue looking for more pickers.

As more workers are hired, total strawberry output continues to increase, but not nearly as fast. Although the later hires work just as hard, the limited availability of land and capital constrain their marginal physical product. One problem is the number of boxes. There are only a dozen boxes, and the additional pickers often have to wait for an empty box. The time spent waiting depresses marginal physical product. The worst problem is space: as additional workers are crowded onto the one-acre patch, they begin to get in one another's way. The picking process is slowed, and marginal physical product is further depressed. Note that the MPP of the fifth picker is 2 boxes per hour, while the MPP of the sixth picker is only 1 box per hour. By the time we get to the seventh picker, marginal physical product actually falls to zero, as no further increases in total strawberry output take place.

Things get even worse if the grower hires still more pickers. If 8 pickers are employed, total output actually *declines,* because the pickers can no longer work efficiently under such crowded conditions. Hence the MPP of the eighth worker is *negative,* no matter how ambitious or hard-working this person may be. Figure 29.4 illustrates this decline in marginal physical product.

Our observations on strawberry production are similar to those made in most industries. In general, ***the marginal physical product of labor declines as the quantity of labor employed increases.*** This is the **law of diminishing returns** we first encountered in Chapter 20. It is based on the simple observation that an increasing number of workers leaves each worker with less land and capital to work with.

Diminishing MRP   As marginal *physical* product diminishes, so does marginal *revenue* product (MRP). As noted earlier, marginal revenue product is the increase in the *value* of total output associated with an added unit of labor (or other input). In our example, it refers to the increase in strawberry revenues associated with one additional picker.

law of diminishing returns:
The marginal physical product of a variable factor declines as more of it is employed with a given quantity of other (fixed) inputs.

FIGURE 29.4
Diminishing Marginal Physical Product

The marginal physical product of labor is the increase in total production that results when one additional worker is hired. Marginal physical product tends to fall as additional workers are hired in any given production process. This decline occurs because each worker has increasingly less of other factors (e.g., land) with which to work.

When the second worker (*George*) is hired, total output increases from 5 to 10 boxes per hour. Hence the second worker's MPP equals 5 boxes per hour. Thereafter, capital and land constraints diminish marginal physical product.

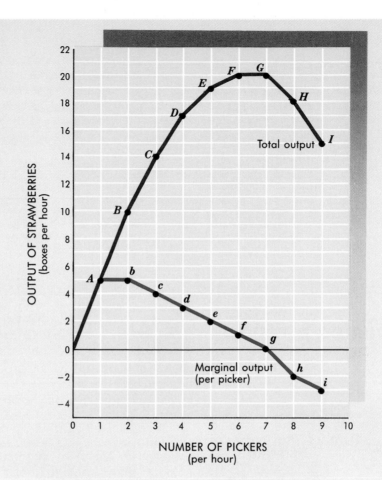

	Number of pickers (per hour)	Total strawberry output (boxes per hour)	Marginal physical product (boxes per hour)
A	1 (Marvin)	5	5
B	2 (George)	10	5
C	3	14	4
D	4	17	3
E	5	19	2
F	6	20	1
G	7	20	0
H	8	18	-2
I	9	15	-3

The decline in marginal revenue product mirrors the drop in marginal physical product. Recall that a box of strawberries sells for $2. With this price and the output statistics of Figure 29.4, we can readily calculate marginal revenue product, as summarized in Table 29.2. As the growth of output diminishes, so does marginal revenue product. Marvin's marginal revenue product of $10 an hour has fallen to $4 by the time 4 pickers are employed and reaches zero when 7 pickers are employed.[4]

[4]Marginal revenue product would fall even faster if the price of strawberries declined as increasing quantities were supplied. We are assuming that the grower's output does not influence the market price of strawberries, and hence that the grower is a *competitive* producer.

TABLE 29.2   Diminishing Marginal Revenue Product

Marginal revenue product (MRP) measures the change in total revenue that occurs when one additional worker is hired. At constant product prices, MRP equals MPP × price. Hence MRP declines along with MPP.

Numbers of pickers (per hour)	Total strawberry output (in boxes per hour)	×	Price of strawberries (per box)	=	Total strawberry revenue (per hour)	Marginal revenue product
0	0		$2		0	—
1 (Marvin)	5		2		$10	$10
2 (George)	10		2		20	10
3	14		2		28	8
4	17		2		34	6
5	19		2		38	4
6	20		2		40	2
7	20		2		40	0
8	18		2		36	−4
9	15		2		30	−6

THE HIRING DECISION

The tendency of marginal revenue product to diminish will clearly cool the strawberry grower's eagerness to hire 1,000 pickers. We still don't know, however, how many pickers will be hired.

Firm vs. Market Demand

Our earlier discussion of labor supply indicated that more workers are available only at higher wage rates. But that is true only for the *market* supply. A single producer may be able to hire an unlimited number of workers at the prevailing wage rate—if the firm is perfectly competitive in the labor market. In other words, *a firm that is a perfect competitor in the labor market can hire all the labor it wants at the prevailing market wage.*

Let us assume that the strawberry grower is so small that his hiring decisions have no effect on local wages. As far as he is concerned, there is an unlimited supply of strawberry pickers willing to work for $3 an hour. His only decision is how many of these willing pickers to hire at that wage rate.

Figure 29.5 provides the answer. We already know that the grower is eager to hire pickers whose marginal revenue product exceeds their wage. He will therefore hire at least 1 worker at that wage, because the MRP of the first picker is $10 an hour (point *A* in Figure 29.5). A second worker will be hired as well, because that picker's MRP (point *B* in Figure 29.5) also exceeds the going wage rate. In fact, *the grower will continue hiring pickers until the MRP has declined to the level of the market wage rate.* Figure 29.5 indicates that this intersection (point *C*) occurs after 5 pickers are employed. Hence we can conclude that the grower will be willing to hire—will *demand*— 5 pickers if wages are $3 an hour.

The folly of hiring more than 5 pickers is also apparent in Figure 29.5. The marginal revenue product of the sixth worker is only $2 an hour (point *D*). Hiring a sixth picker will cost more in wages than the picker brings in as revenue. The *maximum* number of pickers the grower will employ at prevailing wages is $5\frac{1}{2}$ (point *C*).

FIGURE 29.5
The Marginal Revenue Product Curve is the Labor-Demand Curve

The MRP curve tells us how many workers an employer would want to hire at various wage rates. An employer is willing to pay a worker no more than his or her marginal revenue product. In this case, a grower would gladly hire a second worker, because that worker's MRP (point *B*) exceeds the wage rate ($3). The sixth worker will not be hired at that wage rate, however, since his MRP (at point *D*) is less than $3. The MRP curve is the labor–demand curve.

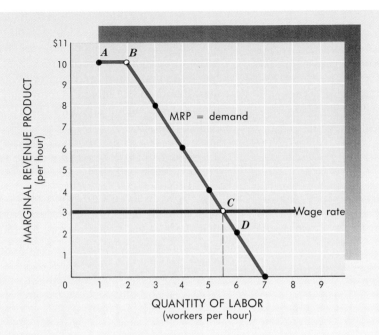

In The News

MARGINAL REVENUE PRODUCT

Where the Really Big Money Is

New Lawyers Get $65,000 a Year; Investment Bankers Pocket $100,000

Perry Mason didn't have it as good, and he rarely lost a case. Salaries for new lawyers are reaching a stratosphere once the exclusive province of masters of business administration. Blue-chip New York law firms are paying more than $65,000 this year to lure 24-year-olds straight from the classroom, with some firms paying a $10,000-to-$20,000 bonus for working a year or two as a judge's clerk.

Call it Economics 101: Demand for well-trained but untried attorneys apparently outstrips the supply of top-ranking graduates of elite schools. Another reason for the escalating salaries is fear of massive defections to investment banks—where first-year earnings can reach six figures. Median investment-banking base salary for 1986 Harvard Business School graduates is $50,000 plus a $3,000-to-$90,000 bonus.

When the investment banks aren't being blamed for the high salaries, the target is Cravath, Swaine & Moore, one of the nation's most prestigious law firms. It raised pay for its 42 new associates $12,000 to $65,300 this year, including a $1,000-a-month housing allowance for all associates. Paul, Weiss, Rifkind, Wharton & Garrison followed suit with $65,000. Not to be outdone, Shearman & Sterling bid $67,000, and, though it won't say so, Sullivan & Cromwell reportedly upped the ante to $70,000.

Are the new lawyers worth it? "In terms of motivation, dedication and ability to quickly pick up the necessary skills, we're looking at the same kind of justification as businesses hiring M.B.A.'s from the top schools," says Shearman & Sterling partner Arthur Field. At a major firm, a new associate who bills for 2,100 hours of service a year at $75 an hour would generate $157,500 for the firm. . . .

—Beth Brophy

U.S. News & World Report, June 16, 1986, p. 49. Copyright © 1986 U.S. News & World Report.

The law of diminishing returns also implies that all of the 5 pickers will be paid the same wage. Once 5 pickers are employed, we cannot say that any single picker is responsible for the observed decline in marginal revenue product. Marginal revenue product of labor diminishes because each worker has less capital and land to work with, not because the last worker hired is less able than the others. Accordingly, the "fifth" picker cannot be identified as any particular individual. Once 5 pickers are hired, Marvin's *MRP* is no higher than any other picker's. ***Each (identical) worker is worth no more than the marginal revenue product of the last worker hired, and all workers are paid the same wage rate.***

Changes in Wage Rates

The grower's decision to hire only 5 pickers is not unalterable. If the wage rate were to drop, more pickers would be hired. Suppose for the moment that the pickers agree to work for only $2 an hour. The grower will now be able to hire a sixth worker without sacrificing any profits. Figure 29.6*a* illustrates the effect of a reduction in wage rates. When wages drop, the employer moves down the labor-demand curve to a larger quantity of labor. Hence the labor-demand curve obeys the law of demand.

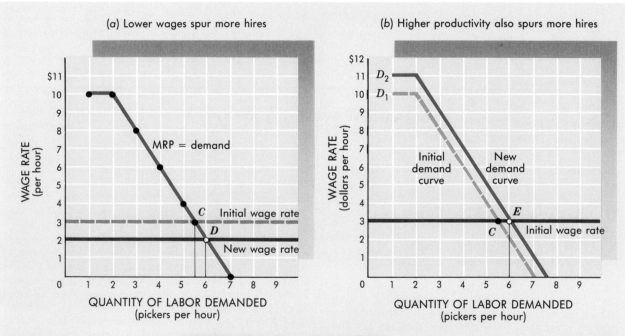

FIGURE 29.6 Incentives to Hire

(*a*) If the wage rate drops, an employer will be willing to hire additional workers (*ceteris paribus*). At $3 an hour, only 5½ pickers per hour would be demanded (point *C*). If the wage rate dropped to $2 an hour, 6 pickers per hour would be demanded (point *D*).

(*b*) The willingness of an employer to hire labor at any specific wage rate is based on labor's marginal revenue product. If the marginal revenue product of labor improves, the employer will be willing to hire a greater quantity of labor at any given wage rate. The labor–demand curve will shift to the right (e.g., from D_1 to D_2). In this case, an increase in MRP leads the employer to hire 6 workers (point *E*) rather than only 5½ workers (point *C*) at $3 per hour.

Changes in Productivity

Reductions in wages are not the only path to increased employment of strawberry pickers. The hiring decision involves a comparison of marginal revenue product and the wage rate. Accordingly, an increase in MRP can be just as effective as a wage (W) reduction in increasing employment.

Suppose that Marvin and his friends all enroll in a local agricultural extension course and learn new methods of strawberry picking. With these new methods, the marginal physical product of each picker increases by 1 box per hour. With the price of strawberries still at $2 a box, this productivity improvement implies an increase in marginal *revenue* product of $2 per worker. This change causes a rightward *shift* of the labor-demand (MRP) curve, as in Figure 29.6*b*.

Notice that the old wage rate of $3 an hour, when combined with the new labor-demand curve, leads to the employment of a sixth picker. Hence *either an increase in productivity or a fall in wage rates can bring about an increase in the quantity of labor demanded.* Naturally, the pickers are happier when the additional employment comes about through increased productivity, because in that case they don't suffer a wage reduction.

MARKET EQUILIBRIUM

The principles that guide the hiring decisions of a single strawberry grower can be extended to the entire labor market. This suggests that the *market* demand for labor depends on

- The number of employers

- The marginal revenue product of labor in each firm and industry

Increases in either the demand for final products or the productivity of labor will tend to increase the demand for labor.

On the supply side of the labor market we have already observed that the market supply of labor depends on

- The number of workers

- Each worker's willingness to work at alternative wage rates

The supply decisions of each worker are in turn a reflection of tastes, income, wealth, expectations, other prices, and taxes.

Equilibrium Wage

equilibrium wage: The wage at which the quantity of labor supplied in a given time period equals the quantity of labor demanded.

Figure 29.7 brings these market forces together. ***The intersection of the market supply and demand curves establishes the* equilibrium wage.** This is the only wage at which the quantity of labor supplied equals the quantity of labor demanded. Everyone who is willing and able to work for this wage will find a job.

If the labor market is perfectly competitive, all employers will be able to hire as many workers as they want at the equilibrium wage. Like our strawberry grower, every competitive firm is assumed to have no discernible effect on market wages. ***Competitive employers act like price takers with respect to wages as well as prices.*** This phenomenon is also portrayed in Figure 29.7.

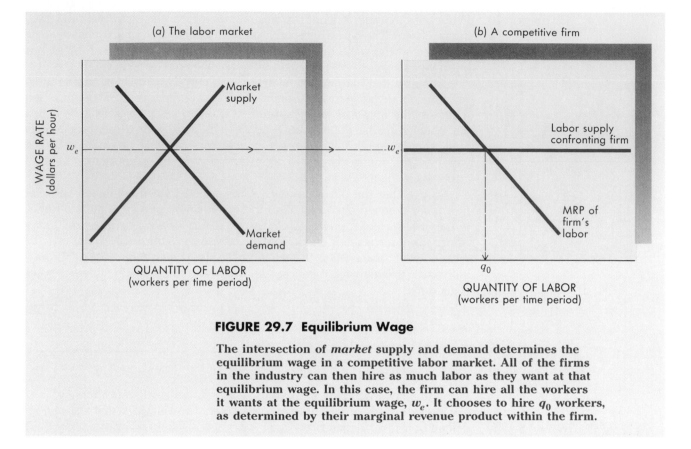

FIGURE 29.7 Equilibrium Wage

The intersection of *market* supply and demand determines the equilibrium wage in a competitive labor market. All of the firms in the industry can then hire as much labor as they want at that equilibrium wage. In this case, the firm can hire all the workers it wants at the equilibrium wage, w_e. It chooses to hire q_0 workers, as determined by their marginal revenue product within the firm.

Many people may be unhappy with the equilibrium wage. Employers may grumble that wages are too high. Workers may complain that wages are too low. Nevertheless, the equilibrium wage is the only one that clears the market. Attempts to enforce any other wage rate inevitably cause unemployment or labor shortages. This conclusion also applies to minimum wage laws that require above-equilibrium wage rates (see In the News).

CHOOSING AMONG INPUTS

The principles determining the shape and position of the demand curve for labor can be extended to rationalize the choice among various factors of production. Suppose that someone invents a mechanical strawberry picker that can pick berries twice as fast as Marvin. Who will the grower hire, Marvin or the mechanical picker?

At first it would seem that the grower would choose the mechanical picker. But the choice isn't so obvious. So far, all we know is that the mechanical picker's MPP is twice as large as Marvin's. But we haven't said anything about the *cost* of the mechanical picker.

Cost Efficiency Suppose that a mechanical picker can be rented for $10 an hour, while Marvin is still willing to work for $3 an hour. Will this difference in hourly cost change the grower's input choice?

In The News

DISEQUILIBRIUM

Minimum Wage Goes Up

The minimum wage rose from $3.35 to $3.80 in April 1990 and jumped another 45 cents to $4.25 per hour in April 1991. These hikes in the minimum wage were the first increases since 1981. Throughout the 1980s President Reagan rejected congressional proposals for minimum wage hikes, fearing that higher minimum wages would increase unemployment. President Bush also vetoed a minimum wage hike but later compromised with Congress on a two-year, 90 cents per hour increase.

Economists agree that an above-equilibrium wage will create unemployment. Some workers end up with higher wages, but others find themselves jobless. In the accompanying graph, the surplus workers represented by the difference between the quantities supplied (q_s) and demanded (q_d) do not get jobs. Those left out are the least skilled, with low marginal productivity.

The actual size of the job loss is hotly debated. In the early 1980s the consensus estimate was that a 10 percent increase in the minimum wage would cause a 1 percent reduction in employment. Between 1981 and 1990, however, the minimum was stuck at $3.35 an hour while average wages increased 30 percent. Hence the minimum wage became a less important constraint. By 1989 the federal minimum may have actually been below the equilibrium wage. Ten states had already increased *their* wage floors above the federal minimum. Moreover, fast-food chains were already paying wages above the federal minimum in 1989. Accordingly, the most recent hikes in the minimum wage had far less serious employment effects than earlier feared.

Minimum Wage History

Oct. '38	$0.25	May '74	$2.00
Oct. '39	0.30	Jan. '75	2.10
Oct. '45	0.40	Jan. '76	2.30
Jan. '50	0.75	Jan. '78	2.65
Mar. '56	1.00	Jan. '79	2.90
Sept. '61	1.15	Jan. '80	3.10
Sept. '63	1.25	Jan. '81	3.35
Feb. '67	1.40	Apr. '90	3.80
Feb. '68	1.60	Apr. '91	4.25

If the minimum wage exceeds the equilibrium wage, a labor surplus will result: more workers will be willing to work at that wage rate than employers will be prepared to hire. Some workers will end up with higher wages, but others will end up unemployed.

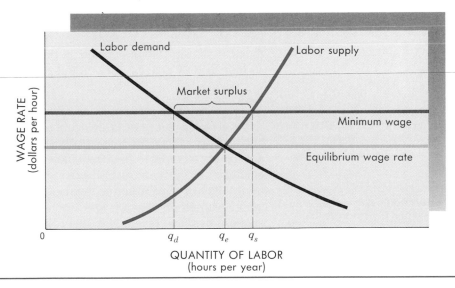

To determine the relative desirability of hiring Marvin or renting the mechanical picker, the grower must compare the ratio of their marginal physical products to their cost.[5] This ratio of marginal product to cost expresses the **cost efficiency** of an input—that is,

cost efficiency: The amount of output associated with an additional dollar spent on input; the MPP of an input divided by its price (cost).

[5]Note that it doesn't matter whether we are dealing with marginal physical product or marginal revenue product, because we are only comparing the productivity of two inputs used to produce the same good.

$$\bullet \quad \text{Cost efficiency} = \frac{\text{marginal physical product of an input}}{\text{cost of an input}}$$

Marvin's MPP is 5 boxes of strawberries per hour and his cost (wage) is $3. Thus the return on each dollar of wages paid to Marvin is

$$\begin{matrix} \text{Cost} \\ \text{efficiency} \\ \text{of labor} \end{matrix} = \frac{\text{MPP}_{\text{labor}}}{\text{cost}_{\text{labor}}} = \frac{5 \text{ boxes}}{\$3} = 1.67 \text{ boxes per } \$1 \text{ of cost}$$

By contrast, the mechanical picker has an MPP of 10 boxes per hour and costs $10 per hour; thus

$$\begin{matrix} \text{Cost} \\ \text{efficiency of} \\ \text{mechanical} \\ \text{picker} \end{matrix} = \frac{\begin{matrix}\text{MPP of} \\ \text{mechanical} \\ \text{picker}\end{matrix}}{\begin{matrix}\text{cost of} \\ \text{mechanical} \\ \text{picker}\end{matrix}} = \frac{10 \text{ boxes}}{\$10} = 1 \text{ box per } \$1 \text{ of cost}$$

These calculations indicate that Marvin is more cost-effective than the mechanical picker. From this perspective, the grower is better off hiring Marvin than renting a mechanical picker.

From the perspective of cost efficiency, the "cheapness" of a productive input is measured not by its price but by the amount of output it delivers for that price. Thus *the most cost-efficient factor of production is the one that produces the most output per dollar.*

The concept of cost efficiency helps to explain why American firms don't move en masse to Haiti, where peasants are willing to work for as little as 10 cents an hour. Although this wage rate is far below the minimum wage in the United States, the marginal physical product of Haitian peasants is even further below American standards. American workers remain more cost-efficient than the "cheap" labor available in Haiti and other less developed countries, so long as they deliver more output per dollar of wages.

Alternative Production Processes

Typically a producer does not choose between individual inputs but rather between alternative production processes. General Motors, for example, cannot afford to compare the cost efficiency of each job applicant with the cost efficiency of mechanical tire mounters. Instead, GM compares the relative desirability of a **production process** that is labor-intensive (uses a lot of labor) with others that are less labor-intensive. GM ignores individual differences in marginal revenue product. Nevertheless, the same principles of cost efficiency guide the decision.

production process: A specific combination of resources used to produce a good or service.

The Efficiency Decision

Let us return to the strawberry patch to see how the choice of an entire production process is made. We shall again assume that strawberries can be picked by either human or mechanical hands. Now, however, we shall assume that one ton of strawberries can be produced by only one of the three production processes described in Table 29.3. Process *A* uses the most labor and thus keeps more human pickers employed. By contrast, process *C* uses the most mechanical pickers and provides the least employment to human pickers. Process *B* falls between these two extremes.

TABLE 29.3 Alternative Production Processes

One ton of strawberries can be produced with varying input combinations. Which process is most efficient? What information is missing?

Input	Alternative processes for producing one ton of strawberries		
	Process A	Process B	Process C
Labor (hours)	400	270	220
Machinery (hours)	13	15	18
Land (acres)	1	1	1

Which of these three production processes should the grower use? If he used process *A*, he would demand the largest quantity of labor, and in this sense do the pickers a real favor. But his goal is to maximize profits, so we assume he will choose the production process that best serves this objective. That is to say, he will choose the *least-cost* process to produce one ton of strawberries.

But which of the production processes in Table 29.3 is least expensive? We really can't tell on the basis of the information provided. To determine the relative cost of each process—and thus to understand the producer's choice—we have to know something more about costs. In particular, we have to know how much an hour of mechanical picking costs and how much an hour of human picking (labor) costs. Then we can determine which combination of inputs is least expensive in producing one ton of strawberries—that is, which is most *cost-efficient*. Note that we don't have to know how much the land costs, because the same amount of land is used in all three production processes. Thus land costs will not affect our efficiency decision.

Suppose that strawberry pickers are still paid $3 an hour and that mechanical pickers can be rented for $10 an hour. The acre of land rents for $500 per year. With this information we can now calculate the total dollar cost of each production process and quickly determine the most cost-efficient. Table 29.4 summarizes the required calculations.

TABLE 29.4 The Least-Cost Combination

A producer wants to produce a given rate of output for the least cost. Choosing the least expensive production process is the efficiency decision. In this case, process *C* represents the most cost-efficient production process for producing one ton of strawberries.

Input	Cost calculation	
Process A		
Labor	400 hours at $3 per hour	= $1,200
Machinery	13 hours at $10 per hour	= 130
Land	1 acre at $500	= 500
	Total cost	$1,830
Process B		
Labor	270 hours at $3 per hour	= $ 810
Machinery	15 hours at $10 per hour	= 150
Land	1 acre at $500	= 500
	Total cost	$1,460
Process C		
Labor	220 hours at $3 per hour	= 660
Machinery	18 hours at $10 per hour	= 180
Land	1 acre at $500	= 500
	Total cost	$1,340

The calculations performed in Table 29.4 clearly identify production process *C* as the least expensive way of producing one ton of strawberries. Process *A* entails a total cost of $1,830, whereas process *C* costs only $1,340 to produce the same quantity of output. As a profit maximizer, the grower will choose process *C*, even though it implies less employment for strawberry pickers.

The choice of an appropriate production process—the decision about *how* to produce—is called the **efficiency decision.** As we have seen, a producer seeks to use the combination of resources that produces a given rate of output for the least cost. The efficiency decision requires the producer to find that particular least-cost combination.

---

efficiency decision: The choice of a production process for any given rate of output.

POLICY INSIGHTS:

COMPARABLE WORTH—A CHALLENGE TO WAGE THEORY

The concepts of marginal productivity and cost efficiency can be used to help explain the very different wages paid to individuals in our economy. The theory of labor demand suggests that workers are evaluated in terms of their *marginal revenue product.* Individuals who contribute the most to the revenues of a firm will be paid the highest wage rates. Those workers whose MRP is low will be paid little. As we observed at the beginning of this chapter, the chairman of General Motors is paid over $2 million a year. Why are GM's stockholders willing to pay him so much? The only rational explanation is that his marginal revenue product exceeds $2 million. Presumably his managerial skills and knowledge of the automobile market are considered to be so vast that GM's total revenues might fall by at least $2 million a year if he departed. While this might sound extraordinary, it is certainly not impossible in the case of a firm with over $120 *billion* in annual revenues.

GM does not pay all its employees so handsomely, of course. The worker who tightens the bolts on the left rear wheel of every Chevette rolling down the assembly line earns close to $18 an hour—a good wage, but a far cry from the $1,000 an hour GM's chairman is paid. This difference in wage rates is explained in part by their respective marginal revenue products. GM has discovered that tight rear-wheel bolts aren't an essential determinant of car sales and represent a very small proportion of total cost. No matter how hard the bolt tighteners work, they have very little influence on GM's total revenues. The marginal revenue product and the wage rate of bolt tighteners are comparatively low.

The fantastic incomes of top entertainers and athletes can also be explained in terms of marginal revenue product. In 1990 boxer Mike Tyson earned over $6 million for just an hour's work. This wage reflected the fact that boxing fans were *willing to pay* high prices to see Tyson fight Buster Douglas in a heavyweight championship bout. Thousands of fans paid as much as $1,500 per seat to watch the fight at ringside in Tokyo. Another million or so fans paid $35 each to watch the fight on closed-circuit television. Total revenue from the fight exceeded $70 million. If a pair of nobodies were fighting, total revenue might equal only a few hundred dollars, but with Tyson and Douglas in the ring, total revenues soared. This increased revenue represented Tyson's MRP and thus set the limit to the wage the fight promoters were *willing to pay* for Tyson's labor. After he *lost* the fight (his first-ever loss as a professional boxer) his marginal revenue product actually *increased:* *Everybody,* it seemed, wanted to see a Douglas–Tyson rematch.

In The News

MARGINAL REVENUE PRODUCT

Louisville's Two Coaches Priceless

Cardinals Pay Premium for Top-Notch Basketball, Football Programs

Call it the mother lode of college coaching.

The University of Louisville wants a top-of-the-line basketball program. And as soon as possible—a football program to match.

The strategy: Shell out the needed bucks for top-of-the-line coaches.

- For basketball coach Denny Crum, whose teams have won two national championships in his 14 years at the

school, a package that includes $110,022 in base salary, a minimum of $80,000 a year from television and radio shows and a 10-year annuity worth $1 million.

- For football coach Howard Schnellenberger, hired a year after he won a national title at the University of Miami (Fla.) in 1982, a base salary of $72,100, the same radio and TV guarantee plus a share of those profits, a $500,000 annuity and even a say in who his new boss would be. . . .

—Steve Wieberg

USA TODAY, 1986. Copyright © 1986 USA TODAY. Excerpted with permission.

The same considerations induced the University of Louisville to pay its basketball and football coaches over $250,000 per year (see In the News). After Howard Schnellenberger was hired, average attendance at Louisville football games increased from 24,000 to over 27,000. In the first year of his coaching reign, the football program generated a profit of about $350,000, reversing losses of earlier years. Coach Schnellenberger's marginal revenue product thus exceeded his salary. The same was true for Denny Crum, who helped boost Louisville's basketball attendance, television coverage, and sponsorship.

Unmeasured MRP

Although marginal revenue principles offer a fairly convincing explanation for wage disparities, they don't explain all wages. We noted earlier that the president of the United States is paid $200,000 a year. Can we argue that this salary represents his marginal revenue product? For that matter, how would one begin to measure the MRP of the president? The wage we pay the president of the United States is less a reflection of his contribution to total output than a matter of custom. His salary also reflects the price voters believe is required to induce competent individuals to forsake private-sector jobs and assume the responsibilities of the presidency. In this sense, the wage paid to the president and other public officials is set by their **opportunity wage**—that is, the wage they could earn in private industry.

opportunity wage: The highest wage an individual would earn in his or her best alternative job.

The same kinds of considerations influence the wages of college professors. The marginal revenue product of a college professor is not easy to measure. Is it the number of students he or she teaches, the amount of knowledge conveyed, or something else? Confronted with such problems, most universities tend to pay college professors according to their opportunity wage—that is, the amount the professors could earn elsewhere.

Opportunity wages also help explain the difference between the wage rate paid to GM's president and that paid to its rear-wheel bolt tighteners. The low wage of bolt tighteners reflects not only their marginal revenue product at General Motors but also the fact that they are not trained for many other jobs. That is to say, their opportunity wages are low. By contrast, GM's president has impressive managerial skills that are in demand by many corporations; his opportunity wages are high.

Discrimination   Although marginal productivity theory and opportunity costs explain much inequality, they do not fully account for all wage differentials. Two individuals of equal productivity may command very different wages simply because of race or sex. Black and female workers are consistently paid less than white males. Does this reflect differences in innate ability, or are women and minority workers denied equal access to better jobs and wages?

The Equal Pay Act of 1963 requires that all workers performing the same job be paid identical wages. This act precludes blatant discrimination by race and sex. Women's-rights advocates argue, however, that the enforcement of equal pay for equal work is not enough. They contend that women have been excluded from the jobs that pay high wages. They see women segregated into "women's" jobs and excluded from "men's." In their view, this occupational sex discrimination makes a mockery of marginal revenue product theory.

Examples of apparent inequities abound. At the University of Washington, the nursing faculty—which is overwhelmingly female—is paid substantially less than the faculty in male-dominated departments such as engineering. The nursing instructors claimed that their research and teaching were as important as that of other faculty members. They viewed their work as *comparable* if not identical to that of other departments, and they demanded equivalent pay.

In The News

COMPARABLE WORTH

Typist = Driver

Los Angeles Adjusts Its Salaries

Los Angeles Mayor Tom Bradley said he was sending "a message to all cities across this country." Flanked by union officials and city aides, he announced last week that municipal pay scales would be adjusted so that salaries for jobs held mainly by women would be comparable to those for positions traditionally held by males. Los Angeles thus became the largest city to adopt the controversial system of "comparable worth," which attempts to calculate the value of different jobs, from secretary to warehouseman, based on factors such as education, responsibilities, and work conditions. Claimed Gerald McEntee, president of the American Federation of State, County and Municipal Employees: "The momentum in eliminating sex bias from public-sector wage scales is now irreversible."

Federal law requires that workers in the same job cannot be paid differently because of their sex or race. Comparable worth takes "equal pay for equal work" a long step further, requiring similar pay for jobs of similar value. The problem, and a devilishly difficult one, is to decide which jobs are comparable. In Los Angeles, for instance, stenographers and typists have been paid about 15% less than drivers and warehouse workers. Under the new system painstakingly negotiated by AFSCME and the city, all are considered to be doing comparable work. The agreement, which will cost $12 million in salary hikes for 3,900 workers, was supported by male employees, who will not lose any pay in the process.

Many "women's" jobs have historically paid less than "men's" jobs. But correcting these differentials through comparable-worth rulings will substantially alter the workings of the labor market, allowing theoretical calculations and arbitrary rulings by a new tier of bureaucrats to supplant the forces of supply and demand. The U.S. Commission on Civil Rights last month rejected comparable worth, saying it would lead to "a radical reordering of our economic system." Nevertheless, it has already been adopted, at least in principle, by Minnesota and New York. In addition, studies are under way in 25 other states to determine how such adjustments could be made.

Time, May 20, 1985, p. 23. Copyright 1985 Time Inc. Reprinted by permission.

The same kind of charge led to a strike at Yale University. Yale's clerical and technical workers, who are predominantly female, earn significantly less than the university's maintenance workers (predominantly male). An administrative assistant, for example, earned $13,424 in 1984, while a university truck driver earned $18,470. The clerical workers demanded equal pay to reflect the claim that their work was at least as valuable to the university as was that of truck drivers.

These demands for comparable wages strike at the very core of wage theory. Economic theory tells us that wages will reflect supply and demand. Marginal revenue product will set a ceiling to the wage rate for any occupation. The actual wage paid will depend on how many people are able and willing to work (supply labor) at various wages. If wages are "too low," the employers will not be able to hire all the workers they want. As employers bid for scarce labor, wages will rise.

Comparable-worth advocates want a different mechanism for establishing wages. They want every job to be evaluated on the basis of its importance to society, the skills required to perform it, the administrative burdens assumed, and its (un)pleasantness. Wages would then reflect the "score" assigned to each job.

Comparable-worth principles are not a viable substitute for market-determined wages. The implementation of comparable worth would require highly subjective assessments of every job. More important, those subjective assessments might not coincide with the realities of supply and demand. What if we paid nurses more and engineers less than at present? The number of applicants for nursing positions would increase significantly, while the number of engineering faculty supplied would diminish. How would the resulting surpluses and shortages be resolved? Sooner or later, wage differentials would have to be reintroduced. Those differentials would again reflect the respective demand and supply for each profession. The comparable-worth dilemma is similar to the plight of the strawberry pickers we discussed at the outset of this chapter. The wages of lower-paid workers will rise only if (1) the demand for the product they produce increases, (2) they become more productive, or (3) their supply diminishes. To date, the courts have rejected comparable-worth claims, in recognition of those wage-setting forces of the marketplace. The resulting wages may not be "fair," but they are efficient in allocating labor to its best uses.

SUMMARY

- The motivation to work arises from a variety of social, psychological, and economic forces. People need income to pay their bills, but they also need to feel they have a role in society's efforts, and to attain a sense of achievement. As a consequence, people are willing to work—to supply labor.

- There is an opportunity cost involved in working—namely, the amount of leisure one sacrifices. By the same token, the opportunity cost of not working (leisure) is the income and related consumption possibilities thereby forgone. Thus each person confronts a tradeoff between leisure and income.

- Increases in wage rates raise the marginal utility of labor and tend to induce people to work more—that is, to substitute labor for leisure. But this substitution effect may be offset by an income effect. Higher wages also enable a person to work fewer hours with no loss of income. When income effects outweigh substitution effects, the labor-supply curve begins to bend backward.

• A firm's demand for labor reflects labor's marginal revenue product. The greater the marginal revenue product of labor, the larger the quantity of labor a firm is willing to hire at any given wage.

• The marginal revenue product of labor also establishes a limit to the wage rate that firms willingly pay. A profit-maximizing employer will not pay a worker more than the worker produces.

• The marginal revenue product of labor tends to diminish as additional workers are employed on a particular job (the law of diminishing returns). This decline occurs because additional workers have to share existing land and capital, leaving each worker with less land and capital to work with.

• A producer seeks to get the most output for every dollar spent on inputs. This means getting the highest ratio of marginal product to input price. Accordingly, a profit-maximizing producer will always choose the most cost-efficient input (not necessarily the one with the cheapest price).

• The efficiency decision involves the choice of the least-cost production process and is also made on the basis of cost efficiency. A producer seeks the least expensive process to produce a given rate of output.

• Differences in marginal revenue product are an important explanation of wage inequalities. But the difficulty of measuring MRP in many instances leaves many wage rates to be determined by custom, power, discrimination, or opportunity wages.

Terms to Remember

Define the following terms:

labor supply	marginal revenue product
substitution effect of wages	(MRP)
income effect of wages	law of diminishing returns
market supply of labor	equilibrium wage
elasticity of labor supply	cost efficiency
demand for labor	production process
derived demand	efficiency decision
marginal physical product (MPP)	opportunity wage

Questions for Discussion

1. Why are you doing this homework? What are you giving up? What utility do you expect to gain?

2. Would you continue to work after winning a lottery prize of $50,000 a year for life? Would you change schools, jobs, or career objectives? What factors besides income influence work decisions?

3. If all individual workers had backward-bending supply curves, could the market supply of labor still be positively sloped? Explain.

4. Is this course increasing your marginal productivity? If so, in what way?

5. Suppose George is making $13 an hour installing transistorized digital chips in electronic calculators. Would your offer to work for $8 an hour get you the job? Why might a profit-maximizing employer turn down your generous offer?

6. Explain why marginal physical product would diminish as
   (a) More secretaries are hired in an office
   (b) More professors are hired in the economics department
   (c) More construction workers are hired to build a school

7. Why are professors of computer science paid more than professors of English literature?

Problems

1. The following table depicts the number of grapes that can be picked in an hour with varying amounts of labor.

Number of pickers (per hour)	1	2	3	4	5	6	7	8
Output of grapes (in flats)	20	38	53	64	71	74	74	70

Using these data, determine how many pickers will be hired if the wage rate is $10 per hour and a flat of grapes sells for $1.25. Illustrate graphically.

2. Reread the article about law school graduates, "Where the Really Big Money Is," on page 735.
   (a) At Shearman & Sterling, the marginal revenue product of a new associate who bills for 2,100 hours of service a year at $75 an hour is $157,500. What is the difference between the marginal revenue product of a new law school graduate and the salary he or she receives from that firm?
   (b) Given similar differences at other law firms, are the salaries of law school graduates likely to rise even higher than is reported in the article? Why?
   (c) The article provides information on earnings in investment banking. What, is the article suggesting, is the opportunity wage of a law school graduate?
   (d) How might the marginal revenue product of law school graduates eventually be brought into line with their equilibrium salary?

CHAPTER 30

Power in Labor Markets

Labor markets are no different in concept from other markets. Market supply and market demand interact to determine the quantity of labor hired and its price (the wage rate). And like all markets, labor markets can be distorted by market power. Power may reside on the supply side of the market (labor unions) or on the demand side (large employers). In either case, the objective of those who hold market power is to alter wages and employment conditions. This chapter focuses on the extent of **market power** in the U.S. labor market, the kinds of confrontations that occur, and the impact of labor-market power on our economic welfare. We address the following questions:

market power: The ability to alter the market price of a good or service.

- How do large and powerful employers affect market wages?
- How do labor unions alter wages and employment?
- What outcomes are possible from collective bargaining between management and unions?

In the process of answering these questions, we look at the nation's most powerful unions and their actual behavior.

THE LABOR MARKET

labor supply: The willingness and ability to work specific amounts of time at alternative wage rates in a given time period, *ceteris paribus*.

demand for labor: The quantities of labor employers are willing and able to hire at alternative wage rates in a given time period, *ceteris paribus*.

To gauge the impact of labor-market power on wages and employment, we can review the nature of a competitive labor market. On the supply side, we have all those individuals who are willing to work—to supply labor—at various wage rates. By counting the number of individuals who are willing to work at each and every wage rate, we can construct a *market* **labor-supply** curve, as in Figure 30.1.

The willingness of producers (firms) to hire labor is reflected in the market labor-demand curve. The curve itself is constructed by simply counting the number of workers each firm says it is willing and able to hire at each and every wage rate. The curve illustrates the market **demand for labor.**

**FIGURE 30.1
Competitive Equilibrium
in the Labor Market**

The market labor–supply curve
includes all persons willing to
work at various wage rates.
The labor–demand curve
tells us how many workers
employers are willing to hire.
In a competitive market, the
intersection of the labor-
supply and labor-demand
curves (point C) determines
the equilibrium wage rate
(w_e) and the amount of
employment (q_e).

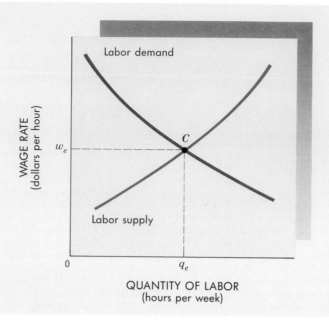

**Competitive
Equilibrium**

equilibrium wage: The wage
rate at which the quantity of
labor supplied in a given time
period equals the quantity of
labor demanded.

The intersection of the labor-supply and labor-demand curves (point C in Figure 30.1) reveals the **equilibrium wage** rate (w_e): the wage rate at which the quantity of labor supplied equals the quantity demanded. At this wage rate, every job seeker who is willing and able to work for the wage w_e is employed. In addition, firms are able to acquire all the labor they are willing and able to hire at that wage.

Not everyone is employed in equilibrium. Workers who demand wages in excess of w_e are unable to find jobs. By the same token, employers who refuse to pay a wage as high as w_e are unable to attract workers.

Local Labor Markets

Figure 30.1 appears to suggest that there is only *one* labor market and thus only one equilibrium wage. But this is a gross oversimplification. Although the concept of a national labor market is important and useful, it is more appropriate to think in terms of localized labor markets. If you were looking for a job in Tulsa, Oklahoma, you would have little interest in employment prospects or power configurations in New York City. You would be more concerned about the available jobs and wages in Tulsa—that is, the condition of the *local* labor market.

Even within a particular geographical area, interest usually focuses on particular classes of jobs and workers rather than on all the people supplying labor. If you were looking for work as a disco dancer, you would have little interest in the employment situation for carpenters or dentists. Rather, you would want to know how many discos or nightclubs had job vacancies, and what wages and working conditions they offered. By the same token, people in the construction industry or in dentistry would probably have no more than a passing interest in the job market for disco dancers. Accordingly, local labor markets are defined not only by geography, but also by industries and occupations.

The distinction among various geographical, occupational, and industrial labor markets provides a more meaningful basis for analyzing labor-market power. The tremendous size of the national labor market, with over 125 million workers, precludes anyone from acquiring control of the entire market. The largest private employer in the United States (General Motors) employs less than 0.5 percent of the labor force. The top 500 industrial corporations employ only 20 percent of all workers. The situation on the supply side is similar. The largest labor union (the Teamsters) represents less than 2 percent of all workers in the country. All unions together represent less than one-fifth of the labor force. This does not mean that the actions of particular employers or unions have no important effects on our general economic welfare. It suggests, however, that *power in labor markets is likely to be more effective in specific areas, occupations, and industries.*

LABOR UNIONS

Types of Unions

The immediate objective of labor unions is to alter the equilibrium wage and employment conditions in specific labor markets. *To be successful, unions must be able to exert control over the market-supply curve.* For this purpose, workers have organized themselves along either industry or occupational craft lines. *Industrial unions* include workers in a particular industry (the United Auto Workers, for example). *Craft unions* represent workers with a particular skill (e.g., the International Brotherhood of Electrical Workers), regardless of the industry in which they work.

The purpose of both types of labor unions is to coordinate the actions of thousands of individual workers, thereby achieving control of market supply. If a union is able to control the supply of workers in a particular industry or occupation, the union acquires a monopoly in that market. Like most monopolies, unions attempt to use their market power to increase their incomes.

Union Objectives

A primary objective of unions is to raise the wages of union members. But union objectives also include improved working conditions, job security, and other nonwage forms of compensation, such as retirement (pension) benefits, vacation time, and health insurance. The Players Association and the National Football League have bargained about the use of artificial turf, early retirement, player fines, television revenues, game rules, the use of team doctors, drug tests, pensions, and the number of players permitted on a team. In 1987 the foremost concern of the United Auto Workers (UAW) was job security. Cutbacks and plant closings had eliminated more than 400,000 auto-industry jobs in the 1980s. When UAW negotiators sat down with Ford and GM in 1987, they were more concerned about preserving the jobs that remained than about pay boosts. Unions boycotted Coors beer for ten years (1977–87) over the issue of union recognition and organization rights. The same issue of union recognition caused the United Farm Workers' grape strike of 1956–70. The UFW was striking to force the growers into bilateral negotiations—to discuss employment issues with the workers' representatives.

Although union objectives tend to be as broad as the concerns of union members, we focus here on just one objective, wage rates. This is not too great a simplification, because most nonwage issues can be translated into their effective impact on wage rates. In 1987, for example, the UAW won an increase in basic hourly wages that amounted to only 40 cents over three years. But the auto workers won many other benefits also (see In the News).

In The News

What Auto Workers Won

After two months of negotiations, the UAW and GM signed a new three-year contract in September 1987. The contract included these provisions:

- *Wages.* A basic wage increase of 3 percent in the first year; lump-sum performance bonus payments in the second and third years; cost-of-living wage adjustments at the rate of 1 percent per hour for every 0.26-point rise in the consumer price index.

- *Profit sharing.* Workers to receive a share of GM's before-tax profits that exceed 1.8 percent of sales; profit share to vary between 7.5 percent and 16 percent of profits above that level.

- *Legal services.* GM to contribute 7.2 cents for each labor hour worked to legal services fund.

- *Insurance.* Life insurance benefit increased by $3,000; extended disability benefit increased by $165–$200 per month.

- *Pension.* Basic retirement benefit increased by $4.20 per month for each year of service; maximum monthly benefit increased from $1,350 to $1,500.

- *Dental.* Dental benefits increased to $1,200 per year (from $1,000); lifetime limit on orthodontic work increased to $1,125 (from $800).

- *Eye care.* Benefits for contact lenses increased from $35 to $55.

- *Substance abuse.* Maximum of 90 days for substance abuse treatment, including residential centers, halfways houses, and detoxification centers.

- *Relocation allowance.* Expense allowance for workers transferring to another plant increased 20 percent, to a maximum of $2,770.

- *Holidays.* Birthday of Martin Luther King, Jr. made a company holiday, creating a total of 14 paid holidays a year.

- *Job security.* Company to limit outsourcing of components and to give the union more advance notice of plans to purchase rather than make components; company to provide a $1.3 billion fund to guarantee "secure employment levels" in the event of production cutbacks.

These additional benefits cost GM another $3.65 an hour. Hence the increase in total wage costs was $4.05 per hour. Accordingly, our simple two-dimensional illustration of union objectives can be used to convey the nature and substance of most collective-bargaining situations. What we seek to determine is whether and how unions can raise wage rates in a specific labor market by altering the competitive equilibrium depicted in Figure 30.1.

THE POTENTIAL USE OF POWER

In a competitive labor market, each worker makes a labor-supply decision on the basis of his or her own perceptions of the relative values of labor and leisure (Chapter 29). Whatever decision is made will not alter the market wage. One worker simply isn't that significant in a market composed of thousands. Once a market is unionized, however, these conditions no longer hold. A union must evaluate job offers on the basis of the *collective* interests of its members. In particular, it must be concerned with the effects of increased employment on the wage rate paid to its members. *Like all monopolists, unions have to worry about the downward slope of the demand curve.* In the case of labor markets, a larger quantity of labor can be "sold" only at lower wage rates.

The Marginal Wage

Suppose that the workers in a particular labor market confront the market labor-demand schedule depicted in Figure 30.2. This schedule tells us that employers are not willing to hire any workers at a wage rate of $6 per hour (row *S*) but will hire 1 worker per hour if the wage rate is $5 (row *T*). At still lower wage rates, the quantity of labor demanded increases; 5 workers per hour are demanded at a wage of $1 per hour.

An individual worker offered a wage of $1 an hour would have to decide whether such wages merited the sacrifice of an hour's leisure. But a union would evaluate the offer differently. A union must consider how the hiring of one more worker will affect the wages of all the workers.

Notice that when 4 workers are hired at a wage rate of $2 an hour (row *W*), total wages are $8 per hour. In order for a fifth worker to be employed, however, the wage rate must drop to $1 an hour (row *X*). At wages of $1 per hour, the *total* wages paid to the 5 workers amount to only $5 per hour. Thus total wages paid to the workers actually *fall* when a fifth worker is employed. Collectively the workers would be better off sending only 4 workers to work at the higher wage of $2 an hour and paying the fifth worker $1 an hour to stay home!

The basic mandate of a labor union is to evaluate wage and employment offers from this collective perspective. To do so, **a union must distinguish the marginal wage from the market wage.** The market wage is simply the

FIGURE 30.2
The Marginal Wage

The *marginal wage* is the change in *total wages* (paid to all workers) associated with the employment of an additional worker. If the wage rate is $4 per hour, only 2 workers will be hired. The wage rate must fall to $3 per hour if 3 workers are to be hired. In the process, *total* wages paid rise from $8 ($4 × 2 workers) to $9 ($3 × 3 workers). The *marginal* wage of the third worker is only $1.

The graph illustrates the relationship of the marginal wage to labor demand. The marginal wage curve lies below the labor–demand curve, because the marginal wage is less than the nominal wage. Compare the marginal wage (point *v*) and the nominal wage (point *V*) of the third worker.

	Wage rate (per hour)	×	Number of workers demanded (per hour)	=	Total wages paid (per hour)	Marginal wage (per labor hour)
S	$6		0		$0	$0
T	5		1		5	5
U	4		2		8	3
V	3		3		9	1
W	2		4		8	−1
X	1		5		5	−3

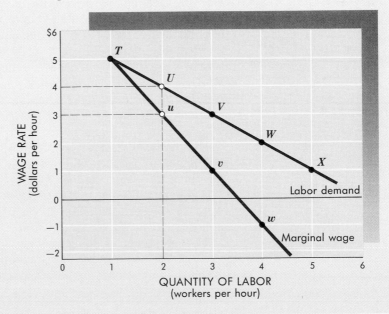

marginal wage: The change in total wages paid associated with a one-unit increase in the quantity of labor employed.

current wage rate paid by the employer; it is the wage received by individual workers. The **marginal wage,** on the other hand, is the change in *total* wages paid (to all workers) when an additional worker is hired—that is,

$$\text{Marginal wage} = \frac{\text{change in total wages paid}}{\text{change in quantity of labor employed}}$$

The distinction between marginal wages and market wages arises from the downward slope of the labor-demand curve. It is analogous to the distinction we made between marginal revenue and price for monopolists in product markets. The distinction simply reflects the law of demand: as wages fall, the number of workers hired increases.

The impact of increased employment on marginal wages is also illustrated in Figure 30.2. According to the labor-demand curve, 1 worker will be hired at a wage rate of $5 an hour (point T); 2 workers will be hired only if the market wage falls to $4 an hour (point U), at which point the first and second workers will each be getting $4 an hour.[1] Thus the increased wages of the second worker (from zero to $4) will be partially offset by the reduction in the wage rate paid to the first worker (from $5 to $4). *Total* wages paid will increase by only $3; this is the *marginal* wage (point u). The marginal wage actually becomes negative at some point, when the implied wage loss to workers already on the job begins to exceed the wages of a newly hired worker.

Monopolistic Equilibrium

A union never wants to accept a negative marginal wage, of course. At such a point, union members would be better off paying someone to stay home. The question, then, is what level of (positive) marginal wage the union should accept.

We can answer this question by looking at the labor-supply curve. The labor-supply curve tells us how much labor workers are *willing to supply* at various wage rates. The question then becomes: What wage are they really being offered? From their collective perspective, the wage that union members are getting for additional labor is the *marginal* wage, not the nominal (market) wage. Hence the marginal wage curve, not the labor-demand curve, is the one of immediate interest to the union.

What the union seeks is that level of employment which equates the marginal wage with the supply preferences of union members. In Figure 30.3, *the intersection of the marginal wage curve with the labor-supply curve identifies the optimal level of employment for the union.* In Figure 30.3 this intersection occurs at point u, yielding total employment of 2 workers per hour.

The marginal wage at point U is $3. However, the union members will get a higher actual wage than that. Look up from point u on the marginal wage curve to point U on the employer's labor-demand curve. Point U tells us that the employer is *willing to pay* a wage rate of $4 an hour to employ two workers. Hence the union knows it can demand and get $4 an hour if it supplies only two workers to the firm.

What the union is doing here is choosing a point on the labor-demand curve that the union regards as the optimal combination of wages and employment. In a competitive market, point C would represent the equilibrium

---

[1]Recall that the decline in wage rates reflects the law of diminishing marginal productivity and is not caused by any particular worker (see Chapter 29).

FIGURE 30.3
The Union Wage Objective

The intersection of the marginal wage and labor-supply curves (point *u*) determines the union's desired employment. Employers are willing to pay a wage rate of $4 per hour for that many workers, as revealed by point *U* on the labor-demand curve.

More workers (*N*) are willing to work at $4 per hour than employers demand (*U*). To maintain that wage rate, the union must exclude some workers from the market. In the absence of such power, wages would fall to the competitive equilibrium (point *C*).

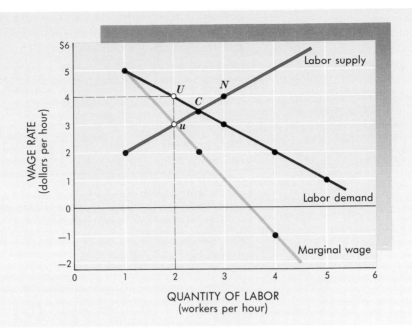

combination of wages and employment. But the union forces employers to point *U,* thereby attaining a higher wage rate and reducing employment. The union's motivation for moving to point *U* arises from its recognition of the *marginal wage*—that is, the impact of increased employment on the total wages of its members.

Exclusion

The union's ability to maintain a wage rate of $4 an hour depends on its ability to exclude some workers from the market. Figure 30.3 suggests that three workers are willing and able to work at the union wage of $4 an hour (point *N*), whereas only two are hired (point *U*). If the additional worker were to offer his or her services, the wage rate would be pushed down the labor-demand curve (to $3 per hour). Hence *to maintain a noncompetitive wage, the union must be able to exercise some control over the labor-supply decisions of individual workers.* The essential force here is union solidarity. Once unionized, the individual workers in an industry or occupation must agree not to compete among themselves by offering their labor at nonunion wage rates. Instead, the workers must agree to withhold labor—to strike, if necessary—if wage rates are too low, and to supply labor only if a specified wage rate is offered.

Unions attempt to solidify their control of the labor supply by establishing **union shops,** workplaces where workers must join the union within thirty days after being employed. In this way, the unions gain control of all the workers employed in a particular company or industry and thereby reduce the number of workers available for employment during a strike. Stiff penalties (such as loss of seniority or pension rights) and general union solidarity ensure that only nonunion workers will "fink" or "scab"—take the job of a worker on strike. When the United Auto Workers (UAW) threatens a strike, the Big Three auto makers know that nonunion automotive workers will be hard to find and thus take the UAW threat seriously. But the grape growers in California ignored the UFW strike for five years, because unionization

union shop: An employment setting in which all workers must join the union within thirty days after being employed.

among farm workers was minimal and substitute labor (including Mexican *braceros*) was readily available. Professional football players faced the same problem in 1987. When they went out on strike, hundreds of other players rushed in for the chance to play pro football. The ready supply of substitute players forced the National Football League Players Association to abandon their strike.

THE EXTENT OF UNION POWER

Early Growth

The first labor unions in America were organized as early as the 1780s, and the first worker protests as early as 1636. Union power was not a significant force in labor markets, however, until the 1900s, when heavily populated commercial centers and large-scale manufacturing became common. Only then did large numbers of workers begin to view their employment situations from a common perspective.

The period 1916–20 was one of particularly fast growth for labor unions, largely because of the high demand for labor resulting from World War I. All of these membership gains were lost, however, when the Great Depression threw millions of people out of work. By 1933 union membership had dwindled to the levels of 1915.

As the Depression lingered on, public attitudes and government policy changed. Too many people had learned the meaning of layoffs, wage cuts, and prolonged unemployment. Moreoever, the notion was growing that layoffs and wage cuts were not appropriate solutions to economic recessions. Accordingly, as the country began to work its way out of the Depression, the labor-union movement was infused with renewed vigor. In 1933 the National Industrial Recovery Act (NIRA) established the right of employees to bargain collectively with their employers. When the NIRA was declared unconstitutional by the Supreme Court in 1935, its labor provisions were incorporated into a new law, the Wagner Act. With this legislative encouragement, union membership doubled between 1933 and 1937. Unions continued to gain in strength as the production needs of World War II increased the demand for labor (and its marginal revenue product). The tremendous spurt of union activity between the depths of the Depression and the height of World War II is reflected in Figure 30.4.

Union Power Today

Since World War II, union membership has continued to grow, but not as fast as the labor force. This reflects the changing structure of the U.S. economy, with a growing services sector and a relative decline in manufacturing (where unions are strongest). As a consequence, union power, expressed as the percentage of workers belonging to labor unions, has fallen. Today roughly 17 percent of the labor force is enrolled in labor unions.[2]

unionization ratio: The percentage of the labor force belonging to a union.

Although a **unionization ratio** of 17 percent is an impressive basis for market (and political) power, union strength varies greatly from labor market to labor market. As noted before, the national labor market is really a mix of thousands of distinguishable labor markets, each defined by geographical, industrial, or occupational characteristics. Concentrations of union power in

[2]These and the following figures include membership in the professional associations (such as the National Education Association), which function much like unions.

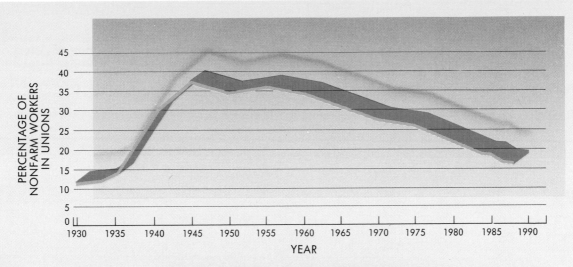

FIGURE 30.4 Unionization of the Labor Force

Unions grew most rapidly during the decade 1935–45. Since that time, the growth of unions has not kept pace with the growth of the U.S. labor force.

Source: U.S. Department of Labor, Bureau of Labor Statistics.

any of these localized labor markets can be far greater than the national average. Moreover, these local concentrations can have tremendous influence on related economic outcomes. This situation is analogous to concentration among producers. As noted in Chapter 25, concentration in particular product markets is much higher and of more immediate consequence than national averages sometimes suggest.

Table 30.1 provides an overview of union power in various industries. As is apparent, there is tremendous variation in labor-supply concentration among industries. In group *A*, labor-supply concentration is so high (75–100 percent) as to confer monopoly powers on particular unions. The Teamsters, Longshoremen, and United Mine Workers stand out in this regard. The unions in group *B* also have great market power, because they represent over half the workers in each industry. Many of the unions are well known from their many confrontations with business over the exercise of market power.

Although Table 30.1 provides a convenient index to who's who on the supply side of the labor market, some additional observations are in order. Each industry classification depicted in the table represents a broad assortment of firms and products. Accordingly, a low degree of unionization for an industry may mask very high levels of supply concentration in particular labor markets. The "service industry" (group *D*), for example, has a relatively low level of unionization but includes such disparate workers as professional football players, laundry workers, barbers, and broadcasters. Obviously, the low level of unionization reflected in the industry average is of little relevance to you when you go to get a haircut. It certainly offers no comfort to the owners of NFL football teams when they have to negotiate retirement benefits. Even relatively small unions may have great market power if they control labor supply for a particular area, company, product, or occupation.

One labor organization conspicuously absent from the table is the AFL-

TABLE 30.1 Union Power

A union's power may be measured by the percentage of the related work force that it controls. The Teamsters, for example, have substantial market power because most truck drivers belong to that union.

Degree of unionization	Industry	Principal unions
A: 75–100 percent	Transportation	Teamsters
		Longshoremen
		Maritime
		Railway unions
	Contract construction	Carpenters
		Painters
		Plumbers
	Mining	United Mine Workers
B: 50–75 percent	Transportation equipment	United Auto Workers
		Marine and Shipbuilding
	Primary metals	Steelworkers
	Apparel	Amalgamated Clothing Workers
		Garment Workers
		Ladies Garment Workers
	Electrical machinery	International Brotherhood of Electrical Workers (IBEW)
		International Union of Electrical Workers
	Federal government	Government Employees (AFGE)
		Letter Carriers
		Post Office Clerks
C: 25–50 percent	Rubber	Rubber Workers
	Lumber	Coopers
		Woodworkers
	Leather	Shoe Workers
	Electric, gas, utilities	Electrical (IBEW)
	Government (state and local)	Teachers
		Fire Fighters
	Telephone and telegraph	Communications Workers
		Electrical (IBEW)
	Food and kindred products	Bakery Workers
		Brewery
		Meat Cutters
D: less than 25 percent	Textiles	Textile Workers
	Service	Hotel
		Laundry Workers
	Finance	Insurance Agents
	Agriculture and fishing	Teamsters
		United Farm Workers
	Trade	Retail Clerks
	Printing, publishing	Newspaper Guild
		Printing Pressmen
		Typographers

Source: U.S. Department of Labor, Bureau of Labor Statistics, *Directory of National Unions and Employee Associations.*

CIO (the American Federation of Labor–Congress of Industrial Organizations). The AFL-CIO is not a separate union, but a representational body of 120 national unions. It does not represent or negotiate for any particular group of workers but focuses instead on issues of general labor interest. The AFL-CIO's role is to act as a spokesman for the labor movement and represent labor's interest in legislative areas. It is the primary vehicle for political action. In addition, the AFL-CIO may render economic assistance to member unions or to groups of workers who wish to organize into an AFL-CIO affiliate.

EMPLOYER POWER

The impressive power possessed by labor unions in various areas and industries seldom exists in a power vacuum. Tremendous power exists on the demand side of labor markets, too. The United Auto Workers confront GM, Ford, and Chrysler; the Steelworkers confront USX, Bethlehem, and LTV; the Teamsters confront the Truckers' Association; the Communications Workers confront AT&T; and so on. An imbalance of power often exists on one side of the market or the other (as with, say, the Carpenters versus individual construction contractors). Labor markets with significant power on both sides, however, are common. To understand how wage rates and employment are determined in such markets, we have to consider the nature and potential of market power possessed by employers.

Monopsony

monopsony: A market in which there is only one buyer.

Power on the demand side of a market belongs to a *buyer* who is able to influence the market price of a good. With respect to labor markets, market power on the demand side implies the ability of a single employer to alter the market wage rate. The extreme case of such power is a **monopsony,** a situation in which one employer is the only buyer in a particular market. The classic example of a monopsony is a company town—that is, a town that depends for its livelihood on the decisions of a single employer.

There are many degrees of market power, and they can be defined in terms of *buyer concentration.* When buyers are many and of limited market power, the demand for resources is likely to be competitive. When only one buyer has access to a particular resource market, a monopsony exists. Between the two extremes lie the various degrees of imperfect competition, including the awkward-sounding but empirically important case of oligopsony. In an oligopsony only a few buyers account for most of the purchases of a particular resource. The similarity of these definitions to those used to characterize power on the supply side of product markets should be obvious.

The Potential Use of Power

Firms with power in labor markets generally have the same objective as all other firms—to maximize profits. What distinguishes them from competitive (powerless) firms is their ability to attain and keep economic profits. Firms with monopsony power can exploit the market supply curve, and end up using fewer resources and paying less for them than competitive firms would. In labor markets, this means using fewer workers and paying them lower wages than a firm in a competitive market would have to do.

The distinguishing characteristic of labor-market monopsonies is the fact that their hiring decisions influence the market wage rate. In a competitive labor market, no single employer has any direct influence on the market wage rate; each firm can hire as much labor as it needs at the prevailing wage. But a monopsonist recognizes that an increase in the quantity of labor demanded

In The News

MONOPSONY

Free Agents in Sports: A Threat to Monopsony

Prior to 1976 the owners of professional baseball, football, and basketball teams enjoyed monopsonistic power. This power was bestowed by the "reserve clause" included in player contracts. Individual players were permitted to negotiate with only one team. Once signed, they could not move to another team without their owner's permission. The player's only option was to "take it or leave"—that is, to accept his team's wage offer or quit playing altogether for at least one season. Team owners used the reserve clause to hold down player salaries. Although pro basketball, football, and baseball players were paid huge salaries, those salaries were far below their marginal revenue product.

The reserve clause began to unravel in 1975, when an arbitration panel ruled it was too restrictive. In 1976 baseball players won the right to become "free agents"—to negotiate and play for any team—after six years of major-league experience. In 1977 pro football players

also won the right to become free agents, but under more restrictive conditions (the team losing a free agent had to be "compensated" with draft choices). Pro basketball players first won limited mobility rights in 1976 and became true free agents in 1980.

The weakening of monopsonistic power led to dramatically higher player salaries. The average baseball salary soared from about $51,000 in 1976 to $600,000 in 1990. Pro basketball players enjoyed the same kind of wage gain, attaining an *average* salary of over $750,000 in 1990. Only pro football players lagged behind. Their more limited free-agent rights kept a lid on average football salaries. Football players went out on strike in 1982 to secure higher salaries and ultimately got wages much closer to their marginal revenue products. The formation of a second league—the United States Football League—weakened the monopsonistic power of the NFL team owners and therefore contributed to this wage adjustment. By 1987, however, the USFL had collapsed, and free agency was again a central issue. A football players' strike in that year failed to weaken the team owners' monopsonistic power.

---

will force him to climb up the labor-supply curve in search of additional workers. In other words, *a monopsonist can hire additional workers only if he offers a higher wage rate.*

Marginal factor cost Any time the price of a resource (or product) changes as a result of a firm's purchases, a distinction between marginal cost and price (average cost) must be made. Making this distinction is one of the little headaches—and potential sources of profit—of a monopsonist. In the case of labor, we distinguish between the **marginal factor cost (MFC)** of labor and its wage rate.

Suppose for the moment that the graph and table in Figure 30.5 accurately describe the labor-supply schedule confronting a monopsonist. It is evident that the monopsonist will have to pay a wage of at least $2 an hour if it wants any labor. But even at that wage rate (row *F* of the supply schedule), only 1 worker will be willing to work. If the firm wants more labor, it will have to pay higher wages.

Two things happen when the firm raises its wage offer to $3 an hour (row *G*). First, the quantity of labor supplied increases (to 2 workers per hour). Second, the total wages paid rise by $4. This high *marginal* cost of labor is attributable to the fact that the first worker's wages rise when the wage rate is increased to attract additional workers. If all the workers perform the same job, the first worker will demand to be paid the new (higher) wage rate. Thus *the marginal factor cost exceeds the wage rate, because additional workers can be hired only if the wage rate for all workers is increased.*

marginal factor cost (MFC): The change in total costs that results from a one-unit increase in the quantity of a factor employed.

FIGURE 30.5
Marginal Factor Cost

More workers can be attracted only if the wage rate is increased. As it rises, all workers must be paid the higher wage. Consequently, the change in *total* wage costs exceeds the actual wage paid to the last worker. In the table, notice that in row *I*, for example, the marginal factor cost of the fourth worker ($8) exceeds the wage actually paid to that worker ($5). Thus the marginal factor cost curve lies above the labor-supply curve.

In the graph, the intersection of the marginal factor cost and labor-demand curves (point *U*) indicates the quantity of labor a monopsonist will want to hire. The labor-supply curve (at point *G*) indicates the wage rate that must be paid to attract the desired number of workers. This is the monopsonist's desired wage ($3). In the absence of market power, an employer would end up at point *C* (the competitive equilibrium), paying a higher wage and employing more workers.

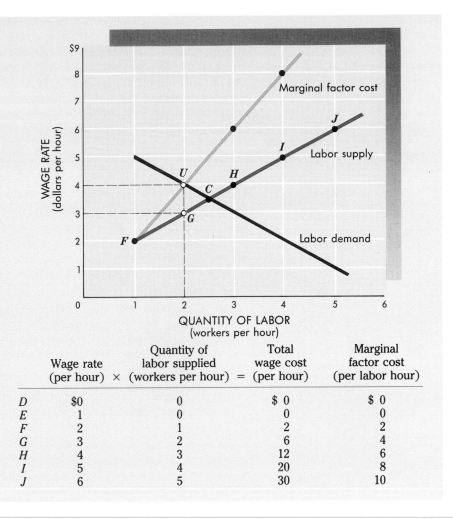

	Wage rate (per hour)	×	Quantity of labor supplied (workers per hour)	=	Total wage cost (per hour)	Marginal factor cost (per labor hour)
D	$0		0		$ 0	$ 0
E	1		0		0	0
F	2		1		2	2
G	3		2		6	4
H	4		3		12	6
I	5		4		20	8
J	6		5		30	10

marginal revenue product (MRP): The change in total revenue associated with one additional unit of input.

Monopsonistic equilibrium   The marginal factor cost curve confronting this monopsonist is shown in the upper half of Figure 30.5. It starts at the bottom of the labor-supply curve and rises above it. The monopsonist must now decide how many workers to hire, given the impact of this hiring decision on the market wage rate.

Remember from Chapter 29 that the labor-demand curve reflects labor's **marginal revenue product,** that is, the increase in total revenue attributable to the employment of one additional worker.

As we have emphasized, the profit-maximizing producer always seeks to equalize marginal revenue and marginal cost. Accordingly, the monopsonistic employer will seek to hire the amount of labor at which the marginal revenue product of labor equals its marginal factor cost—that is,

- Profit-maximizing level of input use : marginal revenue product of input (MRP) = marginal factor cost of input (MFC)

In Figure 30.5, this objective is illustrated by the intersection of the marginal factor cost and labor-demand curves at point *U*.

At point *U* the monopsonist is *willing to hire* 2 workers per hour at a wage rate of $4. But he doesn't have to pay this much. The labor-supply curve informs us that 2 workers are *willing to work* for only $3 an hour. Hence the firm first decides how many workers it wants to hire (at point *U*), then looks at the labor-supply curve (point *G*) to see what it has to pay them. As we suspected, a monopsonistic employer ends up hiring fewer workers at a lower wage rate than would prevail in a competitive market (point *C*).

COLLECTIVE BARGAINING

bilateral monopoly: A market with only one buyer (a monopsonist) and one seller (a monopolist).

collective bargaining: Direct negotiations between employers and unions to determine labor-market outcomes.

The potential for conflict between a powerful employer and a labor union should be evident. The objective of a labor union (Figure 30.3) is to establish a wage rate that is *higher* than the competitive wage. A monopsonistic employer, on the other hand, seeks to establish a wage rate that is *lower* than competitive standards (Figure 30.5). The resultant clash is often exciting.

The confrontation of power on both sides of the labor market is referred to as **bilateral monopoly.** In such a market, wages and employment are not determined simply by supply and demand. Rather, economic outcomes must be determined by **collective bargaining**—that is, direct negotiations between employers and labor unions for the purpose of determining wages, employment, working conditions, and related issues.

Possible Agreements

In a typical labor–business confrontation, the two sides begin by stating their preferences for equilibrium wages and employment. The *demands* laid down by the union are likely to revolve around point *U* in Figure 30.6; the *offer* enunciated by management is likely to be at point *G*.[3] Thus the boundaries of a potential settlement—a negotiated final equilibrium—are usually established at the outset of collective bargaining.

[3]Even though points *U* and *G* may not be identical to the initial bargaining positions, they represent the positions of maximum attainable benefit for both sides. Points outside the demand or supply curve will be rejected out of hand by one side or the other.

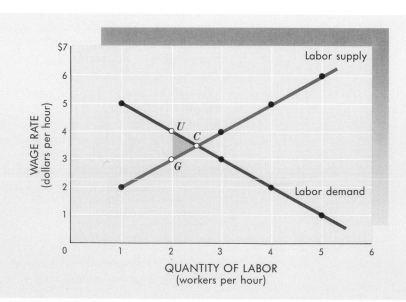

**FIGURE 30.6
The Boundaries of
Collective Bargaining**

Firms with power in the labor market seek to establish wages and employment levels corresponding to point *G*. Unions, on the other hand, seek to establish an equilibrium at point *U*. The competitive equilibrium is at point *C*. The function of collective bargaining is to identify a compromise between these points—that is, to locate an equilibrium somewhere in the shaded area.

The interesting part of collective bargaining is not the initial bargaining positions but the negotiation of the final settlement. The speed with which a settlement is reached and the nature of the compromise it embodies depend on the patience, tactics, and resources of the negotiating parties. The fundamental source of negotiating power for either side is its ability to withhold labor or jobs. The union can threaten to strike, thereby cutting off the flow of union labor to the employer. The employer can impose a lockout, thereby cutting off jobs and paychecks previously available to union members. In practice, each weapon constitutes an ultimate threat to the other side of the collective-bargaining negotiations. The effectiveness of those threats depends on the availability of substitute workers or jobs and the credibility of the strike or lockout threat.

The Pressure to Settle

Labor and management both suffer from either a strike or a lockout, no matter who initiates the work stoppage. The strike benefits paid to workers are rarely comparable to wages they would otherwise have received, and the payment of those benefits depletes the union treasury. By the same token, the reduction in labor costs and other expenses rarely compensates the employer for lost profits.

In a sixty-seven–day strike in 1970, General Motors lost $90 million a day in sales, while the United Auto Workers spent $160 million in strike benefits. In 1987, neither GM nor the UAW could afford such losses. Although GM and Ford were enjoying billion-dollar profits in 1987, they were worried about increased import competition. A strike, they feared, would lead consumers to buy still more imported cars. On the labor side, the UAW was still reeling from the loss of 400,000 members and was fearful of further job cutbacks. The two sides settled their differences quickly, without a strike (see In the News, p. 752).

The steel industry did not move to settlement so quickly. The nation's longest steel strike—a six-month walkout at United Steel (USX) Corporation—ended in 1987 only after state- and company-paid unemployment and health benefits began to run out and the company's inventory and orders began to dry up. By then the company had lost almost $600 million, and the union's strike fund was nearly depleted. In the Soviet and Appalachian coal strikes of 1989 (see World View), differences in the pressure to settle had a dramatic effect on the outcomes.

Because potential income losses are usually high, both labor and management try to avoid a strike or lockout if they can. In fact, over 90 percent of all collective-bargaining agreements are concluded without recourse to a strike, and often without even the explicit threat of one.

The Final Settlement

The built-in pressures for settlement help to resolve collective bargaining. They do not tell us, however, what the dimensions of that final settlement will be. All we know is that the settlement will be located within the boundaries established in Figure 30.6, and that the relative pressures on each side will determine whether the final equilibrium is closer to the union or the management position.

In the 1987 National Football League strike, the pressures to settle were very one-sided. The average pro football player was losing $14,375 per missed game. But the team owners were actually making *more* profit during the strike than before it. Although their revenues from ticket sales, parking, and food

W●RLD VIEW

PRESSURES TO SETTLE

Coal Miner Strikes in Siberia and Appalachia

In 1989 some 1,700 United Mine Workers went on strike in Appalachia and over 300,000 coal miners went on strike in the Soviet Union. The two miners' strikes illustrate some of the common elements in collective bargaining—and important differences as well.

	In Appalachia	In the Soviet Union
The strikers:	1,700 union coal miners in Virginia, West Virginia, and Kentucky. Sympathy walkouts spread to 46,000 workers in ten states	100,000 coal miners in Siberia, another 200,000 in the Ukraine
Their adversary:	The Pittston Coal Company	The government (there are no private coal companies)
Their demands:	Maintenance of 100 percent health insurance, pension benefits, and work rules	Greater availability of consumer products (particularly meat, milk, soap, and housing) Some profit sharing Local reinvestment of export revenues Government to study grievances
Offer:	Company offered a $1 per hour wage increase in return for reduced health benefits and "flextime" work schedules	
Pressures to settle:	Company had other mines, many of them nonunion Coal price depressed, reducing any potential loss of profits Union share of national coal production down Union had $95 million strike fund Union regarded demands as "must-win" situation for survival	Soviet industry highly dependent on coal Memories of Polish coal strike and later toppling of Communist party raised fears that the first labor protest in Soviet history would create political instability Strikers' demands strengthened Gorbachev's calls for economic reform
Outcome:	*Duration* Strike continues for eleven months *Wages* increased by $1.20 per hour over three years to maximum of $17.52 an hour *Health benefits* Company to pay 100 percent of health coverage *Flexible hours* Company may operate mines continuously, with Sundays and ten-hour shifts added *Job security* Laid-off union members to have hiring priority at nonunion mines and subcontractors *Bonus* Immediate back-to-work bonus of $1,000	*Duration* Strike ended in two weeks *Consumer Goods* Government provided over $8 billion worth of benefits including special consignments of meat, soap, vodka, sewing machines *Reforms* Political and economic reforms implemented

concessions fell, weekly television revenues of $1 million per team continued to pour in. Those revenues, together with the sharply lower costs of replacement teams, led to higher profits. It didn't take long for the striking players to capitulate and accept the team owners' offer.

The baseball dispute in 1990 presented very different pressures. At the outset, the owners demanded that the players accept an entirely new salary system. When the Major League Players Association balked at that proposal, the owners staged a spring-training lockout. Neither the owners nor the players get paid for spring training anyway. But as the scheduled season opening approached, the owners began to worry about their recently signed $1.5 billion TV contract. The players, too, worried about losing monthly installments on their $600,000 (average) season paychecks. A compromise was reached just prior to opening day.

The final settlement almost always necessitates hard choices on both sides. The union will usually have to choose between a slight increase in job security or slightly higher pay. In other words, higher wage rates may be acceptable to management only if the labor force is reduced. For the union, this would mean a cutback in employment and possibly even union membership, a potentially stiff price to pay. A union must also consider how management will react in the long run to higher wages. That is, the union must consider the likelihood that management will introduce new technology that reduces its dependence on labor.

POLICY INSIGHTS:

THE IMPACT OF UNIONS

Stepping back from the negotiations that take place between individual unions and companies, we may ask whether the presence of unions has altered economic outcomes in general. We do know that unions tend to raise wage rates in individual companies, industries, and occupations. This, after all, is one of their basic objectives. But can we be equally sure that unions have raised wages in general? If the UAW is successful in raising wages in the autmobile industry, what, if anything, happens to wages in the breakfast cereals industry? Or what, for that matter, happens to car prices when auto workers' wages go up? If car prices rise in step with UAW wage rates, labor and management in the auto industry will get proportionally larger slices of the economic pie. At the same time, workers in other industries will be burdened with higher car prices.

Relative Wages One measure of union impact is *relative* wages—the wages of union members in comparison with those of nonunion workers. As we have noted, unions seek to control the supply of labor in a particular industry or occupation and thereby increase union wages. In their efforts to control labor supply, they restrict the number of people who can compete for available jobs, forcing those workers who are excluded to seek work elsewhere. As a result of this labor-supply imbalance, wages tend to be higher in unionized industries than in nonunionized industries. Figure 30.7 illustrates this effect.

Although the theoretical impact of union exclusionism on relative wages is clear, empirical estimates of that impact are fairly rare. We do know that union wages in general are significantly higher than nonunion wages ($497 versus $372 per week in 1989). But part of this differential is due to the fact that unions are more common in industries that have always been more capital-intensive and paid relatively high wages. When comparisons are made within particular industries or sectors, the differential narrows considerably. Nevertheless, there is a general consensus that unions have managed to in-

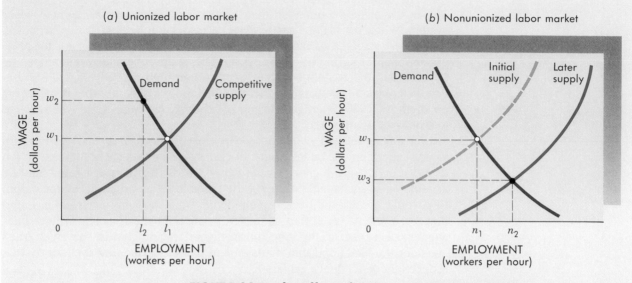

FIGURE 30.7 The Effect of Unions on Relative Wages

In the absence of unions, the average wage rate would be equal to w_1. As unions take control of the market, however, they seek to raise wage rates to w_2, in the process reducing the amount of employment in that market from l_1 to l_2. The workers displaced from the unionized market will seek work in the nonunionized market, thereby shifting the nonunion supply curve to the right. The result will be a reduction of wage rates (to w_3) in the nonunionized market. Thus union wages end up higher than nonunion wages.

crease their relative wages from 15 to 20 percent. Some unions, of course, have been markedly more successful than others, as a comparison of the wages received by Teamsters and United Farm Workers attests.

Labor's Share of Total Income

Even though unions have been successful in redistributing some income from nonunion to union workers, the question still remains as to whether they have increased labor's share of *total* income. The *labor share* of total income is the proportion of income received by all workers, in contrast to the share of income received by owners of capital (the *capital share*). If unions are effective in excluding nonunion workers from highly productive industries and also in increasing their share of income in those industries, the total labor share will grow. In this case, unions redistribute from capital owners to workers. Thus the increase in relative union wages is the result of two factors: redistribution from capital to labor and union exclusion of nonunion workers.

Evidence of unions' impact on labor's share is almost as difficult to assemble as evidence on relative wages, and for much the same reasons. Labor's share has risen dramatically, from only 56 percent in 1919 to over 74 percent in 1990 (see Chapter 31). But there have been tremendous changes in the mix of output during that same period. The proportion of output composed of personal services (accountants, teachers, electricians) is much larger now than it was in 1919. The labor share of income derived from personal services is and always was close to 100 percent. Accordingly, most of the rise in labor's share of total income is due to changes in the structure of the economy rather than to unionization.

Prices

Closely related to the issue of the labor share is the question of union impact on product prices. If all union wage increases were reflected in product prices, the ability of unions to increase the labor share of income would be limited severely. In such a case, the additional money firms needed to pay their workers would come out of increased prices, not out of profits. Accordingly, the ability of firms to "pass on" wage increases to consumers is a major determinant of their ability to maintain their capital share. If they are successful, they may contribute to cost-push inflation. At this juncture, we may note that the cause of price increases, especially in oligopolistic market situations, is usually very difficult to identify. Undoubtedly, however, unions have provided an incentive for firms to increase product prices faster than they otherwise would have done.

Productivity

productivity: Output per unit of input, e.g., output per labor hour.

Unions also affect prices indirectly, via changes in **productivity.** Unions bargain not only for wages but also for work rules that specify how goods should be produced. Work rules may limit the pace of production, restrict the type of jobs a particular individual can perform, or require a minimum number of workers to accomplish a certain task. A factory carpenter, for example, may not be permitted to change a light bulb that burns out in his shop area. And the electrician who is summoned may be required to have an apprentice on all work assignments. Such restrictive work rules would make it very costly to change a burnt-out light bulb.

Not all work rules are so restrictive. In general, however, work rules are designed to protect jobs and maximize the level of employment at any given rate of output. From this perspective, work rules directly restrain productivity and thus inflate costs and prices.

Work rules may also have some beneficial effects, however. The added job security provided by work rules and seniority provisions tends to reduce labor turnover (quitting) and thus saves recruitment and training costs. Protective rules may also make workers more willing to learn new tasks and to train others in specific skills.

In any given firm, the net effect of unions on productivity will depend on how restrictive the work rules and seniority provisions are. For the economy as a whole, there is a strong suspicion but little hard evidence that unions have restrained productivity growth.

Political Impact

Perhaps more important than any of these specific union effects is the general impact the union movement has had on our economic, social, and political institutions. Unions are a major political force in the United States. They not only have provided critical electoral and financial support for selected political candidates, but they have also fought hard for important legislation. Unions have succeeded in establishing minimum wage laws, work and safety rules, and retirement benefits. They have also actively lobbied for such things as civil rights legislation and health and education programs. Whatever one may think of any particular union or specific union action, it is clear that our institutions and national welfare would be very different in their absence.

SUMMARY

• Power in labor markets is the ability to alter market wage rates. Most often, such power is evident in local labor markets defined by geographical, occupational, or industrial boundaries.

• Power on the supply side of labor markets is typically manifested by labor unions, organized along either industry or craft lines. The basic function of a union is to evaluate employment offers in the light of the *collective* interest of its members.

• The downward slope of the labor-demand curve creates a distinction between the marginal wage and the market wage. The marginal wage is the change in *total* wages occasioned by employment of one additional worker and is less than the market wage.

• Unions seek to establish that rate of employment at which the marginal wage curve intersects the labor-supply curve. The desired union wage is then found by following the labor-demand curve to the wage that employers are willing to pay for that number of workers.

• Power on the demand side of labor markets is manifested in buyer concentrations such as monopsony and oligopsony. Such power is usually found among the same firms that exercise market power in product markets.

• By definition, power on the demand side implies some direct influence on market wage rates; additional hiring by a monopsonist will force up the market wage rate. Hence a monopsonist must recognize a distinction between the marginal factor cost of labor and its (lower) market wage rate.

• The goal of a monopsonistic employer is to hire the number of workers indicated by the point at which the marginal factor cost of labor equals its marginal revenue product. The employer then looks at the labor-supply curve to determine the wage rate that must be paid for that number of workers.

• The desire of unions to establish a wage rate that is higher than competitive wages directly opposes the desire of powerful employers to establish lower wage rates. In bilateral monopolies, in which power exists on both sides of the labor market, unions and employers engage in collective bargaining to negotiate a final settlement.

• The impact of unions on the economy is difficult to measure. It appears, however, that they have increased their own relative wages and contributed to rising prices. They have also had substantial political impact.

Terms to Remember   Define the following terms:

market power	monopsony
labor supply	marginal factor cost (MFC)
demand for labor	marginal revenue product (MRP)
equilibrium wage	bilateral monopoly
marginal wage	collective bargaining
union shop	productivity
unionization ratio	

Questions for Discussion

1. Collective-bargaining sessions often start with "unreasonable" demands and "categorical" rejections. Why do unions and employers tend to begin bargaining from extreme positions?

2. Does a strike for a 5-cents-an-hour raise make any sense? What kinds of long-term benefits might a union gain from such a strike?

3. Are large and powerful firms easier targets for union organization than small firms? Why, or why not?

4. Nonunionized firms tend to offer wage rates that are close to rates paid by unionized firms in the same industry. How do you explain this?

5. In 1973 a group of priests in Milwaukee sought to establish a union to bargain over wages and retirement benefits. With whom would the priests negotiate, and what kinds of tactics could they use to achieve their demands?

Problems

1. Suppose that the following supply and demand schedules apply in a particular labor market.

Wage rate (per hour)	$4	$5	$6	$7	$8	$9	$10
Quantity of labor supplied (workers per hour)	2	3	4	5	6	7	8
Quantity of labor demanded (workers per hour)	6	5	4	3	2	1	0

Graph the relevant curves and identify:
(a) The competitive wage rate
(b) The union wage rate
(c) The monopsonist's wage rate

2. At the time of the National Football League strike in 1987, the football owners made available the following data:

	Before the strike	During the strike
Revenues		
Television	$973,000	$973,000
Stadium gate	526,000	126,000
Luxury box seats	255,000	200,000
Concessions	60,000	12,000
Radio	40,000	40,000
Players' salaries and associated costs	854,000	230,000
Nonplayer costs (coaches' salaries)	200,000	200,000

(a) Compute total revenues, total expenses, and profits both before and during the strike.
(b) If the owners were choosing the alternative that would maximize profits, would they prefer the strike or not?
(c) Why would the owners ever agree to settle the strike under these conditions?

CHAPTER 31

Rent, Interest, and Profit

*C*hapters 29 and 30 focused on only one factor of production—labor. The emphasis on labor reflects the fact that wages and salaries account for nearly three-fourths of total national income. Hence the level and distribution of wages and salaries largely determine *for whom* our output is produced. Nevertheless, the share of income received by capital (one-fourth) is not negligible, and its distribution significantly affects our collective answer to the basic question of *FOR WHOM* to produce.

The capital share of income consists of rent, interest, and profit. Our objective in this chapter is to determine the nature of each of these income flows and the forces that determine their size. We pursue answers to the following questions:

- What is "economic rent" and how is its level determined?

- What function do interest rates serve, and how is their level determined?

- What justifies an economic profit?

We will also try to figure out what venture capitalists do to earn exceptionally high incomes. All of these questions are motivated by the desire to understand how the market distributes total income among the various factors of production (land, labor, and capital). Chapter 32 takes a closer look at the *individuals* who receive these income flows and the *personal* income distribution that results.

THE FUNCTIONAL DISTRIBUTION OF INCOME

Karl Marx believed that capitalism was doomed by the ceaseless conflict between workers and capitalists for their respective shares of output. Marx recognized that incomes varied *within* the capitalist and proletariat (laboring) classes. He believed, however, that the distinction *between* those who owned the means of production (the capitalists) and those whose labor was exploited (the proletariat) overwhelmed all other differences. He predicted that the capitalists would continue to accumulate wealth, power, and income, steadily increasing their share of total output. Ultimately, those who had little would vastly outnumber those who had much and would come to resent them. This resentment at inequality would lead to a proletarian revolution.

771

functional distribution of income: The division of income among factors of production, especially between capital and labor.

factor share: The proportion of total income received by a factor of production.

The division of total income between labor and capital is now called the **functional distribution of income.** No one is quite sure what the functional distribution looked like in the mid-nineteenth century (when Marx was writing). Recent estimates suggest, however, that wage and salary workers were getting less than 40 percent of total output. This low labor share was explained largely by the prevalence of small farmers, whose income was derived primarily from their own labor and was not paid in wages and salaries. No matter how poor, the small family farmer has always been considered part of the capitalist class.

By 1929 labor's share of total income was 60 percent (see Table 31.1). Since then, labor's share of total income has increased further and now accounts for nearly three-fourths of total income. In part this trend is explained by the substantial shift in our GNP away from heavy manufacturing (which is capital-intensive) to labor-intensive services (including government services and education). As the mix of output continues to shift toward goods and services that use little capital and much labor, labor's share of total income—its **factor share**—may be expected to rise.

Another force that has helped to boost labor's share of total income is labor unionism. Unions have reduced the size of the labor force (by demanding earlier retirements, longer school attendance, and tougher immigration restrictions) and have shortened the working day. These actions have served to make labor a scarcer resource and thus more valuable.

Finally, we may note that the supply of capital has expanded much more quickly than the supply of labor. While the labor force has grown at a rate of something like 1 percent a year, the stock of capital has grown by 3–4 percent a year. This disparity makes capital relatively abundant and thus cheaper, while making labor relatively scarce and thus expensive.

The capital share of income depicted in Table 31.1 includes several distinct types of income. The rest of this chapter assesses how the "price" of each of these factors is determined, and what economic function each serves. As we will see, the components of the capital share are not as simple as they might seem.

TABLE 31.1 The Functional Distribution of Income, 1929–89

Labor's share of total income has risen substantially in the last fifty years. Much of this increase is due to the shift away from manufacturing to more labor-intensive service industries. Increased capital investment, education, skill training, and labor organization have also contributed to a rising labor share of income.

Year	Total labor share (percent)	Total capital share	Farmers	Nonfarm proprietors	Rental income	Corporate profits	Interest income
1929	60.3	39.7	7.2	9.8	5.8	11.3	5.5
1933	75.1	24.9	6.3	7.4	5.1	$-3.8^\dagger$	10.4
1943	64.6	35.4	7.0	9.9	2.7	14.1	1.6
1953	68.6	31.4	4.2	9.9	3.5	12.3	1.4
1963	69.1	30.9	2.4	9.1	3.4	12.7	3.3
1973	72.4	27.6	3.0	7.6	1.6	10.1	5.3
1983	74.3	25.7	0.5	6.5	0.5	7.9	10.3
1989	73.7	26.3	1.1	7.2	0.2	7.0	10.8

Header spanning: "Capital share (percent)*" spans Total capital share, Farmers, Nonfarm proprietors, Rental income, Corporate profits, and Interest income columns.

*Includes income of farmers, landowners, and landlords, as well as those who own plant and equipment.
†In 1933, corporate profits were negative, as was net investment.
Source: *Economic Report of the President,* 1990.

RENT

Rental income is the smallest item in the capital share of income. As used in the national-income accounts (Table 31.1), rent refers to payments made to landlords for the use of shelter, offices, and factories. However, this is not the concept of rent used in economic theory. The term "rent" as used by economists does not necessarily refer to "capital." Nor does it even refer to the monthly payments made by tenants to landlords. In other words, *economists use the term "rent" differently from the way it is used by almost everyone else in the world.*

The origins of this confusion go back to nineteenth-century England. At that time, there was great concern about the rapidly increasing price of cereal grains, which the English called "corn." In looking for an explanation for the rising price of corn, many Englishmen pointed to the escalating prices being demanded and paid for agricultural land. The landlords, it appeared, were the villains responsible for the plight of the working masses. By raising land rents, they were driving up the price of corn and pushing the population of England into poverty.

Not so, argued David Ricardo, one of the great Classical economists: "Corn is not high because a rent is paid, but a rent is paid because corn is high." Were landlords to reduce their rents, Ricardo noted, this action would only increase the incomes of tenant farmers; the price of corn itself would not drop.

Ricardo's view of land rents as *price-determined* rather than *price-determining* can be explained in terms of either the corn market or the land market.

The Price of Corn   The market price of corn, like that of any other product, is determined by the intersection of market supply and demand curves. In Figure 31.1, the price p_1 prevails as long as D_1 and S_1 represent the market demand and supply curves for corn.

In essence, the nineteenth-century debate over corn prices focused on the effect of rising land prices on the market supply of corn. Those who blamed landlords for rising corn prices were implicitly arguing that increasing

FIGURE 31.1
The Price of Corn

The market price of corn is established by the intersection of market supply and demand. The corn controversy in nineteenth-century England was based on the assumption that rising land rents shifted the corn supply curve upward (to S_2). This was not true, however, because supply decisions are based on marginal costs, not fixed costs. Rising corn prices led to rising land prices, not vice versa.

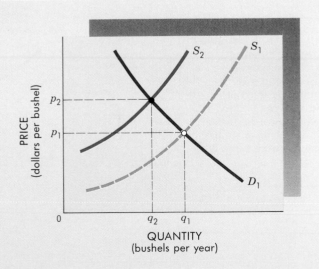

land rents caused an upward *shift* of the corn supply curve, to S_2. The increased costs associated with S_2, they argued, led to a reduction in the quantity of corn supplied (q_2) and a higher corn price (p_2).

But Ricardo argued that rising land rents would *not* shift the corn supply curve. His argument was based on the concept of **marginal cost.** In his own words, "The reason why raw produce rises in comparative value (price) is because more labor is employed in the production of the last portion obtained, and not because a rent is paid to the landlord." In other words, *marginal costs* determine the supply price of competitively produced goods.

We saw in Chapter 21 that producers will be willing to produce and sell goods in competitive markets as long as price exceeds marginal cost. In fact, the short-run supply curve of a competitive firm is identical to its marginal cost curve. Hence the market supply curve for corn (a competitively produced good) will shift upward only if the marginal cost of producing a given quantity of output changes. An increase in land rent will not alter the market supply or price of corn, because land rent is a **fixed cost** for farmers.

As Ricardo himself concluded, an increase in land rent served only to redistribute income from farmers to landlords. In his own words again, "No reduction would take place in the price of corn, although [even if] landlords should forgo the whole of their rent. Such a measure would only enable some farmers to live like gentlemen, but would not diminish the quantity of labor necessary to raise raw produce on the least productive land in cultivation."[1]

marginal cost: The increase in total cost associated with a one-unit increase in production.

fixed costs: Costs of production that do not change when the rate of output is altered, e.g., the cost of basic plant and equipment.

The Price of Land

Landlords do not have the power to raise rents indiscriminately. Land rents, too, are determined by market supply and demand. As Figure 31.2 reveals, however, the supply curve of land has an unconventional shape: it is vertical.

Typically, we expect producers to respond positively to increased prices. That is, we expect the **price elasticity of supply** to be greater than zero; the quantity supplied increases as prices rise, as in Figure 31.1. In the case of

price elasticity of supply: The percentage change in quantity supplied divided by the percentage change in price.

[1] Ricardo blamed the high price of English corn on the Corn Laws of 1815, which placed high tariffs (taxes) on imported grains, forcing domestic farmers to expand output into the range of substantially higher marginal cost. The impact of international trade restrictions on domestic prices is discussed in Chapter 35.

FIGURE 31.2
The Price of Land

The quantity of land available to the market is essentially fixed (Q_1). Hence changes in the price of land will be determined by market demand. In this case, land rents increase from R_1 to R_2 as a result of an upward shift of the demand curve from D_1 to D_2.

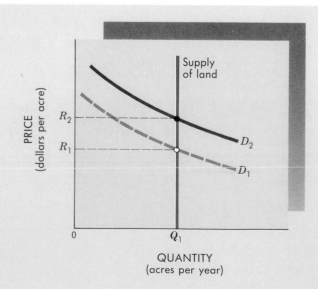

land, however, few such possibilities exist. Although some possibilities exist for increasing the amount of cultivable land through swamp drainage or filling in tidal areas, the quantity of land available is basically fixed. As a consequence, the quantity of land supplied *cannot* increase in response to rising prices. The supply of land is perfectly price inelastic, as illustrated by the vertical supply curve of Figure 31.2.

Because the supply of land is price inelastic, changes in the price of land must be completely determined by market demand. Notice that the initial price of land in Figure 31.2 is R_1, as determined by the intersection of D_1 and the land supply curve. If the demand for land were to shift upward, to D_2, the price of land would rise to R_2. But no additional land would be supplied, and no less. This is exactly the kind of situation that occurred in Ricardo's time: when the demand for corn rose, the (derived) demand for agricultural land increased. The increased demand for land caused rents to rise. In the News illustrates how these same forces alter the price of U.S. farmland.

Economic Rent

market mechanism: The use of market prices and sales to signal desired outputs (or resource allocations).

The function of price increases is to signal consumers' desire for more of a particular good or service. Indeed, price signals are the central feature of the **market mechanism.** In the case of land, however, the price signals have no effect: the quantity of land is unchanged. In this sense, rising prices for land exceed the amount required to call forth the available quantity of land. In fact, the land would be available even if no price were paid for it! Hence any rent paid for the use of land exceeds the price required to call forth the available supply; in this sense, all rent is "surplus" payment.

rent: Payments to a factor of production in excess of the amount required to call forth a given quantity of the factor.

The term "economic rent" is used to refer to such surplus payments, whether they are paid for land or for any other factor of production. Specifically, *economic* **rent** *is a factor payment above the minimum necessary to attract a given quantity of an input.* In the case of "pure," unimproved land, all payments made are regarded as economic rent.

In The News

LAND PRICES

U.S. Farm Incomes and Land Prices

In 1972–73 the demand for U.S. farm output increased substantially as a consequence of poor harvests elsewhere in the world. U.S. farm output could not expand fast enough to keep pace with demand. As a result, the price of farm products increased dramatically; the average price of farm output rose by nearly 40 percent in one year.

The rising prices of farm goods sharply increased farm incomes. They also made farmland more valuable. The resultant competition for farmland pushed land prices up more than 25 percent in 1973–74. The rest of the 1970s continued to be good for farmland. Crop prices generally increased faster than inflation, and the value of farmland more than tripled.

The 1980s were not so good for farm prices. The prices of major agricultural products started to fall in 1980, as a consequence of huge harvests and generally weak demand. Net farm income fell dramatically between 1979 and 1983 as cost increases greatly outpaced price increases (see Chapter 28). In response to this diminishing income potential, the price of farmland started falling as well. From 1981 to 1985 farmland prices fell sharply. In the 1984–85 season alone, average farm prices fell 13 percent. The decline in land prices was reversed in 1987 when crop prices and farm incomes increased substantially.

Clearly, "pure" rent, as defined by economists, is not the same thing as the rent people pay for their homes or apartments. Rental payments made to landlords typically include compensation for the use of capital (the building structure) and labor (building maintenance and management), and for the use of utility services (water, electricity, gas). In most cases, a very small fraction of the rental payment represents pure economic rent, as defined here.

Even in Ricardo's time, a distinction was drawn between "pure," "natural" land and land that had been improved through cultivation, irrigation, or fencing. Land improvements entail resource costs and will not be made unless a sufficient compensation (price) is offered. Only the land itself will be there at any price. Hence the rental payments made by nineteenth-century farmers included economic rent as well as compensation for the use of labor and capital in improving the land.

The concept of pure rent applies to other factors of production besides land. The demand for the services of Madonna, Sting, Michael Jackson, and Will Clark (see In the News) is very high, because these performers can generate substantial revenues for an athletic or musical event. In other words, their **marginal revenue product (MRP)** is high in certain situations. As a result, sports and music promoters are willing to pay very high prices for performances by such individuals.

Marginal revenue product only establishes a *limit* to a factor's price, however. To determine the market price of the factor, we have to examine the supply curve as well. We find that the supply curves of individual performers are relatively vertical, much like that in Figure 31.2. They can perform only a limited number of times in a given time period. Consequently, these performers are getting economic rent—that is, payments in excess of the amount required to call forth their services. If all baseball players' wages were cut in half, Will Clark, for example, would probably continue to play just as well and just as often. Whatever he is being paid in excess of the amount required to get him to play baseball is economic rent.

marginal revenue product (MRP): The change in total revenue associated with one additional unit of input.

In The News

ECONOMIC RENT

Giants' Clark: $15 Million

Four-Year Deal Sets Record

SAN FRANCISCO, Jan. 22—Will Clark jumped to the top of baseball's salary list today when he agreed to a $15 million, four-year contract with the San Francisco Giants that calls for the first $4 million salary in baseball history.

Clark, the most valuable player of the National League playoffs, will average $3.75 million a season in the new deal, topping the $3.5 million a year that Oakland's Dave Stewart will get in the two-year extension he agreed to last week.

"It definitely overwhelms you to know that baseball has this much money," Clark said. "I did not get into it to try to rob the bank, I got into it because I love the game."

The 25-year-old first baseman gets a $2 million signing bonus, $1.75 million in 1990, $3.25 million in 1991, $3.75 million in 1992 and $4.25 million in 1993. Clark, who got a four-year no-trade provision, can make $100,000 if he is named the NL's MVP, $50,000 each for being named MVP of the playoffs or World Series, and $25,000 for making the all-star team.

The Washington Post, January 23, 1990, p. E7. Reprinted by permission of The Associated Press.

Rents as an allocation mechanism Although rising economic rents do not increase the quantity of a factor supplied, they do serve an economic function. Why have all the farmers left Manhattan, where much of the land was once used for pasture and crops? The answer is simple. The rising price of land drove the fixed costs of farming so high that farmers could no longer earn a profit in New York City. In the long run, as they made new investment decisions, the farmers migrated to less expensive land in the Midwest.

The farmers were initially replaced by modest homes, rooming houses, and factories, and ultimately by skyscraping office buildings. Each step in the evolutionary process was propelled in part by increasing rents. Firms and individuals with more valuable uses for the scarce land offered increasingly high prices for its use. In turn, the high rents forced others to move their firms or households to other locations. Accordingly, ***rents serve to allocate a scarce factor among competing uses. The most valuable use will determine the market rent.*** People seeking to make less valuable use of the scarce factor will not be able to pay the price and will therefore not acquire it. Michael J. Fox will not make a guest appearance in your economics class because his talent is valued more highly elsewhere. The market mechanism determines how society's scarce resources will be allocated: whoever bids the most for a scarce resource gets it.

Rent Control   Many people are unhappy with the prices and resource allocations determined by the market. Tenants, for example, are always complaining that housing rents are too high. They want lower rents and often demand that government agencies step in to control the actions of "greedy" landlords. Elected officials sometimes respond with rent controls. Rent control places a limit on the amount of rent a landlord can charge.

Although apartment rents and economic rents are not the same thing, the theory behind rent control is related to the concept of economic rent. In cities such as New York there isn't much room for new apartment buildings. Yet the city's population keeps growing. This implies that apartment rents will keep escalating in the manner of Figure 31.2. Upward shifts of demand, together with an inelastic supply of apartments, will drive apartment prices up. In the process, landlords will reap extraordinary gains (economic rents).

Rent control is imposed to prevent apartment rents from becoming economic rents. It is based on the assumption that the supply of apartments is highly inelastic. This is not a valid assumption. The supply of apartments *can* change over time, as new and larger buildings replace old, smaller ones. In the short run, the supply of habitable apartments also depends on continued maintenance. If landlords earn below-average incomes as a consequence of rent control, they will not build new apartments or maintain old ones. (Landlords will also want to convert rent-controlled apartments into uncontrolled condominiums.) Over time, the quantity of apartments will fall, thereby aggravating the market shortage.

Rent control also implies a windfall gain for people who already occupy rent-controlled apartments. If rents are kept below their equilibrium price, the quantity demanded will exceed the quantity available. People who are lucky enough to live in rent-controlled apartments will be able to "sell" their leases to others. The "price" of occupancy rights will be determined by market forces. Those consumers most able and willing to "buy" occupancy will get the scarce apartments. In this case, the initial occupants, rather than the landlord, get the *economic* rent. New occupants still pay higher (equilibrium) rents; only the form of the payments is changed.

INTEREST

Interest payments are a second major form of property income and are also included in the capital share of income. In 1989 interest income exceeded $460 billion. In its purest form, interest is simply the amount of money paid for using someone else's money; typically, it is expressed in percentage terms, as the **interest rate.** An interest rate of 9 percent means that the borrower must pay $9 yearly for every $100 borrowed until the loan is repaid.

interest rate: The price paid for the use of money.

The Loanable Funds Market

The rate of interest may be determined through a study of supply and demand forces in the loanable funds market. Some people and firms (particularly banks) are willing and able to lend money at alternative interest rates. From a customer's point of view, lending money entails the sacrifice of some immediate consumption possibilities and thus real opportunity costs. As interest rates climb, however, the tradeoff between future consumption and present consumption tilts in the direction of future consumption. In other words, high interest rates make it appealing to sacrifice some consumption now for more consumption later. As a consequence, the quantity of loanable funds *supplied* increases as interest rates rise, as indicated by the upward slope of the supply curve in Figure 31.3. (This situation contrasts with that of land, which entails a vertical supply curve. Higher interest rates *do* call forth larger quantities of loanable funds.)

The quantity of loanable funds *demanded* has the familiar downward slope, as Figure 31.3 illustrates. From an individual consumer's perspective, borrowing money at high interest rates implies sacrificing a relatively large amount of future consumption possibilities (when the loan must be paid back) for a smaller increase in present consumption. As the implied cost of borrowing diminishes, the quantity of loanable funds demanded increases.

**FIGURE 31.3
The Loanable Funds Market**

The market rate of interest (r_e) is determined by the intersection of the curves representing supply of and demand for loanable funds. The rate of interest represents the price paid for the use of money.

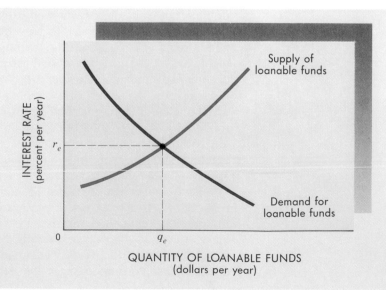

QUANTITY OF LOANABLE FUNDS
(dollars per year)

From a potential investor's point of view, increases in interest rates represent an increase in investment costs. Hence high interest rates reduce the net revenues of any potential investment. Here again we anticipate an increase in the quantity of loanable funds demanded as interest rates decline (*ceteris paribus*).

The Rate of Return to Capital

Although we can readily determine the equilibrium rate of interest by studying the supply and demand for loanable funds, the significance of the interest rate for factor prices is not always apparent. After all, money is not a factor of production; it cannot produce anything. Instead, money is a medium of exchange that can be used to acquire goods and services. ***When people lend or borrow money, they are really lending or borrowing access to goods and services.***

People who use their own or someone else's money to build an apartment house or factory are making the same kind of sacrifice a lender makes. They are giving up the opportunity to spend their income on consumer goods, choosing instead to build, buy, or lease plant and equipment. As compensation for this use of funds, an investor expects increased consumption opportunities in the future. Essentially, the investor expects to be paid interest on his or her investment. In this case, however, the resultant payments represent *returns to capital*—that is, payments for the use of real plant and equipment.

Typically, an investment is made for many years. A person who builds a factory does not begin to receive any income back until the factory is constructed and in use. The same is true of an apartment building. It may take a year to construct an apartment building and years more before rent payments equal the owner's original investment. Such investments return a *flow* of income over time. To compute the rate of return to capital in these situations, that future flow of income must be summarized in a meaningful way.

Suppose that the cost of constructing an apartment building is $1 million. After completion, the apartments will generate net rent payments (after expenses) of $100,000 per year, forever. Is this a good investment?

One way to answer this question is to calculate the implicit rate of return. Rent payments of $100,000 per year represent a 10 percent return on a million-dollar investment. This is a "good" investment so long as funds can be borrowed for less than 10 percent. If, for example, $1 million could be borrowed at 9 percent, the landlord would have to make annual interest payments of $90,000. But annual rent payments would total $100,000, so the landlord could pocket the difference of $10,000 per year. Hence ***it pays to invest so long as the return on capital exceeds the cost of money.***

Present Discounted Value

Another way to evaluate the attractiveness of an investment is to *discount* the future stream of rental income to a lump-sum figure. Suppose you are entitled to receive a payment of $100,000 exactly one year from today. Naturally, you'd rather have that income now, so you could start spending or investing it. But how much less would you accept in return for an earlier payment? Discounting provides an objective answer.

To determine the *present* value of a *future* payment, we consider the available rate of interest. What we want to find is the amount of money that, if received today and permitted to earn interest all year long would total $100,000 by year's end. In other words, the **present value** *of a future payment is discounted by potential interest accumulation.*

present discounted value: The value today of future payments, adjusted for interest accumulation.

In this case, where we are contemplating a single payment of $100,000 a year from today, the discounting computation is simple:

- $$\text{Present value of income to be received in one year} = \frac{\text{income to be received}}{1 + \text{interest rate}}$$

Suppose the market rate of interest is 9 percent. The present-value computation is then

$$\text{Present value} = \frac{\$100,000}{1 + 0.09} = \frac{\$100,000}{1.09} = \$91,743$$

In other words, if the rate of interest is 9 percent, $100,000 received one year from today is worth only $91,743 today. This is because money earns interest. If we had $91,743 today, we could deposit it and earn interest. If the interest rate were 9 percent, our $91,743 deposit would be worth $100,000 at year's end. Hence "discounting" involves adjusting future income receipts for forgone interest. ***By discounting, we translate future receipts into present values.***

The preceding computation applies to a single payment to be made one year from today. Typically, however, we are concerned with multiple future payments, stretched out over many years. Our apartment building, for example, generates $100,000 in income *each* year, not just the first. Hence we need to discount the *entire* future stream of rent payments, not just the first year's.

To compute the present value of a *stream* of future payments, we need to discount each year's payment, then add them up. The computation looks like this:

- $$\text{Present value of future income} = \Sigma \frac{\text{payment in year } t}{(1 + \text{interest rate})^t}$$

where the Greek letter Σ represents the "sum of" and t refers to specific years in the future. In the case of $100,000 rent payments to be made in every future year, the required computation is

$$\text{Present discounted value} = \frac{\$100,000}{1.09} + \frac{\$100,000}{(1.09)^2}$$
$$+ \frac{\$100,000}{(1.09)^3} + \cdots + \frac{\$100,000}{(1.09)^t}$$
$$= \$91,743 + \$84,168 + \$77,218 + \cdots$$

All this formula does is discount each future year's rent back to today's value, then adds the values up. The second year's income of $100,000 must be discounted back two years; therefore, the interest rate in the denominator is squared. If the investment income stretches far into the future (t is large), this sum equals $1,111,111.

The formula for computing present discounted values can be simplified. If the same income is received every year into the indefinite future, the formula becomes

$$\text{Present discounted value} = \frac{\text{annual income}}{\text{interest rate}} = \frac{\$100,000}{0.09} = \$1,111,111$$

This is the same answer we got before. It means that the future stream of annual $100,000 rental payments is worth $1.11 million when it is discounted at 9 percent. Since the cost of the investment is only $1 million, the investment is attractive. The In the News story shows how this discounting technique can also be used to compute the true value of a lottery jackpot.

People will continue to invest as long as the present discounted value of future returns exceeds their cost. Alternatively, we may conclude that people will continue to invest as long as the rate of return exceeds the interest rate. Once the rate of return and rate of interest are equal, it no longer pays to invest. Accordingly, *in equilibrium, the rate of return to capital will be equal to the rate of interest.* Likewise, the present discounted value of future income will equal the cost of the investment.

The logic of this conclusion becomes clearer when you think what would happen if an inequality existed. So long as the rate of interest is less than the rate of return to capital, people will continue to borrow and invest. This will drive up interest rates and lower the rate of return to capital. On the other hand, if the rate of interest were higher than the rate of return to capital, investors would simply lend out funds, rather than purchase plant and equipment. By doing so, they would increase their future incomes. As the quantity of loanable funds increased, the market rate of interest would fall. At the same time, the rate of investment would slow, because investors were lending their funds, rather than buying plant and equipment. With less new investment, marginal revenue product and thus the returns to capital would increase. Ultimately the rate of interest and the rate of return to capital would converge, eliminating motives for any further changes in investor behavior.

PROFIT

economic profit: The difference between total revenues and total economic costs.

The last major form of income is profit. As with rent, its *economic* definition differs from common perceptions of the term. As we saw in Chapter 21, **economic profit** is the difference between total revenues and all factor pay-

In The News

PRESENT DISCOUNTED VALUE

$55 Million Lottery Worth Only $28 Million!

In September 1988 the jackpot in the Florida lottery reached $55 million. Mrs. Sheelah Ryan, a sixty-three-year-old real estate agent, won it all, becoming America's biggest lottery winner. Mrs. Ryan did not get the jackpot in cash, however. Instead, she was to be paid $2.8 million a year for twenty years.

The delayed payouts of the jackpot greatly reduced its value. If $55 million were received in cash, it could be deposited in a bank or money market fund, where it could earn interest. An interest rate of 10 percent would generate *interest* payments of $5.5 million a year, nearly *twice* the size of the lottery payouts.

The actual value of the $55 million jackpot can be figured by computing the present discounted value of the annual payouts. With an interest rate of 10 percent, the present value of twenty annual payouts of $2.8 million is approximately $28 million. Hence the actual value of a $55 million jackpot paid out over twenty years is only $28 million. Despite its smaller present value, Mrs. Ryan says she gets a steady stream of marriage offers, business proposals, and appeals for charity.

economic cost: The value of all resources used to produce a good or service; opportunity cost.

ments, whether explicitly made or not. It is an above-average rate of return—a residual that remains after all **economic costs** have been subtracted.

Entrepreneurship

In view of the fact that economic profit is a residual that remains after all factors of production have been paid, the question arises as to what profit "buys" in the market. Wages, for example, buy the use of labor, interest rates buy the use of money and capital, and rent buys the use of land. But what does society get in return for profits paid to business?

Economic profits are usually regarded as the reward for *entrepreneurship,* the ability and willingness to take risks, to organize factors of production, and to produce something society desires. From this perspective, profit represents a return to an intangible but vitally important "fourth factor of production." Profit represents the payoff for making an "extra" effort, over and above "normal" factor payments. In the absence of such additional compensation, few people would want to make the extra effort required.

Risk

It is also important to observe that the *potential* for profit is not a *guarantee* of profit. Quite the contrary. Substantial risks are attached to starting and operating a business. Thousands of businesses fail every year and still more suffer economic losses. From this perspective, profit represents compensation for risks incurred.

The risks associated with a new business are particularly high when new products or processes are being developed. The microcomputer industry, discussed in Chapters 22–24, was developed on the basis of repeated technological improvements, each of which required substantial investments of labor and capital. Who would have risked such investments without some potential for high profits? In the end, more companies lost money—suffered economic losses—than made money in microcomputers. Without the chance of making huge profits, how many of those firms would have entered the market?

The In the News story lists some of the entrepreneurial hits and misses of the 1980s. People who invested in premium ice creams, minivans, and sunscreens raked in economic profits. People who risked their time and resources on home banking services, preroasted chickens, or smokeless cigarettes suffered economic losses. Society as a whole benefited from all this activity, however, by gaining access to a broader array of goods and services.

Monopoly Profits

Although profits serve an important function in stimulating economic activity, not all profits can be justified on that basis. In many situations, profits may result from the exercise of market power that inhibits rather than encourages economic progress. Monopolies provide a classic example. As we observed in Chapter 23, a monopoly can maintain economic profits by limiting the market output of a good or service. Such profits take on the appearance of economic rent, as high prices and profit do not necessarily call forth a greater quantity supplied. The same kind of quasi-rent is obtained by firms and unions that possess market power even though they are not monopolies.

In The News

ENTREPRENEURIAL RISK

Marketing Milestones of the Decade

Hits

IBM PC: Big Blue claimed the power to set industry standards.

Microwave food: It's changing our definition of good food.

Diet Coke: Brilliant brand extension.

Lean Cuisine: Pricey diet entrees launched at the height of the recession. Caught the fit-but-fast wave.

Macintosh computer: Apple computer's new design changed the way people use these machines.

Super-premium ice cream: Häagen-Dazs, Ben & Jerry's, DoveBar, the perfect end to low-calorie meals.

Chrysler minivans: These station wagons of the '80s created a new category of cars.

Tartar Control Crest: P&G's efforts to teach consumers about nasty tooth deposits helped restore its toothpaste market share.

Athletic footwear: After stumbling in 1986, Nike slam-dunked rival Reebok by winning the favor of big-city kids.

USA Today: The colorful national daily is still mired in red ink, but it's changed the way many newspapers look and act.

Swatch watches: A new look at an old product made watches into hot fashion accessories.

Nintendo video games: Games like Super Mario Brothers continue so strong they're zapping the rest of the toy business.

SPF sunscreens: Do you need SPF 5 or SPF 15? High-tech sunscreens sell well to aging baby boomers.

Misses

New Coke: Fixed what wasn't broken; customers immediately clamored for the original.

Premier cigarette: "Smokeless" cigarette couldn't be lit with matches.

IBM PCjr: A problematic keyboard contributed to its demise.

Yugo: Yugoslavian minicar was billed as cheapest new car in America, and it showed.

LA Beer: Despite the New Sobriety, the market for reduced-alcohol beer has little fizz.

Home banking: Consumers weren't ready for this complicated "service."

Pontiac Fiero: Looked great, but was discontinued after problems with engine fires.

Disk camera: Kodak's Edsel.

RCA's SelectaVision: Bad timing for the videodisk player once lauded as RCA's premier product of the '80s.

Generic products: An '80s flop, if not an '80s innovation; consumers felt queasy about their quality.

Fab 1 Shot: Colgate-Palmolive Co.'s pre-measured laundry detergent means consumers can't use just enough for a small load.

Holly Farms roasted chickens: Consumers liked these fully cooked birds, but retailers balked at their short shelf life.

The Wall Street Journal, November 28, 1989, p. B1. Reprinted by permission of *The Wall Street Journal,* © Dow Jones & Company, Inc. (1989). All Rights Reserved.

POLICY INSIGHTS:

VENTURE CAPITALISTS

One of the proven paths to high incomes and wealth is entrepreneurship. Most of the great American fortunes originated in entrepreneurial ventures, for example, building railroads, mass-producing automobiles, introducing new computers, or perfecting mass-merchandising techniques. These successful ventures, however, required more than just a great idea. To convert the original idea into actual output requires the investment of real resources.

Recall that Apple Computer got started in a garage, with a minimum of resources (Chapter 22). The idea of packaging a personal computer was novel and few resources were required to demonstrate that it could be done. But Steven Jobs could not have become a multimillionaire by building just a couple of dozen computers a month. To reap huge economic profits from his idea, he needed much greater production capacity. He also needed resources for marketing the new Apples to a broader customer base. In other words, Steven Jobs needed lots of economic resources—land, labor, and capital—to convert his entrepreneurial dream into a profit-making reality.

Steven Jobs and his partner, Steve Wozniak, had few resources of their own. In fact, they had sold Jobs's Volkswagen and Wozniak's scientific calculator to raise the finances for their first computer. To go any further, they needed financial support from others. Loans were hard to obtain, however, since the new company had no assets, no financial history, and no certainty of success. Jobs needed people who were willing to share the *risks* associated with a new venture. He found one such person in A. C. Markkula, who put up $250,000 and became a partner in the new venture. Shortly thereafter, other venture capitalists provided additional financing. With this start-up financing, Jobs was able to acquire more resources and make the Apple Computer Company a reality.

This is a classic case study of venture capitalism. Venture capitalists provide initial funding for entrepreneurial ventures. In return for their financial backing, the venture capitalists are entitled to a share of any profits that result. If the venture fails, however, they get nothing. Thus **venture capitalists provide financial support for entrepreneurial ideas and share in the risks and rewards.** Even Christopher Columbus needed venture capitalists to fund his risky expeditions to the New World, as we will see in Chapter 34. We merely note here that venture capitalists are a critical link between entrepreneurial ideas and market reality.

SUMMARY

- Total income in the economy includes payments for labor, capital, land, and entrepreneurship. The functional distribution of income indicates how much income goes to each factor of production.

- Economic rent is defined as payments for a factor of production in excess of the amount required to call forth the desired supply. Because the quantity of "pure," unimproved land is fixed—cannot respond to increases in prices—all payments for the use of unimproved land represent economic rent. Rents are also paid for the use of other factors whose supply is essentially fixed.

- Economic rent does not attract a larger quantity of the fixed factor for which it is paid. The "surplus" factor payments, however, do serve to allocate the fixed resource among competing uses.

- Interest payments are the price paid for the use of money. Interest rates measure the opportunity cost of investing one's funds in plant and equipment. The payments made for the use of such capital are the returns to capital.

- Interest rates are used to "discount" future payments to their present-value equivalent. In equilibrium, the returns to capital will equal the market rate of interest.

• Economic profits are the income that remains after all economic costs have been accounted for. These above-normal profits represent a reward for entrepreneurship and compensation for its risks. When market power or other institutional barriers inhibit economic activity, however, profits may take on the appearance of economic rent.

• Venture capitalists provide funding for entrepreneurial ideas and share in the risks and rewards of those ventures.

Terms to Remember   Define the following terms:

functional distribution of income	**rent**
factor share	**marginal revenue product (MRP)**
marginal cost	**interest rate**
fixed costs	**present discounted value**
price elasticity of supply	**economic profit**
market mechanism	**economic cost**

Questions for Discussion

1. Mike Tyson was paid over $6 million for his 1990 boxing loss to Buster Douglas. How much of this payment represented economic rent?

2. A Rand Corporation study of rent control in Los Angeles concluded that "rent control confers its benefits early and exacts its costs late." What is meant by this statement?

3. What functions, if any, do economic profits perform? Do they help allocate any scarce resources?

4. Henry George, a nineteenth-century printer, author, and politician, advocated adoption of a single property tax that would replace all other taxes. What economic arguments might be used to defend or reject such a tax?

5. Why do lenders charge interest on loans? Why are borrowers willing to pay it?

Problems

1. Suppose that the following figures summarize the annual revenues and costs of operating a Baskin-Robbins ice cream store:

(a) Investment in store equipment and franchise	$100,000
(b) Annual sales	
Ice creams	180,000
Other confections	32,000
(c) Cost of goods	134,000
(d) Lease expenses ($600 per month)	_____
(e) Employee wages (4 workers @ $8,000 per year each)	_____
(f) The owner-manager works in the store 50 hours per week except for a two-week vacation; his opportunity wage ($8 per hour)	_____
(g) Interest (9 percent)	_____

Compute the totals for d–g. Then, using the figures in the right-hand column, determine the net revenue and economic profit of the store's owner-operator. Assume that half of the initial investment is borrowed.

2. Suppose the economy is entering a recession but interest rates have remained at 10 percent. A manager of a firm faces three choices over what to do with a subsidiary:
   (*a*) Sell it immediately for $250,000 in cash
   (*b*) Sell it for a deferred price of $300,000, with payments of $100,000 for each of the next three years
   (*c*) Hold on to the subsidiary and sell it at the end of three years for $350,000

   Which of the choices results in the highest present value of the subsidiary?

3. Compute the present value of the lottery jackpot noted in In the News (p. 781), assuming
   (*a*) An interest rate of 5 percent
   (*b*) An interest rate of 3 percent
   Why is the jackpot more valuable at lower interest rates?

FACTOR MARKETS:
Issues

Efficiency and equity are central concerns of every society. We seek to get as much output as possible from the resources we use. We also want the fruits of our labor to be distributed fairly. These goals may conflict, however. If we use taxes to redistribute incomes, incentives to produce may be impaired. Similarly, if we provide income support for the poor, people may choose to work less. The enormous gains available in financial markets also raise concerns for both equity and efficiency. These are the issues examined in Chapters 32–34.

Taxes:
Equity vs. Efficiency

Insistence on carving the pie into equal slices would shrink the size of the pie. That fact poses the tradeoff between economic equality and economic efficiency.

–Arthur M. Okun

*C*raig McCaw, the 40-year-old chairman of McCaw Cellular Communications, earned $54 million in 1989. That was enough income to bring over 15,000 low-income families out of poverty. But Mr. McCaw didn't share his income, so all those families remained poor.

The market mechanism generates a unique answer to the basic FOR WHOM question. The wages, profits, interest, and rents generated in the marketplace determine how much income everyone gets. Those incomes, in turn, provide access to the goods and services produced.

But is the market-determined distribution of income fair? Should some people own vast fortunes while others seek shelter in abandoned cars? Or do the inequalities that result in the product and factor markets violate our notions of equity? If the market's answer to the FOR WHOM question is not right, some form of government intervention to redistribute incomes may be desired.

The tax system is the government's primary lever for redistributing income. But taxing Peter to pay Paul may affect more than just income shares. If taxed too heavily, Peter may stop producing so much and leave us all with less income to share. Paul, too, may work less if assured of government support. In other words, taxes affect production as well as distribution. This creates a potential tradeoff between our goal of equity and our goal of efficiency.

In this chapter we examine the equity–efficiency tradeoff. The following questions guide the examination:

- How are incomes distributed in the United States?

- How do taxes alter that distribution?

- How do taxes affect the rate and mix of output?

WHAT IS "INCOME"?

Personal Income

personal income (PI): Income received by households before payment of personal taxes.

Before examining the distribution of income in the United States, we have to decide what to include in our concept of "income" and what to omit. There are several possibilities. The most obvious choice is **personal income (PI)**— the flow of annual income received by households before payment of personal income taxes. Personal income includes wages and salaries, corporate dividends, rent, interest, Social Security benefits, welfare payments, and any other form of money income.

Personal income is not a completely satisfactory basis for measuring the distribution of income, however. Measures of the distribution of income should tell us *for whom* our output is produced. The distribution of personal income does not fully answer this question. Many goods and services are distributed directly as **in-kind income,** rather than through market purchases. Many poor people, for example, live in public housing and pay little or no rent. As a consequence, they receive a larger share of total output than their money incomes imply. People with low incomes also receive food stamps that allow them to purchase more food than their money incomes would allow. In this sense, food-stamp recipients are better off than the distribution of personal income (which omits food stamps) implies.

in-kind income: Goods and services received directly, without payment in a market transaction.

Similarly, students who attend public schools and colleges consume more goods and services than they directly pay for; public education is subsidized by all taxpayers. As a consequence, the distribution of money income understates the share of output received by students in public schools.

So long as some goods and services need not be purchased in the marketplace, *the distribution of money income is not synonymous with the distribution of goods and services.* Accordingly, the distribution of money receipts is not a complete answer to the question of FOR WHOM we produce. This measurement problem is particularly important when comparisons are made over time. For example, the federal government officially classifies people as "poor" if their money income is below a certain threshold. By this standard, we have made little progress in reducing the number of poor people in America during the last fifteen years. In that time, however, we have provided a vastly increased amount of in-kind benefits to low-income people. Hence their *real* incomes have risen much more than the *money* statistics indicate. In this case, money statistics give a misleading picture of the changing income distribution.

The distinction between money incomes and real incomes also affects international comparisons. Many people in less developed countries rely more on home production than on market participation for essential goods and services. As a consequence, the measured distribution of money income may look more unequal than it really is. This overstatement affects comparisons between the United States and such countries as Sweden and Great Britain. In those countries, the governments provide more direct goods and services (e.g., housing, medical care) than the U.S. government does. Hence *real* income is more evenly distributed in those countries than money incomes imply.

Wealth and Happiness

wealth: The market value of assets.

Concentration on money incomes raises still other problems. If our real concern is access to goods and services, the distribution of wealth is also important. **Wealth** refers to the market value of the assets (e.g., houses, bank accounts) people own. Hence *wealth represents a stock of potential pur-*

chasing power; income statistics tell us only how this year's flow of purchasing power (income) is being distributed. Yet goods and services can be purchased with income saved in previous years (or generations, through inheritance). That is to say, ownership of wealth implies greater access to goods and services than income alone permits. Accordingly, to provide a complete answer to the FOR WHOM question, we have to know how wealth, as well as income, is distributed. In general, wealth tends to be distributed much less equally than income. The Internal Revenue Service estimates that 3 percent of the adult population owns 30 percent of all personal wealth in the United States.

Finally, we have to confront a very basic question about the importance of income and wealth. By focusing on access to goods and services, we are implicitly asserting that material things are primary determinants of individual well-being. Does money really buy happiness? Apparently so. In a study of attitudes and income in nineteen countries, Richard Easterlin of the University of Pennsylvania came to the following conclusion:

> Does greater happiness go with higher income? The answer is, quite clearly, yes. This does not mean there are no unhappy people among the rich and no happy people among the poor. On the average, however, higher-income people are happier than the poor.[1]

Professor Easterlin also noted, however, that entire societies don't become happier as their abundance grows. What matters to people is their *relative* position in society, not the absolute quantity of goods and services they consume. A "rich" fisherman in Sri Lanka might feel better off than a "poor" American, even though the American has access to far more goods and services. What matters is how many goods and services one has compared to one's neighbors.

THE SIZE DISTRIBUTION OF INCOME

How many goods and services one has is largely, though not completely, determined by one's income. We need to know, therefore, how total income is distributed.

size distribution of income: The way total personal income is divided up among households or income classes.

The most common measure of the income shares received by individuals is the **size distribution of income.** This measure tells us how large a share of total personal income is received by various households, grouped by income class. Imagine for the moment that the entire population is lined up in order of income, with lowest-income recipients in front and highest-income recipients at the end of the line. We want to know how much income the people in front get in comparison with those at the back. Table 32.1 provides the answer.

The figures in Table 32.1 indicate that no household in the first (lowest) fifth, or quintile, of the line received more than $11,382 in 1988; thus $11,382 was the upper boundary for the lowest income class. Note also that this class received only 3.8 percent of total income, despite the fact that it included 20 percent of all households (the lowest fifth). Thus the **income share** of the people in the lowest group (3.8 percent) was much smaller than their proportion in the total population (20 percent).

income share: The proportion of total income received by a particular group.

[1]Richard A. Easterlin, "Does Money Buy Happiness?," *Public Interest,* Winter 1973.

TABLE 32.1   Size Distribution of Personal Income, 1988

The size distribution of income indicates how total income is distributed among income classes. That fifth of our population with the lowest incomes received only 3.8 percent of total income. The highest-income class (fifth) received over 46 percent of total income.

Income group	1988 income (dollars)	Aggregate income (billions of dollars)	Share of total income (percent)
Lowest fifth	0–11,382	120	3.8
Second fifth	11,383–21,500	303	9.6
Third fifth	21,501–33,506	505	16.0
Fourth fifth	33,507–50,593	764	24.2
Highest fifth	above 50,593	1,462	46.3

Source: U.S. Department of Commerce, Bureau of the Census.

Moving back to the end of the line, we observe that a family needed $50,594 in annual income to make it into the highest income class in 1988. Naturally, many families in that class made much more than $50,000, some even millions of dollars. But $50,594 was at least enough to get into the top fifth.

The top fifth of all families obviously fared much better than everyone else. The extent of their prosperity is indicated by their relative income share. They got 46.3 percent of total income and, by implication, that much of total output. This was twelve times as much income as the lowest class received.

The Lorenz Curve

The size distribution of income provides the kind of information we need to determine how total personal income is distributed. A more convenient summary of that same information is often desired, however. For this purpose we can draw a Lorenz curve, first suggested by an American statistician, Max Otto Lorenz, in 1905.

Lorenz curve: A graphic illustration of the cumulative size distribution of income; contrasts complete equality with the actual distribution of income.

A **Lorenz curve** for the United States is illustrated in Figure 32.1. Our lineup of individuals is on the horizontal axis, with the lowest income earners on the left. On the vertical axis we depict the cumulative share of income received by people in our income line. Consider the lowest fifth of the distribution again—that is, the people in front of our income line. They are represented on the horizontal axis at 20 percent. What we want to know is how large a share of income they receive. If their share of income was identical to their share of population, they would get 20 percent of total income. This would be represented by point *C* in the figure. In fact, the lowest quintile gets much less than 20 percent of total income. They get only 3.8 percent, as indicated by point *A*. We already knew this from Table 32.1, of course.

Past point *A*, the Lorenz curve starts to provide a bit more information. Point *B*, for example, tells us that the *cumulative* share of income received by the lowest three-fifths of the population was 29.4 percent. We could have gotten this information from Table 32.1 as well, but it would have required a little addition.

The really handy feature of the Lorenz curve is the way it contrasts the actual distribution of income with an absolutely equal one. If incomes were distributed equally, all income shares would be identical. In that case, the first 20 percent of the people in line would be getting exactly 20 percent of all income, and the Lorenz curve would run through point *C*. Indeed, the

FIGURE 32.1
The Lorenz Curve

The Lorenz curve illustrates the extent of income inequality. If all incomes were equal, each fifth of the population would receive one-fifth of total income. In this case, the diagonal line through point C would represent the cumulative size distribution of income. In reality, though, incomes are not distributed equally. Point A, for example, indicates that 20 percent of the population with the lowest income receives only 3.8 percent of total income.

Source: Table 32.1

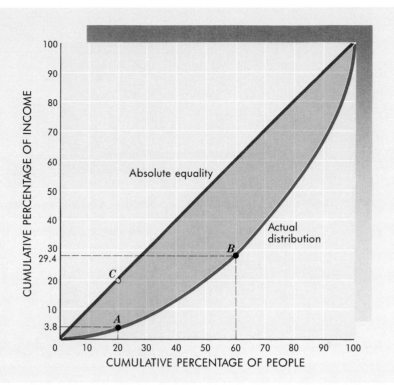

W🌐RLD VIEW

INEQUALITY

Income Share of the Rich

Incomes are distributed much less equally in poor countries than in rich ones. In most developing countries the top tenth of all households receives 30–50 percent of all income. In the United States and other developed countries inequality is much less severe.

Country	Percentage of total income received by highest decile
Brazil	50.6
Zambia	46.4
Kenya	45.8
Malaysia	39.8
Philippines	37.0
Australia	30.5
Sweden	28.1
France	26.4
United States	**23.3**
Japan	22.4
Belgium	21.5

Source: World Bank, data for various years, 1975–81.

Reprinted by permission of the *San Francisco Chronicle*. Artist: Robert Graysmith.

Lorenz "curve" would be a straight line along the diagonal. The fact that the actual Lorenz curve lies below the diagonal indicates that our national income is not distributed equally. In fact, the area between the diagonal and the actual Lorenz curve (the shaded area in Figure 32.1) is a convenient measure of the degree of inequality. ***The greater the area between the Lorenz curve and the diagonal, the more inequality exists.***[2]

THE FEDERAL INCOME TAX

Many people believe that the distribution of income generated by the market is too unequal. Incomes should be equalized, they argue, with high taxes on the rich and generous income transfers for the poor. By levying taxes on the basis of "ability to pay," the government could reshape the Lorenz curve.

The federal income tax is designed on the ability-to-pay principle. Specifically, the federal income tax is designed to be **progressive**—that is, to impose higher tax rates on high incomes than on low ones. Progressivity is achieved by imposing increasing **marginal tax rates** on higher incomes. The *marginal* tax rate refers to the tax rate imposed on the last (marginal) dollar of income. Prior to 1987, the personal income tax specified sixteen different marginal tax rates, ranging from zero to a top rate of 50 percent. The more income a person had, the higher the tax bracket and thus the higher the

progressive tax: A tax system in which tax rates rise as incomes rise.

marginal tax rate: The tax rate imposed on the last (marginal) dollar of income.

[2]The ratio of the shaded area to the area of the triangle formed by the diagonal and the axes is often used as a numerical summary of the Lorenz curve. This ratio, called the "Gini coefficient," was 0.426 in 1988.

marginal tax rate. Single individuals with $20,000 of taxable income, for example, confronted a marginal tax rate of 26 percent on any additional income they received. Single people with $90,000 worth of taxable income confronted a marginal tax rate of 50 percent. Hence the high-income individual paid not only more taxes, but also a larger percentage of his or her income.

Efficiency? The seemingly progressive tax rates imposed by the federal income tax raised two basic objections, one regarding efficiency, the other, equity. The efficiency objection focused on the top marginal tax rate. Why should anyone work hard if Uncle Sam is going to take half of every extra dollar earned? Certainly ***the incentive to work more, produce more, or invest more is reduced by high marginal tax rates.*** Critics argued that the top rates were too high. A reduction in tax rates, they claimed, would increase productivity and output, resulting in more goods and services for all of us.

Equity? A second objection to the federal tax system was motivated by equity concerns. Although the tax system looked very progressive, many people with high incomes were able to escape high tax rates. They weren't breaking any laws, just taking advantage of "loopholes" in the tax system.

Loopholes The progressive tax rates described in the tax code apply to "taxable" income, not to all income. The so-called loopholes in the system arise from the way Congress defines taxable income. The tax laws permit one to subtract certain exemptions and deductions from gross income in computing taxable income—that is,

- $$\frac{\text{Taxable}}{\text{income}} = \frac{\text{gross}}{\text{income}} - \text{exemptions and deductions}$$

Exemptions are permitted for dependent children, spouses, old age, and disabilities. Prior to the 1986 law, deductions were also permitted for home mortgage interest, work-related expenses, child care, depreciation of investments, oil exploration, interest payments, union dues, medical expenses, and many other items.

The purpose of these many itemized deductions was to encourage specific economic activities and reduce potential hardship. The deduction for mortgage interest payments, for example, encourages people to buy their own homes. The deduction for medical expenses helps relieve the financial burden of illness.

Whatever the merits of specific exemptions and deductions, they created potential inequities. People with high incomes could avoid high taxes by claiming large exemptions and deductions. Each year the Internal Revenue Service discovered individuals earning million-dollar incomes and paying little or no taxes. They weren't doing anything illegal, just taking advantage of the many deductions Congress permitted. Nevertheless, this meant that some people with high incomes could end up paying less tax than people with lower incomes. This **vertical inequity** was contrary to the progressive intent of taxing people on the basis of their ability to pay.

vertical equity: Principle that people with higher incomes should pay more taxes.

Table 32.2 illustrates vertical inequality. Mr. Jones's income is three times larger than Ms. Smith's. However, Mr. Jones also has huge deductions that reduce his *taxable* income dramatically. In fact, Mr. Jones ends up with less taxable income than Ms. Smith! As a result, he also ends up paying lower taxes.

TABLE 32.2   Vertical Inequity

Tax exemptions and deductions create a gap between total income and *taxable* income. In this case, Mr. Jones has both a higher income and extensive deductions. He ends up with less taxable income than Ms. Smith and so pays less taxes. This vertical inequity is reflected in the effective tax rates paid by each person.

	Mr. Jones	Ms. Smith
1. Total income	$90,000	$30,000
2. Less exemptions and deductions	70,000	5,000
3. Taxable income	$20,000	$25,000
4. Tax	$4,000	$5,500
5. Nominal tax rate (= row 4 ÷ row 3)	20%	22%
6. Effective tax rate (= row 4 ÷ row 1)	4.4%	18.3%

horizontal equity: Principle that people with equal incomes should pay equal taxes.

The deductions that create the vertical inequity between Mr. Jones and Ms. Smith could also create **horizontal inequities**—that is, people with the *same* incomes paying different amounts of income tax. These horizontal inequities likewise contradicted the basic notions of fairness expressed in the ability-to-pay principle.

Nominal vs. effective tax rates   The loopholes created by exemptions, deductions, and tax credits create a distinction between gross economic income and taxable income. That distinction, in turn, requires us to distinguish between nominal tax rates and effective tax rates. The term **nominal tax rate** refers to the taxes actually paid as a percentage of taxable income. By contrast, the **effective tax rate** is the tax paid divided by *total* economic income without regard to exemptions, deductions, or other intricacies of the tax laws. As noted in Table 32.2, a single individual with a gross income of $90,000 might end up with a very low *taxable* income, thanks to the benefits of various tax deductions and exemptions. Mr. Jones ended up with a taxable income of $20,000 and a tax bill of $4,000. We could then characterize this individual's tax burden in two ways:

nominal tax rate: Taxes paid divided by taxable income.

effective tax rate: Taxes paid divided by total income.

$$\bullet \quad \frac{\text{Nominal}}{\text{tax rate}} = \frac{\text{tax paid}}{\text{taxable income}}$$

$$= \frac{\$4,000}{20,000} = 20 \text{ percent}$$

or, alternatively,

$$\bullet \quad \frac{\text{Effective}}{\text{tax rate}} = \frac{\text{tax paid}}{\text{total economic income}}$$

$$= \frac{\$4,000}{90,000} = 4.4 \text{ percent}$$

This huge gap between the nominal tax rate (20 percent) and the effective tax rate (4.4 percent) is a reflection of loopholes in the tax code. It is also the source of the vertical and horizontal inequities discussed earlier. Notice that Ms. Smith, with much less income, ends up with an effective tax rate (18.3 percent) that is over four times higher than Mr. Jones's (4.4 percent).

Tax-induced misallocations A further unwelcome by-product of tax loopholes is resource misallocation. Ideally, we want the mix of output to reflect a balance between social preferences and opportunity costs. In principle, the market mechanism helps us achieve the optimal mix by signaling consumer demands and the marginal costs of producing various goods. But the tax code adds a new dimension to the decision-making process. By offering preferential treatment for some activities, the tax code reduces their relative accounting cost. In so doing, *tax preferences induce resource shifts into tax-preferred activities.*

These resource allocations are, of course, a principal objective of tax preferences. By 1986, however, the accumulation of exemptions, deductions, and credits had become so unwieldy and complex that tax considerations were overwhelming economic considerations in many investment and consumption decisions. The resulting mix of output, many observers felt, was decidedly inferior to a "pure" market outcome. From this viewpoint, the federal income tax was promoting both inequity and inefficiency.

tax base: The amount of income or property directly subject to nominal tax rates.

A shrinking tax base The loopholes in the tax code were creating yet another problem. As the **tax base** got smaller and smaller, it became increasingly difficult to sustain, much less increase, tax revenues. The tax arithmetic is simple:

$$\bullet \quad \text{Tax revenue} = \frac{\text{average}}{\text{tax rate}} \times \frac{\text{tax}}{\text{base}}$$

As deductions, exemptions, and credits accumulated, the tax base (taxable income) kept shrinking. This implied that tax rates would have to go up, which threatened to discourage production and investment still more. To keep tax rates low—or to reduce them further—Congress had to stop this erosion of the tax base.

THE 1986 TAX REFORM ACT

Rising discontent with a shrinking tax base, horizontal and vertical inequities, and tax-distorted resource allocations led to a major reform of federal taxes in 1986. The basic features of the Tax Reform Act (TRA) of 1986 included

- *Loophole closing.* Major loopholes were closed or reduced.

- *Reductions in marginal tax rates.* The top marginal tax rate was reduced from 50 percent to 28 percent.

- *Fewer tax brackets.* The number of tax brackets was reduced from sixteen to two.

- *Tax relief for the poor.* Increases in the personal exemption and standard deduction removed nearly 5 million poor people from the tax rolls.

- *A shift from personal to corporate taxes.* The direct tax burden on individuals was reduced, while the corporate tax burden was increased.

Base Broadening The elimination or reduction of scores of tax preferences increased the tax base almost 25 percent. By broadening the tax base to encompass more economic income, the TRA eliminated the source of many horizontal and vertical inequities. This loophole closing also tended to make the tax system more progressive, since tax preferences disproportionately benefited higher-income families.

Rate Reductions

By broadening the tax base, the TRA made it possible to reduce tax rates. This was of particular concern to those who feared that high marginal tax rates were inhibiting labor supply, investment, and production. The cut in the top marginal tax rate from 50 percent to 28 percent was intended to stimulate a greater supply of labor and capital, and thus promote our efficiency goal.

Reducing tax rates and simplifying tax brackets (to two instead of sixteen) tends to reduce the progressivity of the tax system. However, this equity sacrifice was offset by the loophole closing and the elimination of the federal tax burden for most poor families. A shift of the tax burden from individuals to corporations also increased progressivity, since corporate owners tend to have higher incomes.[3] Table 32.3 shows how the Tax Reform Act of 1986 changed the tax burdens of different income classes. The tax burden of the 10 percent of individuals with the lowest incomes (the lowest-income decile) fell 16 percent, while the tax burden of individuals in the highest decile increased 2 percent.

Table 32.4 displays the *effective* federal income tax rates for 1988 for different income classes. Nominally, there are only two tax brackets and rates (15 and 28 percent) in the revised tax code. However, numerous exemptions and deductions are still permitted. Hence effective tax rates vary considerably. On average, however, ***the federal income tax is progressive.*** Individuals with less than $5,000 of income now confront a *negative* tax; they receive a tax credit from Uncle Sam. Above that income threshold, people confront increasingly higher tax rates. President Bush paid an effective tax rate of 21.7 percent on his 1989 income of $466,244 (see In the News). For people with million-dollar incomes, the effective tax rate is now 24.5 percent—one-quarter of their income goes to the U.S. Treasury.

[3]Taxes on corporations are ultimately paid by individuals, in the form of reduced dividends, lower wages, or higher prices for goods produced.

TABLE 32.3   The Change in Tax Burdens

The Tax Reform Act of 1986 increased the progressivity of the federal tax system. The federal tax burden of the lowest-income decile (tenth of the population) fell by 16 percent, while the tax burden of the highest decile increased by 2 percent.

Income decile	Change in federal taxes (percent)
Highest	+2
Ninth	−4
Eighth	−3
Seventh	−4
Sixth	−4
Fifth	−6
Fourth	−7
Third	−10
Second	−11
Lowest	−16

Source: Joseph A. Pechman, "Tax Reform: Theory and Practice," *Journal of Economic Perspectives,* Summer 1987.

TABLE 32.4   Effective Tax Rates, 1988

The federal income tax is progressive, with effective rates ranging from −1 percent (a net credit) for incomes under $5,000 to 24.5 percent for million-dollar incomes. Effective rates depend on two factors: the nominal tax rate and the amount of exemptions, deductions, and tax credits available to reduce one's taxable income.

Adjusted gross income (dollars)	Effective average tax rate (percent)
0–5,000	−1.0
5,000–10,000	0.4
10,000–15,000	3.5
15,000–20,000	6.1
20,000–25,000	7.7
25,000–35,000	9.1
35,000–50,000	10.9
50,000–100,000	14.9
100,000–500,000	21.6
500,000–1,000,000	23.6
1,000,000 and over	24.5
Average	12.0

Source: Joseph A. Pechman, "Tax Reform: Theory and Practice," *Journal of Economic Perspectives*, Summer 1987.

In The News

EFFECTIVE TAX RATES

The President's Taxes

President and Mrs. Bush had a total income of $466,244 in 1989. Deductions and exemptions reduced their *taxable* income to $358,078, however. The $101,382 tax bill they paid represented 28.3 percent of taxable income, but only 21.7 percent of total income. (Note: The Bushes later amended their tax return to include an additional $26,250 in income and $7,497 more in taxes.)

INCOME	466,244
Salary	196,810
Blind trust income	182,211
Book royalties	14,282
Capital gains	36,068
Dividends	9,997
Interest	16,876
DEDUCTIONS	94,702
State income tax	2,479
Property tax	19,528
Personal property tax	207
Interest paid	324
Charitable contributions	37,866
Legal and accounting fees	20,492
Moving expense	3,856
Tax preparation fee	1,600
Miscellaneous deductions	8,350
EXEMPTIONS	13,464
Tax-exempt interest	9,464
Personal exemption	4,000
TAXABLE INCOME	$358,078
TAX	$101,382

Source: The White House.

PAYROLL, STATE, AND LOCAL TAXES

The federal income tax is only one of many taxes the average taxpayer must pay. For many families, in fact, the federal income tax is the smallest of many tax bills. Other tax bills come from the U.S. Social Security Administration and state and local governments. These taxes also affect both efficiency and equity.

Sales and Property Taxes

regressive tax: A tax system in which tax rates fall as incomes rise.

As we observed in Chapter 3, *sales taxes* are the major source of revenue for *state* governments. Many *local* governments also impose sales taxes, but most cities rely on *property taxes* for the bulk of their tax receipts. Both of these taxes hit the poor hardest. In other words, sales and property taxes are **regressive**—they impose higher tax rates on lower incomes.

At first glance, a 5 percent sales tax doesn't look very regressive. After all, the same 5 percent tax is imposed on virtually all goods. But we are interested in *people,* not goods and services. So **we gauge tax burdens in relation to people's incomes.** A tax is regressive if it imposes a proportionally larger burden on lower incomes.

This is exactly what a uniform sales tax does. To see this, we have to look not only at how much tax is levied on each dollar of consumption but also at *what percentage of income* is spent on consumer goods.

Low-income families spend everything they've got (and sometimes more) on basic consumption. As a result, most of their income ends up subject to sales tax. By contrast, higher-income families save more. As a result, a smaller proportion of their income is subject to a sales tax. Table 32.5 illustrates this regressive feature of a sales tax.

Property taxes are regressive also, and for the same reason. Low-income families spend a higher percentage of their incomes for shelter. A uniform property tax thus ends up taking a larger fraction of their income than it does of the incomes of high-income families.

tax incidence: Distribution of the real burden of a tax.

Tax incidence It may sound strange to suggest that low-income families bear the brunt of property taxes. After all, the tax is imposed on the landlords who *own* property, not on people who *rent* apartments and houses. However, here again we have to distinguish between the nominal payee and the individual whose income is actually reduced by the tax. **Tax incidence** refers to the actual burden of a tax—that is, who really ends up paying it.

TABLE 32.5   The Regressivity of Sales Taxes

A sales tax is imposed on consumer purchases. Although the sales tax itself is uniform (here at 5 percent), the taxes paid represent different proportions of high and low incomes. In this case, the low-income family's *sales tax* bill equals 4.7 percent of its *income*. The high-income family has a sales tax bill equal to only 3 percent of its income.

	High-income family	Low-income family
Income	$50,000	$15,000
Consumption	$30,000	$14,000
Saving	$20,000	$1,000
Sales tax paid (5% of consumption)	$1,500	$700
Effective tax rate (sales tax ÷ income)	3.0%	4.7%

In general, people who rent apartments pay higher rents as a result of property taxes. In other words, landlords tend to pass along to tenants any property taxes they must pay. Thus to a large extent, ***the burden of property taxes is reflected in higher rents.*** Tenants pay property taxes *indirectly* via these higher rents. The incidence of the property tax thus falls on renters, in the form of higher rents, rather than on the landlords who write checks to the local tax authority.

Payroll Taxes

The actual distribution of sales, property, and payroll taxes depends on market conditions. Specifically, the incidence of a tax depends on the elasticity of supply and demand for the taxed good. Consider, for example, the Social Security payroll tax. Nominally, the Social Security payroll tax consists of two parts—half paid by employees and half by employers. But do employers really pay their half? Or do they end up paying lower wages to compensate for their tax share? If so, employees end up paying *both* halves of the Social Security payroll tax.

Figure 32.2 illustrates how the tax incidence of the payroll tax is distributed. The supply of labor reflects the ability and willingness of people to work for various wage rates. Labor demand reflects the **marginal revenue product (MRP)** of labor; it sets a *limit* to the wage an employer is willing to pay.

marginal revenue product (MRP): The change in total revenue associated with one additional unit of input.

The employer's half of the payroll tax increases the nominal cost of labor. Thus the S + tax curve lies above the labor-supply curve. It incorporates the wages that must be paid to workers *plus* the payroll tax that must be paid to the Social Security Administration. This total labor cost is the one that will determine how many workers are hired. Specifically, the intersection of the S + tax curve and the labor-demand curve determines the equilibrium level of employment (L_1). The employer will pay the amount w_1 for this much labor. But part of that outlay ($w_1 - w_2$) will go to the public treasury in the form of payroll taxes. Workers will receive only w_2 in wages. This is less than they would get in the absence of the payroll tax (compare w_0 and w_2). Thus ***fewer workers are employed and the net wage is reduced when a payroll tax is imposed.***

**FIGURE 32.2
The Incidence
of a Payroll Tax**

Some portion of a payroll tax imposed on employers may actually be borne by workers. The tax raises the cost of labor and so shifts the supply curve upward (to *S* + tax). The intersection of this tax-burdened supply curve with the labor-demand curve determines a new equilibrium of employment (L_1). At that level, employers pay w_1 in wages and taxes, but workers get only w_2 in wages. The wage reduction from w_0 to w_2 is a real burden of the payroll tax, and it is borne by workers.

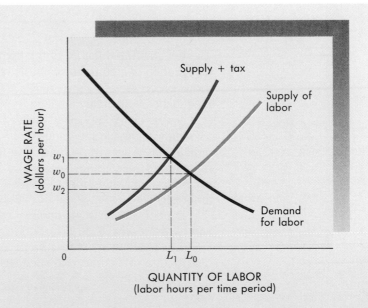

These reflections on tax incidence do not imply that payroll taxes are necessarily bad. They do emphasize, however, that the apparent taxpayer is not necessarily the individual who bears the real burden of a tax.

TAXES AND INEQUALITY

A Proportional System

The regressivity of the Social Security payroll tax and of many state and local taxes offsets most of the progressivity of the federal income tax. When all is said and done, the tax system as a whole ends up being nearly proportional. High-income families end up paying roughly the same percentage of their income in taxes as do low-income families. The tax system does reduce inequality somewhat—but the redistributive impact is quite small.

The Impact of Transfers

income transfers: Payments to individuals for which no current goods or services are exchanged, e.g., Social Security, welfare, unemployment benefits.

The tax system tells only half the redistribution story. It tells whose income was taken away. Equally important is who gets the income the government collects. The government completes the redistribution process by *transferring* income to consumers. The **income transfers** may be explicit, as in the case of welfare benefits, Social Security payments, and unemployment insurance. Or the transfers may be indirect, as in the case of public schools, farm subsidies, and student loans. The direct transfers are more likely to be progressive—that is, to increase the income share of lower-income households. This progressivity results from the fact that low-income status is often a requirement for a direct income transfer. By contrast, most indirect transfers are ostensibly designed to fulfill other purposes (e.g., education, agricultural stability). As a consequence, they are less likely to be progressive and may even be regressive in some cases. A recent study of "social welfare" expenditures (including all direct transfers, housing, and education) attempted to assess the share of such transfers going to the poor. It found that only half of federal transfers and even a smaller proportion (30 percent) of state and local transfers go to the poor.[4] Were indirect transfers to be included, the proportions would be smaller yet.

WHAT IS "FAIR"?

The demonstrated failure of the tax-transfer system to alter substantially the distribution of income raises basic questions. Should we make the tax system more progressive? Do we really want greater equality? Or are the existing inequalities sufficiently justified to preclude further efforts at redistribution?

Nearly everyone has an answer to these questions, but the answers vary as widely as people's incomes. "Fairness" is a subjective concept that is often indistinguishable from self-interest. Rich people, for example, can rattle off as many good reasons for preserving income inequalities as poor people can recite for eliminating them. People in the middle-income brackets tend to be ambivalent.

Economists are not uniquely qualified to overcome self-interest, much less to divine what a fair distribution of income might look like. But economists are in a position to assess some of the costs and benefits of altering the distribution of income, and such assessments can facilitate policy decisions.

[4]Robert Plotnicle and Felicity Skidmore, *Progress Against Poverty* (New York: Academic Press, 1975).

The Costs of Greater Equality

The greatest potential cost of a move toward greater equality is the reduced incentives it might leave in its wake. People *are* motivated by income. In factor markets, higher wages call forth more workers and may induce them to work longer hours. In fields where earnings are exceptionally high, as in the medical and legal professions, people are willing to spend years of their lives and many thousands of dollars acquiring the skills such earnings require. Could we really expect people to make such sacrifices in a market that paid everyone the same wage?

The same problem exists in product markets. The willingness of producers to supply us with goods and services depends on their expectation of profits. Why should they work hard and take risks to produce goods and services if their efforts will not make them any better off? If incomes were in fact distributed equally, producers might just as well sit back and enjoy the fruits of someone else's labor.

The essential economic problem that absolute income equality poses is that it breaks the market link between effort and reward. If all incomes were equal, it would no longer pay to make an above-average effort. If people stopped making such efforts, total output would decline, and we would have less income to share. Not that all high incomes are attributable to great skill or effort. Such factors as luck, market power, and family connections also influence incomes. It remains true, however, that the promise of higher income encourages work effort. Moreover, we can reach our production-possibilities curve only if we are efficient, highly motivated producers. Absolute income equality threatens those conditions.

The argument for preserving income inequalities is thus anchored in a concern for productivity. From this perspective, income inequalities are the driving force behind much of our production. By preserving such inequalities, we not only enrich the fortunate few but also, by providing incentives to increase total output, make more goods and services available to lower income groups. Thus everyone is potentially better off, even if only a few end up rich.

The Benefits of Greater Equality

Although the potential benefits of inequality are impressive, *there is a tradeoff between efficiency and equality.* Moreover, many people are convinced that the terms of the tradeoff are exaggerated and the benefits of greater equality are ignored. These rebuttals are both economic and non-economic.

The economic arguments for greater equality also focus on incentives. The first argument is that the present degree of inequality is more than necessary to maintain work incentives. Upper-class incomes need not be twelve times as large as those of the lowest-income classes; perhaps *five* times as large would do as well.

The second argument is that low-income earners might actually work harder if incomes were distributed more fairly. As matters now stand, the low-income worker sees little chance of making it big. Extremely low income can also inhibit workers' ability to work by subjecting them to poor health, malnutrition, or inadequate educational opportunities. Accordingly, some redistribution of income to the poor might improve the productivity of low-income workers and compensate for reduced productivity among the rich.

Finally, we have noted that the maze of loopholes that preserve inequality also distorts economic incentives. Labor and investment decisions are influenced by tax considerations, not just economic benefits and costs. If greater

"*I suppose one could say it favors the rich, but, on the other hand it's a great incentive for everyone to make two hundred grand a year.*"

Drawing by Lorenz; © 1985 The New Yorker Magazine, Inc.

equality was achieved via tax simplification, a more efficient allocation of resources might result.

There are noneconomic arguments for greater equality as well. To the extent that high incomes go hand in hand with political power, an unequal distribution of income weakens the democratic process. Inequalities may also tend to distort our values by their very emphasis on material reward. By the same token, the anxieties and frustrations created by the quest for upper-

In The News

INCENTIVES

Cut the Capital Gains Tax?

In 1989, President Bush proposed a cut in the capital gains tax. Congressional Democrats objected to the proposal, calling it a giveaway to the rich.

Capital gains are increases in the value of assets. When stocks, land, or other assets are sold, any resulting gain is counted as regular income. As such, it is subject to a marginal tax rate of 28 percent. The administration argues that this tax discourages people from investing. A lower tax rate would stimulate more investment and also encourage people to reallocate their assets more often, thus increasing economic efficiency. Many countries—

including Japan, Italy, South Korea, Taiwan, and the Netherlands—do not levy any taxes on capital gains. The rest of the European Community and Canada impose lower capital gains taxes than does the United States.

Critics argue that a capital gains tax cut would overwhelmingly favor the rich, who own most stocks, property, and other wealth. This inequity, they assert, would outweigh any efficiency gains, which are themselves unproven. They also point out that the tax code permits people to pass assets on to their heirs without paying any capital gains tax. No tax cut should be enacted, they argue, unless this loophole is closed.

income positions may actually make us less happy as a society, even if somewhat richer. The accompanying In the News illustrates how these arguments for greater equality and efficiency define the two sides of the battle over capital gains tax cuts.

SUMMARY————————————————————

- The distribution of income is a vital economic issue because incomes largely determine access to the goods and services we produce. Wealth distribution is important for the same reason.

- The size distribution of income tells us how incomes are divided up among individuals. The Lorenz curve provides a graphic summary of the cumulative size distribution of income.

- Personal incomes are distributed quite unevenly in the United States. At present, the highest income group (the top 20 percent) gets twelve times as much income as the lowest income group.

- The progressivity of the federal income tax is weakened by various loopholes (exemptions, deductions, and credits). These create a distinction between nominal and effective tax rates and cause vertical and horizontal inequities.

- The Tax Reform Act of 1986 broadened the tax base (by eliminating many deductions), reduced tax rates, and shifted the tax burden onto corporations. The reforms made federal taxes a bit more progressive.

- Mildly progressive federal income taxes are offset by regressive payroll, state, and local taxes. Overall, the tax system redistributes little income; most redistribution occurs through transfer payments.

- Tax incidence refers to the real burden of a tax. In many cases, reductions in wages, increases in rent, or other real income changes represent the true burden of a tax.

- There is a tradeoff between efficiency and equality. If all incomes are equal, there is no economic reward for superior productivity. On the other hand, a more equal distribution of incomes might increase the productivity of lower income groups and serve important noneconomic goals as well. The actual terms of this tradeoff between equality and efficiency are not known, however, and the debate on income distribution continues.

Terms to Remember   Define the following terms:

personal income (PI)	horizontal equity
in-kind income	nominal tax rate
wealth	effective tax rate
size distribution of income	tax base
income share	regressive tax
Lorenz curve	tax incidence
progressive tax	marginal revenue product (MRP)
marginal tax rate	income transfers
vertical equity	

Questions for Discussion

1. What goods or services do you and your family receive without directly paying for them? How do these goods affect the distribution of economic welfare?

2. Why are incomes distributed so unevenly? Identify and explain three major causes of inequality.

3. Do inequalities stimulate productivity? In what ways? Provide two specific examples.

4. Do loopholes in the tax system serve any social purpose? How else might the same purpose be achieved?

Problems

1. Using the numbers in Table 32.1 as a base, calculate the average tax rates that would have to be imposed on each income class to bring about absolute equality across income classes.

2. For the 1986 tax year, the federal tax liability of single individuals was computed with formulas that included the following:

If your taxable income is above:	But below:	Then your tax is computed as:
$11,650	$13,920	$1297.70 + 18% of anything over $11,650
$13,920	$16,190	$1706.30 + 20% of anything over $13,920

(*a*) Compute the taxable income and taxes for the following taxpayers:

Taxpayer	Gross income	Exemptions and deductions
1	$20,000	$7,000
2	$20,000	$4,000
3	$40,000	$28,000

(*b*) Rank each taxpayer on the basis of the nominal tax rate, effective tax rate, and marginal tax rate.

(*c*) What can be said about the vertical and horizontal equity of this tax system?

3. Following are hypothetical data on the size distribution of income and wealth for each quintile (one-fifth) of a population:

Quintile	Lowest	Second	Third	Fourth	Highest
Income	5%	10%	15%	25%	45%
Wealth	2%	8%	12%	20%	58%

(*a*) Draw the line of absolute equality; then draw a Lorenz curve for income, and shade the area between the two curves.

(*b*) In the same diagram, draw a Lorenz curve for wealth. Is there more inequality in the distribution of wealth than of income, or less? How do you know?

(*c*) The difference in inequality between income and wealth is quite typical of most economies. What might be the reason?

CHAPTER 33

Work vs. Welfare

The war on poverty is not a struggle simply to support people, to make them dependent on the generosity of others. It is a struggle to give people a chance. It is an effort to allow them to develop and use their capacities, as we have been allowed to develop and use ours, so that they can share, as others share, in the promise of this nation.

—Lyndon B. Johnson, 1964

[Welfare is] a cancer that is destroying those it should succor and threatening society itself.

—Ronald Reagan, 1971

Public policy toward the poor has been plagued by a persistent dilemma. Should we provide poor people with enough income to buy "adequate" nutrition, housing, and clothing? Or should we instead provide them with improved opportunities to earn their own incomes? Quite simply, should we offer welfare or work to low-income families?

It is tempting to respond that *both* welfare and work are needed. In practice, however, the two policy options often conflict. The availability of welfare benefits reduces the need to work. All too often, welfare also lessens the *incentives* to work. On the other hand, not everyone who is poor has the ability or opportunity to earn an adequate income.

The tradeoff between work and welfare is examined in this chapter. Specifically, we address the following questions:

- How many Americans are poor?

- How much assistance do they get from the welfare system?

- Does the welfare system discourage work and so perpetuate the welfare problem?

Our main objective here is to identify the tradeoffs that exist between the goals of providing income assistance to poor people and encouraging their financial independence. As we shall discover, the notion of "helping the poor" is fraught with contradictions. Because of the inevitable tradeoffs between "more welfare" and "more work," there is no easy solution to the "welfare mess."

THE EXTENT OF POVERTY

To be counted as poor in America, an individual or family must be unable to provide for the essential needs of food, shelter, and clothing. Naturally, there is not going to be universal agreement about how little is not enough. Much effort has been expended in trying to establish an acceptable standard of poverty. Large families clearly have greater needs than do smaller families and thus could be regarded as poor even if they had slightly more income than a smaller, nonpoor family. A husband and wife with six children and an annual income of $12,000 are demonstrably in greater financial straits than a childless couple earning $10,000 a year or a college student earning $8,000. In recognition of these differences in need, *the official poverty index is based on a comparison of income and family size.*

Table 33.1 presents the official poverty standards for 1990. A single person was counted as poor in 1990 if he or she received less than $6,559 in income. A family of four, on the other hand, could have received up to $13,167 in 1990 and still been counted among the poor. A family of six with as much as $17,500 was included in the poverty count. Although there is some degree of arbitrariness in these "poverty lines," they are based on the costs of providing a subsistence food budget and other needs. They serve as a convenient yardstick for measuring the dimensions of poverty in the United States. (See World View for much lower Soviet poverty standards.)

Cash vs. In-Kind Income

According to the poverty standards depicted in Table 33.1, we can determine whether a household is poor simply by counting the number of people it contains and tallying up the income it takes in. The latter task is not so simple, however. To begin with, people are reluctant or reveal all their income and are often successful in concealing it. In addition, not all income is received in cash. This problem is particularly acute in low-income families, who receive **in-kind transfers**—that is, direct transfers of goods and services rather than cash. Some of the more important in-kind transfers are food stamps, Medicaid, and housing assistance.

in-kind transfers: Direct transfers of goods and services rather than cash, e.g., food stamps, Medicaid, and housing subsidies.

TABLE 33.1 Federal Poverty Standards, by Family Size, 1990

The official definition of poverty relates current income to the "minimal" needs of a family. The poverty standard varies with family size and age of the household head (over or under age sixty-five). Age distinctions for one- and two-person households are ignored here.

Number of family members	Family income
1	$6,559
2	8,389
3	10,274
4	13,167
5	15,577
6	17,584
7	19,870
8	22,082
9 or more	26,278

Source: U.S. Department of Commerce, Bureau of the Census; updated by author.

W RLD VIEW

COMPARATIVE POVERTY

Soviet Poverty

Roughly one-seventh of the Soviet population was living in poverty in 1988, the Moscow News reported.

The progressive weekly said most of those below the official poverty line were in the strife-torn southern republics. In Tadzhik, bordering Afghanistan, a staggering 59% were below the poverty line, the paper said. The republics with the fewest poor were Latvia, Lithuania and Estonia, where poverty averaged 3.6%.

The report dramatized the plight of the poor by giving case histories of a single mother, an invalid and a family of seven. Accompanying photographs included a shot of an old woman rummaging through garbage for food.

According to the report, 41 million of the Soviet Union's approximately 280 million people have incomes equaling less than $125 a month—the official poverty level—making the poverty rate 14.6%. The 1988 U.S. poverty rate was 13.1%, with the poverty threshold defined as $12,092 per year for a family of four.

The Wall Street Journal, March 15, 1990, p. A11. Reprinted by permission of The Wall Street Journal, © Dow Jones & Company, Inc. (1990). All Rights Reserved.

Food stamps   Food stamps are simply coupons that may be used to purchase food. Food stamps are given to poor families, who use them like regular money at the grocery store. The grocer, in turn, cashes the stamps in at a local bank, which redeems them at face value from the government. Thus food stamps increase the *real* income of poor families by increasing the amount of goods and services they can consume at any given level of *cash* income. In 1990 a poor family of four could receive a food-stamp allotment of up to $331 a month ($3,972 a year). The actual value of the stamps a family gets depends on its needs, as measured by family size and cash income.

Medicaid   Even larger than the food-stamp program is Medicaid, a program that provides medical services to the poor. Under Medicaid, an eligible person can use the services of a doctor or hospital just like anyone else. The difference is that the Medicaid patient simply passes the bill on to the government rather than paying it or submitting it to a private insurance company. Obviously, the amount of benefit a poor family gets from Medicaid depends on the amount of medical treatment it requires. Nearly all public-welfare recipients make some use of Medicaid, as do many others who have incomes just above the poverty standard. The average value of the services received exceeds $1,500 per family.

Housing assistance   In addition to food and medical services, a poor family can receive housing assistance. Such assistance is provided in the form of public housing (usually large housing projects owned and operated by the government) or rent subsidies for privately owned apartments. In either case, recipients are paying less than the market value of their apartments and thus receiving an income transfer. Over 4 million families receive an average rent subsidy of $2,000 a year.

Table 33.2 provides a summary of these major in-kind transfers. In 1989 alone, nearly $90 billion was spent on such in-kind transfers.

TABLE 33.2 In-Kind Transfers, 1989

The government transfers billions of dollars to the poor in the form of in-kind benefits. None of these benefits is counted, however, in Census surveys of the poverty population. Hence the official count of poverty is too high.

Program	Number of recipients (millions)	Average benefit per recipient (per month)	Total annual (billions of dollars)
Food stamps	19.5	$ 52	$12.9
Medicaid	25.0	204	61.2
Housing assistance	4.3	222	11.5
Nutrition programs (including school lunches)	27.7	23	7.6

Source: U.S. Congress, Committee on Ways and Means.

Two Poverty Counts   In view of the amount of in-kind transfers received by the poor, the government measures poverty in two ways. The first measure takes into account only *cash* income; the second includes both cash and in-kind income in deciding who is "poor." Figure 33.1 depicts the "official" poverty counts, using these alternative measures of income. If only cash income is counted, nearly 32 million people—1 out of every 8 Americans—were poor in 1988. In-kind income reduced the number of poor people to about 29 million or less.[1]

POLICY OPTIONS

Even after adjustments for in-kind transfers, there are still lots of poor people in the United States. Moreover, there appears to be a persistent public desire to aid the poor. The question is: What form should that assistance take? Should we encourage poor people to *earn* more income? Or should we simply provide them with income transfers?

[1] There are actually several poverty counts, each incorporating different ways of valuing in-kind transfers. The tabulation here values food stamps and housing subsidies at market value and assigns no value to medical benefits.

**FIGURE 33.1
The Extent of Poverty**

The official poverty count is based on a comparison of estimated need and cash income. By this criterion, over 30 million Americans are poor. If in-kind income (e.g., food stamps) is counted, the poverty population shrinks by 4 million to 5 million people. The number of people counted as poor under either definition varies from year to year as economic conditions change.

Source: U.S. Bureau of the Census.

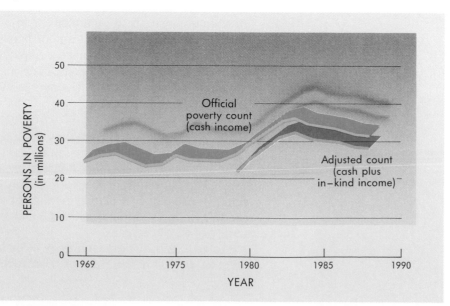

More Work

Encouraging poor people to work is a generally acceptable policy option. There are limits, however, to the effectiveness of this approach. Many poor people are too old or too sick to participate in the labor market. Others have full-time child-care responsibilities that make it difficult to hold a steady job. It is estimated that over 3 million poor people are over age 65 and another 12 million live in single-parent households.

We must also be careful to note that labor-force participation itself is no ticket out of poverty. Approximately 40 percent of the families in poverty participate in the labor force at some point during the year. Over 2 million poor families are headed by individuals who hold full-time jobs all year long.

One reason even **labor-force participants** remain poor is that they have inadequate *human capital*. **Human capital** is the bundle of skills and abilities that a person carries into the labor market. Such capital may include specialized vocational skills, a high level of general education, or simply raw talent. The impact of human capital on employment prospects is evident from our earlier discussion (Chapter 29) of **marginal productivity.** The more human capital an individual has to offer, the greater will be his or her marginal productivity in any given production process. By the same token, individuals with little human capital offer less productivity and are more likely to receive low wages and experience unemployment.

Having the "right" amount of human capital is itself no guarantee of job success, however. Such assets as education merely define the characteristics of the supply of labor. It is equally important to examine the nature of the *demand* for labor. Of particular concern is **cyclical unemployment.** When the demand for labor is inadequate, there aren't enough jobs to go around. Hence even people with "adequate" human capital discover that their earnings are too low.

Discrimination also precludes full use of human capital. Minority groups, women, and the offspring of the poor are generally not given an equal chance to acquire the "right" set of human-capital characteristics. Nor do they have an equal chance to use those characteristics in the labor market. Hence race, sex, and class discrimination have significant impact on both the distribution and the extent of poverty.

Assuring "more work," for the poor, then, isn't a simple task. At the *macroeconomic* level, it requires the attainment of full employment. Professor Harry Johnson summarized the point well: "In the absence of a policy of raising the demand for labor . . . , ad hoc policies for remedying poverty by piecemeal assaults on particular poverty-associated characteristics are likely to prove both ineffective and expensive. The most effective way to attack poverty is to attack unemployment, not the symptoms of it."[2]

At the *microeconomic* level, government policy may focus on structural barriers to success. This means developing human capital and training programs, dismantling discriminatory barriers, and improving the flow of information about job vacancies and workers.

More Welfare

A two-pronged (macro and micro) approach to more jobs would undoubtedly reduce poverty. But some people would remain poor even under the best of employment/human-capital policies. People also object that the provision of education, training, and even jobs is too expensive and too uncertain, and entails too much government intervention. If we really want to eliminate pov-

labor-force participant: Someone who is either employed for pay or actively seeking paid employment.

human capital: The bundle of skills an individual possesses.

marginal productivity: The change in total output that results from employment of one additional unit of input (e.g., one more worker).

cyclical unemployment: Unemployment attributable to a lack of job vacancies—i.e., to an inadequate level of aggregate demand.

[2]Harry G. Johnson, "Poverty and Unemployment," in *The Economics of Poverty,* ed. Burton Weisbrod (Englewood Cliffs, N.J.: Prentice-Hall, 1965), p. 170.

income transfers: Payments to individuals for which no current goods or services are exchanged; e.g., Social Security, welfare, unemployment benefits.

erty, why not just provide more generous **income transfers?** The existing poverty gap—that is, the difference between the cash income poor people now have and what the government says they need—is only $53 billion, or roughly 1 percent of GNP. In-kind transfers reduce this gap even further. It appears, then, that a relatively small increase in income transfers might put an end to poverty.

Unfortunately, eliminating poverty isn't that easy. There are two basic objections to increasing welfare payments:

- Welfare benefits perpetuate dependence, since they don't increase human capital or job opportunities.

- Welfare benefits may *worsen* the poverty problem by discouraging recipients from working.

THE WORK–WELFARE DILEMMA

Suppose we guaranteed everyone an income equal to the 1990 poverty standard of roughly $13,000 for a family of four. Any family earning less than this amount would receive an income-transfer payment to make up the difference, thus eliminating all existing poverty.

A guaranteed income floor like this creates a strong incentive for persons just above the poverty line to leave the labor market. If offered an income transfer, people working at dead-end, low-paying jobs may abandon employment and join the ranks of the nonworking poor. Recall (from Chapter 29) that the decision to work is largely a response to the financial and psychological rewards associated with employment. People in dull, dirty, low-paying jobs get little of either. By quitting their jobs, declaring themselves poor, and accepting a guaranteed income transfer, they would gain much more leisure at little financial or psychological cost.

People already counted as poor would have a similar incentive. By substituting welfare checks for paychecks, they could work less while still maintaining their incomes. Accordingly, ***the provision of income transfers may conflict with established work incentives.*** Both the size of the poverty population and the "need" for income transfers may be sensitive to the particular form our income-transfer policies take.

The AFDC Program

This basic work–welfare dilemma can be illustrated by examining a specific welfare program. Aid to Families with Dependent Children (AFDC) is by far the largest cash welfare program in the United States. It provides monthly benefits to over 11 million poor people, at a cost of $17 billion per year.

As its name implies, AFDC is available only to families with children. Moreover, eligibility is restricted largely to single-parent families. Although all states must also offer AFDC benefits to two-parent families, restrictions on assets and employment keep most two-parent families off welfare. Over 90 percent of AFDC households are female-headed.

The Work-Incentive Problem

Until 1967 a family receiving AFDC payments had very little financial incentive to seek employment. This was not because welfare represented the "good life," however. Welfare benefits have always been below poverty standards. Rather, welfare regulations prohibited a family from improving its standard

In The News

PUBLIC PERCEPTIONS

Breaking Through the Welfare Myths

From remarks by Secretary of Health, Education and Welfare Joseph A. Califano Jr. before the Washington Press Club April 27:

Past debates about welfare have too often focused on pernicious myths about the poor in America. These myths have been perpetrated and perpetuated by ignorance, by incoherent and demagogic discussion by public officials, and inadequate reporting by the media. It is imperative that the forthcoming national debate on welfare not focus on phony issues, false choices or unrealistic expectations that have so clouded past discussions....

Five myths have come to distort public understanding of the poor and welfare.

Myth No. 1—the most pernicious and most widespread—is that people are poor because they don't work and don't want to work, that the welfare rolls are replete with lazy loafers.

The facts are quite different.

Nearly 71 per cent of the 26 million poor Americans are people that we do not normally ask to work: children and young people under 16, the aged, the severely disabled, students or mothers with children under six. Another 19 per cent of the poor population works either full-time or part-time. Thus, 90 per cent of poor Americans either work full- or part-time or are people no civilized society would force to work....

Only 2 per cent of the 26 million poor people even resemble the mythical welfare stereotype—non-aged, non-disabled males who do not work. But census figures indicate that most of this group is between 62 and 64, ill, or looking for work....

Myth No. 2 is that most of the poor are poor for life—that they represent a permanent stagnant group.

The fact is that the poverty poulation is extremely fluid—with sizable numbers of people moving in and out of poverty with remarkable frequency. Each year about 7.5 to 10 million people move above the poverty line, and a like number become poor.

Over the period 1967 through 1972, only 3 per cent of the American population was poor in every one of those 6 years. More than one-fifth—21 per cent—of the American population was poor in at least one of those 6 years....

Most of the poor are poor, not because of some inherent character flaw or personal failing, but because of events they cannot control. And many of them do, in fact, regain higher incomes and climb back out of poverty.

Myth No. 3 is that the poor are mostly black and non-white. The fact is that 69 per cent of the American poor are white.

Myth No. 4 is that the poor don't know how to spend their money. The evidence we have shows that low-income people spend a somewhat greater proportion—about 88 per cent—of their income on food, clothing, housing, medical care and transportation than do people with higher incomes.

Myth No. 5 is that many welfare families receive payments that are far too high. The fact is that in 24 states, the combined benefits of Aid for Families with Dependent Children and food stamps total less than three-fourths of the official poverty-income level.

The Washington Post, May 1, 1977. Reprinted with permission of Joseph A. Califano.

---

of living by working. Such a regulation might appear absurd, but it was simply the consequence of the way in which a family's benefits were calculated.

When a family applies for welfare, it is obliged to report any income at its disposal. A woman with small children, for example, might earn $100 a month by babysitting and ironing for neighbors. Until 1967 the welfare authorities subtracted any such income from the family's needs (as determined by the local welfare department) and provided only the difference. This *residual* method of computing welfare benefits was simply

- $$\frac{\text{Welfare}}{\text{benefit}} = \frac{\text{need}}{\text{standard}} - \text{income}$$

Suppose the welfare authorities concluded that Mrs. Jones and her three children needed $400 a month. Knowing that Mrs. Jones herself could earn $100, they would pay her only $300. This policy distributed welfare funds equitably among needy recipients, but it destroyed all motivation for self-help. When every dollar of income reduces the welfare benefits by a dollar, additional work effort merely substitutes wages for welfare benefits, without increasing the income of the family. Thus a *residual method of computing welfare benefits imposes a 100 percent marginal tax rate.*

Clearly, not many people would be eager to work if they confronted a **marginal tax rate** of 100 percent. In this case, labor provides no net increase in income. Thus a person would have no economic incentive to work.

Improved incentives   This glaring failure of the AFDC program to reinforce work incentives prompted some improvements in the welfare system. In 1967 Congress adopted a new procedure for calculating benefits.

Consider the case of Mrs. Jones again. The welfare department figures she needs $400 per month to feed, clothe, and shelter her family. So if she doesn't work at all, they will give her $4,800 per year in welfare benefits. Now suppose she decides to accept a job as a nurse's aide, working 10 hours a week (500 hours a year) at a wage of $5 an hour. Under the old AFDC system, the welfare department would have noted that she was earning $2,500 per year and reduced her welfare benefit accordingly:

$$\text{Welfare benefit} = \$4{,}800 - \$2{,}500 = \$2{,}300$$

This would have left her with a *total income* of

Welfare benefit	= $2,300
Earnings	= 2,500
Total income	= $4,800

Whether she worked or not, she still ended up with $4,800. In fact, by working she was likely to be worse off, since she would have to pay work expenses (e.g., transportation, clothing, child care).

In 1967 Congress improved work incentives by reducing the 100 percent marginal tax rate implicit in the residual method of computing welfare benefits. First, it recognized that there are certain costs associated with working. To ensure that Mrs. Jones's spendable income is not reduced by the amount of these work-related expenses, the welfare department "disregards" that much income in calculating her welfare benefits. Hence her welfare benefits are not reduced until she is earning at least enough income to cover her work expenses. Thus her welfare benefit is now computed as

$$\bullet \quad \frac{\text{Welfare}}{\text{benefit}} = \frac{\text{need}}{\text{standard}} - (\text{income} - \text{``disregards''})$$

These "disregards" are just like the deductions people take in computing their income-tax liability (Chapter 32). In this case, the "deductions" are used to slow the loss of welfare benefits.

Congress decided to disregard not only legitimate work expenses, but also an *additional* $30 a month plus one-third of any remaining income. This improved the work incentives still more, although it complicated the benefit computation. The new benefit computation became

$$\bullet \quad \frac{\text{Welfare}}{\text{benefit}} = \frac{\text{need}}{\text{standard}} - \left[\text{income} - \left(\frac{\text{work}}{\text{expenses}} + \$30/\text{mo.} + \tfrac{1}{3}\,\text{income}\right)\right]$$

which can also be written as

$$\bullet \quad \frac{\text{Welfare}}{\text{benefit}} = \frac{\text{need}}{\text{standard}} - \tfrac{2}{3}\left[\text{income} - \left(\frac{\text{work}}{\text{expenses}} + \$30/\text{mo.}\right)\right]$$

Two things should be noted at this juncture. First, the calculation of welfare benefits has become very complex. Second, the marginal tax rate *has* been reduced.

Figure 33.2 illustrates these changes. Suppose that Mrs. Jones's work expenses total $200 per month ($2,400 per year). She can now earn this much income without losing any welfare benefits. She can also earn an additional $360 per year without losing any welfare benefits, thanks to the $30-per-month "disregard." Hence Mrs. Jones can now earn as much as $2,760 per year without losing any welfare benefits. In other words, the marginal tax rate on her first $2,760 of earnings is zero. By working 500 hours per year, Mrs. Jones now moves from point *A* to point *C*, keeping $4,800 in welfare benefits *and* $2,500 in wages. This contrasts sharply with the pre-1967 system, which left Mrs. Jones at point *B*, with only $2,300 in welfare benefits and $2,500 in wages.

The welfare department begins to "tax" Mrs. Jones's earnings (reduce her welfare benefits) only after her wages exceed the "disregard" of $360 per year plus work expenses. Even at that point, however, the marginal tax rate is "only" 67 percent, rather than 100 percent. Hence Mrs. Jones has an economic incentive to work more than 500 hours per year. She will get to keep 33 cents out of every additional dollar she earns. The incentive is still modest, to be sure, but nevertheless greater than the one (nothing) that existed earlier.

Suppose now that Mrs. Jones wants to increase her work effort to 20 hours per week. If she worked 1,000 hours per year, she could earn $5,000.

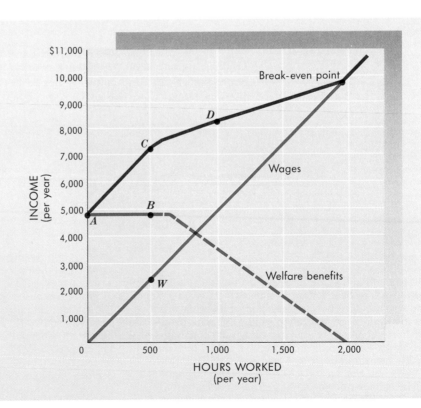

FIGURE 33.2
Work and Welfare: 1967–81 Cash Options

To encourage more work effort, welfare authorities have disregarded some income in computing a family's benefits. Until 1981, when the system was changed again, a welfare mother could earn $30 per month plus enough income to cover work expenses before her benefits were reduced. In this case, wages of $2,500 (point *W*) do not reduce welfare benefits at all, so gross income rises to $7,300 (point *C*). The family stays on welfare until its income exceeds $9,700.

What would happen to her welfare benefits? The formula for calculating her benefit is

Welfare benefit
$$= \$4,800 - \tfrac{2}{3}\text{ (wages in excess of work expenses and disregard)}$$
$$= \$4,800 - \tfrac{2}{3}\,[\$5,000 - (\$2,400 + \$360)]$$
$$= \$4,800 - \$1,493$$
$$= \$3,307$$

Hence by doubling her work effort, Mrs. Jones would move from point C to point D in Figure 33.2. At point D she would receive $5,000 in wages plus $3,307 in welfare benefits. By her own efforts, then, Mrs. Jones is able to increase her family's income.

CONFLICTING WELFARE GOALS

It is comforting to know that Mrs. Jones can increase her family's income from $4,800 to $8,307 a year by working as a nurse's aide 20 hours a week. It might be nicer still if the welfare department would let her keep a little more of the money she earns from making beds, emptying bedpans, and sterilizing bandages. After all, the life of a nurse's aide is not exactly glamorous, and Mrs. Jones obviously needs the money. So why not lower the marginal tax rate from 67 percent to, say, 25 percent, or even zero? Such a reduction in the marginal tax rate would solve two problems. First, it would give Mrs. Jones an even greater incentive to work (see Figure 33.3). Second, it would enable Mrs. Jones to achieve a higher standard of living.

Incentives vs. Costs Unfortunately, a reduction in the marginal tax rate would also increase welfare costs. Suppose that we actually eliminated the marginal tax rate on Mrs. Jones's earnings, thus allowing her to keep everything she earned. Her total income would then rise to $9,800 ($4,800 in benefits plus $5,000 in wages).

In The News

WORK INCENTIVES

Does Welfare Reduce Work?

The potential disincentives associated with cash and in-kind welfare benefits are substantial. Debate continues, however, on just how large an impact these disincentives actually have on the labor supply of poor people. Do welfare recipients work less as a result of high marginal tax rates and income guarantees? If so, by how much?

To answer these questions, the U.S. Department of Health and Human Services funded several income-maintenance experiments. In these experiments, one group of poor people (the "welfare" group) was provided with income guarantees and high marginal tax rates, while an-

other group received nothing. The behavior of both groups was then observed for several years to determine whether the "welfare" group worked less than the "non-welfare" group.

Income-maintenance experiments were conducted in New Jersey; North Carolina; Gary, Indiana; Denver; and Seattle. In general, the results indicate that high marginal tax rates *do* reduce the quantity of labor supplied, just as our theory predicts. In one experiment (Denver and Seattle) the labor supply of husbands declined by 5 percent as a result of income transfers. The labor supply of wives fell by 22 percent.

FIGURE 33.3
The Effects of Welfare on Labor Supply

The availability of welfare benefits reduces the need to work and so shifts the labor supply curve to the left (to S_2). Work effort is further reduced by the high marginal tax rate on wages. In the absence of welfare, q_1 hours of labor would be supplied. With welfare benefits, the quantity supplied drops to q_2. The implied 67 percent tax rate contained in the benefit formula transforms a gross wage of $6 to a *net* wage of $2 per hour. At that wage only q_3 hours of labor are supplied.

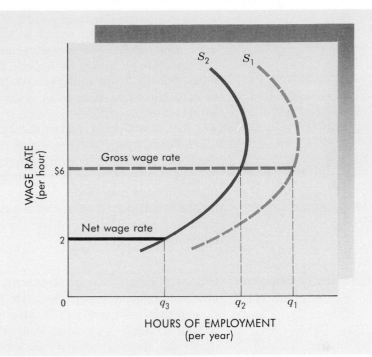

Terrific. But should we still be providing $4,800 in welfare payments to someone who earns $5,000 on her own? How about someone earning $10,000? $20,000? Where should we draw the line? Clearly, ***if we don't impose a marginal tax rate at some point, everyone will be eligible for full welfare benefits.***

While the thought of giving everyone a welfare check might sound like a great idea, it would turn out to be incredibly expensive. In the end, we would have to take those checks back, in the form of increased taxes, in order to pay for the vastly expanded program. We must recognize, then, a basic dilemma:

- Low marginal tax rates encourage more work effort but make more people eligible for welfare.

- High marginal tax rates discourage work effort but make fewer people eligible for welfare.

The conflict between work incentives and the desire to limit welfare costs and eligibility can be summarized in a neat little equation:

- $$\text{Break-even level of income} = \frac{\text{basic benefits}}{\text{marginal tax rate}} + \text{earnings disregards}$$

The break-even level of income is the amount of income a person can earn before losing all welfare benefits. In Mrs. Jones's case, the annual income disregard was $2,760 ($2,400 for work expenses plus $30 per month) and the basic welfare benefit was $4,800 per year. Hence she could earn as much as $9,700 per year before losing all her welfare benefits. In other words, she could virtually hold a full-time job and still collect some welfare benefits. Thus low marginal tax rates and earnings disregards encourage work but make it difficult to get completely off welfare.

If the marginal tax rate were 100 percent, as under the pre-1967 system, the break-even point would be $4,800 ($4,800 ÷ 1.00). In that case, people who earned $4,800 on their own would get no assistance from welfare. Fewer people would be eligible for welfare, but those who drew benefits would have no incentive to work. Under our rejected proposal to lower marginal tax rates to zero, the break-even point would rise to infinity ($4,800 ÷ 0), and we would all be on welfare.

As this arithmetic makes apparent, ***there is a basic conflict between work incentives (low marginal tax rates) and welfare containment (smaller welfare rolls and outlays).*** We can achieve a lower break-even level of income (less welfare eligibility) only by sacrificing low marginal tax rates, earnings disregards, or higher income floors. Hence welfare costs can be minimized only if we sacrifice income provision or work incentives. The same problems affect Social Security benefits and the work decisions of older individuals (see In the News).

The Family Support Act of 1988

President Reagan was among those who were unhappy with the tradeoffs inherent in the welfare system. He thought that welfare rules discouraged poor people from working. He also felt that the break-even level of income was far too high. A welfare recipient could easily end up with more income (cash and in-kind benefits) than a person who was working. Moreover, the welfare recipient could enjoy an income in excess of the poverty standard. Reagan argued that this was inequitable and wasteful. He proposed to focus the welfare system more narrowly on the "truly needy." He also sought to encourage people to move off welfare and into jobs.

In 1981 the Reagan administration succeeded in changing the rules for welfare eligibility and benefits. The Reagan reforms sacrificed work incentives for stricter limits on welfare caseloads. The 100 percent marginal tax rate was

In The News

WORK INCENTIVES

Older Workers: "It Still Doesn't Pay to Work"

People used to die with their boots on. Nowadays, people are more likely to die with a Social Security check in their bank account.

Prior to the Social Security Act of 1934, older people had to support themselves by working or drawing on their savings, their children, or charity. Today things are different. The federal government provides Social Security benefits to just about every older person. With benefits for a retired couple reaching as high as $1,000 per month, there is less pressure to continue working. Most older people retire as soon as they become eligible for Social Security benefits.

Those who want to continue working quickly conclude that employment no longer pays. In 1989 older workers could earn only $8,880 and still receive all their Social Security benefits. If they earned more, the government reduced their Social Security benefits by $1 for every $2 of wages. Social Security thus "taxed" wages at a marginal rate of 50 percent. On top of that, older workers also had to pay the Social Security payroll tax (7.65 percent) and all federal, state, and local taxes. When all is said and done, taxes took 70 percent or more of an older worker's paycheck.

In 1990 the implicit tax rate on Social Security benefits was reduced to $33\frac{1}{3}$ percent. The reduced "tax" rate gives older workers more incentive to continue working. But the total tax bite still approaches 60 percent. Small wonder that older people still choose to retire rather than keep working.

reintroduced and earnings disregards were reduced. A ceiling on gross income was also introduced so that people could not achieve high break-even levels of income.

Workfare

To overcome the disincentive features of the new welfare rules, President Reagan proposed that the "carrot" of low marginal tax rates be replaced by the "stick" of compulsory employment. The administration proposed that welfare recipients be required to "work off" their benefits by doing community-service work. With such compulsory **workfare,** a welfare recipient could not choose between some work and no work. Rather, the choice would be between community service (at the minimum wage) and any private-sector job that was available. In this case, the issue of work incentives, as measured by marginal tax rates, would be secondary.

workfare: Mandatory community-service program for welfare recipients.

Initially, Congress refused to adopt a national workfare plan but did allow states to experiment with their own versions of workfare. Between 1981 and 1988 nearly two-thirds of the states experimented with mandatory community-service programs. Although most of these experiments were quite limited, they did have some positive results. The workfare program did reduce welfare caseloads somewhat. Moreover, both participants and their communities claimed to be satisfied with the nature of the work and the fairness of the participation rules.

EDfare

Although the workfare concept met with some success, critics argued that it was more punitive than productive. If the goal is to foster self-help, they proposed to require education and training activities, rather than mandatory community service. A central goal is to compel recipients to develop their human capital by participating in education and training programs. These so-called EDfare proposals broaden the choice of activities but still *require* the recipient to participate in some educational or work program as a condition for receiving benefits.

Congress concluded the decade of welfare experimentation with a legislative compromise. The Family Support Act of 1988 shifted the focus of welfare policy to the obligations of the poor to help themselves. By 1995 at least 20 percent of adult AFDC recipients in each state must be enrolled in some kind of self-help program (EDfare). Moreover, at least one parent in two-parent welfare families must perform sixteen hours of community service (workfare) per week. These changes, together with the earlier tightening of the benefit formula, made self-help more of an obligation than an incentive.

SUMMARY

- On the basis of cash incomes, approximately 30 million people are officially counted as poor. In-kind transfers, however, substantially reduce the true poverty count.

- Welfare benefits are provided to many, but not all, poor people. Cash benefits are largely restricted to female-headed families with children.

- A reduction in welfare benefits that occurs when a recipient takes a job is an implicit tax. The rate at which welfare benefits are reduced when recipients earn wages represents the marginal tax rate.

• Marginal tax rates illustrate the work–welfare dilemma. High tax rates discourage work but restrict welfare eligibility. Low tax rates encourage work but enlarge the potential welfare population.

• The 1981 welfare reforms restricted welfare eligibility but also lessened work incentives. Families must be more impoverished to get welfare, and they lose eligibility sooner after securing employment.

• Compulsory work and training programs sidestep the work-incentive issue. Workfare and EDfare programs *require* welfare recipients to perform work or develop human capital.

Terms to Remember   Define the following terms:

in-kind transfers	cyclical unemployment
labor-force participant	income transfers
human capital	marginal tax rate
marginal productivity	workfare

Questions for Discussion

1. Negative income tax (NIT) plans are distinguished by their promise of universal eligibility, based only on income standards (without regard for "employability" or other demographic factors). How would such plans differ from our current welfare system?

2. Three goals are associated with welfare: adequacy, work incentives, and cost minimization. What compromise of these three welfare goals do you regard as most appropriate? How high would you set marginal tax rates?

3. Would it be wise to eliminate the Social Security "earnings test" by eliminating the benefit-reduction penalty (see In the News, p. 818)? What would we gain? What would we lose?

4. Are marginal tax rates irrelevant when workfare or EDfare requirements exist?

Problem

1. Using the rules of the post-1981 (Reagan) welfare system, complete the following table relating income to hours worked. Assume the welfare recipient can earn $6 per hour and receives $1,000 each of Medicaid, food stamps, and housing aid so long as she is on welfare. She loses Medicaid when welfare benefits cease, and her food stamp benefits are reduced by 30 cents for every wage dollar received.

Hours worked	Wages	Cash welfare benefits	Total cash income	In-kind benefits	Total real income
0					
500					
1,000					
2,000					

Financial Markets

*I*n 1987 the brokerage firm of Drexel Burnham Lambert paid Michael Milken, its top bond trader, $550 million—more than the president of the United States and all the members of the United States Congress are paid for ten *years* of service. For Milken, that one year's income worked out to roughly $250,000 per *hour!*

To most people, the incomes Wall Street traders, investment bankers, and stockbrokers earn are incomprehensible. They inspire not only envy, but also curiosity. What could anyone *do* to earn so much income? What is "produced" by Wall Street? Do Wall Streeters contribute in any way to the real economy? Or are they just members of a select club, playing a get-rich-quick game? How do the intricacies of Wall Street relate to the reality of Main Street?

Government regulators have been asking the same kinds of questions. Indeed, Milken was later convicted for illegal insider trading. The government has also intervened to restrict massive "buyouts" of major corporations and to monitor more closely trading practices in the stock, bond, and commodity markets.

The objective of this chapter is to see how financial markets work. What is traded in these markets and how does it affect the basic issues of WHAT, HOW, and FOR WHOM to produce? These specific questions are addressed:

- How do financial markets relate to the "real" product and resource markets?

- What causes stock, bond, and commodity prices to fluctuate?

- What risks does "insider" trading pose for the economy?

To answer these questions, we look at three major financial markets: the stock market, the bond market, and the futures market (where everything from frozen pork bellies to U.S. Treasury bonds are traded).

THE ROLE OF FINANCIAL MARKETS

A central question for every economy is WHAT to produce. Suppose you came up with a particular answer. Suppose, in particular, that you invented a laser scanner that could detect any and all mechanical, structural, or electrical defects in airplanes. On the basis of extensive tests, you are convinced that the Air Scanner, as you call it, will eliminate all risk of mechanically caused airline accidents.

821

Clearly, this idea has great potential to save lives and reduce the anxieties of travelers. It also might make you a millionaire. But there are still a few steps that must be taken to make your dream a reality. The first obstacle is resources. To produce Air Scanners you need a manufacturing plant, workers, and materials. You will also want to obtain a patent to protect your invention from would-be competitors. Additionally, you will need a research and development lab for continuous testing and improvement as well as a marketing department to demonstrate and sell the scanners.

Resource Allocation

From a broader economic perspective, what you have here is a resource allocation problem. At present, all of society's land, labor, and capital are devoted to the production of other goods and services. What you have to do is acquire some of these resources for the production of Air Scanners. This basic reallocation dilemma is defined in terms of *real* resources—the land, labor, and **capital** that can actually *produce* Air Scanners. Your immediate problem, however, is defined in far simpler terms—hard cash. To acquire real resources, you must have some means of payment.

capital: Goods produced for use in producing other goods, e.g., machinery, factory.

Financial Intermediaries

For those without a great inheritance, the problem of raising start-up funds boils down to two options: either borrowing the necessary funds or inviting other people to invest in the new venture. But how do you pursue these options? You could ask your relatives and friends for a loan, or even go door-to-door in the neighborhood. This method of raising funds is not likely to achieve your goals, however, unless you have friends and relatives who are both rich and generous.

Fortunately for you and other budding entrepreneurs, most households save some fraction of their income. This flow of **saving** creates an enormous pool of loanable funds. In 1990 alone, American households saved over $150 billion and had accumulated wealth measured in trillions of dollars. Your problem is figuring out how to tap that pool to get enough funds to start building Air Scanners.

saving: That part of disposable income not spent on current consumption; disposable income less consumption.

Access to the economy's savings is provided by **financial intermediaries**, institutions that bring savers and dissavers together. The income set aside by savers may be deposited in banks, used to purchase stocks and bonds, or placed with other financial institutions (e.g., firms managing retirement or pension plans, insurance companies). All of these financial intermediaries help put those savings back into the circular flow. Specifically, *the function of financial intermediaries is to transfer income from savers to dissavers.* They do this by lending or investing the savings entrusted to them.

financial intermediary: Institution (e.g., bank, stock market) that makes savings available to dissavers (e.g., investors).

Financial intermediaries produce several important services. Financial intermediaries greatly reduce the cost of locating loanable funds. Their pools of savings offer a clear economy of scale compared to the alternative of door-to-door solicitations. Financial intermediaries also reduce the cost to savers of finding suitable lending or investment opportunities. Few individuals have the time, resources, or interest to search for the best loans or investments. With huge pools of amassed savings, however, financial intermediaries have the incentive to acquire and analyze information on lending and investment opportunities. Hence *financial intermediaries reduce search and information costs* in the financial markets. In so doing, they make the allocation of resources more efficient.

The pivotal role played by financial intermediaries in the allocation of society's resources is illustrated in Figure 34.1. Consumers, businesses, and

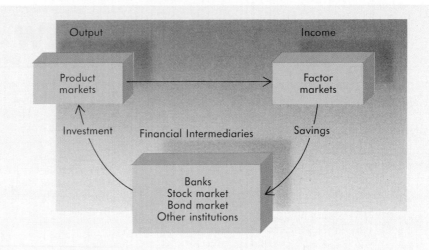

**FIGURE 34.1
Financial Intermediaries**

The central purpose of financial markets is to help channel the savings of consumers and businesses into productive investments. A variety of financial intermediaries, including bankers, bond dealers, and stockbrokers, participate in this transfer of purchasing power.

even some government agencies generate savings. Foreigners also hold savings. Financial intermediaries make these idle funds available to investors, that is, people who want to manufacture Air Scanners, build airplanes, or breed catfish. With these funds, potential investors acquire tangible resources (e.g., capital) and change the mix of output.

Although financial intermediaries make the job of acquiring start-up funds a lot easier, there is no guarantee that you will acquire the funds you need. You still have to convince the intermediaries to allocate some of their financial resources to your project. They will have to be convinced that your idea is sound and that Air Scanners can generate a profit. And they will want to protect themselves against calamitous losses in case the whole idea flops. You will get your chance to build Air Scanners only if you get their financial backing.

Risk Management

Your chances of getting funds for Air Scanners are considerably increased by the ability of financial intermediaries to spread the risks of many ventures. They can afford to back a risky project like Air Scanners because they also undertake many less risky projects. By diversifying their portfolios, they can select any degree of *average* risk they prefer.

This ability to manage the risks of failure increases the potential for new discoveries and products. Columbus might never have discovered America if the entire financial risk of the expedition had to be borne by Queen Isabella (see World View). Similarly, Air Scanners might never be produced if the person who invented them had to bear all the risks of production or if individual investors were forced to put all their eggs in one basket. By spreading the risks, each participant can assume only as much risk as he or she desires.

THE STOCK MARKET

Stock markets are one of the institutions that serve as financial intermediaries. Stock markets help channel savings into investment and permit individuals to manage the risks of diverse assets. Although most people immediately think of Wall Street when they hear "stock exchange," the stock market is highly dispersed. The New York Stock Exchange is a specific building (11 Wall Street

W🌐RLD VIEW

RISK MANAGEMENT

Financing Columbus

Columbus might never have discovered America were it not for financial intermediaries. He did not have enough wealth to pay for the expedition himself. For several years he tried to convince King Ferdinand of Spain to provide the necessary funds. But the king had other commitments and did not want to risk so much wealth on a single venture. Twice he turned Columbus down.

Genoese merchant bankers in Seville came to Columbus's rescue. Convinced that Columbus's "enterprise of the Indies" might bring back "pearls, precious stones, gold, silver, spiceries," and other valuable merchandise,

they guaranteed repayment of the funds granted to Columbus. With that guarantee in hand, the Duke of Medina Sidonia in April 1492 offered to lend 1,000 maravedis (about $25,000 in 1990 dollars) to Queen Isabella for the purpose of funding Columbus's expedition. With no personal financial risk, King Ferdinand then agreed to the proposal and granted Columbus the funds and authority for a royal expedition. Columbus himself was granted one-tenth of any profits, with an option to gain another eighth share of future voyages if he invested a proportionate amount.

Gerald R. Crone, *The Discovery of America* (London: Hamish Hamilton, 1969).

---

in New York City) where lots of trading takes place. But there are other stock exchanges in the United States and over a hundred additional exchanges in other countries (see World View, p. 825). In addition to these physical locations, traders may contact each other in the "over-the-counter" markets, that is, telephone and computer networks that facilitate trading without any central location.

Corporate Ownership

What people buy and sell on the stock exchanges are ownership shares of corporations. Recall that a business may take one of three legal forms, namely:

- proprietorship
- partnership
- corporation

corporation: A business organization having a continuous existence independent of its members (owners) and power and liabilities distinct from those of its members.

corporate stock: Shares of ownership in a corporation.

As noted in Chapter 25, a **corporation** tends to be the largest type of enterprise, with average asset values measured in millions of dollars.

The ownership of a corporation is defined in terms of stock shares. Each share of **corporate stock** represents partial ownership of the business. IBM, for example, has 585 million shares of stock outstanding (i.e., held by the public). Hence each share of IBM stock represents 1/585,000,000 of the IBM Corporation. Potentially, that means that as many as 585 million people own IBM. In reality, however, individuals own hundreds of shares and institutions own thousands of shares. Indeed, some of the largest pension funds in America own over a *million* shares of IBM.

People holding shares of IBM and other corporations hope to realize a financial gain from these assets. Just as a business's primary goal is to make profits, the primary motivation for holding stock is to share in the profits of that business. As part owners, shareholders are entitled to any profits the corporation makes. In 1989, for example, IBM had a profit of $5.3 billion. This profit accrued to IBM owners, the people holding the 585 million shares of common stock. Thus each share of IBM implicitly earned a profit of $9.05.

W🌐RLD VIEW

MARKETS

The Global Stock Market

Want to play the stock markets? At last count, there were 115 exchanges operating in the 26 countries listed here. There are 17 different exchanges in the United States alone and 15 in India. International investors move funds from one market to another with an electronic signal. The interplay of these global markets enhances efficiency by increasing the sources of funds and investment opportunities.

The following list indicates the number of exchanges in each country and the location of the largest exchanges.

Australia (6)
  Sydney, Melbourne
Brazil (9)
  São Paulo, Rio de Janeiro
Canada (5)
  Toronto, Montreal
Denmark (1)
  Copenhagen
France (7)
  Paris
West Germany (8)
  Frankfurt, Düsseldorf
Hong Kong (1)
India (15)
  Bombay, Calcutta
Indonesia (1)
  Jakarta

Ireland (1)
  Dublin
Italy (10)
  Milan, Rome
Japan (8)
  Tokyo, Osaka
South Korea (1)
  Seoul
Luxembourg (1)
Malaysia (1)
  Kuala Lumpur
Netherlands (1)
  Amsterdam
New Zealand (4)
  Auckland, Wellington
Portugal (2)
  Lisbon, Oporto
Singapore (1)

South Africa (1)
  Johannesburg
Spain (4)
  Madrid, Barcelona
Sweden (1)
  Stockholm
Switzerland (7)
  Zurich, Geneva
Taiwan (1)
  Taipei
United Kingdon (1)
  London
United States (17)
  New York (New York and American exchanges), Chicago (Midwest), San Francisco (Pacific), Philadelphia

Source: Spicer & Oppenheim International, *Guide to Securities Markets Around the World* (New York: Wiley, 1988).

Dividends   Shareholders do not necessarily receive their share of the company's profits in cash. The corporation may wish to use some of the profits for investment in new plant or equipment. It may also want to retain some of the profits for operational needs or unforeseen contingencies. ***The corporation may choose to retain earnings or pay them out to shareholders as* dividends.** Any profits not paid out to shareholders are referred to as *retained earnings.* Thus

dividend: Amount of corporate profits paid out to each share of stock.

- Dividends = corporate profits − retained earnings

In 1989 IBM paid quarterly dividends amounting to $4.84 for the year. Thus shareholders received about 53 percent of their accrued profits in dividend checks; the rest of the $9.05 per-share profit was retained by IBM for future investment.

Capital gains   If IBM invests its retained earnings wisely, the corporation may reap even larger profits in the future. As the company grows and prospers, each share of ownership may become more valuable. This will be reflected in higher market prices for shares of IBM stock. These increases represent a **capital gain** for shareholders. Capital gains directly increase shareholder wealth.

There are two motivations for buying and holding stocks—the expectation of dividends and anticipated capital gains. If a stock paid no

capital gain: An increase in the market value of an asset.

dividends and had no prospects for price appreciation (i.e., capital gain), you would be better advised to hold your savings in a different form (e.g., another stock or maybe an interest-earning bank account).

Initial Public Offering

initial public offering (IPO): The first issuance (sale) to the general public of stock in a corporation.

When a corporation is formed, its future sales and profits are uncertain. When shares are *first* offered to the public, the seller is the company itself. By "going public," the corporation seeks to raise funds for investment and growth. A true "start-up" company like Air Scanners may have nothing more than a good idea, a couple of dedicated employees, and Big Plans. To fund these plans, it sells shares of itself in an **initial public offering (IPO).** The individuals who buy the newly issued stock are putting their savings directly into the corporation's accounts.[1] As new owners, they stand to profit from the corporation's business or take their lumps if the company fails. Because the company is incorporated, these new owners are at risk only for however much money they pay for their shares.

The number of shares initially offered by a corporation is determined when the firm is first incorporated. Suppose, for example, that you opted to incorporate your venture and created Air Scanners, Inc. (ASI). When filing the incorporation papers with the Securities and Exchange Commission, you have to designate how many shares of ownership will exist. The owners of these shares will own the company. In the process of going public, the company must also set a price for each share of stock.

In reality, no one knows exactly what the demand curve for the new stock looks like. Typically, the company's managers will rely on investment bankers to "sound out" potential buyers and suggest an initial price for the stock. In effect, the company and its bankers are trying to discern the position of the demand curve for the new issue. Figure 34.2 simplifies this job by constructing a hypothetical demand curve. According to this curve, the public will be willing and able to buy 100,000 shares of your new venture for $20 a share. Hence the company will offer 100,000 shares of ASI to the public at that price. That will bring $2 million (less fees for bankers, lawyers, etc.) into the company's coffers.

The Walt Disney Company used the same financial mechanisms to raise nearly $1 billion for building the new Euro Disneyland near Paris (see World View, p. 827). Once the IPO is sold, a corporation can begin acquiring land, labor, and capital to start production of Air Scanners, Disneyland rides, or any other output. In all such instances, the IPO facilitates the process of resource reallocation. Even managers in the Soviet Union have come to recognize how important stock markets are for this basic economic function (see World View, p. 828).

The After Market

Once a stock has been sold to the public, the corporation no longer participates in continuing stock trades. In the so-called after (secondary) market (e.g., the New York Stock Exchange) the shares in the company are traded between members of the general public. When Mr. Dow bought ASI stock in the initial offering for $20, the corporation was the seller and received the proceeds of the transaction. If Mr. Dow later sells his shares to Ms. Jones, the company gets nothing more: ownership of the shares simply passes from Mr.

[1]In reality, some of the initial proceeds will go to stockbrokers and investment bankers as compensation for their services as financial intermediaries. The entrepreneur who started the company, other company employees, and any venture capitalists who helped fund the company before the public offering may also get some of the IPO receipts by selling shares they acquired before the company went public. Venture capitalists are discussed in Chapter 31.

FIGURE 34.2
Pricing an Initial Offering

A company "goes public" by selling shares of itself. The company's objective in the Initial Public Offering (IPO) is to maximize proceeds of the stock sale. This also maximizes the market value of the company. In this case, $20 is the highest price the public is willing and able to pay for 100,000 shares. If the shares were offered at a higher price (e.g., $30), the company would not sell all the stock it offered, and its total proceeds would be lower. If the price was set below $20 (e.g., point *B*), those individuals lucky enough to get the stock would be able to resell it at the higher equilibrium price (point *C*).

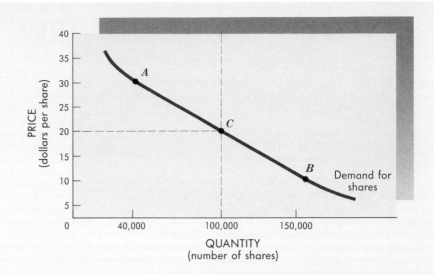

Dow to Ms. Jones. Virtually all of the trading that takes place on the major stock exchanges consists of such "after-market" transactions.

Although the corporation does not participate in these after-market transactions, it does have an indirect interest in their outcome. If the price of its stock rises, the market value of the corporation increases. A higher stock

W RLD VIEW

AN IPO

Euro Disney's IPO

In 1988 the Walt Disney Company began transforming 4,800 acres of sugar beet farmland near Paris into a gigantic theme park and resort. This new "Euro Disneyland," scheduled to open in 1992, will cost roughly $3 billion to develop.

To pay for the new park, Disney could have used its own funds, borrowed funds, or issued new stock. The company used all three financing mechanisms. For the equity part of the financing the company offered 51 percent of the newly founded corporation to European investors. The Walt Disney Company retained a 49 percent share of Euro Disneyland.

Although a Disneyland near Paris might seem like a great idea, it does entail risks. Mickey Mouse would have to master several languages to attract vacationers from all over Europe. The weather, too, is a problem: Paris

does not have nearly as many warm, sunny days as Orlando or Anaheim. There is also competition from other theme parks, at least three of them in France already.

On the other hand, Disneylands in Orlando, Anaheim, and Tokyo have made huge profits. And the Disney Company enjoys instant recognition and proven marketing success. The company itself emphasized these points in a ten-city promotion tour and advertisements in thirty-five European newspapers.

European investors apparently decided that potential profits outweighed the risks. In October 1989 the initial public offering (IPO) of Euro Disneyland sold out quickly. The shares offered were sold at 72 francs (approximately $11.50) each, raising over $1 billion in equity financing. Shares in Euro Disneyland now trade on the Paris and London stock exchanges and can be purchased in U.S. over-the-counter markets.

W☼RLD VIEW

RESOURCE ALLOCATION

Soviet Shareholders May Get the Vote

First political protest. Then McDonald's. Now the Soviet Union may be opening the door on yet another hallmark of democracy and free enterprise: shareholder rights.

Nikolai Bekh, director of Kamaz, the Soviet Union's biggest maker of heavy trucks, told *Pravda* Monday that Kamaz can compete in world markets—but must raise 6 billion rubles ($600 million at unofficial exchange rates) to modernize. Getting it from Moscow is out of the question, he told the Communist Party daily: "Only one hope remains—the financial market."

Kamaz wants to raise money by selling stock—a 49% stake, to be exact. And to entice buyers, it proposes giving stockholders a say in running the company and part of the profits.

That would be a first. Soviet enterprises have been permitted to issue shares since 1988, primarily to plant workers. And foreigners are allowed to own up to 49% of Soviet joint ventures. But neither worker-owners nor foreign investor-owners are allowed any voice in management or any claim to dividends.

—Ed Gregory

USA Today, May 22, 1990, p. B1. Copyright © 1990 USA TODAY. Excerpted with permission.

---

price signals that market participants place high value on the assets, products, and/or management of the company. This will make it easier for the company to raise additional funds, either by borrowing funds or by issuing new stock. Rising stock prices also make shareholders (the owners) more disposed to grant the company's managers (the employees) higher salaries and bonuses. Hence *changes in the price of the company's stock will have a continuing impact on resource allocation by making it more or less difficult to attract additional land, labor, and capital.*

Expectations

What makes stock prices rise or fall is the interplay of demand and supply in the financial markets. As in other markets, prices tend to be stable until either demand or supply shifts. If demand for the stock increases—that is, a rightward *shift in demand* occurs—the stock's price will tend to rise (*ceteris paribus*). Similarly, a leftward shift in supply—an increasing reluctance of owners to sell—would push the stock's price higher.

The determinants of demand for a stock are essentially the same as those for real goods and services:

- Tastes
- Income
- Other goods
- Expectations

portfolio decision: The choice of how (where) to hold idle funds.

In this case, "other goods" refers to alternative uses of one's funds, earlier defined as the *opportunity cost* of buying this stock. A person with available savings confronts a continuing **portfolio decision**, i.e., choices about where to place available funds. Leaving the funds in a bank or money-market account ensures a steady accumulation of interest payments. By buying stocks instead, one forsakes those interest payments. That forgone interest may be viewed as the opportunity cost of purchasing stocks.

Individuals who buy newly issued Air Scanner stock evidently expect to earn a higher return in ASI than they would in interest-bearing deposits or other stocks. Since ASI has no output, sales, or profits yet, that decision must be based solely on *expectations*. All of the people who buy ASI initially *anticipate* future sales and profit. They *expect* to benefit from *future* dividends and capital gains.

Expectations are so important to portfolio decisions that they also explain most changes in stock prices. Specifically, ***changes in expectations imply shifts in supply and demand for a company's stock.*** The increased demand illustrated in Figure 34.3 reflects increased expectations for the IBM Corporation after it announced substantial cost-cutting initiatives on December 4, 1989. The resulting increase in the price of IBM stock acted as a market signal that IBM was expected to become more profitable after these efforts.

Table 34.1 shows what IBM's price rise looked like in the newspaper. Notice that IBM paid a dividend of $4.84 to its shareholders and was earning a profit of $9.02 per share at the time it announced its cost cuts. In the short run, then, shareholders were paying dearly for IBM stock in terms of foregone income since the stock's yield (4.9 percent) was below even the interest rate on passbook savings accounts. However, *expectations* of future profits were strong enough to spur purchases of IBM stock.

The demand for IBM stock would also shift if other determinants of demand changed. A general decline in interest rates, for example, would reduce the opportunity cost of holding stocks. The *relative* return on stocks (e.g., their dividend payouts) rises when interest rates decline. Hence the demand for IBM and all other stocks would tend to shift rightward when interest rates fall.

FIGURE 34.3
Shifts Change Stock Prices

In December 1989 the IBM Corporation announced that it was reducing its work force by 10,000 people and undertaking other cost–cutting moves. Market participants quickly recognized that these cost reductions would increase IBM's profits. Accordingly, they sought to share in the anticipated profits by buying IBM stock. This increased demand pushed the price of IBM stock up by 2 points in one day. That increase raised the value of the IBM Corporation by over $1 billion ($2 × 585 million shares). A leftward shift of supply—an increased reluctance to sell—could also increase share prices. (Note: Once a stock is trading in the after market, its supply curve is no longer vertical. Shareholders will offer a larger number of shares only at higher share prices.)

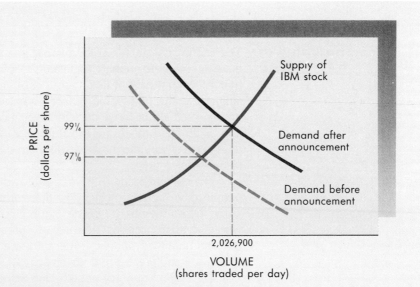

TABLE 34.1 Reading Stock Quotes

The financial pages of the daily newspaper summarize the trading activity in corporate stocks. The following quotation summarizes trading in IBM Corporation at the New York Stock Exchange on December 4, 1989:

| 52-Weeks | | | | | | | Vol | | | | Net |
Hi	Lo	Stock	Sym	Div	Yld%	PE	100s	HI	Lo	Close	Chg
130⅞	96	IBM	IBM	4.84	4.9	11	20269	99½	97⅜	99¼	+2⅛

The information provided by this quotation includes:

52-Weeks Hi and Lo: The highest and lowest prices paid for a share of IBM stock in the previous year.

Stock: The name of the corporation whose shares are being traded.

Sym: The symbol used as a shorthand description for the stock.

Div: A dividend is the amount of profit paid out by the corporation in the preceding year for each share of stock. In 1989 IBM paid a dividend of $4.84 for each share of stock.

Yld%: The yield is the dividend paid per share divided by the price of a share. in this case the yield is $4.84 ÷ 99.25, or 4.9 percent.

PE: The price of the stock (P) divided by the earnings (profit) per share (E). This indicates how much a purchaser is effectively paying for each dollar of profits. IBM has a profit per share of $99.25 ÷ 11, or $9.02. Just over half of this profit was paid out in dividends.

Vol 100s: The number of shares traded in hundreds. Over 2 million shares of IBM were bought and sold on the previous day.

Hi: The highest price paid for IBM stock on the previous day.

Lo: The lowest price paid for IBM stock on the previous day.

Close: The price paid for IBM stock in the last trade of the day as the market was closing.

Net Chg: The change in the closing price yesterday vs. the previous day's closing price. In one day IBM stock rose in price by $2.125 per share. With 585 million shares outstanding, this price rise increased the market value of IBM over $1 billion.

The Value of Information

The abrupt rise in the price of IBM stock highlights a critical dimension of financial markets, namely, the value of information. In hindsight, it is obvious that information about IBM's new cost-cutting moves had a high value. In that single day, the total value of IBM's stock increased over $1 billion. Whoever first learned about those decisions was best positioned to buy the stock early and profit from this jump in value. Likewise, those who can correctly anticipate interest-rate movements will be in the best position to reap capital gains in the stock market.

The evident value of information raises the question of access. Do some people have better information than others? Do they get their information fairly? Or do they have "inside" sources (e.g., company scientists, managers) who give them preferential access to information? If so, these insiders would have an unfair advantage in the marketplace and could alter the distribution of income and wealth in their favor.

The value of information also explains the demand for information services. People pay hundreds and even thousands of dollars for newsletters, wire services, and on-line computer services that provide up-to-date information on companies and markets. They also pay for the services of investment bankers, advisers, and brokers to help keep them informed. These services help disseminate information quickly, thereby helping financial markets operate efficiently (i.e., providing the best possible "signal" of changing resource values).

Booms and Busts If stock markets are so efficient at computing the present value of future profits, why does the entire market make abrupt moves every so often? The Dow Jones industrial average (see Table 34.2) "crashed" on October 17, 1987, falling 504 points. This represented a 24 percent decline in the value of the average stock. In October 1989 (on Friday the thirteenth, no less!) the Dow fell 190 points. Do these abrupt stock-market moves have anything to do with our careful computations of expected profits or the underlying problem of resource allocation?

Fundamentally, the same factors that determine the price of a single stock influence the broader stock-market averages as well. An increase in interest rates, for example, raises the opportunity cost of holding stocks. Hence higher interest rates should cause stock prices to fall, *ceteris paribus*. Stocks might decline even further if higher interest rates are expected to curtail investment and consumption, thus reducing future sales and profits. Such a double whammy can cause the whole stock market to tumble.

Other factors also affect the relative desirability of holding stock. Congressional budget and deficit decisions, monetary policy, consumer confidence, business investment plans, international trade patterns, and new inventions are just a few of the factors that may alter present and future profits. These ***broad changes in the economic outlook will tend to push all stock prices up or down at the same time.***

Broad changes in the economic outlook, however, seldom occur overnight. Moreover, these changes are rarely of a magnitude that could precipitate a stock-market boom or bust. In reality, the stock market often changes more abruptly than the economic outlook. These exaggerated movements in the stock market are caused by sudden and widespread changes in expectations. Keep in mind that the value of a stock depends on anticipated *future* profits and expectations for interest rates and the economic outlook. No ele-

---

TABLE 34.2 Stock-Market Averages

Over 1,600 stocks are listed (traded) on the New York Stock Exchange and many times that number are traded in other stock markets. To gauge changes in so many stocks, people refer to various indices, like the Dow Jones industrial average. The "Dow" and similar indices make it easier to keep track of the market's ups and downs. Some of the most frequently quoted indices are

Dow Jones
  Industrial average An arithmetic average of the prices of 30 "blue chip" industrial stocks traded on the New York Stock Exchange (NYSE).
  Transportation average An average of 20 transportation stocks traded on the NYSE.
  Utilities average An average of 15 utility stocks traded on the NYSE.
S&P 500 An index compiled by Standard and Poor's of 500 stocks drawn from major stock exchanges as well as over-the-counter stocks. The S&P 500 includes 400 industrial companies, 40 utilities, 20 transportation companies, and 40 financial institutions.
New York Stock Exchange composite index This "Big Board" index includes all 1,600-plus stocks traded on the NYSE.
Nikkei index An index of 225 stocks traded on the Tokyo stock market.

In The News

EARLY TRADING

Origins of the New York Stock Exchange

The origins of the New York Stock Exchange go back to the mid-1700s when auctioneers, buyers, and sellers began gathering in the coffee houses on Wall Street (so named for the wall built in 1653 by Dutch colonists to protect the area to its south from Indians and the English). The early trading was chiefly in corn and slaves. In the later 1700s most of the trading was in government bonds. Alexander Hamilton was a major trader; he got rich by buying bonds cheaply then, with the aid of Thomas Jefferson, convincing the new U.S. government to redeem them at full value.

In March 1792, twenty-four brokers from seven firms organized a governing board and changed the name of the trading site from Jonathan's Coffee House to the Stock Exchange. The brokers established trading rules and commission rates, and newspapers started reporting trading activity. Most of the stocks traded were shares in banks, insurance companies, canal companies, and construction or mining firms.

In the early 1800s only 450 shares traded on a typical day. On March 16, 1830, only 31 shares traded all day! In today's market, by comparison, over 200 *million* shares are traded on a busy day.

Just a normal day at the nation's most important financial institution . . .

KAL, *The Baltimore Sun*. Copyright © 1990 Cartoonists & Writers Syndicate.

ments of the future are certain. Instead, people use present clues to try to discern the likely course of future events. In other words, *all information must be filtered through people's expectations.*

The central role of expectations implies that the economy can change more gradually than the stock market. If, for example, interest rates start rising, market participants may regard the increase as temporary or inconsequential. Their expectations for the future may not change. If interest rates keep rising, however, greater doubts may arise. At some point, the market participants may begin to revise their expectations. Stock prices may falter. The faltering prices may act as a signal to revise expectations. A herding instinct may surface, sending expectations and stock prices abruptly lower. So-called technical analysts try to anticipate such movements by monitoring changes in stock prices and buying or selling whenever a trend is discerned. By contrast, "fundamentalists" focus on economic and corporate performance, expecting stock prices to reflect the underlying value of their respective corporations.

THE BOND MARKET

bond: A certificate acknowledging a debt and the amount of interest to be paid each year until repayment; an IOU.

The bond market operates much like the stock market. The major difference is in the kind of paper traded. *In the stock market, people buy and sell shares of corporate ownership. In the bond market, people buy and sell promissory notes ("IOUs").* A **bond** is simply an IOU, a written promise to repay a loan. The bond itself specifies the terms of repayment, noting both the amount of interest to be paid each year and the maturity date (the date on which the borrower is to repay the entire debt). The borrower may be a corporation ("corporate bonds"), local governments ("municipal bonds"), the federal government ("treasury bonds"), and other institutions.

Bond Issuance

A bond is first issued when an institution wants to borrow money. Recall the start-up problem for Air Scanners. The company had great ideas but not enough resources to start production. Previously, we solved this problem by issuing stock, thereby allowing other people to buy ownership in the new venture. Now we have a second alternative for raising the necessary funds—that is, by *borrowing* money. The advantage of borrowing funds rather than issuing stock is that we can keep control of the company. Lenders are not owners, but shareholders are. On the other hand, if we borrow, we have to pay the lenders back, with interest. Shareholders do not get interest and are not promised to get back all the money they paid for their stock.

par value: The face value of a bond; the amount to be repaid when the bond is due.

If ASI decides to use borrowed funds to get started, it will "issue" bonds. This simply means that it prints formal IOUs called bonds. Typically, each bond certificate will have a **par value** (face value) of $1,000. The bond certificate will also specify the rate of interest to be paid and the promised date of repayment. An ASI bond issued in 1991, for example, might specify repayment in ten years, with annual interest payments of $100. The individual who buys the bond from ASI is lending $1,000 for ten years and will receive annual interest payments of $100. Thus *the initial bond purchaser lends funds directly to the bond issuer* (ASI in this case). The borrower (e.g., ASI, General Motors, or the U.S. Treasury) can then use those funds to acquire real resources. Thus the bond market also functions as a financial intermediary, transferring available savings (wealth) to those who want to acquire more resources (invest).

As in the case of IPOs of stock, the critical issue here is the "price" of the bond. How many people will be willing and able to lend funds to the company? What rate of interest will they charge?

Figure 34.4 illustrates a hypothetical supply of bond-market funds for ASI. At low rates of interest no one is willing to lend funds to the company. Why lend your savings to a risky venture like ASI when more secure bonds and even banks pay higher interest rates? ASI might not sell many Air Scanners and later **default** (not pay) on its obligations. Potential lenders will want to be compensated for this extra risk with above-average interest rates. According to Figure 34.4, ASI will have to offer at least 15 percent interest if it wants to borrow $2 million. Accordingly, the ASI bonds will be issued with an initial interest rate—the so-called **coupon rate**—of 15 percent.

default: Failure to make scheduled payments of interest or principal on a bond.

coupon rate: Interest rate set for bond at time of issuance.

Bond Trading

Once a bond has been issued, the initial lenders do not have to wait ten years to get their money back. They cannot go back to the company and demand early repayment. They can, however, sell their bonds to someone else. This *liquidity* is an important consideration for prospective bondholders. If a person had no choice but to wait ten years for repayment, he or she might be less willing to buy a bond (lend funds). *By facilitating resales, the bond market increases the availability of funds to new ventures and other borrowers.* As is the case with stocks, most of the action in the bond markets consists of such after-market trades—that is, the buying and selling of bonds issued at some earlier time. The company that first issued the bonds does not participate in these trades.

The portfolio decision in the bond market is motivated by the same factors that influence stock purchases. The *opportunity cost* of buying any particular bond is the best alternative rate of return (e.g., the interest rate on other bonds or money market mutual funds). *Expectations* also play a role, in gauging both likely changes in opportunity costs and the ability of the

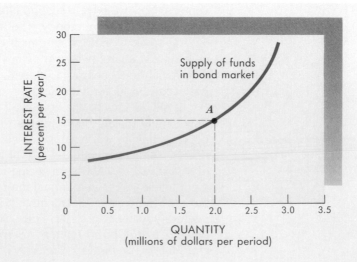

FIGURE 34.4
Selecting the Coupon Rate

The quantity of funds available to a potential borrower depends on the interest rate offered. More people are willing to buy bonds (lend their funds) if the promised interest rate is high. By examining market conditions (the supply of available funds) a borrower can determine the rate that must be paid to raise the desired funds. In this case, the company must offer 15 percent interest if it wants to raise (borrow) $2 million in the bond market.

borrower to redeem (pay off) the bond when it is due. ***Changes in expectations or opportunity costs will shift the bond supply and demand curves,*** thereby altering market interest rates.

Risk and Uncertainty

risk premium: The difference between the interest rate paid on a particular asset and the rate paid on relatively safe assets, e.g., Treasury bonds.

Recall that ASI had to offer 15 percent interest in order to induce enough people to lend the company (buy bonds worth) $2 million. This was far higher than the 8 percent the U.S. Treasury was paying on its bonds (borrowed funds). The difference between the rate paid by ASI and the rate paid on a safe bond like those of the U.S. Treasury is the **risk premium.** The risk premium reflected lenders' fears that Air Scanner, Inc. might not be able to convert its great ideas into actual sales in a timely and profitable manner. In lending their funds to ASI, they incurred a risk of never getting their wealth back.

Suppose that ASI actually gets off to a good start and begins producing and selling laser scanners. Then the risk of a bond default will diminish and people will be more willing to lend it funds. This change in the availability of loanable funds is illustrated by the rightward shift of the supply curve in Figure 34.5.

According to the new supply curve in Figure 34.5, ASI could now borrow $2 million at 10 percent interest (point *B*) rather than paying 15 percent (point *A*). Unfortunately, ASI already borrowed the funds and is obliged to continue paying $150 per year in interest on each bond.[2] Hence the company does not benefit directly from the supply shift.

The change in the equilibrium value of ASI bonds must show up somewhere, however. People who hold ASI bonds continue to get $150 per year in interest (15 percent of $1,000). Now there are lots of people who would be willing to lend funds to ASI at that rate. These people want to hold ASI bonds themselves. To get them, they will have to buy them in the market from

[2]Some bonds have a "call option" that permits the issuer to redeem the bonds early. That option is not included here.

FIGURE 34.5
Risk and Interest Rates

If the creditworthiness of a borrower improves, people will be more willing to lend funds to this borrower. In this case, the supply of available funds increases (shifts to S_2) when the company begins to show concrete prospects for sales and profits. The company could now borrow $2 million at 10 percent interest (point *B*), rather than the 15 percent it confronted when its prospects were less certain (point *A*). This changed equilibrium will be reflected in the (resale) price of the company's bonds (see Table 34.3).

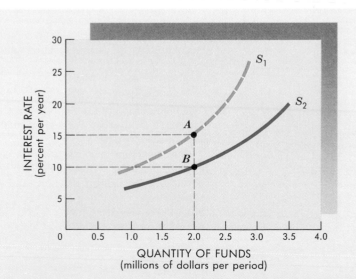

yield: The rate of return on a bond; the annual interest payment divided by the bond's price.

existing bondholders. Thus the ***increased willingness to lend funds is reflected in an increased demand for bonds.*** This increased demand will push up the price of ASI bonds. As bond prices rise, their implied effective interest rate (**yield**) falls. Table 34.3 illustrates this relationship.

Changing bond prices and yields are important market signals for resource allocation. In our example, the rising price of ASI bonds reflects increased optimism for the company's sales prospects. The collective assessment of the marketplace is that Air Scanners will be a profitable venture. The change in the price of ASI bonds will make it easier and less costly for the company to borrow additional funds. This bond market signal will facilitate the production of additional Air Scanners.

Leveraged Buyouts and Junk Bonds

Bonds may be issued for a variety of purposes besides new investment. One is to finance the purchase of an existing company. People may decide that a corporation is undervalued in the stock market. Its current value may be low because of poor management, undervalued assets or a subpar product mix. A potential buyer may see opportunities for higher profits if new management is installed, product lines are rearranged, or new business ventures are developed.

To exploit these perceived opportunities, a person needs to gain control of the corporation, not just a few shares of its stock. That will require an

---

TABLE 34.3 BOND PRICE AND YIELDS

Price of bond	Annual interest payment	Current yield
$ 600	$150	25.0%
800	150	18.8
1,000	150	15.0
1,200	150	12.5

The annual interest payments on a bond are fixed at the time of issuance. Accordingly, only the market (resale) prices of the bond can change. An increase in the price of the bond lowers its *effective* interest rate, or yield. The formula for computing the current yield on a bond is

$$\text{Yield} = \frac{\text{annual interest payment}}{\text{market (resale) price of bond}}$$

Thus higher bond prices imply lower yields (effective interest rates), as confirmed in the table. Bond prices and yields vary with changes in expectations and opportunity costs.

The quotation below shows how changing bond prices and yields are reported. This General Motors (GMA) bond was issued with a coupon rate (nominal interest rate) of $8\frac{1}{4}$ percent. Hence GM promised to pay $80.25 in interest each year until it redeemed (paid off) the $1,000 bond in the year 2006 (06). In February 1990, however, the market price of the bond was only $897.50 ($89\frac{3}{4}$). This created a yield of 9.2 percent.

Bond	Current yield	Volume	Close	Net change
GMA $8\frac{1}{4}$ 06	9.2	1	$89\frac{3}{4}$	$+\frac{3}{4}$

enormous financial outlay. Even the wealthiest "corporate raider" may need to borrow funds for such a buyout. Or he may simply want to reduce his own risks by using other people's funds as well as his own. In either case, the potential buyer may issue bonds to raise the necessary buyout funds.

The buyout of an existing corporation is a risky venture. The most obvious risk is that the raider's assessment is wrong—that the corporation is not as undervalued as he perceives. Even if he is right, there is no assurance that the raider will be able to fix all the company's problems once he gains control. Finally, there is no assurance that he will even gain control. He may end up paying huge fees to investment bankers, lawyers, and brokers—and still fail to acquire controlling interest in the company. In 1989 United Airlines paid over $50 million in fees in trying to execute a management-led buyout that failed.

Potential lenders will want to be compensated for these risks. They will require a high *risk premium* for the funds they lend. Accordingly, bonds issued for corporate buyouts tend to have very high yields and short terms. These and other bonds entailing unusual risk are popularly called **junk bonds.** They are considered "below investment grade," i.e., riskier than the bonds traditionally rated and monitored by bond-appraisal services (e.g., Moody's or Standard & Poor's). In reality, so-called junk bonds have financed not only leveraged buyouts but also enormous amounts of real investment.

junk bonds: Bonds carrying greater risk due to their speculative purpose and lack of security; unrated bonds.

Asset Leverage

In buyout situations, potential lenders are particularly concerned about how the raider will pay them back. If all of the borrowed funds are used to buy the corporation's stock, where will the funds come from to pay off the junk bonds? In many cases, the raider promises to sell some of the corporation's assets once he gains control. Recall that the basic premise of the buyout is that the company is undervalued. The raider hopes to profit from this undervaluation by selling off some of the company's land, labor, or capital at higher prices. He can then use the proceeds of those sales to redeem (repay) the junk bonds. Hence the raider is using the assets of the target company itself to guarantee repayment of junk bonds. This is called a *leveraged* buyout.[3]

It is important to understand the basic economic functions of this transaction. The key thing to remember is that ***a corporate buyout is motivated by the conviction that the opportunity cost of a company's resources exceed their value to the company.*** In effect, a raider is saying that the market has *misallocated* the economy's scarce resources. He hopes to prove this by reallocating the resources more profitably, either by selling them or using (managing) them better. If he is right, not only will he profit, but society will end up with a more desirable mix of output. If the raider is wrong, both he and society will suffer a loss.[4] The accompanying In the News identifies some of the big successes and failures of the 1980s.

---

[3]A leveraged buyout can also be financed with more conventional loans (e.g., from banks). The choice of junk bonds will depend on the availability and cost of alternative funds.

[4]Corporate raiders and insider buyouts sometimes profit from preferential compensation agreements. Preferential tax treatment may also yield financial gain even in the absence of efficiency gains.

In The News

Biggest Buyouts of the 1980s

Junk bonds helped finance many of the multibillion-dollar buyouts of the 1980s. Some of the acquirers (e.g., R. J. Reynolds, number 22) later became targets (number 1) themselves. In many cases the buyouts enhanced efficiency and profits (e.g., General Electric's acquisition of RCA). In other cases, however (e.g., Campeau, Grand Metropolitan), the buyout failed to generate sufficient gains to offset the high costs (including debt service) of the leveraged buyout.

	Acquirer	Target	Price (in billions)
1	Kohlberg Kravis Roberts	RJR Nabisco	$24.6
2	Beecham Group (UK)	SmithKline Beckman	16.1
3	Chevron	Gulf Oil	13.2
4	Philip Morris	Kraft	13.1
5	Bristol-Myers	Squibb	12.0
6	Time Inc.	Warner Communications	11.7
7	Texaco	Getty Oil	0.2
8	Du Pont	Conoco	8.0
9	British Petroleum	Standard Oil (45%)	7.8
10	USX	Marathon Oil	6.6
11	Campeau	Federated Department Stores	6.5
12	General Electric	RCA	6.0
13	Mobil Oil	Superior Oil	5.7
14	Grand Metropolitan (UK)	Pillsbury	5.6
15	Philip Morris	General Foods	5.6
16	Royal Dutch/Shell (UK-Neth.)	Shell Oil (30.5%)	5.5
17	Kohlberg Kravis Roberts	Beatrice	5.4
18	BAT Industries (UK)	Farmers Group	5.2
19	Eastman Kodak	Sterling Drug	5.1
20	Santa Fe Industries	Southern Pacific	5.1
21	General Motors	Hughes Aircraft	5.0
22	R. J. Reynolds	Nabisco Brands	4.9
23	Sovran Financial	Citizens & Southern	4.5
24	Allied	Signal	4.5
25	Burroughs	Sperry	4.4

FUTURES MARKETS

Futures markets provide yet another mechanism for (re)allocating resources and managing risk. In futures markets people buy and sell things that are to be "delivered" in the future at prices agreed on today. The earliest futures markets were organized to facilitate trading of farm products like wheat and corn. In the absence of a futures market, farmers had to wait until harvest, then find buyers for their crops. This subjected them to uncertainty about the prices their crops would fetch. Beginning in 1848, the Chicago Board of Trade offered a more efficient alternative. It provided a central location for buyers and sellers, standard units and measures of quality, and the opportunity for buying and selling *future* deliveries. The futures markets have expanded enormously since then and now trade everything from real commodities (e.g., wheat, corn, livestock, gold) to currencies, interest rates, and even future stock prices (see Table 34.4).

Price Discovery   The core function of any market is to increase the flow of information between buyers and sellers. In the absence of a central market, commodity prices would tend to fluctuate sharply with harvests, buyer or seller information, location, and time. Such price instability would greatly increase the risks to the farmer as well as potential buyers. Each would be hoping for a more favorable price at the time of sale, and thus *gambling* on the eventual market outcome.

A futures market eliminates some of this risk by locating equilibrium prices. Futures markets permit continuous trading in commodities that are to be delivered in a future period. Such trading facilitates continuous price adjustments to changing circumstances. Futures contracts also make it possible for a buyer or seller to eliminate the risk of future price changes. A farmer,

TABLE 34.4   Traded Futures Contracts (1990)

Everything from pork bellies to Dutch guilders are traded in futures markets. The purpose of such trading is to manage the risks of price changes in the underlying commodities and financial instruments.

Agriculture	Metal and fuels	Foreign currencies	Financial instruments
Barley	Crude oil	Australian dollar	Treasury bills
Corn	Fuel oil	Belgian franc	Treasury bonds
Soybeans	Heating oil	British pound	Eurodollars
Sorghum	Gasoline	Canadian dollar	Municipal bonds
Oats	Propane	Deutsche mark	Mortgage bonds
Rye	Aluminum	Dutch guilder	NYSE index
Wheat	Copper	French franc	Comex stock index
Broilers	Gold	Italian lira	Pacific stock index
Cattle	Palladium	Japanese yen	Amex major market
Pork bellies	Platinum	Mexican peso	index
Hams	Silver	Swiss franc	S&P stock price index
Turkeys	Silver coins		Value Line stock index
Hogs	Zinc		Certificates of deposit
Sugar			
Lumber			
Sunflower seeds			
Soybean oil			
Butter			
Cocoa			
Coffee			
Coconut oil			
Cotton			
Eggs			
Frozen orange juice			
Potatoes			
Rubber			
Palm oil			
Wool			
Plywood			

Source: Commodity Futures Trading Commission.

for example, can sell crops *before* they are harvested by signing (selling) a futures contract. For an agreed price, the farmer promises to deliver crops to the buyer on some specific date in the future. Once the futures contract is signed, neither the farmer nor the buyer has to worry about changes in the price of wheat.

The predictability (certainty) of future prices greatly reduces one risk to an individual farmer. The reduced risk, in turn, will tend to stimulate more agricultural investment and a more dependable flow of farm products. Futures contracts reduce risk for commodity purchasers as well, making it easier to develop investment and production plans.

Risk Assumption

Although futures markets make life easier for the farmer and consumer, they do not *eliminate* market risks. Instead, futures markets help *manage* risks by shifting the burden of risk from those who want to minimize risk to those who are willing to take greater risks. Suppose a severe drought curtailed the wheat harvest. The resulting reduction in supply would cause the price of wheat to rise, as in Figure 34.6. Inevitably, some people are going to gain from the price increase and others are going to lose. What the futures market does is redistribute those gains and losses according to the risks each individual is willing to bear.

We have assumed that the farmer has reduced his risk by preselling his harvest for the price p_1. Hence he will not profit from the drought-induced price increase. In all likelihood, the person who contracted to purchase his future crop was a speculator who was willing to assume the risks of future price changes. Such a buyer was hoping that the price of wheat would rise, creating a profit on the wheat she had agreed to buy at a fixed price. The speculator could then resell the wheat at a higher price. The futures trader, rather than the farmer, profits from the price increase in this case. Perhaps that seems unfair. On the other hand, if the price of wheat had *fallen*, the speculator, not the farmer, would have suffered a loss. ***The individual will-***

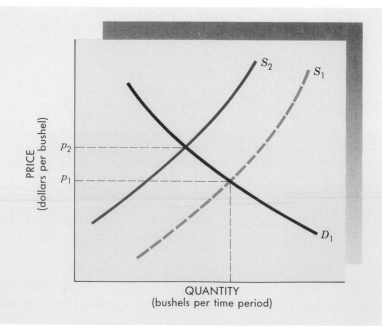

FIGURE 34.6
Changing Commodity Prices

The equilibrium price of a commodity depends on its underlying supply and demand. In this case, a drought reduces supply (to S_2) and pushes wheat prices up. However, the futures market enabled the farmers to "presell" their crops at the initial price p_1, with futures traders assuming the risks and rewards associated with subsequent price changes. In the futures market the price will increase from p_1 to p_2 gradually, as more traders become convinced of the drought's severity.

ing to assume the risks of price changes gets the resulting rewards or losses.

Even the speculator can reduce her risks in the futures market. Suppose she bought wheat futures at $3.20 a bushel. Once a dry spell sets in, people will start worrying about droughts and higher prices. This will increase the demand for wheat futures, pushing their prices up. Rather than waiting to see if drought occurs, the speculator may resell her futures contract before delivery is due. Then she can pocket a small profit and stop worrying about the weather and wheat prices. By passing the risk of further price changes to someone else, she gives up the chance to make greater gains but also eliminates further risk. Most of the trading in futures markets entails these "secondhand" trades; few trades result in actual delivery of a commodity. Just as in the bond and stock markets, the opportunity to resell futures contracts allows people to select the level of risk they prefer.

Market Signaling

As noted earlier, the risk management made possible by the futures markets tends to stabilize production. Farmers and other commodity producers are more willing to invest in seasonal crops and other commodities if they can reduce the risks of abrupt price changes.

Futures markets also help guide investment and production decisions by signaling market expectations. If wheat futures are rising in price, a farmer can "see" the collective expectations of the marketplace for wheat prices. This may induce him to plant more wheat at the next opportunity. Conversely, a decline in wheat futures signals an expected oversupply of wheat and may induce the farmer to plant soybeans instead. *Changing futures prices act as market signals to guide investment, production, and consumption decisions.*

POLICY INSIGHTS:

INSIDER TRADING

The core economic function of financial markets is to facilitate an optimal mix of output. Financial markets serve this purpose by

- Mobilizing savings
- Managing risk
- Signaling desired resource allocations

Hence *efficient financial markets are a prerequisite for efficient economic outcomes.* If the financial markets fail to mobilize and direct society's resources, the economy is likely to produce not only the wrong mix of output, but also less total output than it is capable of. Accordingly, the public has a critical stake in the efficiency of financial markets.

The public also has a legitimate interest in the equity of financial markets. Our basic economic goals encompass not only WHAT and HOW to produce, but also FOR WHOM to produce. As we have observed, a person can make a lot of income in the financial markets. That income would grant significant command over real goods and services. This raises two questions. First, was the income obtained fairly? Second, should a person be permitted to retain huge economic profits and the economic power they imply?

Inequity   The phenomenon of "insider trading" illustrates how financial markets may fail to promote either efficiency or equity. In general, insider trading refers to the exploitation of information not available to the general public. A corporate manager, for example, might discover that the company's products are faulty. With such "insider" information he could sell stock in the corporation before the rest of the world (the "outsiders") finds out. This would enable him to benefit financially at the expense of the company's owners (other shareholders).

The same kind of inequity may arise when a corporate director learns that a "raider" is interested in buying the company. The director may hear this from the raider or from the raider's investment bankers. A director of a corporation is obligated to represent the interests of the shareholders. With privileged (inside) information, however, the director might purchase shares from existing shareholders, thereby depriving them of the opportunity to benefit from the pending buyout. In the process, of course, he would be enriching himself by buying stock at cheaper prices before knowledge of the pending buyout is public.

The government alleged that much of the $550 million Michael Milken made in 1987 and other years derived from insider trading. Milken helped arrange junk bond financing for leveraged buyouts. As a key intermediary, he learned of pending deals. This gave him extraordinary inside information since he knew not only who intended to buy what, but also whether they would have enough financing to complete the deal. The government charged that Milken had a particularly close relationship with Ivan Boesky, a leading corporate raider. Boesky was convicted of insider trading, fined over $100 million, and sent to jail. Milken's firm paid over $600 million in penalties and Milken himself later paid $600 million in penalties as well.

In The News

INSIDER TRADING

Ivan Boesky's Last Deal

Ivan Boesky seemed to have a magic touch on Wall Street. Not long after he purchased stock in a company, its stock started rising. Before long, a corporate raider would come forth and offer to buy the company at premium prices. By being in the right place at the right time, Boesky racked up trading profits measured in hundreds of millions of dollars. He acquired a 200-acre estate in a posh New York suburb, a stretch limousine with three telephones, two antique Rolls-Royces, a wine cellar, Impressionist paintings, and servants. *Forbes* magazine estimated his wealth in 1986 to be $250 million.

Boesky's good fortune, it turns out, was not the result of brilliance or even luck. He was getting advance information on pending corporate takeovers from investment bankers and lawyers. He used this insider information to buy up the stock of target companies, then he resold it for huge gains once the merger or acquisition was announced. He paid his "inside" informants with hundreds of thousands of dollars stuffed in suitcases. He was alleged to have paid one brokerage house (Drexel Burnham Lambert) over $5 million for information on a spate of insider deals.

Boesky's good fortune began to unravel when one of Drexel's top traders, Dennis Levine, was charged with insider trading. Levine paid $11.6 million in fines and started naming names to the Securities and Exchange Commission. The SEC soon charged Boesky with insider trading. In November 1986 he confessed and agreed to pay $100 million in fines. He, too, started naming names. In return for cooperation Boesky was given a shorter prison sentence.

Inefficiency   Insider trading gives some market participants an unfair advantage in answering the FOR WHOM question. This is not exclusively an equity issue, however. The *efficiency* of the market is also damaged by insider trading. The general public may conclude that the stock market is a rigged game in which insiders always win and outsiders always lose. They may decide to stop playing the game. That will reduce the flow of funds going into the financial markets. As the markets shrink, the ability of the economy to mobilize its savings and reallocate resources may be impaired.

SUMMARY

- Financial markets help mobilize and allocate scarce resources. They also enable people to manage risk by holding their wealth in many different forms.

- Financial intermediaries serve as a bridge between savers and investors. They reduce the costs of information and search, increasing market efficiency.

- Shares of stock represent ownership in a corporation. The shares are initially issued to raise funds, then traded on the stock exchanges.

- Changes in the value of a corporation's stock reflect changing expectations and opportunity costs. Share-price changes, in turn, act as market signals to direct more or fewer resources to a company.

- Bonds are IOUs issued when a company (or government agency) borrows funds. After issuance, bonds are traded in the after (secondary) market.

- The interest (coupon) rate on a bond is fixed at the time of issuance. The price of the bond itself, however, varies with changes in expectations (perceived risk) and opportunity cost. Yields vary inversely with bond prices.

- In futures markets people buy and sell contracts for future delivery of commodities and resources. The futures market permits the risks of price changes to be transferred from risk averters to risk takers.

- Abrupt moves in the stock, bond, and futures markets are the result of changed expectations. Expectations often change more abruptly than underlying economic forces and can cause booms and busts if many market participants alter their outlook simultaneously.

- Efficient utilization of society's resources requires effective financial markets. Government seeks to ensure their effectiveness by curbing trading abuses (e.g., insider trading).

Terms to Remember

capital	portfolio decision
saving	bond
financial intermediary	par value
corporation	default
corporate stock	coupon rate
dividend	risk premium
capital gain	yield
initial public offering (IPO)	junk bonds

Questions for Discussion

1. If there were no organized financial markets, how would an entrepreneur acquire resources to develop and produce a new product?

2. Why would anyone buy shares of a corporation that had no profits and paid no dividends? What is the highest price a person would pay for such a stock?

3. Why would anyone sell a bond for less than its par value?

4. If you could finance a new venture with either a stock issue or bonds, which option would you choose? What are their respective (dis)advantages?

Problems

1. Compute the market price of the GM bond described in Table 34.3 if the yield goes to 12 percent.

2. Compute the expected return on Columbus's expedition assuming that he had a 50 percent chance of discovering valuables worth $1 million, a 25 percent chance of bringing home only $10,000 and a 25 percent chance of sinking.

3. Locate the stock quotation for General Motors Corporation in today's newspaper (traded on the New York Stock Exchange). From the information provided, determine:
   (a) Yesterday's percentage change in the price of GM stock
   (b) How much profit ("earnings") GM made last year for each share of stock
   (c) How much of that profit was paid out in dividends
   (d) How much profit was retained by GM for investment

INTERNATIONAL ECONOMICS AND COMPARATIVE SYSTEMS

CHAPTER 35

International Trade

*T*he 1989 World Series between the Oakland Athletics and the San Francisco Giants was played with Japanese gloves, Haitian baseballs, and Mexican bats. Most of the players were wearing shoes made in Korea, and all of them had played regular season games on artificial grass made in Taiwan. Baseball, it seems, has become something less than the "all-American" game.

Imported goods have made inroads into other activities as well. All VCRs are imported, as are most televisions, fax machines, personal computers, and calculators. Every year American consumers also spend a lot of their income on French racing bikes, Japanese cars, Italian sweaters, Swiss chocolates, Colombian coffee, Russian vodka, and Venezuelan oil.

Most of these imported goods could have been produced in the United States, and many were. Why did we purchase them from other countries? For that matter, why did the rest of the world buy computers, tractors, chemicals, airplanes, and wheat from us rather than produce such products for themselves? Wouldn't we all be better off relying on ourselves for the goods we consume (and the jobs we need), rather than buying and selling products in international markets? Or is there some advantage to be gained from international trade? If so, what is the nature of that advantage, and who reaps the benefits?

In this chapter we first survey the nature of international trade patterns — what goods we trade, and with whom. Then we address some basic issues related to such trade, namely:

• What benefit, if any, do we get from international trade?

• How much harm do imports cause, and to whom?

• Should we protect ourselves from "unfair" trade by limiting some or all imports?

After examining the arguments for and against international trade, we try to draw some general conclusions about optimal trade policy. As we shall see, international trade tends to increase our *average* incomes, although it may diminish the job and income opportunities of specific industries and workers.

U.S. TRADE PATTERNS

Imports

imports: Goods and services purchased from foreign sources.

In 1989 the United States imported over $475 billion of merchandise. These **imports** included the consumer items mentioned earlier, as well as capital equipment, raw materials, and food. Table 35.1 provides a sampler of the goods and services we purchase from foreign suppliers.

Although imports represent only 9 percent of total GNP, they account for larger shares of specific product markets. Coffee is a familiar example. Since all coffee is imported, Americans would have a harder time staying awake without imports. Likewise, there would have been no aluminum if we hadn't imported bauxite, no chrome bumpers if we hadn't imported chromium, no

TABLE 35.1 A U.S. Trade Sampler

The United States imports and exports a staggering array of goods and services. Most of our imports could be produced domestically. Foreign nations are also able to produce many of the goods we export to them. Why, then, do countries trade?

Country	Imports from	Exports to
Australia	Lobster tails Alumina Wood	Beverage syrups Fuel oil Whiskey
Belgium	Synthetic rubber Optical glass Yarn	Cigarettes Diamonds Outboard motors
Canada	Newsprint Soybean oil Car tires	Car radios Jet fuel Fish
Egypt	Carpets Wools Cotton fabric	Corn Chickens Flour
Germany	Sausage casings Vitamin C Glass tumblers	Coffee Antibiotics Bourbon
Japan	Cars Stereo equipment Machine tools	Tobacco China clay Gasoline
Netherlands	Beer and ale Benzene Unsweetened cocoa	Soybeans Naphtha Steel drums
South Korea	Microwave ovens Leather handbags Men's suits	Down feathers Telephones Iron ingots and oxides
Taiwan	Electric fans Peeled shrimp Jewelry boxes	Apples Cotton Logs
Soviet Union	Silicon Vodka Sable furs	Engine oil Wheat Cotton drapes

Source: U.S. Department of Commerce.

tin cans without imported tin, and a lot fewer computers without imported components. We couldn't even play the all-American game of baseball without imports, since baseballs are no longer made in the United States!

Exports

exports: Goods and services sold to foreign buyers.

While we are buying baseballs, coffee, bauxite, computer components, and oil from the rest of the world, foreigners are buying our **exports.** In 1989, we exported $362 billion of goods, including farm products (wheat, corn, soybeans), tobacco, machinery (computers), aircraft, automobiles and auto parts, raw materials (lumber, iron ore), and chemicals (see Table 35.1 for a sampler of U.S. exports).

As with our imports, our merchandise exports represent a relatively modest fraction of total GNP. Whereas we export about 7 percent of total output, other developed countries export as much as one-fourth of their output (see World View). Here again, however, the relatively low ratio of exports to total sales disguises our heavy dependence on exports in specific industries. We export 25–50 percent of our rice, corn, and wheat production each year, and still more of our soybeans. Clearly, a decision by foreigners to stop eating American agricultural products could devastate a lot of American farmers. Such companies as Boeing (planes), Caterpillar Tractor (construction and farm machinery), Weyerhaeuser (logs, lumber), Eastman Kodak (film), Dow (chemicals), and Sun Microsystems (computer workstations) sell over one-fourth of their output in foreign markets. Pepsi and Coke are battling it out in the soft-drink markets of such unlikely places as Egypt, Abu Dhabi, and the Soviet Union.

Trade Balances

As the figures indicate, our imports and exports were not equal in 1989. Quite the contrary: we had a large imbalance in our trade flows, with many more imports than exports. The trade balance is computed simply as the difference between exports and imports; that is,

$$\bullet \quad \frac{\text{Trade}}{\text{balance}} = \text{exports} - \text{imports}$$

trade deficit: The amount by which the value of imports exceeds the value of exports in a given time period.

trade surplus: The amount by which the value of exports exceeds the value of imports in a given time period.

During 1989, we imported more than we exported and so had a negative trade balance. A negative trade balance is called a **trade deficit.** In 1989, the U.S. merchandise trade deficit totaled $113 billion.[1]

If the United States has a trade deficit with the rest of the world, then other countries must have an offsetting **trade surplus.** On a global scale, imports must equal exports, since every good exported by one country must be imported by another. Hence *any imbalance in America's trade must be offset by reverse imbalances elsewhere.*

The U.S. trade balance has been in deficit since the mid-1970s, and the deficit first reached $100 billion levels only in the mid-1980s. Prior to that, America generally exported more goods than it imported. Hence the United States was a net exporter and the rest of the world was a net importer. Today, the trade imbalances are reversed.

Whatever the overall balance in our trade accounts, bilateral balances vary greatly. Table 35.2 shows, for example, that our 1989 trade deficit incorporated a huge bilateral trade deficit with Japan and large deficits with Taiwan, Germany, and Canada also. In the same year, however, we had trade

[1]Traditionally the trade deficit (surplus) refers to merchandise only. Imports and exports of services are added to compute the "current account" balance. In 1989 the current account deficit was smaller than the trade deficit, since service exports (e.g., air travel) exceeded service imports. The current account and other international balances are discussed in Chapter 36.

W🌐RLD VIEW

EXPORT RATIOS

Exports in Relation to GNP

Merchandise exports account for 6.7 percent of total U.S. output. Although substantial, this trade dependence is relatively low by international standards. Germany, for example, exports 37 percent of its total output, while Taiwan exports 50 percent of its annual production.

Source: Central Intelligence Agency (1988 data).

Trade in 1989

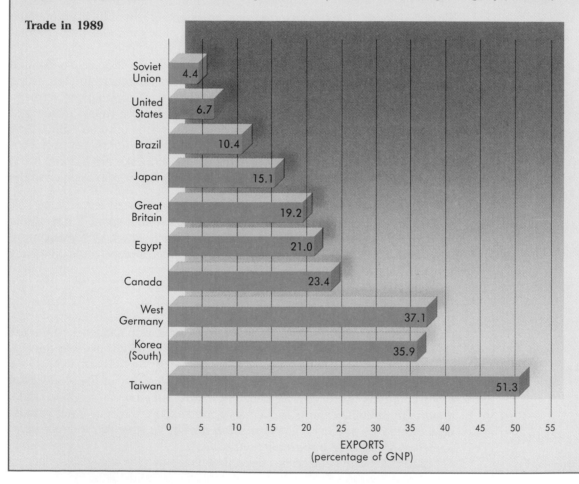

Soviet Union	4.4
United States	6.7
Brazil	10.4
Japan	15.1
Great Britain	19.2
Egypt	21.0
Canada	23.4
West Germany	37.1
Korea (South)	35.9
Taiwan	51.3

EXPORTS
(percentage of GNP)

surpluses with Belgium, Egypt, Australia, and the Soviet Union. Table 35.2 and the World View on page 852 also indicate that most of our trade was conducted with developed nations, and that trade with Eastern Europe has been relatively small.

MOTIVATION TO TRADE

Many people wonder why we trade so much, particularly since (1) we import many of the things we also export (e.g., computers, airplanes, clothes); (2) we *could* produce many of the other things we import; and (3) we seem to

TABLE 35.2   Bilateral Trade Balances of the United States

The U.S. trade deficit of $113 billion in 1989 was the net result of bilateral deficits and surpluses. We had a very large trade deficit with Japan, for example, but small trade surpluses with Belgium, Australia, and the Soviet Union. International trade is multinational, with surpluses in some countries being offset by trade deficits elsewhere.

Country or region	Exports to (in millions of dollars)	Imports from (in millions of dollars)	Trade balance
Canada	80,451	88,960	− 8,509
Japan	43,899	93,621	−49,722
Germany	16,411	24,688	− 8,277
Belgium and Luxembourg	8,592	4,556	+ 4,036
Mexico	24,676	27,066	− 2,390
Taiwan	10,999	24,302	− 13,303
Korea	13,139	19,812	− 6,673
Africa	7,747	14,002	− 6,255
Eastern Europe	5,547	2,059	+ 3,488
Australia	8,124	3,892	+ 4,232

Source: U.S. Department of Commerce.

worry so much about imports and trade imbalances. Why not just import those few things that we cannot produce ourselves, and export just enough to balance that trade?

Although it might seem strange to be importing goods we could or do produce ourselves, such trade is imminently rational. Indeed, our decision to trade with other countries arises from the same considerations that motivate individuals to specialize in production, satisfying their remaining needs in the marketplace. Why don't you become self-sufficient, growing all your own food, building your own shelter, recording your own songs? Presumably because you have found that you can enjoy a much higher standard of living (and better music) by producing only a few goods and buying the rest in the marketplace. When countries engage in international trade, they are expressing the same kind of commitment to specialization, and for the same reason: ***specialization increases total output.***

To demonstrate the economic gains obtainable from international trade, we may examine the production possibilities of two countries. We want to demonstrate that two countries that trade can together produce more output than they could in the absence of trade. If they can, ***the gain from trade will be increased world output and thus a higher standard of living in both countries.*** This is the essential message of the *theory of comparative advantage.*

Production and Consumption Without Trade

production possibilities: The alternative combinations of final goods and services that could be produced in a given time period with all available resources and technology.

Consider the production and consumption possibilities of just two countries—say, the United States and France. For the sake of illustration, we shall assume that both countries produce only two goods, bread and wine. We shall also set aside worries about the law of diminishing returns and the substitutability of resources, thus transforming the familiar **production-possibilities** curve into a straight line, as in Figure 35.1.

The "curves" in Figure 35.1 and our own intuition suggest that the United States is capable of producing much more bread than France is. After all, we have a greater abundance of labor, land, and other factors of production. With these resources, we assume that the United States is capable of producing

W🌐RLD VIEW

TRADE PATTERNS

Partners in Trade

Most U.S. trade is with other developed countries. Canada alone accounts for 20 percent of U.S. trade (exports plus imports). Western Europe and Japan account for another 40 percent of U.S. trade. Trade with Eastern Europe is relatively small but growing rapidly.

Trade in 1989

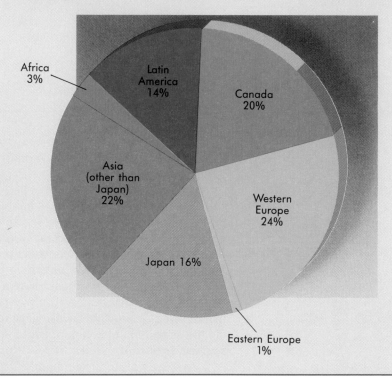

up to 100 zillion loaves of bread per year, if we devote all of our resources to that purpose. This capability is indicated by point *A* in Figure 35.1*a* and the accompanying production-possibilities schedule. France (Figure 35.1*b*), on the other hand, confronts a *maximum* bread production of only 15 zillion loaves per year (point *G*) because it has little available land, less fuel, and fewer potential workers.

The capacities of the two countries for wine production are 50 zillion barrels for us (point *F*) and 60 zillion for France (point *L*), largely reflecting France's greater experience in tending vines. Both countries are also capable of producing alternative *combinations* of bread and wine, as evidenced by their respective production-possibilities curves (points *B–E* for the United States and *H–K* for France).

In the absence of contact with the outside world, the production-possibilities curve for each country also defines its **consumption possibilities.**

consumption possibilities: The alternative combinations of goods and services that a country could consume in a given time period.

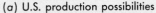

U.S. production possibilities			
	Bread (zillions of loaves)	+	Wine (zillions of barrels)
A	100	+	0
B	80	+	10
C	60	+	20
D	40	+	30
E	20	+	40
F	0	+	50

French production possibilities			
	Bread (zillions of loaves)	+	Wine (zillions of barrels)
G	15	+	0
H	12	+	12
I	9	+	24
J	6	+	36
K	3	+	48
L	0	+	60

(a) U.S. production possibilities

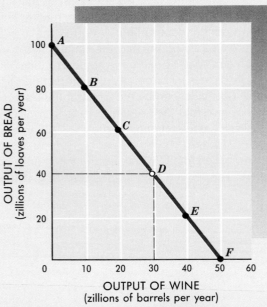

OUTPUT OF BREAD (zillions of loaves per year)

OUTPUT OF WINE (zillions of barrels per year)

(b) French production possibilities

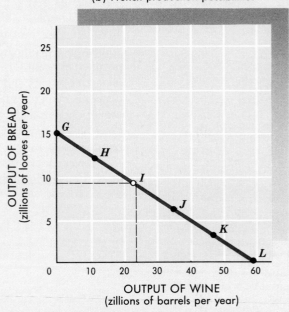

OUTPUT OF BREAD (zillions of loaves per year)

OUTPUT OF WINE (zillions of barrels per year)

FIGURE 35.1
Consumption Possibilities Without Trade

In the absence of trade, a country's consumption possibilities are identical to its production possibilities. The assumed production possibilities of the United States and France are illustrated in the graphs and the corresponding schedules. Before entering into trade, the United States chose to produce and consume at point *D*, with 40 zillion loaves of bread and 30 zillion barrels of wine. France chose point *I* on its own production-possibilities curve. By trading, each country hopes to increase its consumption beyond these levels.

Without imports, neither country can consume more than it produces.[2] Thus the burning issue in each country is which mix of output to choose—*what* to produce—out of the infinite number of choices available.

Assume that Americans choose point *D* on their production-possibilities curve. At point *D* we would produce and consume 40 zillion loaves of bread

[2]If a country has inventories of consumer goods, consumption can exceed production for a brief period. The option is short-lived, however.

and 30 zillion barrels of wine each year. The French, on the other hand, prefer the mix of output represented by point *I* on their production-possibilities curve. At that point they produce and consume 9 zillion loaves of bread and 24 zillion barrels of wine.

Our primary interest here is in the combined annual output of the United States and France. In this case (points *D* and *I*), total world output comes to 49 zillion loaves of bread and 54 zillion barrels of wine. What we want to know is whether world output would increase if France and the United States abandoned their isolation and started trading. Could either country, or both, be made better off by engaging in a little trade?

Production and Consumption with Trade

In view of the fact that both countries are saddled with limited production possibilities, trying to eke out a little extra wine and bread from this situation might not appear very promising. Such a conclusion is unwarranted, however. Take another look at the production possibilities confronting the United States, as reproduced in Figure 35.2. Suppose that the United States were to produce at point *C* rather than point *D*. At point *C* we could produce 60 zillion loaves of bread and 20 zillion barrels of wine. That combination is clearly possible, even if less desirable (as evidenced by the fact that the United States earlier chose point *D*). Suppose also that the French were to move from point *I* to point *K*, producing 48 zillion barrels of wine and only 3 zillion loaves of bread.

Two observations are now called for. The first is simply that output mixes have changed in each country. The second, and more interesting, is that total

**FIGURE 35.2
Consumption
Possibilities With Trade**

A country can increase its consumption possibilities through international trade. Each country alters its mix of domestic output to produce more of the good it produces best. As it does so, total world output increases, and each country enjoys more consumption. In this case, trade allows U.S. consumption to move from point *D* to point *N*. France moves from point *I* to point *M*.

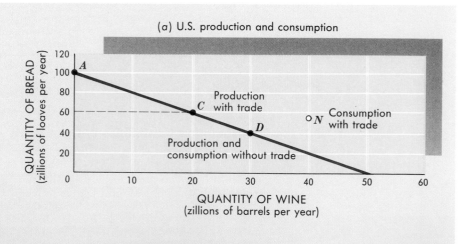

(a) U.S. production and consumption

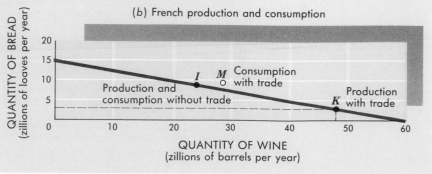

(b) French production and consumption

world output has increased. When the United States and France were at points *D* and *I,* their *combined* annual output consisted of:

	BREAD (ZILLIONS OF LOAVES)	WINE (ZILLIONS OF BARRELS)
U.S. (at point *D*)	40	30
France (at point *I*)	9	24
Total output	49	54

After moving along their respective production-possibilities curves to points *C* and *K,* the combined world output becomes:

	BREAD (ZILLIONS OF LOAVES)	WINE (ZILLIONS OF BARRELS)
U.S. (at point *C*)	60	20
France (at point *K*)	3	48
Total output	63	68

Total world output has increased by 14 zillion loaves of bread and 14 zillion barrels of wine. Just by changing the mix of output in each country, we have increased *total* world output. This additional output creates the potential for making both countries better off than they were in the absence of trade.

The reason the United States and France weren't producing at points *C* and *K* before is that they simply didn't want to consume those particular combinations of output. The United States wanted a slightly more liquid combination than that represented by point *C* and the French could not survive long at point *K.* Hence they chose points *D* and *I.* Nevertheless, our discovery that points *C* and *K* result in greater total output suggests that everybody can be happier if we all cooperate. The obvious thing to do is to trade, to start exchanging wine for bread and vice versa.

Suppose that we are the first to discover the potential benefits that result from trade. Using Figure 35.2 as our guide, we suggest to the French that they move their mix of output from point *I* to point *K.* As an incentive for making such a move, we promise to give them 6 zillion loaves of bread in exchange for 20 zillion barrels of wine. This would leave them at point *M,* with as much bread to consume as they used to have, plus an extra 4 zillion barrels of wine. At point *I* they had 9 zillion loaves of bread and 24 zillion barrels of wine. At point *M* they can have 9 zillion loaves of bread and 28 zillion barrels of wine. Thus by altering their mix of output (from point *I* to point *K*) and then trading (point *K* to point *M*), the French end up with more goods and services than they had in the beginning. Notice in particular that the new consumption possibility made available through international trade (point *M*) lies *outside* France's domestic production-possibilities curve.

The French will obviously be quite pleased with their limited trading experience, but where does this leave us? Do we gain from trade as well? The answer is yes. By trading, we too end up consuming a mix of output that lies outside our production-possibilities curve.

Note that at point *C* we *produce* 60 zillion loaves of bread per year and 20 zillion barrels of wine. We then export 6 zillion loaves to France. This leaves us with 54 zillion loaves of bread to consume. In return for our exported bread, the French give us 20 zillion barrels of wine. These imports, plus our domestic production, permit us to *consume* 40 zillion barrels of wine. Hence we end up *consuming* at point *N*, enjoying 54 zillion loaves of bread and 40 zillion barrels of wine. Thus by first changing our mix of output (from point *D* to point *C*), then trading (point *C* to point *N*), we end up with 14 zillion more loaves of bread and 10 zillion more barrels of wine than we started with! International trade has made us better off, too.

There is no sleight of hand going on here. Rather, the gains from trade are due to specialization in production. When each country goes it alone, it is a prisoner of its own production-possibilities curve; it must take its production decisions on the basis of its own consumption desires. When international trade is permitted, however, each country can concentrate on the exploitation of its production capabilities. Each country produces those goods it makes best. Then the countries trade with each other to acquire the goods they desire to consume.

In other words, international trade allows each country to focus on what it does best, with the resultant specialization increasing total world output. In this way each country is able to escape the confines of its own production-possibilities curve, to reach beyond it for a larger basket of consumption goods. ***When a country engages in international trade, its consumption possibilities always exceed its production possibilities.*** These additional consumption possibilities are emphasized by the position of points *N* and *M outside* the production-possibilities curves (Figure 35.2). If it were not possible for countries to increase their consumption by trading, there would be no incentive for trading, and thus no trade.

PURSUIT OF COMPARATIVE ADVANTAGE

Although international trade can make everyone better off, it is not so obvious what goods should be traded, or on what terms. In our previous illustration, the United States ended up trading bread for wine on terms that were decidedly favorable to us. Why did we choose to export bread rather than wine, and how did we end up getting such a good deal?

Opportunity Costs

comparative advantage: The ability of a country to produce a specific good at a lower opportunity cost than its trading partners.

opportunity cost: The most desired goods or services that are forgone in order to obtain something else.

The decision to export bread is based on **comparative advantage,** that is, the *relative* cost of producing different goods. Recall that we can produce a maximum of 100 zillion loaves of bread per year or 50 zillion barrels of wine. Thus the domestic opportunity cost of producing 100 zillion loaves of bread is the 50 zillion barrels of wine we forsake in order to devote our resources to bread production. In fact, at every point on the U.S. production-possibilities curve (Figure 35.2*a*), the **opportunity cost** of a loaf of bread is one-half barrel of wine. That is to say, we are effectively paying half a barrel of wine to get a loaf of bread.

Although the opportunity costs of bread production in the United States might appear outrageous, note the even higher opportunity costs that prevail in France. According to Figure 35.2*b*, the opportunity cost of producing a loaf of bread in France is a staggering 4 barrels of wine. To produce a loaf of bread, the French must use factors of production that could have been used to produce 4 barrels of wine.

A comparison of the opportunity costs prevailing in each country exposes the nature of what we call comparative advantage. The United States has a comparative advantage in bread production because less wine has to be given up to produce bread in the United States than in France. In other words, the opportunity costs of bread production are lower in the United States than in France. *Comparative advantage refers to the relative (opportunity) costs of producing particular goods.*

A country should specialize in what it is *relatively* efficient at producing, that is, goods for which it has the lowest opportunity costs. In this case, the United States should produce bread because its opportunity cost ($\frac{1}{2}$ barrel of wine) is less than France's (4 barrels of wine). Were you the production manager for the whole world, you would certainly want each country to exploit its relative abilities, thus maximizing world output. Each country can arrive at that same decision itself by comparing its own opportunity costs to those prevailing elsewhere and offering to trade to mutual advantage. *World output, and thus the potential gains from trade, will be maximized when each country pursues its comparative advantage.* It does so by exporting goods that entail relatively low domestic opportunity costs and importing goods that involve relatively high domestic opportunity costs.

Absolute Costs Don't Count

absolute advantage: The ability of a country to produce a specific good with fewer resources (per unit of output) than other countries.

In assessing the nature of comparative advantage, notice that we needn't know anything about the actual costs involved in production. Have you seen any data suggesting how much labor, land, or capital is required to produce a loaf of bread in either France or the United States? For all you and I know, the French may be able to produce both a loaf of bread and a barrel of wine with fewer resources than we are using. Such an **absolute advantage** in production might exist because of their much longer experience in cultivating both grapes and wheat, or simply because they have more talent.

We can envy such productivity, and even try to emulate it, but it should not alter our production and international trade decisions. All we really care about are *opportunity costs*—what we have to give up in order to get more of a desired good. If we can get a barrel of imported wine for less bread than we have to give up to produce that wine ourselves, we have a comparative advantage in producing bread. In other words, as long as we have a *comparative* advantage in bread production we should exploit it. It doesn't matter to us whether France could produce either good with fewer resources. For that matter, even if France had an absolute advantage in *both* goods, we would still have a *comparative* advantage in bread production, as we have already confirmed. The absolute costs of production were omitted from the previous illustration because they were irrelevant.

To clarify the distinction between absolute advantage and comparative advantage, consider this example. When Charlie Osgood joined the Willamette Warriors' football team, he was the fastest runner ever to play football in Willamette. He could also throw the ball farther than most people could see. In other words, he had an *absolute advantage* in both throwing and running that made all other football players look like second-string water boys. Without extolling Charlie's prowess any further, let it stand that Charlie would have made the greatest quarterback *or* the greatest end ever to play football. *Would have.* The problem was that he could play only one position at a time, just as our resources can be used to produce only one good at a time. Thus the Willamette coach had to play Charlie either as a quarterback or as an end. He reasoned that Charlie could throw only a bit farther than some of the other top quarterbacks but could far outdistance all the other ends. In other words, Charlie had a *comparative advantage* in running and was assigned to play as an end.

TERMS OF TRADE

terms of trade: The rate at which goods are exchanged; the amount of good *A* given up for good *B* in trade.

It definitely pays to pursue one's comparative advantage and trade with the rest of the world on that basis. It may not yet be clear, however, how we got such a good deal with France. We are clever traders, to be sure. But beyond that, is there any way to determine the **terms of trade,** the quantity of good *A* that must be given up in exchange for good *B*? In our previous illustration, the terms of trade were very favorable to us; we exchanged only 6 zillion loaves of bread for 20 zillion barrels of wine. The terms of trade were thus 6 loaves = 20 barrels.

Limits to the Terms of Trade

The terms of trade with France were determined by our offer and France's ready acceptance. France was willing to accept our offer because the attendant terms of trade permitted France to increase its wine consumption without giving up any bread consumption. In other words, our offer to trade 6 loaves for 20 barrels was an improvement over France's domestic opportunity costs. France's domestic possibilities required her to give up 24 barrels of wine in order to produce 6 loaves of bread (see Figure 35.2*b*).[3] Getting bread via trade was simply cheaper for France than producing bread at home. As a result, France ended up with an extra 4 zillion barrels of wine.

Our first clue to the terms of trade, then, lies in each country's domestic opportunity costs. A country will not trade unless the terms of trade are superior to domestic opportunities. In our example, the opportunity cost of wine in the United States is 2 loaves of bread. Accordingly, we will not export bread unless we get at least 1 barrel of wine in exchange for every 2 loaves of bread we ship overseas. In other words, we will not play the game unless the terms of trade are superior to our own opportunity costs, thus providing us with some benefit.

No country will trade unless the terms of exchange are better than its domestic opportunity costs. Hence we can predict that ***the terms of trade between any two countries will lie somewhere between their respective opportunity costs in production.*** That is to say, a loaf of bread in international trade will be worth at least $\frac{1}{2}$ barrel of wine (the U.S. opportunity cost) but no more than 4 barrels (the French opportunity cost). In point of fact, the terms of trade ended up at 1 loaf = 3.33 barrels (that is, at 6 loaves = 20 barrels). This represented a very large gain for the United States and a small gain for France. This outcome and several other possibilities are illustrated in Figure 35.3.

The Role of Markets and Prices

Relatively little trade is subject to such direct negotiations between countries. More often than not, the decision to import or export a particular good is left up to the market decisions of individual consumers and producers. There are exceptions, as is illustrated by much of our trade with centrally planned economies and frequent trade intervention by government agencies. But before we look at those exceptions, it is important to note the role that individual consumers and producers play in trade decisions.

Individual consumers and producers are not much impressed by such abstractions as comparative advantage. Market participants tend to focus on

[3]People sometimes use the term "domestic terms of trade" to refer to opportunity costs in production. In this case, we would say that France will trade only if the international terms of trade are superior to the domestic terms of trade.

FIGURE 35.3
Searching for the Terms of Trade

Trade creates the conditions for increasing our consumption possibilities. Note in part *a* that the United States is capable of producing 100 zillion loaves of bread per year (point *A*). If we reduce bread production to only 85 zillion loaves of bread per year, we could move down the production-possibilities curve to point *X*. At point *X* we could produce and consume 7.5 zillion barrels of wine per year and 85 zillion loaves of bread. On the other hand, if we continued to produce 100 zillion loaves of bread, we might be able to trade 15 zillion loaves to France in exchange for as much as 60 zillion barrels of wine. This would leave us producing at point *A* but consuming at point *Y*. At point *Y* we have more wine and no less bread than we had at point *X*. Hence consumption possibilities with trade exceed our production possibilities.

A country will end up on its consumption-possibilities curve only if it gets *all* of the gains from trade. It will remain on its own production-possibilities curve only if it gets *none* of the gains from trade. In reality, the terms of trade determine how the gains from trade are distributed, and thus at what point in the shaded area each country ends up.

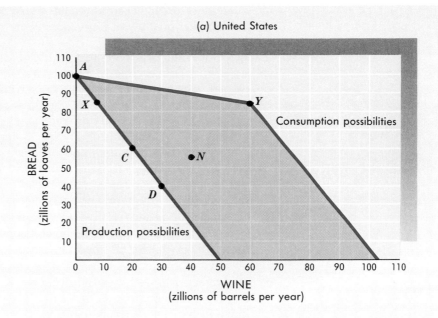

(a) United States

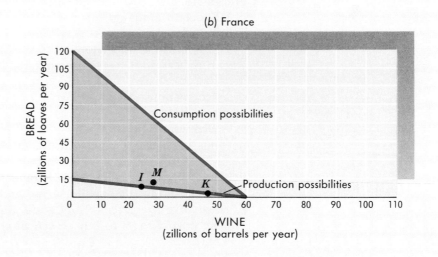

(b) France

prices, always trying to allocate their resources in order to maximize profits or personal satisfaction. As a result, consumers tend to buy the products that deliver the most utility per dollar of expenditure, while producers try to get the most output per dollar of cost. Everybody's looking for a bargain.

So what does this have to do with international trade? Well, suppose that Henri, an enterprising Frenchman, visited the United States before the advent of international trade and observed our market behavior. He noticed that bread was relatively cheap, while wine was relatively expensive, the opposite of the price relationship prevailing in France. These price comparisons brought to his mind the opportunity for making a fast franc. All he had to do was bring over some French wine and trade it in the United States for a large quantity of bread. Then he could return to France and exchange the bread for a greater quantity of wine. *Alors!* Were he to do this a few times, he would amass substantial profits.

Our French entrepreneur's exploits will not only enrich him but will also move each country toward its comparative advantage. The United States ends up exporting bread to France and France ends up exporting wine to the United States, exactly as the theory of comparative advantage suggests. The activating agent is not the Ministry of Trade and its 620 trained economists, however, but simply one enterprising French trader. He is aided and encouraged, of course, by the consumers and producers in each country. The American consumers are happy to trade their bread for his wines. They thereby end up paying less for wine (in terms of bread) than they would otherwise have to. In other words, the terms of trade Henri offers are more attractive than the prevailing (domestic) relative prices. On the other side of the Atlantic, Henri's welcome is equally warm. French consumers are able to get a better deal by trading their wine for his imported bread than by trading with the local bakers.

Even some producers are happy. The wheat farmers and bakers in America are eager to deal with Henri. He is willing to buy a lot of bread and even to pay a premium price for it. Indeed, bread production has become so profitable in the United States that a lot of people who used to grow and mash grapes are now starting to grow wheat and knead dough. This alters the mix of U.S. output in the direction of more bread, exactly as suggested earlier in Figure 35.2*a*.

In France the opposite kind of production shift is taking place. French wheat farmers start to plant grapes so they can take advantage of Henri's generous purchases. Thus Henri is able to lead each country in the direction of its comparative advantage, while raking in a substantial profit for himself along the way.

Where the terms of trade and the volume of exports and imports end up depends in part on how good a trader Henri is. It will also depend on the behavior of the thousands of individual consumers and producers who participate in the market exchanges. In other words, trade flows depend on both the supply and the demand for bread and wine in each country. ***The terms of trade, like the price of any good, will depend on the willingness of market participants to buy or sell at various prices.***

PROTECTIONIST PRESSURES

Although the potential gains from world trade are perhaps clear, we should not conclude that everyone will be smiling at the Franco-American trade celebration. On the contrary, some people will be very upset about the trade routes that Henri has established. They will not only boycott the celebration but actively seek to discourage us from continuing to trade with France.

Microeconomic Pressures

Consider, for example, the winegrowers in western New York. Do you think they are going to be very happy about Henri's entrepreneurship? Recall that Americans can now buy wine more cheaply from France than they can from New York. New York winegrowers are apt to be outraged at some foreigner cutting into their market. Before long we may hear talk about unfair foreign

In The News

Whining over Wine

A new type of wine bar has sprung up on Capitol Hill, and it's not likely to tickle the palate of a dedicated oenophile. California wine makers are hawking a bill that could slap higher tariffs on imported wine, and Congress shows some sign of becoming intoxicated with what the wine makers have to offer. First introduced last summer, the Wine Equity Act, as the measure is called, is already sponsored by 345 Congressmen and 60 Senators.

The wine makers aren't putting all their grapes into one bottle. Behind the scenes they have been making common cause with the American Grape Growers Alliance for Fair Trade, a group that represents many of the farmer cooperatives that supply domestic wineries. In a suit they filed with the Commerce Department and International Trade Commission in January, the growers complained that the Europeans, and particularly the Italians, are unfairly subsidizing their wine producers. If their suit is upheld, the ITC could impose stiff duties on the imports. The importers say there is no good evidence of substantial government subsidies.

competition or about the greater nutritional value of American grapes (see In the News). The New York winegrowers may also emphasize the importance of maintaining an adequate grape supply and a strong wine industry at home, just in case of nuclear war.

Joining with the growers will be the farm workers and all of the other workers, producers, and merchants whose livelihood depends on the New York wine industry. If they are aggressive and clever enough, the growers will also get the governor of the state to join their demonstration. After all, the governor must recognize the needs of his people, and his people definitely don't include the wheat farmers in Kansas who are making a bundle from international trade. New York consumers are, of course, benefiting from lower wine prices, but they are unlikely to demonstrate over a few cents a bottle. On the other hand, those few extra pennies translate into millions of dollars for domestic wine producers.

The winegrowers in western New York (not to mention those in California) will gather additional support from abroad. The wheat farmers in France are no happier about international trade than are the winegrowers in the United States. They would dearly love to sink all those boats bringing wheat from America, thereby protecting their own market position.

If we are to make sense of international trade policies, then, we must recognize one central fact of life: some producers have a vested interest in restricting international trade. In particular, ***workers and producers who compete with imported products—who work in import-competing industries—have an economic interest in restricting trade.*** This helps to explain why GM, Ford, and Chrysler are unhappy about trade in Toyotas and Mercedes, and why workers in Massachusetts want to end the importation of Italian shoes. It also explains why the textile producers in South Carolina think Taiwan and Korea are behaving irresponsibly when they sell cotton shirts and dresses in the United States.

Microeconomic resistance to international trade, then, arises from the fact that imports typically mean fewer jobs and less income for some domestic

In The News

TRADE RESISTANCE

A Litany of Losers

Some excerpts from congressional hearings on trade:

In the past few years, sales of imported table wines . . . have soared at an alarming rate. . . . Unless this trend is halted immediately, the domestic wine industry will face economic ruin. . . . Foreign wine imports must be limited.

—Wine Institute

The apparel industry's workers have few other alternative job opportunities. They do want to work and earn a living at their work. Little wonder therefore that they want their jobs safeguarded against the erosion caused by the increasing penetration of apparel imports.

—International Ladies' Garment Workers' Union

We are never going to strengthen the dollar, cure our balance of payments problem, lick our high unemployment, eliminate an ever-worsening inflation, as long as the U.S. sits idly by as a dumping ground for shoes, TV sets, apparel, steel and automobiles, etc. It is about time that we told the Japanese, the Spanish, the Italians, the Brazilians, and the Argentinians, and others who insist on flooding our country with imported shoes that enough is enough.

—United Shoe Workers of America

We want to be friends with Mexico and Canada. . . . We would like to be put in the same ball game with them. . . . We are not trying to hinder foreign trade . . . (but) plants in Texas go out of business (17 in the last 7 years) because of the continued threat of fly-by-night creek bed, river bank Mexican brick operations implemented overnight.

—Brick Institute of America

Trade policy should not be an absolute statement of how the world ought to behave to achieve a textbook vision of "free trade" or "maximum efficiency." It should . . . attempt to achieve the best results for Americans. . . .

—United Auto Workers

industries. At the same time, however, exports represent increased jobs and incomes for other industries. Producers and workers in export industries gain from trade. Thus on a microeconomic level, there are identifiable gainers and losers from international trade. ***Trade not only alters the mix of output but also redistributes income from import-competing industries to export industries.*** This potential redistribution is the source of political and economic friction.

We must be careful to note, however, that the microeconomic gains from trade are greater than the microeconomic losses. It's not simply a question of robbing Peter to enrich Paul. On the contrary, we must remind ourselves that consumers in general are able to enjoy a higher standard of living as a result of international trade. As we saw earlier, trade increases world efficiency and total output. Accordingly, we end up slicing up a larger pie rather than just reslicing the same old smaller pie. Although this may be little consolation to the producer or worker who ends up getting a smaller slice than before, it does point up an essential fact. The gains from trade are large enough to make everybody better off if we so choose. Whether we actually choose to undertake such a distribution of the gains from trade is a separate question, to which we shall return shortly. We note here, however, that ***trade restrictions designed to protect specific microeconomic interests reduce the total gains from trade.*** Trade restrictions leave us with a smaller pie to split up.

Additional Pressures

Import-competing industries are the principal obstacle to expanded international trade. Selfish micro interests are not the only source of trade restrictions, however. Other arguments are also used to restrict trade.

National security   The national-security argument for trade restrictions is twofold. On the one hand, it is argued that we cannot depend on foreign suppliers to provide us with essential defense-related goods, because that would leave us vulnerable in time of war. The machine-tool industry successfully used this argument in 1986 to protect itself from imports. Much earlier, the oil industry had used the national-security argument to persuade President Dwight Eisenhower to curtail oil imports in the 1950s. As a result, we used up our "essential" reserves faster than we would have in the context of unrestricted trade. The domestic oil industry, of course, reaped enormous benefit from Eisenhower's decision to protect our national security.[4]

The second part of the national-security argument relates to our export of defense-related goods. There is some doubt about the wisdom of shipping nuclear submarines or long-range missiles to a potential enemy, even for a high price. The case for limited trade restriction is again evident. But here also the argument can be overextended, as when we forbade the export to the Soviet Union of sugar-coated cereals and of machinery for making pantyhose.

Dumping   Another set of arguments against trade arises from the practice of *dumping.* Foreign producers "dump" their goods when they sell them in the United States at prices lower than those prevailing in their own country, perhaps even below the costs of production. Should the foreign producers continue this practice indefinitely, dumping would represent a great gain for us, because we would be getting foreign products for very low prices. These bargains might not last, however. Foreign producers might hold prices down only until the domestic import-competing industry is driven out of business. Then we might be compelled to pay the foreign producers higher prices for their products. In that case, dumping could consolidate market power and lead to monopoly-type pricing. The fear of dumping, then, is analogous to the fear of predatory price cutting by powerful corporations.

The potential costs of dumping are serious and merit some policy response. It is not always easy to prove dumping when it occurs, however. Those who compete with imports have an uncanny ability to associate any and all low prices with predatory dumping. Accusations of dumping are readily leveled whenever a domestic producer loses sales to a foreign competitor. Such an outcome may also reflect greater productivity, better quality, or more innovative marketing, however. Thus responsible policymakers must take special care to confirm that dumping has occurred before attempting to restrict trade. If it has, taxes or penalties can be imposed on the foreign producer (see World View on Canada's penalties for Hyundai dumping).

Infant industries   Dumping threatens to damage already established domestic industries. Even normal import prices, however, may make it difficult or impossible for a new domestic industry to develop. Infant industries are often burdened with abnormally high start-up costs. These high costs may arise from the need to train a whole work force and the expenses of establishing new marketing channels. With time to grow, however, an infant industry might experience substantial cost reductions and establish a new comparative advantage. In such cases, trade restrictions are sought to nurture an

---

[4]The Mandatory Oil Import Program was terminated in 1973, when our domestic oil production could no longer satisfy domestic demand.

W◍RLD VIEW

DUMPING

Canada Rules Hyundai Dumped Cars, Imposes Stiff Provisional Import Duties

OTTAWA—Canada's revenue department ruled that Hyundai cars have been dumped on the Canadian market and imposed stiff provisional impact duties on the South Korean vehicles.

The department's investigation was prompted by a complaint from two Canadian auto makers, General Motors at Canada Ltd., a unit of General Motors Corp., De-

troit, and Ford Motor Co., of Canada Ltd., a subsidiary of Dearborn, Mich.-based Ford Motor Co.

Dumping occurs when goods are sold in a foreign market at prices below those in the home market.

The provisional duties are to offset the margin of dumping, which the department estimated at 37.3% for Hyundai's Pony car, 36.6% for the Stellar car, and 35% for the Excel model. . . .

—John Urquhart

industry in its infancy. Trade restrictions are justified, however, only if there is tangible evidence that the industry can develop reasonably quickly and expand the gains from trade.

Improving the terms of trade   One final argument for restricting trade rests on our earlier discussion of the way the gains from trade are distributed. As we observed, the distribution of the gains from trade depends on the terms of trade. That is, it depends on the quantity of exports that must be given up in order to get a given quantity of imports. If we buy fewer imports, foreign producers may lower their prices. If they do, the terms of trade will move in our favor, and we will end up with a larger share of the gains from trade.

One way to bring about this sequence of events is to put restrictions on imports, making it more difficult or expensive for Americans to buy foreign products. This kind of intervention will tend to cut down on import purchases, thereby inducing foreign producers to lower their prices. Unfortunately, this kind of stratagem is available to everyone, so our trading partners are likely to follow suit if we pursue such a course of action. Retaliatory restrictions on imports, each designed to improve the terms of trade, will ultimately eliminate all trade and therewith all of the gains people were competing for in the first place.

BARRIERS TO TRADE

The microeconomic losses associated with imports give rise to a constant clamor for trade restrictions. People whose jobs and incomes are threatened by international trade tend to organize quickly and air their grievances. Moreover, they are assured of a reasonably receptive hearing, both because of the political implications of well-financed organizations and because the gains from trade are widely diffused. If successful, such efforts can lead to a variety of trade restrictions.

Embargoes

The sure-fire way to restrict trade is simply to eliminate it. To do so, a country need only impose an embargo on exports, imports, or both. An **embargo** is nothing more than a prohibition against trading particular goods.

In 1951 Senator Joseph McCarthy convinced the U.S. Senate to impose an embargo on Soviet mink, fox, and five other furs. Senator McCarthy argued that such imports helped finance world communism. Senator McCarthy also represented the state of Wisconsin, where most U.S. minks are raised. The Reagan administration tried to end the fur embargo in 1987 but met with stiff congressional opposition. By then, U.S. mink ranchers had developed a $120 million per year industry.

The United States has also maintained an embargo on Cuban goods since 1959, when Fidel Castro took power there. This embargo severely damaged Cuba's sugar industry and deprived American smokers of the famed Havana cigars. In 1985 President Reagan imposed a similar embargo on trade with Nicaragua. It was lifted by President Bush only after a friendlier government was elected in 1990.

Tariffs

One of the most popular and visible restrictions on trade is the **tariff,** a special tax imposed on imported goods. Tariffs, also called "customs duties," were once the principal source of revenue for governments. In the eighteenth century, tariffs on tea, glass, wine, lead, and paper were imposed on the American colonies to provide extra revenue for the British government. The tariff on tea led to the Boston Tea Party in 1773 and gave added momentum to the independence movement. In modern times, tariffs have been used primarily as a means of import protection to satisfy specific microeconomic or macroeconomic interests. The current U.S. tariff code specifies tariffs on 8,753 different products—nearly 70 percent of all U.S. imports. Although the average tariff is only 5 percent, individual tariffs vary widely. The tariff on cars, for example, is only 2.5 percent, while polyester sweaters confront a 34.6 percent tariff.

The attraction of tariffs to import-competing industries should be obvious. *A tariff on imported goods makes them more expensive to domestic consumers, and thus less competitive with domestically produced goods.* Among familiar tariffs in effect in 1990 were $0.50 per gallon on Scotch whiskey and $1.17 per gallon on imported champagne. These tariffs made American-produced spirits look like relatively good buys and thus contributed to higher sales and profits for domestic distillers and grape growers. In the same manner, imported baby food is taxed at 34.6 percent, orange juice at 36 percent, footwear at 20 percent, and imported stereos at rates ranging from 4 to 6 percent. In each of these cases, domestic producers in import-competing industries gain. The losers are domestic consumers, who end up paying higher prices; foreign producers, who lose business; and world efficiency, as trade is reduced.

Job protection? Microeconomic interests are not the only source of pressure for tariff protection. Imports represent leakage from the domestic circular flow and a potential loss of jobs at home. In the same way, exports represent increased aggregate demand and more jobs. From this perspective, the curtailment of imports looks like an easy solution to the problem of domestic unemployment. Just get people to "buy American" instead of buying imported products, it is argued, and domestic output and employment will expand. Congressman Willis Hawley used this argument in 1930. He assured his colleagues that higher tariffs would "bring about the growth and development in this country that has followed every other tariff bill, bringing as it does a new prosperity in which all people, in all sections, will increase their comforts, their enjoyment, and their happiness."[5] Congress responded by passing the Hawley-Smoot Tariff Act of 1930, which raised tariffs to an average of nearly 60 percent. The Hawley-Smoot Tariff effectively cut off most imports and contributed to the Great Depression.

Tariffs designed to expand domestic employment are more likely to fail than to succeed. If a tariff is successful in limiting imports, it effectively transfers the unemployment problem to other countries, a phenomenon often referred to as "beggar-thy-neighbor." The resultant loss of business in other countries leaves them less able to purchase our exports. The imported unemployment also creates intense economic and political pressures for retaliatory action. That is exactly what happened in the 1930s. Other countries erected trade barriers to compensate for the effects of the Hawley-Smoot Tariff. World trade subsequently fell from $60 billion in 1928 to a mere $25 billion in 1938. In the process, all countries suffered from reduced demand (see World View).

Quotas

quota: A limit on the quantity of a good that may be imported in a given time period.

Tariffs help to reduce the flow of imports by raising import prices. As an alternative barrier to trade, a country can impose import **quotas,** restrictions on the quantity of a particular good that may be imported. The United States maintained a quota on imported petroleum from 1959 to 1973. Other goods that have been (and most of which still are) subject to import quotas in the United States are sugar, meat, dairy products, textiles, cotton, peanuts, steel, cloth diapers, and even ice cream. According to the U.S. Department of State, approximately 12 percent of our imports are subject to import quotas.

Quotas, like all barriers to trade, reduce world efficiency and invite retaliatory action. Moreover, quotas are especially pernicious because of their impact on competition and the distribution of income. To see this impact, we may compare market outcomes in four different contexts: no trade, free trade, tariff-restricted trade, and quota-restricted trade.

Figure 35.4a depicts the supply-and-demand relationships that would prevail in an economy that imposed a trade *embargo* on textiles. In this situation, the **equilibrium price** of textiles is completely determined by domestic demand and supply curves. The equilibrium price is p_1, and the quantity of textiles consumed is q_1.

equilibrium price: The price at which the quantity of a good demanded in a given time period equals the quantity supplied.

Suppose now that the embargo is lifted and foreign producers are allowed to sell textiles in the American market. The immediate effect of this decision will be a rightward shift of the market supply curve, as foreign supplies are added to domestic supplies (Figure 35.4b). If an unlimited quantity of textiles can be bought in world markets at a price of p_2, the new supply curve will look like S_2 (infinitely elastic at p_2). The new supply curve (S_2) intersects the old demand curve (D_1) at a new equilibrium price of p_2 and an expanded consumption of q_2. At this new equilibrium, domestic producers are supplying the quantity q_d while foreign producers are supplying the rest ($q_2 - q_d$). Comparing the new equilibrium to the old one, we see that the initiation of trade results in reduced prices and increased consumption.

[5]*New York Times,* June 15, 1930, p. 25.

W🌐RLD VIEW

RETALIATORY TARIFFS

"Beggar Thy Neighbor" Policies in the 1930s

The Great Depression of the 1930s is usually blamed on the crash of the U.S. stock market and bad monetary policies in the United States and Europe. Restrictive trade policies, most notably the U.S. Smoot-Hawley tariff of 1930 and the retaliation which followed, also contributed to the worldwide depression, however.

Some policymakers in the late 1920s understood the threat to world and national welfare posed by the use of high tariffs. In 1927 and again in 1930 the World Economic Conference met to urge nations to stop raising tariffs. But it was already too late. The Smoot-Hawley tariff was signed into law on June 17, 1930. It raised the effective rate of tariffs in the United States by almost 50 percent between 1929 and 1932. Other nations responded in kind:

- Spain passed the Wais tariff in July in reaction to U.S. tariffs on grapes, oranges, cork, and onions.

- Switzerland, objecting to new U.S. tariffs on watches, embroideries, and shoes, boycotted American exports.

- Italy retaliated against tariffs on hats and olive oil with high tariffs on U.S. and French automobiles in June 1930.

- Canada reacted to high duties on many food products, logs, and timber by raising tariffs threefold in August 1932.

- Australia, Cuba, France, Mexico, and New Zealand also joined in the tariff wars.

Other "beggar thy neighbor" policies, including currency depreciations and foreign exchange controls, were used in attempts to improve domestic economies at the expense of foreign countries. The attempt by all countries to run a trade surplus by cutting imports led to a breakdown of the entire system of trade.

As a result of these policies, all countries suffered from idle productive capacity and low prices. The increased domestic demand for U.S. farm products protected by high tariffs, for example, was more than offset by the loss of export markets. Exports of U.S. agricultural products dropped 66 percent from 1929 to 1932. This aggravated the decline in farm prices, which in turn contributed to rural bank failures.

While a consensus on the causes of the Depression is yet to be reached, it is probable that the beggar thy neighbor trade policies at least added to the severity of the Depression and contributed to the breakdown of international trade.

World Bank, *World Development Report,* 1987.

Domestic textile producers are unhappy, of course, with their foreign competition. In the absence of trade, the domestic producers would sell more output (q_1) and get higher prices (p_1). Once trade is opened up, the willingness of foreign producers to sell unlimited quantities of textiles at the price p_2 puts a limit on the price behavior of domestic producers. Accordingly, we can anticipate some lobbying for trade restrictions.

Figure 35.4c illustrates what would happen to prices and sales if the United Textile Producers were successful in persuading the government to impose a tariff. Let us assume that the tariff has the effect of raising imported textile prices from p_2 to p_3,[6] making it more difficult for foreign producers to undersell so many domestic producers. Domestic production expands from q_d to q_t, imports are reduced from $q_2 - q_d$ to $q_3 - q_t$, and the market price of textiles rises. Domestic textile producers are clearly better off, whereas consumers and foreign producers are worse off. In addition, the U.S. Treasury will be better off as a result of increased tariff revenues.

[6]Import prices will not necessarily rise by the full amount of a tariff, as foreign producers may lower their export prices somewhat to maintain sales. Thus the impact of a tariff on import prices depends in part on the price elasticity of foreign supply. In this case, we have assumed that foreign supplies are perfectly elastic, so that the difference $p_3 - p_2$ measures both the tariff and the ultimate price change.

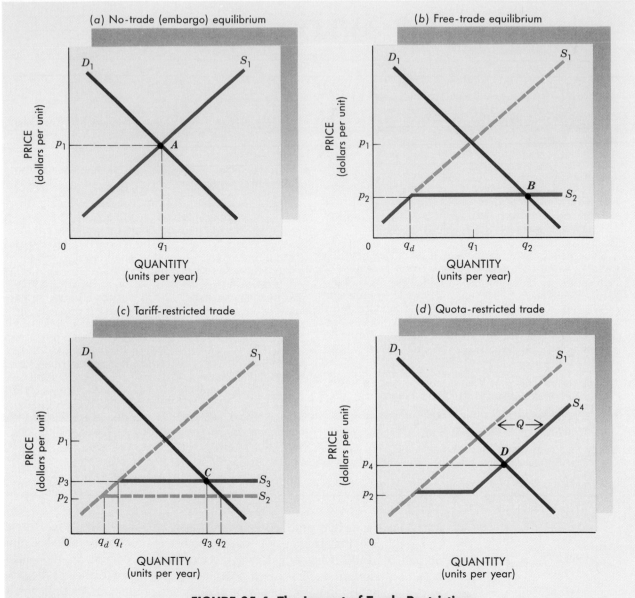

FIGURE 35.4 The Impact of Trade Restrictions

In the *absence of trade*, the domestic price and sales of a good will be determined by domestic supply and demand curves (point *A* in part *a*). Once trade is permitted, the market supply curve will be altered by the availability of imports. With *free trade* and unlimited availability of imports at price p_2, a new market equilibrium will be established at world prices (point *B*).

Tariffs raise domestic prices and reduce the quantity sold (point *C*). *Quotas* put an absolute limit on imported sales and thus give domestic producers a great opportunity to raise the market price (point *D*).

Now consider the impact of a textile *quota*. Suppose that we eliminate tariffs but decree that imports cannot exceed the quantity Q. Because the quantity of imports can never exceed Q, the supply curve is effectively shifted

"TELL ME AGAIN HOW THE QUOTAS ON JAPANESE CARS HAVE PROTECTED US"

—from HERBLOCK AT LARGE (Pantheon Books, 1987).

to the right by that amount. The new curve S_4 (Figure 35.4d) indicates that no imports will occur below the world price p_2, and that above that price the quantity Q will be imported. Thus the *domestic* demand curve determines subsequent prices. Foreign producers are precluded from selling greater quantities as prices rise further. This outcome is in marked contrast to that of tariff-restricted trade (Figure 35.4c), which at least permits foreign producers to respond to rising prices. Accordingly, ***quotas are a much greater threat to competition than tariffs, because quotas preclude additional imports at any price.*** The World View on page 870 suggests how costly such protection can be.

Voluntary Restraint Agreements

voluntary restraint agreement (VRA): An agreement to reduce the volume of trade in a specific good; a "voluntary" quota.

A slight variant of quotas has been used in recent years. Rather than imposing quotas on imports, the U.S. government asks foreign producers to "voluntarily" limit their exports. These so-called **voluntary restraint agreements** have been negotiated with producers in Japan, South Korea, Taiwan, China, the European Community, and other countries. Korea, for example, agreed to reduce its annual shoe exports to the United States from 44 million pairs to 33 million pairs. Taiwan reduced its shoe exports from 156 million pairs to 122 million pairs per year. In 1989 China agreed to slow its exports of clothing, limiting its sales growth to 3 percent a year. For their part, the Japanese agreed to reduce sales of color television sets in the United States from 2.8 million

W🌐RLD VIEW

IMPORT QUOTAS

Sugar Quota a Sour Deal

Very little sugar cane is grown in the United States. Most domestically produced sugar comes from beet sugar. The rest of our sugar is imported from tropical countries.

The 12,000 domestic beet-sugar growers have convinced Congress to protect their industry to ensure a secure supply of sugar in a war. The U.S. Department of Agriculture guarantees the beet-sugar growers a minimum of 18 cents per pound for their output. To keep prices at that level, the U.S. Congress limits sugar imports. As a result, domestic sugar prices are typically twice as high as world sugar prices. In early 1990, the price of sugar in U.S. markets was 22 cents per pound, versus only 10 cents in world markets. This price difference cost American consumers nearly $1 billion in 1990

alone. Foreign producers and workers who were excluded from the U.S. market also lost out. Between 1983 and 1990, over 400,000 workers in Caribbean nations lost their jobs as a result of shrinking U.S. sugar quotas.

Who benefits from these sugar quotas? The list includes

• The 12,000 American beet-sugar farmers

• Producers of sugar substitutes (e.g., corn syrups)

• Those nations and producers that get a share of the U.S. quota

• Former and current members of Congress who receive fees and campaign contributions for perpetuating the sugar quota system

to 1.75 million per year. In 1989 President Bush extended voluntary restraint agreements on foreign steel exports, limiting imported steel to 18.4 percent of total U.S. sales.

All of these "voluntary export restraints," as they are often called, represented an informal type of quota. The only difference is that they are negotiated rather than imposed, and they often include provisions for later increases in sales. But these differences are lost on consumers, who end up paying higher prices for these goods. The voluntary limit on Japanese auto exports to the United States alone cost consumers $15.7 billion in only four years (see World View, p. 871).

Nontariff Barriers   Embargoes, export controls, tariffs, and quotas are the most visible barriers to trade, but they are far from the only ones. Indeed, the variety of protectionist measures that have been devised is testimony to the ingenuity of the human mind. At the turn of the century, the Germans were committed to a most-favored-nation policy, a policy of extending equal treatment to all trading partners. The Germans, however, wanted to lower the tariff on cattle imports from Denmark without extending the same break to Switzerland. Such a preferential tariff would have violated the most-favored-nation policy. Accordingly, the Germans created a new and higher tariff on "brown and dappled cows reared at a level of at least 300 meters above sea level and passing at least one month in every summer at an altitude of at least 800 meters." The new tariff was, of course, applied equally to all countries. But Danish cows never climb that high, so they were not burdened with the new tariff.

Trading Blocs   The effort of the Germans to favor Danish over Swiss cows has its counterpart in bilateral trade agreements and the formation of trading blocs. The twelve nations of the European Community (EC), for example, have eliminated vir-

W🌐RLD VIEW

EXPORT RESTRAINT

Japanese Cars: Voluntary Export Restraint

In 1980 U.S. auto companies sold 1 million fewer cars than in the prior year. Because of their high fixed costs, the Big Three auto companies (GM, Ford, and Chrysler) collectively lost over $4 billion that year.

U.S. producers were quick to blame Japan for their plight. Although imports of Japanese-made cars increased by only 100,000 in 1980 (only one-tenth of the domestic sales decline), the Big Three demanded import protection. They claimed to need "breathing room" to retool for smaller cars, to cut costs, and to update production processes.

Fearing more severe protectionist measures, the Japanese Ministry of International Trade and Industry (MITI) agreed to a "voluntary" three-year freeze on auto exports to the United States. Japanese producers would ship only 1.65 million cars a year, equal to about 20 percent of total U.S. sales.

In April 1984 Japan's voluntary export restraint was scheduled to end. But Detroit demanded continued protection, and Congress debated stricter measures. Japan instead agreed to extend the export restraint for another year, at the slightly higher level of 1.85 million cars a year.

The Japanese export restraint helped U.S. auto producers greatly. Between 1981 and 1985, domestic car prices rose by an average of more than $2,000. Robert Crandall of the Brookings Institution attributes at least $450 of this price increase to the Japanese export limit. The Big Three's profits jumped to $6 billion in 1983 and $10 billion in 1984. Producers and importers of Japanese cars also reaped high profits, as their prices jumped as much as $2,500 per car.

With all the auto makers gaining, who lost? American consumers, of course. Consumers paid higher prices for their cars, had a smaller selection, and had to wait longer for delivery. The U.S. International Trade Commission figured that the higher car prices alone cost consumers $15.7 billion between 1981 and 1985.

tually all trade barriers among themselves. This dismantling of internal trade barriers will stimulate trade and efficiency within the EC. The EC expects economic growth to accelerate 1 percent a year as a result of this market integration. At the same time, however, the EC trading bloc might put non-EC nations at a disadvantage. Differential market access could prevent more efficient producers from exploiting their comparative advantage. The same kinds of gains and risks apply to the bilateral free-trade agreement signed in 1987 by the United States and Canada.

The disadvantage of trading blocs was most apparent in Eastern Europe prior to the dismantling of the Berlin Wall. The members of the East bloc did most of their trading internally, often at prices set by central planners. There was little outside competition and no market test of efficiency. When the Iron Curtain was removed in 1989, the countries of Eastern Europe saw how much such trade barriers and distortions had cost them. They sought to redirect their trade patterns in accordance with comparative advantage, thereby increasing efficiency and living standards.

GATT   Over forty years ago, most of the world's industrialized nations agreed to pursue *multilateral* trade policy, extending most-favored status (equal access) to one another's markets. The General Agreement on Tariffs and Trade (GATT), first signed in 1947, commits the world's trading partners to pursue free-trade policies. In pursuit of that objective, GATT signatories have negotiated seven agreements to lower tariffs. As tariffs have fallen, however, non-tariff barriers to trade continued to grow. Italy, for example, has long discouraged auto imports by imposing a road tax based on weight and axle width. Not surprisingly, the tax resulted in increased levies on imported cars. The Japanese use complex and time-consuming licensing regulations and standards to keep out imports, thus sheltering domestic producers from competition. The United States is no less imaginative when it comes to nontariff barriers to trade. For example, we tax all distilled spirits entering this country as though they were 100 proof, thus effectively raising the tariff on an 86-proof bottle of Scotch. Domestic producers are thereby sheltered a bit from competition, while the rest of us pay more for a drink.

The GATT countries started the most recent round of discussions on trade barriers in November 1986. The focus of the so-called Uruguay Round was nontariff barriers, including export subsidies. The Uruguay Round of GATT negotiations also sought to extend free-trade agreements to services (e.g., air transport, banking, insurance), which now account for one-third of all trade. Earlier GATT agreements covered only manufactured goods. The United States also used the Uruguay Round to gain more protection for "intellectual property," that is, copyrighted books, music, and computer software. Unauthorized production ("piracy") of these goods in developing nations was depriving American producers of $40 billion a year in sales.

After four years of negotiations, the Uruguay Round made only modest progress in dismantling these trade barriers erected by vested interests in the GATT nations. Nevertheless, it did reduce tariffs on manufactured goods further (see World View) and helped focus public attention on other trade barriers and their associated costs.

POLICY INSIGHTS:

TRADE ADJUSTMENT

adjustment assistance: Compensation to market participants for losses imposed by international trade.

The microeconomic pressures for trade barriers arise from the economic losses inflicted on import-competing industries. If those losses could be avoided or compensated for, no such pressures would arise. The strategy to pursue in this case is some form of **adjustment assistance.**

W🌐RLD VIEW

GATT AGREEMENT

Trade Talks Lead to Way to Lower Tariffs by 30%

GENEVA—World trade negotiators agreed on a compromise approach to cutting import tariffs at least 30%. . . .

The 30% target was agreed to by trade ministers meeting in Montreal in December 1988.

The compromise approach allows the 96 GATT members to select their own method of cutting tariffs, one of the main ways of protecting domestic industries from foreign competition.

The U.S. has said it wants to negotiate reductions on an individual product sector basis, including agriculture.

This would enable Washington to keep traditionally high customs duties for its sensitive textiles sector.

The 12-nation European trading group has pressed for across-the-board tariff cuts for industrial products, saying this will prevent countries from keeping high levels of protection in individual sectors. However, the EC insists that agriculture should not be included in this package.

The difference in approaches prevented progress in the tariff talks last year.

The Wall Street Journal, January 31, 1990, p. A14. Reprinted by permission of *The Wall Street Journal,* © Dow Jones & Company, Inc. (1990). All Rights Reserved.

The objective of trade, we should remember, is to reallocate resources in such a way to increase world output and domestic consumption. To this end, each country is expected to shuffle its capital and labor from one industry to another, in the direction of comparative advantage (see In the News). As we observed in Figures 35.2 and 35.3, this simply entails a move from one point on the production-possibilities curve to another point. Unfortunately, such shuffling from one industry to another is more difficult in practice than it is along the dimensions of a textbook graph.

In our previous illustration of Franco-American trade, vineyards were transformed instantaneously into wheat fields, vats into ovens, and grape pickers into wheat threshers. A nice trick if you can manage it, but few people can. Indeed, were such instantaneous resource reallocations possible, there would be no microeconomic resistance to international trade. Everyone would be able to share in the jobs and profits associated with comparative advantage. *The resistance to trade arises from the fact that resource reallocations are difficult and costly in practice,* both in human and in financial terms. The nature of resistance to trade is evident in a few grim statistics. In a recent survey of workers who lost their jobs as a result of import competition, it was found that 26 percent had gone for at least a year without work. Those who had found jobs had worked, on the average, only 50 percent of the time.

Worker Assistance   The objective of adjustment assistance is to speed up the reallocation of resources and to make the transition less painful for affected workers. For this purpose, workers may be taught new skills, assisted in finding new jobs, aided in moving to new areas, and provided with interim income maintenance. In the case of older workers whose skills are not easily transferred, early

In The News

RESOURCE SHIFTS

Reallocating Labor: Comparative Advantage at Work

Between 1972 and 1984, imports displaced workers from some industries while growing exports created new jobs elsewhere. These figures depict some of the major trade-related job losses and gains. By reallocating our labor in this way, we altered the mix of output in the direction of comparative advantage.

Labor moved out of these industries:	Jobs lost
Steel mill products	− 229,700
Textile products	− 216,000
Apparel	− 127,000
Shoes	− 73,800
Radios and television sets	− 38,500
Tires and inner tubes	− 37,000
And into these industries:	Jobs gained
Electronic computing equipment	+ 218,200
Medical and dental instruments	+ 208,800
Communications equipment	+ 196,400
Aerospace	+ 115,100
Oil field machinery	+ 26,600
Biological products	+ 13,300

Source: U.S. International Trade Administration.

retirement and pension benefits may be the most efficient kind of adjustment assistance.

All such assistance is expensive, of course. The Trade Expansion Act of 1962 permitted displaced workers to receive 70 percent of their previous wages for a period of up to 18 months, plus training and relocation allowances. Between 1975 and 1981 over 1 million workers received nearly $3 billion in such assistance. Nevertheless, many labor unions have dismissed the program as "burial insurance." They argue that benefits are too low, and that in any case many workers can neither return nor relocate without considerable hardship. As John Mara, head of the Boot and Shoe Workers' Union, put it after seeing ninety shoe factories shut down in Massachusetts: "Retraining for what? I want the economists to tell me what alternatives are available. Picking tomatoes in California?" ***The critical issue in trade adjustment is whether alternative jobs exist and whether we are prepared to help workers get them.*** Income maintenance, retraining assistance, job-search aid, relocation subsidies, and a strong economy are all required for a smooth transition.

Industry Subsidies

Not only workers but employers as well are adversely affected by import competition. When the competition from abroad is too great, a plant may have to shut down and its owners absorb a loss on their investment. Even though the owners may not need adjustment assistance as badly as the displaced workers, they are going to be a source of protectionist pressure. Furthermore, their loss may leave an entire community without a major source of economic support. For both of these reasons, some adjustment assistance may be necessary or appropriate.

The most common form of adjustment assistance to import-competing firms is a subsidy, a direct payment from the public treasury to the affected firm. Ideally, such a subsidy will be provided for the purpose of converting a plant to more profitable lines of production. When the plant cannot be easily converted, the subsidy should be temporary, with the explicit intent of simply slowing, not obstructing, the process of adjustment to comparative advantage. The Trade Act of 1974 provided for loans of up to $1 million for affected companies and another $3 million in loan guarantees, but few companies accepted such aid. They argued that it was both inadequate and too encumbered with red tape.

The Reagan administration, too, concluded that trade-adjustment assistance was not effective, but for different reasons. The administration concluded that special benefits to trade-impacted workers and industries slow the adjustment process more often than they facilitate it. It reduced the level of special "adjustment" benefits and required recipients to enroll in training.

1988 Trade Act

The market share of imports continued to increase in many industries in the early 1980s (see Table 35.3). The affected industries demanded more protection and more adjustment assistance. They got a little more of both in the Trade Act of 1988. That act requires the president to retaliate with quotas or tariffs when foreign governments "unfairly" subsidize exports or protect their own domestic markets. Yet the act also expands U.S. export subsidy and promotion. The act also provides more generous adjustment assistance to firms and workers injured by import competition. Thus the 1988 Trade Act walked a thin line between protectionism and adjustment.

TABLE 35.3 Import Penetration

Imports compete directly with domestic producers of many goods. Foreign producers have gained an increasing share of total U.S. sales of shoes, apparel, televisions, and many other goods. These rising import shares prompt domestic producers to demand trade protection.

Imported products	Percentage of total industry sales	
	1972	1984
Shoes	17	50
Autos	8	16
Steel	10	17
Textile machinery	37	46
Apparel	7	20
Radios and TV sets	35	58
Machine tools	8	30
Copper	8	17
Farm machinery	9	14

Source: U.S. International Trade Administration.

SUMMARY

- International trade permits each country to concentrate its resources on those goods it can produce relatively efficiently. This kind of productive specialization increases world output. For each country, the gains from trade are reflected in the fact that its consumption possibilities exceed its production possibilities.

- In determining what to produce and offer in trade, each country will exploit its comparative advantage—its *relative* efficiency in producing various goods. One way to determine where comparative advantage lies is to compare the quantity of good A that must be given up in order to get a given quantity of good B from domestic production. If the same quantity of B can be obtained for less A by engaging in world trade, we have a comparative advantage in the production of good A. Comparative advantage rests on a comparison of relative opportunity costs.

- The terms of trade—the rate at which goods are exchanged—are subject to the forces of international supply and demand. The terms of trade will lie somewhere between the opportunity costs of the trading partners. Once established, the terms of trade will help to determine the share of the gains from trade received by each trading partner.

- Resistance to trade emanates from workers and firms that must compete with imports. Even though the country as a whole stands to benefit from trade, these individuals and companies may lose jobs and incomes in the process.

- The means of restricting trade are many and diverse. Embargoes are outright prohibitions against import or export of particular goods. Quotas limit the quantity of a good imported or exported. Tariffs, on the other hand, discourage imports by making them more expensive. Other nontariff barriers make trade too costly or time-consuming.

- Trade-adjustment assistance is a mechanism for compensating people who incur economic losses as a result of international trade; thus it represents an alternative to trade restrictions.

Terms to Remember Define the following terms:

imports	absolute advantage
exports	terms of trade
trade deficit	embargo
trade surplus	tariff
production possibilities	quota
consumption possibilities	equilibrium price
comparative advantage	voluntary restraint agreement (VRA)
opportunity cost	adjustment assistance

Questions for Discussion

1. Suppose a lawyer can type faster than any secretary. Should the lawyer do her own typing? Can you demonstrate the validity of your answer?

2. How much adjustment assistance should a displaced worker receive? For how long?

3. In what sense does international trade restrain the exercise of domestic market power?

4. Suppose we refused to sell goods to any country that reduced or halted its exports to us. Who would benefit and who would lose from such retaliation? Can you suggest alternative ways to ensure import supplies?

5. Domestic producers often base their claim for import protection on the fact that workers in country X are paid substandard wages. Is this a valid argument for protection?

Problems

1. Suppose the following table reflects the domestic supply and demand for compact discs (CDs):

Price ($)	16	14	12	10	8	6	4	2
Quantity supplied	8	7	6	5	4	3	2	1
Quantity demanded	2	4	6	8	10	12	14	16

(*a*) Graph these market conditions and identify the equilibrium price and sales.

(*b*) Now suppose that foreigners enter the market, offering to sell an unlimited supply of CDs for $6 apiece. Illustrate and identify (1) the market price, (2) domestic consumption, and (3) domestic production.

(*c*) If a tariff of $2 per CD is imposed, what will happen to (1) the market price, (2) domestic consumption, and (3) domestic production?

2. Alpha and Beta, two tiny islands off the east coast of Tricoli, produce pearls and pineapples. The production-possibilities schedules at the top of the opposite page describe their potential output in tons per year:

Alpha		Beta	
Pearls	Pineapples	Pearls	Pineapples
0	30	0	20
2	25	10	16
4	20	20	12
6	15	30	8
8	10	40	4
10	5	45	2
12	0	50	0

(a) Graph the production possibilities confronting each island.

(b) What is the opportunity cost of pineapples on each island (before trade)?

(c) Which island has a comparative advantage in pearl production?

(d) Graph the consumption possibilities of each island if unrestricted trade is permitted.

3. Suppose the two islands in problem 2 agree that the terms of trade will be 1 pineapple for 1 pearl and that trade soon results in an exchange of 10 pearls for 10 pineapples.

(a) If Alpha produced 6 pearls and 15 pineapples while Beta produced 30 pearls and 8 pineapples before they decided to trade, how much would each be producing after trade became possible? Assume that the two countries specialize just enough to maintain their consumption of the item they export, and make sure each island trades the item for which it has a comparative advantage.

(b) How much would each island be consuming after specializing and trading?

(c) How much would the combined production of pineapples increase for the two islands due to trade? How much would the combined production of pearls increase?

(d) How could both countries produce and consume even more?

(e) Assume the two islands are able to trade as much as they want with the rest of the world, with the terms of trade at 1 pineapple for 1 pearl. Draw the ultimate consumption-possibilities curve for each island.

International Finance

*W*hen the Berlin Wall was torn down in 1989, East Germans rushed to West Berlin to buy toys, clothes, fresh fruit, and other goods unavailable in the East. They soon encountered another obstacle to their shopping plans, however. Ostmarks, the East German currency, were not accepted as a form of payment. Shopkeepers in West Berlin wanted to be paid in Deutschemarks, the currency of West Germany. Hence the East German shoppers first had to exchange their Ostmarks for Deutschemarks before they could buy Western goods and services. They ended up in the foreign exchange market, buying one national currency (Deutschemarks) with another (Ostmarks).

Americans who travel abroad also participate in foreign-exchange markets. In most places, you must exchange your dollars for the local currency before you go shopping or pay your hotel bill. Even Americans who never leave these shores indirectly participate in foreign-exchange markets. Every time you buy an imported product, you set off a chain of transactions that ultimately entails exchanging one currency (the dollars you pay) for another (the foreign currency paid to foreign producers).

International trade would be clumsy and inefficient without foreign-exchange markets. If national currencies couldn't be exchanged for one another, all trade would have to be bartered. You could buy foreign products only by offering equally desired products in exchange.

For traders, travelers, and Germans, the key concerns about international finance are

- What determines the value of one country's money in terms of other national currencies?

- What causes the international value of currencies to change?

- Can we limit the fluctuations in the value of the dollar, and should we try to do so?

EXCHANGE RATES: THE CRITICAL LINK

In Chapter 35 we observed that we import and export a staggering array of goods and services, including French wine. What makes international trade so easy is that we are able to *exchange* dollars for francs, for yen, or for any other national currency we may desire. If you want to buy French wines directly from the growers, you can exchange your dollars for francs at the Bank of France or almost any commercial bank in France. With your newly acquired francs, you can proceed to the vineyards. There you may dicker with the growers over the price of their Beaujolais and buy as much wine as your income permits.

In fact, if you have no great desire to visit the vineyards but still enjoy Beaujolais, you can stay in the United States and simply go to your local liquor store. In this case, you pay for the wine in dollars. The person who imported the wine attends to the problems of exchanging your dollars for French francs and dickering with the growers.

No matter who actually haggles with the growers or brings the wine back to the United States, however, someone is going to have to exchange dollars for francs. The critical question for everybody concerned is how many francs we can get for our dollars—that is, what the **exchange rate** is. If we can get five francs for every dollar, the exchange rate is 5 francs = 1 dollar. Alternatively, we could note that the price of a French franc is 20 cents when the exchange rate is 5 to 1. Thus *an exchange rate is simply the price of one currency in terms of another.*

exchange rate: The price of one country's currency expressed in terms of another's; the domestic price of a foreign currency.

FOREIGN-EXCHANGE MARKETS

Most exchange rates are determined in foreign-exchange markets. Stop thinking of money as some sort of magical substance and view it instead as a useful commodity that can facilitate market exchanges. From that perspective, an exchange rate—the price of money—is subject to the same influences that determine all market prices: demand and supply.

The Demand for Foreign Currency

With the possible exception of coin collectors and speculators, few people have much demand for foreign currencies per se. Foreign currencies, including French francs and German Deutschemarks, are demanded not for their intrinsic value but for what they can buy. Hence *the demand for foreign currency is primarily an expression of the demand for foreign goods and services.*

The demand for foreign currency originates in many ways. First and foremost, there is a demand for imported products, such as French wines, German cars, and Japanese stereo equipment. To acquire these things, we need foreign money.

Foreign travel by Americans also generates a demand for foreign currency. When you are traveling, you need foreign currency to pay for transportation, hotel rooms, food, and anything else you wish to buy and can afford. Even if you use U.S. dollars or traveler's checks on occasion, the recipients of such money will ultimately exchange them for local money, thereby reflecting your demand for foreign currency.

U.S. corporations demand foreign exchange, too. General Motors builds cars in Germany, Coca-Cola produces Coke in China, Exxon produces and refines oil all over the world. In nearly every such case, the U.S. firm must first build or buy some plant and equipment, using another country's factors of production. This activity requires foreign currency and thus becomes another component of our demand for foreign currency.

Investment opportunities work both ways. Foreign producers often make direct investments in the United States. Shell and BP gas stations are a familiar example of direct foreign investment here, as are foreign auto plants, such as Honda in Ohio and Volvo in Virginia. In making such investments, foreign firms must first demand U.S. currency that can be used to buy our factors of production. Sooner or later, however, the foreign firms will want to reverse the flow of money, taking some of their profits back to their own banks and stockholders. In doing so, they create a demand for foreign currency as they convert the dollars they have earned in the United States into the currencies their stockholders and creditors can spend at home.

The other sources of the U.S. demand for foreign currency include transfers (typically by foreign workers who send home some of their U.S. income), U.S. military installations abroad (which are fed and housed with foreign goods and services), and foreign aid (which is often used to buy foreign goods).

The Supply of Foreign Currency

Foreigners have the same kind of demand for U.S. dollars that we have for foreign currencies. They buy our merchandise (our exports, their imports), travel in the United States, and invest in productive resources located within our borders. When Mitsubishi, a Japanese corporation, bought Rockefeller Center in 1989, it paid in dollars (846 million of them). Likewise, the Sony Corporation needed 3.4 billion dollars to buy Columbia Pictures. All such purchases of American assets create a demand for dollars. The Japanese had to exchange their yen for dollars before acquiring the property. In offering to buy dollars, they were simultaneously offering to sell yen. In other words, ***demands for U.S. dollars also represent a supply of foreign currencies.*** That is to say, foreigners offer to exchange (supply) foreign currency when they desire (demand) U.S. dollars.

Another source of demand for U.S. dollars is the overseas profits of American firms. As we observed earlier, a company that invests in a foreign country wants to get some of its profits out sooner or later. U.S. firms have accumulated a tremendous investment in foreign countries. These investments now generate a steady flow of profits and dividends back to the United States. This flow requires the conversion of foreign currencies into U.S. dollars (supply of foreign currencies, demand for U.S. dollars).

U.S. dollars are also demanded for foreign purchases of U.S. securities. Foreign investors and governments buy a huge volume of U.S. Treasury bonds, which offer both good security and a relatively high rate of interest. Foreigners also buy shares of stock in U.S. corporations and sometimes entire companies. They need U.S. dollars for all these investments.

Balance of Payments

balance of payments: A summary record of a country's international economic transactions in a given period of time.

With so many different sources of supply and demand for U.S. dollars, we need some sort of summary measure of international money flows. That summary is contained in the **balance of payments**—an accounting statement of all international money flows in a given period of time.

Table 36.1 depicts the U.S. balance of payments for 1989. Notice first of all how the millions of separate transactions are classified into a few summary measures. The trade balance refers to the difference between exports and imports of goods (merchandise). In 1989 the United States imported $475 billion of merchandise but exported only $362 billion. This created a **trade deficit** of $113 billion. That trade deficit represents a net outflow of dollars to the rest of the world.

trade deficit: The amount by which the value of imports exceeds the value of exports in a given time period.

- Trade balance = $\dfrac{\text{merchandise}}{\text{exports}} - \dfrac{\text{merchandise}}{\text{imports}}$

TABLE 36.1 The U.S. Balance of Payments, 1989

The balance of payments is a summary statement of a country's international transactions. The major components of that activity are the trade balance (merchandise exports minus merchandise imports), the current-account balance (trade, services, and transfers), and the capital-account balance. The net total of these balances must equal zero, since the quantity of dollars paid must equal the quantity received.

Item	Amount (in billions)
1. Merchandise exports	$362
2. Merchandise imports	(475)
Trade Balance (1 minus 2)	−113
3. Service exports	114
4. Service imports	(93)
5. Income from U.S. overseas investments	125
6. Income outflow for foreign U.S. investments	(124)
7. Net U.S. government grants	(10)
8. Net private transfers and pensions	(4)
Current-Account Balance (items 1–8)	−105
9. U.S. capital inflow	189
10. U.S. capital outflow	(101)
11. Decrease in U.S. official reserves	(25)
12. Increase in foreign official assets in U.S.	7
Capital-Account Balance (items 9–12)	70
13. Statistical discrepancy	35
Net Balance (items 1–13)	0

Source: U.S. Department of Commerce.

The excess supply of dollars created by the trade gap was offset by other net inflows. Our service exports (e.g., air travel, insurance, banking) were larger than our service imports, creating a small net inflow of dollars. Profits from U.S. overseas investments just about matched the outgoing profits to foreign investors.

The current-account balance is a subtotal in Table 36.1.

$$\text{Current-account balance} = \text{trade balance} + \text{services balance} + \text{unilateral transfers}$$

The current-account balance is the most comprehensive summary of our trade relations. As indicated in Table 36.1, the United States had a current-account deficit of $105 billion in 1989.

The current-account deficit is offset by the capital-account surplus. The capital-account balance takes into consideration assets bought and sold across international borders; that is,

$$\text{Capital-account balance} = \text{foreign purchases of U.S. assets} - \text{U.S. purchases of foreign assets}$$

As Table 36.1 shows, foreigners demanded 189 billion worth of dollars in 1989 to buy Rockefeller Center and Columbia Pictures, as well as U.S. bonds, stocks, buildings, farmland, and other investments (item 9). This exceeded the flow of U.S. dollars going overseas to purchase foreign assets (item 10). In addition, the U.S. and foreign governments bought and sold dollars, creating an additional outflow of dollars (items 11 and 12).

The net capital inflows were essential in financing the U.S. trade deficit (negative trade balance). As in any market, the number of dollars demanded must equal the number of dollars supplied. Thus *the capital-account surplus must equal the current-account deficit.* In other words, there can't be any dollars left lying around unaccounted for. Item 13 in Table 36.1 reminds us that our accounting system isn't perfect—that we can't identify every transaction. Nevertheless, all of the accounts must eventually "balance out":

$$\bullet \quad \begin{matrix} \text{Net} \\ \text{balance} \\ \text{of payments} \end{matrix} = \begin{matrix} \text{current-} \\ \text{account} \\ \text{balance} \end{matrix} + \begin{matrix} \text{capital} \\ \text{account} \\ \text{balance} \end{matrix} = 0$$

Supply and Demand Curves

Table 36.1 provides a reasonably complete view of the quantity of money that flowed through foreign-exchange markets in 1989. But such summary statistics can be misleading, because they don't convey how much those flows would have changed had exchange rates been different. Americans surely would have bought fewer imported goods in 1989 if foreign currencies had been more expensive. In other words, we should anticipate that the quantity of foreign currency demanded or supplied, like the quantity of any good traded in markets, depends on its price.

What this means is that both the **demand for foreign exchange** (foreign currencies) and the **supply of foreign exchange** should be represented as curves, not as single points. In particular, we should recognize that the demand for foreign exchange is likely to have the familiar downward slope, while the supply of foreign exchange will have the usual upward slope. These two curves are illustrated in Figure 36.1.

The demand curve The explanations for the shape of the curves in Figure 36.1 should sound familiar. Consider the U.S. demand for any foreign product—say, BMWs. Even people who have never heard of foreign-exchange markets, or haven't the vaguest idea of what a Deutschemark is, buy BMWs. All they know and care about is that they are willing to pay so many dollars for a BMW and will buy something else when BMWs are too expensive. Hence the U.S. demand curve for BMWs will slope downward, reflecting the law of demand—the fact that the number of people willing and eager to buy a BMW increases as BMW prices drop.

Once we know the U.S. sales price for BMWs, we can use the demand curve to determine how many BMWs will be purchased and thus how much foreign exchange will be demanded. Two factors influence the U.S. price of BMWs. The first is the willingness of the BMW company to sell its cars for various amounts of the West German monetary unit—the Deutschemark

demand for foreign exchange:
The quantities of foreign currency demanded in a given time period at alternative exchange rates, *ceteris paribus.*

supply of foreign exchange:
The quantities of foreign currency supplied (offered) in a given time period at alternative exchange rates, *ceteris paribus.*

FIGURE 36.1
The Foreign-Exchange Market

The foreign–exchange market operates like other markets. In this case, the "good" bought and sold is money (foreign exchange). The price and quantity of foreign exchange are determined by market supply and demand.

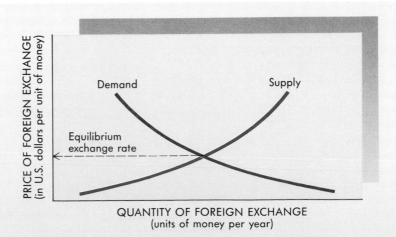

(DM). Remember that the BMW producer and his workers want to be paid in their own currency—in Deutschemarks. The second factor is the number of Deutschemarks that can be purchased for a dollar—that is, the *exchange rate* between Deutschemarks and dollars. Hence the U.S. price of BMWs is

$$\text{Dollar price of BMW} = \text{mark price of BMW} \times \text{dollar price of German mark}$$

Suppose that the BMW company is prepared to sell a BMW for DM100,000, and that the current exchange rate is DM2 = $1. At these rates, a BMW will cost you

$$\text{Dollar price of BMW} = \text{DM100,000} \times \frac{\$1}{\text{DM2}}$$
$$= \$50,000$$

If you are willing to pay this much for a shiny new BMW, you may do so at current exchange rates.

Now suppose that the exchange rate changes from DM2 = $1 to DM1 = $1. *A higher dollar price for German marks will raise the dollar costs of German goods.* In this case, the dollar price of a mark increases from $0.50 to $1. At this new exchange rate, the BMW company is still willing to sell BMWs at DM100,000 apiece. And German consumers continue to buy BMWs at that price. But this constant mark price now translates into a higher *dollar* price. Thus a BMW now costs you $100,000. (The price of Japanese Hondas in the U.S. went up for the same reason when the value of the yen rose; see World View.)

As the U.S. price of a BMW rises, the number of BMWs sold in the United States will decline. As BMW sales decline, the quantity of German marks demanded may decline as well. Thus the quantity of foreign currency demanded declines when the exchange rate rises because foreign goods become more expensive and imports decline.[1] When the dollar price of the German mark actually increased in 1986 and 1987 BMW expresssed considerable alarm.

[1]The extent to which imports decline as the cost of foreign currency rises depends on the *price elasticity of demand* (see Chapter 19).

W🌐RLD VIEW

IMPORT PRICES

Honda Raises Prices for Its Cars, Citing Slide in U.S. Dollar

GARDENA, Calif.—Honda Motor Co. said it raised base prices on its Honda division cars an average of 2.2% and its Acura division cars an average of 2.8% to compensate for the U.S. dollar's slide against the Japanese yen.

The price boosts took effect yesterday upon their announcement by Honda's U.S. sales arm, American Honda Motor Co. They marked the ninth time Honda has raised its prices since the yen began its climb against the dollar in 1985. Prices of Honda division cars have gone up an average of 29.2% in that time, while Acura prices have increased an average of 18.4% since their May 1986 introduction in the U.S. . . .

The Wall Street Journal, January 22, 1988, p. 12. Reprinted by permission of *The Wall Street Journal,* © Dow Jones & Company, Inc. (1988). All Rights Reserved.

The supply curve The supply of foreign exchange can be explained in similar terms. Remember that the supply of foreign exchange arises from the foreign demand for dollars. If the exchange rate moves from DM2 = $1 to DM1 = $1, the mark price of dollars will fall. As dollars become cheaper for Germans, all American exports effectively fall in price. Thus we anticipate that Germans will want to buy more American products and therefore demand a greater quantity of dollars. In addition, foreign investors will perceive in a cheaper dollar the opportunity to buy American stocks, businesses, and property at fire-sale prices. Accordingly, they join foreign consumers in demanding more dollars and supplying more marks. Not all of these behavioral responses will occur overnight, but they are reasonably predictable over a brief period of time.[2]

MARKET DYNAMICS

equilibrium price: The price at which the quantity of a good demanded in a given time period equals the quantity supplied.

Given a neat and orderly demand curve and an equally neat and orderly supply curve, we can predict the **equilibrium price** of any commodity; that is, the price at which the quantity demanded will equal the quantity supplied. This prediction requires very little effort, since anyone can figure out where the two curves cross in Figure 36.1.

The interesting thing about markets is not their character in equilibrium but the fact that prices and quantities are always changing in response to shifts in demand and supply. The American demand for BMWs shifted overnight when Japan introduced a new line of sleek, competitively priced cars. This *shift* in demand threw the demand curve in Figure 36.1 out of place and sent foreign-exchange specialists, GM executives, and worried BMW managers back to the drawing boards. When the Iron Curtain was lifted in 1989, the demand for German goods increased significantly. This increased demand shifted the supply of foreign exchange to the right (and the foreign demand for Deutschemarks to the right as well). Such shocks to the foreign-exchange market are illustrated in Figure 36.2.

Depreciation and Appreciation

depreciation (currency): A fall in the price of one currency relative to another.

appreciation: A rise in the price of one currency relative to another.

Exchange-rate changes have their own terminology. **Depreciation** of a currency refers to the fact that one currency has become cheaper in terms of another currency. In our earlier discussion of exchange rates, for example, we assumed that the exchange rate between Deutschemarks and dollars changed from DM2 = $1 to DM1 = $1, making the price of a dollar cheaper. In this case the dollar depreciated with respect to the mark.

The other side of depreciation is **appreciation,** an increase in value of one currency as expressed in another country's currency. *Whenever one currency depreciates, another currency must appreciate.* When the exchange rate changed from DM2 = $1 to DM1 = $1, not only did the mark price of a dollar fall, but the dollar price of a mark rose. Hence the mark appreciated as the dollar depreciated.

Figure 36.3 illustrates actual changes in exchange rates since 1973. During the 1970s the German mark and Japanese yen appreciated substantially relative to the U.S. dollar. At the same time, the British pound depreciated. Hence

[2]If the demand for our exports is relatively price inelastic, the percentage change in quantity demanded will be smaller than the percentage change in price. In this case, the quantity of foreign exchange supplied may actually decline as the dollar becomes cheaper. In such a case the supply curve in Figure 36.1 would bend backward at higher exchange rates.

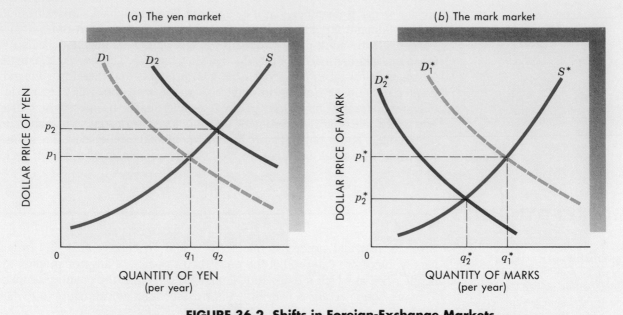

FIGURE 36.2 Shifts in Foreign-Exchange Markets

When Japan started selling more luxurious cars in the United States, the demand for BMWs and German marks shifted to the left (from D_1^* to D_2^* in part *b*), while the demand for Japanese yen shifted to the right (from D_1 to D_2 in part *a*). The dollar price of marks fell from p_1^* to p_2^* in part *b*; the dollar price of yen rose from p_1 to p_2 in part *a*.

German and Japanese goods got more expensive, while the dollar price of British goods fell. These trends were reversed in the early 1980s, and then reversed again after 1985.

Also shown in Figure 36.3 is the trade-adjusted value of the U.S. dollar. This is the (weighted) average of all exchange rates for the dollar. In general, the dollar lost value in the late 1970s but recovered in the early 1980s. Between 1980 and 1984 the U.S. dollar appreciated over 50 percent. This appreciation greatly reduced the price of imports and thus increased their quantity. At the same time, the dollar appreciation raised the foreign price of U.S. exports and so reduced their volume. A huge trade deficit resulted.

The value of the dollar reversed course after 1985, falling sharply against the yen and the mark. This set in motion forces that reduced the trade deficit in the late 1980s and early 1990s.

Market Forces   Exchange rates change for the same reasons that any market price changes; the underlying supply or demand (or both) has shifted. Among the more important sources of such shifts are

- ***Relative income changes.*** If incomes are increasing faster in country *A* than in country *B*, consumers in *A* will tend to spend more, thus increasing the demand for *B*'s exports and currency. *B*'s currency will appreciate.

- ***Relative price changes.*** If domestic prices are rising rapidly in country *A*, consumers will seek out lower-priced imports. The demand for *B*'s exports and currency will increase. *B*'s currency will appreciate.

Exchange rates

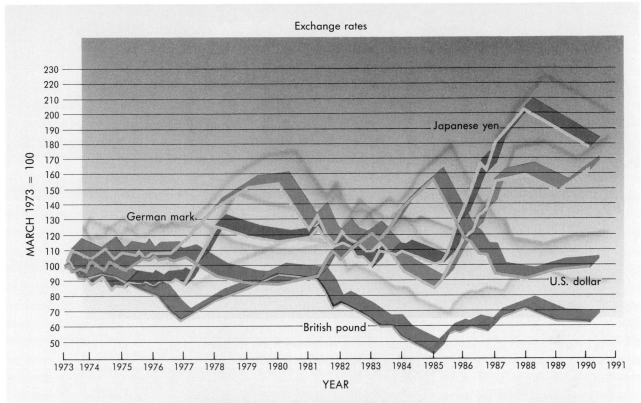

FIGURE 36.3 Changing Exchange Rates

Since 1973, exchange rates have been flexible (not fixed). As a result, exchange rates have reflected international differences in unemployment, inflation, interest rates, and economic growth. The relatively strong growth of the U.S. economy in the mid–1980s raised the American demand for imports and, with it, the price of foreign currencies. This is reflected in the depreciating dollar (beginning in 1985).

Source: *Economic Report of the President*, 1990.

- *Changes in product availability.* If country *A* experiences a disastrous wheat-crop failure, it will have to increase its food imports. *B*'s currency will appreciate.

- *Relative interest-rate changes.* If interest rates rise in country *A*, people in country *B* will want to move their deposits to *A*. Demand for *A*'s currency will rise and it will appreciate.

- *Speculation.* If speculators anticipate an increase in the price of *A*'s currency, for the preceding reasons or any other, they will begin buying it, thus pushing its price up. *A*'s currency will appreciate.

All of these kinds of changes are taking place every minute of every day, thus keeping **foreign-exchange markets** active. On an average day, over $650 *billion* of foreign exchange is bought and sold in the market. Significant changes occur in currency values, however, only when several of these forces move in the same direction at the same time.

foreign-exchange markets: Places where foreign currencies are bought and sold.

W🌐RLD VIEW

IMPORT PRICES

Canadian Dollar's Rise Spurs Imports, Producing First Trade Deficit in 13 Years

OTTAWA—Canada recorded its first trade deficit in more than 13 years in October, as the strong Canadian dollar spurred increased imports from the U.S. and elsewhere.

The October deficit totaled 420.9 million Canadian dollars (US$363 million), compared with a September surplus of C$133.9 million, said Statistics Canada, a federal agency. Imports rose 5.5% in October from September, while exports grew only 0.6%. . . .

The Canadian dollar's recent strength has sent Canadian shoppers flocking to stores in such U.S. cities as Buffalo, Syracuse and Watertown in New York, Sault Ste. Marie, Mich., and Diluth, Minn. A Greater Watertown Chamber of Commerce spokeswoman said the hotels in the city of 30,000 have been filled with Canadian shoppers in recent weeks. The chamber and Watertown merchants have been soliciting Canadians with "Watertown Bucks," a scrip that gives Canadian shoppers a 15% discount on their purchases. The promotion has been advertised in a Canadian newspaper, the *Ottawa Citizen*.

—John Urquhart

RESISTANCE TO EXCHANGE-RATE CHANGES

Exchange-rate changes are resisted by a broad assortment of microeconomic and macroeconomic interests. The resistance to changes in the value of the dollar is analogous to the resistance to trade flows based on comparative advantage. In fact, many of the same vested interests that seek to "protect" U.S. trade also seek to "protect" the U.S. dollar.

Micro Interests The microeconomic resistance to changes in the value of the dollar arises from two general concerns. First, people who trade or invest in world markets like to have some basis for forecasting future costs, prices, and profits. Forecasts are always uncertain, but they are even less dependable when the value of money is subject to change. An American firm that invests $20 million in a tire factory in Brazil expects not only to make a profit on the production there, but also to return that profit to the United States. If the Brazilian cruzeiro depreciates sharply in the interim, however, the profits amassed in Brazil may dwindle to a mere trickle, or even a loss, when the cruzeiros are exchanged back into dollars. From this perspective, the uncertainty associated with fluctuating exchange rates is an unwanted and unnecessary burden.

Even when the direction of an exchange-rate move is certain, those who stand to lose from the change are prone to resist. *A change in the price of a country's money automatically alters the price of all of its exports and imports.* When the U.S. dollar appreciated from 1981 to 1985, for example, the foreign price of all U.S. exports rose and the domestic price of all U.S. imports fell. U.S. importers were pleased, but U.S. exporters were upset. Feelings were reversed when the dollar depreciated from 1985 to 1988.

In general, exporters are hostile to appreciations of their domestic currency. Appreciation makes exports more expensive, and therefore reduces sales. The workers associated with such exports are equally hostile to such exchange-rate movements, because their very jobs are at stake.

Even in the country whose currency becomes cheaper, there will be opposition to exchange-rate movements. When the U.S. dollar appreciates, Americans buy more foreign products. This increased U.S. demand for imports may drive up prices in other countries. In addition, foreign firms may take advantage of the reduced American competition by raising their prices. In either case, some inflation will result. The consumer's insistence that the government "do something" about rising prices may turn into a political force for "correcting" foreign-exchange rates.

Macro Interests

Any microeconomic problem that becomes widespread enough can turn into a macroeconomic problem. The huge U.S. trade deficits of the 1980s effectively exported jobs to foreign nations. Although the U.S. economy expanded rapidly in 1983–85, the unemployment rate stayed high. This was due in part to the fact that American consumers were spending more of their income on imports. Yet fear of renewed inflation precluded more stimulative fiscal and monetary policies.

The U.S. trade deficits of the 1980s were offset by huge capital account surpluses. Foreign investors sought to participate in the U.S. economic expansion by buying land, plant and equipment, and by lending money in U.S. financial markets. These capital inflows complicated monetary policy, however, and greatly increased U.S. foreign debt and interest costs.

U.S. a Net Debtor

The inflow of foreign investment also raised anxieties about "selling off" America. As Japanese and other foreign investors increased their purchases of farmland, factories, and real estate (e.g., Rockefeller Center), many Americans worried that foreigners were taking control of the U.S. economy. A Gallup poll in 1989 revealed that Americans were much more worried about foreign economic domination than foreign military threats.

Fueling these fears was the dramatic change in America's international financial position. From 1914 to 1984 the United States had been a net creditor in the world economy. We owned more assets abroad than foreigners owned in the United States. Our financial position changed in 1985. Continuing trade deficits and offsetting capital inflows transformed the United States to a net debtor in that year (see World View, p. 890). Since then, foreigners have owned more U.S. assets than Americans own of foreign assets.

America's new debtor status can complicate domestic policy. A sudden flight from U.S. assets could severely weaken the dollar and disrupt the domestic economy. To keep that from happening, U.S. policymakers have to consider the impact of their decisions on foreign investors. This may necessitate difficult policy choices.

There is a silver lining to this cloud, however. The inflow of foreign investment is a reflection of confidence in the U.S. economy. Foreign investors want to share in our growth and profitability. In the process, their investments (e.g., new auto plants) expand America's production possibilities and stimulate still more economic growth.

Foreign investors actually assume substantial risk when they invest in the United States. If the dollar falls, the foreign value of their U.S. investments will decline. Hence foreigners who have already invested in the United States have no incentive to start a flight from the dollar. On the contrary, a strong dollar protects the value of their U.S. holdings.

W🌐RLD VIEW

NET DEBTOR STATUS

U.S. Solidified No. 1 Debtor Rank in '86 as Investment Gap More Than Doubled

WASHINGTON—The U.S. international investment position dropped further into the red last year, reinforcing the country's status as the world's largest debtor nation.

The difference between the amount of U.S. assets held by foreigners and the amount of foreign assets held by U.S. investors more than doubled last year to $263.65 billion, the Commerce Department said.

Foreign investors held $1.331 trillion in assets in this country, while U.S. investors owned $1.068 trillion in assets overseas. The latest net investment position compares with a revised figure of $111.88 billion in 1985, when the U.S. became a net debtor for the first time since 1914. The 1985 figures also made the U.S. the largest debtor nation. As recently as 1982, the U.S. was the world's largest creditor.

Foreigners "Optimistic"

"The U.S. has grown dependent on foreign funds to finance the large borrowing that the Treasury and the rest of us are doing," said David Wyss, senior vice president at Data Resources Inc. in Lexington, Mass. "We clearly can't continue to borrow more and more from overseas."

He and other economists contend that the huge debt means Americans standard of living will decline as the U.S. is forced to make interest payments to foreigners. Also, some fear that foreigners have gained too much control over the U.S. economy.

Commerce Undersecretary Robert Ortner, however, said the rise in foreign ownership of U.S. assets is a measure of foreign confidence in the U.S. economy. "They hold money in bank deposits or they buy stocks and bonds because they're optimistic about the U.S.," he said.

—Rose Gutfeld

The Wall Street Journal, June 24, 1987, p. 4. Updated by author. Reprinted by permission of *The Wall Street Journal,* © Dow Jones & Company, Inc. (1987). All Rights Reserved.

Deeper in the Red

U.S. net international investment position

Source: Commerce Department.

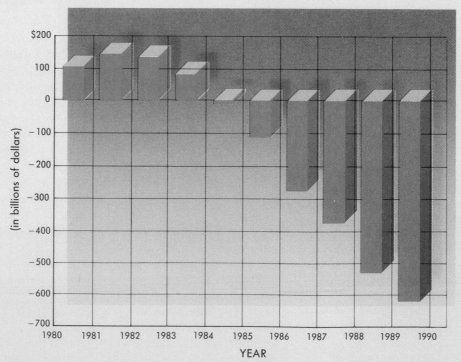

POLICY INSIGHTS:

EXCHANGE-RATE INTERVENTION

Given the potential opposition to exchange-rate movements, governments often feel compelled to intervene in foreign-exchange markets. The intervention is usually intended to achieve greater exchange-rate stability. But such stability may itself give rise to undesirable micro- and macroeconomic effects, and may even compound rather than solve economic problems.

Fixed Exchange Rates

One way to eliminate fluctuations in exchange rates is to fix their value. To fix exchange rates, each country may simply proclaim that its currency is "worth" so much in relation to that of other countries. The easiest way to do this is for each country to define the worth of its currency in terms of some common standard. The standard that has been most popular is gold. Under a **gold standard,** each country determines that its currency is worth so much gold. In so doing, it implicitly defines the worth of its currency in terms of all other currencies, which also have a fixed gold value. In 1944, for example, the major trading nations met at Bretton Woods, New Hampshire, and agreed that each currency was worth so much gold. The value of the U.S. dollar was defined as being equal to 0.0294 ounces of gold, while the British pound was defined as being worth 0.0823 ounces of gold. Thus the exchange rate between British pounds and U.S. dollars was effectively fixed at $1 = 0.357 pounds, or 1 pound = $2.80 (or $2.80/0.0823 = $1/0.0294).

gold standard: An agreement by countries to fix the price of their currencies in terms of gold; a mechanism for fixing exchange rates.

Balance-of-payments problems   It is one thing to proclaim the worth of a country's currency; it is quite another to *maintain* the fixed rate of exchange. As we have observed, foreign-exchange rates are subject to continual and often unpredictable changes in supply and demand. Hence two countries that seek to stabilize their exchange rate at some fixed value are going to find it necessary either to eliminate or to compensate for such foreign-exchange market pressures.

Suppose that the exchange rate officially established by the United States and Great Britain is equal to e_1, as illustrated in Figure 36.4. As is apparent,

**FIGURE 36.4
Fixed Rates and
Market Imbalance**

If exchange rates are fixed, they cannot adjust to changes in market supply and demand. Suppose the exchange rate is initially fixed at e_1. When the demand for British pounds increases (shifts to the right), an excess demand for pounds emerges. More pounds are demanded (q_D) at the rate e_1 than are supplied (q_S). This causes a balance–of–payments deficit for the United States.

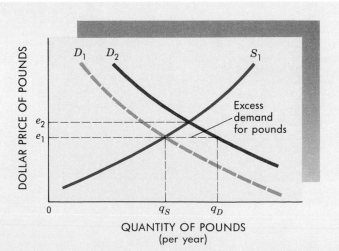

that particular exhange rate is consistent with the then-prevailing demand and supply conditions in the foreign-exchange market (as indicated by curves D_1 and S_1).

Now suppose that Americans suddenly acquire a greater taste for British cars and start spending more income on Jaguars and the like. As U.S. purchases of British goods increase, the demand for British currency will *shift* from D_1 to D_2 in Figure 36.4. Were exchange rates allowed to respond to market influences, the dollar price of a British pound would rise, in this case to the rate e_2. But government intervention has fixed the exchange rate at e_1. Unfortunately, at e_1, American consumers want to buy more pounds (q_D) than the British are willing to supply (q_S). The difference between the quantity demanded and the quantity supplied in the market at the rate e_1 represents a **market shortage** of British pounds.

The excess demand for pounds implies a **balance-of-payments deficit** for the United States: more dollars are flowing out of the country than into it. The same disequilibrium represents a **balance-of-payments surplus** for Britain, because its outward flow of pounds is less than its incoming flow.

Basically, there are only two solutions to balance-of-payments problems brought about by the attempt to fix exchange rates:

- Allow exchange rates to rise to e_2 (Figure 36.4), thereby eliminating the excess demand for pounds.

- Alter market supply or demand so that they intersect at the fixed rate e_1.

Since fixed exchange rates were the initial objective of policy, only the second alternative is of immediate interest.

The need for reserves   One way to alter market conditions would be for someone simply to supply British pounds to American consumers. The U.S. Treasury could have accumulated a reserve of foreign exchange in earlier periods. By selling some of those **foreign-exchange reserves** now, the Treasury could help to stabilize market conditions at the officially established exchange rate. In Figure 36.5 the sale of accumulated British pounds—and related purchase of U.S. dollars—by the U.S. Treasury is illustrated by the rightward shift of the pound supply curve. (In 1989, the U.S. Treasury actually accumulated foreign-exchange reserves; item 12 in Table 36.1 is negative.)

market shortage: The amount by which the quantity demanded exceeds the quantity supplied at a given price; excess demand.

balance-of-payments deficit: An excess demand for foreign currency at current exchange rates.

balance-of-payments surplus: An excess demand for domestic currency at current exchange rates.

foreign-exchange reserves: Holdings of foreign exchange by official government agencies, usually the central bank or treasury.

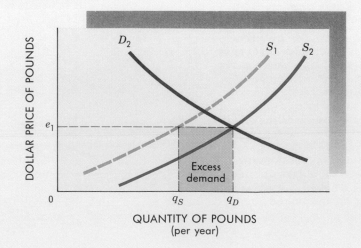

FIGURE 36.5
The Impact of Monetary Intervention

If the U.S. Treasury holds reserves of British pounds, it can use them to buy U.S. dollars in foreign–exchange markets. As it does so, the supply of pounds will shift to the right, to S_2, thereby maintaining the desired exchange rate, e_1. The Bank of England could bring about the same result by offering to buy U.S. dollars with pounds.

Although foreign-exchange reserves can be used to fix exchange rates, such reserves may not be adequate. Indeed, Figure 36.6 should be testimony enough to the fact that today's deficit is not always offset by tomorrow's surplus. One of the principal reasons that fixed exchange rates did not live up to their expectations is that the United States had balance-of-payments deficits for twenty-two consecutive years. This long-term deficit overwhelmed our stock of foreign-exchange reserves and led to a search for other measures to balance foreign-exchange markets at officially fixed rates.

The role of gold   Gold reserves represent a potential substitute for foreign-exchange reserves. As long as each country's money has a value defined in terms of gold, we can use gold to buy British pounds, thereby restocking our foreign-exchange reserves. Or we can simply use the gold to purchase U.S. dollars in foreign-exchange markets. In either case, the exchange value of the dollar will tend to rise. However, we must have **gold reserves** available for this purpose. Unfortunately, the continuing U.S. balance-of-payments deficits recorded in Figure 36.6 exceeded even the hoards of gold buried under Fort Knox. As a consequence, our gold reserves lost their credibility as a potential "guarantee" of fixed exchange rates.

Domestic adjustments   The supply and demand for foreign exchange can also be shifted by changes in basic fiscal, monetary, or trade policies. With respect to trade policy, *trade protection can be used to prop up fixed exchange rates.* We could eliminate the excess demand for pounds (Figure 36.4), for example, by imposing quotas and tariffs on British goods. Such trade restrictions would reduce British imports to the United States and thus the demand for British pounds. In August 1971 President Nixon imposed an emergency 10 percent surcharge on all imported goods to help reduce the payments deficit that fixed exchange rates had spawned. Such restrictions on

gold reserves: Stocks of gold held by a government to purchase foreign exchange.

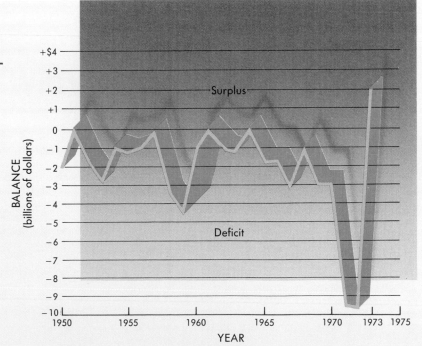

**FIGURE 36.6
The U.S. Balance of
Payments, 1950–73**

The United States had a balance-of-payments deficit for twenty-two consecutive years. During this period, the foreign-exchange reserves of the U.S. Treasury were sharply reduced. Fixed exchange rates were maintained by the willingness of foreign countries to accumulate large reserves of U.S. dollars. However, neither the Treasury's reserves nor foreigners' willingness to accumulate dollars were unlimited. In 1973, fixed exchange rates were abandoned.

international trade, however, violate the principle of comparative advantage and thus reduce total world output. Trade protection also invites retaliatory trade restrictions.

Fiscal policy provides another way out of the imbalance. An increase in U.S. income-tax rates will reduce disposable income and have a negative effect on the demand for all goods, including imports. A reduction in government spending will have similar effects. In general, ***deflationary (or restrictive) policies help correct a balance-of-payments deficit by lowering domestic incomes and thus import demands.***

Monetary policies in a deficit country could follow the same restrictive course. A reduction in the money supply will tend to raise interest rates. The balance of payments will benefit in two ways. The resultant slowdown in spending will help to reduce import demands and may induce domestic producers to focus more attention on export possibilities. In addition, higher interest rates may induce international investors to move some of their funds out of other countries into the deficit country. Such moves will provide immediate relief to the payments imbalance.

A surplus country may also help solve the balance-of-payments problem. By pursuing expansionary—even inflationary—fiscal and monetary policies, a surplus country could stimulate the demand for imports. If domestic prices rise, the relative attractiveness of imports will increase. Moreover, any inflation at home will reduce the competitiveness of exports, thereby helping to restrain the inflow of foreign demand. Taken together, such efforts would help reverse an international-payments imbalance.[3] The accompanying World View describes the United States' attempt to persuade Japan to pursue such expansionary policies.

[3]Before 1930, not only were foreign-exchange rates fixed, but domestic monetary supplies were tied to gold stocks as well. Countries experiencing a balance-of-payments deficit were thus forced to contract their money supply, and countries experiencing a payments surplus were forced to expand their money supply by a set amount. Monetary authorities were powerless to control domestic money supplies except by erecting barriers to trade. The system was abandoned when the world economy collapsed into the Great Depression.

W RLD VIEW

DOMESTIC ADJUSTMENTS

Japan's Big Economic Debate

TOKYO, April 29—American pressures on Japan to stimulate its domestic economy—urgings likely to be renewed this week at the Bonn summit conference—have rekindled a debate about Japan's fundamental economic policies.

Although most economists attribute Japan's large and growing trade surpluses to the strong dollar and other macroeconomic factors, United States officials, most recently Secretary of State George P. Schultz, have suggested that a more expansionary posture domestically would help to reverse trade and currency imbalances.

If Japan took steps to stimulate its domestic economy, the argument runs, consumers would have more money to spend on imports and corporations would invest more money in Japan rather than in the United States Treasury bills they now favor. Less demand for the dollar might also spur its fall against the yen, making American products less expensive in Japan, and Japanese products more expensive in the United States.

—Susan Chira

The New York Times, April 30, 1985, p. Y29. Copyright © 1985 The New York Times Company. Reprinted by permission.

Domestic economic adjustments can cure balance-of-payments problems. There are obvious costs involved, however, particularly in terms of full employment and price stability. In effect, ***domestic adjustments to payments imbalances require a deficit country to forsake full employment and a surplus country to forsake price stability.*** These are sacrifices few countries are willing to make. Accordingly, balance-of-payments problems typically lead to protracted arguments about who should adjust, repeated hopes that the imbalances will go away, and frequent "crises" ending in exchange-rate adjustments. There is no easy way out of this impasse. Market imbalances caused by fixed exchange rates can be corrected only with abundant supplies of foreign-exchange reserves or deliberate changes in fiscal, monetary, or trade policies.

Flexible Exchange Rates

flexible exchange rates: A system in which exchange rates are permitted to vary with market supply and demand conditions; floating exchange rates.

Balance-of-payments problems would not arise in the first place if exchange rates were allowed to respond to market forces. Under a system of **flexible exchange rates** (often called "floating" exchange rates), the exchange rate moves up or down to choke off any excess supply of or demand for foreign exchange. Notice again in Figure 36.4 that the exchange-rate move from e_1 to e_2 prevents any excess demand from emerging. ***With flexible exchange rates, the quantity of foreign exchange demanded always equals the quantity supplied,*** and there is no imbalance. For the same reason, there is no need for foreign-exchange reserves.

Although flexible exchange rates eliminate balance-of-payments and foreign-exchange-reserves problems, they do not solve all of a country's international trade problems. ***Exchange-rate movements associated with flexible rates alter relative prices and may disrupt import and export flows.*** As noted before, depreciation of the dollar raises the price of all imported goods. The price increases may contribute to domestic cost-push inflation. Also, domestic businesses that sell imported goods or use them as production inputs may suffer sales losses. On the other hand, appreciation of the dollar raises the foreign price of U.S. goods and reduces the sales of American exporters. Hence ***someone is always hurt (and others are helped) by exchange-rate movements.*** The resistance to flexible exchange rates originates in these potential losses. Such resistance creates pressure for official intervention in foreign-exchange markets or increased trade barriers.

The United States and its major trading partners abandoned fixed exchange rates in 1973. Although exchange rates are now able to fluctuate freely, it should not be assumed that they necessarily undergo wild gyrations. On the contrary, experience with flexible rates since 1973 suggests that some semblance of stability is possible even when exchange rates are free to change in response to market forces. In 1984 the Council of Economic Advisers concluded that flexible exchange rates had worked reasonably well. Indeed, the council observed, "It is nearly impossible to imagine the world economy going through the past 10 years in the straitjacket of fixed exchange rates. Given the events of this period, notably the large changes in oil prices and the divergent macroeconomic policies among the industrialized countries, floating exchange rates have performed well."[4] In 1990 President Bush's council came to much the same conclusion, despite the greater volatility of exchange rates in the 1980s (see Figure 36.3).

[4]*Economic Report of the President,* 1984, p. 50.

"*Damn it! How can I relax, knowing that out there, somewhere, somehow, someone's attacking the dollar?*"

Drawing by Lorenz. Copyright © 1973 The New Yorker Magazine, Inc.

Speculation   One force that often helps to maintain stability in a flexible-exchange-rate system is speculation. Speculators often counteract short-term changes in foreign-exchange supply and demand. If an exchange rate temporarily rises above its long-term equilibrium, speculators will move in to sell foreign exchange. By selling at high prices and later buying at lower prices, speculators hope to make a profit. In the process, they also help to stabilize foreign-exchange rates.

Speculation is not always stabilizing, however. Speculators may not correctly gauge the long-term equilibrium. Instead, they may move "with the market" and help push exchange rates far out of kilter. This kind of destabilizing speculation sharply lowered the international value of the U.S. dollar in 1987, forcing the Reagan administration to intervene in foreign-exchange markets, borrowing foreign currencies to buy U.S. dollars.

Managed Exchange Rates

managed exchange rates: A system in which governments intervene in foreign-exchange markets to limit but not eliminate exchange-rate fluctuations; "dirty floats."

Governments can intervene in foreign-exchange markets without completely fixing exchange rates. That is, they may buy and sell foreign exchange for the purpose of narrowing rather than eliminating exchange-rate movements. Such limited intervention in foreign-exchange markets is referred to as **managed exchange rates,** or, more popularly, "dirty floats."

The basic objective of exchange-rate management is to provide a stabilizing force. The U.S. Treasury, for example, may use its foreign-exchange reserves to buy dollars when they are depreciating too much. Or it will buy foreign exchange if the dollar is rising too fast. From this perspective, exchange-rate management appears as a fail-safe system for the private market. Unfortunately, the motivation for official intervention is sometimes suspect. Private speculators buy and sell foreign exchange for the sole purpose of making a profit. But government sales and purchases may be motivated by other considerations. A falling exchange rate increases the competitive advantage of a country's exports. A rising exchange rate makes international investment less expensive. Hence a country's efforts to "manage" exchange-

In The News

INTERVENTION

Fed Intervention

U.S. monetary authorities bought $4.14 billion in foreign-exchange markets to support the dollar in November, December, and January, the heaviest intervention since 1979, a report said yesterday.

The concerted purchases were only partially successful. The dollar plummeted to record lows at the end of December in spite of heavy intervention, but then par-tially rebounded in the first days of the new year as market psychology shifted.

The purchases were disclosed by the Federal Reserve Bank of New York, which carries out foreign-exchange operations on behalf of the Federal Reserve and the Treasury Department.

The Washington Post, March 5, 1988, p. G-1. Copyright © 1988 The Washington Post.

rate movements may arouse suspicion and outright hostility in its trading partners.

In 1987, the United States and its major trading partners spent over $100 billion of reserves trying to prop up the falling dollar. Throughout the process there were constant arguments about the "correct" value of the dollar and which country should undertake the steps necessary to ensure that value. The Germans, Japanese, and British lambasted the United States for not reducing its budget deficit and import appetite. For its part, the United States blamed the falling dollar on the slow growth policies of its trading partners. In the end, the dollar fell still further, especially after the stock market crash of October 1987 and the resultant loss of confidence in U.S. investments.

When the stock market took another nosedive in November 1989, people again became anxious about the value of the dollar. There was fear that investors would flee U.S. assets, causing the dollar to tumble. Central bank intervention, led by the Federal Reserve, succeeded in supporting the dollar and investor confidence.

Although managed exchange rates would seem to be an ideal compromise between fixed rates and flexible rates, they can work only when some acceptable "rules of the game" and a condition of mutual trust have been established. As Sherman Maisel, a former governor of the Federal Reserve Board, put it: "Monetary systems are based on credit and faith: if these are lacking a . . . crisis occurs."[5]

SUMMARY

- Money serves the same purposes in international trade as it does in the domestic economy—namely, to facilitate productive specialization and market exchanges. The basic problem of international finance is to create acceptable standards of value from the various currencies maintained by separate countries.

- Exchange rates are the basic mechanism for translating the value of one national currency into the quivalent value of another. An exchange rate of $1 = DM3 means that one dollar is worth three German marks and can be purchased at that price in foreign-exchange markets.

[5]Sherman Maisel, *Managing the Dollar* (New York: W. W. Norton, 1973), p. 196.

• Foreign currencies have value because they can be used to acquire goods and resources from other countries. Accordingly, the supply of and demand for foreign currency reflect the demands for imports and exports, for international investment, and for overseas activities of governments.

• The balance of payments summarizes a country's international transactions. Its components are the trade balance, the current-account balance, and the capital-account balance. The current and capital accounts must offset each other.

• The equilibrium exchange rate is subject to any and all shifts of supply and demand for foreign exchange. If relative incomes, prices, or interest rates change, the demand for foreign exchange will be affected. A depreciation is a change in market exchange rates that makes one country's currency cheaper in terms of another currency. An appreciation is the opposite kind of change.

• Changes in exchange rates are often resisted. Producers of export goods do not want their currencies to rise in value (appreciate); importers and people who travel dislike it when their currencies fall in value (depreciate).

• Under a system of fixed exchange rates, changes in the supply and demand for foreign exchange cannot be expressed in exchange-rate movements. Instead, such shifts will be reflected in excess demand for or excess supply of foreign exchange. Such market imbalances are referred to as balance-of-payments deficits or surpluses.

• To maintain fixed exchange rates, monetary authorities must enter the market to buy and sell foreign exchange. In order to do so, deficit countries must have foreign-exchange reserves. In the absence of sufficient reserves, a country can maintain fixed exchange rates only if it is willing to alter basic fiscal, monetary, or trade policies.

• Flexible exchange rates eliminate balance-of-payments problems and the crises that accompany them. But complete flexibility can lead to excessive changes. To avoid this contingency, many countries prefer to adopt managed exchange rates—that is, rates determined by the market but subject to government intervention.

Terms to Remember

Define the following terms:

exchange rate	gold standard
balance of payments	market shortage
trade deficit	balance-of payments deficit
demand for foreign exchange	balance-of payments surplus
supply of foreign exchange	foreign-exchange reserves
equilibrium price	gold reserves
depreciation	flexible exchange rates
appreciation	managed exchange rates
foreign-exchange markets	

Questions for Discussion

1. How would rapid inflation in Mexico alter our demand for travel to Mexico and for Mexican imports? Does it make any difference whether the exchange rate between pesos and dollars is fixed or flexible?

2. Under what conditions would a country welcome a balance-of-payments deficit? When would it *not* want a deficit?

3. In what sense do fixed exchange rates permit a country to "export its inflation"?

4. In 1988 U.S. exports increased sharply. How did the dollar's depreciation contribute to this development? What else might have caused exports to rise?

5. Under a managed-exchange-rate system, exchange rates can vary by small degrees. When should more significant rate changes be permitted or encouraged?

Problems

1. The following schedules summarize the supply and demand for trifflings, the national currency of Tricoli.

Triffling price (U.S. dollars per triffling)	0	$4	$8	$12	$16	$20	$24
Quantity demanded (per year)	40	38	36	34	32	30	28
Quantity supplied (per year)	1	11	21	31	41	51	61

Using the above schedules:
(a) Graph the supply and demand curves.
(b) Determine the equilibrium exchange rate.
(c) Determine the size of the excess supply or excess demand that would exist if the Tricolian government fixed the exchange rate at $22 = 1 triffling.
(d) How might this imbalance be remedied?

2. For each of the following possible events, indicate whether the demand or supply curve for dollars would shift, the direction of the shift, the determinant of the change, the inflow or outflow effect on the balance of payments (and the specific account that would be affected), and the resulting movement of the equilibrium exchange rate for the value of the dollar.
(a) American cars become suddenly more popular abroad.
(b) Inflation rates in the United States accelerate while they remain low in other countries.
(c) The United States falls into a depression, while other countries enjoy continued growth.
(d) Interest rates in the United States drop, while interest rates abroad remain constant.
(e) The United States suddenly experiences rapid increases in productivity, while other countries continue to experience slow increases.
(f) Anticipating a return to the gold standard, Americans suddenly rush to buy gold from the two big producers, South Africa and the Soviet Union.
(g) War is declared in the Middle East, and foreigners rush to buy American weapons.
(h) The stock markets in the United States suddenly collapse, and foreigners rush to repatriate their portfolio investments.

CHAPTER 37

International Development

*I*n 1950 the per capita income of Haiti was $300 (in 1990 dollars), or about one-sixteenth the per capita income of the United States at that time. By 1990, U.S. per capita income had more than doubled, but incomes in Haiti were no higher than they had been in 1950. Haiti remained desperately poor, while the gap between rich and poor countries widened.

The economic stagnation of Haiti is extreme but not unique. According to the World Bank, 3 billion people—over half of the world's population—live in countries where the average income is still under $500 per year (compared to over $21,000 in the United States!). Worse yet, living standards in many of these countries actually *declined* in the 1980s while ours continued to advance.

Low incomes and slow growth are the hallmarks of the "Third World." There are substantial differences, however, in economic conditions among these developing countries. In addition, there is another spectrum of nations existing between the extremes of Third World poverty and affluent industrialized nations. These "middle players" include the newly industrialized countries (NICs) of the Pacific Rim (e.g., Korea, Taiwan, Singapore) and the rapidly transforming economies of Eastern Europe. In these countries average incomes range from $3,000 to $10,000.

What accounts for these tremendous disparities in living standards? How have some nations prospered while others have stayed on the brink of starvation? This chapter provides some perspective on the global gap between rich and poor by examining these issues:

- Why has the Third World stayed so poor?

- How did some countries manage to grow so quickly?

- What policies would promote still faster growth?

In seeking to answer these questions, our ambitions must necessarily be modest. As Professor Theodore Schultz has written, "Being rich makes it hard to comprehend the economic behavior of poor people."[1] It is also difficult to comprehend just how poor the Third World is.

[1]Theodore Schultz, "Knowledge Is Power in Agriculture," *Challenge,* September–October 1981, p. 6.

THIRD WORLD INCOMES

GNP per Capita

GNP per capita: Total GNP divided by total population; average GNP.

The common denominator of all Third World countries is low income. As Table 37.1 reminds us, the United States enjoys a per capita income of over $20,000. Other "rich" countries include Japan, most of Western Europe, and a couple of oil-rich nations. The average incomes in this handful of countries far exceed living standards everywhere else. Three-fourths of the world's population struggles along with less than $1,500 of **per capita GNP.** Even in some of the seemingly rich Third World countries (e.g., Kuwait) most of the population lives in relative poverty.

Statistics on per capita income are a fundamental measure of a country's economic development. The figures themselves, however, can never convey the dimensions of poverty experienced in many of these countries. Can you really imagine living on only 1 *percent* of your income, as do many of the people in the world's poorest countries?

Basic Human Needs

The reality of Third World poverty is also reflected in statistics on life expectancy, literacy, and social conditions. In Haiti, life expectancy at birth is 55 years; in Ethiopia, it is only 48 years. By contrast, babies born in the United States have a life expectancy of nearly 76 years. Hence a fundamental consequence of underdevelopment is shortened life.

One reason people live such short lives in less developed countries is that they have so little to eat. The World Health Organization estimates that an average person requires a minimum intake of 2,600 calories per day for basic nutrition. People in the United States are well above this threshold, consuming an average of 3,600 calories per day. But people in Haiti try to survive on only 1,900 calories per day. The World Bank estimates that 80

TABLE 37.1   Incomes Around the World
(in 1988 U.S. dollars)

The primary distinction between "developed" and "less developed" countries is reflected in average incomes. However, there is great variety in living standards within each of these broad groupings. Here the countries of the world are classified into five groups, on the basis of per capita GNP.

Rich countries (GNP per capita over $10,000)		Poor countries ($500–1,500)	
United States	Japan	Peru	Honduras
Kuwait	Germany (West)	Colombia	Egypt
Canada	Australia	Thailand	Philippines
Sweden	Great Britain	Nigeria	

Moderate-income countries ($5,000–10,000)		Extremely poor countries (under $500 per capita)	
Singapore	Germany (East)	Pakistan	Indonesia
New Zealand	Israel	China	Burma
Spain	Czechoslovakia	Haiti	Mozambique
		Kenya	Ethiopia
Low-income countries ($1,500–5,000)		India	
Greece	Mexico		
Venezuela	Yugoslavia		
Algeria	Malayasia		
Korea (South)	Brazil		

Source: World Bank.

other countries of the world also suffer from inadequate food consumption. Moreover, the water in most less developed countries (LDCs) is unsafe to drink. In Ethiopia, only 6 percent of the population has access to safe drinking water. In Haiti, only 14 percent of the people can find safe water.

When people in LDCs get sick, they are not likely to find a doctor, a hospital, or even medicine. Haiti has only one doctor for every 13,000 people; Ethiopia has only one doctor for every 88,000 people. By comparison, the United States has one doctor for every 500 people. As for hospitals, the United States has one hospital bed for every 152 people. Haiti has one bed for every 1,169 people and Ethiopia has one for every 3,081. Medical care may be expensive in the United States, but at least you can get it when you need it.

Life expectancy, food consumption, the availability of doctors, access to safe water, and literacy are all indicators of the extent to which *basic human needs* are being fulfilled. The gap between rich and poor countries is enormous, even on this basis. The gap grows larger still when more conventional measures of development are considered. Perhaps the most telling measure of economic development is energy consumption. Although Americans are learning to use energy more efficiently, we still rely on nonhuman energy to do much of the work entailed in consumption and production. In LDCs, virtually all of the work is done by people, using their own energy. This is evident in statistics on *per capita* energy consumption. The average Haitian uses only 66 kilograms of (coal-equivalent) energy per year; the average American uses 12,350 kilograms.

GNP Growth   The kind of poverty that most of the Third World endures is not unknown in the history of countries that are now affluent. All of the "rich" countries of the world today were once poor. What distinguishes today's developed countries is their past ability to *grow*—in particular, to increase output faster than population growth. Even the growth of developed countries, however, is a fairly recent phenomenon. For centuries, per capita incomes grew imperceptibly in Europe. It was not until the Industrial Revolution that Europe really began to grow. In this historical context, the LDCs are not very far behind. This historical view is of little comfort to the world's poor, however. It would take more than a *hundred* years of average economic growth (3 percent per year) to raise the average income in Haiti to today's American poverty standards.

Even that projection may be optimistic. Will today's LDCs experience steady economic growth in the future? Or are growth prospects in the LDCs so fundamentally different that poverty is a permanent condition?

Table 37.2 provides a quick summary of recent growth experiences around the world. The table classifies countries according to their relative incomes, then indicates their respective GNP and population growth rates in the 1980s. A number of observations can be made. First, it is evident that developed countries are still growing. GNP per capita in rich countries is growing at a rate of 2–3 percent per year. This growth rate is the result of moderate output growth combined with very slow population growth.

At the other end of the income spectrum GNP per capita is almost stagnant. The output of the poorest countries is increasing. But in many cases their populations are increasing just as fast. Hence GNP per capita is barely growing. In some countries (e.g., Haiti, Ethiopia, Peru, the Philippines) per capita GNP is actually falling. If these trends continued, the poorest LDCs would never develop, much less catch up with the rest of the world.

TABLE 37.2   Growth Rates in Selected Countries, 1980–88

Most countries continue to experience economic growth. But the relationship between GNP growth and population growth is very different in rich and poor countries. The populations of rich countries are growing very slowly, and gains in per capita GNP are easily achieved. In the poorest countries, population is still increasing rapidly, making it difficult to raise living standards.

Country	GNP growth	Population growth	Per capita growth
Rich countries			
United States	3.1	1.0	2.1
Sweden	2.0	0.1	1.9
Japan	4.0	0.6	3.4
Germany (West)	1.8	−0.1	2.0
Moderate-income countries			
New Zealand	1.6	1.0	0.6
Israel	3.2	1.7	1.5
Spain	2.6	0.5	2.0
Low-income countries			
Yugoslavia	0.5	0.7	−0.1
Algeria	3.0	3.1	0.0
Korea (South)	9.2	1.4	7.7
Mexico	0.7	2.2	−1.4
Brazil	3.4	2.2	1.2
Poor countries			
Peru	1.0	2.2	−1.2
Nigeria	−1.0	3.4	−4.3
Thailand	5.8	1.9	3.8
Honduras	1.8	3.6	−1.7
Egypt	5.6	2.7	2.8
Philippines	0.0	2.4	−2.4
Extremely poor countries			
Pakistan	6.3	3.1	3.0
Kenya	3.9	4.2	−0.2
China	10.5	1.2	9.2
Senegal	3.2	2.9	0.3
Haiti	−0.3	1.8	−2.1
India	5.5	2.1	3.3
Ethiopia	1.1	2.5	−1.4

Source: World Bank.

Between the extremes of rich and poor are many LDCs with low incomes but better growth records. People in the Pacific Rim and Eastern Europe still confront low GNP per capita. But their incomes are growing rapidly, generating some hope for substantial improvement in living standards. Even if such rapid growth rates were maintained, however, it would take another century or so for even these countries to catch up to the ever-increasing income levels of the rich countries.

BARRIERS TO GROWTH

The information in Tables 37.1 and 37.2 suggests that the LDCs may never catch up with the rich countries of the world. Nevertheless, their growth prospects are still of great concern. Growth in Third World GNP per capita implies rising standards of living, even if it doesn't lead to equality with the more developed economies. Before growth can accelerate, though, the present barriers to growth must be identified and overcome.

Labor Resources

One constraint on faster growth of per capita GNP is already evident from Table 37.2: Third World populations are increasing so rapidly that it is difficult to raise average incomes.

Disguised unemployment   The problem here entails more than simple arithmetic. With relatively little land or capital available, a growing population soon presses against its productive capacity. Additional workers simply don't have enough resources to work with. This shortage of capital and land effectively creates a surplus of labor. Part of this surplus shows up as conventional unemployment, where job seekers are unable to find jobs. In subsistence agriculture, however, the surplus labor is more likely to show up as "disguised" unemployment. **Disguised unemployment** is a situation in which people are employed but contribute little or nothing to total output.

disguised unemployment:
People are employed but contribute little or nothing to total output.

State enterprises   Disguised unemployment is not confined to agriculture. In many low- and moderate-income countries, state-owned enterprises often hire more workers than they need. The extra jobs help solidify political support. Economically, however, the "excess" jobs may contribute little or nothing to output. Instead, the disguised employment will push up costs and prices or require higher taxes and subsidies. This kind of disguised unemployment plagued many centrally planned economies in Eastern Europe. Such hidden labor surpluses have also been a drag on productivity and growth in many Latin American and African countries.

Human capital development   Low incomes and rapidly growing populations also retard human capital development. Every dollar of available income must be spent on immediate consumption, just to keep families fed. As a

W🌐RLD VIEW

LIMITING POPULATION GROWTH

China to Levy Tax as Birth Check

PEKING—China, a land of almost 1 billion people, will begin taxing families who have too many children, a top government official said Saturday. The goal is to achieve zero population growth by the year 2000.

Vice Premier Chen Muhua, in an article in the Communist Party newspaper People's Daily, said birth control was an "urgent problem" in China.

She said the population plan has two stages: lowering the birth rate from 12 per thousand to five per thousand by 1985, then lowering it further to achieve a balance between births and deaths—zero population growth—by the end of the century.

One birth per couple will be encouraged, she said. She said the government would "resolutely check three births."

The government will adopt a family planning law that will provide "a series of economic measures to check the birth rate," the vice premier said. "People who refuse to be persuaded and insist on having more children will be taxed."

—Victoria Graham

Oregonian, August 12, 1979. Reprinted by permission of The Associated Press.

consequence, no resources are left over for savings or investment. Nor is there enough income to permit extended schooling or any other significant investments in human capital. In other words, people in abject poverty tend to be caught in a vicious circle of deprivation.

The problems of rapid population growth are often compounded by cultural and social values. Additional children are viewed as economic assets in many LDCs, especially among the vast majority of families that subsist in agriculture. More children mean more hands to till the soil and harvest the crop. And those little hands are sent to the fields at a very early age. Children are also viewed as a form of income security for old age, since extended families are still the norm in most LDCs. Unfortunately, those same children restrict income-earning opportunities and ultimately growth of per capita incomes.

Rapid population growth is only one dimension of the labor problem. Ironically, the other dimension consists of a labor shortage. In LDCs there is typically a severe shortage of *skilled* labor and managers. This is partially a consequence of the problems previously noted. Relatively few children in the poorest LDCs stay in school very long. In Haiti, less than 16 percent of children attend secondary school. Sixty percent of the population is illiterate: they cannot read and write a short simple statement about everyday life. There are few schools or teachers, little educational material is available, and the children are needed to help produce income.

The lack of trained labor also reflects a paucity of public support for vocational education, owing to insufficient resources and a frequent disdain for "commercial" education (see World View on India's college system). In addition, many LDCs have discovered that the first thing newly skilled labor does is leave the country for better opportunities elsewhere. This "brain drain" poses a persistent threat to both the public and private human capital investment.

Capital Resources

productivity: Output per unit of input; e.g., output per labor hour.

Internal savings   A lack of capital resources poses a second major barrier to growth. The LDCs are desperate for plant and equipment that will raise the **productivity** of labor. But their average incomes are so low that they can rarely afford to save enough to finance the required investments. Most of the population lives at the subsistence level, struggling to survive until the next harvest. There is little margin for saving. As a consequence, the question of *WHAT* to produce is determined largely by subsistence needs. Figure 37.1 illustrates the resulting mix of output.

Even the meager saving that does occur is not effectively mobilized. Peasant farmers have a traditional distrust of banks and even paper money. In Haiti, for example, the most valuable crop is coffee. In years of good harvest and high prices, the peasant farmers often have more income than they need for immediate consumption. But they rarely convert that surplus income into money. Instead, they simply store the extra coffee beans. In this way they avoid the risks associated with both paper money and the local banks, and they avoid potential taxes as well. Moreover, they can use the beans to **barter** for desired goods. By holding their savings in this form, however, the peasants also prevent conventional investment financing, whereby savings held in banks are used to finance loans to investors.

barter: The direct exchange of one good for another, without the use of money.

In the absence of conventional financing mechanisms, LDCs must often resort to other saving mechanisms. In centrally planned economies the government may force high saving rates via taxes or controlled prices and wages.

W🌐RLD VIEW

HUMAN CAPITAL

In Third World India, College Students Study Humanities, Not Skills

CALCUTTA—At 102 Amherst St. there is a sagging old school, grimy from Calcutta's appalling pollution, scarred by years of overuse.

From 6:15 to 10:45 a.m. this is Rammohan College for 3,280 girls. From 10:45 to 5:15 p.m. it's City College for 2,500 boys. And from 5:15 to 9 p.m. it is Anandamohan College for 1,300 night students.

All three are part of the University of Calcutta, the biggest university in the world. There are 200,000 students at Calcutta and 257 colleges stretched over three states; 75,000 undergraduates sit for degree exams every year, and there are 13,000 students in graduate school.

In a country as poor as India, a university might be expected to offer the flicker of possibility, the intellectual means to move the nation ahead. So why is it that with its colleges working triple shifts, India still labors among the most backward countries in the world?

Out of Focus

The British founded the University of Calcutta, the first in India, 125 years ago because they needed a few educated Indians to help them administer this huge back yard of their empire. Rich rajahs built the first campus, but the British wrote the curriculum, which was heavy on humanities, light on science and completely in English—perfect for turning out clerks, the Indians say.

But 34 years after independence, the University of Calcutta hasn't done much to change. The education ministry says a million Indians are studying the humanities; another half-million are going to college to become clerks.

"A poor country can't afford the luxury of an education in the humanities," argues J. D. Sethi, a New Delhi professor and former government education planner. Adds Barun De, the head of a social-science research center in Calcutta, "Our people are fairly well educated but totally unemployable."

What They Want

Jobs are scarce in India: Only 23 million of the country's 680 million people hold paying jobs (two-thirds of the population live on subsistence farms). So there's a spurt in interest in college courses that teach skills. At Presidency College, the most prestigious of Calcutta's colleges, 300 students a year apply for admission to the chemistry and physics departments.

But change comes at a hobbled march here. Presidency has room for only 36 chemistry students and 36 physics students. It had the same number in 1938 when B. S. Basak, Presidency's principal, was a student there himself. And even when chemistry applications climbed to 750 one year, Presidency wouldn't expand the department because "our requirements might change again some day," Prof. Basak says. . . .

Glacial Pace

It's a ponderous system. Calcutta's economics syllabus hasn't changed since 1975. . . .

India, ancient as civilization itself, is suspicious of change, and its smothering bureaucracy is resistant to it. Many students, too, oppose a shift to more practical studies. "Withdraw job-oriented education," demands a sign plastered in a Presidency College stairway.

So in this developing country, Calcutta doesn't have a program in rural development. There isn't a course in small-business administration, even though small businesses turn out countless products from fabric to steel. . . .

—June Kronholz

The central planners may also restrict the production of consumer goods. With few goods to buy, consumers are compelled to save more of their income. The Soviet Union and China have been extraordinarily successful with these techniques, having achieved investment ratios of 30 percent even at low levels of per capita income (see Chapter 38). The resultant pressure on living standards, however, helped stir unrest in those countries and topple governments in Eastern Europe.

Another mechanism for financing investment is inflation. In general, inflation tends to redistribute income and wealth. LDC governments use this redistributive feature to transfer a larger share of income into the hands of investors (e.g., via loans at low real rates of interest and preferential tax

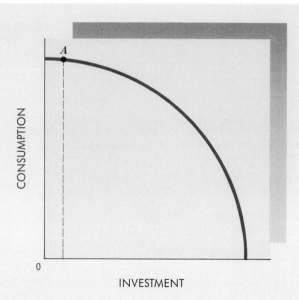

FIGURE 37.1
Hunger Limits Investment

In most LDCs the productive capacity of the country is barely sufficient to feed, clothe, and house the population. As a consequence, most available resources must be allocated to basic consumption. Very few resources are available for investment. Hence the mix of output tends to gravitate toward point *A*, a very low level of investment. This low investment ratio inhibits economic growth.

treatment). In the process, the real incomes of consumers are reduced. This forced saving effectively alters the mix of output. Latin American countries have financed much of their investment in this way, with substantial success.

Capital flight   Even where the pool of internal savings is adequate, there is no guarantee that it will be used for domestic investment. Ironically, much of the wealth generated in developing countries is invested in *developed* nations. Gaping inequalities, unstable governments, wild inflation, and unpredictable changes in tax laws, currency values, and institutions create a sense of anxiety about wealth. Too many people have seen their savings and investments wiped out by inflation or confiscated by governments. They prefer to hold their wealth in safe havens (e.g., U.S. bank accounts) and more productive investments (e.g., in growing industrialized economies). The desire to conceal wealth accumulated through corruption, drugs, or other illegal activity also increases the **capital flight** from poor countries. In the Philippines, former president Ferdinand Marcos was reputed to have secreted billions of dollars abroad, in Swiss banks, U.S. real estate, and other assets. Every dollar of such capital flight limits the potential for much-needed imports and investment. According to the World Bank, capital flight from Latin American countries in the 1980s substantially offset the inflow of foreign aid and loans.

capital flight: The outflow of funds motivated by domestic economic and political instability or illegal activity.

External financing   LDCs are not completely dependent on internal savings for new investment. They can also draw on external sources. Foreign investors are one such source. Foreign investors typically provide not only skilled management and labor, but also scarce plant and capital equipment. By encouraging such investments, an LDC can significantly increase its investment rate without reducing current consumption. In other words, foreign investment represents an immediate outward shift of the **production-possibilities** curve (see Figure 37.2). The shift results not only from the increased availability of capital, but also from the improvements in management, technology, and labor training that typically accompany foreign investment.

production possibilities: The alternative combinations of final goods and services that could be produced in a given time period with all available resources and technology.

Despite its substantial benefits, foreign investment is often discouraged by LDC governments. In part, this resistance reflects a fear of becoming too

FIGURE 37.2
External Financing
of Investment

An inflow of capital, skilled labor, or technology from abroad expands an LDC's production possibilities. Such an inflow permits an LDC to increase its rate of investment (from I_1 to I_2) without reducing its consumption level (C_1). Foreign investment, loans, and foreign aid are all sources of external financing.

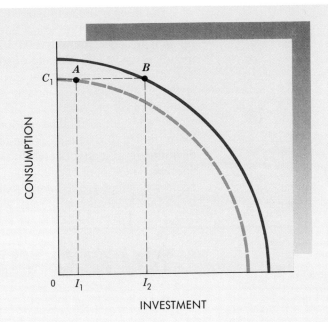

dependent on foreign investors for continuing growth. Such dependence has often entailed political risks, both domestically and internationally. Also, the citizens of LDCs are frequently hostile to the notion of permitting foreigners to own key resources or industries. On top of all this, there is often a widespread conviction that foreign investors take out (in profits) more than they put in (in investment capital), leaving the country worse off than before. This perspective ignores, of course, all the other income generated in the production process. It also suggests that sound investments should reap no profits.

Even when profits are recognized as a legitimate reward to risk and entrepreneurship, the resulting outflow of income is often resented. LDCs need "**hard**" **currencies** to buy new capital and other imported resources. But foreign investors also expect to take their profits home in hard currency. They have no use at home for foreign currencies that are not widely used in international markets and whose value is unstable. They want to take home their profits in U.S. dollars, Japanese yen, British pounds, or German marks. These same hard currencies are scarce in developing countries, however. Exports generate hard currency, but imports and capital flight use it up. Hence LDCs typically try to limit the outflow of hard currency profits. This perspective tends to be short-sighted, since the foreign investments are often the source of the hard-currency earnings.

The myopic view many LDCs have of foreign investment often results in several limitations on the extent and form of foreign investment and on the return ("repatriation") of profits. Popular hostility to foreign investment also leads on occasion to outright expropriation of foreign-owned assets, with or without compensation. The threat of such actions impedes increased foreign investment.

Loans   A second source of external financing for domestic investment is loans. Private banks, national governments, and international organizations all make loans to LDCs. Like foreign investment, loans represent an opportunity to increase current investment without sacrificing current consumption.

hard currency: Any national currency widely accepted in payment in international markets.

The most prominent lending agency is the World Bank. Through its several organizations, the World Bank makes loans to LDCs for specific development projects. The World Bank group (see World View below) also provides technical assistance to help ensure the success of the projects it finances. The other multinational banks provide similar financial and technical assistance, although on a smaller scale. As a group, the multinational development banks provided over $25 billion in new loans in 1990.

In addition to multilateral loans, the LDCs also have access to bilateral loans. In fact, the dollar volume of bilateral loans greatly exceeds the volume of multilateral loans. Bilateral loans are made directly from one country to another. The U.S. Agency for International Development (AID) is the principal agent for official U.S. bilateral loans.

LDCs have often professed a preference for multilateral loans over bilat-

W⊕RLD VIEW

MULTILATERAL LENDING

Multinational Development Banks

Several multilateral development banks provide loans, grant, and technical assistance to less developed countries.

World Bank Group
The World Bank was created at the Bretton Woods Conference in 1944 to facilitate world trade and economic development. There are three separate agencies within the World Bank Group:

- *International Bank for Reconstruction and Development (IBRD).* The IBRD is a profit-making institution that makes "hard" loans to LDCs for specific development projects. LDC borrowers are expected to repay the loans within twenty years, as scheduled. The IBRD raises capital for the loans by borrowing funds in private money markets. In 1990 the IBRD lent approximately $15 billion to LDCs. The IBRD also provides technical assistance on specific projects and consultation on general economic policies.

- *International Development Association (IDA).* The IDA makes "soft" loans to the poorest LDCs. The loans are "soft" in the sense that no interest is charged, and they may be repaid over a period of fifty years. IDA funds are obtained through contributions ("quotas") from developed countries and the earnings of the IBRD. In 1990 the IDA lent approximately $5 billion to poor LDCs.

- *International Finance Corporation (IFC).* The IFC makes equity investments as well as loans. It encourages the development of the private sector and often manages private co-financing of specific projects. The IFC attempts to provide a mix of financial, technical,

and management assistance. In 1990 the IFC lent over $1 billion.

Inter-American Development Bank (IDB)
Forty-three nations provide contributions to promote public and private investments in Latin America. Additional funds are raised in private money markets (via bonds). Like the other multilateral banks, the IDB also provides technical assistance on specific development projects. In 1990 the IDB made over $3 billion in loans.

Asian Development Bank (ADB)
The ADB, with headquarters in the Philippines, provides loans to LDCs in Asia. Because the loans are at market rates, most ADB loans go to the more developed LDCs. In 1990 the ADB lent over $3 billion.

African Development Bank (AFDB)
The AFDB, with headquarters in the Ivory Coast, focuses on Africa and attaches a high priority to agricultural development. In 1990 it lent less than $1 billion.

International Monetary Fund (IMF)
Strictly speaking, the IMF is not a development bank. The IMF's function is to lend money to countries that are having short-term balance-of-payments problems. However, these problems are often a result of structural difficulties and slow growth of exports. The IMF typically makes conditional loans requiring debtor countries to implement macroeconomic policies or structural reforms that will alleviate balance-of-payments problems. In 1990 the leading industrial countries agreed to increase the IMF's funding to $180 billion for loans to both Eastern Europe and the Third World.

eral ones. Bilateral loans, it is argued, often are extended with too many economic and political strings attached. The lending country may insist on changes in basic trade, monetary, or tax policies. The loan may also be tied to projects or specific purchases of greater priority to the lending country than to the borrowing country. The LDC is forced to make a "take it or leave it" decision. LDCs also feel that there is an implicit political agenda to bilateral loans and aid. Polish authorities, for example, claimed that Western countries (and banks) were unfairly using their financial leverage in 1982 to coerce the government into altering its internal policies. After the Communist government was ousted by Solidarity in 1989, the availability of Western loans increased tremendously.

Multilateral loans usually have strings attached, too. The World Bank and International Monetary Fund often insist on "responsible" fiscal and monetary policies as a condition for their development and foreign-exchange loans. These policies typically are more restrictive than the borrowing country desires and can cause political problems domestically. In one sensational case, the IMF refused to extend a loan to Zaire until that country agreed to let the IMF install its own experts at Zaire's national bank so that it could monitor Zaire's finances (and corruption). In 1985 the IMF cut off loans to Argentina and Brazil until those countries demonstrated a commitment to slowing runaway inflation (see World View below).

In addition to official multilateral and bilateral loans, LDCs can also borrow from private banks. In the 1970s the LDCs took out so many private loans that private banks became the biggest single source of LDC foreign capital. However, private banks are least likely to lend money to the poorest LDCs.

W RLD VIEW

LOAN CONDITIONS

IMF Cuts Off Argentina from Financial Aid

Cites Non-compliance with Pact

Argentina has been cut off from further financial aid by the International Monetary Fund until it brings its economic program into compliance with an agreement it reached with the multilateral lending agency only three months ago, banking sources reported yesterday.

The cutoff is a major setback to cash-starved Argentina, which also is nearing completion of a $4.2 billion loan from commercial banks. The banks had hoped to disburse several billion dollars of the loan to Argentina within weeks, but the commercial banks will not make loans to debtor nations that are out of compliance with IMF programs.

International banking sources said the IMF took the action because Argentina has made no headway at all in reducing its rampant inflation, which is running at an annual rate of 800 percent.

Last month the IMF took a similar action against Brazil, the developing world's largest debtor, because the country had failed to take steps to reduce inflation and had permitted its money supply to explode. A new civilian government took over in Brazil last week and has begun negotiations with the IMF to develop an anti-inflation program acceptable to the agency.

Argentina, which owes foreigners more than $45 billion, received nearly $500 million from the IMF last January, about three weeks after the IMF's executive board approved the Argentine economic program.

Negotiations between Argentina and the IMF had dragged on for more than a year because Argentina was reluctant to take the kinds of austerity measures needed to control inflation, reduce its budget deficit and, ultimately, reduce its need to borrow from foreigners.

—James L. Rowe, Jr.

The Washington Post, March 23, 1985, p. 1. Copyright © 1985 The Washington Post.

Debt servicing   Even in the best of political and economic situations, there is a limit to the ability of LDCs to borrow. A loan requires repayment. Hence LDCs that borrow to finance domestic investment must have the capability to "service" (repay) that debt. At a minimum, the economy of the LDC must grow at least enough to generate a surplus for **debt servicing.** Otherwise, debt servicing will require cutbacks in consumption, a contingency the loans were originally intended to avoid.

> **debt servicing:** The interest required to be paid each year on outstanding debt.

Even rapid economic growth, however, does not guarantee adequate debt-servicing capability. Most loans to LDCs are made in hard currencies, such as U.S. dollars, and creditors expect to be paid back in the same way. As a consequence, ***the ability of LDCs to borrow money depends on their capacity to earn hard currency.*** They earn foreign currency by selling exports. Hence debt servicing requires an LDC to increase its export potential. Export-related projects (e.g., a new harbor or factory) must take precedence over more domestic projects (e.g., new schools, improved sewage systems).

The Debt Crisis

During the 1980s the LDCs nearly doubled their external debt, to over $1.3 trillion. Annual servicing on these loans exceeded $170 billion. This was well within the payment capacity of the LDCs: debt service claimed only one-fourth of their export earnings. But averages are very misleading in this case. Much of the debt was incurred by a few very large borrowers, such as Mexico and Brazil. These and other Latin American countries borrowed heavily in the 1970s to finance new industries, oil exploration, and rising living standards. In the 1980s, however, their economies stagnated. A devastating combination of worldwide recession (1981–82), plummeting oil prices, rising interest rates, declining commodity (export) prices, and an appreciating dollar decimated their export earnings. The ratio of debt servicing to export earnings increased dramatically.

By 1985 many Latin American countries were barely taking in enough export earnings to meet their debt-servicing requirements. To make interest payments, they had to cut back imports of needed capital goods (for investment) and desired consumer goods. These hard choices created political and economic crises throughout Latin America. After several years of declining investment, per capita GNP, and growth, some of the major debtor nations declared a moratorium on debt repayment. First Mexico (1985) then Brazil and Peru (1987) announced that they were stopping or reducing debt servicing.

The suspension of debt servicing gave some of the LDCs some "breathing room." They could use this temporary relief to channel more of their export earnings into investment, thereby enhancing their growth and earnings capacity. They could also use the opportunity, however, to reallocate scarce resources to domestic consumption, thereby winning short-term political favor but doing nothing to improve their debt-servicing capacity. In either case, their unilateral refusal to repay debt threatened access to future foreign loans, which are critical to economic development.

The United States and other developed countries also stood to lose from the debt crisis. The private banks that had lent funds to developing countries had the most to lose if loan repayment ceased. Export industries—for example, farm products and equipment, machinery—also worried that the debt crisis would cripple the ability of developing countries to buy imported goods. Thus the developed (creditor) countries and the developing (debtor) nations had a joint interest in resolving the debt crisis. The resolution has included

- Increased exports by developing countries

- A reduction in imports of developing countries

- Greater priority to investment and growth in LDCs

- More loans and aid from developing countries

Although these actions have not eliminated the debt crisis, they have kept it from getting worse. Brazil was able to resume paying debt service in early 1988 and other developing countries have followed its lead. Nevertheless, huge debt loads remain a major barrier to increased investment and growth in many developing countries (especially Mexico, Brazil, and Argentina).

Foreign Aid
The developing nations could grow faster and continue to repay their debts if developed countries gave them more foreign aid. Unlike loans, *foreign aid* refers to money or resources given to LDCs for which no repayment is required. Foreign aid is given on a bilateral basis or through multinational agencies (e.g., the United Nations).

Although foreign aid to LDCs has not been insignificant, it is not a viable substitute for other sources of external financing. In 1989, total foreign aid to LDCs was $50 billion. This was not even enough to pay their debt-servicing requirements, much less fund substantial economic growth. The LDCs, of course, would like more aid. They point out, for example, that the United States allocates only 0.25 percent of total GNP to official development assistance. This was below the norm of most other developed countries (see Table 37.3) and much less than the 0.7 percent goal established by the United Nations.

TABLE 37.3 Foreign Aid in Relation to GNP, 1988

Although the United States provides more development assistance (bilaterally and multilaterally) than any other country, its contribution is modest in relation to its GNP. In 1974 the United Nations set an aid goal equal to 0.7 percent of GNP. Few developed countries have attained that goal.

Country	Millions of U.S. dollars	As a percentage of GNP
United States	$12,170	0.25
Japan	8,528	0.31
France	6,959	0.73
Germany (West)	4,700	0.39
United Kingdom	2,615	0.32
Canada	2,340	0.50
Netherlands	2,231	0.98
Sweden	1,534	0.87
Australia	1,091	0.46
Norway	988	1.12
Denmark	922	0.89
Switzerland	615	0.32
New Zealand	57	0.27
Total foreign aid	$49,730	Average 0.36

Source: World Bank; total includes other developed countries.

The LDCs also complain that foreign aid has too many strings attached. The aid may be conditional on political policies. Or it may require the recipient country to buy products from the donor country. Because of this and the perceived problems of all external financing, the LDCs have petitioned for "trade, not aid." They assert that if we would simply buy more of the goods they produce, the LDCs could increase their export earnings and finance more investment themselves. We shall examine trade problems shortly.

Technology

Capital and labor are basic factors of production. However, technology is also a primary determinant of production possibilities. Indeed, technological advances have been the primary source of rising GNP per capita in the United States. LDCs, too, could greatly increase their growth with improved technology.

In principle, technological advances should be relatively easy in LDCs. The rich countries of the world have already developed advanced technology. LDCs can increase their own productivity simply by utilizing available research and innovation. Many LDCs have in fact benefited greatly from such transfers of technology. South Korea, Taiwan, and Singapore have all learned to copy and adapt American electronics technology. Japan, too, fueled much of its rapid growth with borrowed technology. Even the oil-exporting LDCs have benefited directly from American technological advances in oil exploration, production, and refining.

Technology transfers have also transformed agricultural productivity in much of the Third World. The "Green Revolution" of the 1950s and 1960s spread high-yielding, disease-resistant seeds all over the world. Improved fertilizers and irrigation techniques also generated substantial increases in output.

Although technology transfers have had enormous impact on the growth of LDCs, many observers feel we have only scratched the surface of potential growth. Theodore Schultz, who won a Nobel Prize for his agricultural studies, is one such observer. As he sees it, a major barrier to the growth of LDCs is their failure to disseminate and adapt new technologies in the agricultural sector (where the vast majority of LDC populations live and work). There is too much emphasis on capital improvements (physical technology) and too little on the education and training of farmers (human capital). There is also a tendency to focus on big, glamorous industrial projects rather than small but cumulative improvements in organization and technology. China epitomized this problem with its "Great Leap Forward" in the mid-1970s (see Chapter 38).

Institutional Structure

Another pervasive problem in LDCs is a lack of infrastructure. *Infrastructure* consists of the physical and institutional features that facilitate economic activity. Roads, telephones, schools, hospitals, and electricity are all essential ingredients of a viable economy. Yet most of these bare essentials are simply nonexistent in much of the Third World. As a consequence, productive regions of the country remain isolated and underutilized. The lack of infrastructure is also a serious impediment to foreign investment. Foreign investors want to be assured not only of electricity, water, and roads, but also of housing, schools, and other amenities for their workers, especially for the skilled employees they import from home.

The institutional structure also encompasses the legal and political structure of an economy. In many LDCs legal protection is a luxury, and government corruption is pervasive. Political unrest is common, and governments are frequently overthrown. Under these circumstances, there are substantial risks attached to any long-term investments.

market mechanism: The use of market prices and sales to signal desired outputs (or resource allocations).

Finally, many LDCs are reluctant to rely on the **market mechanism** to allocate resources and distribute incomes. They prefer to use nonmarket prices to pursue specific economic or political objectives. This strategy is seen most commonly in the maintenance of low prices on agricultural products. By regulating prices and distribution LDC governments often try to keep food prices low. The low prices raise the real incomes of consumers, particularly those in urban areas. At the same time, however, low food prices reduce farmers' incentives to produce. Hence the quantity demanded increases while the quantity supplied falls. The end result is a **market shortage,** often accompanied by government rationing of basic foods. This distortion of market processes and outcomes has been a barrier to growth in countries as diverse as China, Poland, Algeria, and Senegal. Eastern European nations are hoping that their new reliance on market pricing will overcome these inefficiencies and accelerate economic growth.

market shortage: The amount by which the quantity demanded exceeds the quantity supplied at a given price; excess demand.

GROWTH STRATEGIES

The array of barriers confronting LDCs looks formidable enough to stop any growth strategy. Indeed, many economists have concluded that the LDCs will not be able to achieve sustained economic growth until they can muster enough resources to overcome all of these barriers simultaneously. Walter W. Rostow popularized this notion by identifying five stages of economic development:

- *Stage 1: Traditional society.* Rigid institutions, low productivity, little infrastructure, dependence on subsistence agriculture

- *Stage 2: Preconditions for takeoff.* Improved institutional structure, increased agricultural productivity, emergence of an entrepreneurial class

- *Stage 3: Takeoff into sustained growth.* Increased saving and investment, rapid industrialization, growth-enhancing policies

- *Stage 4: Drive to maturity.* Spread of growth process to lagging industrial sectors

- *Stage 5: High mass consumption.* High per capita GNP attained and accessible to most of population.

The critical stage in this conception is Stage 2, which develops the essential preconditions for takeoff. The implication is that some minimum set of circumstances must exist before the economy can take off.

Although the need for some preconditions is plausible, their exact nature is usually not evident until the growth process is already under way. In the meantime, LDCs must decide what growth strategies to pursue so as to maximize the probabilities of a takeoff and sustained growth. These strategic questions entail a variety of choices and difficult tradeoffs.

Agriculture vs. Industry

Ultimately the LDCs want to develop industrialized economies with high per capita GNP. It isn't clear, however, whether an early emphasis on industrialization is the fastest route to that objective. Industrialization cannot occur until an adequate flow of food and labor from the agricultural sector is assured. This flow cannot begin until agricultural productivity increases enough to generate a marketable surplus that will feed urban populations and permit some saving in rural communities. Agricultural productivity must rise even more if a surplus is to be maintained once farm workers migrate to urban industries. From this perspective, increased agricultural productivity looks like a precondition for an industrial takeoff. If it is, LDC governments should focus their limited managerial and capital resources on agricultural development rather than on early industrialization.

The massive concentration of LDC populations in the agricultural sector is another reason to give agriculture a higher priority than industry. More than 70 percent of the people in LDCs work in agriculture. Accordingly, agricultural development has the potential to spread the benefits of growth broadly in a short span of time.

Agricultural development also has the potential to improve the balance of trade. Increased agricultural productivity lessens the need for food imports and also creates the potential for additional exports. By contrast, industrialization typically requires an early inflow of foreign resources and may not generate exportable output.

Balanced vs. Unbalanced Growth

The choice between agriculture and industry is a reflection of a broader question about "balanced" growth. Should an LDC pursue growth in many sectors simultaneously? Or should the growth effort be focused on only one or more "leading" sectors?

Ideally, a country would develop its agriculture, its industry, and all of its other component sectors at the same time. But this ideal is generally unattainable. We must remember the limited capacity of most LDCs for any growth effort. A country that pursued balanced growth would end up allocating a minuscule amount of resources to each of many industries. Moreover, it would find that it did not have the management capacity to keep track of these diverse investments. As a consequence, a truly balanced growth strategy is likely to generate no growth. Moreover, the failure of such a strategy is apt to disillusion consumers, savers, and investors, making subsequent growth policies less credible and therefore more difficult.

The pursuit of unbalanced growth, then, is a virtual necessity. That is to say, an LDC must concentrate the limited human and physical resources available for growth on only a few industries. In choosing an appropriate target for growth, an LDC must consider a variety of factors. Among the most important are bottlenecks and linkages. The industries selected must be ones that are not subject to overwhelming bottlenecks caused by shortages of skilled labor, essential inputs, or technology. In other words, they must have some reasonable capacity to grow.

The second criterion for targeting unbalanced growth relates to the cumulative effects on an industry's development. Does the industry have significant linkages to other industries and sectors? If so, the growth of the target industry will stimulate the growth of other industries, thus ultimately promoting more balanced growth. Growth of the agricultural sector, for example, typically stimulates demand for fertilizer and farm equipment.

External vs. Domestic Markets

Another general criterion for targeting growth entails a choice between external and internal markets. Should an LDC rely on export markets for the growth of leading sectors? Or should it promote industries that primarily serve the domestic market? There are significant risks associated with either choice.

W🌐RLD VIEW

POLICY CHOICES

Senegal: A Subsistence Struggle

According to World Bank estimates, Senegal is one of the world's poorest countries, with a per capita income of roughly $400 a year. Even this low figure, however, greatly exaggerates the living standard of most Senegalese. In the small, urbanized area around the capital, Dakar, the average annual income is $850. But in rural areas—where 70 percent of the population lives—the average income is $150 per year. Rapid population growth (officially 2.7 percent a year, but unofficially estimated to be 3.3 percent) combined with minimal economic growth has kept the economy at subsistence levels. Most Senegalese are constantly at the brink of starvation, in mortal fear of recurrent droughts that will reduce their subsistence harvests. Average life expectancy is only 47 years.

Senegal is a resource-poor country, with extremely fragile and depleted soil. It is located in the Sahel, the region just south of the Sahara, where droughts are a recurrent phenomenon. Although it is crossed by two great rivers, Senegal has never built a substantial irrigation system. It has no significant mineral deposits and little known oil. There are iron-ore deposits in the southeastern part of the country, but no roads go there. Since French colonial times, Senegal's principal export crop has been peanuts.

Although a lack of resources constrains Senegal's production possibilities, its growth has been further retarded by government policies. The first president of Senegal, Léopold Sédar Senghor, enjoyed broad political support for twenty years. But this support was based in part on policies that curtailed economic growth. One of Senghor's first goals after independence was achieved in 1960 was to reduce foreign ownership and control of Senegal's crops, industry, and exports. The Senegalese government bought out most foreign investors and assumed control of their investments. In the process, however, the government overextended its management resources and skills, and business activity declined. The government's socialist stance also discouraged new inflows of foreign capital.

Another popular but ultimately self-defeating policy was the government's commitment to cheap food for the cities. The government imposed price and marketing controls on the agriculture sector. The aim of the controls was to hold urban food prices down. However, the low prices so discouraged farmers that they stopped marketing their output. Millet and rice are the principal food crops. But the farmers brought only 2 percent of their rice crop to the government-run markets in the late 1970s. As a consequence, Senegal had to import increasing quantities of food to feed its urban population.

Although Senegal desperately needed investment, the government tried to maintain consumption levels even when the economy was declining. In 1979 consumption absorbed 97 percent of gross domestic product. To further buttress consumption, the government increased the money supply rapidly and allowed consumer-goods imports to increase.

In 1979–80 an economic crisis developed. Senegal's trade deficit had reached alarming proportions as a result of a poor peanut harvest, higher oil prices, and increased consumer imports. The government was unable to meet its own payroll in June 1980 without emergency outside assistance.

In response to this crisis, a new economic strategy was adopted in the sixth five-year plan (1981–85). The new president, Abdou Diouf, vowed to curtail consumption and stimulate agricultural production. To this end, he raised tariffs on imported goods an average of 50 percent, raised food prices (e.g., the price of bread increased 60 percent), increased farm prices for peanuts and cotton, expanded agricultural training and extension services, and provided greater incentives for food exports. Diouf also cut government employment and spending, restricted money and credit growth, and reduced governmental intervention in product markets.

The World Bank, the IMF, and several developed countries helped Diouf formulate the *Plan de Redressement* embodied in this five-year plan. In recognition of Diouf's commitment to economic development, these institutions granted Senegal extraordinary new assistance. Senegal is still desperately poor, but it now has some prospect of economic growth.

Export markets   The advantage of focusing on export markets is twofold. First, every LDC needs foreign exchange (hard currency), and exports are the way to earn it. By promoting exports, an LDC effectively trades domestic resources for the capital and technology of other countries. The second advantage of exports is that they tap a ready market. World export markets are vastly larger than domestic ones, particularly those in poor LDCs. Hence exports confront a market with high levels of purchasing power.

All of the more successful LDCs have relied heavily on exports as the primary engine of growth. The "newly industrialized countries" (NICs) of Asia epitomize this export-led growth strategy. Korea, for example, paid off its debts and acquired advanced technology by exporting as much as 40 percent of its output. Brazil and most Eastern European countries are also using exports as the principal engine of growth.

Relying on exports for growth, however, is not a riskless strategy. The manufactured goods an LDC produces are likely to be of inferior quality and higher cost, given the scarcity of skilled labor, capital, modern technology, and experience. Hence an LDC may find that its manufactured exports are not competitive with goods produced in developed countries. To get a foothold in the export market, an LDC may need preferential treatment (purchases) from developed countries. The "Four Tigers" of Asia (South Korea, Taiwan, Hong Kong, and Singapore) got (and still enjoy) such preferential access to Western markets. The countries of Eastern Europe may also benefit from preferential access to the European community.

> **quota:** A limit on the quantity of a good that may be imported in a given time period.

Not all LDCs are able to gain such market access. Producers in developed countries dislike the added competition from LDC exports. Particularly successful LDC export campaigns are likely to result in trade restrictions of one kind or another (e.g., quotas and tariffs). The most notable example of such restrictions is probably the multination **quotas** on textiles. Many LDCs developed a **comparative advantage** in textile manufacturing and expected to accelerate their economic growth with earnings from textile exports. But the higher-cost textile manufacturers in the United States and elsewhere have successfully limited textile imports from LDCs, thus constraining their growth potential. The same kinds of restrictions are common on shoes, steel, and an assortment of other manufactured goods. These kinds of restrictions are the primary motivation for the LDCs' demand for "trade, not aid."

> **comparative advantage:** The ability of a country to produce a specific good at a lower opportunity cost than its trading partners.

Agricultural exports entail substantial risks also. Here again, the threat of trade restrictions is always present. The U.S. quotas on imported sugar exemplify the problem. As noted in the World View on p. 870, the primary goal of the U.S. sugar quotas is to raise the income of domestic sugar producers. In the process, however, U.S. consumers are denied access to cheaper imported sugar, and LDCs are shut out of a critical export market. The shrinking quotas have severely reduced the export earnings of Australia, Brazil, the Philippines, and several Caribbean countries.

> **price elasticity of demand:** The percentage change in quantity demanded divided by the percentage change in price.

Another risk associated with agricultural exports is their inherent instability. The quantity of food supplied in any year is as erratic as the weather. Yet the demand for food is relatively **price-inelastic.** As a consequence, farm prices and incomes tend to fluctuate greatly. Haiti again provides a convenient illustration. Coffee is Haiti's most important product, accounting for over 70 percent of its total export earnings. In 1977 the world price of coffee more than doubled when a frost in Brazil greatly reduced the quantity of coffee supplied in world markets. Haitian export earnings increased 50 percent, and it looked as though a takeoff into growth might be possible. Two years later, however, coffee prices fell abruptly, and Haiti's export earnings declined to their previous levels. Virtually every LDC has had a similar experience—even those LDCs that export oil (e.g., Nigeria and Mexico).

Many LDCs have tried to stabilize their export earnings by organizing producer cartels. In theory, the cartels could limit exports in years of excess supply or reduced demand, thereby maintaining a mutually agreeable price (and income). However, all such cartels tend to be fragile. Each member country is confronted by an all but irresistible temptation to underprice the cartel when a market surplus develops. And importing countries confront an all but irresistible temptation to disavow any "gentlemen's agreement" to maintain prices in such circumstances. Even OPEC was weakened by these market pressures.

Domestic markets   Given the risks of international trade, many LDCs have assigned greater priority to domestic markets. Of particular interest here are import-competing industries—that is, industries which produce goods that are being imported by the LDC. The attraction here is twofold. First of all, a market for the product already exists, as evidenced by the imports. Second, by producing rather than importing the goods in question, an LDC can reduce its outflow of precious foreign exchange. Rather than trying to earn additional export income to pay for imports, the strategy here is to reduce the need for imports directly.

As alluring as the import-substitution strategy is, it too entails significant costs. Newly developed domestic industries are not likely to be competitive with imported goods. To get started, they will probably need some protection, in the form of trade restrictions. This is the classic *infant industry* argument we encountered in Chapter 35. As is always the case, however, the nurture of infant industries implies higher costs to domestic consumers. These higher costs may in turn make other domestic industries less competitive in their own export markets. There is also the risk that the infant industry may never grow up, thus requiring perpetual subsidies and trade protection.

Should an LDC decide to promote a domestic industry that doesn't compete with imports, the problem of inadequate demand reemerges. Markets in LDCs tend to be very small and very poor. Accordingly, a growth strategy built on a leading domestic industry may flounder for lack of demand.

More Aid   With all the problems inherent in any growth strategy, the prospects for development of poor LDCs hardly look good. One wonders, however, how awful the growth prospects of today's developed countries looked a couple of hundred years ago. Growth certainly is still possible, despite the substantial barriers that impede the process. At the same time, however, it is evident that some of the poorest LDCs are going to flounder for a very long time if they don't receive more aid. Even the "middle-income" countries of Eastern and Central Europe realized that foreign aid and loans were needed to accelerate their growth. Foreign aid is not a substitute for long-term development strategies or structural reform. It is, however, the only immediate source of financing for increased investment in most of the Third World.

In the 1970s the United Nations set a goal for foreign aid, asking industrialized nations to commit 1 percent of their GNP to foreign aid. That goal was later reduced to 0.7 percent. Most rich countries give considerably less, however (Table 37.3), with the average aid share amounting to less than 0.4 percent of GNP.

SUMMARY

- GNP per capita provides a summary index of economic development. Most LDCs are characterized by both low GNP per capita and slow income growth. They are also far less able to satisfy basic human needs (e.g., food, shelter, medical care).

• High birth rates limit a country's ability to raise GNP per capita. Rapid population growth also tends to retard education, saving, and investment.

• Disguised unemployment in farming and state-owned enterprises tends to reduce productivity, raise prices, and require higher taxes and subsidies. Reducing such surpluses, however, is politically risky and requires alternative opportunities.

• LDCs are chronically short of skilled labor, management, capital, and technology. Although domestic saving can finance some of these inputs, external financing is usually required. Foreign investment, loans, and aid are all sources of external financing.

• Capital flight is induced by political and economic instability and illegal activity. The loss of such funds (especially hard currency) severely restricts investment and imports in many LDCs.

• During the 1980s debt-servicing requirements grew while export earnings fell, especially in Latin America. This debt crisis created difficult policy choices and prompted some LDCs to stop debt servicing temporarily.

• In the short run, many of the poorest LDCs must choose between agricultural development and industrialization. Agricultural development typically promises a greater payoff because the vast majority of the population works in agriculture, at low productivity. Improved farm productivity can create food, labor, and capital surpluses for industrialization.

• LDCs generally have no choice but to pursue unbalanced growth, that is, the concerted development of only a few leading industries.

• In seeking a leading industry, LDCs must choose between export promotion and domestic markets. Exports have the potential to earn needed foreign exchange but may also encounter unstable and protectionist markets. On the other hand, production for domestic markets may entail high costs or limited demand.

• There is no single "correct" strategy for economic development. Each country confronts a unique set of barriers and growth possibilities. All LDCs, however, could benefit from more foreign aid.

Terms to Remember   Define the following terms:

GNP per capita	debt servicing
disguised unemployment	market mechanism
productivity	market shortage
barter	quota
capital flight	comparative advantage
production possibilities	price elasticity of demand
hard currency	

Questions for Discussion

1. Why do LDCs prefer trade over aid? Why don't developed countries buy more products from LDCs?

2. Should LDCs restrict the profits of foreign investors? What are the gains and costs of such restrictions?

3. Identify an LDC and discuss its recent growth experience. What explains its growth rate?

4. Did the United States experience "balanced" growth, or were there notable "leading sectors" in our early development?

5. How did the United States finance its early investments when its production possibilities were very limited?

Problems

1. To promote growth, an LDC decides to develop tourist facilities. Its plans include the construction of a larger airport and more hotels. To do this, however, it must borrow $20 million from a U.S. bank.

   The bank's lending rules require an LDC to have a dollar income equal to at least four times the annual debt service (required interest plus principal repayments). Debt service is equal to 15 percent of the loan.

   Suppose that all of the LDC's dollar earnings come from tourists, who spend an average of $500 per visit. How many tourists must the LDC attract each year in order to qualify for the loan?

2. Reread the article about IMF aid to Argentina (p. 911). In 1986 Argentina's debt was more than four times larger than its export earnings. Argentina must finance its debt payments from the difference between its export earnings and its import payments.
   (a) How large can its imports be if it pays interest on its debt at the rate of 10 percent per year?
   (b) How high could the interest rate go before interest payments would theoretically prevent Argentina from importing anything?

CHAPTER 38

The Collapse of Communism

One cannot work without a plan designed for the long run.

—Lenin

*T*here is a Russian joke about Lenin's resurrection. It is 1990 and Lenin is resurrected "back to the future." Through an error in the guidance systems, however, he emerges on a street in New York City rather than in Moscow. Upon seeing the glass and steel skyscrapers, the flashy new cars, the stores overflowing with high-tech and luxury goods, and the obvious wealth of the people, Lenin proclaims: "This is exactly how I pictured our communist future."

The Moscow skyline of 1990 wasn't nearly so impressive, nor did the streets carry many flashy cars. In Russian stores the shelves were mostly empty; where consumer goods were available, long lines of anxious consumers waited. Muscovites weren't wealthy; the government itself said that 40 percent of the population was poor. The average Soviet consumer had cramped housing, few consumer durables, no telephone, no car. Even basics like soap, sugar, and salt were rationed. Seventy years after the revolution, Lenin's vision of a communist utopia remained unfulfilled. The revolution did not deliver the goods it had promised. This realization set off a wave of radical political and economic changes throughout the communist world.

This chapter examines these structural changes, particularly the transformations from centrally planned to market-oriented economies. We start by looking at the grand design of the communist vision, then at the economic difficulties actually encountered. These are the key questions:

- What is the appeal of central planning?

- What are the basic problems of central planning?

- What advantages do decentralized markets offer?

In pursuing these questions, we also look at the tradeoffs involved. The basic restructuring of an entire economy entails significant economic, social, and political costs. Although Karl Marx proclaimed that "economics is everything," the other costs cannot be ignored. They are important in explaining why some communist countries (e.g., the Soviet Union) are slow to change and others (e.g., Cuba) choose not to change at all.

THE PROMISE

Marx's Vision

Working with his good friend and later benefactor Friedrich Engels, Karl Marx described how capitalist systems would be destroyed. From his perspective, all history was a sequence of class strife, with class identities based on economic relationships. In the words of the *Communist Manifesto,* "The history of all existing society is the history of class struggles. Freeman and slave, patrician and plebeian, lord and serf, guildmaster and journeyman, in a word, oppressor and oppressed." **Capitalist** systems, Marx claimed, followed the same pattern; only the class identities were changed. In this case, the oppressors—the capitalists—owned the means of production, and the oppressed—the proletariat—were their modern-day serfs. The "natural" antagonism between these two classes arose out of the capitalist's unrelenting quest for profits and the attendant desire to pay workers as little as possible. This continued exploitation would eventually drive the working class to revolt and would come to an end with a "spontaneous" revolution.

capitalism: An economy in which the factors of production (e.g., land, capital) are owned by individuals; basic allocation decisions are made by market forces.

Once the capitalists were sent packing (if they were so fortunate), the working class itself, the proletariat, would take over the means of production. There would be no more class strife, because there would be only one class, with everyone sharing equally in access to the means of production and the output it yielded. The abolition of private property would mean that nobody would have any means of exploiting anybody else. The motivating principles of the **communism** Marx envisioned would be "from each according to his ability, to each according to his need." In that idealized society, there would be no central authority—no state—because the only function of a state was to express and pursue the interests of the dominant class. Since only one class would exist, in Marx's vision, no state would be necessary.

communism: A stateless, classless economy in which there is no private property and everyone shares in production and consumption according to individual abilities and needs.

The Socialist Transition

Marx was not very specific about exactly how a classless, stateless, communist society and economy would function. His immediate concern was with the continuing exploitation of the working class, the widespread poverty, sickness, and degradation that he himself had experienced in the early stages of the Industrial Revolution. Marx died some twenty-five years before the first successful communist revolution, and before he was able to complete *Das Kapital,* his voluminous study of the way capitalist systems functioned.[1]

Although he concentrated on the internal flaws of capitalism and the awakening of working-class interests, Marx also provided some sketches of the kind of society that would follow the revolution. He foresaw that a central government (the state) would be required for some time to give direction to the new society. The proletariat would not be prepared to embrace fully the basic tenets of communism, nor would it have the technical expertise required to organize the means of production. In the interim period, a central authority, a **socialist** state, would have to solidify class consciousness, reorganize property and production rights, expand output, and plan the transition to a truly communist society. As society moved along in that direction, the state would become increasingly unnecessary and would gradually wither away.

socialism: An economy in which all nonlabor means of production are owned by the state, which exercises control over resource allocaation.

[1]Marx never forgave capitalism for driving him into the relentless research (most of it undertaken in the British Museum) and political activism that exhausted his finances and health. On publication of the first volume of *Das Kapital,* he wrote to Engels, "I hope that the bourgeoisie as long as they live will have cause to remember my carbuncles" (cited in *Fortune,* May 1946, p. 146).

From Marx's perspective, then, the demise of capitalism would be succeeded by two further stages, socialism and communism. In both stages of development, the means of production would be publicly owned. Under socialism, however, the state would play an important role in allocating resources, and goods would be distributed in part according to each person's work effort. The economy would enter the final stage of development, communism, only after goods were in such abundance that everyone's needs could be satisfied. In that final stage—the communist utopia—people would work for the common good and need not be prodded with the promise of personal gain.

The communist revolutions that later took place—in Russia in 1917, in China in 1949, and elsewhere—did not follow Marx's scenario in every respect. Indeed, Marx would have been surprised to see the revolutions occur in countries as underdeveloped as Russia was in 1917 and as China was in 1949. Nevertheless, most "communist" countries heeded Marx's admonition to exert strong central authority, to use the state as an instrument for developing and reforming society. Indeed, most "communist" countries refer to themselves as "socialist," with communism expressed as a goal, not a description.[2]

CENTRAL PLANNING

Outlining ideals and carrying them out, however, are very different tasks. Imagine that you have led a successful revolution and must now organize the economy to fulfill the revolution's goals. This is the kind of dilemma Nikolai Lenin and his comrades confronted in 1917 and Mao Zedong faced in 1949.

In general, you want to ensure greater equality for all the people, because that was a motivating force behind the revolution. And you want to improve the standard of living, both to satisfy revolutionary aspirations and to reassure the proletariat that they have bet on the right horse. Finally, you want to build up the country's defenses to protect yourself against counterrevolution from within and aggression from without. How are you going to attain these goals, and what do you have to work with?

Production Possibilities

production possibilities: The alternative combinations of final goods and services that could be produced in a given time period with all available resources and technology.

The starting point for all planning is the concept of **production possibilities.** By adding up all of society's productive resources and surveying available technology, you could conceivably determine what production possibilities exist. The solid line in Figure 38.1 might be an adequate description of those possibilities. We are assuming that all goods can be lumped into two major categories, here referred to as "consumption goods" and "investment goods." The variety of goods producible is, of course, infinitely larger, but some sort of summary is useful, not to mention more manageable.

The first dilemma we have to confront is the fact that our production possibilities are probably no larger immediately after the revolution than they were just before it. In fact, they are probably smaller. A lot of buildings and

[2]How long one must wait for the stateless society is the subject of considerable debate. Lenin emphasized the need for the state to guard against "capitalist encirclement," implying some form of eternal vigilance. Echoing these thoughts, Joseph Stalin declared in 1939 that Russians could expect to achieve a stateless society only when socialism had been established all over the world and "there is no more danger of attack." This issue is more political than economic.

**FIGURE 38.1
Postrevolutionary
Production Possibilities**

All countries confront limited production possibilities. A revolution may even destroy capital, land, or labor, thus reducing immediate production possibilities (to the solid curve). Deciding what to produce with available resources and technology is a basic planning issue. To increase the production of consumer goods (e.g., from point A to point B) will require cutbacks in investment.

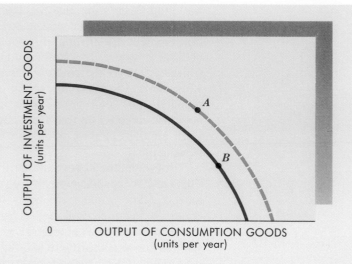

OUTPUT OF INVESTMENT GOODS (units per year)

OUTPUT OF CONSUMPTION GOODS
(units per year)

equipment were destroyed in the revolt, many workers have been wounded, and most of the capitalists and their lackeys are either dead or fled.[3] Accordingly, our immediate production possibilities probably look more like the solid curve in Figure 38.1 than the larger, dashed one that prevailed earlier.

In the face of unchanged or even smaller production possibilities, it is evident that we are going to have a difficult time delivering on the revolution's promises. Any immediate improvement of living standards for the masses will have to come about through *redistribution* of output rather than from *added* output. It is unlikely, however, that there will be sufficient stockpiles of basic goods—food, housing, clothes—to satisfy consumer demands through redistribution of existing output.[4]

What to produce The only viable option for increasing consumption levels is to change the mix of output. In the two-dimensional economy of Figure 38.1, this means cutting back on the production of **investment** goods. By altering the mix of output in favor of more consumption goods, we could deliver an immediate improvement of living standards. Such a change in the output mix is illustrated by the move from point A to point B in Figure 38.1.

Although this move might satisfy the need to deliver quickly on revolutionary promises, it poses difficulties for the years ahead. Some investment is needed simply to maintain and replace existing plant and equipment. Additional *net* investment is required to achieve **economic growth**—to *expand* our productive capacity. Accordingly, ***one of the most basic decisions central planners must confront is what proportion of resources to devote to investment and what proportion to present consumption.*** The tradeoff

investment: Expenditures on (production of) new plant and equipment (capital) in a given time period, plus changes in business inventories.

economic growth: An increase in output (real GNP); an expansion of production possibilities.

[3]At the time the Communists took control of China in 1949, industrial output was one-half its prewar peak. Agricultural output was similarly depressed. In addition, the transportation system was partially destroyed, many skilled technicians and managers had fled, and the government's foreign-exchange reserves had been moved to Taiwan.

[4]Following the Bolshevik revolution of 1917, the mansions of many Russian aristocrats and affluent capitalists were converted into multifamily dwellings; but the number of mansions is obviously limited. Redistribution possibilities may have been slightly greater in China, where the landlord-gentry class had diverted a lot of output to personal consumption, including reserves of rice and other food.

is a difficult one, especially in a country where living standards are abnormally low and we need to increase *both* consumption and investment. In the Soviet Union, the decision was made—first by Lenin and then even more forcefully by Joseph Stalin—to shift the mix of output in favor of investment. Both leaders were well aware that this decision implied reduced living standards in the short run. Investment goods have accounted for as much as one-third of Russian output, approximately double the investment ratio that has prevailed in the United States. One consequence of this emphasis was a faster rate of economic growth in the Soviet Union than in the United States, particularly in the 1930s and again in the 1950s.

The political leaders of China decided that they could not afford such high rates of investment, although they needed it even more than did the Soviets. In 1949 the Chinese people were on the brink of starvation. GNP per capita was less than $200 (in 1990 U.S. dollars). Accordingly, the Chinese leaders had to devote a larger share of total output to consumption, especially such basic foodstuffs as wheat, rice, and cooking oil. Less than 10 percent of total output was devoted to investment in the early postrevolutionary years. Only after minimal consumption standards were ensured did the share of output devoted to investment increase (to as high as 25 percent in the early 1970s).

Resource Allocation

Selecting a mix of output is the easy part of central planning. The hard part is assuring that the desired mix gets produced. There are two critical steps toward fulfilling the central plan:

- Choosing the best production processes

- Allocating the right amount of resources to each sector

In a market economy, these decisions are made by independent producers, each of whom is making production decisions and bidding for scarce resources. A pure socialist state, however, does not permit private ownership, profit accumulation, or "exploitive" wage relationships. Moreover, decisions made by market participants might not conform to the central plan (the designated output mix). ***In a socialist state, central planners assume the resource allocation responsibilities.*** They designate how many resources will go to each industry. The central planners also decide where each person will work (see World View).

This resource allocation task is critical to the success of central planning—and fraught with complexity. Two-dimensional production-possibilities curves will no longer suffice. Now we have to start thinking about widgets and ball bearings, plows and threshers. Even in a socialist economy, the production of goods entails the coordination and completion of several distinct steps. Neither swords nor plowshares will appear out of thin air just because we specify a particular mix of output as being desirable.

Recall that just about any good can be produced in a variety of ways. Such alternative **production processes** burden us with increasingly difficult decisions. We must decide first how many of each output we want, then which combination of inputs is most efficient for producing that quantity. Finally, we must be sure that the input requirements we derive from these calculations do not exceed the quantity of resources we have available.

production process: A specific combination of resources used to produce a good or service.

W☉RLD VIEW

PLANNED EMPLOYMENT

Soviets Find Job for Every College Grad

MOSCOW—"It's like their wedding day," the university rector said happily.

A graduating senior disagreed. "It's terrible," he said. "Everyone is taking tranquilizers."

The occasion was the Day of Distribution, which is far more emotional than Graduation Day at the 900 or so institutions of higher learning in the Soviet Union. On the Day of Distribution, graduates get their first job assignments.

By the end of June, virtually all of the 800,000 young men and women graduating from universities and other university-level institutions will have met with a placement commission and will know which job is waiting for them.

The system is a creature of this country's planned economy.

In the United States, collegians choose their specialties and take their chances in the job market after graduation. In the Soviet Union, the system cranks out cars, bombs and paper clips according to government decree, and it produces diplomas the same way.

"They give us money, we give them specialists," Arnold Koop, rector of Tartu University in Soviet Estonia, summed up.

Most Soviet students, even though they would probably balk at trading their security for what they see as the chaotic rough-and-tumble of the American job market, are not entirely happy with their system.

Eager to begin enjoying the good life that a college degree virtually assures in this society, many see the first job assignment as a way station at best.

When they scrawl "I consent" at the bottom of the placement commission's decision. Soviet graduates technically commit themselves to work at their first job for at least three years, repaying the state for a free education.

But they resent the fact that many assigned jobs are far from home, in the provinces, where life is often primitive and their talents are sometimes not appreciated. And many wind up with jobs only remotely related to their studies.

—Dan Fisher

Input–Output Analysis

The kind of calculations required for efficient resource allocation would give you an unbelievable headache, even if you were equipped with high-speed computers. A sense of how painful such an effort might be is only suggested by Table 38.1, which indicates a few input–output relationships for the Soviet economy. Input–output coefficients, as displayed in the table, indicate how much output from one industry will be required to provide inputs for another industry.

You can discover by reading down the column marked "Automobiles," for example, that the production of 1 ruble's worth of automobiles required 0.08503 ruble's worth of ferrous ores and metals, 0.02649 ruble's worth of nonferrous ores and metals, and so forth. Incredibly boring statistics, to be sure. But if you're in charge of allocating the people's resources, you'd better be certain that you allocate the right amount of resources to the production of such inputs.

Prices

market economy: An economy that relies on markets for basic decisions about WHAT to produce, HOW to produce it, and FOR WHOM to produce.

You might be thinking that markets and prices could help solve some of these problems, thereby relieving you and your planners of an immense burden. But such thoughts merely demonstrate that you have not yet cleansed your mind of its bourgeois capitalist prejudices. It is of course true that ***a basic function of prices in a* market economy *is to signal to producers and consumers that some products are relatively scarce or plentiful.*** These signals are expected to call forth appropriate supply and demand responses.

TABLE 38.1 Soviet Input–Output Relationships

Nothing can be produced unless the required inputs are available in the correct quantities. An input–output table such as this describes the production requirements of various goods. The production of one automobile, for example, requires inputs of 0.08503 unit of ferrous ores and metals, 0.02649 unit of nonferrous ores, and so on. Central planning agencies use such tables to determine what goods and services can be produced with available resources and technology.

Sector number	Inputs	Automobiles	Tractors and agricultural machinery	Bread, flour, and confections	Electric and thermal power
			Input requirement per unit of:		
1	Ferrous ores and metals	0.08503	0.13637	0.00024	0.00137
2	Nonferrous ores and metals	0.02649	0.01685	0.00018	0.00000
3	Coke products and refractory materials	0.00173	0.00382	0.00002	0.00024
4	Industrial metal products	0.00954	0.00828	0.00015	0.00089
5	Coal	0.00216	0.00187	0.00238	0.20491
6	Oil extraction and refining	0.00524	0.00475	0.00065	0.06132
7	Gas	0.00332	0.00303	0.00083	0.05900
8	Peat and oil shales	0.00019	0.00011	0.00014	0.02763
9	Electric and thermal power	0.01171	0.01935	0.00284	0.00153
10	Energy and power machinery	0.00021	0.00065	0.00001	0.00174
11	Electrical machinery and cable products	0.01705	0.01571	0.00026	0.00153
12	Metalworking machinery	0.00155	0.00229	0.00000	0.00000
13	Tools and dies	0.00272	0.00506	0.00009	0.00013
14	Precision instruments	0.00080	0.00147	0.00004	0.00048
15	Mining and metallurgical machinery	0.00000	0.00000	0.00000	0.00000
16	Pumps and compressors	0.00123	0.00122	0.00001	0.00012
17	Tractors and agricultural machinery	0.00026	0.18826	0.00001	0.00008
18	Bearings	0.00841	0.01723	0.00002	0.00009
19	Other machine-building	0.02052	0.02061	0.00041	0.00307
20	Other metalworking	0.00585	0.01013	0.00061	0.00035
21	Repair of machinery	0.00101	0.00153	0.00053	0.00533
22	Abrasives	0.00106	0.00195	0.00001	0.00007
23	Synthetic resins and plastics	0.00240	0.00065	0.00004	0.00040
24	Paints and lacquers	0.00703	0.00626	0.00012	0.00029
25	Rubber and asbestos products	0.08596	0.03779	0.00017	0.00040
26	Woodworking	0.00677	0.01067	0.00401	0.00039
27	Paper and pulp	0.00173	0.00107	0.00225	0.00009
28	Construction materials	0.00136	0.00084	0.00023	0.00044
29	Glass and porcelain	0.00393	0.00074	0.00004	0.00016
30	Textiles	0.00621	0.00296	0.00083	0.00037
31	Sugar	0.00000	0.00006	0.05334	0.00000
32	Bread, flour, and confections	0.00000	0.00000	0.23885	0.00000
33	Crops	0.00002	0.00002	0.31794	0.00000
34	Transportation and communications	0.05446	0.06347	0.01214	0.00054
35	Trade and distribution	0.02239	0.00761	0.07199	0.00005

Source: U.S. Congress, *Soviet Economic Prospects for the Seventies,* a compendium of papers submitted to the Joint Economic Committee, June 27, 1973 (Washington, D.C.: U.S. Government Printing Office, 1973).

Thus one way to solve the resource-allocation problem might be to let prices respond to shortages. If somebody in the Administration for Tires and Rubber Products messed up her homework and left us without enough tires, tire prices would rise. This price increase would provide an early warning of

market mechanism: The use of market prices and sales to signal desired outputs (or resource allocations).

trouble and give tire producers a strong incentive to increase production. In this way, the tire shortage might be alleviated before it got too serious.

But such "efficiency" is not welcome in a planned socialist economy. The **market mechanism** has been rejected for three principal reasons. First, were prices allowed to function as market signals and help distribute goods and resources accordingly, we could no longer be assured that our planning goals would be achieved. Second, if prices are free to respond to market forces and producers are free to react accordingly, some people are going to make a lot of money. Producers will profit from market imbalances and their efforts to correct them. That kind of behavior threatens to unbalance the distribution of income. This is a very serious matter: to suggest that market prices could help to solve our allocation problems is tantamount to condoning profiteering.

Someone might object, however, that any excesses of profit could be taxed away, thereby fulfilling the allocation objective without disturbing the income distribution. But that idea only demonstrates an incomplete understanding of capitalist economics. We simply can't have it both ways. If we enshrine the profit motive as an acceptable means of solving allocation problems, we violate the principle of "from each according to his ability, to each according to his need." Private gain, not communal effort, becomes the motivating force. If we try to correct these excesses by steeply progressive income and profit taxes, we will sanction selfish motives. We will also reduce marginal profits so much that they will lose their effectiveness as motivating forces. (Remember all those squabbles the capitalists had about marginal tax rates and work incentives?)

Distributing output Shall we completely abolish prices, then? No. Unless we are prepared to ration everything from basic resources to final consumer goods, prices will have to be an essential ingredient of our plans. But central planners do not use prices the same way the capitalists do. *In a planned economy, prices are used to reconcile the mix of goods demanded to the centrally planned supply.* The mix of goods supplied is itself determined by the state plan. Prices are not permitted to have an independent influence on resource allocation. The central planners do not permit the high prices attached to some consumer goods, for example, to act as an incentive for increased production. Prices are used solely to control demand. Specifically, *high prices on luxury goods are used to limit the quantity demanded.* Those prices are maintained with high retail taxes, while producers are paid very little for their output of consumer goods. This strategy effectively dampens both consumer demand and producer incentives.

The central planners also use low prices to encourage certain kinds of consumer behavior or to ensure that everyone can afford basic staples. In China and the Soviet Union, for example, the prices of food, housing, and health services are kept very low. Rent on a two-room apartment in China costs something like $100 a year, a visit to the doctor 10 cents, and an abortion only $1.00.[5] The same kind of pricing was evident in Eastern Europe prior to the dismantling of the planning apparatus. In 1989 rent on a three-bedroom apartment in East Berlin was only 70 Ostmarks per month; in West Berlin rents were at least five times higher. In Moscow, bread cost 15 cents a loaf in 1989, the price set by the central planners in 1954. Such *low prices for*

---

[5]The low price of an abortion is consistent with China's growing anxiety about its burgeoning population—estimated at 1.1 billion in 1990 and growing by 9 million or so people a year! It is also hoped that pervasive indoctrination and social counseling, including a prohibition against premarital sex, will restrain the demand for such services.

necessities are intended to assure everyone access to basic consumer goods.

Measuring performance   Centrally planned prices are also used as a convenient measure of efficiency. How are we going to know whether the People's Bicycle Factory at Tientsin is producing as many bicycles as it can with the resources available to it? It would be a horrendous task to inventory all the separate inputs used, then to compare those input–output relationships with those of the People's Bicycle Factory at Kwangchow. And how do you know which factory is better serving the people if you can do no more than observe basic inputs and outputs? Say that the Tientsin factory produced 27 bikes last month and used 18 pounds of aluminum, 7 pounds of rubber, $1\frac{1}{2}$ gallons of lacquer, and 13 pounds of steel. At the same time the Kwangchow factory produced 33 bikes, using 21 pounds of aluminum, $6\frac{1}{2}$ pounds of rubber, 4 gallons of lacquer, and 12 pounds of steel. Some summary sort of measure is clearly necessary. Far better if we attach prices to all those inputs and simply see how much total cost goes into the production of so many bicycles. Prices will allow us to measure performance. We can also use relative prices to discourage the use of relatively scarce inputs such as aluminum and rubber, or whatever resources we desire to ration carefully.[6]

Income Distribution   Insofar as planning objectives are concerned, the question of *income distribution* is readily resolved. We want all our people to be equal. In material terms, this means that we want to move closer to a situation wherein all people enjoy the same standard of living, whatever their respective abilities. Disparities in income serve to create jealousies, anxieties, and social friction. If such disparities are large enough, they can lead to conspicuous social stratification—that is to say, to socioeconomic *classes*. That is clearly inconsistent with the stateless, classless society envisioned by Marx. Hence we shall strive to ensure that everyone receives a more equal share of total income. To ensure further that people do not use their income for purposes of indulgent consumption, we will limit the availability of basic commodities and ration them equally among the people. And we shall price conspicuous consumption goods, such as automobiles, so high that there is little chance of anyone acquiring them.

PROBLEMS OF IMPLEMENTATION

At this point, we may have mixed feelings about central planning. On the one hand, central planning offers the potential to reshape both the mix of output and the distribution of income. In theory, central planners can achieve the utopian vision of communism. On the other hand, that vision may be obscured and ultimately destroyed by the inherent flaws of central planning.

Complexity   To begin with, we have to recognize just how complicated the planning process can become. The input–output relationships in Table 38.1 are just a hint of that complexity. ***The more specific output targets become, the more complex the central plans must be.*** In the Soviet Union, Gosplan establishes production targets for 70,000 items and sets 200,000 prices each year. One of

[6]Many luxury goods and basic commodities are explicitly rationed in China. Rationing further reduces the use of such goods.

the planners' foremost concerns is to confirm that all the planning details are *consistent*—that all inputs and outputs match up in the style of Table 38.1. This is a complex and onerous task, fraught with opportunities for error.

Taking our chances, let us dismiss problems of planning detail and give some thought to the problems of implementation. How are we going to communicate our plans to the masses? What assurances do we have that our plans will be carried out? We're going to look pretty foolish if we advertise grandiose goals and nobody pays any attention to them. The bourgeois press will naturally try to exploit such a situation. They will claim that we have lost the support of the people, that we are out of touch, and that we have started moving our personal fortunes into Swiss bank accounts.

Incentives

The critical question is how to motivate the workers, the farmers, and the managers of our plants to fulfill the specific objectives of our plans. They may not possess the same revolutionary zeal and far-sightedness that we do and may thus have a difficult time understanding and accepting their roles in the master plan. And we can be certain that input–output coefficients will mean as little to them as they do to economics students in capitalist societies. How, then, can we get the masses to contribute to output in the form and quantity we desire?

People's willingness to supply labor—to work—is predicated on a variety of psychological, sociological, and economic considerations. In market economies, the greatest emphasis is placed on economic considerations. Material rewards in the form of higher wages, prices, or profits are used as carrots to call forth the desired supply responses. But such an emphasis is clearly less appropriate for a socialist state. As we have emphasized, ***material incentives lead to income inequalities*** and nurture selfish interests rather than social interests.

Having rejected market incentives, central planners must find other ways to motivate workers. Typically, the only alternatives are exhortation or brute force. Neither alternative is an adequate substitute for material incentives, however. Neither "reeducation" campaigns nor forced labor (e.g., forced collectivization of farms) has succeeded in generating efficiency, much less creativity. Workers in state-owned enterprises find that it is easier—and no less rewarding—to just "get by" than to challenge production decisions or pursue innovation.

Recognizing this shortcoming, most communist governments have experimented with material incentives. In the Soviet Union, for example, workers are coaxed into "fulfilling and overfulfilling" plan targets by a variety of bonuses. In the industrial sector, such bonuses may be direct supplements to wages and account for as much as 30 percent of take-home pay.

In the agricultural sector, the Soviet appeal to private gain takes two forms. On collective farms (*kolkhozy*), all workers are expected to contribute to the fulfillment of output targets. If actual output exceeds those targets, the surplus may be distributed to the workers, much like an industrial bonus. In addition, agricultural workers are allowed to cultivate their own private garden plots. The output from such plots may be consumed directly or sold in farmers' markets, as in capitalist market economies.

Goal conflicts The use of even these limited material incentives conflicts with the egalitarian goals of communist ideology. Mao Zedong repeatedly denounced this Soviet "revisionism." Mao made a much greater effort to rely exclusively on nonmaterial incentives. For over two decades, Chinese workers were urged to "develop the socialist economy, carry the revolution through to the end" by banners hung in every office and factory (together with photographs of Marx, Lenin, and Mao). Thoughts of personal gain were regarded as counterrevolutionary.

Such dedication was difficult to maintain, however. Over time, the Chinese leaders permitted limited use of material incentives (including private garden plots). But this was inconsistent with Mao's basic dictum that "politics must come before economics." This tension led to the Great Proletarian Cultural Revolution (1966–69), a widespread and sometimes violent reaction to "creeping materialism." The Cultural Revolution was designed to reassert revolutionary ideals and communal aspirations.

After Mao's death in 1976, the pendulum swung back toward an emphasis on rapid development. The eight-year plan drawn up in 1978 called for a "new long march" that would make China a major industrial power by the year 2000. This entailed the "Four Modernizations"—of agriculture, industry, technology, and defense. To achieve these ambitious goals, the Chinese planners introduced a "contract" system in both agriculture and industry. Each collective farm and state enterprise was given a production quota (contract). This quota had to be sold to the state at prices fixed by the planners. Any output in excess of the quota, however, could be sold on the open market—at market-determined prices. This two-tier system gave farmers and urban workers a material incentive to increase output. In defending this use of material incentives, Deng Xiaoping explained that "it doesn't matter whether the cat is black or white as long as it catches mice." In other words, a little capitalism would be tolerated if it produced economic gains.

W RLD VIEW

INEFFICIENCIES

Soviets Outline Dramatic Farm Deficiencies

MOSCOW—A confidential study prepared for the top Soviet leadership has outlined a nearly disastrous decline in the Soviet Union's ability to feed itself, demonstrating a compelling need for agricultural and other economic reforms.

The study, made available here, provided figures that showed a tenfold increase in Soviet food imports during the past decade, staggering levels of mishandling of agricultural equipment and "direct losses" of harvested crops due to negligence and lack of storage or drying facilities.

The document, prepared by a special government commission during the past year, said one-fifth of the grain harvest is lost because it is harvested late or left to rot.

The study said one-third of the country's potato crop is left to rot, and experts who took part in drafting the document put the losses even higher. They said about half of potato production—or the equivalent of the annual American production—is lost each year because of a chaotic distribution system and lack of storage facilities.

As a result, the study said, an average Soviet citizen is poorly fed, consuming 54 pounds of meat per year less than required by medical standards.

The commission, which prepared the study in cooperation with the state planning commission and 38 ministries and scientific institutes, concluded that "the existing economic mechanism does not provide necessary economic incentives for production increases and fuller use of the potentially available land.". . .

—Dusko Doder

The Washington Post, May 23, 1982. Copyright © 1982 The Washington Post.

Shortages

Even if material incentives helped increase output, a basic market imbalance would remain. One of the principal goals of a socialist state is to assure greater economic equality. Centrally controlled wages and prices are the chief mechanisms for achieving this goal. Material bonuses create wage inequalities but leave centrally controlled prices intact. As we have noted, the central planners use low prices on basic consumer goods to ensure everyone access to these goods.

Figure 38.2 illustrates the consequences of this pricing policy. The demand for meat in socialist countries conforms to the law of demand: larger quantities are demanded at lower prices. The supply of meat is fixed, however, at a level determined by the central planners. In a market economy, the price of meat would reflect underlying supply and demand. In the figure, p_m would be the market price of meat. At that price, however, meat would be consumed only by those consumers who had a greater ability or willingness to pay. Material bonuses (wage inequalities) might result in unequal access to food. To avoid such inequality, the central planners set the price of meat at p_c. At that low price everyone can afford meat.

Not everyone gets meat, however. Socialist consumers confront a **market shortage:** the quantity demanded at p_c greatly exceeds the quantity supplied; thus the meat disappears from the stores long before everyone who is willing and able to buy it at the controlled price gets a chance to do so.

The symptoms of market shortages are empty shelves and long lines of consumers waiting for a chance to buy scarce goods. Such lines are commonplace in the Soviet Union and China. In 1981 they grew to epidemic proportions in Poland. The government itself estimated that the average Pole was spending four hours a day standing in food lines! The Polish government tried to increase the supply of food but failed. It then turned to rationing. In the fall of 1981 the average Pole was allowed an allotment of only $6\frac{1}{2}$ pounds of meat per month, 2 pounds of sugar, 2 pounds of flour, 12 packs of ciga-

market shortage: The amount by which the quantity demanded exceeds the quantity supplied at a given price; excess demand.

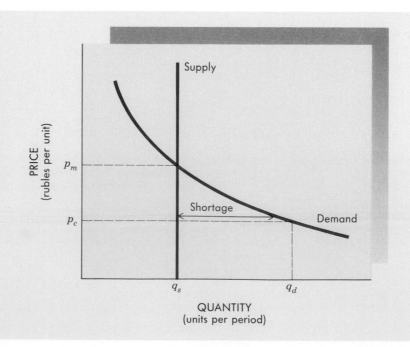

**FIGURE 38.2
Suppressed Inflation**

Socialist planners set low prices on basic consumer goods to ensure that everyone can afford them. At the controlled price (p_c), however, the quantity demanded (q_d) exceeds the supply fixed by the planners (q_s). In a market economy the resulting market shortage would push the price up to equilibrium (p_m). The central planners do not permit price increases, however. As a result, the inflationary pressure causes empty shelves, long lines, and black markets—all symptoms of suppressed inflation.

rettes, and a pint of vodka. Even rationing, however, could not ensure "adequate" supplies. Ultimately the frustrations caused by persistent food shortages helped to spark a workers' strike and political confrontation in Poland.

The same kind of market shortages occur in all centrally planned economies (see World View). In 1990 the Soviet Union was still rationing salt, sugar, soap, butter, and other basic necessities. Rental prices for apartments were still at the level set by the central planners in 1928! The low rents, however, did not guarantee access to housing. Most Russians lived in cramped and often shared quarters while waiting for an opportunity to rent more adequate housing. As recently as 1987, one-fourth of Soviet households had no hot water; 15 percent of urban households shared kitchens or bathrooms with other families. With housing construction controlled by the planners, consumers could only wait for promised improvements in housing. To alleviate critical market shortages of other consumer goods, the Soviet Union had to spend $16 billion on "emergency" imports in 1989, including 1.5 billion razor blades, 40 million tubes of shaving cream, 1.7 million pairs of shoes, 50 million pairs of pantyhose, and tons of toothpaste. Tea, cigarettes, sausage, and meat all remained scarce.

Suppressed inflation   Because prices are centrally controlled, prices do not rise to reflect these market imbalances. In fact, the planners take public credit for the absence of inflation. However, the imbalances have to show up somewhere. The inflationary pressures are manifest in empty shelves, long lines, and rationing—rather than higher prices. These are the symptoms of **suppressed inflation,** that is, inflationary imbalances reflected in nonprice forms. Suppressed inflation also spills over into black markets, where goods and services are exchanged at higher prices without official sanction.

suppressed inflation: Inflationary imbalances reflected in nonprice forms (e.g., market shortages, rationing) when prices are not permitted to rise.

W🌐RLD VIEW

RATIONING

Pork, Sugar Rationing Reimposed in Beijing

Move Comes Months After Party Pledges to Raise Living Standards

BEIJING, Dec. 1—The government reimposed pork and sugar rationing today in the Chinese capital only a month after the Communist Party held a major congress promising further economic reforms aimed at raising the country's living standards.

Beijing today joined a number of other Chinese cities in rationing pork, the main meat eaten in China. The rationing is intended to make up for shortages and prevent profiteers from reselling the meat at higher prices. Grain and cooking oil have been rationed in China since the early 1950s, but the rationing of a number of items; including pork, was stopped in the early 1980s.

"This is not a good sign coming so soon after the congress," said one Chinese intellectual, surveying a nearly empty meat counter at the Dongdan food market.

A dozen Chinese gazed in consternation at three cuts of lean pork on the counter. Only two persons in the group, an elderly man and an elderly woman, were qualified to buy pork in this market, and what they bought was meant to last for an entire month.

Each was allowed one kilogram—about 2.2 pounds—of lean meat at a price of 5 yuan—about $1.35.

Beijing also reimposed rationing on sugar today, allowing each three-person family a kilogram of sugar per month.

—Daniel Southerland

The Washington Post, December 2, 1987, p. A27. Copyright © 1987 The Washington Post.

Involuntary Savings

The shortages of consumer goods not only frustrate consumers, but also weaken production incentives. Socialist countries introduced material bonuses to spur production. However, the basic allure of material bonuses is not the money per se, but the increased consumption implied by greater income. Hence ***material incentives will fail if there is nothing to buy with the added income.***

Recall that the central planners determine the mix of output. They use material incentives only to coax more productivity from the workers. If successful, economic growth will accelerate and more output will be produced. But what about the supply of consumer goods? If the central planners are striving to increase investment or defense output, the increased output may not include additional consumer goods. The workers will have fatter paychecks but nothing more to buy. Before long, they will realize that the material rewards to extra effort are an illusion. As workers in many communist countries have observed: "We pretend to work and they pretend to pay us." Output stagnates and savings accumulate. Such **involuntary saving,** however, frustrates workers and ultimately undermines the bonus system.

Soviet planners began to grapple with this problem in the 1970s. The ninth five-year plan (1971–75) asserted that "the main task" was "to ensure a significant increase in the people's material and cultural standard of living."[7] That goal was submerged by defense needs in the tenth plan, however, and by investment needs (particularly new gas lines) in the eleventh plan. Consumers did not again get priority until the twelfth plan (1986–90). By that time, however, Soviet consumers had accumulated over 100 *billion* unspent and unwanted rubles. They couldn't even buy soap or salt with their rubles, much less consumer appliances, televisions, or a good pair of jeans. In these circumstances, Soviet people saw no purpose in working hard to accumulate still more rubles. As Abel Aganbegyan, chief economist in the Soviet Academy of Sciences, acknowledged in March 1989: "Now there is no incentive to earn a lot of money, because it is very difficult to spend in a legal way."[8]

When the Siberian and Ukrainian coal miners went out on strike in July 1989, their primary concern was not higher wages. They too had more rubles than they could spend. What the coal miners wanted were more goods to buy: more meat, fresh fruit and vegetables, soap, vodka, and sewing machines. Gorbachev persuaded the miners to go back to work by supplying them with special consignments of these and other consumer goods. He thereby averted an energy crisis that would have virtually shut down the Soviet economy (which is heavily dependent on coal-based power). But *redistributing* goods could not placate the entire Soviet work force, since the total production of consumer goods was still restricted.

The same problem afflicted East Germany and Poland. By the end of 1989, East German workers had accumulated 150 billion Ostmarks (about $83 billion) in savings. But the shelves in state stores were bare. East Germans could not purchase an automobile (waiting lists were fifteen years), a better apartment (apartments were rationed), or even a telephone (waiting lists of several years). In Poland, there was little meat or sausage available, and farmers were holding back the supply of food because controlled prices were too low.

involuntary saving: Consumer saving compelled by shortages of consumer goods.

---

[7]*Pravda,* December 19, 1972, cited by Keith Bush in *Soviet Economic Prospects for the Seventies,* a compendium of papers submitted to the Joint Economic Committee of Congress, June 27, 1973.
[8]Cited in *Newsweek,* March 13, 1989, p. 30.

Nonconvertible Currency

In principle, the shortage of consumer goods could be alleviated by imports. However, the inherent difficulties of central planning also affect international trade relations. To begin with, how are consumers to gain access to imported goods? All domestic production and prices are controlled by the state. There is no network of importers, distributors, and retail outlets for selling imported goods. Moreoever, the viability of such a network would depend on profitability—an alien notion. Furthermore, if consumers could purchase imported goods, they might not buy the output produced by the state enterprises. They might even begin making unfavorable comparisons about the quality and price of imported and domestic products.

Fear of competition and a revulsion to profits are not the only forces blocking imports. There is also the problem of *money.* How is the country to pay for imports? Centrally planned prices don't conform to market prices. Hence the currency of communist nations has no foundation in market realities. Foreigners will have little opportunity or incentive to spend Soviet rubles, Polish zlotys, or Chinese yuan. If they take these currencies in payment, they may end up with the same involuntary savings accumulated by consumers in planned economies. To avert this fate, foreign producers will want to be paid in **hard currency**—U.S. dollars and other currencies that are widely exchanged in international markets.

hard currency: Any national currency widely accepted in payment in international markets.

But how will central planners or consumers in communist states acquire hard currency? Like other nations, they will have to *export* goods to earn foreign exchange. But exports aren't part of the central plan. To produce exports, the central planners will have to divert scarce resources from domestic investment or consumption to export-producing industries. This will frustrate planning objectives. Furthermore, there is no guarantee that the goods produced for export will be sold, or at what price (the central planners can't control prices in world markets).

Bartered trade   All of these problems tend to "close" communist economies to international markets. Most of their trade is among themselves and dictated by the central planners. The countries of Eastern Europe, for example, were expected to ship specific quotas of food (Romania), machinery (East Germany), and manufactured goods (Hungary) to the Soviet Union. They were paid for these goods in rubles, at prices established by the central planners. These countries were then "permitted" to buy oil, natural gas, and other resources from the Soviet Union. These bilateral agreements were essentially forms of **barter,** in which specific goods were exchanged.

barter: The direct exchange of one good for another, without the use of money.

Both sides of these bartered deals complained that they were being mistreated. The Soviets complained that they were getting shoddy goods from Eastern Europe. The Europeans complained that the centrally dictated prices favored the Soviets (see World View, p. 938).

Trade with the rest of the world was essentially limited to barter deals as well. Foreign producers who wanted to sell products or build factories in communist countries typically had to accept payment in kind—that is, in oil, coal, diamonds, or other Soviet resources. These barter arrangements greatly limited trading opportunities. As a result, the communist countries could not exploit their **comparative advantage** and associated efficiencies. The relatively small East Germany economy (1990 population of 16 million: GNP of $211 billion), for example, produced 80 percent of the total variety of industrial goods available in the world. With greater specialization and trade, East Germany could have achieved greater efficiency and higher living standards.

comparative advantage: The ability of a country to produce a specific good at a lower opportunity cost than its trading partners.

W⊕RLD VIEW

BARTERED TRADE

Hungary Tells U.S.S.R. It Wants Trade in Dollars

BUDAPEST, Dec. 7—The Hungarian government told the Soviet Union this week that it wants trade between the two countries to be counted in dollars, rather than the ruble, which it says is artificially valued by the Soviets to penalize Hungary.

"It will help the Hungarian economy and create a world market economy here," said Tamas Istvan, deputy director general in the Ministry of Trade specializing in Soviet affairs.

The Hungarian request is likely to be repeated by other East Bloc nations, underscoring the rapid changes taking place in Eastern Europe as countries move away from communism to become free market economies. The Hungarian economic weekly, Heti Vilaggazdasag, reported that most members of Comecon, the Soviet-led trading bloc of communist states, indicated at a September conference that they wanted widespread reforms. Only two remaining hard-line states—Cuba and Romania—wanted to keep the present system.

Hungarian economists believe ruble trade is based on unrealistic prices, set by planners every five years, and amounts to barter since the Soviet currency is not accepted by other nations.

—Stuart Auerbach

The Washington Post, December 8, 1989, p. D12. Copyright © 1989 The Washington Post.

THE COLLAPSE

With so many inherent inefficiencies, the collapse of communism seemed inevitable. However, the upheavals of 1989 were neither widely predicted nor easily explained. After all, the communist system, however creaky and inefficient, had functioned for over seventy years in the Soviet Union and over forty years in Eastern Europe and China. Moreover, some of these countries had achieved remarkable economic growth in earlier years. Stalin's forced industrialization of its economy made the Soviet Union a world power. Along the way, the average Soviet consumer also enjoyed a substantial improvement in living standards. Even China—where living standards are among the world's lowest—had managed to feed, clothe, and house a billion people. As poor as the average Chinese individual was in 1989 (GNP per capita of $330), living standards were much higher than they had been in 1949. Much of this improvement was due to the ability of the government to mobilize and allocate scarce resources, forcing the economy to attain high investment rates. From *within* these countries, growth often looked impressive.

Increasing Pressures

The successes of centrally planned economies were overtaken by their failures as time progressed. As communist economies advanced, they became more complex. As resource allocation problems multiplied, the risk of planning breakdowns increased. Each breakdown not only reduced output, but also raised public doubts about the efficacy of the system.

The incentive issue also loomed larger over time. In the early stages of forced development, the "belt tightening" required of consumers was made palatable by the vision of a better future. But the promised higher consumption levels kept getting postponed. In the absence of tangible rewards, the motivation to work diminished. Declining oil and gold prices plus poor harvests in the 1980s made it increasingly difficult for the Soviet Union to even maintain, much less improve living standards. Severe shortages of soap, sugar, matches, shoes, and fruit and vegetables in the late 1980s eliminated all pretense of improved living standards (see World View below).

Glaring Disparities   The stagnation of consumption levels in communist economies contrasted sharply with rising levels of affluence in market economies. In 1989 Soviet GNP per capita was only half American levels. But the gap in *consumption* levels was far greater. Soviet citizens had few goods to buy; what was available was terribly expensive. Table 38.2 provides some comparisons of the quantities of goods available in the United States, the Soviet Union, and China.

W🌐RLD VIEW

PRESSURE TO REFORM

The Soviet Economy in Shambles

Perestroika *Hasn't Delivered the Goods, and the Nation's Patience Is Running Short*

Seventy-two years after the Russian Revolution, antique Soviet trains, paralyzed by breakdowns, stand silent against a frozen landscape. In the countryside, more than one fifth of this year's grain harvest lies rotting where it fell or sits waiting for trucks that never arrived. In the cities, shelves are mostly bare, and the legendary patience of the masses, who queue up for hours to wait for food, is giving way to anger. *Glasnost* has come back to haunt its creator. During last week's celebrations of the October 1917 socialist revolution, 10,000 people gathered for an unprecedented "alternative" demonstration a few miles from the official one in Red Square. "Seventy-two years on the way to nowhere," read the inscription on one marcher's placard. "Workers of the world, forgive us," pleaded another. . . .

Soviet citizens are understandably pessimistic about the future. Hoarding has become a national obsession, the black market is booming and an overabundance of rubles has made the currency nearly worthless. Unemployment, inflation and corruption are growing. And daily life too often involves a harsh struggle.

Poverty

An estimated 28 percent of the population now lives below the official Soviet poverty line—$1,920 a year at the basic official exchange rate. At the black-market rate, that is more like $240 a year. Meat and dairy-product consumption for all Soviets is on the decline; among the poor, it has plummeted 30 percent since 1970.

Health

More than 30 million Soviets must drink water that is not considered potable. A decline in the life expectancy of Soviet men, caused by rampant alcohol consumption, has only recently been arrested. An estimated 65 percent of the roughly 4,000 rural hospitals have no hot water, and 27 percent lack sewerage. Disposable syringes, commonplace in the West, are a luxury in the Soviet Union: Only 7.8 million were produced last year, despite plans to make 100 million, and the needles are routinely cleaned with steel wool and re-used. Thirty percent of Soviet hospitals have no indoor toilets.

Housing

As of 1987, less than 74 percent of Soviet housing had hot water, and 15 percent of the urban population still share kitchens and bathrooms. Fifteen percent of the total population have no bathrooms at all.

Environment

One out of 5 urban residents breathes dangerously polluted air.

Work

Absenteeism is rampant, much of it related to alcoholism. In 1987, even as Gorbachev was pressing his anti-alcohol campaign, an estimated 20 million Soviet workers needed some time off for alcohol-related problems. More than 10,000 people died in 1987 from drinking alcohol surrogates such as perfume, shoe polish and fuels. The work ethic, in any event, is a foreign concept. The joke is an old one and still valid: "We pretend to work and they pretend to pay us."

U. S. News and World Report, November 20, 1989, p. 29. Copyright © 1989 U.S. News & World Report.

TABLE 38.2   Consumption Levels

Living standards in planned economies are lower than even GNP comparisons suggest. Central planners have generally allocated many resources to industry, defense, and space—leaving little for the production of consumer goods. As a result, consumers in the Soviet Union and China have few of the goods American consumers take for granted.

Product	United States	Soviet Union	China
Wheat (kilograms per capita)	329	322	63
Meat (kilograms per capita)	74	47	20
Automobiles (per thousand persons)	555	42	1
Washing machines in use (percentage of households)	74	55	n.a.
Television sets in use (per thousand persons)	798	296	9
Radio receivers in use (per thousand persons)	2,101	656	113
Crude steel (million metric tons)	80	155	47
Energy (per capita, in coal equivalent)	9,563	5,549	693
Civil aviation (million miles)	4,137	125	65
Telephones (per 1,000 persons)	791	113	1
Personal computers (per 1,000 persons)	229	2	n.a.

Source: *Statistical Abstract of the United States,* 1988.

Differences between East and West Germany were equally revealing. The average East German had to work nearly five months to earn enough income to buy a TV; a West German worker could buy a TV with just a third of one month's pay. Table 38.3 provides other 1989 comparisons of purchasing power between East and West Germany.

As communications and travel between market and command economies increased, these disparities became apparent. The evident gap in living standards encouraged thousands of East Germans to flee to the West. In 1989 over 300,000 East Germans resettled in the West. During the first two months of 1990, the exodus increased to over 2,000 people a day. As more and more skilled workers left, the East's economy sagged even further.

Almost simultaneously, the peoples of Eastern Europe and the Soviet Union came to the same conclusion: communism had failed. Central planning could not deliver the quantity or quality of goods and services people wanted.

TABLE 38.3   German Disparities

When the Berlin Wall was torn down in 1989, the disparities in living standards between the centrally planned East and free-market West were readily apparent. The wages of East German workers bought few goods. In the East, the average worker needed over ten *years'* wages to buy a car. A car in West Germany cost the equivalent of ten *months'* salary. The East German car was of much poorer quality as well.

Product	Price as a percentage of average monthly income	
	In West Germany	In East Germany
Color TV	38%	588%
Washing machine	48	365
Car (VW Polo; Trabant)	1,143	11,765
Beef (kilogram)	0.7	1.0
Jeans	3	15
Women's shoes	4	14

Source: *US News and World Report,* November 27, 1989, p. 43. Copyright © 1989 U.S. News & World Report.

THE MARKET TRANSITION

Once the failure of communism was publicly acknowledged, most centrally planned economies looked to the market mechanism to achieve more and better output. Virtually all of the communist countries had dabbled with market incentives before. As noted earlier, Soviet "revisionism" had offered bonus payments to enterprises and workers who "fulfilled and overfulfilled" their production quotas. The Soviets have also permitted farmers to sell whatever they produced on small "garden" plots set aside for personal use. By 1989 these private plots, encompassing only 3 percent of all farmland, were producing 30 percent of the Soviet supply of food. Market incentives clearly worked. In China, the central planners had effectively dismantled collective farms altogether. The return to individualized farming (via two-tier production quotas and open market sales) led to a huge increase in Chinese farm output during the 1980s. Industrial output also leaped during the 1980s, giving China one of the world's fastest growth rates for that decade.

Perestroika   Gorbachev accelerated the transition from central planning to the market mechanism. His perestroika (restructuring) program, unveiled in June 1987, called for fundamental changes in prices, incentives, markets, and even private ownership. The countries of Eastern Europe adopted and further accelerated these transition plans.

Price Reform   A key component of the transition was price reform. The distorted prices dictated by central planners generated the wrong market signals. If the market mechanism is to function efficiently, price signals must reflect underlying supply and demand conditions. To correct these signals, communist countries had to raise previously subsidized prices. Higher prices for basic (subsidized) goods were needed to increase the quantity supplied and reduce the quantity demanded (see Figure 38.2). Poland was the first communist nation to restructure its prices in this way. Upon taking office, the new Solidarity-led government abruptly eliminated price subsidies on most consumer goods. The price of bread rose 40 percent in the first week of January 1990. Ham prices went up 55 percent; electricity and cooking gas climbed 400 percent, and the price of gasoline doubled. Although these price increases immediately reduced the real wages of Polish workers, they also had a positive effect. Suddenly more goods appeared on Polish shelves. Overnight, shortages disappeared. Polish workers had to pay more for basic goods, but at least they could find them.

Currency Reform   The restructuring of prices also changed the purchasing power of money. In Poland, the price restructuring caused averaged prices to leap 70 percent in only three months (December 1989–February 1990). This intense inflation undermined the official value of the zloty. In the process, the artificiality of "planned" exchange rates became apparent. The official exchange value of the Polish zloty was 0.03 cents in November 1989; its (black) market value was only 0.01 cents, however. To make the zloty *convertible*—a more acceptable form of payment in both domestic and international markets—the Polish government had to abandon the fiction of "official" values. It did this by sharply devaluing the zloty (by 50 percent), then letting its value be determined by the marketplace.

East Germany confronted the same problem. The official value of the Ostmark was equal to one West German Deutschemark. However, the street (market) exchange rate was as low as 20 to 1. The artificially high official value inhibited East German exports and even slowed domestic market activity. East Germany ultimately eliminated the Ostmark, adopting the Deutschemark as a common currency for all Germany. In October 1989 the Soviet Union also adjusted its exchange rates to market realities by reducing the dollar price of the ruble from $1.63 to only 16 cents. All such currency reforms facilitate international trade and investment.

Private Property

---

profit: The difference between total revenue and total cost.

Price and currency reforms laid the foundation for the market mechanism. To function effectively, however, the market also had to offer *incentives*. This was the most difficult issue for communists. To encourage, or even permit private gain was contrary to the very principles of socialism. As a practical matter, however, the new governments of Eastern Europe recognized that market incentives were the key to faster growth. This meant that **profits** would have to be permitted. It also implied that individuals, rather than the state, could own the means of production. Individuals, not only the state, would have to be permitted to buy and hold property, build and operate factories, hire and fire labor, and accumulate profits. In other words, communism would have to permit capitalism if it wanted more goods and services.

In his presidential acceptance speech of March 15, 1990, Gorbachev emphasized the need for "radical economic reform." As he saw it, the command (central planning) system had to be replaced by the "economic leverage" (market) system. "Nothing less than a breakthrough is needed" he asserted. To achieve that breakthrough, "it is imperative to bring out the immense constructive potential that is inherent in . . . ownership . . . I see [this] as a prime presidential task."[9] As Gorbachev went on to explain, the state could still maintain substantial control over the mix of output and the distribution of income. But it would do so indirectly, using tax, spending, and monetary policies rather than centrally planned prices and output. As such reforms advance, the distinction between communism and capitalism begins to fade. Indeed, such reforms helped eliminate the distinction between East Germany and West Germany.

GOAL TRADEOFFS

The transition from command economies to "demand" (market) economies has been the most important economic story of the 1990s. As spectacular as the reforms have been, however, they are far from universal. Many leaders and citizens in socialist countries are reluctant to embrace the market mechanism. The Soviet Congress gave Gorbachev only 59 percent of its votes in 1990, even though he was the sole candidate for president. In East Germany, only 48 percent of the voters chose the coalition that advocated rigorous reform and union with West Germany. China and Cuba both rejected wholesale restructuring and declared themselves loyal to socialist principles.

Equity vs. Efficiency

Much of the opposition to market reforms originates in the core issue of egalitarianism. ***The ultimate justification for communist rule was not economic efficiency, but social justice.*** "From each according to his ability,

[9]Quoted in the *New York Times,* March 16, 1990, p. A6.

to each according to his need" is a basic principle of communism. The inequalities spawned by private property and markets gave impetus to the communist movement. For many socialists, the goal of egalitarianism is still cherished. They fear that market-based incentives will again generate widening inequalities, destroying the very fabric of socialist society.

China had grappled with this tradeoff many times. The Cultural Revolution of 1966–76 was an explicit reaction to the inequalities and incentives spawned by material incentives. During that period, private entrepreneurs were humiliated, imprisoned, and "re-educated." These same forces re-emerged in 1989–90. The successes bred by the 1979 reforms created a new class of successful entrepreneurs and farmers. Increasing inequalities, however, spurred envy and unrest. A Marxian backlash against market reforms accused entrepreneurs of being "capitalist roaders." The Chinese government started backpedaling on reforms. Echoing the Cultural Revolution, the government initiated a re-education campaign that gave socialist principles priority over material incentives (see World View below).

Security vs. Uncertainty

The broad goal of egalitarianism has very tangible dimensions in most socialist countries. Everyone is guaranteed a job, health care, a pension, and access to subsidized goods and services. This "cradle-to-grave" security is hard to give up. When East Germany started moving toward reunification with West Germany, many workers worried about their socialist pensions, health care, and other welfare benefits (see World View, p. 944). Although the inefficiencies of central planning constrained the quality and quantity of social services, at least *some* benefits were guaranteed to socialist workers.

On top of all this concern about welfare benefits was a widespread fear of unemployment. The dismantling of state enterprises and the quest for

W🌐RLD VIEW

TRADEOFFS

China Striving to Rebuild "Socialist Ideals"

BEIJING, March 5—The Chinese Communist Party has conscripted millions of its citizens to participate in a drive to rebuild "socialist ideals" in the largest government-directed mass campaign seen in this country in well over a decade.

The campaign, entitled "Study Lei Feng," is designed to persuade Chinese to emulate the supposed virtues of a long-deceased model soldier—total selflessness and unquestioning loyalty to the Communist Party, rare traits in China in recent years.

As part of the effort, children have swept streets, soldiers have given free haircuts and provincial leaders have brought boiled water to thirsty train passengers. Lei's portrait is being hoisted on placards and his name pro-

claimed over loudspeakers from one end of China to the other.

The officially stated purpose of the campaign is to "encourage people to practice plain living and hard working and help them to resist the effect of bourgeois liberalization," the term used by Beijing to describe Western political ideas that the party says influenced students during last spring's unprecedented democracy movement. . . .

To some Chinese, the campaign is beneficial in Chinese society, where a money-first mentality has burgeoned along with reforms designed to free up part of China's centralized economy. Said a worker in Chengdu, capital of southwest Sichuan Province, "People in China these days are looking too much to money."

—Daniel Southerland

The Washington Post, March 6, 1990, p. 1. Copyright © 1990 The Washington Post.

W🌐RLD VIEW

EQUITY VS. EFFICIENCY

East German Freedom Has a Price

Many Await Higher Costs, Less Security

BERLIN—East Germans are looking past the coalition problems of their newly elected Parliament to the future—excited but uncertain about what lies ahead.

Long used to the security of a cradle-to-the-grave social state, they fear the loss of their broad and generous social welfare system.

If the expensive deutsche mark becomes the currency of the East—and such a move may happen by July—it could mean higher costs for now-subsidized rents, pensions, medical bills and jobs.

"Unification must come, of course," says Martin Mueller, a 49-year-old electrician. "But when you have been brought up in this system and you've been educated in it, what's coming is a bit frightening to many of us."

Social Services

Hildegard Knobloch, an eloquent 84-year-old, is one of 250 people at the Heckelberger Ring Home. "Once I was an honest and dedicated member of the Communist Party," she says. "But then you know what happened and I still can't comprehend what it is the party did to us and why. For me, it's as if everything just broke down.

"I don't see anything good for us coming out of these elections. . . . You'll see that once they eliminate all our subsidies, things will get much more expensive and many people like me and others here will suffer for that."

Now, she pays about $20.75 monthly for everything.

"You know, despite of what everybody says now, things weren't all bad here and we have social programs which people in the Federal Republic wish they had."

Unemployment

Everyone had a job until recently, when the government began to unravel. Now, there is some unemployment.

Health Care

Rolf Arnold, 47, and Dieter Markwartt, 50, share a room in Berlin's Weissensee Hospital.

Arnold, a cab driver, suffers from an intestinal inflammation while Markwartt, a civilian army driver, has heart problems.

"Right now I don't have to worry about medicines, hospital costs and all of this," says Arnold, waving his arm. "I hope it stays that way. I couldn't imagine it not being so for us," he says of benefits he receives at a monthly cost of $12.

Adds Markwartt, 50: "My biggest worry is my job because I don't know what'll happen to the army. I don't want to be without a job. We've never had that."

—Juan J. Walte

USA Today, March 21, 1990, p. A4. Copyright © 1990 USA TODAY. Reprinted with permission.

---

greater efficiency would inevitably entail layoffs and plant closings. In Poland, the new Solidarity-led government estimated that at least 400,000 workers would lose jobs as state enterprises were restructured or closed. The same kind of dislocations were expected to accompany the dismantling and sale of East Germany's 126 state monopolies.

Politics vs. Economics   Economic restructuring also threatened established political structures. As Marx had correctly foreseen, economics is everything. Economic deprivation had helped bring Communist parties to power. In 1989 the same forces were at work. Every government in Eastern Europe was toppled by the reform movement. Market freedom, it seems, spawned greater demands for political freedom. This was a frightening prospect for the established political leadership. The Chinese leadership opted to suppress political unrest. They were willing to halt or even reverse the transition to a market economy in order to preserve the existing political order. Cuban leaders came to the same conclusion.

These economic and political tradeoffs constrain economic transitions in communist countries. In Poland, the Solidarity government reintroduced

W🌐RLD VIEW

SLOWING THE TRANSITION

Gorbachev Slows Economic Change

Shift to Market Pricing Delayed

MOSCOW, April 23—After three weeks of brainstorming with close advisers, Soviet President Mikhail Gorbachev has watered down proposals for radical economic change, apparently because of fears of major social disorder.

Signs that the Soviet Union's transition to a market economy will be slower than earlier indicated have emerged over the weekend in accounts of an expanded meeting of Gorbachev's presidential council to discuss economic reform. They were reinforced at a Kremlin news conference today at which the president's chief spokesman ruled out the application of "shock therapy" to the economy.

"Unemployment is unacceptable under socialism," said Arkady Maslennikov, chief of the presidential press office. "Socialists cannot develop an economy at the expense of ordinary people. You cannot mechanically copy the methods of Mrs. Thatcher in the Soviet Union. This way is closed for us," he said, referring to the market-driven polices of British Prime Minister Margaret Thatcher. . . .

The rapid adoption of market mechanisms could have led to increased social tensions because of the phasing out of price subsidies and the closure of unprofitable factories. A newspaper sponsored by the association of cooperatives, or semi-private businesses, predicted that the introduction of a market economy could result in 20 million unemployed, or 15 percent of the able-bodied population.

In an interview with the government newspaper Izvestia last weekend, one of Gorbachev's leading economic advisers said the Soviet Union could not afford to follow the Hungarian or Polish paths toward a market economy. Prices were freed almost overnight in Poland at the beginning of January, causing a temporary surge in inflation and unemployment but putting an end to chronic consumer shortages.

"Those who say that by 1990-92 we can already have an entirely new economy are, to my mind, simply adventurists," said Stanislav Shatalin, widely regarded as one of the most radical members of Gorbachev's presidential council. He added that the next two years should be devoted to laying the basis for subsequent changes in the economy.

—Michael Dobbs

The Washington Post, April 24, 1990, p. 1. Copyright © 1990 The Washington Post.

"temporary" subsidies for bread and meat shortly after it adopted market prices. In the Soviet Union, the thirteenth five-year plan (1990–94) postponed most price reforms until at least 1992. The plan also sought to relieve pressures for reform by calling for an increase in the centrally planned output of consumer goods (see World View above). This gradualism is unlikely to stop the process of economic restructuring, however. The pace of restructuring will likely be set by its results. The more successful market reforms become, the greater the pressure will be for further restructuring. By the same token, any setbacks—such as prolonged recessions, runaway inflation, or political unrest—will slow the transition to market economies.

SUMMARY

- Marx's vision of communism foresaw an egalitarian society in which individuals would selflessly contribute to output and everyone's material needs would be satisfied.

- To achieve the desired mix of output and distribution of income, the state owns and directs the means of production. Central planning is the key mechanism for deciding WHAT, HOW, and FOR WHOM in a socialist economy.

- Central planning requires detailed knowledge of input–output relationships. As the variety of goods and the specificity of production goals increase, the risk of miscalculation rises.

- Centrally planned prices are used to achieve specific planning goals, for example, to discourage consumption of luxury goods or ensure access to necessities. Resource allocations (production decisions) are determined by central planners, however; prices do not function as conventional market signals.

- The low quality and quantity of planned consumption output force consumers to accumulate involuntary savings. The lack of consumer goods also creates market shortages, long lines, and pressure for reform.

- Incentives are a basic problem in planned economies. Most socialist countries reluctantly adopted limited material incentives (e.g., bonuses, garden plots) to spur production.

- To achieve greater efficiency and growth, most socialist economies are restructuring. The transition to a market-based economy requires price reforms, currency reform, market-based incomes, and the introduction of private property rights.

- The transition from command to market systems entails significant social, economic, and political costs.

Terms to Remember   Define the following terms:

capitalism	**market mechanism**
communism	**market shortage**
socialism	**suppressed inflation**
production possibilities	**involuntary saving**
investment	**hard currency**
economic growth	**barter**
production process	**comparative advantage**
market economy	**profit**

Questions for Discussion

1. Suppose that an increase in agricultural output were a major objective of economic policy. What policy tools would the U.S. Congress use to bring about this result? What tools would the Soviet Gosplan use?

2. What are the advantages of consumer sovereignty? The disadvantages?

3. The unavailability of consumer luxury items in the Soviet Union has helped to equalize living standards. How will the recent expansion of Soviet automobile production affect equality? The incentive to work?

4. Would you plan to work less or choose to enter a different occupation if everyone were paid equal wages regardless of the work they do? What would be the incentive to work under such circumstances?

Problem   The following schedule depicts the daily supply of and demand for television sets on a small island:

Price	$200	$150	$100	$50
Quantity demanded	0	5	10	15
Quantity supplied	20	15	10	5

Graph the supply and demand curves.

(*a*) If the government sets the price of television sets at $50, how will the quantity demanded compare to the quantity supplied? What kind of behavior would you expect from the buyers? from the suppliers?

(*b*) How might the government intervene with taxes or subsidies to eliminate such behavior?

(*c*) If the government requires the suppliers to provide 20 television sets per day, and the suppliers comply, what will be the market price of a set?

(*d*) If the government requires everyone who receives a set to pay no more than $150 for it, will there be a surplus or a shortage of sets, and how much will quantity demanded differ from the 20 sets being provided by the suppliers? What will happen to inventories of television sets?

(*e*) Because of inventory problems, the government drops its minimum price of $150 and decides to institute the full tax or subsidy necessary to provide 20 sets per day. Would the government have to subsidize or tax? How much would the tax or subsidy be, per set?

(*f*) Because of all the problems surrounding television sets, a new government is elected, and it decides to let the market make all the decisions about television sets. How many sets will be sold each day, and at what price will they be sold?

Numbers in parentheses indicate the chapters in which the definitions appear.

absolute advantage: The ability of a country to produce a specific good with fewer resources (per unit of output) than other countries. *(35)*

acreage set-aside: Land withdrawn from production as part of policy to increase crop prices. *(28)*

adjustment assistance: Compensation to market participants for losses imposed by international trade. *(35)*

aggregate demand: The total quantity of output demanded at alternative price levels in a given time period, *ceteris paribus. (5)(8)(14)*

aggregate spending: The rate of total expenditure desired at alternative levels of income, *ceteris paribus. (8)(10)(12)*

aggregate supply: The total quantity of output producers are willing and able to supply at alternative price levels in a given time period, *ceteris paribus. (5)(8)(15)*

antitrust: Government intervention to alter market structure or prevent abuse of market power. *(3)(23)(25)(26)*

appreciation: A rise in the price of one currency relative to another. *(36)*

arithmetic growth: An increase in quantity by a constant amount each year. *(16)*

asset: Anything having exchange value in the marketplace; wealth. *(11)*

average fixed cost (AFC): Total fixed cost divided by the quantity produced in a given time period. *(20)*

average propensity to consume (APC): Total consumption in a given period divided by total disposable income. *(8)*

average total cost (ATC): Total cost divided by the quantity produced in a given time period. *(20)(22)(23)*

average variable cost (AVC): Total variable cost divided by the quantity produced in a given time period. *(20)*

automatic stabilizer: Federal expenditure or revenue item that automatically responds countercyclically to changes in national income, e.g., unemployment benefits, income taxes. *(10)(17)*

balance of payments: A summary record of a country's international economic transactions in a given period of time. *(36)*

balance-of-payments deficit: An excess demand for foreign currency at current exchange rates. *(36)*

balance-of-payments surplus: An excess demand for domestic currency at current exchange rates. *(36)*

bank reserves: Assets held by a bank to fulfill its deposit obligations. *(12)*

barriers to entry: Obstacles that make it difficult or impossible for would-be producers to enter a particular market; e.g., patents. *(22)(23)(25)(26)(28)*

barter: The direct exchange of one good for another, without the use of money. *(12)(37)(38)*

bilateral monopoly: A market with only one buyer (a monopsonist) and one seller (a monopolist). *(30)*

bond: A certificate acknowledging a debt and the amount of interest to be paid each year until repayment; an IOU. *(13)(34)*

bracket creep: The movement of taxpayers into higher tax brackets (rates) as nominal incomes grow. *(7)*

budget constraint: A line depicting all combinations of goods that are affordable with a given income and given prices. *(19)*

budget deficit: The amount by which government expenditures exceed government revenues in a given time period. *(11)*

budget surplus: An excess of government revenues over government expenditures in a given time period. *(10)*

business cycle: Alternating periods of economic growth and contraction. *(5)(17)*

capital: Goods produced for use in producing other goods, e.g., machinery, factory. *(34)*

capital deficit: The amount by which the capital outflow exceeds the capital inflow in a given time period. *(18)*

capital flight: the outflow of funds motivated by domestic economic and political instability or illegal activity. *(37)*

capital gain: An increase in the market value of an asset. *(34)*

capitalism: An economy in which the factors of production (e.g., land, capital) are owned by individuals; basic allocation decisions are made by market forces. *(38)*

capital surplus: The amount by which the capital inflow exceeds the capital outflow in a given time period. *(18)*

categorical grants: Federal grants to state and local governments for specific expenditure purposes. *(3)*

ceteris paribus: The assumption of nothing else changing. *(1)(2)(19)*

collective bargaining: Direct negotiations between employers and unions to determine labor-market outcomes. *(30)*

collusion: Explicit agreements among producers to limit competition among them. *(24)*

communism: A stateless, classless economy in which there is no private property and everyone shares in production and consumption according to individual abilities and needs. *(38)*

comparative advantage: The ability of a country to produce a specific good at a lower opportunity cost than its trading partners. *(35)(37)(38)*

competitive firm: A firm without market power, with no ability to alter the market price of the goods it produces. *(21)*

competitive market: A market in which no buyer or seller has market power. *(22)*

complementary goods: Goods frequently consumed in combination; when the price of good *X* rises, the demand for good *Y* falls, *ceteris paribus. (19)*

concentration ratio: The proportion of total industry output produced by the largest firms (usually the four largest). *(25)*

conglomerate: A firm that produces significant quantities of output in several industries. *(25)*

constant returns to scale: Increases in plant size do not affect minimum average cost; minimum per-unit costs are identical for small plants and large plants. *(20)*

Consumer Price Index (CPI): A measure (index) of changes in the average price of consumer goods and services. *(7)*

consumption: Expenditure by consumers on final goods and services. *(8)*

consumption function: A mathematical relationship indicating the rate of desired consumer spending at various income levels. *(8)(9)*

consumption possibilities: The alternative combinations of goods and services that a country could consume in a given time period. *(35)*

contestable market: An imperfectly competitive industry subject to potential entry if prices or profits increase. *(23)(24)(25)(26)*

corporate stock: Shares of ownership in a corporation. *(34)*

corporation: A business organization having a continuous existence independent of its members (owners) and power and liabilities distinct from those of its members. *(34)*

cost efficiency: The amount of output associated with an additional dollar spent on input; the MPP of an input divided by its price (cost). *(29)*

cost-of-living adjustment (COLA): Automatic adjustments of nominal income to the rate of inflation. *(7)*

cost-push inflation: An increase in the price level initiated by an increase in the cost of production. *(7)(15)*

coupon rate: Interest rate set for bond at time of issuance. *(34)*

cross-price elasticity: Percentage change in the quantity demanded of *X* divided by percentage change in price of *Y*. *(19)*

cross-subsidization: Use of high prices and profits on one product to subsidize low prices on another product. *(26)*

crowding out: A reduction in private-sector borrowing (and spending) necessitated by increased government borrowing. *(10)(11)(14)(16)*

cyclical unemployment: Unemployment attributable to a lack of job vacancies—i.e., to an inadequate level of aggregate demand. *(6)(8)(9)(33)*

debt ceiling: An explicit, legislated limited on the amount of outstanding national debt. *(11)*

debt servicing: The interest required to be paid each year on outstanding debt. *(11)(37)*

default: Failure to make scheduled payments of interest or principal on a bond. *(34)*

deficiency payment: Income transfer paid to farmers for difference between target and support prices. *(28)*

deficit ceiling: An explicit, legislated limitation on the size of the budget deficit. *(11)*

deficit spending: A situation wherein government expenditures exceed government revenues. *(10)*

deflation: A decrease in the average level of prices of goods and services *(7)*

demand: The ability and willingness to buy specific quantities of a good at alternative prices in a given time period, *ceteris paribus.* *(2)(19)*

demand curve: A curve describing the quantities of a good a consumer is willing and able to buy at alternative prices in a given time period, *ceteris paribus.* *(2)(19)*

demand deposit: Checking-account balance. *(12)*

demand for foreign exchange: The quantities of foreign currency demanded in a given time period at alternative exchange rates, *ceteris paribus.* *(36)*

demand for labor: The quantities of labor employers are willing and able to hire at alternative wage rates in a given time period, *ceteris paribus.* *(29)(30)*

demand for money: The quantities of money people are willing and able to hold at alternative interest rates, *ceteris paribus.* *(14)*

demand-pull inflation: An increase in the price level initiated by excessive aggregate demand. *(7)(8)(9)*

demand schedule: A table showing the quantities of a good a consumer is willing and able to buy at alternative prices in a given time period, *ceteris paribus.* *(2)*

deposit creation: The creation of transactions deposits by bank lending. *(12)*

depreciation: The consumption of capital in the production process; the wearing out of plant and equipment. *(4)*

depreciation (currency): A fall in the price of one currency relative to another. *(36)*

derived demand: The demand for labor and other factors of production results from (depends on) the demand for final goods and services produced by these factors. *(8)(15)(29)*

discount rate: The rate of interest charged by the Federal Reserve banks for lending reserves to private banks. *(13)*

discounting: Federal Reserve lending of reserves to private banks. *(13)*

discouraged worker: An individual who is not actively seeking employment but would look for or accept a job if one were available. *(6)*

discretionary fiscal spending: Those elements of the federal budget not determined by past legislative or executive commitments. *(10)*

disguised unemployment: People are employed but contribute little or nothing to total output. *(37)*

disposable income (DI): After-tax income of consumers; personal income less personal taxes. *(4)(8)(10)*

dissaving: Consumption expenditure in excess of disposable income; a negative saving flow. *(8)*

dividend: Amount of corporate profits paid out to each share of stock. *(34)*

economic cost: The value of all resources used to produce a good or service; opportunity cost. *(20)(21)(31)*

economic growth: An increase in output (real GNP); an expansion of production possibilities. *(1)(16)(38)*

economic profit: The difference between total revenues and total economic costs. *(21)(22)(24)(26)(28)(31)*

economics: The study of how best to allocate scarce resources among competing uses. *(1)*

economies of scale: Reductions in minimum average costs that come about through increases in the size (scale) of plant and equipment. *(20)(23)(26)*

effective tax rate: Taxes paid divided by total income. *(32)*

efficiency (technical): Maximum output of a good from the resources used in production. *(20)(22)*

efficiency decision: The choice of a production process for any given rate of output. *(27)(29)*

elasticity of labor supply: The percentage change in the quantity of labor supplied divided by the percentage change in wage rate. *(29)*

embargo: A prohibition on exports or imports. *(35)*

emission charge: A fee imposed on polluters, based on the quantity of pollution. *(27)*

equation of exchange: Money supply (M) times velocity of circulation (V) equals level of aggregate spending ($P \times Q$). *(14)(15)*

equilibrium (macro): The combination of price level and real output that is compatible with both aggregate demand and aggregate supply. *(5)(8)*

equilibrium GNP: Output at which the rate of desired spending equals the rate of production. *(9)(10)*

equilibrium price: The price at which the quantity of a good demanded in a given time period equals the quantity supplied. *(2)(22)(35)(36)*

equilibrium rate of interest: The interest rate at which the quantity of money demanded in a given time period equals the quantity of money supplied. *(14)*

equilibrium wage: The wage rate at which the quantity of labor supplied in a given time period equals the quantity of labor demanded. *(29)(30)*

excess reserves: Bank reserves in excess of required reserves. *(12)(13)*

exchange rate: The price of one country's currency, expressed in terms of another's; the domestic price of a foreign currency. *(18)(36)*

exports: Goods and services sold to foreign buyers. *(4)(18)(35)*

external debt: U.S. government debt (Treasury bonds) held by foreign households and institutions. *(11)*

externalities: Costs (or benefits) of a market activity borne by a third party; the difference between the social and private costs (benefits) of a market activity. *(1)(3)(27)*

factor market: Any place where factors of production (e.g., land, labor, capital) are bought and sold. *(2)*

factor share: The proportion of total income received by a factor of production. *(31)*

factors of production: Resource inputs used to produce goods and services, e.g., land, labor, capital. *(1)(20)*

financial intermediary: Institution (e.g., bank, stock market) that makes savings available to dissavers (e.g., investors). *(34)*

fine-tuning: Adjustments in economic policy designed to counteract small changes in economic outcomes; continuous responses to changing economic conditions. *(17)*

fiscal policy: The use of government taxes and spending to alter macroeconomic outcomes. *(5)(10)(17)*

fiscal year (FY): The twelve-month period used for accounting purposes; begins October 1 for federal government. *(3)(10)*

fixed costs: Costs of production that do not change when the rate of output is altered, e.g., the cost of basic plant and equipment. *(20)(21)(31)*

flexible exchange rates: A system in which exchange rates are permitted to vary with market supply and demand conditions; floating exchange rates. *(36)*

foreign-exchange markets: Places where foreign currencies are bought and sold. *(36)*

foreign-exchange reserves: Holdings of foreign exchange by official government agencies, usually the central bank or treasury. *(36)*

free rider: An individual who reaps direct benefits from someone else's purchase (consumption) of a public good. *(3)*

frictional unemployment: Brief periods of unemployment experienced by people moving between jobs or into the labor markets. *(6)*

full employment. The lowest rate of unemployment compatible with price stability; variously estimated at between 4 and 6 percent unemployment. *(6)*

full-employment GNP: The total market value of final goods and services that could be produced in a given time period at full employment; potential GNP. *(6)(8)*

functional distribution of income: The division of income among factors of production, especially between capital and labor. *(31)*

geometric growth: An increase in quantity by a constant proportion each year. *(16)*

GNP gap: The difference between full-employment GNP and actual GNP. *(6)*

GNP per capita: Total GNP divided by total population; average GNP. *(4)(16)(37)*

gold reserves: Stocks of gold held by a government to purchase foreign exchange. *(36)*

gold standard: An agreement by countries to fix the price of their currencies in terms of gold; a mechanism for fixing exchange rates. *(36)*

government failure: Government intervention that fails to improve economic outcomes. *(1)(2)(3)(26)(27)*

gross investment: Total investment expenditure in a given time period. *(4)*

gross national product (GNP): The total market value of all final goods and services produced in a given time period. *(4)*

growth rate: Percentage change in real GNP from one period to another. *(16)*

growth recession: A period during which real GNP grows, but at a rate below the long-term trend of 3 percent. *(5)(17)*

hard currency: Any national currency widely accepted in payment in international markets. *(37)(38)*

Herfindahl-Hirshman Index: Measure of industry concentration that accounts for number of firms and size of each. *(25)*

horizontal equity: Principle that people with equal incomes should pay equal taxes. *(32)*

imports: Goods and services purchased from foreign sources. *(4)(18)(35)*

income effect of wages: An increased wage rate allows a person to reduce hours worked without losing income. *(29)*

income elasticity of demand: The percentage change in quantity demanded divided by the percentage change in income. *(19)(28)*

income share: The proportion of total income received by a particular group. *(32)*

income transfers: Payments to individuals for which no current goods or services are exchanged; e.g., Social Security, welfare, unemployment benefits. *(32)(33)*

income velocity of money (V): The number of times per year, on average, a dollar is used to purchase final goods and services; $PQ \div M$. *(14)*

indifference curve: A curve depicting alternative combinations of goods that yield equal satisfaction. *(19)*

indifference map: The set of indifference curves that depicts all possible levels of utility attainable from various combinations of goods. *(19)*

inferior good: Good for which demand decreases when income rises. *(19)*

inflation: An increase in the average level of prices of goods and services. *(3)(4)(5)(7)*

inflation rate: The annual rate of increase in the average price level. *(7)*

inflationary gap: The amount by which desired spending at full employment exceeds full-employment output. *(8)(9)(10)(17)*

initial public offering (IPO): The first issuance (sale) to the general public of stock in a corporation. *(34)*

in-kind income: Goods and services received directly, without payment in a market transaction. *(32)*

in-kind transfers: Direct transfers of goods and services rather than cash, e.g., food stamps, Medicaid, and housing subsidies. *(33)*

institutional production possibilities: The alternative combinations of final goods and services that could be produced in a given time period within the limits imposed by resources, technology, and social constraints on their use. *(6)*

interest: Payments made for the use of borrowed money. *(3)*

interest rate: The price paid for the use of money. *(14)(31)*

intermediate goods: Goods or services purchased for use as input in the production of final goods or services. *(4)*

internal debt: U.S. government debt (Treasury bonds) held by American households and institutions. *(11)*

investment: Expenditures on (production of) new plant and equipment (capital) in a given time period, plus changes in business inventories. *(4)(8)(15)(38)*

investment decision: The decision to build, buy, or lease plant and equipment; to enter or exit an industry. *(21)(22)(23)*

involuntary saving: Consumer saving compelled by shortages of consumer goods. *(38)*

junk bonds: Bonds carrying greater risk due to their speculative purpose and lack of security; unrated bonds. *(34)*

labor force: All persons over age sixteen who are either working for pay or actively seeking paid employment. *(6)(15)(16)*

labor-force participant: Someone who is either employed for pay or actively seeking paid employment. *(33)*

labor productivity: Amount of output produced by a worker in a given period of time; output per hour (or day, etc.). *(15)*

labor supply: The willingness and ability to work specific amounts of time at alternative wage rates in a given time period, *ceteris paribus*. *(29)(30)*

Laffer curve: A graph depicting the relationship of tax rates to total tax revenues. *(15)*

laissez faire: The doctrine of "leave it alone," of nonintervention by government in the market mechanism. *(2)(26)*

law of demand: The quantity of a good demanded in a given time period increases as its price falls, *ceteris paribus*. *(2)(5)(19)(24)*

law of diminishing marginal utility: The marginal utility of a good declines as more of it is consumed in a given time period. *(19)*

law of diminishing returns: The marginal physical product of a variable input declines as more of it is employed with a given quantity of other (fixed) inputs. *(20)(29)*

law of increasing opportunity costs: In order to get more of any good in a given time period, society must sacrifice ever-increasing amounts of other goods. *(1)*

law of supply: The quantity of a good supplied in a given time period increases as its price increases, *ceteris paribus*. *(2)(21)*

leakage: Income not spent directly on domestic output, but instead diverted from the circular flow, e.g., saving, imports, taxes. *(8)(18)*

liability: An obligation to make future payment; debt. *(11)*

liquidity trap: The portion of the money-demand curve that is horizontal; people are willing to hold unlimited amounts of money at some (low) interest rate. *(14)*

long run: A period of time long enough for all inputs to be varied (no fixed costs). *(20)(21)*

long-run competitive equilibrium: $p = MC$ = minimum ATC. *(22)*

Lorenz curve: A graphic illustration of the cumulative size distribution of income; contrasts complete equality with the actual distribution of income. *(32)*

macroeconomics: The study of aggregate economic behavior, of the economy as a whole. *(1)(5)*

managed exchange rates: A system in which governments intervene in foreign-exchange markets to limit but not eliminate exchange-rate fluctuations; "dirty floats." *(36)*

marginal cost (MC): The increase in total cost associated with a one-unit increase in production. *(20)(21)(22)(31)*

marginal cost pricing: The offer (supply) of goods at prices equal to their marginal cost. *(22)(23)(24)(26)*

marginal factor cost (MFC): The change in total costs that results from a one-unit increase in the quantity of a factor employed. *(30)*

marginal physical product (MPP): The change in total output associated with one additional unit of input. *(20)(29)*

marginal productivity: The change in total output that results from employment of one additional unit of input (e.g., one more worker). *(33)*

marginal propensity to consume (MPC): The fraction of each additional (marginal) dollar of disposable income spent on consumption; the change in consumption divided by the change in disposable income. *(8)(9)*

marginal propensity to import (MPM): The fraction of each additional (marginal) dollar of disposable income spent on imports. *(18)*

marginal propensity to save (MPS): The fraction of each additional (marginal) dollar of disposable income not spent on consumption; $1 - MPC$. *(8)(9)(10)(18)*

marginal rate of substitution: The rate at which a consumer is willing to exchange one good for another; the relative marginal utilities of two goods. *(19)*

marginal revenue (MR): The change in total revenue that results from a one-unit increase in the quantity sold. *(21)(23)(24)*

marginal revenue product (MRP): The change in total revenue associated with one additional unit of input. *(29)(30)(31)(32)*

marginal tax rate: The tax rate imposed on the last (marginal) dollar of income. *(15)(32)(33)*

marginal utility: The change in total utility obtained from an additional (marginal) unit of a good or service consumed. *(19)*

marginal wage: The change in total wages paid associated with a one-unit increase in the quantity of labor employed. *(30)*

market demand: the total quantities of a good or service people are willing and able to buy at alternative prices in a given time period; the sum of individual demands. *(2)*

market economy: An economy that relies on markets for basic decisions about WHAT to produce, HOW to produce it, and FOR WHOM to produce. *(38)*

market failure: An imperfection in the market mechanism that prevents optimal outcomes. *(1)(3)(25)(26)(27)*

market mechanism: The use of market prices and sales to signal desired outputs (or resource allocations). *(1)(2)(3)(22)(31)(37)(38)*

market power: The ability to alter the market price of a good or service. *(3)(15)(21)(23)(25)(28)(30)*

market share: The percentage of total market output produced by a single firm. *(24)(25)*

market shortage: The amount by which the quantity demanded exceeds the quantity supplied at a given price; excess demand. *(2)(36)(37)(38)*

market supply: The total quantities of a good that sellers are willing and able to sell at alternative prices in a given time period (*ceteris paribus*). *(2)(21)(22)*

market supply of labor: The total quantity of labor that workers are willing and able to supply at alternative wage rates in a given time period, *ceteris paribus*. *(29)*

market surplus: The amount by which the quantity supplied exceeds the quantity demanded at a given price; excess supply. *(2)(28)*

microeconomics: The study of individual behavior in the economy, of the components of the larger economy. *(1)*

mixed economy: An economy that uses both market and nonmarket signals to allocate goods and resources. *(1)*

monetary policy: The use of money and credit controls to influence macroeconomic activity. *(5)(13)(14)(17)*

money: Anything generally accepted as a medium of exchange. *(12)*

money illusion: The use of nominal dollars rather than real dollars to gauge changes in one's income or wealth. *(7)*

money multiplier: The number of deposit (loan) dollars that the banking system can create from $1 of excess reserves; equal to 1 ÷ required reserve ratio. *(12)(13)*

money supply (M1): Currency held by the public, plus balances in transactions accounts. *(12)*

monopolistic competition: A market in which many firms produce similar goods or services but each maintains some independent control of its own price. *(24)*

monopoly: A firm that produces the entire market supply of a particular good or service. *(3)(23)(24)*

monopsony: A market in which there is only one buyer. *(30)*

multiplier: The multiple by which an initial change in aggregate spending will alter total expenditure after infinite number of spending cycles; $1/(1 - MPC)$. *(9)(10)(17)(18)*

national debt: Accumulated debt of the federal government. *(11)*

national income (NI): Total income earned by current factors of production; GNP less depreciation and indirect business taxes. *(4)*

national-income accounting: The measurement of aggregate economic activity, particularly national income and its components. *(4)*

natural monopoly: An industry in which one firm can achieve economies of scale over the entire range of market supply. *(23)(26)*

natural rate of unemployment: Long-term rate of unemployment determined by structural forces in labor and product markets. *(14)(17)*

net exports: Exports minus imports: $(X - M)$. *(18)*

net investment: Gross investment less depreciation. *(4)(16)*

net national product (NNP): GNP less depreciation. *(4)*

nominal GNP: The value of final output produced in a given period, measured in the prices of that period (current prices). *(4)(16)*

nominal income: The amount of money income received in a given time period, measured in current dollars. *(7)*

nominal tax rate: Taxes paid divided by taxable income. *(32)*

normal good: Good for which demand increases when income rises. *(19)*

normal profit: The opportunity cost of capital; the average rate of return. *(21)*

oligopoly: A market in which a few firms produce all or most of the market supply of a particular good or service. *(24)(25)*

open-market operations: Federal Reserve purchases and sales of government bonds for the purpose of altering bank reserves. *(13)*

opportunity cost: The most desired goods or services that are forgone in order to obtain something else. *(1)(2)(3)(11)(19)(20)(22)(26)(27)(35)*

opportunity wage: The highest wage an individual would earn in his or her best alternative job. *(29)*

optimal consumption: The mix of consumer purchases that maximizes the utility attainable from available income. *(19)*

optimal mix of output: The most desirable combination of output attainable with existing resources, technology, and social values. *(3)(11)*

optimal rate of pollution: The rate of pollution that occurs when the marginal social benefit of pollution control equals its marginal social cost. *(27)*

par value: The face value of a bond; the amount to be repaid when the bond is due. *(34)*

parity: The relative price of farm products in the period 1910–1914. *(28)*

perfect competition: A market in which no buyer or seller has market power. *(24)*

personal income (PI): Income received by households before payment of personal taxes. *(4)(32)*

Phillips curve: A historical (inverse) relationship between the rate of unemployment and the rate of inflation; commonly expresses a tradeoff between the two. *(15)*

physical production possibilities: The alternative combinations of final goods and services that could be produced in a given time period within the limits imposed by resources and technology. *(6)*

portfolio decision: The choice of how (where) to hold idle funds. *(13)(14)(34)*

precautionary demand for money: Money held for unexpected market transactions or for emergencies. *(14)*

predatory price cutting: Temporary price reductions designed to alter market shares or drive out competition. *(25)*

present discounted value: The value today of future payments, adjusted for interest accumulation. *(31)*

price ceiling: Upper limit imposed on the price of a good. *(2)*

price discrimination: The sale of an identical good at different prices to different consumers by a single seller. *(23)*

price elasticity of demand: The percentage change in quantity demanded divided by the percentage change in price. *(19)(23)(28)(37)*

price elasticity of supply: The percentage change in quantity supplied divided by the percentage change in price. *(31)*

price fixing: Explicit agreements among producers regarding the price(s) at which a good is to be sold. *(25)*

price floor: Lower limit imposed on the price of a good. *(2)*

price leadership: An oligopolistic pricing pattern that allows one firm to establish the (market) price for all firms in the industry. *(24)(25)*

price stability: The absence of significant changes in the average price level; officially defined as a rate of inflation of less than 3 percent. *(7)*

private costs: The costs of an economic activity directly borne by the immediate producer or consumer (excluding externalities). *(27)*

private good: A good or service whose consumption by one person excludes consumption by others. *(3)*

product differentiation: Features that make one product appear different from competing products in the same market. *(24)(25)(26)*

product market: Any place where finished goods and services (products) are bought and sold. *(2)*

production decision: The selection of the short-run rate of output (with existing plant and equipment). *(21)(22)(23)(27)*

production function: A technological relationship expressing the maximum quantity of a good attainable from different combinations of factor inputs. *(20)*

production possibilities: The alternative combinations of final goods and services that could be produced in a given time period with all available resources and technology. *(1)(3)(4)(11)(16)(35)(37)(38)*

production process: A specific combination of resources used to produce a good or service. *(29)(38)*

productivity: Output per unit of input, e.g., output per labor hour. *(16)(18)(20)(30)(37)*

profit: The difference between total revenue and total cost. *(21)(28)(38)*

profit-maximization rule: Produce at that rate of output where marginal revenue equals marginal cost. *(21)(23)(24)*

profit per unit: Total profit divided by the quantity produced in a given time period; price minus average total cost. *(22)*

profit-push inflation: An increase in the price level initiated by attempts of producers to raise profit margins. *(15)*

progressive tax: A tax system in which tax rates rise as incomes rise. *(32)*

public choice: Theory of public-sector behavior emphasizing rational self-interest of decision makers and voters. *(3)*

public good: A good or service whose consumption by one person does not exclude consumption by others. *(3)*

quota: A limit on the quantity of a good that may be imported in a given time period. *(35)(37)*

quantity demanded: The amount of a product a consumer is willing and able to buy at a specific price in a given time period, *ceteris paribus*. *(24)*

rational expectations: Hypothesis that people's spending decisions are based on all available information, including the anticipated effects of government intervention. *(17)*

real GNP: The value of final output produced

in a given period, measured in the prices of a base period (constant prices). *(4)(5)(16)*

real income: Income in constant dollars; nominal income adjusted for inflation. *(7)*

real rate of interest: The nominal rate of interest minus anticipated inflation rate. *(14)*

recession: A decline in total output (real GNP) for two or more consecutive quarters. *(5)*

recessionary gap: The amount by which desired spending at full employment falls short of full-employment output. *(8)(9)(10)(17)*

refinancing: The issuance of new debt in payment of debt issued earlier. *(11)*

regressive tax: A tax system in which tax rates fall as incomes rise. *(3)(32)*

regulation: Government intervention to alter the behavior of firms, e.g., in pricing, output, advertising. *(3)(26)*

relative price: The price of one good in comparison with the price of other goods. *(7)*

rent: Payments to a factor of production in excess of the amount required to call forth a given quantity of the factor. *(31)*

required reserves: The minimum amount of reserves a bank is required to hold by government regulation; equal to required reserve ratio times transactions deposits. *(12)(13)*

reserve ratio: The ratio of a bank's reserves to its total transactions deposits. *(12)*

risk premium: The difference between the interest rate paid on a particular asset and the rate paid on relatively safe assets, e.g., Treasury bonds. *(34)*

saving: That part of disposable income not spent on current consumption; disposable income less consumption. *(4)(8)(15)(34)*

Say's Law: Supply creates its own demand. *(5)*

seasonal unemployment: Unemployment due to seasonal changes in employment or labor supply. *(6)*

shift in demand: A change in the quantity demanded at any (every) given price. *(2)*

short run: The period in which the quantity (and quality) of some inputs cannot be changed. *(20)(21)*

short-run competitive equilibrium: $p = MC.$ *(22)*

shutdown point: That rate of output where price equals minimum AVC. *(21)(22)*

size distribution of income: The way total personal income is divided up among households or income classes. *(32)*

social costs: The full resource costs of an economic activity, including externalities. *(27)*

socialism: An economy in which all nonlabor means of production are owned by the state, which exercises control over resource allocation. *(38)*

speculative demand for money: Money held for speculative purposes, for later financial opportunities. *(14)*

stagflation: The simultaneous occurrence of substantial unemployment and inflation. *(15)*

structural deficit: Federal revenues at full employment minus expenditures at full employment under prevailing fiscal policy. *(10)(17)*

structural unemployment: Unemployment caused by a mismatch between the skills (or location) of job seekers and the requirements (or location) of available jobs. *(6)(15)*

substitute goods: Goods that substitute for each other; when the price of good X rises, the demand for good Y increases, *ceteris paribus.* *(19)*

substitution effect: The replacement of one resource (or good) with another in response to changing relative prices. *(16)*

substitution effect of wages: An increased wage rate encourages people to work more hours (to substitute labor for leisure). *(29)*

supply: The ability and willingness to sell (produce) specific quantities of a good at alternative prices in a given time period, *ceteris paribus.* *(2)*

supply curve: A curve describing the quantities of a good a producer is willing and able to sell (produce) at alternative prices in a given time period, *ceteris paribus.* *(21)*

supply of foreign exchange: The quantities of foreign currency supplied (offered) in a given time period at alternative exchange rates, *ceteris paribus.* *(36)*

supply-side policy: The use of tax rates, (de)regulation, and other mechanisms to increase the ability and willingness to produce goods and services. *(5)(17)*

suppressed inflation: Inflationary imbalances reflected in nonprice forms (e.g., market shortages, rationing) when prices are not permitted to rise. *(38)*

tariff: A tax (duty) imposed on imported goods. *(35)*

tax base: The amount of income or property directly subject to nominal tax rates. *(32)*

tax elasticity of supply: The percentage change in quantity supplied divided by the percentage change in tax rates. *(15)*

tax incidence: Distribution of the real burden of a tax. *(32)*

tax rebate: A lump-sum refund of taxes paid. *(15)*

terms of trade: The rate at which goods are exchanged; the amount of good A given up for good B in trade. *(35)*

total cost: The market value of all resources used to produce a good or service. *(20)*

total revenue: The price of a product multiplied by the quantity sold in a given time period: $p \times q.$ *(19)(21)*

total utility: The amount of satisfaction obtained from entire consumption of a product. *(19)*

trade deficit: The amount by which the value of imports exceeds the value of exports in a given time period. *(18)(35)(36)*

trade surplus: The amount by which the value of exports exceeds the value of imports in a given time period. *(18)(35)*

transactions account: A bank account that permits direct payment to a third party (e.g., with a check). *(12)*

transactions demand for money: Money held for the purpose of making everyday market purchases. *(14)*

transfer payment: Payments to individuals for which no current goods or services are exchanged, e.g., Social Security, welfare, unemployment benefits. *(3)(10)(11)(15)*

Treasury bonds: Promissory notes (IOUs) issued by the U.S. Treasury. *(11)*

underemployment: People seeking full-time paid employment work only part-time or are employed at jobs below their capability. *(6)*

unemployment: The inability of labor-force participants to find jobs. *(3)(6)*

unemployment rate: The proportion of the labor force that is unemployed. *(6)*

union shop: An employment setting in which all workers must join the union within thirty days after being employed. *(30)*

unionization ratio: The percentage of the labor force belonging to a union. *(30)*

unit labor cost: Hourly wage rate divided by output per labor-hour. *(15)*

user charge: Fee paid for the user of a public-sector good or service. *(3)*

utility: The pleasure or satisfaction obtained from a good or service. *(19)*

value added: The increase in the market value of a product that takes place at each stage of the production process. *(4)*

variable costs: Costs of production that change when the rate of output is altered, e.g., labor and material costs. *(20)(21)*

velocity of money (V): The number of times per year, on average, that a dollar is used to purchase final goods and services; $PQ \div M.$ *(17)*

vertical equity: Principle that people with higher incomes should pay more taxes. *(32)*

voluntary restraint agreement (VRA) An agreement to reduce the volume of trade in a specific good; a "voluntary" quota. *(35)*

wage-price controls: Direct governmental restraints on the wage and price decisions of market participants. *(15)*

wealth: The market value of assets. *(32)*

workfare: Mandatory community-service program for welfare recipients. *(33)*

yield: The rate of return on a bond; the annual interest payment divided by the bond's price. *(13)(34)*

INDEX

Note: Page numbers followed by *n* indicate footnotes. **Boldface** indicates glossary terms defined in the text.

CONSUMER PRICE INDEX, 1913–89
(1982–84 = 100)

Year	Index (all items)	Percent change
1913	9.9	1.0
1914	10.0	2.0
1915	10.1	12.6
1916	10.9	18.1
1917	12.8	20.4
1918	15.1	14.5
1919	17.3	
1920	20.0	2.6
1921	17.9	−10.8
1922	16.8	−2.3
1923	17.1	2.4
1924	17.1	0.0
1925	17.5	3.5
1926	17.7	−1.1
1927	17.4	−2.3
1928	17.1	−1.2
1929	17.1	0.6
1930	16.7	−6.4
1931	15.2	−9.3
1932	13.7	−10.3
1933	13.0	0.8
1934	13.4	1.5
1935	13.7	3.0
1936	13.9	1.4
1937	14.4	2.9
1938	14.1	−2.8
1939	13.9	0.0
1940	14.0	0.7
1941	14.7	9.9
1942	16.3	9.0
1943	17.3	3.0
1944	17.6	2.3
1945	18.0	2.2
1946	19.5	18.1
1947	22.3	8.8
1948	24.1	3.0
1949	23.8	−2.1
1950	24.1	5.9
1951	26.0	6.0
1952	26.5	0.8
1953	26.7	0.7
1954	26.9	−0.7
1955	26.8	0.4
1956	27.2	3.0
1957	28.1	2.9
1958	28.9	1.8
1959	29.1	1.7
1960	29.6	1.4
1961	29.9	0.7
1962	30.2	1.3
1963	30.6	1.6
1964	31.0	1.0
1965	31.5	1.9
1966	32.4	3.5
1967	33.4	3.0
1968	34.8	4.7
1969	36.7	6.2
1970	38.8	5.6
1971	40.5	3.3
1972	41.8	3.4
1973	44.4	8.7
1974	49.3	12.3
1975	53.8	6.9
1976	56.9	4.9
1977	60.6	6.7
1978	65.2	9.0
1979	72.6	13.3
1980	82.4	12.5
1981	90.9	8.9
1982	96.5	3.8
1983	99.6	3.8
1984	103.9	3.9
1985	107.6	3.8
1986	109.6	1.1
1987	113.6	4.4
1988	118.3	4.6
1989	124.0	4.6

Note: Data beginning 1978 are for all urban consumers; earlier data are for urban wage earners and clerical workers.

Source: Department of Labor, Bureau of Statistics.

PRICE DEFLATORS FOR GROSS NATIONAL PRODUCT, 1929–89
(1982 = 100)

Year	Index	Percent change[1]
1929	14.6	—
1933	11.2	−2.2
1939	12.7	−.8
1940	13.0	2.0
1941	13.8	6.2
1942	14.7	6.6
1943	15.1	2.6
1944	15.3	1.4
1945	15.7	2.9
1946	19.4	22.9
1947	22.1	13.9
1948	23.6	7.0
1949	23.5	−.5
1950	23.9	2.0
1951	25.1	4.8
1952	25.5	1.5
1953	25.9	1.6
1954	26.3	1.6
1955	27.2	3.2
1956	28.1	3.4
1957	29.1	3.6
1958	29.7	2.1
1959	30.4	2.4
1960	30.9	1.6
1961	31.2	1.0
1962	31.9	2.2
1963	32.4	1.6
1964	32.9	1.5
1965	33.8	2.7
1966	35.0	3.6
1967	35.9	2.6
1968	37.7	5.0
1969	39.8	5.6
1970	42.0	5.5
1971	44.4	5.7
1972	46.5	4.7
1973	49.5	6.5
1974	54.0	9.1
1975	59.3	9.8
1976	63.1	6.4
1977	67.3	6.7
1978	72.2	7.3
1979	78.6	8.9
1980	85.7	9.0
1981	94.0	9.7
1982	100.0	6.4
1983	103.9	3.9
1984	107.7	3.7
1985	111.2	3.2
1986	114.1	2.6
1987	117.5	3.2
1988	121.4	3.3
1989	126.4	4.1

[1] Changes are based on unrounded data and therefore may differ slightly from changes computed from data shown here.

Source: Department of Commerce, Bureau of Economic Analysis.

INTEREST RATES, 1929–89
(Percent per annum)

Year	Prime rate charged by banks	Discount rate, Federal Reserve Bank of New York
1929	5.50–6.00	5.16
1933	1.50–4.00	2.56
1939	1.50	1.00
1940	1.50	1.00
1941	1.50	1.00
1942	1.50	1.00
1943	1.50	1.00
1944	1.50	1.00
1945	1.50	1.00
1946	1.50	1.00
1947	1.50–1.75	1.00
1948	1.75–2.00	1.34
1949	2.00	1.50
1950	2.07	1.59
1951	2.56	1.75
1952	3.00	1.75
1953	3.17	1.99
1954	3.05	1.60
1955	3.16	1.89
1956	3.77	2.77
1957	4.20	3.12
1958	3.83	2.15
1959	4.48	3.36
1960	4.82	3.53
1961	4.50	3.00
1962	4.50	3.00
1963	4.50	3.23
1964	4.50	3.55
1965	4.54	4.04
1966	5.63	4.50
1967	5.61	4.19
1968	6.30	5.16
1969	7.96	5.87
1970	7.91	5.95
1971	5.72	4.88
1972	5.25	4.50
1973	8.03	6.44
1974	10.81	7.83
1975	7.86	6.25
1976	6.84	5.50
1977	6.83	5.46
1978	9.06	7.46
1979	12.67	10.28
1980	15.27	11.77
1981	18.87	13.42
1982	14.86	11.02
1983	10.79	8.50
1984	12.04	8.80
1985	9.93	7.69
1986	8.33	6.33
1987	8.21	5.66
1988	9.32	6.20
1989	10.87	6.93

Source: Board of Governors of the Federal Reserve System.